NEW

ANNUAL 1999-2000

Published by Invincible Press, an imprint of HarperCollins*Publishers*,
77-85 Fulham Crystal Palace Road, Hammersmith, London W6 8JB

First published 1887

© Invincible Press 1999

The copyrights of the League Fixture Lists are owned by The Football Association,
Football League, Scottish Football Association and Scottish League, and these fixtures
have been reproduced with their permission.

Editorial compilation by Hayters, Humatt House, 146-148 Clerkenwell Road,
London EC1R 5DP

Typesetting by Letterpart Limited, Reigate, Surrey

Printed and bound in Great Britain

Distributed by The Magazine Marketing Company, Octagon House, White Hart
Meadows, Ripley, Woking, Surrey GU23 6HR. Telephone (01483) 211222

ISBN 0 00 218883 X

FRONT COVER

ALEX FERGUSON and his Manchester United players celebrate with the European Cup,
Barcelona, May 1999.

(Cover picture © PA News Photolibrary)

CONTENTS

CALM TO FOLLOW THE STORMS ?
By Eric Brown

British football desperately requires a period of stability as we enter the new **Millennium**.
During the 1998-99 season a wind of change howled through the game like a gale, sweeping away the Football Association hierarchy as well as bringing down England coach **Glenn Hoddle**. Wales manager **Bobby Gould** and Scotland stalwart **Jim Farry** were other distinguished victims.

At the time of writing England, Scotland, Northern Ireland and Wales all have much to do to qualify for the century's first major tournament finals. British eyes may once more be cast enviously towards Ireland as Belgium and Holland prepare to stage **Euro 2000**.

Yet the reputation of English club football continues to climb after the barren post-Heysel years. **Manchester United** were crowned Kings of Europe in both footballing and financial terms. Their breathtaking late rally to wrench the **European Cup** from Bayern Munich's grasp on the 90th anniversary of patriarch Sir Matt Busby's birth completed a magnificent treble.

Manager **Alex Ferguson's** knighthood added to the Old Trafford honours – a sharp contrast to the previous season when United won nothing!

If Ferguson can maintain – or even improve – the formidable Old Trafford squad it will surely be well into the new Millennium before United finish another season empty-handed.

Arsenal gave United a run for their money in the Premier League. They might even have retained their title had Dennis Bergkamp not suffered a mid-season dip in form or Nwankwo Kanu arrived earlier. But manager Arsene Wenger does not possess the squad depth of Utd. and may face major reconstruction work as his famous Highbury rearguard approaches its sell-by date.

David O'Leary is confronted by the reverse problem at **Leeds United** where his prospects hinge on how quickly a squad of promising youngsters mature.

Chelsea were nearly men, finishing third after challenging for some time and also relinquishing the Cup Winners' Cup.

In Scotland, **Rangers** registered a domestic treble after drawing a blank the previous season. But they continue to find European rewards elusive.

Maybe that will change in the new Millennium. What other developments can we expect? My strictly-for-fun predictions are:

★ TV cameras installed in players boots to give viewers 'virtual reality' of goals scored.

★ Three referees to control each match with the aid of instant TV replays.

★ Securicor van standing by at matches to rush players' wages to their banks.

★ Banks owned by top footballers.

★ Matches staged every day of week from August to July and twice on Sundays.

★ World Cup Finals staged annually.

★ July reserved for players' holidays.

★ Two new European competitions introduced to fill players' holidays.

★ Robots introduced to replace players.

Hopefully this annual will be around to chart all the developments. Production is a team effort. I am hugely indebted to former editor **Albert Sewell** for his diligent preparation of the records section and general advice. Thanks also go to **Stuart Barnes**, **Joel Miller** and colleagues at Hayters, **David Barber** of the Football Association, **Nick Sutherland** of the Premier League, **Chris Hull** of the Football League, **David Thompson** of the Scottish League and **Sean Creedon**, for his summary of Irish football; to clubs, correspondents and Leagues for their co-operation and to **Chris Leggett** at the production end.

KEEGAN FACING TEST OF CREDIBILITY IN CRUCIAL SEASON

By Alex Montgomery

News of the World **Chief Football Reporter**

To say this will be the most important season in the managerial career of Kevin Keegan is in no way overstating the importance of the task he must meet and overcome in the months ahead.

He will be forgiven, just, if England fail to qualify for Euro 2000 – it will after all be his first full season in charge of the national team.

The hope must be that the enthusiasm he inspires will be enough to drive England on to victory in the remaining qualifiers against Luxembourg and Poland and then to aggregate victory against which ever country they are paired with in a two leg play-off.

Should they stumble further, should they falter in the European Championships, and the signs it has to be said leave considerable reason for doubt, then it will be how he re-establishes his own and the country's credibility which will decide his fate.

Keegan took over a squad from Glenn Hoddle which had under-achieved in the World Cup finals and looked but a shadow of the one Terry Venables bequeathed the nation after Euro 96.

They appeared to have made the breakthrough under Venables, to be on the verge of returning to the international top table with a sophisticated approach which exploited the strengths of England's top players.

But there has been a gradual decline which climaxed last season in the team's poor performances, losing against Sweden in Stockholm, drawing with them at Wembley under Keegan, a tie they could easily have lost, and even more abysmally against Bulgaria in Sofia four days later.

Keegan, to be scrupulously fair, was without a number of what would have been his first choice players through injury and UEFA suspension.

But the country expected the ones left would, with Wembley advantage, have been good enough to overcome the Swedes and travel to Bulgaria on a winning mission which should have been well within their capacity to accomplish successfully.

These ties did come at the end of another horrendously exhausting year, but sheer tiredness, playing two matches too many, was never going to save them from criticism or be accepted as an excuse.

There is a great groundswell of support for Keegan from the critics as well as the man in the street.

Everyone wants to see a successful England, for Keegan's team to qualify not just for the European finals but the World Cup two years further down the line.

It is the expectations which add a sharp edge to the criticism any international manager of any country with a footballing pedigree must accept and learn to cope with.

The goodwill I believe is strong enough to sustain Keegan in office even should qualification for Euro 2000 be beyond England – but thereafter he must prove there is to be an upturn.

We cannot continue to analyse England performances wondering why the country's finest aren't at their best; there cannot continue to be question marks about England's tactics, doubts about the way the team is set out.

There is a heavy responsibility on the players to produce recognisable levels of performance and there should be enough inner pride for them to make a full contribution without the coach forever carrying the blame.

Keegan has set his standards; he wants an England team representing the excellence of the Premier League, a team capable of winning Euro 2000 and the World Cup in 2002. It's exactly what the country wants and if it can't be achieved at the very least they expect a run for their money – not something which embarrasses them.

SOCCER DIARY 1998-99

JULY 1998

1 Former **Rangers** boss **Walter Smith** becomes manager of **Everton**. **John Hollins** takes over at **Swansea City**. **Brentford** owner **Ron Noades** also becomes manager of the Third Division club. **2 Steve Bruce** is appointed **Sheffield Utd.** manager. **Wes Saunders** takes over at **Torquay Utd. 3** Dion **Dublin** agrees to stay at **Coventry City** for another four years. **6 Danny Wilson** leaves **Barnsley** to join **Sheffield Wed. John Hendrie** takes over at **Oakwell. Chelsea** are fined £4,000 by UEFA for their supporters' behaviour during a Cup-Winners' Cup match. **7** Former England captain **David Platt** announces his retirement from football at the age of 32. **8 Gary Pallister** ends nine years at **Manchester Utd.** to join **Middlesbrough** for £2.5m. **12 France** win the **World Cup** with a 3-0 victory over Brazil. **13 Arsenal** record goalscorer **Ian Wright** leaves Highbury to join **West Ham Utd. 14 England** share the World Cup Fair Play award with **France**. **15 Rangers** coach **Dick Advocaat** takes his spending to £20m with the £5.5m capture of **Andrei Kanchelskis** from **Fiorentina**. **16 Gerard Houllier** becomes joint manager of **Liverpool** with **Roy Evans**. **Arsenal** striker **Nicolas Anelka** signs a new four-year contract. **17 Celtic** appoint former **Aston Villa** boss **Dr Jozef Venglos**. **19 Manchester Utd.** deny they are joining a European Super League. **22 Alex Ferguson** buys **Jesper Blomqvist** from **Parma** (£4.4m) after a three-year chase. **Ian Snodin** becomes **Doncaster Rov.** manager. **23 AXA** begin four-year sponsorship of **F.A. Cup. 24 Bristol Rov.** buy the Memorial Ground from **Bristol Rugby Club's** receivers. **26 Ireland** win the European Under-18 C'ships with victory over **Germany**. **29** Premier League ask **Manchester Utd., Arsenal** and **Liverpool** for assurance over their Super League intentions.

AUGUST 1998

1 F.A. warn that clubs could be expelled from the Premiership and the F.A. Cup if they join a **Super League. 3 Pierre van Hooijdonk** refuses to train with **Nott'm Forest. Patrick Kluivert** turns down a £9m move to **Manchester Utd.** Premier League receive assurances from **Manchester Utd., Arsenal** and **Liverpool** over Super League. **4 Ray Mathias** becomes **Wigan Athletic** manager for second time. **5 Advocaat's Rangers** spending rises to £28m as **Colin Hendry** joins from **Blackburn Rov.** for £4m. The Glasgow club is fined £10,000 for fans' behaviour during UEFA Cup. **8** Nationwide League season begins. **9** Ron **Atkinson** alleges in his book that drug use is widespread in football. **Charity Shield** (Wembley): **Arsenal** 3 **Manchester Utd.** 0. **10** Forest put an £8m price tag on **van Hooijdonk. 13** F.A. Chief Executive **Graham Kelly** defends **Glenn Hoddle** over his World Cup diary. F.A. give **Shane Nicholson** leave to resume his career after a drugs ban and drop misconduct charges against **Brian Clough. 14 Fan Zhiyi** and **Sun Jihai** become first Chinese players in England when they sign for **Crystal Palace. 17 Arsenal** begin title defence with 2-1 win over **Nott'm Forest. 18** Matt **Jansen** signs six-year deal with **Crystal Palace. 19 David Platt** is appointed assistant to England Under-18 and Under-19 sides. **20 Manchester Utd.** smash their transfer record with £12.6m deal for **Aston Villa's Dwight Yorke. David Unsworth** leaves **Aston Villa** for **Everton** three weeks after joining from **West Ham Utd. 21 Manchester Utd.** agree a price of £5.5m with **Tottenham** for **Ole Gunnar Solskjaer**, but the deal is aborted. **22 Reading** play first game at Madejski Stadium (beat **Luton Town** 3-0). **25** Leaders of main European leagues pledge their allegiance to UEFA. **27 Kenny Dalglish** is sacked by **Newcastle Utd.** and replaced by ex-**Chelsea** manager **Ruud Gullit**.

SEPTEMBER 1998

1 Arsenal fine **Emmanuel Petit** a week's wages for a red card against **Charlton Athletic. 2** Ex-England defender **Mark Wright** retires with a back problem. **Steve Clarke** becomes **Gullit's** deputy at **Newcastle Utd. 3 Efan Ekoku** asks **Wimbledon** for a transfer. **4 Dundee Utd** replace manager **Tommy McLean** with **Paul Sturrock. 5 Christian Gross** is sacked by **Tottenham. Paul Ince** is sent off for **England** in 2-1 defeat by Sweden. **7 Berti Vogts** resigns as German manager. **8 Manchester Utd.** accept a £623m takeover bid from BSkyB. **Paul**

Merson joins **Aston Villa** (£6.75m) after complaining about gambling and drinking culture at M'boro. **10** Carlton admit they are in takeover talks with **Arsenal**. **17** Pierre van Hooijdonk apologises for saying his teammates are not good enough for the Prem. **18** Glenn Hoddle meets the F.A. and receives their backing. John Gregory signs a four-year contract at **Aston Villa**. **19** Southampton finally claim first point of the season against **Tottenham**. **23** Everton buy Tranmere Rov. keeper Steve Simonsen for a price which could rise to £3.3m. Steve McMahon walks out on **Swindon Town** after a pitch protest against him. **24** F.A. announce they will appoint a 'sleaze-buster' after former **Arsenal** scout Steve Burtenshaw is fined £7,500 after a lengthy bungs enquiry. **25** FIFA say they will ban clubs who join a Super League. **26** Sheffield Wed. midfielder Paolo Di Canio pushes over referee Paul Alcock after being sent off v **Arsenal**. **28** Di Canio is charged by the F.A. with misconduct. Ray Harford resigns as manager of Q.P.R. **29** Nott'm Forest ask Premier League for £4m loan until they sell van Hooijdonk. **30** Arsenal play first 'home' fixture at Wembley v Panathinaikos.

OCTOBER 1998

1 George Graham becomes manager at **Tottenham**, who pay Leeds Utd. £3m compensation. **2** Jimmy Quinn is appointed **Swindon Town** manager. **5** Euro qualifier between Ireland and Yugoslavia is postponed for security reasons. PFA chief Gordon Taylor calls for calm after three tunnel incidents in ten days. **6** Nigel Clough is released by **Manchester City**. Aston Villa bid £11m for Chris Sutton but are turned down. UEFA ratify proposals for extended Champions League and unification of Cup-Winners Cup and UEFA Cup. **9** Peter Beardsley turns down player-coach job at Carlisle Utd. **10** Paul Gascoigne is admitted to the Priory Clinic with alcohol-related stress problems. **12** Scottish goalkeeper Jim Leighton announces his retirement from int. football. **West Ham Utd.** striker John Hartson is charged with misconduct by F.A. over training ground attack on teammate Eyal Berkovic. **13** Leicester City reject **Leeds Utd.**'s third offer for manager Martin O'Neill. **16** Gerry Francis begins his second spell as **Q.P.R.** manager. **21** O'Neill pledges his future to **Leicester City**. Tribunal rules that **Aston Villa** will have to pay **Brighton & H.A.** up to £1m for Gareth Barry. **23** Di Canio is given a 12-match ban for pushing over **Alcock**. Leading European clubs give UEFA their assurance over the Super League. **25** David O'Leary becomes **Leeds Utd.** manager on a £750,000-a-year salary. **26** Gascoigne returns to M'boro after his spell in the clinic. **27** Manager John Ward walks out of **Bristol City** when Benny Lennartson is proposed as new Director of Football. **Chester City** escape liquidation when a judge dismisses their winding-up order. **29** Brian Laudrup leaves **Chelsea** to join FC Copenhagen.

NOVEMBER 1998

1 England coach Glenn Hoddle agrees pay rise linked to Euro 2000 results. **2** David Lloyd sells **Hull City** to Sheffield consortium. **5** Mark McGhee leaves **Wolves** by mutual consent. Dion Dublin leaves **Coventry City** for **Aston Villa** in £5.75m deal. **6** Sunderland's Alex Rae admitted to a clinic for alcohol-related stress. **7** Chelsea striker Pierluigi Casiraghi sustains serious knee injury. **9** George Graham's first **Tottenham** signing is Mauricio Taricco (£1.75m from Ipswich Town). **10** Mark Hateley sacked by Hull City. F.A. appoint Graham Bean as 'compliance officer'. **11** Lincoln City sack Shane Westley and chairman John Reames takes over. **Arsenal** suffer worst defeat in 73 years when they lose 5-0 to **Chelsea** in Worthington Cup. **12** Roy Evans departs **Liverpool** to leave Gerard Houllier in sole charge. Peter Schmeichel announces intention to leave **Manchester Utd.** at end of season. **18** Int'l friendly: **England** 2 **Czech Rep.** 0. European qualifiers: **Yugoslavia** 1 **Rep. of Ireland** 0, **Northern Ireland** 2 **Moldova** 2. **20** Warren Joyce takes over at Hull City. **21** Blackburn Rov. sack Roy Hodgson after home defeat to Southampton. **23** Everton record first home win of the season against **Newcastle Utd.** Tony Parkes becomes Blackburn Rov. caretaker-manager for fourth time. **24** Manchester Utd. receive planning permission to increase their capacity by 12,000. **25** Duncan Ferguson joins **Newcastle Utd.** from **Everton** for £8m. **Arsenal** knocked out of Champions League after defeat to **Lens**. **30** Peter Johnson resigns as **Everton** chairman.

DECEMBER 1998

4 Brian Kidd appointed **Blackburn Rov.** manager. **6 Mark Viduka** walks out of **Celtic** after a few days claiming 'depression'. **7 Dean Saunders** signs for **Graeme Souness** for third time when he joins **Benfica** for £500,000. **8 David Batty** returns to **Leeds Utd.** from **Newcastle Utd.** for £4.4m. **Arsene Wenger** signs a new three-and-a-half year contract. **Alex Miller** leaves **Aberdeen**. **Freddy Shepherd** and **Douglas Hall** return to **Newcastle Utd.** board. **11** UEFA promise future European champions will earn over £30m. **14 Paolo Di Canio** misses deadline to return to **Sheffield Wed. Patrick Vieira** fined £20,000 for gesturing to fans but cleared of assaulting police officer during **Arsenal's** game with **Sheffield Wed. 15 Graham Kelly** resigns as **F.A.** chief executive over £3.2m loan to Welsh F.A. **Keith Gillespie** is **Brian Kidd's** first signing (£2.35m from **Middlesbrough**). **16 David Platt** appointed **Sampdoria's** coach. **17 Brian McClair** becomes **Brian Kidd's** assistant at **Blackburn Rov. Stevenage** sack manager **Paul Fairclough** after eight years. **18 Portsmouth** chairman **Martin Gregory** resigns after death threats. **28 Arsenal's Patrick Vieira** sent off for elbowing **Neil Redfearn**. **29 Ashley Ward** leaves **Barnsley** and joins **Blackburn Rov.** for £4.5m. **30 Burnley** break their transfer record with £750,000 move for **Luton Town's Steve Davis**. **31** Deadline for **2006 World Cup** bids passes with **England** one of seven choices.

JANUARY 1999

1 Trevor Brooking (CBE), **Stuart Pearce** (MBE) and **Pat Smith**, the former F.A. deputy chief executive, (OBE) all included in New Year Honours. **3 FIFA** President **Sepp Blatter** proposes **World Cup** every two years. **4 Keith Wiseman** resigns as **F.A. Chairman** after vote of no confidence. **Geoff Thompson** takes over until the summer. **5 Dave Bassett** sacked by **Nott'm Forest**. **Lee Sharpe** becomes **David Platt's** first signing at **Sampdoria. 6 Premier League** announce plans for referees and assistants to wear microphones and earpieces. Inland Revenue issue **Portsmouth** with a winding-up order. **8 Arsenal** sign 15-year-old **Jermaine Pennant** from **Notts Co.** and could pay £2m compensation. **Oldham Athletic** chairman **Ian Stott** admits discussions with **Bury** and **Rochdale** over merger. **11 Ron Atkinson** put in charge of **Nott'm Forest** until end of season. **Neil Smillie** sacked by **Wycombe Wand. 12 UEFA** officials reject **Blatter's** plans for World Cup every two years. **Ian Stott** resigns as **Oldham Athletic** chairman. **13 Swansea City** put **West Ham Utd.** out of F.A. Cup and **Fulham** beat **Southampton**. **15 Wimbledon** shatter transfer record with £7.5m move for **West Ham Utd.'s John Hartson**. **Terry Venables** ends spell as **Crystal Palace** manager but remains as part-time consultant. **Steve Coppell** takes over as caretaker manager. **18 John Rudge** sacked by **Port Vale** after 15 years in charge. **Carlton Palmer** joins **Nott'm Forest** for £1.1m to become **Ron Atkinson's** first signing. **Mick Tait** is sacked by **Hartlepool Utd. 19 Gary Mabbutt** retires from football because of knee injury. **20 F.A.** announce plans for 500 more drug tests per season. **21 F.A.** announce £15m sponsorship deal for **England** team with Nationwide Building Society. **Steve Wignall** resigns as **Colchester Utd.** manager. **22 Brian Horton** leaves **Brighton & H.A.** to manage **Port Vale. 23 Aston Villa** beaten by **Fulham** in the F.A. Cup. **25 Aston Villa** announce that **Stan Collymore** is seeking stress counselling. **26 Robbie Fowler** signs contract with **Liverpool** until 2003. **Portsmouth** apply to High Court to go into administration. **27 Paolo Di Canio** joins **West Ham Utd.** for £3.5m. **28 Mick Wadsworth** moves from **Scarborough** to **Colchester Utd.** as manager. **29 Steve McManaman** agrees five-year contract with **Real Madrid. 30** Interview with **Glenn Hoddle** appears in **The Times** in which he suggests that disabled people are being punished for sins in a past life.

FEBRUARY 1999

1 John Hartson fined record £20,000 and banned three matches by **F.A.** for kicking **Eyal Berkovic** in face during training. French midfielder **Zinedine Zidane** named FIFA World Player of the Year. **2 Glenn Hoddle's** contract terminated by **F.A.** Technical director **Howard Wilkinson** put in charge for friendly against France. **David Platt** resigns as **Sampdoria** coach. **4 Tottenham** sign **Blackburn Rov.** captain **Tim Sherwood** for £3m. **5 Steve McLaren** appointed **Alex Ferguson's** assistant at **Manchester Utd. Jeff Wood** takes charge at **Brighton & H.A. Lawrie Sanchez** becomes **Wycombe Wand.** manager. **10** Int'l friendlies: **England** 0 **France** 2, **Rep. of Ireland** 2 **Paraguay** 0. Four men arrested at Charlton Athletic's Valley for tampering with floodlights. **11 Mark Hughes** receives additional two-match ban and £2,000 fine as first player to reach 14 bookings. **13 Arsenal** agree to replay F.A. Cup game with **Sheffield Utd.** after **Marc Overmars'** unsporting 'winner'. **14 Fulham** chairman **Mohamed Al Fayed** gives F.A. permission to approach **Kevin Keegan** for England job. **15** Administrators sack nine members of **Portsmouth** staff. **17 Keegan** becomes temporary **England** coach for four games but remains at **Fulham. 19 Leeds Utd.** refuse to release players for World Under-20 Championships. **Luton Town** chairman **David Kohler** resigns after petrol bomb is posted at his home. **22 Colin Addison** becomes **Scarborough** manager. **23 Arsenal** win F.A. Cup replay with **Sheffield Utd. 24 Chris Turner** takes charge at **Hartlepool Utd. 26 Tottenham** appoint **Stewart Houston** as **George Graham's** assistant. **27 Oxford Utd.** play **Sunderland** in first pay-per-view game on British television.

MARCH 1999

1 SFA suspend chief executive **Jim Farry** over irregularities in **Jorge Cadete** transfer to **Celtic. 2 Graeme Le Saux** and **Robbie Fowler** charged with misconduct by **F.A.** after clash at Stamford Bridge three days earlier. **3** Crystal Palace apply for administration with debts of £22m. Wimbledon manager **Joe Kinnear** rushed to hospital after heart attack at Sheffield Wed. **5 Le Saux** issues public apology to **Fowler. 7 Vinnie Jones** announces retirement from football to pursue film career. **8 Jim Farry** is sacked by **SFA. 11 Premier League** sack chief executive **Peter Leaver** and chairman **Sir John Quinton** also goes in row over TV deal with BSkyB. **Aston Villa** buy **Steve Stone** from **Nott'm Forest** for £5.5m. **16 Alan Little** sacked by **York City** and **Neil Thompson** put in temporary charge. **17 Leeds Utd.** and **Wolves** withdraw threat to prevent players going to World Under-20 Championships. **19 Rangers** and **Celtic** complete £13m joint sponsorship deal with NTL. **21** Worthington Cup final: **Leicester City** 0 **Tottenham** 1. **22 Blackburn Rov.** buy **Lee Carsley** from **Derby Co.** for £3.37m. **23 Kevin Campbell** joins **Everton** on loan from Turkish club **Trabzonspor. 24 UEFA** call off Rep. of Ireland trip to Macedonia due to Balkans war. **Stan Collymore** begins full-time treatment for stress. **Bradford City** sign **Lee Sharpe** on loan from **Leeds Utd. UEFA** refuse Chelsea request to move ECWC final to Wembley. **25** Scotland's game in Bosnia postponed. Transfer deadline day is quietest for four years with £5m spent. **UEFA** fine **Alex Ferguson** £2,000 for comments about Inter Milan. **Graham Rix** imprisoned for 12 months for unlawful sex with under-age girl. **Alvin Martin** resigns as **Southend Utd.** manager. **27** Euro qualifiers: **England** 3 **Poland** 1, **Northern Ireland** 0 **Germany** 3. **28** Crystal Palace midfielder **Sasa Curcic** conducts one-man protest against NATO bombing of Serbia. **30 England** Under-21 coach **Peter Taylor** loses job. Former **Norwich City** keeper **Bryan Gunn** announces retirement from football. **31** Euro qualifiers: **Scotland** 1 **Czech Republic** 2, **Switzerland** 2 **Wales** 0, **Moldova** 0 **Northern Ireland** 0. **Crystal Palace** granted High Court administration order.

APRIL 1999

1 London hotelier **Firoz Kassam** takes over **Oxford Utd.** Crystal Palace administrators sack 46 members of staff. **2 Alan Little** takes over as manager of **Southend Utd.** Crystal Palace players threaten to strike over pay. **6 Robbie Fowler** on second misconduct charge for simulating drug-taking during Merseyside derby. **7 Halifax Town** sack manager **Kieran O'Regan. 8 Gary McAllister** retires from Scottish international football. **Liverpool** withdraw interest in Inter-Toto Cup. **West Ham Utd.** defender **Richard Hall** retires at age of 27. **Brighton & H.A.** sack **Jeff Wood. 9 Robbie Fowler** given record £32,000 fine and six-match ban for simulated drug-taking and clash with **Graeme Le Saux** – who is fined £5,000 and banned for one match. **12 Mickey Adams** becomes **Brighton & H.A.** manager. **13 Fulham** win promotion to First Division and **Sunderland** to the Premiership. **14 Willem Korsten** rejects permanent deal with **Leeds Utd. 16 Robbie Fowler** decides not to appeal against six-match ban. **18 Paul Merson** admits to a lapse in his alcohol rehabilitation. Auto Windscreens Shield: **Millwall** 0 **Wigan Athletic** 1. **19 John Hendrie** sacked by **Barnsley. Graeme Souness** told **Benfica** will terminate his contract. **Dennis Wise** escapes UEFA punishment over alleged 'biting' incident against **Real Mallorca**. **20 Brighton & H.A.** granted £500,000 loan by Football Trust to develop Withdean Stadium. **22 Kevin Keegan** calls up six uncapped players to **England** squad. **Arsenal** end 18-year association with JVC and agree sponsorship deal with Sega. **23 West Ham Utd.** announce termination of director of football **Peter Storrie**'s contract. **25 David Ginola** named **PFA** Player of the Year. **Keegan** calls up three more uncapped players to **England** squad. **Ron Atkinson** announces retirement from management. **26 David Richards** takes over as Premier League chairman. **Roy Hodgson** becomes technical director at **Inter Milan**. **Doncaster Rov.** reveal plans for £20m stadium. **28** Int'l friendly: Hungary 1 **England** 1. **Kevin Keegan** commits himself to **England** on full-time basis.

MAY 1999

1 Football holds minute's silence for **Sir Alf Ramsey**. **2** Referee **Hugh Dallas** is struck by coin during Scottish Old Firm derby marred by violence. Croydon secure **women's** league title. **3 Women's F.A. Cup** final: Arsenal 2 Southampton 0. Rochdale sack **Graham Barrow**. **4 Alex Ferguson** signs new three-year contract at Manchester Utd. **Mark Bright** announces retirement. **5 Ian Wright** charged with misconduct by F.A. for damaging referee's dressing-room after receiving red card. **7 Kevin Keegan** leaves Fulham. **8** Goalkeeper **Jimmy Glass** scores injury-time winner to keep Carlisle Utd. in Football League and relegate Scarborough. **9 Bradford City** secure promotion to Prem. **10** Huddersfield Town sack **Peter Jackson**. **11 David Sheepshanks** announces bid for F.A. chairmanship. **Aberdeen** discard caretaker manager Paul Hegarty. **13 David Ginola** signs three-year contract with Tottenham. **14 Kevin Keegan** becomes full-time England manager. **Paul Bracewell** becomes Fulham manager. Blackburn Rov. fine **Kevin Davies** £30,000 for breaking nightclub curfew. **16 Manchester Utd.** claim Prem. title. **17 Steve Bruce** resigns from Sheffield Utd. **Milan Mandaric** completes £4.5m takeover of Portsmouth. Carlisle Utd. sack **Nigel Pearson**. **18** Derby Co. break transfer record to buy **Seth Johnson** (£3m) from Crewe Alexandra. **21** Wigan Athletic sack manager **Ray Mathias**. **22 F.A. Cup Final**: Manchester Utd. 2 Newcastle Utd. 0. **24 Steve Bruce** takes over at Huddersfield Town. **26 Manchester Utd.** win treble with 2-1 European Cup victory over Bayern Munich. **27 Ian Wright** is banned for three matches and fined £17,500 by F.A. for wrecking referee's room. **Dave Bassett** takes over at Barnsley. **28 David Taylor** replaces Jim Farry as SFA chief executive. **30 Football League** threaten financially-troubled Crystal Palace, Portsmouth, Luton Town and Chester City with expulsion. **31 Watford** beat Bolton Wand. in play-off final for promotion to Premiership.

JUNE 1999

1 Joe Kinnear informs Wimbledon of his decision to leave after seven years. **John Benson** takes over at Wigan Athletic. **2** Irish government refuses to grant visas to **Yugoslav** side before Euro 2000 qualifier. **Mark Bosnich** joins Manchester Utd. on free transfer. **Steve Parkin** resigns as Mansfield Town manager. **Mark Lillis** takes over at Halifax Town. **5** Euro qualifiers: England 0 Sweden 0, Faroe Islands 1 Scotland 1, Italy 4 Wales 0. **Bobby Gould** resigns as Wales manager. **Neville Southall** and **Mark Hughes** become caretakers. **6 Peter Reid** named as England Under-21 coach. **Gianluca Vialli** announces retirement from playing football. **7 Liam Daish** retires. **9** Euro qualifiers: Bulgaria 1 England 1, Czech Republic 3 Scotland 2, Rep. of Ireland 1 Macedonia 0, Wales 0 Denmark 2. **Christian Vieri** joins Inter in world record £31m deal. **Egil Olsen** becomes Wimbledon manager. **10 Kenny Dalglish** becomes Celtic direcor of football and **John Barnes** is named head coach. **11 Brian Little** resigns as Stoke City manager. **12** Manchester Utd. manager **Alex Ferguson** knighted. **Tony Adams** and **Robbie Earle** awarded the MBE. **Craig Brown** given a CBE. **Garth Crooks** awarded the OBE. **15** Charlton Athletic defender **Danny Mills** joins Leeds Utd. for £4m. Liverpool sign Dutch goalkeeper **Sander Westerveld** for the same fee, a British record for a goalkeeper. Newcastle Utd. snap up PSG defender **Alain Goma** for £4.75m. Sheffield Utd. name **Adrian Heath** as manager. **17** Aston Villa complete signing of **David James** from Liverpool **20** Manchester Utd. goalkeeper **Peter Schmeichel** joins Sporting Lisbon on a free transfer. Record crowd for a women's game – 78,972 – see U.S. beat Denmark in the opening game of the **Women's World Cup** in New York. **21**

Chelsea sign **Didier Deschamps** for £3m from Juventus. Newcastle Utd. sign Real Mallorca defender **Elena Marcelino** for £5m. **22** Everton striker **Ibrahim Bakayoko** joins Marseille for £4m. **Dimitri Kharine** quits Chelsea for Celtic under the Bosman Ruling. Barcelona sign **Dani Garcia** from Real Mallorca for £9.3m. **24** Arsenal sign **Stefan Malz** for £650,000 from Munich 1860. **25 Geoff Thompson** elected F.A. Chairman, defeating David Sheepshanks. **27** F.A. offer Manchester Utd. chance to pull out of next season's **F.A. Cup** in order to compete in World Club Championship. **28 Gary Megson** sacked as Stockport Co. boss. Replaced by **Andy Kilner**. **Glenn Hoddle** turns down Nott'm. Forest manager's job. **29** Controversial Nott'm. Forest striker **Pierre van Hooijdonk** joins Vitesse Arnhem for £3.5m. Celtic pair Simon Donnelly and Phil O'Donnell complete free transfers to Sheffield Wed. **30 Manchester Utd.** announce their withdrawal from the 1999-2000 F.A. Cup. Gillingham sack manager **Tony Pulis** for gross misconduct.

UNITED CROWNED CASH KINGS

Manchester Utd. were established as the world's richest football club in a survey published by accountants Deloitte and Touche in February 1999.

The survey, which covered cash generation until the end of 1997, showed the Old Trafford giants nearly £30million clear of Barcelona and Real Madrid, clubs who possess much larger grounds.

United's spectacular turnover of almost £88million made them the highest earners on a list including six British clubs among the top 20.

The survey found that aggressive marketing had catapulted Utd. clear although Real Madrid and Barcelona can accommodate up to 110,000 fans.

Perhaps the lure of a David Beckham bedspread or a Ryan Giggs poster helped Utd. outstrip other European giants in the money-making stakes.

All this at a time when Manchester Utd.'s merchandising income dropped by £4.5million in a year. This shortfall was compensated for by a rise in television income.

The survey charted cash generated by gate receipts, sponsorship, television, merchandising and other commercial income. It did not include transfer values which were judged too complex to calculate.

THE TOP 20 CLUBS' TURNOVER

1.	Manchester Utd.	£87.939m
2.	Barcelona	58.862
3.	Real Madrid	55.569
4.	Juventus	53.223
5.	Bayern Munich	51.619
6.	AC Milan	47.480
7.	Borussia Dortmund	42.119
8.	Newcastle Utd.	41.134
9.	Liverpool	39.153
10.	Inter Milan	39.071
11.	Flamengo (Brazil)	37.422
12.	Atletico Madrid	32.382
13.	Paris St Germain	31.697
14.	Glasgow Rangers	31.664
15.	AS Roma	28.215
16.	Tottenham	27.874
17.	Ajax	27.804
18.	Parma	27.756
19.	Lazio	27.332
20.	Arsenal	27.158

FOOTBALLER OF THE YEAR

(Original award by the Football Writers' Association to the 'player who, by precept and example, on the field and off, shall be considered to have done most for football')

1948 Stanley Matthews (Blackpool); **1949** Johnny Carey (Manchester Utd.); **1950** Joe Mercer (Arsenal); **1951** Harry Johnston (Blackpool); **1952** Billy Wright (Wolves); **1953** Nat Lofthouse (Bolton Wand.); **1954** Tom Finney (Preston N.E.); **1955** Don Revie (Manchester City); **1956** Bert Trautmann (Manchester City); **1957** Tom Finney (Preston N.E.); **1958** Danny Blanchflower (Tottenham); **1959** Syd Owen (Luton Town); **1960** Bill Slater (Wolves); **1961** Danny Blanchflower (Tottenham); **1962** Jimmy Adamson (Burnley); **1963** Stanley Matthews (Stoke City); **1964** Bobby Moore (West Ham Utd.); **1965** Bobby Collins (Leeds Utd.); **1966** Bobby Charlton (Manchester Utd.); **1967** Jack Charlton (Leeds Utd.); **1968** George Best (Manchester Utd.); **1969** Tony Book (Manchester City) & Dave Mackay (Derby Co.) – shared; **1970** Billy Bremner (Leeds Utd.); **1971** Frank McLintock (Arsenal); **1972** Gordon Banks (Stoke City); **1973** Pat Jennings (Tottenham); **1974** Ian Callaghan (Liverpool); **1975** Alan Mullery (Fulham); **1976** Kevin Keegan (Liverpool); **1977** Emlyn Hughes (Liverpool); **1978** Kenny Burns (Nott'm Forest); **1979** Kenny Dalglish (Liverpool); **1980** Terry McDermott (Liverpool); **1981** Frans Thijssen (Ipswich Town); **1982** Steve Perryman (Tottenham); **1983** Kenny Dalglish (Liverpool); **1984** Ian Rush (Liverpool); **1985** Neville Southall (Everton); **1986** Gary Lineker (Everton); **1987** Clive Allen (Tottenham); **1988** John Barnes (Liverpool); **1989** Steve Nicol (Liverpool); Special award to the Liverpool players for the compassion shown to bereaved families after the Hillsborough Disaster; **1990** John Barnes (Liverpool); **1991** Gordon Strachan (Leeds Utd.); **1992** Gary Lineker (Tottenham); **1993** Chris Waddle (Sheff. Wed.); **1994** Alan Shearer (Blackburn Rov.); **1995** Jurgen Klinsmann (Tottenham); **1996** Eric Cantona (Manchester Utd.); **1997** Gianfranco Zola (Chelsea); **1998** Dennis Bergkamp (Arsenal); **1999** David Ginola (Tottenham).

P.F.A. AWARDS

Player of the Year: **1974** Norman Hunter (Leeds Utd.); **1975** Colin Todd (Derby Co.); **1976** Pat Jennings (Tottenham); **1977** Andy Gray (Aston Villa); **1978** Peter Shilton (Nott'm Forest); **1979** Liam Brady (Arsenal); **1980** Terry McDermott (Liverpool); **1981** John Wark (Ipswich Town); **1982** Kevin Keegan (Southampton); **1983** Kenny Dalglish (Liverpool); **1984** Ian Rush (Liverpool); **1985** Peter Reid (Everton); **1986** Gary Lineker (Everton); **1987** Clive Allen (Tottenham); **1988** John Barnes (Liverpool); **1989** Mark Hughes (Manchester Utd.); **1990** David Platt (Aston Villa); **1991** Mark Hughes (Manchester Utd.); **1992** Gary Pallister (Manchester Utd.); **1993** Paul McGrath (Aston Villa); **1994** Eric Cantona (Manchester Utd.); **1995** Alan Shearer (Blackburn Rov.); **1996** Les Ferdinand (Newcastle Utd.); **1997** Alan Shearer (Newcastle Utd.); **1998** Dennis Bergkamp (Arsenal); **1999** David Ginola (Tottenham).

Young Player of the Year: **1974** Kevin Beattie (Ipswich Town); **1975** Mervyn Day (West Ham Utd.); **1976** Peter Barnes (Manchester City); **1977** Andy Gray (Aston Villa); **1978** Tony Woodcock (Nott'm Forest); **1979** Cyrille Regis (W.B.A.); **1980** Glenn Hoddle (Tottenham); **1981** Gary Shaw (Aston Villa); **1982** Steve Moran (Southampton); **1983** Ian Rush (Liverpool); **1984** Paul Walsh (Luton Town); **1985** Mark Hughes (Manchester Utd.); **1986** Tony Cottee (West Ham Utd.); **1987** Tony Adams (Arsenal); **1988** Paul Gascoigne (Newcastle Utd.); **1989** Paul Merson (Arsenal); **1990** Matthew Le Tissier (Southampton); **1991** Lee Sharpe (Manchester Utd.); **1992** Ryan Giggs (Manchester Utd.); **1993** Ryan Giggs (Manchester Utd.); **1994** Andy Cole (Newcastle Utd.); **1995** Robbie Fowler (Liverpool); **1996** Robbie Fowler (Liverpool); **1997** David Beckham (Manchester Utd.); **1998** Michael Owen (Liverpool); **1999** Nicholas Anelka (Arsenal).

Merit Awards: **1974** Bobby Charlton & Cliff Lloyd; **1975** Denis Law; **1976** George Eastham; **1977** Jack Taylor; **1978** Bill Shankly; **1979** Tom Finney; **1980** Sir Matt Busby; **1981** John Trollope; **1982** Joe Mercer; **1983** Bob Paisley; **1984** Bill Nicholson; **1985** Ron Greenwood; **1986** England 1966 World Cup-winning team; **1987** Sir Stanley Matthews;

1988 Billy Bonds; 1989 Nat Lofthouse; 1990 Peter Shilton; 1991 Tommy Hutchison; 1992 Brian Clough; 1993 Manchester Utd., 1968 European Champions; Eusebio (Benfica & Portugal); 1994 Billy Bingham; 1995 Gordon Strachan; 1996 Pele; 1997 Peter Beardsley; 1998 Steve Ogrizovic; 1999 Tony Ford.

MANAGER OF THE YEAR (1)

(Chosen by a 17-strong panel including managers, players, media, fan representatives, referees, the England coach and representatives of the Premier League and Football Association.)

1966 Jock Stein (Celtic); 1967 Jock Stein (Celtic); 1968 Matt Busby (Manchester Utd.); 1969 Don Revie (Leeds Utd.); 1970 Don Revie (Leeds Utd.); 1971 Bertie Mee (Arsenal); 1972 Don Revie (Leeds Utd.); 1973 Bill Shankly (Liverpool); 1974 Jack Charlton (Middlesbrough); 1975 Ron Saunders (Aston Villa); 1976 Bob Paisley (Liverpool); 1977 Bob Paisley (Liverpool); 1978 Brian Clough (Nott'm Forest); 1979 Bob Paisley (Liverpool); 1980 Bob Paisley (Liverpool); 1981 Ron Saunders (Aston Villa); 1982 Bob Paisley (Liverpool); 1983 Bob Paisley (Liverpool); 1984 Joe Fagan (Liverpool); 1985 Howard Kendall (Everton); 1986 Kenny Dalglish (Liverpool); 1987 Howard Kendall (Everton); 1988 Kenny Dalglish (Liverpool); 1989 George Graham (Arsenal); 1990 Kenny Dalglish (Liverpool); 1991 George Graham (Arsenal); 1992 Howard Wilkinson (Leeds Utd.); 1993 Alex Ferguson (Manchester Utd.); 1994 Alex Ferguson (Manchester Utd.); 1995 Kenny Dalglish (Blackburn Rov.); 1996 Alex Ferguson (Manchester Utd.); 1997 Alex Ferguson (Manchester Utd.); 1998 Arsene Wenger (Arsenal); 1999 Alex Ferguson (Manchester Utd.).

MANAGER OF THE YEAR (2)

(As chosen by the League Managers' Association and awarded to 'the manager who has made best use of the resources available to him'.)

1993 Dave Bassett (Sheff. Utd.); 1994 Joe Kinnear (Wimbledon); 1995 Frank Clark (Nott'm. Forest); 1996 Peter Reid (Sunderland); 1997 Danny Wilson (Barnsley); 1998 David Jones (Southampton); 1999 Alex Ferguson (Manchester Utd.).

SCOTTISH FOOTBALL WRITERS' ASSOCIATION

Player of the Year: 1965 Billy McNeill (Celtic); 1966 John Greig (Rangers); 1967 Ronnie Simpson (Celtic); 1968 Gordon Wallace (Raith); 1969 Bobby Murdoch (Celtic); 1970 Pat Stanton (Hibernian); 1971 Martin Buchan (Aberdeen); 1972 David Smith (Rangers); 1973 George Connelly (Celtic); 1974 World Cup Squad; 1975 Sandy Jardine (Rangers); 1976 John Greig (Rangers); 1977 Danny McGrain (Celtic); 1978 Derek Johnstone (Rangers); 1979 Andy Ritchie (Morton); 1980 Gordon Strachan (Aberdeen); 1981 Alan Rough (Partick Thistle); 1982 Paul Sturrock (Dundee Utd.); 1983 Charlie Nicholas (Celtic); 1984 Willie Miller (Aberdeen); 1985 Hamish McAlpine (Dundee Utd.); 1986 Sandy Jardine (Hearts); 1987 Brian McClair (Celtic); 1988 Paul McStay (Celtic); 1989 Richard Gough (Rangers); 1990 Alex McLeish (Aberdeen); 1991 Maurice Malpas (Dundee Utd.); 1992 Ally McCoist (Rangers); 1993 Andy Goram (Rangers); 1994 Mark Hateley (Rangers); 1995 Brian Laudrup (Rangers); 1996 Paul Gascoigne (Rangers); 1997 Brian Laudrup (Rangers); 1998 Craig Burley (Celtic); 1999 Henrik Larsson (Celtic).

SCOTTISH P.F.A. AWARDS

Player of the Year: 1978 Derek Johnstone (Rangers); 1979 Paul Hegarty (Dundee Utd.); 1980 Davie Provan (Celtic); 1981 Mark McGee (Aberdeen); 1982 Sandy Clarke (Airdrieonians); 1983 Charlie Nicholas (Celtic); 1984 Willie Miller (Aberdeen); 1985 Jim Duffy (Morton); 1986 Richard Gough (Dundee Utd.); 1987 Brian McClair (Celtic); 1988 Paul McStay (Celtic); 1989 Theo Snelders (Aberdeen); 1990 Jim Bett (Aberdeen); 1991 Paul Elliott (Celtic); 1992 Ally McCoist (Rangers); 1993 Andy Goram (Rangers); 1994 Mark

Hateley (Rangers); **1995** Brian Laudrup (Rangers); **1996** Paul Gascoigne (Rangers); **1997** Paolo Di Canio (Celtic) **1998** Jackie McNamara (Celtic); **1999** Henrik Larsson (Celtic).

Young Player of Year: 1978 Graeme Payne (Dundee Utd.); **1979** Ray Stewart (Dundee Utd.); **1980** John McDonald (Rangers); **1981** Charlie Nicholas (Celtic); **1982** Frank McAvennie (St. Mirren); **1983** Paul McStay (Celtic); **1984** John Robertson (Hearts); **1985** Craig Levein (Hearts); **1986** Craig Levein (Hearts); **1987** Robert Fleck (Rangers); **1988** John Collins (Hibernian); **1989** Billy McKinlay (Dundee Utd.); **1990** Scott Crabbe (Hearts); **1991** Eoin Jess (Aberdeen); **1992** Phil O'Donnell (Motherwell); **1993** Eoin Jess (Aberdeen); **1994** Phil O'Donnell (Motherwell); **1995** Charlie Miller (Rangers); **1996** Jackie McNamara (Celtic); **1997** Robbie Winters (Dundee Utd.); **1998** Gary Naysmith (Hearts); **1999** Barry Ferguson (Rangers).

SCOTTISH MANAGER OF THE YEAR

1987 Jim McLean (Dundee Utd.); **1988** Billy McNeill (Celtic); **1989** Graeme Souness (Rangers); **1990** Andy Roxburgh (Scotland); **1991** Alex Totten (St. Johnstone); **1992** Walter Smith (Rangers); **1993** Walter Smith (Rangers); **1994** Walter Smith (Rangers); **1995** Jimmy Nicholl (Raith); **1996** Walter Smith (Rangers); **1997** Walter Smith (Rangers); **1998** Wim Jansen (Celtic); **1999** Dick Advocaat (Rangers).

EUROPEAN FOOTBALLER OF THE YEAR

(Poll conducted by *France Football*) 1956 Stanley Matthews (Blackpool); **1957** Alfredo di Stefano (Real Madrid); **1958** Raymond Kopa (Real Madrid); **1959** Alfredo di Stefano (Real Madrid); **1960** Luis Suarez (Barcelona); **1961** Omar Sivori (Juventus); **1962** Josef Masopust (Dukla Prague); **1963** Lev Yashin (Moscow Dynamo); **1964** Denis Law (Manchester Utd.); **1965** Eusebio (Benfica); **1966** Bobby Charlton (Manchester Utd.); **1967** Florian Albert (Ferencvaros); **1968** George Best (Manchester Utd.); **1969** Gianni Rivera (AC Milan); **1970** Gerd Muller (Bayern Munich); **1971** Johan Cruyff (Ajax); **1972** Franz Beckenbauer (Bayern Munich); **1973** Johan Cruyff (Barcelona); **1974** Johan Cruyff (Barcelona); **1975** Oleg Blokhin (Dynamo Kiev); **1976** Franz Beckenbauer (Bayern Munich); **1977** Allan Simonsen (Borussia Moenchengladbach); **1978** Kevin Keegan (SV Hamburg); **1979** Kevin Keegan (SV Hamburg); **1980** Karl-Heinz Rummenigge (Bayern Munich); **1981** Karl-Heinz Rummenigge (Bayern Munich); **1982** Paolo Rossi (Juventus); **1983** Michel Platini (Juventus); **1984** Michel Platini (Juventus); **1985** Michel Platini (Juventus); **1986** Igor Belanov (Dynamo Kiev); **1987** Ruud Gullit (AC Milan); **1988** Marco Van Basten (AC Milan); **1989** Marco Van Basten (AC Milan); **1990** Lothar Matthaus (Inter Milan); **1991** Jean-Pierre Papin (Marseille); **1992** Marco Van Basten (AC Milan); **1993** Roberto Baggio (Juventus); **1994** Hristo Stoichkov (Barcelona); **1995** George Weah (AC Milan); **1996** Matthias Sammer (Borussia Dortmund); **1997** Ronaldo (Inter Milan); **1998** Zinedine Zidane (Juventus).

CARLING AWARDS

MANAGER/PLAYER OF THE MONTH 1998-99

Month	Manager	Player
August	Alan Curbishley (Charlton Athletic)	Michael Owen (Liverpool)
September	John Gregory (Aston Villa)	Alan Shearer (Newcastle Utd.)
October	Martin O'Neill (Leicester City)	Roy Keane (Manchester Utd.)
November	Harry Redknapp (West Ham Utd.)	Dion Dublin (Aston Villa)
December	Brian Kidd (Blackburn Rov.)	David Ginola (Tottenham)
January	Alex Ferguson (Manchester Utd.)	Dwight Yorke (Manchester Utd.)
February	Alan Curbishley (Charlton Athletic)	Nicolas Anelka (Arsenal)
March	David O'Leary (Leeds Utd.)	Ray Parlour (Arsenal)
April	Alex Ferguson (Manchester Utd.)	Kevin Campbell (Everton)

LEAGUE CLUB MANAGERS

Figure in brackets = number of managerial changes at club since war.
Date present manager took over shown on right.
Dario Gradi, appointed by Crewe Alexandra in June 1983, currently has the longest service with one club.

F.A. CARLING PREMIERSHIP

Arsenal (11)	Arsene Wenger	October 1996
Aston Villa (16)	John Gregory	February 1998
Bradford City (23)	Paul Jewell	January 1998
Chelsea (17)	Gianluca Vialli	February 1998
Coventry City (21)	Gordon Strachan	November 1996
Derby Co. (14)	Jim Smith	June 1995
Everton (15)	Walter Smith	July 1998
Leeds Utd. (17)	David O'Leary	October 1998
Leicester City (15)	Martin O'Neill	December 1995
Liverpool (9)	Gerard Houllier†	July 1998
Manchester Utd. (8)	Sir Alex Ferguson	November 1986
Middlesbrough (15)	Bryan Robson	May 1994
Newcastle Utd. (16)	Ruud Gullit	August 1998
Sheffield Wed. (18)	Danny Wilson	July 1998
Southampton (11)	David Jones	June 1997
Sunderland (17)	Peter Reid	March 1995
Tottenham (15)	George Graham	October 1998
Watford (21)	Graham Taylor	May 1997
West Ham Utd. (7)	Harry Redknapp	August 1994
Wimbledon (8)	Egil Olsen	June 1999

(Number of Wimbledon changes is since club elected to Football League in 1977;
†Joint-manager until Roy Evans resigned in November 1998).

NATIONWIDE LEAGUE – FIRST DIVISION

Barnsley (12)	Dave Bassett	May 1998
Birmingham City (20)	Trevor Francis	May 1996
Blackburn Rov. (20)	Brian Kidd	December 1998
Bolton Wand. (16)	Colin Todd	January 1996
Charlton Athletic (12)	Alan Curbishley	July 1991
Crewe Alexandra (17)	Dario Gradi	June 1983
Crystal Palace (26)	Steve Coppell	January 1999
Fulham (21)	Paul Bracewell	May 1999
Grimsby Town (23)	Alan Buckley	May 1997
Huddersfield Town (18)	Steve Bruce	May 1999
Ipswich Town (11)	George Burley	December 1994
Manchester City (23)	Joe Royle	February 1998
Norwich City (19)	Bruce Rioch	June 1998
Nott'm. Forest (11)	David Platt	July 1999
Portsmouth (17)	Alan Ball	January 1998
Port Vale (17)	Brian Horton	January 1999
Q.P.R. (20)	Gerry Francis	October 1999
Sheffield Utd. (28)	Adrian Heath	June 1999
Stockport Co. (28)	Andy Kilner	June 1999
Swindon Town (16)	Jimmy Quinn	October 1998
Tranmere Rov. (13)	John Aldridge	April 1996
Walsall (26)	Ray Graydon	May 1998
W.B.A. (23)	Denis Smith	December 1997
Wolves (17)	Colin Lee	November 1998

SECOND DIVISION

Blackpool (20)	Nigel Worthington	July 1997
Bournemouth (17)	Mel Machin	September 1994
Brentford (21)	Ron Noades (chairman-manager)	July 1998
Bristol City (17)	Tony Pulis	July 1999
Bristol Rov. (16)	Ian Holloway	May 1996
Burnley (19)	Stan Ternent	June 1998
Bury (19)	Neil Warnock	June 1998
Cambridge Utd. (11)	Roy McFarland	November 1996
Cardiff City (21)	Frank Burrows	February 1998
Chesterfield (13)	John Duncan	February 1993
Colchester Utd. (18)	Mick Wadsworth	January 1999
Gillingham (16)	Peter Taylor	July 1999
Luton Town (15)	Lennie Lawrence	March 1993
Millwall (20)*	Keith Stevens	May 1998
	Alan McLeary	May 1999
Notts County (22)	Sam Allardyce	January 1997
Oldham Athletic (17)	Andy Ritchie	May 1998
Oxford Utd. (13)	Malcolm Shotton	January 1998
Preston N.E. (20)	David Moyes	January 1998
Reading (14)	Tommy Burns	March 1998
Scunthorpe Utd. (21)	Brian Laws	February 1997
Stoke City (17)		
Wigan Athletic (13)	John Benson	June 1999
Wrexham (16)	Brian Flynn	November 1989
Wycombe Wand. (4)	Lawrence Sanchez	February 1999

(Number of changes shown are since elected to Football League: Oxford Utd. 1962; Cambridge Utd. 1970; Wigan Athletic 1978; Wycombe Wand. 1993. *Joint managers).

THIRD DIVISION

Barnet (6)	John Still	June 1997
Brighton & H.A. (22)	Micky Adams	April 1999
Carlisle Utd. (25)		
Cheltenham Town (–)	Steve Cotterill	January 1997
Chester City (16)	Kevin Ratcliffe	April 1995
Darlington (26)	David Hodgson	November 1996
Exeter City (21)	Peter Fox	June 1995
Halifax Town (2)	Mark Lillis	June 1999
Hartlepool Utd. (25)	Chris Turner	February 1999
Hull City (18)	Warren Joyce	November 1998
Leyton Orient (18)	Tommy Taylor	November 1994
Lincoln City (20)	John Reames (chairman-manger)	November 1998
Macclesfield Town (–)	Sammy McIlroy	June 1993
Mansfield Town (20)	Billy Dearden	June 1999
Northampton Town (20)	Ian Atkins	January 1995
Peterborough Utd. (20)	Barry Fry	May 1996
Plymouth Argyle (24)	Kevin Hodges	June 1998
Rochdale (24)	Steve Parkin	June 1999
Rotherham Utd. (18)	Ronnie Moore	May 1997
Shrewsbury Town (15)	Jake King	May 1997
Southend Utd. (22)	Alan Little	April 1999
Swansea City (23)	John Hollins	July 1998
Torquay Utd. (26)	Wes Saunders	July 1998
York City (17)	Neil Thompson	March 1999

(Number of changes shown are since elected to Football League: Peterborough Utd. 1960; Barnet 1991; Macclesfield Town 1997; since Halifax Town returned to League in 1998).

EXPANDED CHAMPIONS' LEAGUE MEANS MORE LIVE GAMES

Television's stranglehold over the scheduling of matches was due to intensify in 1999/2000.

UEFA's decision to expand the group stages of the Champions' League to 32 teams means the competition will now be stretched over Tuesday and Wednesday evenings.

UEFA have decreed that England's automatic qualifiers – Arsenal and Manchester Utd. – will not play on the same night, allowing both ITV (on Wednesdays) and newcomers ONdigital (on Tuesdays) to each show a plum tie involving one of the English totems in the same week.

The two networks agreed a four year deal, estimated to be worth a total of £250million, with UEFA in February 1999.

BSkyB continue to dominate the live coverage of domestic football in the UK (they will offer more than 250 live matches in 1999-2000), but this season will also show the home matches of all three English clubs in the revamped UEFA Cup – Tottenham, Leeds Utd. and Newcastle Utd.

Last season saw BSkyB's first foray into pay-per-view football coverage, when they charged viewers £7.95 to watch Sunderland's 0-0 draw at Oxford Utd.

Further experiments are planned for 1999-2000, and ONdigital are expected to show Champions' League games on a pay-per-view basis from the start of the 2000-2001 season. The BBC's live football output is dwarfed in terms of airtime by BSkyB's, but they do have the rights to the UEFA Cup Final, and will share coverage of Euro 2000 with ITV.

In 1998-99 Arsenal and Manchester Utd. became the first clubs to make an eight-figure sum from Premiership coverage in one season. Reversing the top two positions in the Premiership standings, Arsenal finished above United in the earnings league. They were shown in Premiership action 12 times by BSkyB; once more than their closest rivals. Coventry City and Southampton made fewest appearances – three each.

Premiership TV earnings for 1998-99 were (1997-98 figures in brackets):

Arsenal	£10,924,957.72	(£9,714,004)
Manchester Utd.	£10,846,205.72	(£9,523,451)
Chelsea	£9,997,012.72	(£8,328,493)
Leeds Utd.	£9,096,176.72	(£7,520,564)
Aston Villa	£8,916,893.72	(£6,718,453)
Liverpool	£8,759,479.72	(£8,771,628)
West Ham Utd.	£7,885,662.72	(£6,471,794)
Middlesbrough	£7,674,120.72	(–)
Tottenham	£7,359,292.72	(£5,833,430)
Derby Co.	£7,169,439.72	(£6,393,453)
Newcastle Utd.	£6,908,919.72	(£6,108,247)
Leicester City	£6,800,393.72	(£5,950,318)
Sheffield Wed.	£6,458,456.72	(£4,666,630)
Everton	£6,116,519.72	(£5,486,300)
Wimbledon	£6,010,748.72	(£5,165,871)
Coventry City	£5,885,830.72	(£6,012,347)
Blackburn Rov.	£5,828,890.72	(£7,245,747)
Charlton Athletic	£5,459,754.72	(–)
Southampton	£5,326,784.72	(£5,653,371)
Nott'm Forest	£4,982,272.72	(–)

TELEVISION COVERAGE IN 1999/2000

Premiership: BSkyB show 60 live games per season; BBC show Saturday night highlights package (Match of the Day).
Nationwide League: BSkyB show 65 live games, including play-offs.
F.A. Cup: BSkyB and ITV share rights to live games and both show the final; BBC show highlights.
Worthington Cup: BSkyB screen majority of live games, including the final; ITV show one leg of one semi-final.
Scotland: BSkyB show 30 matches a year, from the Scottish Premier League, the Scottish Cup and Scotland home internationals.
UEFA Champions' League: ITV will show live games involving English teams played on Wednesdays; ONdigital will show live games involving English teams played on Tuesdays; ITV show the final.
UEFA Cup: BSkyB will cover Newcastle Utd., Tottenham and Leeds Utd. home games live; all channels can bid for away games; BBC will show the final.
European Super Cup: BBC will show Manchester Utd. v Lazio on August 27.
England: BSkyB show home games live; all channels can bid for individual away games. Channel 5 will show England's Euro 2000 qualifier in Poland on September 9 1999.
Euro 2000: BBC and ITV will share live games from European Championships in Belgium and Holland; both will show the final.

LIVE ON SKY IN 1999-2000

AUGUST 1999: Sun 1: Arsenal v Manchester Utd. (Charity Shield), Aberdeen v Celtic. **Sun 8:** Everton v Manchester Utd., Manchester City v Wolves, Dundee v Hibernian. **Mon 9:** Tottenham v Newcastle Utd. **Tue 10:** Derby Co. v Arsenal. **Fri 13:** Huddersfield Town v Blackburn Rov. **Sun 15:** Southampton v Newcastle Utd., Swindon Town v Ipswich Town, Rangers v Motherwell. **Mon 16:** Aston Villa v West Ham Utd. **Fri 20:** W.B.A. v Nott'm. Forest. **Sun 22:** Arsenal v Manchester Utd., Stoke City v Millwall, Hearts v Aberdeen. **Mon 23:** Leeds Utd. v Liverpool. **Fri 27:** Stockport Co. v Birmingham City. **Sun 29:** Sunderland v Coventry City. **Mon 30:** Leicester City v Watford, Blackburn Rov. v Bolton Wand.
SEPTEMBER: Fri 3: Port Vale v Grimsby Town. **Sat 4:** England v Luxembourg (European Championship). **Sun 5:** Bolton Wand. v Birmingham City. **Fri 10:** Barnsley v Stockport Co. **Sat 11:** Liverpool v Manchester Utd. **Sun 12:** Bradford City v Tottenham, Cheltenham v Shrewsbury Town, Kilmarnock v Celtic. **Sun 19:** Leeds Utd. v Middlesbrough, Nott'm. Forest v Wolves. **Mon 20:** Motherwell v Hearts. **Sun 26:** Wimbledon v Tottenham, Ipswich Town v Manchester City. **Mon 27:** Liverpool v Everton.
OCTOBER: Fri 1: Nott'm. Forest v Barnsley. **Sun 3:** Chelsea v Manchester Utd., Crewe Alexandra v Tranmere Rov. **Mon 4:** Southampton v Derby Co. **Tue 5:** Scotland v Bosnia-Herzegovina (European Championship). **Fri 8:** Walsall v Birmingham City. **Sat 9:** Scotland v Lithuania (European Championship). **Sun 10:** England v Belgium, Burnley v Scunthorpe Utd. **Sun 17:** Middlesbrough v West Ham Utd., Bristol City v Bristol Rov., Dundee v Dundee Utd. **Mon 18:** Sunderland v Aston Villa. **Tue 19:** Birmingham City v Manchester City. **Sun 24:** Watford v Middlesbrough, Norwich City v Bolton Wand., St Johnstone v Celtic. **Mon 25:** Newcastle Utd. v Derby Co. **Sun 31:** Coventry City v Watford, Hibernian v Dundee Utd.
NOVEMBER: Mon 1: Liverpool v Bradford City. **Fri 5:** Port Vale v Crewe Alexandra. **Sun 7:** Wimbledon v Leeds Utd., Reading v Oxford Utd., Rangers v Celtic. **Mon 8:** Newcastle Utd. v Everton. **Fri 12:** Gillingham v AFC Bournemouth. **Sun 14:** Nott'm. Forest v Huddersfield Town. **Sun 21:** West Ham Utd. v Sheffield Wed. **Mon 22:** Coventry City v Aston Villa. **Fri 26:** Walsall v Fulham. **Sun 28:** Chelsea v Bradford City, Grimsby Town v Norwich City.
DECEMBER: Fri 3: Wolves v Manchester City. **Sat 4:** Leicester City v Arsenal. **Sun 5:** Tottenham v West Ham Utd., Nott'm. Forest v Ipswich Town. **Mon 6:** Liverpool v Sheffield Wed. **Fri 17:** Wolves v Birmingham City. **Sun 19:** Chelsea v Leeds Utd.,

Sheffield Utd. v Blackburn Rov. **Sun 26**: Coventry City v Arsenal, W.B.A. v Manchester City. **Mon 27**: Celtic v Rangers. **Tue 28**: Sunderland v Manchester Utd., Huddersfield Town v Charlton Athletic. **Wed 29**: Chelsea v Sheffield Wed.
MARCH 2000: Sun 26: Rangers v Celtic.

QUOTE – UNQUOTE

'The way the game is being played just now, especially in England, you need time to recover during the summer' – Arsenal and Holland forward **Dennis Bergkamp**.

'There are certain players who will be more suited to international football than club level and perhaps Scholes is one of those' – former England coach **Glenn Hoddle** on Manchester Utd.'s Paul Scholes.

'Thirty two teams were not too many for the World Cup Finals. We might not have qualified otherwise' – Scotland coach **Craig Brown**.

'I want to prove myself a genuine candidate for the next World Cup' – Blackburn Rov. striker **Kevin Davies**

'Mentally, Paul has a few problems' – **Glenn Hoddle** on Paul Gascoigne.

'Congratulations Glenn Hoddle for making the biggest error of judgement since the captain of the Titanic' – **Letter** to national newspaper on the World Cup axing of Gascoigne.

'Our success can be measured by the teams who want to play us in friendlies. It used to be Purfleet, now it's the likes of the Italian national team' – West Ham Utd. manager **Harry Redknapp**.

'It's hard to say what's going through your mind when you hit the ground and you're sliding on the runway. The plane was like a roller coaster' – Leeds Utd. manager **David O'Leary** on the team's crash landing at Stansted Airport.

'I think his movie career is probably over' – Arsenal manager **Arsene Wenger** after defender Martin Keown suffered a facial injury requiring stitches.

'It's like a gift from God' – **Sasa Curcic** comments on his transfer from Aston Villa to Premiership bottom club Crystal Palace.

'Graham is my right arm. He is beautiful for me' – Chelsea boss **Gianluca Vialli** on assistant Graham Rix.

'Behind the scenes at Maine Road there were some insincere people who tried to blacken my name during my tenancy as chairman. I could have got rid of some of them but when they had gone they would have been an even bigger menace' – **Francis Lee** after quitting as Manchester City chairman.

'People want to find a new Pele. They couldn't. You don't find another Beethoven, you have only one Michaelangelo. In football you have only one Pele' – **Pele**.

'John Gregory would fine you for not wearing flip-flops in the showers' – **Dave Carroll** of Wycombe Wanderers on his former manager.

'Referees have a very hard job, and I don't want you making it any harder' – **Sir Tom Finney** recalling the words of advice his father gave him when he signed professional for Preston North End.

'They'll be back before the postcards' – Former Scotland manager **Tommy Docherty** on Scottish prospects in France '98.

'I might frighten him when I take my teeth out' – Scotland goalkeeper **Jim Leighton** before facing Brazil's Ronaldo in the opening game of France '98.

NEW HOMES OF SOCCER

Winning last season's final match had an effect far beyond Premiership survival for **Southampton**. It meant the club's £30m plan, approved in April by the city council, for a 32,000 capacity, all-seater stadium to be built on the site of a disused gasworks could go ahead.

It had been essential for the club to avoid relegation for the long-awaited move from the cramped Dell to proceed as scheduled. The new ground will be ready for the start of season 2001-2.

Coventry City have received approval to build a 45,000 capacity stadium, costing at least £100m. on a site near the M6 at Foleshill. Plans include a retractable roof over the pitch, which itself will retract when the arena is required for other sporting events and pop concerts.

The complex will have two superstores and its own railway station. Coventry City's first match at their new home is scheduled for August 2001 and Highfield Road, where they have played since 1899, will then be sold.

In **Wigan Athletic's** final season at Springfield Park, their home for 67 years, they were Wembley winners of the Auto Windscreens Shield. For the start of 1999-2000 they have relocated to the new 25,000 all-seat JJB Stadium, at Robin Park, which they will share with the Rugby League club. The old ground will become a housing estate.

Manchester Utd. received permission (November 1998) to turn Old Trafford into Britain's biggest modern-age club stadium. The East stand is being extended by 12,400 seats, raising the overall capacity to 67,400. The cost is estimated at £30m., and the extension should be completed for the start of season 2001-2.

Brighton & H.A. supporters will welcome the club's return to Sussex this season after renting Gillingham's Prestfield Stadium, 75 miles away, for two years since the Goldstone Ground was sold for property development.

At a cost of some £2m., the municipal athletics stadium at Withdean is being converted into a temporary home (capacity 6,000) for the club, pending construction of a community-based stadium at Falmer, next to Sussex University.

Moving back to Sussex will restore Albion's identity with the town, and should begin to provide some desperately-needed stability under the consortium led by Brighton & H.A. fan Dick Knight.

Thriving **Sunderland** have plans to increase their capacity from 42,000 to 60,000 following promotion back to the Premiership as First Division champions with a new English League record of 105 points.

Their Stadium of Light, opened in 1997, was last season voted 'best new stadium' in the country.

Huddersfield Town's state-of-the-art Alfred McAlpine Stadium, unveiled in 1994, was completed on all four sides last season with the opening of the 4,500-seat Panasonic Stand in the previously vacant area behind one goal.

The additional complex gives a ground capacity of 24,000, all seated. It cost £11m. (of which £5.7m. was grant-aided by the National Lottery), and contains executive boxes, conference rooms, health and fitness centre, dance studio, all-day restaurant, cash dispenser and a 6-lane, 25-metre swimming pool.

Debts of £11m., amid collapsed consortiums, meant that work remained half-completed for two seasons from 1997 on **Oxford Utd.'s** proposed new ground at Minchery Farm.

Prospects of eventual completion improved last April when hotelier Firoz Kassam bought a controlling interest in the club and, as part of the take-over, paid off £1m. that was owed to the local council.

But for at least one more season Oxford Utd. must continue the fight for survival at their dilapidated Manor Ground.

Second Division **Reading** became the latest Football League club to move to new headquarters with the opening, last August, of the 25,000 all-seat stadium that is named after chairman John Madejski.

The development cost £37m. and the new stadium also hosted Rugby Union football through the Richmond club transferring to Reading.

Wrexham announced last December a major overhaul that will elevate their Racecourse Ground to an 'ultra modern football venue'. Plans revealed the building of a 3,000-seat stand on the disused Mold Road side.

The redeveloped stadium, scheduled to be ready for the start of this season, will have 11,000 seats and standing accommodation for 4,000.

The club hope that modernisation will lead to the Welsh F.A. bringing some International fixtures back to the oldest ground in Wales.

Swansea City are to move to a new 25,000-seat stadium at the start of season 2000-1. They will leave Vetch Field for a £75m. sports complex in the city.

Shrewsbury Town are to build a new £8.5m. stadium on the outskirts of the town, for the start of season 2000-1. Capacity will be 10,000, all-seated. It will be called New Meadow, and Shrewsbury Town's existing home, Gay Meadow, will become a supermarket and car park.

Newcastle Utd. plan to increase the capacity at St. James' Park from 36,000 to 52,000 by the start season 2000-1.

CHANGES FOR THE NEW MILLENNIUM

The **Football (Nationwide) League** reverts from goals scored to goal difference to separate clubs level on points. Had a similar system applied last season Port Vale, not Bury, would have been relegated from Div. 1.

The Premier League lead is also to be followed with the introduction of **players' names and squad numbers on shirts**.

The Football League also falls in line with the Premiership, the F.A. and UEFA on **substitutes**, increasing the number of players on the bench to five, of whom three may be used.

The Football League will experiment in this season's **Auto Windscreens Shield** (for 2nd/3rd Div. clubs) with the 10-yard rule that was tried in Jersey last season. Referees will advance a free-kick by 10 yards if a player shows dissent, delays the kick or fails to retreat 10 yards.

FIFA will assess the experiment with a view to possible world-wide introduction of the 10-yard rule.

Football League **referees** revert to traditional **black kit** this season, with a change to green to avoid clashing with club colours.

UEFA have decided that, from this season, a player will be suspended after **three yellow cards** (previously two) in the Champions League and UEFA Cup.

The first six rounds of the **F.A. Cup** are being advanced by a month, to create space for the extra games that will be played in the extended European competitions. The 1st Round proper will be on October 30 and the 3rd Round, traditionally played early in January, will take place on December 11.

The **European Cup-Winners Cup** has been scrapped as a separate tournament after 38 years. Cup winners will qualify for an expanded **UEFA Cup** with some matches scheduled for Tuesday afternoons as well as Thursday nights.

Matches in the ever-swelling **Champions League** will be played on Tuesdays and Wednesdays.

Premiership referees receive a 50% pay increase. Their fees go up from £400 to £600 per game. Referees in the **Nationwide League** continue to receive £195 per match. To improve communication and control, referees and their assistants will be connected by microphones and ear-pieces at all Premiership matches.

Football will celebrate the **Millennium** with a week's break, with the Premiership, Nationwide League and Scotland scheduling no fixtures for January 1, 2000.

On June 26, **Geoff Thompson** J.P. 53, was elected chairman of the Football Association at a meeting in Chester. **Ian Stott** of Oldham Athletic was elected vice-chairman.

ATTENDANCES 1998-99

OFFICIAL FIGURES

League attendances last season (Premiership and Nationwide League) totalled 25,435,981 and were the **highest for 22 years** – since 26,182,800 in 1976-77.

Premier League crowds, at an aggregate of 11,620,765 were up by 528,992 (an increase of 4.8%) and Football League gates, totalling 13,815,216, showed a small increase of 227,270, the 13th consecutive season they have risen.

The average attendance in the Premiership climbed above 30,000 for the first time since its inception; and for the first time in the top-flight since 1979-80.

Attendances in the First Division fell by nearly 10% but this was compensated for by the 18.7% and 19.0% increases in the Second and Third Divisions respectively.

The **10 best-supported clubs in the Premier League** were: 1 Manchester Utd., average 55,188; 2 Liverpool 43,321; 3 Arsenal 38,024; 4 Aston Villa 36,322; 5 Newcastle Utd. 36,690; 6 Everton 36,202; 7 Leeds Utd. 35,773; 8 Chelsea 34,777; 9 Middlesbrough 34,386; 10 Tottenham 34,149. The first three finished in the same order as the previous two years.

In **Div. 1**, the top average attendance for the second year running was **Sunderland's** 38,745; in **Div. 2 Manchester City's** 28,261; and in **Div. 3 Cardiff City's** 7,131.

LEAGUE CROWDS SINCE 1980

	Total	Div. One	Div. Two	Div. Three	Div. Four
1979-80	24,623,975	12,163,002	6,112,025	3,999,328	2,349,620
1980-81	21,907,569	11,392,894	5,175,442	3,637,854	1,701,379
1981-82	20,006,961	10,420,793	4,750,463	2,836,915	1,998,790
1982-83	18,766,158	9,295,613	4,974,937	2,943,568	1,552,040
1983-84	18,358,631	8,711,448	5,359,757	2,729,942	1,557,484
1984-85	17,849,835	9,761,404	4,030,823	2,667,008	1,390,600
1985-86	16,498,868	9,037,854	3,555,343	2,495,991	1,409,680
1986-87	17,383,032	9,144,676	4,168,131	2,354,784	1,715,441
1987-88	17,968,887	8,094,571	5,350,754	2,751,275	1,772,287
1988-89	18,477,565	7,809,993	5,827,805	3,048,700	1,791,067
1989-90	19,466,826	7,887,658	6,884,439	2,803,551	1,891,178
1990-91	19,541,341	8,618,709	6,297,733	2,847,813	1,777,086
1991-92	20,487,273	9,989,160	5,809,787	2,993,352	1,694,974

New format	Total	Premier	Div. One	Div. Two	Div. Three
1992-93	20,657,327	9,759,809	5,874,017	3,483,073	1,540,428
1993-94	21,693,889	10,655,059	6,487,104	2,972,702	1,579,024
1994-95	21,856,223	11,213,371	6,044,293	3,037,752	1,560,807
1995-96	21,844,416	10,469,107	6,566,349	2,843,652	1,965,308
1996-97	22,791,527	10,804,762	6,804,606	3,332,451	1,849,708
1997-98	24,679,527	11,091,773	8,330,018	3,503,264	1,767,220
1998-99	25,435,981	11,620,765	7,543,369	4,169,697	2,102,150

Note: All-time record Football League attendance aggregate: 41,271,414 in season 1948-49 (88 clubs). The average was 22,333.

LOWEST CROWDS – BUT ON THE UP AGAIN

Wimbledon have recorded the lowest single-match attendances in all seven years of the Premiership, but the figure moved into five figures for the first time in 1998-99; 11,801 turned up for the game with Leicester City at Selhurst Park on March 6 compared to the 1997 low of 7,668 who saw Barnsley's visit. Back in 1992-93 just 3,039 people attended the clash with Everton. Wimbledon's average crowd rose again in 1998-99, by nearly 10%, from 16,675 to 18,207 – back in 1992-93 it was a lowly 8,405.

F.A. CARLING PREMIERSHIP
RESULTS 1998–99

	Arsenal	Aston Villa	Blackburn Rovers	Charlton Athletic	Chelsea	Coventry City	Derby Co.	Everton	Leeds Utd.	Leicester City
Arsenal	–	1-0	1-0	0-0	1-0	2-0	1-0	1-0	3-1	5-0
Aston Villa	3-2	–	1-3	3-4	0-3	1-4	1-0	3-0	1-2	1-1
Blackburn Rovers	1-2	2-1	–	1-0	3-4	1-2	0-0	1-2	1-0	1-0
Charlton Athletic	0-1	0-1	0-1	–	0-1	1-1	1-2	1-2	1-1	0-0
Chelsea	0-0	2-1	1-1	2-1	–	2-1	2-1	3-1	1-0	2-2
Coventry City	0-1	1-2	1-1	2-1	2-1	–	1-1	3-0	2-2	1-1
Derby Co.	0-0	2-1	1-0	0-2	2-2	0-0	–	2-1	2-2	2-0
Everton	0-2	0-0	0-0	4-1	0-0	2-0	0-0	–	0-0	0-0
Leeds Utd.	1-0	0-0	1-0	4-1	0-0	2-0	4-1	1-0	–	0-1
Leicester City	1-1	2-2	1-1	1-1	2-4	1-0	1-2	2-0	1-2	–
Liverpool	0-0	0-1	2-0	3-3	1-1	2-0	1-2	3-2	1-3	0-1
Manchester Utd.	1-1	2-1	3-2	4-1	1-1	2-0	1-0	3-1	3-2	2-2
Middlesbrough	1-6	0-0	2-1	2-0	0-0	2-0	1-1	2-2	0-0	0-0
Newcastle Utd.	1-1	2-1	1-1	0-0	0-1	4-1	2-1	1-3	0-3	1-0
Nott'm Forest	0-1	2-2	2-2	0-1	1-3	1-0	2-2	0-2	1-1	1-0
Sheffield Wed.	1-0	0-1	3-0	3-0	0-0	1-2	0-1	0-0	0-2	0-1
Southampton	0-0	1-4	3-3	3-1	0-2	2-1	0-1	2-0	3-0	2-1
Tottenham	1-3	1-0	2-1	2-2	2-2	0-0	1-1	4-1	3-3	0-2
West Ham Utd.	0-4	0-0	2-0	0-1	1-1	2-0	5-1	2-1	1-5	3-2
Wimbledon	1-0	0-0	1-1	2-1	1-2	2-1	2-1	1-2	1-1	0-1

Read across for home results, down for away

Liverpool	Manchester Utd.	Middlesbrough	Newcastle Utd.	Nott'm Forest	Sheffield Wed.	Southampton	Tottenham	West Ham Utd.	Wimbledon	
0-0	3-0	1-1	3-0	2-1	3-0	1-1	0-0	1-0	5-1	Arsenal
2-4	1-1	3-1	1-0	2-0	2-1	3-0	3-2	0-0	2-0	Aston Villa
1-3	0-0	0-0	0-0	1-2	1-4	0-2	1-1	3-0	3-1	Blackburn Rovers
1-0	0-1	1-1	2-2	0-0	0-1	5-0	1-4	4-2	2-0	Charlton Athletic
2-1	0-0	2-0	1-1	2-1	1-1	1-0	2-0	0-1	3-0	Chelsea
2-1	0-1	1-2	1-5	4-0	1-0	1-0	1-1	0-0	2-1	Coventry City
3-2	1-1	2-1	3-4	1-0	1-0	0-0	0-1	0-2	0-0	Derby Co.
0-0	1-4	5-0	1-0	0-1	1-2	1-0	0-1	6-0	1-1	Everton
0-0	1-1	2-0	0-1	3-1	2-1	3-0	2-0	4-0	2-2	Leeds Utd.
1-0	2-6	0-1	2-0	3-1	0-2	2-0	2-1	0-0	1-1	Leicester City
–	2-2	3-1	4-2	5-1	2-0	7-1	3-2	2-2	3-0	Liverpool
2-0	–	2-3	0-0	3-0	3-0	2-1	2-1	4-1	5-1	Manchester Utd.
1-3	0-1	–	2-2	1-1	4-0	3-0	0-0	1-0	3-1	Middlesbrough
1-4	1-2	1-1	–	2-0	1-1	4-0	1-1	0-3	3-1	Newcastle Utd.
2-2	1-8	1-2	1-2	–	2-0	1-1	0-1	0-0	0-1	Nott'm Forest
1-0	3-1	3-1	1-1	3-2	–	0-0	0-0	0-1	1-2	Sheffield Wed.
1-2	0-3	3-3	2-1	1-2	1-0	–	1-1	1-0	3-1	Southampton
2-1	2-2	0-3	2-0	2-0	0-3	3-0	–	1-2	0-0	Tottenham
2-1	0-0	4-0	2-0	2-1	0-4	1-0	2-1	–	3-4	West Ham Utd.
1-0	1-1	2-2	1-1	1-3	2-1	0-2	3-1	0-0	–	Wimbledon

NATIONWIDE LEAGUE
RESULTS 1998–99

FIRST DIVISION

	Barnsley	Birmingham City	Bolton Wand.	Bradford City	Bristol City	Bury	Crewe Alexandra	Crystal Palace	Grimsby Town	Huddersfield Town	Ipswich Town	Norwich City
Barnsley	–	0-0	2-2	0-1	2-0	1-1	2-2	4-0	0-0	7-1	0-1	1-3
Birmingham City	0-0	–	0-0	2-1	4-2	1-0	3-1	3-1	0-1	1-1	1-0	0-0
Bolton Wand.	3-3	3-1	–	0-0	1-0	4-0	1-3	3-0	2-0	3-0	1-0	2-0
Bradford City	2-1	2-1	2-2	–	5-0	3-0	4-1	2-1	3-0	2-3	0-0	4-1
Bristol City	1-1	1-2	2-1	2-3	–	1-1	5-2	1-1	4-1	1-2	0-1	1-0
Bury	0-0	2-4	2-1	0-2	0-1	–	1-0	0-0	1-0	1-0	0-3	0-2
Crewe Alexandra	3-1	0-0	4-4	2-1	1-0	3-1	–	0-1	0-0	1-2	0-3	3-2
Crystal Palace	1-0	1-1	2-2	1-0	2-1	4-2	1-1	–	3-1	2-2	3-2	5-1
Grimsby Town	1-2	0-3	0-1	2-0	2-1	0-0	1-1	2-0	–	1-0	0-0	0-1
Huddersfield Town	0-1	1-1	3-2	2-1	2-2	2-2	0-0	4-0	2-0	–	2-2	1-1
Ipswich Town	0-2	1-0	4-3	3-0	3-1	0-0	1-2	3-0	0-1	3-0	–	0-1
Norwich City	0-0	2-0	2-2	2-2	2-1	0-0	2-1	0-1	3-1	4-1	0-0	–
Oxford Utd.	1-0	1-7	0-0	0-1	0-0	0-1	1-1	1-3	0-0	2-2	3-3	2-4
Port Vale	1-0	0-2	0-2	1-1	3-2	1-0	1-0	1-0	0-1	2-0	0-3	1-0
Portsmouth	1-3	0-1	0-2	2-4	0-1	2-1	2-0	1-1	0-1	1-0	0-0	1-2
Q.P.R.	2-1	0-1	2-0	1-3	1-1	0-0	0-1	6-0	1-2	1-1	1-1	2-0
Sheffield Utd.	1-1	0-2	1-2	2-2	3-1	3-1	3-1	1-1	3-2	2-1	1-2	2-1
Stockport Co.	0-1	1-0	0-1	1-2	2-2	0-0	1-1	1-1	2-0	1-1	0-1	0-2
Sunderland	2-3	2-1	3-1	0-0	1-1	1-0	2-0	2-0	3-1	2-0	2-1	1-0
Swindon Town	1-3	0-1	3-3	1-4	3-2	1-1	1-2	2-0	2-0	3-0	0-6	1-1
Tranmere Rov.	3-0	0-1	1-1	0-1	1-1	4-0	3-0	3-1	1-2	2-3	0-2	1-3
Watford	0-0	1-0	2-0	1-0	1-0	0-0	4-2	2-1	1-0	1-1	1-0	1-1
W.B.A.	2-0	1-3	2-3	0-2	2-2	1-0	1-5	3-2	1-1	3-1	0-1	2-0
Wolves	1-1	3-1	1-1	2-3	3-0	1-0	3-0	0-0	2-0	2-2	1-0	2-2

Read across for home results, down for away

Oxford Utd.	Port Vale	Portsmouth	Q.P.R.	Sheffield Utd.	Stockport Co.	Sunderland	Swindon Town	Tranmere Rov.	Watford	W.B.A.	Wolves	
1-0	0-2	2-1	1-0	2-1	1-1	1-3	1-3	1-1	2-2	2-2	2-3	Barnsley
0-1	1-0	4-1	1-0	1-0	2-0	0-0	1-1	2-2	1-2	4-0	0-1	Birmingham City
1-1	3-1	3-1	2-1	2-2	1-2	0-3	2-1	2-2	1-2	2-1	1-1	Bolton Wand.
0-0	4-0	2-1	0-3	2-2	1-2	0-1	3-0	2-0	2-0	1-0	2-1	Bradford City
2-2	2-0	2-2	0-0	2-0	1-1	0-1	3-1	1-1	1-4	1-3	1-6	Bristol City
1-0	0-0	2-1	1-1	3-3	1-1	2-5	3-0	0-0	1-3	2-0	0-0	Bury
3-1	0-0	3-1	0-2	1-2	0-2	1-4	0-2	1-4	0-1	1-1	0-0	Crewe Alexandra
2-0	0-1	4-1	1-1	1-0	2-2	1-1	0-1	1-1	2-2	1-1	3-2	Crystal Palace
1-0	2-2	1-1	1-0	1-2	1-0	0-2	1-0	1-0	2-1	5-1	0-0	Grimsby Town
2-0	2-1	3-3	2-0	1-0	3-0	1-1	1-2	0-0	2-0	0-3	2-1	Huddersfield Town
2-1	1-0	3-0	3-1	4-1	1-0	0-2	1-0	1-0	3-2	2-0	2-0	Ipswich Town
1-3	3-4	0-0	4-2	1-1	0-2	2-2	2-1	2-2	1-1	1-1	0-0	Norwich City
–	2-1	3-0	4-1	0-2	5-0	0-0	2-0	1-2	0-0	3-0	0-2	Oxford Utd.
1-0	–	0-2	2-0	2-3	1-1	0-2	0-1	2-2	1-2	0-3	2-1	Port Vale
2-2	4-0	–	3-0	1-0	3-1	1-1	5-2	1-1	1-2	2-1	1-0	Portsmouth
1-0	3-2	1-1	–	1-2	2-0	2-2	4-0	0-0	1-2	2-1	0-1	Q.P.R.
1-2	3-0	2-1	2-0	–	1-1	0-4	2-1	2-2	3-0	3-0	1-1	Sheffield Utd.
2-0	4-2	2-0	0-0	1-0	–	0-1	2-1	0-0	1-1	2-2	1-2	Stockport Co.
7-0	2-0	2-0	1-0	0-0	1-0	–	2-0	5-0	4-1	3-0	2-1	Sunderland
4-1	1-1	3-3	3-1	2-2	2-3	1-1	–	2-3	1-4	2-2	1-0	Swindon Town
2-2	1-1	1-1	3-2	2-3	1-1	1-0	0-0	–	3-2	3-1	1-2	Tranmere Rov.
2-0	2-2	0-0	2-1	1-1	4-2	2-1	0-1	2-1	–	0-2	0-2	Watford
2-0	3-2	2-2	2-0	4-1	3-1	2-3	1-1	0-2	4-1	–	2-0	W.B.A.
1-1	3-1	2-0	1-2	2-1	2-2	1-1	1-0	2-0	0-0	1-1	–	Wolves

SECOND DIVISION

	Blackpool	Bournemouth	Bristol Rov.	Burnley	Chesterfield	Colchester Utd.	Fulham	Gillingham	Lincoln City	Luton Town	Macclesfield Town	Manchester City
Blackpool	–	0-0	1-2	0-2	1-1	2-1	2-3	2-2	0-1	1-0	2-1	0-0
Bournemouth	1-1	–	1-0	5-0	0-0	2-1	1-1	3-3	2-0	1-0	1-0	0-0
Bristol Rov.	0-2	1-0	–	3-4	0-0	1-1	2-3	0-1	3-0	1-0	0-0	2-2
Burnley	1-0	0-0	2-1	–	1-2	3-1	1-0	0-5	1-1	1-2	4-3	0-6
Chesterfield	1-2	3-1	0-0	1-0	–	3-1	1-0	1-0	3-0	3-1	2-0	1-1
Colchester Utd.	2-2	2-1	0-3	0-4	1-0	–	0-1	1-1	1-3	2-2	1-1	0-1
Fulham	4-0	0-0	1-0	4-0	2-1	2-0	–	3-0	1-0	1-3	1-0	3-0
Gillingham	1-0	2-1	0-0	2-1	3-1	1-1	1-0	–	4-0	1-0	2-2	0-2
Lincoln City	1-2	2-1	1-0	1-1	2-0	0-0	1-2	1-2	–	2-2	1-0	2-1
Luton Town	1-0	2-2	2-0	1-0	1-0	2-0	0-4	1-0	0-1	–	1-2	1-1
Macclesfield Town	0-1	2-2	3-4	2-1	2-0	2-0	0-1	1-0	0-0	2-2	–	0-1
Manchester City	3-0	2-1	0-0	2-2	1-1	2-1	3-0	0-0	4-0	2-0	2-0	–
Millwall	1-0	1-2	1-1	1-2	0-0	2-0	0-1	3-3	2-0	0-1	0-0	1-1
Northampton Town	0-0	2-1	3-1	2-2	1-0	3-3	1-1	0-1	0-0	1-0	0-2	2-2
Notts Co.	0-1	1-2	1-1	0-0	2-0	1-3	1-0	0-1	2-3	1-2	1-1	1-1
Oldham Athletic	3-0	2-3	2-1	1-1	2-0	1-0	1-1	1-4	2-0	1-1	1-2	0-3
Preston N.E.	1-2	0-1	2-2	4-1	2-0	2-0	1-1	1-1	5-0	1-1	2-2	1-1
Reading	1-1	3-3	0-6	1-1	1-2	1-1	1-1	0-0	2-1	3-0	1-0	1-3
Stoke City	1-3	2-0	1-4	1-4	0-0	3-3	0-1	0-0	2-0	3-1	2-0	0-1
Walsall	1-0	1-0	3-3	3-1	1-1	1-1	2-2	2-1	2-1	1-0	2-0	1-1
Wigan Athletic	3-0	2-1	1-0	0-0	3-1	1-1	2-0	4-1	3-1	1-3	2-0	1-1
Wrexham	1-1	0-1	1-0	1-1	0-0	2-4	0-2	2-1	2-1	1-1	2-1	0-1
Wycombe Wand.	2-2	0-2	1-1	2-0	1-0	2-2	1-1	0-2	4-1	0-1	3-0	1-0
York City	1-0	0-1	1-0	3-3	1-2	1-2	0-3	1-1	2-1	3-3	0-2	2-1

Read across for home results, down for away

Millwall	Northampton Town	Notts Co.	Oldham Athletic	Preston N.E.	Reading	Stoke City	Walsall	Wigan Athletic	Wrexham	Wycombe Wand.	York City	
2-3	2-1	1-0	3-0	0-0	2-0	0-1	0-2	1-1	1-1	0-0	1-2	Blackpool
3-0	1-1	2-0	2-0	3-1	0-1	4-0	0-1	1-0	0-0	2-0	2-1	Bournemouth
3-0	1-1	1-1	2-2	2-2	4-1	1-0	3-4	3-2	0-0	0-2	2-0	Bristol Rov.
2-1	0-2	1-1	1-0	0-1	1-1	0-2	0-0	1-1	2-1	1-1	0-1	Burnley
2-1	0-0	3-0	1-3	0-1	1-0	1-1	0-1	1-1	2-1	2-0	2-1	Chesterfield
0-0	1-0	2-1	2-2	1-0	1-1	0-1	1-0	2-1	1-3	2-1	2-1	Colchester Utd.
4-1	2-0	2-1	1-0	3-0	3-1	1-0	4-1	2-0	1-1	2-0	3-3	Fulham
1-1	2-3	4-0	2-1	1-1	2-1	4-0	1-0	2-0	4-0	3-0	3-1	Gillingham
2-0	1-0	0-1	1-3	3-4	2-2	1-2	0-1	1-0	1-0	0-1	1-2	Lincoln City
1-2	1-0	0-1	2-0	1-1	1-1	1-2	0-1	0-4	1-2	3-1	2-1	Luton Town
0-2	0-1	0-1	1-0	3-2	2-1	1-2	1-1	0-1	0-2	1-3	1-2	Macclesfield Town
3-0	0-0	2-1	1-2	0-1	0-1	2-1	3-1	1-0	0-0	1-2	4-0	Manchester City
–	2-1	1-3	1-1	2-2	1-1	2-0	1-2	3-1	3-0	2-1	3-1	Millwall
1-2	–	1-1	1-1	0-1	1-3	0-1	3-3	0-2	1-1	2-1	2-2	Northampton Town
3-1	3-1	–	0-1	2-3	1-1	1-0	2-1	0-1	1-1	1-0	4-2	Notts Co.
0-1	0-1	1-3	–	0-1	2-0	1-0	0-2	2-3	3-2	0-0	0-2	Oldham Athletic
0-1	3-0	1-1	2-1	–	4-0	3-4	1-0	2-2	3-1	2-1	3-0	Preston N.E.
2-0	0-1	1-0	1-1	2-1	–	2-1	0-1	0-1	4-0	2-1	1-0	Reading
1-0	3-1	2-3	2-0	0-1	0-4	–	2-0	2-1	1-3	2-2	2-0	Stoke City
3-0	0-0	3-2	3-1	1-0	0-2	1-0	–	1-2	1-0	2-2	2-3	Walsall
0-1	1-0	3-0	2-0	2-2	4-1	2-3	2-0	–	1-1	5-0	1-1	Wigan Athletic
0-0	1-0	1-0	1-2	0-5	3-0	0-1	2-1	0-2	–	0-2	1-1	Wrexham
0-1	1-2	1-1	3-0	0-1	2-3	0-1	1-2	2-1	3-0	–	1-2	Wycombe Wand.
2-1	1-1	1-1	0-1	0-1	1-1	2-2	1-2	1-3	1-1	3-0	–	York City

THIRD DIVISION

	Barnet	Brentford	Brighton & H.A.	Cambridge Utd.	Cardiff City	Carlisle Utd.	Chester City	Darlington	Exeter City	Halifax Town	Hartlepool Utd.	Hull City
Barnet	–	0-3	0-1	3-0	1-0	1-0	0-0	3-0	0-1	2-2	0-2	4-1
Brentford	3-1	–	2-0	1-0	1-0	1-1	2-1	3-0	3-0	1-1	3-1	0-2
Brighton & H.A.	0-1	3-1	–	1-3	0-2	1-3	2-2	0-4	0-1	0-1	3-2	0-0
Cambridge Utd.	3-2	0-1	2-3	–	0-0	1-0	2-1	2-1	1-1	4-0	1-2	2-0
Cardiff City	1-0	4-1	2-0	0-1	–	2-1	0-0	3-0	1-0	1-1	4-1	1-1
Carlisle Utd.	2-1	0-1	1-0	1-1	0-1	–	1-1	3-3	1-3	0-1	2-1	0-0
Chester City	3-0	1-3	1-1	0-3	2-2	2-1	–	1-0	0-0	2-2	1-1	2-2
Darlington	0-2	2-2	1-2	0-0	3-0	1-1	1-2	–	4-0	2-2	2-0	0-1
Exeter City	1-0	0-1	1-0	0-3	0-2	2-0	0-1	0-0	–	2-1	2-1	3-0
Halifax Town	1-1	1-0	1-0	3-3	1-2	1-0	3-2	0-0	1-1	–	2-1	0-1
Hartlepool Utd.	2-2	0-1	0-0	2-2	1-1	0-0	2-0	2-3	4-3	2-0	–	1-0
Hull City	1-1	2-3	0-2	0-3	1-2	1-0	1-2	1-2	2-1	1-2	4-0	–
Leyton Orient	2-2	2-1	1-0	2-0	1-1	2-1	2-2	3-2	2-0	1-0	1-1	1-2
Mansfield Town	5-0	3-1	2-0	1-3	3-0	1-1	3-0	0-1	0-1	0-1	2-0	2-0
Peterborough Utd.	5-2	2-4	1-2	2-1	2-1	0-1	3-0	0-1	4-1	0-2	1-1	1-1
Plymouth Argyle	2-0	3-0	1-2	2-2	1-1	2-0	2-0	1-2	1-0	1-0	0-0	0-0
Rochdale	0-0	2-0	2-1	0-2	1-1	1-1	3-1	0-0	1-1	0-0	0-1	3-0
Rotherham Utd.	1-1	2-4	2-1	2-0	1-0	3-1	2-4	3-1	0-0	3-1	3-0	3-1
Scarborough	0-0	3-1	1-2	1-5	1-2	3-0	2-4	0-2	1-0	1-0	1-2	1-2
Scunthorpe Utd.	3-1	0-0	3-1	3-2	0-2	3-1	2-1	0-1	2-0	0-4	1-0	3-2
Shrewsbury Town	0-2	2-0	1-3	1-1	0-3	1-1	2-0	3-0	1-1	2-2	0-1	3-2
Southend Utd.	2-3	1-4	3-0	0-1	0-1	0-1	0-1	2-1	0-0	0-0	1-1	0-1
Swansea City	2-1	2-1	2-2	2-0	2-1	1-1	1-1	2-0	2-0	1-2	1-0	2-0
Torquay Utd.	1-1	3-1	1-1	0-1	0-0	2-2	0-3	2-2	1-0	4-0	3-0	2-0

Read across for home results, down for away

	Leyton Orient	Mansfield Town	Peterborough Utd.	Plymouth Argyle	Rochdale	Rotherham Utd.	Scarborough	Scunthorpe Utd.	Shrewsbury Town	Southend Utd.	Swansea City	Torquay Utd.
Barnet	3-2	0-0	1-9	1-1	0-1	4-2	1-0	1-0	2-2	0-2	0-1	3-1
Brentford	0-0	3-0	3-0	3-1	2-1	0-3	1-1	2-1	0-0	4-1	4-1	3-2
Brighton & H.A.	1-2	1-3	1-0	1-3	1-1	4-1	1-0	1-3	1-0	0-2	1-0	2-0
Cambridge Utd.	1-0	7-2	1-1	1-0	1-1	3-2	2-3	0-0	0-0	3-0	2-1	2-0
Cardiff City	0-0	4-2	1-3	1-0	2-1	0-1	1-0	0-0	3-0	2-0	0-0	2-2
Carlisle Utd.	1-1	0-0	1-1	2-1	0-1	0-0	1-0	0-1	2-1	3-0	1-2	3-0
Chester City	0-2	1-1	1-0	3-2	1-1	1-1	1-3	0-2	1-1	1-1	1-1	2-0
Darlington	1-1	5-1	3-0	1-2	3-0	1-2	3-0	3-1	1-0	2-1	2-2	0-2
Exeter City	1-1	2-1	2-0	1-1	2-1	3-0	1-0	2-2	0-1	2-1	4-0	1-1
Halifax Town	1-2	2-2	2-2	2-0	0-0	2-4	1-2	1-0	2-0	3-1	2-0	1-1
Hartlepool Utd.	1-0	1-2	1-2	2-0	0-1	0-0	3-0	1-2	1-1	2-4	1-2	4-1
Hull City	0-1	0-0	1-0	1-0	2-1	1-0	1-1	2-3	1-1	1-1	0-2	1-0
Leyton Orient	–	1-1	1-2	4-3	3-0	1-4	0-3	1-0	6-1	0-3	1-1	2-0
Mansfield Town	1-2	–	1-0	2-0	3-1	0-3	3-2	2-1	1-0	0-0	1-0	2-1
Peterborough Utd.	3-0	1-0	–	0-2	2-0	2-4	3-1	2-1	2-2	1-1	0-1	4-0
Plymouth Argyle	2-4	3-0	0-2	–	2-1	1-0	0-0	5-0	2-0	0-3	1-2	0-0
Rochdale	2-1	1-0	0-3	1-1	–	0-0	0-1	2-2	1-0	1-0	0-3	0-2
Rotherham Utd.	3-1	0-0	2-2	0-2	2-2	–	4-0	0-0	0-1	2-2	1-0	2-2
Scarborough	1-3	2-3	1-1	3-0	1-0	0-4	–	1-4	2-0	1-2	2-1	1-1
Scunthorpe Utd.	2-0	3-2	1-1	0-2	0-1	4-3	5-1	–	3-0	1-1	1-2	2-0
Shrewsbury Town	1-1	1-0	1-1	2-1	3-2	2-3	3-1	2-1	–	3-1	1-0	1-2
Southend Utd.	2-2	1-2	2-0	1-0	1-1	3-0	1-0	0-1	2-1	–	2-0	0-0
Swansea City	1-1	1-0	0-0	2-3	1-1	1-1	2-0	1-2	1-1	3-1	–	0-0
Torquay Utd.	1-1	0-0	0-1	1-1	2-1	2-0	0-1	1-0	0-3	2-0	1-1	–

FINAL TABLES 1998-99

F.A. CARLING PREMIERSHIP

		P	HOME W	D	L	F	A	AWAY W	D	L	F	A	Pts	GD
1	Manchester Utd.	38	14	4	1	45	18	8	9	2	35	19	79	+43
2	Arsenal	38	14	5	0	34	5	8	7	4	25	12	78	+42
3	Chelsea	38	12	6	1	29	13	8	9	2	28	17	75	+27
4	Leeds Utd.	38	12	5	2	32	9	6	7	6	29	25	66	+27
5	West Ham Utd.	38	11	3	5	32	26	5	6	8	14	27	57	−7
6	Aston Villa	38	10	3	6	33	28	5	7	7	18	18	55	+5
7	Liverpool	38	10	5	4	44	24	5	4	10	24	25	54	+19
8	Derby Co.	38	8	7	4	22	19	5	6	8	18	26	52	−5
9	Middlesbrough	38	7	9	3	25	18	5	6	8	23	36	51	−6
10	Leicester City	38	7	6	6	25	25	5	7	7	15	21	49	−6
11	Tottenham	38	7	7	5	28	26	4	7	8	19	24	47	−3
12	Sheffield Wed.	38	7	5	7	20	15	6	2	11	21	27	46	−1
13	Newcastle Utd.	38	7	6	6	26	25	4	7	8	22	29	46	−6
14	Coventry City	38	9	5	5	26	20	3	3	13	13	30	44	−11
15	Everton	38	6	8	5	22	12	5	2	12	20	35	43	−5
16	Wimbledon	38	7	7	5	22	21	3	5	11	18	42	42	−23
17	Southampton	38	9	4	6	29	26	2	4	13	8	38	41	−27
18	Charlton Athletic	38	4	7	8	20	20	4	5	10	21	36	36	−15
19	Blackburn Rov.	38	6	5	8	21	24	1	9	9	17	28	35	−14
20	Nott'm Forest	38	3	7	9	18	31	4	2	13	17	38	30	−34

Manchester Utd., Arsenal and Chelsea qualify for European Champions League Competition; Leeds Utd., Tottenham (Worthington Cup Winners), Newcastle Utd. (F.A. Cup Finalists) for UEFA Cup; West Ham Utd. for InterToto Cup.

Prize Money in the F.A. Carling Premiership 1998-99: 1 £3,690,460; 2 £3,505,937; 3 £3,321,414; 4 £3,136,891; 5 £2,952,368; 6 £2,767,845; 7 £2,583,322; 8 £2,398,799; 9 £2,214,276; 10 £2,029,753; 11 £1,845,230; 12 £1,660,707; 13 £1,476,184; 14 £1,291,661; 15 £1,107,138; 16 £992,613; 17 £738,092; 18 £553,569; 19 £369,046; 20 £184,523.

Carling pay an annual sponsorship fee of £9 million to the Premier League. A total of £7 million is paid in equal shares to every club who competed in the Carling Premiership during that specific season, ie a per club total of £350,000.

Biggest Win: Nott'm. Forest 1, Manchester Utd. 8.

Highest Attendance: 55,316 (Manchester Utd. v Southampton).

Lowest Attendance: 11,717 (Wimbledon v Coventry City).

Top League Scorer: 18 Yorke (Manchester Utd.), Owen (Liverpool), Hasselbaink (Leeds Utd.)

Top Scorer, all Competitions: 29 Yorke (Manchester Utd.)

Carling Manager of Year (£7,500): Alex Ferguson (Manchester Utd.)

Carling Player of Year (£7,500): Dwight Yorke.

Football Writers' Footballer of Year: David Ginola (Tottenham).

PFA Player of Year: David Ginola (Tottenham).

PFA Young Player of Year: Nicolas Anelka (Arsenal).

PFA Divisional Team of Season: Martyn (Leeds Utd.), G. Neville (Manchester Utd.), Campbell (Tottenham), Stam (Manchester Utd.), Irwin (Manchester Utd.); Beckham (Manchester Utd.), Vieira (Arsenal), Petit (Arsenal), Ginola (Tottenham), Anelka (Arsenal), Yorke (Manchester Utd.).

Fair Play Award: Manchester Utd.

Best Behaved Supporters Award: Wimbledon.

Carling Groundsman of Year (£250): Steve Braddock (Arsenal).

NATIONWIDE FOOTBALL LEAGUE

FIRST DIVISION

			HOME				AWAY						
		P	W	D	L	F	A	W	D	L	F	A	Pts	Gls

		P	W	D	L	F	A	W	D	L	F	A	Pts	Gls
1	Sunderland	46	19	3	1	50	10	12	9	2	41	18	105	(91)
2	Bradford City	46	15	4	4	48	20	11	5	7	34	27	87	(82)
3	Ipswich Town	46	16	1	6	37	15	10	7	6	32	17	86	(69)
4	Birmingham City	46	12	7	4	32	15	11	5	7	34	22	81	(66)
5	Watford*	46	12	8	3	30	19	9	6	8	35	37	77	(65)
6	Bolton Wand.	46	13	6	4	44	25	7	10	6	34	34	76	(78)
7	Wolves	46	11	10	2	37	19	8	6	9	27	24	73	(64)
8	Sheffield Utd.	46	12	6	5	42	29	6	7	10	29	37	67	(71)
9	Norwich City	46	7	12	4	34	28	8	5	10	28	33	62	(62)
10	Huddersfield Town	46	11	9	3	38	23	4	7	12	24	48	61	(62)
11	Grimsby Town	46	11	6	6	25	18	6	4	13	15	34	61	(40)
12	W.B.A.	46	12	4	7	43	33	4	7	12	26	43	59	(69)
13	Barnsley	46	7	9	7	35	30	7	8	8	24	26	59	(59)
14	Crystal Palace	46	11	10	2	43	26	3	6	14	15	45	58	(58)
15	Tranmere Rov.	46	8	7	8	37	30	4	13	6	26	31	56	(63)
16	Stockport Co.	46	7	9	7	24	21	5	8	10	25	39	53	(49)
17	Swindon Town	46	7	8	8	40	44	6	3	14	19	37	50	(59)
18	Crewe Alexandra	46	7	6	10	27	35	5	6	12	27	43	48	(54)
19	Portsmouth	46	10	5	8	34	26	1	9	13	23	47	47	(57)
20	Q.P.R.	46	9	7	7	34	22	3	4	16	18	39	47	(52)
21	Port Vale	46	10	3	10	22	28	3	5	15	23	47	47	(45)
22	Bury	46	9	7	7	24	27	1	10	12	11	33	47	(35)
23	Oxford Utd.	46	7	8	8	31	30	3	6	14	17	41	44	(48)
24	Bristol City	46	7	8	8	35	36	2	7	14	22	44	42	(57)

(* Also promoted via play-offs)

Prize money – Champions: Sunderland £50,000; **Runners-up:** Bradford City £25,000.
Biggest Win: Sunderland 7, Oxford Utd. 0.
Highest Attendance: 41,634 (Sunderland v Birmingham City).
Lowest Attendance: 3,436 (Bury v Oxford Utd.).
Top League Scorer: 31 Lee Hughes (WBA).
Top Scorer, all Competitions: 32 Lee Hughes (W.B.A.).
First Division Manager of Year: Peter Reid (Sunderland).
PFA Divisional Team of Season: Wright (Ipswich Town), Rowett (Birmingham City), Gray (Sunderland), Dyer (Ipswich Town), Butler (Sunderland) and Venus (Ipswich Town), Moore (Bradford City), Frandsen (Bolton Wand.), Clark (Sunderland), Hughes (W.B.A.), Quinn (Sunderland), Johnston (Sunderland).
Fair Play Award: Sunderland.
First Division Groundsman of Year: Mick Moore (Oxford Utd.).

SECOND DIVISION

				HOME				AWAY						
		P	W	D	L	F	A	W	D	L	F	A	Pts	Gls
1	Fulham	46	19	3	1	50	12	12	5	6	29	20	101	(79)
2	Walsall	46	13	7	3	37	23	13	2	8	26	24	87	(63)
3	Manchester City*	46	13	6	4	38	14	9	10	4	31	19	82	(69)
4	Gillingham	46	15	5	3	45	17	7	9	7	30	27	80	(75)
5	Preston N.E.	46	12	6	5	46	23	10	7	6	32	27	79	(78)
6	Wigan Athletic	46	14	5	4	44	17	8	5	10	31	31	76	(75)
7	Bournemouth	46	14	7	2	37	11	7	6	10	26	30	76	(63)
8	Stoke City	46	10	4	9	32	32	11	2	10	27	31	69	(59)
9	Chesterfield	46	14	5	4	34	16	3	8	12	12	28	64	(46)
10	Millwall	46	9	8	6	33	24	8	3	12	19	35	62	(52)
11	Reading	46	10	6	7	29	26	6	7	10	25	37	61	(54)
12	Luton Town	46	10	4	9	25	26	6	6	11	26	34	58	(51)
13	Bristol Rov.	46	8	9	6	35	28	5	8	10	30	28	56	(65)
14	Blackpool	46	7	8	8	24	24	7	6	10	20	30	56	(44)
15	Burnley	46	8	7	8	23	33	5	9	9	31	40	55	(54)
16	Notts Co.	46	8	6	9	29	27	6	6	11	23	34	54	(52)
17	Wrexham	46	8	6	9	21	28	5	8	10	22	34	53	(43)
18	Colchester Utd.	46	9	7	7	25	30	3	9	11	27	40	52	(52)
19	Wycombe Wand.	46	8	5	10	31	26	5	7	11	21	32	51	(52)
20	Oldham Athletic	46	8	4	11	26	31	6	5	12	22	35	51	(48)
21	York City	46	6	8	9	28	33	7	3	13	28	47	50	(56)
22	Northampton Town	46	4	12	7	26	31	6	6	11	17	26	48	(43)
23	Lincoln City	46	9	4	10	27	27	4	3	16	15	47	46	(42)
24	Macclesfield Town	46	7	4	12	24	30	4	6	13	19	33	43	(43)

(* Also promoted via play-offs)

Prize money – Champions: Fulham £25,000; **Runners-Up:** Walsall £10,000.
Biggest Win: Reading 0, Bristol Rov. 6; Burnley 0, Manchester City 6.
Highest Attendance: 32,471 (Manchester City v York City).
Lowest Attendance: 1,868 (Macclesfield Town v Gillingham).
Top League Scorer: 25 Jamie Cureton (Bristol Rov.).
Top Scorer, all Competitions: 29 Jamie Cureton (Britol Rov.).
Second Division Manager of Year: Ray Graydon (Walsall).
PFA Divisional Team of Season: Taylor (Fulham), Finnan (Fulham), Brevett (Fulham) and Vincent (Bournemouth), Gregan (Preston N.E.), Davis (Burnley), Coleman (Fulham), Kavanagh (Stoke City), Wrack (Walsall), Stein (Bournemouth), Horsfield (Fulham), Robinson (Bournemouth).
Fair Play Award: Fulham.
Second Division Groundsman of Year: Brian Horner (York City).

THIRD DIVISION

			HOME					AWAY					
		P	W	D	L	F	A	W	D	L	F	A	Pts	Gls
1	Brentford	46	16	5	2	45	18	10	2	11	34	38	85	(79)
2	Camb Utd.	46	13	6	4	41	21	10	6	7	37	27	81	(78)
3	Cardiff City	46	13	7	3	35	17	9	7	7	25	22	80	(60)
4	Scunthorpe Utd.*	46	14	3	6	42	28	8	5	10	27	30	74	(69)
5	Rotherham Utd.	46	11	8	4	41	26	9	5	9	38	35	73	(79)
6	Leyton Orient	46	12	6	5	40	30	7	9	7	28	29	72	(68)
7	Swansea City	46	11	9	3	33	19	8	5	10	23	29	71	(56)
8	Mansfield Town	46	15	2	6	38	18	4	8	11	22	40	67	(60)
9	Peterborough Utd.	46	11	4	8	41	29	7	8	8	31	27	66	(72)
10	Halifax Town	46	10	8	5	33	25	7	7	9	25	31	66	(58)
11	Darlington	46	10	6	7	41	24	8	5	10	28	34	65	(69)
12	Exeter City	46	13	5	5	32	18	4	7	12	15	32	63	(47)
13	Plymouth Argyle	46	11	6	6	32	19	6	4	13	26	35	61	(58)
14	Chester City	46	6	12	5	28	30	7	6	10	29	36	57	(57)
15	Shrewsbury Town	46	11	6	6	36	29	3	8	12	16	34	56	(52)
16	Barnet	46	10	5	8	30	31	4	8	11	24	40	55	(54)
17	Brighton & H.A.	46	8	3	12	25	35	8	4	11	24	31	55	(49)
18	Southend Utd.	46	8	9	6	24	21	6	6	11	28	37	54	(52)
19	Rochdale	46	9	8	6	22	21	4	7	12	20	34	54	(42)
20	Torquay Utd.	46	9	9	5	29	20	3	8	12	18	38	53	(47)
21	Hull City	46	8	5	10	25	28	6	6	11	19	34	53	(44)
22	Hartlepool Utd.	46	8	7	8	33	27	5	5	13	19	38	51	(52)
23	Carlisle Utd.	46	8	8	7	25	21	3	8	12	18	32	49	(43)
24	Scarborough	46	8	3	12	30	39	6	3	14	20	34	48	(50)

(* Also promoted via play-offs)

Prize money – Champions: Brentford £25,000; **Runners-Up:** Cambridge Utd. £10,000.
Third Place: Cardiff City £5,000.
Biggest Win: Barnet 1, Peterborough Utd. 9.
Highest Attendance: 13,949 (Hull City v Scarborough).
Lowest Attendance: 1,056 (Scarborough v Barnet).
Top League Scorer: 24 Marco Gabbiadini (Darlington).
Top scorer, all Competitions: 25 Marco Gabbiadini (Darlington), Lloyd Owusu (Brentford).
Third Division Manager of Year: Roy McFarland (Cambridge Utd.).
PFA Divisional Team of Season: Hallworth (Cardiff City), Delaney (Cardiff City), Gibbs (Plymouth Argyle), Fowler (Cardiff City), Hope (Scunthorpe Utd.), Hreidarsson (Brentford), Minton (Brighton & H.A.), Forrester (Scunthorpe Utd.), Butler (Cambridge Utd.), Evans (Shrewsbury Town), Davies (Peterborough Utd.) and Etherington (Peterborough Utd.)
Fair Play Award: Cambridge Utd.
Third Division Groundsman of Year: Ian Darker (Cambridge Utd.).

NATIONWIDE LEAGUE PLAY-OFFS 1999

Elton John, watching via a personal satellite link in Seattle, must have enjoyed this dogged and courageous performance from his Watford team, who never gave an out of sorts Bolton Wanderers a second to compose or impose themselves in this final.

What Watford lacked in guile they made up for in teamwork and application against a technically superior Bolton Wanderers side. Nick Wright gave them the lead before half time with an overhead kick. Bolton Wanderers created – and missed – several chances but Watford, who had needed penalties to dispose of Birmingham City, were not to be denied.

Allan Smart settled the issue late on to condemn Bolton Wanderers to another year outside the top flight. They can have had few complaints on a day which belonged to Graham Taylor's men.

Manchester City staged a remarkable comeback to win the Second Division final in front of a sell-out 76,935 crowd.

City had looked down and out after second half strikes from Carl Asaba and Robert Taylor put Gillingham 2-0 in front. An 89th minute goal from Kevin Horlock seemed little more than a consolation but deep into injury time Paul Dickov struck a powerful equaliser to save his team.

Neither side could find a goal in extra-time so the Second Division final was settled by a penalty shoot-out for the first time. City keeper Nicky Weaver saved Guy Butters' spot kick to send his side back to the First Division after a one year absence.

Scunthorpe Utd.'s Spanish striker Alex Calvo-Garcia headed the winning goal in the Iron's Third Division clash with Leyton Orient.

Calvo-Garcia converted Gareth Sheldon's cross early in the first half and Scunthorpe Utd. held on despite a late barrage to secure promotion.

SEMI-FINALS

1st legs Saturday, May 15 and Sunday, May 16; 2nd legs Wednesday, May 19 and Thursday, May 20)

Div 1: Watford 1, Birmingham City 0; Birmingham City 1, Watford 0 (aet. Watford won 7-6 on pens.). Bolton Wand. 1, Ipswich Town 0; Ipswich Town 4, Bolton Wand. 3 (aet Bolton Wand. won on away goals).
Div 2: Wigan Athletic 1, Manchester City 1; Manchester City 1, Wigan Athletic 0 (Manchester City won 2-1 on agg.). Preston N.E. 1, Gillingham 1; Gillingham 1, Preston N.E. 0 (Gillingham won 2-1 on agg.).
Div 3: Leyton Orient 0, Rotherham Utd. 0; Rotherham Utd. 0, Leyton Orient 0 (aet. Leyton Orient won 4-2 on pens.). Swansea City 1, Scunthorpe Utd. 0; Scunthorpe Utd. 3, Swansea City 1 (aet. Scunthorpe Utd. won 3-2 on agg.).

FINALS – AT WEMBLEY

Div 3: Sat., May 29 – **Leyton Orient** 0, **Scunthorpe Utd.** 1 (Calvo-Garcia 6). **Att:** 36,985
Leyton Orient: Barrett, R Joseph, Lockwood, Smith, Hicks (Maskell), Clark, Ling, Richards (Inglethorpe), Watts, Simba, Beall. **Sub not used:** Stimson. **Manager:** Tommy Taylor.
Scunthorpe Utd.: Evans, Harsley, Dawson, Logan, Wilcox, Hope, Walker, Forrester (Bull), Sheldon, Gayle (Stamp), Calvo-Garcia (Housham). **Manager:** Brian Laws.
Referee: C Wilkes (Gloucester). **Half-time:** 0-1.

Div 2: Sun., May 30 – **Gillingham** 2 (Asaba 81, Taylor 86), **Manchester City** 2 (Horlock 90, Dickov 90) (aet. After 90 mins 2-2. Manchester City won 3-1 on pens) **Att:** 76,935.
Gillingham: Bartram, Southall, Ashby, Smith, Butters, Pennock, Patterson (Hodge), Hessenthaler, Asaba (Carr), Galloway (Saunders), Taylor. **Manager:** Tony Pulis.
Manchester City: Weaver, Crooks (Taylor), Edghill, Wiekens, Morrison (Vaughan), Horlock, Brown (Bishop), Jeff Whitley, Dickov, Goater, Cooke. **Manager:** Joe Royle.

Referee: M Halsey (Welwyn Garden City). **Half-time:** 0-0.

Div 1: Mon., May 31 – **Watford** 2 (Wright 38, Smart 88), **Bolton Wand.** 0. **Att:** 70,343.
Watford: Chamberlain, Bazeley, Palmer, Page, Robinson, Hyde, Johnson, Kennedy,
Wright (Hazan), Ngonge (Smart), Mooney. **Sub not used:** Day. **Manager:** Graham Taylor.
Bolton Wand.: Banks, Cox, Todd, Fish, Elliott, Johansen (Sellars), Jensen, Frandsen,
Gardner (Hansen), Taylor, Gudjohnsen. **Sub not used:** Bergsson. **Manager:** Colin Todd.
Referee: T Heilbron (Newton Aycliffe). **Half-time:** 1-0.

PLAY-OFF FINALS – HOME & AWAY

1987 Divs 1/2: Charlton Athletic beat Leeds Utd. 2-1 in replay (Birmingham City) after
1-1 agg (1-0h, 0-1a). Charlton Athletic remained in Div.1. Losing semi-finalists:
Ipswich Town and Oldham Athletic. **Divs 2/3: Swindon Town** beat Gillingham 2-0 in
replay (Crystal Palace) after 2-2 agg (0-1a, 2-1h). Swindon Town promoted to Div.2.
Losing semi-finalists: Sunderland and Wigan Athletic; Sunderland relegated to Div.3.
Divs 3/4: Aldershot beat Wolves 3-0 on agg (2-0h, 1-0a) and promoted to Div.3. Losing
semi-finalists: Bolton Wand. and Colchester Utd.; Bolton Wand. relegated to Div.4.

1988 Divs 1/2: Middlesbrough beat Chelsea 2-1 on agg (2-0h, 0-1a) and promoted to
Div.1; Chelsea relegated to Div.2. Losing semi-finalists: Blackburn Rov. and Bradford
City. **Divs 2/3: Walsall** beat Bristol City 4-0 in replay (h) after 3-3 agg (3-1a, 0-2h) and
promoted to Div.2. Losing semi-finalists: Sheffield Utd. and Notts Co; Sheffield Utd.
relegated to Div.3. **Divs 3/4: Swansea City** beat Torquay Utd. 5-4 on agg (2-1h, 3-3a) and
promoted to Div.3. Losing semi-finalists: Rotherham Utd. and Scunthorpe Utd.;
Rotherham Utd. relegated to Div.4.

1989 Div.2: Crystal Palace beat Blackburn Rov. 4-3 on agg (1-3a, 3-0h). Losing
semi-finalists: Watford and Swindon Town. **Div.3: Port Vale** beat Bristol Rov. 2-1 on agg
(1-1a, 1-0h). Losing semi-finalists: Fulham and Preston N.E. **Div.4: Leyton Orient** beat
Wrexham 2-1 on agg (0-0a, 2-1h). Losing semi-finalists: Scarborough and Scunthorpe
Utd.

PLAY-OFF FINALS AT WEMBLEY

1990 Div.2: Swindon Town 1, Sunderland 0 (att: 72,873). Swindon Town promoted, then
demoted for financial irregularities; Sunderland promoted. Losing semi-finalists: Blackburn Rov. and Newcastle Utd. **Div.3: Notts Co.** 2, Tranmere Rov. 0 (att: 29,252). Losing
semi-finalists: Bolton Wand. and Bury. **Div.4: Cambridge Utd.** 1, Chesterfield 0 (att:
26,404). Losing semi-finalists: Maidstone and Stockport Co.

1991 Div.2: Notts Co. 3, Brighton & H.A. 1 (att: 59,940). Losing semi-finalists:
Middlesbrough and Millwall. **Div.3: Tranmere Rov.** 1, Bolton Wand. 0 (att: 30,217).
Losing semi-finalists: Brentford and Bury. **Div.4: Torquay Utd.** 2, Blackpool 2 – Torquay
Utd. won 5-4 on pens (att: 21,615). Losing semi-finalists: Burnley and Scunthorpe
Utd.

1992 Div.2: Blackburn Rov. 1, Leicester City 0 (att: 68,147). Losing semi-finalists: Derby
Co. and Cambridge Utd. **Div.3: Peterborough Utd.** 2, Stockport Co. 1 (att: 35,087).
Losing semi-finalists: Huddersfield Town and Stoke City. **Div.4: Blackpool** 1, Scunthorpe
Utd. 1 – Blackpool won 4-3 on pens (att: 22,741). Losing semi-finalists: Barnet and
Crewe Alexandra.

1993 Div.1; Swindon Town 4, Leicester City 3 (att: 73,802). Losing semi-finalists:
Portsmouth and Tranmere Rov. **Div.2: W.B.A.** 3, Port Vale 0 (att: 53,471). Losing
semi-finalists: Stockport Co. and Swansea City. **Div.3: York City** 1, Crewe Alexandra 1 –
York City won 5-3 on pens (att: 22,416). Losing semi-finalists: Bury and Walsall.

1994 Div.1: **Leicester City** 2, Derby Co. 1 (att: 73,671). Losing semi-finalists: Millwall and Tranmere Rov. **Div.2:** **Burnley** 2, Stockport Co. 1 (att: 44,806). Losing semi-finalists: Plymouth Argyle and York City. **Div.3:** **Wycombe Wand.** 4, Preston N.E. 2 (att: 40,109). Losing semi-finalists: Carlisle Utd. and Torquay Utd.

1995 Div.1: **Bolton Wand.** 4, Reading 3 (att: 64,107). Losing semi-finalists: Tranmere Rov. and Wolves. **Div.2:** **Huddersfield Town** 2, Bristol Rov. 1 (att: 59,175). Losing semi-finalists: Brentford and Crewe Alexandra. **Div.3:** **Chesterfield** 2, Bury 0 (att: 22,814). Losing semi-finalists: Mansfield Town and Preston N.E.

1996 Div.1: **Leicester City** 2, Crystal Palace 1, aet (att: 73,573). Losing semi-finalists: Charlton Athletic and Stoke City. **Div.2:** **Bradford City** 2, Notts Co. 0 (att: 39,972). Losing semi-finalists: Blackpool and Crewe Alexandra. **Div.3:** **Plymouth Argyle** 1, Darlington 0 (att: 43,431). Losing semi-finalists: Colchester Utd. and Hereford.

1997 Div.1: **Crystal Palace** 1, Sheffield Utd. 0, (att: 64,383). Losing semi-finalists: Ipswich Town and Wolves. **Div.2:** **Crewe Alexandra** 1, Brentford 0 (att: 34,149). Losing semi-finalists: Bristol City and Luton Town. **Div.3:** **Northampton Town** 1, Swansea City 0 (att: 46,804). Losing semi-finalists: Cardiff City and Chester City.

1998 Div.1: **Charlton Athletic** 4, Sunderland 4, aet Charlton Athletic won 7-6 on pens. (Att: 77, 739). Losing semi-finalists: Ipswich Town and Sheffield United. **Div.2:** **Grimsby Town** 1, Northampton Town 0 (att: 62,988). Losing semi-finalists: Bristol Rov. and Fulham. **Div.3:** **Colchester Utd.** 1, Torquay Utd. 0 (att: 19,486). Losing semi-finalists: Barnet and Scarborough.

1999 Div.1: **Watford** 2, Bolton Wand. 0, (Att. 70,343). Losing semi-finalists: Ipswich Town and Birmingham City. **Div. 2:** **Manchester City** 2, Gillingham 2, aet Manchester City won 3-1 on pens. (Att. 76,935). Losing semi-finalists: Preston N.E. and Wigan Athletic. **Div. 3:** **Scunthorpe Utd.** 1, Leyton Orient 0, (Att. 36,985). Losing semi-finalists: Rotherham Utd. and Swansea City.

HISTORY OF THE PLAY-OFFS

Play-off matches were introduced by the Football League to decide final promotion and relegation issues at the end of season 1986-87.

A similar series styled "Test Matches" had operated between Divisions 1 and 2 for six seasons from 1893-98, and was abolished when both divisions were increased from 16 to 18 clubs.

Eighty-eight years later, the play-offs were back in vogue. In the first three seasons (1987-88-89), the Finals were played home-and-away, and since they were made one-off matches in 1990, they have featured regularly in Wembley's spring calendar.

Through the years, these have been the ups and downs of the play-offs:

1987 Initially, the 12 clubs involved comprised the one that finished directly above those relegated in Divisions 1, 2 and 3 and the three who followed the sides automatically promoted in each section. Two of the home-and-away Finals went to neutral-ground replays, in which **Charlton Athletic** clung to First Division status by denying Leeds Utd. promotion while **Swindon Town** beat Gillingham to complete their climb from Fourth Division to Second in successive seasons, via the play-offs. **Sunderland** fell into Div.3 and **Bolton Wand.** into Div.4, both for the first time. **Aldershot** went up after finishing only sixth in Div.4; in their Final, they beat Wolves, who had finished nine points higher and missed automatic promotion by one point.

1988 Chelsea were relegated from the First Division after losing on aggregate to Middlesbrough, who had finished third in Div.2. So Middlesbrough, managed by Bruce Rioch, completed the rise from Third Division to First in successive seasons, only two years after their very existence had been threatened by the bailiffs. Also promoted via the play-offs: **Walsall** from Div.3 and **Swansea City** from Div.4. Relegated, besides Chelsea: **Sheffield Utd.** (to Div.3) and **Rotherham Utd.** to Div.4.

1989 After two seasons of promotion-relegation play-offs, the system was changed to involve the four clubs who had just missed automatic promotion in Divs. 2, 3 and 4. That format has remained. Steve Coppell's **Crystal Palace**, third in Div.2, returned to the top flight after eight years, beating Blackburn Rov. 4-3 on aggregate after extra time. Similarly, **Port Vale** confirmed third place in Div.3 with promotion via the play-offs. For **Leyton Orient**, promotion seemed out of the question in Div.4 when they stood 15th. on March 1. But eight wins and a draw in the last nine home games swept them to sixth in the final table, and two more home victories in the play-offs completed their season in triumph.

1990 The play-off Finals now moved to Wembley over three days of the Spring Holiday week-end. On successive afternoons, **Cambridge Utd.** won promotion from Div.4 and **Notts County** from Div.3. Then, on Bank Holiday Monday, the biggest crowd for years at a Football League fixture (72,873) saw Ossie Ardiles' **Swindon Town** beat Sunderland 1-0 to reach the First Division for the first time. A few weeks later, however, Wembley losers **Sunderland** were promoted instead, by default; Swindon Town were found guilty of "financial irregularities" and stayed in Div.2.

1991 Again, the season's biggest League crowd (59,940) gathered at Wembley for the First Division Final in which **Notts Co.** (having missed promotion by one point) still fulfilled their ambition, beating Brighton & H.A. 3-1. In successive years, County had climbed from Third Division to First via the play-offs – the first club to achieve double promotion by this route. Bolton Wand. were denied automatic promotion in Div.3 on goal difference, and lost at Wembley to an extra-time goal by **Tranmere Rov.** The Fourth Division Final made history, with Blackpool beaten 5-4 on penalties by **Torquay Utd.** – first instance of promotion being decided by a shoot-out. In the table, Blackpool had finished seven points ahead of Torquay Utd.

1992 Wembley that Spring Bank Holiday was the turning point in the history of **Blackburn Rov.** Bolstered by Kenny Dalglish's return to management and owner Jack Walker's millions, they beat Leicester City 1-0 by Mike Newell's 45th-minute penalty to achieve their objective – a place in the new Premier League. Newell, who also missed a second-half penalty, had recovered from a broken leg just in time for the play-offs. In the Div.4 Final **Blackpool** (denied by penalties the previous year) this time won a shoot-out 4-3 against Scunthorpe Utd., who were unlucky in the play-offs for the fourth time in five years. **Peterborough Utd.** climbed out of the Third Division for the first time, beating Stockport Co. 2-1 at Wembley.

1993 The crowd of 73,802 at Wembley to see **Swindon Town** beat Leicester City 4-3 in the First Division Final was 11,000 bigger than that for the F.A. Cup Final replay between Arsenal and Sheffield Wed. Leicester City rallied from three down to 3-3 before Paul Bodin's late penalty wiped away Swindon Town's bitter memories of three years earlier, when they were denied promotion after winning at Wembley. In the Third Division Final, **York City** beat Crewe Alexandra 5-3 in a shoot-out after a 1-1 draw, and in the Div.2 decider, **W.B.A.** beat Port Vale 3-0. That was tough on Vale, who had finished third in the table with 89 points – the highest total never to earn promotion in any division. They had beaten Albion twice in the League, too.

1994 Wembley's record turn-out of 158,586 spectators at the three Finals started with a crowd of 40,109 to see Martin O'Neill's **Wycombe Wand.** beat Preston N.E. 4-2. They thus climbed from Conference to Second Division with successive promotions. **Burnley's** 2-1 victory in the Second Division Final was marred by the sending-off of two Stockport Co. players, and in the First Division decider **Leicester City** came from behind to beat Derby Co. and end the worst Wembley record of any club. They had lost on all six previous appearances there – four times in the F.A. Cup Final and in the play-offs of 1992 and 1993.

1995 Two months after losing the Coca-Cola Cup Final to Liverpool, Bruce Rioch's **Bolton Wand.** were back at Wembley for the First Division play-off Final. From two goals down to Reading in front of a crowd of 64,107, they returned to the top company after 15 years, winning 4-3 with two extra-time goals. **Huddersfield Town** ended the first season at their new £15m. home with promotion to the First Division via a 2-1 victory against Bristol Rov. – manager Neil Warnock's third play-off success (after two with Notts Co.). Of the three clubs who missed automatic promotion by one place, only **Chesterfield** achieved it in the play-offs, comfortably beating Bury 2-0.

1996 Under new manager **Martin O'Neill** (a Wembley play-off winner with Wycombe Wand. in 1994), **Leicester City** returned to the Premiership a year after leaving it. They had finished fifth in the table, but in the Final came from behind to beat third-placed Crystal Palace by Steve Claridge's shot in the last seconds of extra time. In the Second Division **Bradford City** came sixth, nine points behind Blackpool (3rd), but beat them (from two down in the semi-final first leg) and then clinched promotion by 2-0 v Notts Co. at Wembley. It was City's greatest day since they won the Cup in 1911. **Plymouth Argyle** beat Darlington in the Third Division Final to earn promotion a year after being relegated. It was manager **Neil Warnock's** fourth play-off triumph in seven seasons after two with Notts Co. (1990 and 1991) and a third with Huddersfield Town in 1995.

1997 High drama at Wembley as **Crystal Palace** left it late against Sheffield Utd. in the First Division play-off final. The match was scoreless until the last 10 seconds when David Hopkin lobbed Blades' keeper Simon Tracey from 25 yards to send the Eagles back to the Premiership after two seasons of Nationwide action. In the Second Division play-off final, **Crewe Alexandra** beat Brentford 1-0 courtesy of a Shaun Smith goal. **Northampton Town** celebrated their first Wembley appearance with a 1-0 victory over Swansea City thanks to John Frain's injury-time free-kick in the Third Division play-off final.

1998 In one of the finest games ever seen at Wembley, **Charlton Athletic** eventually triumphed 7-6 on penalties over Sunderland. For Charlton Athletic, Wearside-born Clive Mendonca scored a hat-trick and Richard Rufus his first career goal in a match that lurched between joy and despair for both sides as it ended 4-4. Sunderland defender Michael Gray's superb performance ill deserved to end with his weakly struck spot kick being saved by Sasa Ilic. In the Third Division, the penalty spot also had a role to play, as **Colchester Utd.**'s David Gregory scored the only goal to defeat Torquay Utd., while in the Second Division a Kevin Donovan goal gave **Grimsby Town** victory over Northampton Town.

PLAY-OFF CROWDS YEAR BY YEAR

YEAR	MATCHES	AGG. ATT.
1987	20	310,000
1988	19	305,817
1989	18	234,393
1990	15	291,428
1991	15	266,442
1992	15	277,684
1993	15	319,907
1994	15	314,817
1995	15	295,317
1996	15	308,515
1997	15	309,085
1998	15	320,795
1999	15	372,969
	207	3,927,163

WAGES SOAR TO RECORD LEVELS

Premiership wages spiralled by an amazing 40 per cent in 12 months according to an April report.

England's top players are earning an average £250,000 a year , the survey by Deloitte and Touche analyst Gerry Boon revealed.

Annual salaries were about £75,000 a year when the Premiership kicked off in 1992. 'Wages now count for more than 50 per cent of a club's revenue,' said Boon. 'That's 37 per cent more than 10 years ago.'

Chelsea's wage bill rose 81 per cent between 1996-97 and 1997-98 to almost £27million while Manchester Utd., Liverpool, Newcastle Utd. and Arsenal also paid their players over £20million.

Top clubs are able to afford such huge sums because of the spectacular appeal of Premiership football. Since it began in 1992 there has been a 350 per cent increase in revenue with the total standing at £2.15 billion and clubs reporting a joint operating profit of just over £100million for the 1997-98 season.

Only Wimbledon, Sheffield Wed. and Crystal Palace failed to report an operating profit.

Salary Table 1997-98

1	Chelsea	£26,982,000
2	Manchester Utd.	£26,897,000
3	Liverpool	£24,102,000
4	Newcastle Utd.	£22,335,000
5	Arsenal	£21,882,000
6	Blackburn Rovers	£19,035,000
7	Tottenham	£16,980,000
8	Leeds Utd.	£15,858,000
9	Everton	£13,845,000
10	Aston Villa	£12,388,000
11	Sheffield Wed.	£11,842,000
12	Derby Co.	£11,465,000
13	Middlesbrough	£11,332,000
14	West Ham Utd.	£11,181,000
15	Coventry City	£10,423,000
16	Leicester City	£10,200,000
17	Nott'm. Forest	£9,713,000
18	Wimbledon	£8,925,000
19	Southampton	£7,251,000

(Table includes Middlesbrough and Nott'm. Forest who were promoted at end of that season but no figures are available for Charlton Athletic.)
★ Chelsea claim their figure includes all staff, not just players.

Top 10 Wage Bill Increases

		1996-97	1997-98	change
1	Chelsea	£14,873,000	£26,982,000	81pc
2	Derby Co.	£6,407,000	£11,465,000	79pc
3	Liverpool	£14,599,000	£24,102,000	65pc
4	Sheffield Wed.	£7,571,000	£11,842,000	56pc
5	Southampton	£4,776,000	£7,251,000	52pc
6	Wimbledon	£6,018,000	£8,925,000	48pc
7	Arsenal	£15,279,000	£21,882,000	43pc
8	Tottenham	£12,057,000	£16,980,000	41pc
9	Everton	£9,787,000	£13,845,000	41pc
10	West Ham Utd.	£8,298,000	£11,181,000	35pc

OTHER COMPETITIONS 1998-99

AUTO WINDSCREENS SHIELD FINAL

MILLWALL 0, WIGAN ATHLETIC 1

Wembley (55,349), Sunday, April 18, 1999

Millwall: B. Roberts, Lavin, Stuart, Nethercott (capt.), Dolan, Ifill, Newman, Cahill, Reid, Harris, Sadlier. **Subs not used:** Shaw, Bowry, Bircham. **Booked:** Lavin, Newman. **Manager:** Keith Stevens

Wigan Athletic: Carroll, Bradshaw (capt.), Sharp, McGibbon, Balmer, Greenall, O'Neill, Rogers, Liddell, Haworth, Barlow (Lee 89). **Subs not used:** Jones, Green. **Scorer:** Rogers (90). **Booked:** Bradshaw, McGibbon, O'Neill. **Manager:** Ray Mathias

Referee: C Wilkes (Gloucester).

FINALS – RESULTS

Associated Members' Cup
1984   (Hull City) Bournemouth 2, Hull City 1.
Freight Rover Trophy
1985   (Wembley) Wigan Athletic 3, Brentford 1.
1986   (Wembley) Bristol City 3, Bolton Wand. 0.
1987   (Wembley) Mansfield Town 1, Bristol City 1 (aet; Mansfield Town won 5-4 on pens.).
Sherpa Van Trophy
1988   (Wembley) Wolves 2, Burnley 0.
1989   (Wembley) Bolton Wand. 4, Torquay Utd. 1.
Leyland Daf Cup
1990   (Wembley) Tranmere Rov. 2, Bristol Rov. 1.
1991   (Wembley) Birmingham City 3, Tranmere Rov. 2.
Autoglass Trophy
1992   (Wembley) Stoke City 1, Stockport Co. 0.
1993   (Wembley) Port Vale 2, Stockport Co. 1.
1994   (Wembley) Huddersfield Town 1, Swansea City 1 (aet; Swansea City won 3-1 on pens.).
Auto Windscreens Shield
1995   (Wembley) Birmingham City 1, Carlisle Utd. 0 (Birmingham City won in sudden-death overtime).
1996   (Wembley) Rotherham Utd. 2, Shrewsbury Town 1.
1997   (Wembley) Carlisle Utd. 0, Colchester Utd. 0 (aet; Carlisle Utd. won 4-3 on pens.)
1998   (Wembley) Grimsby Town 2, Bournemouth 1 (Grimsby Town won with Golden Goal in extra time).
1999   (Wembley) Wigan Athletic 1, Millwall 0.

OTHER LEAGUE CLUBS' CUP COMPETITIONS

FINALS – AT WEMBLEY

Full Members' Cup (Discontinued after 1992)
1985-86   Chelsea 5, Manchester City 4.
1986-87   Blackburn Rov. 1, Charlton Athletic 0.

Simod Cup
1987-88   Reading 4, Luton Town 1.
1988-89   Nott'm. Forest 4, Everton 3.

Zenith Data Systems Cup
1989-90   Chelsea 1, Middlesbrough 0.
1990-91   Crystal Palace 4, Everton 1.
1991-92   Nott'm Forest 3, Southampton 2.

ANGLO-ITALIAN CUP (Discontinued after 1996: * Home club)

1970   *Napoli 0, Swindon Town 3.
1971   *Bologna 1, Blackpool 2 (aet).
1972   *AS Roma 3, Blackpool 1.
1973   *Fiorentina 1, Newcastle Utd. 2.
1993   Derby Co. 1, Cremonese 3 (at Wembley).
1994   Notts Co. 0, Brescia 1 (at Wembley).
1995   Ascoli 1, Notts Co. 2 (at Wembley).
1996   Port Vale 2, Genoa 5 (at Wembley).

F.A. CHALLENGE VASE FINALS (AT WEMBLEY)

1975   Hoddesdon Town 2, Epsom & Ewell 1
1976   Billericay Town 1, Stamford 0*
1977   Billericay Town 2, Sheffield 1 (replay Nottingham, after a 1-1 draw at Wembley)
1978   Blue Star 2, Barton Rov. 1
1979   Billericay Town 4, Almondsbury Greenway 1
1980   Stamford 2, Guisborough Town 0
1981   Whickham 3, Willenhall Town 2*
1982   Forest Green Rov. 3, Rainworth Miners' Welfare 0
1983   V.S. Rugby 1, Halesowen Town 0
1984   Stansted 3, Stamford 2
1985   Halesowen Town 3, Fleetwood Town 1
1986   Halesowen Town 3, Southall 0
1987   St. Helens Town 3, Warrington Town 2
1988   Colne Dynamoes 1, Emley 0*
1989   Tamworth 3, Sudbury Town 0 (replay Peterborough Utd., after a 1-1 draw at Wembley)
1990   Yeading 1, Bridlington 0 (replay Leeds Utd., after 0-0 draw at Wembley)
1991   Guiseley 3, Gresley Rov. 1 (replay Bramall Lane, Sheffield, after a 4-4 draw at Wembley)
1992   Wimborne Town 5, Guiseley 3
1993   Bridlington Town 1, Tiverton Town 0
1994   Diss Town 2, Taunton Town 1*
1995   Arlesey Town 2, Oxford Utd. City 1
1996   Brigg Town 3, Clitheroe 0
1997   Whitby Town 3, North Ferriby Utd. 0
1998   Tiverton Town 1, Tow Law Town 0
1999   Tiverton Town 1, Bedlington Terriers 0

(Sponsors: Carlsberg since 1995; * After extra time)

F.A. CHALLENGE TROPHY FINALS (AT WEMBLEY)

1970   Macclesfield Town 2, Telford Utd. 0
1971   Telford Utd. 3, Hillingdon Middlesbrough 2
1972   Stafford Rangers 3, Barnet 0
1973   Scarborough 2, Wigan Athletic 1*
1974   Morecambe 2, Dartford 1
1975   Matlock Town 4, Scarborough 0
1976   Scarborough 3, Stafford Rangers 2*
1977   Scarborough 2, Dagenham 1
1978   Altrincham 3, Leatherhead 1

1979	Stafford Rangers 2, Kettering Town 0
1980	Dagenham 2, Mossley 1
1981	Bishop's Stortford 1, Sutton Utd. 0
1982	Enfield 1, Altrincham 0*
1983	Telford Utd. 2, Northwich Victoria 1
1984	Northwich Victoria 2, Bangor City 1 (replay Stoke City, after a 1-1 draw at Wembley)
1985	Wealdstone 2, Boston Utd. 1
1986	Altrincham 1, Runcorn 0
1987	Kidderminster Harriers 2, Burton Albion 1 (replay W.B.A., after a 0-0 draw at Wembley)
1988	Enfield 3, Telford Utd. 2 (replay W.B.A., after a 0-0 draw at Wembley)
1989	Telford Utd. 1, Macclesfield Town 0*
1990	Barrow 3, Leek Town 0
1991	Wycombe Wand. 2, Kidderminster Harriers 1
1992	Colchester Utd. 3, Witton Albion 1
1993	Wycombe Wand. 4, Runcorn 1
1994	Woking 2, Runcorn 1
1995	Woking 2, Kidderminster 1
1996	Macclesfield Town 3, Northwich Victoria 1
1997	Woking 1, Dagenham & Redbridge 0*
1998	Cheltenham Town 1, Southport 0
1999	Kingstonian 1, Forest Green Rov. 0

(Sponsors: Umbro since 1995; * After extra time)

F.A. YOUTH CUP WINNERS

Year	Winners	Runners-up	Aggregate
1953	Manchester Utd.	Wolves	9-3
1954	Manchester Utd.	Wolves	5-4
1955	Manchester Utd.	W.B.A.	7-1
1956	Manchester Utd.	Chesterfield	4-3
1957	Manchester Utd.	West Ham Utd.	8-2
1958	Wolves	Chelsea	7-6
1959	Blackburn Rov.	West Ham Utd.	2-1
1960	Chelsea	Preston N.E.	5-2
1961	Chelsea	Everton	5-3
1962	Newcastle Utd.	Wolves	2-1
1963	West Ham Utd.	Liverpool	6-5
1964	Manchester Utd.	Swindon Town	5-2
1965	Everton	Arsenal	3-2
1966	Arsenal	Sunderland	5-3
1967	Sunderland	Birmingham City	2-0
1968	Burnley	Coventry City	3-2
1969	Sunderland	W.B.A.	6-3
1970	Tottenham	Coventry City	4-3
1971	Arsenal	Cardiff City	2-0
1972	Aston Villa	Liverpool	5-2
1973	Ipswich Town	Bristol City	4-1
1974	Tottenham	Huddersfield Town	2-1
1975	Ipswich Town	West Ham Utd.	5-1
1976	W.B.A.	Wolves	5-0
1977	Crystal Palace	Everton	1-0
1978	Crystal Palace	Aston Villa	*1-0
1979	Millwall	Manchester City	2-0
1980	Aston Villa	Manchester City	3-2
1981	West Ham Utd.	Tottenham	2-1

1982	Watford	Manchester Utd.	7-6
1983	Norwich City	Everton	6-5
1984	Everton	Stoke City	4-2
1985	Newcastle Utd.	Watford	4-1
1986	Manchester City	Manchester Utd.	3-1
1987	Coventry City	Charlton Athletic	2-1
1988	Arsenal	Doncaster Rov.	6-1
1989	Watford	Manchester City	2-1
1990	Tottenham	Middlesbrough	3-2
1991	Millwall	Sheffield Wed.	3-0
1992	Manchester Utd.	Crystal Palace	6-3
1993	Leeds Utd.	Manchester Utd.	4-1
1994	Arsenal	Millwall	5-3
1995	Manchester Utd.	Tottenham	†2-2
1996	Liverpool	West Ham Utd.	4-1
1997	Leeds Utd.	Crystal Palace	3-1
1998	Everton	Blackburn Rov.	5-3
1999	West Ham Utd.	Coventry City	9-0

(* One match only; † Manchester Utd. won 4-3 on pens.)

F.A. SUNDAY CUP FINAL

April 25 (at City Ground, Nottingham):
Little Paxton 2, St. Joseph's (Luton) 2 aet (Little Paxton won 4-3 on pens.)

WELSH CUP FINAL

May 9 (at Merthyr):
Inter Cable Tel 1, Carmarthen 1 aet (Inter Cable Tel won 4-2 on pens.)

BECKHAM TOPS ENGLISH EARNINGS LEAGUE

David Beckham's World Cup dismissal against Argentina failed to harm his earning power, according to a survey by France Football magazine.

The Manchester Utd. and England forward was second only to Brazillian striker Ronaldo in an examination of earnings at European clubs.

Beckham's annual income was reported in the April edition of the magazine to be £2.9million.

Inter's Ronaldo headed the table with an annual income of £5.5million in a survey which included salaries, bonuses, sponsorship and advertising deals.

Alan Shearer, Newcastle Utd.'s England captain, and fleetfooted Liverpool striker Michael Owen, are the other English names in the top 10.

Top 10 Earners in Europe (April 1999)

1	Ronaldo (Inter)	£5.5m
2	David Beckham (Manchester Utd.)	£2.9m
3	Christian Vieri (Lazio)	£2.7m
4	Rivaldo (Barcelona)	£2.65m
5	Alessandro Del Piero (Juventus)	£2.6m
6	Roberto Carlos (Real Madrid)	£2.54m
7	Alan Shearer (Newcastle Utd.)	£2.5m
8	Gabriel Batistuta (Fiorentina)	£2.43m
9	Stefan Effenberg (Bayern Munich)	£2.34m
10	Michael Owen (Liverpool)	£2.26m

★ Zinedine Zidane of Juventus and France could not be included because income from a boutique and media deals could not be established.

★ Steve McManaman was scheduled to earn around £3million a year after moving from Liverpool to Real Madrid.

F.A. CHARITY SHIELD
(Sponsors: AXA)

ARSENAL 3, MANCHESTER UNITED 0

Wembley, (67,342), Sunday, August 9, 1998

Arsenal: Seaman, Dixon, Keown, Adams (capt.) (Bould, 80), Winterburn, Parlour, Petit (Boa Morte, 73), Vieira (Grimandi, 84), Overmars (Hughes, 67), Bergkamp (Wreh, 46), Anelka. **Scorers**: Overmars (34), Wreh (57), Anelka (72). **Booked**: Keown, Dixon.

Manchester Utd.: Schmeichel, G Neville, Johnsen, Stam, Irwin, Beckham, Butt, Keane (capt.) (Berg 76), Giggs (P Neville, 70), Scholes (Sheringham, 70), Cole (Cruyff, 70). **Booked**: G Neville, Irwin, P Neville.

Referee: G Poll (Tring). **Half-time**: 1-0.

Man of the Match: Marc Overmars.

● Arsenal's third outright post-War success was their ninth overall.

CHARITY SHIELD RESULTS

Year	Winners	Runners-up	Score
1908	Manchester Utd.	Q.P.R.	4-0
			(after 1-1 draw)
1909	Newcastle Utd.	Northampton Town	2-0
1910	Brighton & H.A.	Aston Villa	1-0
1911	Manchester Utd.	Swindon Town	8-4
1912	Blackburn Rov.	Q.P.R.	2-1
1913	Professionals	Amateurs	7-2
1920	W.B.A.	Tottenham	2-0
1921	Tottenham Hotspur	Burnley	2-0
1922	Huddersfield Town	Liverpool	1-0
1923	Professionals	Amateurs	2-0
1924	Professionals	Amateurs	3-1
1925	Amateurs	Professionals	6-1
1926	Amateurs	Professionals	6-3
1927	Cardiff City	Corinthians	2-1
1928	Everton	Blackburn Rov.	2-1
1929	Professionals	Amateurs	3-0
1930	Arsenal	Sheffield Wednesday	2-1
1931	Arsenal	W.B.A.	1-0
1932	Everton	Newcastle Utd.	5-3
1933	Arsenal	Everton	3-0
1934	Arsenal	Manchester City	4-0
1935	Sheffield Wednesday	Arsenal	1-0
1936	Sunderland	Arsenal	2-1
1937	Manchester City	Sunderland	2-0
1938	Arsenal	Preston N.E.	2-1
1948	Arsenal	Manchester United	4-3
1949	Portsmouth	Wolverhampton Wanderers	*1-1
1950	England World Cup XI	F.A. Canadian Tour Team	4-2
1951	Tottenham	Newcastle Utd.	2-1
1952	Manchester Utd.	Newcastle Utd.	4-2
1953	Arsenal	Blackpool	3-1
1954	Wolverhampton Wanderers	W.B.A.	*4-4
1955	Chelsea	Newcastle Utd.	3-0
1956	Manchester Utd.	Manchester City	1-0

1957	Manchester Utd.	Aston Villa	4-0
1958	Bolton Wand.	Wolverhampton Wanderers	4-1
1959	Wolverhampton Wanderers	Nottingham Forest	3-1
1960	Burnley	Wolverhampton Wanderers	*2-2
1961	Tottenham	F.A. XI	3-2
1962	Tottenham	Ipswich Town	5-1
1963	Everton	Manchester Utd.	4-0
1964	Liverpool	West Ham Utd.	*2-2
1965	Manchester Utd.	Liverpool	*2-2
1966	Liverpool	Everton	1-0
1967	Manchester Utd.	Tottenham	*3-3
1968	Manchester City	W.B.A.	6-1
1969	Leeds Utd.	Manchester City	2-1
1970	Everton	Chelsea	2-1
1971	Leicester City	Liverpool	1-0
1972	Manchester City	Aston Villa	1-0
1973	Burnley	Manchester City	1-0
1974	Liverpool	Leeds Utd.	1-1

(Liverpool won 6-5 on penalties)

1975	Derby Co.	West Ham Utd.	2-0
1976	Liverpool	Southampton	1-0
1977	Liverpool	Manchester Utd.	*0-0
1978	Nott'm. Forest	Ipswich Town	5-0
1979	Liverpool	Arsenal	3-1
1980	Liverpool	West Ham Utd.	1-0
1981	Aston Villa	Tottenham	*2-2
1982	Liverpool	Tottenham	1-0
1983	Manchester Utd.	Liverpool	2-0
1984	Everton	Liverpool	1-0
1985	Everton	Manchester Utd.	2-0
1986	Everton	Liverpool	*1-1
1987	Everton	Coventry City	1-0
1988	Liverpool	Wimbledon	2-1
1989	Liverpool	Arsenal	1-0
1990	Liverpool	Manchester Utd.	*1-1
1991	Arsenal	Tottenham	*0-0
1992	Leeds Utd.	Liverpool	4-3
1993	Manchester Utd.	Arsenal	1-1

(Manchester Utd. won 5-4 on penalties)

1994	Manchester Utd.	Blackburn Rov.	2-0
1995	Everton	Blackburn Rov.	1-0
1996	Manchester Utd.	Newcastle Utd.	4-0
1997	Manchester Utd.	Chelsea	1-1

(Manchester Utd. won 4-2 on penalties)

1998	Arsenal	Manchester Utd.	3-0

(Fixture played at Wembley since 1974. *Trophy shared)

GROOM ZOOMS TO STADIUM OF LIGHT

Stephen Jones, 27, deserted his new bride and wedding guests to watch Sunderland beat Grimsby Town 3-0.

Jones walked out of his wedding reception at Wingate, Co Durham, and ordered the limousine chauffeur to drive him, his best man and the ushers straight to The Stadium of Light. Another 28 guests followed in a mini-bus.

Bride Lisa Brown entertained remaining guests until her husband returned for the rest of the reception. 'He's a Sunderland nut and couldn't bear to miss a match' explained the new Mrs Jones.

HONOURS LIST

F.A. PREMIER LEAGUE

	First	Pts.	Second	Pts.	Third	Pts.
1992-3a	Manchester Utd.	84	Aston Villa	74	Norwich City	72
1993-4a	Manchester Utd.	92	Blackburn Rov.	84	Newcastle Utd.	77
1994-5a	Blackburn Rov.	89	Manchester Utd.	88	Nott'm Forest	77
1995-6b	Manchester Utd.	82	Newcastle Utd.	78	Liverpool	71
1996-7b	Manchester Utd.	75	Newcastle Utd.	68	Arsenal	68
1997-8b	Arsenal	78	Manchester Utd.	77	Liverpool	65
1998-9b	Manchester Utd.	79	Arsenal	78	Chelsea	75

Maximum points: *a*, 126; *b*, 114.

FOOTBALL LEAGUE

FIRST DIVISION

1992-3	Newcastle Utd.	96	West Ham Utd.	88	††Portsmouth	88
1993-4	Crystal Palace	90	Nott'm Forest	83	††Millwall	74
1994-5	Middlesbrough	82	††Reading	79	Bolton Wand.	77
1995-6	Sunderland	83	Derby Co.	79	††Crystal Palace	75
1996-7	Bolton Wand.	98	Barnsley	80	††Wolves	76
1997-8	Nott'm Forest	94	Middlesbrough	91	††Sunderland	90
1998-9	Sunderland	105	Bradford City	87	††Ipswich	86

Maximum points: 138. ††Not promoted after play-offs.

SECOND DIVISION

1992-3	Stoke City	93	Bolton Wand.	90	††Port Vale	89
1993-4	Reading	89	Port Vale	88	††Plymouth Argyle	85
1994-5	Birmingham City	89	††Brentford	85	††Crewe Alexandra	83
1995-6	Swindon Town	92	Oxford Utd.	83	††Blackpool	82
1996-7	Bury	84	Stockport Co.	82	††Luton Town	78
1997-8	Watford	88	Bristol City	85	Grimsby Town	72
1998-9	Fulham	101	Walsall	87	Manchester City	82

Maximum points: 138. †† Not promoted after play-offs.

THIRD DIVISION

1992-3a	Cardiff City	83	Wrexham	80	Barnet	79
1993-4a	Shrewsbury Town	79	Chester City	74	Crewe Alexandra	73
1994-5a	Carlisle Utd.	91	Walsall	83	Chesterfield	81
1995-6b	Preston N.E.	86	Gillingham	83	Bury	79
1996-7b	Wigan Athletic	87	Fulham	87	Carlisle Utd.	84
1997-8b	Notts County	99	Macclesfield Town	82	Lincoln City	75
1998-9b	Brentford	85	Cambridge Utd.	81	Cardiff City	80

Maximum points: *a*, 126; *b*, 138.

FOOTBALL LEAGUE 1888-1992

	First	Pts.	Second	Pts.	Third	Pts.
1888-89a	Preston N.E.	40	Aston Villa	29	Wolves	28
1889-90a	Preston N.E.	33	Everton	31	Blackburn Rov.	27
1890-1a	Everton	29	Preston N.E.	27	Notts Co.	26
1891-2b	Sunderland	42	Preston N.E.	37	Bolton Wand.	36

OLD FIRST DIVISION

	First	Pts.	Second	Pts.	Third	Pts.
1892-3c	Sunderland	48	Preston N.E.	37	Everton	36
1893-4c	Aston Villa	44	Sunderland	38	Derby Co.	36
1894-5c	Sunderland	47	Everton	42	Aston Villa	39
1895-6c	Aston Villa	45	Derby Co.	41	Everton	39
1896-7c	Aston Villa	47	Sheffield Utd.	36	Derby Co.	36
1897-8c	Sheffield Utd.	42	Sunderland	39	Wolves	35
1898-9d	Aston Villa	45	Liverpool	43	Burnley	39
1899-1900d	Aston Villa	50	Sheffield Utd.	48	Sunderland	41
1900-1d	Liverpool	45	Sunderland	43	Notts Co.	40
1901-2d	Sunderland	44	Everton	41	Newcastle Utd.	37
1902-3d	The Wednesday	42	Aston Villa	41	Sunderland	41
1903-4d	The Wednesday	47	Manchester City	44	Everton	43
1904-5d	Newcastle Utd.	48	Everton	47	Manchester City	46
1905-6e	Liverpool	51	Preston N.E.	47	The Wednesday	44
1906-7e	Newcastle Utd.	51	Bristol City	48	Everton	45
1907-8e	Manchester Utd.	52	Aston Villa	43	Manchester City	43
1908-9e	Newcastle Utd.	53	Everton	46	Sunderland	44
1909-10e	Aston Villa	53	Liverpool	48	Blackburn Rov.	45
1910-11e	Manchester Utd.	52	Aston Villa	51	Sunderland	45
1911-12e	Blackburn Rov.	49	Everton	46	Newcastle Utd.	44
1912-13e	Sunderland	54	Aston Villa	50	Sheffield Wed.	49
1913-14e	Blackburn Rov.	51	Aston Villa	44	Middlesbrough	43
1914-15e	Everton	46	Oldham Athletic	45	Blackburn Rov.	43
1919-20f	W.B.A.	60	Burnley	51	Chelsea	49
1920-1f	Burnley	59	Manchester City	54	Bolton Wand.	52
1921-2f	Liverpool	57	Tottenham	51	Burnley	49
1922-3f	Liverpool	60	Sunderland	54	Huddersfield Town	53
1923-4f	*Huddersfield Town	57	Cardiff City	57	Sunderland	53
1924-5f	Huddersfield Town	58	W.B.A.	56	Bolton Wand.	55
1925-6f	Huddersfield Town	57	Arsenal	52	Sunderland	48
1926-7f	Newcastle Utd.	56	Huddersfield Town	51	Sunderland	49
1927-8f	Everton	53	Huddersfield Town	51	Leicester City	48
1928-9f	Sheffield Wed.	52	Leicester City	51	Aston Villa	50
1929-30f	Sheffield Wed.	60	Derby Co.	50	Manchester City	47
1930-1f	Arsenal	66	Aston Villa	59	Sheffield Wed.	52
1931-2f	Everton	56	Arsenal	54	Sheffield Wed.	50
1932-3f	Arsenal	58	Aston Villa	54	Sheffield Wed.	51
1933-4f	Arsenal	59	Huddersfield Town	56	Tottenham	49
1934-5f	Arsenal	58	Sunderland	54	Sheffield Wed.	49
1935-6f	Sunderland	56	Derby Co.	48	Huddersfield Town	48
1936-7f	Manchester City	57	Charlton Athletic	54	Arsenal	52
1937-8f	Arsenal	52	Wolves	51	Preston N.E.	49
1938-9f	Everton	59	Wolves	55	Charlton Athletic	50
1946-7f	Liverpool	57	Manchester Utd.	56	Wolves	56
1947-8f	Arsenal	59	Manchester Utd.	52	Burnley	52
1948-9f	Portsmouth	58	Manchester Utd.	53	Derby Co.	53
1949-50f	*Portsmouth	53	Wolves	53	Sunderland	52
1950-1f	Tottenham	60	Manchester Utd.	56	Blackpool	50
1951-2f	Manchester Utd.	57	Tottenham	53	Arsenal	53
1952-3f	*Arsenal	54	Preston N.E.	54	Wolves	51
1953-4f	Wolves	57	W.B.A.	53	Huddersfield Town	51
1954-5f	Chelsea	52	Wolves	48	Portsmouth	48
1955-6f	Manchester Utd.	60	Blackpool	49	Wolves	49
1956-7f	Manchester Utd.	64	Tottenham	56	Preston N.E.	56
1957-8f	Wolves	64	Preston N.E.	59	Tottenham	51
1958-9f	Wolves	61	Manchester Utd.	55	Arsenal	50

	First	Pts	Second	Pts	Third	Pts
1959-60f	Burnley	55	Wolves	54	Tottenham	53
1960-1f	Tottenham	66	Sheffield Wed.	58	Wolves	57
1961-2f	Ipswich Town	56	Burnley	53	Tottenham	52
1962-3f	Everton	61	Tottenham	55	Burnley	54
1963-4f	Liverpool	57	Manchester Utd.	53	Everton	52
1964-5f	*Manchester Utd.	61	Leeds Utd.	61	Chelsea	56
1965-6f	Liverpool	61	Leeds Utd.	55	Burnley	55
1966-7f	Manchester Utd.	60	Nott'm Forest	56	Tottenham	56
1967-8f	Manchester City	58	Manchester Utd.	56	Liverpool	55
1968-9f	Leeds Utd.	67	Liverpool	61	Everton	57
1969-70f	Everton	66	Leeds Utd.	57	Chelsea	55
1970-1f	Arsenal	65	Leeds Utd.	64	Tottenham	52
1971-2f	Derby Co.	58	Leeds Utd.	57	Liverpool	57
1972-3f	Liverpool	60	Arsenal	57	Leeds Utd.	53
1973-4f	Leeds Utd.	62	Liverpool	57	Derby Co.	48
1974-5f	Derby Co.	53	Liverpool	51	Ipswich Town	51
1975-6f	Liverpool	60	Q.P.R.	59	Manchester Utd.	56
1976-7f	Liverpool	57	Manchester City	56	Ipswich Town	52
1977-8f	Nott'm Forest	64	Liverpool	57	Everton	55
1978-9f	Liverpool	68	Nott'm Forest	60	W.B.A.	59
1979-80f	Liverpool	60	Manchester Utd.	58	Ipswich Town	53
1980-1f	Aston Villa	60	Ipswich Town	56	Arsenal	53
1981-2g	Liverpool	87	Ipswich Town	83	Manchester Utd.	78
1982-3g	Liverpool	82	Watford	71	Manchester Utd.	70
1983-4g	Liverpool	80	Southampton	77	Nott'm Forest	74
1984-5g	Everton	90	Liverpool	77	Tottenham	77
1985-6g	Liverpool	88	Everton	86	West Ham Utd.	84
1986-7g	Everton	86	Liverpool	77	Tottenham	71
1987-8h	Liverpool	90	Manchester Utd.	81	Nott'm Forest	73
1988-9j	†Arsenal	76	Liverpool	76	Nott'm Forest	64
1989-90j	Liverpool	79	Aston Villa	70	Tottenham	63
1990-1j	Arsenal	83	Liverpool	76	Crystal Palace	69
1991-2g	Leeds Utd.	82	Manchester Utd.	78	Sheffield Wed.	75

Maximum points: *a*, 44; *b*, 52; *c*, 60; *d*, 68; *e*, 76; *f*, 84; *g*, 126; *h*, 120; *j*, 114.
*Won on goal average. †Won on goal diff. No comp. 1915-19 – 1939-46

OLD SECOND DIVISION 1892-1992

	First	Pts.	Second	Pts.	Third	Pts.
1892-3a	Small Heath	36	Sheffield Utd.	35	Darwen	30
1893-4b	Liverpool	50	Small Heath	42	Notts Co.	39
1894-5c	Bury	48	Notts County	39	Newton Heath	38
1895-6c	*Liverpool	46	Manchester City	46	Grimsby Town	42
1896-7c	Notts Co.	42	Newton Heath	39	Grimsby Town	38
1897-8c	Burnley	48	Newcastle Utd.	45	Manchester City	39
1898-9d	Manchester City	52	Glossop	46	Leicester Fosse	45
1899-1900d	The Wednesday	54	Bolton Wand.	52	Small Heath	46
1900-1d	Grimsby Town	49	Small Heath	48	Burnley	44
1901-2d	W.B.A.	55	Middlesbrough	51	Preston N.E.	42
1902-3d	Manchester City	54	Small Heath	51	Woolwich Arsenal	48
1903-4d	Preston N.E.	50	Woolwich Arsenal	49	Manchester Utd.	48
1904-5d	Liverpool	58	Bolton Wand.	56	Manchester Utd.	53
1905-6e	Bristol City	66	Manchester Utd.	62	Chelsea	53
1906-7e	Nott'm Forest	60	Chelsea	57	Leicester Fosse	48
1907-8e	Bradford City	54	Leicester Fosse	52	Oldham Athletic	50
1908-9e	Bolton Wand.	52	Tottenham	51	W.B.A.	51
1909-10e	Manchester City	54	Oldham Athletic	53	Hull City	53
1910-11e	W.B.A.	53	Bolton Wand.	51	Chelsea	49
1911-12e	*Derby Co.	54	Chelsea	54	Burnley	52

1912-13e	Preston N.E. 53	Burnley 50	Birmingham City 46
1913-14e	Notts County 53	Bradford City P.A. .. 49	Woolwich Arsenal 49
1914-15e	Derby Co. 53	Preston N.E. 50	Barnsley 47
1919-20f	Tottenham 70	Huddersfield Town .. 64	Birmingham City 56
1920-1f	*Birmingham City .. 58	Cardiff City 58	Bristol City 51
1921-2f	Nott'm Forest 56	Stoke City 52	Barnsley 52
1922-3f	Notts County 53	West Ham Utd. ... 51	Leicester City ... 51
1923-4f	Leeds Utd. 54	Bury 51	Derby Co. 51
1924-5f	Leicester City 59	Manchester Utd. ... 57	Derby Co. 55
1925-6f	Sheffield Wed. 60	Derby Co. 57	Chelsea 52
1926-7f	Middlesbrough 62	Portsmouth 54	Manchester City 54
1927-8f	Manchester City 59	Leeds Utd. 57	Chelsea 54
1928-9f	Middlesbrough 55	Grimsby Town 53	Bradford City 48
1929-30f	Blackpool 58	Chelsea 55	Oldham Athletic 53
1930-1f	Everton 61	W.B.A. 54	Tottenham 51
1931-2f	Wolves 56	Leeds Utd. 54	Stoke City 52
1932-3f	Stoke City 56	Tottenham 55	Fulham 50
1933-4f	Grimsby Town 59	Preston N.E. 52	Bolton Wand. 51
1934-5f	Brentford 61	Bolton Wand. 56	West Ham Utd. 56
1935-6f	Manchester Utd. 56	Charlton Athletic 55	Sheffield Utd. 52
1936-7f	Leicester City 56	Blackpool 55	Bury 52
1937-8f	Aston Villa 57	Manchester Utd. 53	Sheffield Utd. 53
1938-9f	Blackburn Rov. 55	Sheffield Utd. 54	Sheffield Wed. 53
1946-7f	Manchester City 62	Burnley 58	Birmingham City 55
1947-8f	Birmingham City 59	Newcastle Utd. 56	Southampton 52
1948-9f	Fulham 57	W.B.A. 56	Southampton 55
1949-50f	Tottenham 61	Sheffield Wed. 52	Sheffield Utd. 52
1950-1f	Preston N.E. 57	Manchester City 52	Cardiff City 50
1951-2f	Sheffield Wed. 53	Cardiff City 51	Birmingham City 51
1952-3f	Sheffield Utd. 60	Huddersfield Town .. 58	Luton Town 52
1953-4f	*Leicester City 56	Everton 56	Blackburn Rov. 55
1954-5f	*Birmingham City ... 54	Luton Town 54	Rotherham Utd. 54
1955-6f	Sheffield Wed. 55	Leeds Utd. 52	Liverpool 48
1956-7f	Leicester City 61	Nott'm Forest 54	Liverpool 53
1957-8f	West Ham Utd. 57	Blackburn Rov. 56	Charlton Athletic ... 55
1958-9f	Sheffield Wed. 62	Fulham 60	Sheffield Utd. 53
1959-60f	Aston Villa 59	Cardiff City 58	Liverpool 50
1960-1f	Ipswich Town 59	Sheffield Utd. 58	Liverpool 52
1961-2f	Liverpool 62	Leyton Orient 54	Sunderland 53
1962-3f	Stoke City 53	Chelsea 52	Sunderland 52
1963-4f	Leeds Utd. 63	Sunderland 61	Preston N.E. 56
1964-5f	Newcastle Utd. 57	Northampton Town . 56	Bolton Wand. 50
1965-6f	Manchester City 59	Southampton 54	Coventry City 53
1966-7f	Coventry City 59	Wolves 58	Carlisle Utd. 52
1967-8f	Ipswich Town 59	Q.P.R. 58	Blackpool 58
1968-9f	Derby Co. 63	Crystal Palace 56	Charlton Athletic ... 50
1969-70f	Huddersfield Town .. 60	Blackpool 53	Leicester City 51
1970-1f	Leicester City 59	Sheffield Utd. 56	Cardiff City 53
1971-2f	Norwich City 57	Birmingham City ... 56	Millwall 55
1972-3f	Burnley 62	Q.P.R. 61	Aston Villa 60
1973-4f	Middlesbrough 65	Luton Town 50	Carlisle Utd. 49
1974-5f	Manchester Utd. 61	Aston Villa 58	Norwich City 53
1975-6f	Sunderland 56	Bristol City 53	W.B.A. 53
1976-7f	Wolves 57	Chelsea 55	Nott'm Forest 52
1977-8f	Bolton Wand. 58	Southampton 57	Tottenham 56
1978-9f	Crystal Palace 57	Brighton & H.A. 56	Stoke City 56
1979-80f	Leicester City 55	Sunderland 54	Birmingham City ... 53
1980-1f	West Ham Utd. 66	Notts Co. 53	Swansea City 50

1981-2g	Luton Town 88	Watford 80	Norwich City 71
1982-3g	Q.P.R. 85	Wolves 75	Leicester City 70
1983-4g	†Chelsea 88	Sheffield Wed. 88	Newcastle Utd. 80
1984-5g	Oxford Utd. 84	Birmingham City 82	Manchester City 74
1985-6g	Norwich City 84	Charlton Athletic 77	Wimbledon 76
1986-7g	Derby Co. 84	Portsmouth 78	††Oldham Athletic .. 75
1987-8h	Millwall 82	Aston Villa 78	Middlesbrough 78
1988-9j	Chelsea 99	Manchester City 82	Crystal Palace 81
1989-90j	†Leeds Utd. 85	Sheffield Utd. 85	†† Newcastle Utd. .. 80
1990-1j	Oldham Athletic 88	West Ham Utd. 87	Sheffield Wed. 82
1991-2j	Ipswich Town 84	Middlesbrough 80	†† Derby Co. 78

Maximum points: *a*, 44; *b*, 56; *c*, 60; *d*, 68; *e*, 76; *f*, 84; *g*, 126; *h*, 132; *j*, 138. * Won on goal average. † Won on goal difference. †† Not promoted after play-offs.

THIRD DIVISION 1958-92

	First	Pts.	Second	Pts.	Third	Pts.
1958-9	Plymouth Argyle 62		Hull City 61		Brentford 57	
1959-60	Southampton 61		Norwich City 59		Shrewsbury Town ... 52	
1960-1	Bury 68		Walsall 62		Q.P.R. 60	
1961-2	Portsmouth 65		Grimsby Town 62		Bournemouth 59	
1962-3	Northampton Town . 62		Swindon Town 58		Port Vale 54	
1963-4	*Coventry City 60		Crystal Palace 60		Watford 58	
1964-5	Carlisle Utd. 60		Bristol City 59		Mansfield Town 59	
1965-6	Hull City 69		Millwall 65		Q.P.R. 57	
1966-7	Q.P.R. 67		Middlesbrough 55		Watford 54	
1967-8	Oxford Utd. 57		Bury 56		Shrewsbury Town ... 55	
1968-9	*Watford 64		Swindon Town 64		Luton Town 61	
1969-70	Orient 62		Luton Town 60		Bristol Rov. 56	
1970-1	Preston N.E. 61		Fulham 60		Halifax Town 56	
1971-2	Aston Villa 70		Brighton & H.A. 65		Bournemouth 62	
1972-3	Bolton Wand. 61		Notts Co. 57		Blackburn Rov. 55	
1973-4	Oldham Athletic 62		Bristol Rov. 61		York City 61	
1974-5	Blackburn Rov. 60		Plymouth Argyle 59		Charlton Athletic 55	
1975-6	Hereford 63		Cardiff City 57		Millwall 56	
1976-7	Mansfield Town 64		Brighton & H.A. 61		Crystal Palace 59	
1977-8	Wrexham 61		Cambridge Utd. 58		Preston N.E. 56	
1978-9	Shrewsbury Town ... 61		Watford 60		Swansea City 60	
1979-80	Grimsby Town 62		Blackburn Rov. 59		Sheffield Wed. 58	
1980-1	Rotherham Utd. 61		Barnsley 59		Charlton Athletic 59	
†1981-2	*Burnley 80		Carlisle Utd. 80		Fulham 78	
†1982-3	Portsmouth 91		Cardiff City 86		Huddersfield Town .. 82	
†1983-4	Oxford Utd. 95		Wimbledon 87		Sheffield Utd. 83	
†1984-5	Bradford City 94		Millwall 90		Hull City 87	
†1985-6	Reading 94		Plymouth Argyle 87		Derby Co. 84	
†1986-7	Bournemouth 97		Middlesbrough 94		Swindon Town 87	
†1987-8	Sunderland 93		Brighton & H.A. 84		Walsall 82	
†1988-9	Wolves 92		Sheffield Utd. 84		Port Vale 84	
†1989-90	Bristol Rov. 93		Bristol City 91		Notts Co. 87	
†1990-1	Cambridge Utd. 86		Southend Utd. 85		Grimsby Town 83	
†1991-2	Brentford 82		Birmingham City 81		††Huddersfield T 78	

* Won on goal average. † Maximum points 138 (previously 92). †† Not promoted after play-offs.

FOURTH DIVISION 1958-92

	First	Pts.	Second	Pts.	Third	Pts.	Fourth	Pts.
1958-9	Port Vale 64		Coventry City 60		York City 60		Shrewsbury Town 58	
1959-60	Walsall 65		Notts Co. 60		Torquay Utd. 60		Watford 57	

1960-1	Peterborough Utd. .. 66	Crystal Palace 64	Northampton Town . 60	Bradford City P.A. ... 60
1961-2	Millwall 56	Colchester Utd. 55	Wrexham 53	Carlisle Utd. 52
1962-3	Brentford 62	Oldham Athletic 59	Crewe Alexandra ... 59	Mansfield Town 57
1963-4	*Gillingham 60	Carlisle Utd. 60	Workington 59	Exeter City 58
1964-5	Brighton & H.A. 63	Millwall 62	York City 62	Oxford Utd. 61
1965-6	*Doncaster Rov. 59	Darlington 59	Torquay Utd. 58	Colchester Utd. 56
1966-7	Stockport Co. 64	Southport 59	Barrow 59	Tranmere Rov. 58
1967-8	Luton Town 66	Barnsley 61	Hartlepool Utd. 60	Crewe Alexandra ... 58
1968-9	Doncaster Rov. 59	Halifax Town 57	Rochdale 56	Bradford City 56
1969-70	Chesterfield 64	Wrexham 61	Swansea City 60	Port Vale 59
1970-1	Notts Co. 69	Bournemouth 60	Oldham Athletic 59	York City 56
1971-2	Grimsby Town 63	Southend Utd. 60	Brentford 59	Scunthorpe Utd. 57
1972-3	Southport 62	Hereford 58	Cambridge Utd. 57	Aldershot 56
1973-4	Peterborough Utd. .. 65	Gillingham 62	Colchester Utd. 60	Bury 59
1974-5	Mansfield Town 68	Shrewsbury Town ... 62	Rotherham Utd. 58	Chester City 57
1975-6	Lincoln City 74	Northampton Town . 68	Reading 60	Tranmere Rov. 58
1976-7	Cambridge Utd. 65	Exeter City 62	Colchester Utd. 59	Bradford City 59
1977-8	Watford 71	Southend Utd. 60	Swansea City 56	Brentford 59
1978-9	Reading 65	Grimsby Town 61	Wimbledon 61	Barnsley 61
1979-80	Huddersfield Town .. 66	Walsall 64	Newport 61	Portsmouth 60
1980-1	Southend Utd. 67	Lincoln City 65	Doncaster Rov. 56	Wimbledon 55
†1981-2	Sheffield Utd. 96	Bradford City 91	Wigan Athletic 91	Bournemouth 88
†1982-3	Wimbledon 98	Hull City 90	Port Vale 88	Scunthorpe Utd. 83
†1983-4	York City 101	Doncaster Rov. 85	Reading 82	Bristol City 82
†1984-5	Chesterfield 91	Blackpool 86	Darlington 85	Bury 84
†1985-6	Swindon Town 102	Chester City 84	Mansfield Town 81	Port Vale 79
†1986-7	Northampton Town . 99	Preston N.E. 90	Southend Utd. 80	††Wolves 79
†1987-8	Wolves 90	Cardiff City 85	Bolton Wand. 78	††Scunthorpe Utd. . 77
†1988-9	Rotherham Utd. 82	Tranmere Rov. 80	Crewe Alexandra ... 78	††Scunthorpe Utd. . 77
†1989-90	Exeter City 89	Grimsby Town 79	Southend Utd. 75	††Stockport Co. 74
†1990-1	Darlington 83	Stockport Co. 82	Hartlepool Utd. 82	Peterborough Utd. .. 80
1991-2a	Burnley 83	Rotherham Utd. 77	Mansfield Town 77	Blackpool 76

* Won on goal average. Maximum points: †, 138; a, 126; previously 92. †† Not promoted after play-offs.

THIRD DIVISION – SOUTH 1920-58

	First	Pts.	Second	Pts.	Third	Pts.
1920-1a	Crystal Palace 59		Southampton 54		Q.P.R. 53	
1921-2a	*Southampton 61		Plymouth Argyle 61		Portsmouth 53	
1922-3a	Bristol City 59		Plymouth Argyle 53		Swansea City 53	
1923-4a	Portsmouth 59		Plymouth Argyle 55		Millwall 54	
1924-5a	Swansea City 57		Plymouth Argyle 56		Bristol City 53	
1925-6a	Reading 57		Plymouth Argyle 56		Millwall 53	
1926-7a	Bristol City 62		Plymouth Argyle 60		Millwall 56	
1927-8a	Millwall 65		Northampton Town . 55		Plymouth Argyle 53	
1928-9a	*Charlton Athletic ... 54		Crystal Palace 54		Northampton Town . 52	
1929-30a	Plymouth Argyle 68		Brentford 61		Q.P.R. 51	
1930-31a	Notts Co. 59		Crystal Palace 51		Brentford 50	
1931-2a	Fulham 57		Reading 55		Southend Utd. 53	
1932-3a	Brentford 62		Exeter City 58		Norwich City 57	
1933-4a	Norwich City 61		Coventry City 54		Reading 54	
1934-5a	Charlton Athletic 61		Reading 53		Coventry City 51	
1935-6a	Coventry City 57		Luton Town 56		Reading 54	
1936-7a	Luton Town 58		Notts Co. 56		Brighton & H.A. 53	
1937-8a	Millwall 56		Bristol City 55		Q.P.R. 53	
1938-9a	Newport 55		Crystal Palace 52		Brighton & H.A. 49	
1946-7a	Cardiff City 66		Q.P.R. 57		Bristol City 51	
1947-8a	Q.P.R. 61		Bournemouth 57		Walsall 51	

	First	Pts.	Second	Pts.	Third	Pts.
1948-9a	Swansea City	62	Reading	55	Bournemouth	52
1949-50a	Notts Co.	58	Northampton Town	51	Southend Utd.	51
1950-1d	Nott'm Forest	70	Norwich City	64	Reading	57
1951-2d	Plymouth Argyle	66	Reading	61	Norwich City	61
1952-3d	Bristol Rov.	64	Millwall	62	Northampton Town	62
1953-4d	Ipswich Town	64	Brighton & H.A.	61	Bristol City	56
1954-5d	Bristol City	70	Leyton Orient	61	Southampton	59
1955-6d	Leyton Orient	66	Brighton & H.A.	65	Ipswich Town	64
1956-7d	*Ipswich Town	59	Torquay Utd.	59	Colchester Utd.	58
1957-8d	Brighton & H.A.	60	Brentford	58	Plymouth Argyle	58

THIRD DIVISION – NORTH 1921-58

	First	Pts.	Second	Pts.	Third	Pts.
1921-2b	Stockport Co.	56	Darlington	50	Grimsby Town	50
1922-3b	Nelson	51	Bradford P.A.	47	Walsall	46
1923-4a	Wolves	63	Rochdale	62	Chesterfield	54
1924-5a	Darlington	58	Nelson	53	New Brighton	53
1925-6a	Grimsby Town	61	Bradford P.A.	60	Rochdale	59
1926-7a	Stoke City	63	Rochdale	58	Bradford P.A.	57
1927-8a	Bradford P.A.	63	Lincoln City	55	Stockport Co.	54
1928-9a	Bradford City	63	Stockport Co.	62	Wrexham	52
1929-30a	Port Vale	67	Stockport Co.	63	Darlington	50
1930-1a	Chesterfield	58	Lincoln City	57	Wrexham	54
1931-2c	*Lincoln City	57	Gateshead	57	Chester City	50
1932-3a	Hull City	59	Wrexham	57	Stockport Co.	54
1933-4a	Barnsley	62	Chesterfield	61	Stockport Co.	59
1934-5a	Doncaster Rov.	57	Halifax Town	55	Chester City	54
1935-6a	Chesterfield	60	Chester City	55	Tranmere Rov.	54
1936-7a	Stockport Co.	60	Lincoln City	57	Chester City	53
1937-8a	Tranmere Rov.	56	Doncaster Rov.	54	Hull City	53
1938-9a	Barnsley	67	Doncaster Rov.	56	Bradford City	52
1946-7a	Doncaster Rov.	72	Rotherham Utd.	64	Chester City	56
1947-8a	Lincoln City	60	Rotherham Utd.	59	Wrexham	50
1948-9a	Hull City	65	Rotherham Utd.	62	Doncaster Rov.	50
1949-50a	Doncaster Rov.	55	Gateshead	53	Rochdale	51
1950-1d	Rotherham Utd.	71	Mansfield Town	64	Carlisle Utd.	62
1951-2d	Lincoln City	69	Grimsby Town	66	Stockport Co.	59
1952-3d	Oldham Athletic	59	Port Vale	58	Wrexham	56
1953-4d	Port Vale	69	Barnsley	58	Scunthorpe Utd.	57
1954-5d	Barnsley	65	Accrington	61	Scunthorpe Utd.	58
1955-6d	Grimsby Town	68	Derby Co.	63	Accrington	59
1956-7d	Derby Co.	63	Hartlepool Utd.	59	Accrington	58
1957-8d	Scunthorpe Utd.	66	Accrington	59	Bradford City	57

Maximum points: *a*, 84; *b*, 76; *c*, 80; *d*, 92. * Won on goal average.

CHAMPIONSHIP WINNERS

F.A. PREMIER LEAGUE
Manchester Utd.	5
Blackburn Rov.	1
Arsenal	1

FOOTBALL LEAGUE
DIV.1 (NEW)
Sunderland	2
Bolton Wand.	1
Crystal Palace	1
Middlesbrough	1

Newcastle Utd.	1
Nott'm Forest	1

DIV.1 (ORIGINAL)
Liverpool	18
Arsenal	10
Everton	9
Aston Villa	7
Manchester Utd.	7
Sunderland	6
Newcastle Utd.	4

Sheffield Wed.	4
Huddersfield Town	3
Leeds Utd.	3
Wolves	3
Blackburn Rov.	2
Burnley	2
Derby Co.	2
Manchester City	2
Portsmouth	2
Preston N.E.	2
Tottenham	2

Chelsea	1
Ipswich Town	1
Nott'm Forest	1
Sheffield Utd.	1
W.B.A.	1

DIV.2 (NEW)

Birmingham City	1
Bury	1
Fulham	1
Reading	1
Stoke City	1
Swindon Town	1
Watford	1

DIV.2 (ORIGINAL)

Leicester City	6
Manchester City	6
Sheffield Wed.	5

Birmingham City	4
Derby Co.	4
Liverpool	4
Ipswich Town	3
Leeds Utd.	3
Middlesbrough	3
Notts County	3
Preston N.E.	3
Aston Villa	2
Bolton Wand.	2
Burnley	2
Chelsea	2
Grimsby Town	2
Manchester Utd.	2
Norwich City	2
Nott'm Forest	2
Stoke City	2
Tottenham	2
W.B.A.	2
West Ham Utd.	2

Wolves	2
Blackburn Rov.	1
Blackpool	1
Bradford City	1
Brentford	1
Bristol City	1
Bury	1
Coventry City	1
Crystal Palace	1
Everton	1
Fulham	1
Huddersfield Town	1
Luton Town	1
Millwall	1
Newcastle Utd.	1
Oldham Athletic	1
Oxford Utd.	1
Q.P.R.	1
Sheffield Utd.	1
Sunderland	1

APPLICATIONS FOR RE-ELECTION

(System discontinued 1987)

14	Hartlepool Utd.	4	Norwich City	2	Oldham Athletic
12	Halifax Town	3	Aldershot	2	Q.P.R.
11	Barrow	3	Bradford City	2	Rotherham Utd.
11	Southport	3	Crystal Palace	2	Scunthorpe Utd.
10	Crewe Alexandra	3	Doncaster Rov.	2	Southend Utd.
10	Newport	3	Hereford	2	Watford
10	Rochdale	3	Merthyr Tyd.	1	Blackpool
8	Darlington	3	Swindon Town	1	Brighton & H.A.
8	Exeter City	3	Torquay Utd.	1	Bristol Rov.
7	Chester City	3	Tranmere Rov.	1	Cambridge Utd.
7	Walsall	2	Aberdare	1	Cardiff City
7	Workington	2	Ashington	1	Carlisle Utd.
7	York City	2	Bournemouth	1	Charlton Athletic
6	Stockport Co.	2	Brentford	1	Mansfield Town
5	Accrington	2	Colchester Utd.	1	Port Vale
5	Gillingham	2	Durham C.	1	Preston N.E.
5	Lincoln City	2	Gateshead	1	Shrewsbury Town
5	New Brighton & H.A.	2	Grimsby Town	1	Swansea City
4	Bradford City P.A.	2	Millwall	1	Thames
4	Northampton Town	2	Nelson	1	Wrexham

RELEGATED CLUBS (TO 1992)

1892-3	In Test matches, Darwen and Sheffield Utd. won promotion in place of Accrington and Notts Co.
1893-4	Tests, Liverpool and Small Heath won promotion. Darwen and Newton Heath relegated.
1894-5	After Tests, Bury promoted, Liverpool relegated.
1895-6	After Tests, Liverpool promoted, Small Heath relegated.
1896-7	After Tests, Notts Co. promoted, Burnley relegated.
1897-8	Test system abolished after success of Burnley and Stoke City, League extended. Blackburn Rov. and Newcastle Utd. elected to First Division. Automatic promotion and relegation introduced.

FIRST DIVISION TO SECOND DIVISION

1898-9	Bolton Wand., Sheffield Wed.
1899-00	Burnley, Glossop
1900-1	Preston N.E., W.B.A.
1901-2	Small Heath, Manchester City
1902-3	Grimsby Town, Bolton Wand.
1903-4	Liverpool, W.B.A.
1904-5	League extended. Bury and Notts Co., two bottom clubs in First Division, re-elected.
1905-6	Nott'm Forest, Wolves
1906-7	Derby Co., Stoke City
1907-8	Bolton Wand., Birmingham City
1908-9	Manchester City, Leicester Fosse
1909-10	Bolton Wand., Chelsea
1910-11	Bristol City, Nott'm Forest
1911-12	Preston N.E., Bury
1912-13	Notts Co., Woolwich Arsenal
1913-14	Preston N.E., Derby Co.
1914-15	Tottenham, *Chelsea
1919-20	Notts Co., Sheffield Wed.
1920-1	Derby Co., Bradford P.A.
1921-2	Bradford City, Manchester Utd.
1922-3	Stoke City, Oldham Athletic
1923-4	Chelsea, Middlesbrough
1924-5	Preston N.E., Nott'm Forest
1925-6	Manchester City, Notts Co.
1926-7	Leeds Utd., W.B.A.
1927-8	Tottenham, Middlesbrough
1928-9	Bury, Cardiff City
1929-30	Burnley, Everton
1930-1	Leeds Utd., Manchester Utd.
1931-2	Grimsby Town, West Ham Utd.
1932-3	Bolton Wand., Blackpool
1933-4	Newcastle Utd., Sheffield Utd.
1934-5	Leicester City, Tottenham
1935-6	Aston Villa, Blackburn Rov.
1936-7	Manchester Utd., Sheffield Wed.
1937-8	Manchester City, W.B.A.
1938-9	Birmingham City, Leicester City
1946-7	Brentford, Leeds Utd.
1947-8	Blackburn Rov., Grimsby Town
1948-9	Preston N.E., Sheffield Utd.
1949-50	Manchester City, Birmingham City
1950-1	Sheffield Wed., Everton
1951-2	Huddersfield Town, Fulham
1952-3	Stoke City, Derby Co.
1953-4	Middlesbrough, Liverpool
1954-5	Leicester City, Sheffield Wed.
1955-6	Huddersfield Town, Sheffield Utd.
1956-7	Charlton Athletic, Cardiff City
1957-8	Sheffield Wed., Sunderland
1958-9	Portsmouth, Aston Villa
1959-60	Luton Town, Leeds Utd.
1960-61	Preston N.E., Newcastle Utd.
1961-2	Chelsea, Cardiff City
1962-3	Manchester City, Leyton Orient
1963-4	Bolton Wand., Ipswich Town
1964-5	Wolves, Birmingham City

1965-6	Northampton Town, Blackburn Rov.
1966-7	Aston Villa, Blackpool
1967-8	Fulham, Sheffield Utd.
1968-9	Leicester City, Q.P.R.
1969-70	Sheffield Wed., Sunderland
1970-1	Burnley, Blackpool
1971-2	Nott'm Forest, Huddersfield Town
1972-3	W.B.A., Crystal Palace
1973-4	Norwich City, Manchester Utd., Southampton
1974-5	Chelsea, Luton Town, Carlisle Utd.
1975-6	Sheffield Utd., Burnley, Wolves
1976-7	Tottenham, Stoke City, Sunderland
1977-8	Leicester City, West Ham Utd., Newcastle Utd.
1978-9	Q.P.R., Birmingham City, Chelsea
1979-80	Bristol City, Derby Co., Bolton Wand.
1980-1	Norwich City, Leicester City, Crystal Palace
1981-2	Leeds Utd., Wolves, Middlesbrough
1982-3	Manchester City, Swansea City, Brighton & H.A.
1983-4	Birmingham City, Notts Co., Wolves
1984-5	Norwich City, Sunderland, Stoke City
1985-6	Ipswich Town, Birmingham City, W.B.A.
1986-7	Leicester City, Manchester City, Aston Villa
1987-8	Chelsea**, Portsmouth, Watford, Oxford Utd.
1988-9	Middlesbrough, West Ham Utd., Newcastle Utd.
1989-90	Sheffield Wed., Charlton Athletic, Millwall
1990-1	Sunderland, Derby Co.
1991-2	Luton Town, Notts Co., West Ham Utd.

* Subsequently re-elected to First Division when League extended after the war.
** Relegated after play-offs.

SECOND DIVISION TO THIRD DIVISION

1920-1	Stockport Co.
1921-2	Bradford City, Bristol City
1922-3	Rotherham Utd., Wolves
1923-4	Nelson, Bristol City
1924-5	Crystal Palace, Coventry City
1925-6	Stoke City, Stockport Co.
1926-7	Darlington, Bradford City
1927-8	Fulham, South Shields
1928-9	Port Vale, Clapton Orient
1929-30	Hull City, Notts County
1930-1	Reading, Cardiff City
1931-2	Barnsley, Bristol City
1932-3	Chesterfield, Charlton Athletic
1933-4	Millwall, Lincoln City
1934-5	Oldham Athletic, Notts Co.
1935-6	Port Vale, Hull City
1936-7	Doncaster Rov., Bradford City
1937-8	Barnsley, Stockport Co.
1938-9	Norwich City, Tranmere Rov.
1946-7	Swansea City, Newport
1947-8	Doncaster Rov., Millwall
1948-9	Nott'm Forest, Lincoln City
1949-50	Plymouth Argyle, Bradford City P.A.
1950-1	Grimsby Town, Chesterfield
1951-2	Coventry City, Q.P.R.
1952-3	Southampton, Barnsley

1953-4	Brentford, Oldham Athletic
1954-5	Ipswich Town, Derby Co.
1955-6	Plymouth Argyle, Hull City
1956-7	Port Vale, Bury
1957-8	Doncaster Rov., Notts Co.
1958-9	Barnsley, Grimsby Town
1959-60	Bristol City, Hull City
1960-1	Lincoln City, Portsmouth
1961-2	Brighton & H.A., Bristol Rov.
1962-3	Walsall, Luton Town
1963-4	Grimsby Town, Scunthorpe Utd.
1964-5	Swindon Town, Swansea City
1965-6	Middlesbrough, Leyton Orient
1966-7	Northampton Town, Bury
1967-8	Plymouth Argyle, Rotherham Utd.
1968-9	Fulham, Bury
1969-70	Preston N.E., Aston Villa
1970-1	Blackburn Rov., Bolton Wand.
1971-2	Charlton Athletic, Watford
1972-3	Huddersfield Town, Brighton & H.A.
1973-4	Crystal Palace, Preston N.E., Swindon Town
1974-5	Millwall, Cardiff City, Sheffield Wed.
1975-6	Portsmouth, Oxford Utd., York City
1976-7	Carlisle Utd., Plymouth Argyle, Hereford
1977-8	Hull City, Mansfield Town, Blackpool
1978-9	Sheffield Utd., Millwall, Blackburn Rov.
1979-80	Fulham, Burnley, Charlton Athletic
1980-1	Preston N.E., Bristol City, Bristol Rov.
1981-2	Cardiff City, Wrexham, Orient
1982-3	Rotherham Utd., Burnley, Bolton Wand.
1983-4	Derby Co., Swansea City, Cambridge Utd.
1984-5	Notts Co., Cardiff City, Wolves
1985-6	Carlisle Utd., Middlesbrough, Fulham
1986-7	Sunderland**, Grimsby Town, Brighton & H.A.
1987-8	Sheffield Utd.**, Reading, Huddersfield Town
1988-9	Shrewsbury Town, Birmingham City, Walsall
1989-90	Bournemouth, Bradford City, Stoke City
1990-1	W.B.A., Hull City
1991-2	Plymouth Argyle, Brighton & H.A., Port Vale

** Relegated after play-offs.

THIRD DIVISION TO FOURTH DIVISION

1958-9	Rochdale, Notts Co., Doncaster Rov., Stockport Co.
1959-60	Accrington, Wrexham, Mansfield Town, York City
1960-1	Chesterfield, Colchester Utd., Bradford City, Tranmere Rov.
1961-2	Newport, Brentford, Lincoln City, Torquay Utd.
1962-3	Bradford City P.A., Brighton & H.A., Carlisle Utd., Halifax Town
1963-4	Millwall, Crewe Alexandra, Wrexham, Notts Co.
1964-5	Luton Town, Port Vale, Colchester Utd., Barnsley
1965-6	Southend Utd., Exeter City, Brentford, York City
1966-7	Doncaster Rov., Workington, Darlington, Swansea City
1967-8	Scunthorpe Utd., Colchester Utd., Grimsby Town, Peterborough Utd. (demoted)
1968-9	Oldham Athletic, Crewe Alexandra, Hartlepool Utd., Northampton Town
1969-70	Bournemouth, Southport, Barrow, Stockport Co.
1970-1	Gillingham, Doncaster Rov., Bury, Reading
1971-2	Mansfield Town, Barnsley, Torquay Utd., Bradford City

1972-3	Scunthorpe Utd., Swansea City, Brentford, Rotherham Utd.
1973-4	Cambridge Utd., Shrewsbury Town, Rochdale, Southport
1974-5	Bournemouth, Watford, Tranmere Rov., Huddersfield Town
1975-6	Aldershot, Colchester Utd., Southend Utd., Halifax Town
1976-7	Reading, Northampton Town, Grimsby Town, York City
1977-8	Port Vale, Bradford City, Hereford, Portsmouth
1978-9	Peterborough Utd., Walsall, Tranmere Rov., Lincoln City
1979-80	Bury, Southend Utd., Mansfield Town, Wimbledon
1980-1	Sheffield Utd., Colchester Utd., Blackpool, Hull City
1981-2	Wimbledon, Swindon Town, Bristol City, Chester City
1982-3	Reading, Wrexham, Doncaster Rov., Chesterfield
1983-4	Scunthorpe Utd., Southend Utd., Port Vale, Exeter City
1984-5	Burnley, Orient, Preston N.E., Cambridge Utd.
1985-6	Lincoln City, Cardiff City, Wolves, Swansea City
1986-7	Bolton Wand.**, Carlisle Utd., Darlington, Newport
1987-8	Doncaster Rov., York City, Grimsby Town, Rotherham Utd.**
1988-9	Southend Utd., Chesterfield, Gillingham, Aldershot
1989-90	Cardiff City, Northampton Town, Blackpool, Walsall
1990-1	Crewe Alexandra, Rotherham Utd., Mansfield Town
1991-2	Bury, Shrewsbury Town, Torquay Utd., Darlington

** Relegated after play-offs.

DEMOTED FROM FOURTH DIVISION TO GM VAUXHALL CONFERENCE

1987	Lincoln City
1988	Newport
1989	Darlington
1990	Colchester Utd.
1991	No demotion
1992	No demotion

DEMOTED FROM THIRD DIVISION TO GM VAUXHALL CONFERENCE

1993	Halifax Town
1994-6	No demotion
1997	Hereford
1998	Doncaster Rov.
1999	Scarborough

RELEGATED CLUBS (SINCE 1993)

1993

Premier League to Div. 1: Crystal Palace, Middlesbrough, Nott'm Forest
Div. 1 to Div. 2: Brentford, Cambridge Utd., Bristol Rov.
Div. 2 to Div. 3: Preston N.E., Mansfield Town, Wigan Athletic, Chester City

1994

Premier League to Div. 1: Sheffield Utd., Oldham Athletic, Swindon Town
Div. 1 to Div. 2: Birmingham City, Oxford Utd., Peterborough Utd.
Div. 2 to Div. 3: Fulham, Exeter City, Hartlepool Utd., Barnet

1995

Premier League to Div. 1: Crystal Palace, Norwich City, Leicester City, Ipswich Town
Div. 1 to Div. 2: Swindon Town, Burnley, Bristol City, Notts Co.
Div. 2 to Div. 3: Cambridge Utd., Plymouth Argyle, Cardiff City, Chester City, Leyton Orient

1996

Premier League to Div. 1: Manchester City, Q.P.R., Bolton Wand.
Div. 1 to Div. 2: Millwall, Watford, Luton Town
Div. 2 to Div. 3: Carlisle Utd., Swansea City, Brighton & H.A., Hull City

1997

Premier League to Div. 1: Sunderland, Middlesbrough, Nott'm Forest
Div. 1 to Div. 2: Grimsby Town, Oldham Athletic, Southend Utd.
Div. 2 to Div. 3: Peterborough Utd., Shrewsbury Town, Rotherham Utd., Notts Co.

1998

Premier League to Div. 1: Bolton Wand., Barnsley, Crystal Palace.
Div. 1 to Div. 2: Manchester City, Stoke City, Reading.
Div. 2 to Div. 3: Brentford, Plymouth Argyle, Carlisle Utd., Southend Utd.

1999

Premier League to Div. 1: Charlton Athletic, Blackburn Rov., Nott'm Forest.
Div. 1 to Div. 2: Bury, Oxford Utd., Bristol City.
Div. 2 to Div. 3: York City, Northampton Town, Lincoln City, Macclesfield Town.

BASSETT FALLS VICTIM TO PLAYER POWER

Dave Bassett lost his job as manager of Nott'm. Forest a few months after Pierre van Hooijdonk walked out claiming the club lacked ambition.

Van Hooijdonk returned to Holland upset by the sale of Kevin Campbell and accusing the club of failing to buy quality replacements.

The star striker eventually came back to The City ground but by then Forest were sliding towards relegation. Weeks later Bassett discovered his fate on a car radio while driving to the ground.

He said: 'Van Hooijdonk destroyed me. He's still at the club. I'm not. I've gone because he was a bigger investment than me. It doesn't take long for people to jump on a bandwagon and if a strike is seen to succeed the next thing you know players will be dictating how many matches they play.

'Players have more power, individually and collectively than ever before. They can make it known they're not happy, give out vibes that things are not right. Unless you have a solid board behind you, with directors who are not prepared to listen to any nonsense, you are in trouble.

'Basically the players don't have to have a brain because they've got so much money so early. They're the new rich. They are controlled by agents and don't have to think. When you are talking to them you can see them thinking: "I've got my house and my cars. I don't need you." In the end they don't have to care. It's the disease of greed.

'The new breed of directors think we are like lightbulbs, interchangeable. A manager in the English game has a shelf life of about two years.

'Football is so elitist it is now nigh on impossible for someone to do what I did and go through the League with a single club. The media encourages Premiership directors to go for a big name, instead of thinking long term, and finding someone to build a club.

'International players with managerial ambitions won't serve their time at a Rochdale or Scunthorpe Utd. They're rich enough not to need that. The dream has been lost. At least when I started at Wimbledon there was room for a romantic story like Graham Taylor taking Watford from the Fourth to the First. Now the gulf is almost unbridgeable.

'Things are so ridiculous now you've got schoolboys coming to you with their agents.

'There are times you get a bit stressed out. I like going on long walks. It is only recently that I've noticed things like the trees budding in spring or the leaves falling in autumn.'

FA CUP 1998-99

FIRST ROUND

Basingstoke 1, Bournemouth 2
Bedlington Terriers 4, Colchester Utd. 1
Boreham Wood 2, Luton Town 3
Brentford 5, Camberley 0
Bristol Rov. 3, Welling Utd. 0
Cardiff City 6, Chester City 0
Cheltenham 0, Lincoln City 1
Darlington 3, Burnley 2
Dulwich 0, Southport 1
Emley 1, Rotherham Utd. 1
Enfield 2, York City 2
Fulham 1, Leigh RMI 1
Hartlepool Utd. 2, Carlisle Utd. 1
Hednesford 3, Barnet 1
Hendon 0, Notts Co. 0
Kingstonian 1, Burton Albion 0
Rushden & Diamonds 2, Shrewsbury T. 0
Leyton Orient 4, Brighton & H.A. 2
Manchester City 3, Halifax Town 0
Macclesfield Town 2, Slough 1
Mansfield Town 2, Hayes 1
Northampton Town 2, Lancaster 1
Oldham Athletic 2, Gillingham 1
Plymouth Argyle 0, Kidderminster 0
Preston N.E. 3, Ford Utd 0
Reading 0, Stoke City 1
Runcorn 1, Stevenage 1
Salisbury 0, Hull City 2
Scarborough 1, Rochdale 1
Southend Utd. 0, Doncaster Rov. 1
Swansea City 3, Millwall 0
Tamworth 2, Exeter City 2
Telford 0, Cambridge Utd. 2
Walsall 1, Gresley Rov. 0
Wigan Athletic 4, Blackpool 3
Woking 0, Scunthorpe Utd. 1
Worcester 0, Torquay Utd. 1
Wrexham 1, Peterborough Utd. 0
Wycombe Wand. 1 Chesterfield 0
Yeovil 2, West Auckland 2

FIRST ROUND – REPLAYS

Exeter City 4, Tamworth 1
Kidderminster 0, Plymouth Argyle 0*
(Plymouth Argyle won 5-4 on pens)

Leigh RMI 0, Fulham 2
Notts Co. 3, Hendon 0
Rochdale 2, Scarborough 0
Rotherham Utd. 3, Emley 1
Slough 1, Macclesfield Town 1*
(Macclesfield Town won 9-8 on pens)
Stevenage 2, Runcorn 0
West Auckland 1, Yeovil 1*
(Yeovil won 5-3 on pens)
York City 2, Enfield 1

SECOND ROUND

Cardiff City 3, Hednesford 2
Darlington 1, Manchester City 1
Doncaster Rov. 0, Rushden & Diamonds 0
Exeter City 2, Bristol Rov. 2
Fulham 4, Hartlepool Utd. 2
Notts Co. 1, Wigan Athletic 1
Kingstonian 0, Leyton Orient 0
Lincoln City 4, Stevenage 1
Luton Town 1, Hull City 2
Macclesfield Town 4, Cambridge Utd. 1
Mansfield Town 1, Southport 2
Oldham Athletic 1, Brentford 1
Preston N.E. 2, Walsall 0
Rochdale 0, Rotherham Utd. 0
Scunthorpe Utd. 2, Bedlington Terriers 0
Swansea City 1, Stoke City 1
Torquay Utd. 0, Bournemouth 1
Wrexham 2, York City 1
Wycombe Wand. 1, Plymouth Argyle 1
Yeovil 0, Northampton Town 0

SECOND ROUND – REPLAYS

Brentford 2, Oldham Athletic 2*
(Oldham Athletic won 4-2 on pens)
Bristol Rov. 5, Exeter City 0
Leyton Orient 2, Kingstonian 1
Manchester City 1, Darlington 0*
Plymouth Argyle 3, Wycombe Wand. 2
Rotherham Utd. 4, Rochdale 0
Rushden & Diamonds 4, Doncaster Rov. 2
Wigan Athletic 0, Notts Co. 0*
(Notts Co. won 4-2 on pens)

(*After extra time.)

The Association of Football Statisticians
(FORMED 1978)
Full details from: Ray Spiller,
22 Bretons, Basildon, Essex SS15 5BY

MANCHESTER UNITED COMPLETE THIRD DOUBLE IN SIX SEASONS

THIRD ROUND (January 2)	FOURTH ROUND (January 23)	FIFTH ROUND (February 13)	SIXTH ROUND (March 6)	SEMI-FINALS (April 11)	FINAL (May 22)
*Manchester Utd. 3	*Manchester Utd. 2				
Middlesbrough 1		*Manchester Utd. 1			
Liverpool 3	Liverpool 1		*Manchester Utd. 0:2		
*Port Vale 0					Manchester Utd. 2
Fulham 1:1	Fulham 2	Fulham 0			
*Southampton 1:0					
*Aston Villa 3	*Aston Villa 0			Manchester Utd. ... †0:†2	
Hull City 0					
Chelsea 2	Chelsea 1	Chelsea 1			
*Oldham Athletic 1:4					
Oxford Utd. 3	*Oxford Utd. 1:2		Chelsea 0:0		
*Crewe Alexandra 1					
*Sheffield Wed. 4	*Sheffield Wed. 1	*Sheffield Wed. 0			
Norwich City 1					
Stockport Co. 3	Stockport Co. 0				
*Bury 0					
Arsenal 4	Arsenal 2	*Arsenal 2			
*Preston N.E. 2			*Arsenal 1		
Wolves 2	Wolves 1				
*Bolton Wand. .... 1:†4					
*Sheffield Utd. 1:3	*Sheffield Utd. 4	Sheffield Utd. 1:1			
Notts Co. .... 1:†2				Arsenal 0:1	
*Cardiff City 1:1	*Cardiff City 1				
Yeovil 1					
Derby Co. 3	Derby Co. 3	Derby Co. 2:3			
*Plymouth Argyle 0			Derby Co. 0		
Swansea City 1:1	*Swansea City 0				
*West Ham Utd. 1:0					
Huddersfield Town 1	Huddersfield T 1:2	*Huddersfield T 2:1			
*Q.P.R. 0					
*Wrexham 4	*Wrexham 1:1				
Scunthorpe Utd. 3					

60

Leyton Orient 2	Leyton Orient 0				
*Southport 0					
Bristol Rov. 1	*Bristol Rov. 3	Bristol Rov. 1			
*Rotherham Utd. 0					
*Bournemouth 1	Bournemouth 1		*Barnsley 0		
W.B.A. 0					
Barnsley 0:3	*Barnsley 3	*Barnsley 4			
*Swindon Town 0:1					
Portsmouth 1	*Portsmouth 1			Tottenham .... †0	
*Nott'm Forest 0					
Leeds Utd. 0:3	Leeds Utd. 5	*Leeds Utd 1:0			
*Rushden & D. 0:1					
*Wimbledon 1	*Wimbledon 1:0		Tottenham 1		
Man. City 0					
*Tottenham 5	Tottenham 1:3	Tottenham 1:2			
Watford 2					
*Leicester City 4	*Leicester City 0				**Newcastle Utd.** 0
Birmingham City 2					
*Coventry City 7	Coventry City 3	Coventry City 1			
Macclesfield Town 0					
Ipswich Town 1	Ipswich Town 0		Everton 1		
*Tranmere Rov. 0					
Everton 2	*Everton 1	*Everton 2			
*Bristol City 0					
Sunderland 1	Sunderland 0			**Newcastle Utd.** 2	
*Lincoln City 0					
*Blackburn Rov. 2	*Blackburn Rov. 1	Blackburn Rov. 0:0			
Charlton Athletic 0					
*Bradford City 2	Bradford City 0		***Newcastle Utd.** 4		
Grimsby Town 1					
Crystal Palace 1	***Newcastle Utd.** 3	**Newcastle Utd.** 0:1			
***Newcastle Utd.** 2					

* Drawn at home. † After extra time. A – Replay ordered by FA after disputed Arsenal goal.
Semi finals: **Manchester Utd.** v **Arsenal** (both matches) at Villa Park (replay April 14) – **Tottenham** v **Newcastle Utd.** at Old Trafford.
Final played at Wembley - Saturday, May 22, 1999. Att:79,101.

F.A. CUP FINAL TEAMS 1900-98

1900 BURY – Thompson; Darrock, Davidson, Pray, Leeming, Ross, Richards, Wood, McLuckie, Sagar, Plant. **SOUTHAMPTON** – Robinson; Meehan, Durber, Meston, Chadwick, Petrie, Turner, Yates, Farrell, Wood, Milward. **Scorers:** Bury – McLuckie 2, Wood, Plant.

1901 TOTTENHAM – Clawley; Erentz, Tait, Norris, Hughes, Jones, Smith, Cameron, Brown, Copeland, Kirwan. **SHEFFIELD UTD.** – Foulke; Thickett, Boyle, Johnson, Morren, Needham, Bennett, Field, Hedley, Priest, Lipsham. **Scorers:** (first match) Tottenham – Brown 2, Sheff. Utd. – Bennett, Priest. **Scorers:** (second match) Tottenham – Cameron, Smith, Brown, Sheff. Utd. – Priest.

1902 SHEFFIELD UTD. – Foulke; Thickett, Boyle, Needham, Wilkinson, Johnson, Barnes, Common, Hedley, Priest, Lipsham. (Bennett injured in first match and Barnes took his place in the replay). **SOUTHAMPTON** – Robinson; C. B. Fry, Molyneux, Bowman, Lee, A. Turner, Wood, Brown, Chadwick, J. Turner, Metson. **Scorers:** (first match) Sheff. Utd. – Common, Southampton – Wood. **Scorers:** (second match) Sheff. Utd. – Hedley, Barnes, Southampton – Brown.

1903 BURY – Monteith; Lindsey, McEwan, Johnson, Thorpe, Ross, Richards, Wood, Sagar, Leeming, Plant. **DERBY CO.** – Fryer; Methven, Morris, Warren, Goodall (A.), May, Warrington, York City, Boag, Richards, Davis. **Scorers:** Bury – Ross, Sagar, Leeming 2, Wood, Plant.

1904 MANCHESTER CITY – Hillman; McMahon, Burgess, Frost, Hynde, S. B. Ashworth, Meredith, Livingstone, Gillespie, Turnbull (A.), Booth. **BOLTON WAND.** – D. Davies; Brown, Struthers, Clifford, Greenhalgh, Freebairn, Stokes, Marsh, Yenson, White, Taylor. **Scorer:** Manchester City – Meredith.

1905 ASTON VILLA – George; Spencer, Miles, Pearson, Leake, Windmill, Brawn, Garratty, Hampton, Bache, Hall. **NEWCASTLE UTD.** – Lawrence; McCombie, Carr, Gardner, Aitken, McWilliam, Rutherford, Howie, Appleyard, Veitch, Gosnell. **Scorer:** Aston Villa – Hampton 2.

1906 EVERTON – Scott; Balmer (W.), Crelly, Makepeace, Taylor, Abbott, Sharp, Bolton Wand., Young, Settle, H. P. Hardman. **NEWCASTLE UTD.** – Lawrence; McCombie, Carr, Gardner, Aitken, McWilliam, Rutherford, Howie, Veitch, Orr, Gosnell. **Scorer:** Everton – Young.

1907 SHEFFIELD WED. – Lyall; Layton, Burton, Brittleton, Crawshaw, Bartlett, Chapman, Bradshaw, Wilson, Stewart, Simpson. **EVERTON** – Scott; Balmer (W.), Balmer (R.), Makepeace, Taylor, Abbott, Sharp, Bolton, Young, Settle, H. P. Hardman. **Scorers:** Sheff. Wed. – Stewart, Simpson, Everton – Sharp.

1908 WOLVES – Lunn; Jones, Collins, Rev. K. R. G. Hunt, Wooldridge, Bishop, Harrison, Shelton, Hedley, Radford, Pedley. **NEWCASTLE UTD.** – Lawrence; McCracken, Pudan, Gardner, Veitch, McWilliam, Rutherford, Howie, Appleyard, Speedle, Wilson. **Scorers:** Wolves – Hunt, Hedley, Harrison, Newcastle Utd. – Howie.

1909 MANCHESTER UTD. – Moger; Stacey, Hayes, Duckworth, Roberts, Bell, Meredith, Halse, Turnbull (J.), Turnbull (A.), Wall. **BRISTOL CITY** – Clay; Annan, Cottle, Hanlin, Wedlock, Spear, Staniforth, Hardy, Gilligan, Burton, Hilton. **Scorer:** Manchester Utd. – Turnbull (A.).

1910 NEWCASTLE UTD. – Lawrence; McCracken, Carr, Veitch, Low, McWilliam, Rutherford, Howie, Shepherd, Higgins, Wilson. (Whitson was injured in first match and Carr took his place in the replay). **BARNSLEY** – Mearns; Downs, Ness, Glendinning, Boyle, Utley, Bartrop, Gadsby, Lillycrop, Tufnell, Forman. **Scorers:** (first match) Newcastle Utd. – Rutherford, Barnsley – Tufnell. **Scorer:** (second match) Newcastle Utd. – Shepherd 2 (1 pen.).

1911 BRADFORD CITY – Mellors; Campbell, Taylor, Robinson, Torrance, McDonald, Logan, Spiers, O'Rourke, Devine, Thompson. (Gildea played centre half in the first match). **NEWCASTLE UTD.** – Lawrence; McCracken, Whitson, Veitch, Low, Willis, Rutherford, Jobey, Stewart, Higgins, Wilson. **Scorer:** Bradford City – Spiers.

1912 BARNSLEY – Cooper; Downs, Taylor, Glendinning, Bratley, Utley, Bartrop, Tufnell, Lillycrop, Travers, Moore. **W.B.A.** – Pearson; Cook, Pennington, Baddeley, Buck, McNeal, Jephcott, Wright, Pailor, Bower, Shearman. **Scorer:** Barnsley – Tufnell.

1913 ASTON VILLA – Hardy; Lyons, Weston, Barber, Harrop, Leach, Wallace, Halse, Hampton, Stephenson (C.), Bache. **SUNDERLAND** – Butler; Gladwin, Ness, Cuggy, Thompson, Low, Mordue, Buchan, Richardson, Holley, Martin. **Scorer:** Aston Villa – Barber.

1914 BURNLEY – Sewell; Bamford, Taylor, Halley, Boyle, Watson, Nesbit, Lindley, Freeman, Hodgson, Mosscrop. **LIVERPOOL** – Campbell; Longworth, Pursell, Fairfoul, Ferguson, McKinlay, Sheldon, Metcalfe, Miller, Lacey, Nicholl. **Scorer:** Burnley – Freeman.

1915 SHEFFIELD UTD. – Gough; Cook, English, Sturgess, Brelsford, Utley, Simmons, Fazackerley, Kitchen, Masterman, Evans. **CHELSEA** – Molyneux; Bettridge, Harrow, Taylor, Logan, Walker, Ford, Halse, Thompson, Croal, McNeil. **Scorers:** Sheff. Utd. – Simmons, Fazackerley, Kitchen.

1920 ASTON VILLA – Hardy; Smart, Weston, Ducat, Barson, Moss, Wallace, Kirton, Walker, Stephenson (C.), Dorrell. **HUDDERSFIELD TOWN** – Mutch; Wood, Bullock, Slade, Wilson, Watson, Richardson, Mann, Taylor, Swan, Islip. **Scorer:** Aston Villa – Kirton.

1921 TOTTENHAM – Hunter; Clay, McDonald, Smith, Walters, Grimsdell; Banks, Seed, Cantrell, Bliss, Dimmock. **WOLVES** – George; Woodward, Marshall, Gregory, Hodnett, Riley, Lea, Burrill, Edmonds, Potts, Brooks. **Scorer:** Tottenham – Dimmock.

1922 HUDDERSFIELD TOWN – Mutch; Wood, Wadsworth, Slade, Wilson, Watson, Richardson, Mann, Islip, Stephenson, Smith (W.H.). **PRESTON N.E.** – J. F. Mitchell; Hamilton, Doolan, Duxbury, McCall, Williamson, Rawlings, Jefferis, Roberts, Woodhouse, Quinn. **Scorer:** Huddersfield Town – Smith (pen.).

1923 BOLTON WAND. – Pym; Haworth, Finney, Nuttall, Seddon, Jennings, Butler, Jack, Smith (J. R.), Smith (J.), Vizard. **WEST HAM UTD.** – Hufton; Henderson, Young, Bishop, Kay, Tresadern, Richards, Brown, Watson (V.), Moore, Ruffell. **Scorers:** Bolton Wand. – Jack, Smith (J. R.).

1924 NEWCASTLE UTD. – Bradley; Hampson, Hudspeth, Mooney, Spencer, Gibson, Low, Cowan, Harris, McDonald, Seymour. **ASTON VILLA** – Jackson; Smart, Mort, Moss, Dr. V. E. Milne, Blackburn, York, Kirton, Capewell, Walker, Dorrell. **Scorers:** Newcastle Utd. – Harris, Seymour.

1925 SHEFFIELD UTD. – Sutcliffe; Cook, Milton, Pantling, King, Green, Mercer, Boyle, Johnson, Gillespie, Tunstall. **CARDIFF CITY** – Farquharson; Nelson, Blair, Wake, Keenor, Hardy, Davies (W.), Gill, Nicholson, Beadles, Evans (J.). **Scorer:** Sheff. Utd. – Tunstall.

1926 BOLTON WAND. – Pym; Haworth, Greenhalgh, Nuttall, Seddon, Jennings, Butler, Jack, Smith (J. R.), Smith (J.), Vizard. **MANCHESTER CITY** – Goodchild; Cookson, McCloy, Pringle, Cowan, McMullan, Austin, Browell, Roberts, Johnson, Hicks. **Scorer:** Bolton Wand. – Jack.

1927 CARDIFF CITY – Farquharson; Nelson, Watson, Keenor, Sloan, Hardy, Curtis, Irving, Ferguson, Davies (L.), McLachlan. **ARSENAL** – Lewis; Parker, Kennedy, Baker, Butler, John, Hulme, Buchan, Brain, Blyth, Hoar. **Scorer:** Cardiff City – Ferguson.

1928 BLACKBURN ROV. – Crawford; Hutton, Jones, Healless, Rankin, Campbell, Thornewell, Puddefoot, Roscamp, McLean, Rigby. **HUDDERSFIELD TOWN** – Mercer; Goodall, Barkas, Redfern, Wilson, Steele, Jackson (A.), Kelly, Brown, Stephenson, Smith (W.H.). **Scorers:** Blackburn Rov. – Roscamp 2, McLean, Huddersfield Town – Jackson.

1929 BOLTON WAND. – Pym; Haworth, Finney, Kean, Seddon, Nuttall, Butler, McClelland, Blackmore, Gibson, Cook (W.). **PORTSMOUTH** – Gilfillan; Mackie, Bell, Nichol, McIlwaine, Thackeray, Forward, Smith (J.), Weddle, Watson, Cook (F.). **Scorers:** Bolton Wand. – Butler, Blackmore.

1930 ARSENAL – Preedy; Parker, Hapgood, Baker, Seddon, John, Hulme, Jack, Lambert, James, Bastin. **HUDDERSFIELD TOWN** – Turner; Goodall, Spence, Naylor, Wilson, Campbell, Jackson (A.), Kelly, Davies, Raw, Smith (W. H.). **Scorers:** Arsenal – James, Lambert.

1931 W.B.A. – Pearson; Shaw, Trentham, Magee, Richardson (W.), Edwards, Glidden, Carter, Richardson (W. G.), Sandford, Wood. **BIRMINGHAM** – Hibbs; Liddell, Barkas, Cringan, Morrall, Leslie, Briggs, Crosbie, Bradford, Gregg, Curtis. **Scorers:** W.B.A. – Richardson (W. G.) 2, Birmingham City – Bradford.

1932 NEWCASTLE UTD. – McInroy; Nelson, Fairhurst, McKenzie, Davidson, Weaver, Boyd, Richardson, Allen, McMenemy, Lang. **ARSENAL** – Moss; Parker, Hapgood, Jones (C.), Roberts, Male, Hulme, Jack, Lambert, Bastin, John. **Scorers:** Newcastle Utd. – Allen 2, Arsenal – John.

1933 EVERTON – Sagar; Cook, Cresswell, Britton, White, Thomson, Geldard, Dunn, Dean, Johnson, Stein. **MANCHESTER CITY** – Langford; Cann, Dale, Busby, Cowan, Bray, Toseland, Marshall, Herd, McMullan, Brook. **Scorers:** Everton – Stein, Dean, Dunn.

1934 MANCHESTER CITY – Swift; Barnett, Dale, Busby, Cowan, Bray, Toseland, Marshall, Tilson, Herd, Brook. **PORTSMOUTH** – Gilfillan; Mackie, Smith (W.), Nichol, Allen, Thackeray, Worrall, Smith (J.), Weddle, Easson, Rutherford. **Scorers:** Manchester City – Tilson 2, Portsmouth – Rutherford.

1935 SHEFFIELD WED. – Brown; Nibloe, Catlin, Sharp, Millership, Burrows, Hooper, Surtees, Palethorpe, Starling, Rimmer. **W.B.A.** – Pearson; Shaw, Trentham, Murphy, Richardson (W.), Edwards, Glidden, Carter, Richardson (W. G.), Sandford, Boyes. **Scorers:** Sheff. Wed. – Rimmer 2, Palethorpe, Hooper, W.B.A. – Boyes, Sandford.

1936 ARSENAL – Wilson; Male, Hapgood, Crayston, Roberts, Copping, Hulme, Bowden, Drake, James, Bastin. **SHEFFIELD UTD.** – Smith; Hooper, Wilkinson, Jackson, Johnson, McPherson, Barton, Barclay, Dodds, Pickering, Williams. **Scorer:** Arsenal – Drake.

1937 SUNDERLAND – Mapson; Gorman, Hall, Thomson, Johnston, McNab, Duns, Carter, Gurney, Gallacher, Burbanks. **PRESTON N.E.** – Burns; Gallimore, Beattie (A.), Shankly, Tremelling, Milne, Dougal, Beresford, O'Donnell (F.), Fagan, O'Donnell (H). **Scorers:** Sunderland – Gurney, Carter, Burbanks, Preston N.E. – O'Donnell (F.).

1938 PRESTON N.E. – Holdcroft; Gallimore, Beattie (A.), Shankly, Smith, Batey, Watmough, Mutch, Maxwell, Beattie (R.), O'Donnell (H.). **HUDDERSFIELD TOWN** – Hesford; Craig, Mountford, Willingham, Young, Boot, Hulme, Isaac, McFadyen, Barclay, Beasley. **Scorer:** Preston N.E. – Mutch (pen.).

1939 PORTSMOUTH – Walker; Morgan, Rochford, Guthrie, Rowe, Wharton, Worrall, McAlinden, Anderson, Barlow, Parker. **WOLVES** – Scott; Morris, Taylor, Galley, Cullis, Gardiner, Burton, McIntosh, Westcott, Dorsett, Maguire. **Scorers:** Portsmouth – Barlow, Anderson, Parker 2, Wolves – Dorsett.

1946 DERBY CO. – Woodley; Nicholas, Howe, Bullions, Leuty, Musson, Harrison, Carter, Stamps, Doherty, Duncan. **CHARLTON ATHLETIC** – Bartram; Phipps, Shreeve, Turner (H.), Oakes, Johnson, Fell, Brown, A. A. Turner, Welsh, Duffy. **Scorers:** Derby Co. – Turner (H.) (o.g.), Doherty, Stamps 2, Charlton Athletic – Turner (H.).

1947 CHARLTON ATHLETIC – Bartram; Croker (P.), Shreeve, Johnson, Phipps, Whittaker, Hurst, Dawson, Robinson (W.), Welsh, Duffy. **BURNLEY** – Strong; Woodruff, Mather, Attwell, Brown, Bray, Chew, Morris, Harrison, Potts, F. ·P. Kippax. **Scorer:** Charlton Athletic – Duffy.

1948 MANCHESTER UTD. – Crompton; Carey, Aston, Anderson, Chilton, Cockburn, Delaney, Morris, Rowley, Pearson, Mitten. **BLACKPOOL** – Robinson; Shimwell, Crosland, Johnston, Hayward, Kelly, Matthews, Munro, Mortensen, Dick, Rickett. **Scorers:** Manchester Utd. – Rowley 2, Pearson, Anderson, Blackpool – Shimwell (pen.), Mortensen.

1949 WOLVES – Williams; Pritchard, Springthorpe, Crook (W.), Shorthouse, Wright, Hancocks, Smyth, Pye, Dunn, Mullen. **LEICESTER CITY** – Bradley; Jelly, Scott, Harrison (W.), Plummer, King, Griffiths, Lee, Harrison (J.), Chisholm, Adam. **Scorers:** Wolves – Pye 2, Smyth, Leicester City – Griffiths.

1950 ARSENAL – Swindin; Scott, Barnes, Forbes, Compton (L.), Mercer, Cox, Logie, Goring, Lewis, Compton (D.). **LIVERPOOL** – Sidlow; Lambert, Spicer, Taylor, Hughes, Jones, Payne, Baron, Stubbins, Fagan, Liddell. **Scorer:** Arsenal – Lewis 2.

1951 NEWCASTLE UTD. – Fairbrother; Cowell, Corbett, Harvey, Brennan, Crowe, Walker, Taylor, Milburn, Robledo (G.), Mitchell. **BLACKPOOL** – Farm; Shimwell, Garrett, Johnston, Hayward, Kelly, Matthews, Mudie, Mortensen, W. J. Slater, Perry. **Scorer:** Newcastle Utd. – Milburn 2.

1952 NEWCASTLE UTD. – Simpson; Cowell, McMichael, Harvey, Brennan, Robledo (E.), Walker, Foulkes, Milburn, Robledo (G.), Mitchell. **ARSENAL** – Swindin; Barnes, Smith (L.), Forbes, Daniel, Mercer, Cox, Logie, Holton, Lishman, Roper. **Scorer:** Newcastle Utd. – Robledo (G.).

1953 BLACKPOOL – Farm; Shimwell, Garrett, Fenton, Johnston, Robinson, Matthews, Taylor, Mortensen, Mudie, Perry. **BOLTON WAND.** – Hanson; Ball, Banks (R.), Wheeler, Barrass, Bell, Holden, Moir, Lofthouse, Hassall, Langton. **Scorers:** Blackpool – Mortensen 3, Perry, Bolton Wand. – Lofthouse, Moir, Bell.

1954 W.B.A. – Sanders; Kennedy, Millard, Dudley, Dugdale, Barlow, Griffin, Ryan, Allen, Nicholls, Lee. **PRESTON N.E.** – Thompson; Cunningham, Walton, Docherty, Marston, Forbes, Finney, Foster, Wayman, Baxter, Morrison. **Scorers:** W.B.A. – Allen 2 (1 pen.), Griffin, Preston N.E. – Morrison, Wayman.

1955 NEWCASTLE UTD. – Simpson; Cowell, Batty, Scoular, Stokoe, Casey, White, Milburn, Keeble, Hannah, Mitchell. **MANCHESTER CITY** – Trautmann; Meadows, Little, Barnes, Ewing, Paul, Spurdle, Hayes, Revie, Johnstone, Fagan. **Scorers:** Newcastle Utd. – Milburn, Mitchell, Hannah, Manchester City – Johnstone.

1956 MANCHESTER CITY – Trautmann; Leivers, Little, Barnes, Ewing, Paul, Johnstone, Hayes, Revie, Dyson, Clarke. **BIRMINGHAM CITY** – Merrick; Hall, Green, Newman, Smith, Boyd, Astall, Kinsey, Brown, Murphy, Govan. **Scorers:** Manchester City – Hayes, Dyson, Johnstone, Birmingham City – Kinsey.

1957 ASTON VILLA – Sims; Lynn, Aldis, Crowther, Dugdale, Saward, Smith, Sewell, Myerscough, Dixon, McParland. **MANCHESTER UTD.** – Wood; Foulkes, Byrne, Colman, Blanchflower, Edwards, Berry, Whelan, Taylor (T.), Charlton, Pegg. **Scorers:** Aston Villa – McParland 2, Manchester Utd. – Taylor.

1958 BOLTON WANDERERS – Hopkinson; Hartle, Banks (T.), Hennin, Higgins, Edwards, Birch, Stevens, Lofthouse, Parry, Holden. **MANCHESTER UTD.** – Gregg; Foulkes, Greaves, Goodwin, Cope, Crowther, Dawson, Taylor (E.), Charlton, Viollet, Webster. **Scorer:** Bolton Wand. – Lofthouse 2.

1959 NOTT'M FOREST – Thomson; Whare, McDonald, Whitefoot, McKinlay, Burkitt, Dwight, Quigley, Wilson, Gray, Imlach. **LUTON TOWN** – Baynham; McNally, Hawkes, Groves, Owen, Pacey, Bingham, Brown, Morton, Cummins, Gregory. **Scorers:** Nott'm. Forest – Dwight, Wilson, Luton Town – Pacey.

1960 WOLVES – Finlayson; Showell, Harris, Clamp, Slater, Flowers, Deeley, Stobart, Murray, Broadbent, Horne. **BLACKBURN ROV.** – Leyland; Bray, Whelan, Clayton, Woods, McGrath, Bimpson, Dobing, Dougan, Douglas, MacLeod. **Scorers:** Wolves – McGrath (o.g.), Deeley 2.

1961 TOTTENHAM – Brown; Baker, Henry, Blanchflower, Norman, Mackay, Jones, White, Smith, Allen, Dyson. **LEICESTER CITY** – Banks; Chalmers, Norman, McLintock, King, Appleton, Riley, Walsh, McIlmoyle, Keyworth, Cheesebrough. **Scorers:** Tottenham – Smith, Dyson.

1962 TOTTENHAM – Brown; Baker, Henry, Blanchflower, Norman, Mackay, Medwin, White, Smith, Greaves, Jones. **BURNLEY** – Blacklaw; Angus, Elder, Adamson, Cummings, Miller, Connelly, McIlroy, Pointer, Robson, Harris. **Scorers:** Tottenham – Greaves, Smith, Blanchflower (pen.), Burnley – Robson.

1963 MANCHESTER UTD. – Gaskell; Dunne, Cantwell, Crerand, Foulkes, Setters, Giles, Quixall, Herd, Law, Charlton. **LEICESTER CITY** – Banks; Sjoberg, Norman, McLintock, King, Appleton, Riley, Cross, Keyworth, Gibson, Stringfellow. **Scorers:** Manchester Utd. – Law, Herd 2, Leicester City – Keyworth.

1964 WEST HAM UTD. – Standen; Bond, Burkett, Bovington, Brown, Moore, Brabrook, Boyce, Byrne, Hurst, Sissons. **PRESTON N.E.** – Kelly; Ross, Smith, Lawton, Singleton, Kendall, Wilson, Ashworth, Dawson, Spavin, Holden. **Scorers:** West Ham Utd. – Sissons, Hurst, Boyce, Preston N.E. – Holden, Dawson.

1965 LIVERPOOL – Lawrence; Lawler, Byrne, Strong, Yeats, Stevenson, Callaghan, Hunt, St. John, Smith, Thompson. **LEEDS UTD.** – Sprake; Reaney, Bell, Bremner, Charlton, Hunter, Giles, Storrie, Peacock, Collins, Johanneson. **Scorers:** Liverpool – Hunt, St. John, Leeds Utd. – Bremner.

1966 EVERTON – West; Wright, Wilson, Gabriel, Labone, Harris, Scott, Trebilcock, Young, Harvey, Temple. **SHEFFIELD WED.** – Springett; Smith, Megson, Eustace, Ellis, Young, Pugh, Fantham, McCalliog, Ford, Quinn. **Scorers:** Everton – Trebilcock 2, Temple, Sheff. Wed. – McCalliog, Ford.

1967 TOTTENHAM – Jennings; Kinnear, Knowles, Mullery, England, Mackay, Robertson, Greaves, Gilzean, Venables, Saul. **CHELSEA** – Bonetti; Harris (A.), McCreadie, Hollins, Hinton, Harris (R.), Cooke, Baldwin, Hateley, Tambling, Boyle. **Scorers:** Tottenham – Robertson, Saul, Chelsea – Tambling.

1968 W.B.A. – Osborne; Fraser, Williams, Brown, Talbut, Kaye (Clarke), Lovett, Collard, Astle, Hope, Clark. **EVERTON** – West; Wright, Wilson, Kendall, Labone, Harvey, Husband, Ball, Royle, Hurst, Morrissey. **Scorer:** W.B.A. – Astle.

1969 MANCHESTER CITY – Dowd; Book, Pardoe, Doyle, Booth, Oakes, Summerbee, Bell, Lee, Young, Coleman. **LEICESTER CITY** – Shilton; Rodrigues, Nish, Roberts, Woollett, Cross, Fern, Gibson, Lochhead, Clarke, Glover (Manley). **Scorer:** Manchester City – Young.

1970 CHELSEA – Bonetti; Webb, McCreadie, Hollins, Dempsey, Harris (R.) (Hinton), Baldwin, Houseman, Osgood, Hutchinson, Cooke. **LEEDS UTD.** – Sprake; Madeley, Cooper, Bremner, Charlton, Hunter, Lorimer, Clarke, Jones, Giles, Gray. **Scorers:** Chelsea – Houseman, Hutchinson, Leeds Utd. – Charlton Athletic, Jones. **Replay: CHELSEA** – Bonetti; Harris (R.), McCreadie, Hollins, Dempsey, Webb, Baldwin, Cooke, Osgood (Hinton), Hutchinson, Houseman. **LEEDS UTD.** – Harvey; Madeley, Cooper, Bremner, Charlton, Hunter, Lorimer, Clarke, Jones, Giles, Gray. **Scorers:** Chelsea – Osgood, Webb, Leeds Utd. – Jones.

1971 ARSENAL – Wilson; Rice, McNab, Storey (Kelly), McLintock, Simpson, Armstrong, Graham, Radford, Kennedy, George. **LIVERPOOL** – Clemence; Lawler, Lindsay, Smith, Lloyd, Hughes, Callaghan, Evans (Thompson), Heighway, Toshack, Hall. **Scorers:** Arsenal – Kelly, George, Liverpool – Heighway.

1972 LEEDS UTD. – Harvey; Reaney, Madeley, Bremner, Charlton, Hunter, Lorimer, Clarke, Jones, Giles, Gray. **ARSENAL** – Barnett; Rice, McNab, Storey, McLintock, Simpson, Armstrong, Ball, Radford (Kennedy), George, Graham. **Scorer:** Leeds Utd. – Clarke.

1973 SUNDERLAND – Montgomery; Malone, Guthrie, Horswill, Watson, Pitt, Kerr, Hughes, Halom, Porterfield, Tueart. **LEEDS UTD.** – Harvey; Reaney, Cherry, Bremner, Madeley, Hunter, Lorimer, Clarke, Jones, Giles, Gray (Yorath). **Scorer:** Sunderland – Porterfield.

1974 LIVERPOOL – Clemence; Smith, Lindsay, Thompson, Cormack, Hughes, Keegan, Hall, Heighway, Toshack, Callaghan. **NEWCASTLE UTD.** – McFaul; Clark, Kennedy, McDermott, Howard, Moncur, Smith (Gibb), Cassidy, Macdonald, Tudor, Hibbitt. **Scorers:** Liverpool – Keegan (2), Heighway.

1975 WEST HAM UTD. – Day; McDowell, Lampard, Bonds, Taylor (T.), Lock, Jennings, Paddon, Taylor (A.), Brooking, Holland. **FULHAM** – Mellor; Cutbush, Fraser, Mullery, Lacy, Moore, Mitchell, Conway, Busby, Slough, Barrett. **Scorer:** West Ham Utd. – Taylor (A.) 2.

1976 SOUTHAMPTON – Turner; Rodrigues, Peach, Holmes, Blyth, Steele, Gilchrist, Channon, Osgood, McCalliog, Stokes. **MANCHESTER UTD.** – Stepney; Forsyth, Houston, Daly, Greenhoff (B.), Buchan, Coppell, McIlroy, Pearson, Macari, Hill (McCreery). **Scorer:** Southampton – Stokes.

1977 MANCHESTER UTD. – Stepney; Nicholl, Albiston, McIlroy, Greenhoff (B.), Buchan, Coppell, Greenhoff (J.), Pearson, Macari, Hill (McCreery). **LIVERPOOL** – Clemence; Neal, Jones, Smith, Kennedy, Hughes, Keegan, Case, Heighway, McDermott, Johnson (Callaghan). **Scorers:** Manchester Utd. – Pearson, Greenhoff (J.), Liverpool – Case.

1978 IPSWICH TOWN – Cooper; Burley, Mills, Talbot, Hunter, Beattie, Osborne (Lambert), Wark, Mariner, Geddis, Woods. **ARSENAL** – Jennings; Rice, Nelson, Price, O'Leary, Young, Brady (Rix), Sunderland, Macdonald, Stapleton, Hudson. **Scorer:** Ipswich Town – Osborne.

1979 ARSENAL – Jennings; Rice, Nelson, Talbot, O'Leary, Young, Brady, Sunderland, Stapleton, Price (Walford), Rix. **MANCHESTER UTD.** – Bailey; Nicholl, Albiston,

McIlroy, McQueen, Buchan, Coppell, Greenhoff (J.), Jordan, Macari, Thomas. **Scorers:** Arsenal – Talbot, Stapleton, Sunderland, Manchester Utd. – McQueen, McIlroy.

1980 WEST HAM UTD. – Parkes; Stewart, Lampard, Bonds, Martin, Devonshire, Allen, Pearson, Cross, Brooking, Pike. **ARSENAL** – Jennings; Rice, Devine (Nelson), Talbot, O'Leary, Young, Brady, Sunderland, Stapleton, Price, Rix. **Scorer:** West Ham Utd. – Brooking.

1981 TOTTENHAM – Aleksic; Hughton, Miller, Roberts, Perryman, Villa (Brooke), Ardiles, Archibald, Galvin, Hoddle, Crooks. **MANCHESTER CITY** – Corrigan; Ranson, McDonald, Reid, Power, Caton, Bennett, Gow, Mackenzie, Hutchison (Henry), Reeves. **Scorer:** Tottenham – Hutchison (o.g.), Manchester City – Hutchison. **Replay: TOTTENHAM** – Aleksic; Hughton, Miller, Roberts, Perryman, Villa, Ardiles, Archibald, Galvin, Hoddle, Crooks. **MANCHESTER CITY** – Corrigan; Ranson, McDonald (Tueart), Reid, Power, Caton, Bennett, Gow, Mackenzie, Hutchison, Reeves. **Scorers:** Tottenham – Villa 2, Crooks, Manchester City – Mackenzie, Reeves (pen.).

1982 TOTTENHAM – Clemence; Hughton, Miller, Price, Hazard (Brooke), Perryman, Roberts, Archibald, Galvin, Hoddle, Crooks. **Q.P.R.** – Hucker; Fenwick, Gillard, Waddock, Hazell, Roeder, Currie, Flanagan, Allen (Micklewhite), Stainrod, Gregory. **Scorers:** Tottenham – Hoddle, Q.P.R. – Fenwick. **Replay: TOTTENHAM** – Clemence; Hughton, Miller, Price, Hazard (Brooke), Perryman, Roberts, Archibald, Galvin, Hoddle, Crooks. **Q.P.R.** – Hucker; Fenwick, Gillard, Waddock, Hazell, Neill, Currie, Flanagan, Micklewhite (Burke), Stainrod, Gregory. **Scorer:** Tottenham – Hoddle (pen.).

1983 MANCHESTER UTD. – Bailey; Duxbury, Albiston, Wilkins, Moran, McQueen, Robson, Muhren, Stapleton, Whiteside, Davies. **BRIGHTON & H.A.** – Moseley; Ramsey (Ryan), Pearce, Grealish, Gatting, Stevens, Case, Howlett, Robinson, Smith, Smillie. **Scorers:** Manchester Utd. – Stapleton, Wilkins, Brighton & H.A. – Smith, Stevens. **Replay: MANCHESTER UTD.** – Bailey; Duxbury, Albiston, Wilkins, Moran, McQueen, Robson, Muhren, Stapleton, Whiteside, Davies. **BRIGHTON & H.A.** – Moseley; Gatting, Pearce, Grealish, Foster, Stevens, Case, Howlett (Ryan), Robinson, Smith, Smillie. **Scorers:** Manchester Utd. – Robson 2, Whiteside, Muhren (pen.).

1984 EVERTON – Southall; Stevens, Bailey, Ratcliffe, Mountfield, Reid, Steven, Heath, Sharp, Gray, Richardson. **WATFORD** – Sherwood; Bardsley, Price (Atkinson), Taylor, Terry, Sinnott, Callaghan, Johnston, Reilly, Jackett, Barnes. **Scorers:** Everton – Sharp, Gray.

1985 MANCHESTER UTD. – Bailey; Gidman, Albiston (Duxbury), Whiteside, McGrath, Moran, Robson, Strachan, Hughes, Stapleton, Olsen. **EVERTON** – Southall; Stevens, Van den Hauwe, Ratcliffe, Mountfield, Reid, Steven, Sharp, Gray, Bracewell, Sheedy. **Scorer:** Manchester Utd. – Whiteside. **Sent-off:** Moran.

1986 LIVERPOOL – Grobbelaar; Lawrenson, Beglin, Nicol, Whelan, Hansen, Dalglish, Johnston, Rush, Molby, MacDonald. **EVERTON** – Mimms; Stevens (Heath), Van den Hauwe, Ratcliffe, Mountfield, Reid, Steven, Lineker, Sharp, Bracewell, Sheedy. **Scorers:** Liverpool – Rush 2, Johnston, Everton – Lineker.

1987 COVENTRY CITY – Ogrizovic; Phillips, Downs, McGrath, Kilcline (Rodger), Peake, Bennett, Gynn, Regis, Houchen, Pickering. **TOTTENHAM** – Clemence; Hughton (Claesen), Thomas (M.), Hodge, Gough, Mabbutt, Allen (C.), Allen (P.), Waddle, Hoddle, Ardiles (Stevens). **Scorers:** Coventry City – Bennett, Houchen, Mabbutt (o.g.), Tottenham – Allen (C.), Mabbutt.

1988 WIMBLEDON – Beasant; Goodyear, Phelan, Jones, Young, Thorn, Gibson (Scales), Cork (Cunningham), Fashanu, Sanchez, Wise. **LIVERPOOL** – Grobbelaar; Gillespie, Ablett, Nicol, Spackman (Molby), Hansen, Beardsley, Aldridge (Johnston), Houghton, Barnes, McMahon. **Scorer:** Wimbledon – Sanchez.

1989 LIVERPOOL – Grobbelaar; Ablett, Staunton (Venison), Nicol, Whelan, Hansen, Beardsley, Aldridge (Rush), Houghton, Barnes, McMahon. **EVERTON** – Southall; McDonald, Van den Hauwe, Ratcliffe, Watson, Bracewell (McCall), Nevin, Steven, Sharp, Cottee, Sheedy (Wilson). **Scorers:** Liverpool – Aldridge, Rush 2, Everton – McCall 2.

1990 MANCHESTER UTD. – Leighton; Ince, Martin (Blackmore), Bruce, Phelan, Pallister (Robins), Robson, Webb, McClair, Hughes, Wallace. **CRYSTAL PALACE** – Martyn; Pemberton, Shaw, Gray (Madden), O'Reilly, Thorn, Barber (Wright), Thomas, Bright,

Salako, Pardew. **Scorers:** Manchester Utd. – Robson, Hughes 2, Crystal Palace – O'Reilly, Wright 2. **Replay: MANCHESTER UTD.** – Sealey; Ince, Martin, Bruce, Phelan, Pallister, Robson, Webb, McClair, Hughes, Wallace. **CRYSTAL PALACE** – Martyn; Pemberton, Shaw, Gray, O'Reilly, Thorn, Barber (Wright), Thomas, Bright, Salako (Madden), Pardew. **Scorer:** Manchester Utd. – Martin.

1991 TOTTENHAM – Thorstvedt; Edinburgh, Van den Hauwe, Sedgley, Howells, Mabbutt, Stewart, Gascoigne (Nayim), Samways (Walsh), Lineker, Allen. **NOTT'M FOREST** – Crossley; Charles, Pearce, Walker, Chettle, Keane, Crosby, Parker, Clough, Glover (Laws), Woan (Hodge). **Scorers:** Tottenham – Stewart, Walker (o.g.), Nott'm. Forest – Pearce.

1992 LIVERPOOL – Grobbelaar; Jones (R.), Burrows, Nicol, Molby, Wright, Saunders, Houghton, Rush (I.), McManaman, Thomas. **SUNDERLAND** – Norman; Owers, Ball, Bennett, Rogan, Rush (D.) (Hardyman), Bracewell, Davenport, Armstrong (Hawke), Byrne, Atkinson. **Scorers:** Liverpool – Thomas, Rush (I.).

1993 ARSENAL – Seaman; Dixon, Winterburn, Linighan, Adams, Parlour (Smith), Davis, Merson, Jensen, Wright (O'Leary), Campbell. **SHEFFIELD WED.** – Woods; Nilsson, Worthington, Palmer, Hirst, Anderson (Hyde), Waddle (Bart-Williams), Warhurst, Bright, Sheridan, Harkes. **Scorers:** Arsenal – Wright, Sheff. Wed. – Hirst. **Replay: ARSENAL** – Seaman; Dixon, Winterburn, Linighan, Adams, Davis, Jensen, Merson, Smith, Wright (O'Leary), Campbell. **SHEFFIELD WED.** – Woods; Nilsson (Bart-Williams), Worthington, Palmer, Hirst, Wilson (Hyde), Waddle, Warhurst, Bright, Sheridan, Harkes. **Scorers:** Arsenal – Wright, Linighan, Sheff. Wed. – Waddle.

1994 MANCHESTER UTD. – Schmeichel; Parker, Bruce, Pallister, Irwin (Sharpe), Kanchelskis (McClair), Keane, Ince, Giggs, Cantona, Hughes. **CHELSEA** – Kharine; Clarke, Johnsen, Kjeldbjerg, Sinclair, Burley (Hoddle), Newton, Wise, Peacock, Stein (Cascarino), Spencer. **Scorers:** Manchester Utd. – Cantona 2 (2 pens.), Hughes, McClair.

1995 EVERTON – Southall; Jackson, Watson, Unsworth, Ablett, Horne, Parkinson, Hinchcliffe, Stuart, Limpar (Amokachi), Rideout (Ferguson). **MANCHESTER UTD.** – Schmeichel; Neville (G.), Bruce (Giggs), Pallister, Irwin, Butt, Keane, Ince, Sharpe (Scholes), McClair, Hughes. **Scorer:** Everton – Rideout.

1996 MANCHESTER UTD. – Schmeichel; Irwin, May, Pallister, Neville (P.), Beckham (Neville, G.), Keane, Butt, Giggs, Cantona, Cole (Scholes). **LIVERPOOL** – James; McAteer, Scales, Wright, Babb, Jones (Thomas), McManaman, Redknapp, Barnes, Collymore (Rush), Fowler. **Scorer:** Manchester Utd. – Cantona.

1997 CHELSEA – Grodas; Sinclair, Lebouef, Clarke, Minto, Petrescu, Di Matteo, Newton, Wise, Zola (Vialli), Hughes (M.). **MIDDLESBROUGH** – Roberts; Blackmore, Pearson, Festa, Fleming, Stamp, Emerson, Mustoe (Vickers), Hignett (Kinder), Juninho, Ravanelli, (Beck). **Scorers:** Chelsea – Di Matteo, Newton.

1998 ARSENAL – Seaman; Dixon, Adams, Keown, Winterburn, Parlour, Petit, Vieira, Overmars, Wreh (Platt), Anelka. **NEWCASTLE** – Given; Barton (Watson), Dabizas, Howey, Pearce (Andersson), Pistone, Batty, Lee, Speed, Shearer, Ketsbaia (Barnes). **Scorers:** Arsenal – Overmars, Anelka.

1999 MANCHESTER UTD. – Schmeichel; Neville (G.), Johnsen, May, Neville (P.); Beckham, Scholes (Stam), Keane (Sheringham), Giggs; Cole (Yorke), Solskjaer. **NEWCASTLE UTD.** – Harper; Griffin, Charvet, Dabizas, Domi; Lee, Hamann (Ferguson), Speed, Solano (Maric); Ketsbaia (Glass), Shearer. **Scorers:** Manchester Utd. – Sheringham, Scholes.

DUNMOW DUNCES

Essex club Dunmow ended the season bottom of the Bishop's Stortford, Stansted and District League Premier Division with minus two points!

They lost all 16 games played, conceding 176 goals in the process, and were deducted two points for failing to fulfil a fixture.

F.A. CUP FINALS – COMPLETE RESULTS

AT KENNINGTON OVAL
1872   The Wanderers beat Royal Engineers (1-0)

AT LILLIE BRIDGE, LONDON
1873   The Wanderers beat Oxford University (2-1)

AT KENNINGTON OVAL
1874   Oxford University beat Royal Engineers (2-0)
1875   Royal Engineers beat Old Etonians (2-0 after a 1-1 draw)
1876   The Wanderers beat Old Etonians (3-0 after a 0-0 draw)
1877††   The Wanderers beat Oxford University (2-1)
1878*   The Wanderers beat Royal Engineers (3-1)
1879   Old Etonians beat Clapham Rov. (1-0)
1880   Clapham Rov. beat Oxford University (1-0)
1881   Old Carthusians beat Old Etonians (3-0)
1882   Old Etonians beat Blackburn Rov. (1-0)
1883††   Blackburn Olympic beat Old Etonians (2-1)
1884   Blackburn Rov. beat Queen's Park (Glasgow) (2-1)
1885   Blackburn Rov. beat Queen's Park (Glasgow) (2-0)
1886†a   Blackburn Rov. beat W.B.A. (2-0 after a 0-0 draw)
1887   Aston Villa beat W.B.A. (2-0)
1888   W.B.A. beat Preston N.E. (2-1)
1889   Preston N.E. beat Wolves (3-0)
1890   Blackburn Rov. beat Sheffield Wed. (6-1)
1891   Blackburn Rov. beat Notts Co. (3-1)
1892   W.B.A. beat Aston Villa (3-0)

AT FALLOWFIELD, MANCHESTER
1893   Wolves beat Everton (1-0)

AT GOODISON PARK, LIVERPOOL
1894   Notts Co. beat Bolton Wand. (4-1)

AT CRYSTAL PALACE
1895   Aston Villa beat W.B.A. (1-0)
1896   Sheffield Wed. beat Wolves (2-1)
1897   Aston Villa beat Everton (3-2)
1898   Nott'm. Forest beat Derby Co. (3-1)
1899   Sheffield Utd. beat Derby Co. (4-1)
1900   Bury beat Southampton (4-0)
1901†††   Tottenham beat Sheffield Utd. (3-1 after a 2-2 draw)
1902   Sheffield Utd. beat Southampton (2-1 after a 1-1 draw)
1903   Bury beat Derby Co. (6-0)
1904   Manchester City beat Bolton Wand. (1-0)
1905   Aston Villa beat Newcastle Utd. (2-0)
1906   Everton beat Newcastle Utd. (1-0)
1907   Sheffield Wed. beat Everton (2-1)
1908   Wolves beat Newcastle Utd. (3-1)
1909   Manchester Utd. beat Bristol City (1-0)
1910*   Newcastle Utd. beat Barnsley (2-0 after a 1-1 draw)
1911b   Bradford City beat Newcastle Utd. (1-0 after a 0-0 draw)
1912c   Barnsley beat W.B.A. (1-0 after a 0-0 draw)
1913   Aston Villa beat Sunderland (1-0)
1914   Burnley beat Liverpool (1-0)

AT OLD TRAFFORD, MANCHESTER

1915   Sheffield Utd. beat Chelsea (3-0)

AT STAMFORD BRIDGE, LONDON

1920††   Aston Villa beat Huddersfield Town (1-0)
1921   Tottenham beat Wolves (1-0)
1922   Huddersfield Town beat Preston N.E. (1-0)

AT WEMBLEY

1923   Bolton Wand. beat West Ham Utd. (2-0)
1924   Newcastle Utd. beat Aston Villa (2-0)
1925   Sheffield Utd. beat Cardiff City (1-0)
1926   Bolton Wand. beat Manchester City (1-0)
1927   Cardiff City beat Arsenal (1-0)
1928   Blackburn Rov. beat Huddersfield Town (3-1)
1929   Bolton Wand. beat Portsmouth (2-0)
1930   Arsenal beat Huddersfield Town (2-0)
1931   W.B.A. beat Birmingham City (2-1)
1932   Newcastle Utd. beat Arsenal (2-1)
1933   Everton beat Manchester City (3-0)
1934   Manchester City beat Portsmouth (2-1)
1935   Sheffield Wed. beat W.B.A. (4-2)
1936   Arsenal beat Sheffield Utd. (1-0)
1937   Sunderland beat Preston N.E. (3-1)
1938††   Preston N.E. beat Huddersfield Town (1-0)
1939   Portsmouth beat Wolves (4-1)
1946††   Derby Co. beat Charlton Athletic (4-1)
1947††   Charlton Athletic beat Burnley (1-0)
1948   Manchester Utd. beat Blackpool (4-2)
1949   Wolves beat Leicester City (3-1)
1950   Arsenal beat Liverpool (2-0)
1951   Newcastle Utd. beat Blackpool (2-0)
1952   Newcastle Utd. beat Arsenal (1-0)
1953   Blackpool beat Bolton Wand. (4-3)
1954   W.B.A. beat Preston N.E. (3-2)
1955   Newcastle Utd. beat Manchester City (3-1)
1956   Manchester City beat Birmingham City (3-1)
1957   Aston Villa beat Manchester Utd. (2-1)
1958   Bolton Wand. beat Manchester Utd. (2-0)
1959   Nott'm. Forest beat Luton Town (2-1)
1960   Wolves beat Blackburn Rov. (3-0)
1961   Tottenham beat Leicester City (2-0)
1962   Tottenham beat Burnley (3-1)
1963   Manchester Utd. beat Leicester City (3-1)
1964   West Ham Utd. beat Preston N.E. (3-2)
1965††   Liverpool beat Leeds Utd. (2-1)
1966   Everton beat Sheffield Wed. (3-2)
1967   Tottenham beat Chelsea (2-1)
1968††   W.B.A. beat Everton (1-0)
1969   Manchester City beat Leicester City (1-0)
1970††•   Chelsea beat Leeds Utd. (2-1 after a 2-2 draw)
1971††   Arsenal beat Liverpool (2-1)
1972   Leeds Utd. beat Arsenal (1-0)
1973   Sunderland beat Leeds Utd. (1-0)
1974   Liverpool beat Newcastle Utd. (3-0)
1975   West Ham Utd. beat Fulham (2-0)
1976   Southampton beat Manchester Utd. (1-0)
1977   Manchester Utd. beat Liverpool (2-1)

1978	Ipswich Town beat Arsenal (1-0)
1979	Arsenal beat Manchester Utd. (3-2)
1980	West Ham Utd. beat Arsenal (1-0)
1981	Tottenham beat Manchester City (3-2 after a 1-1 draw)
1982	Tottenham beat Q.P.R. (1-0 after a 1-1 draw)
1983	Manchester Utd. beat Brighton & H.A. (4-0 after a 2-2 draw)
1984	Everton beat Watford (2-0)
1985††	Manchester Utd. beat Everton (1-0)
1986	Liverpool beat Everton (3-1)
1987††	Coventry City beat Tottenham (3-2)
1988	Wimbledon beat Liverpool (1-0)
1989††	Liverpool beat Everton (3-2)
1990	Manchester Utd. beat Crystal Palace (1-0 after a 3-3 draw)
1991††	Tottenham beat Nott'm. Forest (2-1)
1992	Liverpool beat Sunderland (2-0)
1993††	Arsenal beat Sheffield Wed. (2-1 after a 1-1 draw)
1994	Manchester Utd. beat Chelsea (4-0)
1995	Everton beat Manchester Utd. (1-0)
1996	Manchester Utd. beat Liverpool (1-0)
1997	Chelsea beat Middlesbrough (2-0)
1998	Arsenal beat Newcastle Utd. (2-0)
1999	Manchester Utd. beat Newcastle Utd. (2-0)

†† After extra time. * Won outright but restored to the Association. *a* Replayed at Baseball Ground, Derby Co. † A special trophy was awarded for the third consecutive win. ††† Replayed at Burnden Park, Bolton Wand. ** Replayed at Goodison Park, Liverpool. *b* Replayed at Old Trafford, Manchester, new trophy provided. *c* Replayed at Bramall Lane, Sheffield. • Replayed at Old Trafford.
(All replays since 1981 played at Wembley.)

1999 F.A. CUP FINAL

(Competition sponsored by AXA)

MANCHESTER UNITED 2, NEWCASTLE UNITED 0

Wembley, Saturday May 22. Attendance: 79,101. Estimated receipts: £2.5m

Manchester Utd.: (red shirts): Schmeichel; G Neville, May, Johnsen, P Neville; Beckham, Keane (Sheringham 9), Scholes (Stam 77), Giggs; Cole (Yorke 60), Solskjaer. **Scorers:** Sheringham 11 mins, Scholes 53 mins. **Subs not used:** Blomqvist, Van der Gouw. **Manager:** Alex Ferguson.

Newcastle Utd.: (black and white striped shirts): Harper; Griffin, Dabizas, Charvet, Domi; Lee, Hamann (Ferguson 46), Speed, Solano (Maric 68), Shearer, Ketsbaia (Glass 78). **Subs not used:** Barton, Given. **Booked:** Hamann. **Manager:** Ruud Gullit.

Referee: Peter Jones (Loughborough). **Half-time:** 1-0. **Kick-off:** 3.0 (ITV, Sky).

Guest of Honour: HRH Prince Charles.

Conditions: Hot and sunny, pitch excellent.

Manchester United duly completed their third League and F.A. Cup Double of the decade with a comfortable win over a **Newcastle United** side which was almost as poor as the one that lost by the same scoreline to Arsenal 12 months earlier.

United manager Alex Ferguson showed where his priorities lay by resting Dwight Yorke and Nicky Butt in view of the European Cup final four days later, while Jaap Stam returned to the bench after injury.

The wider public seemed to share Ferguson's analysis of the situation. The match was again screened live by both ITV and Sky and though viewing figures were up by 25% on last year's ratings, which were the lowest for over 30 years, the combined audience was still below 11 million, more than four million fewer than the number who tuned in to the game in Barcelona.

Newcastle began aggressively and a fierce Gary Speed tackle forced Roy Keane out of the game in the eighth minute. But the Magpies' approach backfired spectacularly as the Irishman was replaced by Teddy Sheringham, who put his side ahead less than two minutes later after a neat exchange of passes with Paul Scholes.

Newcastle responded and Dieter Hamann forced a fine save low to his right from Peter Schmeichel but Sheringham could have doubled the lead with headers.

The game was effectively ended as a contest ten minutes into the second-half. Ole Gunnar Solskjaer picked up a poor clearance from Nicos Dabizas and fed Sheringham who astutely laid the ball back for Scholes to drive a left-footed shot past Steve Harper.

To their credit Newcastle kept fighting and Timuri Ketsbaia hit the post before Silvio Maric fired wide when clean through but Ferguson's side were worthy winners despite never having to engage top gear.

Indeed Sheringham was just inches away from capping a superb display with another goal when his delicate chip late on grazed the crossbar.

Manchester United's celebrations were tempered by the knowledge that a far sterner test awaited them in Barcelona, while Newcastle's under-achieving players were again unworthy of the remarkable support they received.

To underline the winners' remarkable strength in depth the following eleven did not start at Wembley: Van der Gouw, Irwin, Brown, Berg, Stam, Curtis, Blomqvist, Butt, Greening, Yorke, Sheringham.

With Manchester United guaranteed a place in the Champions' League, Ruud Gullit's side qualified for the revamped UEFA Cup; the second successive season they earned a place in Europe by losing the FA Cup final.

Ticket prices ranged from £10-15 for seats with a restricted view through to £110-125 in the Olympic Gallery. Receipts were estimated at £2.5 million. The programme again cost £6. Officials' fees: Referee £350, assistants each £165 and souvenir gold medals all round.

ANDY TONGUE

HOW THEY REACHED THE FINAL

MANCHESTER UNITED

3rd Round: W 3-1 home to Middlesbrough (Cole, Giggs, Irwin pen)
4th Round: W 2-1 home to Liverpool (Yorke, Solskjaer)
5th Round: W 1-0 home to Fulham (Cole)
6th Round: D 0-0 home to Chelsea
Replay: W 2-0 away to Chelsea (Yorke 2)
Semi-final (Villa Park): D 0-0 v Arsenal aet
Replay (Villa Park): W 2-1 v Arsenal aet (Beckham, Giggs)

NEWCASTLE UNITED

3rd Round: W 2-1 home to Crystal Palace (Speed, Shearer)
4th Round: W 3-0 home to Bradford City (Hamann, Shearer, Ketsbaia)
5th Round: D 0-0 home to Blackburn Rov.
Replay: W 1-0 away to Blackburn Rov. (Saha)
6th Round: W 4-1 home to Everton (Ketsbaia 2, Shearer, Georgiadis)
Semi-final (Old Trafford): W 2-0 v Tottenham aet (Shearer 2; 1 pen)

SUMMARY OF F.A. CUP WINS

Manchester Utd. 10	Sheffield Wed. 3	Charlton Athletic 1
Tottenham 8	West Ham Utd. 3	Clapham Rov. 1
Aston Villa 7	Bury 2	Coventry City 1
Arsenal 7	Chelsea 2	Derby Co. 1
Blackburn Rov. 6	Nottingham Forest 2	Huddersfield Town 1
Newcastle Utd. 6	Old Etonians 2	Ipswich Town 1
Everton 5	Preston N.E. 2	Leeds Utd. 1
Liverpool 5	Sunderland 2	Notts Co. 1
The Wanderers 5	Barnsley 1	Old Carthusians 1
W.B.A 5	Blackburn Olympic 1	Oxford University 1
Bolton Wand. 4	Blackpool 1	Portsmouth 1
Manchester City 4	Bradford City 1	Royal Engineers 1
Sheffield Utd. 4	Burnley 1	Southampton 1
Wolves 4	Cardiff City 1	Wimbledon 1

APPEARANCES IN FINALS

(Figures do not include replays)

Manchester Utd. 15	The Wanderers* 5	Clapham Rov. 2
Arsenal 13	Derby Co. 4	Notts Co. 2
Newcastle Utd. 13	Leeds Utd. 4	Queen's Park (Glas.) 2
Everton 12	Leicester City 4	Blackburn Olympic* 1
Liverpool 11	Oxford University 4	Bradford City* 1
W.B.A. 10	Royal Engineers 4	Brighton & H.A. 1
Aston Villa 9	Sunderland 4	Bristol City 1
Tottenham Hotspur 9	West Ham Utd. 4	Coventry City* 1
Blackburn Rov. 8	Blackpool 3	Crystal Palace 1
Manchester City 8	Burnley 3	Fulham 1
Wolves 8	Nottingham Forest 3	Ipswich Town* 1
Bolton Wand. 7	Portsmouth 3	Luton Town 1
Preston N.E. 7	Southampton 3	Middlesbrough 1
Old Etonians 6	Barnsley 2	Old Carthusians* 1
Sheffield Utd. 6	Birmingham City 2	Q.P.R. 1
Sheffield Wed. 6	Bury* 2	Watford 1
Chelsea 5	Cardiff City 2	Wimbledon* 1
Huddersfield Town 5	Charlton Athletic 2	(* Denotes undefeated)

APPEARANCES IN SEMI-FINALS

(Figures do not include replays)

Everton 23, Manchester Utd. 22, Arsenal 20, Liverpool 20, W.B.A. 19, Aston Villa 18, Blackburn Rov. 16, Sheffield Wed. 16, Tottenham H. 16, Newcastle Utd. 15, Wolves 14, Chelsea 13, Derby Co. Co. 13, Bolton Wand. W. 12, Nott'm Forest 12, Sheffield Utd. 12, Sunderland 11, Manchester City 10, Preston N.E. 10, Southampton 10, Birmingham City 9, Burnley 8, Leeds Utd. 8, Huddersfield Town 7, Leicester City 7, Old Etonians 6, Oxford University 6, West Ham Utd. 6, Fulham 5, Notts Co. 5, Portsmouth 5, The Wanderers 5, Luton Town 4, Queen's Park (Glasgow) 4, Royal Engineers 4, Blackpool 3, Cardiff City 3, Clapham Rov. 3, *Crystal Palace 3, Ipswich Town 3, Millwall 3, Norwich City 3, Old Carthusians 3, Oldham Athletic 3, Stoke City 3, The Swifts 3, Watford 3, Barnsley 2, Blackburn Olympic 2, Bristol City 2, Bury 2, Charlton Athletic 2, Grimsby Town 2, Swansea City Town 2, Swindon Town 2, Wimbledon 2, Bradford City 1, Brighton & H.A. 1, Cambridge University 1, Chesterfield 1, Coventry City 1, Crewe Alexandra 1, Darwen 1, Derby Co. Junction 1, Hull City 1, Marlow 1, Middlesbrough 1, Old Harrovians 1, Orient 1, Plymouth Argyle 1, Port Vale 1, Q.P.R. 1, Rangers (Glasgow) 1, Reading 1, Shropshire Wand. 1, York City 1.

*(*A previous and different Crystal Palace club also reached the semi-final in season 1871-72)*

WEMBLEY'S F.A. CUP FINALS – THE TOP MEN

Year	Winners	Manager	Captain	Referee
1923	Bolton Wand.	Charles Foweraker	Joe Smith	D.H. Asson (West Bromwich)
1924	Newcastle Utd.	No manager	Frank Hudspeth	W.E. Russell (Swindon)
1925	Sheffield Utd.	John Nicholson	Billy Gillespie	G.N. Watson (Nottingham)
1926	Bolton Wand.	Charles Foweraker	Joe Smith	I. Baker (Crewe)
1927	Cardiff City	Fred Stewart	Fred Keenor	W.F. Bunnell (Preston)
1928	Blackburn Row.	Bob Crompton	Harry Healless	T.G. Bryan (Willenhall)
1929	Bolton Wand.	Charles Foweraker	Jimmy Seddon	A. Josephs (South Shields)
1930	Arsenal	Herbert Chapman	Tom Parker	T. Crew (Leicester)
1931	W.B.A.	Fred Everiss	Tommy Glidden	A.H. Kingscott (Long Eaton)
1932	Newcastle Utd.	Andy Cunningham	Jimmy Nelson	W.P. Harper (Stourbridge)
1933	Everton	No manager	W.R. ('Dixie') Dean	E. Wood (Sheffield)
1934	Manchester City	Wilf Wild	Sam Cowan	S.F. Rous (Watford)
1935	Sheffield Wed.	Billy Walker	Ronnie Starling	A.E. Fogg (Bolton)
1936	Arsenal	George Allison	Alex James	H. Nattrass (Seaham, Co. Durham)
1937	Sunderland	Johnny Cochrane	Raich Carter	G. Rudd (Kenton, Middlesex)
1938	Preston N.E.	Tom Smith	Tom Smith	T. Thompson (Lemington-on-Tyne)
1939	Portsmouth	Jack Tinn	Jimmy Guthrie	A.J. Jewell (London)
1946	Derby Co.	Stuart McMillan	Jack Nicholas	E.D. Smith (Whitehaven)
1947	Charlton Athletic	Jimmy Seed	Don Welsh	J.M. Wiltshire (Sherborne)
1948	Manchester Utd.	Matt Busby	Johnny Carey	C.J. Barrick (Northampton)
1949	Wolves	Stan Cullis	Billy Wright	R.A. Mortimer (Huddersfield)
1950	Arsenal	Tom Whittaker	Joe Mercer	H. Pearce (Luton)
1951	Newcastle Utd.	Stan Seymour (Snr.)	Joe Harvey	W. Ling (Stapleford, Cambs.)
1952	Newcastle Utd.	Stan Seymour (Snr.)	Joe Harvey	A.E. Ellis (Halifax)
1953	Blackpool	Joe Smith	Harry Johnston	B.M. Griffiths (Newport, Mon.)
1954	W.B.A.	Vic Buckingham	Len Millard	A.W. Luty (Leeds)
1955	Newcastle Utd.	Dugald Livingstone	Jimmy Scoular	R.J. Leafe (Nottingham)
1956	Manchester City	Les McDowall	Roy Paul	A. Bond (Fulham)
1957	Aston Villa	Eric Houghton	Johnny Dixon	F. Coultas (Hull)
1958	Bolton Wand.	Bill Ridding	Nat Lofthouse	J. Sherlock (Sheffield)
1959	Nott'm Forest	Billy Walker	Jack Burkitt	J.H. Clough (Bolton)
1960	Wolves	Stan Cullis	Bill Slater	K. Howley (Middlesbrough)
1961	Tottenham	Bill Nicholson	Danny Blanchflower	J. Kelly (Chorley)
1962	Tottenham	Bill Nicholson	Danny Blanchflower	J. Finney (Hereford)

Year	Winners	Manager	Captain	Referee
1963	Manchester Utd.	Matt Busby	Noel Cantwell	K.G. Aston (Ilford, Essex)
1964	West Ham Utd.	Ron Greenwood	Bobby Moore	A. Holland (Barnsley)
1965	Liverpool	Bill Shankly	Ron Yeats	W. Clements (West Bromwich)
1966	Everton	Harry Catterick	Brian Labone	J.F. Taylor (Wolverhampton)
1967	Tottenham	Bill Nicholson	Dave Mackay	K. Dagnall (Bolton)
1968	W.B.A.	Alan Ashman	Graham Williams	L. Callaghan (Merthyr Tydfil)
1969	Manchester City	Joe Mercer	Tony Book	G. McCabe (Sheffield)
1970	Chelsea (Rep. Old Trafford)	Dave Sexton	Ron Harris	E. Jennings (Stourbridge)
1971	Arsenal	Bertie Mee	Frank McLintock	N. Burtenshaw (Gt. Yarmouth)
1972	Leeds Utd.	Don Revie	Billy Bremner	D. Smith (Gloucester)
1973	Sunderland	Bob Stokoe	Bobby Kerr	K. Burns (Stourbridge)
1974	Liverpool	Bill Shankly	Emlyn Hughes	C.G. Kew (Amersham)
1975	West Ham Utd.	John Lyall	Billy Bonds	P. Partridge (Durham)
1976	Southampton	Lawrie McMenemy	Peter Rodrigues	C. Thomas (Treorchy)
1977	Manchester Utd.	Tommy Docherty	Martin Buchan	R. Matthewson (Bolton)
1978	Ipswich Town	Bobby Robson	Mick Mills	D.R.G. Nippard (Bournemouth)
1979	Arsenal	Terry Neill	Pat Rice	R. Challis (Tonbridge)
1980	West Ham Utd.	John Lyall	Billy Bonds	G. Courtney (Spennymoor)
1981	Tottenham	Keith Burkinshaw	Steve Perryman	K. Hackett (Sheffield)
1982	Tottenham	Keith Burkinshaw	Steve Perryman	C. White (Harrow)
1983	Manchester Utd.	Ron Atkinson	Bryan Robson	A. Grey (Gt. Yarmouth)
1984	Everton	Howard Kendall	Kevin Ratcliffe	J. Hunting (Leicester)
1985	Manchester Utd.	Ron Atkinson	Bryan Robson	P. Willis (Co. Durham)
1986	Liverpool	Kenny Dalglish	Alan Hansen	A. Robinson (Waterlooville)
1987	Coventry City	John Sillett (Coach)	Brian Kilcline	N. Midgley (Salford)
1988	Wimbledon	Bobby Gould	Dave Beasant	B. Hill (Kettering)
1989	Liverpool	Kenny Dalglish	Ronnie Whelan	J. Worrall (Warrington)
1990	Manchester Utd.	Alex Ferguson	Bryan Robson	A. Gunn (Sussex)
1991	Tottenham	Terry Venables	Gary Mabbutt	R. Milford (Bristol)
1992	Liverpool	Graeme Souness	Mark Wright	P. Don (Middlesex)
1993	Arsenal	George Graham	Tony Adams	K. Barratt (Coventry)
1994	Manchester Utd.	Alex Ferguson	Steve Bruce	D. Elleray (Harrow)
1995	Everton	Joe Royle	Dave Watson	G. Ashby (Worcester)
1996	Manchester Utd.	Alex Ferguson	Eric Cantona	D. Gallagher (Banbury)
1997	Chelsea	Ruud Gullit	Dennis Wise	S. Lodge (Barnsley)
1998	Arsenal	Arsene Wenger	Tony Adams	P. Durkin (Portland)
1999	Manchester Utd.	Alex Ferguson	Roy Keane	P. Jones (Loughborough)

75

TOTTENHAM'S THIRD LEAGUE CUP TRIUMPH

SECOND ROUND	THIRD ROUND	FOURTH ROUND	FIFTH ROUND	SEMI-FINALS	FINAL
Tottenham 3:3	Tottenham 3				
*Brentford 2:2		Tottenham 3			
*Northampton Town .. 2:0	*Northampton Town .. 1		*Tottenham 3		
West Ham Utd. .. 0:1					
Bye●	*Liverpool 3				
		*Liverpool 1			
*Fulham 1:1	Fulham 1			*Tottenham 0:1	
Southampton 1:0					
Bye●	*Manchester Utd. .. †2				
		*Manchester Utd. .. 2			
*Bury 3:1	Bury 0		Manchester Utd. 1		
Crystal Palace 0:2					
Nott'm Forest 5:0	*Nott'm Forest .. †A3				
*Leyton Orient 1:0		Nott'm Forest 1			Tottenham 1
*Sheffield Wed. 0:1	Cambridge Utd. 3				
Cambridge Utd. 1:1					
Wimbledon .... 1:†4	Wimbledon 2				
*Portsmouth 2:1		*Wimbledon 2			
Birmingham City 3:6	*Birmingham City .. 1				
*Macclesfield Town .. 0:0			*Wimbledon 2		
*Bolton Wand. 3:3	Bolton Wand. .... †B1				
Hull City 1:2		*Bolton Wand. 1			
*Norwich City 1:3	*Norwich City 1			Wimbledon 0:0	
Wigan Athletic 0:2					
Bye●	*Chelsea 4				
		Chelsea 5			
Bye●	Aston Villa 1		Chelsea 1		
Bye●	Arsenal 2				
		*Arsenal 0			
*Derby Co. 1:1	*Derby Co. 1				
Manchester City .. 1:0					

*Sunderland 3:1
Chester City .... 0:0 — *Sunderland .... †2
Grimsby Town .... 1:†2 — Grimsby Town .... 1 — Sunderland .... †C1
*Sheff. Utd 2:0
Everton .... 1:1 — Everton .... 1 — *Everton .... 1 — *Sunderland 3
*Huddersfield Town .... 1:2 — *Middlesbrough 2
*Middlesbrough 2:1
Wycombe Wand. 0:1
Luton Town .... 1:†4 — *Luton Town .... 2 — *Luton Town .... 1 — Luton Town 0
*Ipswich Town .... 2:2 — Coventry City .... 0 — Barnsley 0
*Coventry City 1:4
Southend Utd. 0:0
*Barnsley .... 3:1 — *Barnsley 2
Reading 0:1
*Bournemouth .... 1:2 — Bournemouth 1
Wolves 1:1

Bye●
Crewe Alexandra .... 1:2 — Blackburn Rov. .... 1 — Blackburn Rov. .... †D1 — Blackburn Rov. 0
*Bristol City .... 1:0 — *Crewe Alexandra 0
Bye●
Tranmere Rov. .... 1:3 — Newcastle Utd. .... 1 — *Newcastle Utd. 1
*Blackpool .... 2:1 — *Tranmere Rov. 0
Bye●
Bradford City .... 2:3 — *Leeds Utd. .... 1 — Leeds Utd. .... 1 — *Leicester City 1
*Halifax Town .... 1:1 — Bradford City 0
Charlton Athletic .... 2:1 — *Charlton Athletic .... 1 — *Leicester City 1
Q.P.R. 0:0
Chesterfield .... 0:1 — *Leicester City 2
Leicester City 3:3

Semi-final:
*Sunderland 1:1
Leicester City 2:1

Final:
Leicester City 0

* Drawn at home: in 2nd round and semi-finals, drawn at home in first leg. † After extra time. ● Given a bye into the 3rd round because of European Competitions. **Final** played at Wembley – Sunday, March 21 1999. Att: 99,999. A – Nott'm Forest won 4-3 on pens. B – Bolton Wand. won 3-1 on pens. C – Sunderland won 5-4 on pens. D – Blackburn Rov. won 4-2 on pens.)

WORTHINGTON CUP 1998-99

FIRST ROUND (TWO LEGS)

Barnsley 4 Scarborough 0 (3-0h, 1-0a); Birmingham City 3 Millwall 1 (2-0h, 1-1a); Blackpool 2 Scunthorpe Utd. 1 (1-0h, 1-1a); Bolton Wand. 4 Hartlepool Utd. 0 (1-0h, 3-0a); Bournemouth 4 Colchester Utd. 3 (2-0h, 2-3a); Bradford City 2 Lincoln City 1 (1-1h, 1-0a); Brentford 4 W.B.A. 2 (3-0h, 1-2a); Bristol City 7 Shrewsbury Town 4 (4-0h, 3-4a); Bury 5 Burnley 2 (1-1h, 4-1a);

Cambridge Utd. 2 Watford 1 (1-0h, 1-1a); Chester City 4 Port Vale 3 (2-2h, 2-1a); Chesterfield 3 Rotherham Utd. 0 (2-0h, 1-0a); Crewe Alexandra 4 Oldham Athletic 3 (2-0h, 2-3a); Crystal Palace 3 Torquay Utd. 2* (2-1h, 1-1a); Fulham 4 Cardiff City 2 (2-1h, 2-1a); Grimsby Town 0 Preston N.E. 0* (0-0h, 0-0a, Grimsby Town won 7-6 on pens.); Halifax Town 2 Wrexham 2* (0-2h, 2-0a, Halifax Town won 4-2 on pens.); Huddersfield Town 4 Mansfield Town 3 (3-2h, 1-1a); Hull City 2 Stockport Co. 2* (0-0h, 2-2a, Hull City won on away goals);

Ipswich Town 6 Exeter City 2 (5-1h, 1-1a); Leyton Orient 3 Bristol Rov. 2* (1-1h, 2-1a); Luton Town 5 Oxford Utd. 4 (2-3h, 3-1a); Macclesfield Town 3 Stoke City 2 (3-1h, 0-1a); Manchester City 9 Notts. County 1 (7-1h, 2-0a); Northampton Town 3 Brighton & H.A. 2* (2-1h, 1-1a); Norwich City 2 Swansea City 1* (1-0h, 1-1a); Portsmouth 6 Plymouth Argyle 3 (3-2h, 3-1a); Reading 3 Peterborough Utd. 1 (2-0h, 1-1a);

Q.P.R. 3 Walsall 1* (3-1h, 0-0a); Sheff. Utd. 5 Darlington 3* (3-1h, 2-2a); Southend Utd. 2 Gillingham 0 (1-0h, 1-0a); Sunderland 4 York City 1 (2-1h, 2-0a); Tranmere Rov. 4 Carlisle Utd. 0 (3-0h, 1-0a); Wigan Athletic 2 Rochdale 0 (1-0h, 1-0a); Wolves 6 Barnet 2 (5-0h, 1-2a); Wycombe Wand. 3 Swindon Town 2 (2-0h, 1-2a).

* After extra time

LEAGUE CUP FINALS

1961*	Aston Villa beat Rotherham Utd. 3-2 on agg. (0-2a, 3-0h)
1962	Norwich City beat Rochdale 4-0 on agg. (3-0a, 1-0h)
1963	Birmingham City beat Aston Villa 3-1 on agg. (3-1h, 0-0a)
1964	Leicester City beat Stoke City 4-3 on agg. (1-1a, 3-2h)
1965	Chelsea beat Leicester City 3-2 on agg. (3-2h, 0-0a)
1966	W.B.A. beat West Ham Utd. 5-3 on agg. (1-2a, 4-1h)

AT WEMBLEY

1967	Q.P.R. beat W.B.A. (3-2)
1968	Leeds Utd. beat Arsenal (1-0)
1969*	Swindon Town beat Arsenal (3-1)
1970*	Manchester City beat W.B.A. (2-1)
1971	Tottenham beat Aston Villa (2-0)
1972	Stoke City beat Chelsea (2-1)
1973	Tottenham beat Norwich City (1-0)
1974	Wolves beat Manchester City (2-1)
1975	Aston Villa beat Norwich City (1-0)
1976	Manchester City beat Newcastle Utd. (2-1)
1977†*	Aston Villa beat Everton (3-2 after 0-0 and 1-1 draws)
1978††	Nott'm. Forest beat Liverpool (1-0 after 0-0 draw)
1979	Nott'm. Forest beat Southampton (3-2)
1980	Wolves beat Nott'm. Forest (1-0)
1981†††	Liverpool beat West Ham Utd. (2-1 after 1-1 draw)

MILK CUP

1982*	Liverpool beat Tottenham (3-1)
1983*	Liverpool beat Manchester Utd. (2-1)
1984**	Liverpool beat Everton (1-0 after *0-0 draw)

| 1985 | Norwich City beat Sunderland (1-0) |
| 1986 | Oxford Utd. beat Q.P.R. (3-0) |

LITTLEWOODS CUP

1987	Arsenal beat Liverpool (2-1)
1988	Luton Town beat Arsenal (3-2)
1989	Nott'm. Forest beat Luton Town (3-1)
1990	Nott'm. Forest beat Oldham Athletic (1-0)

RUMBELOWS CUP

| 1991 | Sheffield Wed. beat Manchester Utd. (1-0) |
| 1992 | Manchester Utd. beat Nott'm. Forest (1-0) |

COCA-COLA CUP

1993	Arsenal beat Sheffield Wed. (2-1)
1994	Aston Villa beat Manchester Utd. (3-1)
1995	Liverpool beat Bolton Wand. (2-1)
1996	Aston Villa beat Leeds Utd. (3-0)
1997	Leicester City beat Middlesbrough (*1-0 after *1-1 draw) ★
1998	Chelsea beat Middlesbrough (2-0)

WORTHINGTON CUP

| 1999 | Tottenham beat Leicester City (1-0) |

* After extra time. † First replay at Hillsborough, second replay at Old Trafford. ††
Replayed at Old Trafford. ††† Replayed at Aston Villa Park. ** Replayed at Maine
Road. ★ Replayed at Hillsborough

WORTHINGTON (LEAGUE) CUP FINAL

TOTTENHAM 1 (Nielsen 90) **LEICESTER CITY 0**

Wembley, (77,892), Sunday, March 21, 1999. Kick-off 3.0 (Sky live)

Tottenham: Walker, Carr, Vega, Campbell (Capt), Edinburgh, Anderton, Freund, Nielsen, Ginola (Sinton 90), Ferdinand, Iversen. **Subs not used:** Armstrong, Dominguez, Young, Baardsen (gk). **Booked:** Vega **Sent-off:** Edinburgh (63)

Leicester City: Keller, Ullathorne, Elliott, Walsh (Capt), Taggart, Guppy, Savage (Zagorakis 90), Izzet, Lennon, Heskey (Marshall 75), Cottee. Subs not used: Campbell, Kaamark, Arphexad (gk). **Booked:** Elliott, Savage.

Referee: T. Heilbron (Newton Aycliffe). **Receipts:** £3.03m (estimated, competition record).

Guest of Honour: Lennart Johansson, President of UEFA.

NIELSEN STRIKES SILVER

Allan Nielsen scored a dramatic late winner to earn Tottenham their first piece of silverware in eight years.

Danish international Nielsen, in the side because Tim Sherwood was cup-tied, settled a tepid encounter by diving to head home after Leicester City goalkeeper Kasey Keller parried Steffen Iversen's injury-time cross-shot.

The goal could not have been better timed for Tottenham as they faced the prospect of playing extra-time with ten men following the 63rd minute dismissal of left-back Justin Edinburgh.

Edinburgh, the only survivor from the last Tottenham team to win a major trophy – the 1991 FA Cup – received his marching orders when he retaliated after a challenge by Robbie Savage.

79

In a disappointing game of few openings, Leicester City's Emile Heskey was well placed in the first-half to repeat his goalscoring performance of the 1997 final but hesitated in front of goal and allowed Ramon Vega to avert the danger.

A further 30 minutes seemed inevitable until Nielsen intervened to cap a man-of-the-match performance and take the cup to White Hart Lane for the third time.

SUMMARY OF LEAGUE CUP WINNERS

Aston Villa 5	Manchester City 2	Oxford Utd. 1
Liverpool 5	Norwich City 2	Q.P.R. 1
Nott'm. Forest 4	Wolves 2	Sheffield Wed. 1
Tottenham 3	Birmingham City 1	Stoke City 1
Arsenal 2	Leeds Utd. 1	Swindon Town 1
Chelsea 2	Luton Town 1	W.B.A. 1
Leicester City 2	Manchester Utd. 1	

LEAGUE CUP FINAL APPEARANCES

7 Aston Villa, Liverpool; **6** Nott'm. Forest; **5** Arsenal; **4** Manchester Utd., Leicester City, Norwich City, Tottenham; **3** Chelsea, Manchester City, W.B.A.; **2** Everton, Leeds Utd., Luton Town, Middlesbrough, Q.P.R., Sheffield Wed., Stoke City, West Ham Utd., Wolves; **1** Birmingham City, Bolton Wand., Newcastle Utd., Oldham Athletic, Oxford Utd., Rochdale, Rotherham Utd., Southampton, Sunderland, Swindon Town. **(Figures do not include replays).**

LEAGUE CUP SEMI-FINAL APPEARANCES

10 Aston Villa, Liverpool; **9** Arsenal, Tottenham; **7** Manchester Utd., West Ham Utd.; **6** Chelsea, Nott'm. Forest; **5** Leeds Utd., Manchester City, Norwich City; **4** Leicester City, Middlesbrough, W.B.A.; **3** Birmingham City, Burnley, Everton, Q.P.R., Sheffield Wed., Sunderland, Swindon Town, Wolves; **2** Blackburn Rov., Bolton Wand., Bristol City, Coventry City, Crystal Palace, Ipswich Town, Luton Town, Oxford Utd., Plymouth Argyle, Southampton, Stoke City, Wimbledon; **1** Blackpool, Bury, Cardiff City, Carlisle Utd., Chester City, Derby Co., Huddersfield Town, Newcastle Utd., Oldham Athletic, Peterborough, Rochdale, Rotherham Utd., Shrewsbury Town, Stockport Co., Tranmere Rov., Walsall, Watford. **(Figures do not include replays).**

HOT SHOT REFEREE ON MURDER CHARGE

Referee Lebogang Mokgethi, 34, was charged with murder after allegedly pulling out a gun and shooting dead a protesting player during a match near Johannesburg.

A 600-strong crowd saw Wallabies' Isaac Mkhwetha, 20, charge at the referee with a knife after the official allowed a goal by a team called Try Agains.

The referee was alleged to have whipped out a pistol and shot the player in the chest. He died later.

RECORD FOR CARD-SHARP REF

Referee Antonio Lopez set a new Spanish record with 16 yellow cards plus two reds for second bookable offences during Atletico Madrid's 2-1 win over Athletic Bilbao. There were only 33 fouls in the match.

SCOTTISH FINAL TABLES 1998-99

BANK OF SCOTLAND PREMIER LEAGUE

		P	W	D	L	F	A	W	D	L	F	A	Pts
			HOME					AWAY					
1	Rangers	36	12	5	1	32	11	11	3	4	46	20	77
2	Celtic	36	14	2	2	49	12	7	6	5	35	23	71
3	St Johnstone	36	8	7	3	24	18	7	5	6	15	20	57
4	Kilmarnock	36	8	7	3	24	15	6	7	5	23	14	56
5	Dundee	36	7	4	7	18	23	6	3	9	18	33	46
6	Hearts	36	8	2	8	27	26	3	7	8	17	24	42
7	Motherwell	36	6	5	7	20	31	4	6	8	15	23	41
8	Aberdeen	36	6	4	8	24	35	4	3	11	19	36	37
9	Dundee Utd	36	2	8	8	13	22	6	2	10	24	26	34
10	Dunfermline	36	4	7	7	18	29	0	9	9	10	30	28

FIRST DIVISION

		P	W	D	L	F	A	W	D	L	F	A	Pts	GD
			HOME					AWAY						
1	Hibernian	36	16	1	1	45	13	12	4	2	39	20	89	+51
2	Falkirk	36	9	5	4	28	18	11	1	6	32	20	66	+22
3	Ayr	36	8	4	6	38	23	11	1	6	28	19	62	+24
4	Airdrie	36	6	2	10	17	29	12	3	3	25	14	59	−1
5	St Mirren	36	10	2	6	26	25	4	8	6	16	18	52	−1
6	Morton	36	5	5	8	20	24	9	2	7	25	17	49	+4
7	Clydebank	36	5	6	7	17	18	6	7	5	19	20	46	−2
8	Raith	36	5	5	8	19	27	3	6	9	18	30	35	−20
9	Hamilton	36	3	5	10	13	26	3	5	10	17	36	28	−32
10	Stranraer	36	2	2	14	14	31	3	0	15	15	43	17	−45

SECOND DIVISION

		P	W	D	L	F	A	W	D	L	F	A	Pts	GD
			HOME					AWAY						
1	Livingston	36	13	4	1	32	12	9	7	2	34	23	77	+31
2	Inverness CT	36	14	4	0	44	20	7	5	6	36	28	72	+32
3	Clyde	36	10	4	4	28	16	5	4	9	18	26	53	+4
4	Queen of S	36	7	8	3	26	17	6	1	11	24	28	48	+5
5	Alloa	36	8	3	7	41	30	5	4	9	24	26	46	+9
6	Stirling	36	7	3	8	27	28	5	5	8	23	35	44	−13
7	Arbroath	36	7	4	7	19	25	5	4	9	18	27	44	−15
8	Partick	36	7	4	7	18	19	5	3	10	18	26	43	−9
9	East Fife	36	7	3	8	22	31	5	3	10	20	33	42	−22
10	Forfar	36	6	3	9	31	34	2	4	12	17	36	31	−22

THIRD DIVISION

				HOME				AWAY						
		P	W	D	L	F	A	W	D	L	F	A	Pts	GD
1	Ross Co.	36	12	1	5	39	16	12	4	2	48	26	77	+45
2	Stenhousemuir	36	9	2	7	34	26	10	5	3	28	16	64	+20
3	Brechin	36	7	6	5	21	19	10	2	6	26	24	59	+4
4	Dumbarton	36	6	5	7	25	21	10	4	4	28	19	57	+13
5	Berwick	36	7	3	8	28	27	5	11	2	25	22	50	+4
6	Queen's Park	36	6	7	5	22	21	5	4	9	19	25	44	−5
7	Albion	36	5	4	9	22	36	7	4	7	21	27	44	−20
8	East Stirling	36	4	10	4	27	22	5	3	10	23	26	40	+2
9	Cowdenbeath	36	5	2	11	19	30	3	5	10	15	35	31	−31
10	Montrose	36	5	4	9	26	31	3	2	13	16	43	30	−32

SCOTTISH HONOURS LIST

PREMIER DIVISION

	First	Pts.	Second	Pts.	Third	Pts.
1975-6	Rangers	54	Celtic	48	Hibernian	43
1976-7	Celtic	55	Rangers	46	Aberdeen	43
1977-8	Rangers	55	Aberdeen	53	Dundee Utd.	40
1978-9	Celtic	48	Rangers	45	Dundee Utd.	44
1979-80	Aberdeen	48	Celtic	47	St. Mirren	42
1980-81	Celtic	56	Aberdeen	49	Rangers	44
1981-2	Celtic	55	Aberdeen	53	Rangers	43
1982-3	Dundee Utd.	56	Celtic	55	Aberdeen	55
1983-4	Aberdeen	57	Celtic	50	Dundee Utd.	47
1984-5	Aberdeen	59	Celtic	52	Dundee Utd.	47
1985-6	*Celtic	50	Hearts	50	Dundee Utd.	47
1986-7	Rangers	69	Celtic	63	Dundee Utd.	60
1987-8	Celtic	72	Hearts	62	Rangers	60
1988-9	Rangers	56	Aberdeen	50	Celtic	46
1989-90	Rangers	51	Aberdeen	44	Hearts	44
1990-1	Rangers	55	Aberdeen	53	Celtic	41
1991-2	Rangers	72	Hearts	63	Celtic	62
1992-3	Rangers	73	Aberdeen	64	Celtic	60
1993-4	Rangers	58	Aberdeen	55	Motherwell	54
1994-5	Rangers	69	Motherwell	54	Hibernian	53
1995-6	Rangers	87	Celtic	83	Aberdeen	55
1996-7	Rangers	80	Celtic	75	Dundee Utd.	60
1997-8	Celtic	74	Rangers	72	Hearts	67

PREMIER LEAGUE

	First	Pts.	Second	Pts.	Third	Pts.
1998-99	Rangers	77	Celtic	71	St. Johnstone	57

Maximum points: 72 except 1986-8, 1991-4 (88) and from 1994 (108).
* Won on goal difference.

FIRST DIVISION (Scottish Championship until 1975-76)

	First	Pts.	Second	Pts.	Third	Pts.
1890-1a	††Dumbarton	29	Rangers	29	Celtic	24
1891-2b	Dumbarton	37	Celtic	35	Hearts	30

Season						
1892-3a	Celtic	29	Rangers	28	St Mirren	23
1893-4a	Celtic	29	Hearts	26	St Bernard's	22
1894-5a	Hearts	31	Celtic	26	Rangers	21
1895-6a	Celtic	30	Rangers	26	Hibernian	24
1896-7a	Hearts	28	Hibernian	26	Rangers	25
1897-8a	Celtic	33	Rangers	29	Hibernian	22
1898-9a	Rangers	36	Hearts	26	Celtic	24
1899-1900a	Rangers	32	Celtic	25	Hibernian	24
1900-1c	Rangers	35	Celtic	29	Hibernian	25
1901-2a	Rangers	28	Celtic	26	Hearts	22
1902-3b	Hibernian	37	Dundee	31	Rangers	29
1903-4d	Third Lanark	43	Hearts	39	Rangers	38
1904-5a	†Celtic	41	Rangers	41	Third Lanark	35
1905-6a	Celtic	46	Hearts	39	Rangers	38
1906-7f	Celtic	55	Dundee	48	Rangers	45
1907-8f	Celtic	55	Falkirk	51	Rangers	50
1908-9f	Celtic	51	Dundee	50	Clyde	48
1909-10f	Celtic	54	Falkirk	52	Rangers	49
1910-11f	Rangers	52	Aberdeen	48	Falkirk	44
1911-12f	Rangers	51	Celtic	45	Clyde	42
1912-13f	Rangers	53	Celtic	49	Hearts	41
1913-14g	Celtic	65	Rangers	59	Hearts	54
1914-15g	Celtic	65	Hearts	61	Rangers	50
1915-16g	Celtic	67	Rangers	56	Morton	51
1916-17g	Celtic	64	Morton	54	Rangers	53
1917-18f	Rangers	56	Celtic	55	Kilmarnock	43
1918-19f	Celtic	58	Rangers	57	Morton	47
1919-20h	Rangers	71	Celtic	68	Motherwell	57
1920-1h	Rangers	76	Celtic	66	Hearts	56
1921-2h	Celtic	67	Rangers	66	Raith	56
1922-3g	Rangers	55	Airdrieonians	50	Celtic	40
1923-4g	Rangers	59	Airdrieonians	50	Celtic	41
1924-5g	Rangers	60	Airdrieonians	57	Hibernian	52
1925-6g	Celtic	58	Airdrieonians	50	Hearts	50
1926-7g	Rangers	56	Motherwell	51	Celtic	49
1927-8g	Rangers	60	Celtic	55	Motherwell	55
1928-9g	Rangers	67	Celtic	51	Motherwell	50
1929-30g	Rangers	60	Motherwell	55	Aberdeen	53
1930-1g	Rangers	60	Celtic	58	Motherwell	56
1931-2g	Motherwell	66	Rangers	61	Celtic	48
1932-3g	Rangers	62	Motherwell	59	Hearts	50
1933-4g	Rangers	66	Motherwell	62	Celtic	47
1934-5g	Rangers	55	Celtic	52	Hearts	50
1935-6g	Celtic	68	Rangers	61	Aberdeen	61
1936-7g	Rangers	61	Aberdeen	54	Celtic	52
1937-8g	Celtic	61	Hearts	58	Rangers	49
1938-9f	Rangers	59	Celtic	48	Aberdeen	46
1946-7f	Rangers	46	Hibernian	44	Aberdeen	39
1947-8g	Hibernian	48	Rangers	46	Partick	46
1948-9i	Rangers	46	Dundee	45	Hibernian	39
1949-50i	Rangers	50	Hibernian	49	Hearts	43
1950-1i	Hibernian	48	Rangers	38	Dundee	38
1951-2i	Hibernian	45	Rangers	41	East Fife	37
1952-3i	*Rangers	43	Hibernian	43	East Fife	39
1953-4i	Celtic	43	Hearts	38	Partick	35
1954-5f	Aberdeen	49	Celtic	46	Rangers	41
1955-6f	Rangers	52	Aberdeen	46	Hearts	45
1956-7f	Rangers	55	Hearts	53	Kilmarnock	42

1957-8f	Hearts 62	Rangers 49	Celtic 46
1958-9f	Rangers 50	Hearts 48	Motherwell 44
1959-60f	Hearts 54	Kilmarnock 50	Rangers 42
1960-1f	Rangers 51	Kilmarnock 50	Third Lanark 42
1961-2f	Dundee 54	Rangers 51	Celtic 46
1962-3f	Rangers 57	Kilmarnock 48	Partick 46
1963-4f	Rangers 55	Kilmarnock 49	Celtic 47
1964-5f	*Kilmarnock 50	Hearts 50	Dunfermline 49
1965-6f	Celtic 57	Rangers 55	Kilmarnock 45
1966-7f	Celtic 58	Rangers 55	Clyde 46
1967-8f	Celtic 63	Rangers 61	Hibernian 45
1968-9f	Celtic 54	Rangers 49	Dunfermline 45
1969-70f	Celtic 57	Rangers 45	Hibernian 44
1970-1f	Celtic 56	Aberdeen 54	St Johnstone 44
1971-2f	Celtic 60	Aberdeen 50	Rangers 44
1972-3f	Celtic 57	Rangers 56	Hibernian 45
1973-4f	Celtic 53	Hibernian 49	Rangers 48
1974-5f	Rangers 56	Hibernian 49	Celtic 45

* Won on goal average. †Won on deciding match. ††Title shared.
Competition suspended 1940-46 (Second World War).

SCOTTISH CHAMPIONSHIP WINS

Rangers *48	Hibernian 4	Kilmarnock 1
Celtic 36	Dumbarton *2	Motherwell 1
Aberdeen 4	Dundee 1	Third Lanark 1
Hearts 4	Dundee Utd. 1	(* Incl. 1 shared)

FIRST DIVISION

(Since formation of Premier Division)

	First .... Pts.	Second .... Pts.	Third .... Pts.
1975-6d	Partick 41	Kilmarnock 35	Montrose 30
1976-7j	St. Mirren 62	Clydebank 58	Dundee 51
1977-8j	*Morton 58	Hearts 58	Dundee 57
1978-9j	Dundee 55	Kilmarnock 54	Clydebank 54
1979-80j	Hearts 53	Airdrieonians 51	Ayr 44
1980-1j	Hibernian 57	Dundee 52	St. Johnstone 51
1981-2j	Motherwell 61	Kilmarnock 51	Hearts 50
1982-3j	St. Johnstone 55	Hearts 54	Clydebank 50
1983-4j	Morton 54	Dumbarton 51	Partick 46
1984-5j	Motherwell 50	Clydebank 48	Falkirk 45
1985-6j	Hamilton 56	Falkirk 45	Kilmarnock 44
1986-7k	Morton 57	Dunfermline 56	Dumbarton 53
1987-8k	Hamilton 56	Meadowbank 52	Clydebank 49
1988-9j	Dunfermline 54	Falkirk 52	Clydebank 48
1989-90j	St. Johnstone 58	Airdrieonians 54	Clydebank 48
1990-1j	Falkirk 54	Airdrieonians 53	Dundee 52
1991-2k	Dundee 58	Partick 57	Hamilton 57
1992-3k	Raith 65	Kilmarnock 54	Dunfermline 52
1993-4k	Falkirk 66	Dunfermline 65	Airdrieonians 54
1994-5l	Raith 69	Dunfermline 68	Dundee 68
1995-6l	Dunfermline 71	Dundee Utd. 67	Greenock Morton 67
1996-7l	St. Johnstone 80	Airdrieonians 60	Dundee 58
1997-8l	Dundee 70	Falkirk 65	Raith 60
1998-9l	Hibernian 89	Falkirk 66	Ayr 62

Maximum points: a, 36; b, 44; c, 40; d, 52; e, 60; f, 68; g, 76; h, 84; i, 60; j, 78; k, 88; l, 108. * Won on goal difference.

SECOND DIVISION

	First	Pts.	Second	Pts.	Third	Pts.
1921-2a	Alloa	60	Cowdenbeath	47	Armadale	45
1922-3a	Queen's Park	57	Clydebank	52	St. Johnstone	50
1923-4a	St. Johnstone	56	Cowdenbeath	55	Bathgate	44
1924-5a	Dundee Utd.	50	Clydebank	48	Clyde	47
1925-6a	Dunfermline	59	Clyde	53	Ayr	52
1926-7a	Bo'ness	56	Raith	49	Clydebank	45
1927-8a	Ayr	54	Third Lanark	45	King's Park	44
1928-9b	Dundee Utd.	51	Morton	50	Arbroath	47
1929-30a	*Leith Athletic	57	East Fife	57	Albion	54
1930-1a	Third Lanark	61	Dundee Utd.	50	Dunfermline	47
1931-2a	*East Stirling	55	St. Johnstone	55	Stenhousemuir	46
1932-3c	Hibernian	55	Queen of South	49	Dunfermline	47
1933-4c	Albion	45	Dunfermline	44	Arbroath	44
1934-5c	Third Lanark	52	Arbroath	50	St. Bernard's	47
1935-6c	Falkirk	59	St. Mirren	52	Morton	48
1936-7c	Ayr	54	Morton	51	St. Bernard's	48
1937-8c	Raith	59	Albion	48	Airdrieonians	47
1938-9c	Cowdenbeath	60	Alloa	48	East Fife	48
1946-7d	Dundee Utd.	45	Airdrieonians	42	East Fife	31
1947-8e	East Fife	53	Albion	42	Hamilton	40
1948-9e	*Raith	42	Stirling	42	Airdrieonians	41
1949-50e	Morton	47	Airdrieonians	44	St. Johnstone	36
1950-1e	*Queen of South	45	Stirling	45	Ayr	36
1951-2e	Clyde	44	Falkirk	43	Ayr	39
1952-3e	Stirling	44	Hamilton	43	Queen's Park	37
1953-4e	Motherwell	45	Kilmarnock	42	Third Lanark	36
1954-5e	Airdrieonians	46	Dunfermline	42	Hamilton	39
1955-6b	Queen's Park	54	Ayr	51	St. Johnstone	49
1956-7b	Clyde	64	Third Lanark	51	Cowdenbeath	45
1957-8b	Stirling	55	Dunfermline	53	Arbroath	47
1958-9b	Ayr	60	Arbroath	51	Stenhousemuir	46
1959-60b	St. Johnstone	53	Dundee Utd.	50	Queen of South	49
1960-1b	Stirling	55	Falkirk	54	Stenhousemuir	50
1961-2b	Clyde	54	Queen of South	53	Morton	44
1962-3b	St. Johnstone	55	East Stirling	49	Morton	48
1963-4b	Morton	67	Clyde	53	Arbroath	46
1964-5b	Stirling	59	Hamilton	50	Queen of South	45
1965-6b	Ayr	53	Airdrieonians	50	Queen of South	47
1966-7b	Morton	69	Raith	58	Arbroath	57
1967-8b	St. Mirren	62	Arbroath	53	East Fife	49
1968-9b	Motherwell	64	Ayr	53	East Fife	48
1969-70b	Falkirk	56	Cowdenbeath	55	Queen of South	50
1970-1b	Partick	56	East Fife	51	Arbroath	46
1971-2b	*Dumbarton	52	Arbroath	52	Stirling	50
1972-3b	Clyde	56	Dunfermline	52	Raith	47
1973-4b	Airdrieonians	60	Kilmarnock	58	Hamilton	55
1974-5b	Falkirk	54	Queen of South	53	Montrose	53

SECOND DIVISION (MODERN)

	First	Pts.	Second	Pts.	Third	Pts.
1975-6d	*Clydebank	40	Raith	40	Alloa	35
1976-7f	Stirling	55	Alloa	51	Dunfermline	50
1977-8f	*Clyde	53	Raith	53	Dunfermline	48
1978-9f	Berwick	54	Dunfermline	52	Falkirk	50

1979-80*f*	Falkirk	50	East Stirling	49	Forfar	46
1980-1*f*	Queen's Park	50	Queen of South	46	Cowdenbeath	45
1981-2*f*	Clyde	59	Alloa	50	Arbroath	50
1982-3*f*	Brechin	55	Meadowbank	54	Arbroath	49
1983-4*f*	Forfar	63	East Fife	47	Berwick	43
1984-5*f*	Montrose	53	Alloa	50	Dunfermline	49
1985-6*f*	Dunfermline	57	Queen of South	55	Meadowbank	49
1986-7*f*	Meadowbank	55	Raith	52	Stirling	52
1987-8*f*	Ayr	61	St. Johnstone	59	Queen's Park	51
1988-9*f*	Albion	50	Alloa	45	Brechin	43
1989-90*f*	Brechin	49	Kilmarnock	48	Stirling	47
1990-1*f*	Stirling	54	Montrose	46	Cowdenbeath	45
1991-2*f*	Dumbarton	52	Cowdenbeath	51	Alloa	50
1992-3*f*	Clyde	54	Brechin	53	Stranraer	53
1993-4*f*	Stranraer	56	Berwick	48	Stenhousemuir	47
1994-5*g*	Greenock Morton	64	Dumbarton	60	Stirling	58
1995-6*g*	Stirling	81	East Fife	67	Berwick	60
1996-7*g*	Ayr	77	Hamilton	74	Livingston	64
1997-8*g*	Stranraer	61	Clydebank	60	Livingston	59
1998-9*g*	Livingston	77	Inverness Cal.	72	Clyde	53

Maximum points: *a*, 76; *b*, 72; *c*, 68; *d*, 52; *e*, 60; *f*, 78; *g*, 108. * Won on goal average.

THIRD DIVISION (MODERN)

	First	Pts.	Second	Pts.	Third	Pts.
1994-5	Forfar	80	Montrose	67	Ross County	60
1995-6	Livingston	72	Brechin	63	Caledonian Th.	57
1996-7	Inverness Cal.T.	76	Forfar	67	Ross County	77
1997-8	Alloa	76	Arbroath	68	Ross County	67
1997-8	Ross County	77	Stenhousemuir	64	Brechin	59

Maximum points: 108.

RELEGATED FROM PREMIER DIVISION

1975-6	Dundee, St. Johnstone	1987-8	Falkirk, Dunfermline, Morton
1976-7	Kilmarnock, Hearts	1988-9	Hamilton
1977-8	Ayr, Clydebank	1989-90	Dundee
1978-9	Hearts, Motherwell	1990-1	No relegation
1979-80	Dundee, Hibernian	1991-2	St. Mirren, Dunfermline
1980-1	Kilmarnock, Hearts	1992-3	Falkirk, Airdrieonians
1981-2	Partick, Airdrieonians	1993-4	St. J'stone, Raith, Dundee
1982-3	Morton, Kilmarnock	1994-5	Dundee Utd.
1983-4	St. Johnstone, Motherwell	1995-6	Falkirk, Partick Thistle
1984-5	Dumbarton, Morton	1996-7	Raith
1985-6	No relegation	1997-8	Hibernian
1986-7	Clydebank, Hamilton	1998-9	Dunfermline

RELEGATED FROM FIRST DIVISION

1975-6	Dunfermline, Clyde	1981-2	East Stirling, Queen of South
1976-7	Raith, Falkirk	1982-3	Dunfermline, Queen's Park
1977-8	Alloa, East Fife	1983-4	Raith, Alloa
1978-9	Montrose, Queen of South	1984-5	Meadowbank, St. Johnstone
1979-80	Arbroath, Clyde	1985-6	Ayr, Alloa
1980-1	Stirling, Berwick	1986-7	Brechin, Montrose

1987-8	East Fife, Dumbarton	1994-5	Ayr, Stranraer
1988-9	Kilmarnock, Queen of South	1995-6	Hamilton, Dumbarton
1989-90	Albion, Alloa	1996-7	Clydebank, East Fife
1990-1	Clyde, Brechin	1997-8	Partick, Stirling Alb.
1991-2	Montrose, Forfar	1998-9	Hamilton, Stranraer
1992-3	Meadowbank, Cowdenbeath		
1993-4	Dumbarton, Stirling Alb., Clyde, Morton, Brechin		

RELEGATED FROM SECOND DIVISION

1993-4	Alloa, Forfar, E. Stirling, Montrose, Queen's Park, Arbroath, Albion, Cowdenbeath	1995-6	Forfar, Montrose
		1996-7	Dumbarton, Berwick
		1997-8	Stenhousemuir, Brechin
1994-5	Meadowbank, Brechin	1998-9	East Fife, Forfar

QUOTE – UNQUOTE

'He's got the sort of chest they used to put gold in to take it overseas. It's huge' – ITV pundit **Kevin Keegan** on Brazil's Junior Baiano during the France '98 World Cup game against Morocco.

'I was devastated, hurt and upset. My stomach turned over so many times it was unbelievable' – Manchester Utd.'s **David Beckham** on being axed from England's World Cup France '98 team.

'I love tackling. It's better than sex. A great tackle gets everybody pumped up' – England's **Paul Ince**.

'I have a blank sheet of paper to redesign the way footballers are developed in this country' – **Les Reed**, the Football Association's new Director of Youth Development.

'In 10 years I want to see England World Cup squads containing 70 to 80 per cent of players coming through the new system' – **Les Reed**, the Football Association's Director of Youth Development.

'You judge a performance by how much your goalkeeper has to do. David Seaman could have been smoking cigars out there' – BBC pundit **Alan Hansen** on England's World Cup '98 victory over Colombia.

'It was like losing your virginity. It was my first time and I was feeling very, very nervous' – Brazil's **Edmundo** on his World Cup debut.

'I'm proud of what we have accomplished. We have shown that US soccer has a great future' – USA coach **Steve Sampson**, who resigned after losing all three matches in France '98.

'We were so poor that sometimes when there was nothing on the table I'd go next door to get fed' – **Dwight Yorke** reflects on early days in Trinidad after his £12.5million transfer from Aston Villa to Manchester Utd.

'England are out of the World Cup' – Message on the **Football Association** 50p per minute phone line on August 28, almost two months after Glenn Hoddle's team made their exit.

'If Graham Taylor hadn't invited me to Villa Park I'd probably be a beach bum, hiring out boats and windsurf boards to the tourists' – Manchester Utd.'s £12.5 million man **Dwight Yorke**.

'At least it will boost my football pension' – **Bruce Grobbelaar** on his £200 match fee for Rymans League club Chesham Utd.

SCOTTISH LEAGUE RESULTS 1998-99

PREMIER LEAGUE

	Aberdeen	Celtic	Dundee	Dundee Utd.	Dunfermline	Hearts	Kilmarnock	Motherwell	Rangers	St. Johnstone
Aberdeen	–	3-2	2-2	0-3	2-1	2-0	0-1	1-1	1-1	0-1
	–	1-5	1-2	0-4	3-1	2-5	2-1	1-1	2-4	1-0
Celtic	2-0	–	6-1	2-1	5-0	1-1	1-1	2-0	5-1	0-1
	3-2	–	5-0	2-1	5-0	3-0	1-0	1-0	0-3	5-0
Dundee	0-2	1-1	–	2-2	1-0	1-0	1-1	1-0	0-4	0-1
	1-2	0-3	–	1-3	3-1	2-0	2-1	1-0	1-1	0-1
Dundee Utd.	1-0	1-1	0-1	–	1-1	0-0	0-2	2-2	0-0	1-1
	3-0	1-2	0-2	–	1-1	1-3	0-0	0-3	1-2	0-1
Dunfermline	1-1	2-2	2-0	2-1	–	1-1	0-3	1-1	0-2	1-1
	1-2	1-2	2-0	2-2	–	0-0	0-6	1-2	0-3	1-0
Hearts	2-0	2-1	0-2	0-1	2-1	–	2-1	3-0	2-1	1-1
	0-2	2-4	1-2	4-1	2-0	–	2-2	0-2	2-3	0-2
Kilmarnock	4-0	2-0	2-1	2-0	0-0	3-0	–	0-0	1-3	2-2
	4-2	0-0	0-0	2-0	0-0	1-0	–	0-1	0-5	1-1
Motherwell	2-2	1-2	2-1	1-0	0-0	3-2	0-0	–	1-0	1-0
	1-1	1-7	1-2	2-0	1-1	0-4	1-2	–	1-5	1-2
Rangers	2-1	0-0	1-0	2-1	1-1	3-0	1-0	2-1	–	4-0
	3-1	2-2	6-1	0-1	1-0	0-0	1-1	2-1	–	1-0
St. Johnstone	2-0	2-1	1-1	1-3	1-1	1-1	0-0	5-0	0-7	–
	4-1	1-0	1-0	1-0	1-1	0-0	0-1	0-0	3-1	–

Read across for home results, down for away

FIRST DIVISION

	Airdrieonians	Ayr	Clydebank	Falkirk	Greenock Morton	Hamilton Acad.	Hibernian	Raith Rov.	St. Mirren	Stranraer
Airdrieonians	–	0-2	0-0	0-3	0-1	3-2	1-3	0-1	1-0	3-2
	–	0-2	2-0	1-2	0-2	1-0	1-4	2-2	0-3	2-0
Ayr	1-2	–	4-1	4-2	1-0	2-3	3-3	0-2	1-1	7-1
	0-1	–	0-0	1-2	1-0	5-0	1-3	1-0	2-2	4-0
Clydebank	0-1	0-1	–	0-1	2-1	0-0	2-2	1-1	1-0	2-1
	0-1	2-1	–	1-2	1-2	0-0	2-0	0-0	2-2	1-2
Falkirk	0-1	1-0	2-2	–	2-1	2-1	1-1	1-1	1-1	1-0
	1-1	3-0	0-2	–	1-2	6-1	1-2	1-0	1-0	3-2
Greenock Morton	0-0	1-2	2-2	0-3	–	1-2	0-1	2-0	0-1	3-0
	0-2	1-4	1-1	3-2	–	3-0	1-3	1-1	0-0	1-0
Hamilton Acad.	1-1	1-3	1-2	2-1	0-0	–	2-2	3-2	0-0	1-2
	0-2	0-2	0-1	0-2	0-2	–	0-2	1-2	0-0	1-0
Hibernian	1-0	4-2	2-1	2-1	2-1	0-0	–	3-1	4-1	1-2
	3-0	3-0	3-0	2-1	2-1	4-0	–	5-1	2-1	2-0
Raith Rov.	1-3	0-0	0-1	1-1	0-0	0-2	1-3	–	1-0	2-0
	0-1	2-4	2-1	2-1	1-3	1-1	1-3	–	1-1	3-2
St. Mirren	1-5	0-2	0-0	0-2	1-0	3-2	2-0	2-1	–	1-0
	3-0	1-0	1-1	0-3	1-5	1-0	1-2	3-1	–	5-1
Stranraer	1-2	0-1	0-2	1-2	2-3	2-1	0-1	2-2	0-1	–
	1-2	0-2	0-2	0-1	0-1	2-2	0-4	2-0	1-2	–

Read across for home results, down for away

SECOND DIVISION

	Alloa	Arbroath	Clyde	East Fife	Forfar	Inverness CT	Livingston	Partick Thistle	Queen of South	Stirling Albion
Alloa	–	1-1	3-0	5-1	1-2	1-1	3-4	3-1	2-1	7-0
	–	1-2	1-0	3-1	3-1	1-4	1-3	0-1	3-5	2-2
Arbroath	0-2	–	0-0	0-2	2-1	0-1	2-2	1-0	2-1	0-3
	1-2	–	0-3	2-1	2-2	3-1	1-1	2-1	0-2	1-0
Clyde	2-1	3-0	–	0-0	3-1	4-1	1-1	1-2	2-0	2-1
	0-1	1-1	–	1-0	1-0	1-1	0-3	0-1	2-1	4-1
East Fife	2-2	0-3	0-0	–	1-0	1-5	2-3	1-3	2-0	2-3
	0-4	1-2	2-1	–	2-1	3-2	1-1	1-0	0-1	1-0
Forfar	1-2	1-3	2-2	1-2	–	2-2	1-2	0-1	1-0	1-2
	3-1	5-2	3-1	2-4	–	0-3	1-2	2-1	2-1	3-3
Inverness CT	3-2	2-1	1-1	4-2	2-2	–	2-1	3-2	3-2	3-1
	1-1	2-0	3-0	4-0	2-0	–	3-1	3-2	1-0	2-2
Livingston	2-1	2-1	2-0	3-1	1-1	2-1	–	1-0	2-0	1-1
	1-0	1-0	2-0	1-0	5-0	4-3	–	1-1	1-2	0-0
Partick Thistle	1-0	2-0	0-2	0-1	2-0	0-1	1-3	–	2-2	1-0
	2-1	0-0	0-1	2-2	1-0	2-1	1-1	–	1-3	0-1
Queen of South	2-1	0-0	2-1	0-0	3-0	2-2	0-1	0-0	–	2-3
	0-0	3-0	2-1	2-0	0-3	1-1	2-2	2-2	–	3-0
Stirling Albion	4-2	0-1	1-2	3-2	3-1	0-1	1-3	2-0	1-0	–
	1-1	2-1	2-3	0-1	2-2	1-5	0-0	3-0	1-3	–

Read across for home results, down for away

THIRD DIVISION

	Albion Rov.	Berwick Rangers	Brechin City	Cowdenbeath	Dumbarton	East Stirling	Montrose	Queen's Park	Ross Co.	Stenhousemuir
Albion Rov.	–	1-1	1-4	0-1	0-2	3-1	4-1	2-1	0-8	1-3
	–	0-3	4-1	1-1	0-2	0-2	0-0	1-0	3-3	1-2
Berwick Rangers	2-1	–	3-0	3-1	3-1	1-2	1-1	0-3	0-2	1-2
	1-1	–	2-3	2-1	0-1	1-2	4-1	0-2	2-2	2-1
Brechin City	1-0	1-1	–	2-1	0-0	0-0	3-0	2-2	0-1	1-0
	3-1	0-3	–	1-1	3-3	1-0	2-3	1-0	0-1	0-2
Cowdenbeath	2-3	1-1	0-1	–	0-2	2-1	4-1	0-3	1-2	0-2
	0-2	1-2	0-2	–	2-1	3-2	1-0	0-0	2-3	0-2
Dumbarton	2-0	0-0	1-2	5-0	–	2-2	0-2	1-0	1-2	0-2
	1-1	1-1	2-0	6-1	–	0-2	2-1	0-1	0-0	1-4
East Stirling	0-1	0-0	1-1	1-1	1-2	–	3-1	1-1	2-2	1-1
	4-1	3-3	4-1	0-0	1-2	–	2-1	1-1	1-2	1-1
Montrose	1-2	1-1	1-2	1-1	1-1	2-0	–	1-0	3-6	0-0
	2-3	0-3	1-3	1-2	4-2	1-0	–	3-0	2-3	1-2
Queen's Park	0-0	1-1	1-1	2-0	0-1	0-4	3-0	–	4-2	0-0
	0-0	1-1	0-2	2-1	1-1	2-1	1-2	–	0-3	4-1
Ross Co.	1-2	3-1	0-1	2-0	2-0	1-0	3-1	5-1	–	0-1
	2-0	6-0	2-1	1-0	1-2	4-2	3-0	1-2	–	2-2
Stenhousemuir	4-1	1-2	0-1	1-2	0-3	1-0	4-0	2-1	2-4	–
	1-2	1-1	1-0	4-1	0-2	2-2	3-1	4-1	3-2	–

Read across for home results, down for away

RANGERS COMPLETE DOMESTIC TREBLE WITH 28th SCOTTISH CUP WIN

SECOND ROUND	THIRD ROUND	FOURTH ROUND	SEMI-FINALS	FINAL
*Rangers 2				
Stenhousemuir ... 0	Rangers 6			
*St. Mirren ... 1:0		*Rangers 2		
Hamilton 1:1	*Hamilton 0			
*Stranraer ... 1	*Stranraer 1		Rangers 4	
East Stirling ... 0		Falkirk 1		
*Falkirk 2	Falkirk 2			
Huntly 0				Rangers 1
*Motherwell ... 3	*Motherwell 2			
Hearts 1		*Motherwell 0		
*Hibernian ... 1:1	Stirling 0			
Stirling 1:2			St. Johnstone ... 0	
*Aberdeen 0	*Livingston 1			
Livingston 1		St. Johnstone ... 2		
*St. Johnstone ... 0	St. Johnstone ... 3			
Forfar 0				
*Ayr Utd. 3	*Ayr Utd. 1			
Kilmarnock 0		*Ayr Utd. 0:1		
*Brechin 1:1	Albion 0			
Albion 1:3			Dundee Utd. 0	
*Clydebank ... 1:1†3	*Clydebank 2:0			
Ross County ... 1:2		Dundee Utd. 0:2		
*Queen's Park ... 0:0	Dundee Utd. 2:3			
Dundee Utd. 0:1				

*Gr. Morton 2			
Dundee 1	*Gr. Morton 0		
*Raith Row. 0		Celtic 0	
Clyde 4	Clyde 1		
*Partick 1		*Gr. Morton 0	
Dunfermline 2	Dunfermline 0	Celtic 2	
Airdrie 1		Celtic 3	
*Celtic 3	*Celtic 4		

FIRST ROUND: Arbroath 1, Partick 2; Dumbarton 1, Livingston 1; Queen's Park 2, Berwick 0; Stenhousemuir 1, Alloa 0. **REPLAYS:** Alloa 0, Stenhousemuir 1; Livingston 3, Dumbarton 0.

SECOND ROUND: Civil Service 0, Albion 3; Dalbeattie 1, East Stirling 2; Forfar 2, East Fife 2; Huntly 3, Peterhead 0; Inverness C.T. 1, Livingston 2; Keith 0, Brechin 1; Montrose 0, Stirling 0; Partick 5, Cowdenbeath 2; Queen of the South 1, Ross County 3; Queen's Park 1; Clachnacuddin 1; Spartans 1, Clyde 1; Whitehill 1, Stenhousemuir 1. **REPLAYS:** Brechin 3, Keith 1; Clachnacuddin 2, Queen's Park 3; Clyde 5, Spartans 0; East Fife 0, Forfar 1; Stenhousemuir 2, Whitehill 0; Stirling 2, Montrose 1.

(*Drawn at home. †After extra time.)

Semi-finals: **Rangers** v St. Johnstone at Celtic Park – Dundee Utd. v **Celtic** at Ibrox

TENNENT'S SCOTTISH CUP FINAL

RANGERS 1 (Wallace 48), **CELTIC 0**

Hampden Park (52,670), Saturday, May 29, 1999

Rangers: Klos, Porrini, (Kanchelskis 77), Amoruso (Capt.), Hendry, Vidmar, McCann (I. Ferguson 67), McInnes, Van Bronckhorst, Wallace, Amato (Wilson 90), Albertz. **Booked:** Wallace. **Manager:** Dick Advocaat.

Celtic: Gould, Boyd (Capt.), Mahe (O'Donnell 78), Stubbs, Larsson, Wieghorst, Lambert, Annoni (Johnson 60), Blinker, Moravcik, Mjallby. **Booked:** Mjallby, Blinker, Wieghorst, Boyd. **Manager:** Jozef Venglos.

Referee: H. Dallas (Motherwell). **Half-time:** 0-0.

RANGERS 21st SCOTTISH LEAGUE CUP TRIUMPH

SECOND ROUND	THIRD ROUND	FOURTH ROUND	SEMI-FINALS	FINAL
Bye●	*Rangers 4			
*Dundee 0	Alloa 0	Rangers 2		
Alloa 1			Rangers 5	
*East Fife ...... †0	*Motherwell 0			
Motherwell 1	Ayr Utd. 2	Ayr Utd. 0		
*St. Mirren 1				Rangers 2
Ayr Utd. 3				
Bye●	*Kilmarnock ...... †3			
*Livingston ...... †1	Livingston 1	Kilmarnock 0		
Dunfermline 0			Airdrie 0	
*Stenhousemuir 0	*Airdrie 1			
Airdrie 2	Celtic 0	Airdrie ...... †1		
Bye●	*Hearts ...... †4			
Bye●	Raith 2	*Hearts ...... H†1		
*Raith 2			Hearts 0	
Clydebank 0	*Ross County ...... †2			
*Morton 1	Dundee Utd. 0	Ross County 1		
Ross County ...... †2				
*Dundee Utd. ...... †D2				
Stirling Albion 0				

*Hamilton 1
Hibernian 2

   *Hibernian 1

*Inverness Cal. 0
Aberdeen 3

   Aberdeen 0

      Hibernian 0

*Berwick 1
Falkirk 5

   *Falkirk 0

*Stranraer 0
St. Johnstone 1

   St. Johnstone 1

      St. Johnstone 3

         *St. Johnstone 4

           St. Johnstone 1

FIRST ROUND: Arbroath 0, Clydebank 1; Brechin 2, Hamilton 2† (Brechin won 4-3 on pens.); Clyde 1, Berwick 1† (Berwick won 4-3 on pens.); Cowdenbeath 0, Livingston 2; Dumbarton 0, Alloa 4; East Fife 3, Patrick 2†; Forfar 0, Stirling Albion 1; Queen of the South 1, Inverness Cal. 4; Queen's Park 1 Ayr Utd 3; Ross County 4, Montrose 1; Stenhousemuir 1, East Stirling 0; Stranraer 1 Albion Rovers 1† (Stranraer won 3-2 on pens.).

* Drawn at home. † After extra time. H – Hearts won 3-0 on pens. D – Dundee Utd. won 3-0 on pens. ● Given a bye into 3rd round because of European competitions.

Semi-finals: **Rangers** v Airdrie at Celtic Park – **Hearts** v **St. Johnstone** at Easter Road.
Final at Celtic Park, Sunday November 29, 1998.

SCOTTISH LEAGUE CUP FINAL

RANGERS 2 (Guivarc'h 6, Albertz 38), **ST. JOHNSTONE 1** (Dasovic 7)

Celtic Park (45,542), Sunday, November 29, 1998

Rangers: Niemi; Porrini, Hendry, Amoruso (capt.), Numan, B.Ferguson, Albertz (I.Ferguson), Van Bronckhorst, Kanchelskis, Wallace, Guivarc'h (Durie). **Manager:** Dick Advocaat.

St. Johnstone: Main (capt.); McQuillan, Dods, Kernaghan, Bollan, O'Neil (Preston), Kane, Scott, Dasovic, Simao (Grant), O'Boyle (Lowndes).
Booking: Dasovic. **Manager:** Sandy Clark.

Referee: H. Dallas (Motherwell). **Half-time:** 2-1.

SCOTTISH CUP FINALS

1874	Queen's Park beat Clydesdale (2-0)
1875	Queen's Park beat Renton (3-0)
1876	Queen's Park beat Third Lanark (2-0 after 1-1 draw)
1877	Vale of Leven beat Rangers (3-2 after 0-0, 1-1 draws)
1878	Vale of Leven beat Third Lanark (1-0)
1879	Vale of Leven awarded Cup (Rangers withdrew after 1-1 draw)
1880	Queen's Park beat Thornlibank (3-0)
1881	Queen's Park beat Dumbarton (3-1)
1882	Queen's Park beat Dumbarton (4-1 after 2-2 draw)
1883	Dumbarton beat Vale of Leven (2-1 after 2-2 draw)
1884	Queen's Park awarded Cup (Vale of Leven withdrew from Final)
1885	Renton beat Vale of Leven (3-1 after 0-0 draw)
1886	Queen's Park beat Renton (3-1)
1887	Hibernian beat Dumbarton (2-1)
1888	Renton beat Cambuslang (6-1)
1889	Third Lanark beat Celtic (2-1)
1890	Queen's Park beat Vale of Leven (2-1 after 1-1 draw)
1891	Hearts beat Dumbarton (1-0)
1892	Celtic beat Queen's Park (5-1)
1893	Queen's Park beat Celtic (2-1)
1894	Rangers beat Celtic (3-1)
1895	St. Bernard's beat Renton (2-1)
1896	Hearts beat Hibernian (3-1)
1897	Rangers beat Dumbarton (5-1)
1898	Rangers beat Kilmarnock (2-0)
1899	Celtic beat Rangers (2-0)
1900	Celtic beat Queen's Park (4-3)
1901	Hearts beat Celtic (4-3)
1902	Hibernian beat Celtic (1-0)
1903	Rangers beat Hearts (2-0 after 0-0, 1-1 draws)
1904	Celtic beat Rangers (3-2)
1905	Third Lanark beat Rangers (3-1 after 0-0 draw)
1906	Hearts beat Third Lanark (1-0)
1907	Celtic beat Hearts (3-0)
1908	Celtic beat St. Mirren (5-1)
1909	Cup withheld because of riot after two drawn games in Final between Celtic and Rangers (2-2, 1-1)
1910	Dundee beat Clyde (2-1 after 2-2, 0-0 draws)
1911	Celtic beat Hamilton Academical (2-0 after 0-0 draw)
1912	Celtic beat Clyde (2-0)
1913	Falkirk beat Raith Rov. (2-0)
1914	Celtic beat Hibernian (4-1 after 0-0 draw)
1915-19	No competition (World War 1)
1920	Kilmarnock beat Albion Rov. (3-2)
1921	Partick Thistle beat Rangers (1-0)
1922	Morton beat Rangers (1-0)
1923	Celtic beat Hibernian (1-0)
1924	Airdrieonians beat Hibernian (2-0)
1925	Celtic beat Dundee (2-1)
1926	St. Mirren beat Celtic (2-0)
1927	Celtic beat East Fife (3-1)
1928	Rangers beat Celtic (4-0)
1929	Kilmarnock beat Rangers (2-0)
1930	Rangers beat Partick Thistle (2-1 after 0-0 draw)
1931	Celtic beat Motherwell (4-2 after 2-2 draw)
1932	Rangers beat Kilmarnock (3-0 after 1-1 draw)

1933	Celtic beat Motherwell (1-0)
1934	Rangers beat St. Mirren (5-0)
1935	Rangers beat Hamilton Academical (2-1)
1936	Rangers beat Third Lanark (1-0)
1937	Celtic beat Aberdeen (2-1)
1938	East Fife beat Kilmarnock (4-2 after 1-1 draw)
1939	Clyde beat Motherwell (4-0)
1940-6	No competition (World War 2)
1947	Aberdeen beat Hibernian (2-1)
1948†	Rangers beat Morton (1-0 after 1-1 draw)
1949	Rangers beat Clyde (4-1)
1950	Rangers beat East Fife (3-0)
1951	Celtic beat Motherwell (1-0)
1952	Motherwell beat Dundee (4-0)
1953	Rangers beat Aberdeen (1-0 after 1-1 draw)
1954	Celtic beat Aberdeen (2-1)
1955	Clyde beat Celtic (1-0 after 1-1 draw)
1956	Hearts beat Celtic (3-1)
1957†	Falkirk beat Kilmarnock (2-1 after 1-1 draw)
1958	Clyde beat Hibernian (1-0)
1959	St. Mirren beat Aberdeen (3-1)
1960	Rangers beat Kilmarnock (2-0)
1961	Dunfermline Athletic beat Celtic (2-0 after 0-0 draw)
1962	Rangers beat St. Mirren (2-0)
1963	Rangers beat Celtic (3-0 after 1-1 draw)
1964	Rangers beat Dundee (3-1)
1965	Celtic beat Dunfermline Athletic (3-2)
1966	Rangers beat Celtic (1-0 after 0-0 draw)
1967	Celtic beat Aberdeen (2-0)
1968	Dunfermline Athletic beat Hearts (3-1)
1969	Celtic beat Rangers (4-0)
1970	Aberdeen beat Celtic (3-1)
1971	Celtic beat Rangers (2-1 after 1-1 draw)
1972	Celtic beat Hibernian (6-1)
1973	Rangers beat Celtic (3-2)
1974	Celtic beat Dundee Utd. (3-0)
1975	Celtic beat Airdrieonians (3-1)
1976	Rangers beat Hearts (3-1)
1977	Celtic beat Rangers (1-0)
1978	Rangers beat Aberdeen (2-1)
1979†	Rangers beat Hibernian (3-2 after two 0-0 draws)
1980†	Celtic beat Rangers (1-0)
1981	Rangers beat Dundee Utd. (4-1 after 0-0 draw)
1982†	Aberdeen beat Rangers (4-1)
1983†	Aberdeen beat Rangers (1-0)
1984†	Aberdeen beat Celtic (2-1)
1985	Celtic beat Dundee Utd. (2-1)
1986	Aberdeen beat Hearts (3-0)
1987†	St. Mirren beat Dundee Utd. (1-0)
1988	Celtic beat Dundee Utd. (2-1)
1989	Celtic beat Rangers (1-0)
1990†	Aberdeen beat Celtic (9-8 on pens. after 0-0 draw)
1991†	Motherwell beat Dundee Utd. (4-3)
1992	Rangers beat Airdrieonians (2-1)
1993	Rangers beat Aberdeen (2-1)
1994	Dundee Utd. beat Rangers (1-0)
1995	Celtic beat Airdrieonians (1-0)
1996	Rangers beat Hearts (5-1)

1997	Kilmarnock beat Falkirk (1-0)
1998	Hearts beat Rangers (2-1)
1999	Rangers beat Celtic (1-0)

(† After extra time; Cup sponsored by Tennents since season 1989-90)

SUMMARY OF SCOTTISH CUP WINNERS

Celtic 30, Rangers 28, Queen's Park 10, Aberdeen 7, Hearts 6, Clyde 3, Kilmarnock 3, St. Mirren 3, Vale of Leven 3, Dunfermline Ath. 2, Falkirk 2, Hibernian 2, Motherwell 2, Renton 2, Third Lanark 2, Airdrieonians 1, Dumbarton 1, Dundee 1, Dundee Utd. 1, East Fife 1, Morton 1, Partick Thistle 1, St. Bernard's 1.

SCOTTISH LEAGUE CUP FINALS

1946	Aberdeen beat Rangers (3-2)
1947	Rangers beat Aberdeen (4-0)
1948	East Fife beat Falkirk (4-1 after 0-0 draw)
1949	Rangers beat Raith Rov. (2-0)
1950	East Fife beat Dunfermline Athletic (3-0)
1951	Motherwell beat Hibernian (3-0)
1952	Dundee beat Rangers (3-2)
1953	Dundee beat Kilmarnock (2-0)
1954	East Fife beat Partick Thistle (3-2)
1955	Hearts beat Motherwell (4-2)
1956	Aberdeen beat St. Mirren (2-1)
1957	Celtic beat Partick Thistle (3-0 after 0-0 draw)
1958	Celtic beat Rangers (7-1)
1959	Hearts beat Partick Thistle (5-1)
1960	Hearts beat Third Lanark (2-1)
1961	Rangers beat Kilmarnock (2-0)
1962	Rangers beat Hearts (3-1 after 1-1 draw)
1963	Hearts beat Kilmarnock (1-0)
1964	Rangers beat Morton (5-0)
1965	Rangers beat Celtic (2-1)
1966	Celtic beat Rangers (2-1)
1967	Celtic beat Rangers (1-0)
1968	Celtic beat Dundee (5-3)
1969	Celtic beat Hibernian (6-2)
1970	Celtic beat St. Johnstone (1-0)
1971	Rangers beat Celtic (1-0)
1972	Partick Thistle beat Celtic (4-1)
1973	Hibernian beat Celtic (2-1)
1974	Dundee beat Celtic (1-0)
1975	Celtic beat Hibernian (6-3)
1976	Rangers beat Celtic (1-0)
1977†	Aberdeen beat Celtic (2-1)
1978†	Rangers beat Celtic (2-1)
1979	Rangers beat Aberdeen (2-1)
1980	Dundee Utd. beat Aberdeen (3-0 after 0-0 draw)
1981	Dundee Utd. beat Dundee (3-0)
1982	Rangers beat Dundee Utd. (2-1)
1983	Celtic beat Rangers (2-1)
1984†	Rangers beat Celtic (3-2)
1985	Rangers beat Dundee Utd. (1-0)

1986	Aberdeen beat Hibernian (3-0)
1987	Rangers beat Celtic (2-1)
1988†	Rangers beat Aberdeen (5-3 on pens. after 3-3 draw)
1989	Rangers beat Aberdeen (3-2)
1990†	Aberdeen beat Rangers (2-1)
1991†	Rangers beat Celtic (2-1)
1992	Hibernian beat Dunfermline Athletic (2-0)
1993†	Rangers beat Aberdeen (2-1)
1994	Rangers beat Hibernian (2-1)
1995	Raith Rov. beat Celtic (6-5 on pens. after 2-2 draw)
1996	Aberdeen beat Dundee (2-0)
1997	Rangers beat Hearts (4-3)
1998	Celtic beat Dundee Utd. (3-0)
1999	Rangers beat St. Johnstone (2-1)

(† After extra time; Skol Cup 1985-93, Coca-Cola Cup 1995-97)

SUMMARY OF SCOTTISH LEAGUE CUP WINNERS

Rangers	21	Dundee	3	Motherwell	1
Celtic	10	East Fife	3	Partick Thistle	1
Aberdeen	6	Dundee Utd.	2	Raith Rov.	1
Hearts	4	Hibernian	2		

QUOTE – UNQUOTE

'He won headers, came out with pace and was just like a Rolls Royce' – West Ham Utd. manager **Harry Redknapp** on his England defender Rio Ferdinand.

'I won't be buying a Ruud Gullit doll and sticking pins in it' – **Kenny Dalglish** on his replacement as Newcastle Utd. manager by the Dutchman.

'It seems you can get sacked for farting in the wrong direction at the moment' – Wimbledon boss **Joe Kinnear**'s reaction to the Dalglish departure.

'If I'd had a gun I'd have shot him' – Aston Villa manager **John Gregory** on the departing Dwight Yorke.

'It was a genuine slip. I'm not going to stick bamboo shoots up his fingernails' – Manager **Gordon Strachan** on defender Marc Edworthy's blunder which cost Coventry City a first away League win of the season at Charlton Athletic.

'I just had to pack in drinking. I was letting it get on top of me. I'm quite happy being off the drink and feel better for it' – **Paul Gascoigne** on being on the wagon.

'Do you think your surname will be a help or hindrance in your career? I don't know, I've never had any other to compare with' – BBC 'Match of the Day' exchange between **Jon Champion** and Newcastle Utd.'s **Paul Dalglish**, son of Kenny.

'We had lost 4-1, I found my car had been broken into for the third time and there I was driving round the M25 with rain soaking me through the broken window. I felt as miserable as sin and thought "someone is trying to tell me something here" ' – **Ray Harford** on his resignation as manager after winning only five of 34 League games with Q.P.R.

'If my head had been a football it would have ended up in the top corner of the net. There is something wrong with someone who kicks another player' – West Ham Utd.'s **Eyal Berkovic** on the training ground bust-up when John Hartson used his head for shooting practice.

IRISH FOOTBALL 1998-99

FAI NATIONAL LEAGUE

PREMIER DIVISION

		P	W	D	L	F	A	Pts
1	St. Patrick's Ath.	33	22	7	4	58	21	73
2	Cork City	33	21	7	5	62	25	70
3	Shelbourne	33	13	8	12	37	35	47
4	Finn Harps	33	12	10	11	39	40	46
5	Derry City	33	12	9	12	34	32	45
6	U.C.D.	33	10	12	11	31	32	42
7	Waterford Utd.	33	11	9	13	21	37	42
8	Shamrock Rov.	33	9	13	11	34	40	40
9	Sligo Rov.	33	9	11	13	37	50	38
10	Bohemians	33	10	7	16	28	37	37
11	Bray Wanderers	33	8	8	17	30	45	32
12	Dundalk	33	6	9	18	23	40	27

Top Scorer: 15 Trevor Molloy (St. Patrick's Ath.); **Player of Year:** Paul Osram (St. Patrick's Ath.); **Young Player of Year:** Richie Baker (Shelbourne); **Personality of Year:** Paul Osram (St. Patrick's Ath.)

FIRST DIVISION

		P	W	D	L	F	A	Pts
1	Drogheda Utd.	36	17	13	6	57	32	64
2	Galway Utd.	36	16	16	4	53	34	64
3	Cobh Ramblers	36	37	7	12	55	43	58
4	Longford Town	36	15	9	12	41	33	54
5	Kilkenny City	36	14	11	11	49	46	53
6	Limerick R.C.	36	13	13	10	39	35	52
7	Monaghan Utd.	36	10	14	12	44	44	44
8	Athlone Town	36	10	10	16	45	61	40
9	Home Farm/Everton	36	11	5	20	42	54	38
10	St. Francis	36	2	12	22	25	68	18

Top Scorer: 16 Tony Izzi (Cobh Ramblers); **Player of Year:** Tony Izzi (Cobh Ramblers)

FAI HARP LAGER CUP FINAL

Bray Wanderers 0 Finn Harps 0;

Bray Wanderers 2 (O'Connor, O'Brien) **Finn Harps 2** (Speak, Mohan) after extra time.

Bray Wanderers 2 (Byrne 2) **Finn Harps 1** (Speak).

All matches at Tolka Park, Dublin, May 9, May 15, May 20.

Bray Wanderers: Walsh; Tresson, Keogh, Lynch, Doohan, Farrell (Smyth), O'Connor, Byrne, O'Brien, Fox, Kenny.

Finn Harps: McKenna; Scanlon (R. Boyle), Minnock, D. Boyle, Dykes, O'Brien, Mohan (Bradley), McGranaghan (Sheridan), Speak, Mulligan, Harkin.

Referee: J. McDermott (Dublin).

FAI HARP LAGER LEAGUE CUP FINAL

Shamrock Rov. 1 (Mooney o.g.) Cork City 1 (Barry Murphy).

1st Leg, Tolka Park, Dublin, December 8

Cork City 1 (Hartigan), Shamrock Rov. 0

2nd Leg, Turner's Cross, Cork, December 30

Cork City won 2-1 on aggregate.

SMIRNOFF IRISH LEAGUE

PREMIER DIVISION

		P	W	D	L	F	A	Pts
1	Glentoran	36	24	6	6	74	35	78
2	Linfield	36	20	10	6	68	39	70
3	Crusaders	36	18	8	10	48	39	62
4	Newry	36	17	9	10	52	46	60
5	Glenavon	36	13	12	11	49	35	51
6	Ballymena Utd.	36	11	8	17	40	42	41
7	Coleraine	36	10	9	17	34	53	39
8	Portadown	36	9	10	17	41	47	37
9	Cliftonville	36	7	14	15	31	47	35
10	Omagh	36	5	6	25	25	79	21

Top scorer: 19 Vinny Arkins (Portadown); **Player of Year:** John Devine (Glentoran); **Young Player of Year:** Richard Clarke (Portadown); **Manager of Year:** Roy Coyle (Glentoran).

FIRST DIVISION

		P	W	D	L	F	A	Pts
1	Distillery	28	17	4	7	44	30	55
2	Ards	28	16	1	11	47	34	49
3	Bangor	28	15	3	10	37	35	48
4	Ballyclare Com.	28	11	5	12	55	44	38
5	Dungannon Swifts	28	11	5	12	36	46	38
6	Carrick Rangers	28	10	4	14	41	41	34
7	Larne	28	9	5	14	28	32	32
8	Limavady	28	6	7	15	37	63	25

Top Scorer: 21 Darren Armour (Distillery); **Player of Year:** Darren Armour (Distillery); **Manager of Year:** Paul Kirk (Distillery).

BASS IRISH CUP FINAL

Portadown v Cliftonville (Windsor Park, Belfast, May 1)

Portadown walk-over; Cliftonville were deemed to have used an illegal player in their semi-final win over Linfield.

COCA COLA LEAGUE CUP FINAL

Linfield 2 (Ferguson 2), **Glentoran** 1 (Young)

(Windsor Park, Belfast May 4)

OTHER LEAGUES 1998-99

NATIONWIDE CONFERENCE

		P	W	D	L	F	A	W	D	L	F	A	Pts	GD
1	Cheltenham Town	42	11	9	1	35	14	11	5	5	36	22	80	+35
2	Kettering Town	42	11	5	5	31	16	11	5	5	27	21	76	+21
3	Hayes	42	12	3	6	34	25	10	5	6	29	25	74	+13
4	Rushden & Diamonds	42	11	4	6	41	22	9	8	4	30	20	72	+29
5	Yeovil Town	42	8	4	9	35	32	12	7	2	33	22	71	+14
6	Stevenage Borough	42	9	9	3	37	23	8	8	5	25	22	68	+17
7	Northwich Victoria	42	11	3	7	29	21	8	6	7	31	30	66	+9
8	Kingstonian	42	9	7	5	25	19	8	6	7	25	30	64	+1
9	Woking	42	9	5	7	27	20	9	4	8	24	25	63	+6
10	Hednesford Town	42	9	8	4	30	24	6	8	7	19	20	61	+5
11	Dover Athletic	42	7	9	5	27	21	8	4	9	27	27	58	+6
12	Forest Green Rov.	42	9	5	7	28	22	6	8	7	27	28	58	+5
13	Hereford Utd.	42	9	5	7	25	17	6	5	10	24	29	55	+3
14	Morecambe	42	9	5	7	31	29	6	3	12	29	47	53	-16
15	Kidderminster Harriers	42	9	4	8	32	22	5	5	11	24	30	51	+4
16	Doncaster Rov.	42	7	5	9	26	26	5	7	9	25	29	48	-4
17	Telford Utd.	42	7	8	6	24	24	3	8	10	20	36	46	-16
18	Southport	42	6	9	6	29	28	4	6	11	18	31	45	-12
19	Barrow†	42	7	5	9	17	23	4	5	12	23	40	43	-23
20	Welling Utd.†	42	4	7	10	18	30	5	7	9	26	35	41	-21
21	Leek Town	42	5	5	11	34	42	3	3	15	14	34	32	-28
22	Farnborough Town	42	6	5	10	29	48	1	6	14	12	41	32	-48

• Cheltenham Town promoted to Football League.
† Barrow relegated, unable to guarantee fulfilling commitments. Welling re-elected.

Prize money: Champions: Cheltenham Town £5,000; Kettering Town (Runners-up) £3,000; Hayes (third) £2,000.
Manager of the Year: Steve Cotterill (Cheltenham Town), £1,000 award.
Player of Year: Neil Grayson (Cheltenham Town).
Goalscorer of Year: 26 Carl Alford (Stevenage Borough).
Relegated: Farnborough Town to Ryman League, Leek Town to Unibond League.
Promoted to Conference: Sutton Utd. (Ryman League), Altrincham (Unibond League), Nuneaton Borough (Dr. Martens League). They are joined as new members by Scarborough Town (relegated from Nationwide League).

GM VAUXHALL CONFERENCE CHAMPIONS

1979-80	Altrincham	1989-90*	Darlington
1980-81	Altrincham	1990-91*	Barnet
1981-82	Runcorn	1991-92*	Colchester Utd.
1982-83	Enfield	1992-93*	Wycombe Wand.
1983-84	Maidstone Utd.	1993-94	Kidderminster H.
1984-85	Wealdstone	1994-95	Macclesfield Town
1985-86	Enfield	1995-96	Stevenage Borough
1986-87*	Scarborough	1996-97*	Macclesfield Town
1987-88*	Lincoln City	1997-98*	Halifax Town
1988-89*	Maidstone Utd.	1998-99*	Cheltenham Town

(* Promoted to Football League)
Conference – Record Attendance: 9,432, Lincoln City v Wycombe Wand., May 2, 1988.

PONTIN'S LEAGUE

PREMIER DIVISION

		P	W	D	L	F	A	Pts
1	Sunderland	24	14	7	3	46	18	49
2	Liverpool	24	13	7	4	28	16	46
3	Manchester Utd.	24	13	4	7	48	28	43
4	Nott'm. Forest	24	11	6	7	35	26	39
5	Everton	24	11	5	8	35	28	38
6	Blackburn Rov.	24	8	7	9	31	26	31
7	Leeds Utd.	24	9	3	12	40	43	30
8	Leicester City	24	8	6	10	30	41	30
9	Aston Villa	24	8	5	11	36	37	29
10	Stoke City	24	7	7	10	24	32	28
11	Preston N.E.	24	7	5	12	20	42	26
12	Birmingham City	24	5	9	10	24	34	24
13	Derby Co.	24	3	7	14	26	52	16

DIVISION ONE

		P	W	D	L	F	A	Pts
1	Coventry City	24	12	6	6	36	21	42
2	Oldham Athletic	24	13	3	8	36	31	42
3	Middlesbrough	24	12	5	7	48	38	41
4	Port Vale	24	11	4	9	31	30	37
5	Manchester City	24	10	6	8	53	38	36
6	Sheffield Wed.	24	9	8	7	26	23	35
7	W.B.A.	24	8	9	7	35	32	33
8	Wolves	24	10	3	11	43	45	33
9	Tranmere Rov.	24	10	2	12	41	32	32
10	Bolton Wand.	24	8	4	12	25	35	28
11	Barnsley	24	6	9	9	27	35	27
12	Burnley	24	6	8	10	20	35	26
13	Grimsby Town	24	5	5	14	20	46	20

DIVISION TWO

		P	W	D	L	F	A	Pts
1	Newcastle Utd.	24	15	5	4	48	17	50
2	Huddersfield Town	24	13	5	6	41	25	44
3	Shrewsbury Town	24	9	9	6	29	24	36
4	Wrexham	24	11	3	10	41	37	36
5	Bradford City	24	10	4	10	41	41	34
6	Sheffield Utd.	24	9	7	8	27	29	34
7	Stockport Co.	24	9	6	9	41	32	33
8	York City	24	8	9	7	35	28	33
9	Rotherham Utd.	24	9	6	9	33	36	33
10	Scarborough	24	9	4	11	30	39	31
11	Notts Co.	24	7	6	11	31	48	27
12	Lincoln City	24	7	3	14	31	47	24
13	Blackpool	24	3	8	13	25	48	17

DIVISION THREE

		P	W	D	L	F	A	Pts
1	Scunthorpe Utd.	22	13	5	4	48	27	44
2	Walsall	22	12	6	4	49	26	42
3	Hartlepool Utd.	22	11	6	5	44	32	39
3	Rochdale	22	10	6	6	33	27	36
4	Bury	22	10	5	7	42	33	35
5	Chesterfield	22	10	4	8	28	30	34
6	Wigan Athletic	22	9	4	9	32	30	31
7	Darlington	22	9	3	10	36	37	30
8	Halifax Town	22	5	5	12	29	43	20
9	Chester City	22	5	5	12	23	47	20
10	Hull City	22	4	7	11	21	38	19
11	Carlisle Utd.	22	5	2	15	31	46	17

FOOTBALL COMBINATION

Sponsors: Avon Insurance

		P	W	D	L	F	A	GD	Pts
1	Charlton Athletic	28	19	3	6	60	24	+36	60
2	Tottenham	28	18	3	7	56	24	+32	57
3	Chelsea	28	18	3	7	39	22	+17	57
4	Ipswich Town	28	17	4	7	62	32	+30	55
5	Watford	28	14	9	5	56	29	+27	51
6	Southampton	28	15	4	9	53	37	+16	49
7	Peterborough Utd.	28	14	6	8	50	35	+15	48
8	Fulham	28	14	5	9	63	44	+19	47
9	Arsenal	28	13	6	9	47	32	+15	45
10	Colchester Utd.	28	13	4	11	46	43	+03	43
11	West Ham Utd.	28	11	8	9	56	40	+16	41
12	Norwich City	28	12	5	11	38	34	+04	41
13	Northampton Town	28	12	5	11	35	41	-06	41
14	Luton Town	28	11	7	10	45	43	+02	40
15	Q.P.R.	28	11	5	12	44	34	+10	38
16	Portsmouth	28	11	5	12	40	37	+03	38
17	Wimbledon	28	9	11	8	37	36	+01	38
18	Brighton & H.A.	28	9	10	9	27	31	-04	37
19	Bournemouth	28	10	6	12	43	39	+04	36
20	Crystal Palace	28	9	6	13	43	50	-07	33
21	Oxford Utd.	28	10	3	15	33	52	-19	33
22	Reading	28	9	4	15	31	42	-11	31
23	Swindon Town	28	8	6	14	26	47	-21	30
24	Cambridge Utd.	28	8	6	14	41	65	-24	30
25	Barnet	28	8	5	15	33	65	-32	29
26	Millwall	28	7	6	15	33	58	-25	27
27	Brentford	28	5	7	16	25	58	-31	22
28	Wycombe Wand.	28	5	7	16	24	58	-34	22
29	Gillingham	28	4	5	19	21	57	-36	17

*Arsenal, Charlton Athletic, Chelsea, Crystal Palace, Southampton, Tottenham, West Ham Utd., Wimbledon, Reading and Brentford all resigned. Southend Utd.'s application has been accepted.

SOUTH EAST COUNTIES LEAGUE

		P	W	D	L	F	A	Pts	GD
1	Luton Town	30	20	6	4	59	25	66	+34
2	Leyton Orient	30	19	7	4	67	32	64	+35
3	Brentford	30	19	4	7	74	34	61	+40
4	Cambridge Utd.	30	12	9	9	57	53	45	+4
5	Bristol Rov.	30	12	7	11	52	51	43	+1
6	Barnet	30	12	7	11	40	44	43	−4
7	Reading	30	9	12	9	36	38	39	−2
8	Wycombe Wand.	30	9	11	10	35	37	38	−2
9	Brighton & H.A.	30	10	7	13	48	47	37	+1
10	Swindon Town	30	10	7	13	41	43	37	−2
11	Colchester Utd.	30	11	3	16	47	49	36	−2
12	Portsmouth	30	8	10	12	41	56	34	−15
13	Oxford Utd.	30	9	7	14	36	52	34	−16
14	AFC Bournemouth	30	10	3	17	43	66	33	−23
15	Southend Utd.	30	8	5	17	37	55	29	−18
16	Gillingham	30	7	5	18	35	66	26	−31

* League disbanded at end of season.

DEATH OF SOUTH EAST COUNTIES LEAGUE

The league which acted as a non-stop production line for a host of international stars has folded after 44 years.

The South East Counties League was a 'nursery' for talent in the south with many future stars developing their skills as teenagers within its ranks.

Over 2,500 full international caps were won by players who began their careers in the South East Counties League including England's 1966 World Cup winners Bobby Moore, Martin Peters, Geoff Hurst and George Cohen.

Chelsea legend Jimmy Greaves, who later joined Tottenham, was the League's first footballer of the year in 1958 while former England coach Glenn Hoddle and ex-England under-21 coach Peter Taylor also appeared in the league's Saturday morning matches.

More than 700 players 'bred' in the league gained international honours. John Hartson, Rio Ferdinand, Nick Barmby, Jamie Redknapp, Ian Walker, Andy Cole, Steve Morrow, Tony Adams, Martin Keown and current England captain Alan Shearer are among them.

The League's management committee included legendary former Tottenham manager Bill Nicholson and ex-England chief Bobby Robson. Secretary Alan Leather served in three separate capacities during the League's 44 years.

The two division league decided to wind up after losing the majority of its members to the new FA Premier Youth Academy Leagues.

RULEBENDERS PAY THE PENALTY

Two teams battling to reach a cup final experienced the mental anguish of negotiating 22 penalties in a shoot out before they realised competition rules demanded a replay first.

Morwenstow of North Cornwall beat Dolton on penalties after drawing 2-2 following extra time – and won 2-1 without the aid of extra time in the replay.

LEAGUE OF WALES

PREMIER DIVISION

		P	W	D	L	F	A	Pts
1	Barry Town	32	23	7	2	82	23	76
2	Inter Cable Tel	32	19	6	7	61	26	63
3	Cwmbran Town	32	17	6	9	72	44	57
4	Aberystwyth	32	16	9	7	59	48	57
5	Caernarfon	32	13	11	8	45	46	50
6	Newtown	32	13	11	8	45	35	49
7	Conwy Utd.	32	14	7	11	55	49	49
8	TNS Llansantffraid	32	12	11	9	55	42	47
9	Carmarthen Town	32	13	8	11	46	46	47
10	Caerses	32	12	8	12	49	55	44
11	Bangor City	32	11	6	15	44	49	39
12	Connah's Quay	32	10	8	14	44	47	38
13	Haverfordwest	32	9	7	16	43	60	34
14	Afan Lido	32	7	10	15	28	45	31
15	Rhayader Town	32	5	11	16	29	54	26
16	Rhyl	32	7	2	23	41	81	23
17	Holywell Town	32	3	9	20	38	86	18

DR. MARTENS LEAGUE

PREMIER DIVISION

		P	W	D	L	F	A	Pts
1	Nuneaton Borough	42	27	9	6	91	33	90
2	Boston Utd.	42	17	16	9	69	51	67
3	Ilkeston Town	42	18	13	11	72	59	67
4	Bath City	42	18	11	13	70	44	65
5	Hastings Town*	42	18	11	13	57	49	65
6	Gloucester City	42	18	11	13	57	52	65
7	Worcester City	42	18	9	15	58	54	63
8	Halesowen Town	42	17	11	14	72	61	62
9	Tamworth	42	19	5	18	62	67	62
10	King's Lynn	42	17	10	15	53	46	61
11	Crawley Town	42	17	10	15	57	58	61
12	Salisbury City	42	16	12	14	56	61	60
13	Burton Albion	42	17	7	18	58	52	58
14	Weymouth	42	14	14	14	56	55	56
15	Merthyr Tydfil	42	15	8	19	52	62	53
16	Atherstone Utd.	42	12	14	16	47	52	50
17	Grantham Town	42	14	8	20	51	58	50
18	Dorchester Town	42	11	15	16	49	63	48
19	Rothwell Town	42	13	9	20	47	67	48
20	Cambridge City	42	11	12	19	47	68	45
21	Gresley Rov.	42	12	8	22	49	73	44
22	Bromsgrove Rov.	42	8	7	27	39	84	31

* Hastings withdrew to join Southern Division. Rothwell Town remain in Premier Division.

MIDLAND DIVISION

		P	W	D	L	F	A	Pts
1	Clevedon Town	42	28	8	6	83	35	92
2	Newport AFC	42	26	7	9	92	51	85
3	Redditch Utd.*	42	22	12	8	81	45	75
4	Hinckley Utd.	42	20	12	10	58	40	72
5	Stafford Rangers	42	21	8	13	92	61	71
6	Bilston Town	42	20	11	11	79	69	71
7	Solihull Borough	42	19	12	11	76	53	69
8	Moor Green	42	20	7	15	70	61	67
9	Blakenall	42	17	14	11	65	54	65
10	Shepshed Dynamo	42	17	12	13	62	54	63
11	Sutton Coldfield	42	17	8	17	46	57	59
12	Stourbridge	42	16	10	16	60	54	58
13	Evesham Utd.	42	16	9	17	64	63	57
14	Wisbech Town	42	16	9	17	59	66	57
15	Weston-Super-Mare	42	15	10	17	59	56	55
16	Bedworth Utd.	42	15	9	18	63	52	54
17	Cinderford Town	42	13	8	21	61	74	47
18	Stamford	42	13	7	22	60	75	46
19	Paget Rangers	42	11	12	19	49	58	45
20	VS Rugby	42	12	9	21	53	74	45
21	Racing Club Warwick	42	5	8	29	38	93	23
22	Bloxwich Town	42	1	2	39	26	151	5

* Points deducted

SOUTHERN DIVISION

		P	W	D	L	F	A	Pts
1	Havant & Waterlooville	42	29	7	6	85	32	94
2	Margate	42	27	8	7	84	33	89
3	Folkestone Invicta	42	26	8	8	92	47	86
4	Newport IoW	42	23	7	12	68	40	76
5	Chelmsford City	42	20	12	10	91	51	72
6	Raunds Town	42	19	13	10	87	50	70
7	Ashford Town	42	17	12	13	59	54	63
8	Baldock Town	42	17	9	16	60	59	60
9	Fisher Athletic	42	16	11	15	58	52	59
10	Bashley	42	17	7	18	74	77	58
11	Witney Town	42	15	12	15	56	48	57
12	Cirencester Town	42	16	8	18	61	66	56
13	Sittingbourne	42	12	18	12	54	56	54
14	Dartford	42	14	10	18	48	54	52
15	Erith & Belvedere	42	15	7	20	48	64	52
16	Tonbridge Angels	42	12	15	15	48	59	51
17	St Leonards	42	14	8	0	57	72	50
18	Fleet Town	42	12	11	19	54	72	47
19	Corby Town	42	10	10	22	48	73	40
20	Yate Town	42	10	7	25	37	79	37
21	Andover*	42	6	10	26	48	115	28
22	Brackley Town†	42	6	8	28	41	105	26

* Andover resigned.
† Brackley expelled.

UNIBOND LEAGUE

PREMIER DIVISION

		P	W	D	L	F	A	Pts
1	Altrincham	42	23	11	8	67	33	80
2	Worksop Town	42	22	10	10	66	48	76
3	Guiseley	42	21	9	12	64	47	72
4	Bamber Bridge	42	18	15	9	63	48	69
5	Gateshead	42	18	11	13	69	58	65
6	Gainsborough Trinity	42	19	8	15	65	59	65
7	Whitby Town	42	17	13	12	77	62	64
8	Leigh RMI	42	16	15	11	63	54	63
9	Hyde Utd.	42	16	11	15	61	48	59
10	Stalybridge Celtic	42	16	11	15	71	63	59
11	Winsford Utd.	42	14	15	13	56	52	57
12	Runcorn	42	12	19	11	46	49	55
13	Emley	42	12	17	13	47	49	53
14	Blyth Spartans	42	14	9	19	56	64	51
15	Colwyn Bay	42	12	13	17	60	71	49
16	Frickley Athletic	42	11	15	16	55	71	48
17	Marine	42	10	17	15	61	69	47
18	Spennymoor Utd.	42	12	11	19	52	71	47
19	Lancaster City	42	11	13	18	50	62	46
20	Bishop Auckland	42	10	15	17	49	67	45
21	Chorley	42	8	15	19	45	68	39
22	Accrington Stanley	42	9	9	24	47	77	36

RYMAN LEAGUE

PREMIER DIVISION

		P	W	D	L	F	A	Pts
1	Sutton Utd.	42	27	7	8	89	39	88
2	Aylesbury Utd.	42	23	8	11	67	38	77
3	Dagenham & Redbridge	42	20	13	9	71	44	73
4	Purfleet	42	22	7	13	71	52	73
5	Enfield	42	21	9	12	73	49	72
6	St Albans City	42	17	17	8	71	52	68
7	Aldershot Town	42	16	14	12	83	48	62
8	Basingstoke Town	42	17	10	15	63	53	61
9	Harrow Borough	42	17	9	16	72	66	60
10	Gravesend & Northfleet	42	18	6	18	54	53	60
11	Slough Town	42	16	11	15	60	53	59
12	Billericay Town	42	15	13	14	54	56	58
13	Hendon	42	16	9	17	70	71	57
14	Boreham Wood	42	14	15	13	59	63	57
15	Chesham Utd.	42	15	9	18	58	79	54
16	Dulwich Hamlet	42	14	8	20	53	63	50
17	Heybridge Swifts	42	13	9	20	51	85	48
18	Walton & Hersham	42	12	7	23	50	77	43
19	Hampton	42	10	12	20	41	71	42
20	Carshalton Athletic	42	10	10	22	47	82	40
21	Bishop's Stortford	42	9	10	23	49	90	37
22	Bromley	42	8	11	23	50	72	35

Div. 1 – 1 Canvey Island; 2 Hitchin; 3 Wealdstone.

JEWSON WESSEX LEAGUE

DIVISION ONE

		P	W	D	L	F	A	Pts
1	Lymington & N Milton	38	27	6	5	92	31	87
2	Thatcham Town	38	23	9	6	92	46	78
3	AFC Newbury	38	22	11	5	81	39	77
4	Eastleigh	38	22	8	8	69	43	74
5	Christchurch	38	22	7	9	72	53	73
6	Wimborne Town	38	18	14	6	81	34	68
7	Cowes Sports	38	19	8	11	76	54	65
8	Money Fields	38	17	8	13	69	61	59
9	AFC Totton	38	15	10	13	60	50	55
10	Bemerton HH	38	17	4	17	59	54	55
11	Brockenhurst	38	14	7	17	52	61	49
12	Bournemouth	38	12	10	16	46	63	46
13	Fareham Town	38	11	12	15	58	67	45
14	Gosport Bor	38	11	11	16	66	71	44
15	BAT Sports	38	10	13	15	65	43	43
16	E Cowes Vics	38	10	4	24	48	103	34
17	Hamble ASSC	38	6	9	23	37	68	27
18	Portsmouth RN	38	6	9	23	42	81	27
19	Whitchurch Utd.	38	5	11	22	36	76	26
20	Downton	38	4	7	27	40	111	19

JEWSON EASTERN COUNTIES LEAGUE

PREMIER DIVISION

		P	W	D	L	F	A	Pts	GD
1	Wroxham	42	27	10	5	88	36	91	+52
2	Fakenham Town	42	25	10	7	96	50	85	+46
3	Gt Yarmouth Town	42	23	9	10	69	36	78	+33
4	Histon	42	19	17	6	80	53	74	+27
5	Lowestoft Town	42	19	12	11	78	53	69	+25
6	Felixstowe P&T	42	20	9	13	78	56	69	+22
7	Soham Town Rangers	42	19	12	11	77	73	69	+4
8	Newmarket Town	42	19	11	12	70	55	68	+15
9	Sudbury Town	42	20	8	14	75	67	68	+8
10	Sudbury Wand.	42	17	8	17	72	62	59	+10
11	Bury Town	42	15	14	13	47	46	59	+1
12	Diss Town	42	14	15	13	53	59	57	−6
13	Maldon Town	42	16	8	18	69	69	56	0
14	Halstead Town	42	14	11	17	59	71	53	−12
15	Warboys Town	42	14	10	18	70	88	52	−18
16	Stowmarket Town	42	12	11	19	59	72	47	−13
17	Gorleston	42	12	10	20	52	77	46	−25
18	Harwich & Parkeston	42	9	14	19	42	63	41	−21
19	Woodbridge Town	42	9	11	22	49	73	38	−24
20	Watton Utd.	42	9	10	23	53	83	37	−30
21	Ipswich Wand.	42	5	13	24	49	81	28	−32
22	Ely City	42	3	11	28	38	100	20	−62

UHL UNITED COUNTIES

		P	W	D	L	F	A	Pts
1	Spalding Utd.	38	30	3	5	106	30	93
2	Desborough Town	38	24	6	8	82	41	78
3	Cogenhoe Utd.	38	23	5	10	89	47	74
4	Northampton Spencer	38	20	6	12	79	46	66
5	S & L Corby	38	19	9	10	70	45	66
6	Bourne Town	38	18	9	11	75	69	63
7	Stotfold	38	17	11	10	57	43	62
8	Boston Town	38	17	10	11	68	44	61
9	Buckingham Town	38	17	9	12	71	53	60
10	Yaxley	38	18	5	15	87	75	59
11	Wellingborough Town	38	16	6	16	58	57	54
12	Blackstone	38	16	5	17	59	56	53
13	St Neots Town	38	15	6	17	70	73	51
14	St Wootton Blue Cross	38	13	8	17	54	76	47
15	Holbeach Utd.	38	12	10	16	62	65	46
16	Ford Sports	38	12	9	17	50	57	45
17	Kempston Rov.	38	10	6	22	45	75	36
18	Eynesbury Rov.	38	6	7	25	42	100	25
19	Long Buckby	38	3	6	29	26	99	15
20	Potton Utd.	38	2	8	28	21	120	14

UNIJET SUSSEX

		P	W	D	L	F	A	Pts
1	Burgess Hill Town	38	28	5	5	106	24	89
2	Saltdean Utd.	38	26	8	4	100	35	86
3	Horsham YMCA	38	24	7	7	97	50	79
4	Langney Sports	38	20	6	12	69	43	66
5	Shoreham	38	19	8	11	80	57	65
6	Wick	38	18	7	13	65	49	61
7	East Preston	38	18	6	14	69	58	60
8	Eastbourne Utd.	38	17	8	13	59	51	59
9	Pagham	38	16	11	11	42	39	59
10	Eastbourne Town	38	14	12	12	61	62	54
11	Redhill	38	14	11	13	79	60	53
12	Portfield	38	12	13	13	62	66	49
13	Hassocks	38	13	7	18	51	51	46
14	Whitehawk	38	11	10	17	50	61	43
15	Chichester City	38	10	11	17	44	67	41
16	Littlehampton Town	38	10	7	21	38	87	37
17	Ringmer	38	8	11	19	35	64	35
18	Selsey	38	7	8	23	42	93	29
19	Hailsham Town	38	7	4	27	40	101	25
20	Broadbridge Heath	38	4	8	26	32	105	20

SCREWFIX WESTERN

		P	W	D	L	F	A	Pts
1	Taunton Town	38	33	3	2	134	33	102
2	Tiverton Town	38	29	4	5	118	27	91
3	Chippenham Town	38	25	7	6	93	41	82
4	Melksham Town	38	20	10	8	73	44	70
5	Paulton Rov.	38	18	12	8	70	42	66
6	Brislington	38	18	10	10	74	44	64
7	Yeovil Town Res	38	18	4	16	70	66	58
8	Bridport	38	16	7	15	61	68	55
9	Bridgwater Town	38	15	9	14	68	51	54
10	Backwell Utd.	38	15	7	16	56	48	52
11	Mangotsfield Utd.	38	14	9	15	60	58	51
12	Barnstaple Town	38	14	8	16	72	55	50
13	Bristol Manor Farm	38	15	4	19	61	57	49
14	Elmore	38	14	6	18	68	82	48
15	Bishop Sutton	38	12	7	19	65	81	43
16	Westbury Utd.	38	9	8	21	42	103	35
17	Bideford	38	10	1	27	40	108	31
18	Odd Down	38	5	15	18	44	86	30
19	Keynsham Town	38	6	7	25	33	99	25
20	Calne Town	38	3	4	31	34	143	13

COMPLETE MUSIC HELLENIC

		P	W	D	L	F	A	Pts
1	Burnham	36	26	6	4	88	31	84
2	Carterton Town	36	25	6	5	82	34	81
3	Highworth Town	36	21	6	9	92	47	69
4	Banbury Utd.	36	20	9	7	73	33	69
5	North Leigh	36	18	11	7	77	44	65
6	EFC Cheltenham	33	17	5	11	60	36	56
7	Abingdon Utd.	36	17	5	14	61	55	56
8	Tuffley Rov.	36	16	6	14	63	55	54
9	Didcot Town	36	16	5	15	58	52	53
10	Bicester Town	36	15	8	13	58	60	53
11	Cirencester Acad	36	12	11	13	42	56	47
12	Hallen	36	9	14	12	45	48	41
13	Fairford Town	36	10	10	16	42	50	40
14	Swindon Supermarine	36	10	9	17	41	59	39
15	Shortwood Utd.	36	9	11	16	37	61	38
16	Almondsbury Town	36	8	7	21	47	82	31
17	Wantage Town	36	8	5	23	36	90	29
18	*Kintbury Rangers	36	8	8	20	48	89	26
19	Harrow Hill	36	4	2	30	31	99	14

* Points deducted

BOB A JOB

The players at cash-strapped Mansfield Town washed cars at £3 a time at a local shopping centre, raising £800 to stay overnight in Torquay before their crucial Easter Monday Third Division promotion clash. They faced a 4am start to avoid the Bank Holiday traffic.

NORTH WESTERN TRAINS NORTH WEST COUNTIES LEAGUE

DIVISION ONE

		P	W	D	L	F	A	Pts	GD
1	Workington R	40	27	9	4	86	28	90	+58
2	Mossley	40	27	7	6	91	38	88	+53
3	Vauxhall GM	40	26	7	7	92	40	85	+52
4	Newcastle Town	40	25	9	6	86	33	84	+53
5	Kidsgrove Athletic	40	24	7	9	90	47	79	+43
6	Prescot Cables	40	21	9	10	78	44	72	+34
7	Skelmersdale Utd.	40	21	8	11	82	50	71	+32
8	St. Helens Town	40	22	5	13	77	58	71	+19
9	Leek CSOB	40	14	11	15	52	58	53	–6
10	Salford City	40	15	7	18	63	73	52	–10
11	Ramsbottom Utd.	40	14	8	18	54	64	50	–10
12	Clitheroe	40	14	6	20	68	58	48	+10
13	Maine Road	40	14	6	20	50	71	48	–21
14	Rossendale Utd.	40	14	5	21	59	81	47	–22
15	Nantwich Town	40	12	6	22	56	68	42	–12
16	Glossop North End	40	12	6	22	53	81	42	–28
17	Cheadle Town	40	12	6	22	56	97	42	–41
18	Atherton LR	40	10	9	21	45	73	39	–28
19	Atherton Collieries	40	9	7	24	50	88	34	–38
20	Bootle	40	9	7	24	41	84	34	–43
21	Holker Old Boys	40	4	3	33	21	116	15	–95

ARNOTT INSURANCE NORTHERN LEAGUE

DIVISION ONE

		P	W	D	L	F	A	Pts	GD
1	Bedlington Terriers	38	33	2	3	128	37	101	+91
2	Tow Law Town	38	23	6	9	80	48	75	+32
3	Chester-le-Street	38	17	14	7	72	47	65	+25
4	West Auckland Town	38	19	8	11	67	59	65	+8
5	Dunston F.B.	38	18	10	10	75	53	64	+22
6	Guisborough Town	38	18	5	15	69	66	59	+3
7	Seaham Red Star	38	16	7	15	62	59	55	+3
8	Consett	38	15	7	16	72	64	52	+8
9	Morpeth Town	38	15	6	17	54	60	51	–6
10	Stockton	38	15	6	17	67	76	51	–9
11	*Billingham Syn	38	15	7	16	60	56	49	+4
12	Marske Utd.	38	13	9	16	58	63	48	–5
13	Crook Town	38	13	7	18	52	61	46	–9
14	*Billingham Town	38	13	9	16	66	81	45	–15
15	South Shields	38	9	16	13	54	66	43	–12
16	Jarrow Roofing	38	11	10	17	62	85	43	–23
17	Newcastle Blue Star	38	12	5	21	59	83	41	–24
18	Easington Colliery	38	11	6	21	67	78	39	–11
19	*Penrith	38	10	8	20	60	83	35	–23
20	Shildon	38	6	8	24	48	107	26	–59

* 3 points deducted

NORTHERN COUNTIES EAST LEAGUE

PREMIER DIVISION

		P	W	D	L	F	A	Pts	GD
1	Ossett Albion	38	23	5	10	86	50	74	+36
2	Ossett Town	38	22	7	9	76	44	73	+32
3	Brigg Town	38	20	12	6	78	43	72	+35
4	Hallam	38	22	5	11	95	63	71	+32
5	North Ferriby Utd.	38	19	12	7	92	50	69	+42
6	Liversedge	38	21	4	13	87	63	67	+24
7	Arnold Town	38	19	7	12	78	56	64	+22
8	Denaby Utd.	38	15	12	11	66	60	57	+6
9	Garforth Town	38	15	9	14	74	70	54	+4
10	Buxton	38	14	10	14	54	53	52	+1
11	Selby Town	38	15	7	16	59	61	52	−2
12	Sheffield	38	15	6	17	55	58	51	−3
13	Armthorpe MW	38	13	11	14	46	50	50	−4
14	Glasshoughton W	38	13	9	16	58	71	48	−13
15	Thackley	38	14	5	19	65	77	47	−12
16	Eccleshill Utd.	38	12	6	20	56	74	42	−18
17	Staveley MW*	38	9	11	18	50	84	36	−34
18	Maltby MW**	38	8	6	24	51	87	26	−36
19	Pontefract Coll*	38	7	7	24	37	86	26	−49
20	Pickering Town	38	5	7	26	44	107	22	−63

* 2 points deducted   ** 4 points deducted

HIGHLAND LEAGUE

		P	W	D	L	F	A	Pts
1	Peterhead	30	24	4	2	89	19	76
2	Huntly	30	23	3	4	86	37	72
3	Keith	30	22	4	4	92	41	70
4	Elgin City	30	21	1	6	72	39	64
5	Fraserburgh	30	18	9	6	86	39	60
6	Clachnacuddin	30	16	10	8	79	45	56
7	Cove R	30	16	5	9	87	48	53
8	Forres Mechs	30	11	6	13	60	61	39
9	Brora R	30	11	5	14	61	63	38
10	Deveronvale	30	11	4	15	57	72	37
11	Rothes	30	8	5	17	46	64	29
12	Buckie Thistle	30	8	4	17	36	60	28
13	Lossiemouth	30	8	4	17	40	66	28
14	Wick Acad	30	9	2	18	33	85	23
15	Nairn Co	30	3	2	25	32	114	11
16	Fort William	30	1	1	27	24	127	4

SCHWEPPES ESSEX SENIOR LEAGUE

PREMIER DIVISION

		P	W	D	L	F	A	Pts
1	Bowers Utd.	26	21	3	2	78	16	66
2	Great Wakering Rov	26	20	2	4	73	26	62
3	Saffron Walden Town	26	16	8	2	49	20	56
4	Burnham Ramblers	26	14	6	6	61	25	48
5	Basildon Utd.	26	13	5	8	46	35	44
6	Southend Manor	26	11	9	6	49	40	42
7	Ilford	26	13	3	10	49	44	42
8	Concord Rangers	26	8	7	11	33	48	31
9	Hullbridge Sports	26	8	3	15	42	38	27
10	Brentwood	26	5	6	15	30	60	21
11	Stansted	26	6	3	17	40	88	21
12	East Ham Utd.	26	5	5	16	33	88	20
13	Sawbridgeworth Town	26	4	6	16	19	47	18
14	Eton Manor	26	3	4	19	36	63	13

HOOLIGAN HOTLINE

If you have any information, any time, about any person involved in football hooliganism, the **National Criminal Intelligence Service** await your call on free-phone number 0800-515495.

WOMEN'S FOOTBALL

AXA WOMEN'S CUP FINAL

Arsenal 2 Southampton 0
Monday May 3 (at Charlton Athletic att: 6,450).

AXA WOMEN'S PREMIER LEAGUE CUP FINAL

Arsenal 3 Everton 1
Sunday March 28 (at Tranmere Rov. att: 3,000).

WOMEN'S WORLD CUP FINAL

USA 0 China 0 (aet USA won 5-4 on pens)
Saturday July 10 (at Pasadena Rose Bowl, att: 90,185).

AXA F.A. WOMEN'S PREMIER LEAGUE

NATIONAL DIVISION

		P	W	D	L	F	A	Pts
1	Croydon	18	14	4	0	53	11	46
2	Arsenal	18	13	4	1	59	15	43
3	Doncaster Belles	18	9	6	3	32	19	33
4	Everton	18	10	2	6	30	20	32
5	Tranmere Rov.	18	8	3	7	29	32	27
6	Liverpool	18	6	2	10	28	27	20
7	Southampton Saints	18	5	3	10	20	35	18
8	Millwall Lionesses	18	3	6	9	14	26	15
9	Bradford City	18	2	4	12	15	68	10
10	Ilkeston Town	18	2	2	14	14	51	8

SOUTHERN DIVISION

		P	W	D	L	F	A	Pts
1	Reading Royals	18	13	2	3	60	21	41
2	Whitehawk	18	12	3	3	56	15	39
3	Three Bridges	18	11	2	5	35	27	35
4	Brighton & H.A.	18	9	6	3	35	21	33
5	Wimbledon	18	9	1	8	41	45	28
6	Barry Town	18	7	5	6	21	27	26
7	Langford	18	7	2	9	34	28	23
8	Barnet	18	4	3	11	28	52	15
9	Leyton Orient	18	3	2	13	24	58	11
10	Ipswich Town	18	2	0	16	22	62	6

NORTHERN DIVISION

		P	W	D	L	F	A	Pts
1	Aston Villa	18	14	3	1	57	14	45
2	Blyth Spartans Kestrels	18	11	4	3	44	17	37
3	Leeds Utd.	18	9	5	4	67	29	32
4	Wolves	18	9	5	4	40	25	32
5	Sheffield Wed.	18	9	4	5	49	28	31
6	Garswood Saints	18	8	5	5	39	29	29
7	Berkhamsted Town	18	7	1	10	35	54	22
8	Coventry City	18	3	1	14	14	63	10
9	Huddersfield Town	18	2	3	13	24	67	9
10	Arnold Town	18	1	3	14	10	53	6

BARE-FACED CHEEK

Nigerian prostitutes threatened nude protests at the World Youth Cup in April after they were banned from hotels by the tournament organisers. The Nigerian government and tournament organising committee had ordered a clean-up.

SCHOOLS FOOTBALL

ESFA NATIONAL FINALS

Under-14 Heinz Ketchup Cup (At Arsenal, May 17)
Cardinal Newman (Luton) 2 Kingsdown (Swindon) 1

Under-16 United Norwest Co-op Cup (At Tranmere Rovers, May 14)
Individual schools (girls)
Meole Brace (Shropshire) 4 Holmfirth (W. Yorkshire) 1 (at Tranmere Rovers)

Under-16 United Norwest Co-op Trophy (At Tranmere Rov., May 14)
Inter county (girls)
Hampshire 3 Durham 1

Under-19 Premier League (At Berwick Rangers, May 13)
Inter county (boys)
Northumberland 0 Dorset 0 a.e.t-trophy shared

Under-19 Individual Schools (At W.B.A. May 10)
Boys, for the Mars Trophy
Ardingly College (Sussex) 2 Archbishop Beck (Merseyside) 1

Under-19 Schools and Colleges (At W.B.A. May 10)
Individual Schools and Colleges (boys), for the Snickers Trophy
Cirencester College 2 Sheffield College 0

Under-11 Adidas Predator Premier (At Wembley, May 8)
District Associations 7-a-side
Vale of White Horse 0 Carlisle 0 – Trophy shared

Under-11 Adidas Predator (At Wembley, May 8)
Individual schools (6-a-side)
St Mary's (Hendon) 2 Avondale (Darwen) 1

Under-16 Premier League (At Middlesbrough, May 4)
Inter county (boys)
Northumberland 3 Essex 2

Under-16 Individual (At Wolves, May 2)
Individual schools (boys) for the Goodyear Trophy
Cramlington HS (Northumberland) 4 Crown Woods (London) 1

Under-11 Small Primary Schools (At Leicester City, March 29)
Individual schools 6-a-side
Holy Cross (Nottingham) 2 Great Dalby (Leics) 1 a.e.t

Under-12 Wagonwheels (At Aston Villa, March 6)
Individual schools (Indoor 5-a-side)
Boys: Meadows (Chesterfield) 3 Welling (Kent) 0
Girls: Abraham Darby (Telford) 4 Eastlea (Newham) 1

Under-15 Heinz Trophy (two legs)
First leg (At Mansfield Town, May 11)
South Notts 3 Bishop Auckland 0
Second leg (At Bishop Auckland, May 19)
Bishop Auckland 0 South Notts 0. St. Notts win 3-0 on agg.

ADIDAS VICTORY SHIELD (UNDER-15)

Wales 2 England 4
Scotland 4 Northern Ireland 1
Northern Ireland 1 Wales 1
Scotland 1 Wales 1
Northern Ireland 1 England 3
England 0 Scotland 1

FINAL TABLE

		P	W	D	L	F	A	Pts
1	Scotland	3	2	1	0	6	2	5
2	England	3	2	0	1	7	4	4
3	Wales	3	0	2	1	4	6	2
4	Northern Ireland	3	0	1	2	3	8	1

BOODLE AND DUNTHORNE I.S.F.A CUP
FIRST ROUND

Ardingly 7 Kimbolton 0
Bolton 4 K.E.S, Whitley 0
Bradfield 4 Alleyn's 2 a.e.t
Charterhouse 2 Latymer Upper 3
Chigwell 0 Lancing 3
City of London 2 Victoria College, Jersey 2
Eton 5 Forest 1
Grange 1 Shrewsbury 3
Haileybury 1 St. Bede's 5
Hampton 2 Q.E.G.S., Blackburn 1
Highgate 2 Manchester G.S. 3
Hulme G.S. 1 Bury G.S. 0
Repton 2 Brentwood 2 a.e.t (Repton won 6-5 on penalties)
Wellingborough 1 Westminster 2
Wolverhampton G.S. 3 Malvern 2

SECOND ROUND

Eton 1 Ardingly 1 a.e.t (Ardingly won 4-2 on penalties)
Hampton 2 King's School, Chester 1
Hulme G.S. 2 Manchester G.S. 1 a.e.t
Lancing 0 Wolverhampton G.S 4
Latymer Upper 2 Bradfield 2 a.e.t (Bradfield won 5-4 on penalties)
Repton 5 St. Bede's 1 a.e.t
Shrewsbury 9 Victoria College, Jersey 2
Westminster 1 Bolton 1 a.e.t (Bolton won 5-4 on penalties)

THIRD ROUND

Ardingly 1 Hulme G.S 0
Hampton 1 Bradfield 0
Repton 1 Bolton 0
Shrewsbury 1 Wolverhampton G.S. 2

SEMI-FINALS

Hampton 2 Ardingly 0
Repton 3 Wolverhampton G.S. 3 a.e.t (Wolverhampton won 5-4 on penalties)

FINAL

Hampton 2 Wolverhampton G.S. 1

FIFA WORLD FOOTBALL RANKINGS

Top 100 FIFA world soccer rankings at June, 1999. Figs in brackets = change since May list.

1	Brazil	51	Switzerland (–1)
2	France	52	Kuwait (–3)
3	Czech Republic (+2)	53	Bolivia (–3)
4	Italy	54	China (–1)
5	Germany (–2)	55	Latvia (+8)
6	Spain (+2)	56	Australia (–2)
7	Croatia (–1)	56	DR Congo (+2)
8	Argentina (–1)	58	Finland (–2)
9	Romania (+1)	59	Georgia (–3)
10	Netherlands (–1)	60	Trinidad/Tobago (+10)
11	Norway (+1)	61	UAE (–1)
12	Portugal (+3)	62	Angola (–3)
13	**England** (–2)	62	Slovenia (+10)
14	Mexico (–1)	64	FYR Macedonia
15	Sweden (–1)	65	Cyprus (–3)
16	Yugoslavia	65	Peru (+1)
17	Denmark (+1)	67	Costa Rica (2)
18	Morocco (+1)	68	Nigeria (–7)
19	Austria (–2)	69	**Northern Ireland**
20	Slovakia (+4)	70	Honduras
21	Paraguay (–1)	71	Gabon (+5)
22	Israel (+10)	72	Algeria (–4)
23	Poland (+6)	72	Mali (+2)
23	Russia (+10)	74	Uruguay (–7)
25	Ukraine (–4)	75	Guatemala (–2)
26	Tunisia (+2)	76	Burkina Faso
27	**Scotland** (–6)	77	Thailand (–2)
28	South Africa (–4)	78	Togo
29	Chile (–6)	79	Qatar (–1)
30	Belgium (–3)	80	Namibia (+3)
31	United States (–7)	81	Guinea (–1)
32	Colombia (–1)	82	Cuba (+19)
33	Bulgaria (–3)	83	Zimbabwe (–2)
34	Zambia (+2)	84	**Wales** (–2)
35	**Republic of Ireland** (+3)	85	Uzbekistan (–1)
36	Greece (+1)	86	Armenia (+4)
37	Turkey (+5)	86	El Salvador (+1)
38	Korea Republic (–4)	88	Estonia (–3)
39	Egypt (–4)	88	Senegal (–1)
40	Saudi Arabia (–2)	90	Bosnia-Herzegovina (+6)
41	Jamaica (–1)	91	Mozambique
42	Japan (–1)	91	Oman (–5)
43	Ivory Coast (+2)	93	Belarus (–4)
44	Iran (+3)	94	Albania (–2)
45	Ghana	95	Canada (–2)
46	Hungary (–4)	96	Congo (–2)
46	Iceland (+2)	97	Azerbaijan (+6)
48	Cameroon (–6)	98	Moldova (+2)
49	Ecuador (+6)	99	Liberia (–5)
50	Lithuania (+3)	100	Kenya (–3)

NATIONAL REFEREES 1999-2000

Steve Bennett (Orpington), Andy D'Urso (Billericay), Mark Halsey (Welwyn Garden City), Barry Knight (Orpington) and Alan Wiley (Burntwood) are all promoted to a 22-man Premier League list.

Match fees – Premier League and F.A. Cup (from 3rd round) referees £600 (previously £400); assistant referees £225 (£175). Nationwide Football League referees (unchanged) £195 ; assistant referees (unchanged) £95.

▲ ALCOCK, Paul (Halstead, Kent)
　 BAINES, Steve (Chesterfield)
†▲ BARBER, Graham (Tring, Herts)
▲ BARRY, Neale (Scunthorpe)
　 BATES, Tony (Stoke-on-Trent)
★ BEEBY, Richard (Northampton)
▲ BENNETT, Steve (Orpington, Kent)
　 BRANDWOOD, John (Lichfield, Staffs.)
　 BURNS, Bill (Scarborough)
　 BUTLER, Alan (Sutton-in-Ashfield)
　 CABLE, Lee (Woking)
　 CAIN, George (Seaforth, Merseyside)
　 COWBURN, Mark (Blackpool)
　 CRICK, David (Worcester Park, Surrey)
　 DANSON, Paul (Leicester)
　 DEAN, Mike (Heswall, Wirral)
　 DOWD, Phil (Stoke-on-Trent)
†▲ DUNN, Steve (Bristol)
†▲ DURKIN, Paul (Portland, Dorset)
▲ D'URSO, Andy (Billericay, Essex)
†▲ ELLERAY, David (Harrow-on-the-Hill)
　 FLETCHER, Mick (Warley, West Midlands)
　 FOY, Chris (St Helens, Merseyside)
　 FRANKLAND, Graham (Middlesbrough)
　 FURNANDIZ, Roger (Doncaster)
†▲ GALLAGHER, Dermot (Banbury, Oxon)
　 HALL, Andy (Birmingham)
★▲ HALSEY, Mark (Welwyn Garden City, Herts.)
▲ HARRIS, Rob (Oxford)
　 HEILBRON, Terry (Newton Aycliffe)
　 HILL, Keith (Royston, Herts)
　 JONES, Michael (Chester)
†▲ JONES, Peter (Loughborough)
　 JONES, Trevor (Barrow-in-Furness)
　 JORDAN, Bill (Tring, Herts)
★ JOSLIN, Phil (Newark, Nottinghamshire)

★ KAYE, Alan (Wakefield)
　 KIRKBY, John (Sheffield)
▲ KNIGHT, Barry (Orpington, Kent)
　 LAWS, David (Whitley Bay)
　 LAWS, Graham (Whitley Bay)
　 LEACH, Ken (Codsall, Staffs)
　 LEAKE, Tony (Darwen, Lancashire)
▲ LODGE, Steve (Barnsley)
　 LOMAS, Eddie (Manchester)
　 LYNCH, Kevin (Kirk Hammerton, Nr York)
　 MATHIESON, Scott (Stockport)
　 MESSIAS, Matt (York)
　 OLIVER, Ray (Sutton Coldfield)
★ PARKES, Trevor (Birmingham)
　 PEARSON, Roy (Peterlee, Durham)
　 PIKE, Mike (Barrow-in-Furness)
†▲ POLL, Graham (Tring, Hertfordshire)
　 PUGH, David (Bebington, Wirral)
▲ REED, Mike (Birmingham)
　 REJER, Paul (Tipton, West Midlands)
▲ RENNIE, Uriah (Sheffield)
　 RICHARDS, Phil (Preston)
†▲ RILEY, Mike (Leeds)
　 ROBINSON, Paul (Hull)
★ RYAN, Michael (Preston)
　 STRETTON, Frazer (Nottingham)
　 STYLES, Rob (Waterlooville, Hants.)
　 TAYLOR, Paul (Cheshunt, Hertfordshire)
★ TOMLIN, Steve (Lewes, East Sussex)
　 WALTON, Peter (Long Buckby, Northants)
　 WARREN, Mark (Walsall)
▲ WILEY, Alan (Burntwood, Staffs.)
　 WILKES, Clive (Gloucester)
▲ WILKIE, Alan (Chester-le-Street)
†▲ WILLARD, Gary (Worthing, W. Sussex)
▲ WINTER, Jeff (Stockton-on-Tees)
　 WOLSTENHOLME, Eddie (Blackburn)

(† FIFA list; ▲ Premier League; ★ First season)

EUROPEAN CUP FINALS

1956	Real Madrid 4, Rheims 3 (Paris)
1957	Real Madrid 2, Fiorentina 0 (Madrid)
1958†	Real Madrid 3, AC Milan 2 (Brussels)
1959	Real Madrid 2, Rheims 0 (Stuttgart)
1960	Real Madrid 7, Eintracht Frankfurt 3 (Glasgow)
1961	Benfica 3, Barcelona 2 (Berne)
1962	Benfica 5, Real Madrid 3 (Amsterdam)
1963	AC Milan 2, Benfica 1 (Wembley)
1964	Inter Milan 3, Real Madrid 1 (Vienna)
1965	Inter Milan 1, Benfica 0 (Milan)
1966	Real Madrid 2, Partizan Belgrade 1 (Brussels)
1967	Celtic 2, Inter Milan 1 (Lisbon)
1968†	Manchester Utd. 4, Benfica 1 (Wembley)
1969	AC Milan 4, Ajax 1 (Madrid)
1970†	Feyenoord 2, Celtic 1 (Milan)
1971	Ajax 2, Panathinaikos 0 (Wembley)
1972	Ajax 2, Inter Milan 0 (Rotterdam)
1973	Ajax 1, Juventus 0 (Belgrade)
1974	Bayern Munich 4, Atletico Madrid 0 (replay Brussels, after a 1-1 draw, Brussels)
1975	Bayern Munich 2, Leeds Utd. 0 (Paris)
1976	Bayern Munich 1, St. Etienne 0 (Glasgow)
1977	Liverpool 3, Borussia Moenchengladbach 1 (Rome)
1978	Liverpool 1, Brugge 0 (Wembley)
1979	Nott'm. Forest 1, Malmo 0 (Munich)
1980	Nott'm. Forest 1, Hamburg 0 (Madrid)
1981	Liverpool 1, Real Madrid 0 (Paris)
1982	Aston Villa 1, Bayern Munich 0 (Rotterdam)
1983	SV Hamburg 1, Juventus 0 (Athens)
1984†	Liverpool 1, AS Roma 1 (Liverpool won 4-2 on penalties) (Rome)
1985	Juventus 1, Liverpool 0 (Brussels)
1986†	Steaua Bucharest 0, Barcelona 0 (Steaua won 2-0 on penalties) (Seville)
1987	Porto 2, Bayern Munich 1 (Vienna)
1988†	PSV Eindhoven 0, Benfica 0 (PSV won 6-5 on penalties) (Stuttgart)
1989	AC Milan 4, Steaua Bucharest 0 (Barcelona)
1990	AC Milan 1, Benfica 0 (Vienna)
1991†	Red Star Belgrade 0, Marseille 0 (Red Star won 5-3 on penalties) (Bari)
1992	Barcelona 1, Sampdoria 0 (Wembley)
1993	Marseille 1, AC Milan 0 (Munich)
1994	AC Milan 4, Barcelona 0 (Athens)
1995	Ajax 1, AC Milan 0 (Vienna)
1996†	Juventus 1, Ajax 1 (Juventus won 4-2 on penalties) (Rome)
1997	Borussia Dortmund 3, Juventus 1 (Munich)
1998	Real Madrid 1, Juventus 0 (Amsterdam)
1999	Manchester Utd. 2, Bayern Munich 1 (Barcelona)

(† After extra time)

EUROPEAN CUP FINAL

Bayern Munich 1, Manchester Utd. 2

Nou Camp, Barcelona, (90,000), Wednesday May 26, 1999

Bayern Munich: Kahn (Capt.), Matthaus (Fink 79), Babbel, Linke, Kuffour, Tarnat, Jeremies, Effenberg, Basler (Salihamidzic 88), Jancker, Zickler (Scholl 70). **Scorer:** Basler (6). **Booked:** Effenberg.

Manchester Utd.: Schmeichel (Capt.), G. Neville, Irwin, Stam, Johnsen, Beckham, Giggs, Butt, Blomqvist (Sheringham 66), Cole (Solskjaer 80), Yorke. **Scorers:** Sheringham (90), Solskjaer (90).

Referee: P Collina (Italy). **Half-time:** 1-0.

CUP-WINNERS' CUP FINALS

1961	Fiorentina beat Rangers 4-1 on agg. (2-0 Glasgow first leg, 2-1 Florence second leg)
1962	Atletico Madrid beat Fiorentina 3-0 (replay Stuttgart, after a 1-1 draw, Glasgow)
1963	Tottenham beat Atletico Madrid 5-1 (Rotterdam)
1964	Sporting Lisbon beat MTK Budapest 1-0 (replay Antwerp, after a 3-3 draw, Brussels)
1965	West Ham Utd. beat Munich 1860 2-0 (Wembley)
1966†	Borussia Dortmund beat Liverpool 2-1 (Glasgow)
1967†	Bayern Munich beat Rangers 1-0 (Nuremberg)
1968	AC Milan beat SV Hamburg 2-0 (Rotterdam)
1969	Slovan Bratislava beat Barcelona 3-2 (Basle)
1970	Manchester City beat Gornik Zabrze 2-1 (Vienna)
1971†	Chelsea beat Real Madrid 2-1 (replay Athens, after a 1-1 draw, Athens)
1972	Rangers beat Moscow Dynamo 3-2 (Barcelona)
1973	AC Milan beat Leeds Utd. 1-0 (Salonika)
1974	Magdeburg beat AC Milan 2-0 (Rotterdam)
1975	Dynamo Kiev beat Ferencvaros 3-0 (Basle)
1976	Anderlecht beat West Ham Utd. 4-2 (Brussels)
1977	SV Hamburg beat Anderlecht 2-0 (Amsterdam)
1978	Anderlecht beat Austria WAC 4-0 (Paris)
1979†	Barcelona beat Fortuna Dusseldorf 4-3 (Basle)
1980†	Valencia beat Arsenal 5-4 on penalties after a 0-0 draw (Brussels)
1981	Dynamo Tbilisi beat Carl Zeiss Jena 2-1 (Dusseldorf)
1982	Barcelona beat Standard Liege 2-1 (Barcelona)
1983†	Aberdeen beat Real Madrid 2-1 (Gothenburg)
1984	Juventus beat Porto 2-1 (Basle)
1985	Everton beat Rapid Vienna 3-1 (Rotterdam)
1986	Dynamo Kiev beat Atletico Madrid 3-0 (Lyon)
1987	Ajax beat Lokomotiv Leipzig 1-0 (Athens)
1988	Mechelen beat Ajax 1-0 (Strasbourg)
1989	Barcelona beat Sampdoria 2-0 (Berne)
1990	Sampdoria beat Anderlecht 2-0 (Gothenburg)
1991	Manchester Utd. beat Barcelona 2-1 (Rotterdam)
1992	Werder Bremen beat Monaco 2-0 (Lisbon)
1993	Parma beat Royal Antwerp 3-1 (Wembley)
1994	Arsenal beat Parma 1-0 (Copenhagen)
1995†	Real Zaragoza beat Arsenal 2-1 (Paris)

1996	Paris St. Germain beat Rapid Vienna 1-0 (Brussels)
1997	Barcelona beat Paris St. Germain 1-0 (Rotterdam)
1998	Chelsea beat VfB Stuttgart 1-0 (Stockholm)
1999	Lazio beat Real Mallorca 2-1 (Villa Park, Birmingham)

(† After extra time)

CUP-WINNERS' CUP FINAL

Lazio 2, Real Mallorca 1

Villa Park, Birmingham, (33,021), Wednesday, May 19, 1999

Lazio: Marchegiani, Pancaro, Nesta (Capt.), Mihajlovic, Favalli, D. Stankovic (Conceicao 56), Mancini (Couto 90), Almeyda, Nedved (Lombardo 84), Vieri, Salas. **Scorers:** Vieri (7), Nedved (81). **Booked:** Mihajlovic, Vieri, Marchegiani.

Real Mallorca: Roa, Olaizola, Marcelino, Siviero, Miguel Soler (Capt.), Lauren, Ibagaza, Engonga, J. Stankovic, Dani, Biagini (Paunovic 74). **Scorer:** Dani (11). **Booked:** Siviero.

Referee: G Benko (Austria). **Half-time:** 1-1.

UEFA CUP FINALS

1972	Tottenham beat Wolves 3-2 on agg. (2-1a, 1-1h)
1973	Liverpool beat Borussia Moenchengladbach 3-2 on agg. (3-0h, 0-2a)
1974	Feyenoord beat Tottenham 4-2 on agg. (2-2a, 2-0h)
1975	Borussia Moenchengladbach beat Twente Enschede 5-1 on agg. (0-0h, 5-1a)
1976	Liverpool beat Brugge 4-3 on agg. (3-2h, 1-1a)
1977	Juventus beat Atletico Bilbao on away goals after 2-2 agg. (1-0h, 1-2a)
1978	PSV Eindhoven beat Bastia 3-0 on agg. (0-0a, 3-0h)
1979	Borussia Moenchengladbach beat Red Star Belgrade 2-1 on agg. (1-1a, 1-0h)
1980	Eintracht Frankfurt beat Borussia Moenchengladbach on away goals after 3-3 agg. (2-3a, 1-0h)
1981	Ipswich Town beat AZ 67 Alkmaar 5-4 on agg. (3-0h, 2-4a)
1982	IFK Gothenburg beat SV Hamburg 4-0 on agg. (1-0h, 3-0a)
1983	Anderlecht beat Benfica 2-1 on agg. (1-0h, 1-1a)
1984	Tottenham beat Anderlecht 4-3 on penalties after 2-2 agg. (1-1a, 1-1h)
1985	Real Madrid beat Videoton 3-1 on agg. (3-0a, 0-1h)
1986	Real Madrid beat Cologne 5-3 on agg. (5-1h, 0-2a)
1987	IFK Gothenburg beat Dundee Utd. 2-1 on agg. (1-0h, 1-1a)
1988	Bayer Leverkusen beat Espanol 3-2 on penalties after 3-3 agg. (0-3a, 3-0h)
1989	Napoli beat VfB Stuttgart 5-4 on agg. (2-1h, 3-3a)
1990	Juventus beat Fiorentina 3-1 on agg. (3-1h, 0-0a)
1991	Inter Milan beat AS Roma 2-1 on agg. (2-0h, 0-1a)
1992	Ajax beat Torino on away goals after 2-2 agg. (2-2a, 0-0h)
1993	Juventus beat Borussia Dortmund 6-1 on agg. (3-1a, 3-0h)
1994	Inter Milan beat Salzburg 2-0 on agg. (1-0a, 1-0h)
1995	Parma beat Juventus 2-1 on agg. (1-0h, 1-1a)
1996	Bayern Munich beat Bordeaux 5-1 on agg. (2-0h, 3-1a)

1997	FC Schalke beat Inter Milan 4-1 on penalties after 1-1 agg. (1-0h, 0-1a)
1998	Inter Milan beat Lazio 3-0 (one match only)
1999	Parma beat Marseille 3-0 (one match only)

FAIRS CUP FINALS

(As UEFA Cup previously known)

1958	Barcelona beat London 8-2 on agg. (2-2a, 6-0h)
1960	Barcelona beat Birmingham 4-1 on agg. (0-0a, 4-1h)
1961	AS Roma beat Birmingham City 4-2 on agg. (2-2a, 2-0h)
1962	Valencia beat Barcelona 7-3 on agg. (6-2h, 1-1a)
1963	Valencia beat Dynamo Zagreb 4-1 on agg. (2-1a, 2-0h)
1964	Real Zaragoza beat Valencia 2-1 (Barcelona)
1965	Ferencvaros beat Juventus 1-0 (Turin)
1966	Barcelona beat Real Zaragoza 4-3 on agg. (0-1h, 4-2a)
1967	Dynamo Zagreb beat Leeds Utd. 2-0 on agg. (2-0h, 0-0a)
1968	Leeds Utd. beat Ferencvaros 1-0 on agg. (1-0h, 0-0a)
1969	Newcastle Utd. beat Ujpest Dozsa 6-2 on agg. (3-0h, 3-2a)
1970	Arsenal beat Anderlecht 4-3 on agg. (1-3a, 3-0h)
1971	Leeds Utd. beat Juventus on away goals after 3-3 agg. (2-2a, 1-1h)

UEFA CUP FINAL

Parma 3, Marseille 0

Luzhniki Stadium, Moscow, (61,000), Wednesday, May 12, 1999

Parma: Buffon, Thuram, Sensini, Cannavaro (Capt.), Fuser, D. Baggio, Boghossian, Vanoli, Veron (Fiore 76), Chiesa (Balbo 72), Crespo (Asprilla 84). **Scorers:** Crespo (26), Vanoli (36), Chiesa (55). **Booked:** Asprilla.

Marseille: Porato, Blondeau, Blanc (Capt.), Domoraud, Edson da Silva (Camara 46), Pires, Brando, Issa, Bravo, Gourvennec, Maurice. **Booked:** Blondeau.

Referee: H Dallas (Scotland). **Half-time:** 2-0.

BRITISH AND IRISH CLUBS IN EUROPE 1998-99

EUROPEAN CUP

For details see separate section.

CUP-WINNERS' CUP

Qualifying round: Hearts beat FC Lantana Tallinn (Est) 6-0 (5-0h, 1-0a), CSKA Kiev (Ukr) beat **Cork City** (Rep. of Ireland) 3-2 (2-0h, 1-2a), FC Haka (Fin) beat **Bangor City** (Wales) 3-0 (1-0h, 2-0a), Maccabi Haifa (Israel) beat **Glentoran** 3-1 (2-1h, 1-0a)

First round: Chelsea beat Helsingborgs (Swe) 1-0 (1-0h, 0-0a), Partizan Belgrade beat **Newcastle Utd.** on away goals 2-2 (1-0h, 1-2a), Real Mallorca beat **Hearts** 2-1 (1-1h, 1-0a)

Second round: Chelsea beat FC Copenhagen 2-1 (1-1h, 1-0a)

Quarter-final: Chelsea beat Valerenga (Nor) 6-2 (3-0h, 3-2a)

Semi-final: Real Mallorca beat **Chelsea** 2-1 (1-0h, 1-1a)

UEFA CUP

First qualifying round: Rangers beat **Shelbourne** (Rep. of Ireland) 7-3 (2-0h, 5-3a), **Kilmarnock** beat Zeljeznicar Sarajevo (Bos) 2-1 (1-0h, 1-1a), Wisla Krakow (Pol) beat **Newtown** (Wales) 7-0 (7-0h, 0-0a), Omonia Nicosia (Cyp) beat **Linfield** 8-6 (5-1h, 3-5a)

Second qualifying round: Rangers beat PAOK (Gre) 2-0 (2-0h, 0-0a), Sigma Olomouc (Czech) beat **Kilmarnock** 4-0 (2-0h, 2-0a)

First round: Liverpool beat FC Kosice (Slovakia) 8-0 (5-0h, 3-0a), **Aston Villa** beat Stromsgodset (Nor) 6-2 (3-2h, 3-0a), **Leeds Utd.** beat Maritimo (Por) 4-1 on pens (1-0h, 0-1a), **Rangers** beat Beitar Jerusalem (Israel) 5-3 (4-2h, 1-1a), **Celtic** beat Vitoria Guimaraes (Por) 4-2 (2-1h, 2-1a), Lyon beat **Blackburn Rov.** 3-2 (2-2h, 1-0a)

Second round: Liverpool beat Valencia on away goals 2-2 (0-0h, 2-2a), Celta Vigo (Sp) beat **Aston Villa** 3-2 (0-1h, 3-1a), **Rangers** beat Bayer Leverkusen 3-2 (1-1h, 2-1a), Roma beat **Leeds Utd.** 1-0 (1-0h, 0-0a), FC Zurich beat **Celtic** 5-3 (4-2h, 1-1a)

Third round: Celta Vigo (Sp) beat **Liverpool** 4-1 (3-1h, 1-0a), Parma beat **Rangers** 4-2 (3-1h, 1-1a)

WORLD CLUB CUP 1998 FINAL
(Sponsored by Toyota)

REAL MADRID (Spain) 2, VASCO DA GAMA (Brazil) 1

Tokyo (51,514), Tuesday, December 1, 1998

Real Madrid: Illgner, Panucci, Hierro, Sanchis, Sanz, Roberto Carlos, Redondo, Seedorf, Raul, Savio, Mijatovic. **Scorers**: Naza (og 25) Raul (83). **Coach**: Guus Hiddink.

Vasco da Gama: Carlos Germano, Mauro Galvao, Odvan, Felipe, Luizinho, Naza, Ramon, Vagner, Juninho, Donizete, Luizao. **Scorer**: Juninho (57). **Coach**: Antonio Lopes.

COMPLETE RESULTS

Year	Winners	Runners-up	Score		
1960	Real Madrid (Spa.)	Penarol (Uru.)	0-0	5-1	
1961	Penarol (Uru.)	Benfica (Por.)	0-1	2-1	5-0
1962	Santos (Bra.)	Benfica (Por.)	3-2	5-2	
1963	Santos (Bra.)	AC Milan (Ita.)	2-4	4-2	1-0
1964	Inter Milan (Ita.)	Independiente (Arg.)	0-1	2-0	1-0
1965	Inter Milan (Ita.)	Independiente (Arg.)	3-0	0-0	

1966	Penarol (Uru.)	Real Madrid (Spa.)	2-0 2-0
1967	Racing (Arg.)	Celtic (Sco.)	0-1 2-1 1-0
1968	Estudiantes (Arg.)	Manchester Utd. (Eng.)	1-0 1-1
1969	AC Milan (Ita.)	Estudiantes (Arg.)	3-0 1-2
1970	Feyenoord (Hol.)	Estudiantes (Arg.)	2-2 1-0
1971	Nacional (Uru.)	Panathanaikos (Gre.)*	1-1 2-1
1972	Ajax (Hol.)	Independiente (Arg.)	1-1 3-0
1973	Independiente (Arg.)	Juventus (Ita.)*	1-0 #
1974	Atletico Madrid (Spa.)*	Independiente (Arg.)	0-1 2-0
1975	Not played		
1976	Bayern Munich (W.Ger.)	Cruzeiro (Bra.)	2-0 0-0
1977	Boca Juniors (Arg.)	Borussia Mönchengladbach (W.Ger.)*	2-2 3-0
1978	Not played		
1979	Olimpia Asuncion (Par.)	Malmö (Swe.)*	1-0 2-1
1980	Nacional (Arg.)	Nott'm. Forest (Eng.)	1-0
1981	Flamengo (Bra.)	Liverpool (Eng.)	3-0
1982	Penarol (Uru.)	Aston Villa (Eng.)	2-0
1983	Porto Alegre (Bra.)	SV Hamburg (W.Ger.)	2-1
1984	Independiente (Arg.)	Liverpool (Eng.)	1-0
1985	Juventus (Ita.)	Argentinos Juniors (Arg.)	2-2 (aet)
	(Juventus won 4-2 on penalties)		
1986	River Plate (Arg.)	Steaua Bucharest (Rum.)	1-0
1987	Porto (Por.)	Penarol (Uru.)	2-1 (aet)
1988	Nacional (Uru.)	PSV Eindhoven (Hol.)	1-1 (aet)
	(Nacional won 7-6 on penalties)		
1989	AC Milan (Ita.)	Nacional (Col.)	1-0 (aet)
1990	AC Milan (Ita.)	Olimpia Asuncion (Par.)	3-0
1991	Red Star (Yug.)	Colo Colo (Chi.)	3-0
1992	Sao Paulo (Bra.)	Barcelona (Spa.)	2-1
1993	Sao Paulo (Bra.)	AC Milan (Ita.)	3-2
1994	Velez Sarsfield (Arg.)	AC Milan (Ita.)	2-0
1995	Ajax (Hol.)	Gremio (Bra.)	0-0 (aet)
	(Ajax won 4-3 on penalties)		
1996	Juventus (Ita.)	River Plate (Arg.)	1-0
1997	Borussia Dortmund (Ger.)	Cruzeiro (Arg.)	2-0
1998	Real Madrid (Spa.)	Vasco da Gama (Bra.)	2-1

Played as a single match in Tokyo since 1980
* European Cup runners-up. # One match only.
Summary: 37 contests; South America 20 wins, Europe 17 wins.

TAYLOR TOPS EARNINGS LEAGUE

Gordon Taylor of the Professional Footballers' Association emerged as the highest paid union boss in England according to a report published in March.

The annual report of the Official Certification Officer revealed that figures taken from 1998 union accounts placed Taylor top with a £252,704 salary plus benefits worth £120,000.

Taylor finished way ahead of union chiefs like Doug McAvoy (National Union of Teachers-£72,249) and Arthur Scargill (National Union of Mineworkers-£69,642).

EUROPE'S TOP CLUBS 1998-99

AIK Stockholm achieved the remarkable feat of winning their national championship despite scoring only 25 goals in 26 matches. All the other 13 top-division clubs in Sweden scored more, but AIK finished two points clear of Helsingborg – and won the Swedish Cup as well.

This is thought to be the first time a club has won a title without averaging better than a goal a game.

Rosenborg Trondheim won the Norwegian championship for the seventh successive season. Porto won the Portuguese title for the fifth time running, and the eighth in the 1990s.

Country	Champions	P	W	D	L	F	A	P
Austria	Sturm Graz	36	23	4	9	73	32	70
Belgium	Genk	34	22	7	5	74	38	73
Bulgaria	Litex Lovech	30	24	4	2	83	25	76
Czech Republic	Sparta Prague	30	17	9	4	63	23	60
Denmark	AaB	33	17	13	3	65	30	64
England	Manchester Utd.	38	22	13	3	80	37	79
France	Bordeaux	34	22	6	6	66	29	72
Georgia	Dinamo Tbilisi	30	24	5	1	91	17	77
Germany	Bayern Munich	34	24	6	4	76	28	78
Greece	Olympiakos	34	27	4	3	82	21	85
Holland	Feyenoord	34	25	5	4	76	38	80
Hungary	MTK Hungaria	32	26	2	4	75	25	80
Israel	Hapoil Haifa	30	22	5	3	66	23	71
Italy	AC Milan	34	20	10	4	59	34	70
Malta	Valletta	27	23	1	3	71	23	70
Northern Ireland	Glentoran	36	24	6	6	74	35	78
Norway	Rosenborg Trondheim	26	20	3	3	79	23	63
Poland	Wislaw Krakow	30	23	4	3	75	23	73
Portugal	Porto	34	24	7	3	85	26	79
Rep. of Ireland	St. Patrick's	33	22	7	4	58	21	73
Romania	Rapid Bucharest	34	28	5	1	79	18	89
Russia	Spartak Moscow	30	17	8	5	58	27	59
Scotland	Rangers	36	23	8	5	78	31	77
Spain	Barcelona	36	24	7	7	87	43	79
Sweden	AIK Stockholm	26	11	13	2	25	15	46
Turkey	Galatasaray	34	23	9	2	85	30	78
Ukraine	Kiev Dynamo	30	23	5	2	75	17	74
Wales	Barry Town	32	23	7	2	82	23	76
Yugoslavia	Partizan Belgrade	24	21	3	0	59	11	66*

* Programme abandoned with ten games still to play.

Others: **Albania**, FK Tirana; **Andorra**, CE Principat; **Armenia**, Ararat Yerevan; **Azerbaijan**, Kapaz Ganja; **Belarus**, Dnepr-Transmash; **Croatia**, Croatia Zagreb; **Cyprus**, Anorthosis Famagusta; **Estonia**, Flora Tallinn; **Faroe Islands**, IB Torshavn; **Iceland**, IBV Vestmannaeyjar; **Latvia**, Skonto Riga; **Lithuania**, Zalgiris Vilnius; **Luxembourg**, Jeunesse Esch; **Macedonia**, Sloga Jugomagnat Skopje; **Moldova**, Zimbrau Chisinau; **San Marino**, Faetano; **Slovakia**, Slovan Bratislava; **Slovenia**, Maribor Teatanic.

EUROPEAN CHAMPIONSHIP GUIDE

COUNTDOWN TO EURO 2000 – BELGIUM AND HOLLAND

The first European Championship finals of the new Millennium will see the tournament hosted jointly for the first time in its 42-year history. The expansion of UEFA produced a **record entry** of 51 teams, an increase of three from 1996. Two of these, Bosnia-Herzegovina (who beat Italy in a friendly in November 1996) and Andorra, are new to European competition.

Only 16 countries qualify for the finals, including hosts Holland and Belgium, the same number as competed in England in Euro 96. The tournament now has twice as many teams as it did in Sweden in 1992, when there were eight countries and 15 matches.

The countdown to the finals will begin in earnest after the two-legged **play-offs** for the group runners-up, which complete the qualifying stage. The first leg play-off matches will take place on November 13 and 14 and the return legs on November 17. The **draw for the finals** will take place at 3pm on December 12 at the Exhibition Park in Brussels. It will last about 35 minutes and be broadcast across Europe. Belgium will play the first match of the finals on Saturday June 10, 2000, in the King Baudoin Stadium in Brussels.

In the beginning: UEFA's executive committee appointed Holland and Belgium as co-hosts for Euro 2000 in July 1995. The draw for the qualifying round was made in the Belgian city of Ghent on January 18, 1998, by Johan Cruyff and former Belgian international Paul van Himst. The opening fixture, Estonia v Faroe Islands (5-0), was played on June 4 1998.

The eight **grounds** to be used for the finals are: Amsterdam Arena, Amsterdam; Feyenoord Stadium, Rotterdam; Gelredome, Arnhem; Philips Stadium, Eindhoven; Jan Breydel Stadium, Bruges; King Baudoin Stadium, Brussels; Stade Communal, Charleroi; Sclessin Stadium, Liege.

Holland and Belgium will share the group and knock-out matches equally, with the Dutch staging the final at Feyenoord Stadium in Rotterdam.

Qualification: With the two co-hosts qualifying automatically, there are only 14 qualifying places available, a reduction from fifteen in Euro 96. There are nine qualifying groups in all, an increase from eight for Euro 96, with five groups of five teams and four groups of six. The qualifiers for the finals will be the nine group winners, the second placed team with the best record and the winners of four two-legged play-off matches between the other eight group runners-up.

If teams finish **equal** on points after all the group matches the following criteria will be used to determine placings. 1. Greater number of points obtained in the matches between the teams in question. 2. Goal difference resulting from the matches between the teams in question. 3. Greater number of goals scored away from home in the matches between the teams in question. 4. Goal difference (all matches). 5. Greater number of goals scored (all matches). 6. Greater number of goals scored away from home (all matches). 7. Fair play conduct. 8. Drawing of lots.

When the second-placed teams are ranked to determine the teams to qualify for the final round or play-off matches, only the results against teams placed first, third and fourth in the group apply. The criteria are as follows. 1. Number of points obtained against teams placed first, third and fourth in the group. 2. Goal difference from these matches. 3. Greater number of goals scored in these matches. 4. Greater number of goals scored away from home in these matches. 5. Fair play conduct.

FINALS FORMULA

The 16 countries will be drawn in four groups of four. Four countries will be seeded, including Holland, who will be in Group D, and Belgium, in Group B. If Germany qualify for the finals, they will, as reigning European Champions, be seeded as well. The fourth seed (and possibly third seed should Germany not qualify) will be determined based on the results of the qualifying matches for France 98 and EURO 2000.

There will be 24 group fixtures, with the top two teams in each group going through to the quarter-final knock-out stage. Twelve of the 24 group matches will be played in Belgium and 12 in Holland. The quarter finals will take place in Amsterdam, Bruges, Brussels and Rotterdam. The semi finals will be played in Brussels and in Amsterdam. Each stadium will host three first round matches.

Points in the group matches will be 3 for a win, 1 for a draw. **Sudden death** will apply in the knock-out stages when scores are level after 90 minutes – first goal in extra time will end play. **Shoot outs:** If there is no decision after 30 minutes extra time, the tie will be decided on penalties.

Tickets: Around 1.2million tickets will be available for the 31 matches. Demand far exceeded supply when the first batch of 400,000 tickets (34% of total stadium capacity) went on sale in March 1999 and there were applications for 1,050,000 tickets. By June 1999, 15 of the 31 matches were already sold out and more than 80 per cent of tickets destined for the general public had been sold, with applicants entered into a draw to decide who would be successful. Ticket information on 00 31 900 0055(Holland) or 00 32 900 00299(Belgium).

Euro 2000 betting (William Hill): 4-1 Holland; 5-1 Italy; 13-2 France; 8-1 Germany; 9-1 Spain; 12-1 Sweden; 20-1 England, Czech Republic, Norway, Portugal, Yugoslavia; 25-1 Belgium, Romania; 28-1 Ukraine, 33-1 Croatia, Russia; 50-1 Poland; 80-1 Republic of Ireland; 100-1 bar.

EURO 2000: SCHEDULE OF MATCHES

Group A: Liege, Charleroi, Eindhoven, Rotterdam, Arnhem.
Group B: Brussels, Arnhem, Eindhoven.
Group C: Rotterdam, Charleroi, Amsterdam, Liege, Bruges, Arnhem.
Group D: Amsterdam, Rotterdam, Bruges, Liege.

FIRST ROUND

No.	Date	Match	Venue	Time
1.	Saturday June 10	B1 v B2	King Baudoin Stadium	8.45pm
2.	Sunday June 11	B3 v B4	Gelredome	2.30pm
3.		D3 v D4	Jan Breydel Stadium	6pm
4.		D1 v D2	Amsterdam Arena	8.45pm
5.	Monday June 12	A1 v A2	Sclessin Stadium	6pm
6.		A3 v A4	Philips Stadium	8.45pm
7.	Tuesday June 13	C1 v C2	Feyenoord Stadium	6pm
8.		C3 v C4	Stade Communal	8.45pm
9.	Wednesday June 14	B4 v B1	King Baudoin Stadium	8.45pm
10.	Thursday June 15	B2 v B3	Philips Stadium	8.45pm
11.	Friday June 16	D2 v D3	Jan Breydel Stadium	6pm
12.		D4 v D1	Feyenoord Stadium	8.45pm
13.	Saturday June 17	A2 v A3	Gelredome	6pm
14.		A4 v A1	Stade Communal	8.45pm
15.	Sunday June 18	C4 v C1	Amsterdam Arena	6pm
16.		C2 v C3	Sclessin Stadium	8.45pm
17.	Monday June 19	B3 v B1	King Baudoin Stadium	8.45pm
18.		B4 v B2	Philips Stadium	8.45pm
19.	Tuesday June 20	A4 v A2	Stade Communal	8.45pm
20.		A3 v A1	Feyenoord Stadium	8.45pm
21.	Wednesday June 21	C3 v C1	Jan Breydel Stadium	6pm
22.		C4 v C2	Gelredome	6pm
23.		D4 v D2	Sclessin Stadium	8.45pm
24.		D3 v D1	Amsterdam Arena	8.45pm

QUARTER-FINALS

25.	Saturday June 24	BII v AI	Amsterdam Arena	6pm
26.		BI v AII	King Baudoin Stadium	8.45pm
27.	Sunday June 25	DI v CII	Feyenoord Stadium	6pm
28.		CI v DII	Jan Breydel Stadium	8.45pm

SEMI-FINALS

| 29. | Wednesday June 28 | 25 v 28 | King Baudoin Stadium | 8.45pm |
| 30. | Thursday June 29 | 26 v 27 | Amsterdam Arena | 8.45pm |

FINAL

| 31. | Sunday July 2 | | Feyenoord Stadium | 6pm |

KEY: B1 – Belgium, D1 – Holland

HISTORY

After the World Cup, the European Championship is football's most prestigious tournament. It was launched in 1958 and the trophy is the Henri Delaunay Cup, named after its French founder.

Later known as the Nations Cup and, since 1966, as the European Championship, the tournament spans two years, with the final exactly midway between one World Cup and the next. Eight countries have won the ten finals, with Germany (previously playing as West Germany) the only country to have won it more than once with victories in 1972, 1980 and 1996. They completed their third triumph in 1996 when Oliver Bierhoff scored the first ever extra time 'Golden Goal' in a 2-1 win over the Czech Republic at Wembley.

Year	Venue	Winners	Runners-up
1960	Paris	*U.S.S.R 2	Yugoslavia 1
1964	Madrid	Spain 2	U.S.S.R 1
1968	Rome	Italy 2	Yugoslavia 0
(replay, after 1-1 draw)			
1972	Brussels	West Germany 3	U.S.S.R 0
1976	Belgrade	*Czechoslovakia 2	West Germany 2
(Czechoslovakia won 5-3 on penalties)			
1980	Rome	West Germany 2	Belgium 1
1984	Paris	France 2	Spain 0
1988	Munich	Holland 2	U.S.S.R 0
1992	Gothenburg	Denmark 2	Germany 0
1996	London	+Germany 2	Czech Republic 1*
(*After extra time; +decided in overtime)			

Record scorer in the European Championship final series: Michel Platini with 9 goals when he captained France to victory in 1984. He scored in all five games.

QUALIFYING GROUPS

(As at start of season 1999-2000)

GROUP 1

	P	W	D	L	F	A	Pts
Italy	6	4	2	0	11	2	14
Denmark	6	2	2	2	6	5	8
Switzerland	5	2	2	1	4	3	8
Wales	6	2	0	4	5	13	6
Belarus	5	0	2	3	3	6	2

Results: Wales 0 Italy 2, Belarus 0 Denmark 0, Denmark 1 Wales 2, Italy 2 Switzerland 0, Wales 3 Belarus 2, Switzerland 1 Denmark 1, Belarus 0 Switzerland 1, Denmark 1 Italy 2, Switzerland 2 Wales 0, Italy 1 Belarus 1, Denmark 1 Belarus 0, Italy 4 Wales 0, Wales 0 Denmark 2, Switzerland 0 Italy 0.
To play: Sept. 4 Belarus v Wales, Denmark v Switzerland; Sept. 8 Italy v Denmark, Switzerland v Belarus; Oct. 9 Belarus v Italy, Wales v Switzerland.

GROUP 2

	P	W	D	L	F	A	Pts
Norway	7	5	1	1	14	8	16
Slovenia	6	3	2	1	8	6	11
Latvia	7	3	2	2	7	5	11
Greece	7	2	3	2	8	7	9
Georgia	7	1	1	5	4	12	4
Albania	6	0	3	3	3	6	3

Results: Georgia 1 Albania 0, Greece 2 Slovenia 2, Norway 1 Latvia 3, Latvia 1 Georgia 0, Slovenia 1 Norway 2, Greece 3 Georgia 0, Norway 2 Albania 2, Slovenia 1 Latvia 0, Albania 0 Greece 0, Greece 0 Norway 2, Georgia 1 Slovenia 1, Latvia 0 Greece 0, Latvia 0 Albania 0, Georgia 1 Norway 4, Norway 1 Georgia 0, Albania 1 Norway 2, Latvia 1 Slovenia 2, Georgia 1 Greece 2, Albania 0 Slovenia 1, Greece 1 Latvia 2.
To play: Aug. 18 Slovenia v Albania; Sept. 4 Norway v Greece, Albania v Latvia, Slovenia v Georgia; Sept. 8 Greece v Albania, Georgia v Latvia, Norway v Slovenia; Oct. 9 Slovenia v Greece, Latvia v Norway, Albania v Georgia.

GROUP 3

	P	W	D	L	F	A	Pts
Germany	5	4	0	1	14	3	12
Turkey	5	4	0	1	11	5	12
Finland	6	2	1	3	8	10	7
N Ireland	5	1	2	2	3	8	5
Moldova	7	0	3	4	6	16	3

Results: Finland 3 Moldova 2, Turkey 3 N Ireland 0, N Ireland 1 Finland 0, Turkey 1 Germany 0, Turkey 1 Finland 3, Moldova 1 Germany 3, N Ireland 2 Moldova 2, N Ireland 0 Germany 3, Turkey 2 Moldova 0, Moldova 0 N Ireland 0, Germany 2 Finland 0, Germany 6 Moldova 1, Finland 2 Turkey 4, Moldova 0 Finland 0.
To play: Sept. 4 N Ireland v Turkey, Finland v Germany; Sept. 8 Germany v N Ireland, Moldova v Turkey; Oct. 9 Finland v N Ireland, Germany v Turkey.

GROUP 4

	P	W	D	L	F	A	Pts
Ukraine	7	4	3	0	12	3	15
France	7	4	2	1	11	6	14
Russia	7	4	0	3	17	10	12
Iceland	7	3	3	1	7	3	12
Armenia	7	1	2	4	3	10	5
Andorra	7	0	0	7	2	20	0

Results: Armenia 3 Andorra 1, Iceland 1 France 1, Ukraine 3 Russia 2, Andorra 0 Ukraine 2, Armenia 0 Iceland 0, Russia 2 France 3, Iceland 1 Russia 0, Ukraine 2 Armenia 0, France 2 Andorra 0, Andorra 0 Iceland 2, Armenia 0 Russia 3, France 0 Ukraine 0, Russia 6 Andorra 1, Ukraine 1 Iceland 1, France 2 Armenia 0, Iceland 2 Armenia 0, Ukraine 4 Andorra 0, France 2 Russia 3, Russia 1 Iceland 0, Armenia 0 Ukraine 0, Andorra 0 France 1
To play: Sept. 4 Ukraine v France, Russia v Armenia, Iceland v Andorra; Sept. 8 Armenia v France, Iceland v Ukraine, Andorra v Russia; Oct. 9 France v Iceland, Russia v Ukraine, Andorra v Armenia.

GROUP 5

	P	W	D	L	F	A	Pts
Sweden	5	4	1	0	6	1	13
Poland	6	4	0	2	12	6	12
England	6	2	3	1	8	4	9
Bulgaria	6	1	2	3	3	7	5
Luxembourg	5	0	0	5	2	13	0

Results: Sweden 2 England 1, Bulgaria 0 Poland 3, England 0 Bulgaria 0, Poland 3 Luxembourg 0, Bulgaria 0 Sweden 1, Luxembourg 0 England 3, England 3 Poland 1, Sweden 2 Luxembourg 0, Luxembourg 0 Bulgaria 0, Poland 0 Sweden 1, Poland 2 Bulgaria 0, England 0 Sweden 0, Bulgaria 1 England 1, Luxembourg 2 Poland 3
To play: Sept. 4 Sweden v Bulgaria, England v Luxembourg; Sept. 8 Poland v England, Luxembourg v Sweden; Oct. 9 Sweden v Poland; Oct. 10 Bulgaria v Luxembourg.

GROUP 6

	P	W	D	L	F	A	Pts
Spain	5	4	0	1	28	4	12
Israel	5	3	1	1	15	3	10
Austria	6	3	1	2	15	16	10
Cyprus	5	3	0	2	8	8	9
San Marino	7	0	0	7	1	36	0

Results: Austria 1 Israel 1, Cyprus 3 Spain 2, Cyprus 0 Austria 3, San Marino 0 Israel 5, San Marino 1 Austria 4, Israel 1 Spain 2, San Marino 0 Cyprus 1, Cyprus 4 San Marino 0, Spain 9 Austria 0, Israel 3 Cyprus 0, San Marino 0 Spain 6, Austria 7 San Marino 0, Spain 9 San Marino 0, Israel 5 Austria 0
To play: Sept. 4 Austria v Spain; Sept. 5 Cyprus v Israel; Sept. 8 Spain v Cyprus, Israel v San Marino; Oct. 9 Spain v Israel; Oct. 10 Austria v Cyprus.

GROUP 7

	P	W	D	L	F	A	Pts
Portugal	7	6	0	1	27	2	18
Romania	7	5	2	0	16	1	17
Slovakia	7	3	2	2	8	4	11
Hungary	7	2	2	3	11	7	8
Azerbaijan	7	1	0	6	5	21	3
Liechtenstein	7	1	0	6	2	34	3

Results: Romania 7 Liechtenstein 0, Slovakia 3 Azerbaijan 0, Hungary 1 Portugal 3, Liechtenstein 0 Slovakia 4, Azerbaijan 0 Hungary 4, Portugal 0 Romania 1, Liechtenstein 2 Azerbaijan 1, Hungary 1 Romania 1, Slovakia 0 Portugal 3, Portugal 7 Azerbaijan 0, Hungary 5 Liechtenstein 0, Romania 0 Slovakia 0, Slovakia 0 Hungary 0, Azerbaijan 0 Romania 1, Liechtenstein 0 Portugal 5, Azerbaijan 4 Liechtenstein 0, Portugal 1 Slovakia 0, Romania 2 Hungary 0, Hungary 0 Slovakia 1, Portugal 8 Liechtenstein 0, Romania 4 Azerbaijan 0.
To play: Sept. 3 Azerbaijan v Portugal; Sept. 4 Liechtenstein v Hungary, Slovakia v Romania; Sept. 8 Slovakia v Liechtenstein, Romania v Portugal, Hungary v Azerbaijan; Oct. 9 Liechtenstein v Romania, Azerbaijan v Slovakia; Oct. 10 Portugal v Hungary.

GROUP 8

	P	W	D	L	F	A	Pts
Yugoslavia	3	3	0	0	8	1	9
Rep of Ireland	4	3	0	1	8	1	9
F.Y.R. Macedonia	5	2	1	2	9	6	7
Croatia	4	2	1	1	8	6	7
Malta	6	0	0	6	3	22	0

Results: Rep of Ireland 2 Croatia 0, Macedonia 4 Malta 0, Malta 1 Croatia 4, Croatia 3 Macedonia 2, Rep of Ireland 5 Malta 0, Yugoslavia 1 Rep of Ireland 0, Malta 1 Macedonia 2, Malta 0 Yugoslavia 3, Macedonia 1 Croatia 1, Yugoslavia 4 Malta 1, Rep of Ireland 1 Macedonia 0.
To play: Aug. 18 Yugoslavia v Croatia; Sept. 4 Croatia v Rep of Ireland, Yugoslavia v Macedonia; Sept. 8 Malta v Rep of Ireland, Macedonia v Yugoslavia; Oct. 10 Croatia v Yugoslavia, Macedonia v Rep of Ireland; tba Croatia v Malta, Rep of Ireland v Yugoslavia.

GROUP 9

	P	W	D	L	F	A	Pts
Czech Rep	7	7	0	0	17	5	21
Scotland	6	2	2	2	9	9	8
Bosnia-Herzegovina	6	2	2	2	9	10	8
Lithuania	7	2	2	3	7	9	8
Estonia	7	2	1	4	12	13	7
Faroe Islands	7	0	3	4	4	12	3

Results: Estonia 5 Faroe Islands 0, Bosnia-Herzegovina 1 Faroe Islands 0, Lithuania 0 Scotland 0, Bosnia-Herzegovina 1 Estonia 1, Faroe Islands 0 Czech Rep 1, Scotland 3 Estonia 2, Bosnia-Herzegovina 1 Czech Rep 3, Lithuania 0 Faroe Islands 0, Czech Rep 4 Estonia 1, Scotland 2 Faroe Islands 1, Lithuania 4 Bosnia-Herzegovina 2, Czech Rep 2 Lithuania 0, Lithuania 1 Estonia 2, Scotland 1 Czech Rep 2, Faroe Islands 1 Scotland 1, Estonia 0 Czech Rep 2, Bosnia-Herzegovina 2 Lithuania 0, Faroe Islands 2 Bosnia-Herzegovina 2, Estonia 1 Lithuania 2, Czech Rep 3 Scotland 2.
To play: Sept. 4 Bosnia-Herzegovina v Scotland, Faroe Islands v Estonia, Lithuania v Czech Republic, Sept. 8 Estonia v Scotland, Faroe Islands v Lithuania, Czech Republic v Bosnia-Herzegovina; Oct. 5 Scotland v Bosnia-Herzegovina; Oct. 9 Czech Republic v Faroe Islands, Scotland v Lithuania, Estonia v Bosnia-Herzegovina.

ANDY FRASER

EUROPEAN CHAMPIONS LEAGUE 1998-99

First Qualifying Round: Celtic beat **St Patrick's** (Rep. Of Ireland) 2-0 (0-0h, 2-0a), Dynamo Kiev beat **Barry Town** (Wales) 10-1 (8-0h, 2-1a), FC Kosice beat **Cliftonville** (N. Ireland) 13-1 (8-0h, 5-1a).

Second Qualifying Round: Croatia Zagreb beat **Celtic** 3-1 (3-0h, 0-1a), Manchester Utd. beat LKS Lodz 2-0 (2-0h, 0-0a). **Celtic** to UEFA Cup.

GROUP A

September 16, 1998
FC Porto 2 (Zahovic 64, Jardel 85) **Olympiakos** 2 (Giannakopoulos 87, Gogic 90) Att: 37,000
Croatia Zagreb 0 **Ajax** 0 Att: 30,000

September 30, 1998
Ajax 2 (Rudy 62, Litmanen 86 pen) **FC Porto** 1 (Zahovic 69) Att: 40,000
Olympiakos 2 (Alexandris 22, Gogic 81) **Croatia Zagreb** 0 Att: 60,000

October 21, 1998
FC Porto 3 (Doriva 33, Zahovic 42, 75) **Croatia Zagreb** 0 Att: 20,000
Olympiakos 1 (Alexandris 38) **Ajax** 0 Att: 80,000

November 4, 1998
Ajax 2 (Witschge 32, Gorre 88) **Olympiakos** 0 Att: 45,000
Croatia Zagreb 3 (Mikic 7, Rukavina 37, Mujcin 61) **FC Porto** 1 (Jardel 39) Att: 10,000

November 25, 1998
Ajax 0 **Croatia Zagreb** 1 (Simic 68) Att: 30,000
Olympiakos 2 (Gogic 18, Djordjevic 55) **FC Porto** 1 (Zahovic 76) Att: 70,000

December 9, 1998
Croatia Zagreb 1 (Jelicic 35) **Olympiakos** 1 (Giannakopoulos 64) Att: 25,000
FC Porto 3 (Zahovic 54, 73, Drulovic 80) **Ajax** 0 Att: 20,000

FINAL TABLE (Quarter-final qualifier in capitals)

	P	W	D	L	F	A	Pts
OLYMPIAKOS	6	3	2	1	8	6	11
Croatia Zagreb	6	2	2	2	5	7	8
FC Porto	6	2	1	3	11	9	7
Ajax	6	2	1	3	4	6	7

GROUP B

September 16, 1998
Athletic Bilbao 1 (Etxeberria 5) **Rosenborg** 1 (Strand 66) Att: 37,000
Juventus 2 (Inzaghi 17, Birindelli 68) **Galatasaray** 2 (Sukur 42, Davala Sumit 63) Att: 22,000

September 30, 1998
Galatasaray 2 (Buruk 15, Hagi 90) **Athletic Bilbao** 1 (Urzaiz 16) Att: 25,000
Rosenborg 1 (Skammelsrud 69 pen) **Juventus** 1 (Inzaghi 27) Att: 15,385

October 21, 1998
Athletic Bilbao 0 **Juventus** 0 Att: 40,000
Rosenborg 3 (Rushfeldt 68, 86, 90) **Galatasaray** 0 Att: 17,372

November 4, 1998
Galatasaray 3 (Sukur 55, 73, Erdem 65) **Rosenborg** 0 Att: 25,000
Juventus 1 (Lasa 69 o.g.) **Athletic Bilbao** 1 (Guerrero 45) Att: 25,000

November 25, 1998
Rosenborg 2 (Sorensen 2, 50) **Athletic Bilbao** 1 (Perez 90) Att: 15,454

December 2, 1998
Galatasaray 1 (Suat 90) **Juventus** 1 (Amoruso 78) Att: 25,000

December 9, 1998
Athletic Bilbao 1 (Guerrero 44) **Galatasaray** 0 Att: 25,000
Juventus 2 (Inzaghi 16, Amoruso 36) **Rosenborg** 0 Att: 10,000

FINAL TABLE (Quarter-final qualifier in capitals)

	P	W	D	L	F	A	Pts
JUVENTUS	6	1	5	0	7	5	8
Galatasaray	6	2	2	2	8	8	8
Rosenborg	6	2	2	2	7	8	8
Athletic Bilbao	6	1	3	2	5	6	6

GROUP C

September 16, 1998
Real Madrid 2 (Hierro 79 pen, Seedorf 90) **Inter Milan** 0 Att: 42,000
Sturm Graz 0 **Spartak Moscow** 2 (Titov 62, Tsymbalar 64) Att: 12,500

September 30, 1998
Inter Milan 1 (Djorkaeff 90) **Sturm Graz** 0 Att: 24,800
Spartak Moscow 2 (Tsymbalar 71, Titov 78) **Real Madrid** 1 (Raul 64) Att: 80,000

October 21, 1998
Inter Milan 2 (Ventola 32, Ronaldo 59) **Spartak Moscow** 1 (Tsymbalar 65) Att: 65,000
Real Madrid 6 (Savio 12, 90, Raul 22, Jarni 60, 79, Popovic 66 o.g.) **Sturm Graz** 1
(Vastic 8) Att: 12,000

November 4, 1998
Spartak Moscow 1 (Tikhonov 68) **Inter Milan** 1 (Simeone 89) Att: 70,000

November 5, 1998
Sturm Graz 1 (Haas 4) **Real Madrid** 5 (Panucci 7, 61, Mijatovic 35, Seedorf 57, Suker
74) Att: 14,500

November 25, 1998
Spartak Moscow 0 **Sturm Graz** 0 Att: 25,000
Inter Milan 3 (Zamorano 50, Baggio 86, 90) **Real Madrid** 1 (Seedorf 59) Att: 77,829

December 9, 1998
Real Madrid 2 (Raul 34, Bortolini 65) **Spartak Moscow** 1 (Khlestov 89) Att: 55,000
Sturm Graz 0 **Inter Milan** 2 (Zanetti 64, Baggio 80) Att: 14,000

FINAL TABLE (Quarter-final qualifiers in capitals)

	P	W	D	L	F	A	Pts
INTER MILAN	6	4	1	1	9	5	13
REAL MADRID	6	4	0	2	17	8	12
Spartak Moscow	6	2	2	2	7	6	8
Sturm Graz	6	0	1	5	2	16	1

GROUP D

September 16, 1998
Brondby 2 (Hansen 88, Ravn 90) **Bayern Munich** 1 (Babbel 75) Att: 30,378
Manchester Utd. 3 (Giggs 17, Scholes 24, Beckham 64) **Barcelona** 3 (Anderson 47, Giovanni 60 pen, Luis Enrique 71 pen)
Manchester Utd.: Schmeichel, G. Neville, Irwin (P. Neville 79), Stam, Berg, Beckham, Keane, Giggs (Blomqvist 84), Scholes, Yorke, Solskjaer (Butt 55). **Sent-off:** Butt (70). Att: 53,601

September 30, 1998
Barcelona 2 (Anderson 42, 85) **Brondby** 0 Att: 70,000
Bayern Munich 2 (Elber 11, 90) **Manchester Utd.** 2 (Yorke 29, Scholes 48)
Manchester Utd.: Schmeichel, G. Neville, Irwin, Stam, P. Neville, Beckham, Keane, Scholes, Yorke, Sheringham, Blomqvist (Cruyff 69). Att: 53,000

October 21, 1998
Bayern Munich 1 (Effenberg 45) **Barcelona** 0 Att: 56,000
Brondby 2 (Daugaard 35, Sand 90) **Manchester Utd.** 6 (Giggs 2, 21, Cole 27, Keane 55, Yorke 60, Solskjaer 63)
Manchester Utd.: Schmeichel, Brown, G. Neville, P. Neville, Stam, Keane, Scholes, Blomqvist, Cole (Solskjaer 60), Yorke (Wilson 65), Giggs (Cruyff 60). Att: 40,315

November 4, 1998
Barcelona 1 (Giovanni 28 pen) **Bayern Munich** 2 (Zickler 48, Salihamidzic 87) Att: 100,000
Manchester Utd. 5 (Beckham 7, Cole 13, P. Neville 15, Yorke 27, Scholes 63) **Brondby** 0
Manchester Utd.: Schmeichel, G. Neville, P. Neville (Brown 32), Stam, Irwin, Beckham, Scholes, Keane, Blomqvist (Cruyff 46), Yorke, Cole (Solskjaer 55). Att: 53,250

November 25, 1998
Barcelona 3 (Anderson 1, Rivaldo 57, 73) **Manchester Utd.** 3 (Yorke 25, 68, Cole 53)
Manchester Utd.: Schmeichel, G. Neville, Irwin, Stam, Beckham (Butt 81), Brown, Blomqvist, Keane, Cole, Yorke, Scholes. Att: 67,650
Bayern Munich 2 (Jancker 51, Basler 57) **Brondby** 0 Att: 34,000

December 9, 1998
Brondby 0 **Barcelona** 2 (Figo 4, Rivaldo 35) Att: 40,892
Manchester Utd. 1 (Keane 43) **Bayern Munich** 1 (Salihamidzic 56)
Manchester Utd.: Schmeichel, G. Neville, Irwin (Johnsen 46), Stam, Beckham, Cole, Giggs, Keane, Scholes, Yorke (Butt 64), Brown. Att: 54,434

FINAL TABLE (Quarter-final qualifiers in capitals)

	P	W	D	L	F	A	Pts
BAYERN MUNICH	6	3	2	1	9	6	11
MAN UTD	6	2	4	0	20	11	10
Barcelona	6	2	2	2	11	9	8
Brondby	6	1	0	5	4	18	3

GROUP E

September 16, 1998
Lens 1 (Vairelles 90) **Arsenal** 1 (Overmars 51)
Arsenal: Seaman, Dixon, Winterburn, Vieira, Keown, Adams, Petit (Hughes 73), Parlour, Anelka, Bergkamp (Garde 90), Overmars. Att: 36,000
Panathinaikos 2 (Mykland 57, Liberopoulos 69) **Dynamo Kiev** 1 (Rebrov 31) Att: 35,000

September 30, 1998
Arsenal 2 (Adams 64, Keown 72) **Panathinaikos** 1 (Mauro 87)
Arsenal: Seaman, Dixon, Winterburn, Vieira, Keown, Adams, Overmars, Garde (Vivas 79), Petit, Bergkamp, Anelka. Att: 73,455
Dynamo Kiev 1 (Shevchenko 61) **Lens** 1 (Vairelles 62) Att: 50,000

October 21, 1998
Arsenal 1 (Bergkamp 74) **Dynamo Kiev** 1 (Rebrov 90)
Arsenal: Seaman, Dixon, Winterburn, Keown, Adams, Bergkamp, Anelka (Vivas 84), Overmars, Hughes, Parlour, Garde. Att: 73,256
Lens 1 (Eloi 81) **Panathinaikos** 0 Att: 30,000

November 4, 1998
Dynamo Kiev 3 (Rebrov 26 pen, Horovko 61, Shevchenko 72) **Arsenal** 1 (Hughes 84)
Arsenal: Seaman, Dixon, Keown, Bould (Grimandi 44), Winterburn, Parlour, Vieira, Petit, Vivas (Garde 84), Wreh, Boa Morte (Hughes 67). Att: 80,000
Panathinaikos 1 (Vokolos 53) **Lens** 0 Att: 52,000

November 25, 1998
Arsenal 0 **Lens** 1 (Debeve 72)
Arsenal: Seaman, Dixon, Winterburn, Adams (Bould 46), Anelka, Overmars, Wreh (Boa Morte 67), Keown, Parlour, Hughes, Garde (Vivas 67). **Sent-off:** Parlour (90). Att: 73,707
Dynamo Kiev 2 (Rebrov 72, Basinas 79 o.g.) **Panathinaikos** 1 (Lagonikakis 35) Att: 35,000

December 9, 1998
Lens 1 (Smicer 78) **Dynamo Kiev** 3 (Kaladze 60, Vaschuk 76, Shevchenko 85) Att: 41,000
Panathinaikos 1 (Sypniewski 74) **Arsenal** 3 (Mendez 66, Anelka 79, Boa Morte 86)
Arsenal: Seaman, Vivas, Vernazza, Bould, Upson, Mendez (M. Black 78), Grondin, Grimandi, Boa Morte, Anelka, Wreh. Att: 45,000

FINAL TABLE (Quarter-final qualifier in capitals)

	P	W	D	L	F	A	Pts
DYNAMO KIEV	6	3	2	1	11	7	11
Lens	6	2	2	2	5	6	8
Arsenal	6	2	2	2	8	8	8
Panathinaikos	6	2	0	4	6	9	6

* Arsenal played their home games at Wembley Stadium.

GROUP F

September 16, 1998
PSV Eindhoven 2 (Ooijer 59, Bruggink 90) **HJK Helsinki** 1 (Kottila 31) Att: 15,000
Kaiserslautern 1 (Wagner 41) **Benfica** 0 Att: 31,112

September 30, 1998
Benfica 2 (Gomes 47, Joao Pinto 77) **PSV Eindhoven** 1 (Rommedahl 70) Att: 50,000
HJK Helsinki 0 **Kaiserslautern** 0 Att: 21,000

October 21, 1998
HJK Helsinki 2 (Lehkosuo 19 pen, Kottila 68) **Benfica** 0 Att: 25,000
PSV Eindhoven 1 (Khokhlov 78) **Kaiserslautern** 2 (Riedl 63, Rische 83) Att: 25,000

November 4, 1998
Benfica 2 (Nuno Gomes 78, Calado 81) **HJK Helsinki** 2 (Minto 5 o.g, Luiz Antonio) Att: 35,000
Kaiserslautern 3 (Rische 68, Reich 77, Hristov 90) **PSV Eindhoven** 1 (Van Nistelrooij 18) Att: 31,444

November 25, 1998
HJK Helsinki 1 (Lehkosuo 70 pen) **PSV Eindhoven** 3 (Van Nistelrooij 30, 67, 82 pen) Att: 34,000
Benfica 2 (Nuno Gomes 31, Pinto 69) **Kaiserslautern** 1 (Rische 90) Att: 20,000

December 9, 1998
Kaiserslautern 5 (Rosler 43, 61, 80, Marschall 49, Rische 85) **HJK Helsinki** 2 (Ilola 29, Luiz Antonio 68) Att: 25,000
PSV Eindhoven 2 (Khokhlov 41, Van Nistelrooij 89) **Benfica** 2 (Nuno Gomes 47 pen, 65) Att: 25,000

FINAL TABLE (Quarter-final qualifier in capitals)

	P	W	D	L	F	A	Pts
KAISERSLAUTERN	6	4	1	1	12	6	13
Benfica	6	2	2	2	8	9	8
PSV Eindhoven	6	2	1	3	10	11	7
HJK Helsinki	6	1	2	3	8	12	5

QUARTER FINALS

1st leg: Wednesday March 3, Old Trafford
Manchester Utd. 2 (Yorke, 6, 45), **Inter Milan** 0 Att: 54,430
Manchester Utd.: Schmeichel, G Neville, Johnsen (Berg 46), Stam, Irwin, Beckham, Keane, Scholes (Butt 69), Giggs, Yorke, Cole.
Inter Milan: Pagliuca, Bergomi, Colonnese, Galante, Zanetti, Simeone, Winter, Cauet, Djorkaeff, Baggio (Pirlo 79), Zamorano (Ventola 68).

2nd leg: Wednesday, March 17, San Siro, Milan
Inter Milan 1 (Ventola, 63), **Manchester Utd.** 1 (Scholes, 88) Att: 79,528
Inter Milan: Pagliuca, Bergomi, West, Colonnese, Zanetti, Simeone, Silvestre, Cauet, Baggio, Ronaldo, Zamorano.
Manchester Utd.: Schmeichel, G Neville, Berg, Stam, Irwin, Beckham, Keane, Johnsen (Scholes 77), Giggs, (P Neville 82), Yorke, Cole.

SEMI FINALS

1st leg: Wednesday, April 7, 1999, Old Trafford
Manchester Utd. 1 (Gigs 90), **Juventus** 1 (Conte 25) Att: 54,487
Manchester Utd.: Schmeichel, G. Neville, Irwin, Stam, Beckham, Cole, Giggs, Keane, Scholes, Yorke (Sheringham 79), Berg (Johnsen 46).
Juventus: Peruzzi, Mirkovic, Montero (Ferrara 68), Di Livio (Tacchinardi 77), Conte, Inzaghi (Esnaider 88), Juliano, Deschamps, Pessotto, Zidane, Davids.

2nd leg: Wednesday, April 21, 1999, Stadio Delle Alpi, Turin
Juventus 2 (inzaghi 6, 11), **Manchester Utd.** 3 (keane 24, Yorke 34, Cole 84) Att: 64,500
Juventus: Peruzzi, Birindelli (Amoruso 46), Ferrara, Juliano (Montero 46), Pessotto, Conte, Deschamps, Davids, Di Livio (Fonseca 80), Zidane, Inzaghi.
Manchester Utd.: Schmeichel, G. Neville, Irwin, Johnsen, Stam, Beckham, Keane, Butt, Blomqvist (Scholes 68), Yorke, Cole.

EUROPEAN LEAGUE TABLES

BELGIUM

		P	W	D	L	F	A	Pts
1	Genk	34	22	7	5	74	38	73
2	Club Bruges	34	22	5	7	65	38	71
3	Anderlecht	34	21	7	6	76	39	70
4	Excelsior	34	19	9	6	76	47	66
5	Lokeren	34	17	6	11	69	41	57
6	Standard Liege	34	17	3	14	55	47	54
7	Lierse	34	16	6	12	72	47	54
8	Ghent	34	14	10	10	55	59	52
9	Sint-Truiden	34	14	9	11	52	46	51
10	Germinal Ekeren	34	14	7	13	48	46	49
11	Harelbeke	34	10	11	13	44	46	41
12	Westerlo	34	11	7	16	56	62	40
13	Eendracht Aaist	34	9	8	17	48	66	35
14	Charleroi	34	7	11	16	39	54	32
15	Beveren	34	8	6	20	33	60	30
16	Lommel	34	7	7	20	33	55	28
17	Kortrijk	34	6	7	21	49	81	25
18	Ostend	34	4	10	20	27	79	22

Cup winners: Lierse.

FINLAND

		P	W	D	L	F	A	Pts
1	Haka Valkeakoski	27	13	9	5	46	31	48
2	VPS Baasa	27	12	9	6	42	27	45
3	PK-35 Helsinki	27	11	11	5	36	24	44
4	HJK Helsinki	27	9	11	7	33	31	38
5	Jazz Pori	27	9	8	10	37	36	35
6	TPS Turku	27	8	10	9	25	31	34
7	MyPa Anjalankoski	27	8	8	11	35	39	32
8	RoPS Rovaniemi	27	6	14	7	27	31	32
9	FinnPa Helsinki	27	5	11	11	37	43	26
10	Jaro Pietarsaari	27	4	9	14	25	50	21

Cup winners: HJK.

FRANCE

		P	W	D	L	F	A	Pts
1	Bordeaux	34	22	6	6	66	29	72
2	Marseille	34	21	8	5	56	28	71
3	Lyon	34	18	9	7	51	31	63
4	Monaco	34	18	8	8	52	32	62
5	Rennes	34	17	8	9	45	38	59
6	RC Lens	34	14	7	13	46	43	49
7	Nantes	34	12	12	10	40	34	48
8	Montpellier	34	11	10	13	53	50	43
9	Paris St Germain	34	10	9	15	34	35	39
10	Metz	34	9	12	13	28	37	39
11	Nancy	34	10	9	15	35	45	39
12	Strasbourg	34	8	14	12	30	36	38
13	Bastia	34	10	8	16	37	46	38
14	Auxerre	34	9	10	15	40	45	37
15	Le Havre	34	8	11	15	23	38	35
16	Lorient	34	8	11	15	33	49	35
17	Sochaux	34	6	15	13	30	54	33
18	Toulouse	34	6	11	17	24	53	29

Cup winners: Nantes.

GERMANY

		P	W	D	L	F	A	Pts
1	Bayern Munich	34	24	6	4	76	28	78
2	Bayer Leverkusen	34	17	12	5	61	30	63
3	Hertha Berlin	34	18	8	8	59	32	62
4	Bor Dortmund	34	16	9	9	48	34	57
5	Kaiserslautern	34	17	6	11	51	47	57
6	Wolfsburg	34	15	10	9	54	49	55
7	Hamburg	34	13	11	10	47	46	50
8	MSV Duisburg	34	13	10	11	48	45	49
9	1860 Munich	34	11	8	15	49	56	41
10	Schalke	34	10	11	13	41	54	41
11	VfB Stuttgart	34	9	12	13	41	48	39
12	SC Freiburg	34	10	9	15	35	44	39
13	Werder Bremen	34	10	8	16	41	47	38
14	Hansa Rostock	34	9	11	14	49	57	38
15	Eintracht Frankfurt	34	9	10	15	44	54	37
16	FC Nurnberg	34	7	16	11	40	50	37
17	VfL Bochum	34	7	8	19	40	65	29
18	Bor M'gladbach	34	4	9	21	41	79	21

Cup winners: Werder Bremen.

HOLLAND

		P	W	D	L	F	A	Pts
1	Feyenoord	34	25	5	4	76	38	80
2	Willem II Tilburg	34	20	5	9	69	46	65
3	PSV Eindhoven	34	17	10	7	87	55	61
4	Vitesse Arnhem	34	18	7	9	61	44	61
5	Roda JC K'rade	34	17	9	8	59	40	60
6	Ajax Amsterdam	34	16	9	9	73	41	57
7	Heerenveen	34	14	12	8	53	41	54
8	Twente E'chede	34	13	13	8	51	45	52
9	AZ Alkmaar	34	12	12	10	52	60	48
10	Fortuna Sittard	34	12	8	14	49	56	44
11	NEC Nijmegen	34	10	9	15	42	56	39
12	Utrecht	34	10	8	16	54	64	38
13	Graafschap D	34	8	12	14	40	57	36
14	MVV Maastricht	34	7	11	16	42	63	32
15	Cambuur L	34	7	11	16	37	64	32
16	RKC Waalwijk	34	6	9	19	41	62	27
17	Sparta R'dam	34	7	5	22	37	71	26
18	NAC Breda	34	4	11	19	41	61	23

Cup winners: Ajax.

ITALY

		P	W	D	L	F	A	Pts
1	AC Milan	34	20	10	4	59	34	70
2	Lazio	34	20	9	5	65	31	69
3	Fiorentina	34	16	8	10	55	41	56
4	Parma	34	15	10	9	55	36	55
5	Roma	34	15	9	10	69	49	54
6	Juventus	34	15	9	10	42	36	54
7	Udinese	34	16	6	12	52	52	54
8	Internazionale	34	13	7	14	59	54	46
9	Bologna	34	11	11	12	44	47	44
10	Bari	34	9	15	10	39	44	42
11	Venezia	34	11	9	14	38	45	42
12	Cagliari	34	11	8	15	49	49	41
13	Piacenza	34	11	8	15	47	49	41
14	Perugia	34	11	6	17	43	61	39
15	Salernitana	34	10	8	16	37	51	38
16	Sampdoria	34	9	10	15	38	55	37
17	Vincenza	34	8	9	17	27	47	33
18	Empoli*	34	4	10	20	26	63	20

*Empoli deducted 2pts for attempted match fixing.
Cup winners: Empoli.

NORWAY

		P	W	D	L	F	A	Pts
1	Rosenborg	26	20	3	3	79	23	63
2	Molde	26	16	6	4	70	34	54
3	Stabaek	26	16	5	5	63	29	53
4	Viking	26	14	4	8	66	44	46
5	Bodo/Glimt	26	9	9	8	47	47	36
6	Brann	26	9	8	9	44	39	35
7	Valerenga	26	10	3	13	44	48	33
8	Lillestrom	26	9	6	11	41	49	33
9	Moss	26	10	2	14	36	55	32
10	Stromsgodset	26	9	5	12	40	61	32
11	Tromso	26	7	7	12	39	48	28
12	Kongsvinger	26	7	5	14	35	59	26
13	Haugesund	26	6	5	15	41	55	23
14	Sogndal	26	4	4	18	26	80	16

Cup winners: Rosenborg.

PORTUGAL

		P	W	D	L	F	A	Pts
1	Porto	34	24	7	3	85	26	79
2	Boavista	34	20	11	3	57	29	71
3	Benfica	34	19	8	7	71	29	65
4	Sporting Lisbon	34	17	12	5	64	32	63
5	Vitoria Setubal	34	15	8	11	37	38	53
6	Uniao Leiria	34	14	10	10	36	29	52
7	Vitoria Guimaraes	34	14	8	12	53	41	50
8	Estrela Amadora	34	11	12	11	33	40	45
9	Braga	34	10	12	12	38	50	42
10	Maritimo	34	10	11	13	44	45	41
11	Farense	34	10	9	15	39	54	39
12	Salguerios	34	7	17	10	45	55	38
13	Campomaiorense	34	10	7	17	41	51	37
14	Rio Ave	34	8	11	15	26	47	35
15	Alverca	34	8	11	15	36	50	35
16	Beira Mar	34	6	15	13	36	53	33
17	Chaves	34	5	10	19	39	70	25
18	Academica	34	4	9	21	30	71	21

Cup winners: Beira Mar.

SPAIN

		P	W	D	L	F	A	Pts
1	Barcelona	38	24	7	7	87	43	79
2	Real Madrid	38	21	5	12	77	62	68
3	Mallorca	38	20	6	12	48	31	66
4	Valencia	38	19	8	11	63	39	65
5	Celta Vigo	38	17	13	8	69	41	64
6	Deportivo	38	17	12	9	55	43	63
7	Espanyol	38	16	13	9	49	38	61
8	Athletic Bilbao	38	17	9	12	53	47	60
9	Real Zaragoza	38	16	9	13	57	46	57
10	Real Sociedad	38	14	12	12	47	43	54
11	*Real Betis	38	14	7	17	47	58	49
12	Valladolid	38	13	9	16	35	44	48
13	Atletico Madrid	38	12	10	16	54	50	46
14	Oviedo	38	11	12	15	41	57	45
15	Racing Santander	38	10	12	16	41	53	42
16	Alaves	38	11	7	20	36	63	40
17	Extremadura	38	9	12	17	27	53	39
18	Villarreal	38	8	12	18	47	63	36
19	Tenerife	38	7	13	18	41	63	34
20	Salamanca	38	7	6	25	29	66	27

*Real Betis awarded three points and a 3-0 victory over Valladolid who fielded an ineligible player.

Cup winners: Valencia.

SWEDEN

		P	W	D	L	F	A	Pts
1	AIK	26	11	13	2	25	15	46
2	Helsingborg IF	26	12	8	6	43	28	44
3	Hammarby IF	26	11	9	6	39	34	42
4	Halmstad BK	26	12	5	9	42	40	41
5	Völunda	26	10	8	8	29	31	38
6	Örebro SK	26	10	6	10	35	38	36
7	IFK Norrköping	26	9	8	9	43	35	35
8	IFK Göteborg	26	9	8	9	27	29	35
9	Malmö FF	26	9	6	11	35	30	33
10	Elfsborg IF	26	8	9	9	36	33	33
11	Trelleborg FF	26	8	8	10	31	35	32
12	Örgryte IS	26	7	7	12	35	36	28
13	BK Häcken	26	7	6	13	27	46	27
14	Östers IF	26	5	7	14	26	43	22

Cup winners: AIK.

WORLD CUP 2002

South Korea and Japan will make World Cup history on two counts when they jointly host the finals of the 17th World Cup in 2002. Their nomination on May 31, 1996 made them the first countries to co-host a World Cup, as well as the first Asian nations to stage the finals.

World Cup 2002 will be contested by 32 countries. France, as holders, qualify automatically, along with 14 other European nations. There will be five teams from Africa, four from Asia (including co-hosts Japan and South Korea), three from the CONCACAF group and four from South America, with a fifth South American side playing off against the Oceania group winners. The organisers have, however, called for a larger allocation of Asian teams, and the FIFA executive will meet to rule on the proposal.

The draw for the qualifying competition will be made on December 7, 1999 at the Tokyo International Forum in Japan. The qualifying round is scheduled from March 1, 2000 to November 11, 2001. The dates for the finals have yet to be finalised, but the opening game will be staged in Seoul and the final in Tokyo.

The emblem for the 2002 finals is a symbol of the World Cup inside a circle.

Michel Platini, president of the organising committee at France 98, reported that the finals made a pre-tax profit of 505 million francs (£54.1million).

The five candidates bidding to stage the 2006 finals are England, Germany, Brazil, South Africa and Morocco. After considerable debate that an African bid would be weakened if too many countries tried to host the finals, Nigeria, Ghana and Egypt decided not to enter the race. The host nation will be chosen in July 2000.

WORLD CUP FINALS 1-2-3

Year	Venue	Winners	Runners-up	Third
1930	Montevideo	Uruguay	Argentina	–
1934	Rome	Italy*	Czechoslovakia	Germany
1938	Paris	Italy	Hungary	Brazil
1950•	Rio de Janeiro	Uruguay	Brazil	–
1954	Berne	Germany	Hungary	Austria
1958	Stockholm	Brazil	Sweden	France
1962	Santiago	Brazil	Czechoslovakia	Chile
1966	Wembley	England*	West Germany	Portugal
1970	Mexico City	Brazil	Italy	West Germany
1974	Munich	West Germany	Holland	Poland
1978	Buenos Aires	Argentina*	Holland	Brazil
1982	Madrid	Italy	West Germany	Poland
1986	Mexico City	Argentina	West Germany	France
1990	Rome	West Germany	Argentina	Italy
1994	Los Angeles	Brazil†	Italy	Sweden
1998	Paris	France	Brazil	Croatia

(•Final played on pool basis; *After extra time; †On penalties, after extra time)

World champions: 4 – Brazil; 3 – Italy, West Germany; 2 – Argentina, Uruguay; 1 – England, France. **Next finals:** 2002 in Japan and South Korea.

WORLD CUP-WINNING MANAGERS/COACHES

1930 Uruguay, **Alberto Supicci; 1934** Italy, **Vittorio Pozzo; 1938** Italy, **Vittorio Pozzo; 1950** Uruguay, **Juan Lopez; 1954** West Germany, **Sepp Herberger; 1958** Brazil, **Vicente Feola; 1962** Brazil, **Aimore Moreira; 1966** England, **Alf Ramsey; 1970** Brazil, **Mario Zagallo; 1974** West Germany, **Helmut Schoen; 1978** Argentina, **Cesar Luis Menotti; 1982** Italy, **Enzo Bearzot; 1986** Argentina, **Carlos Bilardo; 1990** West Germany, **Franz Beckenbauer; 1994** Brazil, **Carlos Alberto Parreira; 1998** France, **Aime Jacquet.**

WORLD CUP SUMMARIES 1930-98

1930 IN URUGUAY

WINNERS: Uruguay. RUNNERS-UP: Argentina. THIRD: U.S.A.
Other countries taking part: Belgium, Bolivia, Brazil, Chile, France, Mexico, Paraguay, Peru, Rumania, Yugoslavia. **Total entries**: 13.
Venue: All matches played in Montevideo.
Top scorer: Stabile (Argentina) 8 goals.
Final (30.7.30): **Uruguay 4** (Dorado 12, Cea 55, Iriarte 64, Castro 89), **Argentina 2** (Peucelle 29, Stabile 35). **Att**: 90,000.
Uruguay: Ballesteros; Nasazzi (Capt.), Mascheroni, Andrade, Fernandez, Gestido, Dorado, Scarone, Castro, Cea, Iriarte.
Argentina: Botasso; Della Torre, Paternoster, Evaristo (J.), Monti, Suarez, Peucelle, Varallo, Stabile, Ferreira (Capt.), Evaristo (M.).
Referee: Langenus (Belgium). **Half-time**: 1-2.

1934 IN ITALY

WINNERS: Italy. RUNNERS-UP: Czechoslovakia. THIRD: Germany.
Other countries in finals: Argentina, Austria, Belgium, Brazil, Egypt, France, Holland, Hungary, Romania, Spain, Sweden, Switzerland, U.S.A. **Total entries**: 29 (16 qualifiers).
Venues: Bologna, Florence, Genoa, Milan, Naples, Rome, Trieste, Turin.
Top scorers: Conen (Germany), Nejedly (Czechoslovakia), Schiavio (Italy), each 4 goals.
Final (Rome, 10.6.34): **Italy 2** (Orsi 82, Schiavio 97), **Czechoslovakia 1** (Puc 70), **after extra time. Att**: 50,000.
Italy: Combi (Capt.); Monzeglio, Allemandi, Ferraris, Monti, Bertolini, Guaita, Meazza, Schiavio, Ferrari, Orsi.
Czechoslovakia: Planicka (Capt.); Zenisek, Ctyroky, Kostalek, Cambal, Krcil, Junek, Svoboda, Sobotka, Nejedly, Puc.
Referee: Eklind (Sweden). **Half-time**: 0-0. **90 mins**: 1-1.

1938 IN FRANCE

WINNERS: Italy. RUNNERS-UP: Hungary. THIRD: Brazil.
Other countries in finals: Belgium, Cuba, Czechoslovakia, Dutch East Indies, France, Germany, Holland, Norway, Poland, Rumania, Sweden, Switzerland. **Total entries**: 25 (15 qualifiers).
Venues: Antibes, Bordeaux, Le Havre, Lille, Marseilles, Paris, Reims, Strasbourg, Toulouse.
Top scorer: Leonidas (Brazil) 8 goals.
Final (Paris, 19.6.38): **Italy 4** (Colaussi 6, 36, Piola 15, 81), **Hungary 2** (Titkos 7, Sarosi 65). **Att**: 45,000.
Italy: Olivieri; Foni, Rava, Serantoni, Andreolo, Locatelli, Biavati, Meazza (Capt.), Piola, Ferrari, Colaussi.
Hungary: Szabo; Polgar, Biro, Szalay, Szucs, Lazar, Sas, Vincze, Sarosi (Capt.), Szengeller, Titkos.
Referee: Capdeville (France). **Half-time**: 3-1.

1950 IN BRAZIL

WINNERS: Uruguay. RUNNERS-UP: Brazil. THIRD: Sweden.
Other countries in finals: Bolivia, Chile, England, Italy, Mexico, Paraguay, Spain, Switzerland, U.S.A., Yugoslavia. **Total entries**: 29 (13 qualifiers).
Venues: Belo Horizonte, Curitiba, Porto Alegre, Recife, Rio de Janeiro, Sao Paulo.
Top scorer: Ademir (Brazil) 9 goals.
Deciding Match (Rio de Janeiro, 16.7.50): **Uruguay 2** (Schiaffino 64, Ghiggia 79), **Brazil 1** (Friaca 47). **Att**: 199,850.

(For the only time, the World Cup was decided on a final pool system, in which the winners of the four qualifying groups met in a six-match series. So, unlike previous and subsequent tournaments, there was no official Final as such, but Uruguay v Brazil was the deciding final match in the final pool).
Uruguay: Maspoli; Gonzales, Tejera, Gambetta, Varela (Capt.), Andrade, Ghiggia, Perez, Miguez, Schiaffino, Moran.
Brazil: Barbosa; Augusto (Capt.), Juvenal, Bauer, Danilo, Bigode, Friaca, Zizinho, Ademir, Jair, Chico.
Referee: Reader (England). **Half-time**: 0-0.

1954 IN SWITZERLAND

WINNERS: West Germany. RUNNERS-UP: Hungary. THIRD: Austria.
Other countries in finals: Belgium, Brazil, Czechoslovakia, England, France, Italy, Korea, Mexico, Scotland, Switzerland, Turkey, Uruguay, Yugoslavia. **Total entries**: 35 (16 qualifiers).
Venues: Basle, Berne, Geneva, Lausanne, Lugano, Zurich.
Top scorer: Kocsis (Hungary) 11 goals.
Final (Berne, 4.7.54): **West Germany 3** (Morlock 12, Rahn 17, 84), **Hungary 2** (Puskas 4, Czibor 9). **Att**: 60,000.
West Germany: Turek; Posipal, Kohlmeyer, Eckel, Liebrich, Mai, Rahn, Morlock, Walter (O.), Walter (F.) (Capt.), Schaefer.
Hungary: Grosics; Buzansky, Lantos, Bozsik, Lorant, Zakarias, Czibor, Kocsis, Hidegkuti, Puskas (Capt.), Toth (J.).
Referee: Ling (England). **Half-time**: 2-2.

1958 IN SWEDEN

WINNERS: Brazil. RUNNERS-UP: Sweden. THIRD: France.
Other countries in finals: Argentina, Austria, Czechoslovakia, England, Hungary, Mexico, Northern Ireland, Paraguay, Scotland, Soviet Union, Wales, West Germany, Yugoslavia. **Total entries**: 47 (16 qualifiers).
Venues: Boras, Eskilstuna, Gothenburg, Halmstad, Helsingborg, Malmo, Norrkoping, Orebro, Sandviken, Stockholm, Vasteras.
Top scorer: Fontaine (France) 13 goals.
Final (Stockholm, 29.6.58): **Brazil 5** (Vava 10, 32, Pele 55, 88, Zagalo 76), **Sweden 2** (Liedholm 4, Simonsson 83). **Att**: 49,737.
Brazil: Gilmar; Santos (D.), Santos (N.), Zito, Bellini (Capt.), Orlando, Garrincha, Didi, Vava, Pele, Zagalo.
Sweden: Svensson; Bergmark, Axbom, Boerjesson, Gustavsson, Parling, Hamrin, Gren, Simonsson, Liedholm (Capt.), Skoglund.
Referee: Guigue (France). **Half-time**: 2-1.

1962 IN CHILE

WINNERS: Brazil. RUNNERS-UP: Czechoslovakia. THIRD: Chile.
Other countries in finals: Argentina, Bulgaria, Colombia, England, Hungary, Italy, Mexico, Soviet Union, Spain, Switzerland, Uruguay, West Germany, Yugoslavia. **Total entries**: 53 (16 qualifiers).
Venues: Arica, Rancagua, Santiago, Vina del Mar.
Top scorer: Jerkovic (Yugoslavia), 5 goals.
Final (Santiago, 17.6.62): **Brazil 3** (Amarildo 17, Zito 69, Vava 77), **Czechoslovakia 1** (Masopust 16). **Att**: 68,679.
Brazil: Gilmar; Santos (D.), Mauro (Capt.), Zozimo, Santos (N.), Zito, Didi, Garrincha, Vava, Amarildo, Zagalo.
Czechoslovakia: Schroiff; Tichy, Novak, Pluskal, Popluhar, Masopust (Capt.), Pospichal, Scherer, Kvasnak, Kadraba, Jelinek.
Referee: Latychev (Soviet Union). **Half-time**: 1-1.

1966 IN ENGLAND

WINNERS: England. RUNNERS-UP: West Germany. THIRD: Portugal.
Other countries in finals: Argentina, Brazil, Bulgaria, Chile, France, Hungary, Italy, Mexico, North Korea, Soviet Union, Spain, Switzerland, Uruguay. **Total entries**: 53 (16 qualifiers).
Venues: Birmingham (Villa Park), Liverpool (Goodison Park), London (Wembley and White City), Manchester (Old Trafford), Middlesbrough, Sheffield (Hillsborough), Sunderland.
Top scorer: Eusebio (Portugal) 9 goals.
Final (Wembley, 30.7.66): **England 4** (Hurst 19, 100, 120, Peters 78), **West Germany 2** (Haller 13, Weber 89), **after extra time. Att**: 93,802.
England: Banks; Cohen, Wilson, Stiles, Charlton (J.), Moore (Capt.), Ball, Hurst, Hunt, Charlton (R.), Peters.
West Germany: Tilkowski; Hottges, Schnellinger, Beckenbauer, Schulz, Weber, Haller, Held, Seeler (Capt.), Overath, Emmerich.
Referee: Dienst (Switzerland). **Half-time**: 1-1. **90 mins**: 2-2.

1970 IN MEXICO

WINNERS: Brazil. RUNNERS-UP: Italy. THIRD: West Germany.
Other countries in finals: Belgium, Bulgaria, Czechoslovakia, El Salvador, England, Israel, Mexico, Morocco, Peru, Romania, Soviet Union, Sweden, Uruguay. **Total entries**: 68 (16 qualifiers).
Venues: Guadalajara, Leon, Mexico City, Puebla, Toluca.
Top scorer: Muller (West Germany) 10 goals.
Final (Mexico City, 21.6.70): **Brazil 4** (Pele 18, Gerson 66, Jairzinho 71, Carlos Alberto 87), **Italy 1** (Boninsegna 38). **Att**: 107,412.
Brazil: Felix; Carlos Alberto (Capt.), Brito, Piazza, Everaldo, Clodoaldo, Gerson, Jairzinho, Tostao, Pele, Rivelino.
Italy: Albertosi; Burgnich, Facchetti (Capt.), Cera, Rosato, Bertini (Juliano 72), Domenghini, De Sisti, Mazzola, Boninsegna (Rivera 84), Riva.
Referee: Glockner (East Germany). **Half-time**: 1-1.

1974 IN WEST GERMANY

WINNERS: West Germany. RUNNERS-UP: Holland. THIRD: Poland.
Other countries in finals: Argentina, Australia, Brazil, Bulgaria, Chile, East Germany, Haiti, Italy, Scotland, Sweden, Uruguay, Yugoslavia, Zaire. **Total entries**: 98 (16 qualifiers).
Venues: Berlin, Dortmund, Dusseldorf, Frankfurt, Gelsenkirchen, Hamburg, Hanover, Munich, Stuttgart.
Top scorer: Lato (Poland) 7 goals
Final (Munich, 7.7.74): **West Germany 2** (Breitner 25 pen., Muller 43), **Holland 1** (Neeskens 2 pen.). **Att**: 77,833.
West Germany: Maier; Vogts, Schwarzenbeck, Beckenbauer (Capt.), Breitner, Bonhof, Hoeness, Overath, Grabowski, Muller, Holzenbein.
Holland: Jongbloed; Suurbier, Rijsbergen (De Jong 69), Haan, Krol, Jansen, Van Hanegem, Neeskens, Rep, Cruyff (Capt.), Rensenbrink (Van der Kerkhof (R.) 46).
Referee: Taylor (England). **Half-time**: 2-1.

1978 IN ARGENTINA

WINNERS: Argentina. RUNNERS-UP: Holland. THIRD: Brazil.
Other countries in finals: Austria, France, Hungary, Iran, Italy, Mexico, Peru, Poland, Scotland, Spain, Sweden, Tunisia, West Germany. **Total entries**: 102 (16 qualifiers).
Venues: Buenos Aires, Cordoba, Mar del Plata, Mendoza, Rosario.
Top scorer: Kempes (Argentina) 6 goals.

Final (Buenos Aires, 25.6.78): **Argentina 3** (Kempes 38, 104, Bertoni 115), **Holland 1** (Nanninga 82), **after extra time. Att**: 77,000.
Argentina: Fillol; Passarella (Capt.), Olguin, Galvan, Tarantini, Ardiles (Larrosa 66), Gallego, Ortiz (Houseman 74), Bertoni, Luque, Kempes.
Holland: Jongbloed; Krol (Capt.), Poortvliet, Brandts, Jansen (Suurbier 73), Haan, Neeskens, Van der Kerkhof (W.), Rep (Nanninga 58), Van der Kerkhof (R.), Rensenbrink.
Referee: Gonella (Italy). **Half-time**: 1-0. **90 mins**: 1-1.

1982 IN SPAIN

WINNERS: Italy. RUNNERS-UP: West Germany. THIRD: Poland.
Other countries in finals: Algeria, Argentina, Austria, Belgium, Brazil, Cameroon, Chile, Czechoslovakia, El Salvador, England, France, Honduras, Hungary, Kuwait, New Zealand, Northern Ireland, Peru, Scotland, Soviet Union, Spain, Yugoslavia. **Total entries**: 109 (24 qualifiers).
Venues: Alicante, Barcelona, Bilbao, Coruna, Elche, Gijon, Madrid, Malaga, Oviedo, Seville, Valencia, Valladolid, Vigo, Zaragoza.
Top scorer: Rossi (Italy) 6 goals.
Final (Madrid, 11.7.82): **Italy 3** (Rossi 57, Tardelli 69, Altobelli 81), **West Germany 1** (Breitner 84). **Att**: 90,089.
Italy: Zoff (Capt.); Bergomi, Scirea, Collovati, Cabrini, Oriali, Gentile, Tardelli, Conti, Rossi, Graziani (Altobelli 18 – Causio 88).
West Germany: Schumacher; Kaltz, Stielike, Forster (K-H.), Forster (B.), Dremmler (Hrubesch 63), Breitner, Briegel, Rummenigge (Capt.) (Muller 70), Fischer, Littbarski.
Referee: Coelho (Brazil). **Half-time**: 0-0.

1986 IN MEXICO

WINNERS: Argentina. RUNNERS-UP: West Germany. THIRD: France.
Other countries in finals: Algeria, Belgium, Brazil, Bulgaria, Canada, Denmark, England, Hungary, Iraq, Italy, Mexico, Morocco, Northern Ireland, Paraguay, Poland, Portugal, Scotland, South Korea, Soviet Union, Spain, Uruguay. **Total entries**: 118 (24 qualifiers).
Venues: Guadalajara, Irapuato, Leon, Mexico City, Monterrey, Nezahualcoyotl, Puebla, Queretaro, Toluca.
Top scorer: Lineker (England) 6 goals.
Final (Mexico City, 29.6.86): **Argentina 3** (Brown 23, Valdano 56, Burruchaga 85), **West Germany 2** (Rummenigge 74, Voller 82). **Att**: 115,026.
Argentina: Pumpido; Cuciuffo, Brown, Ruggeri, Olarticoechea, Batista, Giusti, Maradona (Capt.), Burruchaga (Trobbiani 89), Enrique, Valdano.
West Germany: Schumacher; Berthold, K-H.Forster, Jakobs, Brehme, Briegel, Eder, Matthaus, Magath (Hoeness 62), Allofs (Voller 45), Rummenigge (Capt.).
Referee: Filho (Brazil). **Half-time**: 1-0.

1990 IN ITALY

WINNERS: West Germany. RUNNERS-UP: Argentina. THIRD: Italy.
Other countries in finals: Austria, Belgium, Brazil, Cameroon, Colombia, Costa Rica, Czechoslovakia, Egypt, England, Holland, Rep. of Ireland, Romania, Scotland, Spain, South Korea, Soviet Union, Sweden, United Arab Emirates, U.S.A., Uruguay, Yugoslavia. **Total entries**: 103 (24 qualifiers).
Venues: Bari, Bologna, Cagliari, Florence, Genoa, Milan, Naples, Palermo, Rome, Turin, Udine, Verona.
Top scorer: Schillaci (Italy) 6 goals.
Final (Rome, 8.7.90): **Argentina 0, West Germany 1** (Brehme 85 pen.). **Att**: 73,603.
Argentina: Goycochea; Ruggeri (Monzon 45), Simon, Serrizuela, Lorenzo, Basualdo, Troglio, Burruchaga (Calderon 53), Sensini, Maradona (Capt.), Dezotti. **Sent-off**: Monzon (65), Dezotti (86) – first players ever to be sent off in World Cup Final.

West Germany: Illgner; Berthold (Reuter 75), Buchwald, Augenthaler, Kohler, Brehme, Matthaus (Capt.), Littbarski, Hassler, Klinsmann, Voller.
Referee: Codesal (Mexico). **Half-time:** 0-0.

1994 IN U.S.A.

WINNERS: Brazil. RUNNERS-UP: Italy. THIRD: Sweden.
Other countries in finals: Argentina, Belgium, Bolivia, Bulgaria, Cameroon, Colombia, Germany, Greece, Holland, Mexico, Morocco, Nigeria, Norway, Rep. of Ireland, Romania, Russia, Saudi Arabia, South Korea, Spain, Switzerland, U.S.A. **Total entries:** 144 (24 qualifiers).
Venues: Boston, Chicago, Dallas, Detroit, Los Angeles, New York City, Orlando, San Francisco, Washington.
Top scorers: Salenko (Russia), Stoichkov (Bulgaria), each 6 goals.
Final (Los Angeles, 17.7.94): **Brazil 0, Italy 0,** after extra time; **Brazil** won 3-2 on pens. **Att:** 94,194.
Brazil: Taffarel; Jorginho (Cafu 21), Aldair, Marcio Santos, Branco, Mazinho, Mauro Silva, Dunga (Capt.), Zinho (Viola 105), Romario, Bebeto.
Italy: Pagliuca; Mussi (Apolloni 35), Baresi (Capt.), Maldini, Benarrivo, Berti, Albertini, D. Baggio (Evani 95), Donadoni, R. Baggio, Massaro.
Referee: Puhl (Hungary).
Shoot-out: Baresi over, Marco Santos saved, Albertini 1-0, Romario 1-1, Evani 2-1, Branco 2-2, Massaro saved, Dunga 2-3, R Baggio over.

1998 IN FRANCE

WINNERS: France. RUNNERS-UP: Brazil. THIRD: Croatia.
Other countries in finals: Argentina, Austria, Belgium, Bulgaria, Cameroon, Chile, Colombia, Denmark, England, Germany, Holland, Iran, Italy, Jamaica, Japan, Mexico, Morocco, Nigeria, Norway, Paraguay, Romania, Saudi Arabia, Scotland, South Africa, South Korea, Spain, Tunisia, U.S.A., Yugoslavia. **Total entries:** 172 (32 qualifiers).
Venues: Bordeaux, Lens, Lyon, Marseille, Montpellier, Nantes, Paris (St Denis, Parc des Princes), Saint-Etienne, Toulouse.
Top scorer: Davor Suker (Croatia) 6 goals.
Final (Paris St Denis, 12.7.98): **Brazil 0, France 3** (Zidane 27, 45, Petit 90). **Att:** 75,000.
Brazil: Traffarel; Cafu, Junior Baiano, Aldair, Roberto Carlos; Dunga, Leonardo (Denilson 46), Cesar Sampaio (Edmundo 74), Rivaldo; Bebeto, Ronaldo.
France: Barthez; Thuram, Leboeuf, Desailly, Lizarazu; Karembeu (Boghossian 56), Deschamps, Petit, Zidane, Djorkaeff (Viera 75); Guivarc'h (Dugarry 66). **Sent-off:** Desailly (68).
Referee: S Belqola (Morocco). **Half-time:** 0-2.

FIFA WORLD PLAYER OF THE YEAR
(Voted by National Coaches)

1991	Lothar Matthaus (Inter Milan and Germany)
1992	Marco van Basten (AC Milan and Holland)
1993	Roberto Baggio (Juventus and Italy)
1994	Romario (Barcelona and Brazil)
1995	George Weah (Milan and Liberia)
1996	Ronaldo (Barcelona and Brazil)
1997	Ronaldo (Barcelona, Inter Milan and Brazil)
1998	Zinedine Zidane (Juventus and France)

BRITISH AND IRISH INTERNATIONALS
1998-99

Note: In the senior Internationals that follow, * = new cap.

EUROPEAN CHAMPIONSHIP – QUALIFYING ROUND

SWEDEN 2, ENGLAND 1
Stockholm, (35,000), Saturday, September 5, 1998

Sweden: Hedman, R. Nilsson, Kaamark (Lucic 83), P. Anderssen, Bjorklund, Schwarz, Mjallby, A. Anderssen (D. Anderssen 90), Ljungberg, Larsson, Pettersson. **Scorers:** A. Anderssen (31), Mjallby (33). **Booked:** Schwarz.

England: Seaman (Arsenal), Southgate (Aston Villa), Adams (Arsenal), Campbell (Tottenham) (Merson, Middlesbrough, 75), Anderton (Tottenham) (Lee, Newcastle Utd., 42), Le Saux (Chelsea), Scholes (Manchester Utd.) (Sheringham, Manchester Utd., 87), Ince (Liverpool), Redknapp (Liverpool), Shearer (Newcastle Utd., Capt), Owen (Liverpool). **Scorer:** Shearer (2). **Booked:** Ince, Owen, Redknapp. **Sent-off:** Ince (67)
Referee: P. Collina (Italy). **Half-time:** 2-1.

WALES 0, ITALY 2
Anfield, (23,160), Saturday, September 5, 1998

Wales: Jones (Southampton), Robinson (Charlton Athletic), Barnard (Barnsley), Symons (Fulham), Williams (Wolves), Coleman (Fulham), *Johnson (Nott'm Forest), Speed (Newcastle Utd.), Blake (Bolton Wand.) (Saunders, Sheff. Utd., 65), M. Hughes (Southampton) (Savage, Leicester City, 80), Giggs (Manchester Utd.). **Booked:** Blake, Speed.

Italy: Peruzzi, Panucci, Pessotto, D. Baggio, Cannavaro, Juliano, Fuser, Albertini (Di Biagio 67), Vieri, Del Piero (R. Baggio 74), Di Francesco (Serena 85). **Scorers:** Fuser (20), Vieri (77).

Referee: T. Hauge (Norway). **Half-time:** 0-1.

TURKEY 3, NORTHERN IRELAND 0
Istanbul, (26,500), Saturday, September 5, 1998

Turkey: Rustu, Mert, Saffet, Tayfun, Alpay, Abdullah, Okan (Arif 87), Tugay (Oguz 75), Sukur, Sergen, Oktay (Hami 78). **Scorers:** Oktay (19, 58), Tayfun (49 pen).

Northern Ireland: Fettis (Blackburn Rov.), Horlock (Manchester City), Hill (Northampton Town), A. Hughes (Newcastle Utd.), Morrow (Q.P.R.), Rowland (Q.P.R.) (Quinn, W.B.A., 46), Lennon (Leicester City), Mulryne (Manchester Utd.), Gillespie (Newcastle Utd.) (Jim Whitley, Manchester City, 73), M. Hughes (Wimbledon), Dowie (Q.P.R.). **Booked:** Lennon.

Referee: R. Wojcik (Poland). **Half-time:** 1-0.

REPUBLIC OF IRELAND 2, CROATIA 0
Lansdowne Road, Dublin, (34,001), Saturday, September 5, 1998

Rep. of Ireland: Given (Newcastle Utd.), Irwin (Manchester Utd.), Staunton (Liverpool), Babb (Liverpool), Cunningham (Wimbledon), Roy Keane (Manchester Utd.) (Carsley, Derby Co., 62), McAteer (Liverpool), Kinsella (Charlton Athletic), O'Neill (Norwich City) (Cascarino, Nancy, 9), Robbie Keane (Wolves), Duff (Blackburn Rov.) (Kenna, Blackburn Rov., 46). **Scorers:** Irwin (4 pen), Roy Keane (16)

Croatia: Ladic, Simic (Panic 46), Stanic, Soldo (Tokic 77), Stimac, Asanovic, Tudor (Krpan 62), Maric, Boban, Jurcic, Jarni. **Sent-off:** Stanic (70), Jurcic (72)

Referee: V. Melo Pereira (Portugal). **Half-time:** 2-0.

LITHUANIA 0, SCOTLAND 0
Vilnius, (4,800), Saturday, September 5, 1998

Lithuania: Stauche, Skerla, Shemberas, Zhutautus, Baltushnikas, Zhvirgzhdauskus, Mikulenas (Shlerys 90), Shugzhda (Biutkus 61), Preikshaitis, Skarbalius, Jankauskas. **Booked:** Shemberas, Skarbalius.

Scotland: Leighton (Aberdeen), Hendry (Rangers), Boyd (Celtic), Calderwood (Tottenham) (*Davidson, Blackburn Rov., 71), Dailly (Blackburn Rov.), Lambert (Celtic), Collins (Everton), Jackson (Celtic) (*B. Ferguson, Rangers, 56), Gallacher (Blackburn Rov.), McCoist (Kilmarnock) (*McCann, Hearts, 82), Elliott (Leicester City). **Booked:** Gallacher, Davidson.

Referee: C. Zotta (Romania).

ENGLAND 0, BULGARIA 0
Wembley, (72,974), Saturday, October 10, 1998

England: Seaman (Arsenal), G. Neville (Manchester Utd.), Southgate (Aston Villa), Campbell (Tottenham), Lee (Newcastle Utd.), Hinchcliffe (Sheff. Wed.) (Le Saux, Chelsea, 34), Anderton (Tottenham) (Batty, Newcastle Utd., 67), Redknapp (Liverpool), Shearer (Newcastle Utd.), Owen (Liverpool), Scholes (Manchester Utd.) (Sheringham, Manchester Utd., 77). **Booked:** Anderton, Redknapp.

Bulgaria: Zdravkov, Kishishev, Zagorcic, Naidenov, Yordanov, Kirilov, Yankov, Stoichkov (Batchev 60), Hristov (G. Ivanov 90), M. Petkov, Iliev (Gruev 63). **Booked:** Kishishev.

Referee: L. Vagner (Hungary).

DENMARK 1, WALES 2
Copenhagen, (41,500), Saturday October 10, 1998

Denmark: Krogh, Toefting, Rieper, J. Hogh, Heintze, Helveg, S. Nielsen, Frandsen (Gravesen 76), Frederiksen, Jorgensen, Beck (Sand 67). **Scorer:** Frederiksen (57).

Wales: Jones (Southampton), Barnard (Barnsley), Savage (Leicester City), Symons (Fulham), Williams (Wolves), Coleman (Fulham), M. Hughes (Southampton), Speed (Newcastle Utd.), Johnson (Nott'm Forest) (Pembridge, Benfica, 64), Blake (Bolton Wand.) (Bellamy, Norwich City, 69), Saunders (Sheff. Utd.) (Robinson, Charlton Athletic, 80). **Scorers:** Williams (58), Bellamy (87). **Booked:** Savage, Speed.

Referee: S. Pillar (Hungary). **Half-time:** 0-0.

NORTHERN IRELAND 1, FINLAND 0
Windsor Park, Belfast, (7,000), Saturday October 10, 1998

Northern Ireland: Fettis (Blackburn Rov.), A. Hughes (Newcastle Utd.), Rowland (Q.P.R.) (Quinn, W.B.A., 88), Mulryne (Manchester Utd.), Patterson (Dundee Utd.), Morrow (Q.P.R.), Gillespie (Newcastle Utd.) (McCarthy, Birmingham City, 70), Lennon (Leicester City), Dowie (Q.P.R.) (O'Boyle, St Johnstone, 79), M. Hughes (Wimbledon), Horlock (Manchester City). **Scorer:** Rowland (31).

Finland: Niemi, Ylonen, Reini, Hyypia, Kautonen, Riihilahti (Litmanen 75), Iloia, Valakari, Paatelainen, Kolkka, Johansson.

Referee: Z. Arsic (Yugoslavia). **Half-time:** 1-0.

SCOTLAND 3, ESTONIA 2
Tynecastle, Edinburgh, (16,930), Saturday October 10, 1998

Scotland: Leighton (Aberdeen), Weir (Hearts), Boyd (Celtic), Calderwood (Tottenham) (Donnelly, Celtic, 56), Hendry (Rangers), Davidson (Blackburn Rov.), Gallacher (Blackburn Rov.) (Jackson, Celtic, 17), B. McKinlay (Blackburn Rov.), McCoist (Kilmarnock) (Dodds, Dundee Utd. 69), Durrant (Kilmarnock), *Johnston (Sunderland). **Scorers:** Dodds (70, 85), Hohlev-Simson o. g. (79). **Booked:** Jackson, Dodds, Donnelly, Weir.

Estonia: Poom, Smirnov, Kirs, Hohlev-Simson, M. Rooba, Alonen, Terehhov, Oper, Kristal, Reim, Zelinski (Viikmae 88). **Scorers:** Hohlev-Simson (34), Smirnov (76). **Booked:** Alonen, Kristal, Kirs, M. Rooba. **Sent-off:** Kristal (83).

Referee: J. Marques (Portugal). Half-time: 0-1.

LUXEMBOURG 0, ENGLAND 3
Stade Josy Barthel, Luxembourg, (8,200), Wednesday October 14, 1998

Luxembourg: Koch, Ferron, Funck, L. Deville, Strasser, Theis (Holtz 62), F. Deville (Alverdi 85), Saibene, Christophe (Amodio 78), Cardoni, Posing. **Booked:** Cardoni.

England: Seaman (Arsenal), R. Ferdinand (West Ham Utd.), Campbell (Tottenham), Southgate (Aston Villa), Beckham (Manchester Utd.), Batty (Newcastle Utd.), Scholes (Manchester Utd.) (I. Wright, West Ham Utd., 77), Anderton (Tottenham) (Lee, Newcastle Utd., 64), P. Neville (Manchester Utd.), Shearer (Newcastle Utd.), Owen (Liverpool). **Scorers:** Owen (19), Shearer (40 pen), Southgate (90). **Booked:** Beckham.

Referee: S. Vorgias (Greece). Half-time: 0-2.

WALES 3, BELARUS 2
Ninian Park, Cardiff, (11,000), Wednesday October 14, 1998

Wales: Jones (Southampton), Robinson (Charlton Athletic), Barnard (Barnsley), Savage (Leicester City), Symons (Fulham), Coleman (Fulham), Johnson (Nott'm Forest), Saunders (Sheff. Utd.), Blake (Bolton Wand.), M. Hughes (Southampton), Pembridge (Benfica). **Scorers:** Robinson (16), Coleman (50), Symons (84). **Booked:** Robinson.

Belarus: Satsunkevich, Iakhimovitch, Ostrovski, Satanuk, Gerashchenko (Romaschenko 88), Gurenko, Khatskevich, Baranov (Gerasimets 70), Belkevich, Makovski (Katchouro 73), Lavrik. **Scorers:** Gurenko (21), Belkevich (49). **Booked:** Gurenko, Khatskevich, Gerashchenko.

Referee: L. Sammut (Malta). Half-time: 1-1.

REPUBLIC OF IRELAND 5, MALTA 0
Lansdowne Road, Dublin, (34,500), Wednesday October 14, 1998

Rep. of Ireland: Given (Newcastle Utd.), Kenna (Blackburn Rov.), Staunton (Liverpool), Breen (Coventry City), Cunningham (Wimbledon), Roy Keane (Manchester Utd.), McAteer (Liverpool) (Carsley, Derby Co., 84), Kinsella (Charlton Athletic), Robbie Keane (Wolves) (Kennedy, Wimbledon, 82), Quinn (Sunderland) (Cascarino, Nancy, 73), Duff (Blackburn Rov.). **Scorers:** Robbie Keane (19, 21), Roy Keane (53), Quinn (61), Breen (80).

Malta: Cini, Sixsmith (Camilleri 76), Chetcuti, Spiteri, Debono, Buttigieg, Turner, Carabott, Suda (Aquis 65), Brincat, Zahra (Zammit 70).

Referee: R. Olsen (Norway). Half-time: 2-0.

Robbie Keane became Ireland's youngest full international goalscorer at 18 years and 98 days.

SCOTLAND 2, FAROE ISLANDS 1
Pittodrie, Aberdeen, (18,517), Wednesday October 14, 1998

Scotland: Sullivan (Wimbledon), Weir (Hearts), Boyd (Celtic), Elliott (Leicester City), Hendry (Rangers), Davidson (Blackburn Rov.), B. McKinlay (Blackburn Rov.) (Durrant, Kilmarnock, 46), Burley (Celtic), Donnelly (Celtic), Dodds (Dundee Utd.), Johnston (Sunderland) (*Glass, Newcastle Utd., 79). **Scorers:** Burley (21), Dodds (45). **Booked:** Elliott, Dodds.

Faroe Islands: Mikkelsen, Johannsen, J. K. Hansen, Thorsteinsson, H. Hansen, Jonsson, H. Jarnskor (John Hansen 79), J. Johnsson, Arge (Borg 68), Petersen, S. Johnsson. **Scorer:** Petersen (86 pen). **Booked:** H. Hansen, H. Jarnskor, Arge.

Referee: C. Kapitanis (Cyprus). Half-time: 2-0.

NORTHERN IRELAND 2, MOLDOVA 2

Windsor Park, Belfast, (11,137), Wednesday November 18, 1998

Northern Ireland: Fettis (Blackburn Rov.), Griffin (St Johnstone), Lomas (West Ham Utd.), *Kennedy (Watford), Patterson (Dundee Utd.), Morrow (Q.P.R.), Gillespie (Newcastle Utd.) (McCarthy, Birmingham City, 88), Lennon (Leicester City), Dowie (Q.P.R.), M. Hughes (Wimbledon), Rowland (Q.P.R.) (Gray, Luton Town, 77). **Scorers:** Dowie (49), Lennon (64). **Booked:** Kennedy, Gillespie.

Moldova: Dinov, Fistikan, Rebeza, Tistimitanu (V. Maievici 86), Guzun (Pusca 66), Stroienco, Curtiean, G. Stratulat (Sukharev 66), Gaidamasciuc, Epuryanu, Clescenco. **Scorers:** Gaidamasciuc (22), Tistimitanu (57). **Booked:** Curtiean, Tistimitanu, G. Skratulat, Dinov. **Sent-off:** Curtiean (66).

Referee: V. Hrinak (Slovakia). **Half-time:** 0-1.

YUGOSLAVIA 1, REPUBLIC OF IRELAND 0

Belgrade, (44,000), Wednesday November 18, 1998

Yugoslavia: Kralj, J. Stankovic, Djorovic, D. Stankovic, Mihajlovicj, Djukic, Jokanovic, Jugovic (Grozdic 85), Mijatovic, Milosevic (Drulovic 76), Stojkovic (Kovacevic 46). **Scorer:** Mijatovic (64). **Booked:** Djukic.

Rep. of Ireland: Given (Newcastle Utd.), Irwin (Manchester Utd.), Kinsella (Charlton Athletic), McAteer (Liverpool) (O'Neill, Norwich City, 83), Roy Keane (Manchester Utd.), Cunningham (Wimbledon), Breen (Coventry City), Staunton (Liverpool), McLoughlin (Portsmouth) (Cascarino, Nancy, 71), Duff (Blackburn Rov.), Quinn (Sunderland) (Connolly, Wolves, 71).

Referee: K. Nilsson (Sweden). **Half-time:** 0-0.

ENGLAND 3, POLAND 1

Wembley, (73,836), Saturday, March 27, 1999

England: Seaman (Arsenal), G. Neville (Manchester Utd.), Le Saux (Chelsea), Keown (Arsenal), Campbell (Tottenham), *Sherwood (Tottenham), Beckham (Manchester Utd.) (P. Neville, Manchester Utd., 78), Scholes (Manchester Utd.) (Redknapp, Liverpool, 82), McManaman (Liverpool) (*Parlour, Arsenal, 69), Cole (Manchester Utd.), Shearer (Newcastle Utd.). **Scorer:** Scholes (11, 21, 70). **Booked:** Sherwood, Scholes.

Poland: Matysek, Bak, Lapinski, Ratajczyk, Zielinski, Hajto, Swierczewski (Klos 46), Iwan, Siadaczki (Kowalczyk 64), Brzeczek, Trzeciak (Juskowiak 82). **Scorer:** Brzeczek (29). **Booked:** Ratajczyk, Hajto.

Referee: V. Melo Pereira (Portugal). **Half-time:** 2-1.

NORTHERN IRELAND 0, GERMANY 3

Windsor Park, Belfast, (14,270), Saturday, March 27, 1999

Northern Ireland: *Taylor (Fulham), Patterson (Dundee Utd.), Horlock (Manchester City), Lomas (West Ham Utd.), *Williams (Chesterfield), Morrow (Q.P.R.), Gillespie (Blackburn Rov.) (McCarthy, Birmingham City, 83), Lennon (Leicester City) (Sonner, Sheffield Wed., 68), Dowie (Q.P.R.), M. Hughes (Wimbledon), Rowland (Q.P.R.) (Kennedy, Watford, 68). **Booked:** Patterson.

Germany: Kahn, Babbel, Heinrich, Worns, Strunz, Jeremies, Neuville (Jancker 68), Hamann, Bierhoff, Matthaus (Nowotny 46), Bode (Preetz 77). **Scorers:** Bode (11, 42), Hamann (62). **Booked:** Bode, Worns.

Referee: G. Cesari (Italy). **Half-time:** 0-2.

SWITZERLAND 2, WALES 0

Zurich, (13,500), Wednesday March 31, 1999

Switzerland: Brunner, Jeanneret, Fournier, Henchoz, Wolf, Vogel, Muller, Wicky, Chapuisat, Sforza, Cornisetti (Buhlmann 67). **Scorer:** Chapuisat (4, 70). **Booked:** Vogel.

Wales: Jones (Southampton) (Crossley, Nott'm. Forest, 26), Robinson (Charlton Athletic), Pembridge (Benfica), Savage (Leicester City), Symons (Fulham), Coleman (Fulham), Johnson (Nott'm. Forest), Saunders (Benfica), Blake (Blackburn Rov.) (Hartson, Wimbledon, 64), Hughes (Southampton) (Bellamy, Norwich City, 75), Speed (Newcastle Utd.). **Booked:** Hughes, Savage.

Referee: M. Liba (Czech Republic). **Half-time:** 1-0.

MOLDOVA 0, NORTHERN IRELAND 0
Chisinau, (9,237), Wednesday, March 31, 1999

Moldova: Dinov, Fistikan, Rebeza, Sosnovschii, Guzun, Stroienco, Suharev, Oprea (Stratulat 90), Gaidamascuic, Epureanu, Clescenco.

Northern Ireland: Taylor (Fulham), Patterson (Dundee Utd.) (A. Hughes, Newcastle Utd., 63), Horlock (Manchester City), Lomas (West Ham Utd.), Williams (Chesterfield), Morrow (Q.P.R.), Gillespie (Blackburn Rov.), Dowie (Q.P.R.), Lennon (Leicester City), Robinson (Bournemouth), M. Hughes (Wimbledon). **Booked:** M. Hughes, Dowie, Horlock.

Referee: E. Trivcovic (Croatia).

SCOTLAND 1, CZECH REPUBLIC 2
Celtic Park, (44,513), Wednesday, March 31, 1999

Scotland: Sullivan (Wimbledon), Weir (Everton), Boyd (Celtic), Lambert (Celtic), Elliott (Leicester City), Davidson (Blackburn Rov.) (Johnston, Sunderland, 52), Burley (Celtic), Hopkin (Leeds Utd.), Jess (Aberdeen), McAllister (Coventry City) (Hutchison, Everton, 64), McCann (Rangers). **Scorer:** Jess 68. **Booked:** Hopkin.

Czech Republic: Srnicek, Votava, Suchoparek, Nedved, Hornak, Hasek, Nemec, Poborsky (Rada 76), Lokvenc (Kuka 70), Smicer (Baranek 84), Berger. **Scorers:** Elliott o.g. (27), Smicer (35). **Booked:** Baranek.

Referee: M. Nielsen (Denmark). **Half-time:** 0-2.

Scotland's first defeat for 12 years in a home qualifying tie.

ENGLAND 0, SWEDEN 0
Wembley, (75,824), Saturday, June 5, 1999

England: Seaman (Arsenal), P. Neville (Manchester Utd.), Le Saux (Chelsea) (Gray, Sunderland, 45), Campbell (Tottenham), Keown (Arsenal) (Ferdinand, West Ham Utd., 34), Beckham (Manchester Utd.) (Parlour, Arsenal, 76), Batty (Leeds Utd.), Sherwood (Tottenham), Scholes (Manchester Utd.), Cole (Manchester Utd.), Shearer (Newcastle Utd.). **Booked:** Scholes, Cole, Shearer, Batty. **Sent-off:** Scholes (51).

Sweden: Hedman, R. Nilsson, Bjorklund, Kaamark, P. Anderssen, Ljungberg, Schwarz, Mild (Alexandersson 7), Mjallby (D. Anderssen 83), Larsson (Svensson 70), K. Anderssen. **Booked:** Hedman, Schwarz, K. Anderssen.

Referee: J. Garcia-Aranda (Spain).

ITALY 4, WALES 0
Bologna, (12,392), Saturday, June 5, 1999

Italy: Buffon, Panucci, Cannavaro, Negro, Maldini, Fuser (Di Livio 67), Albertini, Conte, Di Francesco, Vieri (Montella 45), Inzaghi (Chiesa 81). **Scorers:** Vieri (6), Inzaghi (36), Maldini (39), Chiesa (89).

Wales: Jones (Southampton), Page (Watford), Melville (Fulham), Williams (Wolves), Robinson (Charlton Athletic) (Jenkins, Huddersfield Town, 76), Hughes (Southampton), Speed (Newcastle Utd.), Bellamy (Norwich City) (Pembridge, Benfica, 80), Barnard (Barnsley), Saunders (Benfica) (Hartson, Wimbledon, 65), Giggs.

Referee: E. Steinborn (Germany). **Half-time:** 3-0.

Bobby Gould resigned as Wales manager after the game.

FAROE ISLANDS 1, SCOTLAND 1
Toftir, (4,500), Saturday, June 5, 1999

Faroe Islands: Mikkelsen, Johannsen, H. Hansen, Thorsteinsson, O. Hansen (J. Hansen 86), Johnsson, J. Joensen (Borg 69), S. Joensen, Moerkore, Jonsson, Petersen (Arge 79). **Scorer:** H. Hansen (90). **Booked:** Borg.

Scotland: Sullivan (Wimbledon), Weir (Everton), Boyd (Celtic), Calderwood (Aston Villa), Elliott (Leicester City), Davidson (Blackburn Rov.), Dodds (Dundee Utd.), Lambert (Celtic), Gallacher (Blackburn Rov.) (Jess, Aberdeen, 89), Durrant (Kilmarnock) (Cameron, Hearts, 45), Johnston (Sunderland) (Gemmill, Everton, 86). **Scorer:** Johnston (38). **Booked:** Johnston. **Sent-off:** Elliott (45).

Referee: P. Kalt (France). **Half-time:** 0-1.

Craig Brown's 50th match in charge of Scotland.

BULGARIA 1, ENGLAND 1
Sofia, (22,000), Wednesday, June 9, 1999

Bulgaria: Ivankov, Markov, Kirilov, Zagorcic, Stoilov, Kischischev, Illiev (Borimov 60), S. Petrov, Petkov, Stoichkov (Batchev 75), Yovov (M. Petrov 45). **Scorer:** Markov (18). **Booked:** M. Petrov. **Sent-off:** M. Petrov (58).

England: Seaman (Arsenal), *Woodgate (Leeds Utd.) (Parlour, Arsenal, 65), Southgate (Aston Villa), Campbell (Tottenham), P. Neville (Manchester Utd.), Gray (Sunderland), Redknapp (Liverpool), Batty (Leeds Utd.), Sheringham (Manchester Utd.), Shearer (Newcastle Utd.), Fowler (Liverpool) (Heskey, Leicester City, 81). **Scorer:** Shearer (13). **Booked:** Southgate, Sheringham, Fowler, Campbell.

Referee: M. Van der Ende (Holland). **Half-time:** 1-1.

WALES 0, DENMARK 2
Anfield, (10,956), Wednesday, June 9, 1999

Wales: Jones (Southampton), Jenkins (Huddersfield Town), Melville (Fulham), Coleman (Fulham), Barnard (Barnsley) (Legg, Cardiff City, 90), Robinson (Charlton Athletic) (Pembridge, Benfica, 85), Hughes (Southampton), Speed (Newcastle Utd.), Saunders (Benfica), Hartson (Wimbledon) (Bellamy, Norwich City, 88), Giggs (Manchester Utd.). **Booked:** Hartson.

Denmark: Schmeichel, Colding, Henriksen, Hogh, Heintze, Jorgensen (Frandsen 89), A. Nielsen (Tofting 83), Goldbaek, Gronkjaer, Molnar (Tomasson 70), Sand. **Scorers:** Tomasson (84), Tofting (90 pen).

Referee: A. Ancion (Belgium). **Half-time:** 0-0.

Neville Southall and Mark Hughes joint-caretaker managers for the game.

REPUBLIC OF IRELAND 1, MACEDONIA 0
Lansdowne Rd, Dublin, (28,108), Wednesday, June 9, 1999

Rep. of Ireland: Kelly (Sheffield Utd.), Carr (Tottenham), Cunningham (Wimbledon), Breen (Coventry City), Irwin (Manchester Utd.), Kennedy (Wimbledon), Carsley (Blackburn Rov.), Kinsella (Charlton Athletic), Duff (Blackburn Rov.) (Kilbane, W.B.A., 64), Quinn (Sunderland) (Connolly, Wolves, 81), Robbie Keane (Wolves) (Cascarino, Nancy, 68). **Scorer:** Quinn (67).

Macedonia: Milosevski, Trajcov (Nedmedin 45), Stavreski, Nikolovski, Stojanoski, Babunski, Sainovski (Sedloski 71), Trenevski (Hristrov 77), Sakiri, Ciric, Micevski. **Booked:** Hristov.

Referee: U. Meier (Switzerland). **Half-time:** 0-0.

Tony Cascarino equalled Paul McGrath's record of 83 Rep. of Ireland caps.

CZECH REPUBLIC 3, SCOTLAND 2

Prague, (22,000), Wednesday, June 9, 1999

Czech Republic: Srnicek, Hornak, Suchoparek, Repka, Poborsky (Kuka 65), Nedved (Koller 65), Hasek (Baranek 60), Berger, Nemec, Lokvenc, Smicer. **Scorers:** Repka (65), Kuka (75), Koller (87). **Booked:** Suchoparek, Poborsky, Smicer.

Scotland: Sullivan (Wimbledon), Weir (Everton), Boyd (Celtic), Ritchie (Hearts), Calderwood (Aston Villa), Lambert (Celtic), Davidson (Blackburn Rov.), Durrant (Kilmarnock) (Jess, Aberdeen, 71), Johnston (Sunderland), Gallacher (Blackburn Rov.), Dodds (Dundee Utd.). **Scorers:** Ritchie (30), Johnston (62). **Booked:** Davidson, Ritchie, Dodds.

Referee: H. Krug (Germany). **Half-time:** 0-1.

Scotland's 600th international.

FRIENDLY INTERNATIONALS

ENGLAND 2, CZECH REPUBLIC 0

Wembley, (33,535), Wednesday November 18, 1998

England: Martyn (Leeds Utd.), Campbell (Tottenham), Keown (Arsenal), R. Ferdinand (West Ham Utd.), Butt (Manchester Utd.), Le Saux (Chelsea), Anderton (Tottenham), Beckham (Manchester Utd.), Dublin (Aston Villa), I. Wright (West Ham Utd.) (Fowler, Liverpool, 71), Merson (Aston Villa) (*Hendrie, Aston Villa, 71). **Scorers:** Anderton (22), Merson (40).

Czech Republic: Kouba, Latal (Kotulek 46), Votava, Novotny (Baranek 46), Repka, Berger, Nemec (Vonasek 46), Poborsky, Kuka (Sloncik 74), Smicer (Lokvenc 46), Bejbl.

Referee: L. Meier (Switzerland). **Half-time:** 2-0

ENGLAND 0, FRANCE 2

Wembley, (74,111), Wednesday February 10, 1999

England: Seaman (Arsenal) (Martyn, Leeds Utd., 46), Dixon (Arsenal) (R. Ferdinand, West Ham Utd., 72), Le Saux (Chelsea), Ince (Liverpool), Keown (Arsenal) (Scholes, Manchester Utd., 86), Adams (Arsenal), Beckham (Manchester Utd.), Redknapp (Liverpool) (Wilcox, Blackburn Rov., 86), Shearer (Newcastle Utd.), Owen (Liverpool) (Cole, Manchester Utd., 66), Anderton (Tottenham).

France: Barthez, Thuram, Lizarazu, Desailly, Blanc (Leboeuf 46), Zidane, Djorkaeff (Wiltord 84), Deschamps (Candela 90), Petit, Pires (Dugarry 46), Anelka (Vieira 84). **Scorer:** Anelka (69, 76).

Referee: H. Krug (Germany). **Half-time:** 0-0.

Howard Wilkinson in charge of England as caretaker-coach.

REPUBLIC OF IRELAND 2, PARAGUAY 0

Lansdowne Road, Dublin, (27,600), Wednesday February 10, 1999

Rep. of Ireland: Given (Newcastle Utd.) (A. Kelly, Sheff. Utd., 66), Irwin (Manchester Utd.), Cunningham (Wimbledon), Breen (Coventry City), Harte (Leeds Utd.) (Babb, Liverpool, 71), McAteer (Blackburn Rov.) (McLoughlin, Portsmouth, 81), Roy Keane (Manchester Utd.), Kinsella (Charlton Athletic) (Carsley, Derby Co., 66), Quinn (Sunderland) (Cascarino, Nancy, 69), Robbie Keane (Wolves) (Connolly, Wolves, 66), Duff (Blackburn Rov.). **Scorers:** Irwin (39 pen), Connolly (73).

Paraguay: Tavarelli, Valdez, Rolon, Ortiz, Caniza, Acosta, Aguilera, Paredes, Caballero (Britez 71), Franco (Esquivel 79), Roman (Peralta 63). **Booked:** Rolon.

Referee: G. F. Orrason (Iceland). **Half-time:** 1-0.

NORTHERN IRELAND 1, CANADA 1
Windsor Park, Belfast, (7,663), Tuesday, April 27, 1999

Northern Ireland: Taylor (Fulham) (Wright, Manchester City, 45), A. Hughes (Newcastle Utd.), Horlock (Manchester City), Lomas (West Ham Utd.), Williams (Chesterfield), Hunter (Reading), McCarthy (Birmingham City) (*Hamill, Glentoran, 60), Mulryne (Norwich City) (Sonner, Sheffield Wed., 81), Dowie (Q.P.R.) (*Ferguson, Glentoran, 74), *Coote (Norwich City) (*McVeigh, Tottenham, 74), Rowland (Q.P.R.). **Scorer:** McVeigh (90).

Canada: Forrest, Clarke, Parker, Watson, Devos, Xausa (Bircham 58), Stalteri (Kusch 65), Dasovic, Peschisolido, Bent, Brennan. **Scorer:** Bircham 67.

Referee: T. McCurry (Scotland). **Half-time:** 0-0.

HUNGARY 1, ENGLAND 1
Budapest, (20,000), Wednesday, April 28, 1999

Hungary: Kiraly, Hrutka, A. Korsos (Toth 65) (Herczeg 90), Matyus, Sebok, Halmai, Dombi, Dardai, Pisont (Somogyi 45), Illis, G. Korsos. **Scorer:** Hrutka (79).

England: Seaman (Arsenal), *Brown (Manchester Utd.) (*Gray, Sunderland, 74), P. Neville (Manchester Utd.), Batty (Leeds Utd.), Ferdinand (West Ham Utd.) (*Carragher, Liverpool, 62), Keown (Arsenal), Butt (Manchester Utd.), Sherwood (Tottenham), Shearer (Newcastle Utd.), *Phillips (Sunderland) (*Heskey, Leicester City, 83), McManaman (Liverpool) (Redknapp, Liverpool, 85). **Scorer:** Shearer (22 pen).

Referee: L. Frohlich (Germany). **Half-time:** 0-1.

REPUBLIC OF IRELAND 2, SWEDEN 0
Lansdowne Rd, Dublin, (29,300), Wednesday, April 28, 1999

Rep. of Ireland: Given (Newcastle Utd.), *Carr (Tottenham), Staunton (Liverpool), McLoughlin (Portsmouth), Cunningham (Wimbledon), Breen (Coventry City) (Babb, Liverpool, 45), McAteer (Blackburn Rov.) (Kavanagh, Stoke City, 45), Kinsella (Charlton Athletic) (Kilbane, W.B.A., 45), Quinn (Sunderland) (Robbie Keane, Wolves, 79), Connolly (Wolves) (Cascarino, Nancy, 71), Kennedy (Wimbledon) (Duff, Blackburn Rov., 79). **Scorers:** Kavanagh (75), Kennedy (77).

Sweden: Kihlstedt, Kaamark, P. Anderssen, Bjorklund (Jakobsson 45), Lucic, Schwarz, Mild (Alexandersson 45), D. Anderssen, Blomqvist, Larsson, Pettersson (Jonsson 82). **Referee:** P. Garibian (France). **Half-time:** 0-0.

GERMANY 0, SCOTLAND 1
Bremen, (27,000), Wednesday, April 28, 1999

Germany: Lehmann, Nowotny, Matthaus, Worns, Strunz (Jancker 86), Hamann (Ballack 57), Jeremies (Ramelow 46), Heinrich, Neuville, Bierhoff (Kirsten 57), Heldt.

Scotland: Sullivan (Wimbledon), Weir (Everton), Hendry (Rangers) (*Ritchie, Hearts, 66), Boyd (Celtic), Gemmill (Everton) (Jess, Aberdeen, 57), Durrant (Kilmarnock) (*Winters, Aberdeen, 72), Lambert (Celtic) (*Cameron, Hearts, 84), Johnston (Sunderland) (O'Neil, VFL Wolfsburg, 86), Davidson (Blackburn Rov.) (Whyte, Aberdeen, 79), Hutchison (Everton), Dodds (Dundee Utd.). **Scorer:** Hutchison (65). **Booked:** Durrant.

Referee: U. Meier (Switzerland). **Half-time:** 0-0.

REPUBLIC OF IRELAND 0, NORTHERN IRELAND 1
Lansdowne Rd, Dublin, (12,100), Saturday, May 29, 1999

Rep. of Ireland: Given (Newcastle Utd.), Carr (Tottenham), Cunningham (Wimbledon), Babb (Liverpool), Maybury (Leeds Utd.), Kennedy (Wimbledon), Kinsella (Charlton Athletic) (Kavanagh, Stoke City, 82), Carsley (Blackburn Rov.) (McLoughlin, Portsmouth, 45), Robbie Keane (Wolves), Quinn (Sunderland) (Cascarino, Nancy, 71), Duff (Blackburn Rov.).

Northern Ireland: Taylor (Fulham) (Carroll, Wigan Athletic, 45), Patterson (Dundee Utd.), Williams (Chesterfield), Hunter (Reading), A. Hughes (Newcastle Utd.), McCarthy (Birmingham City), Robinson (Bournemouth), Lennon (Leicester City) (Griffin, St. Johnstone, 79), Rowland (Q.P.R.) (*Johnson, Blackburn Rov., 74), Quinn (W.B.A.), Dowie (Q.P.R.) (Coote, Norwich City, 45). **Scorer:** Griffin (85).

Referee: K. Richards (Wales). **Half-time:** 0-0.

Benefit match for victims of the Omagh bombing.

EUROPEAN U-21 CHAMPIONSHIP

(Qualifying Round)

SWEDEN 0, ENGLAND 2
Sundsvall, (5,260), Friday, September 4, 1998

England: Wright (Ipswich Town), Carragher (Liverpool), Dyer (Ipswich Town), (Curtis, Manchester Utd., 78), Lampard (West Ham Utd.), Ball (Everton), Brown (Manchester Utd.), Upson (Arsenal), Hendrie (Aston Villa), (Clemence, Tottenham, 88), Jansen (Crystal Palace), (Euell, Wimbledon, 81), Heskey (Leicester City), Mills (Charlton Athletic).

Scorers – England: Carragher (8), Lampard (86 pen). **Half-time:** 0-1.

WALES 1, ITALY 2
Wrexham, (2,000), Friday, September 4, 1998

Wales: Anthony Williams (Blackburn Rov.), Green (Wolves) (Price, Swansea City, 23), Roberts (Liverpool), Jones (Leeds Utd.), Jarman (Cardiff City), Hughes (Aston Villa), Llewellyn (Norwich City), Bellamy (Norwich City) (Roberts, Wrexham, 87) Haworth (Coventry City), Oster (Everton), Andrew Williams (Southampton).

Scorers – Wales: Bellamy (45 pen). **Italy:** Grandoni (14), Camandini (25). **Sent-off – Wales:** Oster (77). **Italy:** Ambrosini (77). **Half-time:** 1-2.

TURKEY 2, NORTHERN IRELAND 0
Kocaeli, (3,739), Friday, September 4, 1998

Northern Ireland: Carroll (Wigan Athletic), Griffin (St Johnstone), McGlinchey (Port Vale), Feeney (Linfield), Burns (Port Vale), Waterman (Portsmouth), Johnson (Blackburn Rov.) (Lyttle, Peterborough Utd., 89), McVeigh (Tottenham) (McKnight, Rangers, 75), Coote (Norwich City) (Fitzgerald, Rangers, 75), Jeff Whitley (Manchester City), Friars (Ipswich Town).

Scorers – Turkey: Halit (57), Erhan (69). **Half-time:** 0-0.

REPUBLIC OF IRELAND 2, CROATIA 2
Buckley Park, Kilkenny, (4,000), Friday, September 4, 1998

Rep. of Ireland: O'Reilly (West Ham Utd.), Worrell (Blackburn Rov.), Coughlan (Cork City) (Darcy, Tottenham, 50), Ryan (Millwall), Boxall (Brentford) (Folan, Crystal Palace, 86), Morgan (St Patrick's Athletic), Inman (Peterborough Utd.), Mahon (Tranmere Rov.) (Baker, Middlesbrough, 50), Kilbane (W.B.A.), Clare (Grimsby Town), Conlon (Manchester City).

Scorers – Rep. of Ireland: Conlon (2), Baker (59). **Croatia:** Tomic (56), Sokota (77). **Sent-off – Rep. of Ireland:** Conlon (43). **Half-time:** 1-0.

LITHUANIA 0, SCOTLAND 0
Vilnius (500) Friday, September 4, 1998

Scotland: Alexander (Livingston), McEwan (Raith), Buchan (Aberdeen), McCluskey (St Johnstone), Archibald (Partick), Brebner (Reading), Easton (Dundee Utd.), Strachan (Coventry City) (Mason, Manchester City, 73), Burchill (Celtic) (Notman, Manchester Utd., 85), Graham (Rangers) (Elliot, Celtic, 45), Campbell (Leicester City).

ENGLAND 1, BULGARIA 0
Upton Park, (11,000), Friday, October 9, 1998

England: Wright (Ipswich Town), Carragher (Liverpool), Dyer (Ipswich Town) (Mills, Charlton Athletic, 63), Lampard (West Ham Utd.), Ball (Everton), Brown (Manchester Utd.), Upson (Arsenal), Hendrie (Aston Villa), Jansen (Crystal Palace) (Morris, Chelsea, 75), Heskey (Leicester City) (Euell, Wimbledon, 90), Curtis (Manchester Utd.).

Scorer – England: Lampard (55 pen). **Half-time:** 0-0.

DENMARK 2, WALES 2
Odense, (3,000), Friday, October 9, 1998

Wales: Anthony Williams (Blackburn Rov.), Price (Swansea City), Roberts (Liverpool), Green (Wolves) (Andrew Williams, Southampton, 65), Danny Williams (Liverpool), Gabbidon (W.B.A.), Davies (Peterborough Utd.), Jones (Leeds Utd.) (Wright, Oxford Utd., 69), Haworth (Coventry City), Llewellyn (Norwich City), Thomas (Blackburn Rov.) (Gibson, Tranmere Rov., 79).

Scorers – Wales: Haworth (8), Thomas (44). **Denmark:** Rommedahl (16), Madsen (62). **Half-time:** 1-2.

SCOTLAND 2, ESTONIA 0
Airdrie, (5,676), Friday, October 9, 1998

Scotland: Alexander (Livingston), R. Anderson (Aberdeen) (McEwan, Raith, 27) Naysmith (Hearts), Easton (Dundee Utd.), Wilson (Rangers), Buchan (Aberdeen), Campbell (Leicester City) (Notman, Manchester Utd., 67), Strachan (Coventry City), Dargo (Raith) (Burchill, Celtic, 79), Brebner (Reading), Dalglish (Newcastle Utd.).

Scorers – Scotland: Dargo (6), Dalglish (74). **Half-time:** 1-0.

NORTHERN IRELAND 1, FINLAND 1
Ballymena, (2,000), Friday, October 9, 1998

Northern Ireland: Carroll (Wigan Athletic), Griffin (St Johnstone), McGlinchey (Port Vale), Jeff Whitley (Manchester City), Burns (Port Vale), Waterman (Portsmouth), Johnson (Blackburn Rov.), Feeney (Linfield), Coote (Norwich City), Fitzgerald (Rangers) (Graham, Q.P.R., 64), Friars (Ipswich Town) (Elliott, Glentoran, 87).

Scorers – Northern Ireland: Coote (17). **Finland:** Niemi (29). **Half-time:** 1-1.

WALES 0, BELARUS 0
Jenner Park, Barry, (400), Tuesday, October 13, 1998

Wales: Anthony Williams (Blackburn Rov.), Price (Swansea City), Roberts (Liverpool), Green (Wolves), Danny Williams (Liverpool), Gabbidon (W.B.A.), Davies (Peterborough Utd.), Jones (Leeds Utd.), Haworth (Coventry City) Llewellyn (Norwich City), Thomas (Blackburn Rov.) (Gibson, Tranmere Rov., 68).

LUXEMBOURG 0, ENGLAND 5
Luxembourg, (500), Tuesday, October 13, 1998

England: Wright (Ipswich Town), Carragher (Liverpool), Mills (Charlton Athletic), Lampard (West Ham Utd.) (Johnson, Crewe Alexandra, 75), Ball (Everton), Brown (Manchester Utd.), Upson (Arsenal), Hendrie (Aston Villa) (Morris, Chelsea, 49), Jansen (Crystal Palace) (Cort, Wimbledon, 59), Heskey (Leicester City), Curtis (Manchester Utd.).

Scorers – England: Hendrie (27), Upson (45), Lampard (52), Cort (65, 85). **Sent-off –
England:** Morris (68). **Half-time:** 0-2.

REPUBLIC OF IRELAND 2, MALTA 1
Lamberton Park, Arklow, (4,500), Tuesday, October 13, 1998

Rep. of Ireland: O'Reilly (West Ham Utd.), Boxall (Brentford), Hawkins (St Patrick's
Athletic), Worrell (Blackburn Rov.), Ryan (Millwall), Inman (Peterborough Utd.) (Folan,
Brentford, 78), Morgan (St Patrick's Athletic), Mahon (Tranmere Rov.) (McPhail, Leeds
Utd., 56), Kilbane (W.B.A.), Clare (Grimsby Town), Lee (Aston Villa).

Scorers – Rep. of Ireland: Clare (29), Worrell (90). **Malta:** Licari (27) **Half-time:** 1-1.

BELGIUM 2, SCOTLAND 0
Ghent, (1,000), Wednesday, October 14, 1998

Scotland: Alexander (Livingston), McEwan (Raith), Naysmith (Hearts), Easton (Dundee
Utd.) (Paterson, Dundee Utd., 62), Wilson (Rangers), Buchan (Aberdeen), Campbell
(Leicester City) (Dargo, Raith, 83), Strachan (Coventry City), Burchill (Celtic), Brebner
(Reading), Dalglish (Newcastle Utd.) (Notman, Manchester Utd., 69).

Scorers – Belgium: Morhaye (37, 43). **Half-time:** 2-0

NORTHERN IRELAND 1, MOLDOVA 1
Coleraine, (1,920), Tuesday, November 17, 1998

Northern Ireland: Carroll (Wigan Athletic), Lyttle (Peterborough Utd.), McGlinchey (Port
Vale), Jeff Whitley (Manchester City), Burns (Port Vale), Waterman (Portsmouth),
Graham (Q.P.R.) (Healy, Manchester Utd., 65), Feeney (Linfield), Coote (Norwich City),
McVeigh (Tottenham) (McKnight, Rangers, 65), Friars (Ipswich Town).

Scorers – Northern Ireland: Healy (74). **Moldova:** Lungu (43). **Half-time:** 0-1.

SCOTLAND 2, BELGIUM 2
St Mirren Park, Paisley, (5,087), Wednesday, November 18, 1998

Scotland: Alexander (Livingston), McEwan (Raith), Naysmith (Hearts), Ferguson (Rang-
ers) (Easton, Dundee Utd., 65), Anderson (Aberdeen), Wilson (Rangers), Campbell
(Leicester City) (Notman, Manchester Utd., 82), Strachan (Coventry City) (Paterson,
Dundee Utd., 45), Dargo (Raith), Burchill (Celtic), Brebner (Reading).

Scorers – Scotland: Dargo (41, 69). **Belgium:** Somers (8), Vandepaar (pen), (14). **Sent-off
– Scotland:** Easton (84). **Half-time:** 1-2.

YUGOSLAVIA 1, REPUBLIC OF IRELAND 1
Smederevo, (5,550), Wednesday, November 18, 1998

Rep. of Ireland: O'Reilly (West Ham Utd.), Boxall (Brentford) (Murphy, Cork City, 43),
Coughlan (Cork City) (Darcy, Tottenham, 39), Worrell (Blackburn Rov.), Ryan (Millwall),
Dunne (Everton), Mahon (Tranmere Rov.) (Inman, Peterborough Utd., 57), Morgan (St
Patrick's Athletic), Lee (Aston Villa), Baker (Middlesbrough), Kilbane (W.B.A.).

Scorers – Yugoslavia: Ivic (6). **Rep. of Ireland:** Kilbane (pen), (90). **Half-time:** 1-0. **Sent-off
– Rep. of Ireland:** Ryan (32), Baker (52)

ENGLAND 5, POLAND 0
The Dell, Southampton, (15,202), Friday, March 26, 1999

England: Wright (Ipswich Town), Carragher (Liverpool), Mills (Charlton Athletic), Ball
(Everton), Brown (Manchester Utd.), Bowyer (Leeds Utd.), Lampard (West Ham Utd.)
(Mullins, Crystal Palace, 79), Hendrie (Aston Villa) (Curtis, Manchester Utd., 73),
Johnson (Crewe Alexandra), Jansen (Blackburn Rov.) (Euell, Wimbledon, 61), Beattie
(Southampton).

Scorers – England: Bowyer (40, 80), Lampard (54 pen, 59), Hendrie (71). **Half-time:** 1-0.

NORTHERN IRELAND 1, GERMANY 0
The Oval, Belfast, (2,534), Friday, March 26, 1999

Northern Ireland: Carroll (Wigan Athletic), Griffin (St. Johnstone), McGlinchey (Port Vale), Jeff Whitley (Manchester City), Burns (Port Vale), Waterman (Portsmouth), Johnson (Blackburn Rov.) (Feeney, Rangers, 80), McVeigh (Tottenham), Coote (Norwich City) (Healy, Manchester Utd., 85), Mulryne (Norwich City), Friars (Ipswich Town).

Scorer – Northern Ireland: Coote (52). **Half-time:** 0-0.

SWITZERLAND 1, WALES 0
Winterthur, (1,050), Tuesday, March 30, 1999

Wales: Anthony Williams (Blackburn Rov.), Green (Wolves), Andrew Williams (Southampton), Gabbidon (W.B.A.), Hughes (Aston Villa), Jones (Leeds Utd.), S. Roberts (Swansea City) (Maxwell, Liverpool, 65), Davies (Peterborough Utd.), Haworth (Wigan Athletic), Jeanne (Q.P.R.) (Tipton, Oldham Athletic, 65), D. Williams (Wrexham).

Scorer – Switzerland: Yakin (2). **Half-time:** 1-0.

MOLDOVA 0, NORTHERN IRELAND 0
Speia, (3,000), Tuesday, March 30, 1999

Northern Ireland: Carroll (Wigan Athletic), Griffin (St. Johnstone), McGlinchey (Port Vale), Lyttle (Peterborough Utd.), Burns (Port Vale), Waterman (Portsmouth), Johnson (Blackburn Rov.), McVeigh (Tottenham), Coote (Norwich City), Mulryne (Norwich City), Friars (Ipswich Town).

SCOTLAND 0, CZECH REPUBLIC 1
Fir Park, Motherwell, (3,681), Tuesday, March 30, 1999

Scotland: Alexander (Livingston), McEwan (Raith) (Teale, Ayr Utd., 87), Naysmith (Hearts), Hughes (Bournemouth), Lauchlan (Kilmarnock), Buchan (Aberdeen), Campbell (Leicester City), (Young, Aberdeen, 79), Dalglish (Newcastle Utd.), McCulloch (Motherwell) (Dargo, Raith, 79), Brebner (Reading), Burchill (Celtic).

Scorer – Czech Republic: Sionko (47). **Half-time:** 0-0.

ENGLAND 3, SWEDEN 0
McAlpine Stadium, Huddersfield, (13,045), Friday, June 4, 1999

England: Wright (Ipswich Town), Carragher (Liverpool), Robinson (Watford), Mills (Charlton Athletic), Brown (Manchester Utd.), Lampard (West Ham Utd.), Johnson (Derby Co.), Woodhouse (Sheffield Utd.) (Curtis, Manchester Utd., 57), Dyer (Ipswich Town), Cort (Wimbledon), Cresswell (Sheffield Wed.) (Greening, Manchester Utd., 71).

Scorers – England: Cort (30, 80), Cresswell (45). **Half-time:** 2-0.

ITALY 6, WALES 2
Ferrara, (6,864), Friday, June 4, 1999

Wales: Anthony Williams (Blackburn Rov.), Green (Wolves), Andrew Williams (Southampton), Jones (Leeds Utd.), Hughes (Aston Villa), D. Williams (Wrexham) (Gabbidon, W.B.A., 79), Jeanne (Q.P.R.), Earnshaw (Cardiff City) (Evans, Leeds Utd., 55) (S. Roberts, Swansea City, 79), Llewellyn (Norwich City), S. Davies (Peterborough Utd.), Maxwell (Liverpool).

Scorers – Italy: Ventola (9, 72, 86), Pirlo (62), Comandini (76), Vannucchi (78). **Wales:** Jeanne (28), Jones (67). **Sent-off – Wales:** Jeanne (28). **Half-time:** 1-1.

BULGARIA 0, ENGLAND 1
Vratsa, (20,000), Tuesday, June 8, 1999

England: Simonsen (Everton), Robinson (Watford), Curtis (Manchester Utd.), Carragher (Liverpool), Brown (Manchester Utd.), Johnson (Derby Co.), Mullins (Crystal Palace), Woodhouse (Sheffield Utd.), Greening (Manchester Utd.), Cort (Wimbledon), Cresswell (Sheffield Wed.) (Morris, Sheffield Utd., 72).

Scorer – England: Cort (87). **Half-time:** 0-0.

WALES 1, DENMARK 2
Racecourse Ground, Wrexham, (881), Tuesday, June 8, 1999

Wales: A. Williams (Blackburn Rov.), Gabbidon (W.B.A.), G. Roberts (Panionis), Holloway (Exeter City), D. Williams (Wrexham), Evans (Leeds Utd.), S. Roberts (Swansea City) (C. Roberts, Cardiff City, 16), S. Davies (Peterborough Utd.), Martin (Crystal Palace) (D. Davies, Barry Town, 63), Green (Wolves), Earnshaw (Cardiff City) (Jellyman, Peterborough Utd., 82).

Scorers – Wales: Evans (12). **Denmark:** Smith (2), Alkkag (73). **Half-time:** 1-1.

REPUBLIC OF IRELAND 0, MACEDONIA 0
Terryland Park, Galway, (2,000), Tuesday, June 8, 1999

Rep. of Ireland: O'Reilly (West Ham Utd.), Boxall (Brentford), Worrell (Dundee Utd.), Hawkins (St. Patrick's Athletic), Ferguson (Coventry City), Rowlands (Brentford), Quinn (Coventry City) (McClare, Barnsley, 78), McPhail (Leeds Utd.), Mahon (Tranmere Rov.), Grant (Stockport Co.), Fenn (Tottenham) (Molloy, St. Patrick's Athletic, 66).

CZECH REPUBLIC 3, SCOTLAND 2
Teplice, (3,150), Tuesday, June 8, 1999

Scotland: Gallacher (Dundee Utd.), R. Anderson (Aberdeen) (Nicholson, Rangers, 86), Naysmith (Hearts) (O'Brien, Blackburn Rov., 89), Rae (Dundee), Wilson (Rangers), Lauchlan (Kilmarnock), Hughes (Bournemouth), Burchill (Celtic), Thompson (Dundee Utd.), Brebner (Reading), I. Anderson (Dundee) (Campbell, Leicester City, 55).

Scorers – Czech Republic: Doser (7), Heinz (72), Sionko (85). **Scotland:** Thompson (50), Hughes (68). **Half-time:** 1-0.

OTHER U-21 INTERNATIONALS

TRIANGULAR TOURNAMENT

SCOTLAND 1, REPUBLIC OF IRELAND 0
Borough Briggs, Elgin, (3,816), Monday, May 31, 1999

Scotland: Gallacher (Dundee Utd.), R. Anderson (Aberdeen), Naysmith (Hearts), Hughes (Bournemouth), Wilson (Rangers), Buchan (Aberdeen), Campbell (Leicester City) (Teale, Ayr Utd., 46), Burchill (Celtic) (Rae, Dundee, 83), Thompson (Dundee Utd.), Brebner (Reading), I. Anderson (Dundee) (O'Brien, Blackburn Rov., 58).

Rep. of Ireland: O'Reilly (West Ham Utd.), Boxall (Brentford), Maybury (Leeds Utd.), Quinn (Coventry City), Hawkins (St. Patrick's Athletic), Worrell (Dundee Utd.), McPhail (Leeds Utd.), Fenn (Tottenham), Lee (Aston Villa) (Conlon, Southend Utd., 66), Rowlands (Brentford), Mahon (Tranmere Rov.) (McKeever, Sheffield Wed., 50).

Scorer – Scotland: Thompson (44). **Half-time:** 1-0.

REPUBLIC OF IRELAND 1, NORTHERN IRELAND 0
Caledonian Stadium, Inverness, (605), Wednesday, June 2, 1999

Rep. of Ireland: O'Connor (Bradford Park Avenue), Worrell (Dundee Utd.) (Maybury, Leeds Utd., 62), Ryan (Millwall), Hawkins (St. Patrick's Athletic) (Mahon, Tranmere Rov., 62), Ferguson (Coventry City), McClare (Barnsley), Folan (Brentford), Barry-Murphy (Cork City), McKeever (Sheffield Wed.) (McPhail, Leeds Utd., 75), Conlon (Southend Utd.), Molloy (St. Patrick's Athletic).

Northern Ireland: Carroll (Wigan Athletic), Griffin (St. Johnstone), McGlinchey (Port Vale), Burns (Port Vale), Waterman (Portsmouth), Jeff Whitley (Manchester City), Johnson (Blackburn Rov.), Feeney (Rangers) (Graham, Crystal Palace, 68), Coote (Norwich City), McVeigh (Tottenham) (Healy, Manchester Utd., 68), Elliott (Glentoran) (Clarke, Portadown, 77).

Scorer – Rep. of Ireland: Ferguson (6). **Half-time:** 1-0.

SCOTLAND 1, NORTHERN IRELAND 1
Caledonian Stadium, Inverness, (2,569), Friday, June 4, 1999

Scotland: Gallacher (Dundee Utd.), Nicholson (Rangers), Hughes (Bournemouth), Rae (Dundee), R. Anderson (Aberdeen), Lauchlan (Kilmarnock), Campbell (Leicester City) (Tarrant, Aston Villa, 73), Burchill (Celtic) (Dargo, Raith, 86), Thompson (Dundee Utd.) (O'Brien, Blackburn Rov., 79), Brebner (Reading), I. Anderson (Dundee).

Northern Ireland: Wells (Barry Town), Lyttle (Peterborough Utd.), McGlinchey (Port Vale), Griffin (St. Johnstone), Morgan (Preston N.E.), Jeff Whitley (Manchester City), Feeney (Rangers), Graham (Crystal Palace), Kirk (Hearts), Healy (Manchester Utd.), Clarke (Portadown).

Scorers – Scotland: Burchill (35). **Northern Ireland:** Healy (11). **Half-time:** 1-1.

FRIENDLY INTERNATIONALS

ENGLAND 0, CZECH REPUBLIC 1
Portman Road, (13,768), Tuesday, November 17, 1998

England: Simonsen (Everton), Carragher (Liverpool), Dyer (Ipswich Town), Lampard (West Ham Utd.), Ball (Everton) (Beattie, Southampton, 79), Brown (Manchester Utd.) (Johnson, Crewe Alexandra, 79), Curtis (Manchester Utd.), Morris (Chelsea) (Dunn, Blackburn Rov., 70), Cort (Wimbledon) (Cadamarteri, Everton, 70), Barry (Aston Villa), Davies (Blackburn Rov.) (Upson, Arsenal, 45).

Scorers – Czech Republic: Dosek (41). **Half-time:** 0-1.

PORTUGAL 3, WALES 0
Braganca, (500), Wednesday, November 18, 1998

Wales: Williams (Blackburn Rov.), Price (Swansea City), Roberts (Liverpool) (Hopkins, Wrexham, 70), Gibson (Tramere), Gabbidon (W.B.A.), Jarman (Cardiff City), Low (Bristol Rov.) Holloway (Exeter City), Roberts (Wrexham), Tipton (Oldham Athletic) (Jeanne, Q.P.R., 70), Thomas (Blackburn Rov.) (Earnshaw, Cardiff City, 57).

Scorers – Portugal: Soares (19), Pacheco (38), Moreira (88). **Half-time:** 2-0.

ENGLAND 2, FRANCE 1
Pride Park, Derby, (32,865), Tuesday, February 9, 1999

England: Simonsen (Everton), Barry (Aston Villa) (Johnson, Crewe Alexandra, 45), O'Brien (Bradford City), Carragher (Liverpool), Upson (Arsenal) (Marshall, Norwich City, 87), Curtis (Manchester Utd.), Williams (Sunderland), Hendrie (Aston Villa), Lampard (West Ham Utd.) (Jansen, Blackburn Rov., 45), Bowyer (Leeds Utd.) (Cresswell, York City, 68), Bridges (Sunderland) (Beattie, Southampton, 45).

Scorers – England: Bowyer (54), Upson (62). **France:** Christanval (21). **Half-time:** 0-1.

HUNGARY 2, ENGLAND 2
Budapest, (5,000), Tuesday, April 27, 1999

England: Wright (Ipswich Town), Mills (Charlton Athletic), Curtis (Manchester Utd.), Young (Tottenham), Barry (Aston Villa) (Vassell, Aston Villa, 60), Griffin (Newcastle Utd.) (Bridge, Southampton, 28), Mullins (Crystal Palace), Woodhouse (Sheffield Utd.), Greening (Manchester Utd.), Euell (Wimbledon) (Cresswell, Sheffield Wed., 45), Beattie (Southampton) (Cort, Wimbledon, 67).

Scorers – Hungary: Rosa (3, 25). **England:** Mills (53), Beattie (56 pen). **Half-time:** 2-0.

GERMANY 2, SCOTLAND 1
Meppen, (4,000) Tuesday, April 27, 1999

Scotland: Alexander (Livingston) (Mathieson, Queen of the South, 71), Nicholson (Rangers) (Young, Aberdeen, 65), Naysmith (Hearts), R. Anderson (Aberdeen), Wilson (Rangers), Lauchlan (Kilmarnock) (McAnespie, St Johnstone, 45), Campbell (Leicester City) (Teale, Ayr Utd., 79), Buchan (Aberdeen) (McEwan, Raith, 87), Dargo (Raith) (I. Anderson, Dundee, 65), Brebner (Reading), McCulloch (Motherwell) (Thompson, Dundee Utd., 71).

Scorers – Germany: Nehrbauer (20), Reich (88 pen). **Scotland:** Thompson (89). **Half-time:** 1-0.

REPUBLIC OF IRELAND 0, SWEDEN 3
Birr Town, (1,800), Tuesday, April 27, 1999

Rep. of Ireland: O'Connor (Bradford Park Avenue), Worrell (Dundee Utd.) (Baker, Shelbourne, 63), Barry-Murphy (Cork City), O'Brien (Bradford City), Hawkins (St. Patrick's Athletic) (Lynch, UCD, 59), Maybury (Leeds Utd.), Morgan (St. Patrick's Athletic) (Cummins, Middlesbrough, 45), Mahon (Tranmere Rov.), McKeever (Sheffield Wed.) (Armstrong, Brighton & H.A., 59), Fenn (Tottenham) (Molloy, St. Patrick's Athletic, 60), Clare (Grimsby Town) (Grant, Stockport Co., 63).

Scorers – Sweden: Andersson (24), Wallerstedt (55, 90). **Half-time:** 0-1.

Bradford City's Andrew O'Brien appeared for Ireland having already played for England U-21's against France earlier in the season.

KEEGAN'S FIRST SQUAD

Kevin Keegan, Fulham's chief operating officer, accepted the post of England caretaker-coach on February 16. His first game in charge was the European Championship qualifier against Poland at Wembley on March 27 and his original squad was:

David Seaman (Arsenal), Nigel Martyn (Leeds Utd.), Tony Adams (Arsenal), Sol Campbell (Tottenham), Rio Ferdinand (West Ham Utd.), Martin Keown (Arsenal), Gary Neville (Manchester Utd.), Phil Neville (Manchester Utd.), Graeme Le Saux (Chelsea), Andy Hinchcliffe (Everton), Gareth Southgate (Aston Villa), Ray Parlour (Arsenal), Paul Scholes (Manchester Utd.), David Beckham (Manchester Utd.), David Batty (Leeds Utd.), Steve McManaman (Liverpool), Darren Anderton (Tottenham), Tim Sherwood (Tottenham), Jamie Redknapp (Liverpool), Andy Cole (Manchester Utd.), Alan Shearer (Newcastle Utd.), Michael Owen (Liverpool), Robbie Fowler (Liverpool), Chris Sutton (Blackburn Rov.)

Hinchcliffe, Batty, Anderton, Owen, Fowler and Sutton subsequently withdrew through injuries. Chris Armstrong (Tottenham) was called up.

OTHER BRITISH INTERNATIONAL RESULTS
ENGLAND

v. ALBANIA

		E	A
1989	Tirana (W.C.)	2	0
1989	Wembley (W.C.)	5	0

v. ARGENTINA

		E	A
1951	Wembley	2	1
1953*	Buenos Aires	0	0
1962	Rancagua (W.C.)	3	1
1964	Rio de Janeiro	0	1
1966	Wembley (W.C.)	1	0
1974	Wembley	2	2
1977	Buenos Aires	1	1
1980	Wembley	3	1
1986	Mexico City (W.C.)	1	2
1991	Wembley	2	2
1998†	St Etienne (W.C.)	2	2

(* Abandoned after 21 mins. – rain)
(† England lost 3-4 on pens.)

v. AUSTRALIA

		E	A
1980	Sydney	2	1
1983	Sydney	0	0
1983	Brisbane	1	0
1983	Melbourne	1	1
1991	Sydney	1	0

v. AUSTRIA

		E	A
1908	Vienna	6	1
1908	Vienna	11	1
1909	Vienna	8	1
1930	Vienna	0	0
1932	Stamford Bridge	4	3
1936	Vienna	1	2
1951	Wembley	2	2
1952	Vienna	3	2
1958	Boras (W.C.)	2	2
1961	Vienna	1	3
1962	Wembley	3	1
1965	Wembley	2	3
1967	Vienna	1	0
1973	Wembley	7	0
1979	Vienna	3	4

v. BELGIUM

		E	B
1921	Brussels	2	0
1923	Highbury	6	1
1923	Antwerp	2	2
1924	W.B.A.	4	0
1926	Antwerp	5	3
1927	Brussels	9	1

		E	B
1928	Antwerp	3	1
1929	Brussels	5	1
1931	Brussels	4	1
1936	Brussels	2	3
1947	Brussels	5	2
1950	Brussels	4	1
1952	Wembley	5	0
1954	Basle (W.C.)	4	4
1964	Wembley	2	2
1970	Brussels	3	1
1980	Turin (E.C.)	1	1
1990	Bologna (W.C.)	1	0
1998*	Casablanca	0	0

(* England lost 3-4 on pens.)

v. BOHEMIA

		E	B
1908	Prague	4	0

v. BRAZIL

		E	B
1956	Wembley	4	2
1958	Gothenburg (W.C.)	0	0
1959	Rio de Janeiro	0	2
1962	Vina del Mar (W.C.)	1	3
1963	Wembley	1	1
1964	Rio de Janeiro	1	5
1969	Rio de Janeiro	1	2
1970	Guadalajara (W.C.)	0	1
1976	Los Angeles	0	1
1977	Rio de Janeiro	0	0
1978	Wembley	1	1
1981	Wembley	0	1
1984	Rio de Janeiro	2	0
1987	Wembley	1	1
1990	Wembley	1	0
1992	Wembley	1	1
1993	Washington	1	1
1995	Wembley	1	3
1997	Paris (T.F.)	0	1

v. BULGARIA

		E	B
1962	Rancagua (W.C.)	0	0
1968	Wembley	1	1
1974	Sofia	1	0
1979	Sofia (E.C.)	3	0
1979	Wembley (E.C.)	2	0
1996	Wembley	1	0
1998	Wembley (E.C.)	0	0
1999	Sofia (E.C.)	1	1

v. CAMEROON

		E	C
1990	Naples (W.C.)	3	2
1991	Wembley	2	0
1997	Wembley	2	0

v. CANADA

		E	C
1986	Vancouver	1	0

v. CHILE

		E	C
1950	Rio de Janeiro (W.C.)	2	0
1953	Santiago	2	1
1984	Santiago	0	0
1989	Wembley	0	0
1998	Wembley	0	2

v. CHINA

		E	C
1996	Beijing	3	0

v. C.I.S.
(formerly Soviet Union)

		E	C
1992	Moscow	2	2

v. COLOMBIA

		E	C
1970	Bogota	4	0
1988	Wembley	1	1
1995	Wembley	0	0
1998	Lens (W.C.)	2	0

v. CROATIA

		E	C
1995	Wembley	0	0

v. CYPRUS

		E	C
1975	Wembley (E.C.)	5	0
1975	Limassol (E.C.)	1	0

v. CZECH REPUBLIC

		E	C
1998	Wembley	2	0

v. CZECHOSLOVAKIA

		E	C
1934	Prague	1	2
1937	Tottenham	5	4
1963	Bratislava	4	2
1966	Wembley	0	0
1970	Guadalajara (W.C.)	1	0
1973	Prague	1	1
1974	Wembley (E.C.)	3	0
1975*	Bratislava (E.C.)	1	2
1978	Wembley (E.C.)	1	0
1982	Bilbao (W.C.)	2	0
1990	Wembley	4	2
1992	Prague	2	2

(* Aband. 0-0, 17 mins. prev. day – fog)

v. DENMARK

		E	D
1948	Copenhagen	0	0
1955	Copenhagen	5	1
1956	W'hampton (W.C.)	5	2
1957	Copenhagen (W.C.)	4	1
1966	Copenhagen	2	0
1978	Copenhagen (E.C.)	4	3
1979	Wembley (E.C.)	1	0
1982	Copenhagen (E.C.)	2	2
1983	Wembley (E.C.)	0	1
1988	Wembley	1	0
1989	Copenhagen	1	1
1990	Wembley	1	0
1992	Malmo (E.C.)	0	0
1994	Wembley	1	0

v. EAST GERMANY

		E	EG
1963	Leipzig	2	1
1970	Wembley	3	1
1974	Leipzig	1	1
1984	Wembley	1	0

v. ECUADOR

		E	Ec
1970	Quito	2	0

v. EGYPT

		E	Eg
1986	Cairo	4	0
1990	Cagliari (W.C.)	1	0

v. F.I.F.A.

		E	F
1938	Highbury	3	0
1953	Wembley	4	4
1963	Wembley	2	1

v. FINLAND

		E	F
1937	Helsinki	8	0
1956	Helsinki	5	1
1966	Helsinki	3	0
1976	Helsinki (W.C.)	4	1
1976	Wembley (W.C.)	2	1
1982	Helsinki	4	1
1984	Wembley (W.C.)	5	0
1985	Helsinki (W.C.)	1	1
1992	Helsinki	2	1

v. FRANCE

		E	F
1923	Paris	4	1
1924	Paris	3	1
1925	Paris	3	2
1927	Paris	6	0
1928	Paris	5	1
1929	Paris	4	1
1931	Paris	2	5
1933	Tottenham	4	1
1938	Paris	4	2
1947	Highbury	3	0
1949	Paris	3	1
1951	Highbury	2	2
1955	Paris	0	1

		E	F
1957	Wembley	4	0
1962	Sheffield (E.C.)	1	1
1963	Paris (E.C.)	2	5
1966	Wembley (W.C.)	2	0
1969	Wembley	5	0
1982	Bilbao (W.C.)	3	1
1984	Paris	0	2
1992	Wembley	2	0
1992	Malmo (E.C.)	0	0
1997	Montpellier (T.F.)	1	0
1999	Wembley	0	2

v. GEORGIA

		E	G
1996	Tbilisi (W.C.)	2	0
1997	Wembley (W.C.)	2	0

v. GERMANY/ WEST GERMANY

		E	G
1930	Berlin	3	3
1935	Tottenham	3	0
1938	Berlin	6	3
1954	Wembley	3	1
1956	Berlin	3	1
1965	Nuremberg	1	0
1966	Wembley	1	0
1966	Wembley (W.C.F.)	4	2
1968	Hanover	0	1
1970	Leon (W.C.)	2	3
1972	Wembley (E.C.)	1	3
1972	Berlin (E.C.)	0	0
1975	Wembley	2	0
1978	Munich	1	2
1982	Madrid (W.C.)	0	0
1982	Wembley	1	2
1985	Mexico City	3	0
1987	Dusseldorf	1	3
1990*	Turin (W.C.)	1	1
1991	Wembley	0	1
1993	Detroit	1	2
1996†	Wembley (E.C.)	1	1

(* England lost 3-4 on pens.)
(† England lost 5-6 on pens.)

v. GREECE

		E	G
1971	Wembley (E.C.)	3	0
1971	Athens (E.C.)	2	0
1982	Salonika (E.C.)	3	0
1983	Wembley (E.C.)	0	0
1989	Athens	2	1
1994	Wembley	5	0

v. HOLLAND

		E	H
1935	Amsterdam	1	0
1946	Huddersfield Town	8	2
1964	Amsterdam	1	1
1969	Amsterdam	1	0
1970	Wembley	0	0
1977	Wembley	0	2
1982	Wembley	2	0
1988	Wembley	2	2
1988	Dusseldorf (E.C.)	1	3
1990	Cagliari (W.C.)	0	0
1993	Wembley (W.C.)	2	2
1993	Rotterdam (W.C.)	0	2
1996	Wembley (E.C.)	4	1

v. HUNGARY

		E	H
1908	Budapest	7	0
1909	Budapest	4	2
1909	Budapest	8	2
1934	Budapest	1	2
1936	Highbury	6	2
1953	Wembley	3	6
1954	Budapest	1	7
1960	Budapest	0	2
1962	Rancagua (W.C.)	1	2
1965	Wembley	1	0
1978	Wembley	4	1
1981	Budapest (W.C.)	3	1
1981	Wembley (W.C.)	1	0
1983	Wembley (E.C.)	2	0
1983	Budapest (E.C.)	3	0
1988	Budapest	0	0
1990	Wembley	1	0
1992	Budapest	1	0
1996	Wembley	3	0
1999	Budapest	1	1

v. ICELAND

		E	I
1982	Reykjavik	1	1

v. REPUBLIC OF IRELAND

		E	RI
1946	Dublin	1	0
1950	Goodison Park	0	2
1957	Wembley (W.C.)	5	1
1957	Dublin (W.C.)	1	1
1964	Dublin	3	1
1977	Wembley	1	1
1978	Dublin (E.C.)	1	1
1980	Wembley (E.C.)	2	0
1985	Wembley	2	1
1988	Stuttgart (E.C.)	0	1
1990	Cagliari (W.C.)	1	1
1990	Dublin (E.C.)	1	1
1991	Wembley (E.C.)	1	1
1995*	Dublin	0	1

(* Abandoned 27 mins. – crowd riot)

v. ISRAEL

		E	I
1986	Tel Aviv	2	1

		E	I
1988	Tel Aviv	0	0

		E	M
1997	Wembley	2	0

v. ITALY

		E	I
1933	Rome	1	1
1934	Highbury	3	2
1939	Milan	2	2
1948	Turin	4	0
1949	Tottenham	2	0
1952	Florence	1	1
1959	Wembley	2	2
1961	Rome	3	2
1973	Turin	0	2
1973	Wembley	0	1
1976	New York City	3	2
1976	Rome (W.C.)	0	2
1977	Wembley (W.C.)	2	0
1980	Turin (E.C.)	0	1
1985	Mexico City	1	2
1989	Wembley	0	0
1990	Bari (W.C.)	1	2
1996	Wembley (W.C.)	0	1
1997	Nantes (T.F.)	2	0
1997	Rome (W.C.)	0	0

v. JAPAN

		E	J
1995	Wembley	2	1

v. KUWAIT

		E	K
1982	Bilbao (W.C.)	1	0

v. LUXEMBOURG

		E	L
1927	Luxembourg	5	2
1960	Luxembourg (W.C.)	9	0
1961	Highbury (W.C.)	4	1
1977	Wembley (W.C.)	5	0
1977	Luxembourg (W.C.)	2	0
1982	Wembley (E.C.)	9	0
1983	Luxembourg (E.C.)	4	0
1998	Luxembourg (E.C.)	3	0

v. MALAYSIA

		E	M
1991	Kuala Lumpur	4	2

v. MALTA

		E	M
1971	Valletta (E.C.)	1	0
1971	Wembley (E.C.)	5	0

v. MEXICO

		E	M
1959	Mexico City	1	2
1961	Wembley	8	0
1966	Wembley (W.C.)	2	0
1969	Mexico City	0	0
1985	Mexico City	0	1
1986	Los Angeles	3	0

v. MOLDOVA

		E	M
1996	Kishinev	3	0
1997	Wembley (W.C.)	4	0

v. MOROCCO

		E	M
1986	Monterrey (W.C.)	0	0
1998	Casablanca	1	0

v. NEW ZEALAND

		E	NZ
1991	Auckland	1	0
1991	Wellington	2	0

v. NIGERIA

		E	N
1994	Wembley	1	0

v. NORWAY

		E	N
1937	Oslo	6	0
1938	Newcastle Utd.	4	0
1949	Oslo	4	1
1966	Oslo	6	1
1980	Wembley (W.C.)	4	0
1981	Oslo (W.C.)	1	2
1992	Wembley (W.C.)	1	1
1993	Oslo (W.C.)	0	2
1994	Wembley	0	0
1995	Oslo	0	0

v. PARAGUAY

		E	P
1986	Mexico City (W.C.)	3	0

v. PERU

		E	P
1959	Lima	1	4
1961	Lima	4	0

v. POLAND

		E	P
1966	Goodison Park	1	1
1966	Chorzow	1	0
1973	Chorzow (W.C.)	0	2
1973	Wembley (W.C.)	1	1
1986	Monterrey (W.C.)	3	0
1989	Wembley (W.C.)	3	0
1989	Katowice (W.C.)	0	0
1990	Wembley (E.C.)	2	0
1991	Poznan (E.C.)	1	1
1993	Chorzow (W.C.)	1	1
1993	Wembley (W.C.)	3	0
1996	Wembley (W.C.)	2	1
1997	Katowice (W.C.)	2	0
1999	Wembley (E.C.)	3	1

v. PORTUGAL

		E	P
1947	Lisbon	10	0
1950	Lisbon	5	3
1951	Goodison Park	5	2
1955	Oporto	1	3
1958	Wembley	2	1
1961	Lisbon (W.C.)	1	1
1961	Wembley (W.C.)	2	0
1964	Lisbon	4	3
1964	Sao Paulo	1	1
1966	Wembley (W.C.)	2	1
1969	Wembley	1	0
1974	Lisbon	0	0
1974	Wembley (E.C.)	0	0
1975	Lisbon (E.C.)	1	1
1986	Monterrey (W.C.)	0	1
1995	Wembley	1	1
1998	Wembley	3	0

v. ROMANIA

		E	R
1939	Bucharest	2	0
1968	Bucharest	0	0
1969	Wembley	1	1
1970	Guadalajara (W.C.)	1	0
1980	Bucharest (W.C.)	1	2
1981	Wembley (W.C.)	0	0
1985	Bucharest (W.C.)	0	0
1985	Wembley (W.C.)	1	1
1994	Wembley	1	1
1998	Toulouse (W.C.)	1	2

v. SAN MARINO

		E	SM
1993	Wembley (W.C.)	6	0
1994	Bologna (W.C.)	7	1

v. SAUDI ARABIA

		E	SA
1988	Riyadh	1	1
1998	Wembley	0	0

v. SOUTH AFRICA

		E	SA
1997	Old Trafford	2	1

v. SOVIET UNION
(see also C.I.S.)

		E	SU
1958	Moscow	1	1
1958	Gothenburg (W.C.)	2	2
1958	Gothenburg (W.C.)	0	1
1958	Wembley	5	0
1967	Wembley	2	2
1968	Rome (E.C.)	2	0
1973	Moscow	2	1
1984	Wembley	0	2
1986	Tbilisi	1	0
1988	Frankfurt (E.C.)	1	3
1991	Wembley	3	1

v. SPAIN

		E	S
1929	Madrid	3	4
1931	Highbury	7	1
1950	Rio de Janeiro (W.C.)	0	1
1955	Madrid	1	1
1955	Wembley	4	1
1960	Madrid	0	3
1960	Wembley	4	2
1965	Madrid	2	0
1967	Wembley	2	0
1968	Wembley (E.C.)	1	0
1968	Madrid (E.C.)	2	1
1980	Barcelona	2	0
1980	Naples (E.C.)	2	1
1981	Wembley	1	2
1982	Madrid (W.C.)	0	0
1987	Madrid	4	2
1992	Santander	0	1
1996*	Wembley (E.C.)	0	0

(* England won 4-2 on pens.)

v. SWEDEN

		E	S
1923	Stockholm	4	2
1923	Stockholm	3	1
1937	Stockholm	4	0
1948	Highbury	4	2
1949	Stockholm	1	3
1956	Stockholm	0	0
1959	Wembley	2	3
1965	Gothenburg	2	1
1968	Wembley	3	1
1979	Stockholm	0	0
1986	Stockholm	0	1
1988	Wembley (W.C.)	0	0
1989	Stockholm (W.C.)	0	0
1992	Stockholm (E.C.)	1	2
1995	Elland Road	3	3
1998	Stockholm (E.C.)	1	2
1999	Wembley (E.C.)	0	0

v. SWITZERLAND

		E	S
1933	Berne	4	0
1938	Zurich	1	2
1947	Zurich	0	1
1949	Highbury	6	0
1952	Zurich	3	0
1954	Berne (W.C.)	2	0
1962	Wembley	3	1
1963	Basle	8	1
1971	Basle (E.C.)	3	2
1971	Wembley (E.C.)	1	1
1975	Basle	2	1
1977	Wembley	0	0
1980	Wembley (W.C.)	2	1
1981	Basle (W.C.)	1	2
1988	Lausanne	1	0
1995	Wembley	3	1

		E	S
1996	Wembley (E.C.)	1	1
1998	Berne	1	1

v. TUNISIA

		E	T
1990	Tunis	1	0
1998	Marseille (W.C.)	2	0

v. TURKEY

		E	T
1984	Istanbul (W.C.)	8	0
1985	Wembley (W.C.)	5	0
1987	Izmir (E.C.)	0	0
1987	Wembley (E.C.)	8	0
1991	Izmir (E.C.)	1	0
1992	Wembley (E.C.)	1	0
1992	Wembley (W.C.)	4	0
1993	Izmir (W.C.)	2	0

v. URUGUAY

		E	U
1953	Montevideo	1	2
1954	Basle (W.C.)	2	4
1964	Wembley	2	1
1966	Wembley (W.C.)	0	0
1969	Montevideo	2	1
1977	Montevideo	0	0
1984	Montevideo	0	2
1990	Wembley	1	2

		E	U
1995	Wembley	0	0

v. U.S.A.

		E	USA
1950	Belo Horizonte (W.C.)	0	1
1953	New York City	6	3
1959	Los Angeles	8	1
1964	New York City	10	0
1985	Los Angeles	5	0
1993	Boston	0	2
1994	Wembley	2	0

v. YUGOSLAVIA

		E	Y
1939	Belgrade	1	2
1950	Highbury	2	2
1954	Belgrade	0	1
1956	Wembley	3	0
1958	Belgrade	0	5
1960	Wembley	3	3
1965	Belgrade	1	1
1966	Wembley	2	0
1968	Florence (E.C.)	0	1
1972	Wembley	1	1
1974	Belgrade	2	2
1986	Wembley (E.C.)	2	0
1987	Belgrade (E.C.)	4	1
1989	Wembley	2	1

ENGLAND'S RECORD

England's first international was a 0-0 draw against Scotland in Glasgow, on the West of Scotland cricket ground, Partick, on November 30, 1872. Now, 127 years on, their complete International record, at the start of 1999-2000, is:

P	W	D	L	F	A
758	429	183	146	1730	782

ENGLAND "B" TEAM RESULTS
(England score shown first)

1949	Finland (A)	4	0	1954	Switzerland (A)	0	2
1949	Holland (A)	4	0	1955	Germany (H)	1	1
1950	Italy (A)	0	5	1955	Yugoslavia (H)	5	1
1950	Holland (H)	1	0	1956	Switzerland (H)	4	1
1950	Holland (A)	0	3	1956	Scotland (A)	2	2
1950	Luxembourg (A)	2	1	1957	Scotland (H)	4	1
1950	Switzerland (H)	5	0	1978	W. Germany (A)	2	1
1952	Holland (A)	1	0	1978	Czechoslovakia (A)	1	0
1952	France (A)	1	7	1978	Singapore (A)	8	0
1953	Scotland (A)	2	2	1978	Malaysia (A)	1	1
1954	Scotland (H)	1	1	1978	N. Zealand (A)	4	0
1954	Germany (A)	4	0	1978	N. Zealand (A)	3	1
1954	Yugoslavia (A)	1	2	1978	N. Zealand (A)	4	0

1979	Austria (A)	1	0
1979	N. Zealand (H)	4	1
1980	U.S.A. (H)	1	0
1980	Spain (H)	1	0
1980	Australia (H)	1	0
1981	Spain (A)	2	3
1984	N. Zealand (H)	2	0
1987	Malta (A)	2	0
1989	Switzerland (A)	2	0
1989	Iceland (A)	2	0
1989	Norway (A)	1	0
1989	Italy (H)	1	1
1989	Yugoslavia (H)	2	1
1990	Rep. of Ireland (A)	1	4

1990	Czechoslovakia (H)	2	0
1990	Algeria (A)	0	0
1991	Wales (A)	1	0
1991	Iceland (H)	1	0
1991	Switzerland (H)	2	1
1991	Spanish XI (A)	1	0
1992	France (H)	3	0
1992	Czechoslovakia (A)	1	0
1992	C.I.S. (A)	1	1
1994	N. Ireland (H)	4	2
1995	Rep. of Ireland (H)	2	0
1998	Chile (H)	1	2
1998	Russia (H)	4	1

GREAT BRITAIN V. REST OF EUROPE (F.I.F.A.)

		GB	RofE				GB	RofE
1947	Glasgow	6	1	1955	Belfast		1	4

SCOTLAND

v. ARGENTINA

		S	A
1977	Buenos Aires	1	1
1979	Glasgow	1	3
1990	Glasgow	1	0

v. AUSTRALIA

		S	A
1985*	Glasgow (W.C.)	2	0
1985*	Melbourne (W.C.)	0	0
1996	Glasgow	1	0
(* World Cup play-off)

v. AUSTRIA

		S	A
1931	Vienna	0	5
1933	Glasgow	2	2
1937	Vienna	1	1
1950	Glasgow	0	1
1951	Vienna	0	4
1954	Zurich (W.C.)	0	1
1955	Vienna	4	1
1956	Glasgow	1	1
1960	Vienna	1	4
1963*	Glasgow	4	1
1968	Glasgow (W.C.)	2	1
1969	Vienna (W.C.)	0	2
1978	Vienna (E.C.)	2	3
1979	Glasgow (E.C.)	1	1
1994	Vienna	2	1
1996	Vienna (W.C.)	0	0
1997	Glasgow (W.C.)	2	0
(* Abandoned after 79 minutes)

v. BELARUS

		S	B
1997	Minsk (W.C.)	1	0
1997	Aberdeen (W.C.)	4	1

v. BELGIUM

		S	B
1947	Brussels	1	2
1948	Glasgow	2	0
1951	Brussels	5	0
1971	Liege (E.C.)	0	3
1971	Aberdeen (E.C.)	1	0
1974	Brugge	1	2
1979	Brussels (E.C.)	0	2
1979	Glasgow (E.C.)	1	3
1982	Brussels (E.C.)	2	3
1983	Glasgow (E.C.)	1	1
1987	Brussels (E.C.)	1	4
1987	Glasgow (E.C.)	2	0

v. BRAZIL

		S	B
1966	Glasgow	1	1
1972	Rio de Janeiro	0	1
1973	Glasgow	0	1
1974	Frankfurt (W.C.)	0	0
1977	Rio de Janeiro	0	2
1982	Seville (W.C.)	1	4
1987	Glasgow	0	2
1990	Turin (W.C.)	0	1
1998	St. Denis (W.C.)	1	2

v. BULGARIA

		S	B
1978	Glasgow	2	1
1986	Glasgow (E.C.)	0	0

		S	B
1987	Sofia (E.C.)	1	0
1990	Sofia (E.C.)	1	1
1991	Glasgow (E.C.)	1	1

v. CANADA

		S	C
1983	Vancouver	2	0
1983	Edmonton	3	0
1983	Toronto	2	0
1992	Toronto	3	1

v. CHILE

		S	C
1977	Santiago	4	2
1989	Glasgow	2	0

v. C.I.S.
(formerly Soviet Union)

		S	C
1992	Norrkoping (E.C.)	3	0

v. COLOMBIA

		S	C
1988	Glasgow	0	0
1996	Miami	0	1
1998	New York City	2	2

v. COSTA RICA

		S	C
1990	Genoa (W.C.)	0	1

v. CYPRUS

		S	C
1968	Nicosia (W.C.)	5	0
1969	Glasgow (W.C.)	8	0
1989	Limassol (W.C.)	3	2
1989	Glasgow (W.C.)	2	1

v. CZECH REPUBLIC

		S	C
1999	Glasgow (E.C.)	1	2
1999	Prague (E.C.)	2	3

v. CZECHOSLOVAKIA

		S	C
1937	Prague	3	1
1937	Glasgow	5	0
1961	Bratislava (W.C.)	0	4
1961	Glasgow (W.C.)	3	2
1961*	Brussels (W.C.)	2	4
1972	Porto Alegre	0	0
1973	Glasgow (W.C.)	2	1
1973	Bratislava (W.C.)	0	1
1976	Prague (W.C.)	0	2
1977	Glasgow (W.C.)	3	1

(* World Cup play-off)

v. DENMARK

		S	D
1951	Glasgow	3	1
1952	Copenhagen	2	1

		S	D
1968	Copenhagen	1	0
1970	Glasgow (E.C.)	1	0
1971	Copenhagen (E.C.)	0	1
1972	Copenhagen (W.C.)	4	1
1972	Glasgow (W.C.)	2	0
1975	Copenhagen (E.C.)	1	0
1975	Glasgow (E.C.)	3	1
1986	Neza (W.C.)	0	1
1996	Copenhagen	0	2
1998	Ibrox	0	1

v. EAST GERMANY

		S	EG
1974	Glasgow	3	0
1977	East Berlin	0	1
1982	Glasgow (E.C.)	2	0
1983	Halle (E.C.)	1	2
1986	Glasgow	0	0
1990	Glasgow	0	1

v. ECUADOR

		S	E
1995	Toyama, Japan	2	1

v. EGYPT

		S	E
1990	Aberdeen	1	3

v. ESTONIA

		S	E
1993	Tallinn (W.C.)	3	0
1993	Aberdeen	3	1
1996	Tallinn (W.C.)	* No result	
1997	Monaco (W.C.)	0	0
1997	Kilmarnock (W.C.)	2	0
1998	Edinburgh (E.C.)	3	2

(* Estonia absent)

v. FAROE ISLANDS

		S	F
1994	Glasgow (E.C.)	5	1
1995	Toftir (E.C.)	2	0
1998	Aberdeen (E.C.)	2	1
1999	Toftir (E.C.)	1	1

v. FINLAND

		S	F
1954	Helsinki	2	1
1964	Glasgow (W.C.)	3	1
1965	Helsinki (W.C.)	2	1
1976	Glasgow	6	0
1992	Glasgow	1	1
1994	Helsinki (E.C.)	2	0
1995	Glasgow (E.C.)	1	0
1998	Edinburgh	1	1

v. FRANCE

		S	F
1930	Paris	2	0
1932	Paris	3	1
1948	Paris	0	3

Year	Venue	S	F
1949	Glasgow	2	0
1950	Paris	1	0
1951	Glasgow	1	0
1958	Orebro (W.C.)	1	2
1984	Marseilles	0	2
1989	Glasgow (W.C.)	2	0
1990	Paris (W.C.)	0	3
1997	St. Etienne	1	2

v. GERMANY/ WEST GERMANY

Year	Venue	S	G
1929	Berlin	1	1
1936	Glasgow	2	0
1957	Stuttgart	3	1
1959	Glasgow	3	2
1964	Hanover	2	2
1969	Glasgow (W.C.)	1	1
1969	Hamburg (W.C.)	2	3
1973	Glasgow	1	1
1974	Frankfurt	1	2
1986	Queretaro (W.C.)	1	2
1992	Norrkoping (E.C.)	0	2
1993	Glasgow	0	1
1999	Bremen	1	0

v. GREECE

Year	Venue	S	G
1994	Athens (E.C.)	0	1
1995	Glasgow	1	0

v. HOLLAND

Year	Venue	S	H
1929	Amsterdam	2	0
1938	Amsterdam	3	1
1959	Amsterdam	2	1
1966	Glasgow	0	3
1968	Amsterdam	0	0
1971	Amsterdam	1	2
1978	Mendoza (W.C.)	3	2
1982	Glasgow	2	1
1986	Eindhoven	0	0
1992	Gothenburg (E.C.)	0	1
1994	Glasgow	0	1
1994	Utrecht	1	3
1996	Birmingham City (E.C.)	0	0

v. HUNGARY

Year	Venue	S	H
1938	Glasgow	3	1
1955	Glasgow	2	4
1955	Budapest	1	3
1958	Budapest	1	1
1960	Budapest	3	3
1980	Budapest	1	3
1987	Glasgow	2	0

v. ICELAND

Year	Venue	S	I
1984	Glasgow (W.C.)	3	0
1985	Reykjavik (W.C)	1	0

v. IRAN

Year	Venue	S	I
1978	Cordoba (W.C.)	1	1

v. REPUBLIC OF IRELAND

Year	Venue	S	RI
1961	Glasgow (W.C.)	4	1
1961	Dublin (W.C.)	3	0
1963	Dublin	0	1
1969	Dublin	1	1
1986	Dublin (E.C.)	0	0
1987	Glasgow (E.C.)	0	1

v. ISRAEL

Year	Venue	S	I
1981	Tel Aviv (W.C.)	1	0
1981	Glasgow (W.C.)	3	1
1986	Tel Aviv	1	0

v. ITALY

Year	Venue	S	I
1931	Rome	0	3
1965	Glasgow (W.C.)	1	0
1965	Naples (W.C.)	0	3
1988	Perugia	0	2
1992	Glasgow (W.C.)	0	0
1993	Rome (W.C.)	1	3

v. JAPAN

Year	Venue	S	J
1995	Hiroshima	0	0

v. LATVIA

Year	Venue	S	L
1996	Riga (W.C.)	2	0
1997	Celtic Park (W.C.)	2	0

v. LITHUANIA

Year	Venue	S	L
1998	Vilnius (E.C.)	0	0

v. LUXEMBOURG

Year	Venue	S	L
1947	Luxembourg	6	0
1986	Glasgow (E.C.)	3	0
1987	Esch (E.C.)	0	0

v. MALTA

Year	Venue	S	M
1988	Valletta	1	1
1990	Valletta	2	1
1993	Glasgow (W.C.)	3	0
1993	Valletta (W.C.)	2	0
1997	Valletta	3	2

v. MOROCCO

		S	M
1998	St. Etienne (W.C.)	0	3

v. NEW ZEALAND

		S	NZ
1982	Malaga (W.C.)	5	2

v. NORWAY

		S	N
1929	Bergen	7	3
1954	Glasgow	1	0
1954	Oslo	1	1
1963	Bergen	3	4
1963	Glasgow	6	1
1974	Oslo	2	1
1978	Glasgow (E.C.)	3	2
1979	Oslo (E.C.)	4	0
1988	Oslo (W.C.)	2	1
1989	Glasgow (W.C.)	1	1
1992	Oslo	0	0
1998	Bordeaux (W.C.)	1	1

v. PARAGUAY

		S	P
1958	Norrkoping (W.C.)	2	3

v. PERU

		S	P
1972	Glasgow	2	0
1978	Cordoba (W.C.)	1	3
1979	Glasgow	1	1

v. POLAND

		S	P
1958	Warsaw	2	1
1960	Glasgow	2	3
1965	Chorzow (W.C.)	1	1
1965	Glasgow (W.C.)	1	2
1980	Poznan	0	1
1990	Glasgow	1	1

v. PORTUGAL

		S	P
1950	Lisbon	2	2
1955	Glasgow	3	0
1959	Lisbon	0	1
1966	Glasgow	0	1
1971	Lisbon (E.C.)	0	2
1971	Glasgow (E.C.)	2	1
1975	Glasgow	1	0
1978	Lisbon (E.C.)	0	1
1980	Glasgow (E.C.)	4	1
1980	Glasgow (W.C.)	0	0
1981	Lisbon (W.C.)	1	2
1992	Glasgow (W.C.)	0	0
1993	Lisbon (W.C.)	0	5

v. ROMANIA

		S	R
1975	Bucharest (E.C.)	1	1
1975	Glasgow (E.C.)	1	1
1986	Glasgow	3	0
1990	Glasgow (E.C.)	2	1
1991	Bucharest (E.C.)	0	1

v. RUSSIA

		S	R
1994	Glasgow (E.C.)	1	1
1995	Moscow (E.C.)	0	0

v. SAN MARINO

		S	SM
1991	Serravalle (E.C.)	2	0
1991	Glasgow (E.C.)	4	0
1995	Serravalle (E.C.)	2	0
1995	Glasgow (E.C.)	5	0

v. SAUDI ARABIA

		S	SA
1988	Riyadh	2	2

v. SOVIET UNION
(see also C.I.S. and RUSSIA)

		S	SU
1967	Glasgow	0	2
1971	Moscow	0	1
1982	Malaga (W.C.)	2	2
1991	Glasgow	0	1

v. SPAIN

		S	Sp
1957	Glasgow (W.C.)	4	2
1957	Madrid (W.C.)	1	4
1963	Madrid	6	2
1965	Glasgow	0	0
1975	Glasgow (E.C.)	1	2
1975	Valencia (E.C.)	1	1
1982	Valencia	0	3
1985	Glasgow (W.C.)	3	1
1985	Seville (W.C.)	0	1
1988	Madrid	0	0

v. SWEDEN

		S	Swe
1952	Stockholm	1	3
1953	Glasgow	1	2
1975	Gothenburg	1	1
1977	Glasgow	3	1
1980	Stockholm (W.C.)	1	0
1981	Glasgow (W.C.)	2	0
1990	Genoa (W.C.)	2	1
1995	Solna	0	2
1996	Glasgow (W.C.)	1	0
1997	Gothenburg (W.C.)	1	2

v. SWITZERLAND

		S	Sw
1931	Geneva	3	2
1948	Berne	1	2
1950	Glasgow	3	1
1957	Basle (W.C.)	2	1
1957	Glasgow (W.C.)	3	2

	S	Sw
1973 Berne	0	1
1976 Glasgow	1	0
1982 Berne (E.C.)	0	2
1983 Glasgow (E.C.)	2	2
1990 Glasgow (E.C.)	2	1
1991 Berne (E.C.)	2	2
1992 Berne (W.C.)	1	3
1993 Aberdeen (W.C.)	1	1
1996 Birmingham (E.C.)	1	0

v. TURKEY

	S	T
1960 Ankara	2	4

v. U.S.A.

	S	USA
1952 Glasgow	6	0
1992 Denver	1	0
1996 New Britain, Conn	1	2
1998 Washington	0	0

v. URUGUAY

	S	U
1954 Basle (W.C.)	0	7
1962 Glasgow	2	3
1983 Glasgow	2	0
1986 Neza (W.C.)	0	0

v. YUGOSLAVIA

	S	Y
1955 Belgrade	2	2
1956 Glasgow	2	0
1958 Vaasteras (W.C.)	1	1
1972 Belo Horizonte	2	1
1974 Frankfurt (W.C.)	1	1
1984 Glasgow	6	1
1988 Glasgow (W.C.)	1	1
1989 Zagreb (W.C.)	1	3

v. ZAIRE

	S	Z
1974 Dortmund (W.C.)	2	0

WALES

v. ALBANIA

	W	A
1994 Cardiff City (E.C.)	2	0
1995 Tirana (E.C.)	1	1

v. ARGENTINA

	W	A
1992 Gifu (Japan)	0	1

v. AUSTRIA

	W	A
1954 Vienna	0	2
1955 Wrexham	1	2
1975 Vienna (E.C.)	1	2
1975 Wrexham (E.C.)	1	0
1992 Vienna	1	1

v. BELARUS

	W	B
1998 Cardiff (E.C.)	3	2

v. BELGIUM

	W	B
1949 Liege	1	3
1949 Cardiff City	5	1
1990 Cardiff City (E.C.)	3	1
1991 Brussels (E.C.)	1	1
1992 Brussels (W.C.)	0	2
1993 Cardiff City (W.C.)	2	0
1997 Cardiff City (W.C.)	1	2
1997 Brussels (W.C.)	2	3

v. BRAZIL

	W	B
1958 Gothenburg (W.C.)	0	1
1962 Rio de Janeiro	1	3
1962 Sao Paulo	1	3
1966 Rio de Janeiro	1	3
1966 Belo Horizonte	0	1
1983 Cardiff City	1	1
1991 Cardiff City	1	0
1997 Brasilia	0	3

v. BULGARIA

	W	B
1983 Wrexham (E.C.)	1	0
1983 Sofia (E.C.)	0	1
1994 Cardiff City (E.C.)	0	3
1995 Sofia (E.C.)	1	3

v. CANADA

	W	C
1986 Toronto	0	2
1986 Vancouver	3	0

v. CHILE

	W	C
1966 Santiago	0	2

v. COSTA RICA

	W	C
1990 Cardiff City	1	0

v. CYPRUS

	W	C
1992 Limassol (W.C.)	1	0
1993 Cardiff City (W.C.)	2	0

v. CZECHOSLOVAKIA
(see also R.C.S.)

	W	C
1957 Cardiff City (W.C.)	1	0
1957 Prague (W.C.)	0	2

		W	C
1971	Swansea City (E.C.)	1	3
1971	Prague (E.C.)	0	1
1977	Wrexham (W.C.)	3	0
1977	Prague (W.C.)	0	1
1980	Cardiff City (W.C.)	1	0
1981	Prague (W.C.)	0	2
1987	Wrexham (E.C.)	1	1
1987	Prague (E.C.)	0	2

v. DENMARK

		W	D
1964	Copenhagen (W.C.)	0	1
1965	Wrexham (W.C.)	4	2
1987	Cardiff City (E.C.)	1	0
1987	Copenhagen (E.C.)	0	1
1990	Copenhagen	0	1
1998	Copenhagen (E.C.)	2	1
1999	Anfield (E.C.)	0	2

v. EAST GERMANY

		W	EG
1957	Leipzig (W.C.)	1	2
1957	Cardiff City (W.C.)	4	1
1969	Dresden (W.C.)	1	2
1969	Cardiff City (W.C.)	1	3

v. ESTONIA

		W	E
1994	Tallinn	2	1

v. FAROE ISLANDS

		W	FI
1992	Cardiff City (W.C.)	6	0
1993	Toftir (W.C.)	3	0

v. FINLAND

		W	F
1971	Helsinki (E.C.)	1	0
1971	Swansea City (E.C.)	3	0
1986	Helsinki (E.C.)	1	1
1987	Wrexham (E.C.)	4	0
1988	Swansea City (W.C.) ...	2	2
1989	Helsinki (W.C.)	0	1

v. FRANCE

		W	F
1933	Paris	1	1
1939	Paris	1	2
1953	Paris	1	6
1982	Toulouse	1	0

v. GEORGIA

		W	G
1994	Tbilisi (E.C.)	0	5
1995	Cardiff City (E.C.)	0	1

v. GERMANY/
WEST GERMANY

		W	G
1991	Cardiff City (E.C.)	1	0
1968	Cardiff City	1	1

		W	G
1969	Frankfurt	1	1
1977	Cardiff City	0	2
1977	Dortmund	1	1
1979	Wrexham (E.C.)	0	2
1979	Cologne (E.C.)	1	5
1989	Cardiff City (W.C.)	0	0
1989	Cologne (W.C.)	1	2
1991	Cardiff City (E.C.)	1	0
1991	Nuremberg (E.C.)	1	4
1995	Dusseldorf (E.C.)	1	1
1995	Cardiff City (E.C.)	1	2

v. GREECE

		W	G
1964	Athens (W.C.)	0	2
1965	Cardiff City (W.C.)	4	1

v. HOLLAND

		W	H
1988	Amsterdam (W.C.)	0	1
1989	Wrexham (W.C.)	1	2
1992	Utrecht	0	4
1996	Cardiff City (W.C.)	1	3
1996	Eindhoven (W.C.)	1	7

v. HUNGARY

		W	H
1958	Sanviken (W.C.)	1	1
1958	Stockholm (W.C.)	2	1
1961	Budapest	2	3
1963	Budapest (E.C.)	1	3
1963	Cardiff City (E.C.)	1	1
1974	Cardiff City (E.C.)	2	0
1975	Budapest (E.C.)	2	1
1986	Cardiff City	0	3

v. ICELAND

		W	I
1980	Reykjavik (W.C.)	4	0
1981	Swansea City (W.C.) ...	2	2
1984	Reykjavik (W.C.)	0	1
1984	Cardiff City (W.C.)	2	1
1991	Cardiff City	1	0

v. IRAN

		W	I
1978	Tehran	1	0

v. REPUBLIC OF IRELAND

		W	RI
1960	Dublin	3	2
1979	Swansea City	2	1
1981	Dublin	3	1
1986	Dublin	1	0
1990	Dublin	0	1
1991	Wrexham	0	3
1992	Dublin	1	0
1993	Dublin	1	2
1997	Cardiff City	0	0

v. ISRAEL

		W	I
1958	Tel Aviv (W.C.)	2	0
1958	Cardiff City (W.C.)	2	0
1984	Tel Aviv	0	0
1989	Tel Aviv	3	3

v. ITALY

		W	I
1965	Florence	1	4
1968	Cardiff City (W.C.)	0	1
1969	Rome (W.C.)	1	4
1988	Brescia	1	0
1996	Terni	0	3
1998	Anfield (E.C.)	0	2
1999	Bologna (E.C.)	0	4

v. JAMAICA

		W	J
1998	Cardiff City	0	0

v. JAPAN

		W	J
1992	Matsuyama	1	0

v. KUWAIT

		W	K
1977	Wrexham	0	0
1977	Kuwait City	0	0

v. LUXEMBOURG

		W	L
1974	Swansea City (E.C.)	5	0
1975	Luxembourg (E.C.)	3	1
1990	Luxembourg (E.C.)	1	0
1991	Luxembourg (E.C.)	1	0

v. MALTA

		W	M
1978	Wrexham (E.C.)	7	0
1979	Valletta (E.C.)	2	0
1988	Valletta	3	2
1998	Valletta	3	0

v. MEXICO

		W	M
1958	Stockholm (W.C.)	1	1
1962	Mexico City	1	2

v. MOLDOVA

		W	M
1994	Kishinev (E.C.)	2	3
1995	Cardiff City (E.C.)	1	0

v. NORWAY

		W	N
1982	Swansea City (E.C.)	1	0
1983	Oslo (E.C.)	0	0
1984	Trondheim	0	1
1985	Wrexham	1	1
1985	Bergen	2	4
1994	Cardiff City	1	3

v. POLAND

		W	P
1973	Cardiff City (W.C.)	2	0
1973	Katowice (W.C.)	0	3
1991	Radom	0	0

v. PORTUGAL

		W	P
1949	Lisbon	2	3
1951	Cardiff City	2	1

v. R.C.S.
(formerly Czechoslovakia)

		W	RCS
1993	Ostrava (W.C.)	1	1
1993	Cardiff City (W.C.)	2	2

v. REST OF UNITED KINGDOM

		W	UK
1951	Cardiff City	3	2
1969	Cardiff City	0	1

v. ROMANIA

		W	R
1970	Cardiff City (E.C.)	0	0
1971	Bucharest (E.C.)	0	0
1983	Wrexham	5	0
1992	Bucharest (W.C.)	1	5
1993	Cardiff City (W.C.)	1	2

v. SAN MARINO

		W	SM
1996	Serravalle (W.C.)	5	0
1996	Cardiff City (W.C.)	6	0

v. SAUDI ARABIA

		W	SA
1986	Dahran	2	1

v. SOVIET UNION

		W	SU
1965	Moscow (W.C.)	1	2
1965	Cardiff City (W.C.)	2	1
1981	Wrexham (W.C.)	0	0
1981	Tbilisi (W.C.)	0	3
1987	Swansea City	0	0

v. SPAIN

		W	S
1961	Cardiff City (W.C.)	1	2
1961	Madrid (W.C.)	1	1
1982	Valencia	1	1
1984	Seville (W.C.)	0	3
1985	Wrexham (W.C.)	3	0

v. SWEDEN

		W	S
1958	Stockholm (W.C.)	0	0
1988	Stockholm	1	4
1989	Wrexham	0	0
1990	Stockholm	2	4
1994	Wrexham	0	2

v. SWITZERLAND

		W	S
1949	Berne	0	4
1951	Wrexham	3	2
1996	Lugano	0	2
1999	Zurich (E.C.)	0	2

v. TUNISIA

		W	T
1998	Tunis	0	4

v. TURKEY

		W	T
1978	Wrexham (E.C.)	1	0
1979	Izmir (E.C.)	0	1
1980	Cardiff City (W.C.)	4	0
1981	Ankara (W.C.)	1	0
1996	Cardiff City (W.C.)	0	0

		W	T
1997	Istanbul (W.C.)	4	6

v. URUGUAY

		W	U
1986	Wrexham	0	0

v. YUGOSLAVIA

		W	Y
1953	Belgrade	2	5
1954	Cardiff City	1	3
1976	Zagreb (E.C.)	0	2
1976	Cardiff City (E.C.)	1	1
1982	Titograd (E.C.)	4	4
1983	Cardiff City (E.C.)	1	1
1988	Swansea City	1	2

NORTHERN IRELAND

v. ALBANIA

		NI	A
1965	Belfast (W.C.)	4	1
1965	Tirana (W.C.)	1	1
1983	Tirana (E.C.)	0	0
1983	Belfast (E.C.)	1	0
1992	Belfast (W.C.)	3	0
1993	Tirana (W.C.)	2	1
1996	Belfast (W.C.)	2	0
1997	Zurich (W.C.)	0	1

v. ALGERIA

		NI	A
1986	Guadalajara (W.C.)	1	1

v. ARGENTINA

		NI	A
1958	Halmstad (W.C.)	1	3

v. ARMENIA

		NI	A
1996	Belfast (W.C.)	1	1
1997	Yerevan (W.C.)	0	0

v. AUSTRALIA

		NI	A
1980	Sydney	2	1
1980	Melbourne	1	1
1980	Adelaide	2	1

v. AUSTRIA

		NI	A
1982	Madrid (W.C.)	2	2
1982	Vienna (E.C.)	0	2
1983	Belfast (E.C.)	3	1
1990	Vienna (E.C.)	0	0
1991	Belfast (E.C.)	2	1
1994	Vienna (E.C.)	2	1
1995	Belfast (E.C.)	5	3

v. BELGIUM

		NI	B
1976	Liege (W.C.)	0	2
1977	Belfast (W.C.)	3	0
1997	Belfast (W.C.)	3	0

v. BRAZIL

		NI	B
1986	Guadalajara (W.C.)	0	3

v. BULGARIA

		NI	B
1972	Sofia (W.C.)	0	3
1973	Sheffield (W.C.)	0	0
1978	Sofia (E.C.)	2	0
1979	Belfast (E.C.)	2	0

v. CANADA

		NI	C
1995	Edmonton	0	2
1999	Belfast	1	1

v. CHILE

		NI	C
1989	Belfast	0	1
1995	Edmonton, Canada	0	2

v. COLOMBIA

		NI	C
1994	Boston, USA	0	2

v. CYPRUS

		NI	C
1971	Nicosia (E.C.)	3	0
1971	Belfast (E.C.)	5	0
1973	Nicosia (W.C.)	0	1
1973	Fulham (W.C.)	3	0

v. CZECHOSLOVAKIA

		NI	C
1958	Halmstad (W.C.)	1	0
1958	Malmo (W.C.)	2	1

v. DENMARK

		NI	D
1978	Belfast (E.C.)	2	1
1979	Copenhagen (E.C.)	0	4
1986	Belfast	1	1
1990	Belfast (E.C.)	1	1
1991	Odense (E.C.)	1	2
1992	Belfast (W.C.)	0	1
1993	Copenhagen (W.C.)	0	1

v. FAROE ISLANDS

		NI	FI
1991	Belfast (E.C.)	1	1
1991	Landskrona, Sw. (E.C.)	5	0

v. FINLAND

		NI	F
1984	Pori (W.C.)	0	1
1984	Belfast (W.C.)	2	1
1998	Belfast (E.C.)	1	0

v. FRANCE

		NI	F
1951	Belfast	2	2
1952	Paris	1	3
1958	Norrkoping (W.C.)	0	4
1982	Paris	0	4
1982	Madrid (W.C.)	1	4
1986	Paris	0	0
1988	Belfast	0	0

v. GERMANY/ WEST GERMANY

		NI	G
1958	Malmo (W.C.)	2	2
1960	Belfast (W.C.)	3	4
1961	Berlin (W.C.)	1	2
1966	Belfast	0	2
1977	Cologne	0	5
1982	Belfast (E.C.)	1	0
1983	Hamburg (E.C.)	1	0
1992	Bremen	1	1
1996	Belfast	1	1
1997	Nuremberg (W.C.)	1	1
1997	Belfast (W.C.)	1	3
1999	Belfast (E.C.)	0	3

v. GREECE

		NI	G
1961	Athens (W.C.)	1	2
1961	Belfast (W.C.)	2	0
1988	Athens	2	3

v. HOLLAND

		NI	H
1962	Rotterdam	0	4
1965	Belfast (W.C.)	2	1
1965	Rotterdam (W.C.)	0	0
1976	Rotterdam (W.C.)	2	2
1977	Belfast (W.C.)	0	1

v. HONDURAS

		NI	H
1982	Zaragoza (W.C.)	1	1

v. HUNGARY

		NI	H
1988	Budapest (W.C.)	0	1
1989	Belfast (W.C.)	1	2

v. ICELAND

		NI	I
1977	Reykjavik (W.C.)	0	1
1977	Belfast (W.C.)	2	0

v. REPUBLIC OF IRELAND

		NI	RI
1978	Dublin (E.C.)	0	0
1979	Belfast (E.C.)	1	0
1988	Belfast (W.C.)	0	0
1989	Dublin (W.C.)	0	3
1993	Dublin (W.C.)	0	3
1993	Belfast (W.C.)	1	1
1994	Belfast (E.C.)	0	4
1995	Dublin (E.C.)	1	1
1999	Dublin	1	0

v. ISRAEL

		NI	I
1968	Jaffa	3	2
1976	Tel Aviv	1	1
1980	Tel Aviv (W.C.)	0	0
1981	Belfast (W.C.)	1	0
1984	Belfast	3	0
1987	Tel Aviv	1	1

v. ITALY

		NI	I
1957	Rome (W.C.)	0	1
1957	Belfast	2	2
1958	Belfast (W.C.)	2	1
1961	Bologna	2	3
1997	Palermo	0	2

v. LATVIA

		NI	L
1993	Riga (W.C.)	2	1
1993	Belfast (W.C.)	2	0
1995	Riga (E.C.)	1	0
1995	Belfast (E.C.)	1	2

v. LIECHTENSTEIN

		NI	L
1994	Belfast (E.C.)	4	1
1995	Eschen (E.C.)	4	0

v. LITHUANIA

		NI	L
1992	Belfast (W.C.)	2	2
1993	Vilnius (W.C.)	1	0

v. MALTA

		NI	M
1988	Belfast (W.C.)	3	0

		NI	M
1989	Valletta (W.C.)	2	0

v. MEXICO

		NI	M
1966	Belfast	4	1
1994	Miami	0	3

v. MOLDOVA

		NI	M
1998	Belfast (E.C.)	2	2
1999	Kishinev (E.C.)	0	0

v. MOROCCO

		NI	M
1986	Belfast	2	1

v. NORWAY

		NI	N
1974	Oslo (E.C.)	1	2
1975	Belfast (E.C.)	3	0
1990	Belfast	2	3
1996	Belfast	0	2

v. POLAND

		NI	P
1962	Katowice (E.C.)	2	0
1962	Belfast (E.C.)	2	0
1988	Belfast	1	1
1991	Belfast	3	1

v. PORTUGAL

		NI	P
1957	Lisbon (W.C.)	1	1
1957	Belfast (W.C.)	3	0
1973	Coventry City (W.C.)	1	1
1973	Lisbon (W.C.)	1	1
1980	Lisbon (W.C.)	0	1
1981	Belfast (W.C.)	1	0
1994	Belfast (E.C.)	1	2
1995	Oporto (E.C.)	1	1
1997	Belfast (W.C.)	0	0
1997	Lisbon (W.C.)	0	1

v. ROMANIA

		NI	R
1984	Belfast (W.C.)	3	2
1985	Bucharest (W.C.)	1	0
1994	Belfast	2	0

v. SLOVAKIA

		NI	S
1998	Belfast	1	0

v. SOVIET UNION

		NI	SU
1969	Belfast (W.C.)	0	0
1969	Moscow (W.C.)	0	2
1971	Moscow (E.C.)	0	1
1971	Belfast (E.C.)	1	1

v. SPAIN

		NI	S
1958	Madrid	2	6
1963	Bilbao	1	1
1963	Belfast	0	1
1970	Seville (E.C.)	0	3
1972	Hull City (E.C.)	1	1
1982	Valencia (W.C.)	1	0
1985	Palma, Majorca	0	0
1986	Guadalajara (W.C.)	1	2
1988	Seville (W.C.)	0	4
1989	Belfast (W.C.)	0	2
1992	Belfast (W.C.)	0	0
1993	Seville (W.C.)	1	3
1998	Santander	1	4

v. SWEDEN

		NI	S
1974	Solna (E.C.)	2	0
1975	Belfast (E.C.)	1	2
1980	Belfast (W.C.)	3	0
1981	Stockholm (W.C.)	0	1
1996	Belfast	1	2

v. SWITZERLAND

		NI	S
1964	Belfast (W.C.)	1	0
1964	Lausanne (W.C.)	1	2
1998	Belfast	1	0

v. THAILAND

		NI	T
1997	Bangkok	0	0

v. TURKEY

		NI	T
1968	Belfast (W.C.)	4	1
1968	Istanbul (W.C.)	3	0
1983	Belfast (E.C.)	2	1
1983	Ankara (E.C.)	0	1
1985	Belfast (W.C.)	2	0
1985	Izmir (W.C.)	0	0
1986	Izmir (E.C.)	0	0
1987	Belfast (E.C.)	1	0
1998	Istanbul (E.C.)	0	3

v. UKRAINE

		NI	U
1996	Belfast (W.C.)	0	1
1997	Kiev (W.C.)	1	2

v. URUGUAY

		NI	U
1964	Belfast	3	0
1990	Belfast	1	0

v. YUGOSLAVIA

		NI	Y
1975	Belfast (E.C.)	1	0
1975	Belgrade (E.C.)	0	1
1982	Zaragoza (W.C.)	0	0
1987	Belfast (E.C.)	1	2

		NI	Y
1987	Sarajevo (E.C.)	0	3
1990	Belfast (E.C.)	0	2

		NI	Y
1991	Belgrade (E.C.)	1	4

REPUBLIC OF IRELAND

v. ALBANIA

		RI	A
1992	Dublin (W.C.)	2	0
1993	Tirana (W.C.)	2	1

v. ARGENTINA

		RI	A
1951	Dublin	0	1
1979*	Dublin	0	0
1980	Dublin	0	1
1998	Dublin	0	2

(* Not regarded as full Int.)

v. AUSTRIA

		RI	A
1952	Vienna	0	6
1953	Dublin	4	0
1958	Vienna	1	3
1962	Dublin	2	3
1963	Vienna (E.C.)	0	0
1963	Dublin (E.C.)	3	2
1966	Vienna	0	1
1968	Dublin	2	2
1971	Dublin (E.C.)	1	4
1971	Linz (E.C.)	0	6
1995	Dublin (E.C.)	1	3
1995	Vienna (E.C.)	1	3

v. BELGIUM

		RI	B
1928	Liege	4	2
1929	Dublin	4	0
1930	Brussels	3	1
1934	Dublin (W.C.)	4	4
1949	Dublin	0	2
1950	Brussels	1	5
1965	Dublin	0	2
1966	Liege	3	2
1980	Dublin (W.C.)	1	1
1981	Brussels (W.C.)	0	1
1986	Brussels (E.C.)	2	2
1987	Dublin (E.C.)	0	0
1997*	Dublin (W.C.)	1	1
1997*	Brussels (W.C.)	1	2

(* World Cup play-off)

v. BOLIVIA

		RI	B
1994	Dublin	1	0
1996	East Rutherford, N.J.	3	0

v. BRAZIL

		RI	B
1974	Rio de Janeiro	1	2

v. BULGARIA

		RI	B
1982	Uberlandia	0	7
1987	Dublin	1	0

		RI	B
1977	Sofia (W.C.)	1	2
1977	Dublin (W.C.)	0	0
1979	Sofia (E.C.)	0	1
1979	Dublin (E.C.)	3	0
1987	Sofia (E.C.)	1	2
1987	Dublin (E.C.)	2	0

v. CHILE

		RI	C
1960	Dublin	2	0
1972	Recife	1	2
1974	Santiago	2	1
1982	Santiago	0	1
1991	Dublin	1	1

v. CROATIA

		RI	C
1996	Dublin	2	2
1998	Dublin (E.C.)	2	0

v. CYPRUS

		RI	C
1980	Nicosia (W.C.)	3	2
1980	Dublin (W.C.)	6	0

v. CZECHOSLOVAKIA/ CZECH REPUBLIC

		RI	C
1938	Prague	2	2
1959	Dublin (E.C.)	2	0
1959	Bratislava (E.C.)	0	4
1961	Dublin (W.C.)	1	3
1961	Prague (W.C.)	1	7
1967	Dublin (E.C.)	0	2
1967	Prague (E.C.)	2	1
1969	Dublin (W.C.)	1	2
1969	Prague (W.C.)	0	3
1979	Prague	1	4
1981	Dublin	3	1
1986	Reykjavik	1	0
1994	Dublin	1	3
1996	Prague	0	2
1998	Olomouc	1	2

v. DENMARK

		RI	D
1956	Dublin (W.C.)	2	1
1957	Copenhagen (W.C.)	2	0

		RI	D
1968*	Dublin (W.C.)	1	1
1969	Copenhagen (W.C.)	0	2
1969	Dublin (W.C.)	1	1
1978	Copenhagen (E.C.)	3	3
1979	Dublin (E.C.)	2	0
1984	Copenhagen (W.C.)	0	3
1985	Dublin (W.C.)	1	4
1992	Copenhagen (W.C.)	0	0
1993	Dublin (W.C.)	1	1

(* Abandoned after 51 mins. – fog)

v. ECUADOR

		RI	E
1972	Natal	3	2

v. EGYPT

		RI	E
1990	Palermo (W.C.)	0	0

v. FINLAND

		RI	F
1949	Dublin (W.C.)	3	0
1949	Helsinki (W.C.)	1	1
1990	Dublin	1	1

v. FRANCE

		RI	F
1937	Paris	2	0
1952	Dublin	1	1
1953	Dublin (W.C.)	3	5
1953	Paris (W.C.)	0	1
1972	Dublin (W.C.)	2	1
1973	Paris (W.C.)	1	1
1976	Paris (W.C.)	0	2
1977	Dublin (W.C.)	1	0
1980	Paris (W.C.)	0	2
1981	Dublin (W.C.)	3	2
1989	Dublin	0	0

v. GERMANY/ WEST GERMANY

		RI	G
1935	Dortmund	1	3
1936	Dublin	5	2
1939	Bremen	1	1
1951	Dublin	3	2
1952	Cologne	0	3
1955	Hamburg	1	2
1956	Dublin	3	0
1960	Dusseldorf	1	0
1966	Dublin	0	4
1970	Berlin	1	2
1979	Dublin	1	3
1981	Bremen	0	3
1989	Dublin	1	1
1994	Hanover	2	0

v. HOLLAND

		RI	H
1932	Amsterdam	2	0

		RI	H
1934	Amsterdam	2	5
1935	Dublin	3	5
1955	Dublin	1	0
1956	Rotterdam	4	1
1980	Dublin (W.C.)	2	1
1981	Rotterdam (W.C.)	2	2
1982	Rotterdam (E.C.)	1	2
1983	Dublin (E.C.)	2	3
1988	Gelsenkirchen (E.C.)	0	1
1990	Palermo (W.C.)	1	1
1994	Tilburg	1	0
1994	Orlando (W.C.)	0	2
1995*	Anfield (E.C.)	0	2
1996	Rotterdam	1	3

(* Qual. Round play-off)

v. HUNGARY

		RI	H
1934	Dublin	2	4
1936	Budapest	3	3
1936	Dublin	2	3
1939	Cork	2	2
1939	Budapest	2	2
1969	Dublin (W.C.)	1	2
1969	Budapest (W.C.)	0	4
1989	Budapest (W.C.)	0	0
1989	Dublin (W.C.)	2	0
1992	Gyor	2	1

v. ICELAND

		RI	I
1962	Dublin (E.C.)	4	2
1962	Reykjavik (E.C.)	1	1
1982	Dublin (E.C.)	2	0
1983	Reykjavik (E.C.)	3	0
1986	Reykjavik	2	1
1996	Dublin (W.C.)	0	0
1997	Reykjavik (W.C.)	4	2

v. IRAN

		RI	I
1972	Recife	2	1

v. ISRAEL

		RI	I
1984	Tel Aviv	0	3
1985	Tel Aviv	0	0
1987	Dublin	5	0

v. ITALY

		RI	I
1926	Turin	0	3
1927	Dublin	1	2
1970	Florence (E.C.)	0	3
1971	Dublin (E.C.)	1	2
1985	Dublin	1	2
1990	Rome (W.C.)	0	1
1992	Boston, USA	0	2
1994	New York City (W.C.)	1	0

v. LATVIA

		RI	L
1992	Dublin (W.C.)	4	0
1993	Riga (W.C.)	2	0
1994	Riga (E.C.)	3	0
1995	Dublin (E.C.)	2	1

v. LIECHTENSTEIN

		RI	L
1994	Dublin (E.C.)	4	0
1995	Eschen (E.C.)	0	0
1996	Eschen (W.C.)	5	0
1997	Dublin (W.C.)	5	0

v. LITHUANIA

		RI	L
1993	Vilnius (W.C.)	1	0
1993	Dublin (W.C.)	2	0
1997	Dublin (W.C.)	0	0
1997	Zalgiris (W.C.)	2	1

v. LUXEMBOURG

		RI	L
1936	Luxembourg	5	1
1953	Dublin (W.C.)	4	0
1954	Luxembourg (W.C.)	1	0
1987	Luxembourg (E.C.)	2	0
1987	Luxembourg (E.C.)	2	1

v. MACEDONIA

		RI	M
1996	Dublin (W.C.)	3	0
1997	Skopje (W.C.)	2	3
1999	Dublin (E.C.)	1	0

v. MALTA

		RI	M
1983	Valletta (E.C.)	1	0
1983	Dublin (E.C.)	8	0
1989	Dublin (W.C.)	2	0
1989	Valletta (W.C.)	2	0
1990	Valletta	3	0
1998	Dublin (E.C.)	1	0

v. MEXICO

		RI	M
1984	Dublin	0	0
1994	Orlando (W.C.)	1	2
1996	New Jersey	2	2
1998	Dublin	0	0

v. MOROCCO

		RI	M
1990	Dublin	1	0

v. NORWAY

		RI	N
1937	Oslo (W.C.)	2	3
1937	Dublin (W.C.)	3	3
1950	Dublin	2	2
1951	Oslo	3	2
1954	Dublin	2	1
1955	Oslo	3	1
1960	Dublin	3	1
1964	Oslo	4	1
1973	Oslo	1	1
1976	Dublin	3	0
1978	Oslo	0	0
1984	Oslo (W.C.)	0	1
1985	Dublin (W.C.)	0	0
1988	Oslo	0	0
1994	New York City (W.C.)	0	0
1999	Dublin	2	0

v. POLAND

		RI	P
1938	Warsaw	0	6
1938	Dublin	3	2
1958	Katowice	2	2
1958	Dublin	2	2
1964	Cracow	1	3
1964	Dublin	3	2
1968	Dublin	2	2
1968	Katowice	0	1
1970	Dublin	1	2
1970	Poznan	0	2
1973	Wroclaw	0	2
1973	Dublin	1	0
1976	Poznan	2	0
1977	Dublin	0	0
1978	Lodz	0	3
1981	Bydgoscz	0	3
1984	Dublin	0	0
1986	Warsaw	0	1
1988	Dublin	3	1
1991	Dublin (E.C.)	0	3
1991	Poznan (E.C.)	3	3

v. PORTUGAL

		RI	P
1946	Lisbon	1	3
1947	Dublin	0	2
1948	Lisbon	0	2
1949	Dublin	1	0
1972	Recife	1	2
1992	Boston, USA	2	0
1995	Dublin (E.C.)	1	0
1995	Lisbon (E.C.)	0	3
1996	Dublin	0	1

v. ROMANIA

		RI	R
1988	Dublin	2	0
1990*	Genoa	0	0
1997	Bucharest (W.C.)	0	1
1997	Dublin (W.C.)	1	1

(* Rep. won 5-4 on pens.)

v. RUSSIA
(See also Soviet Union)

		RI	R
1994	Dublin	0	0
1996	Dublin	0	2

v. SOVIET UNION
(See also Russia)

		RI	SU
1972	Dublin (W.C.)	1	2
1973	Moscow (W.C.)	0	1
1974	Dublin (E.C.)	3	0
1975	Kiev (E.C.)	1	2
1984	Dublin (W.C.)	1	0
1985	Moscow (W.C.)	0	2
1988	Hanover (E.C.)	1	1
1990	Dublin	1	0

v. SPAIN

		RI	S
1931	Barcelona	1	1
1931	Dublin	0	5
1946	Madrid	1	0
1947	Dublin	3	2
1948	Barcelona	1	2
1949	Dublin	1	4
1952	Madrid	0	6
1955	Dublin	2	2
1964	Seville (E.C.)	1	5
1964	Dublin (E.C.)	0	2
1965	Dublin (W.C.)	1	0
1965	Seville (W.C.)	1	4
1965	Paris (W.C.)	0	1
1966	Dublin (E.C.)	0	0
1966	Valencia (E.C.)	0	2
1977	Dublin	0	1
1982	Dublin (E.C.)	3	3
1983	Zaragoza (E.C.)	0	2
1985	Cork	0	0
1988	Seville (W.C.)	0	2
1989	Dublin (W.C.)	1	0
1992	Seville (W.C.)	0	0
1993	Dublin (W.C.)	1	3

v. SWEDEN

		RI	S
1949	Stockholm (W.C.)	1	3
1949	Dublin (W.C.)	1	3
1959	Dublin	3	2
1960	Malmo	1	4
1970	Dublin (E.C.)	1	1
1970	Malmo (E.C.)	0	1
1999	Dublin	2	0

v. SWITZERLAND

		RI	S
1935	Basle	0	1
1936	Dublin	1	0
1937	Berne	1	0
1938	Dublin	4	0
1948	Dublin	0	1
1975	Dublin (E.C.)	2	1
1975	Berne (E.C.)	0	1
1980	Dublin	2	0
1985	Dublin (W.C.)	3	0
1985	Berne (W.C.)	0	0
1992	Dublin	2	1

v. TRINIDAD & TOBAGO

		RI	T&T
1982	Port of Spain	1	2

v. TUNISIA

		RI	T
1988	Dublin	4	0

v. TURKEY

		RI	T
1966	Dublin (E.C.)	2	1
1967	Ankara (E.C.)	1	2
1974	Izmir (E.C.)	1	1
1975	Dublin (E.C.)	4	0
1976	Ankara	3	3
1978	Dublin	4	2
1990	Izmir	0	0
1990	Dublin (E.C.)	5	0
1991	Istanbul (E.C.)	3	1

v. URUGUAY

		RI	U
1974	Montevideo	0	2
1986	Dublin	1	1

v. U.S.A.

		RI	USA
1979	Dublin	3	2
1991	Boston	1	1
1992	Dublin	4	1
1992	Washington	1	3
1996	Boston	1	2

v. YUGOSLAVIA

		RI	Y
1955	Dublin	1	4
1988	Dublin	2	0
1998	Belgrade (E.C.)	0	1

INTERNATIONAL APPEARANCES
SINCE THE WAR (1946-99)

(As at start of season 1999-2000. Year shown = season, ie. 1999 = season 1998-9.
*Also a pre-war International player. Totals include appearances as substitute).

ENGLAND

A'Court, A. (Liverpool, 1958-9) 5
Adams, T. (Arsenal, 1987-99) 57
Allen, A. (Stoke City, 1960) 3
Allen, C. (Q.P.R., Tottenham,
   1984-8) 5
Allen, R. (W.B.A., 1952-5) 5
Anderson, S. (Sunderland, 1962) 2
Anderson, V. (Nott'm Forest, Arsenal,
   Manchester Utd., 1979-88) 30
Anderton, D. (Tottenham, 1994-9) ... 27
Angus, J. (Burnley, 1961) 1
Armfield, J. (Blackpool, 1959-66) 43
Armstrong, D. (Middlesbrough,
   Southampton, 1980-4) 3
Armstrong, K. (Chelsea, 1955) 1
Astall, G. (Birmingham City, 1956) ... 2
Astle, J. (W.B.A., 1969-70) 5
Aston, J. (Manchester Utd.,
   1949-51) 17
Atyeo, J. (Bristol City, 1956-7) 6

Bailey, G. (Manchester Utd., 1985) ... 2
Bailey, M. (Charlton Athletic,
   1964-5) 2
Baily, E. (Tottenham, 1950-3) 9
Baker, J. (Hibernian, Arsenal,
   1960-6) 8
Ball, A. (Blackpool, Everton, Arsenal,
   1965-75) 72
Banks, G. (Leicester City, Stoke City,
   1963-72) 73
Banks, T. (Bolton Wand., 1958-9) 6
Bardsley, D. (Q.P.R., 1993) 2
Barham, M. (Norwich City, 1983) 2
Barlow, R. (W.B.A., 1955) 1
Barmby, N. (Tottenham, Middlesbrough,
   1995-7) 10
Barnes, J. (Watford, Liverpool,
   1983-96) 79
Barnes, P. (Manchester City, W.B.A.,
   Leeds Utd., 1978-82) 22
Barrass, M. (Bolton Wand., 1952-3) ... 3
Barrett, E. (Oldham Athletic, Aston Villa,
   1991-3) 3
Barton, W. (Wimbledon, Newcastle Utd.,
   1995) 3
Batty, D. (Leeds Utd., Blackburn Rov.,
   Newcastle Utd., Leeds Utd.,
   1991-9) 40

Baynham, R. (Luton Town, 1956) 3
Beardsley, P. (Newcastle Utd., Liverpool,
   Newcastle Utd., 1986-96) 59
Beasant, D. (Chelsea, 1990) 2
Beattie, K. (Ipswich Town, 1975-8) ... 9
Beckham, D. (Manchester Utd.,
   1997-9) 23
Bell, C. (Manchester City, 1968-76) . 48
Bentley, R. (Chelsea, 1949-55) 12
Berry, J. (Manchester Utd., 1953-6) ... 4
Birtles, G. (Nott'm Forest, 1980-1) ... 3
Blissett, L. (Watford, AC Milan,
   1983-4) 14
Blockley, J. (Arsenal, 1973) 1
Blunstone, F. (Chelsea, 1955-7) 5
Bonetti, P. (Chelsea, 1966-70) 7
Bould, S. (Arsenal, 1994) 2
Bowles, S. (Q.P.R., 1974-7) 5
Boyer, P. (Norwich City, 1976) 1
Brabrook, P. (Chelsea, 1958-60) 3
Bracewell, P. (Everton, 1985-6) 3
Bradford City, G. (Bristol Rov., 1956) . 1
Bradley, W. (Manchester Utd., 1959) .. 3
Bridges, B. (Chelsea, 1965-6) 4
Broadbent, P. (Wolves, 1958-60) 7
Broadis, I. (Manchester City, Newcastle
   Utd., 1952-4) 14
Brooking, T. (West Ham Utd.,
   1974-82) 47
Brooks, J. (Tottenham, 1957) 3
Brown, A. (W.B.A., 1971) 1
Brown, K. (West Ham Utd., 1960) 1
Brown, W. (Manchester Utd., 1999) ... 1
Bull, S. (Wolves, 1989-91) 13
Butcher, T. (Ipswich Town, Rangers,
   1980-90) 77
Butt, N. (Manchester Utd., 1997-8) ... 6
Byrne, G. (Liverpool, 1963-6) 2
Byrne, J. (Crystal Palace, West Ham
   Utd., 1962-5) 11
Byrne, R. (Manchester Utd.,
   1954-8) 33

Callaghan, I. (Liverpool, 1966-78) 4
Campbell, S. (Tottenham, 1996-9) ... 27
Carragher, J. (Liverpool, 1999) 1
*Carter, H. (Derby Co., 1947) 7
Chamberlain, M. (Stoke City,
   1983-5) 8

184

NORTHERN IRELAND

190

Whitley, Jeff (Manchester City, 1997-8) 3
Whitley, Jim (Manchester City, 1998-9) 2
Williams, M. (Chesterfield, 1999) 4
Williams, P. (W.B.A., 1991) 1
Wilson, D. (Brighton & H.A., Luton Town, Sheffield Wed., 1987-92) ... 24
Wilson, K. (Ipswich Town, Chelsea, Notts Co., Walsall, 1987-95) 42

SCOTLAND

Aird, J. (Burnley, 1954) 4
Aitken, G. (East Fife, 1949-54) 8
Aitken, R. (Celtic, Newcastle Utd., St. Mirren, 1980-92) 57
Albiston, A. (Manchester Utd., 1982-6) 14
Allan, T. (Dundee, 1974) 2
Anderson, J. (Leicester City, 1954) 1
Archibald, S. (Aberdeen, Tottenham, Barcelona, 1980-6) 27
Auld, B. (Celtic, 1959-60) 3

Baird, H. (Airdrie, 1956) 1
Baird, S. (Rangers, 1957-8) 7
Bannon, E. (Dundee Utd., 1980-6) .. 11
Bauld, W. (Hearts, 1950) 3
Baxter, J. (Rangers, Sunderland, 1961-8) 34
Bell, W. (Leeds Utd., 1966) 2
Bernard, P. (Oldham Athletic, 1995) .. 2
Bett, J. (Rangers, Lokeren, Aberdeen, 1982-90) 26
Black, E. (Metz, 1988) 2
Black, I. (Southampton, 1948) 1
Blacklaw, A. (Burnley, 1963-6) 3
Blackley, J. (Hibernian, 1974-7) 7
Blair, J. (Blackpool, 1947) 1
Blyth, J. (Coventry City, 1978) 2
Bone, J. (Norwich City, 1972-3) 2
Booth, S. (Aberdeen, Borussia Dortmund, 1993-8) 16
Bowman, D. (Dundee Utd., 1992-4) ... 6
Boyd, T. (Motherwell, Chelsea, Celtic, 1991-9) 64
Brand, R. (Rangers, 1961-2) 8
Brazil, A. (Ipswich Town, Tottenham, 1980-3) 13
Bremner, D. (Hibernian, 1976) 1
Bremner, W. (Leeds Utd., 1965-76) . 54
Brennan, F. (Newcastle Utd., 1947-54) 7
Brogan, J. (Celtic, 1971) 4
Brown, A. (East Fife, Blackpool, 1950-4) 14
Brown, H. (Partick, 1947) 3
Brown, J. (Sheffield Utd., 1975) 1

Wilson, S. (Glenavon, Falkirk, Dundee, 1962-8) 12
Wood, T. (Walsall, 1996) 1
Worthington, N. (Sheffield Wed., Leeds Utd., Stoke City, 1984-97) 66
Wright, T. (Newcastle Utd., Nott'm Forest, Reading, Manchester City, 1989-99) 30

Brown, R. (Rangers, 1947-52) 3
Brown, W. (Dundee, Tottenham, 1958-66) 28
Brownlie, J. (Hibernian, 1971-6) 7
Buchan, M. (Aberdeen, Manchester Utd., 1972-8) 34
Buckley, P. (Aberdeen, 1954-5) 3
Burley, C. (Chelsea, Celtic, 1995-9) . 30
Burley, G. (Ipswich Town, 1979-82) . 11
Burns, F. (Manchester Utd., 1970) 1
Burns, K. (Birmingham City, Nott'm Forest, 1974-81) 20
Burns, T. (Celtic, 1981-8) 8

Calderwood, C. (Tottenham, Aston Villa, 1995-9) 34
Caldow, E. (Rangers, 1957-63) 40
Callaghan, T. (Dunfermline, 1970) 2
Cameron, C. (Hearts, 1999) 3
Campbell, R. (Falkirk, Chelsea, 1947-50) 5
Campbell, W. (Morton, 1947-8) 5
Carr, W. (Coventry City, 1970-3) 6
Chalmers, S. (Celtic, 1965-7) 5
Clark, J. (Celtic, 1966-7) 4
Clark, R. (Aberdeen, 1968-73) 17
Clarke, S. (Chelsea, 1988-94) 6
Collins, J. (Hibernian, Celtic, Monaco, Everton, 1988-99) 54
Collins, R. (Celtic, Everton, Leeds Utd., 1951-65) 31
Colquhoun, E. (Sheffield Utd, 1972-3) 9
Colquhoun, J. (Hearts, 1988) 1
Combe, J. (Hibernian, 1948) 3
Conn, A. (Hearts, 1956) 1
Conn, A. (Tottenham, 1975) 2
Connachan, E. (Dunfermline, 1962) ... 2
Connelly, G. (Celtic, 1974) 2
Connolly, J. (Everton, 1973) 1
Connor, R. (Dundee, Aberdeen, 1986-91) 4
Cooke, C. (Dundee, Chelsea, 1966-75) 16
Cooper, D. (Rangers, Motherwell, 1980-90) 22

Malpas, M. (Dundee Utd., 1984-93) 55
Marshall, G. (Celtic, 1992) 1
Martin, B. (Motherwell, 1995) 2
Martin, F. (Aberdeen, 1954-5) 6
Martin, N. (Hibernian, Sunderland, 1965-6) 3
Martis, J. (Motherwell, 1961) 1
Mason, J. (Third Lanark, 1949-51) 7
Masson, D. (Q.P.R., Derby Co., 1976-8) 17
Mathers, D. (Partick, 1954) 1
McAllister, B. (Wimbledon, 1997) 3
McAllister, G. (Leicester City, Leeds Utd., Coventry City, 1990-9) 58
McAvennie, F. (West Ham Utd., Celtic, 1986-8) 5
McBride, J. (Celtic, 1967) 2
McCall, S. (Everton, Rangers, 1990-8) 40
McCalliog, J. (Sheffield Wed., Wolves, 1967-71) 5
McCann, N. (Hearts, Rangers, 1999) .. 2
McCann, R. (Motherwell, 1959-61) 5
McClair, B. (Celtic, Manchester Utd., 1987-93) 30
McCloy, P. (Rangers, 1973) 4
McCoist, A. (Rangers, Kilmarnock, 1986-99) 61
McColl, I. (Rangers, 1950-8) 14
McCreadie, E. (Chelsea, 1965-9) 23
McDonald, J. (Sunderland, 1956) 2
McFarlane, W. (Hearts, 1947) 1
McGarr, E. (Aberdeen, 1970) 2
McGarvey, F. (Liverpool, Celtic, 1979-84) 7
McGhee, M. (Aberdeen, 1983-4) 4
McGinlay, J. (Bolton Wand., 1995-7) 14
McGrain, D. (Celtic, 1973-82) 62
McGrory, J. (Kilmarnock, 1965-6) 3
McInally, A. (Aston Villa, Bayern Munich, 1989-90) 8
McInally, J. (Dundee Utd., 1987-93) 10
McKay, D. (Celtic, 1959-62) 14
McKean, R. (Rangers, 1976) 1
McKenzie, J. (Partick, 1954-6) 9
McKimmie, S. (Aberdeen, 1989-96) . 40
McKinlay, T. (Celtic, 1996-8) 22
McKinlay, W. (Dundee Utd., Blackburn Rov., 1994-9) 29
McKinnon, R. (Rangers, 1966-71) ... 28
McKinnon, R. (Motherwell, 1994-5) ... 3
McLaren, A. (Preston N.E., 1947-8) ... 4
McLaren, A. (Hearts, Rangers, 1992-6) 24
McLean, G. (Dundee, 1968) 1

McLean, T. (Kilmarnock, Rangers, 1969-71) 6
McLeish, A. (Aberdeen, 1980-93) 77
McLintock, F. (Leicester City, Arsenal, 1963-71) 9
McMillan, I. (Airdrie, 1952-61) 6
McNamara, J. (Celtic, 1997-8) 10
McNaught, W. (Raith, 1951-5) 5
McNeill, W. (Celtic, 1961-72) 29
McPhail, J. (Celtic, 1950-4) 5
McPherson, D. (Hearts, Rangers, 1989-93) 27
McQueen, G. (Leeds Utd., Manchester Utd., 1974-81) 30
McStay, P. (Celtic, 1984-97) 76
Millar, J. (Rangers, 1963) 2
Miller, W. (Celtic, 1946-7) 6
Miller, W. (Aberdeen, 1975-90) 65
Mitchell, R. (Newcastle Utd., 1951) .. 2
Mochan, N. (Celtic, 1954) 3
Moir, W. (Bolton Wand., 1950) 1
Moncur, R. (Newcastle Utd., 1968-72) 16
Morgan, W. (Burnley, Manchester Utd., 1968-74) 21
Morris, H. (East Fife, 1950) 1
Mudie, J. (Blackpool, 1957-8) 17
Mulhall, G. (Aberdeen, Sunderland, 1960-4) 3
Munro, F. (Wolves, 1971-5) 9
Munro, I. (St. Mirren, 1979-80) 7
Murdoch, R. (Celtic, 1966-70) 12
Murray, J. (Hearts, 1958) 5
Murray, S. (Aberdeen, 1972) 1

Narey, D. (Dundee Utd., 1977-89) ... 35
Nevin, P. (Chelsea, Everton, Tranmere Rov., 1987-96) 26
Nicholas, C. (Celtic, Arsenal, Aberdeen, 1983-9) 20
Nicol, S. (Liverpool, 1985-92) 27

O'Donnell, P. (Motherwell, 1994) 1
O'Hare, J. (Derby Co., 1970-2) 13
O'Neil, B. (Celtic, VfL Wolfsburg, 1996-9) 2
Ormond, W. (Hibernian, 1954-9) 6
Orr, T. (Morton, 1952) 2

Parker, A. (Falkirk, Everton, 1955-6) 15
Parlane, D. (Rangers, 1973-7) 12
Paton, A. (Motherwell, 1952) 2
Pearson, T. (Newcastle Utd., 1947) ... 2
Penman, A. (Dundee, 1966) 1
Pettigrew, W. (Motherwell, 1976-7) ... 5
Plenderleith, J. (Manchester City, 1961) 1

Younger, T. (Hibernian, Liverpool,
  1955-8) 24

WALES

REPUBLIC OF IRELAND

202

O'Reilly, J. (Cork Utd., 1946) 3

Peyton, G. (Fulham, Bournemouth,
Everton, 1977-92) 33
Peyton, N. (Shamrock R., Leeds Utd.,
1957-61) 6
Phelan, T. (Wimbledon, Manchester City,
Chelsea, Everton, 1992-7) 38

Quinn, N. (Arsenal, Manchester City,
Sunderland, 1986-99) 69

Richardson, D. (Shamrock R.,
Gillingham, 1972-80) 3
Ringstead, A. (Sheffield Utd.,
1951-9) 20
Robinson, M. (Brighton & H.A.,
Liverpool, Q.P.R., 1981-6) 23
Roche, P. (Shelbourne, Manchester Utd.,
1972-6) 8
Rogers, E. (Blackburn Rov., Charlton
Athletic, 1968-73) 19
Ryan, G. (Derby Co., Brighton & H.A.,
1978-85) 16
Ryan, R. (W.B.A., Derby Co.,
1950-56) 16

Savage, D. (Millwall, 1996) 5
Saward, P. (Millwall, Aston Villa,
Huddersfield Town, 1954-63) 18
Scannell, T. (Southend Utd., 1954) 1
Scully, P. (Arsenal, 1989) 1
Sheedy, K. (Everton, Newcastle Utd.,
1984-93) 46
Sheridan, J. (Leeds Utd., Sheffield
Wed., 1988-96) 34
Slaven, B. (Middlesbrough, 1990-3) ... 1
Sloan, P. (Arsenal, 1946) 2
Smyth, M. (Shamrock R., 1969) 1
Staunton, S. (Liverpool, Aston Villa,
Liverpool, 1989-99) 78

Stapleton, F. (Arsenal, Manchester Utd.,
Ajax, Derby Co., Le Havre, Blackburn
Rov., 1977-90) 71
*Stevenson, A. (Everton, 1947-9) 6
Strahan, F. (Shelbourne, 1964-5) 5
Swan, M. (Drumcondra, 1960) 1
Synnott, N. (Shamrock R., 1978-9) 3

Thomas, P. (Waterford, 1974) 2
Townsend, A. (Norwich City, Chelsea,
Aston Villa, Middlesbrough,
1989-97) 70
Traynor, T. (Southampton, 1954-64) ... 8
Treacy, R. (W.B.A., Charlton Athletic,
Swindon Town, Preston N.E.,
Shamrock R., 1966-80) 43
Tuohy, L. (Shamrock R., Newcastle Utd.,
Shamrock R., 1956-65) 8
Turner, A. (Celtic, 1963) 2

Vernon, J. (Belfast Celtic, 1946) 2

Waddock, G. (Q.P.R., Millwall,
1980-90) 21
Walsh, D. (W.B.A., Aston Villa,
1946-54) 20
Walsh, J. (Limerick, 1982) 1
Walsh, M. (Blackpool, Everton, Q.P.R.,
Porto, 1976-85) 21
Walsh, M. (Everton, Norwich City,
1982-3) 5
Walsh, W. (Manchester City,
1947-50) 9
Waters, J. (Grimsby Town, 1977-80) ... 2
Whelan, R. (St. Patrick's Ath., 1964) . 2
Whelan, R. (Liverpool, Southend Utd.,
1981-95) 53
Whelan, L. (Manchester Utd.,
1956-7) 4
Whittaker, R. (Chelsea, 1959) 1

INTERNATIONAL GOALSCORERS 1946-99

(As at start of season 1999-2000)

ENGLAND

Charlton, R 49	Keegan 21	Douglas 11
Lineker 48	Peters 20	Mannion 11
Greaves 44	Haynes 18	Clarke, A 10
Finney 30	Hunt, R 18	Flowers, R 10
Lofthouse 30	Lawton 16	Gascoigne 10
Platt 28	Taylor, T 16	Lee, F 10
Robson, B 26	Woodcock 16	Milburn 10
Hurst 24	Chivers 13	Wilshaw 10
Shearer 24	Mariner 13	Beardsley 9
Mortensen 23	Smith, R 13	Bell 9
Channon 21	Francis, T 12	Bentley 9
	Barnes, J 11	Hateley 9

N. IRELAND

Casey ... 2
Clements ... 2
Doherty, P ... 2
Harkin ... 2
Finney ... 2
Lennon ... 2
Lomas ... 2
McMahon ... 2
Neill, W ... 2
O'Neill, J ... 2
Peacock ... 2
Penney ... 2
Stewart, I ... 2
Barr ... 1
Black ... 1
Blanchflower, J ... 1
Brennan ... 1
Campbell, W ... 1
Caskey ... 1
Cassidy ... 1
Cochrane, T ... 1
Crossan, E ... 1
D'Arcy ... 1
Doherty, L ... 1
Elder ... 1
Ferguson ... 1
Ferris ... 1
Gillespie ... 1
Griffin ... 1
Hill, C ... 1
Humphries ... 1
Hunter, A ... 1
Hunter, B ... 1
Johnston ... 1
Jones, J ... 1
McClelland (1961) ... 1
McCrory ... 1
McCurdy ... 1
McGarry ... 1
McVeigh ... 1
Moreland ... 1
Morrow ... 1
Mulryne ... 1
Nelson ... 1
Nicholl, J ... 1
O'Boyle ... 1
O'Kane ... 1
Patterson, D ... 1
Rowland ... 1
Quinn, S.J. ... 1
Stevenson ... 1
Walker ... 1
Welsh ... 1
Wilson, D ... 1

SCOTLAND

Dalglish ... 30
Law ... 30

Reilly ... 22
McCoist ... 19
Johnston, M ... 14
Gilzean ... 12
Steel ... 12
Collins, J ... 11
Jordan ... 11
Collins, R ... 10
Johnstone, R ... 10
Stein ... 10
McStay ... 9
Mudie ... 9
St. John ... 9
Brand ... 8
Gallacher ... 8
Gemmill, A ... 8
Leggat ... 8
Robertson, J (1978-84) ... 8
Wilson, D ... 8
Durie ... 7
Gray, A ... 7
Wark ... 7
Brown, A ... 6
Cooper ... 6
Gough ... 6
Liddell ... 6
Rioch ... 6
Waddell ... 6
Booth ... 5
Henderson, W ... 5
Macari ... 5
Masson ... 5
McAllister G. ... 5
McQueen ... 5
Murdoch ... 5
Nevin ... 5
Nicholas ... 5
O'Hare ... 5
Scott, A ... 5
Strachan ... 5
Young, A ... 5
Archibald ... 4
Caldow ... 4
Dodds ... 4
Hamilton ... 4
Hartford ... 4
Herd, D. ... 4
Jackson, D ... 4
Johnstone, J ... 4
Lorimer ... 4
Mackay, D ... 4
Mason ... 4
McGinlay ... 4
McKinlay, W. ... 4
McLaren ... 4
Smith, G ... 4
Souness ... 4
Baxter ... 3
Bremner, W ... 3

Burley, C ... 3
Chalmers ... 3
Gibson ... 3
Graham, G ... 3
Gray, E ... 3
Greig ... 3
Lennox ... 3
MacDougall ... 3
McInally, A ... 3
McNeill ... 3
McPhail ... 3
Morris ... 3
Robertson, J (1991-5) ... 3
Sturrock ... 3
White ... 3
Baird, S ... 2
Bauld ... 2
Flavell ... 2
Fleming ... 2
Graham, A ... 2
Harper ... 2
Hewie ... 2
Holton ... 2
Hopkin ... 2
Houliston ... 2
Jess ... 2
Johnstone, A. ... 2
Johnstone, D. ... 2
McClair ... 2
McGhee ... 2
McMillan ... 2
Pettigrew ... 2
Ring ... 2
Robertson, D ... 2
Shearer, D ... 2
Aitken, R ... 1
Bannon ... 1
Bett ... 1
Bone ... 1
Boyd ... 1
Brazil ... 1
Buckley ... 1
Burns ... 1
Calderwood ... 1
Campbell, R ... 1
Combe ... 1
Conn ... 1
Craig ... 1
Crawford ... 1
Curran ... 1
Dailly ... 1
Davidson ... 1
Docherty ... 1
Duncan, M ... 1
Fernie ... 1
Gray, F ... 1
Gemmell, T ... 1
Henderson, J ... 1
Hendry ... 1

Howie 1
Hughes, J 1
Hunter, W 1
Hutchison, D 1
Hutchison, T 1
Jackson, C 1
Jardine 1
Johnstone, L 1
Linwood 1
Mackay, G 1
MacLeod 1
McAvennie 1
McCall 1
McCalliog 1
McKenzie 1
McKimmie 1
McKinnon 1
McLean 1
McLintock 1
Miller, W 1
Mitchell 1
Morgan 1
Mulhall 1
Murray, J 1
Narey 1
Ormond 1
Orr 1
Parlane 1
Provan, D 1
Quinn 1
Ritchie, P 1
Sharp 1
Stewart, R 1
Thornton 1
Wallace, I 1
Weir, A 1

WALES

Rush 28
Allchurch, I 23
Ford 23
Saunders 21
Hughes, M 16
Charles, John 15
Jones, C 15
Toshack 13
James, L 10
Davies, R.T. 8
James, R 8
Vernon 8
Davies, R.W. 7
Flynn 7
Walsh, I 7
Charles, M 6
Curtis, A 6
Griffiths, A 6
Medwin 6
Clarke, R 5

Giggs 5
Leek 5
Pembridge 5
Coleman 4
Deacy 4
Edwards, I 4
Tapscott 4
Thomas, M 4
Woosnam 4
Allen, M 3
Bodin 3
Bowen, M 3
England 3
Melville 3
Palmer, D 3
Rees, R 3
Speed 3
Bellamy 2
Davies, G 2
Blake 2
Durban, A 2
Dwyer 2
Edwards, G 2
Giles, D 2
Godfrey 2
Griffiths, M 2
Hartson 2
Hodges 2
Horne 2
Jones, Barrie 2
Jones, Bryn 2
Lowrie 2
Nicholas 2
Phillips, D 2
Reece, G 2
Robinson 2
Slatter 2
Symons 2
Yorath 2
Barnes 1
Blackmore 1
Bowen, D 1
Boyle, T 1
Burgess, R 1
Charles, Jeremy 1
Evans, I 1
Foulkes 1
Harris, C 1
Hewitt, R 1
Hockey 1
Jones, A 1
Jones, D 1
Jones, J 1
Krzywicki 1
Lovell 1
Mahoney 1
Moore, G. 1
O'Sullivan 1
Paul 1

Powell, A 1
Powell, D 1
Price, P 1
Roberts, P 1
Savage 1
Smallman 1
Williams, A 1
Williams, G.E 1
Williams, G.G 1
Young 1

REP. OF IRELAND

Stapleton 20
Aldridge 19
Cascarino 19
Givens 19
Quinn 18
Cantwell 14
Daly 13
Brady 9
Kelly, D 9
Sheedy 9
Curtis 8
Grealish 8
McGrath, P 8
Connolly 7
Fitzsimons 7
Ringstead 7
Townsend 7
Coyne 6
Houghton 6
McEvoy 6
Martin, C 6
Moran 6
Cummins 5
Fagan, F 5
Giles 5
Keane, Roy 5
Lawrenson 5
O'Neill, K 5
Rogers 5
Sheridan 5
Staunton 5
Treacy 5
Walsh, D 5
Byrne, J 4
Irwin 4
McGee 4
Martin, M 4
Robinson 4
Tuohy 4
Breen G 3
Carey, J 3
Coad 3
Conway 3
Farrell 3
Fogarty 3
Haverty 3

O'Flanagan, K 3	O'Connor 2	Kavanagh 1
Ryan, R 3	O'Farrell 2	Kernaghan 1
Waddock 3	O'Reilly, J 2	Mancini 1
Walsh, M 3	Ambrose 1	McAteer 1
Whelan 3	Anderson 1	McCann 1
Conroy 2	Brown 1	Mooney 1
Dennehy 2	Byrne, A 1	Moroney 1
Eglington 2	Carroll 1	Mulligan 1
Fallon 2	Dempsey 1	O'Callaghan, K 1
Fitzgerald, P 2	Duffy 1	O'Keefe 1
Gavin 2	Fitzgerald, J 1	O'Leary 1
Keane, Robbie 2	Fullam, J 1	O'Neill, F 1
Hale 2	Galvin 1	O'Reilly, J. 1
Hand 2	Glynn 1	Ryan, G 1
Harte 2	Grimes 1	Slaven 1
Hurley 2	Holmes 1	Sloan 1
Leech 2	Hughton 1	Strahan 1
McCarthy 2	Kennedy, Mark 1	Waters 1
McLoughlin 2	Kelly, G 1	

QUOTE – UNQUOTE

'The lad didn't have any self-belief in himself' – TV pundit **Ron Atkinson** comments on a Michael Owen miss during the England-Bulgaria game.

'The only thing he ever suffers from is sweat rash' – Aston Villa manager **John Gregory** on new signing Steve Watson's medical history.

'At one point he said he felt like jumping off a train and ending it all' – Workington's **Paul Stewart** on a mobile telephone conversation with former Tottenham colleague Paul Gascoigne.

'The way Simeone reacted was a disgrace. I heard him squealing like a pig when he went down' – **Teddy Sheringham** pays tribute to Argentine midfielder Diego Simeone's farmyard impressions after the incident which led to David Beckham's France '98 red card.

'We've had so many kicks in the teeth here we're wearing gumshields' – Manager **Malcolm Shotton** on the Oxford Utd. financial crisis.

'I didn't really help myself by discovering drink and women. It was like opening Pandora's Box' – Rushden and Diamonds defender **Jim Rodwell** on why he failed to make it at a higher football level.

'I'm delighted with the win but horrified my assistant manager is down at the police station' – Sheffield Utd.'s **Steve Bruce** after the 2-1 win at Q.P.R. when John Deehan was arrested following animated touchline protests.

'I love this club in a way only a Geordie could understand' – **Alan Shearer**, on reports that he is unhappy at Newcastle Utd.

'We won the Double for them last season and when you taste caviar it is difficult to go back to sausage' – Arsenal manager **Arsene Wenger** after fans barracked his team.

'Joey says he loves this club but unless he leaves there may be no club left' – Manager **Malcolm Shotton** on Joey Beauchamp's reluctance to leave Oxford Utd., desperate for his transfer fee to start paying off £13million debts.

'This second half is much more open. Both teams can go on to win it now' – Channel 4 TV pundit **Joe Jordan** predicts a unique result in the Sampdoria-AC Milan match.

HEROES OF '66 MOURN SIR ALF

Sir Alf Ramsey, the only manager to win the World Cup for England, died on April 28, aged 79, plunging members of his triumphant Wembley squad into mourning.

Ramsey, renowned for loyalty to his players, can lay claim to the title of greatest English manager of all time for his unique achievement at Wembley in July 1966.

But his success in transforming a mediocre Ipswich Town side into League Champions was also of huge merit. It helped create the Ramsey legend.

Ramsey, born in Dagenham, Essex, on January 22, 1920, did not become a professional footballer until he was 24, having pursued his ambition to become a grocer after leaving school. Eventually he signed amateur forms with Portsmouth before joining their neighbours Southampton, who spotted him playing for the Duke of Cornwall's Light Infantry. He served briefly in Palestine after the Second World War before returning to the Dell and switching from attacker to right-back.

He became an England international in 1948 and moved to Tottenham soon afterwards, becoming an integral part of Arthur Rowe's push-and-run side which won the Second and First Division titles in successive seasons.

Ramsey won 32 caps in all, captaining his country on three occasions in the absence of Billy Wright. He played in the 1950 defeat by the United States, while the famous 6-3 Wembley defeat at the hands of Puskas's Hungarians three years later was his final international appearance.

In 1955 he became manager of Ipswich Town, then languishing in the obscurity of Division Three South. By 1961 they were Second Division champions and, emulating his feat as a player with Tottenham, captured the First Division title the following year.

In October 1962 Ramsey was offered the England job, although he was not the FA's first-choice to succeed Walter Winterbottom.

His England team was built like the Ipswich Town side, based on solid defence which made it hard to beat. He did away with wingers again, though this was in part due to the lack of available attacking talent in wide positions. More importantly he persuaded Bobby Charlton to move from his favoured left-wing spot into a central midfield role.

As the 1996 World Cup progressed he made another inspired but unpopular decision, leaving out Jimmy Greaves in favour of Geoff Hurst in attack.

His quarter-final outburst against Argentinians he described as 'animals', was motivated by their spitting at his players in the tunnel rather than events on the pitch.

In the final, after the Germans had equalised two minutes from time to force an extra half hour, Ramsey famously exhorted his men "You have won it once – now go and do it again."

That they did but when Hurst broke away in the final seconds to score the fourth goal, ensuring it really was all over, Ramsey sat impassive on his bench, content that he had kept his promise, made to FA committee back in 1962, to win the Cup.

Two years later England lost a bad-tempered European Nations Cup semi-final against Yugoslavia but by the 1970 World Cup finals in Mexico he had moulded a side regarded by most observers as superior to that which ruled the world four years earlier.

Despite losing to Brazil in the group stages, a game which featured the legendary save by Gordon Banks from Pele then the famous Bobby Moore tackle on the same player, Ramsey's side progressed to the verge of a semi-final spot. With a 2-0 lead against West Germany, Ramsey made the mistake of considering the match won. He took off the tiring Charlton, ostensibly to save his legs for the semis, and unwittingly unleashed marker Franz Beckenbauer. The Germans came back to win 3-2 after extra-time, with goalkeeper Peter Bonetti, deputising for Gordon Banks, blamed for two of the goals.

That marked the beginning of the end for Ramsey. England were beaten again by the Germans in the 1972 European Championship quarter-finals then failed to qualify for the 1974 World Cup after the infamous 1-1 draw at home to Poland a year earlier.

He was summarily dismissed in May 1974 and never consulted again in any capacity by the FA despite his experience and incredible record. Of his 113 games in charge he won 69 and lost just 17.

He managed Birmingham City in 1977 but resigned due to ill-health six months later.

ANDY TONGUE

RECORDS SECTION
Compiled by Albert Sewell

INDEX

GOALSCORING
(† Football League pre 1992-3. * Home team)

Highest: *Arbroath 36; Bon Accord (Aberdeen) 0, in **Scottish Cup** 1st Round, Sept. 12, 1885. On same day, also in Scottish Cup 1st Round, Dundee Harp beat Aberdeen Rov. 35-0.

Internationals: England 15, *France 0, in Paris, 1906 (Amateur); England 13 *Ireland 0, in Belfast, Feb. 18, 1882 (record in U.K.); *England 9, Scotland 3, at Wembley, Apr. 15, 1961; Biggest England win at Wembley: 9-0 v Luxembourg (E.Champ), Dec. 15, 1982.

Other record wins: Scotland: 11-0 v Ireland (Glasgow, Feb. 23, 1901); **Northern Ireland:** 7-0 v Wales (Belfast, Feb. 1, 1930); **Wales:** 11-0 v Ireland (Wrexham, Mar. 3, 1888); **Rep. of Ireland:** 8-0 v Malta (E. Champ., Dublin, Nov. 16, 1983).

Record International defeats: England: 1-7 v Hungary (Budapest, May 23, 1954); **Scotland:** 3-9 v England (Wembley, April 15, 1961); **Ireland:** 0-13 v England (Belfast, Feb. 18, 1882); **Wales:** 0-9 v Scotland (Glasgow, March 23, 1878); **Rep. of Ireland:** 0-7 v Brazil (Uberlandia, May 27, 1982).

World Cup: Qualifying round – Maldives 0, Iran 17 (June 2, 1997). **Finals – highest scorers:** Hungary 10, El Salvador 1 (Spain, June 15, 1982); Hungary 9, S. Korea 0 (Switzerland, June 17, 1954); Yugoslavia 9, Zaire 0 (W. Germany, June 18, 1974).

F.A. Cup: *Preston N.E. 26, Hyde 0, 1st Round, Oct. 15, 1887.

League Cup: *West Ham Utd. 10, Bury 0 (2nd Round, 2nd Leg, Oct 25, 1983); *Liverpool 10, Fulham 0 (2nd Round, 1st Leg, Sept. 23, 1986). **Record Aggregates:** Liverpool 13, Fulham 2 (1-0h, 3-2a), Sept. 23-Oct. 7, 1986; West Ham Utd. 12, Bury 1 (2-1a, 10-0h), Oct. 4-25, 1983; Liverpool 11, Exeter City 0 (5-0h, 6-0a), Oct 7-28, 1981.

F.A. Premier League (beginning 1992-3): *Manchester Utd. 9, Ipswich Town 0, Mar. 4, 1995. **Record away win:** Manchester Utd. 8, *Nott'm. Forest 1, Feb. 6, 1999.

Highest aggregate scores in Premier League – 9: Manchester Utd. 9, Ipswich Town 0, Mar. 4, 1995; Nott'm. Forest 1, Manchester Utd. 8, Feb. 6, 1999; Blackburn Rov. 7, Sheff. Wed. 2, Mar. 11, 1999; Southampton 6, Manchester Utd. 3, Oct. 26, 1996.

†Football League (First Division): *Aston Villa 12, Accrington 2, Mar. 12, 1892; *Tottenham 10, Everton 4, Oct. 11, 1958 (highest 1st. Div. aggregate this century); *W.B.A. 12, Darwen 0, Apr. 4, 1892; *Nott'm. Forest 12, Leicester Fosse 0, Apr. 21, 1909. **Record away wins:** Sunderland 9, *Newcastle Utd. 1, Dec. 5, 1908; Wolves 9, *Cardiff City 1, Sept. 3, 1955.

New First Division (beginning 1992-3): *Bolton Wand. 7, Swindon Town 0, Mar. 8, 1997; Sunderland 7, Oxford Utd. 0, Sept. 19, 1998. **Record away win:** Birmingham City 7, *Stoke City 0, Jan. 10, 1998; Birmingham City 7, *Oxford Utd. 0, Dec. 12, 1998.

†Second Division: *Manchester City 11, Lincoln City 3, Mar. 23, 1895; *Newcastle Utd. 13, Newport County 0, Oct. 5, 1946; *Small Heath 12, Walsall Town Swifts 0, Dec. 17, 1892; *Darwen 12, Walsall 0, Dec. 26, 1896; *Small Heath 12, Doncaster Rov. 0, Apr. 11, 1903. **Record away win:** Sheffield Utd. 10, *Burslem Port Vale 0, Dec. 10, 1892.

New Second Division (beginning 1992-3): *Hartlepool Utd. 1, Plymouth Argyle 8, May 7, 1994.

†**Third Division:** *Gillingham 10, Chesterfield 0, Sept. 5, 1987; *Tranmere Rov. 9, Accrington Stanley 0, Apr. 18, 1959; *Brighton & H.A. 9, Southend Utd. 1, Nov. 22, 1965; *Brentford 9, Wrexham 0, Oct. 15, 1963. **Record away win:** Fulham 8, *Halifax Town 0, Sept. 16, 1969.

New Third Division (beginning 1992-3): *Barnet 1, Peterborough Utd. 9, Sept. 5, 1998.

†**Third Division (North):** *Stockport Co. 13, Halifax Town 0 (still joint biggest win in F. League – see Div. 2) Jan. 6, 1934; *Tranmere Rov. 13, Oldham Athletic 4, Dec. 26, 1935. *(17 is highest Football League aggregate score).* **Record away win:** Barnsley 9, *Accrington Stanley 0, Feb. 3, 1934.

†**Third Division (South):** *Luton Town 12, Bristol Rov. 0, Apr. 13, 1936; *Gillingham 9, Exeter City 4, Jan. 7, 1951. **Record away win:** Walsall 8, *Northampton Town 0, Apr. 8, 1947.

†**Fourth Division:** *Oldham Athletic 11, Southport 0, Dec. 26, 1962; *Hartlepool Utd. 10, Barrow 1, Apr. 4, 1959; *Wrexham 10, Hartlepool Utd. 1, Mar. 3, 1962. **Record away win:** Rotherham Utd. 8, *Crewe Alexandra 1, Sept. 8, 1973.

Scottish Premier Division – Highest aggregate: 11 goals – Celtic 8, Hamilton 3, Jan. 3, 1987. **Other highest team scores:** Aberdeen 8, Motherwell 0 (Mar. 26, 1979); Kilmarnock 1, Rangers 8 (Sept. 6, 1980); Hamilton 0, Celtic 8 (Nov. 5, 1988).

Scottish League Div. 1: *Celtic 11, Dundee 0, Oct. 26, 1895. **Record away win:** Hibs 11, *Airdrie 1, Oct. 24, 1959.

Scottish League Div. 2: *Airdrieonians 15, Dundee Wanderers 1, Dec. 1, 1894.

Record British score this century: Stirling Albion 20, Selkirk 0 (Scottish Cup 1st. Round, Dec. 8, 1984). Winger Davie Thompson (7 goals) was one of 9 Stirling players to score.

FOOTBALL LEAGUE – BEST IN SEASON (Before restructure in 1992)

Div.		Goals	Games
1	W.R. (Dixie) Dean, Everton, 1927-8	60	39
2	George Camsell, Middlesbrough, 1926-7	59	37
3(S)	Joe Payne, Luton Town, 1936-7	55	39
3(N)	Ted Harston, Mansfield Town, 1936-7	55	41
3	Derek Reeves, Southampton, 1959-60	39	46
4	Terry Bly, Peterborough Utd., 1960-1	52	46

(Since restructure in 1992)

Div.		Goals	Games
1	Guy Whittingham, Portsmouth, 1992-3	42	46
2	Jimmy Quinn, Reading, 1993-4	35	46
3	Graeme Jones, Wigan Athletic, 1996-7	31	40

F.A. PREMIER LEAGUE – BEST IN SEASON

Andy Cole **34 goals** (Newcastle Utd. – 40 games, 1993-4); Alan Shearer **34 goals** (Blackburn Rov. – 42 games, 1994-5).

FOOTBALL LEAGUE – BEST MATCH HAULS
(Before restructure in 1992)

Div.		Goals
1	Ted Drake (Arsenal), away to Aston Villa, Dec. 14, 1935	7
	James Ross (Preston N.E.) v Stoke City, Oct 6, 1888	7
2	*Neville (Tim) Coleman (Stoke City) v Lincoln City, Feb. 23, 1957 .	7
	Tommy Briggs (Blackburn Rov.) v Bristol Rov., Feb. 5, 1955	7
3(S)	Joe Payne (Luton Town) v Bristol Rov., April 13, 1936	10
3(N)	Robert ('Bunny') Bell (Tranmere Rov.) v Oldham Athletic, Dec. 26, 1935 – he also missed a penalty	9

3	Barrie Thomas (Scunthorpe Utd.) v Luton Town, April 24, 1965	5
	Keith East (Swindon Town) v Mansfield Town, Nov. 20, 1965	5
	Steve Earle (Fulham) v Halifax Town, Sept. 16, 1969	5
	Alf Wood (Shrewsbury Town) v Blackburn Rov., Oct. 2, 1971	5
	Tony Caldwell (Bolton Wand.) v Walsall, Sept 10, 1983	5
	Andy Jones (Port Vale) v Newport Co., May 4, 1987	5
4	Bert Lister (Oldham Athletic) v Southport, Dec. 26, 1962	6

* Scored from the wing

(SINCE RESTRUCTURE IN 1992)

Div. Goals
1   **4** in match – John Durnin (Oxford Utd. v Luton Town, 1992-3); Guy Whit-
      tingham (Portsmouth v Bristol Rov. 1992-3); Craig Russell (Sunderland v
      Millwall, 1995-6).
2   **5** in match – Paul Barnes (Burnley v Stockport Co., 1996-7); Robert Taylor
      (all 5, Gillingham at Burnley, 1998-9).
3   **5** in match – Tony Naylor (Crewe Alexandra v Colchester Utd., 1992-3);
      Steve Butler (Cambridge Utd. v Exeter City, 1993-4); Guiliano Grazioli
      (Peterborough Utd. at Barnet, 1998-9).

F.A. PREMIER LEAGUE – BEST MATCH HAUL

5 goals in match: Andy Cole (Manchester Utd. v Ipswich Town, 1994-5).

SCOTTISH LEAGUE

Div.		Goals
Prem.	Paul Sturrock (Dundee Utd.) v Morton, Nov. 20, 1984	5
1	Jimmy McGrory (Celtic) v Dunfermline Athletic, Jan. 14, 1928	8
1	Owen McNally (Arthurlie) v Armadale, Oct. 1, 1927	8
2	Jim Dyet (King's Park) v Forfar Athletic, Jan. 2,	8
	1930, on his debut for the club	
2	John Calder (Morton) v Raith Rov., April 18, 1936	8
2	Norman Haywood (Raith Rov.) v Brechin, Aug. 20, 1937	8

SCOTTISH LEAGUE – BEST IN SEASON

Prem.	Brian McClair (Celtic, 1986-7)	35
1	William McFadyen (Motherwell, 1931-2)	53
2	*Jimmy Smith (Ayr, 1927-8 – 38 appearances)	66

(*British record)

CUP FOOTBALL

Scottish Cup: John Petrie (Arbroath) v Bon Accord, at Arbroath, 1st Round,
Sept. 12, 1885 .... **13**

F.A. Cup: Ted MacDougall (Bournemouth) v Margate, 1st Round, Nov. 20,
1971 .... **9**

F.A. Cup Final: Billy Townley (Blackburn Rov.) v Sheffield Wed., at Kennington
Oval, 1890; Jimmy Logan (Notts Co.) v Bolton Wand., at Everton, 1894;
Stan Mortensen (Blackpool) v Bolton Wand., at Wembley, 1953 .... **3**

League Cup: Frank Bunn (Oldham Athletic) v Scarborough (3rd Round), Oct.
25, 1989 .... **6**

Scottish League Cup: Jim Fraser (Ayr) v Dumbarton, Aug. 13, 1952 .... **5**

Jim Forrest (Rangers) v Stirling Albion, Aug. 17, 1966 .... **5**

Scottish Cup: Most goals in match since war: **10** by **Gerry Baker** (St. Mirren) in 15-0
win (1st. Round) v Glasgow Univ., Jan 30, 1960; **9** by his brother **Joe Baker** (Hibernian) in 15-1 win (2nd. Round) v Peebles Rov., Feb. 11, 1961.

AGGREGATE LEAGUE SCORING RECORDS

Goals

* Arthur Rowley (1947-65, WBA, Fulham, Leicester City, Shrewsbury Town) **434**
† Jimmy McGrory (1922-38, Celtic, Clydebank) **410**
Hughie Gallacher (1921-39, Airdrieonians, Newcastle Utd., Chelsea, Derby Co.,
  Notts Co., Grimsby Town, Gateshead) **387**
William ('Dixie') Dean (1923-37, Tranmere Rov., Everton, Notts County) **379**
Hugh Ferguson (1916-30, Motherwell, Cardiff City, Dundee) **362**
■ Jimmy Greaves (1957-71, Chelsea, Tottenham, West Ham Utd.) **357**
Steve Bloomer (1892-1914, Derby Co., Middlesbrough, Derby Co.) **352**
George Camsell (1923-39, Durham City, Middlesbrough) **348**
Dave Halliday (1920-35, St. Mirren, Dundee, Sunderland, Arsenal, Manchester City,
  Clapton Orient) **338**
John Aldridge (1979-98, Newport, Oxford Utd., Liverpool, Tranmere Rov.) **329**
John Atyeo (1951-66, Bristol City) **315**
Joe Smith (1908-29, Bolton Wand., Stockport Co.) **315**
Victor Watson (1920-36, West Ham Utd., Southampton) **312**
Harry Johnson (1919-36, Sheffield Utd., Mansfield Town) **309**
Bob McPhail (1923–1939, Airdrie, Rangers) **306**

(* **Rowley** scored 4 for WBA, 27 for Fulham, 251 for Leicester City, 152 for Shrewsbury Town. ■ **Greaves's** 357 is record top-division total (he also scored 9 League goals for AC Milan). **Aldridge** also scored 33 League goals for Real Sociedad. † **McGrory** scored 397 for Celtic, 13 for Clydebank.)

Most League goals for one club: 349 – Dixie Dean (Everton 1925-37); **326 – George Camsell** (Middlesbrough 1925-39); **315 – John Atyeo** (Bristol City 1951-66); **306 – Vic Watson** (West Ham Utd. 1920-35); **291 – Steve Bloomer** (Derby Co. 1892-1906, 1910-14); **259 – Arthur Chandler** (Leicester City 1923-35); **255 – Nat Lofthouse** (Bolton Wand. 1946-61); **251 – Arthur Rowley** (Leicester City 1950-58).

Over 500 Goals: Jimmy McGrory (Celtic, Clydebank and Scotland) scored a total of 550 goals in his first-class career (1922-38).

Over 1,000 goals: Brazil's **Pele** is reputedly the game's all-time highest scorer with 1,282 goals in 1,365 matches (1956-77), but many of them were scored in friendlies for his club, Santos. He scored his 1,000th goal, a penalty, against Vasco da Gama in the Maracana Stadium, Rio, on November 19, 1969. Pele (born Oct. 23, 1940) played regularly for Santos from the age of 16. During his career, he was sent off only once. He played 95 'A' Internationals for Brazil and in their World Cup-winning teams in 1958 and 1970. ● Pele (Edson Arantes do Nascimento) was subsequently Brazil's Minister for Sport. He never played at Wembley, apart from being filmed there scoring a goal for a commercial. Aged 57, Pele received an 'honorary knighthood' (Knight Commander of the British Empire) from the Queen at Buckingham Palace on December 3, 1997.

MOST LEAGUE GOALS IN SEASON: DEAN'S 60

W.R. ('Dixie') Dean, Everton centre-forward, created a League scoring record in 1927-8 with an aggregate of 60 in 39 First Division matches. He also scored three goals in F.A. Cup-ties, and 19 in representative games (total for the season 82).

George Camsell, of Middlesbrough, previously held the record with 59 goals in 37 Second Division matches in 1926-7, his total for the season being 75.

SHEARER'S RECORD 'FIRST'

Alan Shearer (Blackburn Rov.) is the first player to score more than 30 top-division goals in 3 successive seasons since the war: 31 in 1993-4, 34 in 1994-5, 31 in 1995-6.
David Halliday (Sunderland) topped 30 First Div. goals in 4 consecutive seasons with totals of 38, 36, 36 and 49 from 1925-26 to 1928-29.

MOST GOALS IN A MATCH

TOP SCORE by a player in a first-class match is **13** in the Scottish Cup and **10** in the Football League.

September 12, 1885: John Petrie set the all-time British individual record for a first-class match when, in Arbroath's 36-0 win against Bon Accord (Scottish Cup first round), he scored **13**

April 13, 1936: Joe Payne set the still-existing individual record on his debut as a centre-forward, for Luton Town v Bristol Rov. (Div. III South). In a 12-0 win he scored **10**

December 26, 1935: Robert ('Bunny') Bell for Tranmere Rov. v Oldham Athletic (Div. III North) beat Drake's 12-day-old record in a 13-4 win by scoring **9**

October 6, 1888: James Ross for Preston N.E. (7-0 v Stoke City) set a League record in its first season by scoring all **7**

December 14, 1935: Ted Drake for Arsenal in 7-1 win away to Aston Villa (Div. 1). Scored six goals with his first six shots and in all equalled Ross's Football League record by scoring **7**

February 5, 1955: Tommy Briggs for Blackburn Rov. v Bristol Rov. set Second Division record during 8-3 win by scoring **7**

February 23, 1957: Neville ('Tim') Coleman for Stoke City v Lincoln City (8-0) in Second Division set a record as a winger by scoring **7**

OTHER BIG HAULS

Eric Gemmell for Oldham Athletic v Chester City in Third Division North (11-2), January 19, 1952, and **Albert Whitehurst** for Bradford City v Tranmere Rov. (Third Division North) (8-0), March 6, 1929; both scored **seven**.

W.H. (Billy) Minter scored **seven** goals for St. Albans City in replayed F.A. Cup 4th Qualifying Round against Dulwich Hamlet, November 22, 1922. Dulwich won 8-7, and Minter's seven is still the most goals scored in one match by a player in a losing side.

Denis Law scored **seven** but only one counted and he finished a loser in Manchester City's F.A. Cup 4th Round tie at Luton Town in 1961. The original match on January 28 was washed out (69 mins.) when City led 6-2 (Law 6). He scored a seventh when the game was played again, but Luton Town won 3-1.

Louis Page, England outside-left, when tried for the first time as centre-forward, accomplished the **double hat-trick** for Burnley in a First Division match against Birmingham City, at St. Andrews, April 10, 1926. Burnley won 7-1.

Davie Wilson, Rangers outside-left, scored **six** goals from centre-forward at Falkirk in Scottish league, March 17, 1962. Result: 7-1.

Geoff Hurst was the last player to score **six** in a League match, in West Ham Utd.'s 8-0 win v Sunderland (Div. 1) on October 19, 1968.

ROWLEY'S ALL-TIME RECORD

Arthur Rowley is English football's **top club scorer** with a total of 464 goals for WBA, Fulham, Leicester City and Shrewsbury Town (1947-65). They comprised 434 in the League, 26 F.A. Cup, 4 League Cup.

Jimmy Greaves is second with a total of 420 goals for Chelsea, AC Milan, Tottenham and West Ham Utd., made up of 366 League, 35 F.A. Cup, 10 League Cup and 9 in Europe. He also scored nine goals for Italian club AC Milan.

John Aldridge, Tranmere Rovers manager, retired as a player at the end of the season 1997-98 with a career total of 329 Football League goals for Newport, Oxford Utd., Liverpool and Tranmere Rov. (1997-98). In all competitions for those clubs he scored 410 goals in 737 apps. He also scored 45 goals in 63 games for Spanish club Real Sociedad.

MOST GOALS IN INTERNATIONAL FOOTBALL

SEVEN BY

Vivian Woodward for England v France in Amateur International in Paris, November 1, 1906. Result 15-0.

SIX BY

Nat Lofthouse for Football League v Irish League, at Wolves, September 24, 1952. Result: 7-1.
Joe Bambrick for Ireland against Wales, in Belfast, February 1, 1930. Result: 7-0.
W.C. Jordan in Amateur International for England v France, at Park Royal, March 23, 1908. Result: 12-0.
Vivian Woodward for England v Holland in Amateur International, at Chelsea, December 11, 1909. Result: 9-1.

FIVE BY

Oliver Vaughton for England v Ireland (Belfast), February 18, 1882. Result: 13-0.
Steve Bloomer for England v Wales (Cardiff City) March 16, 1896. Result: 9-1.
Hughie Gallacher for Scotland against Ireland (Belfast), February 23, 1929. Result: 7-3.
Willie Hall for England v Ireland, at Old Trafford, Manchester, November 16, 1938. Five in succession (first three in 3½ mins. – fastest International hat-trick). Result: 7-0.
Malcolm Macdonald for England v Cyprus (Wembley) April 16, 1975. Result: 5-0.
Hughie Gallacher for Scottish League against Irish League (Belfast) November 11, 1925. Result: 7-3.
Barney Battles for Scottish League against Irish League (Firhill Park, Glasgow) October 31, 1928. Result: 8-2.
Bobby Flavell for Scottish League against Irish League (Belfast) April 30, 1947. Result: 7-4.
Joe Bradford for Football League v Irish League (Everton) September 25, 1929. Result: 7-2.
Albert Stubbins for Football League v Irish League (Blackpool) October 18, 1950. Result: 6-3.
Brian Clough for Football League v Irish League (Belfast) September 23, 1959. Result: 5-0.

LAST ENGLAND PLAYER TO SCORE . . .

3 goals: Paul Scholes v Poland (3-1), Eur. Champ. qual., Wembley, Mar. 27, 1999.
4 goals: David Platt v San Marino (6-0), World Cup qual., Wembley, Feb. 17, 1992.
5 goals: Malcolm Macdonald v Cyprus (5-0), Eur. Champ. qual., Wembley, Apr. 16, 1975.

INTERNATIONAL TOP SHOTS

		Goals	Games
England	– Bobby Charlton (1958-70)	49	106
N. Ireland	– Colin Clarke (1986-92)	13	38
Scotland	– Denis Law (1958-74)	30	55
	– Kenny Dalglish (1971-86)	30	102
Wales	– Ian Rush (1980-96)	28	73
Rep. of I.	– Frank Stapleton (1977-90)	20	71

ENGLAND'S TOP MARKSMEN

(As at start of season 1999-2000)

	Goals	Games
Bobby Charlton (1958-70)	49	106
Gary Lineker (1984-92)	48	80
Jimmy Greaves (1959-67)	44	57
Tom Finney (1946-58)	30	76
Nat Lofthouse (1950-58)	30	33
Vivian Woodward (1903-11)	29	23
Steve Bloomer (1895-1907)	28	23
David Platt (1989-96)	27	62
Bryan Robson (1979-91)	26	90

Geoff Hurst (1966-72)	24	49
Alan Shearer (1992-99)	24	51
Stan Mortensen (1947-53)	23	25
Tommy Lawton (1938-48)	22	23
Mike Channon (1972-77)	21	46
Kevin Keegan (1972-82)	21	63
Martin Peters (1966-74)	20	67
George Camsell (1929-36)	18	9
'Dixie' Dean (1927-32)	18	16
Johnny Haynes (1954-62)	18	56
Roger Hunt (1962-69)	18	34
Tommy Taylor (1953-57)	16	19
Tony Woodcock (1978-86)	16	42

CONSECUTIVE GOALS FOR ENGLAND

Tinsley Lindley (Cambridge Univ.) scored a total of 12 goals in **NINE** consecutive Internationals for **England** in three seasons (March 1886-March 1888) – three games against each of Ireland, Wales and Scotland.

In modern times, **Paul Mariner** (Ipswich Town) scored in six consecutive **England** appearances (7 goals) between November 1981 and June 1982.

'GOLDEN GOAL' DECIDERS

The Football League, in an experiment to avoid penalty shoot-outs, introduced a new 'golden goal' system in the 1994-95 **Auto Windscreens Shield** to decide matches in the knock-out stages of the competition in which scores were level after 90 minutes. The first goal scored in overtime ended play.

Iain Dunn (Huddersfield Town) became the first player in British football to settle a match by this sudden-death method. His 107th-minute goal beat Lincoln City 3-2 on Nov. 30, 1994, and to mark his 'moment in history' he was presented with a golden football trophy.

The AWS Final of 1995 was decided when **Paul Tait** headed the only goal for Birmingham City against Carlisle Utd. 13 minutes into overtime – the first time a match at Wembley had been decided by the 'golden goal' formula.

First major International tournament match to be decided by sudden death was the final of the **1996 European Championship** at Wembley in which Germany beat Czech Rep. 2-1 by **Oliver Bierhoff's** goal in the 95th minute.

In the 1998 World Cup Finals (2nd Round), host country France beat Paraguay 1-0 on a 'golden goal' (114 mins.).

PREMIERSHIP TOP SHOTS (1992-99)

Alan Shearer	153	Matthew Le Tissier	97
Ian Wright	113	Teddy Sheringham	87
Les Ferdinand	111	Chris Sutton	80
Andy Cole	106	Dwight Yorke	78
Robbie Fowler	106	(As at start of season 1999-2000)	

LEAGUE GOAL RECORDS

The highest goal-scoring aggregates in the Football League, Premier and Scottish League are as follows:

FOR

	Goals	Games	Club	Season
Prem.	82	42	Newcastle Utd.	1993-4
Div. 1	128	42	Aston Villa	1930-1

New Div. 1	100	46	Bolton Wand.	1996-7
Div. 2	122	42	Middlesbrough	1926-7
New Div. 2	88	46	W.B.A.	1992-3
	88	46	Plymouth Argyle	1993-4
Div. 3(S)	127	42	Millwall	1927-8
Div. 3(N)	128	42	Bradford City	1928-9
Div. 3	111	46	Q.P.R.	1961-2
New Div. 3	84	46	Wigan Athletic	1996-7
Div. 4	134	46	Peterborough Utd.	1960-1
Scot. Prem.	101	44	Rangers	1991-2
Scot. L. 1	132	34	Hearts	1957-8
Scot. L. 2	142	34	Raith Rov.	1937-8
Scot. L. 3 (Modern)	87	36	Ross County	1998-9

AGAINST

	Goals	Games	Club	Season
Prem.	100	42	Swindon Town	1993-4
Div. 1	125	42	Blackpool	1930-1
New Div. 1	87	46	Bristol Rov.	1992-3
Div. 2	141	34	Darwen	1898-9
New Div. 2	102	46	Chester City	1992-3
Div. 3(S)	135	42	Merthyr T.	1929-30
Div. 3(N)	136	42	Nelson	1927-8
Div. 3	123	46	Accrington S.	1959-60
New Div. 3	113	46	Doncaster Rov.	1997-8
Div. 4	109	46	Hartlepool Utd.	1959-60
Scot. Prem.	100	36	Morton	1984-5
Scot. Prem.	100	44	Morton	1987-8
Scot. L. 1	137	38	Leith A.	1931-2
Scot. L. 2	146	38	Edinburgh City	1931-2
Scot. L. 3 (Modern)	82	36	Albion Rov.	1994-5

BEST DEFENSIVE RECORDS – *Denotes under old offside law

Div.	Goals Agst.	Games	Club	Season
Prem.	17	38	Arsenal	1998-9
1	16	42	Liverpool	1978-9
1	*15	22	Preston N.E.	1888-9
New Div. 1	28	46	Sunderland	1998-9
2	18	28	Liverpool	1893-4
2	*22	34	Sheffield Wed.	1899-1900
2	24	42	Birmingham City	1947-8
2	24	42	Crystal Palace	1978-9
New Div. 2	32	46	Fulham	1998-9
3(S)	*21	42	Southampton	1921-2
3(S)	30	42	Cardiff City	1946-7
3(N)	*21	38	Stockport Co.	1921-2
3(N)	21	46	Port Vale	1953-4
3	30	46	Middlesbrough	1986-7
New Div. 3	20	46	Gillingham	1995-6
4	25	46	Lincoln City	1980-1

SCOTTISH LEAGUE

Div.	Goals Agst.	Games	Club	Season
Prem.	19	36	Rangers	1989-90
1	*12	22	Dundee	1902-3
1	*14	38	Celtic	1913-14
2	20	38	Morton	1966-7
2	*29	38	Clydebank	1922-3
2	29	36	East Fife	1995-6
New Div. 3	21	36	Brechin	1995-6

TOP SCORERS (LEAGUE ONLY)

		Goals	Div.
1998-9	Lee Hughes (W.B.A.)	31	1
1997-8	Pierre van Hooijdonk (Nott'm Forest)	29	1
	Kevin Phillips (Sunderland)	29	1
1996-7	Graeme Jones (Wigan Athletic)	31	3
1995-6	Alan Shearer (Blackburn Rov.)	31	Prem.
1994-5	Alan Shearer (Blackburn Rov.)	34	Prem.
1993-4	Jimmy Quinn (Reading)	35	2
1992-3	Guy Whittingham (Portsmouth)	42	1
1991-2	Ian Wright (Crystal Palace 5, Arsenal 24)	29	1
1990-1	Teddy Sheringham (Millwall)	33	2
1989-90	Mick Quinn (Newcastle Utd.)	32	2
1988-9	Steve Bull (Wolves)	37	3
1987-8	Steve Bull (Wolves)	34	4
1986-7	Clive Allen (Tottenham)	33	1
1985-6	Gary Lineker (Everton)	30	1
1984-5	Tommy Tynan (Plymouth Argyle)	31	3
	John Clayton (Tranmere Rov.)	31	4
1983-4	Trevor Senior (Reading)	36	4
1982-3	Luther Blissett (Watford)	27	1
1981-2	Keith Edwards (Hull City 1, Sheffield Utd. 35)	36	4
1980-1	Tony Kellow (Exeter City)	25	3
1979-80	Clive Allen (Queens Park Rangers)	28	2
1978-9	Ross Jenkins (Watford)	29	3
1977-8	Steve Phillips (Brentford)	32	4
	Alan Curtis (Swansea City)	32	4
1976-7	Peter Ward (Brighton & H.A.)	32	3
1975-6	Dixie McNeil (Hereford)	35	3
1974-5	Dixie McNeil (Hereford)	31	3
1973-4	Brian Yeo (Gillingham)	31	4
1972-3	Bryan (Pop) Robson (West Ham Utd.)	28	1
1971-2	Ted MacDougall (Bournemouth)	35	3
1970-1	Ted MacDougall (Bournemouth)	42	4
1969-70	Albert Kinsey (Wrexham)	27	4
1968-9	Jimmy Greaves (Tottenham)	27	1
1967-8	George Best (Manchester Utd.)	28	1
	Ron Davies (Southampton)	28	1
1966-7	Ron Davies (Southampton)	37	1
1965-6	Kevin Hector (Bradford P.A.)	44	4
1964-5	Alick Jeffrey (Doncaster Rov.)	36	4
1963-4	Hugh McIlmoyle (Carlisle Utd.)	39	4
1962-3	Jimmy Greaves (Tottenham)	37	1
1961-2	Roger Hunt (Liverpool)	41	2
1960-1	Terry Bly (Peterborough Utd.)	52	4

100 LEAGUE GOALS

Bolton Wand., as First Div. Champions in 1996-7, reached exactly 100 goals, the first (and latest) side to complete a century in League football since 103 by Northampton Town (Div. 4 Champions) in 1986-7.

Last League Champions to reach **100** League goals: **Tottenham** (115 in 1960-1). Last century of goals in the top division: **111** by runners-up **Tottenham** in 1962-3.

In **1930-1**, the Championship top three all scored a century of League goals: 1 Arsenal (127), 2 Aston Villa (128), 3 Sheffield Wed. (102).

100 GOALS AGAINST

Swindon Town, relegated with 100 goals against in 1993-4, were the first top-division club to concede a century of League goals since **Ipswich Town** (121) went down in 1964. Most goals conceded in the top division: 125 by **Blackpool** in 1930-31, but they avoided relegation.

THE DAY IT RAINED GOALS

Saturday, February 1, 1936 has a permanent place in the Football League records, because on that afternoon the **44** matches played in the four divisions produced **209** goals – the most that have ever been scored on one day. They piled up like this: 46 in Div.1; 46 in Div.2; 68 in Div.3 North; 49 in Div.3 South. Three players scored four each and nine scored three each. Two matches in the Northern Section provided no fewer than 23 goals – Chester City 12, York City 0, and Crewe Alexandra 5, Chesterfield 6. There was only one 0-0 result (Aldershot v Bristol City, Div. 3 South).

● The previous record was set four years earlier on January 2, 1932, when 205 goals were scored in 43 League matches: 56 in Div.1, 49 in Div.2, 57 in Div.3 South and 43 in Div.3 North.

MOST GOALS IN TOP DIV. ON ONE DAY

This record has stood since December 26, 1963, when **66 goals** were scored in the ten First Division matches played.

MOST F.A. PREMIER LEAGUE GOALS ON ONE DAY

47, in nine matches on May 8, 1993 (last day of season).

FEWEST FIRST DIV. GOALS ON ONE DAY

For full/near full programme: **Ten goals,** all by home clubs, in ten matches on April 28, 1923 (day of Wembley's first F.A. Cup Final).

SIX-OUT-OF-SIX HEADERS

When **Oxford Utd.** beat Shrewsbury Town 6-0 (Div. 2) on April 23, 1996, all six goals were headers.

FIVE IN A MATCH

Latest players to score 5 goals in a top-division match: **Tony Woodcock** (for Arsenal in 6-2 win away to Aston Villa) and **Ian Rush** (Liverpool 6, Luton Town 0), both on October 29, 1983; **Andy Cole** (Manchester Utd. 9, Ipswich Town 0) on March 4, 1995.

ALL–ROUND MARKSMAN

Alan Cork scored in four divisions of the Football League and in the F.A. Premier League in his 18-season career with Wimbledon, Sheffield Utd., and Fulham (1977-95).

MOST CUP GOALS

F.A. Cup – most goals in one season: 20 by J.D. Ross (Preston N.E., runners-up 1887-8); 15 by Albert (Sandy) Brown (Tottenham, winners 1900-1).

Most F.A. Cup goals in individual careers: 48 by Henry Cursham (Notts Co. 1880-87); this century: 44 by Ian Rush (39 for Liverpool, 4 for Chester City, 1 for Newcastle Utd. 1979-98). Denis Law was the previous highest F.A. Cup scorer this century with 41 goals for Huddersfield Town, Manchester City and Manchester Utd. (1957-74).

Most F.A. Cup Final goals by individual: 5 by Ian Rush for Liverpool (2 in 1986, 2 in 1989, 1 in 1992).

HOTTEST CUP HOT-SHOT

Geoff Hurst scored 21 cup goals in season 1965-66: 11 League Cup, 4 F.A. Cup and 2 Cup-Winners' Cup for West Ham Utd., and 4 in the World Cup for England.

SCORERS IN EVERY ROUND

Twelve players have scored in **every round** of the F.A. Cup in one season, from opening to Final inclusive: **Archie Hunter** (Aston Villa, winners 1887); **Albert (Sandy) Brown** (Tottenham, winners 1901); **Harry Hampton** (Aston Villa, winners 1905); **Harold Blackmore** (Bolton Wand., winners 1929); **Ellis Rimmer** (Sheffield Wed., winners 1935); **Frank O'Donnell** (Preston N.E., beaten 1937); **Stan Mortensen** (Blackpool, beaten 1948); **Jack Milburn** (Newcastle Utd., winners 1951); **Nat Lofthouse** (Bolton Wand., beaten 1953); **Charlie Wayman** (Preston N.E., beaten 1954); **Jeff Astle** (W.B.A., winners 1968); **Peter Osgood** (Chelsea, winners 1970).

Blackmore and the next seven completed their 'set' in the Final at Wembley; Osgood did so in the Final replay at Old Trafford.

Only player to score in every **Football League Cup** round possible in one season: **Tony Brown** for W.B.A., winners 1965-6, with 9 goals in 10 games (after bye in Round 1).

TEN IN A ROW

Dixie McNeill scored for Wrexham in **ten successive** F.A. Cup rounds (18 goals): 11 in Rounds 1-6, 1977-8; 3 in Rounds 3-4, 1978-9; 4 in Rounds 3-4, 1979-80.

Stan Mortensen (Blackpool) scored 25 goals in 16 F.A. Cup rounds out of 17 (1946-51).

TOP MATCH HAULS IN F.A. CUP

Ted MacDougall scored nine goals in the F.A. Cup first round on November 20, 1971, when Bournemouth beat Margate 11-0. On November 23, 1970 he had scored six in an 8-1 first round replay against Oxford City.

Other six-goal F.A. Cup scorers include **George Hilsdon** (Chelsea v Worksop, 9-1, 1907-8), **Ronnie Rooke** (Fulham v Bury, 6-0, 1938-9), **Harold Atkinson** (Tranmere Rov. v Ashington, 8-1, 1952-3), **George Best** (Manchester Utd. v Northampton Town 1969-70, 8-2 away), and **Duane Darby** (Hull City v Whitby, 8-4, 1996-7).

Denis Law scored all **six** for Manchester City at Luton Town (6-2) in an F.A. Cup 4th Round tie on January 28, 1961, but none of them counted – the match was abandoned because of a waterlogged pitch.

Tony Philliskirk scored **five** when Peterborough Utd. beat Kingstonian 9-1 in an F.A. Cup 1st Round replay on November 25, 1992, but had them wiped from the records. With the score at 3-0, the Kingstonian goalkeeper was concussed by a coin thrown from the crowd and unable to play on. The F.A. ordered the match to be replayed at Peterborough Utd. behind closed doors, and Kingstonian lost 1-0.

QUICKEST GOALS AND RAPID SCORING

Six seconds after kick-off by **Albert Mundy** for Aldershot v Hartlepool Utd., October 25, 1958; **Barrie Jones** for Newport County v Torquay Utd., March 31, 1962; **Keith Smith** for Crystal Palace v Derby Co., December 12, 1964.

9.6 seconds by **John Hewitt** for Aberdeen at Motherwell, 3rd Round, January 23, 1982 (fastest goal in Scottish Cup history).

A goal in **4 seconds** was claimed by **Jim Fryatt**, for Bradford P.A. v Tranmere Rov. (Div. 4, April 25, 1965), and by **Gerry Allen** for Whitstable Town v Danson (Kent League, March 3,1989). Backed by filmed evidence, **Damian Mori** scored in 4 seconds for Adelaide City v Sydney Utd. (Australian National League, December 6, 1995).

Colin Cowperthwaite reputedly scored in 3½ **seconds** for Barrow v Kettering (Alliance Premier League) on December 8, 1979, but the timing was unofficial.

Phil Starbuck scored for Huddersfield Town only **3 seconds** after entering the field as 54th min. substitute at home to Wigan Athletic (Div. 2) on Easter Monday, April 12, 1993. A corner-kick was delayed, awaiting his arrival, and he scored with a header.

Malcolm Macdonald scored after **5 seconds** (officially timed) in Newcastle Utd.'s 7-3 win in a pre-season friendly at St. Johnstone on July 29, 1972. From the kick-off, the ball was passed to him, and Macdonald, spotting the goalkeeper off his line, smashed a shot over him and into the net.

Scored first kick: Billy Foulkes (Newcastle Utd.) for Wales v England at Cardiff City, October 20, 1951, in his first International match.

Six goals in seven minutes in Preston N.E.'s record 26-0 F.A. Cup 1st Round win v Hyde, October 15, 1887.

Five in 20 minutes: Frank Keetley in Lincoln City's 9-1 win over Halifax Town in Div. III (North), January 16, 1932; **Brian Dear** for West Ham Utd. v W.B.A. (6-1, Div.1) April 16, 1965.

Four in five minutes: by **John McIntyre** for Blackburn Rov. v Everton (Div. 1), September 16, 1922; **W.G. Richardson** for W.B.A. v West Ham Utd. (Div. 1), November 7, 1931.

Three in three minutes: Billy Lane for Watford v Clapton Orient (Div.3S), December 20, 1933; **Johnny Hartburn** for Leyton Orient v Shrewsbury Town (Div. 3S), January 22, 1955; **Gary Roberts** for Brentford v Newport, (Freight Rover Trophy, South Final), May 17, 1985; **Gary Shaw** for Shrewsbury Town v Bradford City (Div. 3), December 22, 1990.

Three in two minutes: Jimmy Scarth for Gillingham v Leyton Orient (Div. 3S), November 1, 1952.

Arsenal scored six goals in 18 minutes (71-89 mins.) in 7-1 home win v Sheffield Wed., February 15, 1992.

Sunderland scored eight goals in 28 minutes at Newcastle Utd. (9-1 Div 1), December 5, 1908. Newcastle went on to win the championship.

Southend Utd. scored all seven goals in 29 minutes in 7-0 win at home to Torquay Utd. (Leyland Daf Cup, Southern quarter-final), February 26, 1991. Score was 0-0 until 55th. minute.

Six goals in first 19 minutes by Tranmere Rov. when they beat Oldham Athletic 13-4 (Div. 3 North) on December 26, 1935.

Notts Co. scored six second-half goals in 12 minutes (Tommy Lawton 3, Jackie Sewell 3) when they beat Exeter City 9-0 (Div. 3 South) at Meadow Lane on October 16, 1948.

Fastest International goal: 8.3 secs. by **Davide Gualtieri** for San Marino v England (World Cup qual., Bologna, November 17, 1993).

Fastest International hat-trick: 3½ minutes by **Willie Hall** for England v N. Ireland at Old Trafford, Manchester, November 16, 1938. (Hall scored 5 in England's 7-0 win).

Fastest International goal by substitute: 5 seconds by **John Jensen** for Denmark v Belgium (Eur. Champ.), October 12, 1994.

Fastest England goals: 27 seconds by **Bryan Robson** v. France in World Cup at Bilbao, Spain on June 16, 1982; at Wembley: 38 seconds by **Bryan Robson** v Yugoslavia, December 13, 1989; 42 seconds by **Gary Lineker** v Malaysia in Kuala Lumpur, June 12, 1991.

Fastest F.A. Cup Final goals: 30 seconds by **John Devey**, for Aston Villa v W.B.A., 1895; at Wembley: 42 seconds by **Roberto di Matteo**, for Chelsea v Middlesbrough, 1997.

Fastest F.A. Cup hat-tricks: In 3 minutes by **Billy Best** for Southend Utd. v Brentford (2nd. Round, December 7, 1968); 2 minutes 20 seconds by **Andy Locke** for Nantwich v Droylesden (1st. Qual. Round, September 9, 1995).

F.A. Premier League – fastest scoring: Four goals in 4 minutes, 44 seconds by Tottenham at home to Southampton on Sunday, February 7, 1993.

Fastest First Division hat-tricks since war: Graham Leggat, 3 goals in 3 minutes (first half) when Fulham beat Ipswich Town 10-1 on Boxing Day, 1963; **Nigel Clough,** 3 goals in 4 minutes (81, 82, 85 pen) when Nott'm Forest beat Q.P.R. 4-0 on Sunday, December 13, 1987.

F.A. Premier League – fastest hat-trick: 4½ minutes (26, 29, 31) by **Robbie Fowler** in Liverpool 3, Arsenal 0 on Sunday, August 28, 1994.

Fastest Premier League goals: 13 seconds by **Chris Sutton** for Blackburn Rov. at Everton, April 1, 1995; 13 seconds by **Dwight Yorke** for Aston Villa at Coventry City, September 30, 1995.

Fastest Premier League goal by substitute: 13 seconds by **Jamie Cureton** for Norwich City v Chelsea, December 10, 1994.

Four in 13 minutes by Premier League substitute: Ole Gunnar Solskjaer for Manchester Utd. away to Nott'm. Forest, Feb. 6, 1999.

Fastest new-First Division goal: 10 seconds by **Keith O'Neill** for Norwich City v Stoke City, April 12, 1997.

Fastest Scottish hat-trick: 2½ mins. by **Ian St. John** for Motherwell away to Hibernian (Scottish League Cup), August 15, 1959.

Fastest all-time hat-trick: Reported at 1 min. 50 secs. by **Maglioni** for Independiente against Gimnasia de la Plata in Argentina, March 18, 1973.

Fastest own goals: 8 seconds by **Pat Kruse** of Torquay Utd., for Cambridge Utd. (Div. 4), January 3, 1977; in **First Division**, 16 seconds by **Steve Bould** (Arsenal) away to Sheffield Wed., February 17, 1990.

FASTEST GOALS IN WORLD CUP FINAL SERIES

15 secs. by **Vaclav Masek** for Czechoslovakia v Mexico (in Vina, Chile, 1962).
27 secs. by **Bryan Robson** for England v France (in Bilbao, Spain, 1982).

TOP MATCH SCORES SINCE WAR

By English clubs: 13-0 by Newcastle Utd. v Newport (Div. 2, Oct. 1946); **13-2** by Tottenham v Crewe Alexandra (F.A. Cup 4th. Rd. replay, Feb. 1960); **13-0** by Chelsea v Jeunesse Hautcharage, Lux. (Cup-Winners' Cup 1st. Rd., 2nd. Leg, Sept. 1971).

By Scottish club: 20-0 by Stirling Albion v Selkirk (E. of Scotland League) in Scottish Cup 1st. Rd. (Dec. 1984). That is the highest score in British first-class football this century, since Preston N.E. beat Hyde 26-0 in F.A. Cup, Oct. 1887.

GOALS BY WINGERS

	Season (Div. I)	Matches	Goals
Football League			
Cliff Bastin (Arsenal)	1932-3	42	33
Scottish League (Div. I)			
Bob Ferrier (Motherwell)	1929-30	27	32
Scottish League (Div. II)			
Ken Dawson (Falkirk)	1935-6	34	39

GOALS BY GOALKEEPERS

Goalkeepers who have scored with long clearances include:

Pat Jennings for Tottenham away to Manchester Utd. (goalkeeper Alex Stepney) in the F.A. Charity Shield on August 12, 1967.

Peter Shilton for Leicester City at Southampton (goalkeeper Campbell Forsyth) on October 14, 1967 (Div. 1).

Ray Cashley for Bristol City at home to Hull City (goalkeeper Jeff Wealands) on September 18, 1973 (Div. 2).

Steve Sherwood for Watford away to Coventry City (goalkeeper Raddy Avramovic) on January 14, 1984 (Div. 1).

Steve Ogrizovic for Coventry City away to Sheffield Wed. (goalkeeper Martin Hodge) on October 25, 1986 (Div. 1).

Andy Goram for Hibernian at home to Morton (goalkeeper David Wylie) on May 7, 1988 (Scottish Premier Div.).

Andy McLean, on Irish League debut, for Cliftonville v Linfield (goalkeeper George Dunlop) on August 20, 1988.

Alan Paterson for Glentoran against Linfield (goalkeeper George Dunlop) on November 30, 1989 (Roadferry Cup Final at The Oval, Belfast).

Ray Charles for East Fife at Stranraer (goalkeeper Bernard Duffy) on February 28, 1990 (Scottish Div. 2).

Iain Hesford scored Maidstone's winner (3-2 v Hereford, Div. 4, November 2, 1991) with long kick-out that went first bounce past Tony Elliott in opposite goal.

Chris Mackenzie for Hereford at home to Barnet (goalkeeper Mark Taylor) in Div. 3, August 12, 1995.

Aston Villa's **Mark Bosnich** scored the last goal (a penalty) when Australia beat Solomon Islands 13-0 in World Cup Oceania Zone qualifier in Sydney on June 11, 1997.

Most goals by a goalkeeper in a League season: 5 (all penalties) by **Arthur Birch** for Chesterfield (Div. 3 North), 1923-4.

Arthur Wilkie, Reading's goalkeeper at home to Halifax Town (Div. 3) on August 31, 1962, injured a hand, then played as a forward and scored twice in a 4-2 win.

Alex Stepney was Manchester Utd.'s joint top scorer for two months in season 1973-4 with two penalties.

Alan Fettis, N. Ireland goalkeeper, scored twice for Hull City in Div. 2 in season 1994-5: as a substitute in 3-1 home win v Oxford Utd. (Dec. 17) and, when selected outfield, with last-minute winner (2-1) at Blackpool on May 6.

Peter Schmeichel, Manchester Utd.'s goalkeeper, headed an 89th minute equaliser (2-2) from Ryan Giggs' corner in the UEFA Cup 1st. Round, 2nd leg against Rotor Volgograd (Russia) on September 26, 1995, but United lost the tie on away goals.

In League matches for Swansea City, **Roger Freestone** scored with a penalty at Oxford Utd. (Div. 2, April 30, 1995) and, in 1995-6 (Div. 2) with penalties at home to Shrewsbury Town (August 12) and Chesterfield (August 26).

Goalkeeper **Jimmy Glass**, on loan from Swindon Town, scored the winner that kept Carlisle Utd. in the Football League on May 8, 1999. With only ten seconds of injury time left, he went upfield for a corner and shot the goal that beat Plymouth Argyle 2-1 at Brunton Park. It preserved Carlisle Utd.'s League existence since 1928 and sent Scarborough down to the Conference.

MOST SCORERS IN MATCH

Liverpool set a Football League record with **EIGHT** scorers when they beat Crystal Palace 9-0 (Div.1) on September 12, 1989. Their marksmen were: Steve Nicol (7 and 88 mins), Steve McMahon (16), Ian Rush (45), Gary Gillespie (56), Peter Beardsley (61), John Aldridge pen. (67), John Barnes (79) and Glenn Hysen (82).

Fifteen years earlier, **Liverpool** had gone one better with **NINE** different scorers when they achieved their record win, 11-0 at home to Stromsgodset (Norway) in the Cup-Winners' Cup 1st. round, 1st leg on September 17, 1974.

Eight players scored for **Swansea City** when they beat Sliema, Malta, 12-0 in the Cup-Winners' Cup 1st round, 1st leg on September 15, 1982.

Nine **Stirling Albion** players scored in the 20-0 win against Selkirk in the Scottish Cup 1st. Round on December 8, 1984.

LONG SCORING RUNS

The record in England is held by **Bill Prendergast**, who scored in 13 consecutive appearances for Chester City (Div. 3, Sept.-Dec., 1938).

Dixie Dean scored in 12 consecutive games (23 goals) for Everton in Div. 2 in 1930-1.

Danish striker **Finn Dossing** scored in 15 consecutive matches (Scottish record) for Dundee Utd. (Div. 1) in 1964-5.

Marco Negri (Rangers) scored in all the first 10 Premier games of 1997-8 a total of 12 goals.

John Aldridge (Liverpool) scored in 10 successive First Division matches – the last game of season 1986-7 and the first nine in 1987-8.

Kevin Russell (Wrexham) scored in nine consecutive matches in Div. 4, March-May, 1988.

In the F.A. Premier League, **Mark Stein** scored in seven successive matches for Chelsea (Dec. 28, 1993-Feb. 5, 1994). **Alan Shearer** equalled the feat for Newcastle Utd. (Sept. 14-Nov. 30, 1996).

Ian Wright scored on 12 successive first-team appearances, including 7 Premiership, for Arsenal (Sept. 15-Nov. 23, 1994).

50-GOAL PLAYERS

With **52** goals for **Wolves** in 1987-8 (34 League, 12 Sherpa Van Trophy, 3 Littlewoods Cup, 3 F.A. Cup), **Steve Bull** became the first player to score 50 in a season for a League club since **Terry Bly** for 4th Division newcomers Peterborough Utd. in 1960-1. Bly's 54 comprised 52 League goals and 2 in the F.A. Cup, and included 7 hat-tricks, still a post-war League record.

Bull was again the country's top scorer with 50 goals in season 1988-9: 37 League, 2 Littlewoods Cup and 11 Sherpa Van Trophy.

Between Bly and Bull, the highest individual scoring total for a season was 49 by two players: Ted MacDougall (Bournemouth 1970-1, 42 League, 7 F.A. Cup) and Clive Allen (Tottenham 1986-7, 33 League, 12 Littlewoods Cup, 4 F.A. Cup).

HOT SHOTS

Jimmy Greaves was First Division top scorer (League goals) six times in 11 seasons: 32 for Chelsea (1958-9), 41 for Chelsea (1960-1) and, for Tottenham, 37 in 1962-3, 35 in 1963-4, 29 in 1964-5 (joint top) and 27 in 1968-9.

Brian Clough (Middlesbrough) was the Second Division's leading scorer in three successive seasons: 40 goals in 1957-8, 42 in 1958-9 and 39 in 1959-60.

John Hickton (Middlesbrough) was top Div. 2 scorer three times in four seasons: 24 goals in 1967-8, 24 in 1969-70 and 25 in 1970-1.

MOST HAT-TRICKS

Nine by **George Camsell** (Middlesbrough) in Div. 2, 1926-7, is the record for one season. Most League hat-tricks in career: 37 by **Dixie Dean** for Tranmere Rov. and Everton (1924-38).

Most **top division** hat-tricks in a season since last war: six by **Jimmy Greaves** for Chelsea (1960-1). **Alan Shearer** scored five hat-tricks for Blackburn Rov. in the Premier League, season 1995-96.

Frank Osborne (Tottenham) scored three consecutive hat-tricks in Div. 1 in October-November 1925, against Liverpool, Leicester City (away) and West Ham Utd.

Tom Jennings (Leeds Utd.) scored hat-tricks in three successive First Div. matches (Sept-Oct, 1926): 3 goals v Arsenal, 4 at Liverpool, 4 v Blackburn Rov. Leeds Utd. were relegated at the end of the season.

Jack Balmer (Liverpool) scored only three hat-tricks in a 17-year career - in successive First Div. matches (Nov. 1946): 3 v Portsmouth, 4 at Derby Co., 3 v Arsenal.

Gilbert Alsop scored hat-tricks in three successive matches for Walsall in Div. 3 South in April 1939: 3 at Swindon Town, 3 v Bristol City and 4 v Swindon Town.

Alf Lythgoe scored hat-tricks in three successive games for Stockport Co. (Div. 3 North) in March 1934: 3 v Darlington, 3 at Southport and 4 v Wrexham.

TRIPLE HAT-TRICKS

There have been at least three instances of **3 hat-tricks being scored** for **one team** in a Football League match:-

April 21, 1909: Enoch West, Billy Hooper and Arthur Spouncer scored 3 apiece for Nott'm. Forest (12-0 v Leicester Fosse, Div. 1).

March 3, 1962: Ron Barnes, Wyn Davies and Roy Ambler registered hat-tricks in Wrexham's 10-1 win against Hartlepool Utd. (Div. 4).

November 7, 1987: Tony Adcock, Paul Stewart and David White each scored 3 goals for Manchester City in 10-1 win at home to Huddersfield Town (Div. 2).

For the first time in the Premiership, **three hat-tricks** were completed **on one day** (September 23, 1995): Tony Yeboah for Leeds Utd. at Wimbledon; Alan Shearer for Blackburn Rov. v Coventry City; and Robbie Fowler with 4 goals for Liverpool v Bolton Wand.

In the F.A. Cup, **Jack Carr**, **George Elliott** and **Walter Tinsley** each scored 3 in Middlesbrough's 9-3 first round win against Goole in Jan. 1915. **Les Allen** scored 5, **Bobby Smith** 4 and **Cliff Jones** 3 when Tottenham beat Crewe Alexandra 13-2 in a fourth-round replay in February 1960.

HAT-TRICKS v THREE 'KEEPERS

When West Ham Utd. beat Newcastle Utd. 8-1 (Div.1) at home on April 21, 1986 **Alvin Martin** scored 3 goals against different 'keepers: Martin Thomas injured a shoulder and was replaced, in turn, by outfield players Chris Hedworth and Peter Beardsley.

In 1948 **Jock Dodds** of Lincoln City had done the same **against** West Ham Utd., scoring past **Gregory**, **Moroney** and **Dick**. The Hammers lost 3-4.

David Herd (Manchester Utd.) scored against three Sunderland goalkeepers (Montgomery, Hurley and Parke) in 5-0 First Division home win on Nov. 26, 1966.

Brian Clark, of Bournemouth, scored against three Rotherham Utd. goalkeepers (McDonough, Gilbert and Leng twice) in 7-2 win at Rotherham Utd. (Div. 3) on Oct. 10, 1972.

On Oct. 16, 1993 (Div.3) **Chris Pike** (Hereford) scored a hat-trick against different goalkeepers. Opponents Colchester Utd., beaten 5-0, became the first team in League history to have two 'keepers sent off in the same game.

Joe Bradford of Birmingham City scored three hat-tricks in eight days in September 1929-3 v Newcastle Utd. (won 5-1) on the 21st, 5 for the football league v Irish league (7-2) on the 25th, and 3 in his club's 5-7 defeat away to Blackburn Rov. on the 28th.

TON UP – BOTH ENDS

Manchester City are the only club to **score and concede** a century of League goals in the same season. When fifth in the 1957-8 Championship, they scored 104 goals and gave away 100.

HALF AN OWN GOAL EACH

Chelsea's second goal in a 3-1 home win against Leicester City on December 18, 1954 was uniquely recorded as 'shared own goal'. Leicester City defenders **Stan Milburn** and **Jack Froggatt**, both lunging at the ball in an attempt to clear, connected simultaneously and sent it rocketing into the net.

TOURNAMENT TOP SHOTS

Most individual goals in a World Cup Final series: 13 by **Just Fontaine** for France, in Sweden 1958.

Most in European Championship Finals: 9 by **Michel Platini** for France, in France 1984.

MOST GOALS ON CLUB DEBUT

Jim Dyet scored **eight** goals for King's Park against Forfar Athletic (Jan. 2, 1930).

Len Shackleton scored **six** times in Newcastle Utd.'s 13-0 win v Newport County (Div. 2, Oct. 5, 1946) in the week he joined them from Bradford Park Avenue.

MOST GOALS ON LEAGUE DEBUT

Five by **George Hilsdon**, for Chelsea (9-2) v Glossop, Div. 2 Sept. 1, 1906.

Alan Shearer, with three goals for Southampton (4-2) v Arsenal, April 9, 1988, became, at 17, the youngest player to score a First Division hat-trick on his full debut.

CLEAN-SHEET RECORDS

On the way to promotion from Div. 3 in season 1995-6, **Gillingham's** ever-present goalkeeper **Jim Stannard** set a clean-sheet record. In 46 matches, he achieved 29 shut-outs (17 at home, 12 away), beating the 28 by Ray Clemence for Liverpool (42 matches in Div. 1, 1978-9) and the previous best in a 46-match programme of 28 by Port Vale (Div. 3 North, 1953-4). In conceding only 20 League goals in 1995-6, Gillingham created a defensive record for the lower divisions.

Chris Woods, Rangers' England goalkeeper, set a British record in season 1986-7 by going 1,196 minutes without conceding a goal. The sequence began in the UEFA Cup match against Borussia Moenchengladbach on Nov. 26, 1986 and ended when Rangers were sensationally beaten 1-0 at home by Hamilton in the Scottish Cup 3rd. Round on Jan. 31, 1987 with a 70th.-minute goal by Adrian Sprott.

The previous British record of 1,156 minutes without a goal conceded was held by Aberdeen goalkeeper **Bobby Clark** (season 1970-1).

There have been three instances of clubs keeping 11 consecutive clean sheets in the Football League: Millwall (Div. 3 South, 1925-6), York City (Div. 3, 1973-4) and Reading (Div. 4, 1978-9). In that sequence, Reading goalkeeper Steve Death set the existing League shut-out record of 1,103 minutes.

Mark Leonard (Chesterfield) kept a clean sheet in 8 consecutive Div.3 away games (Jan-April 1994). Believed an away-match record in British football.

Sasa Ilic remained unbeaten for over 14 hours with 9 successive shut-outs (7 in FL Div. 1, 2 in play-offs) to equal a Charlton Athletic club record in Apr./May 1998. He had 12 clean sheets in 17 first team games after winning promotion from the reserves with 6 successive clean sheets.

Sebastiano Rossi kept a clean sheet in 8 successive away matches for AC Milan (Nov. 1993-Apr. 1994).

A world record of 1,275 minutes without conceding a goal was set in 1990-1 by **Abel Resino**, the Atletico Madrid goalkeeper. He was finally beaten by Sporting Gijon's Enrique in Atletico's 3-1 win on March 19, 1991.

In International football, the record is held by **Dino Zoff** with a shut-out for Italy (Sept. 1972 to June 1974) lasting 1,142 minutes.

LOW SCORING

Fewest goals by any club in season in Football League: **24** by **Stoke City** (Div. 1, 42 matches, 1984-5); **24** by **Watford** (Div. 2, 42 matches, 1971-2). In 46-match programme, **27** by **Stockport Co.** (Div. 3, 1969-70).

Arsenal were the lowest Premier League scorers in its opening season (1992-3) with 40 goals in 42 matches, but won both domestic cup competitions. In subsequent seasons the lowest Premier League scorers were **Ipswich Town** (35) in 1993-4, **Crystal Palace** (34) in 1994-5, and **Manchester City** (33) in 1995-6, before **Leeds Utd.** set the Premiership's existing fewest-goals record with 28 in 1996-7.

LONG TIME NO SCORE

Longest non-scoring sequences in Football League: 11 matches by **Coventry City** in 1919-20 (Div. 2); 11 matches by **Hartlepool Utd.** in 1992-3 (Div. 2). After beating Crystal Palace 1-0 in the F.A. Cup 3rd round on Jan. 2, they went 13 games and 2 months without scoring (11 League, 1 F.A. Cup, 1 Autoglass Trophy). The sequence ended after 1,227 blank minutes with a 1-1 draw at Blackpool (League) on March 6.

In the **Premier League** (Oct.-Jan. season 1994-5) Crystal Palace failed to score in nine consecutive matches.

The British non-scoring record is held by Scottish club **Stirling Albion**: 14 consecutive matches (13 League, 1 Scottish Cup) and 1,292 minutes play, from Jan. 31, 1981 until Aug. 8, 1981 (when they lost 4-1 to Falkirk in the League Cup).

In season 1971-2, **Mansfield Town** did not score in any of their first nine home games in Div. 3. They were relegated on goal difference of minus two.

F.A. CUP CLEAN SHEETS

Most consecutive F.A. Cup matches without conceding a goal: 12 by **Bradford City**. The sequence spanned 8 rounds, from 3rd. in 1910-11 to 4th. Round 3rd. replay in 1911-12, and included winning the Cup in 1911.

ATTENDANCES

GREATEST WORLD CROWDS

World Cup, Maracana Stadium, Rio de Janeiro, July 16, 1950. Final match (Brazil v Uruguay) attendance 199,850; receipts £125,000.

Total attendance in three matches (including play-off) between Santos (Brazil) and AC Milan for the Inter-Continental Cup (World Club Championship) 1963, exceeded 375,000.

BRITISH RECORD CROWDS

Most to pay: 149,547, Scotland v England, at Hampden Park, Glasgow, April 17, 1937. This was the first all-ticket match in Scotland (receipts £24,000).

At Scottish F.A. Cup Final: 146,433, Celtic v Aberdeen, at Hampden Park, April 24, 1937. Estimated another 20,000 shut out.

For British club match (apart from a Cup Final): 143,470, Rangers v Hibernian, at Hampden Park, March 27, 1948 (Scottish Cup semi-final).

F.A. Cup Final: 126,047, Bolton Wand. v West Ham Utd., at Wembley, April 28, 1923. Estimated 150,000 in stadium.

World Cup Qualifying Ties: 120,000, Cameroon v Morocco, Yaounde, November 29, 1981; 107,580, Scotland v Poland, Hampden Park, October 13, 1965.

European Cup: 135,826, Celtic v Leeds Utd. (semi-final) at Hampden Park, Glasgow, April 15, 1970.

European Cup Final: 127,621, Real Madrid v Eintracht Frankfurt, at Hampden Park, Glasgow, May 18, 1960.

European Cup-Winners' Cup Final: 100,000, West Ham Utd. v TSV Munich, at Wembley, May 19, 1965.

Scottish League: 118,567, Rangers v Celtic, January 2, 1939.

Scottish League Cup Final: 107,609, Celtic v Rangers, at Hampden Park, October 23, 1965.

Football League old format: First Div.: 83,260, Manchester Utd. v Arsenal, January 17, 1948 (at Maine Road); **Second Div.:** 70,302 Tottenham v Southampton, February 25, 1950; **Third Div. South:** 51,621, Cardiff City v Bristol City, April 7, 1947; **Third Div. North:** 49,655, Hull City v Rotherham Utd., December 25, 1948; **Third Div.:** 49,309, Sheffield Wed. v Sheffield Utd., December 26, 1979; **Fourth Div.:** 37,774, Crystal Palace v Millwall, March 31, 1961.

F.A. Premier League: 55,316 Manchester Utd. v Southampton, February 27, 1999.

Football League – New Div. 1: 41,214, Sunderland v Stoke City, April 25, 1998; **New Div. 2:** 19,141, Bristol City v Watford, April 13, 1998; **New Div. 3:** 18,700, Preston N.E. v Exeter City, May 4, 1996.

In English Provinces: 84,569, Manchester City v Stoke City (F.A. Cup 6th Round), March 3, 1934.

Record for Under-21 International: 32,865 England v France at Derby Co., February 9, 1999.

Record for friendly match: 104,679, Rangers v Eintracht Frankfurt, at Hampden Park, Glasgow, October 17, 1961.

Record Football League aggregate (season): 41,271,414 (1948-9) – 88 clubs.

Record Football League aggregate (single day): 1,269,934, December 27, 1949.

Record average home League attendance for season: 57,758 by Manchester Utd. in 1967-8.

Long-ago League attendance aggregates: 10,929,000 in 1906-07 (40 clubs); 28,132,933 in 1937-8 (88 clubs).

Last 1m. crowd aggregate, League: 1,007,200, December 27, 1971.

Record Amateur match attendance: 100,000 for F.A. Amateur Cup Final, Pegasus v Harwich & Parkeston at Wembley, April 11, 1953.

Record Cup-tie aggregate: 265,199, at two matches between Rangers and Morton, in the Scottish Cup Final, 1947-8.

Abandoned match attendance records: In England – 63,480 at Newcastle Utd. v Swansea City F.A. Cup 3rd round, Jan. 10, 1953, abandoned 8 mins (0-0), fog.

In Scotland: 94,596 at Scotland v Austria (4-1), Hampden Park, May 8, 1963. Referee Jim Finney ended play (79 minutes) after Austria had two players sent off and one carried off.

What is still **Colchester Utd.'s** record crowd (19,072) was for the F.A. Cup 1st round tie v Reading on Nov. 27, 1948, abandoned 35 minutes (0-0), fog.

SMALLEST CROWDS

Lowest post-war League attendance: 450 Rochdale v Cambridge Utd. (Div. 3, February 2, 1974).

Lowest F.A. Premier League crowd: 3,039 for Wimbledon v Everton, Jan. 26, 1993 (smallest top-division attendance since war).

Lowest Saturday post-war top-division crowd: 3,231 for Wimbledon v Luton Town, Sept. 7, 1991 (Div. 1).

Lowest Football League crowds, new format – Div. 1: 3,086 Southend Utd. v Bristol City, February 10,1993; **Div. 2:** 1,077, Hartlepool Utd. v Cardiff City, March 22, 1994; **Div. 3:** 739, Doncaster Rov. v Barnet, March 3, 1998.

Other low First Division crowds since the war: 3,121 for Wimbledon v Sheffield W., Oct. 2, 1991; 3,231 for Wimbledon v Luton Town, Sept. 7, 1991; 3,270 for Wimbledon v Coventry City, Dec. 28, 1991; 3,496 for Wimbledon v Luton Town, Feb. 14, 1990.

Lowest top-division crowd at a major ground since the war: 4,554 for Arsenal v Leeds Utd. (May 5, 1966) – fixture clashed with live TV coverage of Cup-Winners' Cup Final (Liverpool v Borussia Dortmund).

Smallest League Cup attendance at top-division ground: 1,987 for Wimbledon v Bolton Wand. (2nd Round, 2nd Leg) Oct. 6, 1992.

Smallest Wembley crowds for England matches: 15,628 v Chile (Rous Cup, May 23, 1989 – affected by Tube strike); 20,038 v Colombia (Friendly, Sept. 6, 1995); 21,432 v Czech. (Friendly, Apr. 25, 1990); 21,142 v Japan (Umbro Cup, June 3, 1995); 23,600 v Wales (British Championship, Feb. 23, 1983); 23,659 v Greece (Friendly, May 17, 1994); 23,951 v East Germany (Friendly, Sept. 12, 1984); 24,000 v N. Ireland (British Championship, Apr. 4, 1984); 25,756 v Colombia (Rous Cup, May 24, 1988); 25,837 v Denmark (Friendly, Sept. 14, 1988).

Other smallest Int. crowds – N.Ireland: 2,500 v Chile (Belfast, May 26, 1989 – clashed with ITV live screening of Liverpool v Arsenal Championship decider); **Scotland:** 7,843 v N.Ireland (Hampden Park, May 6, 1969); **Wales:** 2,315 v N.Ireland (Wrexham, May 27, 1982).

Smallest attendance for any England match: 2,378 v San Marino (World Cup) at Bologna (Nov. 17, 1993). Tie clashed with Italy v Portugal (World Cup) shown live on Italian TV.

F.A. CUP CROWD RECORD (OUTSIDE FINAL)

The first F.A. Cup-tie shown on closed-circuit TV (5th. Round, Saturday, March 11, 1967, kick-off 7pm) drew a total of 105,000 spectators to Goodison Park and Anfield. This is the biggest attendance for a single F.A. Cup match other than the Final. At Goodison, 64,851 watched the match 'for real', while 40,149 saw the TV version on eight giant screens at Anfield. Everton beat Liverpool 1-0.

LOWEST SEMI-FINAL CROWD

The smallest F.A. Cup semi-final attendance since the war was 17,987 for Manchester Utd. v Crystal Palace replay, at Villa Park on April 12, 1995. Crystal Palace supporters largely boycotted tie after a fan died in car-park clash outside pub in Walsall before first match. Previous lowest: 25,963 for Wimbledon v Luton Town, at Tottenham on April 9, 1988.

Lowest quarter-final crowd since the war: 8,735 for Chesterfield v Wrexham on March 9, 1997.

Smallest F.A. Cup 3rd. Round attendances for matches between League clubs: 1,833 for Chester City v Bournemouth (at Macclesfield Town) Jan. 5, 1991; 1,966 for Aldershot v Oxford Utd., Jan. 10, 1987.

PRE-WEMBLEY CUP FINAL CROWDS

AT CRYSTAL PALACE

1895 42,560	1902 48,036	1908 74,967
1896 48,036	Replay 33,050	1909 67,651
1897 65,891	1903 64,000	1910 76,980
1898 62,017	1904 61,734	1911 69,098
1899 73,833	1905 101,117	1912 54,434
1900 68,945	1906 75,609	1913 120,028
1901 110,802	1907 84,584	1914 72,778

AT OLD TRAFFORD

1915 50,000

AT STAMFORD BRIDGE

1920 50,018	1921 72,805	1922 53,000

RECEIPTS RECORDS

Wembley Stadium underwent its first considerable alteration during 1962-3 in preparation for the World Cup in 1966. Higher admission fees at the 1963 F.A. Cup Final resulted in 100,000 spectators paying a record £89,000.

This is how Wembley's receipts records have risen since then:–

1968 F.A. Cup Final (Everton v W.B.A.)	£110,000
1968 European Cup Final (Manchester Utd. v Benfica)	£120,000
1976 F.A. Cup Final (Southampton v Manchester Utd.)	£420,000
1978 F.A. Cup Final (Ipswich Town v Arsenal)	£500,000
1981 England v Hungary (World Cup)	£671,000
1982 F.A. Cup Final (Tottenham v Q.P.R.)	£886,000
(plus £605,000 for replay)	
1984 F.A. Cup Final (Everton v Watford)	£919,000
*1985 F.A. Cup Final (Manchester Utd. v Everton)	£1,100,000
1986 F.A. Cup Final (Liverpool v Everton)	£1,100,000
†1987 League Cup Final (Arsenal v Liverpool)	£1,000,000
1987 F.A. Cup Final (Coventry City v Tottenham)	£1,286,737
1988 F.A. Cup Final (Wimbledon v Liverpool)	£1,422,814
1989 F.A. Cup Final (Liverpool v Everton)	£1,600,000
1990 League Cup Final (Nott'm Forest v Oldham Athletic)	£1,650,000
1990 F.A. Cup Final (Manchester Utd. v Crystal Palace – first match) ..	£2,000,000
1991 League Cup Final (Manchester Utd. v Sheffield Wed.)	£2,000,000
1991 F.A. Cup Final (Nott'm F. v Tottenham)	£2,016,000
1992 F.A. Cup Final (Liverpool v Sunderland)	£2,548,174
1993 F.A. Cup Final (Arsenal v Sheffield W. – first match)	£2,818,000
(Replay took receipts for both matches to £4,695,200)	
1994 F.A. Cup Final record (Manchester Utd. v Chelsea)	£2,962,167
1997 League Cup Final record (Leicester City v Middlesbrough)	£2,750,000
•1998 League Cup Final record (Chelsea v Middlesbrough)	£2,983,000

F.A. Cup Final receipts for last five years: 1995 £2.45m.; 1996 £2.4m.; 1997 £2.4m.; 1998 £2.4m.; 1999 £2.5m.
(* Britain's first £1m. gate; †First £1m. gate for League Cup Final; • British club match receipts record)

Record England match receipts: £4,100,000 (v. Germany, Wembley, European Championship semi-final, June 26, 1992 - att: 75,862)

EARLY CUP FINAL RECEIPTS

1885 Blackburn Rov. v Queens Park £442
1913 Aston Villa v Sunderland £9,406
1923 Bolton Wand. v West Ham Utd., first Wembley Final £27,776
1939 Portsmouth v Wolves £29,000
1946 Derby Co. v Charlton Athletic £45,000

WORLD RECORD MATCH RECEIPTS

£4,300,000 for **World Cup Final**, Argentina v West Germany (Rome, July 8, 1990).

BRITISH CLUB MATCH RECORD RECEIPTS

£2,983,000 at the **1998 League Cup Final**, Chelsea v Middlesborough.

INTERNATIONAL RECORDS

MOST APPEARANCES

Peter Shilton, England goalkeeper, then aged 40, retired from International football after the 1990 World Cup Finals with the then world record number of caps - 125. Previous record (119) was set by **Pat Jennings**, Northern Ireland's goalkeeper from 1964-86, who retired on his 41st birthday during the 1986 World Cup in Mexico. Shilton's England career spanned 20 seasons from his debut against East Germany at Wembley on Nov. 25, 1970.

Four players have completed a century of appearances in full International matches for England. **Billy Wright** of Wolves, was the first, retiring in 1959 with a total of 105 caps.

Bobby Charlton, of Manchester Utd., beat Wright's record in the World Cup match against West Germany in Leon, Mexico, in June 1970 and **Bobby Moore,** of West Ham Utd., overtook Charlton's 106 caps against Italy in Turin, in June 1973. Moore played 108 times for England, a record that stood until **Shilton** reached 109 against Denmark in Copenhagen (June 7, 1989).

Kenny Dalglish became Scotland's first 100-cap International v Romania (Hampden Park, March 26, 1986).

Thomas Ravelli holds the world record for full International caps - 143 for Sweden (1981-97).

Gillian Coultard, England Women's captain (Doncaster Belles) received a special presentation from Geoff Hurst to mark 100 Caps when England beat Holland 1-0 at Upton Park on October 30, 1997. That was her 102nd. Int. (debut at 18 in May 1981).

BRITAIN'S MOST-CAPPED PLAYERS

(As at start of season 1999-2000)

England

Peter Shilton 125
Bobby Moore 108
Bobby Charlton 106
Billy Wright 105

Scotland

Kenny Dalglish	102
Jim Leighton	91
Alex McLeish	77
Paul McStay	76

Wales

Neville Southall	92
Peter Nicholas	73
Ian Rush	73
Mark Hughes	72
Joey Jones	72

Northern Ireland

Pat Jennings	119
Mal Donaghy	91
Sammy McIlroy	88

Republic of Ireland

Tony Cascarino	83
Paul McGrath	83
Pat Bonner	80
Steve Staunton	78
Ray Houghton	73
Liam Brady	72
Frank Stapleton	71

MOST CAPS IN ROW

Most consecutive International appearances: 70 by **Billy Wright**, for England from October 1951 to May 1959. He played 105 of England's first 108 post-war matches. **England captains most times: Billy Wright** and **Bobby Moore**, 90 each.

ENGLAND'S WORLD CUP-WINNERS

At Wembley, July 30, 1966, 4-2 v West Germany (2-2 after 90 mins), scorers Hurst 3, Peters. Team: Banks; Cohen, Wilson, Stiles, Charlton (J.), Moore (Captain), Ball, Hurst, Charlton (R.), Hunt, Peters. Manager **Alf Ramsey** fielded that same eleven in six successive matches (an England record): the World Cup quarter-final, semi-final and Final, and the first three games of the following season. England wore red shirts in the Final and Her Majesty the Queen presented the Cup to Bobby Moore. The players each received a £1,000 bonus, plus £60 World Cup Final appearance money, all less tax, and Ramsey a £6,000 bonus from the F.A. The match was shown live on TV (in black and white).

BRAZIL'S RECORD RUN

Brazil hold the record for the longest unbeaten sequence in International football: 37 matches (30W, 7D, goals 85-18) from December 1993 until they lost 2-0 to Mexico in the CONCACAF Gold Cup Final on January 21, 1996. The previous record of 31 matches undefeated (27W, 4D, goals 139-33) was held by Hungary between June 1950 and July 1954.

ALL-SEATED INTERNATIONALS

The first **all-seated crowd** (30,000) for a full International in Britain saw **Wales** and **West Germany** draw 0-0 at Cardiff City Arms Park on May 31, 1989. The terraces were closed. **England's** first all-seated International at Wembley was against Yugoslavia (2-1) on December 13, 1989 (attendance 34,796). The terracing behind the goals was closed for conversion to seating.

England's first **full-house all-seated** International at Wembley was for England v Brazil (1-0) on March 28, 1990, when a capacity 80,000 crowd paid record British receipts of £1,200,000.

FIRST BLACK CAPS

England's first black player was Nott'm. Forest full-back **Viv Anderson** against Czechoslovakia at Wembley on November 29, 1978.

Aston Villa's **Ugo Ehiogu** was **England's** first black captain (U-21 v Holland at Portsmouth, April 27, 1993).

Paul Ince (Manchester Utd.) became the first black player to captain **England** in a **full International** (v U.S.A., Boston, June 9, 1993).

First black British International was **Eddie Parris** (Bradford Park Avenue) for Wales against N. Ireland in Belfast on December 5, 1931.

PLAYED FOR MORE THAN ONE COUNTRY

Multi-nationals in senior International football include: **Johnny Carey** (1938-53) – caps Rep. of Ireland 29, N. Ireland 7; **Ferenc Puskas** (1945-62) – caps Hungary 84, Spain 4; **Alfredo di Stefano** (1950-6) – caps Argentina 7, Spain 31; **Ladislav Kubala** (1948-58) – caps Hungary 3, Czechoslovakia 11, Spain 19, only player to win full Int. honours with 3 countries. Kubala also played in a fourth Int. team, scoring twice for FIFA v England at Wembley in 1953.

Eleven players, including Carey, appeared for both N. Ireland and the Republic of Ireland in seasons directly after the last war.

Cecil Moore, capped by N. Ireland in 1949 when with Glentoran, played for USA v England in 1953.

John Reynolds (W.B.A.) played for both England and Ireland in the 1890s.

Robert Evans (Sheffield Utd.) had played 10 times for Wales when capped for England, in 1910-11. He was born in Chester of Welsh parents.

In recent years several players have represented USSR and one or other of the breakaway republics. The same applies to Yugoslavia and its component states.

FATHER & SON SAME-DAY CAPS

Iceland made father-and-son Int. history when they beat Estonia 3-0 in Tallin on April 24, 1996. Arnor Gudjohnsen (35) started the match and was replaced (62 mins.) by his 17-year-old son Eidur.

POSTWAR HAT-TRICKS v ENGLAND

November 25, 1953, scorer **Nandor Hidegkuti** (England 3, Hungary 6, Wembley); May 11, 1958, scorer **Aleksander Petakovic** (Yugoslavia 5, England 0, Belgrade); May 17, 1959, scorer **Juan Seminario** (Peru 4, England 1, Lima); June 15, 1988, scorer **Marco Van Basten** (Holland 3, England 1, European Championship, Dusseldorf).

NO-SAVE GOALKEEPERS

Chris Woods did not have one save to make when England beat San Marino 6-0 (World Cup) at Wembley on February 17, 1993. He touched the ball only six times throughout the match.

Gordon Banks had a similar no-save experience when England beat Malta 5-0 (European Championship) at Wembley on May 12, 1971. Malta did not force a goal-kick or corner, and the four times Banks touched the ball were all from back passes.

FIFA PIONEERS

FIFA, now with a membership of 203 countries, began in 1904 with seven founder nations: Belgium, Denmark, France, Holland, Spain, Sweden and Switzerland.

FIFA WORLD YOUTH CHAMPIONSHIP (UNDER-20)

Finals: 1977 (Tunis) Soviet Union 2, Mexico 2 (Soviet won 9-8 on pens.); **1979** (Tokyo) Argentina 3, Soviet Union 1; **1981** (Sydney) W. Germany 4, Qatar 0; **1983** (Mexico City) Brazil 1, Argentina 0; **1985** (Moscow) Brazil 1, Spain 0; **1987** (Santiago) Yugoslavia 1, W. Germany 1 (Yugoslavia won 5-4 on pens.); **1989** (Riyadh) Portugal 2, Nigeria 0; **1991** (Lisbon) Portugal 0, Brazil 0 (Portugal won 4-2 on pens.); **1993** (Sydney) Brazil, 2 Ghana 1; **1995** (Qatar) Argentina 2, Brazil 0; **1997** (Kuala Lumpur) Argentina 2, Uruguay 1; **1999** (Lagos) Spain 4, Japan 0.

FAMOUS CLUB FEATS

The Double: There have been nine instances of a club winning the Football League Premiership title and the F.A. Cup in the same season. Manchester Utd. have done so three times and Arsenal twice:-

Preston N.E. 1888-89; **Aston Villa** 1896-97; **Tottenham** 1960-61; **Arsenal** 1970-71, 1997-98; **Liverpool** 1985-86; **Manchester Utd.** 1993-94, 1995-96, 1998-99.

The Treble: Liverpool were the first English club to win three major competitions in one season when in 1983-84, Joe Fagan's first season as manager, they were League Champions, League Cup winners and European Cup winners.

Alex Ferguson's **Manchester Utd.** achieved an even more prestigious treble in 1998-99, completing the domestic double of Premiership and F.A. Cup and then winning the European Cup.

(See Scottish section for treble feats by Rangers and Celtic.)

Home Runs: Sunderland lost only one home Div. 1 game out of 73 in five seasons, 1891 to 1896. **Brentford** won all 21 home games in 1929-30 in the Third Division (South). Others have won all home games in a smaller programme.

Record Home Run: Liverpool went 85 competitive first-team games unbeaten at home between losing 2-3 to Birmingham City on January 21, 1978 and 1-2 to Leicester City on January 31, 1981. They comprised 63 in the League, 9 League Cup, 7 in European competition and 6 F.A. Cup. Leicester were relegated that season.

Millwall were unbeaten at home in the League for 59 consecutive matches from 1964-67.

Third to First: Charlton Athletic, in 1936, became the first club to advance from the Third to First Division in successive seasons. **Queen's Park Rangers** were the second club to achieve the feat in 1968, and **Oxford Utd.** did it in 1984 and 1985 as Champions of each division. Subsequently, **Derby Co.** (1987), **Middlesbrough** (1988), **Sheffield Utd.** (1990) and **Notts Co.** (1991) climbed from Third Division to First in consecutive seasons.

Watford won successive promotions from the modern Second Division to the Premier League in 1997-8, 1998-9.

Fourth to First: Northampton Town, in 1965 became the first club to rise from the Fourth to the First Division. **Swansea City** climbed from the Fourth Division to the First (three promotions in four seasons), 1977-8 to 1980-1. **Watford** did so in five seasons, 1977-8 to 1981-2. **Carlisle Utd.** climbed from Fourth Division to First, 1964-74.

Non-League to First: When **Wimbledon** finished third in the Second Division in 1986, they completed the phenomenal rise from non-League football (Southern League) to the First Division in nine years. Two years later they won the F.A. Cup.

Tottenham, in 1960-1, not only carried off the First Division Championship and the F.A. Cup for the first time this century but set up other records by opening with 11 successive wins, registering most First Division wins (31), most away wins in the League's history (16), and equalling Arsenal's First Division records of 66 points and 33 away points. They already held the Second Division record of 70 points (1919-20).

Arsenal, in 1993, became the first, and still only, club to win both English domestic cup competitions (F.A. Cup and League Cup) in the same season.

Preston N.E., in season 1888-9, won the first League Championship without losing a match and the F.A. Cup without having a goal scored against them throughout the competition.

Bury, in 1903, also won the F.A. Cup without conceding a goal.

Everton won Div. 2, Div. 1 and the F.A. Cup in successive seasons, 1930-1, 1931-2, 1932-3.

Liverpool won the League Championship in 1964, the F.A. Cup in 1965 and the Championship again in 1966. In 1978 they became the first British club to win the European Cup in successive seasons. **Nott'm. Forest** repeated the feat in 1979 and 1980.

Liverpool won the League Championship six times in eight seasons (1976-83) under **Bob Paisley's** management.

Arsenal supplied seven men (still a record) to the England team v Italy at Highbury on November 14, 1935. They were: Frank Moss, George Male, Eddie Hapgood, Wilf Copping, Ray Bowden, Ted Drake and Cliff Bastin. In addition, Arsenal's Tom Whittaker was England's trainer.

Since then, the most players from one club in an England team was six from **Liverpool** against Switzerland at Wembley in September 1977. The side also included a Liverpool old boy, Kevin Keegan (Hamburg).

Seven **Arsenal** men took part in the England – France (0-2) match at Wembley on February 10, 1999. Goalkeeper David Seaman and defenders Lee Dixon, Tony Adams and Martin Keown lined up for England. Nicolas Anelka (2 goals) and Emmanuel Petit started the match for France and Patrick Vieira replaced Anelka.

COVENTRY UNIQUE

Coventry City are the only club to have played in the Premier League, all four previous divisions of the Football League and in both sections (North and South) of the old Third Division.

Grimsby Town were the other club to play in the four divisions of the Football League and its two Third Division sections.

FAMOUS UPS & DOWNS

Sunderland: Relegated in 1958 after maintaining First Division status since their election to the Football League in 1890. They dropped into Division 3 for the first time in 1987.

Aston Villa: Relegated with **Preston N.E.** to the Third Division in 1970.

Arsenal up: When the League was extended in 1919, Woolwich Arsenal (sixth in Division Two in 1914-15, last season before the war) were elected to Division One. Arsenal have been in the top division ever since.

Tottenham down: At that same meeting in 1919 Chelsea (due for relegation) retained their place in Division One but the bottom club (Tottenham) had to go down to Division Two.

Preston N.E. and Burnley down: Preston N.E., the first League Champions in season 1888-9, dropped into the Fourth Division in 1985. So did Burnley, also among the League's original members in 1888. In 1986, Preston N.E. had to apply for re-election.

Wolves' fall: Wolves, another of the Football League's original members, completed the fall from First Division to Fourth Division in successive seasons (1984-5-6).

Lincoln City out: Lincoln City became the first club to suffer automatic demotion from the Football League when they finished bottom of Div. 4, on goal difference, in season 1986-7. They were replaced by Scarborough, champions of the GM Vauxhall Conference. Lincoln City regained their place a year later.

Swindon Town up and down: In the 1990 play-offs, Swindon Town won promotion to the First Division for the first time, but remained in the Second Division because of financial irregularities.

MOST CHAMPIONSHIP WINS

Liverpool, by winning the First Division in 1976-7, established a record of 10 Championship victories. They later increased the total to 18. **Manchester Utd.** are second with 12 League titles (7 Football League, 5 Premier League).

LONGEST CURRENT MEMBERS OF TOP DIVISION

Arsenal (since 1919), **Everton** (1954), **Liverpool** (1962), **Coventry City** (1967), **Manchester Utd.** (1975), **Southampton** (1978).

CHAMPIONS: FEWEST PLAYERS

Liverpool used only 14 players (five ever-present) when they won the League Championship in season 1965-6. **Aston Villa** also called on no more than 14 players to win the title in 1980-81, with seven ever-present.

MOST PLAYERS USED IN LEAGUE SEASON

46: By Birmingham City in 1995-6. **45**: By **Doncaster Rovers** in 1997-8. **42**: By **Coventry City** and **Sheffield Wed.** (both 1919-20) and by **Hull City** (1946-7), in each case in a season following a break in League football because of war.

BEST OF CENTURY

Arsenal (1990-91) were the first League Champions this century to lose only once (38 matches). **Preston N.E.** were undefeated first Champions in 1888-9, but played only 22 matches.

LEAGUE HAT-TRICKS

Huddersfield Town created a record in 1925-6 by winning the League Championship for the third year in succession.
   Arsenal equalled this League hat-trick in 1933-4-5, and **Liverpool** in 1982-3-4.

'SUPER DOUBLE' WINNERS

Since the war, there have been three instances of players appearing in and then managing F.A. Cup and Championship-winning teams:
   Joe Mercer: Player in Arsenal Championship teams 1948, 1953 and in their 1950 F.A. Cup side; manager of Manchester City when they won Championship 1968, F.A. Cup 1969.
   Kenny Dalglish: Player in Liverpool Championship-winning teams 1979, 1980, 1982, 1983, 1984, player-manager 1986, 1988, 1990: player-manager when Liverpool won F.A. Cup (to complete Double) 1986; manager of Blackburn Rov., Champions 1995.
   George Graham: Played in Arsenal's Double-winning team in 1971, and as manager took them to Championship success in 1989 and 1991 and the F.A. Cup – League Cup double in 1993.

CHAMPIONS IN SUCCESSIVE SEASONS

Preston N.E. (1888-9, 1889-90).
Sunderland (1891-2, 1892-3).
Aston Villa (1895-6, 1896-7, 1898-9, 1899-1900).
Sheffield Wed. (1902-3, 1903-4, 1928-9, 1929-30).
Liverpool (1921-2, 1922-3, 1975-6, 1976-7, 1978-9, 1979-80, 1981-2, 1982-3, 1983-4).
Portsmouth (1948-9, 1949-50).
Manchester Utd. (1955-6, 1956-7, 1992-3, 1993-4, 1995-6, 1996-7).
Wolves (1957-8, 1958-9).

The Second Division Championship and League Championship were won in successive seasons by **Liverpool** (1905-6), **Everton** (1931-2), **Tottenham** (1950-1) and **Ipswich Town** (1961-2).

Oxford Utd. became the first club to win the Third and Second Division Championships in successive years (1984, 1985).

Wolves are the only club to win the Fourth and Third Division Championships in successive years (1988, 1989).

BACK FIRST TIME

The following clubs won promotion the season after losing their position in the First Division of the League (*as Champions):

Sheffield Wed. *1899-1900, *1951-2, *1955-6, *1958-9, 1990-1; **Bolton Wand.** 1899-1900, *1908-9, 1910-11; **W.B.A.** *1901-2; **Manchester City** *1902-3, *1909-10, 1950-1; **Burnley** *1897-8.

Small Heath 1902-3; **Liverpool** *1904-5; **Nott'm. Forest** *1906-7; **Preston N.E.** *1912-13, 1914-15; **Notts Co.** *1913-14; **Derby Co.** *1914-15.

Tottenham *1919-20, 1977-8; **Leeds Utd.** 1927-8, 1931-2; **Middlesbrough** *1928-9; **Everton** *1930-1; **Manchester Utd.** 1937-8, *1974-5; **Huddersfield Town** 1952-3.

Aston Villa *1959-60, 1987-8; **Chelsea** 1962-3; *1988-9; **Norwich City** 1974-5, 1981-2, *1985-6; **Wolves** 1976-7, 1982-3; **Birmingham City** 1979-80, 1984-5.

West Ham Utd., relegated in 1992, won promotion to the **Premier League** in 1993; *Crystal Palace and Nott'm. Forest both returned to the **Premiership** in 1994, a year after relegation; so did **Leicester City** in 1996, *Bolton Wand. in 1997, and *Nott'm Forest and Middlesbrough in 1998.

ORIGINAL TWELVE

The original 12 members of the Football League (formed in 1888) were: **Accrington, Aston Villa, Blackburn Rov., Bolton Wand., Burnley, Derby Co., Everton, Notts Co., Preston N.E., Stoke City, W.B.A.** and **Wolves**.

Results on the opening day (September 8, 1888): Bolton Wand. 3, Derby Co. 6; Everton 2, Accrington 1; Preston N.E. 5, Burnley 2; Stoke City 0, W.B.A. 2; Wolves 1, Aston Villa 1. Preston N.E. had the biggest first-day crowd: 6,000. Blackburn Rov. and Notts Co. did not play that day. They kicked off a week later (September 15) – Blackburn Rov. 5, Accrington 5; Everton 2, Notts Co. 1.

FASTEST CLIMB – FOURTH DIV. TO FIRST

Three promotions in four seasons by two clubs – **Swansea City:** 1978 third in Div.4; 1979 third in Div.3; 1981 third in Div.2; **Wimbledon:** 1983 Champions of Div.4; 1984 second in Div.3; 1986 third in Div.2.

MERSEYSIDE RECORD

Liverpool is the only city to have staged top-division football – through Everton and/or Liverpool – in **every season** since League football began in 1888.

LEAGUE RECORDS

MOST POINTS IN A SEASON

The following records applied before the introduction of three points for a win in the Football League in 1981-2.
Lincoln City set a **Football League** record in season 1975-6 with 74 points from 46 games (including 32 victories) in **Division 4**.
First Division: Liverpool (1978-9), 68 points from 42 matches.

Second Division: Tottenham (1919-20), 70 points from 42 matches.
Third Division: Aston Villa (1971-2) 70 points from 46 matches.

Since 3 points for win (pre-Premier League):
First Division: Everton (1984-5) and Liverpool (1987-8) 90 points: **Second Division:** Chelsea (1988-9) 99 points; **Third Division:** Bournemouth (1986-7) 97 points; **Fourth Division:** Swindon Town (1985-6) 102 points.

Since change of League format:
Premier League: Manchester Utd. (1993-4) 92 points; **First Division:** Sunderland (1998-9) 105 points (record for any division); **Second Division:** Fulham (1998-9) 101 points; **Third Division:** Notts Co. (1997-8) 99 points.

Fewest Points: Doncaster Rov. 8 points (of possible 68) in Second Division, 1904-5. Stirling Albion 6 points (of possible 60) in Scottish League Division A, 1954-5.

DOUBLE CHAMPIONS

Nine men have played in and managed League Championship-winning teams:

Ted Drake Player – Arsenal 1934, 1935, 1938. Manager – Chelsea 1955.
Bill Nicholson Player – Tottenham 1951. Manager – Tottenham 1961.
Alf Ramsey Player – Tottenham 1951. Manager – Ipswich Town 1962.
Joe Mercer Player – Everton 1939, Arsenal 1948, 1953. Manager – Manchester City 1968.
Dave Mackay Player – Tottenham 1961. Manager – Derby Co. 1975.
Bob Paisley Player – Liverpool 1947. Manager – Liverpool 1976, 1977, 1979, 1980, 1982, 1983.
Howard Kendall Player – Everton 1970. Manager – Everton 1985, 1987.
Kenny Dalglish Player – Liverpool 1979, 1980, 1982, 1983, 1984. Player-manager – Liverpool 1986, 1988, 1990. Manager – Blackburn Rov. 1995.
George Graham Player – Arsenal 1971. Manager – Arsenal 1989, 1991.

MOST LEAGUE CHAMPIONSHIP MEDALS

Kenny Dalglish: 9 – 8 for Liverpool (5 as player, 1979-80-82-83-84; 3 as player-manager, 1986-88-90); 1 for Blackburn Rov. (as manager, 1995). As a player he also won 4 Scottish Championship medals with Celtic (1972-73-74-77). **Phil Neal:** 8 for Liverpool (1976-77-79-80-82-83-84-86); **Alan Hansen:** 8 for Liverpool (1979-80-82-83-84-86-88-90).

CANTONA'S FOUR-TIMER

Eric Cantona played in four successive Championship-winning teams: Marseille 1990-1, Leeds Utd. 1991-2, Manchester Utd. 1992-3 and 1993-4.

ARRIVALS AND DEPARTURES

The following are the Football League arrivals and departures since 1923:

Year	In	Out
1923	Doncaster Rov.	Stalybridge Celtic
	New Brighton	
1927	Torquay Athletic	Aberdare Athletic
1928	Carlisle Utd.	Durham City
1929	York City	Ashington
1930	Thames	Merthyr Tydfil
1931	Mansfield Town	Newport County
	Chester City	Nelson
1932	Aldershot	Thames
	Newport County	Wigan Borough
1938	Ipswich Town	Gillingham
1950	Colchester Utd.	
	Gillingham	
	Scunthorpe Utd.	

	Shrewsbury Town	
1951	Workington	New Brighton
1960	Peterborough Utd.	Gateshead
1962	Oxford Utd.	Accrington Stanley (resigned)
1970	Cambridge Utd.	Bradford P.A.
1972	Hereford Utd.	Barrow
1977	Wimbledon	Workington
1978	Wigan Athletic	Southport
1987	Scarborough	Lincoln City
1988	Lincoln City	Newport County
1989	Maidstone Utd.	Darlington
1990	Darlington	Colchester Utd.
1991	Barnet	
1992	Colchester Utd.	Aldershot, Maidstone (resigned)
1993	Wycombe Wand.	Halifax Town
1997	Macclesfield Town	Hereford Utd.
1998	Halifax Town	Doncaster Rov.
1999	Cheltenham Town	Scarborough

Leeds City were expelled from Div. 2 in October, 1919; Port Vale took over their fixtures.

EXTENSIONS TO FOOTBALL LEAGUE

Clubs	Season	Clubs	Season
12 to 14	1891-2	44 to 66+	1920-1
14 to 28*	1892-3	66 to 86†	1921-2
28 to 31	1893-4	86 to 88	1923-4
31 to 32	1894-5	88 to 92	1950-1
32 to 36	1898-9	92 to 93	1991-2
36 to 40	1905-6	(Reverted to 92 when Aldershot closed,	
40 to 44	1919-20	March 1992)	

* Second Division formed. + Third Division (South) formed from Southern League clubs.
† Third Division (North) formed.
Football League reduced to 70 clubs and three divisions on the formation of the F.A.
Premier League in 1992; increased to 72 season 1994-5, when Premier League
reduced to 20 clubs.

RECORD RUNS

Nott'm. Forest hold the record unbeaten sequence in the Football League – 42 matches spanning the last 26 of season 1977-8 and the first 16 of 1978-9. The run began on 19, November 1977 and ended on December 9, 1978 when Forest lost 0-2 at Liverpool. Their sequence comprised 21 wins and 21 draws.

Best debuts: Ipswich Town won the First Division at their first attempt in 1961-2. **Peterborough Utd.** in their first season in the Football League (1960-1) not only won the Fourth Division but set the all-time scoring record for the League of 134 goals. **Hereford Utd.** were promoted from the Fourth Division in their first League season, 1972-3. **Wycombe Wand.** were promoted from the Third Division (via the play-offs) in their first League season, 1993-4.

Record winning sequence: 14 consecutive League victories by three clubs (all in Second Division): **Manchester Utd.** 1904-5, **Bristol City** 1905-6 and **Preston N.E.** 1950-1. Since then, **Reading** have gone closest to equalling this record with 13 successive League wins in Div. 3 from the start of season 1985-6.

Best starts in 'old' First Division: 11 consecutive victories by **Tottenham** in 1960-1; 10 by **Manchester Utd.** in 1985-6. **Newcastle Utd.** won their first 11 matches in the **'new' First Division** in 1992-3.

Longest unbeaten sequence (all competitions): 40 by **Nott'm. Forest**, March-December 1978. It comprised 21 wins, 19 draws (in 29 League matches, 6 League Cup, 4 European Cup, 1 Charity Shield).

Longest unbeaten start to League season: 29 matches – Leeds Utd., Div. 1 1973-4 (19 wins, 10 draws, goals 51-16); Liverpool, Div. 1 1987-8 (22 wins, 7 draws, goals 67-13).

Most consecutive League matches unbeaten in a season: 30 Burnley (21 wins, 9 draws, goals 68-17), September 6, 1920 – March 25, 1921, Div. 1.

Longest winning sequence in Div. 1: 13 matches by Tottenham – last two of season 1959-60, first 11 of 1960-1.

Longest winning one-season sequences in Championship: 13 matches by Preston N.E. in 1891-2 (September 12–January 2); 13 by Sunderland, also in 1891-2 (November 14–April 2).

Premier League – best starts to season: 12 games unbeaten – Nott'm. Forest in 1995-6, Arsenal in 1997-8, Aston Villa in 1998-9.

Premier League – most consecutive wins: 10 by Arsenal, March-April 1998.

Premier League's record unbeaten run: 25 matches (15W, 10D) by Nott'm. Forest (Feb.-Nov. 1995). It ended with a 7-0 defeat at Blackburn Rov.

Record home-win sequences: Bradford Park Avenue won 25 successive home games in Div. 3 North – the last 18 in 1926-7 and the first 7 the following season. Longest run of home wins in the top division is 21 by Liverpool – the last 9 of 1971-2 and the first 12 of 1972-3.

WORST SEQUENCES

Cambridge Utd. experienced the longest run without a win in Football League history in season 1983-4: 31 matches (21 lost, 10 drawn) between October 8 and April 23. They finished bottom of the Second Division.

Previous worst no-win League sequence was 30 by Crewe Alexandra (Div. 3 North) in season 1956-7.

Worst losing start to a League season: 12 consecutive defeats by Manchester Utd. (Div. 1) in 1930-1.

Worst Premier League start: Swindon Town 15 matches without win (6 draws, 9 defeats), 1993-4.

Worst Premier League sequence: Nott'm. Forest 19 matches without win (7 draws, 12 defeats), 1998-9.

Premier League – most consecutive defeats: 8 by Ipswich Town in 1994-5, Manchester City in 1995-6, Crystal Palace in 1997-8, Charlton in 1998-9.

Longest non-winning start to League season: 25 matches (4 draws, 21 defeats) by Newport County, Div. 4 (Aug. 15, 1970 – Jan. 9, 1971). Worst no-win League starts since then: 16 matches by Burnley (9 draws, 7 defeats in Div. 2, 1979-80); 16 by Hull City (10 draws, 6 defeats in Div. 2, 1989-90); 16 by Sheffield Utd. (4 draws, 12 defeats in Div. 1, 1990-91).

Most consecutive League defeats: 18 by Darwen (Div. 1) 1898-9. In modern times: 15 by Walsall (Div. 2, 1988-9), longest such sequence since last War.

Most League defeats in season: 33 by Rochdale (Div. 3 North) 1931-2; by Cambridge Utd. (Div. 3) 1984-5; by Newport County (Div. 4) 1987-8; by Chester City (Div. 2) 1992-3.

Most home League defeats in season: 18 by Cambridge Utd. (Div. 3, 1984-5).

Away League defeats record: 24 in row by Nelson (Div. 3 North) – 3 in April 1930 followed by all 21 in season 1930-31. They then dropped out of the League.

Biggest defeat in Champions' season: During Newcastle Utd.'s Championship-winning season in 1908-9, they were beaten 9-1 at home by Sunderland on December 5.

WORST START BY EVENTUAL CHAMPIONS

Sunderland took only 2 points from their first 7 matches in season 1912-13 (2 draws, 5 defeats). They won 25 of the remaining 31 games to clinch their fifth League title.

UNBEATEN LEAGUE SEASON

Only two clubs have completed a Football League season unbeaten: Preston N.E. (22 matches in 1888-9, the League's first season) and Liverpool (28 matches in Div. 2, 1893-4).

240

100 PER CENT HOME RECORDS

Five clubs have won every home League match in a season, four of them in the old Second Division: **Liverpool** (14) in 1893-4, **Bury** (15) in 1894-5, **Sheffield Wed.** (17) in 1899-1900 and **Birmingham City** (17) in 1902-3. The last club to do it, **Brentford**, won all 21 home games in Div. 3 South in 1929-30.

. **Rotherham Utd.** just failed to equal that record in 1946-7. They won their first 20 home matches in Div. 3 North, then drew the last 3-3 v Rochdale.

WORST HOME RUN

Most consecutive home League defeats: 8 by **Rochdale,** who took only 11 points in Div. 3 North in season 1931-2.

Between November 1958 and October 1959 **Portsmouth** drew 2 and lost 14 out of 16 consecutive home games.

MOST AWAY WINS IN SEASON

Doncaster Rov. won 18 of their 21 away League fixtures when winning the Div. 3 North Championship in 1946-7.

AWAY WINS RECORD

Most **consecutive away League wins: 10 by Tottenham** (Div. 1) – 8 at start of 1960-1, after ending previous season with 2 away victories.

100 PER CENT HOME WINS ON ONE DAY

Div. 1 – All 11 home teams won on Feb. 13, 1926 and on Dec. 10, 1955. **Div. 2** – All 12 home teams won on Nov. 26, 1988. **Div. 3**, all 12 home teams won in the week-end programme of Oct. 18-19, 1968.

NO HOME WINS IN DIV. ON ONE DAY

Div. 1 – 8 away wins, 3 draws in 11 matches on Sept. 6, 1986. **Div. 2** – 7 away wins, 4 draws in 11 matches on Dec. 26, 1987. **Premier League** – 6 away wins, 5 draws in 11 matches on Dec. 26, 1994.

In the week-end **Premiership** programme on Dec. 7-8-9, 1996 there was not one home win in the ten games (4 aways, 6 draws).

MOST DRAWS IN A SEASON (FOOTBALL LEAGUE)

23 by **Norwich City** (Div. 1, 1978-9), **Exeter City** (Div. 4, 1986-7). **Cardiff City** and **Hartlepool Utd.** (both Div. 3, 1997-8). Norwich City played 42 matches, the others 46.

MOST DRAWS IN ONE DIV. ON ONE DAY

On September 18, 1948 **nine** out of 11 First Division matches were drawn.

MOST DRAWS IN PREMIER DIV. PROGRAMME

Over the week-end of December 2-3-4, 1995, seven out of the ten matches finished level.

HIGHEST-SCORING DRAWS IN LEAGUE

Leicester City 6, Arsenal 6 (Div. 1 April 21, 1930) and **Charlton Athletic 6, Middlesbrough 6** (Div 2. October 22, 1960)

Latest 6-6 draw in first-class football was between Tranmere Rov. and Newcastle Utd. in the Zenith Data Systems Cup 1st. Round on October 1, 1991. The score went from 3-3 at 90 minutes to 6-6 after extra time, and Tranmere Rov. won 3-2 on penalties.

Most recent 5-5 draws in top division: Southampton v Coventry City (Div. 1, May 4, 1982); Q.P.R. v Newcastle Utd. (Div. 1, Sept. 22, 1984).

DRAWS RECORDS

Most consecutive drawn matches in Football League: 8 by **Torquay Utd.** (Div. 3), Oct. 25 – Dec. 13, 1969.
   Longest sequence of draws by the same score: six 1-1 results by **Q.P.R.** in season 1957-8.
   Tranmere Rov. became the first club to play **five consecutive 0-0 League draws**, in season 1997-8.

IDENTICAL RECORDS

There is only **one instance** of two clubs in one division finishing a season with identical records. In 1907-8, **Blackburn Rov.** and **Woolwich Arsenal** were bracketed equal 14th. in the First Division with these figures: P38, W12, D12, L14, Goals 51-63, Pts. 36.
   The total of **1195 goals** scored in the Premier League in season 1993-4 was **repeated** in 1994-5.

CHAMPIONS OF ALL DIVISIONS

Wolves and **Burnley** are the only clubs to have won the Championships of the old **Divisions 1, 2, 3 and 4**. Wolves were also **Champions** of the **Third Division North**.

UPS & DOWNS RECORD

Northampton Town went from **Fourth Division** to **First** and back again in nine seasons (1961-9). **Carlisle Utd.** did the same from 1974-87.

NIGHTMARE STARTS

Most goals conceded by a goalkeeper on League debut: 13 by **Steve Milton** when Halifax Town lost 13-0 at Stockport Co. (Div. 3 North) on January 6, 1934.
   Post-war: 11 by Crewe Alexandra's new goalkeeper **Dennis Murray** (Div. 3 North) on September 29, 1951, when Lincoln City won 11-1.

RELEGATION ODD SPOTS

In season 1937-8, **Manchester City** were the highest-scoring team in the First Division with 80 goals (3 more than Champions Arsenal), but they finished in 21st place and were relegated – a year after winning the Championship. They scored more goals than they conceded (77).
   Twelve years earlier, in 1925-6, City went down to Division 2 despite totalling 89 goals – still the most scored in any division by a relegated team. Manchester City also scored 31 F.A. Cup goals that season, but lost the Final 1-0 to Bolton Wand.
   Cardiff City were relegated from Div. 1 in season 1928-9, despite conceding fewest goals in the division (59). They also scored fewest (43).

RELEGATION TREBLES

Two Football League clubs have been relegated three seasons in succession. **Bristol City** fell from First Division to Fourth in 1980-1-2, and **Wolves** did the same in 1984-5-6.

OLDEST CLUBS

Oldest Association Football Club is **Sheffield F.C.** (formed in 1855). The minute book for 1857 is still in existence.
   The oldest Football League clubs are **Notts Co.**, 1862; **Nott'm. Forest**, 1865; and **Sheffield Wed.**, 1866.

FOUR DIVISIONS

In **May, 1957**, the Football League decided to re-group the two sections of the Third Division into Third and Fourth Divisions in **season 1958-9**.

The Football League was reduced to three divisions on the formation of the F.A. Premier League in **1992**.

THREE UP – THREE DOWN

The Football League Annual General Meeting of June 1973 agreed to adopt the promotion and relegation system of three up and three down.

The **new system** came into effect in **season 1973-4** and applied only to the first three divisions; four clubs were still relegated from the Third and four promoted from the Fourth.

It was the first change in the promotion and relegation system for the top two divisions in 81 years.

MOST LEAGUE APPEARANCES

Players with more than 700 Football League appearances (as at end of season 1998-9):-

1005   **Peter Shilton** 1966-97 (286 Leicester City, 110 Stoke City, 202 Nott'm. Forest, 188 Southampton, 175 Derby Co., 34 Plymouth Argyle, 1 Bolton Wand., 9 Leyton Orient).

842   **Tony Ford** 1975-98 (423 Grimsby Town, 9 Sunderland, 112 Stoke City, 114 W.B.A., 5 Bradford City, 76 Scunthorpe Utd., 103 Mansfield Town).

824   **Terry Paine** 1956-77 (713 Southampton, 111 Hereford).

795   **Tommy Hutchison** 1968-91 (165 Blackpool, 314 Coventry City, 46 Manchester City, 92 Burnley, 178 Swansea City). In addition, 68 Scottish League apps. for Alloa 1965-68, giving career League app. total of 863.

782   **Robbie James** 1973-94 (484 Swansea City, 48 Stoke City, 87 Q.P.R., 23 Leicester City, 89 Bradford City, 51 Cardiff City).

777   **Alan Oakes** 1959-84 (565 Manchester City, 211 Chester City, 1 Port Vale).

770   **John Trollope** 1960-80 (all for Swindon Town, record total for one club).

764   **Jimmy Dickinson** 1946-65 (all for Portsmouth).

761   **Roy Sproson** 1950-72 (all for Port Vale).

760   **Mick Tait** 1974-97 (64 Oxford Utd., 106 Carlisle Utd., 33 Hull City, 240 Portsmouth, 99 Reading, 79 Darlington, 139 Hartlepool Utd.).

758   **Billy Bonds** 1964-88 (95 Charlton Athletic, 663 West Ham Utd.).

758   **Ray Clemence** 1966-88 (48 Scunthorpe Utd., 470 Liverpool, 240 Tottenham).

757   **Pat Jennings** 1963-86 (48 Watford, 472 Tottenham, 237 Arsenal).

757   **Frank Worthington** 1966-88 (171 Huddersfield Town, 210 Leicester City, 84 Bolton Wand., 75 Birmingham City, 32 Leeds Utd., 19 Sunderland, 34 Southampton, 31 Brighton & H.A., 59 Tranmere Rov., 23 Preston N.E., 19 Stockport Co.).

749   **Ernie Moss** 1968-88 (469 Chesterfield, 35 Peterborough Utd., 57 Mansfield Town, 74 Port Vale, 11 Lincoln City, 44 Doncaster Rov., 26 Stockport Co., 23 Scarborough, 10 Rochdale).

746   **Les Chapman** 1966-88 (263 Oldham Athletic, 133 Huddersfield Town, 70 Stockport Co., 139 Bradford City, 88 Rochdale, 53 Preston N.E.).

743   **Alan Ball** 1963-84 (146 Blackpool, 208 Everton, 177 Arsenal, 195 Southampton, 17 Bristol Rov.).

743   **John Hollins** 1963-84 (465 Chelsea, 151 Q.P.R., 127 Arsenal).

743   **Phil Parkes** 1968-91 (52 Walsall, 344 Q.P.R., 344 West Ham Utd., 3 Ipswich Town).

737   **Steve Bruce** 1979-99 (205 Gillingham, 141 Norwich City, 309 Manchester Utd. 72 Birmingham City, 10 Sheffield Utd.).

732   **Mick Mills** 1966-88 (591 Ipswich Town, 103 Southampton, 38 Stoke City).

731	**Asa Hartford** 1967-90 (213 W.B.A., 260 Manchester City, 3 Nott'm. F., 81 Everton, 28 Norwich City, 81 Bolton Wand., 45 Stockport Co., 4 Oldham Athletic, 16 Shrewsbury Town).
731	**Ian Callaghan** 1959-81 (640 Liverpool, 76 Swansea City, 15 Crewe Alexandra).
725	**Steve Perryman** 1969-90 (655 Tottenham, 17 Oxford Utd., 53 Brentford).
722	**Martin Peters** 1961-81 (302 West Ham Utd., 189 Tottenham, 207 Norwich City, 24 Sheffield Utd.).
718	**Mike Channon** 1966-86 (511 Southampton, 72 Manchester City, 4 Newcastle Utd., 9 Bristol Rov., 88 Norwich City, 34 Portsmouth).
718	**Phil Neal** 1968-89 (186 Northampton Town, 455 Liverpool, 77 Bolton Wand.).
716	**Ron Harris** 1961-83 (655 Chelsea, 61 Brentford).
716	**Mike Summerbee** 1959-79 (218 Swindon Town, 357 Manchester City, 51 Burnley, 3 Blackpool, 87 Stockport Co.).
714	**Glenn Cockerill** 1976-98 (186 Lincoln City, 26 Swindon Town, 62 Sheffield Utd., 387 Southampton, 90 Leyton Orient, 40 Fulham, 23 Brentford).
705	**John Wile** 1968-86 (205 Peterborough Utd., 500 W.B.A.).

● **Stanley Matthews** made 701 League apps. 1932-65 (322 Stoke City, 379 Blackpool), incl. 3 for Stoke City at start of 1939-40 before season abandoned (war).

● Goalkeeper **John Burridge** made a total of 771 League appearances in a 28-season career in English and Scottish football (1968-96). He played 691 games for 15 English clubs (Workington, Blackpool, Aston Villa, Southend Utd., Crystal Palace, Q.P.R., Wolves, Derby Co., Sheffield Utd., Southampton, Newcastle Utd., Scarborough, Lincoln City, Manchester City and Darlington) and 80 for 5 Scottish clubs (Hibernian, Aberdeen, Dumbarton, Falkirk and Queen of the South).

LONGEST LEAGUE SEQUENCE

Harold Bell, centre-half of Tranmere Rov., was ever-present for the first nine post-war seasons (1946-55), achieving a League record of 401 consecutive matches. Counting F.A. Cup and other games, his run of successive appearances totalled 459.

The longest League sequence since Bell's was 394 appearances by goalkeeper **Dave Beasant** for Wimbledon, Newcastle Utd. and Chelsea. His nine-year run began on August 29, 1981 and was ended by a broken finger sustained in Chelsea's League Cup-tie against Portsmouth on October 31, 1990. Beasant's 394 consecutive League games comprised 304 for Wimbledon (1981-8), 20 for Newcastle Utd. (1988-9) and 70 for Chelsea (1989-90).

Phil Neal made 366 consecutive First Division appearances for Liverpool between December 1974 and September 1983, a remarkable sequence for an outfield player in top-division football.

EVER-PRESENT DEFENCE

The **entire defence** of Huddersfield Town played in all 42 Second Division matches in season 1952-3, namely, Bill Wheeler (goal), Ron Staniforth and Laurie Kelly (full-backs), Bill McGarry, Don McEvoy and Len Quested (half-backs). In addition, Vic Metcalfe played in all 42 League matches at outside-left.

FIRST SUBSTITUTE USED IN LEAGUE

Keith Peacock (Charlton Athletic), away to Bolton Wand. (Div. 2) on August 21, 1965.

FROM PROMOTION TO CHAMPIONS

Clubs who have become Champions of England a year after winning promotion: **Liverpool** 1905, 1906; **Everton** 1931, 1932; **Tottenham** 1950, 1951; **Ipswich Town** 1961, 1962; **Nott'm. Forest** 1977, 1978. The first four were placed top in both seasons: Forest finished third and first.

THREE-NATION CHAMPION

Trevor Steven earned eight Championship medals, in three countries: two with Everton (1985, 1987); five with Rangers (1990, 1991, 1993, 1994, 1995) and one with Marseille in 1992.

LEEDS NO-WAY AWAY

Leeds Utd., in 1992-3, provided the first instance of a club failing to win an away League match in the season following Championship success.

PIONEERS IN 1888 AND 1992

Three clubs among the twelve who formed the Football League in 1888 were also founder members of the F.A. Premier League: **Aston Villa**, **Blackburn Rov.** and **Everton**.

CHAMPIONS (MODERN) WITH TWO CLUBS – PLAYERS

Francis Lee (Manchester City 1968, Derby Co. 1975); **Ray Kennedy** (Arsenal 1971, Liverpool 1979, 1980, 1982); **Archie Gemmill** (Derby Co. 1972, 1975, Nott'm. F. 1978); **John McGovern** (Derby Co. 1972, Nott'm. F. 1978) **Larry Lloyd** (Liverpool 1973, Nott'm. F. 1978); **Peter Withe** (Nott'm. F. 1978, Aston Villa 1981); **John Lukic** (Arsenal 1989, Leeds Utd. 1992); **Kevin Richardson** (Everton 1985, Arsenal 1989); **Eric Cantona** (Leeds Utd. 1992, Manchester Utd. 1993, 1994, 1996, 1997); **David Batty** (Leeds Utd. 1992, Blackburn Rov. 1995), **Bobby Mimms** (Everton 1987, Blackburn Rov. 1995).

CLUB CLOSURES

Four clubs have left the Football League in mid-season: **Leeds City** (expelled Oct. 1919); **Wigan Athletic** (Oct. 1931, debts of £20,000); **Accrington Stanley** (March 1962, debts £62,000); **Aldershot** (March 1992, debts £1.2m.). **Maidstone Utd.**, with debts of £650,000, closed August 1992, on the eve of the season.

FOUR-DIVISION MEN

In season 1986-7, goalkeeper **Eric Nixon**, became the first player to appear in **all four divisions** of the Football League **in one season**. He served two clubs in Div. 1: Manchester City (5 League games) and Southampton (4); in Div. 2 Bradford City (3); in Div. 3 Carlisle Utd. (16); and in Div. 4 Wolves (16). Total appearances: 44.

Harvey McCreadie, a teenage forward, played in four divisions over two seasons inside a calendar year – from Accrington (Div. 3) to Luton Town (Div. 1) in January 1960, to Div. 2 with Luton Town later that season and to Wrexham (Div. 4) in November.

FATHERS & SONS

When player-manager **Ian Bowyer** (39) and **Gary Bowyer** (18) appeared together in the **Hereford Utd.** side at Scunthorpe Utd. (Div.4, April 21, 1990), they provided the first instance of father and son playing in the same team in a Football League match for 39 years. Ian Bowyer played as substitute, and Gary scored Hereford's injury-time equaliser in a 3-3 draw.

Alec (39) and **David** (just 17) **Herd** were the previous father-and-son duo in League football – for **Stockport Co.**, 2-0 winners at Hartlepool Utd. (Div.3 North) on May 5, 1951.

When **Preston N.E.** won 2-1 at Bury in Div. 3 on January 13, 1990, the opposing goalkeepers were brothers: **Alan Kelly** (21) for Preston N.E. and **Gary** (23) for Bury. Their father, **Alan Kelly Senior** (who kept goal for Preston N.E. in the 1964 F.A. Cup Final and won 47 Rep. of Ireland caps) flew from America to watch the sons he taught to keep goal line up on opposite sides.

FATHER & SON ON OPPOSITE SIDES

It happened for the first time in F.A. Cup history (1st. Qual. Round on Sept. 14, 1996) when 21-year-old **Nick Scaife** (Bishop Auckland) faced his father **Bobby** (41), who played for Pickering. Both were in midfield. Home side Bishops won 3-1.

THREE BROTHERS IN DIV. 1 SIDE

Southampton provided the first instance for 65 years of three brothers appearing together in a First Division side when **Danny Wallace** (24) and his 19-year-old twin brothers **Rodney** and **Ray** played against Sheffield Wed.on October 22, 1988. In all, they made 25 appearances together for Southampton until September 1989.

A previous instance in Div. 1 was provided by the Middlesbrough trio, **William**, **John** and **George Carr** with 24 League appearances together from January 1920 to October 1923.

The **Tonner** brothers, **Sam**, **James** and **Jack**, played together in 13 Second Division matches for Clapton Orient in season 1919-20.

SIR TOM DOES THE HONOURS

Sir Tom Finney, England and Preston N.E. legend, opened the Football League's new headquarters on their return to Preston on Feb. 23, 1999. Preston had been the League's original base for 70 years before they moved to Lytham St. Annes in 1959.

SHORTEST MATCH

The 0-0 score in the **Bradford City v Lincoln City Third Division fixture** on May 11, 1985, abandoned through fire after 40 minutes, was subsequently confirmed as a result. It is the shortest officially completed League match on record, and only the third instance in Football League history of the score of an unfinished match being allowed to stand.

The other occasions: **Middlesbrough 4, Oldham Athletic 1** (Div. 1, April 3, 1915), abandoned after 55 minutes when Oldham Athletic defender Billy Cook refused to leave the field after being sent off; **Barrow 7, Gillingham 0** (Div. 4, Oct. 9, 1961), abandoned after 75 minutes because of bad light, the match having started late because of Gillingham's delayed arrival.

The last 60 seconds of **Birmingham City v Stoke City** (Div. 3, 1-1, on Feb. 29, 1992) were played behind locked doors. The ground had been cleared after a pitch invasion.

A First Division fixture, **Sheffield Wed. v Aston Villa** (Nov. 26, 1898), was abandoned through bad light after 79½ mins. with Wed. leading 3-1. The Football League ruled that the match should be completed, and the remaining 10½ minutes were played **four months later** (Mar. 13, 1899), when Wed. added another goal to make the result 4-1.

A crucial **Manchester derby** (Div.1) was abandoned after 85 minutes, and the result stood, on April 27, 1974, when a pitch invasion at Old Trafford followed the only goal, scored for City by Denis Law, which relegated Manchester Utd. – Law's former club.

F.A. CUP RECORDS

CHIEF WINNERS

Ten Times: Manchester Utd.
Eight Times: Tottenham.
Seven Times: Aston Villa, Arsenal.
Three Times in Succession: The Wanderers (1876-7-8) and Blackburn Rov. (1884-5-6).
Trophy Handed Back: The F.A. Cup became the Wanderers' absolute property in 1878, but they handed it back to the Association on condition that it was not to be won outright by any club.
In Successive Years by Professional Clubs: Blackburn Rov. (in 1890 and 1891); Newcastle Utd. (in 1951 and 1952); Tottenham (in 1961 and 1962) and Tottenham again (in 1981 and 1982).

Record Final-tie score: Bury 6, Derby Co. 0 (1903).
Most F.A. Cup wins at Wembley: Manchester Utd. 9, Arsenal 7, Tottenham 6, Newcastle Utd. 5, Liverpool 5.

F.A. CUP: SECOND DIVISION WINNERS

Notts Co. (1894), Wolves (1908), Barnsley (1912), West Bromwich Albion (1931), Sunderland (1973), Southampton (1976), West Ham Utd. (1980). When Tottenham won the Cup in 1901 they were a Southern League club.

THIRD DIVISION SEMI-FINALISTS

Millwall (1937), Port Vale (1954), York City (1955), Norwich City (1959), Crystal Palace (1976), Plymouth Argyle (1984).
   Chesterfield, from the modern Second Division (the old Third), reached the semi-final in 1997.

FOURTH DIVISION QUARTER-FINALISTS

Oxford Utd. (1964), Colchester Utd. (1971), Bradford City (1976), Cambridge Utd. (1990).

F.A. CUP – FOUR TROPHIES

The latest F.A. Cup, first presented at Wembley in 1992, is a replica of the one it replaced, which had been in existence since 1911. 'It was falling apart and was not going to last much longer, said the FA.'
   The new trophy is the fourth F.A. Cup. These were its predecessors:
1895 First stolen from shop in Birmingham while held by Aston Villa. Never seen again.
1910 Second presented to Lord Kinnaird on completing 21 years as F.A. president.
1992 Third 'gracefully retired' after 80 years' service (1911-91).
There are three F.A. Cups currently in existence. The retired model is still used for promotional work. The present trophy stays with the winners until the following March. A third, identical Cup is secreted in the F.A. vaults as cover against loss of the existing trophy.

FINALISTS RELEGATED

Four clubs have reached the F.A. Cup Final in a season of relegation, and all lost at Wembley: Manchester City 1926, Leicester City 1969, Brighton & H.A. 1983, Middlesbrough 1997.

GIANT-KILLING IN F.A. CUP

(* Home team; R = Replay; Season 1999 = 1998-9)

1999	*Bedlington T 4	Colchester Utd. ... 1	1997	*Blackpool 0	Hednesford 1
1999	*Hednesford 3	Barnet 1	1997	*Cambridge Utd. . 0	Woking 2
1999	*Mansfield Town .. 1	Southport 0	1997	*Leyton O. 1	Stevenage 2
1999	*Rushden & D 1	Shrewsbury Town . 0	1997	*Hednesford 1	York City 0
1999	*Southend Utd. ... 0	Doncaster Rov. 1	1997	*Chesterfield 1	Nott'm. Forest 0
1999	*Yeovil Town 2	Northampton T 0	1996	*Hitchin 2	Bristol Rov. 1
1999	*Aston Villa 0	Fulham 2	1996	*Woking 2	Barnet 1R
1998	*Hull City 0	Hednesford 2	1996	*Bury 0	Blyth Spartans ... 2
1998	Lincoln City 3	Emley 3R	1996	*Gravesend 2	Colchester Utd. ... 0
	(at H'field; Emley won on pens).		1995	*Kingstonian 2	Brighton & H.A. ... 1
1998	*Leyton O 0	Hendon 1R	1995	*Enfield 1	Cardiff City 0
1998	*Swindon Town ... 1	Stevenage 2	1995	*Marlow 2	Oxford Utd. 0
1998	*Stevenage 2	C'bridge Utd. 1	1995	*Woking 1	Barnet 0R
1997	*Millwall 0	Woking 1R	1995	*Hitchin 4	Hereford 2R
1997	*Brighton & H.A. .. 1	Sudbury Town ... 1R	1995	*Torquay Utd. 0	Enfield 1R
	(Sudbury won on pens).		1995	*Altrincham 1	Wigan Athletic 0

1995	*Wrexham 2	Ipswich Town 1
1995	*Scarboro' 1	Port Vale 0
1994	*Colchester Utd. .. 3	Sutton 4
1994	*Yeovil 1	Fulham 0
1994	*Torquay Utd. 0	Sutton 1
1994	*Halifax Town 2	W.B.A. 1
1994	*Birmingham C. .. 1	Kid'minster 2
1994	*Stockport Co. 2	Q.P.R. 1
1994	*Liverpool 0	Bristol City 1R
1994	*Arsenal 1	Bolton Wand. 3R
1994	*Leeds Utd. 2	Oxford Utd. 3R
1994	*Luton Town 2	Newcastle Utd. . 0R
1994	*Kidderminster 1	Preston N.E. 0
1994	*Cardiff City 1	Manchester City .. 0
1993	*Hereford 1	Yeovil 2R
1993	*Torquay Utd. 2	Yeovil 5
1993	*Altrincham 2	Chester City 0R
1993	*Cardiff City 2	Bath 3
1993	*Chesterfield 2	Macclesfield 2R
	(Macclesfield Town won on pens.)	
1993	*Marine 4	Halifax Town 1
1993	*Stafford 2	Lincoln City 1R
1993	*Hartlepool Utd. .. 1	Crystal Palace 0
1993	*Liverpool 0	Bolton Wand. 2R
1992	*Fulham 0	Hayes 2
1992	*Crawley 4	Northampton 2
1992	*Telford 2	Stoke City 1R
1992	*Aldershot 0	Enfield 1
1992	*Halifax Town 1	Witton A. 2R
1992	*Maidstone 1	Kettering 2
1992	*Walsall 2	Yeovil 1R
1992	*Farnborough 4	Torquay Utd. 3
1992	*Wrexham 2	Arsenal 1
1991	*Scarboro' 0	Leek 2
1991	*Northampton 0	Barnet 1R
1991	*Hayes 1	Cardiff City 0R
1991	*Chorley 2	Bury 1
1991	*Shrewsbury T 1	Wimbledon 0
1991	*W.B.A. 2	Woking 4
1990	*Aylesbury 1	Southend Utd. 0
1990	*Scarborough 0	Whitley Bay 1
1990	*Welling 1	Gillingham 0R
1990	*Whitley Bay 2	Preston N.E. 0
1990	*Northampton 1	Coventry City 0
1990	*Cambridge Utd. .. 1	Millwall 0R
1989	*Sutton 2	Coventry City 1
1989	*Halifax Town 2	Kettering 3R
1989	*Kettering 2	Bristol Rov. 1
1989	*Bognor 2	Exeter City 1
1989	*Leyton Orient 0	Enfield 1R
1989	*Altrincham 3	Lincoln City 2
1989	*Wrexham 2	Runcorn 3R
1988	*Sutton 3	Aldershot 0
1988	*Peterborough 1	Sutton 3
1988	*Carlisle Utd. 2	Macclesfield 4
1988	*Macc'field 4	Rotherham Utd. ... 0
1988	*Chester City 0	Runcorn 1
1988	*Cambridge Utd. .. 0	Yeovil 1
1987	*Caernarfon 1	Stockport Co. 0

1987	Chorley 3	Wolves 0R
	(at Bolton Wand.)	
1987	*Telford 3	Burnley 0
1987	*York City 1	Caernarfon 2R
1987	*Aldershot 3	Oxford Utd. 0
1987	*Wigan Athletic ... 1	Norwich City 0
1987	*Charlton Ath. 1	Walsall 2
1986	*Stockport Co. 0	Telford 1
1986	*Wycombe W. 2	Colchester Utd. ... 0
1986	*Dagenham 2	Cambridge Utd. .. 1
1986	*Blackpool 1	Altrincham 2
1986	*Birmingham C. ... 1	Altrincham 2
1986	*Peterboro' 1	Leeds Utd. 0
1985	*Telford 2	Lincoln City 1
1985	*Preston N.E. 1	Telford 4
1985	*Telford 2	Bradford City 1
1985	*Telford 3	Darlington 0R
1985	*Blackpool 0	Altrincham 1
1985	*Wimbledon 1	Nott'm. Forest ... 0R
1985	*Orient 2	W.B.A. 1
1985	*Dagenham 1	Peterborough 0
1985	*Swindon Town 1	Dagenham 2R
1985	*York City 1	Arsenal 0
1984	*Halifax Town 1	Whitby 3
1984	*Bournemouth 2	Manchester Utd. .. 0
1984	*Telford 3	Stockport Co. 0
1984	*Telford 3	Northampton 2R
1984	Telford 4	*Rochdale 1
1983	*Cardiff City 2	Weymouth 3
1981	*Exeter City 3	Leicester City ... 1R
1981	*Exeter City 4	Newcastle Utd. . 0R
1980	*Halifax Town 1	Manchester City .. 0
1980	*Harlow 1	Leicester City ... 0R
1980	*Chelsea 0	Wigan Athletic 1
1979	*Newport 2	West Ham Utd. 1
1978	*Wrexham 4	Newcastle 1R
1978	*Stoke City 2	Blyth S 3
1976	*Leeds Utd. 0	Crystal Palace 1
1975	*Brighton & H.A. . 0	Leatherhead 1
1975	*Burnley 0	Wimbledon 1
1972	*Hereford 2	Newcastle 1R
1971	*Colchester Utd. ... 3	Leeds Utd. 2
1969	*Mansfield Town .. 3	West Ham Utd. ... 0
1967	*Swindon Town ... 3	West Ham Utd. . 0R
1967	*Manchester U. ... 1	Norwich City 2
1966	*Ipswich Town 2	Southport 3R
1965	*Peterboro' 2	Arsenal 1
1964	*Newcastle Utd. ... 1	Bedford Town 2
1964	*Aldershot 2	Aston Villa 1R
1961	*Coventry City 1	Kings Lynn 2
1961	*Chelsea 1	Crewe Alex. 2
1960	*Manchester City . 1	South'ton 5
1959	*Norwich City 3	Manchester U 0
1959	*Worcester 2	Liverpool 1
1959	*Tooting 3	Bournemouth 1
1959	*Tooting 2	Northampton 1
1958	*Newcastle Utd. .. 1	Scunthorpe Utd. .. 3
1957	*Wolves 3	Bournemouth 1
1957	*Bournemouth 3	Tottenham 1

248

1957	*Derby Co. 1	N. Brighton 3	1949	*Yeovil Town 2	Sunderland 1

1957 *Derby Co. 1   N. Brighton 3   1949 *Yeovil Town 2   Sunderland 1
1956 *Derby Co. 1   Boston United 6   1948 *Colchester Utd. .. 1   Huddersfield 0
1955 *York City 2   Tottenham 1   1948 *Arsenal 0   Bradford City 1
1955 *Blackpool 0   York City 2   1938 *Chelmsford 4   Southampton 1
1954 *Arsenal 1   Norwich City 2   1933 *Walsall 2   Arsenal 0
1954 *Port Vale 2   Blackpool 0   1922 *Everton 0   Crystal Palace 6
1952 *Everton 1   Leyton Orient 3

YEOVIL TOP GIANT-KILLERS

Yeovil's second round victory against Northampton in season 1998-9 gave them a total of 18 F.A. Cup wins against League opponents. They hold another non-League record by reaching the third round 12 times.

This is Yeovil's triumphant Cup record against League clubs: 1924-5 Bournemouth 3-2; 1934-5 Crystal Palace 3-0, Exeter City 4-1; 1938-9 Brighton & H.A. 2-1; 1948-9 Bury 3-1, Sunderland 2-1; 1958-9 Southend Utd. 1-0; 1960-1 Walsall 1-0; 1963-4 Southend Utd. 1-0, Crystal Palace 3-1; 1970-1 Bournemouth 1-0; 1972-3 Brentford 2-1; 1987-8 Cambridge Utd. 1-0; 1991-2 Walsall 1-0; 1992-3 Torquay Utd. 5-2, Hereford 2-1; 1993-4 Fulham 1-0; 1998-9 Northampton 2-0.

NON-LEAGUE BEST IN F.A. CUP

Since League football began in 1888, three non-League clubs have reached the F.A. Cup Final. **Sheffield Wed.** (Football Alliance) were runners-up in 1890, as were **Southampton** (Southern League) in 1900 and 1902. **Tottenham** won the Cup as a Southern League team in 1901.

Otherwise, the **furthest progress** by non-League clubs has been to the **5th. Round** on 5 occasions: Colchester Utd. 1948, Yeovil 1949, Blyth Spartans 1978, Telford 1985 and Kidderminster 1994.

Greatest number of non-League sides to reach the **3rd. Round** is 6 in 1978: Blyth, Enfield, Scarborough, Tilbury, Wealdstone and Wigan Athletic.

Most to reach **Round 4**: 3 in 1957 (Rhyl, New Brighton, Peterborough Utd.) and 1975 (Leatherhead, Stafford and Wimbledon).

TOP-DIVISION SCALPS

Victories in F.A. Cup by non-League clubs over top-division teams this century include:-
1900-1 (Final, replay); **Tottenham** 3, Sheffield Utd. 1 (Tottenham then in Southern League); 1919-20 **Cardiff City** 2, Oldham Athletic 0, and Sheffield Wed. 0, **Darlington** 2; 1923-4 **Corinthians** 1, Blackburn Rov. 0; 1947-8 **Colchester Utd.** 1, Huddersfield Town 0; 1948-9 **Yeovil Town** 2, Sunderland 1; 1971-2 **Hereford Utd.** 2, Newcastle Utd. 1; 1974-5 Burnley 0, **Wimbledon** 1; 1985-6 Birmingham City 1, **Altrincham** 2; 1988-9 **Sutton Utd.** 2, Coventry City 1.

MOST WEMBLEY FINALS

Seven players have appeared in five F.A. Cup Finals at Wembley, replays excluded:-
- Joe Hulme (Arsenal: 1927, lost; 1930 won; 1932 lost; 1936 won; Huddersfield Town: 1938 lost).
- Johnny Giles (Manchester Utd.: 1963 won; Leeds Utd.: 1965 lost; 1970 drew at Wembley, lost replay at Old Trafford; 1972 won; 1973 lost).
- Pat Rice (all for Arsenal: 1971 won; 1972 lost; 1978 lost; 1979 won; 1980 lost).
- Frank Stapleton (Arsenal: 1978 lost; 1979 won; 1980 lost; Manchester Utd.: 1983 won; 1985 won).
- Ray Clemence (Liverpool: 1971 lost; 1974 won; 1977 lost; Tottenham: 1982 won; 1987 lost).
- Mark Hughes (Manchester Utd.: 1985 won; 1990 won; 1994 won; 1995 lost; Chelsea: 1997 won).
- John Barnes (Watford: 1984 lost; Liverpool: 1988 lost; 1989 won; 1996 lost; Newcastle Utd.: 1998, sub, lost): he was the first player to lose Wembley F.A. Cup Finals with three different clubs.

Stapleton, Clemence and Hughes also played in a replay, making six actual F.A. Cup Final appearances for each of them.

Glenn Hoddle also made six F.A. Cup Final appearances at Wembley: 5 for Tottenham (incl. 2 replays), in 1981, 1982 and 1987, and 1 for Chelsea as sub in 1994.

F.A. CUP SEMI-FINALS AT WEMBLEY

1991 Tottenham 3, Arsenal 1; **1993** Sheffield Wed. 2, Sheffield Utd. 1; Arsenal 1, Tottenham 0; **1994** Chelsea 2, Luton Town 0; Manchester Utd. 1, Oldham Athletic 1.

FIRST F.A. CUP ENTRANTS (1871-2)

Barnes, Civil Service, Crystal Palace, Clapham Rov., Donnington School (Spalding), Hampstead Heathens, Harrow Chequers, Hitchin, Maidenhead, Marlow, Queen's Park (Glasgow), Reigate Priory, Royal Engineers, Upton Park and Wanderers. Total 15. Three scratched.

    Record F.A. Cup entry .... **674 in 1921**

CUP 'FIRSTS'

Out of country: Cardiff City, by defeating Arsenal 1-0 in the 1927 Final at Wembley, became the first and only club to take the F.A. Cup out of England.

    All-English Winning XI: First club to win the F.A. Cup with all-English XI: W.B.A., in 1888 and again in 1931. Others since: Bolton Wand. (1958), Manchester City (1969), West Ham Utd. (1964 and 1975).

    Non-English Winning XI: Liverpool in 1986 (Mark Lawrenson, born Preston N.E., was a Rep. of Ireland player).

    Won both Cups: Old Carthusians won the F.A. Cup in 1881 and the F.A. Amateur Cup in 1894 and 1897. **Wimbledon** won Amateur Cup in 1963, F.A. Cup in 1988.

MOST GAMES NEEDED TO WIN F.A. CUP

Barnsley played a record 12 matches (20 hours' football) to win the F.A. Cup in season 1911-12. All six replays (one in Rd. 1, three in Rd. 4 and one in each of semi-final and Final) were brought about by goalless draws.

    Arsenal played 11 F.A. Cup games when winning the trophy in 1979. Five of them were in the 3rd. Rd. against Sheffield Wed..

LONGEST F.A. CUP TIES

6 matches (11 hours): **Alvechurch v Oxford City** (4th. qual. round, 1971-2). Alvechurch won 1-0.

5 matches (9 hours, 22 mins – record for competition proper): **Stoke City v Bury** (3rd. round, 1954-5). Stoke City won 3-2.

5 matches: Chelsea v Burnley (4th. round, 1955-6). Chelsea won 2-0.

5 matches: Hull City v Darlington (2nd. round, 1960-1). Hull City won 3-0.

5 matches: Arsenal v Sheffield Wed. (3rd. round, 1978-9). Arsenal won 2-0.

Other marathons (qualifying comp., all 5 matches, 9 hours): **Barrow v Gillingham** (last qual. round, 1924-5) – winners Barrow; **Leyton v Ilford** (3rd. qual. round, 1924-5) – winners Leyton; **Falmouth Town v Bideford** (3rd. qual. round, 1973-4) – winners Bideford.

End of Cup Final replays: The F.A. decided that, with effect from 1999, there would be no Cup Final replays. In the event of a draw after extra time, the match would be decided on penalties.

F.A. Cup marathons ended in season 1991-2, when the penalty shoot-out was introduced to decide ties still level after one replay and extra time.

● In 1932-3 **Brighton & H.A.** (Div. 3 South) played 11 F.A. Cup games, including replays, and scored 43 goals, without getting past Rd 5. They forgot to claim exemption and had to play from 1st Qual. Round.

LONGEST ROUND

The longest round in F.A. Cup history was the **third round** in **season 1962-3**. It took 66 days to complete, lasting from January 5 to March 11, and included 261 postponements because of bad weather.

LONGEST UNBEATEN F.A. CUP RUN

23 matches by **Blackburn Rov.** In winning the Cup in three consecutive years (1884-5-6), they won 21 ties (one in a replay), and their first Cup defeat in four seasons was in a first round replay of the next competition.

RE-STAGED F.A. CUP TIES

Sixth round, March 9, 1974: Newcastle Utd. 4, Nott'm. Forest 3. Match declared void by F.A. and ordered to be replayed following a pitch invasion after Newcastle Utd. had a player sent off. Forest claimed the hold-up caused the game to change its pattern. The tie went to two further matches at Goodison Park (0-0, then 1-0 to Newcastle Utd.).

Third round, January 5, 1985: Burton Albion 1, Leicester City 6 (at Derby Co.). Burton goalkeeper Paul Evans was hit on the head by a missile thrown from the crowd, and continued in a daze. The F.A. ordered the tie to be played again, behind closed doors at Coventry City (Leicester City won 1- 0).

First round replay, November 25, 1992: Peterborough 9 (Tony Philliskirk 5), Kingstonian 1. Match expunged from records because, at 3-0 after 57 mins, Kingstonian were reduced to ten men when goalkeeper Adrian Blake was concussed by a 50 pence coin thrown from the crowd. The tie was re-staged on the same ground behind closed doors (Peterborough Utd. won 1-0).

Fifth round: Within an hour of cup-holders Arsenal beating Sheffield Utd. 2-1 at Highbury on February 13, 1999, the Football Association took the unprecedented step of declaring the match void because an unwritten rule of sportsmanship had been broken. With United's Lee Morris lying injured, their goalkeeper Alan Kelly kicked the ball into touch. Play resumed with Arsenal's Ray Parlour throwing it in the direction of Kelly, but Nwankwo Kanu took possession and centred for Marc Overmars to score the 'winning' goal. After four minutes of protests by his team-mate manager Steve Bruce and his players, referee Peter Jones confirmed the goal. Both managers absolved Kanu of cheating but Arsenal's Arsene Wenger offered to replay the match. With the F.A. immediately approving, it was re-staged at Highbury ten days later (ticket prices halved) and Arsenal again won 2-1.

WAR-TIME MARATHON

Match of 203 minutes: Stockport Co.'s second-leg tie with Doncaster Rov. in the Third Division North Cup, March 30, 1946, lasted 203 minutes and a replay was still necessary. Both legs were drawn 2-2 and Doncaster Rov. won the replay 4-0.

F.A. CUP FINAL HAT-TRICKS

There have been only three in the history of the competition: **Billy Townley** (Blackburn Rov., 1890), **Jimmy Logan** (Notts Co., 1894) and **Stan Mortensen** (Blackpool, 1953).

FIVE WINNING MEDALS

The Hon. A.F. Kinnaird (The Wanderers and Old Etonians), **C.H.R. Wollaston** (The Wanderers) and **James Forrest** (Blackburn Rov.) each earned five F.A. Cup winners' medals. Kinnaird, later president of the F.A., played in nine of the first 12 F.A. Cup Finals, and was on the winning side three times for The Wanderers, in 1873 (captain), 1877, 1878 (captain), and twice as captain of Old Etonians (1879, 1882).

MOST WINNING MEDALS THIS CENTURY

4 – Mark Hughes (3 for Manchester Utd., 1 for Chelsea).

3 – 17 players: Dick Pym (3 clean sheets in Finals), **Bob Haworth, Jimmy Seddon, Harry Nuttall, Billy Butler** (all Bolton Wand.); **David Jack** (2 Bolton Wand., 1 Arsenal); **Bob Cowell, Jack Milburn, Bobby Mitchell** (all Newcastle Utd.); **Dave Mackay** (Tottenham); **Frank Stapleton** (1 Arsenal, 2 Manchester Utd.); **Bryan Robson** (3 times winning captain), **Arthur Albiston, Gary Pallister** (all Manchester Utd.); **Bruce Grobbelaar, Steve Nicol, Ian Rush** (all Liverpool).

MOST F.A. CUP APPEARANCES

88 by **Ian Callaghan** (79 for Liverpool, 7 for Swansea City, 2 for Crewe Alexandra); 87 by **John Barnes** (31 for Watford, 51 for Liverpool, 5 for Newcastle Utd.); 86 by **Stanley Matthews** (37 for Stoke City, 49 for Blackpool); 86 by **Peter Shilton** for six clubs (Leicester City, Stoke City, Nott'm. Forest, Southampton, Derby Co. and Plymouth Argyle); 84 by **Bobby Charlton** (80 for Manchester Utd., 4 for Preston N.E.).

THREE-CLUB FINALISTS

Three players have appeared in the F.A. Final for three clubs: **Harold Halse** for Manchester Utd. (1909), Aston Villa (1913) and Chelsea (1915); **Ernie Taylor** for Newcastle Utd. (1951), Blackpool (1953) and Manchester Utd. (1958); **John Barnes** for Watford (1984), Liverpool (1998, 1989, 1996) and Newcastle Utd. (1998).

CUP MAN WITH TWO CLUBS IN SAME SEASON

Stan Crowther, who played for Aston Villa against Manchester Utd. in the 1957 F.A. Cup Final, played for both Aston Villa and United. in the 1957-8 F.A. Cup competition. United signed him directly after the Munich air crash and, in the circumstances, he was given special dispensation to play for them also in the Cup, including the Final.

CAPTAIN'S CUP DOUBLE

Martin Buchan is the only player to have captained Scottish and English F.A. Cup-winning teams – Aberdeen in 1970 and Manchester Utd. in 1977.

MEDALS BEFORE AND AFTER

Two players appeared in F.A. Cup Final teams before and after the war: **Raich Carter** was twice a winner (Sunderland 1937, Derby Co. 1946) and **Willie Fagan** twice on the losing side (Preston N.E. 1937, Liverpool 1950).

STARS WHO MISSED OUT

Internationals who never won an F.A. Cup winner's medal include: **Tommy Lawton, Tom Finney, Johnny Haynes, Gordon Banks, George Best, Terry Butcher, Peter Shilton, Martin Peters, Nobby Stiles, Alan Ball** and **Malcolm Macdonald.**

CUP WINNERS AT NO COST

Not one member of **Bolton's.**' 1958 F.A. Cup-winning team cost the club a transfer fee. Five were Internationals and the eleven each joined the club. for a £10 signing-on fee.

ALL-INTERNATIONAL CUP WINNERS

In **Manchester Utd.'s** 1985 Cup-winning team v Everton, all 11 players were full Internationals, as was the substitute who played. So were ten of Everton's team.

NO-CAP CUP WINNERS

Sunderland, in 1973, were the last F.A. Cup-winning team not to include an International player, although some were capped later.

HIGH-SCORING SEMI-FINALS

The **record team score** in F.A. Cup semi-finals is 6: 1891-2 WBA 6, Nott'm. Forest 2; 1907-8 Newcastle Utd. 6, Fulham 0; 1933-4 Manchester City 6, Aston Villa 1.

Most goals in semi-finals (aggregate): 17 in 1892 (4 matches) and 1899 (5 matches). In modern times: 15 in 1958 (3 matches, including Manchester Utd. 5, Fulham 3 – highest-scoring semi-final since last war); 16 in 1989-90 (Crystal Palace 4, Liverpool 3; Manchester Utd. v Oldham Athletic 3-3, 2-1. **All 16 goals** in those three matches were scored by **different players**.

Last hat-trick in an F.A. Cup semi-final was scored by **Alex Dawson** for Manchester Utd. in 5-3 replay win against Fulham at Highbury in 1958.

FOUR SPECIAL AWAYS

For the only time in F.A. Cup history, **all four quarter-finals** in season 1986-7 were won by the away team.

F.A. CUP – DRAWS RECORD

In season 1985-6, **seven** of the eight F.A. Cup 5th. Round ties went to replays – a record for that stage of the competition.

LUCK OF THE DRAW

In the F.A. Cup on Jan. 11, 1947, eight of **London**'s ten Football League clubs involved in the 3rd. Round were drawn at home (including Chelsea v Arsenal). Only Crystal Palace played outside the capital (at Newcastle Utd.).

Contrast: In the 3rd. Round in Jan. 1992, Charlton Athletic were the only London club drawn at home (against Barnet), but the venue of the Farnborough v West Ham Utd. tie was reversed on police instruction. So Upton Park staged Cup-ties on successive days, with West Ham Utd. at home on the Saturday and Charlton Athletic (who shared the ground) on Sunday.

Arsenal were drawn away in every round on the way to reaching the F.A. Cup Finals of 1971 and 1972. **Manchester Utd.** won the Cup in 1990 without playing once at home.

The 1999 F.A. Cup finalists **Manchester Utd.** and **Newcastle Utd.** were both drawn at home every time in Rounds 3-6.

F.A. CUP: ALL TOP-DIVISION VICTIMS

Only instance of an F.A. Cup-winning club meeting top-division opponents in every round was provided by Manchester Utd. in 1947-8. They beat Aston Villa, Liverpool, Charlton Athletic, Preston N.E., then Derby Co. in the semi-final and Blackpool in the Final.

HOME ADVANTAGE

For the first time in F.A. Cup history, all eight ties in the 1992-3 5th. Round were won (no replays) by the **clubs drawn at home**. Only other instance of eight home wins at the 'last 16' stage of the F.A. Cup was in 1889-90, in what was then the 2nd. Round.

SIXTH-ROUND ELITE

For the first time in F.A. Cup 6th. Round history, dating from 1926, when the format of the competition changed, **all eight quarter-finalists** in 1995-6 were from the top division.

F.A. CUP SEMI-FINAL – DOUBLE DERBIES

There have been only two instances of both F.A. Cup semi-finals in the same year being local derbies: **1950** Liverpool beat Everton 2-0 (Maine Road), Arsenal beat Chelsea 1-0 after 2-2 draw (both at Tottenham); **1993** Arsenal beat Tottenham 1-0 (Wembley), Sheffield Wed. beat Sheffield Utd. 2-1 (Wembley).

CUP FINAL HYMN

'**Abide With Me**' was introduced into the F.A. Cup Final community singing in 1927, and has been sung ever since with the exception of 1959. So many complaints followed its omission that it was restored the following year.

TOP CLUB DISTINCTION

Since the Football League began in 1888, there has never been an F.A. Cup Final in which **neither club** represented the top division.

SPURS OUT – AND IN

Tottenham were banned, pre-season, from the 1994-5 F.A. Cup competition because of financial irregularities, but were readmitted on appeal and reached the semi-finals.

BROTHERS IN F.A. CUP FINAL TEAMS (Modern Times)

1950 Denis and Leslie Compton (Arsenal); **1952** George and Ted Robledo (Newcastle Utd.); **1967** Ron and Allan Harris (Chelsea); **1977** Jimmy and Brian Greenhoff (Manchester Utd.); **1996** and **1999** Gary and Phil Neville (Manchester Utd.)

F.A. CUP – FIRST SPONSORS

Littlewoods Pools became the first sponsors of the F.A. Cup in season 1994-5 in a £14m., 4-year deal.

French insurance giants **AXA** took over (season 1998-9) in a sponsorship worth £25m. over 4 years.

LEAGUE CUP RECORDS

(See also League Cup and Goalscoring Sections)

Highest scores: West Ham Utd. 10-0 v Bury (2nd. Rd., 2nd. Leg 1983-4; agg. 12-1); Liverpool 10-0 v Fulham (2nd. Rd., 1st. Leg 1986-7; agg. 13-2).

Most League Cup goals (career): 49 Geoff Hurst (43 West Ham Utd., 6 Stoke City, 1960-75); 49 Ian Rush (48 Liverpool, 1 Newcastle Utd., 1981-98).

Highest scorer (season): 12 Clive Allen (Tottenham 1986-7 in 9 apps).

Most goals in match: 6 Frank Bunn (Oldham Athletic v Scarborough, 3rd. Rd., 1989-90).

Fewest goals conceded by winners: 3 by Leeds Utd. (1967-8), Tottenham (1970-1), Aston Villa (1995-6).

Most winner's medals: 5 Ian Rush (Liverpool).

Most appearances in Final: 6 Kenny Dalglish (Liverpool 1978-87), Ian Rush (Liverpool 1981-95).

Alan Hardaker Man of the Match Award was introduced in the 1990 Final, in recognition of the League's late secretary who proposed the competition in 1960.

League Cup sponsors: Milk Cup 1981-6, Littlewoods Cup 1987-90, Rumbelows Cup 1991-2, Coca-Cola Cup 1993-8. Bass Brewers took over from season 1998-9 with a 5-year sponsorship of the Worthington Cup worth £23m.

Norwich City unique: In 1985, Norwich City became (and they remain) the only club to win a major domestic cup and be relegated in the same season. They won the League's Milk Cup and went down from the old First Division.

Liverpool's League Cup records: First club to win competition 5 times. **Ian Rush** first player to win 5 times. Rush also first to play in 8 winning teams in Cup Finals **at Wembley**, all with Liverpool (F.A. Cup 1986-89-92; League Cup 1981-82-83-84-95).

DISCIPLINE

SENDINGS-OFF

Season 1998-9 produced a **record total** of 425 dismissals in English first-class domestic football (previous record 376 in 1994-5).

They comprised 70 (top-division record) in the F.A. Carling Premiership; 301 in the Football (Nationwide) League, plus 3 in the play-offs; 31 League club players sent off in the AXA-sponsored F.A. Cup; 15 in the League (Worthington) Cup; 5 in the Auto Windscreens Shield.

After a two-season experiment, the League cup discontinued its self-contained disciplinary system in 1998-9.

Season-by-season dismissals from the Eighties: **1981-2**, 157 (132 League); **1982-3**, 242 (211 League); **1983-4**, 173 (150 League); **1984-5**, 183 (163 League); **1985-6**, 207 (185 League); **1986-7**, 219 (193 League); **1987-8**, 217 (197 League, incl. 2 in play-offs); **1988-9**, 192 (173 League, incl. 1 in play-offs); **1989-90**, 183 (162 in League, incl. 1 in play-offs); **1990-1**, 238 (204 League, incl. 2 in play-offs); **1991-2**, 278 (245 League, incl. 1 in play-offs); **1992-3**, 277 (229 in League, incl. 3 in play-offs); **1993-4**, 288 (239 in League, incl. 6 in play-offs); **1994-5**, 376 (309 in League, incl. 5 in play-offs); **1995-6**, 320 (279 in League, incl. 1 in play-offs); **1996-7**, 341 (300 League, incl. 5 in play-offs); **1997-8**, 321 (313 League, incl. 8 in play-offs); **1998-9**, 425 (304 in League, incl. 3 in play-offs).

November 20, 1982 was the **worst day** for dismissals **in football history** with 15 players sent off (3 League, 12 in the F.A. Cup first round). That was also the blackest day for disciplinary action in the F.A. Cup (previous worst – eight on January 9, 1915).

Most players ordered off in **Anglo-Scottish football on one day**: 17 on Dec. 14, 1985 (13 Football League, 4 Scottish League).

Most players sent off in **English League football on one day**: 15 on Oct. 31, 1998 (2 Prem. League, 13 Nationwide League).

Most players sent off in one **Football League programme**: 15 in week-end of Sat., Dec. 22 (11) and Sun., Dec. 23 (4), 1990.

● In the entire first season of post-war League football (1946-7) only 12 players were sent off, followed by 14 in 1949-50, and the total League dismissals for the first nine seasons after the war was 104.

The worst pre-war total was 28 in each of seasons 1921-2 and 1922-3.

ENGLAND SENDINGS-OFF

Paul Scholes became the seventh player England have had sent off – their first dismissal at Wembley – in international history (1872 to date) when he was shown the red card for two bookable offences in the European Championship qualifier against Sweden on June 5, 1999. The others are:

June 5, 1968 **Alan Mullery**   v Yugoslavia (Florence, Eur. Champ.)
June 6, 1973 **Alan Ball**   v Poland (Chorzow, World Cup qual.)
June 15, 1977 **Trevor Cherry**   v Argentina (Buenos Aires, friendly)
June 6, 1986 **Ray Wilkins**   v Morocco (Monterrey, World Cup Finals)
June 30, 1998 **David Beckham**   v Argentina (St. Etienne, World Cup Finals)
Sept. 5, 1998 **Paul Ince**   v Sweden (Stockholm, Eur. Champ. qual.)
Other countries: Most recent sendings-off of players representing the other Home Countries: **N. Ireland – Iain Dowie** v. Norway (Friendly, Belfast, March 1996); **Scotland – Matt Elliott** v Faroe Islands (European Champ., Toftir, June, 1999); **Wales – Vinnie Jones** v. Georgia (European Champ., Cardiff City, June 1995); **Rep. of Ireland – David Connolly** (v Belgium, World Cup play-off, Brussels, November 1997).

England dismissals at other levels:-
U-23 (4): **Stan Anderson** (v Bulgaria, Sofia, May 19, 1957); **Alan Ball** (v Austria, Vienna, June 2, 1965); **Kevin Keegan** (v E. Germany, Magdeburg, June 1, 1972); **Steve Perryman** (v Portugal, Lisbon, Nov. 19, 1974).
U-21 (12): **Sammy Lee** (v Hungary, Keszthely, June 5, 1981); **Mark Hateley** (v Scotland, Hampden Park, April 19, 1982); **Paul Elliott** (v Denmark, Maine Road, Manchester,

March 26, 1986); **Tony Cottee** (v W. Germany, Ludenscheid, September 8, 1987); **Julian Dicks** (v Mexico, Toulon, France, June 12, 1988); **Jason Dodd** (v Mexico, Toulon, May 29, 1991; 3 Mexico players also sent off in that match); **Matthew Jackson** (v France, Toulon, May 28, 1992); **Robbie Fowler** (v Austria, Kafkenberg, October 11, 1994); **Alan Thompson** (v Portugal, Oporto, September 2, 1995); **Terry Cooke** (v Portugal, Toulon, May 30, 1996); **Ben Thatcher** (v Italy, Rieti, October 10, 1997); **John Curtis** (v Greece, Heraklion, November 13, 1997); **Jody Morris** (v Luxembourg, Grevenmacher, October 13, 1998).

England 'B' (1): Neil Webb (v Algeria, Algiers, December 11, 1990).

FIVE OFF IN ONE MATCH

For the first time since League football began in 1888, **five** players were sent off in one match (two Chesterfield, three Plymouth Argyle) in Div. 2 at Saltergate on **Feb. 22, 1997**. Four were dismissed (two from each side) in a goalmouth brawl in the last minute.

Second instance of **five** sent off in League matches was on **Dec. 2, 1997**: 4 Bristol Rov. players, 1 Wigan Athletic in Div. 2 match at Wigan Athletic. Four of those dismissals came in the 45th minute.

There have been eight instances of **four** Football League club players being sent off in one match:

Jan. 8, 1955 Crewe Alexandra v Bradford City (Div. 3 North), two players from each side.

Dec. 13, 1986 Sheffield Utd. (1 player) v Portsmouth (3) in Div. 2.

Aug. 18, 1987 Port Vale v Northampton Town (Littlewoods Cup 1st. Round, 1st. Leg), two players from each side.

Dec. 12, 1987 Brentford v Mansfield Town (Div. 3), two players from each side.

Sept. 6, 1992 First instance in British first-class football of **four players from one side** being sent off in one match. Hereford Utd.'s seven survivors, away to Northampton Town (Div. 3), held out for a 1-1 draw.

Mar. 1, 1977 Norwich City v Huddersfield Town (Div. 1), two from each side.

Oct. 4, 1977 Shrewsbury Town (1 player), Rotherham Utd. (3) in Div. 3.

Aug. 22, 1998 Gillingham v Bristol Rov. (Div. 2), two from each side, all after injury-time brawl.

Four Stranraer players were sent off away to Airdrie (Scottish Div. 1) on Dec. 3, 1994, and that Scottish record was equalled when **four Hearts men** were ordered off away to Rangers (Prem. Div.) on **Sept. 14, 1996**. Albion Rov. had **four players** sent off (3 in last 8 mins) away to Queen's Park (Scottish Div. 3) on **August 23, 1997**.

Modern instances of **three players from one side** being sent off:

Dec. 13, 1986 Portsmouth (away to Sheffield Utd., Div. 2); **Aug. 23, 1989** Falkirk (home to Hearts, Scottish Skol Cup 3rd. Round); **Apr. 20, 1992** Newcastle Utd. (away to Derby Co., Div. 2); **May 2, 1992** Bristol City (away to Watford, Div. 2); **Nov. 23, 1996** Wycombe Wand. (home to Preston N.E., Div. 2); **Feb. 8, 1997** Darlington (away to Scarborough, Div. 3); **Oct. 4, 1997** Rotherham Utd. (away to Shrewsbury Town, Div. 3); **Mar. 28, 1998** Barnsley (home to Liverpool, Premiership); **Sept. 26, 1998** Southend Utd. (away to Swansea City, Div. 3); **May 1, 1999** West Ham Utd. (home to Leeds Utd., Premiership).

Aug. 24, 1994: Three Sheffield Utd. players, and one from Udinese, were sent off in the Anglo-Italian Cup at Bramall Lane on Aug. 24, 1994. In addition, Utd. manager Dave Bassett was ordered from the bench.

Most dismissals one team, one match: Five players of America Tres Rios in first ten minutes after disputed goal by opponents Itaperuna in Brazilian cup match in Rio de Janeiro on Nov. 23, 1991. Tie then abandoned and awarded to Itaperuna.

Eight dismissals in one match: Four on each side in S. American Super Cup quarter-final (Gremio, Brazil v Penarol, Uruguay) in Oct. 1993.

Five dismissals in one season – Dave Caldwell (2 with Chesterfield, 3 with Torquay Utd.) in 1987-88.

First instance of **four dismissals in Scottish match:** three **Rangers** players (all English – Terry Hurlock, Mark Walters, Mark Hateley) and **Celtic's** Peter Grant in Scottish Cup quarter-final at Parkhead on Mar. 17, 1991 (Celtic won 2-0).

Four players (3 Hamilton, 1 Airdrie) were sent off in Scottish Div. 1 match on Oct. 30, 1993.

Four players (3 Ayr, 1 Stranraer) were sent off in Scottish Div. 1 match on Aug. 27, 1994.

In Scottish Cup first round replays on Dec. 16, 1996, there were two instances of three players of one side sent off: Albion Rov. (away to Forfar) and Huntly (away to Clyde).

FASTEST SENDINGS-OFF

World record – 10 secs: Giuseppe Lorenzo (Bologna) for striking opponent in Italian League match v Parma, December 9, 1990.

Domestic – 19 secs: Mark Smith (Crewe Alexandra goalkeeper at Darlington, Div. 3, Mar. 12, 1994). In Div. 1 – 85 secs: Liam O'Brien (Manchester Utd. at Southampton, Jan. 3, 1987). Premier League – 72 secs: Tim Flowers (Blackburn Rov. goalkeeper v Leeds Utd., Feb. 1, 1995).

In World Cup – 55 secs: Jose Batista (Uruguay v Scotland at Neza, Mexico, June 13, 1986).

In European competition – 90 secs: Sergei Dirkach (Dynamo Moscow v Ghent UEFA Cup 3rd round, 2nd leg, December 11, 1991).

Fastest F.A. Cup dismissal – 52 secs: Ian Culverhouse (Swindon Town defender, deliberate hand-ball on goal-line, away to Everton, 3rd. Round, Sunday Jan. 5, 1997).

Fastest League Cup dismissal – 33 secs: Jason Crowe (Arsenal substitute v Birmingham City, 3rd Round, Oct. 14, 1997).

Fastest Sending-off on debut: See Jason Crowe (above).

MOST SENDINGS-OFF IN CAREER

21 – Willie Johnston (Rangers 7, WBA 6, Vancouver Whitecaps 4, Hearts 3, Scotland 1)
21 – Roy McDonough (13 in Football League, 8 non-league).

WEMBLEY SENDINGS-OFF

Manchester Utd.'s Kevin Moran is the only player to be sent off in the F.A. Cup Final (v Everton, 1985). His dismissal is one of 16 in major matches at Wembley:

Aug. 1948 Boris Stankovic (Yugoslavia) v Sweden, Olympic Games.
July 1966 Antonio Rattin (Argentina captain) v England, World cup q-final.
Aug. 1974 Billy Bremner (Leeds Utd.) and Kevin Keegan (Liverpool), Charity Shield.
Mar. 1977 Gilbert Dresch (Luxembourg) v England, World Cup.
May 1985 Kevin Moran (Manchester Utd.) v Everton, F.A. Cup Final.
Apr. 1993 Lee Dixon (Arsenal) v Tottenham, F.A. Cup semi-final.
May 1993 Peter Swan (Port Vale) v W.B.A., Div. 2 Play-off Final.
Mar. 1994 Andrei Kanchelskis (Manchester Utd.) v Aston Villa, League Cup Final.
May 1994 Mike Wallace and Chris Beaumont (Stockport Co.) v Burnley, Div. 2 Play-off Final.
June 1995 Tetsuji Hashiratani (Japan) v England, Umbro Cup.
May 1997 Brian Statham (Brentford) v Crewe Alexandra, Div. 2 Play-off Final.
Apr. 1998 Carpucho (Portugal) v England, friendly.
Mar. 1999 Justin Edinburgh (Tottenham) v Leicester City, League Cup Final.
June 1999 Paul Scholes (England) v Sweden, European Championship qual.

WEMBLEY'S SUSPENDED CAPTAINS

Suspension prevented four club captains playing at Wembley in modern finals, in successive years.

Three were in F.A. Cup Finals – Glenn Roeder (Q.P.R., 1982), Steve Foster (Brighton & H.A., 1983) and Wilf Rostron (Watford, 1984) – and Sunderland's Shaun Elliott was barred from the 1985 Milk Cup Final.

Roeder was banned from Q.P.R.'s 1982 Cup Final replay against Tottenham, and Foster was ruled out of the first match in Brighton & H.A.'s 1983 Final against Manchester Utd.

BOOKINGS RECORDS

Most players of one Football League club booked in one match is **TEN** – members of the Mansfield Town team away to Crystal Palace in F.A. Cup third round, January 1963.

Fastest bookings – 3 seconds after kick-off, **Vinnie Jones** (Chelsea, home to Sheffield Utd., F.A. Cup fifth round, February 15, 1992); 5 seconds after kick-off: **Vinnie Jones** (Sheffield Utd., away to Manchester City, Div. 1, January 19, 1991). He was sent-off (54 mins) for second bookable offence.

FIGHTING TEAM-MATES

Charlton Athletic's **Mike Flanagan** and **Derek Hales** were sent off for fighting each other five minutes from end of F.A. Cup 3rd Round tie at home to Southern League Maidstone on Jan. 9, 1979.

On Sept. 28, 1994 the Scottish F.A. suspended Hearts players **Graeme Hogg** and **Craig Levein** for ten matches for fighting each other in a pre-season 'friendly' v Raith.

PLAYERS JAILED

Ten professional footballers found guilty of conspiracy to fraud by 'fixing' matches for betting purposes were given prison sentences at Nottingham Assizes on Jan. 26, 1965.

Jimmy Gauld (Mansfield Town), described as the central figure, was given four years. Among the others sentenced, Tony Kay (Sheffield Wed., Everton & England), Peter Swan (Sheffield Wed. & England) and David 'Bronco' Layne (Sheffield Wed.) were suspended from football for life by the F.A.

LONG SUSPENSIONS

The longest suspension in modern times for a player in British football was imposed on Manchester Utd.'s French international captain **Eric Cantona**, following his attack on a spectator as he left the pitch after being sent off at Crystal Palace (Prem. League) on Jan. 25, 1995. He was banned from football for 8 months.

The club immediately suspended him to the end of the season and fined him 2 weeks' wages (est. £20,000). Then, on a disrepute charge, the F.A. fined him £10,000 (February 1995) and extended the ban to September 30 (which FIFA confirmed as world wide).

A subsequent 2-weeks' jail sentence on Cantona for assault was altered, on appeal, to 120 hours' community service, which took the form of coaching schoolboys in the Manchester area.

Mark Dennis, the Q.P.R. defender, was sent off for the 11th time in his career away to Tottenham (Div. 1) on November 14, 1987. (Two of those dismissals were for after-match tunnel offences; in addition, Dennis had then been cautioned 64 times in ten seasons and answered two disrepute charges concerning newspaper articles).

On December 10, the F.A. imposed on him a 53-day suspension, which was amended on appeal (January 25) to an 8-match ban. This was the longest suspension of a Football League player since **Kevin Keegan** (Liverpool) and **Billy Bremner** (Leeds Utd.) were each banned for 5 weeks (10 matches) after being sent off in the F.A. Charity Shield at Wembley in August 1974.

On December 6, 1988 Dennis was sent off for **12th. time** (Q.P.R. v Fulham reserves) and fined £1,000.

Steve Walsh (Leicester City) has been sent off 12 times in his 16-season career (4 times with Wigan Athletic, 8 with Leicester City; 11 times in League, once in F.A. Cup; 11 times away, once at home). His latest dismissal was away to West Ham Utd. on Oct. 19, 1996.

Before the disciplinary points system was introduced in season 1972-73, offenders were suspended for a specific number of weeks. Other lengthy suspensions imposed by the F.A. for on-field offences:

November 1969: Derek Dougan (Wolves) 8 weeks; **John Fitzpatrick** (Manchester Utd.) 8 weeks.

January 1970: Ronnie Rees (Nott'm Forest) 6 weeks; **George Best** (Manchester Utd.) 6 weeks.

January 1971: Peter Osgood (Chelsea) 8 weeks, following second trio of cautions in a year.

December 1971: Kevin Lewis (Manchester Utd.) 5 months; **Denis Hollywood** and **Brian O'Neil** (both Southampton) 9 weeks.

October 1987: Steve Walsh (Leicester City) 9 matches – original ban of 6 games (following the sixth sending-off of his career) increased to 9 when he reached 21 disciplinary points.

April 1988: Chris Kamara (Swindon Town) suspended to end of season (6 matches).

October 1988: Paul Davis (Arsenal) suspended for 9 matches, and fined a record £3,000, for breaking jaw of Glen Cockerill (Southampton) – off-ball incident caught on video.

January 1992: Frank Sinclair (Chelsea) suspended for 9 matches (fined £600) after being found guilty of assault on referee Paul Alcock (clash of heads) while playing for W.B.A. on loan.

January 1993: Alan Gough, Fulham goalkeeper, suspended for 42 days for assaulting referee in Autoglass Trophy match at Gillingham on December 8.

November 1994: Andy Townsend (Aston Villa) suspended for 6 matches (3 for 21 discip. points, 3 for sending-off).

October 26, 1997: Emmanuel Petit (Arsenal) pushes referee Paul Durkin when sent off at home to Aston Villa (Prem.). F.A. impose 3-match ban and £1,000 fine.

August 1998: F.A. suspend **David Batty** (Newcastle Utd.) for first 6 Prem. matches of season 1998-9 and fine him £1,500 for pushing referee David Elleray when sent off at Blackburn Rov. in last game of previous season.

October 1998: Paolo Di Canio (Sheff. Wed.) banned for 11 matches and fined £10,000 for pushing referee Paul Alcock after being sent off at home to Arsenal (Prem.), Sept. 26.

Seven-month ban: Frank Barson, 37-year-old Watford centre-half, sent off at home to Fulham (Div. 3 South) on September 29, 1928, was suspended by the F.A. for the remainder of the season.

Twelve-month ban: Oldham Athletic full-back **Billy Cook** was given a 12-month suspension for refusing to leave the field when sent off at Middlesbrough (Div. 1), on April 3, 1915. The referee abandoned the match with 35 minutes still to play, and the score (4-1 to Middlesbrough) was ordered to stand.

Long Scottish bans: September 1954: Willie Woodburn, Rangers and Scotland centre-half, suspended for rest of career after fifth sending-off in 6 years.

Billy McLafferty, Stenhousemuir striker, was banned (April 14) for 8½ months, to Jan. 1, 1993, and fined £250 for failing to appear at a disciplinary hearing after being sent off against Arbroath on Feb. 1.

Twelve-match ban: On May 12, 1994 Scottish F.A. suspended Rangers forward **Duncan Ferguson** for 12 matches for violent conduct v Raith on Apr. 16. On Oct. 11, 1995, Ferguson (then with Everton) sent to jail for 3 months for the assault (served 44 days); Feb. 1, 1996 Scottish judge quashed 7 matches that remained of SFA ban on Ferguson.

FINES ETC. – MODERN

For space reasons, this section has been condensed. Fuller details appeared seasonally in previous Annuals.

1988 (July) **Chelsea** fined record £75,000 by F.A. following serious crowd trouble at play-off v Middlesbrough in May.

1988 (November) League fine **Tottenham** £15,000 for failing to fulfil opening-day fixture v Coventry City (ground not ready after close-season improvements).

1989 (February) **Brian Clough**, Nott'm. F. manager, fined £5,000 by F.A. (and banned from touchline for rest of season) for striking spectators at League Cup quarter-final v Q.P.R.

1989 (March) **Wimbledon** fined £10,000 by F.A. for making unauthorised loans to players.

1989 (June) League fine **Bradford City** £10,000 for poaching manager Terry Yorath from Swansea City. **1989** (November) **Paul McGrath** (Aston Villa) fined £8,500 by F.A.

(record for disrepute charge against player) following newspaper criticism of former club, Manchester Utd. F.A. fine **Norwich City** £50,000, **Arsenal** £20,000 following player brawl at Highbury.

1989 (December) **West Ham Utd.** and **Wimbledon** each fined £20,000 after player brawl at League Cup-tie.

1990 (February) **Swindon Town** fined £7,500 by F.A., their former manager **Lou Macari** £1,000 and censured, their chairman **Brian Hillier** suspended from football for 3 years for breach of rules re betting on a match (Newcastle Utd. v Swindon Town, F.A. Cup 4th. Round, Jan. 1988).

1990 (June) **Swindon Town** (promoted to Div.1 via play-offs) demoted to Div. 3, then, on appeal, to Div. 2, by League after pleading guilty to 36 charges of irregular payments to players over four-year period.

1990 (September) **Chesterfield** fined £12,500 by League for failing to fulfil League Cup-tie when hit by injuries.

1990 (November) F.A. deduct 2 League points from **Arsenal**, 1 from **Manchester Utd.** and fine both clubs £50,000, following mass player brawl at Old Trafford.

1991 (January) League fine **Chelsea** record £105,000 for making illegal payments to three players.

1991 (April) League fine **Tottenham** £20,000 (£15,000 of it suspended) for late arrival at Chelsea.

1991 (November) League fine **Tottenham** £17,500 for late payment of transfer instalment to Chelsea for Gordon Durie.

1992 (January) **Birmingham City** fined £10,000 by League for fielding ineligible player.

1992 (February) F.A. fine **Michael Thomas** (Liverpool) £3,000 for press criticism of his former manager George Graham (Arsenal).

1992 (April) F. A. fine **Birmingham City** £50,000 (suspended to end of season 1992-3) after pitch invasion v Stoke City.

1992 (August) F.A. fine **Southampton** £20,000 (£15,000 suspended) for previous season's disciplinary record (5 sent off, 80 cautions, 11 suspensions). F.A. fine **Kevin Keegan** (Newcastle Utd. manager) £1,000 on disrepute charge (assistant **Terry McDermott** fined £250) for comments to referee at Derby Co., April 20. F.A. warn **Kenny Dalglish** (Blackburn Rov. manager) on disrepute charge for comments to referee v Wolves, April 14.

1992 (October) *F.A. ban **Gordon Durie** (Tottenham) 3 matches for 'feigning injury' v Coventry City, Aug. 18 (*ban quashed by F.A. Appeal Board, Dec. 16).

1992 (November) F.A give **Joe Kinnear** (Wimbledon manager) 5-match touchline ban and £750 fine (suspended) for comments to referee at Blackburn Rov., Sept. 19. F.A. fine **Vinnie Jones** (Wimbledon) record individual sum of £20,000 on disrepute charge for narrating 'Soccer's hard men' video; Jones also given 6-month playing ban (suspended for 3 years). **Barnet** fined £50,000 by League after investigation into club's financial affairs.

1993 (January) Sequel to League match at Tottenham, Dec. 12: F.A. fine Arsenal manager **George Graham** £500 for remarks to referee, suspend **Ian Wright** for 3 matches for throwing punch at opponent.

1993 (March) F.A. fine **Martin Allen** (West Ham Utd.) £1,000 (4-match ban) as season's first player to reach 41 discip. points (12 bookings). F.A. fine **Eric Cantona** (Manchester Utd.) £1,000 for spitting at spectators at Leeds Utd., Feb. 8.

1993 (April) F.A. fine **Vinnie Jones** (Wimbledon) £1,000 (4-match ban) for reaching 41 discip. points (his 4th suspension of season). F.A. fine **Manchester City** £50,000 (suspended) following F.A. Cup 6th Round pitch invasion v Tottenham, March 7. **Graeme Souness** (Liverpool manager) fined £500 by F.A. and warned for 'insulting behaviour' to referee at Crystal Palace, March 23.

1993 (May) League fine **Barnet** £25,000 for irregular payment to player, and warn that further indiscretion could cost them League status.

1993 (August) F.A. fine **Ian Wright** (Arsenal) £5,000 for 'improper gesture' to linesman at F.A. Cup Final replay v Sheffield Wed. F.A. punish clubs for poor disap. records, season 1992-3: **Southampton** fined £25,000 (suspended), £10,000 of prev. year's fine activated; **Wimbledon** £25,000 (suspended); **Sheffield Utd.** £20,000 (suspended).

1993 (October) F.A. fine **Jim Smith** (Portsmouth manager) £750 for 'insulting comments to referee'; UEFA fine **Cardiff City** £1,000 for coin-throwing incident v Standard Liege (CWC).

1993 (November) F.A. fine **Tottenham** £25,000 for 'poaching' manager Ossie Ardiles from WBA. F. League fine **Watford** £10,000 for illegal approach when signing manager Glenn Roeder from Gillingham. UEFA fine **Aberdeen** £4,500 and **Manchester U.** £2,260 for offences at European matches. F.A. fine **Bristol City** £40,000 (£30,000 suspended for 2 years) for improper claims to Football Trust over ground improvements. F.A. fine **Aston Villa** and **Notts Co.** £30,000 each for breach of rules when signing players from Australia.

1994 (January) FIFA fine **Welsh F.A.** £7,055 over incident at Wales-Romania World Cup match in which a fan was killed by rocket-flare.

1994 (February) F. League fine **Birmingham City** £55,000 for 'poaching' manager Barry Fry from Southend Utd.

1994 (March) F.A. fine **Sunderland** £5,000 for 'poaching' Mick Buxton (manager) from Huddersfield Town. Welsh F.A. fine **Cardiff City** £25,000, **Swansea City** £30,000 (suspended to season's end) for crowd trouble in match at Cardiff City, Dec. 22. **Alex Ferguson** (Manchester Utd. manager) fined £250 by F.A. for remarks to referee at 'A' team match.

1994 (April) F.A. Premier League fine **Everton** record £75,000 (plus £50,000 compensation) for 'poaching' manager Mike Walker from Norwich City.

1994 (June) In **heaviest punishment** ever handed out by F.A., **Tottenham** fined £600,000, deducted 12 Premiership points at start of season 1994-5 and banned from F.A. Cup for same season for 'financial irregularities' involving loans to players during previous administration at club (see Dec. 1994 re appeal). F.A. give **Millwall** 3 sentences (first 2 suspended for 2 years) after crowd trouble at play-off v Derby Co.: fined £100,000; ordered to play 2 matches behind closed doors; 3 League points deducted if further disturbances, home or away, before Dec. 31.

1994 (July) F.A. Appeals Board reduce **Tottenham's** 12-point deduction to 6 points, increase fine from £600,000 to £1.5m., confirm F.A. Cup ban (see Dec. 1994).

1994 (September) F.A. fine **Ian Wright** (Arsenal) £750 for making 'gestures' to fans at Q.P.R., April 27.

1994 (October) Football League fine **Preston N.E.** £2,500 for late arrival at Darlington (Aug. 13). UEFA fine **Aston Villa** £12,500 for pitch invasion, home to Inter Milan (UEFA Cup, Sept. 29).

1994 (November) UEFA fine **Aston Villa** £9,367 for pitch invasion after UEFA home leg v Trabzonspor (Nov. 1). F.A. fine **Des Walker** (Sheffield W.) £1,200, plus 3-match ban, for butting opponent v Ipswich Town (Nov. 16). F.A. fine **John Fashanu** (Aston Villa) £6,000 on misconduct charge (newspaper criticism of Cantona).

1994 (December – see June, July) Tribunal annuls 6-point penalty imposed on **Tottenham** and re-instates them in F.A. Cup.

1994 (December) F.A. suspend **Paul Merson** (Arsenal) 2 months from senior football while under treatment for drug abuse.

1995 (January) F.A. fines: **Ian Wright** (Arsenal) £1,000 (4-match ban) for reaching 41 discip. points; **Terry Hurlock** (Fulham) £350, with total 6-week ban for 51 discip. points; **Alan Ball** (Southampton manager) £500 for comments to linesman at Q.P.R. (Dec. 28); **Joe Jordan** (Bristol City manager) £250 for remarks to match official; **Martin Edwards** (Manchester Utd. chairman) £100 for remarks to referee at Arsenal (Nov. 26).

1995 (March) League fine **Sunderland** £2,500 for fielding ineligible player (Dominic Matteo, loan transfer from Liverpool registered after transfer deadline). F.A. fines (for 41 discip. points): **Steve Bruce** (Manchester Utd.) £750 and 2-match ban; **Mike Milligan** (Norwich City) £500 and 2-match ban; **Francis Benali** (Southampton) £350 and 3-match ban.

1995 (April) F.A. fines: **Robbie Fowler** (Liverpool) £1,000 for hitching shorts to spectators at Leicester City, Dec. 26; **Tim Sherwood** (Blackburn Rov.) £1,000 and 1-match ban (41 discip. points); **Ken Monkou** (Southampton) £350 and 1-match ban (41 discip. points); **Joe Kinnear** (Wimbledon manager) £1,500 and 6-month touchline ban to Oct. 31 on misconduct charges (verbal abuse of referees); **Vinnie Jones** (Wimbledon) £1,750 on misconduct charge (swearing at Newcastle Utd. manager Kevin Keegan after match); **Terry Hurlock** (Fulham) £400 and 4-match suspension (totalling 15-game ban in 1994-5) as first player to reach 61 discip. points in a season.

1995 (May) F.A. fines: **Gary Neville** (Manchester Utd.) and **Carlton Palmer** (Sheffield Wed.) each £1,000 (41 discip. points); **Roy Keane** (Manchester Utd.) £5,000 on disrepute charge after being sent off in F.A. Cup s-final v Crystal Palace

1995 (July) F.A. and FIFA ban sacked Arsenal manager **George Graham** from football for year for taking illegal payment after Arsenal signed Pal Lydersen (Nov. 1991) and John Jensen.

1995 (August) F.A. give suspended fines to 5 clubs for previous season's poor disciplinary records: **Q.P.R.** (£25,000), **Wimbledon** (£25,000), **Burnley** (£10,000), **Chester City** (£10,000), **Fulham** (£10,000).

1995 (September) UEFA suspend **Vinnie Jones** (Wales) for 5 matches (sent off v Georgia, June); UEFA fine **Rangers** £2,500 for supporters' misconduct in Cyprus (E. Cup, August).

1995 (October) F.A. suspend **Julian Dicks** (West Ham) 3 matches on disrepute charge (alleged stamping on Chelsea's John Spencer, Sept. 11).

1995 (November) UEFA fine **Chelsea** £17,000 for misconduct by 'unofficial' supporters away to Real Zaragoza (CWC s-final, April 6); F.A. fine **Robert Fleck** (Norwich City) £1,000 for abuse of official at Sheffield Utd., Sept. 9); Blackburn Rov. fine **Graeme Le Saux** and **David Batty** for brawling with each other away to Spartak Moscow (E. Champions' League, Nov. 22); **UEFA suspend** Le Saux and Batty each for 2 European club matches.

1995 (December) F.A. fine **Bournemouth** £5,000 (suspended) following crowd trouble v Crewe Alexandra (Sept. 16).

1996 (January) **Tottenham** and **Wimbledon** each given 1-year Euro ban (active for 5 years) by UEFA for fielding weak team in last summer's Inter Toto Cup; on appeal, UEFA quash ban, impose fines instead – **Tottenham** £90,000, **Wimbledon** £60,000 (Premier League's 20 clubs each pay £9,000 to cover fines/costs). F.A. fine **Manchester Utd.** £20,000 for illegal approach to 17-year-old David Brown (Oldham Athletic). F.A. fine **Bryan Robson** (player-manager) £750 and Middlesbrough players **Neil Cox** and **Nigel Pearson** each £500 for abusive remarks to referee at Blackburn Rov., Dec. 16.

1996 (February) **Leyton Orient** sack **Roger Stanislaus** after F.A. ban him for 12 months – first British-based player to test positive for taking performance-enhancing drug, cocaine-related). F.A. fine **Vinnie Jones** £2,000 (his 5th. large fine in 3 years) for newspaper attack on Chelsea's Ruud Gullit and foreign players generally; F.A. fine **Gary Megson** (Norwich City manager) £1,000 on disrepute charge (incident at Derby Co., Jan. 1).

1996 (March) F.A. fine **Keith Curle** (Manchester City) £500 for remarks made to referee (v Everton, Feb. 10).

1996 (April) F.A. fine **Mark Hughes** (Chelsea) £1,000, plus 2-match ban, for reaching 45 discip. points (his third suspension of season); F.A. fine **Mark Ford** (Leeds Utd.) £75, with 1-match ban (45 discip. points); **Faustino Asprilla** (Newcastle Utd.) fined £10,000 by F.A. and banned from first match 1996-7, on misconduct charges for elbowing/butting Keith Curle (Manchester City) at Maine Road, Feb. 24 (Curle cleared).

1996 (August) F.A. fine **Neil Ruddock** (Liverpool) £2,000 for exceeding 45 discip. points last season. F.A. fine **Q.P.R.** £25,000 (plus £50,000 suspended) **Wimbledon** £10,000 for prev. season's discip. record and gave suspended fines to 9 clubs: **Mid'bro'** and **Manchester City** each £25,000; **Portsmouth, Luton Town, Millwall, Gillingham, Burnley, Hartlepool Utd.** each £25,000; **Doncaster Rov.** £6,000.

1996 (September) **Sunderland** fined £1,000 for fielding suspended Alex Rae in pre-season reserve match.

1996 (October) F.A. fine **Gary Poole** (Birmingham City) £1,000, plus 4-match suspensions, for assault on referee at Manchester City, Sept. 1; F.A. fine **Bryan Robson** (Mid'bro' manager) £1,500 for remarks to referee at Nott'm. F., Aug. 24; F.A. fine **Graeme Souness** (So'ton manager) £750 for remarks to referee at Leicester City, Aug. 21; F.A. fine **Gordon Strachan** (Coventry City asst-manager) £2,000 for refusing to leave field when sent off in reserve game; F.A. fine Coventry City manager **Ron Atkinson** £750 for remarks to referee at same match.

1996 (November) F.A. fine **Mark Bosnich** (Aston Villa goalkeeper) £1,000 for making 'Hitler salute' gesture to crowd at Tottenham, Oct. 12; F.A. fine **Liam Daish** (Coventry City) £500 for clash with female steward at Chelsea, Aug. 24.

1996 (December) F.A. dock **Brighton & H.A.** 2 points after pitch invasions v Lincoln City, Oct. 1.

1997 (January) Premier League dock **Mid'bro'** 3 points (plus £50,000 fine) for refusing to play at Blackburn Rov., Dec. 21, through injuries; F.A. fine **Gary Megson** (Blackpool manager) £500 for remarks to referee at Millwall, Oct. 30.

1997 (February) F.A. fine **Denis Smith** (Oxford Utd. manager) £250 for remarks to match officials v Wolves, Dec. 26; F.A. fine **Neil Lennon** (Leicester City) £500 for obscene gestures to Newcastle Utd. fans, Oct. 26.

1997 (March) F.A. fine **Norwich City** and **Crystal P.** £40,000 each (£30,000 of it suspended until June 1998) after player-brawl at Norwich City, Dec. 14; UEFA fine **Manchester Utd.** £2,600 after flare thrown on pitch at home to Porto (E. Cup q-final); UEFA fine **Robbie Fowler** (Liverpool) £900 for wearing politically motivated under-shirt at CWC q-final v Brann.

1997 (April) F.A. fine **Bolton Wand.** £40,000 (£30,000 susp.) and **Wolves** £30,000 (£22,500 susp.) after player-brawl at Bolton, Jan. 18; F.A. fine **Stevenage** (Conf.) £25,000 (susp. 2 years) for seeking £30,000 'bung' from Torquay Utd.

1997 (May) F.A. fine **Billy McKinlay** (Blackburn Rov.) £750, **Robbie Mustoe** (Middlesbrough) £500 for reaching 45 discip. points in season.

1997 (June) F.A. fine **Plymouth Argyle** £30,000 (£22,500 susp.) and **Chesterfield** £20,000 (£15,000 susp.) for player-brawl at Chesterfield, Feb. 22.

1997 (July) F.A. fine **Ian Wright** (Arsenal) £15,000 for remarks made to referee v Blackburn Rov. (April 19) and gestures to crowd at Coventry City (April 21). He is severely warned as to his future conduct.

1997 (August) F.A. impose £50,000 suspended fine on **Arsenal** for poor disciplinary record season 1996-7 (6 red cards, 91 yellows). Last year's suspended £25,000 fine activated against **Mid'bro'** (5 red cards, 106 yellow) and another £50,000 suspended penalty imposed. **Norwich City** (10 red cards, season 1996-7) given £30,000 suspended fine. **Portsmouth** (9 red cards, 51 yellow) have half of £10,000 suspended fine activated. **Gillingham** have £10,000 suspended fine activated and new fine of £20,000 imposed.

1997 (September) **Pat Rice**, Arsenal assistant-manager, fined £500 by F.A. for unseemly comments to referee after match at Leicester City, Aug. 27. F.A. fine **Frank Sinclair** (Chelsea) £750 for dropping his shorts after scoring at Coventry City, Aug. 9.

1997 (October) F.A. fine **Portsmouth** and **Peterborough Utd.** each £12,500 (of which £10,000 suspended until June 1, 1998) for mass player brawl at Coca-Cola Cup match, Aug. 12.

1997 (November) F.A. fine **Slaven Bilic** (Everton) £1,000 for remarks to referee at Newcastle Utd., Sept. 24. F.A. fine **Paolo Di Canio** (Sheffield W.) £1,000 for hitching up shorts to spectators after scoring at Wimbledon, Aug. 23. F.A. fine **John Hartson** (West Ham Utd.) £1,000 for criticism of referee Mike Reed at Leicester City Oct. 27. F.A. fine **Emannuel Petit** (Arsenal) £1,000 (plus further 1-match ban) for pushing referee Paul Durkin (home to Aston Villa, Oct. 26).

1997 (December) F.A. hand goalkeepers **Bruce Grobbelaar** and **Hans Segers** each 6-month ban and £10,000 fine (both suspended 2 years) for breaking F.A. rules on betting on matches. Both cleared in court earlier in year of match-fixing charges after helping Far East betting syndicate to predict outcome of matches in which they were not involved.

1998 (January) F.A. fine Brentford manager **Mickey Adams** £500 for verbal abuse against referee v Bristol City, Nov. 8. F.A. fine **Steve Lomas** (West Ham Utd.) £500 (plus further 1-match ban) for 'laying hands on referee' when sent off at Blackburn Rov., Dec. 20.

1998 (February) F.A. fines: **Martin O'Neill** (Leicester City manager) £2,500 for using insulting language to referee Jeff Winter (home to Everton, Dec. 28); **Carlton Palmer** (Southampton) £1,000 (plus 1-match ban) for abusive language to referee Gerald Ashby (home to Derby Co., F.A. Cup. Jan. 3); **Paul Dickov** (Manchester City) £1,000 for abusive language to referee (away to Birmingham City, Dec. 13); **Garry Parker** (Leicester City) £750 for screaming at referee while running line at Oxford Utd. Sunday match; **Samassi Abou** (West Ham Utd.) £1,000 (plus further 1-match ban) for 'making physical contact' with referee when sent off at Tottenham, Jan. 17.

1998 (March) F.A. fine **Bradford City** and **Bury** each £25,000, of which £20,000 suspended to end of season 1998-9, after player brawl at Bradford City, Dec. 13.

Dennis Wise (Chelsea) given 2-match ban by F.A. and fined £1,000 as first Premiership player of season to collect 11 cautions. F.A. fine **Kevin Muscat** (Wolves) £500, plus 2-match ban, for collecting 11 cautions. F.A. fine **Leyton Orient** £20,000 (£12,500 suspended to June 1999) for fielding 3 suspended players (admin. error by club official).

1998 (April) F.A. fine **Les Ferdinand** (Tottenham) £2,500 for criticising referee Gerald Ashby after Cup defeat at Barnsley, Feb. 4. F.A. fine **Aston Villa** £2,000 for illegal approach to former Charlton Athletic youth player Jay Samuel. F.A. fine **Igor Stimac** (Derby Co.) £1,000 for gestures to crowd at Everton, Feb. 14. Football League deduct 3 points from **Leyton Orient** for fielding 3 ineligible players (see March).

1998 (August) F.A. fine **David Batty** (Newcastle Utd.) £1,500 and extend new season's Prem. ban to first 6 matches for 'laying hands' on referee David Elleray when sent off in previous season's final game at Blackburn Rov.

1998 (September) F.A. punish Q.P.R. chief scout **Steve Burtenshaw** with £7,500 fine (plus £2,500 costs) for accepting £35,000 from Norwegian agent Rune Hauge when Arsenal (then Burtenshaw's employers) signed John Jensen from Brondby in 1992.

1998 (October) UEFA add 2-match (E. Champ.) suspension to **Paul Ince's** 1-match England ban for his sending-off v Sweden, Sept. 5. UEFA fine **English F.A.** £27,000 for fans' racist chanting at Henrik Larsson in same match and for damage England fans caused at Rasunda Stadium. UEFA fine **Blackburn Rov.** £3,000 for 'improper conduct' of their players in UEFA Cup at Lyons, Sept. 27 (Jason Wilcox sent off, 5 others booked). F.A. ban **Paolo Di Canio** (Sheff. Wed.) for 11 matches and fine him £10,000 for pushing referee Paul Alcock to ground after being sent off v Arsenal (Sept. 26).

1998 (November) F.A. fine **Paul Ince** £1,500 for gesture when sent off playing for England in Sweden, Sept. 5. F.A. fine **Carlton Palmer** (Southampton) £2,500 for comments to referee Paul Durkin after Worthington Cup match v Fulham (Sept. 23). UEFA ban **Paul Ince** for 3 UEFA Cup matches, **Steve McManaman** for 2 (both sent off for Liverpool in Valencia, Nov. 3).

1998 (December) F.A. fine **Patrick Vieira** (Arsenal) £20,000 for gestures to crowd at Sheff. Wed. (Sept. 26). This equals record player-fine imposed on Vinnie Jones (Wimbledon) in 1992. F.A. fine **Swindon Town** £20,000 and **Sheff. Utd.** £5,000 – half of each fine suspended to end of season 1999-2000 – for 'failing to control their players' (mass brawl in Div. 1 match at Bramall Lane, Aug. 8). F.A. fine **Mark Hughes** (Southampton) £1,000 (with 2-match ban), as first player to receive 11 yellow cards this season (see also Feb. 1999).

1999 (January) F.A. fine **Viv Anderson** (Middlesbrough asst-manager) £750 for remarks to referee Paul Alcock at Southampton, Nov. 7. F.A. give Gillingham manager **Tony Pulis** 28-day touchline ban for incident with referee Alan Wiley at Bournemouth (Oct. 20). F.A. fine Northampton Town manager **Ian Atkins** £750 for involvement in 'fracas' v Preston N.E. (Oct. 24). F.A. fine **Fan Zhiyi** (Crystal Palace's Chinese Int.) £750, with 1-match ban, for 'improper behaviour towards referee' at W.B.A. (Nov. 3). F.A. fine **John Hartson** (now Wimbledon) *£20,000, with 3-match ban, for kicking former West Ham Utd. team-mate Eyal Berkovic in face at training ground (West Ham Utd. had already fined him £10,000. (*equals record player-fines, see December).

1999 (February) F.A. fine **Mark Hughes** (Southampton) £2,000, with 2-match ban, for 14 bookings in matches this season (see December).

1999 (March) For reaching 11 bookings in season, F.A. fine Everton's **Olivier Dacourt** £1,000 with 2-match ban, Middlesbrough's **Paul Gascoigne** £1,000 with 1-match ban, **Alf-Inge Haaland** (Leeds Utd.) £2,500 with 1-match ban. UEFA fine **Alex Ferguson** £2,000 for 'unnecessary provocation before Champions' League q-final 2nd leg away to Inter Milan; **Manchester Utd.** fined £13,000 and **Inter Milan** £21,550 for fireworks offences by fans at match.

1999 (April) Liverpool's **Robbie Fowler**, on double charge from F.A., receives record player fine of £32,000 (with 6-match ban) for provocative clash with **Graeme Le Saux** at Chelsea (Feb. 27) and for cocaine-snorting mime after scoring v Everton (April 3); Liverpool fined Fowler a reported £60,000. **Le Saux**, also charged by F.A. over Fowler incident, fined £5,000 with 1-match suspension. At F.A. inquiry into touchline fracas at Chelsea v Coventry City match on Jan. 19, Coventry manager **Gordon Strachan** fined £1,000 (plus costs); **Mark Nicholls** (Chelsea) and **Noel Whelan** (Coventry City) each fined £750, **Whelan** also fined £1,000 with 1-match suspension for 11 cautions. F.A. fine **Olivier Dacourt** (Everton) £2,500 for reaching 14 bookings (see also March).

1999 (May) F.A. fine **Kevin Ball** (Sunderland) £3,000 for 14 bookings and **Don Hutchison** (Everton) £1,000 (11 cautions). F.A. fine **Ian Wright** (West Ham Utd.) £17,500, with 3-match ban at start of next season, for trashing referee Rob Harris's room after being sent off at home to Leeds Utd., May 1.

TOP FINES

(Details in preceding text)

Clubs: £1,500,000 (increased from original £600,000) Tottenham, Dec. 1994; **£105,000** Chelsea, Jan. 1991; **£90,000** Tottenham, Jan. 1996; **£75,000** Chelsea, July 1988; **£75,000** Everton, Apr. 1994; **£60,000** Wimbledon, Jan. 1996; **£55,000** Birmingham City, Feb. 1994; **£50,000** Norwich City, June 1989; **£50,000** Arsenal, Nov. 1990; **£50,000** Barnet, Nov. 1992; **£50,000** Middlesbrough, Jan. 1997; **£50,000** Arsenal, Aug. 1997.

Players: £32,000 Robbie Fowler (Liverpool), Apr. 1999; **£20,000** Vinnie Jones (Wimbledon), Nov. 1992; **£20,000** Patrick Vieira (Arsenal), Dec. 1998; **£20,000** John Hartson (Wimbledon – offence with West Ham Utd.), Jan. 1999; **£17,500** Ian Wright (West Ham Utd.), May 1999; **£15,000** Ian Wright (Arsenal), July 1997; **£10,000** Paolo Di Canio (Sheff. Wed.), Oct. 1998; **£10,000** Faustino Asprilla (Newcastle Utd.), Apr. 1996; **£10,000** Eric Cantona (Manchester Utd.), Feb. 1995; **£8,500** Paul McGrath (Aston Villa), June 1989; **£6,000** John Fashanu (Aston Villa), Nov. 1994; **£5,000** Ian Wright (Arsenal), Aug. 1993; **£5,000** Roy Keane (Manchester Utd.), May 1995.

Managers: £5,000 Brian Clough (Nott'm. Forest), Feb. 1989; **£2,500** Martin O'Neill (Leicester City), Feb. 1998; **£2,000** Gordon Strachan (Coventry City), Oct. 1996; **£2,000** Alex Ferguson (Manchester Utd.), Mar. 1999; **£1,500** Joe Kinnear (Wimbledon), Apr. 1995; **£1,500** Bryan Robson (Middlesbrough), Oct. 1996; **£1,000** Gordon Strachan (Coventry City), Apr. 1999; **£1,000** Lou Macari (ex-Swindon Town), Feb. 1990; **£1,000** Kevin Keegan (Newcastle Utd.), Aug. 1992; **£1,000** Gary Megson (Norwich City), Feb. 1996.

MANAGERS

INTERNATIONAL RECORDS

(As at start of season 1999-2000)

	P	W	D	L	F	A
Kevin Keegan	4	1	3	0	5	5
(England – appointed Feb. 1999)						
Lawrie McMenemy	10	4	3	3	8	13
(N. Ireland – appointed Feb. 1998)						
Craig Brown	52	23	12	17	64	46
(Scotland – appointed Sept. 1993)						
***Bobby Gould**	24	7	4	13	32	47
(Wales – Aug. 1995 – June 1999)						
Mick McCarthy	31	11	8	12	46	31
(Rep. of Ireland – appointed Feb. 1996)						

*Neville Southall/Mark Hughes joint caretakers for final match season 1998-9 (lost 0-2 v Denmark at Anfield).

ENGLAND'S MANAGERS

		P	W	D	L
1946-62	**Walter Winterbottom**	139	78	33	28
1963-74	**Sir Alf Ramsey**	113	69	27	17

1974	**Joe Mercer**, caretaker	7	3	3	1
1974-77	**Don Revie**	29	14	8	7
1977-82	**Ron Greenwood**	55	33	12	10
1982-90	**Bobby Robson**	95	47	30	18
1990-93	**Graham Taylor**	38	18	13	7
1994-96	**Terry Venables**, coach	23	11	11	1
1996-99	**Glenn Hoddle**, coach	28	17	6	5
1999	**Howard Wilkinson**, caretaker	1	0	0	1
1999	**Kevin Keegan**	4	1	3	0

INTERNATIONAL MANAGER CHANGES

England: Walter Winterbottom 1946-62 (initially coach); **Alf Ramsey** (Feb. 1963-May 1974); **Joe Mercer** (caretaker May 1974); **Don Revie** (July 1974-July 1977); **Ron Greenwood** (Aug. 1977-July 1982); **Bobby Robson** (July 1982-July 1990); **Graham Taylor** (July 1990-Nov. 1993); **Terry Venables**, coach (Jan. 1994-June 1996); **Glenn Hoddle**, coach (June 1996-Feb. 1999); **Howard Wilkinson** (caretaker Feb. 1999); **Kevin Keegan** coach (from Feb. 1999).

N. Ireland (modern): **Billy Bingham** (1967-Aug. 1971); **Terry Neill** (Aug. 1971-Mar. 1975); **Dave Clements** (player-manager Mar. 1975-1976); **Danny Blanchflower** (June 1976-Nov. 1979); **Billy Bingham** (Feb. 1980-Nov. 1993); **Bryan Hamilton** Feb. 1994-Feb. 1998); **Lawrie McMenemy** (since Feb. 1998).

Scotland (modern): **Bobby Brown** (Feb. 1967-July 1971); **Tommy Docherty** (Sept. 1971- Dec. 1972); **Willie Ormond** (Jan. 1973-May 1977); **Ally MacLeod** (May 1977-Sept.1978); **Jock Stein** (Oct. 1978-Sept. 1985); **Alex Ferguson** (caretaker Oct. 1985-June 1986); **Andy Roxburgh**, coach (June 1986-Sept. 1993); **Craig Brown** (since Sept. 1993).

Wales (modern): **Mike Smith** (July 1974-Dec. 1979); **Mike England** (Mar. 1980-Feb. 1988); **David Williams** (caretaker Mar. 1988); **Terry Yorath** (Apr. 1988-Nov. 1993); **John Toshack** (Mar. 1994, one match); **Mike Smith** (Mar. 1994-June 1995); **Bobby Gould** (Aug. 1995-June 1999); **Neville Southall/Mark Hughes** (joint caretakers June 1999).

Rep. of Ireland (modern): **Liam Tuohy** (Sept. 1971-Nov. 1972); **Johnny Giles** (Oct. 1973-Apr. 1980, initially player-manager); **Eoin Hand** (June 1980-Nov. 1985); **Jack Charlton** (Feb. 1986-Dec. 1995); **Mick McCarthy** (since Feb. 1996).

FIRST BLACK ENGLAND MANAGER

Chris Ramsey, 36, in charge of England's U-20 squad for the World Youth Championship in Nigeria, April 1999. He was Brighton & H.A.'s right-back in the 1983 F.A. Cup Final v Manchester Utd.

LONGEST-SERVING LEAGUE MANAGERS – ONE CLUB

Fred Everiss, secretary-manager of W.B.A. for 46 years (1902-48); since last war, **Sir Matt Busby**, in charge of Manchester Utd. for 26 seasons (Oct 1945-June 1971); **Jimmy Seed** at Charlton Athletic for 23 years (1933-56).

SHORT-TERM MANAGERS

		Departed
3 Days	Bill Lambton (Scunthorpe Utd.)	April 1959
7 Days	Tim Ward (Exeter City)	March 1953
7 Days	Kevin Cullis (Swansea City)	February 1996
10 Days	Dave Cowling (Doncaster Rov.)	October 1997
13 Days	Johnny Cochrane (Reading)	April 1939
13 Days	Micky Adams (Swansea City)	October 1997
16 Days	Jimmy McIlroy (Bolton Wand.)	November 1970
20 Days	Paul Went (Leyton Orient)	October 1981
27 Days	Malcolm Crosby (Oxford Utd.)	January 1998
28 Days	Tommy Docherty (Q.P.R.)	December 1968
32 Days	Steve Coppell (Manchester City)	November 1996

41 Days	Steve Wicks (Lincoln City)	October 1995
44 Days	Brian Clough (Leeds Utd.)	September 1974
44 Days	Jock Stein (Leeds Utd.)	October 1978
48 Days	John Toshack (Wales)	March 1994
48 Days	David Platt (Sampdoria coach)	February 1999
49 Days	Brian Little (Wolves)	October 1986
61 Days	Bill McGarry (Wolves)	November 1985
63 Days	Dave Booth (Peterborough Utd.)	January 1991

● In May 1984, Crystal Palace named **Dave Bassett** as manager, but he changed his mind four days later, without signing the contract, and returned to Wimbledon.

EARLY-SEASON MANAGER SACKINGS

1997 Kerry Dixon (Doncaster Rov.) 12 days; **1996** Sammy Chung (Doncaster Rov.) on morning of season's opening League match; **1996** Alan Ball (Manchester City) 12 days; **1994** Kenny Hibbitt (Walsall) and Kenny Swain (Wigan Athletic) 20 days; **1993** Peter Reid (Manchester City) 12 days; **1991** Don Mackay (Blackburn Rov.) 14 days; **1989** Mick Jones (Peterborough Utd.) 12 days; **1980** Bill McGarry (Newcastle Utd.) 13 days; **1979** Dennis Butler (Port Vale) 12 days; **1977** George Petchey (Leyton O.) 13 days; **1977** Willie Bell (Birmingham City) 16 days; **1971** Len Richley (Darlington) 12 days.

FEWEST MANAGERS

West Ham Utd. have had only eight managers in their 103-year history: Syd King, Charlie Paynter, Ted Fenton, Ron Greenwood, John Lyall, Lou Macari, Billy Bonds and Harry Redknapp.

RECORD START FOR MANAGER

Arsenal were unbeaten in 17 League matches from the start of season 1947-8 under new manager Tom Whittaker.

MANAGER DOUBLES

Four managers have won the League Championship with different clubs: **Tom Watson**, secy-manager with Sunderland (1892-3-5) and Liverpool (1901); **Herbert Chapman** with Huddersfield Town (1923-4, 1924-5) and Arsenal (1930-1, 1932-3); **Brian Clough** with Derby Co. (1971-2) and Nott'm. Forest (1977-8); **Kenny Dalglish** with Liverpool (1985-6, 1987-8, 1989-90) and Blackburn Rov. (1994-5).

Managers to win the F.A. Cup with different clubs: **Billy Walker** (Sheffield Wed. 1935, Nott'm. Forest 1959); **Herbert Chapman** (Huddersfield Town 1922, Arsenal 1930).

Kenny Dalglish (Liverpool) and **George Graham** (Arsenal) completed the Championship/F.A. Cup double as both player and manager with a single club. **Joe Mercer** won the Championship as a player with Everton, the Championship twice and F.A. Cup as a player with Arsenal and both competitions as manager of Manchester City.

FIRST CHAIRMAN-MANAGER

On December 20, 1988, after two years on the board, Dundee Utd. manager **Jim McLean** was elected chairman, too. McLean, Scotland's longest-serving manager (appointed by Utd. on November 24, 1971), resigned at end of season 1992-3 (remained chairman).

TOP DIVISION PLAYER-MANAGERS

Les Allen (Q.P.R. 1968-9); Johnny Giles (W.B.A. 1976-7); Howard Kendall (Everton 1981-2); Kenny Dalglish (Liverpool, 1985-90); Trevor Francis (Q.P.R., 1988-9); Terry Butcher (Coventry City, 1990-1), Peter Reid (Manchester City, 1990-93), Trevor Francis (Sheffield Wed., 1991-4), Glenn Hoddle, (Chelsea, 1993-5), Bryan Robson (Middlesbrough, 1994-7), Ray Wilkins (Q.P.R., 1994-6), Ruud Gullit (Chelsea, 1996-8), Gianluca Vialli (Chelsea, 1998-9).

FIRST FOREIGN TRIUMPHS

Former Dutch Int. **Ruud Gullit** became the first foreign manager to win a major English competition when Chelsea took the F.A. Cup in 1997.

In season 1997-8 Chelsea won the Coca-Cola Cup and the Cup-Winners' Cup for Gullit's successor, the Italian **Gianluca Vialli**; Arsenal won the Premiership and F.A. Cup double under Frenchman **Arsene Wenger**; Dutchman **Wim Jansen** took Celtic to triumph in the Scottish Championship and Coca-Cola Cup.

In 1998-9 Rangers completed the Scottish treble under Dutchman **Dick Advocaat**.

MANAGERS OF POST-WAR CHAMPIONS

1947 George Kay (Liverpool); **1948** Tom Whittaker (Arsenal); **1949** Bob Jackson (Portsmouth); **1950** Bob Jackson (Portsmouth); **1951** Arthur Rowe (Tottenham); **1952** Matt Busby (Manchester Utd.); **1953** Tom Whittaker (Arsenal).
1954 Stan Cullis (Wolves); **1955** Ted Drake (Chelsea); **1956** Matt Busby (Manchester Utd.); **1957** Matt Busby (Manchester Utd.); **1958** Stan Cullis (Wolves); **1959** Stan Cullis (Wolves); **1960** Harry Potts (Burnley).
1961 *Bill Nicholson (Tottenham); **1962** Alf Ramsey (Ipswich Town); **1963** Harry Catterick (Everton); **1964** Bill Shankly (Liverpool); **1965** Matt Busby (Manchester Utd.); **1966** Bill Shankly (Liverpool); **1967** Matt Busby (Man Utd.).
1968 Joe Mercer (Manchester City); **1969** Don Revie (Leeds Utd.); **1970** Harry Catterick (Everton); **1971** *Bertie Mee (Arsenal); **1972** Brian Clough (Derby Co.); **1973** Bill Shankly (Liverpool); **1974** Don Revie (Leeds Utd.).
1975 Dave Mackay (Derby Co.); **1976** Bob Paisley (Liverpool); **1977** Bob Paisley (Liverpool); **1978** Brian Clough (Nott'm. Forest); **1979** Bob Paisley (Liverpool); **1980** Bob Paisley (Liverpool); **1981** Ron Saunders (Aston Villa).
1982 Bob Paisley (Liverpool); **1983** Bob Paisley (Liverpool); **1984** Joe Fagan (Liverpool); **1985** Howard Kendall (Everton); **1986** *Kenny Dalglish (Liverpool – player/manager); **1987** Howard Kendall (Everton).
1988 Kenny Dalglish (Liverpool – player/manager); **1989** George Graham (Arsenal); **1990** Kenny Dalglish (Liverpool); **1991** George Graham (Arsenal); **1992** Howard Wilkinson (Leeds Utd.); **1993** Alex Ferguson (Manchester Utd.).
1994 *Alex Ferguson (Manchester Utd.); **1995** Kenny Dalglish (Blackburn Rov.); **1996** *Alex Ferguson (Manchester Utd.); **1997** Alex Ferguson (Manchester Utd.); **1998** *Arsene Wenger (Arsenal); **1999** *Alex Ferguson (Manchester Utd.)
(* Double winners)

ALEX FERGUSON TOP ANGLO MANAGER

With 22 major prizes **Sir Alex Ferguson** has the most successful managerial record with Scottish and English clubs combined. At **Aberdeen** (1978-86) he won ten top prizes: 3 Scottish Championships, 4 Scottish Cups, 1 Scottish League Cup, 1 Cup-Winners' Cup, 1 European Super Cup.

With **Manchester Utd.** he has won 12 major trophies in the last 10 seasons: 1990 F.A. Cup, 1991 Cup-Winners' Cup, 1992 League Cup, 1993 League Championship, 1994 League Championship and F.A. Cup, 1996 Championship and F.A. Cup; 1997 Championship; 1999 Championship, F.A. Cup and European Cup.

Aged 57, he signed a new 3-year contract with Utd. (May 4, 1999), making him **Britain's highest-paid manager**, reputedly at £1.67m. a year.

MOST SUCCESSFUL ENGLISH-CLUB MANAGER

Bob Paisley, with 20 trophies for Liverpool (1974-83): 6 League Championships, 3 European Cups, 3 League Cups, 1 UEFA Cup, 1 European Super Cup, 6 Charity Shields (1 shared).

MANAGERS WITH MOST F.A. CUP WINS

4 Sir Alex Ferguson (Manchester Utd.); **3** Charles Foweraker (Bolton Wand.), John Nickolson (Sheffield Utd.), Bill Nicholson (Tottenham).

RECORD FEE FOR MANAGER

Tottenham paid Leeds Utd. £3m. compensation when they appointed **George Graham** In October 1998.

RELEGATION 'DOUBLES'

Managers associated with two clubs relegated in same season: **John Bond** in 1985-6 (Swansea City and Birmingham City); **Ron Saunders** in 1985-6 (W.B.A. – and their reserve team – and Birmingham City); **Bob Stokoe** in 1986-7 (Carlisle Utd. and Sunderland); **Billy McNeill** in 1986-7 (Manchester City and Aston Villa); **Dave Bassett** in 1987-8 (Watford and Sheffield Utd.); **Mick Mills** in 1989-90 (Stoke City and Colchester Utd.).

WEMBLEY STADIUM

The F.A. Cup Final in May 2000 will be the last at Wembley before the 'home of English football' is knocked down and replaced by a new national stadium.

In a £103m. deal completed in January 1999, Wembley plc sold the 'Venue of Legends' to the English National Stadium Development Company, a subsidiary of the Football Association, so clearing the way for the £320m. redevelopment that will take three years.

Demolition is due to begin after the Charity Shield match in August 2000, and the opening of a 90,000 all-seat high-tech stadium is planned for the F.A. Cup Final in 2003. Until then, from next August alternative venues will have to be found for Cup Finals and England matches.

Whether the symbolic Twin Towers, built in reinforced concrete when the stadium was constructed in 1923, will be integrated in the design of the new structure remains the subject of logistical debate.

It is felt that the 'new Wembley', which will also host major athletics and Rugby League events, is crucial to England's bid to stage the 2006 World Cup.

Over the past decade, more than £80m. was spent on the stadium. Improvements included the conversion to all-seating (capacity 80,000) in season 1989-90, construction of the Olympic Gallery (capacity 4,000) that encircles the stadium, installation of modern box office and walkways linking Wembley Park station to the ground.

ORIGINAL CONTRACT

The **Empire Stadium** was built at a cost of **£750,000**. Its construction included 25,000 tons of concrete, 2,000 tons of steel and 104 turnstiles. The original contract (May 1921) between the F.A. and the British Empire Exhibition was for the Cup Final to be played there for 21 years.

INVASION DAY

Memorable scenes were witnessed at the **first F.A. Cup Final at Wembley, April 28, 1923**, between **Bolton Wand.** and **West Ham Utd.**. An accurate return of the attendance could not be made owing to thousands breaking in, but there were probably more than 200,000 spectators present. The match was delayed for 40 minutes by the crowd invading the pitch. Official attendance was 126,047.

Gate receipts totalled £27,776. The two clubs and the Football Association each received £6,365 and the F.A. refunded £2,797 to ticket-holders who were unable to get to their seats. Admission since has been by ticket only.

ENGLAND'S WEMBLEY DEAL

Under an agreement signed in 1983, the Football Association were contracted to playing **England's home matches***, the F.A. Cup Final and Charity Shield at Wembley Stadium until 2002.

* Exceptions were v Sweden (Umbro Cup) at Elland Road, Leeds, on June 8, 1995 – first England home game played away from Wembley since Poland at Goodison Park on Jan. 5, 1966 – and the match v S. Africa at Old Trafford on May 24, 1997.

England previously played elsewhere on their own soil on May 12, 1973, when they met N. Ireland on Everton's ground. Officially, that was a home fixture for Ireland, but the venue was switched from Belfast for security reasons.

MODERN CAPACITY

Capacity of the now all-seated **Wembley Stadium** is 80,000. The last 100,000 attendance was for the 1985 F.A. Cup Final between Manchester Utd. and Everton.

WEMBLEY'S FIRST UNDER LIGHTS

November 30, 1955 (England 4, Spain 1), when the floodlights were switched on after 73 minutes (afternoon match played in damp, foggy conditions).

First Wembley International played throughout under lights: England 8, N. Ireland 3 on evening of November 20, 1963 (att: 55,000).

MOST WEMBLEY APPEARANCES BY PLAYER

57 by Peter Shilton (52 England, 2 League Cup Finals, 1 F.A. Cup Final, 1 Charity Shield, 1 Football League XI).

WEMBLEY HAT-TRICKS

Three players have scored hat-tricks in major cup finals at Wembley: **Stan Mortensen** for Blackpool v Bolton Wand. (F.A. Cup Final, 1953), **Geoff Hurst** for England v West Germany (World Cup Final, 1966) and **David Speedie** for Chelsea v Manchester City (Full Members Cup, 1985).

ENGLAND'S WEMBLEY DEFEATS

England have lost 17 matches to foreign opponents at Wembley:

Nov.	1953	3-6 v Hungary	Sept.	1983	0-1 v Denmark
Oct.	1959	2-3 v Sweden	June	1984	0-2 v Russia
Oct.	1965	2-3 v Austria	May	1990	1-2 v Uruguay
Apr.	1972	1-3 v W. Germany	Sept.	1991	0-1 v Germany
Nov.	1973	0-1 v Italy	June	1995	1-3 v Brazil
Feb.	1977	0-2 v Holland	Feb.	1997	0-1 v Italy
Mar.	1981	1-2 v Spain	Feb.	1998	0-2 v Chile
May	1981	0-1 v Brazil	Feb.	1999	0-2 v France
Oct.	1982	1-2 v W. Germany			

A further defeat came in **Euro 96**. After drawing the semi-final with Germany 1-1, England went out 6-5 on penalties.

FASTEST GOALS AT WEMBLEY

In first-class matches: **38 seconds** by **Bryan Robson** in England's 2-1 win against Yugoslavia on December 13, 1989; **44 seconds** by **Bryan Robson** for England in 4-0 win v N. Ireland on February 23, 1982; **42 seconds** by **Roberto di Matteo** for Chelsea in the 1997 F.A. Cup Final v Middlesbrough.

Fastest goal in **any** match at Wembley: **20 seconds** by **Maurice Cox** for Cambridge University against Oxford on December 5, 1979.

FOUR WEMBLEY HEADERS

When **Wimbledon** beat Sutton Utd. 4-2 in the F.A. Amateur Cup Final at Wembley on May 4, 1963, Irish centre-forward **Eddie Reynolds** headed all four goals.

ENGLAND POSTPONEMENT

Fog at Wembley on November 21, 1979 caused England's European Championship match against Bulgaria to be postponed 24 hours.

WEMBLEY ONE-SEASON DOUBLES

In 1989, **Nott'm. Forest** became the first club to win two Wembley Finals in the same season (Littlewoods Cup and Simod Cup).

In 1993, **Arsenal** made history there as the first club to win the League (Coca-Cola) Cup and the F.A. Cup in the same season. They beat Sheffield Wed. 2-1 in both finals.

SUDDEN DEATH DECIDERS

First Wembley Final decided on sudden death (first goal scored in overtime): April 23, 1995 – **Birmingham City** beat Carlisle Utd. (1-0, Paul Tait 103 mins.) to win Auto Windscreens Shield.

First instance of a 'golden goal' deciding a major International tournament was at Wembley on June 30, 1996, when **Germany** beat the Czech Republic 2-1 in the European Championship Final with Oliver Bierhoff's goal in the 95th. minute.

WEMBLEY'S 'NEVER' CLUBS

Of the current English League clubs, ten have never played at Wembley: Barnsley, Chester City, Exeter City, Halifax Town, Hartlepool Utd., Hull City, Lincoln City, Rochdale, Walsall and Wrexham.

DOWN WEMBLEY'S MEMORY LANE

April 1923	Wembley's first Cup Final (Bolton Wand. 2, West Ham Utd. 0). The new stadium's capacity is officially 126,000 but more than 200,000 get in.
March 1928	England lose 5-1 to Scotland's 'Wembley Wizards' – 11 men who played together only once.
April 1938	Preston N.E.'s George Mutch sends a penalty in off the underside of the crossbar in the last seconds of extra time – the only goal of the Cup Final against Huddersfield Town.
May 1953	'The Matthews Final,' including a hat-trick by Stan Mortensen in Blackpool's 4-3 win against Bolton Wand.
May 1961	Tottenham (2-0 v Leicester City) do more than win the Cup – they complete the first Double this century.
April 1961	England's record victory over Scotland (9-3), their tally topped by a hat-trick from Jimmy Greaves.
July 1966	Alf Ramsey's England win the World Cup, dramatically beating West Germany 4-2 in extra time. The Queen presents football's greatest prize to Bobby Moore, and there's a knighthood for Alf.
May 1968	Matt Busby's dream comes true: Manchester Utd. 4, Benfica 1 in the European Cup Final.
May 1973	Second Division Sunderland shock Leeds Utd. in the Cup Final. Has Wembley seen a greater save than Jim Montgomery's that keeps out a 'certain' goal by Peter Lorimer?
June 1977	Scotland beat England 2-1 in the Home Championship and their fans go wild, invading the field, pulling down the goalposts and tearing up the pitch.
May 1996	Manchester Utd. beat Liverpool for a record ninth F.A. Cup triumph and become the first English club to do the Double twice.
June 1996	England are just short of reaching the European Championship Final – beaten 6-5 on penalties by Germany.
June 1996	Germany are Kings of Europe for the third time, beating the Czech Republic by the first sudden death goal to decide a major tournament.

| May 1998 | Arsenal beat Newcastle Utd. in F.A. Cup Final and join Manchester Utd. as the only English clubs to do the Double twice. |
| May 1999 | Manchester Utd. beat Newcastle Utd. in F.A. Cup Final and became first English club to complete the Double three times. |

SHADOWS OVER SOCCER

DAYS OF TRAGEDY – CLUBS

Season 1988-9 brought the worst disaster in the history of British sport, with the death of *95 Liverpool supporters (200 injured) at the **F.A. Cup semi-final** against Nott'm. Forest at **Hillsborough, Sheffield**, on Saturday, April 15. The tragedy built up in the minutes preceding kick-off, when thousands surged into the ground at the Leppings Lane end. Many were crushed in the tunnel between entrance and terracing, but most of the victims were trapped inside the perimeter fencing behind the goal. The match was abandoned without score after six minutes' play. The dead included seven women and girls, two teenage sisters and two teenage brothers. The youngest victim was a boy of ten, the oldest 67-year-old Gerard Baron, whose brother Kevin played for Liverpool in the 1950 Cup Final. (*Total became 96 in March 1993, when Tony Bland died after being in a coma for nearly four years).

The two worst disasters in one season in British soccer history occurred at the end of 1984-5. On May 11, the last Saturday of the League season, 56 people (two of them visiting supporters) were burned to death – and more than 200 taken to hospital – when fire destroyed the main stand at the **Bradford City-Lincoln City** match at Valley Parade.

The wooden, 77-year-old stand was full for City's last fixture before which, amid scenes of celebration, the club had been presented with the Third Division Championship trophy. The fire broke out just before half-time and, within five minutes, the entire stand was engulfed.

Eighteen days later, on May 29, at the European Cup Final between **Liverpool** and **Juventus** at the Heysel Stadium, Brussels, 39 spectators (31 of them Italian) were crushed or trampled to death and 437 injured. The disaster occurred an hour before the scheduled kick-off when Liverpool supporters charged a Juventus section of the crowd at one end of the stadium, and a retaining wall collapsed.

The sequel was a 5-year ban by UEFA on English clubs generally in European competition, with a 6-year ban on Liverpool.

On May 26, 1985 ten people were trampled to death and 29 seriously injured in a crowd panic on the way into the **Olympic Stadium, Mexico City** for the Mexican Cup Final between local clubs National University and America.

More than 100 people died and 300 were injured in a football disaster at Nepal's national stadium in Katmandu in March 1988. There was a stampede when a violent hailstorm broke over the capital. Spectators rushed for cover, but the stadium exits were locked, and hundreds were trampled in the crush.

In South Africa, on January 13, 1991 40 black fans were trampled to death (50 injured) as they tried to escape from fighting that broke out at a match in the gold-mining town of Orkney, 80 miles from Johannesburg. The friendly, between top teams **Kaiser Chiefs** and **Orlando Pirates**, attracted a packed crowd of 20,000. Violence erupted after the referee allowed Kaiser Chiefs a disputed second-half goal to lead 1-0.

Disaster struck at the French Cup semi-final (May 5, 1992), with the death of 15 spectators and 1,300 injured when a temporary metal stand collapsed in the Corsican town of Bastia. The tie between Second Division **Bastia** and French Champions **Marseille** was cancelled. **Monaco**, who won the other semi-final, were allowed to compete in the next season's Cup-Winners' Cup.

A total of 318 died and 500 were seriously injured when the crowd rioted over a disallowed goal at the National Stadium in Lima, Peru, on May 24, 1964. **Peru** and **Argentina** were competing to play in the Olympic Games in Tokyo.

That remained sport's heaviest death toll until October 20, 1982, when (it was revealed only in July 1989) 340 Soviet fans were killed in Moscow's Lenin Stadium at the UEFA Cup second round first leg match between **Moscow Spartak** and **Haarlem (Holland)**. They were crushed on an open stairway when a last-minute Spartak goal sent departing spectators surging back into the ground.

Among other crowd disasters abroad: **June 1968** – 74 died in **Argentina**. Panic broke out at the end of a goalless match between River Plate and Boca Juniors at Nunez, Buenos Aires, when Boca supporters threw lighted newspaper torches on to fans in the tiers below.

February 1974 – 49 killed in **Egypt** in crush of fans clamouring to see Zamalek play Dukla Prague.

September 1971 – 44 died in **Turkey**, when fighting among spectators over a disallowed goal (Kayseri v Siwas) led to a platform collapsing.

The then worst disaster in the history of British football, in terms of loss of life, occurred at Glasgow Rangers' ground at **Ibrox Park**, January 2, 1971.

Sixty-six people were trampled to death (100 injured) as they tumbled down Stairway 13 just before the end of the **Rangers v Celtic** New Year's match. That disaster led to the 1975 Safety of Sports Grounds legislation.

The Ibrox tragedy eclipsed even the Bolton Wand. disaster in which 33 were killed and about 500 injured when a wall and crowd barriers collapsed near a corner-flag at the **Bolton Wand. v Stoke City** F.A. Cup sixth round tie on March 9, 1946. The match was completed after half an hour's stoppage.

In a previous crowd disaster at **Ibrox** on April 5, 1902, part of the terracing collapsed during the Scotland v England International and 25 people were killed. The match, held up for 20 minutes, ended 1-1, but was never counted as an official International.

Eight leading players and three officials of **Manchester Utd.** and eight newspaper representatives were among the 23 who perished in the air crash at Munich on February 6, 1958, during take-off following a European Cup-tie in Belgrade. The players were Roger Byrne, Geoffrey Bent, Eddie Colman, Duncan Edwards, Mark Jones, David Pegg, Tommy Taylor and Liam Whelan, and the officials were Walter Crickmer (secretary), Tom Curry (trainer) and Herbert Whalley (coach). The newspaper representatives were Alf Clarke, Don Davies, George Follows, Tom Jackson, Archie Ledbrooke, Henry Rose, Eric Thompson and Frank Swift (former England goalkeeper of Manchester City).

On May 14, 1949, the entire team of Italian Champions **Torino**, 8 of them Internationals, were killed when the aircraft taking them home from a match against Benfica in Lisbon crashed at Superga, near Turin. The total death toll of 28 included all the club's reserve players, the manager, trainer and coach Leslie Lievesley a former Manchester United player.

On February 8, 1981, 24 spectators died and more than 100 were injured at a match **in Greece**. They were trampled as thousands of the 40,000 crowd tried to rush out of the stadium at Piraeus after Olympiakos beat AEK Athens 6-0.

On November 17, 1982, 24 people (12 of them children) were killed and 250 injured when fans stampeded at the end of a match at the Pascual Guerrero stadium in **Cali, Colombia**. Drunken spectators hurled fire crackers and broken bottles from the higher stands on to people below and started a rush to the exits.

On December 9, 1987, the 18-strong team squad of **Alianza Lima,** one of Peru's top clubs, were wiped out, together with 8 officials and several youth players, when a military aircraft taking them home from Puccalpa crashed into the sea off Ventillana, ten miles from Lima. The only survivor among 43 on board was a member of the crew.

On April 28, 1993, 18 members of **Zambia's International** squad and 5 ZFA officials died when the aircraft carrying them to a World Cup qualifying tie against Senegal crashed into the Atlantic soon after take-off from Libreville, Gabon.

On October 16, 1996, 81 fans were crushed to death and 147 seriously injured in the 'Guatemala Disaster' at the World Cup qualifier against Costa Rica in Mateo Flores stadium. The tragedy happened an hour before kick-off, allegedly caused by ticket forgery and overcrowding – 60,000 were reported in the 45,000-capacity ground – and safety problems related to perimeter fencing.

On July 9, 1996, 8 people died, 39 injured in riot after derby match between Libya's two top clubs in Tripoli. Al-Ahli had beaten Al-Ittihad 1-0 by a controversial goal.

On April 6, 1997, 5 spectators were crushed to death at **Nigeria's national stadium** in Lagos after the 2-1 World Cup qualifying victory over Guinea. Only two of five gates were reported open as the 40,000 crowd tried to leave the ground.

It was reported from the **Congo** (October 29, 1998) that a bolt of lightning struck a village match, killing all 11 members of the home team Benatshadi, but leaving the opposing players from Basangana unscathed. It was believed the surviving team wore better-insulated boots.

On January 10, 1999 eight fans died and 13 were injured in a stampede at Egypt's Alexandria Stadium. Some 25,000 spectators had pushed into the ground. Despite the tragedy, the cup-tie between Al-Ittihad and Al-Koroum was completed.

DAYS OF TRAGEDY – PERSONAL

Sam Wynne, Bury right-back, collapsed five minutes before half-time in the First Division match away to Sheffield Utd. on April 30, 1927, and died in the dressing-room.

In the Rangers v Celtic League match on September 5, 1931, **John Thomson**, the 23-year-old Celtic and Scotland goalkeeper, sustained a fractured skull when diving at an opponent's feet just before half-time and died the same evening.

Sim Raleigh (Gillingham), injured in a clash of heads at home to Brighton & H.A. (Div. 3 South) on December 1, 1934, continued to play but collapsed in second half and died in hospital the same night.

James Thorpe, 23-year-old Sunderland goalkeeper, was injured during the First Division match at home to Chelsea on February 1, 1936 and died in a diabetic coma three days later.

Derek Dooley, Sheffield Wed. centre-forward and top scorer in 1951-52 in the Football League with 46 goals in 30 matches, broke a leg in the League match at Preston N.E. on February 14, 1953, and, after complications set in, had to lose the limb by amputation.

John White (27), Tottenham's Scottish International forward, was killed by lightning on a golf course at Enfield, North London in July, 1964.

Two players were killed by lightning during the Army Cup Final replay at Aldershot in April, 1948.

Tommy Allden (23), Highgate Utd. centre-half was struck by lightning during Highgate's Amateur Cup quarter-final with Enfield Town on February 25, 1967. He died the following day. Four other players were also struck but recovered.

Roy Harper died while refereeing the York City–Halifax Town (Div. 4) match on May 5, 1969.

Jim Finn collapsed and died from a heart attack while refereeing Exeter City v Stockport Co. (Div. 4) on September 16, 1972.

Scotland manager **Jock Stein**, 62, collapsed and died at the end of the Wales-Scotland World Cup qualifying match (1-1) at Ninian Park, Cardiff on September 10, 1985.

David Longhurst, 25-year-old York City forward, died after being carried off two minutes before half-time in the Fourth Division fixture at home to Lincoln City on September 8, 1990. The match was abandoned (0-0). The inquest revealed that Longhurst suffered from a rare heart condition.

GREAT SERVICE

'For services to Association Football', **Stanley Matthews** (Stoke City, Blackpool and England), already a C.B.E., became the first professional footballer to receive a knighthood. This was bestowed in 1965, his last season.

Before he retired and five days after his 50th birthday, he played for Stoke City to set a record as the oldest First Division footballer (v. Fulham, February 6, 1965).

Over a brilliant span of 33 years, he played in 886 first-class matches, including 54 full Internationals (plus 31 in war time), 701 League games (including 3 at start of season 1939-40, which was abandoned on the outbreak of war) and 86 F.A. Cup-ties, and scored 95 goals. He was never booked in his career.

Sir Stanley celebrated his 84th birthday last season (February 1, 1999). After spending a number of years in Toronto, he made his home back in the Potteries in

1989, having previously returned to his hometown, Hanley, Stoke-on-Trent in October, 1987 to unveil a life-size bronze statue of himself.

The inscription reads: 'Sir Stanley Matthews, CBE. Born Hanley, 1 February 1915. His name is symbolic of the beauty of the game, his fame timeless and international, his sportsmanship and modesty universally acclaimed. A magical player, of the people, for the people.'

On his home-coming in 1989, Sir Stanley was made President of Stoke City, the club he joined as a boy of 15 and served as a player for 20 years between 1931 and 1965, on either side of his spell with Blackpool.

In July 1992 FIFA honoured him with their 'Gold merit award' for outstanding services to the game.

Former England goalkeeper **Peter Shilton** has made more first-class appearances (1,387) than any other footballer in British history. He played his 1,000th. League game in Leyton Orient's 2-0 home win against Brighton & H.A. on Dec. 22, 1996 and in all played 9 times for Orient in his final season. He retired from International football after the 1990 World Cup in Italy with 125 caps, then a world record.

Shilton's career spanned 32 seasons, 20 of them on the International stage. He made his League debut for Leicester City in May 1966, two months before England won the World Cup.

His 1,387 first-class appearances comprise a record 1,005 in the Football League, 125 Internationals, 102 League Cup, 86 F.A. Cup, 13 for England U-23s, 4 for the Football League and 52 other matches (European Cup, UEFA Cup, World Club Championship, Charity Shield, European Super Cup, Full Members' Cup, Play-offs, Screen Sports Super Cup, Anglo-Italian Cup, Texaco Cup, Simod Cup, Zenith Data Systems Cup and Autoglass Trophy).

Shilton appeared more times at Wembley (57) than any other player: 52 for England, 2 League Cup Finals, 1 F.A. Cup Final, 1 Charity Shield match, and 1 for the Football League. He passed a century of League appearances with each of his first five clubs: Leicester City (286), Stoke City (110), Nott'm. Forest (202), Southampton (188) and Derby Co. (175) and subsequently played for Plymouth Argyle, Bolton Wand. and Leyton Orient.

His club honours, all gained with Nott'm. Forest: League Championship 1978, League Cup 1979, European Cup 1979 and 1980, PFA Player of Year 1978.

Three other British footballers have made more than 1,000 first-class appearances:

Ray Clemence, formerly with Tottenham, Liverpool and England, retired through injury in season 1987-8 after a goalkeeping career of 1,119 matches starting in 1965-6. Clemence played 50 times for his first club, Scunthorpe Utd.; 665 for Liverpool; 337 for Tottenham; his 67 representative games included 61 England caps.

A third great British goalkeeper, **Pat Jennings,** ended his career (1963-86) with a total of 1,098 first-class matches for Watford, Tottenham, Arsenal and N. Ireland. They were made up of 757 in the Football League, 119 full Internationals, 84 F.A. Cup appearances, 72 League/Milk Cup, 55 European club matches, 2 Charity Shield, 3 Other Internationals, 1 Under-23 cap, 2 Texaco Cup, 2 Anglo-Italian Cup and 1 Super Cup. Jennings played his 119th. and final International on his 41st birthday, June 12, 1986, against Brazil in Guadalajara in the Mexico World Cup.

Defender **Graeme Armstrong,** 42-year-old commercial manager for an Edinburgh whisky company and part-time assistant-manager and captain of Scottish Third Division club Stenhousemuir, made the 1000th first team appearance of his career in the Scottish Cup 3rd Round against Rangers at Ibrox on January 23, 1999. He was presented with the Man of the Match award before kick-off.

Against East Stirling on Boxing Day, he had played his 864th League game, breaking the British record for an outfield player set by another Scot, Tommy Hutchison, with Alloa, Blackpool, Coventry City, Manchester City, Burnley and Swansea City.

Armstrong's 24-year career, spent in the lower divisions of the Scottish League, began as a 1-match trialist with Meadowbank Thistle in 1975 and continued via Stirling Albion, Berwick Rangers, Meadowbank and, from 1992, Stenhousemuir.

SEVEN KNIGHTS OF SOCCER

Within three weeks of Manchester Utd. completing the unique treble of Premier League Championship, F.A. Cup and European Cup in May, 1999 manager **Alex Ferguson** received ultimate acclaim with the award of a knighthood in the Queen's Birthday Honours.

He became the seventh player or manager to be so honoured and third associated with Manchester Utd.

The elite list reads: **Stanley Matthews** (1965), **Alf Ramsey** (1967), **Matt Busby** (1968), **Bobby Charlton** (1994), **Tom Finney** (1998), **Geoff Hurst** (1998) and **Alex Ferguson** (1999).

PENALTIES

It is now **108 years** since the **penalty-kick** was introduced to the game, following a proposal to the Irish F.A. in 1890 by William McCrum, son of the High Sheriff for Co. Omagh, and approved by the International Football Board on June 2, 1891.

First penalty scored in a first-class match was by John Heath, for Wolves v Accrington Stanley (5-0 in Div. 1, September 14, 1891).

The greatest influence of the penalty has come since the 1970s, with the introduction of the shoot-out to settle deadlocked ties in various competitions.

Manchester Utd. were the first club to win a competitive match in British football via a shoot-out (4-3 v Hull City, Watney Cup semi-final, August 1970); in that penalty contest, George Best was the first player to score, Denis Law the first to miss.

In season 1991-2, penalty shoot-outs were introduced to decide **F.A. Cup ties** still level after one replay and extra time.

Wembley saw its first penalty contest in the 1974 Charity Shield. Since then many major matches across the world have been settled thus, including:-

1974	**F.A. Charity Shield** (Wembley): Liverpool beat Leeds Utd. 6-5 (after 1-1).
1976	**Eur. Champ. Final** (Belgrade): Czech. beat W. Germany 5-3 (after 2-2).
1980	**Cup-Winners' Cup Final** (Brussels): Valencia beat Arsenal 5-4 (0-0).
1982	**World Cup s-final** (Seville): West Germany beat France 5-4 (after 3-3).
1984	**European Cup Final** (Rome): Liverpool beat AS Roma 4-2 (after 1-1).
1984	**UEFA Cup Final**: Tottenham (home) beat Anderlecht 4-3 (2-2 agg.).
1984	**Eur. Champ. s-final** (Lyon, France): Spain beat Denmark 5-4 (after 1-1).
1986	**European Cup Final** (Seville): Steaua Bucharest beat Barcelona 2-0 (0-0). Barcelona missed all four penalties taken.
1986	**World Cup q-finals** (in Mexico): France beat Brazil 4-3 (after 1-1); West Germany beat Mexico 4-1 (after 0-0); Belgium beat Spain 5-4 (after 1-1).
1987	**Freight Rover Trophy Final** (Wembley): Mansfield Town Town beat Bristol City 5-4 (after 1-1).
1987	**Scottish League (Skol) Cup Final** (Hampden Park): Rangers beat Aberdeen 5-3 (after 3-3).
1988	**European Cup Final** (Stuttgart): PSV Eindhoven beat Benfica 6-5 (after 0-0).
1988	**UEFA Cup Final**: Bayer Leverkusen (home) beat Espanyol 3-2 after 3-3 (0-3a, 3-0h).
1990	**Scottish F.A. Cup Final** (Hampden Park): Aberdeen beat Celtic 9-8 (0-0).
1990	**World Cup** (in Italy): 2nd. Round: Rep. of Ireland beat Romania 5-4 (after 0-0); q-final: Argentina beat Yugoslavia 3-2 (after 0-0); s-finals: Argentina beat Italy 4-3 (after 1-1); West Germany beat England 4-3 (1-1).
1991	**European Cup Final** (Bari): Red Star Belgrade beat Marseille 5-3 (after 0-0).
1991	**Barclays League Play-off** (4th. Div. Final – Wembley): Torquay Utd. beat Blackpool 5-4 (after 2-2).
1992	**F.A. Cup s-final** replay (Villa Park): Liverpool beat Portsmouth 3-1 (after 0-0).
1992	**Barclays League Play-off** (4th. Div. Final – Wembley): Blackpool beat Scunthorpe Utd. 4-3 (after 1-1).
1992	**Eur. Champ. s-final** (Gothenburg): Denmark beat Holland 5-4 (after 2-2).

1993	**Barclays League Play-off:** (3rd Div. Final – Wembley): York City beat Crewe Alexandra 5-3 (after 1-1).
1993	**F.A. Charity Shield** (Wembley): Manchester Utd. beat Arsenal 5-4 (after 1-1).
1994	**League (Coca-Cola) Cup s-final:** Aston Villa beat Tranmere Rov. 5-4 (after 4-4, 1-3a, 3-1h).
1994	**Autoglass Trophy Final** (Wembley): Swansea City beat Huddersfield Town 3-1 (after 1-1).
1994	**World Cup** (in U.S.A.): **2nd. Round:** Bulgaria beat Mexico 3-1 (after 1-1); q-final: Sweden beat Romania 5-4 (after 2-2); **Final:** Brazil beat Italy 3-2 (after 0-0).
1994	**Scottish League (Coca-Cola) Cup Final** (Ibrox Park): Raith beat Celtic 6-5 (after 2-2).
1995	**Cup-Winners' Cup s-final:** Arsenal beat Sampdoria away 3-2 (5-5 agg.)
1995	**Copa America Final** (Montevideo): Uruguay beat Brazil 5-3 (after 1-1).
1996	**European Cup Final** (Rome): Juventus beat Ajax 4-2 (after 1-1).
1996	**European U-21 Champ. Final** (Barcelona): Italy beat Spain 4-2 (after 1-1).
1996	**Eur. Champ. q-finals:** England beat Spain (Wembley) 4-2 after 0-0; France beat Holland (Anfield) 5-4 after 0-0; **s-finals:** Germany beat England (Wembley) 6-5 after 1-1; Czech Republic beat France (Old Trafford) 6-5 after 0-0.
1997	**Auto Windscreens Shield Final** (Wembley): Carlisle Utd. beat Colchester Utd. 4-3 (after 0-0)
1997	**UEFA Cup Final:** FC Schalke beat Inter Milan 4-1 (after 1-1 agg.).
1998	**Nationwide League play-off** (1st Div. Final Wembley): Charlton Athletic beat Sunderland 7-6 (after 4-4).
1998	**World Cup Finals:** Argentina beat England (2nd Round) 4-3 (after 2-2); France beat Italy (Q-final) 4-3 (after 0-0; Brazil beat Holland (S-final) 4-2 (after 1-1).
1999	**Nationwide League play-offs Div. 1 s-final:** Watford beat Birmingham City 7-6 away (after 1-1); **Div. 2 Final (Wembley):** Manchester City beat Gillingham 3-1 (after 2-2).
1999	**Womens World Cup Final** (Rose Bowl, Pasedena, California) U.S.A. beat China 5-4 (after 0-0). **Third/Fourth place play-off** (same venue): Barazil beat Norway 5-4 (after 0-0).

Footnote: Highest-recorded score in a penalty shoot-out between Football League clubs was **Aldershot's 11-10** victory at home to **Fulham** after their 1-1 draw in the Freight Rover Trophy Southern quarter-final on February 10, 1987. Seven spot-kicks were missed or saved in a record 28-penalty shoot-out at senior level.

Longest-recorded penalty shoot-out in first-class matches was in Argentina in 1988 – **Argentinos Juniors** beat **Racing Club 20-19. Genclerbirligi** beat **Galatasaray** 17-16 in a Turkish Cup-tie in 1996.

Highest-scoring shoot-outs in **Int. football:** North Korea beat Hong Kong 11-10 (after 3-3 draw) in an Asian Cup match in 1975; and Ivory Coast beat Ghana 11-10 (after 0-0 draw) in African Nations Cup Final, 1992.

ENGLAND'S CRUCIAL PENALTY SHOOT-OUTS

1990 World Cup Semi-final: Beaten 4-3 by West Germany.
1996 European Champ. Q-final: Beat Spain 4-2
1996 European Champ. S-final: Beaten 6-5 by Germany
1998 World Cup (2nd Round): Beaten 4-3 by Argentina.

F.A. CUP SHOOT-OUTS

In **eight seasons** since the introduction of this method to settle F.A. Cup ties (from Round 1) that are level after two matches, a total of **43 ties** in the competition proper have been decided by such means (5 in 1991-2, 6 in 1992-3, 4 in 1993-4, 4 in 1994-5, 4 in 1995-6; 3 in 1996-7, 12 in 1997-8, 5 in 1998-9).

But the **first** penalty contest in the F.A. Cup took place **27** years ago. In days of the play-off for third place, the 1972 match was delayed until the eve of the following season when losing semi-finalists **Birmingham City** and **Stoke City** met at St. Andrew's on Aug. 5. The score was 0-0 and Birmingham City won 4-3 on penalties.

Highest recorded F.A. Cup shoot-out went to 22 kicks. The first 21 were scored before Marlow beat Littlehampton 11-10 in a first qual. round second replay on Sept. 17, 1997. It ended at 10.45 p.m. when the Littlehampton goalkeeper shot wide.

MISSED CUP FINAL PENALTIES

John Aldridge (Liverpool) became the first player to miss a penalty in the F.A. Cup Final at Wembley – and the second in the competition's history (previously Charlie Wallace, of Aston Villa, in the 1913 Final against Sunderland at Crystal Palace) – when Wimbledon's Dave Beasant saved his shot in May 1988. Seven previous penalties had been scored in this Final at Wembley.

   Tottenham's **Gary Lineker** saw his penalty saved by Nott'm. Forest goalkeeper Mark Crossley in the 1991 F.A. Cup Final.

   Another crucial penalty miss at Wembley was by Arsenal's **Nigel Winterburn**, Luton Town's Andy Dibble saving his spot-kick in the 1988 Littlewoods Cup Final, when a goal would have put Arsenal 3-1 ahead. Instead, they lost 3-2.

   Winterburn was the third player to fail with a League Cup Final penalty at Wembley, following **Ray Graydon** (Aston Villa) against Norwich City in 1975 and **Clive Walker** (Sunderland), who shot wide in the 1985 Milk Cup Final, also against Norwich City (won 1-0). Graydon had his penalty saved by Kevin Keelan, but scored from the rebound and won the cup for Aston Villa (1-0).

   Derby Co.'s Martin Taylor saved a penalty from **Eligio Nicolini** in the Anglo-Italian Cup Final at Wembley on March 27, 1993, but Cremonese won 3-1.

LEAGUE PENALTIES RECORD

Most penalties in Football League match: Five – 4 to Crystal Palace (3 missed), 1 to Brighton & H.A. (scored) in Div. 2 match at Selhurst Park on March 27 (Easter Monday), 1989. Crystal Palace won 2-1. Three of the penalties were awarded in a 5-minute spell. The match also produced 5 bookings and a sending-off.

   Manchester City provided the previous instance of a team missing 3 penalties in a match – against Newcastle Utd. (Div. 1) in January, 1912.

HOTTEST MODERN SPOT-SHOT

Matthew Le Tissier starts season 1999-2000 with the distinction of having netted 47 out of 48 first-team penalties for Southampton. He has scored the last 26 since his only miss when Nott'm. Forest keeper Mark Crossley saved in a Premier League match at The Dell on March 24, 1993.

SPOT-KICK HAT-TRICKS

Danish International **Jan Molby**'s only hat-trick in English football, for Liverpool in their 3-1 win at home to Coventry City (Littlewoods Cup, 4th round replay, Nov. 26, 1986) comprised three goals from the penalty spot.

   It was the first such hat-trick in a major match for two years – since **Andy Blair** scored three penalties for Sheffield Wed. against Luton Town (Milk Cup 4th. round, Nov. 20 1984).

   Portsmouth's **Kevin Dillon** scored a penalty hat-trick in the Full Members Cup (2nd rd.) at home to Millwall (3-2) on Nov. 4, 1986.

   Alan Slough scored a hat-trick of penalties in an away game and was on the losing side, when Peterborough Utd. were beaten 4-3 at Chester City (Div. 3, Apr. 29, 1978).

MOST PENALTY GOALS (LEAGUE) IN SEASON

Thirteen out of 13 by **Francis Lee** for Manchester City (Div. 1) in 1971-2. His goal total for the season was 33. In season 1988-9, **Graham Roberts** scored 12 League penalties for Second Division Champions Chelsea.

PENALTY-SAVE SEQUENCES

Ipswich Town goalkeeper **Paul Cooper** saved eight of the ten penalties he faced in 1979-80. **Roy Brown** (Notts Co.) saved six in a row in season 1972-3.

Andy Lomas, goalkeeper for Chesham Utd. (Diadora League) claimed a record eight **consecutive** penalty saves – three at the end of season 1991-2 and five in 1992-3.

Mark Bosnich (Aston Villa) saved five in two consecutive matches in 1993-4: three in Coca-Cola Cup semi-final penalty shoot-out v Tranmere Rov. (Feb. 26), then two in Premiership at Tottenham (Mar. 2).

MISSED PENALTIES SEQUENCE

Against Wolves in Div. 2 on Sept. 28, 1991, **Southend Utd.** missed their seventh successive penalty (five of them the previous season).

SCOTTISH RECORDS
(See also under 'Goals')

RANGERS' MANY RECORDS

Rangers' record-breaking feats include:-
League Champions: 48 times (once joint holders) – world record.
Winning every match in Scottish League (18 games, 1898-9 season).
Major hat-tricks: Rangers have completed the domestic treble (League Championship, League Cup and Scottish F.A. Cup) a record six times (1948-9, 1963-4, 1975-6, 1977-8, 1992-3, 1998-9).
League & Cup double: 14 times.
Nine successive Championships (1989-97), equalling Celtic's record.

CELTIC'S GRAND SLAM

Celtic's record in 1966-7 was the most successful by a British club in one season. They won the **Scottish League**, the **Scottish Cup**, the **Scottish League Cup** and became the first British club to win the **European Cup**. They also won the **Glasgow Cup**.

Celtic have twice achieved the Scottish treble (League Championship, League Cup and F.A. Cup), in 1966-7 and 1968-9.

They have won the Scottish Cup most times (30), and have completed the League and Cup double 11 times.

Celtic won nine consecutive Scottish League titles (1966-74) under Jock Stein.

SCOTTISH CUP HAT-TRICKS

Aberdeen's feat of winning the Scottish F.A. Cup in 1982-3-4 made them only the third club to achieve that particular hat-trick.

Queen's Park did it twice (1874-5-6 and 1880-1-2), and **Rangers** have won the Scottish Cup three years in succession on three occasions: 1934-5-6, 1948-9-50 and 1962-3-4.

SCOTTISH CUP FINAL DISMISSALS

Three players have been sent off in the Scottish F.A. Cup Final: **Jock Buchanan** (Rangers v. Kilmarnock, 1929), **Roy Aitken** (Celtic .v Aberdeen, 1984) and **Walter Kidd** (Hearts captain v Aberdeen, 1986).

CELTIC'S RECORD 62

Celtic hold the Scottish League record run of success with 62 matches undefeated, from November 13, 1915 to April 21, 1917, when Kilmarnock won 2-0 at Parkhead.

Greenock Morton in 1963-4 were undefeated in home League matches, obtained a record 67 points out of 72 and scored 135 goals, clinching promotion from Div. 2 as early as February 29.

Queen's Park did not have a goal scored against them during the first seven seasons of their existence (1867-74, before the Scottish League was formed).

WORST HOME SEQUENCE

After gaining promotion to Div. 1 in 1992, **Cowdenbeath** went a record 38 consecutive home League matches without a win. They ended the sequence (drew 8, lost 30) when beating Arbroath 1-0 on April 2, 1994, watched by a crowd of 225.

ALLY'S RECORDS

Ally McCoist became the first player to complete 200 goals in the Premier Division when he scored Rangers' winner (2-1) at Falkirk on December 12, 1992. His first was against Celtic in September 1983, and he reached 100 against Dundee on Boxing Day 1987.

When McCoist scored twice at home to Hibernian (4-3) on December 7, 1996, he became Scotland's record post-war League marksman, beating Gordon Wallace's 264. With 7 Premier League goals for Kilmarnock last season, his total of Scottish League goals stands at 280 at the start of 1999-2000.

In his 15 seasons at Ibrox, he scored 355 goals for Rangers and helped them in 10 Championships, 3 Scottish Cups and earned a record 9 League Cup winner's medals.

FIVE IN A MATCH

Paul Sturrock set an individual scoring record for the Scottish Premier Division with 5 goals in Dundee Utd.'s 7-0 win at home to Morton on November 17, 1984. **Marco Negri** equalled the feat with all 5 when Rangers beat Dundee Utd. 5-1 at Ibrox (Premier Division) on August 23, 1997.

SEATS MILESTONE FOR CELTIC

In season 1998-9, **Celtic** became the first British club with an **all-seated** capacity of 60,000.

NEGRI'S TEN-TIMER

Marco Negri scored in Rangers' first ten League matches (23 goals) in season 1997-8 – a Premier Division record. The previous best sequence was 8 by Ally MacLeod for Hibernian in 1978.

DOUBLE SCOTTISH FINAL

Rangers v Celtic drew **129,643** and **120,073** people to the Scottish Cup Final and replay at Hampden Park, Glasgow, in 1963. Receipts for the two matches totalled £50,500.

CHAMPIONS NINE TIMES

Alan Morton won **nine** Scottish Championship medals with Rangers in 1921-23-24-25-27-28-29-30-31. **Ally McCoist** played in the Rangers side that won nine successive League titles (1989-97).

Between 1927 and 1939 **Bob McPhail** helped Rangers win nine Championships, finish second twice and third once. He scored 236 League goals but was never top scorer in a single season.

SCOTTISH CUP – NO DECISION

The **Scottish F.A.** withheld their Cup and medals in 1908-9 after Rangers and Celtic played two drawn games at Hampden Park. Spectators rioted.

HAMPDEN'S £63M. REDEVELOPMENT

On completion of redevelopment costing £63m. **Hampden Park**, home of Scottish football and the oldest first-class stadium in the world, was re-opened full scale for the Rangers-Celtic Cup Final on May 29 last.

Work on the 'new Hampden' (capacity 52,000) began in 1992. The North and East stands were restructured (£12m.); a new South stand and improved West stand cost £51m. The Millennium Commission contributed £23m. and the Lottery Sports Fund provided a grant of £3.75m.

GREAT SCOTS

In February 1988, the Scottish F.A. launched a national **Hall of Fame**, initially comprising the first 11 Scots to make 50 International appearances, to be joined by all future players to reach that number of caps. Each member receives a gold medal, invitation for life at all Scotland's home matches, and has his portrait hung at Scottish F.A. headquarters in Glasgow.

MORE CLUBS IN 2000

The **Scottish Premier League** will be increased from 10 to 12 clubs in season 2000-1.

The **Scottish Football League** will admit two new clubs at the end of season 1999-2000, to provide three divisions of 10 clubs in 2000-1.

NOTABLE SCOTTISH 'FIRSTS'

- The father of League football was a Scot, **William McGregor**, a draper in Birmingham City. The 12-club Football League kicked off in September 1888, and McGregor was its first president.
- **Hibernian** were the first British club to play in the European Cup, by invitation. They reached the semi-final when it began in 1955-6.
- **Celtic** were Britain's first winners of the European Cup, in 1967.
- Scotland's First Division became the **Premier Division** in season 1975-6.
- Football's **first International** was staged at the West of Scotland cricket ground, Partick, on November 30, 1872: Scotland 0, England 0.
- Scotland introduced its **League Cup** in 1945-6, the first season after the war. It was another 15 years before the Football League Cup was launched.
- The Scottish F.A. Cup has been **sponsored** by Tennents for the last ten seasons.
- Scotland pioneered the use in British football of **two substitutes** per team in League and Cup matches.
- The world's **record football score** belongs to Scotland: Arbroath 36, Bon Accord 0 (Scottish Cup first round) on September 12, 1885.
- The Scottish F.A. introduced the **penalty shoot-out** to their Cup Final in 1990.
- On Jan. 22, 1994 all six matches in the **Scottish Premier Division** ended as draws.
- Scotland's new Premier League introduced a **3-week shut-down** in January 1999 – first instance of British football adopting the winter break system that operates in a number of European countries.

SCOTTISH CUP SHOCK RESULTS

1885-86 (1) Arbroath 36, Bon Accord 0
1921-22 (F) Morton 1, Rangers 0
1937-38 (F) East Fife 4, Kilmarnock 2 (replay, after 1-1)
1960-61 (F) Dunfermline 2, Celtic 0 (replay, after 0-0)
1966-67 (1) Berwick Rangers 1, Rangers 0
1979-80 (3) Hamilton 2, Keith 3
1984-85 (1) Stirling Albion 20, Selkirk 0
1984-85 (3) Inverness Thistle 3, Kilmarnock 0
1986-87 (3) Rangers 0, Hamilton 1
1994-95 (4) Stenhousemuir 2, Aberdeen 0
1998-99 (3) Aberdeen 0, Livingston 1

SCOTTISH FINES (MODERN)

1989 (June) fine **Hearts** £93,000, following TV infringement at UEFA Cup q-final.

1990 (May) S.F.A. fine Rangers manager **Graeme Souness** record £5,000 for breaking touchline ban v Hearts on Feb. 17, and extend Souness trackside ban to May 1992.

1991 (February) S.F.A. fine **Rangers** £10,000 and order them to forfeit £13,000 sponsorship money for failing to carry out sponsors' agreement at Cup-tie v Dunfermline in January.

1991 (June) S.F.A. fine **Dundee Utd.** £12,000 for incidents involving referee at Scottish Cup Final defeat by Motherwell.

1992 (October) UEFA fine **Hibernian** £5,730 for crowd trouble at UEFA Cup match v Anderlecht.

1993 (March) UEFA fine **Rangers** £8,000 (later halved) for crowd misconduct away to Bruges in European Cup.

1993 (May) **Rangers** fined £5,000 by League under rule covering 'tapping' of players with other clubs.

1993 (August) S.F.A. fine **Airdrie** £10,000, **Dundee** £5,000 for poor disciplinary records, season 1992-3.

1993 (November) UEFA fine **Aberdeen** £4,500 for fan misconduct v Torino (CWC).

1994 (January) S.F.A. fine **Rangers** coach **John McGregor** £3,000 and ban him from touchline until year 2000 for using foul and abusive language to referee at reserve match.

1994 (August) Scottish League fine **Celtic** record £100,000 for poaching manager Tommy Burns from Kilmarnock.

1994 (August) S.F.A. fines for prev. season's disciplinary records: **Dundee** £10,000; **Cowdenbeath, East Fife, Stranraer** each £1,000.

1994 (November) S.F.A fine **Celtic** manager **Tommy Burns** £2,000 and assistant **Billy Stark** each £2,000 for breach of contract when leaving Kilmarnock.

1995 (March) S.F.A. fine **Celtic** manager **Tommy Burns** £1,000 and ban him from touchline for rest of season (verbal abuse of referee).

1995 (August) S.F.A. fine five clubs for poor disciplinary records in 1994-5: **Dundee Utd.** (£5,000), **Falkirk** (£5,000), **Cowdenbeath, East Fife** and **Stranraer** (each £2,000).

1996 (August) Scottish League fine **Ayr** £12,000 for fielding suspended players in Coca-Cola Cup.

1996 (October) S.F.A. fine **Tommy Burns** (Celtic manager) £3,000 for 'aggressive attitude' to referee in match v Kilmarnock, April 10.

1996 (November) UEFA fine **Celtic** £42,000 and **Alan Stubbs** £28,000 for using unlicensed agents in summer transfer from Bolton Wand.; UEFA ban **Paul Gascoigne** from 4 Champions' League games (sent off away to Ajax, Oct. 17); UEFA fine **Rangers** £2,500 for players' poor discipline v Ajax, Oct. 17.

1996 (December) Scottish League fine **Falkirk** £25,000 for fielding ineligible player and order match v St. Mirren to be replayed.

1997 (January) S.F.A. fine Celtic manager **Tommy Burns** £2,000 for verbal abuse of match officials v Rangers, Nov. 14.

1997 (February) Scottish League fine **Raith** £10,000 for fielding 3 Scandinavian trialists in match (rule permits maximum of 2).

1998 (April) S.F.A. fine Rangers manager **Walter Smith** £500 for comments to referee at match at Celtic, Nov. 19.

1999 (March) S.F.A. fine Rangers manager **Dick Advocaat** £1,000, with 'severe censure', for touchline misbehaviour at Dunfermline, Feb. 7.

MISCELLANEOUS

NATIONAL ASSOCIATIONS FORMED

F.A. on Oct. 26 .... **1863**
F.A. of Wales **1876**
Scottish F.A. **1873**
Irish F.A. **1904**
Federation of International Football Associations (FIFA) **1904**

NATIONAL COMPETITIONS LAUNCHED

F.A. Cup **1871**
Welsh Cup **1877**
Scottish Cup **1873**
Irish Cup **1880**
Football League **1888**
F.A. Premier League **1992**
Scottish League **1890**
Scottish Premiership **1998**
Football League Cup **1960**
Scottish League Cup **1945**
World (Jules Rimet) Cup, at Montevideo **1930**
International Championship **1883-4**
Youth International (16-18 age-groups) **1946-7**
Olympic Games Tournament, at Shepherd's Bush **1908**

INNOVATIONS

Size of Ball: Fixed in **1872.**
Shinguards: Introduced and registered by Sam Weller Widdowson (Nott'm. Forest & England) in **1874.**
Referee's Whistle: First used on Nott'm. Forest's ground in **1878.**
Professionalism: Legalised in England in the summer of **1885** as a result of agitation by Lancashire clubs.
Goal-nets: Invented and patented in **1890** by Mr. J. A. Brodie of Liverpool. They were first used in the North v South match in January, **1891.**
Referees and Linesmen: Replaced umpires and referees in January, **1891.**
Penalty-kick: Introduced at Irish F.A.'s request in the season **1891-2.** The penalty law ordering the goalkeeper to remain on the goal-line came into force in September, **1905,** and the order to stand on his goal-line until the ball is kicked arrived in **1929-30.**
White ball: First came into official use in **1951.**
Floodlighting: First F.A. Cup-tie (replay), Kidderminster Harriers v Brierley Hill Alliance, **1955.**
Electrified pitch to beat frost tried by Everton at Goodison Park in **1958.**
First Soccer Closed-circuit TV: At Coventry City ground in October **1965** (10,000 fans saw their team win at Cardiff City, 120 miles away).
Substitutes (one per team) were first allowed in Football League matches at the start of season **1965-6.** Three substitutes (one a goalkeeper) allowed, two of which could be used, in Premier League matches, **1992-93.** The Football League introduced three substitutes for **1993-94.**
Three points for a win: This was introduced by the Football League in **1981-2,** by FIFA in World Cup games in 1944, and by the Scottish FA in the same year.
Offside law amended, player 'level' no longer offside, and 'professional foul' made sending-off offence, **1990.**
Penalty shoot-outs introduced to decide F.A. Cup ties level after one replay and extra time, **1991-2.**
New back-pass rule – goalkeeper must not handle ball kicked to him by team-mate, **1992.**

Linesmen became 'referees' assistants' in 1998.

CUP AND LEAGUE DOUBLES

League Championship and F.A. Cup: Preston N.E., 1889; Aston Villa, 1897; Tottenham, 1961; Arsenal, 1971; Liverpool 1986; Manchester Utd. 1994, 1996; Arsenal 1998; Manchester Utd. 1999.
F.A. Cup and Promotion: W.B.A., 1931.
F.A. Cup and Football League Cup: Arsenal, 1993
League Championship and Football League Cup: Nott'm Forest, 1978; Liverpool, 1982; Liverpool, 1983; Liverpool, 1984 (also won European Cup).
Scottish League Championship and Cup Double: Rangers, (14): 1928-30-34-35-49-50-53-63-64-76-78-92-93-96. Celtic, (11): 1907-8-14-54-67-69-71-72-74-77-88. Aberdeen, (1): 1984.
Scottish Treble (Championship, Cup, League Cup): Rangers 6 times (1949-64-76-78-93-99); Celtic twice (1967-69) (also won European Cup in 1967).

DERBY DAYS: COMPLETE LEAGUE RESULTS

Arsenal v Tottenham: Played 124 (all in top div.); Arsenal 49 wins, Tottenham 44, Drawn 31.
Aston Villa v Birmingham City: Played 96; Aston Villa 39, Birmingham City 32, Drawn 25.
Everton v Liverpool: Played 160 (all in top div.); Liverpool 57, Everton 53, Drawn 50.
Ipswich Town v Norwich City: Played 66; Ipswich Town 33, Norwich 23, Drawn 10.
Manchester City v Manchester Utd.: Played 124; United 48, City 32, Drawn 44.
Middlesbrough v Newcastle Utd.: Played 92; Newcastle Utd. 35, Middlesbrough 31, Drawn 26.
Newcastle Utd. v Sunderland: Played 118; Newcastle Utd. 43, Sunderland 39, Drawn 36 (incl. 1990 play-offs – Sunderland win and draw).
Nott'm. Forest v Notts Co.: Played 86; Forest 35, County 28, Drawn 23.
Sheffield Utd. v Sheffield Wed.: Played 98; United 37, Wed. 31, Drawn 30.
Port Vale v Stoke City: Played 40; Stoke City 16, Port Vale 12, Drawn 12.
Bristol City v Bristol Rov.: Played 82; City 33, Rov. 23, Drawn 26.
Celtic v Rangers: Played 252; Rangers 100, Celtic 76, Drawn 76.
Dundee v Dundee Utd.: Played 102; United 51, Dundee 31, Drawn 20.
Hearts v Hibernian: Played 214; Hearts 89, Hibernian 62, Drawn 63.

YOUNGEST AND OLDEST

Youngest Caps   *Age*
Norman Whiteside (N. Ireland v Yugoslavia, June 17, 1982)   **17** years, **42** days
Ryan Green (Wales v Malta, June 3, 1998)   **17** years **226** days
James Prinsep (England v Scotland, April 5, 1879)   **17** years **252** days
Denis Law (Scotland v Wales, October 18, 1958)   **18** years **235** days
Jimmy Holmes (Rep. of Ireland v Austria, May 30, 1971)   **17** years **200** days

England's youngest cap this century: Michael Owen (v Chile, Wembley, February 11, 1998) 18 years 59 days.
Youngest England scorer: Michael Owen (18 years, 164 days) v Morocco, Wembley, May 27, 1998.
Youngest England captain: Bobby Moore (v Czech., away, May 29, 1963), 22 years, 47 days.
Youngest player to appear in World Cup Finals: Norman Whiteside (N. Ireland v Yugoslavia in Spain – June 17, 1982, age 17 years and 42 days (record previously held by Pele – 17 years and 237 days when playing for Brazil in 1958 World Cup in Sweden).
Youngest First Division player: Derek Forster (Sunderland goalkeeper v Leicester City, August 22, 1964) aged 15 years, 185 days.
Youngest First Division scorer: At 16 years and 57 days, schoolboy Jason Dozzell (substitute after 30 minutes for Ipswich Town at home to Coventry City on February 4, 1984). Ipswich Town won 3-1 and Dozzell scored their third goal.

Youngest F.A. Premier League player: Neil Finn (West Ham Utd. goalkeeper at Manchester City, January 1, 1996) 17 years, 3 days.

Youngest F.A. Premier League scorer: Andy Turner (Tottenham v Everton, September 5, 1992), 17 years, 166 days.

Youngest First Division hat-trick scorer: Alan Shearer, aged 17 years, 240 days, in Southampton's 4-2 home win v Arsenal (April 9, 1988) on his full debut. Previously, Jimmy Greaves (17 years, 309 days) with 4 goals for Chelsea at home to Portsmouth (7-4), Christmas Day, 1957.

Youngest to complete 100 Football League goals: Jimmy Greaves (20 years, 261 days) when he did so for Chelsea v Manchester City, November 19, 1960.

Youngest Football League scorer: Ronnie Dix (for Bristol Rov. v Norwich City, Div. 3 South, March 3, 1928) aged 15 years, 180 days.

Youngest players in Football League: Albert Geldard (Bradford Park Avenue v Millwall, Div. 2, September 16, 1929) aged 15 years, 158 days; Ken Roberts (Wrexham v Bradford Park Avenue, Div. 3 North, September 1, 1951) also 15 years, 158 days.

Youngest player in Scottish League: Goalkeeper Ronnie Simpson (Queens Park) aged 15 in 1946.

Youngest player in F.A. Cup: Andy Awford, Worcester City's England Schoolboy defender, aged 15 years, 88 days when he substituted in second half away to Boreham Wood (3rd. qual. round) on October 10, 1987.

Youngest player in F.A. Cup proper: Scott Endersby (15 years, 279 days) when he kept goal for Kettering Town v Tilbury in first round on November 26, 1977.

Youngest Wembley Cup Final captain: Barry Venison (Sunderland v Norwich City, Milk Cup Final, March 24, 1985 – replacing suspended captain Shaun Elliott) – aged 20 years, 220 days.

Youngest F.A. Cup-winning captain: Bobby Moore (West Ham Utd., 1964, v Preston N.E.), aged 23 years, 20 days.

Youngest F.A. Cup Final captain: David Nish was 21 years and 212 days old when he captained Leicester City against Manchester City at Wembley on April 26, 1969.

Youngest F.A. Cup Final player: James Prinsep (Clapham Rov. v Old Etonians, 1879) aged 17 years, 245 days.

Youngest F.A. Cup Final player this century: Paul Allen (West Ham Utd. v Arsenal, 1980) aged 17 years, 256 days.

Youngest F.A. Cup Final scorer: Norman Whiteside (Manchester Utd. v Brighton & H.A. in 1983 replay at Wembley), aged 18 years, 19 days.

Youngest F.A. Cup Final managers: Stan Cullis, Wolves (33) v Leicester City, 1949; Steve Coppell, Crystal Palace (34) v Manchester Utd., 1990; Ruud Gullit, Chelsea (34) v Mid'bro', 1997.

Youngest player in Football League Cup: Kevin Davies (Chesterfield sub at West Ham Utd., 2nd Round, 2nd Leg on September 22, 1993) aged 16 years, 180 days.

Youngest Wembley scorer: Norman Whiteside (Manchester Utd. v Liverpool, Milk Cup Final, March 26, 1983) aged 17 years, 324 days.

Youngest Wembley Cup Final goalkeeper: Chris Woods (18 years, 125 days) for Nott'm Forest v Liverpool, League Cup Final on March 18, 1978.

Youngest Wembley F.A. Cup Final goalkeeper: Peter Shilton (19 years, 219 days) for Leicester City v Manchester Utd., April 26, 1969.

Youngest senior International at Wembley: Salomon Olembe (sub for Cameroon v England, November 15, 1997), aged 16 years, 342 days.

Youngest winning manager at Wembley: Roy McDonough, aged 33 years. 6 moths, 24 days as player-manager of Colchester Utd., F.A. Trophy winners on May 10, 1992.

Youngest scorer in full International: Mohamed Kallon (Sierra Leone v Congo, African Nations Cup, April 22, 1995), aged 15 years, 192 days.

Youngest player sent off in World Cup Final series: Rigobert Song (Cameroon v Brazil, in USA, June 1994) aged 17 years, 358 days.

Youngest F.A. Cup Final referee: Kevin Howley, of Middlesbrough, aged 35 when in charge of Wolves v Blackburn Rov., 1960.

Youngest player in England U-23 team: Duncan Edwards (v. Italy, Bologna, January 20, 1954), aged 17 years, 112 days.

Youngest player in England U-21 team: Lee Sharpe (v. Greece, away, February 7, 1989), aged 17 years, 254 days.

Youngest player in Scotland U-21 team: Christian Dailly (v Romania, Hampden Park, Sept. 11, 1990), aged 16 years, 330 days.

Youngest player in senior football: Cameron Campbell Buchanan, Scottish-born outside right, aged 14 years, 57 days when he played for Wolves v W.B.A. in War-time League match, September 26, 1942.

Youngest player in peace-time senior match: Eamon Collins (Blackpool v Kilmarnock, Anglo-Scottish Cup quarter-final 1st. leg, September 9, 1980) aged 14 years, 323 days.

Oldest player to appear in Football League: New Brighton manager Neil McBain (51 years, 120 days) as emergency goalkeeper away to Hartlepool Utd. (Div. 3 North, March 15, 1947).

Other oldest post-war League players: Sir Stanley Matthews (Stoke City, 1965, 50 years, 5 days); Peter Shilton (Leyton Orient 1997, 47 years, 126 days); Alf Wood (Coventry City, 1958, 43 years, 199 days); Tommy Hutchison (Swansea City, 1991, 43 years, 172 days).

Oldest Football League debutant: Andrew Cunningham, for Newcastle Utd. at Leicester City (Div. 1) on February 2, 1929, aged 38 years, 2 days.

Oldest player to appear in First Division: Sir Stanley Matthews (Stoke City v Fulham, February 6, 1965), aged 50 years, 5 days.

Oldest player in Premier League: Goalkeeper John Burridge (Manchester City v Q.P.R., May 14, 1995), aged 43 years, 5 months, 11 days.

Oldest F.A. Cup Final player: Walter (Billy) Hampson (Newcastle Utd. v Aston Villa on April 26, 1924), aged 41 years, 242 days.

Oldest F.A. Cup-winning team: Arsenal 1950 (average age 31 years, 2 months). Eight of the players were over 30, with the three oldest centre-half Leslie Compton 37, and skipper Joe Mercer and goalkeeper George Swindin, both 35.

Oldest World Cup-winning captain: Dino Zoff, Italy's goalkeeper v W. Germany in 1982 Final, aged 40 years, 92 days.

Oldest player capped by England: Stanley Matthews (v. Denmark, Copenhagen, May 15, 1957), aged 42 years, 104 days.

Oldest England scorer: Stanley Matthews (v N. Ireland, Belfast, October 6, 1956), aged 41 years, 248 days.

Oldest British International player: Billy Meredith (Wales v England at Highbury, March 15, 1920), aged 45 years, 228 days.

Oldest 'new cap': Arsenal centre-half Leslie Compton, at 38 years, 64 days when he made his England debut in a 4-2 win against Wales at Sunderland on November 15, 1950. **For Scotland:** Goalkeeper Ronnie Simpson (Celtic) at 36 years, 185 days v England at Wembley, April 15, 1967.

Longest Football League career: This spanned 32 years and 10 months, by Stanley Matthews (Stoke City, Blackpool, Stoke City) from March 19, 1932 until February 6, 1965.

Smallest F.A. Cup-winning captain: 5ft. 4in. – Bobby Kerr (Sunderland v Leeds Utd., 1973).

SHIRT NUMBERING

Numbering players in Football League matches was made compulsory in 1939. Players wore numbered shirts (1-22) in the F.A. Cup Final as an experiment in 1933 (Everton 1-11 v Manchester City 12-22).

Squad numbers for players were introduced by the F.A. Premier League at the start of the season 1993-4. They were optional in the Football League until made compulsory in 1999-2000.

Names on shirts: For first time, players wore names as well as numbers on shirts in League Cup and F.A. Cup Finals, 1993.

SUBSTITUTES

In **1965**, the Football League, by 39 votes to 10, agreed that **one substitute** be allowed for an injured player at any time during a League match.

Two substitutes per team were approved for the League (Littlewoods) Cup and F.A. Cup in season 1986-7 and two were permitted in the Football League for the first time in 1987-8.

Three substitutes (one a goalkeeper), two of which could be used, introduced by the Premier League for 1992-3. The Football League followed suit for 1993-4.

Three substitutes (one a goalkeeper) were allowed at the World Cup Finals for the first time at US '94.

Three substitutes (any position) introduced by Premier League and Football League in 1995-6.

The **first recorded use of a substitute was in 1889** (Wales v Scotland at Wrexham on April 15) when Sam Gillam arrived late – although he was a Wrexham player – and Alf Pugh (Rhostellyn) was allowed to keep goal until he turned up. The match ended 0-0.

When Leigh Roose, the Welsh goalkeeper, was injured against England at Wrexham, March 16, 1908, David Davies (Bolton Wand.) was allowed to take his place as substitute. Thus Wales used 12 players. England won 7-1.

First substitute to score in F.A. Cup Final: Eddie Kelly (Arsenal v Liverpool, 1971).

END OF WAGE LIMIT

Freedom from the maximum wage system – in force since the formation of the Football League in 1888 – was secured by the Professional Footballers' Association in 1961. About this time Italian clubs renewed overtures for the transfer of British stars and Fulham's **Johnny Haynes** became the first British player to earn £100 a week.

GREATEST SHOCKS

Excluding such tragedies as the Munich air crash (Feb. 1958), the Bradford City fire disaster (May 1985), Heysel (May 1985) and Hillsborough (April 1989), here in date order are, arguably, the greatest shocks in football history:

(1)	Jan. 1933	F.A. Cup 3rd. Round: Walsall 2, Arsenal 0.
(2)	Jan. 1949	F.A. Cup 4th. Round: Yeovil 2, Sunderland 1.
(3)	June 1950	World Cup Finals: U.S.A. 1, England 0 (Belo Horizonte, Brazil).
(4)	Nov. 1953	England 3, Hungary 6 (Wembley).
(5)	Sept. 1962	Cup-Winners' Cup 1st. Round, 1st. Leg: Bangor 2, Napoli 0.
(6)	Mar. 1966	World Cup stolen in London (found a week later).
(7)	June 1966	World Cup Finals: N. Korea 1, Italy 0 (Middlesbrough).
(8)	Jan. 1967	Scottish Cup 1st. Round: Berwick Rangers 1, Glasgow Rangers 0.
(9)	Mar. 1969	League Cup Final: Swindon Town 3, Arsenal 1.
(10)	Feb. 1971	F.A. Cup 5th. Round: Colchester Utd. 3, Leeds Utd. 2.
(11)	Jan. 1972	F.A. Cup 3rd. Round: Hereford Utd. 2, Newcastle Utd. 1.
(12)	July 1974	Bill Shankly retires as Liverpool manager.
(13)	May 1973	F.A. Cup Final: Sunderland 1, Leeds Utd. 0.
(14)	May 1976	F.A. Cup Final: Southampton 1, Manchester Utd. 0.
(15)	July 1977	England manager Don Revie defects to coach Utd. Arab Emirates.
(16)	June 1982	World Cup Finals: Algeria 2, West Germany 1 (Gijon, Spain).
(17)	Jan. 1984	F.A. Cup 3rd. Round: Bournemouth 2, Manchester Utd. (holders) 0.
(18)	May 1988	F.A. Cup Final: Wimbledon 1, Liverpool 0 .
(19)	June 1990	World Cup Finals: Cameroon 1, Argentina (World Champions) 0 (Milan).
(20)	Sept. 1990	European Championship (Qual. Round): Faroe Islands 1, Austria 0.
(21)	Feb. 1991	Kenny Dalglish resigns as Liverpool manager.
(22)	Jan. 1992	F.A. Cup 3rd. Round: Wrexham 2, Arsenal 1.
(23)	June 1992	European Championship Final: Denmark 2, Germany (World Champions) 0.
(24)	June 1993	U.S. Cup '93: U.S.A. 2, England 0 (Foxboro, Boston).
(25)	July 1994	World Cup Finals: Bulgaria 2, Germany 1 (New York City).
(26)	Feb. 1998	Conacaf Gold Cup: U.S.A. 1, Brazil 0 (Los Angeles).
(27)	July 1998	World Cup Q-final: Croatia 3 Germany 0.

OTHER INTERNATIONAL SHOCKS

(Read in conjunction with Greatest Shocks above)

1982	Spain 0, N. Ireland 1 (World Cup Finals in Spain).
1990	Scotland 0, Costa Rica 1 (World Cup Finals in Italy).
1990	Sweden 1, Costa Rica 2 (World Cup Finals in Italy).
1993	Argentina 0, Colombia 5 (World Cup qual. round).
1993	France 2, Israel 3 (World Cup qual. round).
1993	San Marino score fastest goal in Int. records: 8.3 secs. v England (World Cup qual. round).
1994	Moldova 3, Wales 0; Georgia 5, Wales 0 (both Euro. Champ. qual. round).
1995	Belarus 1, Holland 0 (European Champ. qual. round).

GREAT RECOVERIES

On December 21, 1957, Charlton Athletic were losing 5-1 against Huddersfield Town (Div. 2) at The Valley with only 28 minutes left, and from the 15th minute, had been reduced to ten men by injury, but they won 7-6, with left-winger Johnny Summers scoring five goals. Huddersfield Town (managed by Bill Shankly) remain the only team to score six times in a League match and lose.

Among other notable comebacks: on November 12, 1904 (Div. 1), Sheffield Wed. were losing 0-5 at home to Everton, but drew 5-5. At Anfield on December 4, 1909 (Div.1), Liverpool trailed 2-5 to Newcastle Utd. at half-time, then won 6-5. On Boxing Day, 1927, in Div. 3 South, Northampton Town won 6-5 at home to Luton Town after being 1-5 down at half-time. On September 22, 1984 (Div. 1), Q.P.R. drew 5-5 at home to Newcastle Utd. after trailing 0-4 at half-time. On April 12, 1993 (Div. 1) Swindon Town were 1-4 down at Birmingham City with 30 minutes left, but won 6-4.

Other astonishing turnabouts in Div.1 include: Grimsby Town (3-5 down) won 6-5 at W.B.A. on Apr. 30, 1932; and Derby Co. beat Manchester Utd. 5-4 (from 1-4) on Sept. 5, 1936.

With 5 minutes to play, Ipswich Town were losing 3-0 at Barnsley (Div. 1, March 9, 1996), but drew 3-3.

On Sunday, Jan. 19, 1997 (Div. 1), Q.P.R. were 0-4 down away to Port Vale at half-time and still trailing 1-4 with 5 minutes left. They drew 4-4.

Celtic trailed 0-2, 1-3 and 2-4 away to Dunfermline (Scottish First Div., Nov. 19,1966) but won 5-4 with a last-minute penalty.

Premier League comebacks: Jan. 4, 1994 – Liverpool were 3 down after 24 mins. at home to Manchester Utd., drew 3-3; Nov. 8, 1997 – Derby Co. led 3-0 after 33 mins. at Elland Road, but Leeds Utd. won 4-3 with last-minute goal.

MATCHES OFF

Worst day for postponements: Feb. 9, 1963, when 57 League fixtures in England and Scotland were frozen off. Only 7 Football League matches took place, and the entire Scottish programme was wiped out

Worst other weather-hit days:

Jan. 12, 1963 and Feb. 2, 1963 – on both those Saturdays, only 4 out of 44 Football League matches were played.

Jan. 1, 1979 – 43 out of 46 Football League fixtures postponed.

Jan. 17, 1987 – 37 of 45 scheduled Football League fixtures postponed; only 2 Scottish matches survived.

Feb. 8-9, 1991 – only 4 of the week-end's 44 Barclays League matches survived the freeze-up (4 of the postponements were on Friday night). In addition, 11 Scottish League matches were off.

Jan. 27, 1996 – 44 Cup and League matches in England and Scotland were frozen off. The ten fixtures played comprised 3 F.A. Cup (4th. Round), 1 in Div. 1, 5 in Scottish Cup (3rd. Round), 1 in Scottish Div. 2.

Fewest matches left on one day by postponements was during the Second World War – Feb. 3, 1940 when, because of snow, ice and fog only one out of 56 regional league fixtures took place. It resulted Plymouth Argyle 10, Bristol City 3.

The Scottish Cup second round tie between Inverness Thistle and Falkirk in season 1978-9 was **postponed 29 times** because of snow and ice. First put off on Jan. 6, it was eventually played on Feb. 22. Falkirk won 4-0.

Pools Panel's busiest days: Jan. 17, 1987 and Feb. 9, 1991 – on both dates they gave their verdict on 48 postponed coupon matches.

FEWEST 'GAMES OFF'

Season 1947-8 was the best since the war for Football League fixtures being played to schedule. Only **six** were postponed.

LONGEST SEASON

The latest that **League** football has been played in a season was **June 7, 1947** (six weeks after the F.A. Cup Final). The season was extended because of mass postponements caused by bad weather in mid-winter.

The latest the **F.A. Cup competition** has ever been completed was in season 1981-2, when Tottenham beat Q.P.R. 1-0 in a Final replay at Wembley on May 27.

Worst winter hold-up was in season 1962-3. The Big Freeze began on Boxing Day and lasted until March, with nearly 500 first-class matches postponed. The F.A. Cup 3rd. Round was the longest on record – it began with only three out of 32 ties playable on January 5 and ended 66 days and 261 postponements later on March 11. The Lincoln City-Coventry City tie was put off 15 times. The Pools Panel was launched that winter, on January 26, 1963.

Hottest day for a Football League programme is believed to have been Saturday, September 1, 1906, when temperatures across the country were over 90°.

LEAGUE SECRETARIES

In February 1989, the Football League confirmed the appointment of **David Dent**, 52, as secretary in succession to Graham Kelly, who became chief executive of the F.A.

Mr. Dent, previously assistant and formerly with Coventry City, is only the **sixth secretary** of the League in its 111-year history, following: **Harry Lockett** (1888-1902), **Tom Charnley** (1902-33), **Fred Howarth** (1933-57), **Alan Hardaker** (1957-79) and **Graham Kelly** (1979-88).

Football League chairman: Peter Middleton (appointed Sept. 1998). **Chief executive:** Richard Scudamore (appointed May 1998).

F.A. Premier League (1992-99): Secretary – Mike Foster. Chairman (appointed April 1999): David Richards (Sheff. Wed.).

FOOTBALL ASSOCIATION SECRETARIES

Ebenezer Morley (1863-66), **Robert Willis** (1866-68), **R.G. Graham** (1868-70), **Charles Adcock** (1870-95, paid from 1887), 1895-1934 **Sir Frederick Wall**, 1934-62 **Sir Stanley Rous**, 1962-73 **Denis Follows**, 1973-89 **Ted Croker** (latterly chief executive), 1989-99 **Graham Kelly** (chief executive).

FOOTBALL'S SPONSORS

Football League: Canon 1983-6; Today Newspaper 1986-7; Barclays 1987-93; Endsleigh Insurance 1993-6; Nationwide Building Society 1996-2001.

League Cup: Milk Cup 1982-6; Littlewoods 1987-90; Rumbelows 1991-2; Coca-Cola Cup 1993-8; Worthington Cup 1998-2003.

Premier League: Carling 1993-2001.

F.A. Cup: Littlewoods 1994-8; AXA 1998-2002.

SOCCER HEADQUARTERS

Football Association: 16 Lancaster Gate, London W2 3LW. Chief Executive – to be appointed.

F.A. Premier League: 16 Lancaster Gate, London W2 3LW.
Football League: Edward VII Quay, Navigation Way, Preston PR2 2YF. Secretary: David Dent. **London Office:** 11 Connaught Place, London W2 2ET.
Professional Footballers' Association: 2 Oxford Utd. Court, Bishopsgate, Manchester M2 3WQ. Chief Executive: Gordon Taylor.
Football Trust: Walkden House, 10 Melton Street, London NW1 2EB. Chief Executive: Peter Lee.
Scottish Football Association: 6 Park Gardens, Glasgow G3 7YF. Chief Executive – to be appointed.
Scottish Football League: 188 West Regent Street, Glasgow G2 4RY. Secretary – Peter Donald.
Irish Football Association: 20 Windsor Avenue, Belfast BT9 6EG. Secretary – David Bowen.
Irish Football League: 96 University Street, Belfast BT7 1HE. Secretary – Harry Wallace.
League of Ireland: 80 Merrion Square, Dublin 2. Secretary – Eamonn Morris.
Republic of Ireland F.A.: 80 Merrion Square, Dublin 2. Secretary: Sean Connolly.
Welsh Football Association: 3 Westgate Street, Cardiff City, S. Glamorgan CF1 1DD. Secretary – David Collins.
Football Conference: Collingwood House, Schooner Court, Crossways, Dartford, Kent DAZ 6QQ.
FIFA: P.O. Box 85, 8030 Zurich, Switzerland.
UEFA: Chemin de la Redoute 54, Case Postale 303, CH-1260, Nyon, Geneva, Switzerland.

WORLD'S LARGEST STADIA

(Source: FIFA NEWS)

Capacity 165,000: Maracana, Rio de Janeiro, Brazil; **150,000** Rungnado Stadium, Pyongyang, North Korea; **125,000** Magalhaes Pinto Stadium, Belo Horizonte, Brazil; **120,000** Morumbi Stadium, Sao Paulo, Brazil; Stadium of Light, Lisbon, Portugal; Krirangan Stadium, Salt Lake, Calcutta; Senayan Stadium, Jakarta, Indonesia; **119,000** Castelao Stadium, Fortaleza, Brazil; **115,000** Arrudao Stadium, Recife, Brazil; Azteca Stadium, Mexico City; Nou Camp, Barcelona, Spain; **114,000** Bernabeu Stadium, Madrid; **100,000** Nasser Stadium, Cairo, Egypt; Azadi Stadium, Tehran, Iran; Red Star Stadium, Belgrade, Yugoslavia; Central Stadium, Kiev, USSR.

NEW HOMES OF SOCCER

Newly-constructed League grounds in Britain since the war: 1946 Hull City (Boothferry Park); 1950 Port Vale (Vale Park); 1955 Southend Utd. (Roots Hall); 1988 Scunthorpe Utd. (Glanford Park); 1988 St. Johnstone (McDiarmid Park); 1990 Walsall (Bescot Stadium); 1990 Wycombe Wand. (Adams Park); 1992 Chester City (Deva Stadium, Bumpers Lane); 1993 Millwall (New Den); 1994 Clyde (Broadwood Stadium); 1994 Huddersfield Town (Alfred McAlpine Stadium, Kirklees); 1994 Northampton Town (Sixfields Stadium); 1995 Middlesbrough (Riverside Stadium); 1997 Bolton Wand. (Reebok Stadium, Horwich); 1997 Derby Co. (Pride Park); Stoke City (Britannia Stadium); Sunderland (Stadium of Light); 1998 Reading (Madejski Stadium); 1999 Wigan Athletic (JJB Stadium).

GROUND-SHARING

Crystal Palace and **Charlton Athletic** (Selhurst Park, 1985-91); **Bristol Rov.** and **Bath City** (Twerton Park, Bath, 1986-96); **Partick Thistle** and **Clyde** (Firhill Park, Glasgow, 1986-91; in seasons 1990-1, 1991-2 **Chester City** shared **Macclesfield Town's** ground (Moss Rose). **Crystal Palace** and **Wimbledon** now share Selhurst Park, starting season 1991-2, when **Charlton Athletic** (tenants) moved to rent Upton Park from **West Ham Utd..** **Clyde** moved to Douglas Park, **Hamilton Academicals'** home, in 1991-2. **Stirling Albion** shared Stenhousemuir's ground, Ochilview Park, in 1992-3. In 1993-4, **Clyde** shared **Partick's** home until moving to their new ground. In 1994-5, **Celtic** shared Hampden Park with **Queen's Park** (while Celtic Park was redeveloped); **Hamilton** shared **Partick's** ground. **Airdrie** shared **Clyde's** Broadwood Stadium. **Bristol Rov.** left Bath City's ground at the start of season 1996-7, sharing Bristol Rugby Club's Memorial Ground. **Dumbarton** and **Clydebank** shared Boghead Park from 1996-7.

ARTIFICIAL TURF

Q.P.R. were the first British club to install an artificial pitch, in 1981. They were followed by **Luton Town** in 1985, and **Oldham Athletic** and **Preston N.E. in 1986**. Q.P.R. reverted to grass in 1988, as did Luton Town and promoted Oldham Athletic in season 1991-2 (when artificial pitches were banned in Div. 1). **Preston N.E.** were the last Football League club playing 'on plastic' in 1993-4, and their Deepdale ground was restored to grass for the start of 1994-5.

Stirling Albion were the **first Scottish club** to play on plastic, in season 1987-8.

F.A. SOCCER SCHOOL

The Football Association's **national soccer school**, at Lilleshall, aimed at providing the backbone of England's World Cup challenge in the 1990s, was opened by the Duke of Kent (President) on September 4, 1984. It was sponsored by GM Motors, and the first intake comprised 25 boys aged fourteen.

The School of Excellence produced England Internationals Nick Barmby, Andy Cole, Sol Campbell, Ian Walker and Michael Owen. It closed in 1999, to be replaced nationwide by academies at leading clubs.

DOUBLE RUNNERS-UP

There have been eight instances of clubs finishing **runner-up in both the League Championship and F.A. Cup in the same season**: 1928 Huddersfield Town; 1932 Arsenal; 1939 Wolves; 1962 Burnley; 1965 and 1970 Leeds Utd.; 1986 Everton; 1995 Manchester Utd.

CORNER-KICK RECORDS

Not a single corner-kick was recorded when **Newcastle Utd.** drew 0-0 at home to **Portsmouth** (Div.1) on December 5, 1931.

The record for **most corners** in a match for one side is believed to be **Sheffield Utd.'s 28** to West Ham Utd.'s 1 in Div.2 at Bramall Lane on October 14, 1989. For all their pressure, Sheffield Utd. lost 2-0.

Nott'm. Forest led Southampton 22-2 on corners (Premier League, Nov. 28, 1992) but lost the match 1-2.

Tommy Higginson (Brentford, 1960s) once passed back to his own goalkeeper from a corner kick.

'PROFESSIONAL FOUL' DIRECTIVE

After the 1990 World Cup Finals, F.I.F.A. dealt with the **'professional foul'**, incorporating this directive into the Laws of the Game: 'If, in the opinion of the referee, a player who is moving towards his opponents' goal, with an obvious opportunity to score, is intentionally impeded by an opponent through unlawful means – thus denying the attacking player's team the aforesaid goalscoring opportunity – the offender should be sent from the field of play.'

SACKED AT HALF-TIME

Leyton Orient sacked **Terry Howard** on his 397th. appearance for the club – at half-time in a Second Division home defeat against Blackpool (Feb. 7, 1995) for 'an unacceptable performance'. He was fined two weeks' wages, given a free transfer and moved to Wycombe Wand.

MOST GAMES BY 'KEEPER FOR ONE CLUB

At the end of 1998-9, **Alan Knight** had made 682 League appearances for Portsmouth, over 22 seasons, a record for a goalkeeper at one club. The previous holder was Peter Bonetti with 600 League games for Chelsea (20 seasons, 1960-79).

COLOURFUL REFS

With the launch of the F.A. Premier League in 1992-3, referees wore **green, purple** or **yellow shirts**. Traditional all-black kit was still used when there was a clash with team colours.

PLAYED TWO GAMES ON SAME DAY

Jack Kelsey played full-length matches for both club and country on Wed., November 26, 1958. In the afternoon he kept goal for Wales in a 2-2 draw against England at Aston Villa Park, and he then drove to Highbury to help Arsenal win 3-1 in a prestigious floodlit friendly against Juventus.

On the same day, winger **Danny Clapton** played for England (against Wales and Kelsey) and then in part of Arsenal's match against Juventus.

On November 11, 1987, **Mark Hughes** played for Wales against Czechoslovakia (European Championship) in Prague, then flew to Munich and went on as substitute that night in a winning Bayern Munich team, to whom he was on loan from Barcelona.

On February 16, 1993 goalkeeper **Scott Howie** played in Scotland's 3-0 U-21 win v Malta at Tannadice Park, Dundee (k.o. 1.30pm) and the same evening played in Clyde's 2-1 home win v Queen of South (Div. 2).

GOING PUBLIC

Manchester Utd. became the fourth British club (after Tottenham, Hibernian and Millwall) to 'go public' with a Stock Exchange share issue in June 1991. Clubs who have since unfolded flotation plans include Chelsea, Preston N.E., Celtic, Leeds Utd., Newcastle Utd., Sunderland, Aston Villa, Birmingham City, West Ham Utd., W.B.A. and Sheffield Utd..

FIRST 'MATCH OF THE DAY'

BBC TV (recorded highlights): Liverpool 3, Arsenal 2 on August 22, 1964. **First complete match to be televised:** Arsenal 3, Everton 2 on August 29, 1936. **First League match televised in colour:** Liverpool 2, West Ham Utd. 0 on November 15, 1969.

'MATCH OF THE DAY' – BIGGEST SCORES

Football League: Tottenham 9, Bristol Rov. 0 (Div. 2, 1977-8). **Premier League:** Nott'm Forest 1, Manchester Utd. 8 (1998-9).

OLYMPIC SOCCER WINNERS

1908 Great Britain (in London); **1912** Great Britain (Stockholm); **1920** Belgium (Antwerp); **1924** Uruguay (Paris); **1928** Uruguay (Amsterdam); **1932** No soccer in Los Angeles Olympics.
1936 Italy (Berlin); **1948** Sweden (London); **1952** Hungary (Helsinki); **1956** USSR (Melbourne); **1960** Yugoslavia (Rome); **1964** Hungary (Tokyo).
1968 Hungary (Mexico); **1972** Poland (Munich); **1976** E. Germany (Montreal); **1980** Czechoslovakia (Moscow); **1984** France (Los Angeles); **1988** USSR (Seoul); **1992** Spain (Barcelona); **1996** Nigeria (Atlanta).
Highest scorer in Final tournament: Ferenc Bene (Hungary) 12 goals, 1964.
Record crowd for Olympic Soccer Final: 108,800 (France v Brazil, Los Angeles 1984).

MOST AMATEUR CUP WINS

Bishop Auckland set the F.A. Amateur Cup record with 10 wins, and in 1957 became the only club to carry off the trophy in three successive seasons. Five wins: Clapton and Crook Town. The competition was discontinued after the Final on April 20, 1974. (Bishop's Stortford 4, Ilford 1, at Wembley).

THE FOOTBALL TRUST

The Football Trust founded in 1975 – an initiative of Pools companies Littlewoods, Vernons and Zetters – has been providing support for the game at every level throughout the UK for 24 years, from kit and equipment for school teams to pitches and dressing rooms for local clubs and safety and improvement work throughout the game.

Grants exceeding £140m. have been made to major ground redevelopment projects across Britain, towards the construction of 150 new/refurbished stands in Premier League, Football League and Scottish League and the opening of new grounds.

The F.A. Premier League will contribute £20m. to the Football Trust from 1997-2001 during which, via the Trust and the Sports Council Lottery Fund, grants of £55m. will be made for essential work at football grounds throughout England.

RECORD TESTIMONIALS

Two nights after Manchester Utd. completed the Double in May, 1994, 42,079 packed Old Trafford for **Mark Hughes'** testimonial (1-3 Celtic). The estimated proceeds of £500,000 equalled the then testimonial record of **Ally McCoist's** match (Rangers 1, Newcastle Utd. 2) on August 3, 1993.

The match for **Bryan Robson**, Manchester Utd. and England captain, against Celtic at Old Trafford on Tuesday, November 20, 1990 was watched by a crowd of 41,658, and receipts of £300,000 were a then record for a testimonial.

Kenny Dalglish's testimonial (Liverpool v Real Sociedad) at Anfield on August 14, 1990 attracted 30,461 spectators, with receipts estimated at £150,000.

On December 4, 1990, **Willie Miller's** testimonial (Aberdeen v World XI) packed Pittodrie to its 22,500 capacity, and raised an estimated £150,000.

The match for 82-year-old **Sir Matt Busby**, between Manchester Utd. and a Rep. of Ireland XI at Old Trafford on Sunday, August 11, 1991 was watched by 35,410 (estimated benefit £250,000).

Ian Rush's testimonial brought an estimated £250,000 from a 25,856 crowd at Anfield on December 6, 1994 (Liverpool 6, Celtic 0).

Three lucrative testimonials were staged in May 1996. Arsenal's **Paul Merson** earned a reported £400,000 (a percentage to charity) from his match against an Int. XI at Highbury (May 9, att: 31,626); the Republic of Ireland's new manager **Mick McCarthy** received an estimated £300,000 from a 40,000 crowd who saw Celtic beaten 3-0 at Lansdowne Road, Dublin on May 26; and **Stuart Pearce** benefited by some £200,000 from a turn-out of 23,815 when Nott'm. Forest beat Newcastle Utd. 6-5 at the City Ground on May 8.

Testimonial sums reported in season 1996-7 included: **Bryan Gunn**, Norwich City goalkeeper, £250,000 for 21,000 sell-out v Manchester Utd., Nov. 4; **Brian McClair**, Manchester Utd., £380,000 v Celtic, April 14.

Among testimonials in 1997-8: A full-house 50,000 at Ibrox paid an estimated £500,000 for retiring manager **Walter Smith** (Rangers 1, Liverpool 0) on March 3, 1998.

Paul McGrath's testimonial at Lansdowne Road, Dublin (May 17, 1998) produced record receipts of £600,000. A crowd of 39,000 saw Jack Charlton's XI beat a Rep. Of Ireland XI 3-2.

A crowd of 49,468 attended Ibrox (Rangers 4, Middlesbrough 4) on March 2, 1999 for former Rangers player **Alan McLaren's** testimonial. His fund benefited by an estimated £500,000.

A capacity crowd of 36,733 packed St. James' Park, paying an estimated £250,000, for **Peter Beardsley's** testimonial (Newcastle Utd. 1, Celtic 3) on Jan. 27, 1999.

WHAT IT USED TO COST

Minimum admission to League football was one shilling in 1939. After the war, it was increased to 1s. 3d. in 1946; 1s. 6d. in 1951; 1s. 9d. in 1952; 2s. in 1955; 2s. 6d. in 1960; 4s. in 1965; 5s. in 1968; 6s. in 1970; and 8s. (40p) in 1972. After that, the fixed minimum charge was dropped.

WHAT THEY USED TO EARN

In the 1930s, First Division players were on £8 a week (£6 in close season) plus bonuses of £2 win, £1 draw. The maximum wage went up to £12 when football resumed post-war in 1946 and had reached £20 by the time the limit was abolishied in 1961.

ENGLAND TOP EURO-PRIZE WINNERS

There have been **124 European club competitions** since the Champions' Cup was launched in season 1955-6; 44 for the European Cup, 41 for the Fairs/UEFA Cup and 39 for the Cup-Winners' Cup.

Despite the five-year enforced absence that followed the Heysel disaster in 1985, **English clubs** jointly head the European prize list, Manchester Utd.'s success in the 1999 European Cup taking the total to 26 triumphs: 9 in the Champions' Cup, 8 in the Cup-Winners' Cup and 9 in the Fairs/UEFA Cup.

Italy have also won 26 Euro prizes, followed by Spain (23) and West Germany/Germany (15). The 124 winners have come from 16 countries.

England's 26 prizes are shared among 13 clubs: Liverpool 6 (4 EC, 2 UEFA); Manchester Utd. 3 (2 EC, 1 CWC); Tottenham 3 (1 CWC, 2 UEFA); Chelsea 2 (2 CWC); Leeds Utd. 2 (2 UEFA); Nott'm. Forest 2 (2 EC); Arsenal 2 (1 UEFA, 1 CWC); Aston Villa 1 (EC); Everton 1 (CWC); Ipswich Town 1 (UEFA); Manchester City 1 (CWC); Newcastle Utd. 1 (UEFA); West Ham Utd. 1 (CWC).

Scotland's three successes have been achieved by Celtic (EC); Rangers and Aberdeen (both CWC).

EUROPEAN TRIUMPHS, COUNTRY BY COUNTRY

	European Cup	Cup-Winners' Cup	UEFA Cup	Total
England	9	8	9	26
Italy	9	7	10	26
Spain	8	7	8	23
West Germany/Germany	5	4	6	15
Holland	6	1	3	10
Belgium	–	3	1	4
Portugal	3	1	–	4
Scotland	1	2	–	3
USSR	–	3	–	3
France	1	1	–	2
Sweden	–	–	2	2
Yugoslavia	1	–	1	2
Czechoslovakia	–	1	–	1
East Germany	–	1	–	1
Hungary	–	–	1	1
Romania	1	–	–	1
Total:	44	39	41	124

EUROPEAN TROPHY WINNERS – SUMMARY

European Cup (44 competitions, 21 different winners): **7** Real Madrid; **5** AC Milan; **4** Ajax Amsterdam, Liverpool; **3** Bayern Munich; **2** Benfica, Inter Milan, Juventus, Manchester Utd., Nott'm. Forest; **1** Aston Villa, Barcelona, Borussia Dortmund, Celtic, Feyenoord, Hamburg SV, Marseille, PSV Eindhoven, FC Porto, Red Star Belgrade, Steaua Bucharest.

Cup-Winners' Cup (39 competitions, 32 different winners): **4** Barcelona; **2** Anderlecht, Chelsea, Dynamo Kiev, AC Milan; **1** Aberdeen, Ajax Amsterdam, Arsenal, Atletico Madrid, Bayern Munich, Borussia Moenchengladbach, Dynamo Tbilisi, Everton, Fiorentina, Hamburg SV, Juventus, Lazio, Magdeburg, Manchester City, Manchester Utd., Mechelen, Paris St. Germain, Parma, Rangers, Real Zaragoza, Sampdoria, Slovan Bratislava, Sporting Lisbon, Tottenham, Valencia, Werder Bremen, West Ham Utd.

UEFA Cup (orig. Fairs Cup) (41 competitions, 27 different winners): **3** Barcelona, Inter Milan, Juventus; **2** Borussia Moenchengladbach, IFK Gothenburg, Leeds Utd., Liverpool, Parma, Real Madrid, Tottenham, Valencia; **1** Ajax Amsterdam, Anderlecht, Arsenal, Bayer Leverkusen, Bayern Munich, Dynamo Zagreb, Eintracht Frankfurt, PSV Eindhoven, Ferencvaros, Feyenoord, Ipswich Town, Napoli, Newcastle Utd., Real Zaragoza, AS Roma, FC Schalke.

● Four clubs have won all three trophies – Barcelona, Bayern Munich, Juventus and Ajax.

BRITAIN'S 29 TROPHIES IN EUROPE

Manchester United's success in the 1998-99 European Cup took the number of **British** club triumphs in European Football to 29:

European Cup (10)	Cup-Winners' Cup (10)	Fairs/UEFA Cup (9)
1967 Celtic	1963 Tottenham	1968 Leeds Utd.
1968 Manchester Utd.	1965 West Ham Utd.	1969 Newcastle Utd.
1977 Liverpool	1970 Manchester City	1970 Arsenal
1978 Liverpool	1971 Chelsea	1971 Leeds Utd.
1979 Nott'm Forest	1972 Rangers	1972 Tottenham
1980 Nott'm Forest	1983 Aberdeen	1973 Liverpool
1981 Liverpool	1985 Everton	1976 Liverpool
1982 Aston Villa	1991 Manchester Utd.	1981 Ipswich Town
1984 Liverpool	1994 Arsenal	1984 Tottenham
1999 Manchester Utd.	1998 Chelsea	

END OF CUP-WINNERS' CUP

The **European Cup-Winners' Cup**, inaugurated in 1960-61, terminated with the 1999 final. The competition has been merged into a revamped, 96-club **UEFA Cup**.

Also with effect from season 1999-2000, the **European Cup/Champions League** has been increased by 8 clubs to 32.

From its inception in 1955, the **European Cup** comprised only championship-winning clubs until 1998-9, when selected runners-up were introduced. Further expansion comes in 1999-2000 with the inclusion of clubs finishing third in certain leagues.

EUROPEAN CLUB COMPETITIONS – SCORING RECORDS

European Cup – Record aggregate: 18-0 by Benfica v Dudelange (Lux) (8-0a, 10-0h), prelim. round, 1965-6.
　　Record single-match score: 12-0 by Feyenoord v KR Reykjavik (Ice), 1st. round, 1st. leg, 1969-70 (aggregate was 16-0).
Cup-Winners' Cup – Record aggregate: 21-0 by Chelsea v Jeunesse Hautcharage (Lux) (8-0a, 13-0h), 1st. round, 1971-2.
　　Record single-match score: 16-1 by Sporting Lisbon v Apoel Nicosia, 2nd. round, 1st. leg, 1963-4 (aggregate was 18-1).

UEFA Cup (prev. Fairs Cup) – Record aggregate: 21-0 by Feyenoord v US Rumelange (Lux) (9-0h, 12-0a), 1st. round, 1972-3.
Record single-match score: 14-0 by Ajax Amsterdam v Red Boys (Lux) 1st. round, 2nd leg, 1984-5 (aggregate also 14-0).
Record British score in Europe: 13-0 by **Chelsea** at home to Jeunesse Hautcharage (Lux) in Cup-Winners' Cup 1st. round, 2nd. leg, 1971-2. Chelsea's overall 21-0 win in that tie is highest aggregate by British club in Europe.
Individual scoring records for European tie (over two legs): **8 goals** by Jose Altafini for AC Milan v US Luxembourg (European Cup, prelim. round, 1962-3, agg. 14-0) and by **Peter Osgood** for Chelsea v Jeunesse Hautcharage (Cup-Winners' Cup, 1st. round 1971-2, agg. 21-0). Altafini and Osgood each scored 5 goals at home, 3 away.
Individual single-match scoring record in European competition: **6 goals** by **Lothar Emmerich** when Borussia Dortmund beat Floriana (Malta) 8-0 in Cup-Winners' Cup 1st. round, 2nd. leg, 1965-6.
Most goals in single European campaign: 15 by Jurgen Klinsmann for Bayern Munich (UEFA Cup 1995-6).
Most goals (career total) **by British player in European competition:** 31 by Peter Lorimer (Leeds Utd., in 9 campaigns).

EUROPEAN FOOTBALL – BIG RECOVERIES

In the 44-year history of European competition, only four clubs have survived a **4-goal** deficit after the first leg had been completed:
1961-2 (Cup-Winners' Cup 1st. Rd.): Leixoes (Portugal) beat Chaux de Fonds (Luxembourg) 7-6 on agg. (lost 2-6a, won 5-0h).
1962-3 (Fairs Cup 2nd. Rd.): Valencia (Spain) beat **Dunfermline** 1-0 in play-off in Lisbon after 6-6 agg. (Valencia won 4-0h, lost 2-6a).
1984-5 (UEFA Cup 2nd. Rd.): Partizan Belgrade beat **Q.P.R.** on away goals (lost 2-6 away, at Highbury, won 4-0 home).
1985-6 (UEFA Cup 3rd. Rd.): Real Madrid beat Borussia Moenchengladbach on away goals (lost 1-5a, won 4-0h) and went on to win competition.

In the **European Cup**, there are eight instances of clubs reaching the next round after **arrears of three goals** in the first leg:
1958-9 (Prel. Rd.): Schalke beat KB Copenhagen (0-3, 5-2, 3-1).
1965-6 (Q-final) Partizan Belgrade beat Sparta Prague (1-4, 5-0).
1970-1 (Q-final) Panathinaikos beat Red Star Belgrade on away goal (1-4, 3-0).
1975-6 (2nd. Rd.) Real Madrid beat **Derby Co.** (1-4, 5-1).
1985-6 (S-final) Barcelona beat IFK Gothenburg on pens. (0-3, 3-0).
1988-9 (1st. Rd.) Werder Bremen beat Dynamo Berlin (0-3, 5-0).
1988-9 (2nd. Rd.) Galatasaray (Turkey) beat Neuchatel Xamax (Switz.) (0-3, 5-0).
1992-3 (1st. Rd.) **Leeds Utd.** beat VfB Stuttgart 2-1 in play-off in Barcelona. Over two legs, VfB won on away goal (3-0h, 1-4 away) but was ordered third match because they broke 'foreigners' rule in team selection.

In the **Cup-Winners' Cup**, six clubs survived a **3-goal** deficit:
1963-4 (Q-final) Sporting Lisbon beat **Manchester Utd.** (1-4, 5-0).
1963-4 (S-final) MTK Budapest beat **Celtic** (0-3, 4-0).
1978-9 (2nd. Rd.) Barcelona beat Anderlecht on pens. (0-3, 3-0).
1980-1 (1st. Rd.) Carl Zeiss Jena beat AS Roma (0-3, 4-0).
1984-5 (Q-final) Rapid Vienna beat Dynamo Dresden (0-3, 5-0).
1989-90 (1st. Rd.) Grasshoppers (Switz.) beat Slovan Bratislava (0-3, 4-0).

In the **Fairs Cup/UEFA Cup**, there have been more than 20 occasions when clubs have survived a deficit of **3 goals**, the most notable example being the 1988 UEFA Cup Final, which Bayer Leverkusen won 3-2 on pens., having lost the first leg 0-3 away to Espyanol and won the return 3-0 to level the aggregate.

Apart from Leeds Utd., two other British clubs have won a European tie from a 3-goal, first leg deficit: **Kilmarnock** 0-3, 5-1 v Eintracht Frankfurt (Fairs Cup 1st. Round, 1964-5); **Hibernian** 1-4, 5-0 v Napoli (Fairs Cup 2nd. Round, 1967-8).

English clubs have three times gone out of the **UEFA Cup** after leading 3-0 from the first leg: 1975-6 (2nd. Rd.) **Ipswich Town** lost 3-4 on agg. to Bruges; 1976-7 (Q-final) **Q.P.R.** lost on pens. to AEK Athens after 3-3 agg; 1977-8 (3rd. Rd.) **Ipswich Town** lost on pens. to Barcelona after 3-3 agg.

HEAVIEST ENGLISH-CLUB DEFEATS IN EUROPE

(Single-leg scores)

European Cup: Ajax 5, Liverpool 1 (2nd. Rd.), Dec. 1966 (agg. 7-3); Real Madrid 5, Derby Co. 1 (2nd. Rd.), Nov. 1975 (agg. 6-5).
Cup-Winners' Cup: Sporting Lisbon 5, Manchester Utd. 0 (Q-final), Mar. 1964 (agg. 6-4).
Fairs/UEFA Cup: Bayern Munich 6, Coventry City 1 (2nd. Rd.), Oct. 1970 (agg. 7-3).

SHOCK ENGLISH-CLUB DEFEATS

1968-69 (E. Cup, 1st. Rd.): Manchester City beaten by Fenerbahce, 1-2 agg.
1971-72 (CWC, 2nd. Rd.): Chelsea beaten by Atvidaberg on away goals.
1993-94 (E. Cup, 2nd. Rd.): Manchester Utd. beaten by Galatasaray on away goals.
1994-95 (UEFA Cup, 1st. Rd.): Blackburn Rov. beaten by Trelleborgs, 2-3 agg.

FIFA'S HALL OF CHAMPIONS (Named on January 12, 1998)

Ten retired players, honoured for 'sporting success that contributed to the positive image of the game' – Sir Stanley Matthews, Sir Bobby Charlton (England), Pele (Brazil), Franz Beckenbauer (W. Germany), Johan Cruyff (Holland), Alfredo di Stefano (Argentina), Eusebio (Portugal), Michel Platini (France), Ferenc Puskas (Hungary), Lev Yashin (Soviet Union).

Managers: Sir Matt Busby (Manchester Utd.), Rinus Michels (Ajax Amsterdam).

100 FOOTBALL LEGENDS

The **Football League** celebrated its 100th season with an 'Evening of Legends' dinner in London (May 1999). To mark the occasion, 100 players were selected by a panel of football writers – footballers who stood out, by reputation and achievement, and graced the League since its inception in 1888:

Tony Adams 1983-99, Ivor Allchurch 1948-64, Ossie Ardiles 1978-90, Jimmy Armfield 1954-71, Alan Ball 1962-84, Gordon Banks 1958-73, John Barnes 1981-99, Billy Bassett 1888-1900, Cliff Bastin 1927-48, Colin Bell 1963-79, Dennis Bergkamp 1995-99, George Best 1963-83, Danny Blanchflower 1948-64, Steve Bloomer 1892-1915, Liam Brady 1973-90, Billy Bremner 1959-82, Charles Buchan 1910-29, George Camsell 1924-39, Eric Cantona 1991-97, Johnny Carey 1937-54.

Raich Carter 1932-53, John Charles 1948-66, Bobby Charlton 1956-75, Ray Clemence 1965-88, Alf Common 1900-15, Wilf Copping 1930-39, Bob Crompton 1896-1921, Kenny Dalglish 1977-1990, Dixie Dean 1923-39, Jimmy Dickinson 1946-65, Peter Doherty 1933-54, Ted Drake 1931-39, Duncan Edwards 1953-58, Tom Finney 1946-60, Trevor Ford 1946-61, Billy Foulke 1894-1908, Trevor Francis 1970-95, Neil Franklin 1946-58, Hughie Gallacher 1925-39, Paul Gascoigne 1984-99.

Ryan Giggs 1990-99, Johnny Giles 1959-77, John Goodall 1888-1904, Jimmy Greaves 1957-71, Alan Hansen 1977-90, Eddie Hapgood 1927-39, George Hardwick 1937-56, Sam Hardy 1902-26, Johnny Haynes 1952-70, Harry Hibbs 1925-39, Glenn Hoddle 1974-96, Archie Hunter 1888-91, Norman Hunter 1962-83, Geoff Hurst 1959-76, David Jack 1920-35, Alex James 1925-38, Pat Jennings 1962-85, Cliff Jones 1952-70, Kevin Keegan 1968-84, Denis Law 1956-74.

Tommy Lawton 1935-57, Billy Liddell 1946-61, Gary Lineker 1978-93, Nat Lofthouse 1946-61, Dave Mackay 1958-72, Wilf Mannion 1936-56, Stanley Matthews 1931-66, Bill McCracken 1904-24, Malcom Macdonald 1968-77, Paul McGrath 1981-98, Jimmy McIlroy 1950-68, Frank McLintock 1959-77, Joe Mercer 1932-54,

Billy Meredith 1893-1925, Jack Milburn 1946-57, Bobby Moore 1958-77, Stan Mortensen 1938-58, Alan Mullery 1958-76, Terry Paine 1956-77, Martin Peters 1960-81.
Alf Ramsey 1946-55, Bryan Robson 1974-97, Arthur Rowley 1946-65, Ian Rush 1978-90, Peter Schmeichel 1991-99, Elisha Scott 1912-34, Len Shackleton 1946-58, Alan Shearer 1987-99, Peter Shilton 1965-97, Frank Swift 1933-51, Tommy Smith 1962-79, Graeme Souness 1972-84, Neville Southall 1980-99, Clem Stephenson 1910-30, Nobby Stiles 1959-74, Tommy Taylor 1950-58, Bert Trautmann 1949-64, Vivian Woodward 1908-15, Billy Wright 1946-59, Alex Young 1960-69.

P.F.A. FAIR PLAY TROPHY (Bobby Moore Fair Play Trophy from 1993)

1988	Liverpool		1994	Crewe Alexandra
1989	Liverpool		1995	Crewe Alexandra
1990	Liverpool		1996	Crewe Alexandra
1991	Nott'm. Forest		1997	Crewe Alexandra
1992	Portsmouth		1998	Cambridge Utd.
1993	Norwich City		1999	Grimsby

RECORD MEDALS SALE

'The **Billy Wright Collection**' – caps, medals and other memorabilia from his illustrious career – fetched over £100,000 at Christies' ninth annual football sale in Glasgow on Nov. 21, 1996.

At the sale in Oct. 1993, trophies, caps and medals earned by **Ray Kennedy**, 42-year-old former England, Arsenal and Liverpool player, fetched a then record total of £88,407. Kennedy, who suffers from Parkinson's Disease, received £73,000 after commission.

The P.F.A. paid £31,080 for a total of 60 lots – including a record £16,000 for his 1977 European Cup winner's medal – to be exhibited at their Manchester museum. An anonymous English collector paid £17,000 for the medal and plaque commemorating Kennedy's part in the Arsenal Double in 1971.

Previous records for one player's medals, shirts etc. collection: £30,000 (**Bill Foulkes**, Manchester Utd. in 1992). The sale of **Dixie Dean**'s medals etc. in 1991 realised £28,000.

A 1966 World Cup winner's-medal belonging to **George Cohen** was withdrawn from sale when it failed to reach its reserve price at an auction in June 1998. The bidding reached £55,000.

VARSITY MATCH

Oxford Utd. beat **Cambridge Utd.** 1-0 in the 115th Varsity soccer match at Fulham on March 28 last. Cambridge Utd. have won 45, Oxford Utd. 44, with 26 draws. The fixture began in 1874.

LONGEST UNBEATEN CUP RUN

Liverpool established the longest unbeaten Cup sequence by a Football League club: 25 successive rounds in the League/Milk Cup between semi-final defeat by Nott'm. Forest (1-2 agg.) in 1980 and defeat at Tottenham (0-1) in the third round on October 31, 1984. During this period Liverpool won the tournament in four successive seasons, a feat no other Football League club has achieved in any competition.

NEAR £1M. RECORD DAMAGES

A High Court judge in Newcastle (May 7, 1999) awarded Bradford City's 28-year-old striker **Gordon Watson** record damages for a football injury: £909,143. He had had his right leg fractured in two places by Huddersfield Town's Kevin Gray on Feb. 1, 1997.

Huddersfield Town were 'proven negligent for allowing their player to make a rushed tackle'. The award was calculated at £202,643 for loss of earnings, £730,500 for 'potential career earnings' if he had joined a Premiership club, plus £26,000 to cover medical treatment and care.

Watson, awarded £50,000 in an earlier legal action, had a 6-inch plate inserted in the leg. He resumed playing for City last season.

F.A. SHOCK DEPARTURES

The Football Association lost three top men in a matter of 50 days in the middle of season 1998-9. On December 15 chief executive **Graham Kelly** resigned, as did chairman **Keith Wiseman** on January 4 – both departures following the grant of £3.2m. to the Welsh F.A. without the authority of the F.A. Council – and on February 2 England coach **Glenn Hoddle** was sacked after making remarks that offended disabled people.

HIGH HALF-TIME SCORES

Tottenham 10, Crewe Alexandra 1 (F.A. Cup 4th. Rd. replay, Feb. 3, 1960; result 13-2); Tranmere Rov. 8, Oldham Athletic 1 (Div. 3N., Dec. 26, 1935; result 13-4); Chester City 8, York City 0 (Div. 3N., Feb. 1, 1936; result 12-0; believed to be record half-time scores in League football).

Stirling Albion led Selkirk 15-0 at half-time (result 20-0) in the Scottish Cup 1st. Rd., Dec. 8, 1984.

● On March 4, 1933 Coventry City beat Q.P.R. (Div. 3 South) 7-0, having led by that score at half-time. This repeated Bristol City's win over Grimsby Town on Dec. 26, 1914.

● Only instance of club failing to win League match after leading 5-0 at half-time: Sheffield Wed. 5, Everton 5 (Div. 1, Nov. 12, 1904; Wed. scored 5 in first half, Everton 5 in second).

TOP SECOND-HALF TEAM

Most goals scored by a team in one half of a League match is eleven. Stockport Co. led Halifax Town 2-0 at half-time in Div. 3 North on Jan. 6, 1934 and won 13-0.

FIVE NOT ENOUGH

Last team to score 5 in League match and lose: Reading, beaten 7-5 at Doncaster Rov. (Div. 3, Sept. 25, 1982).

LONG SERVICE WITH ONE CLUB

Bob Paisley was associated with Liverpool for 57 years from 1939, when he joined them from Bishop Auckland, until he died in February 1996. He served them as player, trainer, coach, assistant-manager, manager, director and vice-president.

Ronnie Moran, who joined Liverpool in as a player 1952, retired from the Anfield coaching staff in season 1998-9.

Ernie Gregory served West Ham Utd. for 52 years as goalkeeper and coach. He joined them as boy of 14 from school in 1935, retired in May 1987.

Ted Sagar, Everton goalkeeper, 23 years at Goodison Park (1929-52, but only 16 League seasons because of War).

Roy Sproson, defender, played 21 League seasons for his only club, Port Vale (1950-71).

Allan Ball, goalkeeper, 20 seasons with Queen of the South (1963-83).

Pat Bonner, goalkeeper, 19 seasons with Celtic (1978-97).

Danny McGrain, defender, 17 years with Celtic (1970-87).

TIGHT AT HOME

Fewest home goals conceded in League season (modern times): 4 by **Liverpool** (Div. 1, 1978-9); 4 by **Manchester Utd.** (Premier League, 1994-5) – both in 21 matches.

TRIBUNAL-FEE RECORDS

Top tribunal fee: £2.5m for **Chris Bart-Williams** (Sheffield Wed. to Nott'm. Forest, June 1995).

Biggest discrepancy: **Andy Walker**, striker, Bolton Wand. to Celtic, June 1994: Bolton Wand. asked £2.2m, Celtic offered £250,000. Tribunal decided £550,000.

LONGEST THROW-IN?

That by Notts Co.'s **Andy Legg** was measured (season 1994-5) at 41 metres (45 yards) and claimed as the longest throw by any footballer in the world, until 1997-8, when **Dave Challinor** (Tranmere Rov.) reached 46.3 metres (50½ yards).

BALL JUGGLING: WORLD RECORD CLAIM

Sam Ik (South Korea) juggled a ball non-stop for 18 hours, 11 minutes, 4 seconds in March 1995.

SUBS' SCORING RECORD

Barnet's 5-4 home win v Torquay Utd. (Div. 3, Dec. 28, 1993) provided the first instance of **all four substitutes** scoring in a major League match in England.

FOOTBALL'S OLDEST ANNUAL

Now in its 113th edition, this publication began as the 16-page *Athletic News Football Supplement & Club Directory* in 1887. From the long-established *Athletic News*, it became the *Sunday Chronicle Annual* in 1946, the *Empire News* in 1956, the *News of the World & Empire News* in 1961 and, since 1965, the *News of the World Annual*.

QUOTE – UNQUOTE

'Dick Knight wouldn't recognise Gareth Barry if he stood on Brighton beach in an Albion shirt with a ball tucked under his arm and a seagull on his head' – Aston Villa manager **John Gregory** on Brighton & H.A. chairman Dick Knight's ability to identify the outstanding youngster who left Albion for Villa Park.

'I knew I was in trouble when I realised the last person to wish me luck as I left the dressing room was the club chaplain' – Charlton Athletic goalkeeper **Mike Salmon** whose one-match loan at Oxford Utd. resulted in a 7-1 beating by Birmingham City.

'If England's coaches got time to work properly on the training pitch it would take just two seasons and they'd wipe the floor with the likes of Real Madrid, Juventus and Barcelona. But in England there's no time to teach players tactics and new skills. The way the FA organise English football is all wrong' – Dutchman **Leo Beenhakker**, who established a reputation as one of the world's leading coaches by winning six League titles in Holland and Spain.

'Our gates just aren't big enough to produce the revenue. Wages are too high and we are quite prepared to go back to part-time football!' – Rotherham Utd. chairman **Ken Booth**.

'It's unbelievable. Maybe Mr Blatter drank too much champagne to welcome the New Year' – Arsenal manager **Arsene Wenger**'s response to Sepp Blatter's call for a biennial World Cup.

'Well, that's a bit of cool panic' – ITV pundit **Ron Atkinson** during the Inter-Manchester Utd. European Cup quarter final.

'There is an obligation on the FA to protect the integrity of the game' – Former Lancaster Gate Chief Executive **Graham Kelly**.

TRANSFER TRAIL

For space reasons, it is no longer possible to include every million-pound transfer involving British clubs since the first such deal: **Trevor Francis** from Birmingham City to Nott'm. Forest (£1,180,000) in Feb. 1979. All deals of £2m and below are not included for the same reason.

Alan Shearer became the world's first £15m. player when he moved from Blackburn Rov. to Newcastle Utd. in July 1996. Key:

★	=	British record fee at that time	H	=	Record paid for winger
A	=	Record all-British deal	J	=	Record received for winger
B	=	Record for goalkeeper	K	=	Record for teenager
C	=	Record for defender	L	=	Most expensive foreign import
D	=	Record deal between English and	M	=	Record English-club signing
		Scottish clubs	N	=	Record British striker
E	=	Record fee paid by Scottish club			(• Fees as at time of transfer, i.e. not
F	=	Record fee to Scottish club			including any subsequent increases)
G	=	Record all-Scottish deal			

	Player	From	To	Date	£
AMN★	Alan Shearer	Blackburn Rov.	Newcastle Utd.	7/96	15,000,000
	Dwight Yorke	Aston Villa	Manchester Utd.	8/98	12,600,000
	Juninho	Middlesbrough	Atl. Madrid	7/97	12,000,000
L C	Jaap Stam	PSV Eindhoven	Manchester Utd.	5/98	10,750,000
	Chris Sutton	Blackburn Rov.	Chelsea	7/99	10,000,000
★	Stan Collymore	Nott'm Forest	Liverpool	6/95	8,500,000
J	Andrei Kanchelskis	Everton	Fiorentina	1/97	8,000,000
★	Dennis Bergkamp	Inter Milan	Arsenal	6/95	7,500,000
	Kevin Davies	Southampton	Blackburn Rov.	6/98	7,500,000
	John Hartson	West Ham Utd.	Wimbledon	1/99	7,500,000
★	Andy Cole	Newcastle Utd.	Manchester Utd.	1/95	7,000,000
	Fabrizio Ravanelli	Juventus	Middlesbrough	7/96	7,000,000
	Stan Collymore	Liverpool	Aston Villa	5/97	7,000,000
H	Marc Overmars	Ajax Amsterdam	Arsenal	6/97	7,000,000
	Duncan Ferguson	Everton	Newcastle Utd.	11/98	7,000,000
	Paul Merson	Middlesbrough	Aston Villa	8/98	6,750,000
	Faustino Asprilla	Parma	Newcastle Utd.	2/96	6,700,000
★	David Platt	Bari	Juventus	6/92	6,500,000
	Olivier Dacourt	Everton	Lens	6/99	6,500,000
★	Paul Ince	Manchester Utd.	Inter Milan	6/95	6,000,000
	Les Ferdinand	Q.P.R.	Newcastle Utd.	6/95	6,000,000
	Les Ferdinand	Newcastle Utd.	Tottenham	7/97	6,000,000
	Faustino Asprilla	Newcastle Utd.	Parma	1/98	6,000,000
	Nick Barmby	Middlesbrough	Everton	10/96	5,750,000
	Dion Dublin	Coventry City	Aston Villa	10/98	5,750,000
★	David Platt	Aston Villa	Bari	7/91	5,500,000
★	Paul Gascoigne	Tottenham	Lazio	6/92	5,500,000
	Fabrizio Ravanelli	Middlesbrough	Marseille	9/97	5,500,000
	Gary Speed	Everton	Newcastle Utd.	2/98	5,500,000
	Georgi Kinkladze	Manchester City	Ajax	5/98	5,500,000
E	Andrei Kanchelskis	Fiorentina	Rangers	7/98	5,500,000
	Steve Stone	Nott'm Forest	Aston Villa	3/99	5,500,000
	Eyal Berkovic	West Ham Utd.	Celtic	7/99	5,500,000
	Pierluigi Casiraghi	Lazio	Chelsea	5/98	5,400,000
	Christian Dailly	Derby Co.	Blackburn Rov.	8/98	5,300,000
	Nick Barmby	Tottenham	Middlesbrough	8/95	5,250,000
	Dieter Hamann	Bayern Munich	Newcastle Utd.	7/98	5,250,000

	Name	From	To	Date	Fee
	David Platt	Juventus	Sampdoria	7/93	5,200,000
F	Trevor Steven	Rangers	Marseille	8/91	5,000,000
	Chris Sutton	Norwich City	Blackburn Rov.	7/94	5,000,000
	Andrei Kanchelskis	Manchester Utd.	Everton	8/95	5,000,000
	Paul Merson	Arsenal	Middlesbrough	7/97	5,000,000
	Graeme Le Saux	Blackburn Rov.	Chelsea	8/97	5,000,000
	Henning Berg	Blackburn Rov.	Manchester Utd.	8/97	5,000,000
	Arthur Numan	PSV Eindhoven	Rangers	7/98	5,000,000
	Elena Marcelino	Real Mallorca	Newcastle Utd.	6/99	5,000,000
	Roberto Di Matteo	Lazio	Chelsea	7/96	4,900,000
	David Platt	Sampdoria	Arsenal	7/95	4,750,000
	Juninho	Sao Paulo	Middlesbrough	10/95	4,750,000
	Alain Goma	Paris St. Germain	Newcastle Utd.	6/99	4,750,000
	Marcel Desailly	AC Milan	Chelsea	6/98	4,600,000
	Chris Armstrong	Crystal Palace	Tottenham	6/95	4,500,000
	Lee Sharpe	Manchester Utd.	Leeds Utd.	8/96	4,500,000
	Gianfranco Zola	Parma	Chelsea	11/96	4,500,000
	Slaven Bilic	West Ham Utd.	Everton	5/97	4,500,000
D	Paolo Di Canio	Celtic	Sheffield Wed.	8/97	4,500,000
	Jason McAteer	Bolton Wand.	Liverpool	9/95	4,500,000
	Alan Thompson	Bolton Wand.	Aston Villa	6/98	4,500,000
	Ibrahim Bakayoko	Montpellier	Everton	10/98	4,500,000
	Jesper Blomqvist	Parma	Manchester Utd.	7/98	4,400,000
	David Batty	Newcastle Utd.	Leeds Utd.	12/98	4,400,000
	Paul Gascoigne	Lazio	Rangers	7/95	4,300,000
	Tomas Brolin	Parma	Leeds Utd.	11/95	4,300,000
	Alessandro Pistone	Inter Milan	Newcastle Utd.	7/97	4,300,000
★	Chris Waddle	Tottenham	Marseille	7/89	4,250,000
	Nathan Blake	Bolton Wand.	Blackburn Rov.	10/98	4,250,000
	Ashley Ward	Barnsley	Blackburn Rov.	11/98	4,250,000
	Ruel Fox	Newcastle Utd.	Tottenham	10/95	4,200,000
	Paul Ince	Inter Milan	Liverpool	7/97	4,200,000
	Emerson	Middlesbrough	Tenerife	1/98	4,200,000
	Gabriel Amato	Real Mallorca	Rangers	7/98	4,200,000
	Matt Jansen	Crystal Palace	Blackburn Rov.	1/99	4,100,000
G	Duncan Ferguson	Dundee Utd.	Rangers	7/93	4,000,000
	Duncan Ferguson	Rangers	Everton	12/94	4,000,000
	Warren Barton	Wimbledon	Newcastle Utd.	6/95	4,000,000
	David Batty	Blackburn Rov.	Newcastle Utd.	2/96	4,000,000
	Emerson	FC Porto	Middlesbrough	5/96	4,000,000
	Jorg Albertz	Hamburg	Rangers	7/96	4,000,000
	Sasa Curcic	Bolton Wand.	Aston Villa	8/96	4,000,000
	Viorel Moldovan	Coventry City	Fenerbache	7/98	4,000,000
	Colin Hendry	Blackburn Rov.	Rangers	8/98	4,000,000
	Steve Watson	Newcastle Utd.	Aston Villa	10/98	4,000,000
	Jason McAteer	Liverpool	Blackburn Rov.	1/99	4,000,000
B	Sander Westerveld	Vitesse Arnhem	Liverpool	6/99	4,000,000
	Danny Mills	Charlton Athletic	Leeds Utd.	6/99	4,000,000
	Ibrahim Bakayoko	Everton	Marseille	6/99	4,000,000
	Michael Mols	Utrecht	Rangers	6/99	4,000,000
	Silvinho	Corinthians	Arsenal	6/99	4,000,000
	Chris Perry	Wimbledon	Tottenham	7/99	4,000,000
	Lorenzo Amoruso	Fiorentina	Rangers	5/97	3,950,000
	Olivier Dacourt	Strasbourg	Everton	7/98	3,800,000
	Roy Keane	Nott'm. Forest	Manchester Utd.	7/93	3,750,000
	Phil Babb	Coventry City	Liverpool	9/94	3,600,000
	Andreas Andersson	AC Milan	Newcastle Utd.	1/98	3,600,000
	John Scales	Wimbledon	Liverpool	9/94	3,500,000
	Savo Milosevic	P'zan. Belgrade	Aston Villa	6/95	3,500,000

	Alan Stubbs	Bolton Wand.	Celtic	5/96	3,500,000
	Gary Speed	Leeds Utd.	Everton	6/96	3,500,000
	Stephane Henchoz	Blackburn Rov.	Liverpool	6/99	3,500,000
	Pierre van Hooijdonk	Nott'm Forest	Vitesse Arnhem	6/99	3,500,000
	Karel Poborsky	Slavia Prague	Manchester Utd.	7/96	3,500,000
	Patrick Vieira	AC Milan	Arsenal	8/96	3,500,000
	Sebastian Rozental	Univ. Cath (Chile)	Rangers	1/97	3,500,000
	Ramon Vega	Cagliari	Tottenham	1/97	3,500,000
	Oyvind Leonhardsen	Wimbledon	Liverpool	6/97	3,500,000
	Marco Negri	Perugia	Rangers	6/97	3,500,000
	Teddy Sheringham	Tottenham	Manchester Utd.	6/97	3,500,000
	Lee Bradbury	Portsmouth	Manchester City	7/97	3,500,000
	Dean Holdsworth	Wimbledon	Bolton Wand.	10/97	3,500,000
	Savo Milosevic	Aston Villa	R. Zaragoza	5/98	3,500,000
	Stephane Guivarc'h	Auxerre	Newcastle Utd.	6/98	3,500,000
	Vegard Heggem	Rosenborg	Liverpool	7/98	3,500,000
	Rino Gattuso	Rangers	Salernitana	10/98	3,500,000
	Marc Vivien Foe	Lens	West Ham Utd.	1/99	3,500,000
	Paul Gascoigne	Rangers	Middlesbrough	3/98	3,450,000
	Tony Yeboah	Eint. F'furt	Leeds Utd.	1/95	3,400,000
	Stephane Guivarc'h	Rangers	Auxerre	6/99	3,400,000
	Lee Carsley	Derby Co.	Blackburn Rov.	3/99	3,375,000
	Robert Jami	Coventry City	Real Madrid	8/98	3,350,000
★	Alan Shearer	Southampton	Blackburn Rov.	7/92	3,300,000
	John Hartson	Arsenal	West Ham Utd.	2/97	3,300,000
	Silvio Maric	Croatia Zagreb	Newcastle Utd.	2/99	3,300,000
	Mark Draper	Leicester City	Aston Villa	7/95	3,250,000
	Patrik Berger	Bor. Dortmund	Liverpool	7/96	3,250,000
	David Hopkin	Crystal Palace	Leeds Utd.	7/97	3,250,000
	Viorel Moldovan	Grasshopper	Coventry City	12/97	3,250,000
	Didier Domi	Paris St. Germain	Newcastle Utd.	12/98	3,250,000
	Keith Gillespie	Newcastle Utd.	Blackburn Rov.	12/98	3,250,000
★	Ian Rush	Liverpool	Juventus	6/87	3,200,000
	Gheorghe Popescu	Tottenham	Barcelona	5/95	3,200,000
	Garry Flitcroft	Manchester City	Blackburn Rov.	3/96	3,200,000
	Fredrik Ljungberg	Halmstad	Arsenal	9/99	3,200,000
	Daniel Amokachi	Bruges	Everton	8/94	3,000,000
	Sebastien Perez	Bastia	Blackburn Rov.	6/98	3,000,000
	Gary McAllister	Leeds Utd.	Coventry City	7/96	3,000,000
	Benito Carbone	Inter Milan	Sheffield Wed.	10/96	3,000,000
	Pierre van Hooijdonk	Celtic	Nott'm. Forest	3/97	3,000,000
	Emmanuel Petit	Monaco	Arsenal	6/97	3,000,000
	Sergio Porrino	Juventus	Rangers	6/97	3,000,000
	Stephan Henchoz	Hamburg	Blackburn Rov.	6/97	3,000,000
	Jorge Cadete	Celtic	Celta Viga	8/97	3,000,000
	Karel Poborsky	Manchester Utd.	Benfica	12/97	3,000,000
	Trevor Sinclair	Q.P.R.	West Ham Utd.	1/98	3,000,000
	David Unsworth	West Ham Utd.	Aston Villa	7/98	3,000,000
	David Unsworth	Aston Villa	Everton	8/98	3,000,000
	Brian Deane	Benfica	Middlesbrough	10/98	3,000,000
	Stephane Guivar'ch	Newcastle Utd.	Rangers	11/98	3,000,000
	Nwankwo Kanu	Inter Milan	Arsenal	1/99	3,000,000
	Tim Sherwood	Blackburn Rov.	Tottenham	2/99	3,000,000
	Seth Johnson	Crewe Alexandra	Derby Co.	5/99	3,000,000
	Didier Deschamps	Juventus	Chelsea	6/99	3,000,000
	Lee Clark	Sunderland	Fulham	7/99	3,000,000
	Marco Materazzi	Everton	Perugia	7/99	3,000,000
★	Dean Saunders	Derby Co.	Liverpool	7/91	2,900,000
	Gheorghe Popescu	PSV Eindhoven	Tottenham	9/94	2,900,000

Ian Rush	Juventus	Liverpool	8/88	2,800,000
Chris Coleman	Crystal Palace	Blackburn Rov.	12/95	2,800,000
Marco Materazzi	Perugia	Everton	7/98	2,800,000
Gary Lineker	Everton	Barcelona	6/86	2,750,000
Andy Sinton	Q.P.R.	Sheffield Wed.	8/93	2,750,000
David Batty	Leeds Utd.	Blackburn Rov.	10/93	2,750,000
Mike Sheron	Stoke City	Q.P.R.	7/97	2,750,000
Valerien Ismael	Strasbourg	Crystal Palace	1/98	2,750,000
Andy Hinchcliffe	Everton	Sheffield Wed.	1/98	2,750,000
Brian Deane	Sheffield Utd.	Leeds Utd.	7/93	2,700,000
Des Walker	Sampdoria	Sheffield Wed.	7/93	2,700,000
Paul Warhust	Sheffield Wed.	Blackburn Rov.	9/93	2,700,000
Darren Peacock	Q.P.R.	Newcastle Utd.	3/94	2,700,000
Basile Boli	Marseille	Rangers	6/94	2,700,000
Andy Booth	Huddersfield Town	Sheffield Wed.	7/96	2,700,000
Gianluca Festa	Inter Milan	Middlesbrough	1/97	2,700,000
Horacio Carbonari	Rosario (Arg)	Derby Co.	5/98	2,700,000
Philippe Albert	Anderlecht	Newcastle Utd.	8/94	2,650,000
Carlton Palmer	Sheffield Wed.	Leeds Utd.	6/94	2,600,000
Ilie Dumitrescu	Steaua Buch.	Tottenham	7/94	2,600,000
K Lee Bowyer	Charlton Athletic	Leeds Utd.	7/96	2,600,000
Jonas Bjorklund	Vicenza	Rangers	7/96	2,600,000
John Scales	Liverpool	Tottenham	12/96	2,600,000
Sammy Hyypia	Willem II	Liverpool	5/99	2,600,000
Rigobert Song	Salernitana	Liverpool	1/99	2,600,000
Robert Jarni	Real Betis	Coventry City	8/98	2,600,000
Keith Curle	Wimbledon	Manchester City	8/91	2,500,000
Ian Wright	Crystal Palace	Arsenal	9/91	2,500,000
Terry Phelan	Wimbledon	Manchester City	8/92	2,500,000
Craig Short	Notts Co.	Derby Co.	9/92	2,500,000
Kevin Gallacher	Coventry City	Blackburn Rov.	3/93	2,500,000
Neil Ruddock	Tottenham	Liverpool	7/93	2,500,000
Bryan Roy	Foggia	Nott'm. Forest	6/94	2,500,000
John Hartson	Luton Town	Arsenal	1/95	2,500,000
Gareth Southgate	Crystal Palace	Aston Villa	6/95	2,500,000
David Ginola	Paris St. Germain	Newcastle Utd.	7/95	2,500,000
Stefan Schwarz	Arsenal	Fiorentina	7/95	2,500,000
Oleg Salenko	Valencia	Rangers	7/95	2,500,000
Kevin Campbell	Arsenal	Nott'm. Forest	6/95	2,500,000
Chris Bart-Williams	Sheffield Wed.	Nott'm. Forest	6/95	2,500,000
Darko Kovacevic	Sheffield Wed.	R. Sociedad	6/96	2,500,000
Frank Lebouef	Strasbourg	Chelsea	6/96	2,500,000
John Spencer	Chelsea	Q.P.R.	11/96	2,500,000
Steffen Iversen	Rosenborg	Tottenham	11/96	2,500,000
Gary Breen	Birmingham City	Coventry City	1/97	2,500,000
Per Pedersen	Odense	Blackburn Rov.	2/97	2,500,000
Jon Daal Tomasson	Herenveen (Holl.)	Newcastle Utd.	4/97	2,500,000
Lee Clark	Newcastle Utd.	Sunderland	6/97	2,500,000
Martin Dahlin	Roma	Blackburn Rov.	7/97	2,500,000
Craig Burley	Chelsea	Celtic	7/97	2,500,000
Gary Pallister	Manchester Utd.	Middlesbrough	7/98	2,500,000
Kevin Campbell	Nott'm Forest	Trabzonspor	7/98	2,500,000
John Collins	Monaco	Everton	7/98	2,500,000
Wim Jonk	PSV	Sheff. W.	7/98	2,500,000
Colin Cooper	Nott'm Forest	M'boro	8/98	2,500,000
Nigel Quashie	Q.P.R.	Nott'm Forest	8/98	2,500,000
Sebastian Perez	Blackburn Rov.	Marseille	5/99	2,500,000
Kaba Diawara	Bordeaux	Arsenal	1/99	2,500,000
Kaba Diawara	Arsenal	Marseille	6/99	2,500,000

Player	From	To	Date	£
Nolberto Solano	Boca Juniors	Newcastle	8/98	2,500,000
Trevor Steven	Marseille	Rangers	7/92	2,400,000
Craig Short	Derby Co.	Everton	7/95	2,400,000
Florin Raducioiu	Espanol	West Ham Utd.	7/96	2,400,000
★ Mark Hughes	Manchester Utd.	Barcelona	5/86	2,300,000
Gary Pallister	Middlesbrough	Manchester Utd.	8/89	2,300,000
Paul Stewart	Tottenham	Liverpool	7/92	2,300,000
Dean Saunders	Liverpool	Aston Villa	9/91	2,300,000
Paul Furlong	Watford	Chelsea	5/94	2,300,000
Andreas Thom	B. Leverkusen	Celtic	7/95	2,300,000
Dan Petrescu	Sheffield Wed.	Chelsea	10/95	2,300,000
Paul Kitson	Newcastle Utd.	West Ham Utd.	2/97	2,300,000
Tommy Johnson	Aston Villa	Celtic	3/97	2,300,000
Moussa Saib	Valencia	Tottenham	2/98	2,300,000
Michael Johansen	FC Copenhagen	Bolton Wand.	6/96	2,280,000
Per Frandsen	FC Copenhagen	Bolton Wand.	6/96	2,280,000
Nigel Clough	Nott'm. Forest	Liverpool	6/93	2,275,000
Ruel Fox	Norwich City	Newcastle Utd.	2/94	2,250,000
Paul Kitson	Derby Co.	Newcastle Utd.	9/94	2,250,000
Nigel Martyn	Crystal Palace	Leeds Utd.	7/96	2,250,000
Celestine Babayaro	Anderlecht	Chelsea	4/97	2,250,000
Ed de Goey	Feyenoord	Chelsea	6/97	2,250,000
Tony Cottee	West Ham Utd.	Everton	7/88	2,200,000
Mark Wright	Derby Co.	Liverpool	7/91	2,200,000
Gordon Durie	Chelsea	Tottenham	8/91	2,200,000
Stan Collymore	Southend Utd.	Nott'm. Forest	6/93	2,200,000
Brian Laudrup	Fiorentina	Rangers	6/94	2,200,000
Vinny Samways	Tottenham	Everton	8/94	2,200,000
Robbie Elliott	Newcastle Utd.	Bolton Wand.	7/97	2,200,000
Albert Ferrer	Barcelona	Chelsea	6/98	2,200,000
Daniel Prodan	Atletico Madrid	Rangers	7/98	2,200,000
Teddy Sheringham	Nott'm. Forest	Tottenham	8/92	2,100,000
Robert Fleck	Norwich City	Chelsea	8/92	2,100,000
Andy Townsend	Chelsea	Aston Villa	7/93	2,100,000
Chris Coleman	Blackburn Rov.	Fulham	12/97	2,100,000

Record stages: Prior to Trevor Francis becoming the subject of the first £1m. transfer, this is how the record was broken, stage by stage from the time of the first £1,000 deal in 1905:

Player	From	To	Date	£
Alf Common	Sunderland	Middlesbrough	2/1905	1,000
Syd Puddefoot	West Ham Utd.	Falkirk	2/22	5,000
Warney Cresswell	S. Shields	Sunderland	3/22	5,500
Bob Kelly	Burnley	Sunderland	12/25	6,500
David Jack	Bolton Wand.	Arsenal	10/28	10,890
Bryn Jones	Wolves	Arsenal	8/38	14,500
Billy Steel	Morton	Derby Co.	9/47	15,000
Tommy Lawton	Chelsea	Notts Co.	11/47	20,000
Len Shackleton	Newcastle Utd.	Sunderland	2/48	20,500
Johnny Morris	Manchester Utd.	Derby Co.	2/49	24,000
Eddie Quigley	Sheffield Wed.	Preston N.E.	12/49	26,500
Trevor Ford	Aston Villa	Sunderland	10/50	30,000
Jackie Sewell	Notts Co.	Sheffield Wed.	3/51	34,500
Eddie Firmani	Charlton Athletic	Sampdoria	7/55	35,000
John Charles	Leeds Utd.	Juventus	4/57	65,000
Denis Law	Manchester City	Torino	6/61	100,000
Denis Law	Torino	Manchester Utd.	7/62	115,000
Allan Clarke	Fulham	Leicester City	6/68	150,000

Allan Clarke	Leicester City	Leeds Utd.	6/69	165,000
Martin Peters	West Ham Utd.	Tottenham	3/70	200,000
Alan Ball	Everton	Arsenal	12/71	220,000
David Nish	Leicester City	Derby Co.	8/72	250,000
Bob Latchford	Birmingham City	Everton	2/74	350,000
Graeme Souness	Middlesbrough	Liverpool	1/78	352,000
Kevin Keegan	Liverpool	Hamburg	6/77	500,000
David Mills	Middlesbrough	W.B.A.	1/79	516,000

• **World's first £1m. transfer:** Guiseppe Savoldi, Bologna to Napoli, July 1975.

TOP FOREIGN SIGNINGS

Player	From	To	Date	£
Christian Vieri	Lazio	Inter Milan	6/99	31,000,000
Denilson	Sao Paulo	Real Betis	7/97	21,400,000
Marcio Amoroso	Udinese	Parma	6/99	21,000,000
Juan Sebastian Veron	Parma	Lazio	6/99	19,800,000
Ronaldo	Barcelona	Inter Milan	6/97	18,000,000
Christian Vieri	Atletico Madrid	Lazio	8/98	16,960,000
Andrei Shevchenko	Dynamo Kiev	AC Milan	6/99	15,700,000
Vincenzo Montella	Sampdoria	Roma	6/99	15,300,000
Ronald de Boer	Ajax	Barcelona	1/99 }	14,000,000
Frank de Boer	Ajax	Barcelona	1/99	
Gianluigi Lentini	Torino	AC Milan	7/92	13,000,000
Gianluca Vialli	Sampdoria	Juventus	6/92	12,500,000
Ronaldo	PSV Eindhoven	Barcelona	7/96	12,500,000
Rivaldo	Dep. La Coruna	Barcelona	8/97	12,500,000
Christian Vieri	Juventus	Atletico Madrid	7/97	12,000,000
Sonny Anderson	Monaco	Barcelona	7/97	12,000,000
Marcelo Salas	River Plate, Arg	Lazio	2/98	12,000,000
Darko Kovacevic	Real Sociedad	Juventus	6/99	12,000,000
Enrico Chiesa	Sampdoria	Parma	7/96	11,000,000
Thierry Henry	Monaco	Juventus	1/99	11,000,000
Stephan Appiah	Udinese	Parma	6/99	11,000,000
Simone Inzaghi	Piacenza	Lazio	6/99	11,000,000
Jay Jay Okocha	Fenerbache	Paris St. Germain	7/98	10,600,000
Angelo Peruzzi	Juventus	Inter Milan	6/99	10,500,000
Enrico Chiesa	Parma	Fiorentina	6/99	10,200,000
Jean-Pierre Papin	Marseille	AC Milan	6/92	10,000,000
Simao Sabrosa	Sporting Lisbon	Barcelona	5/99	9,300,000
Christian Panucci	Real Madrid	Inter Milan	6/99	9,000,000
Patrick Kluivert	AC Milan	Barcelona	8/98	8,750,000
Roberto Rios	Real Betis	Athletic Bilbao	7/97	8,500,000
Alen Boksic	Marseille	Lazio	10/93	8,400,000
Dennis Bergkamp	Ajax	Inter Milan	6/93	8,000,000
Roberto Baggio	Juventus	AC Milan	7/95	8,000,000
Roberto Baggio	Fiorentina	Juventus	5/90	7,700,000
Gianluca Pagliuca	Sampdoria	Inter Milan	8/94	7,500,000
Ariel Ortega	Valencia	Sampdoria	7/98	7,300,000
Diego Simeone	Inter Milan	Lazio	6/99	7,300,000
Daniel Fonseca	Cagliari	Napoli	6/92	7,000,000
Gianluca Zambrotta	Bari	Juventus	6/99	7,000,000
Marco Di Vaio	Salernitana	Parma	6/99	6,800,000
Igor Shalimov	Foggia	Inter Milan	5/92	6,500,000
David Platt	Bari	Juventus	6/92	6,500,000
Ruud Gullit	PSV Eindh'n	AC Milan	6/87	6,000,000
Luca Marchegiani	Torino	Lazio	7/93	6,000,000
Edwin Van der Saar	Ajax	Juventus	5/99	6,000,000

Thomas Hassler	Juventus	Roma	7/91	5,800,000
K.-H. Riedle	Wer. Bremen	Lazio	4/90	5,500,000
Vitor Baia	Porto	Barcelona	7/96	5,500,000
Claudio Caniggia	Atalanta	Roma	5/92	5,500,000
K.-H. Riedle	Lazio	B. Dortmund	7/93	5,500,000
Thomas Hassler	Cologne	Juventus	4/90	5,400,000
Dragan Stojkovic	Red Star	Marseille	7/90	5,250,000
Diego Maradona	Barcelona	Napoli	6/84	5,000,000
Thomas Doll	Hamburg	Lazio	6/91	5,000,000
Christian Karembeu	Nantes	Sampdoria	7/95	5,000,000
Romario	Flamenco	Valencia	7/96	5,000,000
Diego Maradona	Boca Juniors	Barcelona	6/82	4,800,000
Lajos Detari	Eint. F'furt	Olympiakos	7/88	4,700,000
Hristo Stoichkov	Barcelona	Parma	7/95	4,600,000
Diego Maradona	Napoli	Seville	9/92	4,500,000
George Weah	Paris SG	AC Milan	5/95	4,500,000
Clarence Seedorf	Ajax	Sampdoria	7/95	4,500,000
Roberto Carlos	Palmeiras	Inter Milan	7/95	4,500,000
Paulo Futre	At. Madrid	Benfica	1/93	4,200,000

WORLD RECORD GOALKEEPER FEE

£10.5m for **Angelo Peruzzi** (Juventus to Inter Milan, July 1999).

RECORD CONFERENCE FEE

£250,000: **Andy Clarke**, Barnet to Wimbledon, Feb 1991; **Barry Hayles**, Stevenage Borough to Bristol Rov., Aug. 1997; **Jason Roberts**, Hayes to Wolves, Sept. 1997.

RECORD FEE BETWEEN NON-LEAGUE CLUBS

£85,000 for **Carl Alford**, 24-year-old striker from Kettering (GMVC) to neighbours Rushden & Diamonds (Beazer Homes League), March 1996.

WORLD RECORD FEE FOR 17-YEAR OLD

£3.4m for **Roque Santa Cruz** (Olympia Asuncion, Paraguay, to Bayern Munich, June 1999).

PORT VALE HAT-TRICK

Hundreds of Port Vale supporters marched into a match against Huddersfield Town 10 minutes late wearing flat caps as a tribute to sacked manager John Rudge who had been in charge for 843 games.

FOR WHOM THE BELL TOLLS

Irate vicar the Rev Keith Sinclair ordered the bells of his Aston parish church rung throughout the Aston Villa-Chelsea televised game in March because he claimed the Sunday morning match kept people away from services at eight churches.

SNAP!

Southampton defender Francis Benali broke an arm in a match at Leicester City and a month later did it again sweeping up leaves in his garden.

OBITUARIES 1998-99

JULY

JOHN CAMKIN, 75, pipe-smoking football journalist, broadcaster, travel agent, director of Coventry City and, in 1980, founder of the League Managers' Association, of which he was the first chief executive. In 1961 he persuaded Jimmy Hill to enter management with Coventry City, a sequel to which was the club's climb from Third Division to First. Became football correspondent of the *News Chronicle* in 1953 and later wrote for the *Daily Mail*. He reported the World Cups of 1954, 1958 and 1962, and wrote a book commemorating the presence of the four Home Countries at the 1958 Finals in Sweden. He joined Anglia TV in 1962 and also commentated for BBC Radio.

GLADSTONE GUEST, 81, was a clever inside-forward who remains chronicled in Rotherham Utd.'s history as their record scorer with 130 goals in 356 League games from 1946-56. Because of the war, he was 29 before making his League debut, but quickly made up for lost time. He captained Rotherham Utd. to the Division Three North Championship in 1951, and in 1954-55 all but led them to the First Division. With Birmingham City and Luton Town, they totalled 54 points, but missed promotion on goal average.

SEPTEMBER

JOHN 'JACKIE' BLANCHFLOWER, 65, was one of Manchester Utd.'s celebrated 'Busby Babes', but had his career prematurely ended by the Munich air crash in 1958. He suffered multiple injuries and carried the scars for the rest of his life. His 12 caps for N. Ireland (1954-58) were all won alongside his legendary brother Danny. Jackie was a N. Ireland Schoolboy Int. and went to Old Trafford from Belfast junior football in 1949. He played 105 League games (26 goals) at centre-half for Utd., plus six in the F.A. Cup, five European Cup, one Charity Shield. He helped them win the League Championships of 1956 and 1957, and played heroically as emergency goalkeeper when Ray Wood was injured in the 1957 F.A. Cup Final against Aston Villa. Post-Munich, he continued in Manchester as bookmaker and publican, and became a popular after-dinner speaker. He died after a long battle against cancer.

RAYMOND BOWDEN, 89, was the last surviving member of the great Arsenal team of the Thirties, in which five League Championships went to Highbury and the F.A. Cup twice. A Cornishman from Looe, he was signed by Herbert Chapman from Plymouth Argyle for £4,500 in March 1933, and played inside-right between Joe Hulme on the wing and Ted Drake at centre-forward in a line completed by Alex James and Cliff Bastin. Under George Allison, Bowden earned Championship honours in 1933-34 and 1934-35 and an F.A. Cup winner's medal in 1936. The most memorable of his six England caps was as one of a record seven Arsenal players in the side that beat Italy 3-2 in the 'Battle of Highbury' in 1934. He was transferred to Newcastle Utd. for £5,000 in Nov. 1937 and spent two seasons at St. James' Park before retiring on the outbreak of war in 1939.

LAURIE BROWN, 61, former Arsenal and Tottenham centre-half, died at his home near Bishop Auckland. He played for Great Britain in the 1960 Rome Olympics and was an England amateur with Darlington before turning professional with Northampton Town in Oct. 1960. The following August he moved to Arsenal for £3,500. He made 101 League apps. for Arsenal (1961-63), then 62 for Tottenham (1963-66), subsequently playing for Norwich City and as player-manager for Bradford Park Avenue. His career ended in non-League football, and he retired to his native North-east to work as a publican and milkman.

JIMMY CONSTANTINE, 78, was a centre-forward who identified with the all-action style of Millwall in the early post-war years, scoring 75 goals, including many a bullet header, in 141 League apps (1948-52). He played pre-war for Rochdale and Manchester City, resuming with City in season 1946-47, then spent 1947-48 with Bury before moving to Millwall. A wholehearted player whose wages never exceeded £20 a week, he left

Millwall at 32 for non-League Tonbridge and played local football until he was 50. He remained a Millwall fan at heart, and attended matches at The Den until well into the 1990s.

JIM GREGORY, 70, a motor-trade millionaire who had owned Q.P.R. and chaired Portsmouth, died after a long illness. During his 22 years at Loftus Road, he hired 14 managers – including Dave Sexton, Tommy Docherty, Terry Venables and Jim Smith – and Rangers climbed from Third Division to First. They won Wembley's first League Cup Final in 1967 and reached the F.A. Cup Final in 1982. He sold his controlling interest in Q.P.R. after a severe heart attack in 1987 and bought Portsmouth for £3m. a year later.

TOMMY POWELL, 73, was a one-club loyalist with his hometown team, Derby Co. He first played for them as a 16-year-old in war-time, but Army service delayed his League debut until 1948. Mostly on the right wing, he made 489 first-team apps for the club (86 goals) before retiring in 1962. Father of Steve, who played more than 400 senior games for Derby Co.

OCTOBER

STEPHEN BOLER, 55, Manchester City's main share-holder (24%) died in a Johannesburg hospital following a heart attack while visiting South Africa on business.

RON REEVES, 55, a Coventry City steward from Northfield, Birmingham, died in hospital shortly after being crushed by the Arsenal team bus as he was guiding it into a parking space at Highfield Road on Oct. 31.

NOVEMBER

HAROLD BROOK, 78, Sheffield-born, joined his local club Utd. in wartime and in the early post-war years played in every forward position, as well as at wing-half and full-back. He scored 89 goals in 229 League games for The Blades (1946-54), then made 102 League apps. (46 goals) for Leeds Utd. (1954-58), playing in the side promoted to the First Division in 1956. He ended his career with a brief spell at Lincoln City.

HENRY HORTON, 65, belonged to that sporting breed of bygone years, the professional at both cricket and football. Originally an amateur with Worcestershire CCC, he played for Hampshire from 1953-67. On the football field, he was a wing-half with Blackburn Rov. (1947-51, 92 League apps, five goals), Southampton (1951-54, 75/12) and Bradford Park Avenue (1954-55, 26 apps). He was later a first-class umpire and coached Worcs. for two spells between 1968-79.

JOHN OSBORNE, 57, was one of W.B.A.'s finest goalkeepers. Having begun at the 'home of 'keepers,' Chesterfield (1960-67), he played in Albion's F.A. Cup-winning team against Everton in 1968 and made 321 first-team apps. for The Hawthorns club (1967-76). His playing career ended with a brief spell at Walsall, and he then became commercial manager of Worcestershire CCC.

DECEMBER

MATT GILLIES, 77, who managed Leicester City (1958-68) and Nott'm. Forest (1969-72), died in Nottingham on Christmas Eve. His playing career, as a half-back, was spent with Bolton Wand. (1942-52) – beginning while off duty as a navigator with Bomber Command – and Leicester City (1952-56). As Leicester City manager, the courteous Scot won the League Cup in 1964, and took them to the F.A. Cup Finals of 1961 and 1963, to a further League Cup Final in 1965, and to their first European venture, the Cup-Winners' Cup (as runners-up to Tottenham) in 1961. Among players whose careers advanced under his guidance at Filbert Street were Gordon Banks, Frank McLintock and Peter Shilton.

BRIAN LEWIS, 55, was a member of the Colchester Utd. side which famously beat Don Revie's Leeds Utd. 3-2 in the F.A. Cup fifth round at Layer Road in Feb. 1971. They were the sixth club in his League career of 412 first-team apps. (92 goals) that began with Crystal Palace in 1960 and continued via Portsmouth, Coventry City, Luton Town, Oxford Utd., Colchester Utd. and ended in 1974 in a second spell with Portsmouth.

JOHN McGRATH, 60, burly centre-half for Bury, Newcastle Utd., Southampton and England U-23s., and later manager of four League clubs, died of a heart attack on Christmas Day. The Mancunian's playing career (1955-75) began at Bury and spanned a total of 489 League apps., more than 150 of them for both Newcastle Utd. and Southampton. He managed Port Vale (1979-83), Chester City (1984-85), Preston N.E. 1986-90, incl. promotion from Div. Four in 1987) and Halifax Town (1991-92). On leaving football, he became well known on the Northern circuit as an after-dinner speaker and as a soccer pundit on local radio in Lancashire.

ANDY THOMSON, promising Motherwell striker, died suddenly at his 19th. birthday party. As a mark of respect, the following day's Premier League match at home to Dundee was postponed.

JANUARY 1999

SYD OWEN, 76, would have won many more than three England caps had his career at centre-half not coincided with that of Billy Wright, and possibly had he been with a more fashionable club than Luton Town. After five League apps. for Birmingham City in 1946-47, he was transferred for £1,500 to Luton Town, for whom he played 388 League games. His playing career ended with the 1959 F.A. Cup Final and the Footballer of the Year award. He stayed to manage Luton Town (1959-60), was subsequently Leeds Utd. coach (1960-75), assistant-manager at Birmingham City, and finally youth coach and scout at Manchester Utd. before retiring in 1982.

FEBRUARY

JOCK GOVAN, 76, full-back in Hibernian's team of Scottish Champions in 1947-48. He was capped six times by Scotland in 1948-49.

BILL HOULISTON, 77, powerfully-built centre-forward, was capped three times (all wins) in season 1948-49, the only Queen of the South player to earn full Scotland honours. Began his career with Arbroath, scored 67 goals in 154 First Div. apps. for QoS, and was in the Scotland side that beat England 3-1 at Wembley in April 1949 to win the Home Championship. Subsequently played for Berwick Rangers and Third Lanark, and after retiring became a hotelier in Dumfries.

ARTHUR MANN, 51, left-back in Manchester City's League Cup Final victory against WBA in 1970, died in an accident at the scrapyard where he worked. After playing for Hearts in the 1968 Scottish Cup Final against Dunfermline, he moved to Maine Road in November that year for £65,000. He played for Blackpool (1971), Notts Co. (1972-79), Shrewsbury Town (1979) and Mansfield Town (1979-82) and in his five-club English career made an aggregate of 415 League apps. He later assisted manager Alan Buckley at Grimsby Town and WBA.

MARCH

PETER FARRELL, 76, was among the band of early post-war footballers who played for both the Rep. of Ireland (28 caps) and N. Ireland (seven). He scored one of the goals when the Republic became the first 'foreign' country to lower England's colours on home soil (2-1 at Goodison Park, Sept. 1949). Dublin-born, the sturdy wing-half joined Everton from Shamrock Rov. in 1946, and captained them during eleven seasons at Goodison (1946-57, 453 League and Cup apps.). He played a further 114 League games across the Mersey as player-manager of Tranmere Rov. (1957-60).

IGOR NETTO, 69, captain of the Soviet Union in their two biggest triumphs: winners of the European Championship in 1960 following their 1956 Olympic success in Melbourne.

TOMMY PEARSON, 84, held the rare distinction of having played for both England and Scotland in matches between the two. Born in Scotland, he was asked to represent

England in a 1939 wartime home international at St James' Park when Manchester City's Eric Book was involved in a car crash shortly before kick-off. He was not awarded a cap, but received a special certificate commemorating his part in a 2-1 win. A left-winger who played club football for Newcastle Utd. and Aberdeen, he finally got the chance to play for Scotland against England in a 1-1 draw at Wembley in 1947. After winning just one further cap he retired from playing in 1953, but returned to Aberdeen as manager between 1959 and 1965.

DENNIS VIOLLET, 65, one of Manchester Utd.'s 'Busby Babes' and a survivor of the Munich air disaster in 1958, died at his U.S. home in Jacksonville. He had battled against a brain tumour for two years. Born in Manchester, he graduated via Utd.'s prolific youth section, played in their Championship-winning sides of 1955-56 and 1956-57, and scored 178 goals in 291 senior apps. His 32 goals in 36 First Div. matches in 1959-60, when captaining Utd., remain a seasonal record for the club. Within three months of Munich – he sat next to Bobby Charlton as the aircraft crashed on take-off – he had overcome his injuries to play in the Cup Final against Bolton Wand. He was capped twice by England in the early Sixties. He left Old Trafford for Stoke City (£25,000) in Jan. 1962 and, alongside Stanley Matthews, helped them win the Second Div. a year later. He scored 59 goals in 181 League apps. for Stoke City, then spent two years with Baltimore Bays. He returned to England with non-League Witton Albion, and earned an Irish Cup-winner's medal as Linfield's player-coach in 1970. After a coaching spell at Preston N.E., he briefly managed Crewe Alexandra (1971), then went back to USA in charge of Washington Diplomats (1974-77) and as a university coach in Jacksonville.

REG VOWELS, 70, was one of the outstanding amateurs of the Fifties. A red-haired wing-half, he tackled doggedly and was supreme in the air. He captained Cambridge University, earned an Amateur Cup-winners' medal with Pegasus (6-0 v Harwich & Parkeston at Wembley, 1953) and was capped for England's Amateur team v France in 1957. He subsequently played for Corinthian Casuals for 10 seasons.

APRIL

LES BENNETT, 81, was a creative inside-forward with Tottenham in the early post-war years. He played in Arthur Rowe's famous 'push and run' Championship-winning team of 1950-51 and was the club's top scorer in seasons 1948-49 and 1951-52. Locally born, he joined Tottenham from their Northfleet nursery in 1939, but the war delayed his League debut until he was nearly 29. In all he made 295 first-team apps. for the club and scored 118 goals. He moved briefly to West Ham Utd. (£5,000) in Dec. 1954 and after leaving Upton Park became player-manager of Clacton Town.

BRIAN HALL, 59, first manager to complete the Conference/F.A. Trophy double with Wealdstone in season 1984-85. At Wealdstone, he helped launch the careers of Stuart Pearce and Vinnie Jones, and he also managed Yeovil for two spells.

SIR ALF RAMSEY: See index for separate tribute.

MAY

ARTHUR ELLIS, 84, advanced from officiating in the Yorkshire League at 22 to a place among the world's top referees. One of the most cheerful, too, was the brewers' traveller from Halifax. He whistled at three World Cups (1950-54-58) and in more than 40 Internationals, the most bitter of them the World Cup quarter-final between Brazil and Hungary in 1954 ('the battle of Berne'), from which he dismissed three players. He attended the celebration parties of both clubs after the 1952 F.A. Cup Final between Newcastle Utd. and Arsenal, saying: 'I didn't want to show any favouritism.' He took charge of the first European Cup Final, Real Madrid v Reims in 1956 and of the first European Nations Final between USSR and Yugoslavia, also in Paris, four years later. Retired compulsorily from the League list at 47, he became a celebrity on BBC TV as referee in *It's A Knockout* for 18 years, and chaired the Pools Panel.

Complied by ***Albert Sewell***
*(Sources: National and provincial newspapers,
Association of Football Statisticians, World Soccer and FIFA News)*

MILESTONES OF SOCCER

1848 First code of rules compiled at Cambridge Univ.
1855 Sheffield F.C., world's oldest football club, formed.
1862 Notts Co. (oldest League club) formed.
1863 Football Association founded – their first rules of game agreed.
1871 F.A. Cup introduced.
1872 First official International: Scotland 0, England 0. Corner-kick introduced.
1873 Scottish F.A. formed; Scottish Cup introduced.
1874 Shinguards introduced. Oxford v Cambridge, first match.
1875 Crossbar introduced (replacing tape).
1876 F.A. of Wales formed.
1877 Welsh Cup introduced.
1878 Referee's whistle first used.
1880 Irish F.A. founded; Irish Cup introduced.
1883 Two-handed throw-in introduced.
1885 Record first-class score (Arbroath 36, Bon Accord 0 – Scottish Cup). Professionalism legalised.
1886 International Board formed.
1887 Record F.A. Cup score (Preston N.E. 26, Hyde 0).
1888 Football League founded by Wm. McGregor. First matches on Sept. 8.
1889 Preston N.E. win Cup and League (first club to complete Double).
1890 Scottish League and Irish League formed.
1891 Goal-nets introduced. Penalty-kick introduced.
1892 Inter-League games began. Football League Second Division formed.
1893 F.A. Amateur Cup launched.
1894 Southern League formed.
1895 F.A. Cup stolen from Birmingham shop window – never recovered.
1897 First Players' Union formed. Aston Villa win Cup and League.
1898 Promotion and relegation introduced.
1901 Maximum wage rule in force (£4 a week). Tottenham first professional club to take F.A. Cup South. First six-figure attendance (110,802) at F.A. Cup Final.
1902 Ibrox Park disaster (25 killed). Welsh League formed.
1904 F.I.F.A. founded (7 member countries).
1905 First £1,000 transfer (Alf Common, Sunderland to Middlesbrough).
1907 Players' Union revived.
1908 Transfer fee limit (£350) fixed in January and withdrawn in April.
1911 New F.A. Cup trophy – in use to 1991. Transfer deadline introduced.
1914 King George V first reigning monarch to attend F.A. Cup Final.
1916 Entertainment Tax introduced.
1919 League extended to 44 clubs.
1920 Third Division (South) formed.
1921 Third Division (North) formed.
1922 Scottish League (Div. II) introduced.
1923 Beginning of football pools. First Wembley Cup Final.
1924 First International at Wembley (England 1, Scotland 1). Rule change allows goals to be scored direct from corner-kicks.
1925 New offside law.
1926 Huddersfield Town complete first League Championship hat-trick.
1927 First League match broadcast (radio): Arsenal v Sheff. Utd. (Jan 22). First radio broadcast of Cup Final (winners Cardiff City). Charles Clegg, president of F.A., becomes first knight of football.
1928 First £10,000 transfer – David Jack (Bolton Wand. to Arsenal). W.R. ('Dixie') Dean (Everton) creates League record – 60 goals in season. Britain withdraws from F.I.F.A.
1930 Uruguay first winners of World Cup.
1931 W.B.A. win Cup and promotion.
1933 Players numbered for first time in Cup Final (1-22).

1934 Sir Frederick Wall retires as F.A. secretary; successor Stanley Rous. Death of Herbert Chapman (Arsenal manager).

1935 Arsenal equal Huddersfield Town's Championship hat-trick record. Official two-referee trials.

1936 Joe Payne's 10-goal League record (Luton Town 12, Bristol Rov. 0).

1937 British record attendance: 149,547 at Scotland v England match.

1938 First live TV transmission of F.A. Cup Final. F.A.'s 75th anniversary. Football League 50th Jubilee. New pitch marking – arc on edge of penalty-area. Laws of Game re-drafted by Stanley Rous. Arsenal pay record £14,500 fee for Bryn Jones (Wolves).

1939 Compulsory numbering of players in Football League. First six-figure attendance for League match (Rangers v Celtic, 118,567). All normal competitions suspended for duration of Second World War.

1944 Death of Sir Frederick Wall (84), F.A. secretary 1896-1934.

1945 Scottish League Cup introduced.

1946 British associations rejoin F.I.F.A. Bolton Wand. disaster (33 killed) during F.A. Cup tie with Stoke City. Walter Winterbottom appointed England's first director of coaching.

1947 Great Britain beat Rest of Europe 6-1 at Hampden Park, Glasgow. First £20,000 transfer – Tommy Lawton, Chelsea to Notts Co.

1949 Stanley Rous, secretary F.A., knighted. England's first home defeat outside British Champ. (0-2 v Eire).

1950 Football League extended from 88 to 92 clubs. World record crowd (203,500) at World Cup Final, Brazil v Uruguay, in Rio. Scotland's first home defeat by foreign team (0-1 v Austria).

1951 White ball comes into official use.

1952 Newcastle Utd. first club to win F.A. Cup at Wembley in successive seasons.

1953 England's first Wembley defeat by foreign opponents (3-6 v Hungary).

1954 Hungary beat England 7-1 in Budapest.

1955 First F.A. Cup match under floodlights (prelim. round replay, Sept. 14): Kidderminster Harriers v Brierley Hill Alliance.

1956 First F.A. Cup ties under floodlights in competition proper (Jan. 7). First League match by floodlight (Feb. 22, Portsmouth v Newcastle Utd.). Real Madrid win the first European Cup.

1957 Last full Football League programme on Christmas Day. Entertainment Tax withdrawn.

1958 Manchester Utd. air crash at Munich (Feb. 6). League re-structured into four divisions.

1959 Football League establish fixtures copyright; pools must pay for use.

1960 Record transfer fee: £55,000 for Denis Law (Huddersfield Town to Manchester City). Wolves win Cup, miss Double and Championship hat-trick by one goal. For fifth time in ten years F.A. Cup Final team reduced to ten men by injury. F.A. recognise Sunday football. Football League Cup launched.

1961 Tottenham complete the first Championship-F.A. Cup double this century. Maximum wage (£20 a week) abolished in High Court challenge by George Eastham. First British £100-a-week wage paid (by Fulham to Johnny Haynes). First £100,000 British transfer – Denis Law, Manchester City to Torino. Sir Stanley Rous elected president of F.I.F.A.

1962 Manchester Utd. raise record British transfer fee to £115,000 for Denis Law.

1963 F.A. Centenary. Football League's 75th anniversary. Season extended to end of May due to severe winter. First pools panel. English "retain and transfer" system ruled illegal in High Court test case.

1964 Rangers' second great hat-trick – Scottish Cup, League Cup and League. Football League and Scottish League guaranteed £500,000 a year in new fixtures copyright agreement with Pools. First televised 'Match of the Day' (BBC2): Liverpool 3, Arsenal 2 (August 22).

1965 Bribes scandal – ten players jailed (and banned for life by F.A.) for match-fixing 1960-3. Stanley Matthews knighted in farewell season. Arthur Rowley (Shrewsbury Town) retires with record of 434 League goals. Substitutes allowed for injured players in Football League matches (one per team).

1966 England win World Cup (Wembley).

1967 Alf Ramsey, England manager, knighted; O.B.E. for captain Bobby Moore. Celtic become first British team to win European Cup. First substitutes allowed in F.A. Cup Final (Tottenham v Chelsea) but not used. Football League permit loan transfers (two per club).

1968 First F.A. Cup Final televised live in colour (BBC2 – W.B.A. v Everton). Manchester Utd. first English club to win European Cup.

1971 Arsenal win League Championship and F.A. Cup.

1973 Football League introduce 3-up, 3-down promotion/relegation between Divisions 1, 2 and 3 and 4-up, 4-down between Divisions 3 and 4.

1974 First F.A. Cup ties played on Sunday (Jan. 6). League football played on Sunday for first time (Jan. 20). Last F.A. Amateur Cup Final. Joao Havelange (Brazil) succeeds Sir Stanley Rous as F.I.F.A. president.

1975 Scottish Premier Division introduced.

1976 Football League introduce goal difference (replacing goal average).

1977 Liverpool achieve the double of League Championship and European Cup. Don Revie defects to United Arab Emirates when England manager – successor Ron Greenwood.

1978 Freedom of contract for players accepted by Football League. P.F.A. lifts ban on foreign players in English football. Football League introduce Transfer Tribunal. Viv Anderson (Nott'm. Forest) first black player to win a full England cap. Willie Johnston (Scotland) sent home from World Cup Finals in Argentina after failing dope test.

1979 First all-British £500,000 transfer – David Mills, M'bro' to W.B.A. First British million pound transfer (Trevor Francis – B'ham to Nott'm. Forest). Andy Gray moves from Aston Villa to Wolves for a record £1,469,000 fee.

1981 Tottenham win 100th F.A. Cup Final. Liverpool first British side to win European Cup three times. Three points for a win introduced by Football League. Q.P.R. install Football League's first artificial pitch. Sept. 29, death of Bill Shankly, manager-legend of Liverpool 1959-74. Record British transfer – Bryan Robson (W.B.A. to Manchester Utd.), £1,500,000.

1982 Aston Villa become sixth consecutive English winners of European Cup. Tottenham retain F.A. Cup – first club to do so since Tottenham 1961 and 1962. Football League Cup becomes the (sponsored) Milk Cup.

1983 Liverpool complete the League Championship-Milk Cup double for second year running. Manager Bob Paisley retires. Aberdeen first club to do Cup-Winners' Cup and domestic Cup double. Football League clubs vote to keep own match receipts. Football League sponsored by Canon, Japanese camera and business equipment manufacturers – 3-year agreement starting 1983-4. Football League agree 2-year contract for live TV coverage of ten matches per season (5 Friday night, BBC, 5 Sunday afternoon, ITV).

1984 One F.A. Cup tie in rounds 3, 4, 5 and 6 shown live on TV (Friday or Sunday). Aberdeen take Scottish Cup for third successive season, win Scottish Championship, too. Tottenham win UEFA Cup on penalty shoot-out. Liverpool win European Cup on penalty shoot-out to complete unique treble with Milk Cup and League title (as well as Championship hat-trick). N. Ireland win the final British Championship. France win European Championship – their first honour. F.A. National Soccer School opens at Lilleshall. Britain's biggest score this century: Stirling Alb. 20, Selkirk 0 (Scottish Cup).

1985 Bradford City fire disaster – 56 killed. First £1m. receipts from match in Britain (F.A. Cup Final). Kevin Moran (Manchester Utd.) first player to be sent off in F.A. Cup Final. Celtic win 100th Scottish F.A. Cup Final. European Cup Final horror (Liverpool v Juventus, riot in Brussels) 39 die. UEFA ban all English clubs indefinitely from European competitions. No TV coverage at start of League season – first time since 1963 (resumption delayed until January 1986). Sept: first ground-sharing in League history – Charlton Athletic move from The Valley to Selhurst Park (Crystal Palace).

1986 Liverpool complete League and Cup double in player-manager Kenny Dalglish's first season in charge. Swindon Town (4th Div. Champions) set League points record (102). League approve reduction of First Division to 20 clubs by 1988. Everton chairman Philip Carter elected president of Football League. July 18, death of Sir

Stanley Rous (91). 100th edition of *News of the World* Football Annual. League Cup sponsored for next three years by Littlewoods (£2m.). Football League voting majority (for rule changes) reduced from ¾ to ⅔. Wales move HQ from Wrexham to Cardiff City after 110 years. Two substitutes in F.A. Cup and League (Littlewoods) Cup. Two-season League/TV deal (£6.2m.):- BBC and ITV each show seven live League matches per season, League Cup semi-finals and Final. Football League sponsored by *Today* newspaper. Luton Town first club to ban all visiting supporters; as sequel are themselves banned from League Cup. Oldham Athletic and Preston N.E. install artificial pitches, making four in F. League (following Q.P.R. and Luton Town).

1987 May: League introduce play-off matches to decide final promotion/relegation places in all divisions. Re-election abolished – bottom club in Div. 4 replaced by winners of GM Vauxhall Conference. Two substitutes approved for Football League 1987-8. Red and yellow disciplinary cards (scrapped 1981) re-introduced by League and F.A. Football League sponsored by Barclays. First Div. reduced to 21 clubs.

1988 Football League Centenary. First Division reduced to 20 clubs.

1989 Soccer gets £74m. TV deal: £44m. over 4 years, ITV; £30m. over 5 years, BBC/BSB. But it costs Philip Carter the League Presidency. Ted Croker retires as F.A. chief executive; successor Graham Kelly, from Football League. Hillsborough disaster: 95 die at F.A. Cup semi-final (Liverpool v Nott'm. Forest). Arsenal win closest-ever Championship with last kick. Peter Shilton sets England record with 109 caps.

1990 Nott'm. Forest win last Littlewoods Cup Final. Both F.A. Cup semi-finals played on Sunday and televised live. Play-off finals move to Wembley; Swindon Town win place in Div. 1, then relegated back to Div. 2 (breach of financial regulations) – Sunderland promoted instead. Pools betting tax cut from 42½ to 40%. England reach World Cup semi-final in Italy and win F.I.F.A. Fair Play Award. Peter Shilton retires as England goalkeeper with 125 caps (world record). Graham Taylor (Aston Villa) succeeds Bobby Robson as England manager. Int. Board amend offside law (player 'level' no longer offside). F.I.F.A. make "pro foul" a sending-off offence. English clubs back in Europe (Manchester Utd. and Aston Villa) after 5-year exile.

1991 First F.A. Cup semi-final at Wembley (Tottenham 3, Arsenal 1). Bert Millichip (F.A. chairman) and Philip Carter (Everton chairman) knighted. End of artificial pitches in Div. 1 (Luton Town, Oldham Athletic). Scottish League reverts to 12-14-12 format (as in 1987-8). Penalty shoot-out introduced to decide F.A. Cup ties level after one replay.

1992 Introduction of fourth F.A. Cup (previous trophy withdrawn). F.A. launch Premier League (22 clubs). Football League reduced to three divisions (71 clubs). Record TV-sport deal: BSkyB/BBC to pay £304m. for 5-year coverage of Premier League. ITV do £40m., 4-year deal with F. League. Channel 4 show Italian football live (Sundays). F.I.F.A. approve new back-pass rule (goalkeeper must not handle ball kicked to him by team-mate). New League of Wales formed. Record all-British transfer, £3.3m.: Alan Shearer (Southampton to Blackburn Rov.). Charlton Athletic return to The Valley after 7-year absence.

1993 Barclays end 6-year sponsorship of F. League. For first time both F.A. Cup semi-finals at Wembley (Sat., Sun.). Arsenal first club to complete League Cup/F.A. Cup double. Rangers pull off Scotland's domestic treble for fifth time. F.A. in record British sports sponsorship deal (£12m. over 4 years) with brewers Bass for F.A. Carling Premiership, from Aug. Brian Clough retires after 18 years as Nott'm. Forest manager; as does Jim McLean (21 years manager of Dundee Utd.). Football League agree 3-year, £3m. sponsorship with Endsleigh Insurance. Premier League introduce squad numbers with players' names on shirts. Record British transfer: Duncan Ferguson, Dundee Utd. to Rangers (£4m.). Record English-club signing: Roy Keane, Nott'm. Forest to Manchester Utd. (£3.75m.). Graham Taylor resigns as England manager after World Cup exit (Nov.). Death in Feb. of Bobby Moore (51), England World-Cup winning captain 1966.

1994 Death of Sir Matt Busby (Jan.). Terry Venables appointed England coach (Jan.). Manchester Utd. complete the Double. Last artificial pitch in English football goes – Preston N.E. revert to grass, summer 1994. Bobby Charlton knighted. Scottish League format changes to four divisions of ten clubs. Record British transfer: Chris

Sutton, Norwich City to Blackburn Rov. (£5m.). Sept: F.A. announce first sponsorship of F.A. Cup – Littlewoods Pools (4-year, £14m. deal, plus £6m. for Charity Shield). Death of Billy Wright, 70 (Sept).

1995 New record British transfer: Andy Cole, Newcastle Utd. to Manchester Utd. (£7m.). First England match abandoned through crowd trouble (v Rep. of Ireland, Dublin). Blackburn Rov. Champions for first time since 1914. Premiership reduced to 20 clubs. British transfer record broken again (June): Stan Collymore, Nott'm. Forest to Liverpool (£8½m.). Starting season 1995-6, teams allowed to use 3 substitutes per match, not necessarily including a goalkeeper. Dec: European Court of Justice upholds Bosman ruling, barring transfer fees for players out of contract and removing limit on number of foreign players clubs can field.

1996 Death in Feb. of Bob Paisley (77), ex-Liverpool, most successful manager in English Football. F.A. appoint Chelsea manager Glenn Hoddle to succeed Terry Venables as England coach after Euro 96. Manchester Utd. first English club to achieve Double twice (and in 3 seasons). Football League completes £125m., 5-year TV deal with BSkyB starting 1996-7. England stage European Championship, reach semi-finals, lose on pens to tournament winners Germany. Keith Wiseman succeeds Sir Bert Millichip as F.A. Chairman. Linesmen become known as "referees' assistants". Coca-Cola Cup experiment with own disciplinary system (red, yellow cards). Alan Shearer football's first £15m. player (Blackburn Rov. to Newcastle Utd.). Nigeria first African country to win Olympic soccer. Nationwide Building Society sponsor Football League in initial 3-year deal worth £5.25m. Peter Shilton first player to make 1000 League apps.

1997 Howard Wilkinson appointed English football's first technical director. England's first home defeat in World Cup (0-1 v Italy). Ruud Gullit (Chelsea) first foreign coach to win F.A. Cup. Rangers equal Celtic's record of 9 successive League titles. Manchester Utd. win Premier League for fourth time in 5 seasons. New record World Cup score: Iran 17, Maldives 0 (qual. round). Season 1997-8 starts Premiership's record £36m., 4-year sponsorship extension with brewers Bass (Carling).

1998 In French manager Arsene Wenger's second season at Highbury, Arsenal become second English club to complete the Double twice. Chelsea also win two trophies under new player-manager Gianluca Vialli (Coca-Cola Cup, Cup Winners' Cup). France win 16th World Cup competition. In breakaway from Scottish League, top ten clubs form new Premiership under SFA, starting season 1998-9. Football League celebrates its 100th season, 1998-9. New F.A. Cup sponsors – French insurance giants AXA (25m., 4-year deal). League Cup becomes Worthington Cup in £23m., 5-year contract with brewers Bass. Nationwide Building Society's sponsorship of Football League extended to season 2000-1.

1999 F.A. buy Wembley Stadium (£103m.) for £320m. redevelopment (Aug. 2000-March 2003) as new national stadium (Lottery Sports fund contributes £110m.) Scotland's new Premier League takes 3-week mid-season break in January. Sky screen Oxford Utd. v Sunderland (Div. 1, Feb. 27) as first pay-per-view match on TV. F.A. sack England coach Glenn Hoddle; Fulham's Kevin Keegan replaces him at £1m. a year until 2003. Sir Alf Ramsey, England's World Cup-winning manager, dies aged 79. With effect 1999, F.A. Cup Final to be decided on day (via penalties, if necessary). Hampden Park re-opens for Scottish Cup Final after £63m. refit. Alex Ferguson knighted after Manchester Utd. complete Premiership, F.A. Cup, European Cup treble. Starting season 1999-2000, UEFA increase Champions League from 24 to 32 clubs. End of Cup-Winners' Cup (merged into 121-club UEFA Cup).

MANCHESTER CITY TOP CROWD PULLERS

Manchester City attracted last season's top home League crowd at 19 of the 23 clubs they visited in Division 2. The exceptions were Blackpool, Fulham, Lincoln City and Stoke City.

NARROW MAJORITY

Of the 176 players who started the eight Premiership matches on the opening day of season 1998-99, 89 were English and 87 non-English.

ENGLISH LEAGUE ROLL-CALL

APPEARANCES & SCORERS 1998-99

(figures in brackets = appearances as substitute)

F.A. CARLING PREMIERSHIP

ARSENAL

Adams, T 26	Grimandi, G .... 3(5)	Parlour, R 35
Anelka, N .... 34(1)	Grondin, D 1	Petit, E .... 26(1)
Bergkamp, D .... 28(1)	Hughes, S .... 4(10)	Seaman, D 32
Boa Morte, L .... 2(6)	Kanu, N .... 5(7)	Upson, M .... –(5)
Bould, S .... 14(5)	Keown, M 34	Vieira, P 34
Caballero, F .... –(1)	Ljungberg, F .... 10(6)	Vivas, N .... 10(13)
Diawara, K .... 2(10)	Manninger, A 6	Winterburn, N 30
Dixon, L 36	Mendez, A .... –(1)	Wreh, C .... 3(9)
Garde, R .... 6(4)	Overmars, M 37	

League Goals (59): Anelka 17, Bergkamp 12, Kanu 6, Overmars 6, Parlour 6, Petit 4, Vieira 3, Adams 1, Ljungberg 1, Hughes 1, Keown 1, Opponents 1.
Worthington Cup Goals (2): Vivas 1, Opponents 1. **F.A. Cup Goals (12):** Overmars 4, Bergkamp 3, Petit 2, Boa Morte 1, Vieira 1, Kanu 1. **Champions League Goals (7):** Adams 1, Keown 1, Bergkamp 1, Hughes 1, Anelka 1, Boa Morte 1, Mendez 1. **F.A. Charity Shield Goals (3):** Overmars 1, Anelka 1, Wreh 1.
Player of Year: to be announced.
Average home League attendance 1998-99: 38,024.

ASTON VILLA

Barry, G .... 27(5)	Ehiogu, U .... 23(2)	Southgate, G 38
Bosnich, M 15	Grayson, S .... 4(11)	Stone, S .... 9(1)
Calderwood, C 8	Hendrie, L .... 31(1)	Taylor, I .... 31(2)
Charles, G .... 10(1)	Joachim, J .... 29(7)	Thompson, A .... 20(5)
Collymore, S .... 11(9)	Merson, P .... 21(5)	Vassell, D .... –(6)
Delaney, M .... –(2)	Oakes, M 23	Watson, S .... 26(1)
Draper, M .... 13(10)	Rachel, A .... –(1)	Wright, A 38
Dublin, D 24	Scimeca, R .... 16(2)	Yorke, D 1

League Goals (51): Joachim 14, Dublin 11, Merson 5, Taylor 4, Hendrie 3, Barry 2, Draper 2, Ehiogu 2, Scimeca 2, Thompson 2, Charles 1, Collymore 1, Southgate 1, Opponents 1.
Worthington Cup Goals (1): Draper 1. **F.A. Cup Goals (3):** Collymore 2, Joachim 1. **UEFA Cup Goals (8):** Collymore 4, Vassell 2, Charles 1, Joachim 1.
Player of Year: Julian Joachim.
Average home League attendance 1998-99: 36,936.

BLACKBURN ROVERS

Blake, N .... 9(2)	Davies, K .... 9(12)	Gallacher, K .... 13(3)
Broomes, M .... 8(5)	Duff, D .... 18(10)	Gillespie, K .... 13(3)
Carsley, L .... 7(1)	Dunn, D .... 10(5)	Henchoz, S 34
Croft, G .... 10(2)	Fettis, A 2	Jansen, M .... 10(1)
Dahlin, M .... 2(3)	Filan, J 26	Johnson, D .... 14(7)
Dailly, C .... 14(3)	Flitcroft, G 8	Kenna, J .... 22(1)
Davidson, C 34	Flowers, T .... 10(1)	Marcolin, D .... 5(5)

McAteer, J 13	Perez, S .... 4(1)	Taylor, M .... 1(2)
McKinlay, W .... 14(2)	Sherwood, T 19	Ward, A 17
Peacock, D .... 27(3)	Sutton, C 17	Wilcox, J .... 28(2)

League Goals (38): Ward 5, Gallacher 5, Blake 3, Jansen 3, Sherwood 3, Sutton 3, Wilcox 3, Flitcroft 2, Davidson 1, Davies 1, Duff 1, Dunn 1, Gillespie 1, Johnson 1, Marcolin 1, McAteer 1, Peacock 1, Perez 1 , Opponents 1.
Worthington Cup Goals (2): Sutton 1, Sherwood 1. **F.A. Cup Goals (3):** Wilcox 1, Davies 1, Gillespie 1. **UEFA Cup Goals (2):** Perez 1, Flitcroft 1.
Player of Year: John Filan.
Average home League attendance 1998-99: 25,761.

CHARLTON ATHLETIC

Barnes, J .... 2(10)	Kinsella, M 38	Powell, C 38
Barness, A .... –(3)	Konchesky, P .... 1(1)	Pringle, M .... 15(3)
Bowen, M .... 2(4)	Lisbie, K .... –(1)	Redfearn, N .... 29(1)
Bright, M .... 1(5)	Mendonca, C .... 19(6)	Robinson, J .... 27(3)
Brown, S .... 13(5)	Mills, D 36	Royce, S 8
Hunt, A .... 32(3)	Mortimer, P .... 10(7)	Rufus, R 27
Ilic, S 23	Newton, S .... 13(3)	Stuart, G 9
Jones, K .... 13(9)	Parker, S .... –(4)	Tiler, C 27
Jones, S .... 7(18)	Petterson, A .... 7(3)	Youds, E .... 21(1)

League Goals (41): Mendonca 8, Hunt 7, Stuart 4, Pringle 3, Redfearn 3, Kinsella 2, Mills 2, Robinson 2, Youds 2, Bright 1, Jones K 1, Jones S 1, Mortimer 1, Rufus 1, Tiler 1, Opponents 2.
Worthington Cup Goals (4): Newton 1, Youds 1, Mortimer 1, Opponents 1. **F.A. Cup Goals:** None.
Player of Year: Mark Kinsella.
Average home League attendance 1998-99: 19,823.

CHELSEA

Babayaro, C .... 26(2)	Goldbaek, B .... 13(10)	Newton, E 1
Casiraghi, P 10	Hitchcock, K .... 2(1)	Nicholls, M .... –(9)
De Goey, E 35	Kharine, D 1	Petrescu, D .... 23(9)
Desailly, M .... 30(1)	Lambourde, B .... 12(5)	Poyet, G .... 21(7)
Di Matteo, R .... 26(4)	Laudrup, B .... 5(2)	Terry, J .... –(2)
Duberry, M .... 18(7)	Leboeuf, F 33	Vialli, G 9
Ferrer, A 30	Le Saux, G .... 30(1)	Wise, D .... 21(1)
Flo, T .... 18(12)	Morris, J .... 14(4)	Zola, G .... 35(2)
Forssell, M .... 4(6)	Myers, A 1	

League Goals (57): Zola 13, Flo 10, Poyet 10, Goldbaek 5, Leboeuf 4, Petrescu 4, Babayaro 3, Di Matteo 2, Casiraghi 1, Forssell 1, Morris 1 Vialli 1, Opponents 2.
Worthington Cup Goals (10): Vialli 6, Poyet 2, Flo 1, Leboeuf 1. **F.A. Cup Goals (8):** Vialli 2, Forssell 2, Di Matteo 1, Leboeuf 1, Wise 1, Zola 1. **European Super Cup Goals (1):** Poyet 1. **Cup-Winners' Cup Goals (10):** Flo 2, Leboeuf 1, Desailly 1, Laudrup 1, Babayaro 1, Wise 1, Zola 1, Vialli 1, Lambourde 1.
Player of Year: to be announced.
Average home League attendance 1998-99: 34,751.

COVENTRY CITY

Aloisi, J .... 7(9)	Clement, P .... 6(6)	Gioacchini, S .... –(3)
Boateng, G .... 29(4)	Dublin, D 10	Hall, M .... 2(3)
Breen, G .... 21(4)	Edworthy, M .... 16(6)	Hall, P .... 2(7)
Burrows, D 23	Froggatt, S 23	Haworth, S 1

Hedman, M 36	Nilsson, R 28	Soltvedt, T .... 21(6)
Huckerby, D .... 31(3)	Ogrizovic, S 2	Telfer, P .... 30(2)
Jackson, D .... –(3)	Quinn, B .... 6(1)	Walleme, J .... 4(2)
Konjic, M .... 3(1)	Shaw, R .... 36(1)	Whelan, N 31
McAllister, G 29	Shilton, S .... 1(4)	Williams, P .... 20(2)
McSheffrey, G .... –(1)		

League Goals (39): Whelan 10, Huckerby 9, Aloisi 5, Boateng 4, Dublin 3, McAllister 3, Solvedt 2, Telfer 2, Froggatt 1.
Worthington Cup Goals (5): Hall P 1, Boateng 1, Solvedt 1, Whelan 1, Dublin 1. **F.A. Cup Goals (11):** Huckerby 3, Whelan 2, Froggatt 2, Boateng 1, McAllister 1, Telfer 1, Opponents 1.
Player of Year: Richard Shaw.
Average home League attendance 1998-99: 20,778.

DERBY COUNTY

Baiano, F .... 17(5)	Dailly, C 1	Laursen, J 37
Beck, M .... 6(1)	Delap, R .... 21(2)	Murray, A .... –(4)
Boertien, P .... –(1)	Dorigo, L .... 17(1)	Poom, M .... 15(2)
Bohinen, L .... 29(3)	Elliott, S .... 7(4)	Powell, D .... 30(3)
Borbokis, V .... 3(1)	Eranio, S .... 18(7)	Prior, S .... 33(1)
Bridge-Wilkinson, M .. –(1)	Harper, K .... 6(21)	Robinson, M .... –(1)
Burton, D .... 14(7)	Hoult, R 23	Schnoor, S .... 20(3)
Carbonari, H .... 28(1)	Hunt, J .... –(6)	Stimac, I 14
Carsley, L .... 20(2)	Kozluk, R .... 3(4)	Sturridge, D .... 23(6)
Christie, M .... –(2)	Launders, B .... –(1)	Wanchope, P .... 33(2)

League Goals (40): Burton 9, Wanchope 9, Carbonari 5, Sturridge 5, Baiano 4, Schnoor 2, Beck 1, Carsley 1, Dorigo 1, Harper 1, Hunt 1, Prior 1.
Worthington Cup Goals (3): Delap 1, Wanchope 1, Sturridge 1. **F.A. Cup Goals (9):** Burton 3, Baiano 2, Dorigo 2, Eranio 1, Harper 1.
Player of Year: Jacob Laursen.
Average home League attendance 1998-99: 29,194.

EVERTON

Bakayoko, I .... 17(6)	Farley, A .... –(1)	Myhre, T 38
Ball, M .... 36(1)	Farrelly, G .... –(1)	O'Kane, J 2
Barmby, N .... 20(4)	Ferguson, D 13	Oster, J .... 6(3)
Branch, M .... 1(6)	Gemmill, S 7	Short, C 22
Cadamarteri, D ..... 11(19)	Grant, A .... 13(3)	Spencer, J .... 2(1)
Campbell, K 8	Hutchison, D .... 29(4)	Thomas, T .... –(1)
Cleland, A .... 16(2)	Jeffers, F .... 11(4)	Tiler, C 2
Collins, J .... 19(1)	Jevons, P .... –(1)	Unsworth, D .... 33(1)
Dacourt, O .... 28(2)	Madar, M 2	Ward, M .... 4(2)
Degn, P .... –(4)	Materazzi, M .... 26(1)	Watson, D 22
Dunne, R .... 15(1)	Milligan, J .... –(3)	Weir, D .... 11(3)

League Goals (42): Campbell 9, Jeffers 6, Bakayoko 4, Cadamarteri 4, Ferguson 4, Ball 3, Barmby 3, Hutchison 3, Dacourt 2, Collins 1, Gemmill 1, Materazzi 1, Unsworth 1.
Worthington Cup Goals (7): Watson 1, Materazzi 1, Dacourt 1, Ferguson 1, Hutchison 1, Bakayoko 1, Collins 1. **F.A. Cup Goals (6):** Bakayoko 2, Barmby 1, Jeffers 1, Oster 1, Unsworth 1.
Player of Year: to be announced.
Average home League attendance 1998-99: 36,202.

LEEDS UNITED

Batty, D 10	Hopkin, D .... 32(2)	Radebe, L 29
Bowyer, L 35	Jones, M .... 3(5)	Ribeiro, B .... 7(6)
Granville, D .... 7(2)	Kewell, H .... 36(2)	Robinson, P .... 4(1)
Haaland, A .... 24(5)	Korsten, W .... 4(3)	Sharpe, L .... 2(2)
Halle, G .... 14(3)	Lilley, D .... –(2)	Smith, A .... 15(7)
Harte, I .... 34(1)	Martyn, N 34	Wetherall, D .... 14(7)
Hasselbaink, J 36	McPhail, S .... 11(6)	Wijnhard, C .... 11(7)
Hiden, M 14	Molenaar, R 17	Woodgate, J 25

League Goals (62): Hasselbaink 17, Bowyer 9, Smith 7, Kewell 6, Hopkin 4, Harte 4, Wijnhard 3, Haaland 2, Halle 2, Korsten 2, Ribeiro 2, Woodgate 2, Molenaar 1, Opponents 1.
Worthington Cup Goals (2): Kewell 2. **F.A. Cup Goals (9):** Harte 2, Smith 2, Hasselbaink 1, Wijnhard 1, Kewell 1, Wetherall 1, Ribeiro 1. **UEFA Cup Goals (1):** Hasselbaink 1.
Player of Year: Lee Bowyer.
Average home League attendance 1998-99: 35,845.

LEICESTER CITY

Arphexad, P .... 2(2)	Impey, A .... 17(1)	Parker, G .... 2(5)
Campbell, S .... 1(11)	Izzet, M 31	Savage, R .... 29(5)
Cottee, A .... 29(2)	Kaamark, P .... 15(4)	Sinclair, F .... 30(1)
Elliott, M 37	Keller, K 36	Taggart, G .... 9(6)
Fenton, G .... 3(6)	Lennon, N 37	Ullathorne, R 25
Gunnlaugsson, A 5 (4)	Marshall, I .... 6(4)	Walsh, S .... 17(5)
Guppy, S 38	Miller, C .... 1(3)	Wilson, S .... 1(8)
Heskey, E .... 29(1)	Oakes, S .... 2(1)	Zagorakis, T .... 16(3)

League Goals (40): Cottee 10, Heskey 6, Izzet 5, Guppy 4, Walsh 3, Marshall 3, Elliott 3, Savage 1, Zagorakis 1, Sinclair 1, Lennon 1, Opponents 2.
Worthington Cup Goals (14): Cottee 5, Heskey 3, Taggart 1, Wilson 1, Fenton 1, Izzet 1, Parker 1, Lennon 1. **F.A. Cup Goals (4):** Sinclair 1, Guppy 1, Cottee 1, Ullathorne 1.
Player of Year: Tony Cottee.
Average home League attendance 1998-99: 20,468

LIVERPOOL

Babb, P .... 24(1)	Harkness, S .... 4(2)	McManaman, S ...... 25(3)
Berger, P .... 30(2)	Heggem, V .... 27(2)	Murphy, D .... –(1)
Bjornebye, S .... 20(3)	Ince, P 34	Owen, M 30
Carragher, J 34	James, D 26	Redknapp, J .... 33(1)
Dundee, S .... –(3)	Kvarme, B .... 2(5)	Riedle, K .... 16(18)
Ferri, J .... –(2)	Leonhardsen, O .... 7(2)	Song, R .... 10(3)
Fowler, R .... 23(2)	Matteo, D .... 16(4)	Staunton, S 31
Friedel, B 12	McAteer, J .... 6(7)	Thompson, D .... 4(10)
Gerrard, S .... 4(8)		

League Goals (68): Owen 18, Fowler 14, Redknapp 8, Berger 7, Ince 6, Riedle 5, McManaman 4, Heggem 2, Leonhardsen 2, Carragher 1, Matteo 1, Thompson 1.
Worthington Cup Goals (4): Ince 1, Fowler 1, Owen 1, Opponents 1. **F.A. Cup Goals (4):** Owen 2, Ince 1, Fowler 1. **UEFA Cup Goals (11):** Redknapp 2, Berger 2, Fowler 2, Owen 2, Riedle 1, Ince 1, McManaman 1.
Player of Year: to be announced.
Average home League attendance 1998-99: 43,321.

MANCHESTER UNITED

Beckham, D .... 33(1)	Blomqvist, J .... 20(5)	Butt, N .... 22(9)
Berg, H .... 10(6)	Brown, W .... 11(3)	Cole, A .... 26(6)

Cruyff, ... –(5)
Curtis, J .... 1(3)
Giggs, R .... 20(4)
Greening, J .... –(3)
Irwin, D .... 26(3)
Johnsen, R .:........... 19(3)

Keane, R .... 33(2)
May, D .... 4(2)
Neville, G 34
Neville, P .... 19(9)
Schmeichel, P 34
Scholes, P .... 24(7)

Sheringham, E .... 7(10)
Solskjaer, O .... 9(10)
Stam, J 30
Van Der Gouw, R ...... 4(1)
Yorke, D 32

League Goals (80): Yorke 18, Cole 17, Solskjaer 12, Scholes 6, Beckham 6, Johnsen 3, Giggs 3, Butt 2, Cruyff 2, Irwin 2, Keane 2, Sheringham 2, Blomqvist 1, G Neville 1, Stam 1, Opponents 2.
Worthington Cup Goals (5): Solskjaer 3, Sheringham 1, Nevland 1. **F.A. Cup Goals (12):** Yorke 3, Giggs 2, Cole 2, Irwin 1, Scholes 1, Solskjaer 1, Beckham 1, Sheringham 1. **Champions League Goals (31):** Yorke 8, Giggs 5, Cole 5, Scholes 4, Keane 3, Beckham 2, Solskjaer 2, P Neville 1, Sheringham 1. **F.A. Charity Shield Goals:** None.
Player of Year: to be announced.
Average home League attendance 1998-99: 55,188.

MIDDLESBROUGH

Armstrong, A .... –(6)
Baker, S .... 1(1)
Beck, M .... 13(14)
Beresford, M 4
Branca, M .... –(1)
Campbell, A .... 1(7)
Cooper, C .... 31(1)
Cummins, M 1
Deane, B .... 24(2)
Festa, G 25

Fleming, C .... 12(2)
Gavin, J 2
Gascoigne, P .... 25(1)
Gordon, D 38
Harrison, C .... 3(1)
Kinder, V .... –(5)
Maddison, N ...... 10(11)
Merson, P 3
Moore, A .... 3(1)
Mustoe, R .... 32(1)

O'Neill, K .... 4(2)
Pallister, G 26
Ricard, H .... 32(4)
Schwarzer, M 34
Stamp, P .... 5(11)
Stockdale, R .... 17(2)
Summerbell, M .... 7(4)
Townsend, A 35
Vickers, S .... 30(1)

League Goals (48): Ricard 15, Deane 6, Beck 5, Mustoe 4, Gascoigne 3, Gordon 3, Festa 2, Kinder 2, Stamp 2, Armstrong 1, Cooper 1, Fleming 1, Townsend 1, Vickers 1, Opponents 1.
Worthington Cup Goals (5): Ricard 3, Festa 1, Summerbell 1. **F.A. Cup Goals (1):** Townsend 1.
Player of Year: Hamilton Ricard.
Average home League attendance 1998-99: 34,389.

NEWCASTLE UNITED

Albert, P .... 3(3)
Andersson, A .... 11(4)
Barnes, J .... –(1)
Barton, W .... 17(7)
Batty, D .... 6(2)
Beharall, D 4
Brady, G .... 3(6)
Charvet, L .... 30(1)
Dabizas, N .... 25(5)
Dalglish, P .... 6(5)
Domi, D 14
Ferguson, D 7

Georgiadis, G .... 7(3)
Gillespie, K .... 5(2)
Given, S 31
Glass, S .... 18(4)
Griffin, A 14
Guivarc'h, S .... 2(2)
Hamann, D .... 22(1)
Harper, S .... 7(1)
Howey, S 14
Hughes, A .... 12(2)
Ketsbaia, T .... 14(12)

Lee, R .... 20(6)
Maric, S .... 9(1)
McClen, J 1
Pearce, S 12
Pistone, A .... 2(1)
Saha, L .... 5(6)
Serrant, C .... 3(1)
Shearer, A .... 29(1)
Solano, N .... 24(5)
Speed, G .... 34(4)
Watson, S 7

League Goals (48): Shearer 14, Solano 6, Ketsbaia 5, Hamann 4, Speed 3, Dabizas 3, Glass 3, Andersson 2, Ferguson 2, Charvet 1, Dalglish 1, Guivarc'h 1, Saha 1, Opponents 1.
Worthington Cup Goals (2): Dalglish 1, Shearer 1. **F.A. Cup Goals (12):** Shearer 5, Ketsbaia 3, Speed 1, Hamann 1, Saha 1, Georgiadis 1. **Cup-Winners' Cup Goals (2):** Dabizas 1, Shearer 1.

NOTTINGHAM FOREST

Allou, B .... –(2)	Gemmill, S .... 18(2)	Melton, S 1
Armstrong, C .... 20(2)	Gough, R 7	Palmer, C 13
Bart-Williams, C ..... 20(4)	Gray, A .... 3(5)	Porfirio, H .... 3(6)
Beasant, D 26	Harewood, M .... 11(12)	Quashie, N .... 12(4)
Bonalair, T .... 24(4)	Harkes, J 3	Rogers, A 34
Chettle, S .... 32(2)	Hjelde, J .... 16(1)	Shipperley, N .... 12(8)
Crossley, M 12	Hodges, G .... 3(2)	Stensaas, S .... 6(1)
Darcheville, J-C ...... 14(2)	Johnson, A .... 25(3)	Stone, S 26
Doig, C .... 1(1)	Louis-Jean, M .... 15(1)	Thomas, G 5
Edwards, C .... 7(5)	Lyttle, D .... 5(5)	Van Hooijdonk, P .... 19(2)
Freedman, D .... 20(11)	Mattsson, J .... 5(1)	Woan, I .... –(2)

League Goals (35): Freedman 9, Van Hooijdonk 6, Rogers 4, Bart-Williams 3, Stone 3, Chettle 2, Darcheville 2, Shipperley 1, Bonalair 1, Harewood 1, Hjelde 1, Porfirio 1, Thomas 1.
Worthington Cup Goals (9): Freedman 3, Stone 2, Harewood 2, Johnson 1, Armstrong 1.
F.A. Cup Goals: None.
Player of Year: Alan Rogers.
Average home League attendance 1998-99: 24,415.

SHEFFIELD WEDNESDAY

Agogo, M .... –(1)	Hinchcliffe, A 32	Quinn, A 1
Alexandersson, N .... 31(1)	Humphreys, R .... 19(9)	Rudi, P .... 33(1)
Atherton, P 38	Hyde, G .... –(1)	Sanetti, F .... –(3)
Barrett, E .... –(5)	Jonk, W 38	Scott, P .... –(4)
Booth, A 34	Magilton, J .... 1(5)	Sonner, D .... 24(2)
Briscoe, L .... 5(11)	McKeever, M .... 1(2)	Srnicek, P 24
Carbone, B 31	Morrison, J .... –(1)	Stefanovic, D .... 8(3)
Cobian, J .... 7(2)	Newsome, J .... 2(3)	Thome, E 38
Cresswell, R .... 1(6)	Oakes, S .... –(1)	Walker, D 37
Di Canio, P .... 6(1)	Pressman, K .... 14(1)	Whittingham, G .... 1(1)
Haslam, S 2		

League Goals (41): Carbone 8, Booth 6, Rudi 6, Alexandersson 3, Di Canio 3, Hinchcliffe 3, Sonner 3, Atherton 2, Jonk 2, Thome 1, Cresswell 1, Briscoe 1, Humphreys 1, Scott 1.
Worthington Cup Goals (1): Opponents 1. **F.A. Cup Goals (6):** Humphreys 2, Stefanovic 1, Rudi 1, Carbone 1, Thome 1.
Player of Year: Benito Carbone.
Average home League attendance 1998-99: 26,745.

SOUTHAMPTON

Basham, S .... –(4)	Gibbens, K .... 2(2)	Lundekvam, C .... 30(3)
Beattie, J .... 22(13)	Hiley, S .... 27(2)	Marsden, C 14
Benali, F .... 19(4)	Hirst, D .... –(2)	Marshall, S 2
Beresford, J .... 1(3)	Howells, D .... 8(1)	Monk, G 4
Bradley, S .... –(3)	Hughes, P .... 6(3)	Monkou, K 22
Bridge, W .... 15(8)	Hughes, M 32	Moss, N 7
Colleter, P 16	Jones, P 31	Oakley, M .... 21(1)
Dodd, J .... 27(1)	Kachloul, H .... 18(4)	Ostenstad, E .... 27(7)
Dryden, R 4	Le Tisser, M .... 20(10)	Pahars, M .... 4(2)

Palmer, C .... 18(1) Warner, P 5   Williams, A .... –(1)
Ripley, S .... 16(6)

League Goals (37): Le Tissier 7, Ostenstad 7, Kachloul 5, Beattie 5, Pahars 3, Marsden 2, Oakley 2, Basham 1, Dodd 1, Colleter 1, Howells 1, Hughes M 1, Monkou 1.
Worthington Cup Goals (1): Beattie 1. **F.A. Cup Goals (1):** Ostenstad 1.
Player of Year: Ken Monkou.
Average home League attendance 1998-99: 15,139.

TOTTENHAM HOTSPUR

Allen, R .... –(5)   Edinburgh, J .... 14(2)   Scales, J 7
Anderton, D .... 31(1)   Ferdinand, L .... 22(2)   Segers, H 1
Armstrong, C .... 24(10)   Fox, R .... 17(3)   Sherwood, T .... 12(2)
Baardsen, E 12   Freund, S 17   Sinton, A .... 12(10)
Berti, N 4   Ginola, D 30   Taricco, M .... 12(1)
Calderwood, C .... 11(1)   Iversen, S .... 22(5)   Tramezzani, P 6
Campbell, S 37   King, L .... –(1)   Vega, R .... 13(3)
Carr, S 37   Nielsen, A .... 24(4)   Walker, I 25
Clemence, S .... 9(9)   Nilsen, R 3   Young, L .... 14(1)
Dominguez, J .... 2(11)   Saib, M .... –(4)

League Goals (47): Iversen 9, Armstrong 7, Campbell 6, Ferdinand 5, Fox 3, Nielsen 3, Ginola 3, Anderton 3, Vega 2, Dominguez 2, Sherwood 2, Opponents 2.
Worthington Cup Goals (17): Armstrong 5, Nielsen 3, Iversen 2, Campbell 2, Carr 1, Vega 1, Dominguez 1, Scales 1, Ginola 1. **F.A. Cup Goals (13):** Nielsen 3, Ginola 3, Anderton 2, Iversen 2, Fox 1, Sinton 1, Sherwood 1.
Player of Year: to be announced.
Average home League attendance 1998-99: 34,153.

WEST HAM UNITED

Abou, S .... 2(1)   Hartson, J .... 16(1)   Minto, S .... 14(1)
Berkovic, E .... 28(2)   Hislop, S 37   Moncur, J .... 6(8)
Breacker, T .... 2(1)   Hodges, L .... –(1)   Omoyinmi, E .... –(3)
Cole, J .... 2(6)   Holligan, G .... –(1)   Pearce, I 33
Coyne, C .... –(1)   Impey, A .... 6(2)   Potts, S .... 11(8)
Di Canio, P .... 12(1)   Keller, M .... 17(4)   Ruddock, N 27
Dicks, J 9   Kitson, P .... 13(4)   Sinclair, T 36
Ferdinand, R 31   Lampard, F 38   Wright, I 20
Foe, M 13   Lazaridis, S .... 11(4)   Lomas, S 30
Forrest, C .... 1(1)   Margas, J 3

League Goals (46): Wright 9, Sinclair 7, Keller 5, Lampard 5, Di Canio 4, Hartson 4, Berkovic 3, Kitson 3, Pearce 2, Ruddock 2, Lomas 1, Opponents 1.
Worthington Cup Goals (1): Lampard 1. **F.A. Cup Goals (1):** Dicks 1.
Player of Year: Shaka Hislop.
Average home League attendance 1998-99: 25,684.

WIMBLEDON

Ainsworth, G .... 5(3)   Euell, J .... 31(2)   Kennedy, M .... 7(10)
Ardley, N .... 16(7)   Fear, P .... –(2)   Kimble, A .... 22(4)
Blackwell, D .... 27(1)   Gayle, M .... 31(4)   Leaburn, C .... 14(8)
Castledine, S 1   Goodman, J .... –(1)   Perry, C 34
Cort, C .... 6(10)   Hartson, J .... 12(2)   Roberts, A .... 23(5)
Cunningham, K 35   Hughes, C .... 8(6)   Sullivan, N 38
Earle, R 35   Hughes, M .... 28(2)   Thatcher, B 31
Ekoku, E .... 11(11)   Jupp, D .... 3(3)

League Goals (40): Euell 10, Gayle 10, Ekoku 6, Earle 5, Cort 3, Hartson 2, Hughes M 2, Roberts 2.
Worthington Cup Goals (11): Ekoku 3, Ardley 3, Earle 1, Gayle 1, Kennedy 1, Leaburn 1, Hughes M 1. F.A. Cup Goals (2): Cort 1, Earle 1.
Player of Year: Neil Sullivan.
Average home League attendance 1998-99: 18,235.

NATIONWIDE LEAGUE – FIRST DIVISION

BARNSLEY

Ground: Oakwell, Barnsley, South Yorkshire, S71 1ET.
Telephone: 01226 211211. Clubcall: 0891 121152. Club Nickname: Tykes.
First-choice Colours: Red shirts; white shorts; red stockings.

Appleby, M .... 32(1)	Goodman, D .... 5(3)	Moses, A .... 33(1)
Bagshaw, P .... –(1)	Hendrie, J .... 6(2)	McClare, S .... 23(7)
Barnard, D 26	Hignett, C 24	Parkin, J .... –(2)
Blackmore, C .... 4(3)	Hristov, D .... 2(1)	Richardson, K .... 24(2)
Bullock, A 32	Jones, S .... 28(1)	Rose, K .... 2(1)
Bullock, M .... 20(12)	Krizan, A 1	Sheridan, D .... 15(10)
Burton, D 3	Leese, L 8	Sheron, M .... 15(1)
Cuesta, F 2	Liddell, A .... 3(5)	Tinkler, E .... 21(4)
De Zeeuw, A 38	Marcelle, C .... 2(7)	Turner, M .... 2(11)
Dyer, B 28	Markstedt, P 2	Van der Laan, R ..... 13(4)
Eaden, N .... 38(2)	Moore, A .... 4(1)	Ward, A 17
Fjortoft, J .... 9(10)	Morgan, C .... 18(1)	Watson, D 6

League Goals (59): Ward 12, Hignett 9, Dyer 7, Barnard 4, De Zeeuw 4, Fjortoft 3, Jones, 3, McClare 3, Tinkler 3, Sheron 2, Bullock M 2, Sheridan 1, Turner 1, Hendrie 1, Van der Laan 1, Opponents 3.
Worthington Cup Goals (10): Fjortoft 4, Ward 3, Van der Laan 1, Barnard 1, Eaden 1. F.A. Cup Goals (10): Hignett 5, Bullock M 2, Dyer 1, McClare 1, Sheridan 1.
Player of Year: Craig Hignett. Sponsors: ORA.
Average home League attendance 1998-99: 16,270. Capacity for 1999-2000: 23,000.
Record attendance: 40,255 v Stoke City (F.A. Cup 5) 15 February 1936.

BIRMINGHAM CITY

Ground: St Andrews, Birmingham, B9 4NH.
Telephone: 0121 7720101. Clubcall: 0891 121188. Club Nickname: Blues.
First-choice Colours: Blue shirts; white shorts; blue stockings.

Ablett, G .... 23(3)	Gill, J 3	Marsh, S .... 6(1)
Adebola, D .... 33(6)	Grainger, M .... 30(10)	McCarthy, J .... 35(8)
Bass, J .... 9(2)	Holdsworth, D 8	Ndlovu, P .... 38(5)
Bennett, I 10	Holland, C .... 7(7)	O'Connor, M .... 35(2)
Bradbury, L .... 6(1)	Hughes, B .... 20(8)	Poole, K 36
Charlton, S .... 27(1)	Hyde, G 13	Purse, D .... 11(9)
Forinton, H .... –(3)	Johnson, A .... –(4)	Robinson, S .... 20(10)
Forster, N .... 8(25)	Johnson, M .... 43(2)	Rowett, G 42
Furlong, P .... 24(5)	Marsden, C 20	Wassall, D .... –(3)

Play-offs – Appearances: Adebola 1(1), Bradbury 1(1), Furlong 2, Grainger 2, Holdsworth 2, Holland 1(1), Hughes 1, Johnson M 2, McCarthy 2, Ndlovu 1(1), O'Connor 2, Poole 2, Purse –(1), Robinson 1, Rowett 2.
League Goals (66): Adebola 13, Furlong 13, Ndlovu 11, Forster 5, Rowett 5, Grainger 4, Johnson M 4, O'Connor 4, Hughes 3, Marsden 2, Forinton 1, Holdsworth 1. Play-off Goals (1): Adebola.

Worthington Cup Goals (13): Marsden 3, Adebola 2, Johnson M 2, Ndlovu 2, Rowett 2, Forster 1, Opponents 1. **F.A. Cup Goals (2):** Adebola 1, Robinson 1.
Player of Year: Michael Johnson. **Sponsors:** Auto Windscreens.
Average home League attendance 1998-99: 20,794. **Capacity for 1999-2000:** 30,008.
Record attendance: 66,844 v Everton (F.A. Cup 5) 11 February 1939.

BOLTON WANDERERS

Ground: Reebok Stadium, Burnden Way, Lostock, Bolton, Lancashire, BL6 6JW.
Telephone: 01204 673673. **Clubcall:** 0891 121164. **Club Nickname:** Trotters.
First-choice Colours: White shirts; navy shorts; navy stockings.

Aljofree, H .... 1(3)	Fullarton, J 1	Newson, J 6
Banks, S 9	Gardener, R .... 19(11)	Phillips, J .... 14(1)
Bergsson, G .... 15(2)	Gudjohnson, E .... 8(6)	Sellars, S .... 22(3)
Blake, N .... 10(2)	Gunnlaugsson, A .... 21(5)	Strong, G .... 4(1)
Branagan, K 3	Hansen, B .... 1(7)	Taylor, R .... 32(6)
Cox, N .... 42(2)	Holdsworth, D ...... 22(10)	Todd, A .... 18(2)
Elliott, R .... 14(8)	Jaaskelainen, J 34	Warhurst, P .... 17(3)
Fish, M 36	Jensen, C 44	Whitlow, M .... 27(1)
Frandsen, P 44	Johansen, M .... 40(2)	

Play-offs – Appearances: Banks 3, Bergsson –(2), Cox 3, Elliott 3, Fish 3, Frandsen 3, Gardener 3, Gudjohnson 3, Hansen –(3), Jensen 3, Johansen 3, Sellars –(1), Taylor 3, Todd 3, Warhurst –(2).
League Goals (78): Taylor 15, Gunnlaugsson 13, Holdsworth 12, Frandsen 8, Johansen 7, Blake 6, Gudjohnson 5, Cox 4, Sellars 2, Jensen 2, Gardener 2, Fish 1, Strong 1.
Play-off Goals (4): Taylor 2, Frandsen 1, Johansen 1.
Worthington Cup Goals (12): Blake 3, Jensen 2, Elliott 1, Frandsen 1, Gardener 1, Gunnlaugsson 1, Johansen 1, Phillips 1, Taylor 1. **F.A. Cup Goals (1):** Sellars 1.
Player of Year: Michael Johansen. **Sponsors:** Reebok.
Average home League attendance 1998-99: 18,240. **Capacity for 1999-2000:** 25,000.
Record attendance: (Burnden Park) 69,912 v Manchester City (F.A. Cup 5) 18 February 1933; (Reebok Stadium) 25,000 at nine Premiership matches, season 1997-98.

BRADFORD CITY

Ground: The Pulse Stadium, Valley Parade, West Yorkshire, BD8 7DY.
Telephone: 01274 773355. **Clubcall:** 09068 888640. **Club Nickname:** Bantams.
First-choice Colours: Claret and amber shirts; amber shorts; claret stockings.

Beagrie, P 43	McCall, S 43	Todd, L .... 14(2)
Blake, R .... 35(4)	Mills, L 45	Walsh, G 46
Bolland, P 2	Moore, D 43	Watson, G .... 5(13)
Dreyer, J .... 19(2)	O'Brien, A .... 19(12)	Westwood, A .... 17(3)
Edinho .... 1(2)	Pepper, N .... 5(4)	Whalley, G 45
Grant, G .... 1(4)	Rankin, I .... 15(12)	Windass, D .... 6(6)
Jacobs, W .... 42(2)	Ramage, C .... –(3)	Wright, S .... 21(1)
Lawrence, J .... 33(2)	Sharpe, L .... 6(3)	

League Goals (82): Mills 24, Blake 16, Beagrie 12, Rankin 5, Watson 4, Jacobs 3, McCall 3, Moore 3, Windass 3, Sharpe 2, Lawrence 2, Westwood 2, Whalley 2, Pepper 1.
Worthington Cup Goals (7): Beagrie 3, Blake 1, Moore 1, Pepper 1, Rankin 1. **F.A. Cup Goals (2):** Mills 1, Lawrence 1.
Player of Year: Stuart McCall. **Sponsors:** JCT 600.
Average home League attendance 1998-99: 14,265 **Capacity for 1999-2000:** 18,018.
Record attendance: 39,146 v Burnley (F.A. Cup 4) 11 March 1911.

BRISTOL CITY

Ground: Ashton Gate, Bristol, BS3 2EJ.
Telephone: 0117 9630630. **Clubcall:** 09068 121176. **Club Nickname:** Robins.
First-choice Colours: Red shirts; red shorts; white stockings.

Akinbiyi, A 44	Goodridge, G .... 15(14)	Pinamonte, C 1
Andersen, S .... 26(13)	Hale, M .... –(1)	Phillips, S 15
Anderssen, B 10	Heaney, N .... 2(1)	Sebok, V .... 10(2)
Bell, M 33	Hewlett, M 8	Shail, M .... 21(4)
Brennan, J 29	Hill, M .... –(2)	Taylor, S 8
Brown, A 14	Howells, D 8	Tistimetanu, I 8
Carey, L .... 40(1)	Hutchings, C .... 16(5)	Thorpe, A .... 9(7)
Cramb, C .... 4(8)	Jordan, A 1	Torpey, S .... 19(2)
Doherty, T .... 15(8)	Langan, K 1	Tinnion, B .... 32(3)
Dyche, S .... 4(2)	Locke, A .... 26(2)	Watts, J .... 16(1)
Edwards, C 3	Meechan, A .... –(1)	Welch, K 21
Edwards, R .... 19(4)	Murray, S .... 27(5)	Zwijnenberg, C .... 1(2)

League Goals (57): Akinbiyi 19, Andersen S 10, Bell 5, Torpey 4, Locke 3, Murray 3, Goodridge 2, Hutchings 2, Thorpe 2, Brennan 1, Doherty 1, Hewlett 1, Howells 1, Pinamonte 1, Tinnion 1, Watts 1.
Worthington Cup Goals (8): Akinbiyi 4, Andersen S 1, Doherty 1, Hutchings 1, Thorpe 1. **F.A. Cup Goals:** None.
Player of Year: Ade Akinbiyi. **Sponsors:** DAS.
Average home League attendance 1998-99: 12,860. **Capacity for 1999-2000:** 21,497.
Record attendance: 43,335 v Preston N.E. (F.A. Cup 5) 16 February 1935.

BURY

Ground: Gigg Lane, Bury, Lancashire BL9 9HR.
Telephone: 0161 7644881. **Clubcall:** 0930 190003. **Club Nickname:** Shakers.
First-choice Colours: White shirts; blue shorts; white stockings.

Armstrong, G .... –(2)	Foster, J .... 6(1)	Patterson, M .... 9(4)
Avrdiu, K .... –(6)	Grobbelaar, B 1	Preece, A .... 19(20)
Baldry, S .... –(5)	Hall, P 7	Redmond, S 26
Barnes, P .... 6(2)	James, L .... 10(7)	Rigby, A .... 1(1)
Barrick, D .... 16(4)	Jemson, N .... 6(8)	Serrant, C 15
Billy, C .... 34(2)	Johnrose, L .... 26(1)	Souter, R .... –(1)
Bullock, D 12	Kiely, D 45	Swailes, C 42
Daws, N 46	Lilley, D 5	Swailes, D 1
D'Jaffo, L .... 35(2)	Littlejohn, A .... 11(9)	West, D .... 18(5)
Ellis, A .... 3(11)	Lucketti, C 43	Williams, P 14
Forrest, M .... –(1)	Matthews, R .... 12(4)	Woodward, A .... 36(1)

League Goals (35): D'Jaffo 8, Preece 3, Swailes C 3, West 3, Daws 2, Ellis 2, James 2, Johnrose 2, Matthews 2, Avrdiu 1, Barrick 1, Bullock 1, Lilley 1, Littlejohn 1, Lucketti 1, Williams 1, Woodward 1.
Worthington Cup Goals (8): Matthews 3, Johnrose 2, Armstrong 1, Daws 1, D'Jaffo 1. **F.A. Cup Goals:** None.
Player of Year: Chris Swailes. **Sponsors:** Birthdays.
Average home League attendance 1998-99: 5,476. **Capacity for 1999-2000:** 12,300.
Record attendance: 35,000 v Bolton Wand. (F.A. Cup 3) 9 January 1960.

CREWE ALEXANDRA

Ground: Gresty Road, Crewe, Cheshire CW2 6EB
Telephone: 01270 213014. **Clubcall:** 0891 121647. **Club Nickname:** Railwaymen.
First-choice Colours: Red shirts; red shorts; white stockings.

Anthrobus, S .... 16(5)	Kearton, J 46	Smith, P .... –(4)
Bignot, M 26	Lightfoot, C .... 19(3)	Street, K .... 4(19)
Charnock, P .... 40(4)	Little, C .... 27(10)	Smith, S 46
Collins, J .... 5(1)	Lunt, K .... 6(12)	Unsworth, L .... 15(9)
Foran, M .... 4(2)	Macauley S .... 12(8)	Walton, D 38
Foster, S .... –(1)	Murphy, D 16	Wicks, M .... 4(2)
Jack, R .... 37(2)	Newell, M .... 1(3)	Wright, D 20
Johnson, S 42	Rivers, M .... 38(5)	Wright, J 44

League Goals (54): Little 10, Jack 9, Rivers 7, Wright J 5, Johnson 4, Smith S 4, Anthrobus 3, Charnock 2, Street 2, Lightfoot 2, Collins 1, Lunt 1, Walton 1, Wright D 1, Macauley 1, Murphy 1.
Worthington Cup Goals (7): Rivers 3, Jack 2, Little 2. **F.A. Cup Goals (1):** Johnson 1.
Player of Year: Seth Johnson. **Sponsors:** LC Charles.
Average home League attendance 1998-99: 5,269. **Capacity for 1999-2000:** 10,089.
Record attendance: 20,000 v Tottenham (F.A. Cup 4) 30 January 1960.

CRYSTAL PALACE

Ground: Selhurst Park, London SE25 6PU.
Telephone: 0181 768 6000. **Clubcall:** 0891 400333. **Club Nickname:** Eagles.
First-choice Colours: Red and blue shirts; red shorts; red stockings.

Amsalem, D .... 6(4)	Fullarton, J 7	Mullins, H .... 38(2)
Austin, D .... 17(3)	Graham, G .... –(1)	Padovano, M .... –(2)
Bent, M .... 3(9)	Harris, R .... –(1)	Petric, G 18
Bradbury, L .... 19(3)	Hibburt, J .... –(2)	Rizzo, N .... 13(6)
Burton, S .... 18(5)	Hreidarsson, H .... 6(1)	Rodger, S 18
Carlisle, W .... 2(4)	Jansen, M 18	Shipperley, N 3
Crowe, J 8	Jihai, S .... 22(1)	Smith, J 25
Curcic, S .... 4(11)	Linighan, A .... 19(1)	Svensson, M .... 6(2)
Del Rio, W .... 1(1)	Lombardo, A 19	Thomson, S .... 11(5)
Digby, F 18	McKenzie, L .... 10(6)	Turner, A .... –(2)
Dyer, B .... 5(1)	Martin, A .... 1(1)	Tuttle, D .... 17(5)
Edworthy, M .... 1(2)	Miller, K 28	Warhurst, P 5
Evans, S .... –(4)	Moore, C 23	Woozley, D 7
Foster, C .... 30(2)	Morrison, C .... 27(10)	Zhiyi, F .... 28(1)
Frampton, A .... 4(2)		

League Goals (58): Morrison 12, Jansen 7, Mullins 5, Bradbury 4, Curcic 4, Lombardo 3, Moore 3, Dyer 2, Tuttle 2, Zhiyi 2, Austin 1, Burton 1, McKenzie 1, Petric 1, Rizzo 1, Rodger 1, Shipperley 1, Svensson 1, Warhurst 1, Opponents 3.
Worthington Cup Goals (5): Lombardo 2, Morrison 1, Hreidarsson 1, Zhiyi 1. **F.A. Cup Goals (1):** Bradbury 1.
Player of Year: Hayden Mullins. **Sponsors:** to be announced.
Average home League attendance 1998-99: 17,123. **Capacity for 1999-2000:** 26,500.
Record attendance: 51,482 v Burnley (Div. 2) 11 May 1979.

GRIMSBY TOWN

Ground: Blundell Park, Cleethorpes, NE Lincs, DN35 7PY.
Telephone: 01472 605050. **Clubcall:** 09068 555855. **Club Nickname:** Mariners.
First-choice Colours: Black and white stripes; black shorts; black stockings.

Ashcroft, L .... 21(6)	Chapman, B .... –(1)	Donovan, K .... 27(1)
Black, K .... 29(12)	Clare, D .... 7(15)	Gallimore, T 43
Bloomer, M .... –(4)	Coldicott, S .... 35(1)	Groves, P 46
Buckley, A .... –(2)	Croudson, S 2	Handyside, P .... 30(1)
Burnett, W .... 15(5)	Davison, A 35	Lester, J .... 26(6)
Butterfield, D .... 9(3)	Dobbin, J .... –(4)	Lever, M .... 15(9)

Livingstone, S .... 15(8)   Nogan, L .... 30(8)   Smith, R .... 29(1)
Love, A 9   Smith, D .... 30(1)   Widdrington, T ..... 16(10)
McDermott, J 37

League Goals (40): Groves 14, Smith D 5, Black 4, Lester 4, Ashcroft 3, Clare 3, Nogan 2, Handyside 2, Burnett 2, Widdrington 1.
Worthington Cup Goals (4): Ashcroft 1, Groves 1, Clare 1, Nogan 1. **F.A. Cup Goals (1):** McDermott 1.
Player of Year: Paul Groves. **Sponsors:** Dixon Motors PLC.
Average home League attendance 1998-99: 6,216. **Capacity for 1999-2000:** 10,033.
Record attendance: 31,651 v Wolves (F.A. Cup 5) 20 February 1937.

HUDDERSFIELD TOWN

Ground: The Alfred McAlpine Stadium, Leeds Road, Huddersfield, West Yorkshire, HD1 6PX.
Telephone: 01484 484100. **Clubcall:** 0891 121635. **Club Nickname:** Terriers.
First-choice Colours: Blue and white striped shirts; white shorts; white stockings.

Allison, W 44   Edmondson, D .... 1(2)   Johnson, I 36
Armstrong, C 13   Edwards, R 45   Lawson, I .... 2(4)
Baldry, S .... 8(5)   Facey, D .... 5(15)   Mattis, D .... –(2)
Barnes, P .... 2(13)   Francis, S 3   Morrison, A 12
Beech, C .... 13(4)   Gray, K .... 28(6)   Phillips, D .... 15(8)
Beresford, D .... 13(6)   Hamilton, D 10   Richardson, ... 13(2)
Browning, M .... 2(4)   Heary, T 3   Schofield, J 1
Collins, S .... 22(1)   Hessey, S .... 7(3)   Stewart, M 43
Cowan, T 5   Horne, B 20   Thornley, B. .... 32(3)
Dalton, J .... 7(2)   Jackson, M 5   Vaesen, N 43
Dyson, J .... 10(4)   Jenkins, S 36   Vincent, J 7

League Goals (62): Stewart 22, Allison 9, Johnson 4, Thornley 4, Dalton 3, Facey 3, Beech 2, Beresford 2, Edwards 2, Lawson 2, Armstrong 1, Barnes 1, Dyson 1, Gray 1, Hamilton 1, Horne 1, Jenkins 1, Phillips 1, Opponents 1.
Worthington Cup Goals (6): Allison 2, Stewart 2, Dalton 1, Johnson 1. **F.A. Cup Goals (7):** Allison 2, Beech 2, Stewart 2, Thornley 1.
Player of Year: Nico Vaesen. **Sponsors:** Panasonic.
Average home League attendance 1998-99: 12,976. **Capacity for 1999-2000:** 24,413.
Record attendance: (Leeds Road) 67,037 v Arsenal (F.A. Cup 6) 27 February 1932; (McAlpine Stadium) 22,129 v Derby Co. (F.A. Cup 5) 13 February 1999.

IPSWICH TOWN

Ground: Portman Road, Ipswich, Suffolk, IP1 2DA.
Telephone: 01473 400500. **Clubcall:** 0891 121068. **Club Nickname:** Blues.
First-choice Colours: Blue shirts; white shorts; blue stockings.

Abou, S 5   Hunt, J .... 2(4)   Sonner, D .... –(4)
Bramble, T .... 2(2)   Johnson, D .... 41(1)   Stockwell, M 23 (7)
Brown, W .... –(1)   Kennedy, J .... 6(1)   Tanner, A .... 13(6)
Clapham, J .... 45(1)   Logan, R .... –(2)   Taricco, M 16
Cundy, J .... 1(3)   Magilton, J 19   Thetis, M .... 29(2)
Dyer, K .... 36(1)   Mathie, A .... 2(6)   Venus, M 44
Harewood, M .... 5(1)   Mowbray, T 40   Vernazza, P 2
Hodges, L .... –(4)   Naylor, R .... 10(17)   Wilnis, F .... 17(1)
Holland, M 46   Petta, B .... 26(6)   Wright, R 46
Holster, M .... 1(9)   Scowcroft, J 29 (3)

Play-offs – Appearances: Clapham 2, Dyer 2, Holland 2, Johnson 2, Magilton 2, Mowbray 2, Naylor –(2), Petta 1, Scowcroft 2, Stockwell –(1), Thetis 1(1), Venus 2, Wilnis 2, Wright 2.
League Goals (69): Johnson 14, Scowcroft 13, Venus 9, Dyer 5, Holland 5, Naylor 5, Clapham 3, Magilton 3, Mowbray 2, Petta 2, Thetis 2, Stockwell 1, Taricco 1, Mathie 1, Abou 1, Wilnis 1, Harewood 1. **Play-off Goals (4):** Dyer 2, Holland 2.
Worthington Cup Goals (10): Holland 2, Johnson 1, Mason 1, Mathie 1, Scowcroft 1, Stockwell 1, Taricco 1, Thetis 1, Opponents 1. **F.A. Cup Goals (1):** Opponents 1.
Player of Year: Jamie Clapham. **Sponsors:** Greene King.
Average home League attendance 1998-99: 16,920. **Capacity for 1999-2000:** 22,500.
Record attendance: 38,010 v Leeds Utd. (F.A. Cup 6) 8 March 1975.

NORWICH CITY

Ground: Carrow Road, Norwich, Norfolk, NR1 1JE.
Telephone: 01603 760760 **Clubcall:** 0891 121144. **Club Nickname:** Canaries.
First-choice Colours: Yellow shirts; green shorts; yellow stockings.

Adams, N .... 15(3)	Fuglestad, E .... 22(2)	Milligan, M .... 1(1)
Anselin, C 7	Grant, P .... 31(2)	Mulryne, P .... 6(1)
Bellamy, C .... 38(2)	Green, R 2	O'Neill, K .... 14(4)
Brannan, G .... 10(1)	Hughes, P .... 2(2)	Roberts, I .... 40(5)
Carey, S .... 7(2)	Jackson, M .... 36(1)	Russell, D .... 8(5)
Coote, A .... 2(4)	Kenton, D 22	Segura, V .... 2(2)
Dalglish, P .... 3(2)	Llewellyn, C .... 21(10)	Sutch, D .... 34(2)
Eadie, D .... 21(1)	Mackay, M .... 24(4)	Watt, M .... 7(1)
Fleming, C .... 35(2)	Marshall, A 37	Wilson, C .... 14(3)
Forbes, A .... 7(8)	Marshall, L .... 38(6)	

League Goals (62): Roberts 19, Bellamy 17, Adams 3, Eadie 3, Fleming 3, Marshall L 3, Llewellyn 2, Mulryne 2, Anselin 1, Brannan 1, Hughes 1, Jackson 1, Kenton 1, Mackay 1, O'Neill 1, Russell 1, Opponents 2.
Worthington Cup Goals (7): Roberts 3, Bellamy 2, O'Neill 1, Opponents 1. **F.A. Cup Goals (1):** Roberts 1.
Player of Year: Iwan Roberts. **Sponsors:** Colman's.
Average home League attendance 1998-99: 15,760. **Capacity for 1999-2000:** 21,473.
Record attendance: 43,984 v Leicester City (F.A. Cup 6) 30 March 1963.

OXFORD UNITED

Ground: The Manor Ground, Headington, Oxford, OX3 7RS.
Telephone: 01865 761503. **Clubcall:** 0891 440055. **Club Nickname:** U's.
First-choice Colours: Yellow shirts; dark blue shorts; dark blue stockings.

Banger, N .... 22(10)	Lundin, P 7	Thomson, A .... 25(13)
Beauchamp, J .... 31(6)	Murphy, M .... 33(10)	Warren, M 4
Cook, J .... 9(10)	Marsh, D .... 20(1)	Watson, M 23
Davis, S 3	Powell, P .... 40(4)	Weatherstone, S .... 4(8)
Francis, K .... 12(6)	Remy, C .... 10(2)	Whelan, P .... 14(1)
Gerrard, P 16	Robinson, L 44	Williams, M .... –(2)
Gilchrist, P 39	Rose, A .... 1(3)	Whitehead, P 21
Gray, M 40	Salmon, M 1	Wilsterman, B .... 12(5)
Hill, D .... 1(8)	Smith, D .... 19(3)	Windass, D 33
Jackson, E 1	Tait, P 17	Wright, A .... 4(2)

League Goals (48): Windass 15, Thomson 7, Banger 6, Beauchamp 4, Murphy 4, Powell 3, Gilchrist 2, Marsh 2, Wilsterman 2, Cook 1, Francis 1, Remy 1, Weatherstone 1.
Worthington Cup Goals (4): Murphy 2, Weatherstone 1, Whelan 1. **F.A. Cup Goals (6):** Windass 3, Murphy 2, Opponents 1.
Player of Year: Phil Gilchrist. **Sponsors:** to be announced.

Average home League attendance 1998-99: 7,040. **Capacity for 1999-2000:** 9,580 (subject to FL approval).
Record attendance: 22,730 v Preston N.E. (F.A. Cup 6) 29 February 1964.

PORTSMOUTH

Ground: Fratton Park, Frogmore Road, Portsmouth, Hampshire PO4 8RA.
Telephone: 01705 731204. **Clubcall:** 0891 121182. **Club Nickname:** Pompey.
First-choice Colours: Blue shirts; white shorts; red stockings.

Aloisi, J 22	Kyzeridis, N .... 2(2)	Robinson, M .... 27(2)
Andreasson, S .... –(2)	McLoughlin, A 41	Simpson, F .... 38(3)
Awford, A 35	Miglioranzi, S .... 4(3)	Soley, S .... 1(7)
Claridge, S 39	Nightingale, L ...... 6(13)	Thogersen, T .... 29(5)
Durnin, J .... 16(10)	Peron, J .... 37(1)	Thomson, A 14
Flahavan, A 13	Perrett, R .... 12(3)	Vlachos, M 29 (1)
Hillier, D .... 11(5)	Pethick, R .... 4(6)	Waterman, D 10
Igoe, S .... 39(1)	Petterson, A 13	Whitbread, A 33
Knight, A 20	Phillips, M .... 2(15)	Whittingham, G 9

League Goals (57): Aloisi 14, Claridge 9, Durnin 7, McLoughlin 7, Whittingham 7, Igoe 5, Nightingale 3, Awford 1, Peron 1, Phillips 1, Robinson 1, Simpson 1.
Worthington Cup Goals (9): Aloisi 3, McLoughlin 3, Hillier 1, Vlachos 1, Whitbread 1. **F.A. Cup Goals (2):** Claridge 1, Nightingale 1.
Player of Year: Steve Claridge/Jeff Peron (joint). **Sponsors:** to be announced.
Average home League attendance 1998-99: 11,973. **Capacity for 1999-2000:** 19,200.
Record attendance: 51,385 v Derby Co. (F.A. Cup 6) 26 February 1949.

PORT VALE

Ground: Vale Park, Hamil Road, Burslem, Stoke-on-Trent ST6 1AW.
Telephone: 01782 814134. **Clubcall:** 0891 121636. **Club Nickname:** Valiants.
First-choice Colours: White shirts; black shorts; white stockings.

Ainsworth, G 15	Clarke, A .... 2(4)	Mean, S 1
Allen, C .... 2(3)	Corden, W .... 5(12)	Musselwhite, P 38
Aspin, N .... 28(2)	Eyre, R .... 7(3)	Naylor, A .... 14(8)
Barker, S .... 23(3)	Foyle, M .... 32(3)	O'Callaghan, G 4
Barnett, D .... 26(1)	Gardner, A .... 14(1)	Pilkington, K 8
Beadle, P .... 18(5)	Griffiths, C 3	Pounewatchy, S 2
Beesley, P .... 33(2)	Horlaville, C .... 1(1)	Rougier, A .... 8(5)
Bent, M .... 10(5)	Jansson, J .... 5(2)	Russell, C 8
Bernsten, R 1	Koordes, R .... 13(2)	Smith, A .... 7(1)
Bogie, I .... 31(3)	Lee, A .... 7(4)	Snijders, M .... 6(3)
Brammer, D 9	Lyttle, D 7	Talbot, S .... 29(4)
Briscoe, N 1	McGill, D .... –(3)	Tankard, A 37
Burns, L .... 2(2)	McGlinchey, B ...... 10(5)	Walsh, M .... 18(1)
Butler, A 4	McQuade, J .... –(3)	Widdrington, T 8
Carragher, M .... 8(2)		

League Goals (45): Foyle 9, Beadle 6, Ainsworth 5, Naylor 4, Tankard 4, Beesley 3, Barker 2, Bogie 2, Lee 2, Allen 1, Gardner 1, Griffiths 1, McGlinchey 1, Russell 1, Walsh 1, Widdrington 1, Opponents 1.
Worthington Cup Goals (3): Naylor 2, Ainsworth 1. **F.A. Cup Goals:** None.
Player of Year: Martin Foyle. **Sponsors:** Tunstall.
Average home League attendance 1998-99: 6,991. **Capacity for 1999-2000:** to be announced.
Record attendance: 50,000 v Aston Villa (F.A. Cup 5) 20 February 1960.

QUEENS PARK RANGERS

Ground: Rangers Stadium, South Africa Road, Shepherds Bush, London, W12 7PA.
Telephone: 0181 743 0262. **Clubcall:** 0891 121162. **Club Nickname:** R's.
First-choice Colours: Blue and white hoops; white shorts; white stockings.

Baraclough, I .... 41(2)	Kiwomya, C .... 12(4)	Plummer, C .... 8(2)
Breacker, T 18	Kulscar, G 17	Ready, K .... 40(1)
Darlington, J 4	Langley, R .... 7(1)	Rose, M .... 27(2)
Dowie, I .... 7(12)	Linighan, A .... 4(3)	Rowland, K .... 16(14)
Gallen, K .... 41(3)	Maddix, D 37	Scully, T .... 10(13)
Graham, R .... –(2)	Miklosko, J 31	Sheron, M .... 21(2)
Harper, L 15	Morrow, S 24	Slade, S .... 10(10)
Heinola, A 23	Murray, P .... 32(7)	Steiner, R .... 5(7)
Jeanne, L .... 7(3)	Peacock, G .... 41(1)	Yates, S 6
Jones, V .... 1(1)	Perry, M 1	

League Goals (52): Gallen 8, Sheron 8, Peacock 8, Kiwomya 6, Maddix 4, Rowland 3, Steiner 3, Scully 2, Ready 2, Baraclough 1, Breacker 1, Dowie 1, Kulscar 1, Langley 1, Murray 1, Slade 1, Opponents 1.
Worthington Cup Goals (3): Sheron 1, Slade 1, Maddix 1. **F.A. Cup Goals:** None.
Player of Year: Danny Maddix. **Sponsors:** Ericsson.
Average home League attendance 1998-99: 11,820. **Capacity for 1999-2000:** 19,154.
Record attendance: 35,353 v Leeds Utd. (Div 1) 27 April 1974.

SHEFFIELD UNITED

Ground: Bramall Lane, Sheffield, South Yorkshire, S2 4SU.
Telephone: 0114 221 5757. **Clubcall:** 0891 888650. **Club Nickname:** Blades.
First-choice Colours: Red and white shirts; black shorts; black stockings.

Bruce, S 10	Hamilton, I .... 27(3)	O'Connor, J 2
Borbokis, V .... 19(2)	Henry, N .... 3(3)	Quinn, W .... 41(3)
Campbell, A 11	Holdsworth, D 16	Sandford, L .... 34(1)
Cullen, J .... –(2)	Hunt, J .... 12(1)	Saunders, D 19
Dellas, T .... 9(8)	Katchouro, P .... 8(8)	Stuart, G 25
Derry, S .... 23(3)	Kelly, A 22	Taylor, G .... 7(5)
Devlin, P .... 23(10)	Kozluk, R 10	Tebily, O .... 7(1)
Donis, G .... 5(2)	Marcelo .... 26(9)	Tracey, S .... 17(1)
Ford, B .... 26(3)	Marker, N .... 17(1)	Twiss, M .... 2(10)
Goram, A 7	Morris, L .... 14(6)	Wilder, C 4
Hamilton, D 6	Nilsen, R .... 14(3)	Woodhouse, C .... 31(2)

League Goals (71): Marcelo 16, Saunders 7, Katchuoro 6, Morris 6, Stuart 6, Devlin 5, Campbell 3, Dellas 3, Marker 3, Woodhouse 3, Borbokis 2, Hamilton I 2, Hunt 2, Donis 1, Holdsworth 1, Quinn 1, Taylor 1, Twiss 1, Opponents 2.
Worthington Cup Goals (7): Saunders 3, Borbokis 1, Ford 1, Hamilton I 1, Taylor 1. **F.A. Cup Goals (11):** Marcelo 4, Holdsworth 2, Morris 2, Borbokis 1, Devlin 1, Stuart 1.
Player of Year: Curtis Woodhouse. **Sponsors:** to be announced.
Average home League attendance 1998-99: 16,228 **Capacity for 1999-2000:** 30,370.
Record attendance: 68,287 v Leeds Utd. (F.A. Cup 5) 15 February 1936.

STOCKPORT COUNTY

Ground: Edgeley Park, Hardcastle Road, Edgeley, Stockport, Cheshire, SK3 9DD.
Telephone: 0161 2868888. **Clubcall:** 0891 121 638. **Club Nickname:** County or Hatters.
First-choice Colours: Blue and white; to be announced.

Alsaker, P 1	Bennett, T .... 3(4)	Byrne, C 11
Angell, B 42	Branch, G .... 10(4)	Byrne, D 2

Connelly, S	33(2)	Grant, S	1(12)	Nash, C	40
Cook, P	24(1)	Gray, I	3	Phillips, W	7(2)
Cooper, K	27 (11)	McIntosh, M	41	Smith, D	17
Dinning, A	35(6)	Mannion, S	–(1)	Travis, S	1(8)
Ellis, A	16	Matthews, R	19(4)	Wilbraham, A	8(17)
Flynn, M	46	Moore, I	32(6)	Woodthorpe, C	37
Gannon, J	28(10)				

League Goals (49): Angell 17, Ellis 6, Dinning 5, Branch 3, McIntosh 3, Moore 3, Byrne C 2, Matthews 2, Woodthorpe 2, Connelly 1, Cooper 1, Flynn 1, Grant 1, Smith 1, Opponents 1.
Worthington Cup Goals (2): Moore 1, Byrne C 1. **F.A. Cup Goals (3):** Angell 1, Woodthorpe 1, Opponents 1.
Player of Year: Mike Flynn. **Sponsors:** Frederick Robinson Ltd.
Average home League attendance 1998-99: 7,901. **Capacity for 1999-2000:** 11,535.
Record attendance: 27, 833 v Liverpool (F.A. Cup 5) 11 February 1950.

SUNDERLAND

Ground: Stadium of Light, Sunderland, Tyne and Wear SR5 1BT.
Telephone: 0191 5515000. **Clubcall:** 01716 136000. **Club Nickname:** None.
First-choice Colours: Red and white shirts; black shorts, black stockings.

Ball, K	42	Johnston, A	40	Rae, A	12(3)
Bridges, M	13(16)	McCann, G	5(6)	Scott, M	14(1)
Butler, P	44	Makin, C	37(1)	Smith, M	4(3)
Clark, L	26(1)	Marriott, A	1	Sorensen, T	45
Craddock, J	3(3)	Melville, A	44	Summerbee, N	36
Dichio, D	16(20)	Mullin, J	8(2)	Thirlwell, P	1
Gray, M	37(1)	Phillips, K	26	Williams, D	16(9)
Holloway, D	1(5)	Quinn, N	36(3)		

League Goals (91): Phillips 23, Quinn 18, Dichio 10, Bridges 8, Johnston 7, Clark 3, Smith 3, Summerbee 3, Ball 2, Butler 2, Gray 2, Melville 2, Mullin 2, Rae 2, Scott 2, Opponents 2.
Worthington Cup Goals (16): Bridges 4, Quinn 3, Dichio 2, Phillips 2, Johnston 1, McCann 1, Scott 1, Smith 1, Opponents 1. **F.A. Cup Goals (1):** McCann 1.
Player of Year: Niall Quinn. **Sponsors:** to be announced.
Average home League attendance 1998-99: 38,745. **Capacity for 1999-2000:** 42,000.
Record attendance: (Roker Park) 75,118 v Derby Co. (F.A. Cup 6) 8 March 1933; (Stadium of Light) 41,634 v Birmingham City (Div. 1) 9 May 1999.

SWINDON TOWN

Ground: County Ground, County Road, Swindon, Wiltshire SN1 2ED.
Telephone: 01793 430430. **Clubcall:** 0891 121460. **Club Nickname:** Robins.
First-choice Colours: Red shirts; white shorts; red stockings.

Borrows, B	40	Gooden, T	36(2)	Ndah, G	40(1)
Bullock, D	17(5)	Griffin, C	1(4)	Onuora, I	40(3)
Bradley, S	6(1)	Hall, G	39(2)	Reeves, A	23(1)
Campagna, S	–(2)	Hay, C	16(11)	Robinson, M	25(4)
Collins, L	2(2)	Howe, L	20(3)	Talia, F	43
Cowe, S	2(3)	Hulbert, R	7(9)	Taylor, C	18(3)
Cuervo, P	2(4)	Kerslake, D	12(2)	Walters, M	31(7)
Davies, G	6	Leitch, D	23(1)	Watson, K	9(9)
Davis, S	21(4)	Linton, D	7(1)	Willis, A	11
Fenn, N	4	McAreavey, P	–(1)	Williams, J	1(2)
Glass, J	3	McHugh, F	1		

League Goals (59): Onuora 20, Ndah 11, Walters 10, Hay 6, Howe 3, Reeves 2, Gooden 1, Bullock 1, Hall 1, Griffin 1, Opponents 3.
Worthington Cup Goals (2): Ndah 1, Reeves 1. **F.A. Cup Goals (1):** Walters 1.
Player of Year: George Ndah. **Sponsors:** Nationwide.
Average home League attendance 1998-99: 8,651. **Capacity for 1999-2000:** 15,700.
Record attendance: 32,000 v Arsenal (F.A. Cup 3) 15 January 1972.

TRANMERE ROVERS

Ground: Prenton Park, Prenton Road West, Birkenhead, Wirral, CH42 9PY.
Telephone: 0151 608 4194. **Clubcall:** 0891 121646. **Club Nickname:** Rovers.
First-choice Colours: White shirts; navy shorts; white stockings.

Achterberg, J 24	Jones, L .... 18(12)	Santos, G 37
Allen, G 41	Kelly, D .... 16(10)	Sharps, I .... –(1)
Challinor, D .... 29(5)	Koumas, J .... 11(12)	Taylor, S .... 31(5)
Coyne, D 17	McGreal, J 36	Thomson, A 37
Gibson, N .... –(1)	Mahon, A .... 34(5)	Williams, R .... 2(3)
Hill, C 33	Morgan A .... 4(2)	Mellon, M .... 21(3)
Hinds, R .... 1(1)	Morrissey, J .... 5(19)	Russell, C .... 3(1)
Irons, K 43	O'Brien, L .... 18(5)	Shepherd, P .... –(1)
Jones, G .... 15(11)	Parkinson, A .... 20(9)	Simonsen, S 5

League Goals (63): Irons 15, Taylor 9, Mahon 6, Allen 5, Jones G 5, Hill 4, Kelly 4, Koumas 3, Challinor 2, Jones L 2, O'Brien 2, Parkinson 2, Thompson 1, Mellon 1, Santos 1, Opponents 1.
Worthington Cup Goals (8): Irons 3, Kelly 2, Jones, L 1, Koumas 1, Parkinson 1. **F.A. Cup Goals:** None.
Player of Year: Kenny Irons. **Sponsors:** Wirral Borough Council.
Average home League attendance 1998-99: 6,930. **Capacity for 1999-2000:** 16,500.
Record Attendance: 24,424 v Stoke City (F.A. Cup 4) 5 February 1972.

WATFORD

Ground: Vicarage Road Stadium, Vicarage Road, Watford, Herts, WD1 8ER.
Telephone: 01923 496000. **Clubcall:** 0891 104104. **Club Nickname:** Hornets.
First-choice Colours: Yellow shirts with red sleeves; red shorts; red stockings.

Bazeley, D .... 36(4)	Johnson, R 40	Perpetuini, D 1
Bonnot, A .... 1(3)	Kennedy, P 46	Robinson, P .... 26(3)
Chamberlain, A 46	Lee, J 1	Rosenthal, R .... 1(4)
Daley, T .... 6(6)	Millen, K .... 10(1)	Smart, A .... 34(1)
Easton, C 7	Mooney, T .... 20(16)	Smith, T .... 3(5)
Gibbs, N .... 9(1)	Ngonge, M .... 13(9)	Ward, D 1
Gudmundsson, J ...... 6(7)	Noel-Williams, G .... 19(7)	Whittingham, G .... 4(1)
Hazan, A .... 8(15)	Page, R .... 37(2)	Wright, N .... 31(2)
Hyde, M .... 43(1)	Palmer, S .... 40(1)	Yates, D 9
Iroha, B .... 8(2)		

Play-offs – Appearances: Bazeley 3, Chamberlain 3, Gibbs 1, Hazan –(3), Hyde 3, Johnson 3, Kennedy 3, Mooney 3, Ngonge 3, Page 3, Palmer 3, Robinson 3, Smart –(3), Wright 3.
League Goals (65): Noel-Williams 10, Mooney 9, Smart 7, Kennedy 6, Wright 6, Johnson 4, Ngonge 4, Bazeley 2, Gudmundsson 2, Hazan 2, Hyde 2, Palmer 2, Smith 2, Daley 1, Lee 1, Millen 1, Yates 1, Opponents 3. **Play-off Goals (3):** Ngonge 1, Smart 1, Wright 1.
Worthington Cup Goals (1): Ngonge 1. **F.A. Cup Goals (2):** Johnson 1, Kennedy 1.
Player of Year: Steve Palmer. **Sponsors:** to be announced.
Average home League attendance 1998-99: 11,822. **Capacity for 1999-2000:** 22,763.
Record attendance: 34,099 v Manchester Utd. (F.A. Cup 4) 3 February 1969.

WEST BROMWICH ALBION

Ground: The Hawthorns, Halfords Lane, West Bromwich, West Midlands B71 4LF.
Telephone: 0121 525 8888. **Clubcall:** 0891 121193. **Club Nickname:** Baggies.
First-choice Colours: Navy blue and white striped shirts; white shorts; navy blue and white stockings.

Angel, M .... 4(18)	Hughes, L 42	Potter, G .... 19(3)
Bortolazzi, M .... 25(10)	Kilbane, K 44	Quailey, B .... 1(1)
Burgess, D .... 15(5)	Mardon, P .... 12(6)	Quinn, J .... 39(4)
Carbon, M .... 38(1)	Maresca, E .... 9(13)	Raven, P .... 6(1)
De Freitas, F .... 22(15)	McDermott, A 20	Richards, J .... –(1)
Evans, M .... 17(3)	Miller, A 20	Sneekes, R .... 35(5)
Flynn, S .... 33(5)	Murphy, S .... 30(7)	Van Blerk, J 30
Gabbidon, D 2	Oliver, A .... –(1)	Whitehead, P 26
Holmes, P 17		

League Goals (69): Hughes 31, De Freitas 7, Kilbane 6, Quinn 6, Murphy 4, Sneekes 4, Bortolazzi 2, Carbon 2, Evans 2, Flynn 2, Maresca 2, Angel 1.
Worthington Cup Goals (2): Evans 1, Hughes 1. **F.A. Cup Goals:** None.
Player of Year: Lee Hughes. **Sponsors:** West Bromwich Building Society.
Average home League attendance 1998-99: 14,649. **Capacity for 1999-2000:** 24,953.
Record attendance: 64,815 v Arsenal (F.A. Cup 6) 6 March 1937.

WOLVERHAMPTON WANDERERS

Ground: Molineux, Waterloo Road, Wolverhampton, West Midlands WV1 4QR.
Telephone: 01902 655000. **Clubcall:** 0891 121103. **Club Nickname:** Wolves.
First-choice Colours: Gold shirts; black shorts; gold stockings.

Atkins, M 15	Froggatt, S 8	Niestroj, R .... 2(3)
Bull, S .... 11(4)	Gilkes, M .... 24(5)	Osborn, S .... 36(1)
Connolly, D .... 18(14)	Gomez, F .... 18(2)	Richards, D .... 40(1)
Corica, S .... 20(11)	Green, R 1	Robinson, C .... 29(5)
Curle, K 45	Jones, M .... –(2)	Sedgley, S .... 41(3)
Emblen, N .... 30(3)	Keane, R .... 29(3)	Simpson, P .... 8(3)
Ferguson, D .... 2(2)	Muscat, K 37	Stowell, M 46
Flo, H .... 18(1)	Naylor, L .... 17(6)	Whittingham, G .... 9(1)
Foley, D .... 2(3)		

League Goals (58): Keane 11, Robinson 7, Connolly 6, Curle 4, Flo 4, Muscat 4, Bull 3, Richards 3, Sedgley 3, Corica 2, Emblen 2, Foley 2, Gomez 2, Osborn 2, Naylor 1, Simpson 1, Whittingham 1.
Worthington Cup Goals (8): Bull 3, Keane 3, Ferguson 1, Osborn 1. **F.A. Cup Goals (3):** Keane 2, Flo 1.
Player of Year: Kevin Muscat. **Sponsors:** Goodyear.
Average home League attendance 1998-99: 22,260. **Capacity for 1999-2000:** 28,500.
Record attendance: 61,315 v Liverpool (F.A. Cup 5) 11 February 1939.

NATIONWIDE LEAGUE – SECOND DIVISION

AFC BOURNEMOUTH

Ground: Dean Court, Bournemouth, Dorset, BH7 7AF.
Telephone: 01202 395381. **Clubcall:** 0891 121163. **Club Nickname:** Cherries.
First-choice Colours: Red and black shirts; black shorts; black stockings.

Bailey, J .... 30(2)	Cox, I 46	Fletcher, C .... –(1)
Berthe, M .... 12(3)	Day, J .... –(2)	Fletcher, S .... 38(1)
Boli, R .... 5(1)	Dean, M .... 1(8)	Griffin, A .... 1(4)

Hayter, J .... 16(4)	O'Neill, J .... 18(6)	Tindall, J .... 6(11)
Howe, E 45	Ovendale, M 46	Town, D .... 1(9)
Huck, W .... 6(2)	Rawlinson, M .... 5(2)	Vincent, J .... 31(1)
Hughes, R .... 43(1)	Robinson, S 42	Warren, C .... 26(6)
Jenkins, J ....-(1)	Rodrigues, D ....-(5)	Young, N 44
Lovell, S .... 1(6)	Stein, M 43	

League Goals (63): Stein 15, Robinson 13, Fletcher S 8, Cox 5, Warren 5, O'Neill 3, Berthe 2, Howe 2, Vincent 2, Hayter 2, Hughes 1, Tindall 1, Young 1, Opponents 2.
Worthington Cup Goals (8): Stein 5, Fletcher S 1, Howe 1, Robinson 1. **F.A. Cup Goals (5):** Howe 2, O'Neill 1, Robinson 1, Stein 1. **Auto Windscreens Shield Goals (8):** Stein 4, Fletcher S 2, Cox 1, Robinson 1.
Player of Year: Eddie Howe. **Sponsors:** Seaward Rover MG.
Average home League attendance 1998-99: 7,117. **Capacity for 1999-2000:** 15,000 approx.
Record attendance: 28,799 v Manchester Utd. (F.A. Cup 6) 2 March 1957.

BLACKPOOL

Ground: Bloomfield Road, Blackpool, Lancashire FY1 6JJ.
Telephone: 01253 404331. **Clubcall:** 0891 121648. **Club Nickname:** Seasiders.
First-choice Colours: Tangerine shirts; white shorts; tangerine stockings.

Aldridge, M .... 19(3)	Carlisle, C .... 34(5)	Malkin, C .... 24(5)
Banks, S 35	Clarkson, P 44	Nowland, A .... 13(24)
Bardsley, D 29	Coid, D ....-(1)	Ormerod, B .... 30(10)
Barnes, P .... 3(2)	Conroy, M .... 7(1)	Patterson, M 7
Bent, J .... 21(18)	Couzens, A 6	Robinson, P .... 2(3)
Blunt, J .... 1(1)	Garvey, S .... 6(9)	Rogan, A .... 9(5)
Brabin, G .... 5(2)	Hills, J .... 27(1)	Shuttleworth, B .... 12(2)
Bryan, M .... 37(4)	Hughes, I .... 31(2)	Sturridge, S 5
Bushell, S 31	Jarrett, J 2	Thompson, P .... 18(4)
Butler, A 20	Lawson, I 9	Watts, J 9
Caig, A 10		

League Goals (44): Clarkson 9, Ormerod 8, Aldridge 7, Bushell 3, Lawson 3, Nowland 2, Thompson 2, Malkin 1, Bryan 1, Bent 1, Hughes 1, Hills 1, Garvey 1, Shuttleworth 1, Carlisle 1, Sturridge 1, Opponents 1.
Worthington Cup Goals (5): Aldridge 2, Malkin 1, Bent 1, Conroy 1. **F.A. Cup Goals (3):** Aldridge 1, Ormerod 1, Bent 1. **Auto Windscreens Shield Goals:** None.
Player of Year: Brett Ormerod/Steve Banks (joint). **Sponsors:** Telewest Communications.
Average home League attendance 1998-99: 5,116. **Capacity for 1999-2000:** 11,298.
Record attendance: 38,098 v Wolves (Div. 1) 17 September 1955.

BRISTOL ROVERS

Ground: The Memorial Ground, Filton Avenue, Horfield, Bristol BS7 0AQ.
Telephone: 0117 9772000. **Clubcall:** 0891 9772000. **Club Nickname:** Pirates.
First-choice Colours: Blue and white quartered shirts; white shorts; blue stockings.

Andreasson, M 4	Hillier, D 13	McKeever, M .... 5(2)
Andrews, B 3	Holloway I .... 33(4)	Penrice, G .... 10(16)
Basford, L .... 6(3)	Ipoua, G .... 15(9)	Pethick, R 9
Bennett, F .... 1(3)	Johnston, R 1	Phillips, M 2
Challis, T 38	Jones, L 32	Pritchard, D .... 4(1)
Collett, A 3	Kuiper, S 1	Roberts, J .... 32(5)
Cureton, J 46	Lee, D .... 10(1)	Shore, J .... 18(6)
Ellington, N .... 1(9)	Leoni, S .... 25(5)	Smith, M .... 11(3)
Foster, S .... 41(2)	Low, J .... 5(3)	Thomson, A 21
Hayles, B 17	Meaker, M .... 17(3)	Trees, R .... 33(3)

335

Tillson, A 18   Williams, L 9 .... (2)   Zabek, L .... 9(2)
Trought, M .... 6(3)

League Goals (65): Cureton 25, Roberts 16, Hayles 9, Ipoua 3, Shore 2, Tillson 2, Meaker 2, Bennett 1, Ellington 1, Foster 1, Lee 1, Penrice 1, Thomson 1.
Worthington Cup Goals (2): Cureton 1, Hayles 1. **F.A. Cup Goals (15):** Roberts 7, Cureton 2, Shore 2, Lee 1, Penrice 1, Zabek 1, Leoni 1. **Auto Windscreens Shield Goals (2):** Cureton 1, Shore 1.
Player of Year: to be announced. **Sponsors:** Cowlin Construction.
Average home League attendance 1998-99: 6,263. **Capacity for 1999-2000:** 9,300.
Record attendance (At previous ground, Eastville): 38,472 v Preston N.E. (F.A. Cup 4) 30 January 1960. Current ground: 9,274 v Leyton Orient (F.A. Cup 4) 23 January 1999.

BURNLEY

Ground: Turf Moor, Burnley, Lancashire, BB10 4BX.
Telephone: 01282 700000. **Clubcall:** 0891 121153. **Club Nickname:** Clarets.
First-choice Colours: Claret and blue shirts; white shorts; white stockings.

Armstrong, G 40	Hewlett, M 2	Reid, B .... 30(1)
Blatherwick, S 3	Heywood, M .... 11(2)	Robertson, M .... 18(4)
Branch, G .... 14(6)	Howey, L 3	Scott, C .... 9(5)
Brass, C .... 33(1)	Jepson, R .... 3(12)	Smith, C .... 5(5)
Carr-Lawton, C .... 2(2)	Johnrose, L .... 9(3)	Smith, P .... 11(1)
Cook, P 12	Little, G .... 32(2)	Swan, P .... 11(6)
Cooke, A 36	Maylett, B .... –(17)	Vindheim, R 8
Cowan, T 12	Mellon, M 20	Ward, G 17
Crichton, P 29	Moore, N .... 10(2)	Weller, P 1
Davis, S 19	Morgan, S 17	Williams, M 2
Eastwood, P .... 6(7)	O'Kane, J 8	Williamson, J .... –(1)
Ford, M .... 11(1)	Payton, A .... 39(1)	Winstanley, M 1
Henderson, K .... –(7)	Pickering, A 21	

League Goals (54): Payton 20, Cooke 9, Little 5, Davis 3, Reid 3, Mellon 2, Vindheim 2, Armstrong 1, Branch 1, Cook 1, Cowan 1, Eastwood 1, Henderson 1, Jepson 1, Johnrose 1, Pickering 1, Robertson 1.
Worthington Cup Goals (2): Cooke 1, Payton 1. **F.A. Cup Goals (2):** Payton 2. **Auto Windscreens Shield Goals:** None.
Player of Year: Andy Payton. **Sponsors:** P.3 Computers.
Average home League attendance 1998-99: 10,606. **Capacity for 1999-2000:** 22,619.
Record attendance: 54,775 v Huddersfield Town (F.A. Cup 4) 23 February 1924.

CHESTERFIELD

Ground: Recreation Ground, Chesterfield, Derbyshire S40 4SX.
Telephone: 01246 209765. **Clubcall:** 0891 555818. **Club Nickname:** Spireites.
First-choice Colours: Blue shirts; white shorts; blue stockings.

Beaumont, C .... 35(4)	Howard, J .... 34(3)	Nicholson, S .... 23(1)
Blatherwick, S .... 9(4)	Jules, M .... 19(4)	Pearce, G .... –(1)
Breckin, I 44	Leaning, A 2	Perkins, C .... 32(2)
Carss, A .... 2(2)	Lee, J .... 14(8)	Reeves, D .... 37(3)
Curtis, T 24	Lenagh, S .... 6(4)	Simpkins, M .... –(1)
Ebdon, M .... 39(1)	Lomas, J .... 5(2)	Wilkinson, S .... 18(5)
Hewitt, J 40	Mercer, W 44	Williams, M 40
Holland, P .... 32(1)	Morris, A .... –(1)	Willis, R .... 7(10)

League Goals (46): Reeves 10, Howard 8, Wilkinson 6, Holland 4, Curtis 3, Williams 3, Hewitt 2, Beaumont 2, Breckin 2, Ebdon 1, Blatherwick 1, Lee 1, Lenagh 1, Perkins 1, Opponents 1.
Worthington Cup Goals (4): Holland 2, Howard 1, Reeves 1. **F.A. Cup Goals:** None. **Auto Windscreens Shield goals (4):** Hewitt 1, Perkins 1, Wilkinson 1, Williams 1.
Player of Year: Mark Williams. **Sponsors:** Kennings and Brompton Print.
Average home League attendance 1998-99: 4,564. **Capacity for 1999-2000:** 8,880.
Record attendance: 30,698 v Newcastle Utd. (Div. 2) 7 April 1939.

COLCHESTER UNITED

Ground: Layer Road, Colchester, Essex CO2 7JJ.
Telephone: 01206 508800. **Clubcall:** 09068 400222. **Club Nickname:** U's.
First-choice Colours: Blue and white striped shirts; blue shorts; white stockings.

Allen, B 4	Fernandes, T 8	Opara, K .... –(1)
Abrahams, P ...... 13(14)	Forbes, S .... 8(7)	Pounewatchy, S 15
Adcock, A .... –(6)	Germain, S .... 1(5)	Rainford, D .... –(1)
Aspinall, W 15	Greene, D 42	Richard, F 10
Antunes, J 1	Gregory, D 42	Sale, M .... 21(10)
Betts, S .... 22(7)	Gregory, N .... 27(8)	Skelton, A .... 7(2)
Buckle, P .... 39(4)	Haydon, N .... 7(4)	Stamps, S .... 16(2)
Dozzell, J .... 20(6)	Launders, B 1	Walker, A 1
Dublin, K 2	Lock, T .... 15(9)	Wiles, I .... –(1)
Duguid, K .... 24(9)	Lua Lua, L .... 6(7)	Wilkins, R .... 25(1)
Dunne, J .... 32(4)	Okafor, S .... –(1)	Williams, G .... 38(1)
Emberson, C 37		

League Goals (52): Gregory, D 11, Greene 8, Gregory, N 4, Dozzell 4, Duguid 4, Aspinall 3, Abrahams 2, Betts 2, Buckle 2, Forbes 2, Sale 2, Wilkins 2, Allen 1, Pounewatchy 1, Haydon 1, Lock 1, Lua Lua 1, Opponents 1.
Worthington Cup Goals (3): Gregory, D 2, Abrahams 1. **F.A. Cup Goals (1):** Adcock 1. **Auto Windscreen Shield Goals (1):** Gregory, D 1.
Player of Year: David Greene. **Sponsors:** Home – Guardian Direct; Away – Ashby's.
Average home League attendance 1998-99: 4,482. **Capacity for 1999-2000:** 7,555.
Record attendance: 19,072 v Reading (F.A. Cup 1) 27 November 1948.

FULHAM

Ground: Craven Cottage, Stevenage Road, Fulham, London, SW6 6HH.
Telephone: 0171 893 8383. **Clubcall:** 0891 440044. **Club Nickname:** Cottagers.
First-choice Colours: White shirts; black shorts; white stockings.

Albert, P .... 12(1)	Finnan, S .... 22(1)	Neilson, A .... 3(1)
Beardsley, P .... 11(2)	Hayles, B .... 26(4)	Peschisolido, P .... 18(15)
Betsy, K .... 1(4)	Hayward, S .... 42(3)	Salako, J .... 7(3)
Bracewell, P .... 25(1)	Horsfield, G .... 26(2)	Scott, R .... 2(1)
Brazier, M .... 1(1)	Keller, F .... –(1)	Smith, J 8
Brevett, R 45	Lawrence, M 1	Smith, N .... 20(9)
Brooker, P .... –(1)	Lehmann, D .... 16(10)	Symons, K 45
Coleman, C 45	McAnespie, S .... 1(2)	Taylor, M 46
Collins, W .... 18(3)	Moody, P .... 2(5)	Trollope, P .... 16(3)
Cornwall, L .... 1(3)	Morgan, S .... 32(2)	Uhlenbeek, G .... 11(12)
Davis, S .... 1(4)		

League Goals (79): Horsfield 15, Symons 11, Hayles 8, Peschisolido 7, Morgan 5, Coleman 4, Moody 4, Beardsley 3, Hayward 3, Albert 2, Collins 2, Finnan 2, Lehmann 2, Trollope 2, Betsy 1, Bracewell 1, Brevett 1, Cornwall 1, Neilson 1, Salako 1, Smith J 1, Smith N 1, Uhlenbeek 1,

Worthington Cup Goals (7): Lehmann 2, Beardsley 1, Coleman 1, Morgan 1, Peschisolido 1, Salako 1. **F.A. Cup Goals (11):** Hayward 2, Horsfield 2, Morgan 2, Peschisolido 2, Hayles 1, Lehmann 1, Opponents 1. **Auto Windscreens Shield Goals (1):** Trollope 1.
Player of Year: Paul Peschisolido. **Sponsors:** Demon Internet.
Average home League attendance 1998-99: 11,387. **Capacity for 1999-2000:** 19,250.
Record attendance: 49,335 v Millwall (Div. 2) 8 October 1938.

GILLINGHAM

Ground: Priestfield Stadium, Redfern Avenue, Gillingham, Kent ME7 4DD.
Telephone: 01634 851854. **Clubcall:** 0891 332211. **Club Nickname:** Gills.
First choice Colours: Blue and black striped shirts; black shorts; black stockings.

Asaba, C	40(1)	Dobson, A	2	Pennock, A	39(1)
Ashby, B	38	Edge, N	1(5)	Pinnock, J	–(4)
Bartram, V	44	Elliott, S	4(1)	Rolling, F	1
Bryant, M	16(7)	Galloway, M	19(6)	Saunders, M	28(6)
Brown, K	2(3)	Hessenthaler, A	36(3)	Smith, P	45
Browning, M	1(3)	Hodge, J	7(27)	Southall, N	34(8)
Butler, S	4(3)	Lisbie, K	4(3)	Stannard, J	2
Butters, G	23	Nosworthy, N	–(3)	Taylor, R	43
Carr, D	22(7)	Patterson, M	42	Williams, P	9(1)

Play-offs – Appearances: Asaba 3, Ashby 2, Bartram 3, Brown –(1), Butters 3, Carr 1(1), Galloway 3, Hessenthaler 3, Hodge –(3), Patterson 3, Pennock 3, Saunders –(3), Smith 3, Southall 3, Taylor 3.
League Goals (75): Asaba 20, Taylor 16, Hessenthaler 7, Smith 6, Lisbie 4, Saunders 4, Southall 4, Butters 3, Galloway 3, Carr 2, Patterson 2, Ashby 1, Hodge 1, Williams 1, Opponents 1. **Play-off Goals (4):** Taylor 2, Asaba 1, Hessenthaler 1.
Worthington Cup Goals: None. **F.A. Cup Goals:** None. **Auto Windscreens Shield Goals (7):** Taylor 3, Asaba 1, Hessenthaler 1, Pennock 1, Smith 1.
Player of Year: Robert Taylor. **Sponsors:** to be announced.
Average home League attendance 1998-99: 6,339. **Capacity for 1999-2000:** to be announced.
Record attendance: 23,002 v Q.P.R. (F.A. Cup 3) 10 January 1948.

LINCOLN CITY

Ground: Sincil Bank, Lincoln, LN 5 8LD.
Telephone: 01522 880011. **Clubcall:** 0891 555900. **Club Nickname:** Imps.
First-choice Colours: Red and white striped shirts; black shorts; black stockings.

Alcide, C	20(3)	Gain, P	–(4)	Richardson, B	13
Austin, K	38(1)	Gordon, G	21(6)	Smith, P	22(6)
Barnett, J	29	Grobbelaar, B	2	Stant, P	–(3)
Battersby, T	35(4)	Hartfield, C	3	Stones, C	–(1)
Bimson, S	30(1)	Holmes, S	37	Thorpe, L	35(3)
Brabin, G	3(1)	Miller, P	26(6)	Vaughan, J	31
Brown, G	21(1)	Oatway, C	3	Walling, D	–(3)
Fenn, N	–(4)	Peacock, R	3(7)	Watts, J	2
Finnigan, J	36(1)	Perry, L	10(2)	Whitney, J	13
Fleming, T	40(3)	Phillips, D	3	Wilder, C	2(1)
Fortune-West, L	7(2)	Philpott, L	15(9)		

League Goals (42): Thorpe 8, Battersby 7, Holmes 6, Gordon 5, Bimson 2, Miller 2, Smith 2, Whitney 2, Alcide 1, Austin 1, Barnett 1, Brown 1, Finnigan 1, Fortune-West 1, Hartfield 1, Opponents 1.
Worthington Cup Goals (1): Battersby 1. **F.A. Cup Goals (5):** Alcide 1, Battersby 1, Finnigan 1, Holmes 1, Thorpe 1. **Auto Windscreens Shield Goals (5):** Bimson 1, Battersby 1, Holmes 1, Miller 1, Thorpe 1.

LUTON TOWN

Ground: Kenilworth Road Stadium, 1 Maple Road, Luton, Bedfordshire LU4 8AW.
Telephone: 01582 411622. Clubcall: 0891 121123. Club Nickname: Hatters.
First-choice Colours: to be announced.

Abbey, N 2	Evers, S 27	McKinnon, R .... 29(1)
Alexander, G .... 28(1)	Fotiadis, A .... 8(13)	McLaren, P .... 14(9)
Bacque, H .... 2(4)	Fraser, S .... 5(3)	Scarlett, A .... 2(4)
Boyce, E 1	George, L .... 6(6)	Showler, P .... 2(1)
Cox, J .... 3(5)	Gray, P .... 32(3)	Spring, M 45
Davies, S 2	Harrison, G 14	Thomas, M .... 26(7)
Davis, K 44	Johnson, M 42	Thorpe, A .... 7(1)
Davis, S 20	Kandol, T .... 2(2)	White, A .... 18(14)
Doherty, G .... 5(15)	Marshall, D .... 3(1)	Willmott, C .... 13(1)
Douglas, S 42	McGowan, G .... 27(4)	Zahana-Oni, L .... 4(4)
Dyche, S 14	McIndoe, M .... 17(5)	

League Goals (51): Douglas 9, Gray 8, Davis S 6, Doherty 6, Alexander 4, Thorpe 4, Evers 3, Spring 3, Fotiadis 2, McKinnon 2, Dyche 1, Marshall 1, Scarlett 1, White 1. Worthington Cup Goals (13): Gray 3, Alexander 2, Davis S 2, Douglas 2, Evers 1, Fotiadis 1, Johnson 1, McLaren 1. F.A. Cup Goals (4): Davis S 2, Gray 2. Auto Windscreens Shield Goals: None.

MACCLESFIELD TOWN

Ground: Moss Rose Ground, London Road, Macclesfield, Cheshire SK11 7SP.
Telephone: 01625 264686. Clubcall: 0930 555635. Club Nickname: Silkmen.
First-choice Colours: Blue shirts; blue shorts; white stockings.

Askey, J .... 31(7)	Holt, M .... 3(1)	Smith, P 12
Bailey, A .... 5(5)	Howarth, N .... 11(9)	Sodje, E 42
Barclay, D .... 3(6)	Ingram, R .... 23(4)	Soley, S .... 5(5)
Brown, G 5	Landon, R .... 10(4)	Sorvel, N .... 38(3)
Brown, S .... 1(1)	Lomax, M .... −(1)	Tinson, D 37
Davenport, P .... −(1)	Matias, P .... 21(1)	Tomlinson, G .... 15(13)
Davies, S .... 9(3)	McDonald, M 23	Whittaker, S .... 18(9)
Durkan, K .... 23(3)	Payne, S .... 32(6)	Williams, T 4
Griffiths, P 4	Price, R 42	Wood, S .... 29(13)
Hitchen, S 35	Sedgemore, B .... 25(9)	

League Goals (43): Sorvel 5, Tomlinson 4, Askey 4, Wood 4, Sodje 3, Smith 3, Durkan 3, Payne 3, Sedgemore 2, McDonald 2, Landon 2, Davies 2, Matias 1, Barclay 1, Griffiths 1, Holt 1, Whittaker 1, Bailey 1.
Worthington Cup Goals (3): Askey 2, Wood 1. F.A. Cup Goals (7): Tomlinson 4, Askey 1, Sodje 1, Sedgemore 1. Auto Windscreens Shield Goals: None.

MANCHESTER CITY

Ground: Maine Road, Moss Side, Manchester M14 7WN.
Telephone: 0161 2323000. **Clubcall:** 0891 121191. **Club Nickname:** Citizens.
First-choice Colours: Light blue shirts; white shorts; blue stockings.

Allsopp, D .... 3(21)	Fenton, N 15	Shelia, M 3
Bishop, I .... 21(4)	Goater, S .... 41(2)	Tiatto, D .... 8(9)
Bradbury, L .... 11(1)	Greenacre, C 1	Tskhadadze, K 2
Branch, M 4	Horlock, K .... 35(1)	Vaughan, T .... 35(3)
Brown, M .... 26(5)	Mason, G .... 18(1)	Weaver, N 45
Cooke, T 21	Morrison, A .... 21(1)	Whitley, Jeff .... 1(5)
Crooks, L .... 32(2)	Pollock, J .... 25(2)	Whitley, Jim .... 10(10)
Dickov, P .... 22(13)	Robins, M .... –(2)	Wiekens, G 42
Edghill, R 38	Russell, C .... 5(2)	Wright,T 1

Play-offs – Appearances: Allsopp –(1), Bishop –(1), Brown 3, Cooke 3, Crooks 3, Dickov 3, Edghill 3, Goater 3, Horlock 3, Morrison 1, Pollock –(1), Taylor –(3), Vaughan 2(1), Weaver 3, Wiekens 3, Whitley Jeff 3.
League Goals (69): Goater 17, Dickov 10, Horlock 9, Cooke 7, Allsopp 4, Morrison 4, Taylor 4, Bradbury 3, Brown 2, Wiekens 2, Crooks 1, Pollock 1, Russell 1, Tskhadadze 1, Vaughan 1, Whitley Jeff 1, Opponents 1. **Play-off Goals (4):** Dickov 2, Goater 1, Horlock 1.
Worthington Cup Goals (10): Dickov 2, Goater 2, Allsopp 1, Bradbury 1, Mason 1, Tiatto 1, Tskhadadze 1, Whitley Jim 1. **F.A. Cup Goals (5):** Russell 2, Brown 1, Dickov 1, Goater 1. **Auto Windscreens Shield Goals (1):** Allsopp.
Player of Year: Gerard Wiekens. **Sponsors:** to be announced.
Average home League attendance 1998-99: 28,261. **Capacity for 1999-2000:** 33,000.
Record attendance: 84,569 v Stoke City (F.A. Cup 6) 3 March 1934.

MILLWALL

Ground: The New Den, Zampa Road, London SE16 3LN.
Telephone: 0171 232 1222. **Clubcall:** 0891 400300. **Club Nickname:** Lions.
First-choice Colours: White shirts; white shorts; white stockings.

Bircham, M .... 20(8)	Hockton, D .... 1(7)	Roberts, B 11
Bowry, B .... 22(3)	Ifill, P .... 12(3)	Roberts, T 8
Bubb, B .... 1(2)	Lavin, G .... (38)	Roche, S 3
Bull, R 1	Law, B 5	Ryan, R .... 22(4)
Cahill, T .... 34(2)	McDougald, J .... –(1)	Sadlier, R .... 18(13)
Carter, J 16	McLeary, A 2	Savage, P .... –(2)
Cook, A .... 1(2)	Neill, L .... 33(2)	Shaw, P .... 31(3)
Dolan, J 9	Nethercott, S .... 35(2)	Smith, P 5
Fitzgerald, S 32	Newman, R .... 22(2)	Spink, N 22
Grant, K .... 4(12)	Odunsi, L .... 2(1)	Stevens, K .... 1(2)
Harris, N .... 37(2)	Reid, S 25	Stuart, J .... 33(2)
Hicks, M .... –(1)		

League Goals (52): Harris 15, Shaw 10, Cahill 7, Neill 6, Sadlier 5, Grant 3, Dolan 1, Fitzgerald 1, Hockton 1, Ifill 1, Opponents 2.
Worthington Cup Goals (1): Shaw 1. **F.A. Cup Goals:** None. **Auto Windscreens Shield Goals (11):** Harris 3, Shaw 3, Sadlier 2, Cahill 1, Lavin 1, Hockton 1.
Player of Year: Neil Harris. **Sponsors:** Giorgio.
Average home League attendance 1998-99: 6,958. **Capacity for 1999-2000:** 20,146.
Record attendance: (New Den) 20,093 v Arsenal (F.A. Cup 3) 10 January 1994. (The Den) 48,672 v Derby Co. (F.A. Cup 5) 20 February 1937.

NORTHAMPTON TOWN

Ground: Sixfields Stadium, Upton Way, Northampton NN5 5QA.
Telephone: 01604 757773. **Clubcall:** 0930 555970. **Club Nickname:** Cobblers.
First-choice Colours: Claret shirts; white shorts; claret stockings.

Bishop, C 4	Hill, C .... 22(5)	Savage, D .... 18(9)
Clarke, A .... 2(2)	Hodgson, D .... 7(1)	Seal, D .... 5(1)
Clarkson, I .... 3(2)	Hope, R .... 17(2)	Spedding, D .... 15(9)
Corazzin, C .... 36(3)	Howard, S 12	Turley, B 25
Dobson, A .... 8(3)	Howey, L 25	Warburton, R 13
Frain, J .... 40(1)	Hunt, J .... 24(10)	Warner, M .... 5(5)
Francis, S 3	Lee, C .... 9(10)	Wilder, C 1
Freestone, C ...... 17(14)	Matthew, D 1	Wilkinson, P .... 12(3)
Gibb, A .... 30(11)	Parrish, S 33	Wilson, K 8
Heggs, C .... 8(5)	Peer, D .... 21(5)	Witter, A .... 1(3)
Hendon, I 7	Sampson, I 41	Woodman, A 18

League Goals (43): Corazzin 16, Howey 6, Savage 6, Hunt 2, Freestone 2, Heggs 1, Hodgson 1, Hunter 1, Lee 1, Parrish 1, Peer 1, Sampson 1, Spedding 1, Warburton 1, Wilkinson 1, Wilson 1.
Worthington Cup Goals (6): Freestone 3, Heggs 2, Parrish 1. **F.A. Cup Goals (2):** Sampson 2. **Auto Windscreens Shield Goals (2):** Corazzin 1, Freestone 1.
Player of Year: Carlo Corazzin. **Sponsors:** Nationwide.
Average home League attendance 1998-99: 6,073. **Capacity for 1999-2000:** 7,653.
Record attendance: (Sixfields Stadium) 7,557 v Manchester City (Div. 2) 26 September 1998; (County Ground) 24,523 v Fulham (Div. 1) 23 April 1966.

NOTTS COUNTY

Ground: Meadow Lane, Nottingham NG2 3HJ.
Telephone: 0115 9529000. **Clubcall:** 0891 888684. **Club Nickname:** The Magpies.
First-choice Colours: Black and white shirts; black shorts; black stockings.

Beadle, P .... 13(1)	Goram, A 1	Pearce, D .... 31(1)
Billy, C .... 3(3)	Grant, K 6	Quayle, M .... 2(3)
Bolland, P .... 12(1)	Hendon, I 32	Rapley, K .... 10(6)
Creaney, G .... 13(3)	Holmes, R .... 3(5)	Redmile, M .... 39(2)
Devlin, P 5	Hughes, A .... 21(9)	Richardson, I 23
Dudley, C .... –(4)	Jackson, J .... 3(7)	Robson, M .... –(2)
Dyer, A .... 19(10)	Jones, G .... 23(4)	Stallard, M .... 13(1)
Fairclough, C 16	Liburd, R .... 27(8)	Strodder, G .... 8(3)
Farrell, S .... 7(4)	Matthews, L .... 4(1)	Tierney, F .... 13(7)
Finnan, S .... 12(1)	Murray, S .... 32(3)	Torpey, N .... 4(2)
Foley, D 2	Owers, G .... 36(3)	Ward, D 43
Garcia, A .... 10(9)	Parkin, B 1	Warren, M 18
Gibson, P 1		

League Goals (52): Richardson 7, Hendon 6, Stallard 4, Beadle 3, Creaney 3, Farrell 3, Hughes 3, Murray 3, Owers 3, Tierney 3, Garcia 2, Jones 2, Rapley 2, Fairclough 1, Grant 1, Liburd 1, Pearce 1, Redmile 1, Strodder 1, Torpey 1, Opponents 1.
Worthington Cup Goals (1): Torpey 1. **F.A. Cup Goals (8):** Jones 6, Murray 1, Owers 1. **Auto Windscreens Shield Goals:** None.
Player of Year: Ian Richardson/Darren Ward (joint). **Sponsors:** Sapa Aluminium.
Average home League attendance 1998-99: 5,617. **Capacity for 1999-2000:** 20,300.
Record attendance: 47,310 v York City (F.A. Cup 6) 12 March 1955.

OLDHAM ATHLETIC

Ground: Boundary Park, Oldham, Lancashire, OL1 2PA.
Telephone: 0161 6244972. **Clubcall:** 09068 121142. **Club Nickname:** Latics.
First-choice Colours: Blue shirts; blue shorts; blue stockings.

Allott, M .... 32(9)	Kelly, G 45	Ritchie, A .... –(1)
Beavers, P 7	Littlejohn, A .... 11(5)	Salt, P .... 5(6)
Clitheroe, L .... 1(1)	Mardon, P 12	Sheridan, J 30
Duxbury, L 42	McGinlay, J .... 4(3)	Sinnott, L .... 13(4)
Garnett, S .... 36(1)	McLean, I 5	Spooner, N 2
Graham, R 11	McNiven, D .... 1(5)	Sugden, R .... –(2)
Gray, A 4	McNiven, S .... 33(4)	Swan, I 1
Hodgson, D .... –(1)	Miskelly, D 1	Thom, S .... 19(6)
Holt, A .... 39(4)	Orlygsson, T .... 19(3)	Tipton, M .... 15(13)
Hotte, M .... –(1)	Reid, P 40	Walsh, D .... –(1)
Innes, M .... 8(5)	Rickers, P .... 44(1)	Whitehall, S .... 28(8)

League Goals (48): Allott 7, Duxbury 6, Holt 5, Rickers 4, Whitehall 4, Graham 3, Mardon 3, Beavers 2, Garnett 2, Littlejohn 2, Sheridan 2, Tipton 2, Innes 1, McGinlay 1, McNiven S 1, Reid 1, Thom 1, Opponents 1.
Worthington Cup Goals (3): Allott 1, Littlejohn 1, Reid 1. **F.A. Cup Goals (5):** McGinlay 2, Duxbury 1, McNiven S 1, Salt 1. **Auto Windscreens Shield Goals:** None.
Player of Year: John Sheridan. **Sponsors:** Slumberland Plc.
Average home League attendance 1998-99: 5,631. **Capacity for 1999-2000:** 13,657.
Record attendance: 47,761 v Sheffield Wed. (F.A. Cup 4) 25 January 1930.

PRESTON NORTH END

Ground: Deepdale, Lowthorpe Road, Preston PR1 6RU.
Telephone: 01772 902020. **Clubcall:** 0891 660220. **Club Nickname:** Lilywhites.
First-choice Colours: White shirts; navy shorts; white and navy stockings.

Alexander, G 10	Gregan, S .... 40(1)	McGregor, P .... 1(3)
Appleton, M .... 13(12)	Harris, J .... 9(25)	McKenna, P .... 31(5)
Basham, S .... 15(2)	Harrison, C 6	Moilanen, T 16
Byfield, D .... 3(2)	Holt, M .... –(3)	Murdock, C .... 28(5)
Cartwright, L ...... 14(13)	Jackson, M 44	Nogan, K .... 39(3)
Clement, N 4	Kidd, R .... 27(1)	Parkinson, G 27
Darby, J .... 12(8)	Lucas, D 30	Rankine, M 42
Eyres, D .... 33(1)	Ludden, D .... 26(6)	Wright, M 1
Gray, A 5	Macken, J .... 30(12)	

Play-offs – Appearances: Appleton 1(1), Alexander 2, Cartwright 2, Darby –(1), Eyres 2, Gregan 2, Harris –(2), Jackson 2, Lucas 2, Ludden 2, Macken 2, Murdock 2, Nogan 1(1), Rankine 2.
League Goals (78): Nogan 18, Basham 10, Macken 8, Eyres 8, Jackson 8, Harris 6, Cartwright 4, Gregan 3, Kidd 3, Rankine 3, Appleton 2, Murdock 1, Parkinson 1, Darby 1, Byfield 1, Opponents 1. **Play-off Goals (1):** Eyres 1.
Worthington Cup Goals: None. **F.A. Cup Goals (7):** Nogan 3, Rankine 1, Harris 1, Darby 1, McKenna 1. **Auto Windscreens Shield Goals (3):** Darby 1, Macken 1, Parkinson 1.
Player of Year: Michael Jackson. **Sponsors:** Baxi.
Average home League attendance 1998-99: 11,926. **Capacity for 1999-2000:** 22,000.
Record attendance: 42,684 v Arsenal (Div.1) 23 April 1938.

READING

Ground: Madejski Stadium, Bennett Road, Reading, RG2 0FL.
Telephone: 01189 681100. **Clubcall:** 0891 121000. **Club Nickname:** Royals.
First-choice Colours: Blue and white hoops; blue shorts; blue and white stockings.

Asaba, C .... –(1)	Gray, S .... 25(2)	McPherson, K .... 13(2)
Barras, A .... 4(2)	Gurney, A .... 5(3)	Murty, G .... 8(1)
Bernal, A .... 18(4)	Hammond, N 1	Parkinson, P 42
Booty, M .... 7(1)	Hodges, L .... –(1)	Polston, J 4
Bowen, J 1	Houghton, R .... 13(5)	Primus, L 31
Brayson, P .... 13(16)	Howie, S 42	Reilly, M .... 4(2)
Brebner, G .... 36(3)	Hunter, B .... 2(1)	Roach, N .... 3(2)
Caskey, D 42	Kromheer, E 11	Sarr, M .... 18(10)
Casper, C 32	Lambert, J 1	Scott, K .... 5(4)
Clement, N 11	Legg, A 2	Stamp, N .... –(1)
Crawford, J .... 9(1)	Maybury, A 8	Thorpe, A 6
Davies, G 1	McIntyre, J .... 22(10)	Van Der Kwaak, P 3
Evers, S .... –(1)	McKeever, M .... 6(1)	Williams, M .... 20(6)
Fleck, R .... 2(2)	McLaren, A 7	Wright, A .... –(2)
Glasgow, B .... 28(4)		

League Goals (54): Williams 11, Brebner 9, Caskey 7, McIntyre 6, Parkinson 5, Sarr 3, Gray 2, McKeever 2, Scott 2, Barras 1, Clement 1, Fleck 1, Glasgow 1, McLaren 1, Thorpe 1, Opponents 1.
Worthington Cup Goals (4): Caskey 2, Asaba 1, Brebner 1. **F.A. Cup Goals:** None. **Auto Windscreens Shield Goals:** None.
Player of Year: Phil Parkinson. **Sponsors:** to be announced.
Average home League attendance 1998-99: 11,265. **Capacity for 1999-2000:** 25,000.
Record attendance: (Elm Park) 33,042 v Brentford (F.A. Cup 5) 17 February 1927; (Madejski Stadium) 20,555 v Manchester City (Div. 2) 27 March 1999.

STOKE CITY

Ground: Britannia Stadium, Stanley Matthews Way, Stoke-on-Trent, Staffs, ST4 7QW.
Telephone: 01782 592222. **Clubcall:** 0891 121040. **Club Nickname:** Potters.
First-choice Colours: Red and white shirts; white shorts; red and white socks.

Clarke, C 2	Mackenzie, N .... 3(3)	Strong, G 5
Collins, L 4	Mohan, N 15	Sturridge, S .... 1(2)
Connor, P .... 2(1)	Muggleton, C 40	Taaffe, S .... 1(2)
Crowe, D .... 17(19)	O'Connor, J 4	Thorne, P .... 32(1)
Forsyth, R .... 13(5)	Oldfield, D .... 43(3)	Tweed, S .... –(1)
Fraser, S .... –(1)	Petty, B .... 8(2)	Wallace, R .... 11(20)
Heath, R .... 7(3)	Robinson, P .... 39(1)	Ward, G 6
Kavanagh, G 36	Sigurdsson, L 37	Whittle, J .... 9(5)
Kavanagh, J 8	Short, C .... 19(2)	Woods, S 33
Keen, K 43	Small, B .... 35(2)	Wooliscroft, A .... –(1)
Lightbourne, K .... 29(8)		

League Goals (59): Kavanagh G 11, Thorne 9, Crowe 8, Lightbourne 7, Oldfield 6, Sigurdsson 4, Wallace 3, Connor 2, Forsyth 2, Keen 2, Robinson 1, Strong 1, Whittle 1, Opponents 2.
Worthington Cup Goals (2): Kavanagh G 1, Thorne 1. **F.A. Cup Goals (1):** Lightbourne 1.
Auto Windscreens Shield Goals (3): Crowe 1, Kavanagh G 1, Thorne 1.
Player of Year: Kevin Keen. **Sponsors:** Britannia.
Average home League attendance 1998-1999: 12,732. **Capacity for 1999-2000:** 28,000.
Record attendance: (Victoria Ground) 51,380 v Arsenal (Div. 1) 29 March 1937. (Britannia Stadium) 26,663 v Manchester City (Div. 1) 3 May 1998.

WALSALL

Ground: Bescot Stadium, Bescot Crescent, Walsall, West Midlands, WS1 4SA.
Telephone: 01922 622791. **Clubcall:** 09068 555800. **Club Nickname:** Saddlers.
First-choice Colours: Red shirts; black shorts; red stockings.

Brissett, J .... 27(8)	Keister, J 2	Rammell, A 39
Carter, A .... –(1)	Keates,S .... 38(5)	Ricketts, M .... 2(6)
Cramb, C 4	Lambert, J .... 4(2)	Roper, I .... 29(3)
Davis, N .... –(1)	Larusson, B .... 33(3)	Simpson, P 10
Dyer, W .... –(1)	Marsh, C 43	Steiner, R 10
Eyjolfsson, Z .... –(10)	Mavrak, D .... 12(1)	Thomas,W .... 1(11)
Evans, W .... 6(5)	Otta, W .... 6(2)	Viveash, A 40
Gadsby, M .... 3(3)	Platt, C .... 6(1)	Walker, J 46
Green, R .... 22(8)	Pointon, N 43	Watson, A .... 12(9)
Henry, N 8	Porter, G .... 14(1)	Wrack, D 46

League Goals (63): Rammell 18, Wrack 13, Cramb 4, Watson 3, Larusson 3, Otta 3, Steiner 3, Keates 2, Mavrak 2, Marsh 2, Brissett 2, Platt 1, Simpson 1, Green 1, Eyjolfsson 1, Roper 1, Opponents 3.
Worthington Cup Goals (1): Rammell 1. **F.A. Cup Goals (1):** Roper 1. **Auto Windscreens Shield Goals (7):** Eyjolfsson 1, Keates 1, Larusson 1, Otta 1, Rammell 1, Watson 1, Wrack 1.
Player of Year: James Walker. **Sponsors:** Banks's.
Average home League attendance 1998-99: 5,478. **Capacity for 1999-2000:** 9,900.
Record attendance: (Fellows Park) 25,433 v Newcastle Utd. (Div. 2) 29 August 1961. (Bescot Stadium) 10,628 England v Switzerland "B" int., May 20, 1991. Club: 9,517 v Manchester City (Div. 2) 23 January 1999.

WIGAN ATHLETIC

Ground: JJB Stadium, Robin Park, Wigan, Lancashire.
Telephone: 01942 244433. **Clubcall:** 0891 121655. **Club Nickname:** Latics.
First-choice Colours: Blue shirts with green trim; blue shorts; blue stockings.

Balmer, S 38	Haworth, S .... 19(1)	McGibbon, P .... 35(1)
Barlow, S .... 39(1)	Jenkinson, L .... 3(4)	Nixon, E 3
Bradshaw, C 39	Jones, G .... 8(12)	O'Neill, M .... 35(1)
Carroll, R 43	Kilford, I .... 16(7)	Porter, A .... 6(10)
Fitzhenry, N 1	Lee, D .... 20(15)	Rogers, P 42
Green, S .... 30(5)	Liddell, A 28	Sharp, K .... 25(6)
Greenall, C 40	Lowe, D .... 5(11)	Smeets, J .... –(1)
Griffiths, G 20	Martinez, R .... 3(7)	Warne, P .... 8(3)

Play-offs – Appearances: Balmer 2, Barlow 2, Bradshaw 2, Carroll 2, Green 1(1), Greenall 2, Haworth 1, Jones –(2), Kilford –(1), Lee –(2), Liddell 2, Lowe 1, McGibbon 2, O'Neill 1, Porter 2, Sharp 2.
League Goals (75): Barlow 19, Liddell 10, Haworth 10, Bradshaw 6, Greenall 6, Lee 6, McGibbon 5, Jones 3, Rogers 2, Sharp 2, Balmer 1, Lowe 1, Porter 1, Warne 1, Opponents 2. **Play-off Goals (1):** Barlow 1.
Worthington Cup Goals (4): Barlow 1, Griffiths 1, Lee 1, Opponents 1. **F.A. Cup Goals (5):** Lowe 2, Barlow 1, Greenall 1, Haworth 1. **Auto Windscreens Shield Goals (17):** Barlow 4, Haworth 3, O'Neill 3, Balmer 1, Lee 1, Jones 1, Kilford 1, Rogers 1, Sharp 1, Warne 1.
Player of Year: Colin Greenall. **Sponsors:** JJB Sports.
Average home League attendance 1998-99: 4,250. **Capacity for 1999-2000:** 25,000.
Record attendance: (Springfield Park) 27,500 v Hereford Utd. (F.A. Cup 2) 12 December 1953.

WREXHAM

Ground: Racecourse Ground, Mold Road, Wrexham, N.Wales LL11 2AH.
Telephone: 01978 262129. **Clubcall:** 0891 121642. **Club Nickname:** The Robins.
First-choice Colours: Red shirts; white shorts; red stockings.

Barrett, P .... 8(2)	Brammer, D .... 31(3)	Cartwright, M 30
Brace, D .... 15(2)	Carey, B 36	Chalk, M .... 19(9)

Connolly, K .... 43(1)	McGregor, M 43	Russell, K .... 25(6)
Cooke, T 10	Morrell, A .... 4(3)	Skinner, C 12
Edwards, J .... 4(5)	Owen, G 35	Spink, D .... 26(8)
Elliott, S .... 8(1)	Ridler, D .... 35(1)	Thomas, S .... 1(4)
Gibson, R .... 3(4)	Rishworth, S .... –(4)	Ward, P 25
Griffiths, C 4	Roberts, N .... 11(11)	Whitley, J 9
Hardy, P .... 31(2)	Rush, I .... 12(5)	Wright, T 16
Humes, A .... 10(2)		

League Goals (43): Connolly 11, Griffiths 3, Owen 3, Roberts 3, Spink 3, Brammer 2, Carey 2, Russell 2, Skinner 2, Ward 2, Whitley 2, Edwards 1, Gibson 1, McGregor 1, Ridler 1, Opponents 4.
Worthington Cup Goals (2): Connolly 1, Roberts 1. **F.A. Cup Goals (9):** Connolly 5, Brammer 1, Roberts 1, Russell 1, Opponents 1. **Auto Windscreens Shield Goals (10):** Edwards 2, Roberts 2, Brammer 1, Connolly 1, Griffiths 1, Owen 1, Ridler 1, Opponents 1.
Player of Year: Dean Spink. **Sponsors:** Home – Wrexham Lager; Away – Carlsberg.
Average home League attendance 1998-99: 3,938. **Capacity for 1999-2000:** 15,500.
Record attendance: 34,445 v Manchester Utd. (F.A. Cup 4) 26 January 1957.

WYCOMBE WANDERERS

Ground: Adams Park, Hillbottom Road, High Wycombe, Bucks, HP1 4HJ.
Telephone: 01494 472100. **Clubcall:** 09003 446855. **Club Nickname:** Chairboys.
First-choice Colours: Light blue and dark blue quartered shirts; dark blue shorts; dark blue stockings.

Baird, A .... 25(3)	Harkin, M .... 1(1)	Robson, M .... 1(3)
Bates, J 9	Holsgrove, L .... –(1)	Ryan, K .... 26(2)
Beeton, A .... 11(5)	Kavanagh, J .... 14(4)	Scott, K .... 23(2)
Brown, S .... 34(4)	Lawrence, M 34	Senda, D .... –(6)
Bulman, D .... 5(6)	Lee, M .... (2)	Simpson, M .... 31(2)
Carroll, D .... 27(5)	McCarthy, P .... 26(3)	Stallard, M .... 12(3)
Cornforth, J .... 9(4)	McGavin, S .... –(4)	Taylor, M 44
Cousins, J 34	McSporran, J ..... 11(14)	Vinnicombe, C .... 39(2)
Devine, S .... 11(1)	Mohan, N 25	Westhead, M 2
Emblen, P .... 28(7)	Read, P .... 11(5)	Wraight, G 6
Forsyth, M 4		

League Goals (52): Devine 9, Carroll 6, Scott 6, Baird 5, McSporran 4, Simpson 4, Brown 3, Cousins 2, Emblen 2, Lawrence 2, Mohan 2, Stallard 2, Bulman 1, Cornforth 1, McCarthy 1, Read 1, Ryan 1.
Worthington Cup Goals (4): Brown 2, Read 1, Stallard 1. **F.A. Cup Goals (4):** Baird 1, Carroll 1, Read 1, Scott 1. **Auto Windscreens Shield Goals (2):** McSporran 1, Ryan 1.
Player of Year: Jason Cousins. **Sponsors:** Verco Office Furniture.
Average home League attendance 1998-99: 5,121. **Capacity for 1999-2000:** 10,000.
Record attendance: 9,007 v West Ham Utd. (F.A. Cup 3) 7 January 1995.

YORK CITY

Ground: Bootham Crescent, York, North Yorkshire YO3 7AQ.
Telephone: 01904 624447. **Clubcall:** 0891 121643. **Club Nickname:** Minstermen.
First-choice Colours: Red shirts; navy blue shorts; red stockings.

Agnew, S .... 19(1)	Fairclough, C 11	Jordan, S .... 27(5)
Barras, A 24	Garratt, M .... 33(6)	McMillan, A 33
Carruthers, M .... 3(3)	Hall, W .... 26(1)	Mimms, B 35
Connolly, G 28	Himsworth, G .... 12(1)	Pouton, A .... 24(3)
Cresswell, R 36	Hocking, M .... 4(2)	Prendergast, R .... 1(2)
Dawson, A .... 7(4)	Jones, B .... 44(1)	Reed, M .... 8(4)

Rowe, R .... 24(15)	Tinkler, M .... 36(1)	Warrington, A 11
Skinner, C .... 3(2)	Tolson, N .... 17(10)	Williams, M 11
Thompson, N 24		

League Goals (56): Cresswell 16, Rowe 7, Thompson 6, Jordan 5, Connolly 4, Williams 4, Tolson 3, Agnew 2, Jones 2, Tinkler 2, Dawson 1, Garratt 1, Hall 1, Pouton 1, Opponents 1.
Worthington Cup Goals (1): Thompson 1. **F.A. Cup Goals (5):** Cresswell 3, Jordan 2. **Auto Windscreens Shield Goals (2):** Rowe 1, Tolson 1.
Player of Year: Barry Jones. **Sponsors:** Portakabin.
Average home League attendance 1998-99: 3,646. **Capacity for 1999-2000:** 8,975.
Record attendance: 28,123 v Huddersfield Town (F.A. Cup 6) 5 March 1938.

NATIONWIDE LEAGUE – THIRD DIVISION

BARNET

Ground: Underhill Stadium, Barnet Lane, Barnet, Herts EN5 2BE.
Telephone: 0181 441 6932. **Clubcall:** 0891 121544. **Club Nickname:** Bees.
First-choice Colours: Black and amber shirts; black shorts; white stockings.

Alsford, J 9	Ford, J 15	McGleish, S .... 25(11)
Arber, M 34	Gledhill, L .... –(1)	Onwere, U .... 8(5)
Barnes, S .... 3(9)	Goodhind, W 15	Rust, N 2
Basham, M 32	Hackett, W .... 3(4)	Sawyers, R .... 21(1)
Charlery, K .... 40(2)	Harle, M 11	Searle, S .... 33(2)
Currie, D .... 33(5)	Harrison, L 43	Simpson, P .... 11(2)
Dearden, K 1	Heald, G 19	Stockley, S .... 41(1)
Devine, S .... 10(10)	King, M .... 17(5)	Wilson, P 31
Doolan, J .... 39(2)	Manuel, B .... 3(9)	

League Goals (54): Charlery 16, McGleish 8, King 6, Currie 4, Searle 3, Arber 2, Doolan 2, Heald 2, Onwere 2, Wilson 2, Alsford 1, Basham 1, Devine 1, Ford 1, Goodhind 1, Manuel 1, Opponents 1.
Worthington Cup Goals (2): Currie 1, McGleish 1. **F.A. Cup Goals (1):** Currie. **Auto Windscreens Shield Goals (1):** McGleish.
Player of Year: Lee Harrison. **Sponsors:** Loaded.
Average home League attendance 1998-99: 2,107. **Capacity for 1999-2000:** 4,057.
Record attendance: 11,026 v Wycombe Wand. (F.A. Amateur Cup 4) January 1954.

BRENTFORD

Ground: Griffin Park, Braemar Road, Brentford, TW7 6RD.
Telephone: 0181 847 2511. **Clubcall:** 09068 121108. **Club Nickname:** Bees.
First-choice Colours: Red and white shirts; black shorts; black stockings.

Anderson, I .... 35(3)	Folan, A .... 19(9)	Partridge, S .... 12(2)
Aspinall, W .... 17(2)	Fortune-West, L .... 2(9)	Pearcey, J 17
Bates, J 27	Freeman, D .... 16(6)	Powell, D 33
Boxall, D .... 37(1)	Hebel, D .... 6(9)	Quinn, R .... 34(8)
Broughton, D 1	Hreidarsson, H 33	Rapley, K .... 3(9)
Bryan, D .... 9(12)	Jenkins, S .... –(1)	Rowlands, M .... 32(4)
Coyne, C 7	Mahon, G 29	Scott, A .... 31(3)
Cullip, D 2	Oatway, C .... 7(17)	Watson, P 12
Dearden, K 7	Owusu, L .... 42(4)	Woodman, A 22
Evans, P 14		

League Goals (79): Owusu 22, Partridge 7, Scott 7, Freeman 6, Bryan 4, Folan 4, Hreidarsson 4, Mahon 4, Rowlands 4, Evans 3, Rapley 3, Aspinall 2, Powell 2, Quinn 2, Anderson 1, Bates 1, Boxall 1, Opponents 2.
Worthington Cup Goals (8): Owusu 2, Scott 2, Bates 1, Freeman 1, Oatway 1, Rapley 1.
F.A. Cup Goals (8): Folan 2, Freeman 2, Bates 1, Hreidarsson 1, Owusu 1, Quinn 1. **Auto Windscreens Shield Goals (6):** Scott 2, Fortune-West 1, Hreidarsson 1, Quinn 1, Rowlands 1.
Player of Year: Darren Powell. **Sponsors:** G.M.B.
Average home League attendance 1998-99: 5,445. **Capacity for 1999-2000:** 12,763.
Record attendance: 39,626 v Preston N.E. (F.A. Cup 6) 5 March 1938.

BRIGHTON & HOVE ALBION

Ground: Withdean Stadium, Tongdean Lane, Brighton BN1 5JD.
Telephone: 01273 778855. **Clubcall:** 0891 440066. **Club Nickname:** Seagulls.
First-choice Colours: Blue and white striped shirts; white shorts; blue stockings with white trim.

Allan, D .... 21(1)	Doherty, L 3	Moralee, J .... 22(9)
Andrews, B .... –(1)	Hart, G .... 42(2)	Nicholls, K 4
Ansah, A .... 3(8)	Hinshelwood, D .... 3(1)	Ormerod, M 27
Armstrong, P .... 21(7)	Hobson, G .... 12(1)	Ryan,D .... 3(2)
Arnott, A 27	Ifejiagwa, E 2	Smith, P .... 8(6)
Atkinson, G 7	Johnson, R .... 30(4)	Storer, S .... 14(9)
Barker, R .... 33(10)	King, P 3	Sturgess, P .... 28(2)
Bennett, M .... 37(1)	Mayo, K .... 21(4)	Thomas, G .... 2(1)
Browne, A 13	McArthur, D 3	Thomas, R .... 11(1)
Culverhouse, I 35	McPherson, K 10	Tuck, S 2
Davies, D .... –(1)	Minton, J 35	Walton, M 19
Davies, L .... 2(6)	Mills, D .... 1(1)	Westcott, J .... –(4)

League Goals (49): Hart 12, Barker 10, Minton 9, Thomas R 3, Moralee 3, Johnson 2, Armstrong 2, Arnott 2, Mayo 1, Allan 1, Ifejiagwa 1, Nicholls 1, Ryan 1, Opponents 1.
Worthington Cup Goals (2): Barker 1, Storer 1. **F.A. Cup Goals (2):** Barker 1, Mayo 1. **Auto Windscreens Shield Goals (1):** Moralee 1.
Player of Year: Gary Hart. **Sponsors:** Skint.
Average home League attendance 1998-99: 3,253. **Capacity for 1999-2000:** 6,411.
Record attendance: (Goldstone Ground) 36,747 v Fulham (Div. 2) 27 December 1958.

CAMBRIDGE UNITED

Ground: Abbey Stadium, Newmarket Road, Cambridge CB5 8LN.
Telephone: 01223 566500. **Clubcall:** 09068 555885. **Club Nickname:** U's.
First-choice Colours: Amber and black shirts; black shorts; amber and black stockings.

Andrews, W .... 1(1)	Joseph, M .... 28(1)	Russell, A .... 36(1)
Ashbee, L .... 25(6)	Kyd, M .... 5(6)	Preece, D .... 5(9)
Benjamin, T .... 37(5)	MacKenzie, N .... 3(1)	Taylor, J .... 29(11)
Bruce, P .... 2(2)	Marshall, S 19	Van Heusden, A 27
Butler, M 46	McAvoy, L 1	Walker, R .... 7(14)
Campbell, J 45	McCammon, M .... 1(1)	Wanless, P 45
Chenery, B 44	McMahon,S .... 1(2)	Wilde, A 1
Duncan, A 45	McNeil, M .... 4(2)	Youngs, T .... 6(4)
Eustace, S .... 15(1)	Mustoe, N 7	

League Goals (78): Butler 17, Taylor 17, Benjamin 10, Wanless 8, Russell 6, Ashbee 4, Campbell 4, Mustoe 3, Walker 3, Preece 2, Duncan 1, MacKenzie 1, Opponents 2.
Worthington Cup Goals (7): Benjamin 4, Butler 2, Taylor 1. **F.A. Cup Goals (3):** Benjamin 1, Butler 1, Campbell 1. **Auto Windscreens Shield Goals (5):** Benjamin 2, Butler 1, Taylor 1, Walker 1.

Player of Year: Martin Butler. **Sponsors:** Home – C & R Windows; Away – Philips Lighting Systems.
Average home League attendance 1998-99: 4,583. **Capacity for 1999-2000:** 9,237.
Record attendance: 14,000 v Chelsea (Friendly) 1 May 1970.

CARDIFF CITY

Ground: Ninian Park, Sloper Road, Cardiff, South Glamorgan, CF1 8SX.
Telephone: 01222 221001. **Clubcall:** 09068 121171. **Club Nickname:** Bluebirds.
First-choice Colours: Blue shirts; white shorts; white stockings.

Allen, C .... 3(1)	Fowler, J .... 32(5)	O'Sullivan, W .... 38(4)
Bonner, M .... 21(4)	Hallworth, J 41	Penney, D 1
Bowen, J .... 10(7)	Hill, D .... 13(12)	Phillips, L 2
Brazier, M 11	Jarman, L .... 2(4)	Roberts, C .... –(4)
Carpenter, R .... 41(1)	Kelly, S 5	Saville, A 2
Delaney, M 28	Legg, A .... 18(6)	Thomas, D .... 16(8)
Earnshaw, R .... 1(4)	Middleton, C .... 20(15)	Williams, J .... 25(18)
Eckhardt, J .... 31(4)	Mitchell, G 46	Young, S 33
Ford, M 25	Nugent, K 41	

League Goals (60): Nugent 15, Williams 12, Eckhardt 5, Middleton 4, Thomas 4, Fowler 3, Bowen 2, Brazier 2, Hill 2, Legg 2, O'Sullivan 2, Bonner 1, Carpenter 1, Earnshaw 1, Jarman 1, Saville 1, Young 1, Opponents 1.
Worthington Cup Goals (2): Eckhardt 1, Williams 1. **F.A. Cup Goals (13):** Fowler 3, Nugent 3, Williams 3, Middleton 2, Delaney 1, Eckhardt 1. **Auto Windscreens Shield Goals:** None.
Player of Year: Kevin Nugent. **Sponsors:** to be announced.
Average home League attendance 1998-99: 7,131. **Capacity for 1999-2000:** 15,585.
Record attendance: 61,566 Wales v England 14 October 1961. Club: 57,800 v Arsenal (Div. 1) 22 April 1953.

CARLISLE UNITED

Ground: Brunton Park, Warwick Road, Carlisle
Telephone: 01228 526237. **Clubcall:** 0891 230011. **Club Nickname:** Cumbrians.
First-choice Colours: Blue shirts; white shorts; white stockings.

Anthony, G .... 21(5)	Dobie, S .... 26(7)	Ormerod, A 5
Bagshaw, P .... 5(4)	Douglas, A .... –(1)	Paterson, S .... 18(1)
Barr, B .... 21(2)	Finney, S .... 22(11)	Prokas, R .... 33(1)
Bass, D .... 8(1)	Glass, J 3	Scott, R 7
Boertien, P 8	Hopper, A .... 17(6)	Searle, D .... 43(2)
Bowman, R 24	Knight, R 6	Stevens, I .... 31(10)
Bridge-Wilkinson, M . 4(3)	Kubicki, D 7	Thorpe, J .... 6(7)
Brightwell, D 41	McAlindon, G .... 3(13)	Tracey, R .... 10(1)
Caig, A 37	McGregor, P .... 9(1)	Varty, W .... 5(1)
Clark, P .... 35(1)	Mendes, J .... 5(1)	Whitehead, S .... 36(1)
Couzens, A .... 10(5)		

League Goals (43): Stevens 9, Dobie 6, Finney 6, Brightwell 4, McGregor 3, Scott 3, Tracey 3, Searle 2, Glass 1, Mendes 1, Paterson 1, Boertien 1, Bowman 1, Opponents 2.
Worthington Cup Goals: None. **F.A. Cup Goals (1):** Stevens 1. **Auto Windscreens Shield Goals (1):** Searle 1.
Player of Year: Stuart Whitehead. **Sponsors:** to be announced.
Average home League attendance 1998-99: 3,319. **Capacity for 1999-2000:** 16,300.
Record attendance: 27,500 v Birmingham City (F.A. Cup 3) 5 January 1957 and v Middlesbrough (F.A. Cup 5) 7 January 1970.

CHESTER CITY

Ground: Deva Stadium, Bumpers Lane, Chester CH1 4LT.
Telephone: 01244 371376. **Clubcall:** 0891 121633. **Club Nickname:** Blues.
First-choice Colours: Blue and white shirts; blue shorts; blue stockings.

Alsford, J .... 9(1)	Cutler, N 23	Reid, S .... 16(6)
Aiston, S 11	Davidson, R 40	Richardson, N .... 41(2)
Beckett, L .... 24(4)	Fisher, N .... 7(1)	Shelton, A .... 5(17)
Bennett, G .... 5(2)	Flitcroft, D 42	Smeets, J .... 1(2)
Brown, W 23	Jones, J .... 2(6)	Smith, A 10
Carson, D .... 1(1)	Lancaster, M .... 8(3)	Thomas, R .... 3(3)
Conroy, M .... 11(4)	Moss, D .... 5(2)	Woods, M .... 41(2)
Crosby, A 41	Murphy, J .... 41(1)	Wright, D .... 6(11)
Cross, J .... 33(2)	Priest, C 35	

League Goals (57): Murphy 12, Beckett 11, Flitcroft 6, Crosby 4, Priest 4, Conroy 3, Richardson 3, Thomas 3, Smith 2, Alsford 1, Bennett 1, Cross 1, Davidson 1, Reid 1, Shelton 1, Woods 1, Wright 1, Opponents 1.
Worthington Cup Goals (4): Beckett 2, Smith 1, Opponents 1. **F.A. Cup Goals:** None. **Auto Windscreens Shield Goals (1):** Shelton 1.
Player of Year: Ross Davidson. **Sponsors:** to be announced.
Average home League attendance 1998-99: 2,562. **Capacity for 1999-2000:** 6,000.
Record attendance: (Deva Stadium) 5,386 v Preston N.E. (Div. 3) 2 April 1994. (Sealand Road) 20,500 v Chelsea (F.A. Cup 3) 16 January 1952.

DARLINGTON

Ground: Feethams, Darlington, County Durham DL1 5JB.
Telephone: 01325 240240. **Clubcall:** 0891 101555. **Club Nickname:** Quakers.
First-choice Colours: White shirts; black shorts; white stockings.

Atkinson, B .... 42(1)	Duffield, P .... 10(4)	Liddle, C 44
Barnard, M .... 29(4)	Ellison, L .... 3(17)	Naylor, G .... 32(10)
Bennett, G .... 26(3)	Gabbiadini, M 40	Oliver, M .... 33(3)
Brumwell, P .... 24(13)	Gaughan, S .... 12(11)	Pepper, C .... 5(1)
Campbell, P .... 4(3)	Heckingbottom, P 10	Preece, D 46
Carruthers, M 11	Himsworth, G .... 13(1)	Reed, A .... 25(4)
Carter, M 1	Hope, R 8	Roberts, D .... 10(14)
Costa, R .... –(3)	Kilty, M .... –(2)	Scott, K 4
Devos, J 12	Kubicki, D .... 2(2)	Shutt, C .... 8(6)
Dorner, M .... 9(13)	Leah, J 7	Tutill, S .... 33(3)

League Goals (69): Gabbiadini 24, Naylor 9, Roberts 5, Bennett 4, Dorner 3, Liddle 3, Carruthers 2, Devos 2, Duffield 2, Gaughan 2, Reed 2, Shutt 2, Atkinson 1, Barnard 1, Campbell 1, Carter 1, Costa 1, Himsworth 1, Leah 1, Oliver 1, Opponents 1.
Worthington Cup Goals (3): Roberts 1, Devos 1, Opponents 1. **F.A. Cup Goals (4):** Barnard 1, Dorner 1, Atkinson 1, Bennett 1. **Auto Windscreens Shield Goals (1):** Gabbiadini 1.
Player of Year: Marco Gabbiadini. **Sponsors:** Darlington Building Society.
Average home League attendance 1998-99: 3,181. **Capacity for 1999-2000:** 7,200.
Record Attendance: 21,023 v Bolton Wand. (League Cup 3) 14 November 1960.

EXETER CITY

Ground: St. James' Park, Exeter, EX4 6PX.
Telephone: 01392 254073. **Clubcall:** 0891 121634. **Club Nickname:** Grecians.
First-choice Colours: Red and white striped shirts; white shorts; red stockings.

Baddeley, L 23	Blake, N .... 4(3)	Clark, B .... 8(2)
Bayes, A 41	Breslan, G .... 24(10)	Crowe, G .... 3(6)

Curran, C .... 30(4)	McConnell, B .... 15(7)	Rowbotham, D .... 28(4)
Flack, S .... 38(6)	Potter, D 5	Smith, P .... –(1)
Fry, C .... 27(5)	Power, G 40	Speakman, R .... –(1)
Gale, S .... 21(6)	Quailey, B .... 8(4)	Tosh, P .... 8(2)
Gardner, J .... 23(4)	Rees, J 44	Waugh, W .... –(7)
Gittens, J 44	Richardson, J .... 39(1)	Wilkinson, J .... 6(12)
Holloway, C .... 27(7)		

League Goals (47): Flack 11, Rowbotham 7, Breslan 4, Curran 4, McConnell 4, Fry 2, Gittens 2, Quailey 2, Richardson 2, Tosh 2, Wilkinson 2, Holloway 1, Rees 1, Opponents 3.
Worthington Cup Goals (2): Richardson 2. **F.A. Cup Goals (8):** Flack 2, Rowbotham 2, Gardner 1, Gittens 1, Richardson 1, Opponents 1. **Auto Windscreens Shield Goals (4):** Flack 2, Clark 1, Quailey 1.
Player of Year: Ashley Bayes. **Sponsors:** Exeter Friendly Society.
Average home League attendance 1998-99: 3,154. **Capacity for 1999-2000:** 6,000 (reduced while ground is redeveloped to 10,500 capacity).
Record attendance: 20,894 v Sunderland (F.A. Cup 6) 4 March 1931.

HALIFAX TOWN

Ground: The Shay Stadium, Halifax, West Yorkshire, HX1 2YS.
Telephone: 01422 345543. **Clubcall:** 0891 227328. **Club Nickname:** Shaymen.
First-choice Colours: Blue and white shirt; blue shorts; white stockings.

Bradshaw, M 41	Horsfield, G 10	O'Regan, K .... 15(3)
Brown, J .... 31(9)	Hulme, K 30	Paterson, J .... 20(5)
Butler, P 33	Jackson, J 16	Power, L .... 14(4)
Carter, T .... 9(1)	Lucas, R .... 29(7)	Sertori, M .... 39(1)
Duerden, I .... 1(1)	Martin, L 37	Stansfield, J 12
Etherington, C 4	Murphy, J .... 21(2)	Stoneman, P 40
Grant, G .... –(3)	Murphy, S .... 10(3)	Thackeray, A .... 37(1)
Guinan, S 12	Newton, C .... 8(5)	Williams, M .... 18(6)
Hanson, D .... 19(13)		

League Goals (58): Paterson 10, Horsfield 7, Williams 6, Stoneman 5, Thackeray 5, Bradshaw 4, Hulme 4, Power 4, Jackson 3, Guinan 2, Hanson 2, O'Regan 2, Butler 1, Murphy 1, Newton 1, Stansfield 1.
Worthington Cup Goals (4): Hanson 2, Horsfield 1, Paterson 1. **F.A. Cup Goals:** None. **Auto Windscreens Shield Goals (5):** Williams 2, Bradshaw 1, Lucas 1, Hanson 1.
Player of Year: Paul Stoneman. **Sponsors:** Nationwide.
Average home League attendance 1998-99: 3,002. **Capacity for 1999-2000:** 9,900.
Record attendance: 36,885 v Tottenham (F.A. Cup 5) 14 February 1953.

HARTLEPOOL UNITED

Ground: Victoria Park, Clarence Road, Hartlepool, Cleveland TS24 8BZ.
Telephone: 01429 272584. **Clubcall:** None. **Club Nickname:** Pool.
First-choice Colours: Blue and white striped shirts, blue shorts, blue stockings.

Baker, P .... 3(10)	Evans, N .... –(1)	Knowles, D 46
Barron, M 38	Freestone, C .... 9(1)	Lee, G .... 23(1)
Beardsley, P 22	Heckingbottom, P 5	McDonald, C 5
Beech, C 16	Hollund, M 41	McGuckin, I 8
Brightwell, S .... 8(9)	Howard, S .... 25(3)	McKinnon, R 7
Clark, I .... 36(3)	Hughes, D .... 6(2)	Midgley, C .... 26(3)
Davies, L .... 2(1)	Hutt, S .... 2(2)	Miller, T .... 29(5)
Di Lella, G .... 18(5)	Ingram, D 37	Miotto, S 5
Dunwell, M .... –(1)	Irvine, S .... 10(8)	Pemberton, M .... –(4)
Elliott, S 5	Jones, G 12	Rush, D .... 5(5)

Smith, J .... 2(1)	Stokoe, G .... 15(4)	Westwood, C .... 3(2)
Stephenson, P .... 24(3)	Strodder, G 13	

League Goals (52): Beech 9, Midgley 7, Howard 5, Ingram 4, Miller 4, Freestone 3, Lee 3, Stephenson 2, Di Lella 2, Baker 2, Beardsley 2, Clark 2, Brightwell 1, Heckingbottom 1, Barron 1, Irvine 1, Jones 1, Opponents 2.
Worthington Cup Goals: None. **F.A. Cup Goals (4):** Howard 2, Miller 1, Midgley 1. **Auto Windscreen Shield Goals (4):** Miller 2, Howard 1, Brightwell 1.
Player of Year: Michael Barron. **Sponsors:** Camerons Brewery.
Average home League attendance 1998-99: 2,443. **Capacity for 1999-2000:** 7,229.
Record attendance: 17,426 v Manchester Utd. (F.A. Cup 3) 5 January 1957.

HULL CITY

Ground: Boothferry Park, Boothferry Road, Hull HU4 6EU.
Telephone: 01482 575263. **Clubcall:** 09068 888688. **Club Nickname:** Tigers.
First-choice Colours: Black and amber striped shirts; black and amber shorts; black and amber stockings.

Alcide, C 17	French, J .... 9(6)	Oakes, A 19
Bolder, A .... –(1)	Gage, K .... 2(1)	Peacock, R 13 (1)
Bonner, M 1	Gibson, P 4	Perry, J .... 7(1)
Brabin, G 21	Greaves, M .... 18(7)	Rioch, G .... 10(3)
Brown, D .... 38(4)	Harrison, G 8	Saville, A 3
D'Auria, D 42	Hateley, M .... 8(4)	Swales, S .... 20(2)
Darby, D .... 4(4)	Hawes, S .... 18(1)	Whitney, J 21
Dewhurst, R .... 4(4)	Hocking, M .... 24(2)	Whittle, J 24
Dudley, C .... 4(3)	Joyce, W .... 28(1)	Whitworth, N 18
Edwards, M .... 28(2)	Mann, N .... 16(4)	Williams, G .... 24(1)
Ellington, L .... 3(3)	McGinty, B .... 22(10)	Wilson, S 23
Faulconbridge, C ...... 4(6)	Morley, B .... 1(11)	

League Goals (44): Brown 11, Brabin 4, D'Auria 4, McGinty 4, Alcide 3, Hateley 3, Dudley 2, Joyce 2, Peacock 2, Whitworth 2, Bonner 1, Hocking 1, Mann 1, Williams 1, Whitney 1, Whittle 1, Opponents 1.
Worthington Cup Goals (5): Brown 3, McGinty 1, Rioch 1. **F.A. Cup Goals (4):** Dewhurst 1, McGinty 1, Morley 1, Rioch 1. **Auto Windscreens Shield Goals (2):** D'Auria 1, Williams 1.
Player of Year: Justin Whittle. **Sponsors:** to be announced.
Average home League attendance 1998-99: 6,051. **Capacity for 1999-2000:** 12,500.
Record attendance: 55,019 v Manchester Utd. (F.A. Cup 6) 28 February 1949.

LEYTON ORIENT

Ground: Matchroom Stadium, Brisbane Road, Leyton, London E10 5NE.
Telephone: 0181 926 1111. **Clubcall:** 0891 121150. **Club Nickname:** O's.
First-choice Colours: Red and white shirts; black shorts; red stockings.

Ampadu, K 26 (3)	Joseph, M .... 34(1)	Omoyinmi, E .... 3(1)
Barrett, S 20	Joseph, R .... 13(7)	Raynor, P .... 1(3)
Beall, M .... 21(2)	Ling, M 44	Reinelt, R .... 2(5)
Canham, S .... 2(5)	Lockwood, M .... 36(1)	Richards, T .... 28(1)
Clark, S 40	McCormick, S .... 1(3)	Simba, A .... 15(3)
Finney, S .... 2(3)	McDougald, J .... 3(5)	Smith, D 37
Griffiths, C .... 21(3)	MacKenzie, C 26	Stimson, M 2
Harris, J .... 1(1)	Martin, J 1	Walschaerts, W 44
Hicks, S 29	Maskell, C .... 8(7)	Warren, N 10
Inglethorpe, A .... 15(7)	Morrison, D .... 7(16)	Watts, S .... 10(18)

Play-offs – Appearances: Barrett 3, Beall 3, Clark 3, Hicks 1(1), Inglethorpe –(2), Joseph M. 1, Joseph R. 3, Ling 3, Lockwood 3, Maskell –(2), Morrison –(1), Richards 3, Simba 3, Smith 3, Stimson 1(1), Watts 3.
League Goals (68): Simba 10, Smith 9, Griffiths 8, Richards 7, Watts 6, Clark 4, Inglethorpe 4, Ling 4, Lockwood 3, Morrison 3, Walschaerts 3, Beall 2, Ampadu 1, Harris 1, Omoyinmi 1, Opponents 2. **Play-off Goals:** None.
Worthington Cup Goals (4): Inglethorpe 1, Reinelt 1, Richards 1, Warren 1. **F.A. Cup Goals (8):** Richards 3, Walschaerts 2, Griffiths 1, Simba 1, Smith 1. **Auto Windscreens Shield Goals:** None.
Player of Year: Wim Walschaerts. **Sponsors:** Marchpole.
Average home League attendance 1998-99: 4,688. **Capacity for 1999-2000:** 13,500.
Record attendance: 34,345 v West Ham Utd. (F.A. Cup 4) 25 January 1964.

MANSFIELD TOWN

Ground: Field Mill, Quarry Lane, Mansfield.
Telephone: 01623 623567. **Clubcall:** 0891 121311. **Club Nickname:** Stags.
First-choice Colours : Amber and blue shirts; amber and blue shorts; blue stockings.

Adamson, C 2	Harper, S 45	Rose, J .... –(1)
Allardyce, C 6	Hassell, R .... 1(2)	Ryder, S .... 18(4)
Bowling I 37	Kerr, D .... 30(5)	Schofield, J .... 37(5)
Carruthers, M .... –(5)	L'Helgoualch, C ...... 3(1)	Sedlan, J .... 1(4)
Cherry, S 1	Linighan, D 10	Sisson, M .... –(1)
Christie, I .... 18(24)	Lormor, T .... 35(6)	Tallon, G .... 31(5)
Clarke, D .... 24(9)	Naylor, S 6	Walker, J .... 18(19)
Ford, T .... 39(3)	Peacock, L .... 42(3)	Williams, L .... 31(13)
Hackett, W .... 24(2)	Peters, M 37	Willis, A 10

League Goals (60): Peacock 17, Lormor 11, Christie 8, Harper 6, Clarke 5, Ford 2, Kerr 2, Ryder 2, Williams 2, L'Helgoualch 1, Peters 1, Tallon 1, Walker 1, Opponents 1.
Worthington Cup Goals (3): Christie 1, Clarke 1, Peters 1. **F.A. Cup Goals (3):** Lormor 2, Clarke 1. **Auto Windscreens Shield Goals (2):** Peacock 2.
Player of Year: Lee Peacock. **Sponsors:** Home – Ad-mag; Away – GMB.
Average home League attendance 1998-99: 2,963. **Capacity for 1999-2000:** 5,289.
Record attendance: 24,467 v Nott'm Forest (F.A. Cup 3). 10 January 1953.

PETERBOROUGH UNITED

Ground: London Road, Peterborough, Cambridge PE2 8AL.
Telephone: 01733 563947. **Clubcall:** 0891 121654. **Club Nickname:** Posh.
First-choice Colours: Blue shirts; white shorts; blue stockings.

Allardyce, C 4	Etherington, M .... 21(8)	Legg, A 5
Andrews, W .... 8(2)	Farrell, D .... 28(9)	Linton, D 8
Bodley, M 24	Forbes, S .... 1(2)	Martin, J .... –(4)
Broughton, D ...... 14(11)	Gill, M .... 22(4)	McKenzie, L 14
Butler, S .... 13(1)	Grazioli, G .... 21(13)	McMenamin, C .... 4(1)
Carruthers, M .... 13(1)	Green, F .... 3(3)	Payne, D .... 8(1)
Castle, S 26	Griemink, B 17	Quinn, J 7
Chapple, P 1	Hann, M .... –(4)	Rennie, D 9
Cleaver, C .... –(2)	Hanlon, R .... –(3)	Rowe, Z .... –(7)
Connor, D 2	Hooper, D .... 36(2)	Scott, R .... 19(8)
Davies, S 43	Houghton, S .... 7(1)	Shields, A .... 6(3)
De Souza, M 3	Inman, N .... 1(2)	Tyler, M 27
Drury, A .... 39(1)	Koogi, A .... –(1)	Wicks, M 11
Edwards, A 41		

League Goals (72): Grazioli 15, McKenzie 8, Broughton 7, Quinn 5, Andrews 5, Scott 4, Davies 4, Farrell 4, Castle 4, Etherington 3, Carruthers 2, Butler 2, Edwards 2, Hooper 2, Houghton 1, Inman 1, Hanlon 1, Green 1, Opponents 1.
Worthington Cup Goals (1): Carruthers 1. **F.A. Cup Goals:** None. **Auto Windscreens Shield Goals (4):** Edwards 1, McKenzie 1, Broughton 1, Butler 1.
Player of Year: Simon Davies. **Sponsors:** to be announced.
Average home League attendance 1998-99: 5,306. **Capacity for 1999-2000:** 15,500.
Record attendance: 30,096 v Swansea City (F.A. Cup 5) 20 February 1965.

PLYMOUTH

Ground: Home Park, Plymouth, Devon PL2 3DQ.
Telephone: 01752 562561 **Clubcall:** 0839 442270. **Club Nickname:** Pilgrims.
First-choice Colours: Green and black shirts; green shorts; green, black and white stockings.

Ashton, J .... 22(3)	Ford, L .... –(1)	McCall, S .... 14(3)
Barlow, M 45	Forinton, H .... 8(1)	McCarthy, S .... 14(2)
Barrett, A .... –(1)	Gibbs, P 27	McGovern, B .... –(2)
Bastow, D .... 22(8)	Gritton, M .... –(2)	Phillips, L .... 8(7)
Beswetherick, J ...... 18(4)	Guinan, S 11	Power, L .... 7(9)
Branston, G 8	Hargreaves, C .... 30(2)	Sale, M 8
Collins, S 40	Heathcote, M 43	Sheffield, J 39
Crittenden, N .... 15(1)	Jean, E .... 21(8)	Sweeney, T .... 6(7)
Crowe, G .... 3(8)	Marker, N 4	Taylor, C 6
Dungey, J 7	Marshall, D .... 25(3)	Wills, K .... –(2)
Edmondson, D 4	Mauge, R .... 31(1)	Wotton, P .... 32(4)
Flash, R .... 4(1)		

League Goals (58): Marshall 12, Guinan 7, Barlow 5, Forinton 3, Gibbs 3, Heathcote 3, Jean 3, Mauge 3, McCarthy 3, Bastow 2, Collins 2, Hargreaves 2, Branston 1, Crowe 1, Phillips 1, Sale 1, Sweeney 1, Wotton 1, Taylor 1, Opponents 3.
Worthington Cup Goals (3): McCarthy 2, Jean 1. **F.A. Cup Goals (3):** Heathcote 1, Sweeney 1, Wotton 1. **Auto Windscreens Shield Goals:** None.
Player of Year: Mick Heathcote. **Sponsors:** to be announced.
Average home League attendance 1998-99: 5,323. **Capacity for 1999-2000:** 19,200.
Record attendance: 42,684 v Aston Villa (Div. 2) 10 October 1936.

ROCHDALE

Ground: Spotland Stadium, Wilbutts Lane, Rochdale, Lancashire, OL11 5DS.
Telephone: 01706 644648. **Clubcall:** 0891 555858. **Club Nickname:** The Dale.
First-choice Colours: Blue shirts; blue shorts with white trim; blue stockings.

Bailey, M 12 (7)	Hicks, G 1	Morris, A 25
Barlow, A 25 (4)	Hill, K 33	Painter, R 35 (5)
Bayliss, D 22 (3)	Holt, M .... 17(6)	Peake, J .... 36(2)
Bryson, I 31 (8)	Johnson, A .... 13(3)	Priestley, P 1
Carden, P 24 (1)	Jones, G .... 11(9)	Sparrow, A .... 21(4)
De Souza, M 5	Lancashire, G .... 7(4)	Stoker, G .... 11(1)
Diaz, I 12 (2)	Leonard, M .... 2(6)	Stokes, D .... 10(1)
Edwards, N 45	Lydiate, J 14	Stuart, M .... 9(10)
Farrell, A 36 (2)	Monington, M 37	Williams, S .... 11(3)
Gray, D .... –(3)		

League Goals (42) : Holt 7, Morris 7, Painter 6, Peake 5, Lancashire 3, Monington 3, Diaz 2, Sparrow 2, Bailey 1, Barlow 1, Bayliss 1, Hill 1, Lydiate 1, Stoker 1, Williams 1.
Worthington Cup Goals: None. **F.A. Cup Goals (3):** Bryson 2, Monington 1. **Auto Windscreens Shield Goals (4) :** Holt 1, Jones 1, Monington 1, Morris 1.

Player of Year: Mark Monington . **Sponsors:** Carcraft.
Average home League attendance 1998-99: 2,125. **Capacity for 1999 – 2000:** 9,195.
Record attendance: 24,231 v Notts Co. (F.A. Cup 2) 10 December 1949.

ROTHERHAM UNITED

Ground: Millmoor, Rotherham, S60 1HR.
Telephone: 01709 512434. **Clubcall:** 09068 121637. **Club Nickname:** Merry Millers.
First-choice Colours: Red shirts; white shorts; white stockings.

Beech, C 24	Jackson, J 2	Scott, R .... 4(1)
Berry, T .... 10(6)	Knill, A .... 34(1)	Strodder, G 3
Bos, G .... 1(1)	Martindale, G .... 6(4)	Thompson, S .... 27(5)
Dillon, P .... 24(1)	Monkhouse, A .... –(5)	Tracey, R .... –(3)
Fortune-West, L 19	Pollitt, M 45	Varty, W 14
Garner, D 39	Raven, P 11	Warne, P 18
Glover, L .... 18(1)	Richardson, N .... 4(1)	Warner, V 22
Hudson, D .... 19(7)	Roscoe, A .... 26(11)	Whelan, P 13
Hurst, P .... 30(1)	Sedgwick, C .... 24(9)	White, J .... 17(8)
Ingledow, J .... 15(6)	Scott, G 14	Williams, M .... 10(1)

Play-offs – Appearances: Dillon 2, Fortune-West 2, Hudson 2, Hurst 2, Knill 2, Pollitt 2, Roscoe 2, Sedgwick –(1), Scott R 2, Thompson 2, Varty 2, Warne 2, Williams –(2).
League Goals (79): Fortune-West 12, Glover 10, Warne 8, Thompson 5, White 5, Garner 4, Hudson 4, Roscoe 4, Whelan 4, Knill 3, Sedgwick 3, Berry 2, Hurst 2, Ingledow 2, Martindale 2, Raven 2, Whelan 2, Dillon 1, Jackson 1, Monkhouse 1, Scott R 1, Warner 1. **Play-off Goals:** None.
Worthington Cup Goals: None. **F.A. Cup Goals (8):** Garner 2, Glover 2, Berry 1, Hudson 1, Hurst 1, Warne 1. **Auto Windscreens Shield Goals:** None.
Player of Year: Mike Pollitt/Steve Thompson (joint). **Sponsors:** One 2 One.
Average home League attendance 1998-1999: 3,988. **Capacity for 1999-2000:** 11,500.
Record attendance: 25,000 v Sheffield Wed. (Div. 2) 26 January 1952. 25,000 v Sheffield Wed. (Div. 2) 13 December 1952.

SCARBOROUGH

Ground: The McCain Stadium, Seamer Road, Scarborough, North Yorkshire YO12 4HF.
Telephone: 01723 375094. **Clubcall:** 0891 121650. **Club Nickname:** Borough.
First-choice Colours: White shirts; white shorts; white stockings; all with red and green trim.

Atkinson, G 16	Jackson, R .... 19(1)	Radigan, N .... 4(5)
Atkinson, P .... 22(4)	Jones, N .... 8(1)	Rennison, S 15
Brodie, S 43	Kay, J .... 23(1)	Renshaw, I .... –(1)
Bullimore, W .... 33(2)	Lydiate, J .... 26(1)	Roberts, D 18
Campbell, N .... 3(8)	McAuley, S .... 6(1)	Robinson, L .... 17(12)
Carr, G .... 5(4)	McNaughton, M ..... 22(9)	Russell, M .... 19(17)
Dablesteen, T 5	Marinkov, A 22	Saville, A .... –(2)
Elliott, A 20	Milbourne, I .... 2(14)	Tate, C .... 18(7)
Goodlad, M 3	Mountfield, D .... 5(1)	Todd, A .... –(1)
Greenacre, C .... 10(2)	Naisbett, P 2	Weaver, L 6
Hodges, G 1	Parks, A 15	Williams, G 17
Hoyland, J 44	Porter, G .... 11(2)	Worrall, J .... 25(6)

League Goals (50): Brodie 12, Tate 12, Marinkov 4, Roberts 3, Hoyland 3, Robinson 3, Russell 3, Williams 2, Greenacre 2, Atkinson 1, Bullimore 1, Dablesteen 1, Lydiate 1, McNaughton 1, Rennison 1.
Worthington Cup Goals: None. **F.A. Cup Goals (1):** Williams 1. **Auto Windscreens Shield Goals:** None.
Player of Year: Jamie Hoyland. **Sponsors:** Arnott Insurance.

SCUNTHORPE UNITED

Ground: Glanford Park, Doncaster Road, Scunthorpe, North Lincolnshire, DN15 8TD.
Telephone: 01724 848077. **Clubcall:** 0891 121652. **Club Nickname:** Iron.
First-choice Colours: Sky blue and claret shirts; white shorts; white stockings.

Atkinson, G .... –(1)	Forrester, J 46	McAuley, S .... 16(1)
Bull, G .... 4(20)	Gayle, J .... 36(1)	Sheldon, G .... 5(6)
Calvo-Garcia, A ..... 42(1)	Harsley, P .... 32(2)	Stamp, D .... 5(20)
Clarke, T 22	Hope, C 46	Stanton, N .... 3(1)
Dawson, A 24	Housham, S .... 11(5)	Walker, J .... 40(1)
Evans, T 24	Logan, R .... 38(3)	Wilcox, R .... 24(4)
Eyre, J 41	Marshall, L .... 5(14)	Witter, A 14
Fickling, A .... 28(1)		

Play-offs – Appearances: Bull –(1), Calvo-Garcia 3, Clarke 2, Dawson 3, Evans 1, Eyre 2, Fickling 1, Forrester 3, Gayle 3, Harsley 2, Hope 3, Housham 1(2), Logan 2, Sheldon 1(1), Stamp –(1), Walker 3, Wilcox 3.
League Goals (69): Forrester 20, Forrester 15, Calvo-Garcia 9, Logan 6, Hope 5, Gayle 4, Stamp 4, Marshall 1, Sheldon 1, Walker 1, Wilcox 1, Opponents 2. **Play-off Goals (4):** Sheldon 2, Calvo-Garcia 1, Dawson 1.
Worthington Cup Goals (1): Forrester 1. **F.A. Cup Goals (6):** Forrester 2, Eyre 2, Harsley 1, Housham 1. **Auto Windscreens Shield Goals (1):** Walker 1.
Player of Year: Alex Calvo-Garcia. **Sponsors:** Motek.
Average home League attendance 1998-99: 3,741. **Capacity for 1999-2000:** 9,183.
Record attendance: (Glanford Park) 8,775 v Rotherham Utd. (Div. 4) 1 May 1989; (Old Show Ground) 23,935 v Portsmouth (F.A. Cup 4) 30 January 1954.

SHREWSBURY

Ground: Gay Meadow, Shrewsbury, SY2 5AL.
Telephone: 01743 360111. **Clubcall:** 0891 121194. **Club Nickname:** Shrews.
First-choice Colours: to be announced.

Beavers, P 2	Hanmer, G 46	Seabury, K 44
Berkley, A 41	Hayfield, M .... 1(1)	Steele, L .... 33(5)
Brown, M .... 15(19)	Herbert, C .... 6(2)	Thompson, G 1
Cooksey, S 2	Jagielka, S .... 13(18)	Tretton, A .... 22(1)
Craven, D .... 6(4)	Jobling, K 41	Whelan, S .... 8(1)
Drysdale, L 2	Jones, M .... –(1)	White, D .... 7(4)
Edwards, P 43	Kerrigan, S .... 32(5)	Wilding, P 42
Evans, P 32	Preece, R .... 16(4)	Winstanley, M 8
Gayle, B 43	Rutherford, M .... –(3)	

League Goals (52): Steele 13, Kerrigan 10, Berkley 8, Evans 6, Seabury 5, Brown 2, Preece 2, Gayle 1, Jagielka 1, Jobling 1, Opponents 3.
Worthington Cup Goals (4): Evans 3, Jobling 1. **F.A. Cup Goals:** None. **Auto Windscreens Shield Goals:** None.
Player of Year: Paul Edwards. **Sponsors:** Patrick.
Average home League attendance 1998-99: 2,575. **Capacity for 1999-2000:** 8,000.
Record attendance: 18,917 v Walsall (Div. 3) 26 April 1961.

SOUTHEND

Ground: Roots Hall, Victoria Avenue, Southend on Sea, Essex SS2 6NQ
Telephone: 01702 304050. **Clubcall:** 0839 664444.
First-choice Colours: Blue shirts; white shorts; blue stockings.

Beard, M .... 36(1)	Fitzpatrick, T .... 7(16)	Margetson, M 32
Booty, M .... 18(2)	Gooding, M .... 19(4)	McGavin, S .... 4(7)
Burns, A .... 26(5)	Hails, J 11	Morley, D .... 26(1)
Capleton, M 14	Harris, A 1	Newman, R 36
Campbell, N .... 9(3)	Hodges, L 10	Patterson, M 5
Clarke, A .... 14(10)	Houghton, S .... 22(1)	Rapley, K 9
Coleman, S .... 41(1)	Hunter, B 5	Roach, N .... 7(1)
Conlon, B .... 28(6)	Iorfa, D .... –(2)	Roget, L .... 11(3)
Coyne, C .... –(1)	Jones, N .... 5(12)	Stimson, M 17
De Souza, M 2	Livett, S .... 19(4)	Unger, L 14
Dublin, K .... 6(3)	Maher, K 34	Whyte, D .... 14(4)

League Goals (52): Newman 7, Conlon 7, Fitzpatrick 5, Burns 5, Rapley 4, Maher 4, Coleman 4, Clarke 3, Houghton 3, Whyte 2, Hunter 2, Campbell 2, Hodges 1, Hails 1, Roach 1, Livett 1.
Worthington Cup Goals (2): Clarke 1, Newman 1. **F.A. Cup Goals:** None. **Auto Windscreens Shield Goals (1):** Maher 1.
Player of Year: Mark Beard. **Sponsors:** Progressive Printing (UK) Ltd.
Average home League attendance 1998-99: 4,317 **Capacity for 1999-2000:** 12,306
Record attendance: 31,033 v Liverpool (F.A. Cup 3) 10 January 1979.

SWANSEA CITY

Ground: Vetch Field, Swansea, SA1 3SU
Telephone: 01792 474114. **Clubcall:** 0891 543123. **Club Nickname:** The Swans.
First-choice Colours: White shirts; white shorts; white stockings; all with black and maroon trim.

Alsop, J .... 37(4)	Freestone, R 38	O'Leary, K .... 17(1)
Appleby, R .... 36(3)	Gregg, M 5	Phillips, G .... –(1)
Bird, A .... 8(20)	Howard, M .... 38(1)	Price, J .... 25(3)
Bound, M 45	Jenkins, L .... 6(6)	Roberts, S .... 15(17)
Casey, R .... 5(5)	Jones, J 3	Smith, J 42
Clode, M 2	Jones, S .... 31(1)	Thomas, M .... 26(4)
Coates, J .... 30(3)	Lacey, D .... 7(5)	Walker, K 1
Cusack, N .... 42(1)	Newhouse, A .... 5(1)	Watkin, S .... 40(3)
Davies, J .... –(1)	O'Gorman, D .... 2(3)	

Play-offs – Appearances: Alsop 2, Appleby –(2), Bird 1(1), Bound 2, Coates 2, Cusack 2, Freestone 2, Howard 2, Jones S 2, O'Leary –(1), Price –(1), Roberts 2, Smith 2, Thomas 2, Watkin 1.
League Goals (56): Watkin 17, Alsop 10, Price 4, Smith 4, Appleby 3, Bird 3, Roberts 3, Thomas 3, Bound 2, Jones S 2, O'Leary 2, Casey 1, Cusack 1, Howard 1. **Play-off Goals (2):** Bird 1, Bound 1.
Worthington Cup Goals (1): Cusack 1. **F.A. Cup Goals (6):** Thomas 2, Alsop 1, Appleby 1, Price 1, Smith 1. **Auto Windscreens Shield Goals (4):** Bird 2, Appleby 1, Smith 1.
Player of Year: Matthew Bound. **Sponsors:** Silver Shield.
Average home League attendance 1998-99: 5,333. **Capacity for 1999-2000:** 11,837.
Record attendance: 32,786 v Arsenal (F.A. Cup 4) 17 February 1968.

TORQUAY UNITED

Ground: Plainmoor, Torquay, Devon, TQ1 3PS.
Telephone: 01803 328666. **Clubcall:** None. **Club Nickname:** Gulls.
First-choice Colours: to be announced.

Aggrey, J .... 22(3)	Forrester, M .... 1(4)	Hapgood, L .... 11(6)
Bedeau, A .... 28(8)	Gregg, M 11	Harries, P 5
Clayton, G 15	Gurney, A 20	Healy, B .... 16(3)
Donaldson, O .... 7(5)	Hadley, S .... –(2)	Herrera, R .... 39(1)

356

Hill, K .... 22(13)
Jermyn, M .... –(1)
Leadbitter, C 37
Lee, A .... 6(1)
MacFarlane, A .... 6(10)
McGorry, B .... 31(3)
Monk, G 6
Neil, G .... 6(1)

Nicholls, J .... 5(1)
Partridge, S 30
Platts, M .... 7(1)
Robinson, J 29
Russell, L 9
Simb, J-P .... 3(6)
Southall, N 25
Thomas, W 44

Tully, S .... 31(6)
Veysey, K 10
Waddle, C 7
Watson, A 8
Williams, E 7
Witter, A 4
Worthington, M .... –(1)

League Goals (47): Partridge 12, Bedeau 9, Hill 5, Williams 5, MacFarlane 3, Healey 2, Lee 2, Tully 2, Donaldson 1, Gurney 1, Leadbitter 1, McGorry 1, Robinson 1, Simb 1, Thomas 1.
Worthington Cup Goals (2): Bedeau 1, Thomas 1. **F.A. Cup Goals (1):** Partridge 1. **Auto Windscreens Shield Goals (2):** Lee 1, Partridge 1.
Player of Year: Neville Southall. **Sponsors:** Westward Developments.
Average home League attendance 1998-99: 2,600. **Capacity for 1999-2000:** 6,003.
Record attendance: 21,908 v Huddersfield Town (F.A. Cup 4) 29 January 1955.

SCOTTISH LEAGUE ROLL CALL

APPEARANCES & SCORERS 1997-98

Figures in brackets = appearances as substitute

PREMIER LEAGUE

ABERDEEN

Ground: Pittodrie Stadium, Aberdeen. **Capacity:** 22,199 (all-seated).
Telephone: 01224 650400. **Colours:** Red with white. **Nickname:** Dons.

Anderson, R .... 13(3)
Bernard, P .... 8(1)
Bett, B 1
Buchan, J .... 19(4)
Dodds, W 6
Dow, A .... 22(3)
Gillies, R .... 4(7)
Good, I .... –(1)
Hamilton, J .... 6(1)
Hart, M .... 5(9)

Hignett, C 13
Inglis, J .... 16(1)
Jess, E 36
Kiriakov, I .... 17(5)
Leighton, J 22
Mayer, A 13
Newell, M .... 14(9)
Notman, A .... –(2)
Pepper, N .... 7(3)
Perry, M 32

Rowson, D .... 18(4)
Smith, G 30
Stillie, D 8
Warner, A 6
Whyte, D 35
Winters, R 28
Wyness, D .... 6(8)
Young, Darren 11
Young, Derek .... –(4)

League Goals (43): Jess 14, Winters 12, Perry 4, Hignett 2, Dodds 2, Inglis 1, Wyness 1, Bernard 1, Hamilton 1, Opponents 1.
League Cup Goals (3): Dodds 3. **Scottish Cup Goals:** None.

CELTIC

Ground: Celtic Park, Glasgow. **Capacity:** 60,294 (all seated).
Telephone: 0141 556 2611. **Colours:** Green and white. **Nickname:** Bhoys.

Annoni, E .... 9(5)
Blinker, R .... 13(2)
Boyd, T 31
Brattbakk, H .... 16(8)
Burchill, M .... 5(16)

Burley C .... 20(1)
Corr, B .... –(1)
Donnelly, S .... 20(3)
Gould, J 28
Hannah, D .... 5(4)

Healy, C .... 2(1)
Jackson, D .... 4(2)
Johnson, T 3
Kerr, S 4
Lambert, P 33

Larsson, H 35
Mackay, M 1
Mahe, S 24
Marshall, S .... 1(1)
McBride, J-P .... –(1)
McConidchie, A 1

McKinlay, T .... 11(7)
McNamara, J .... 15(1)
Mjallby, J 17
Moravcik, L 14
O'Donnell, P .... 13(2)
Rieper, M 7

Riseth, V .... 26(1)
Stubbs, A .... 22(1)
Viduka, M .... 8(1)
Warner, A 3
Wieghorst, M .... 5(2)

League Goals (84): Larsson 29, Burley 9, Burchill 9, Moravcik 6, Donnelly 5, Viduka 5, Brattbakk 5, Blinker 4, Johnson 3, Riseth 3, O'Donnell 2, Mackay 1, Stubbs 1, Lambert 1, Mjallby 1.
League Cup Goals: None. **Scottish Cup Goals (12):** Larsson 5, Viduka 3, Blinker 1, Brattbakk 1, O'Donnell 1, Opponents 1. **Europe Goals (10):** Larsson 4, Brattbakk 2, Donnelly 1, Jackson 1, O'Donnell 1, Stubbs 1.

DUNDEE

Ground: Dens Park Stadium, Dundee. **Capacity:** 12,085 (all-seated).
Telephone: 01382 826104. **Colours:** Navy blue and white. **Nickname:** Dark Blues.

Adamczuk, D .... 24(2)
Anderson, I .... 17(11)
Annand, E .... 19(10)
Bayne, G .... –(2)
Boyack, S 8
Coyne, T .... 8(8)
Douglas, R 35
Falconer, W .... 31(2)
Fleming, D 1
Garcin, E .... 2(1)
Grady, J .... 20(6)

Grant, B .... –(4)
Hunter, G 3
Irvine, B 33
Langfield, J .... 1(1)
Maddison, L 21
Magee, D .... 1(1)
McCormick, S .... –(1)
McInally, J .... 14(1)
McSkimming, S .... 25(4)
Miller, W 26

O'Driscoll, J .... –(1)
Pounewatchy, S ..... 2(1)
Rae, G .... 23(7)
Raeside, R .... 19(2)
Robertson, H .... 9(1)
Rogers, D .... 7(4)
Sharp, L .... 4(2)
Smith, B .... 29(4)
Strachan, G .... 4(2)
Tweed, S 10

League Goals (36): Annand 9, Adamczuk 6, Falconer 4, Anderson 3, Grady 3, Irvine 3, McSkimming 2, Boyack 2, Rae 1, Sharp 1, Tweed 1, Opponents 1.
League Cup Goals: None. **Scottish Cup Goals (1):** Annand 1.

DUNDEE UNITED

Ground: Tannadice Park, Dundee. **Capacity:** 14,209 (all-seated).
Telephone: 01382 833166. **Colours:** Tangerine and black. **Nickname:** The Terrors.

Boli, R 3
Combe, A 10
Devos, J .... 23(2)
Dijkstra, S .... 26(1)
Dodds, W .... 29(1)
Dolan, J .... 4(1)
Duffy, C .... 12(3)
Easton, C .... 28(2)
Eustace, J .... 8(3)
Jenkins, I .... 5(1)
Jonsson, S .... 12(2)
Hannah, D 13

Malpas, M 31
Mathie, A .... 13(9)
McConalogue, S ..... –(1)
McCulloch, S 9
McLaren, A .... 3(5)
McLaughlin, B .... 1(2)
McNally, M .... 4(1)
McSwegan, G 5
Miller, J .... 14(10)
Mols, T 11
Murray, N .... 2(1)
Olofsson, K .... 32(2)

Partridge, D .... –(1)
Pascual, B 16
Patterson, D .... 17(2)
Paterson, J .... 8(7)
Pedersen, E 6
Skoldmark, M ...... 22(3)
Thompson, S .... 5(10)
Valeriani, J .... –(1)
Winters, R .... 1(2)
Worrall, D .... 3(1)
Zetterlund, L .... 20(1)

League Goals (37): Dodds 17, Olofsson 7, McSwegan 3, Miller 2, Easton 1, Eustace 1, Hannah 1, Jonsson 1, Mathie 1, Thompson 1, Winters 1, Zetterlund 1.
League Cup Goals (2): Boli 1, McSwegan 1. **Scottish Cup Goals (8):** Olofsson 3, Dodds 1, Duffy 1, Murray 1, Patterson 1, Skoldmark 1.

DUNFERMLINE ATHLETIC

Ground: East End Park, Dunfermline. **Capacity:** 12,565 (all-seated).
Telephone: 01383 724295. **Colours:** Black and white. **Nickname:** Pars.

Amaral Neto, E .... 5(4)	French, H .... 15(6)	Nish, C .... –(2)
Boyle, S 1	Graham, D .... 14(7)	Petrie, S .... 19(11)
Britton, G .... 13(8)	Huxford, R .... 22(3)	Shields, G 36
Butler, L 35	Ireland, C .... 21(2)	Squires, J .... 19(2)
Coyle, O 11	Johnson, G 18	Tod, A .... 24(1)
Dair, J .... 9(1)	Linighan, D 1	Smith, A .... 29(6)
Den Bieman, I .... –(2)	Macdonald, W .... –(1)	Shaw, G .... 10(8)
Dolan, J 10	Martin, C .... 2(1)	Templeman, C .... 5(7)
Faulconbridge, C .... 1(5)	McCulloch, S 19	Thomson, S .... 20(1)
Ferguson, D .... 18(3)	McGroarty, C .... 3(1)	Westwater, I 1
Fraser, J .... 2(4)	Millar, M .... 13(8)	

League Goals (28): Smith 8, Britton 2, French 2, Graham 2, Petrie 2, Shaw 2, Squires 2, Thomson 2, Amaral Neto 1, Boyle 1, Coyle 1, McCulloch 1, Millar 1, Tod 1.
League Cup Goals: None. **Scottish Cup Goals (2):** Smith 2.

HEART OF MIDLOTHIAN

Ground: Tynecastle Stadium, Edinburgh. **Capacity:** 18,000 (all-seated).
Telephone: 0131 200 7200. **Colours:** Maroon. **Nickname:** The Jam Tarts.

Adam, S .... 28(1)	James, K .... 1(3)	Murie, D .... –(4)
Berthe, M 1	Jenkinson, L .... 3(2)	Murray, G .... 18(3)
Callaghan, S 2	Kirk, A .... –(5)	Naysmith, G .... 23(3)
Cameron, C .... 10(1)	Lilley, D .... 3(1)	O'Neill, K .... –(3)
Carricondo, J .... 1(10)	Locke, G .... 22(3)	Pressley, S .... 29(1)
Flögel, T .... 18(2)	Makel, L .... 6(8)	Quitongo, J .... 5(7)
Fulton, S 27	McCann, N 8	Ritchie, P 29
Guerin, V .... 9(10)	McKenzie, R 10	Rousset, G 26
Hamilton, J .... 20(5)	McKinnon, R .... 14(2)	Salvatori, S .... 11(1)
Holmes, D .... 1(5)	McPherson, D .... 17(1)	Severin, S .... 5(2)
Jackson, D 9	McSwegan, G .... 17(4)	Weir, D 23

League Goals (44): Adam 10, McSwegan 7, Hamilton 6, Cameron 6, McCann 3, Flögel 2, Fulton 2, Guerin 1, Jackson 1, Lilley 1, Locke 1, Makel 1, Pressley 1, Ritchie 1, Weir 1.
League Cup Goals (5): Adam 1, Fulton 1, Hamilton 1, Holmes 1, McKinnon 1. **Scottish Cup Goals (1):** Hamilton 1. **Europe Goals (7):** Hamilton 2, Flogel 1, Fulton 1, Holmes 1, Makel 1, McCann 1.

KILMARNOCK

Ground: Rugby Park, Kilmarnock. **Capacity:** 18,128 (all-seated).
Telephone: 01563 545300. **Colours:** White and blue. **Nickname:** Killie.

Bagan, D. .... 1(4)	Kerr, D. 16	Mitchell, A. .... 27(5)
Baker, M. 23	Lauchlan, J. 14	Montgomerie, R. 22
Burke, A. .... 2(17)	MacPherson, A. 31	Nevin, P. .... 2(1)
Durrant, I. 36	Mahood, A. .... 16(12)	Reilly, M. .... 17(1)
Hamilton, S. 5	Marshall, G. 36	Roberts, M. .... 9(13)
Henry, J. .... 7(4)	McCoist, A. .... 16(10)	Vareille, J. .... 20(3)
Holt, G. 33	McCutcheon, G. ..... 2(11)	Wright, P. .... 25(8)
Innes, C. 4	McGowne, K. 32	

League Goals (47): McCoist 7, Wright 6, Vareille 5, Durrant 4, McGowne 4, Mitchell 4, Henry 3, Holt 3, Roberts 3, Mahood 2, McCutheon 2, MacPherson 1, Innes 1, Nevin 1, Opponents 1.
League Cup Goals (3): Wright 2, McCoist 1. **Scottish Cup Goals:** None. **Europe Goals (2):** Mahood 1, McGowne 1.

MOTHERWELL

Ground: Fir Park, Motherwell. **Capacity:** 13,742 (all-seated).
Telephone: 01698 333333. **Colours:** Claret and amber. **Nickname:** The Well.

Adams, D .... 11(15)	Halliday, S .... 2(2)	Nicholas, S .... 1(6)
Bacque, H ....–(1)	Kaven, M 16	Nyyssonen, K 3
Brannan, G 25	Matthaei, R .... 14(3)	Ramsay, D ....–(4)
Christie, K .... 4(1)	May, E .... 10(2)	Ross, I .... 8(4)
Coyle, O 26	McClair, B .... 8(3)	Shivute, E ....–(1)
Craigan, S .... 6(4)	McCulloch, L ...... 14(12)	Spencer, J 21
Denham, G ....–(1)	McGowan, J 32	Stirling, J .... 4(1)
Doesburg, M .... 29(1)	McMillan, S 30	Teale, S 29
Goodman, D 8	Michels, J .... 7(3)	Thomas, A 10
Goram, A 13	Miller, G .... 1(3)	Valakari, S 35
Gower, M .... 8(1)	Nevin, P .... 14(16)	Woods, S 7

League Goals (35): Coyle 7, Spencer 7, Brannan 5, Adams 3, McCulloch 3, McMillan 2, Goodman 1, Gower 1, McGowan 1, Stirling 1, Nicholas 1, Nyyssonen 1, Ramsay 1, Teale 1.
League Cup Goals (1): Halliday 1. **Scottish Cup Goals (5):** Brannan 1, Coyle 1, McCulloch 1, Thomas 1, Opponents 1.

RANGERS

Ground: Ibrox Stadium, Glasgow. **Capacity:** 50,411 (all-seated).
Telephone: 0141 427 8500. **Colours:** Royal blue. **Nickname:** The Gers.

Albertz, J .... 33(1)	Hendry, C .... 16(3)	Porrini, S 35
Amato, G .... 13(7)	Johansson, J .... 13(12)	Reyna, C 6
Amoruso, L 33	Kanchelskis, A .... 29(1)	Riccio, L ....–(1)
Charbonnier, L 11	Klos, S 18	Rozental, S ....–(3)
Durie, G .... 1(4)	McCann, N .... 15(4)	Stensaas, S 1
Feeney, L ....–(1)	McInnes, D ....–(7)	Thern, J 1
Ferguson, B 23	Miller, C .... 2(14)	Van Bronckhorst, G 35
Ferguson, I .... 4(9)	Moore, C 8	Vidmar, A .... 26(2)
Gattuso, G .... 3(2)	Nicholson, B .... 3(3)	Wallace, R 34
Graham, D ....–(3)	Niemi, A 7	Wilson, S .... 7(5)
Guivarc'h, S .... 11(3)	Numan, A .... 8(2)	

League Goals (78): Wallace 18, Albertz 11, Johansson 8, Kanchelskis 8, Van Bronckhorst 7, Amato 6, Guivarc'h 5, McCann 5, Miller 3, Porrini 2, Amoruso 1, Ferguson B 1, Moore 1, Vidmar 1, Wilson 1.
League Cup Goals (13): Albertz 3, Wallace 2, Amato 1, Amoruso 1, Durie 1, Ferguson B 1, Ferguson I 1, Guivarc'h 1, Johansson 1, Miller 1. **Scottish Cup Goals (15):** Johansson 3, McCann 3, Wallace 3, Albertz 1, Amoruso 1, Guivarc'h 1, Kanchelskis 1, Van Bronckhorst 1, Vidmar 1. **Europe Goals (19):** Johansson 5, Albertz 4, Wallace 3, Amato 2, Van Bronckhurst 2, Gattuso 1, Kanchelskis 1, Porrini 1.

ST. JOHNSTONE

Ground: McDiarmid Park, Perth. **Capacity:** 10,673 (all-seated).
Telephone: 01738 459090. **Colours:** Royal blue and white. **Nickname:** The Saints.

Bollan, G .... 32(1)
Connolly, P .... 6(3)
Dasovic, N 31
Dods, D 34
Ferguson, A .... 2(1)
Grant, R .... 14(11)
Griffin, D .... 14(5)
Kane, P .... 33(1)
Kernaghan, A 26

Lowndes, N .... 12(17)
Main, A 34
McAnespie, K .... 8(10)
McBride, J-P .... 2(1)
McCluskey, S .... 5(2)
McMahon, G .... 13(6)
McQuillan, J .... 27(1)
O'Boyle, G .... 12(1)

O'Halloran, K .... 10(6)
O'Neil, J 33
Parker, K .... –(2)
Preston, A .... 8(7)
Scott, P .... 14(2)
Simao, M .... 20(6)
Weir, D .... 6(1)
Whiteford, A .... –(1)

League Goals (39): Bollan 4, Grant 4, Simao 4, Kane 3, Kernaghan 3, Dods 2, Lowndes 2, McAnespie 2, O'Boyle 2, O'Neil 2, Scott 2, Connolly 1, Dasovic 1, Griffin 1, McMahon 1, McQuillan 1, O'Halloran 1, Preston 1, Weir 1, Opponents 1.
League Cup Goals (12): Dasovic 2, Lowndes 2, O'Boyle 2, Connolly 1, Kane 1, McMahon 1, O'Halloran 1, O'Neil 1, Preston 1. **Scottish Cup Goals (6):** Grant 2, Dods 1, O'Neil 1, Scott 1, Simao 1.

FIRST DIVISION

AIRDRIEONIANS

Ground: Excelsior Stadium, Airdrie. **Capacity:** 10,166 (all-seated).
Telephone: 01236 622000. **Colours:** White and red. **Nickname:** Diamonds.

Black, K .... 30(1)
Brady, D .... –(1)
Cooper, S .... 25(2)
Easton, S .... 3(4)
Evans, G .... 21(5)
Farrell, D .... 20(4)
Farrell, G .... 6(12)
Greacen, S .... –(1)
Jack, P .... 21(1)

Johnston, F .... 26(5)
Mackay, G .... 4(6)
Martin, J 28
McCann, A .... 27(4)
McCloy, B .... 2(2)
McCormick, S .... 4(8)
McGrillen, P .... 20(3)
McGuire, D .... 2(2)
McKeown, S .... 2(11)

Moore, A .... 21(7)
Sandison, J .... 33(1)
Sissoko, H .... –(1)
Smith, A .... 23(2)
Stewart, A .... 31(1)
Taylor, S .... 8(4)
Thomson, S 8
Wilson, M 31

League Goals (42): Cooper 8, Black 7, Evans 6, McCann 4, Moore 4, McCormick 2, Taylor 2, Wilson 2, Farrell D 1, Farrell G 1, Johnston 1, McGrillen 1, McKeown 1, Sissoko 1, Opponents 1.
League Cup Goals (4): Moore 2, Wilson 2. **Scottish Cup Goals (1):** Cooper 1.

AYR UNITED

Ground: Somerset Park, Ayr. **Capacity:** 12,178.
Telephone: 01292 263435. **Colours:** White and black. **Nickname:** Honest Men.

Agnew, P .... 1(2)
Armstrong, G .... –(2)
Barrick, D 11
Bowman, G .... –(4)
Bradford, J .... 2(3)
Burns, G .... 4(6)
Campbell, M 9
Castilla, D 21
Craig, D 22
Crilly, M .... –(3)
Davies, J .... 27(2)

Dick, J .... 1(3)
Duthie, M .... –(5)
Ferguson, I .... 9(13)
Findlay, W .... 15(7)
Hamilton, B .... 2(1)
Horace, A .... –(4)
Hurst, G 30
Kelly, R .... 7(11)
Lyons, A .... 31(1)
Millen, A 34
Miller, C .... 4(2)

Nelson, C 15
Nolan, J .... –(1)
Reynolds, M .... 11(7)
Robertson, J 21
Scally, N 2
Stewart, D .... –(1)
Teale, G 23
Traynor, J .... 22(7)
Walker, A .... 31(2)
Welsh, S .... 24(1)
Winnie, D 13

League Goals (66): Hurst 18, Walker 15, Ferguson 8, Lyons 8, Teale 4, Davies 3, Craig 2, Findlay 2, Bradford 1, Burns 1, Kelly 1, Millen 1, Reynolds 1, Robertson 1.
League Cup Goals (8): Hurst 2, Armstrong 1, Davies 1, Lyons 1, Walker 1, Welsh 1, Opponents 1. **Scottish Cup Goals (5):** Walker 3, Lyons 1, Teale 1.

CLYDEBANK

Ground: to be confirmed. **Capacity:** to be confirmed.
Telephone: to be confirmed. **Colours:** White and red. **Nickname:** Bankies.

Anthony, M .... 9(4)	McDonald, C ...... 22(8)	Newland, R 1
Brannigan, K 31	McKelvie, D .... –(9)	Nicholls, D 34
Brown, A .... 1(14)	McKinstrey, J .... 7(2)	Ritchie, I .... 11(2)
Callaghan, S 5	McLaughlin, J 32	Robertson, A .... 7(4)
Dobie, S 6	McMillan, A .... 1(1)	Ross, S 3
Docherty, S .... 17(11)	McWilliams, D ...... 5(4)	Scott, C 28
Elliot, B 4	Miller, S .... 28(4)	Smith, T .... 20(1)
Gardner, R .... 24(11)	Morrison, S .... 2(1)	Taggart, M .... 25(10)
Inglis, N 1	Murdoch, S .... 13(3)	Teale, G .... 7(1)
Love, G 7	Naylor, R 1	Wishart, F 32
Lovering, P 12		

League Goals (36): McDonald 9, McLaughlin 3, Miller 3, Smith 3, Brannigan 2, Docherty 2, Elliot 2, Gardner 2, Taggart 2, Teale 2, Anthony 1, Brown 1, Love 1, McWilliams 1, Nicholls 1, Robertson 1.
League Cup Goals (1): McDonald 1. **Scottish Cup Goals (6):** Nicholls 2, Ritchie 2, Gardner 1, McMillan 1.

FALKIRK

Ground: Brockville Park, Falkirk. **Capacity:** 7,576.
Telephone: 01324 624121. **Colours:** Navy blue and white. **Nickname:** Bairns.

Corrigan, M .... 21(3)	James, K .... 11(2)	McStay, G .... 4(6)
Crabbe, S 36	Keith, M .... 27(2)	Morrison, S .... –(1)
Den Bieman, I 24	Kerr, M .... 1(1)	Moss, D .... 16(1)
Duffield, P .... 10(7)	Mathers, P 31	O'Hara, G 2
Hagen, D .... 9(3)	McAllister, K 35	Oliver, N .... 7(1)
Hamilton, B .... 12(4)	McCart, C .... 12(2)	Rennie, S 3
Henry, J .... 11(1)	McKee, C .... 2(2)	Seaton, A .... 16(8)
Hogarth, M 5	McKenzie, S .... 33(2)	Sinclair, D 23
Hutchison, G .... 24(9)	McQuilken, J .... 21(1)	

League Goals (60): Keith 17, Crabbe 10, Hutchison 6, McAllister 6, Henry 5, Moss 5, Corrigan 3, Duffield 3, Hamilton 2, McCart 1, McKenzie 1, McStay 1.
League Cup Goals (5): McKee 2, Crabbe 1, Keith 1, Oliver 1. **Scottish Cup Goals (6):** Moss 3, Crabbe 1, McAllister 1, Opponents 1.

GREENOCK MORTON

Ground: Cappielow Park, Greenock. **Capacity:** 14,891.
Telephone: 01475 723571. **Colours:** Royal blue and white. **Nickname:** Ton.

Aitken, S .... 19(4)	Foster, M .... 14(5)	Morrow, J .... 4(1)
Anderson, D 16	George, M .... 1(3)	Murie, D .... 6(1)
Anderson, J 33	Hawke, W .... 27(4)	Slavin, B .... 11(4)
Archdeacon, O 33	Juttla, J .... 4(4)	Thomas, K 22
Blaikie, A .... 3(9)	MacDonald, S .... –(1)	Twaddle, K 31
Blair, P .... –(2)	Matheson, R ...... 17(14)	Tweedie, G .... 2(1)
Collins, D 18	Maxwell, A 30	Whalen, S .... –(1)
Curran, H 33	McCormick, S .... 3(2)	Wright, K .... 10(6)
Duffield, P .... 2(1)	McPherson, C ...... 20(13)	Wylie, D 6
Fenwick, P 31		

League Goals (45): Thomas 9, Anderson J 6, Wright 6, Curran 5, Fenwick 5, Twaddle 5, Hawke 3, Anderson D 1, Blaikie 1, Matheson 1, McCormick 1, McPherson 1, Opponents 1.
League Cup Goals: None. **Scottish Cup Goals (8):** Archdeacon 2, Thomas 2, Twaddle 2, Anderson J 1, Matheson 1.

HAMILTON ACADEMICAL

Ground: Firhill Stadium, Glasgow. **Capacity:** 14,538.
Telephone: 01698 286103. **Colours:** Red and white. **Nickname:** Accies.

Berry, N .... 14(1)	Kerr, A .... 1(1)	Miller, C .... 7(1)
Bonnar, M .... –(1)	Krivokapic, M .... –(1)	Moore, M .... 3(9)
Clark, G .... 14(11)	Lynn, G 1	Muir, D .... –(1)
Cunnington, E 33	MacFarlane, I 15	Oliver, N 6
Davidson, W .... 3(1)	MacLaren, R .... 12(3)	Rajamaki, K .... 4(3)
Geraghty, M .... 18(5)	Martin, M .... 2(1)	Reid, C 6
Henderson, D 25	McAulay, I .... 21(3)	Renicks, S 32
Henderson, N .... 24(4)	McCormick, S .... 12(9)	Robertson, S 6
Hillcoat, C 25	McFarlane, D .... 5(10)	Tait, T .... 21(1)
Hillcoat, J 9	McGill, D 3	Thomson, S .... 33(1)
Kelly, R .... –(1)	McKenzie, P .... 13(5)	Wales, G .... 28(2)

League Goals (30): Wales 11, Geraghty 5, McCormick 4, Henderson D 3, Berry 1, Cunnington 1, McFarlane 1, Moore 1, Renicks 1, Tait 1, Thomson 1.
League Cup Goals (3): Geraghty 1, MacFarlane 1, Renicks 1. **Scottish Cup Goals (2):** Clark 1, Wales 1.

HIBERNIAN

Ground: Easter Road Stadium, Edinburgh. **Capacity:** 16,032 (all-seated).
Telephone: 0131 6612159. **Colours:** Green and white. **Nickname:** Hibees.

Anderson, D 6	Hartley, P .... 6(7)	Paatelainen, M .... 25(1)
Bannerman, S .... 2(10)	Holsgrove, P .... 9(9)	Paton, E .... 1(3)
Bottiglieri, E .... –(1)	Hughes, J .... 22(1)	Prenderville, B 13
Collins, D 16	Latapy, R 23	Reid, A .... –(1)
Crawford, S .... 28(7)	Lavety, B .... 9(18)	Renwick, M .... 15(1)
Dempsie, M .... 5(3)	Lovell, S .... 26(5)	Rougier, A .... 10(5)
Dennis, S .... 29(2)	Lovering, P 17	Sauzee, F 9
Dietrich, K 1	Marinkov, A 10	Shannon, R 1
Elliot, D 8	McGinlay, P .... 29(1)	Skinner, J 24
Gottskalksson, O 36	McManus, T .... –(1)	Smith, T .... 3(2)
Guggi, P .... 7(1)	Miller, K .... 5(2)	Tosh, P 1
Harper, K .... –(2)		

League Goals (84): Crawford 14, McGinlay 12, Paatelainen 12, Lovell 11, Latapy 6, Hartley 5, Dennis 3, Hughes 3, Guggi 2, Lavety 2, Prenderville 2, Sauzee 2, Skinner 2, Harper 1, Holsgrove 1, Lovering 1, Marinkov 1, Miller 1, Rougier 1, Opponents 2.
League Cup Goals (2): Crawford 1, Lovell 1. **Scottish Cup Goals (2):** Latapy 1, Lovering 1.

RAITH ROVERS

Ground: Stark's Park, Kirkcaldy. **Capacity:** 10,271 (all-seated).
Telephone: 01592 263514. **Colours:** Navy blue and white. **Nickname:** Rovers.

Andrews, M .... 19(5)	Brownlie, P .... 2(7)	Cormack, P 1
Bowman, D 23	Byers, K .... 10(5)	Dair, J 27
Britton, G 5	Cameron, I .... 26(2)	Dair, L .... –(2)
Browne, P .... 31(1)	Clark, A .... –(1)	Dargo, C .... 21(1)

Ellis, L .... 4(5)	McCulloch, G .... 23(8)	Robertson, G .... 3(3)
Fotheringham, G ...... 1(4)	McEwan, C .... 23(3)	Shields, P .... 6(8)
Fotheringham, K 26	McGeown, M 3	Smart, C .... 3(3)
Hartley, P 18	McInally, D 1	Stein, J .... 6(14)
Holmes, D .... 13(1)	McLeish, K .... 1(1)	Tosh, S .... 23(2)
Kirkwood, D .... 5(1)	McPherson, D .... 3(1)	Van de Kamp, G 33
Lennon, D .... 21(4)	McQuade, J .... 3(3)	Venables, R 2
Maughan, R 1	Nicol, K .... 1(1)	Wright, K .... 8(4)

League Goals (37): Dargo 8, Holmes 6, Cameron 5, Hartley 4, Dair J 3, Tosh 3, Wright 2, Andrews 1, Britton 1, Fotheringham K 1, McQuade 1, Stein 1, Opponents 1.
League Cup Goals (4): Dair J 1, Hartley 1, Shields 1, Wright 1. **Scottish Cup Goals:** None.

ST. MIRREN

Ground: St. Mirren Park, Paisley. **Capacity:** 14,935.
Telephone: 0141 8892558. **Colours:** Black and white. **Nickname:** Buddies.

Brown, T .... 23(3)	McNamee, D .... 30(1)	Prentice, A .... 1(5)
Cameron, A .... 3(8)	McQuilter, R 29	Robinson, R .... –(1)
Creaney, G .... 11(1)	McWhirter, N .... 24(1)	Roy, L 17
Drew, C .... 15(1)	Mendes, J .... 13(9)	Rudden, P .... 18(8)
Innes, C 9	Milne, D .... 7(2)	Scrimgour, D 19
Kerr, C .... 24(4)	Murray, H .... 27(2)	Turner, T .... 13(1)
McGarry, S .... 27(7)	Nicolson, I .... 24(6)	Walker, P .... –(1)
McLaughlin, B 23	O'Brien, B .... 17(5)	Yardley, M .... 22(13)

League Goals (42): Yardley 11, McGarry 8, Brown 4, Mendes 4, Nicolson 4, Creaney 3, Cameron 2, Kerr 2, McLaughlin 1, O'Brien 1, Opponents 2.
League Cup Goals (1): Brown 1. **Scottish Cup Goals (1):** Mendes 1.

STRANRAER

Ground: Stair Park, Stranraer. **Capacity:** 5,600.
Telephone: 01776 703271. **Colours:** Royal blue and white. **Nickname:** Blues.

Abbott, S .... 2(2)	George, D .... 17(1)	Meldrum, C 7
Adams, M .... –(2)	Hamilton, B 1	O'Neill, M 1
Archdeacon, P 4	Harty, I .... 13(8)	Ronald, P .... 25(4)
Bell, R .... 12(8)	Jenkins, A .... 9(10)	Skilling, M .... 25(3)
Black, T 26	Johnstone, D .... 21(3)	Smith, J 4
Blaikie, A .... 4(1)	Kinnaird, P 21	Walker, P .... 8(1)
Brownlie, P 2	Knox, K .... 25(1)	Watson, P 36
Bruce, G 11	Matthews, G 18	Wright, F .... –(2)
Campbell, M 26	McIntyre, P .... 22(1)	Young, G .... 17(10)
Friels, G .... 9(10)	McMartin, G 13	Young, J .... 13(2)
Galloway, G .... 4(4)		

League Goals (29): Ronald 5, Young G 5, Campbell 3, Black 2, George 2, Harty 2, Knox 2, Young J 2, Bell 1, Friels 1, Jenkins 1, Kinnaird 1, Skilling 1, Walker 1.
League Cup Goals (1): Ronald 1. **Scottish Cup Goals (2):** Friels 1, Knox 1.

SECOND DIVISION

ALLOA ATHLETIC

Ground: Recreation Park, Alloa. **Capacity:** 3,142.
Telephone: 01259 722695. **Colours:** Black and Gold. **Nickname:** The Wasps.

Allan, G .... 2(1) Gilmour, J .... –(1)   Nelson, M .... 19(7)
Armstrong, G .... 1(1) Haddow, L .... 12(1)   Pew, D .... 21(8)
Beaton, D .... 6 Irvine, W 33   Ramsay, S .... 15(4)
Cairns, M .... 36 Mackay, S .... 6(13)   Sharp, R .... 15(2)
Cameron, M .... 21(7) McAneny, P .... 33(1)   Simpson, P .... 25(8)
Clark, D .... 9 (5) McCulloch, K 6   Valentine, C 34
Cowan, M .... 18 McKechnie, G .... 20(5)   Wilson, M .... 22(3)
Donaghy, M .... 10(1) McLeod, K .... –(2)   Wilson, S .... 27(1)
Duthie, M .... 5(3)

League Goals (65): Cameron 15, Irvine 15, Simpson 10, McKechnie 9, Cowan 3, Clark
2, Duthie 2, Mackay 2, McAneny 2, Pew 1, Ramsay 1, Wilson S 1, Wilson M 1,
Opponents 1.
League Cup Goals (5): McKechnie 2, Cameron 1, Simpson 1, Wilson, M 1. **Scottish Cup
Goals (1):** Cameron 1.

ARBROATH

Ground: Gayfield Park, Arbroath. **Capacity:** 6,488.
Telephone: 01241 872157. **Colours:** Maroon and white. **Nickname:** The Red Lichties.

Arbuckle, D .... 23(5) Grant, B .... 2(6)   O'Driscoll, J .... 3(1)
Burns, K .... –(1) Hinchcliffe, C 25   Peters, S .... 10(2)
Cooper, C .... 13(4) Jones, K .... 22(1)   Scott, S .... 1(2)
Crawford, J .... 35 McAulay, J .... 34(1)   Scott, W .... 15(5)
Devine, C .... 5(1) McGlashan, C 27   Sellers, B .... 22(8)
Donahie, B .... 2(1) McGlashan, J 14   Spence, W .... 5(6)
Elliott, J .... 8(3) McWalter, M .... 3(2)   Thomson, N .... 14(9)
Florence, S .... 24 Mercer, J .... 22(7)   Tindal, K .... 23(8)
Gallagher, J .... 31(1) Mitchell, B 2   Wight, C 11

League Goals (37): McGlashan C 12, Sellers 5, Arbuckle 4, Gallagher 4, Tindal 3,
McGlashan J 2, Crawford 2, Cooper 1, Mercer 1, Peters 1, Opponents 2.
League Cup Goals: None. **Scottish Cup Goals (1):** Gallagher 1.

CLYDE

Ground: Broadwood Stadium, Cumbernauld. **Capacity:** 8,029 (all-seated).
Telephone: 01236 451511. **Colours:** White and Red. **Nickname:** The Bully Wee.

Balfour, R .... 3 Keogh, P .... 34(2)   Mitchell, J .... 2(4)
Barrett, J .... 13(7) McClay, A 29   Murray, D .... 25(4)
Brownlie, P .... –(1) McCusker, R 35   O'Brien, A 15
Campbell, P .... –(4) McDonald, I .... 14(4)   Peters, S .... 1(1)
Carrigan, B .... 19(12) McGhee, G .... –(1)   Rice, B .... 8(10)
Convery, S .... 30 McGraw, M 5   Sexton, D 1
Cranmer, C .... 23(5) McHarg, S .... 7(9)   Smith, B 35
Dillon, J .... –(2) McIntyre, G 2   Spittal, J 35
Grant, A .... 28(6) McMillian, A 9   Wylie, D .... 29(1)
Hay, P .... 6(5) McPhee, G .... 2(2)

League Goals (46): Convery 12, McCusker 10, Keogh 6, Barrett 3, Carrigan 3, O'Brien 3,
McHarg 2, McGraw 2, Grant 2, Cranmer 1, McClay 1, Spittal 1.
League Cup Goals (1): McPhee 1. **Scottish Cup Goals (11):** McCusker 3, Carrigan 2,
Convery 2, McHarg 2, Grant 1, McClay 1.

EAST FIFE

Ground: Bayview Stadium, Methil. **Capacity:** 2,000.
Telephone: 01333 426323. **Colours:** Black with gold stripes. **Nickname:** The Fifers.

Abercromby, M .... 7(3)	Fisher, D .... –(3)	McNeil, J .... 4(7)
Allan, G .... 21(2)	Gartshore, P .... 1(5)	McPherson, G .... 3(6)
Archibald, E .... –(2)	Gibb, R .... 28(3)	Moffat, B 35
Brown, G .... 13(4)	Harrison, T 17	Mooney, R .... 3(2)
Butter, J 2	Honeyman, B .... 2(1)	Munro, K 36
Coyle, R .... 25(1)	Johnston, G 17	Peters, S .... 5(2)
Cusick, J 32	Kirk, S .... 17(10)	Ramsey, S 7
Dair, L .... 13(3)	Lawrie, A 13	Robertson, G 7
Dixon, A 1	MacFarlane, C .... –(1)	Skeldon, K .... 18(4)
Dyer, M .... 4(2)	Martin, J .... 11(9)	Strathdee, J .... 7(4)
Findlay, M 1	McCulloch, W 34	Venables, R .... 12(10)

League Goals (42): Moffat 13, Dair 5, Kirk 5, Allan 3, Brown 3, Martin 3, Honeyman 2, Cusick 1, Dyer 1, Gartshore 1, Gibb 1, Lawrie 1, Robertson 1, Opponents 2.
League Cup Goals (3): Coyle 1, Cusick 1, Kirk 1. **Scottish Cup Goals (2):** Coyle 1, Moffat 1.

FORFAR ATHLETIC

Ground: Station Park, Forfar. **Capacity:** 8,732.
Telephone: 01307 463576/462259. **Colours:** Sky blue and navy. **Nickname:** The Loons.

Allison, J .... 19(8)	Glennie, S .... –(1)	McLean, B .... 12(9)
Bowes, M .... –(1)	Gray, A .... –(2)	Moffat, J 11
Brand, R .... 24(10)	Hamilton, J 5	Nairn, J 22
Cargill, A .... 30(3)	Honeyman, B .... 17(6)	Rattray, A 20
Christe, S .... 1(3)	Johnston, G .... 4(2)	Raynes, S .... 27(5)
Craig, D .... 26(2)	Mann, R 18	Robertson, D 25
Ferguson, G 19	McCheyne, G .... 27(1)	Sharp, R 9
Gibson, A .... 8(1)	McIllravey, P .... 6(3)	Tully, C 6
Gillies, K .... 17(4)	McLauchlan, M ...... 24(9)	Watson, G 19

League Goals (48): Brand 10, Cargill 7, Honeyman 6, McLean 6, McLauchlan 6, McCheyne 2, McIllravey 2, Mann 2, Nairn 2, Rattray 2, Craig 1, Gibson 1, Tully 1.
League Cup Goals: None. **Scottish Cup Goals (3):** Brand 2, Craig 1.

INVERNESS CALEDONIAN THISTLE

Ground: Caledonian Stadium, Inverness. **Capacity:** 5,580.
Telephone: 01463 222880. **Colours:** Royal blue and white. **Nickname:** Caley Thistle.

Addicoat, W .... 5(4)	Fridge, L 14	Robertson, H 12
Allan, A .... 9(4)	Glancy, M .... 9(4)	Robson, B .... 4(11)
Bavidge, M .... 1(7)	Hastings, R 23	Shearer, D .... 21(9)
Calder, J 22	Macarthur, I .... 1(3)	Sherrin, P .... 34(2)
Cherry, P .... 24(3)	Mann, R 13	Stewart, I .... 1(5)
Christie, C .... 33(1)	McCulloch, M .... 32(1)	Teasdale, M 36
Craig, D .... –(1)	McLean, S .... 34(1)	Tokely, R .... 23(1)
Farquhar, G .... 9(3)	Nicol, G .... 1(3)	Wilson, B .... 35(1)

League Goals (80): McClean 19, Wilson 14, Shearer 12, Sheerin 10, Christie 4, McCulloch 4, Teasdale 4, Cherry 3, Glancy 3, Stewart 2, Bavidge 1, Robertson 1, Tokely 1, Opponents 2.
League Cup Goals (4): Cherry 1, McLean 1, Shearer 1, Sheerin 1. **Scottish Cup Goals (1):** Opponents 1.

LIVINGSTON

Ground: West Lothian Courier Stadium, Livingston. **Capacity:** 6,100.
Telephone: 01506 417000. **Colours:** Gold and black. **Nickname:** Livvy's Lions.

Alexander, N 21	Fleming, D .... 14(1)	McManus, A 31
Bennett, J .... 13(7)	Forrest, G .... 2(3)	McMartin, G .... –(4)
Bingham, D 29	Harvey, P .... 1(3)	McPhee, B .... 9(19)
Boyle, J 34	King, C 29	Millar, J 30
Conway, F .... 10(2)	Little, I .... 7(7)	Rajamaki, K .... 3(2)
Coughlan, G 6	Macdonald, W 5	Robertson, J .... 30(6)
Courts, T .... –(1)	Magee, K .... 2(1)	Sherry, J .... 20(2)
Deas, A 35	McCaldon, I 15	Sweeney, S 10
Ferguson, I .... 3(1)	McCormick, M ...... 10(22)	Watson, G .... 26(1)
Feroz, C .... 1(10)		

League Goals (66): Robertson 12, Bingham 11, King 9, McPhee 9, Deas 5, McCormick 4, Millar 4, Sherry 4, Fleming 3, Boyle 1, Deas 1, Little 1, McManus 1, Watson 1.
League Cup Goals (4): Bingham 2, Millar 1, Robertson 1. **Scottish Cup Goals (8):** Bingham 2, Robertson 2, Fleming 1, McCormick 1, Millar 1, Opponents 1.

PARTICK THISTLE

Ground: Firhill Stadium Glasgow. **Capacity:** 14,538.
Telephone: 0141 579 1971. **Colours:** Red and yellow. **Nickname:** The Jags.

Archibald, A 33	Dunn, R .... 26(8)	Martin, A .... –(1)
Arthur, K 26	Flannigan, C .... 8(8)	McArthur, S .... 8(1)
Avdiu, K 6	Frame, A .... 4(3)	McCann, K 1
Bonar, S .... 7(7)	Gaughan, K .... 22(4)	McDonald, P .... 29(2)
Bryce, T .... 18(1)	Hood, G 6	McHarg, S .... 1(1)
Burns, G 6	Houston, S .... –(2)	McKenzie, J .... 3(4)
Callaghan, T .... 14(11)	Howie, W .... –(1)	McKeown, D 30
Callaghan, W .... 7(6)	Jamieson, W 25	Morgan, A .... 12(1)
Connell, G .... 32(1)	Johnston, S .... 4(11)	Ross, S 10
Dair, L 1	Kennedy, D 24	Tosh, P 10
Donaghy, M 1	Lauchlan, M .... 22(5)	

League Goals (36): Dunn 10, Morgan 6, Lauchlan 5, Bryce 3, McDonald 3, Jamieson 2, Archibald 1, Avdiu 1, Connell 1, Flannigan 1, Houston 1, Tosh 1, Opponents 1.
League Cup Goals (2): Lauchlan 1, Morgan 1. **Scottish Cup Goals (8):** Dunn 4, Tosh 4.

QUEEN OF THE SOUTH

Ground: Palmerston Park, Dumfries. **Capacity:** 6,412.
Telephone: 01387 254853. **Colours:** Royal Blue. **Nickname:** The Doonhamers.

Adams, C .... 18(9)	Leslie, S .... 21(1)	Milligan, R 1
Aitken, A .... 27(2)	Lilley, D 27	Moffat, A 2
Armstrong, G .... 4(3)	Love, G 9	Nesovic, A .... 20(3)
Bailey, L .... 16(1)	Macleod, J 4	Potts, C 5
Boyle, D .... 6(5)	Mallan, S .... 24(7)	Rowe, J .... 28(2)
Bryce, T .... 1(5)	Mathieson, D 36	Russell, G .... 5(1)
Caldwell, B .... 2(13)	McAllister, J .... 25(2)	Thomson, J 18
Cleeland, M .... 26(2)	McCaig, J .... 1(1)	Townsley, D .... 21(6)
Doig, K 9	McGuffie, R 1	Turner, T .... (5)
Eadie, K .... 15(5)	McKee, C 2	Weir, M .... 17(2)

League Goals (50): Mallan 15, Townsley 10, Rowe 7, Eadie 5, Adams 4, Nesovic 3, Armstrong 1, Bailey 1, Caldwell 1, Cleeland 1, Leslie 1, Potts 1.
League Cup Goals (1): Eadie 1. **Scottish Cup Goals (1):** Nesovic 1.

STIRLING ALBION

Ground: Forthbank Stadium, Stirling. **Capacity:** 3,808.
Telephone: 01786 450399. **Colours:** Red and white. **Nickname:** The Albion.

Aitken, A .... –(1)	Graham, A 23	McKee, C .... 1(1)
Bell, D .... 1(16)	Grant, B 7	Mortimer, P .... 15(8)
Bone, A .... 27(1)	Hendry, J .... 6(1)	Nicholas, S 27
Bradley, M .... 4(3)	Jackson, C .... 21(1)	Paterson, A 36
Clark, P .... 30(3)	Jaffa, G .... 1(2)	Philliben, J .... 20(2)
Cormack, P 6	Martin, B 33	Price, G .... 14(5)
Donald, G .... 18(4)	McCallion, K .... –(2)	Provan, A .... 8(10)
Forrest, E .... 24(3)	McCallum, D .... 28(2)	Wood, C .... 10(14)
Gow, G 27	McGeown, M 9	

League Goals (50): Bone 21, Graham 5, Nicholas 5, Donald 3, Paterson 3, Price 3, Hendry 2, Wood 2, Grant 1, Jackson 1, Martin 1, McCallum 1, Provan 1, Opponents 1.
League Cup Goals (3): Bone 2, Price 1. **Scottish Cup Goals (5):** Graham 2, Jackson 1, McCallum 1, Nicholas 1.

THIRD DIVISION

ALBION ROVERS

Ground: Cliftonhill Stadium, Coatbridge. **Capacity:** 2,496.
Telephone: 01236 606334. **Colours:** Yellow and red. **Nickname:** Wee Rovers.

Blair, P 12	Limond, W .... 3(2)	McStay, J 32
Bottiglieri, E 10	Lorimer, D .... 31(5)	Melvin, M .... 33(1)
Bruce, D .... 6(1)	McBride, K .... 1(3)	Mitchell, C 1
Diack, I .... 14(5)	McBride, M .... –(1)	Murphy, J .... 11(3)
Docherty, R 6	McColm, N 1	Ross, A 5
Donaldson, E .... 35(1)	McGowan, C .... –(2)	Shaw, M .... 9(12)
Duncan, G 26	McGowan, N 33	Silvestro, C .... 4(1)
Goldie, G .... –(1)	McIlhatton, L .... –(2)	Sinclair, C .... 2(2)
Greenock, R .... 15(7)	McLean, M 35	Smith, J 1
Hamilton, J 23	McLees, J .... 29(2)	Sturrock, G .... 10(11)
Harty, M .... 8(13)	McQuade, K .... –(1)	

League Goals (43): Lorimer 10, McLees 6, Donaldson 5, Melvin 5, Diack 4, McStay 3, Blair 2, Murphy 2, Bottiglieri 1, Bruce 1, Hamilton 1, Ross 1, Shaw 1, Opponents 1.
League Cup Goals (1): Donaldson 1. **Scottish Cup Goals (7):** Lorimer 3, Murphy 2, Diack 1, Melvin 1.

BERWICK RANGERS

Ground: Shelfield Park, Berwick-upon-Tweed. **Capacity:** 4,131.
Telephone: 01289 307424. **Colours:** Black and gold. **Nickname:** Borderers.

Baigrie, J .... 1(7)	Hunter, M .... 12(3)	Rafferty, K .... 24(8)
Beaton, D 28	Irvine, N 2	Ramage, I .... 20(9)
Buglass, K .... –(1)	Laidlaw, S .... 2(2)	Reilly, D .... 1(1)
Burgess, M 1	Leask, M .... 24(6)	Ritchie, I 9
Campbell, C .... 25(1)	McCole, D .... –(1)	Seaton, S .... 4(5)
Clark, J 2	McLeod, J .... 7(1)	Shaw, G .... 14(7)
Cunningham, T 1	McNicoll, G 34	Sinclair, C 2
Dixon, A .... –(4)	Neil, M .... 19(1)	Smith, D .... 9(6)
Forrester, P .... 28(2)	Neill, A 35	Smith, S .... –(3)
Fraser, G .... 26(3)	O'Connor, G 35	Watt, D .... 28(2)
Haddow, L .... –(1)	Quinn, B .... –(11)	

League Goals (53): Leask 12, Forrester 9, Smith D 7, Watt 7, Rafferty 5, Shaw 4, Hunter 2, Neil 2, Ramage 2, Baigrie 1, McNicoll 1, Neill 1.
League Cup Goals (2): Forrester 1, Laidlaw 1. **Scottish Cup Goals:** None.

BRECHIN CITY

Ground: Glebe Park, Brechin. **Capacity:** 3,960.
Telephone: 01356 622856. **Colours:** Red and white. **Nickname:** City.

Bain, K 31	Campbell, S .... 27(1)	MacLeod, I .... –(3)
Black, R .... 32(1)	Christie, G .... 11(5)	McKellar, J .... 22(7)
Boylan, P 6	Dailly, M .... 10(6)	Riley, P 12
Boyle, S 8	Dickson, J .... 34(2)	Smart, C .... 11(1)
Brown, R .... 13(3)	Garden, S 33	Smith, G 26
Buick, G .... 15(7)	Hutcheon, A .... 6(15)	Sorbie, S 31
Butter, J 3	Kerrigan, S .... 14(12)	Williamson, K .... 12(1)
Cairney, H 34	Laing, K 5	

League Goals (48): Dickson 15, Sorbie 12, Bain 5, Kerrigan 4, Black 2, Campbell 2, McKellar 2, Christie 1, Dailly 1, Hutcheon 1, Smart 1, Smith 1, Opponents 1.
League Cup Goals (2): Hutcheon 2. **Scottish Cup Goals (5):** Dickson 2, Sorbie 2, Kerrigan 1.

COWDENBEATH

Ground: Central Park, Cowdenbeath. **Capacity:** 4,370.
Telephone: 01383 610166. **Colours:** Royal blue and white. **Nickname:** Blue Brazil.

Bannatyne, P .... –(3)	Horn, R 8	Mitchell, W .... 13(2)
Blair, D .... 2(1)	Humphreys, M .... 10(3)	Murray, D .... 7(1)
Bowsher, C .... 7(1)	Hunter, G 2	Paterson, G 1
Bradley, M 19	Hutchison, S 27	Pryde, D .... 2(3)
Brown, G .... 23(12)	Lakie, J 1	Ritchie, A .... 4(3)
Bruno, P 1	Lynch .... , J 1	Robertson, M .... 13(4)
Burns, J .... 23(4)	Malcolm, S 4	Smith, P .... –(1)
Carnie, G 8	Martin, A .... –(1)	Snedden, S .... 29(1)
Cuthbert, L .... 15(2)	McKenzie, J 5	Stewart, W .... 26(3)
Dair, L 3	McMillan, A 1	Thomson, R .... 21(1)
Dinse, A 2	McMillan, C .... 7(6)	Urquhart, M .... 11(2)
Findlay, G 5	Melvin, A .... –(6)	Ward, M .... –(2)
Godfrey, R 9	Millar, P .... 1(2)	Welsh, B .... 4(8)
Graham, C .... 11(4)	Milne, K 23	Winter, C 25
Hamilton, A .... 22(4)		

League Goals (34): Stewart 7, Milne 6, Brown 5, Bradley 2, Hamilton 2, Snedden 2, Thomson 2, Winter 2, Bowsher 1, Dair 1, Graham 1, Hunter 1, Robertson 1, Welsh 1.
League Cup Goals: None. **Scottish Cup Goals (2):** Burns 1, Snedden 1.

DUMBARTON

Ground: Boghead Park, Dumbarton. **Capacity:** 3,761.
Telephone: 01389 762569. **Colours:** Yellow and black. **Nickname:** Sons.

Barnes, D 1	Gow, S .... 6(3)	Millar, K .... 2(7)
Bradford, J 4	Grace, A .... 18(2)	Mooney, M .... 28(4)
Brittain, C .... 22(1)	Harvey, P .... 7(2)	Reid, D .... 9(1)
Brown, A .... 2(5)	Jack, S 35	Robertson, J .... 21(5)
Bruce, J 17	King, T 29	Sharp, L 17
Dennison, P 2	McKinnon, C 27	Smith, C .... 3(6)
Finnigan, P .... 1(2)	Meechan, K 33	Stewart, D .... 9(1)
Flannery, P 33	Melvin, M .... 2(9)	Wilkinson, B .... 4(2)
Glancy, M .... 5(5)	Melvin, W .... 24(6)	Wilson, W 35

369

League Goals (53): Flannery 17, Robertson 8, Mooney 4, King 3, McKinnon 3, Melvin W 3, Smith 3, Bradford 2, Sharp 2, Brittain 1, Bruce 1, Glancy 1, Gow 1, Grace 1, Jack 1, Stewart 1, Wilson 1.
League Cup Goals: None. **Scottish Cup Goals (1):** Flannery 1.

EAST STIRLINGSHIRE

Ground: Firs Park, Falkirk. **Capacity:** 816.
Telephone: 01324 623583. **Colours:** Black and white. **Nickname:** Shire.

Abdulrahman, K .... –(1)	Laidlaw, S 14	Ross, B 32
Barr, A .... 23(3)	Lepper, N .... 1(1)	Russell, G .... 13(1)
Brown, M .... 21(6)	McBeth, P .... –(3)	Scott, A .... –(4)
Bruce, G 4	McDougall, G 13	Sime, A .... –(4)
Ferguson, B .... 16(2)	McGoldrick, K ...... 19(1)	Smith, J 28
Hardie, M .... 20(2)	McNeill, W .... 22(6)	Storrar, A .... 21(7)
Hoxley, L .... 1(2)	Millar, D 1	Thompson, B 19
Hunter, S .... –(4)	Muirhead, D 34	Walker, S 25
Kennedy, K .... 7(11)	Patterson, P 36	Ward, H .... 26(5)

League Goals (50): McNeill 8, Laidlaw 6, Muirhead 6, Patterson 5, Ward 5, Walker 4, Barr 3, Hardie 3, Kennedy 3, Smith 3, McGoldrick 2, Opponents 2.
League Cup Goals: None. **Scottish Cup Goals (2):** Walker 2.

MONTROSE

Ground: Links Park Stadium, Montrose. **Capacity:** 4,338.
Telephone: 01674 673200. **Colours:** Royal blue and white. **Nickname:** Gable Endies.

Andrew, B .... 13(11)	Irvine, B .... –(1)	Niddrie, K .... 21(1)
Coulston, D 19	Loney, J .... 14(2)	O'Driscoll, J 9
Craib, M 31	Lyon, M .... 6(3)	Paterson, G 14
Craig, M 15	Magee, K 13	Shand, M .... 9(4)
Duffy, K 21	Mailer, , C 32	Stevenson, C .... 1(4)
Farnan, C .... 30(1)	McGlashan, C 8	Taylor, S .... 30(2)
Fitzpatrick, F .... 21(1)	McWilliam, R ...... 4(13)	Watt, J .... 13(5)
Henry, J .... 3(5)	Meldrum, G 35	Winiarski, S .... 5(2)
Higgins, G 7	Murray, M 15	Wylie, R .... 4(1)
Hutton, D .... 3(3)		

League Goals (42): Taylor 7, Craig 5, Magee 5, Paterson 4, Andrew 3, Coulston 3, Farnan 3, Higgins 2, Lyon 2, Duffy 1, Hutton 1, Loney 1, Mailer 1, McGlashan 1, McWilliam 1, Niddrie 1, Shand 1.
League Cup Goals (1): Andrew 1. **Scottish Cup Goals (1):** Taylor 1.

QUEEN'S PARK

Ground: The National Stadium, Hampden Park, Glasgow. **Capacity:** 52,046 (all-seated).
Telephone: 0141 6321275. **Colours:** Black and white. **Nickname:** Spiders.

Agostini, D .... 5(4)	Ferguson, P .... 11(3)	McColl, B .... 2(9)
Alexander, D .... 24(2)	Ferry, D .... 31(4)	McGhee, D 2
Brown, J .... 13(1)	Finlayson, K .... 27(9)	McGill, D 4
Carmichael, D .... 12(1)	Finlayson, R .... –(1)	McGuffie, R .... 5(6)
Caven, R 27	Graham, D .... 19(1)	Monaghan, M 2
Chalmers, J 17	Hamilton, W .... –(3)	Orr, G .... 4(2)
Connaghan, D .... 26(4)	Inglis, N 11	Parks, G .... 7(13)
Cook, B 6	Little, ... T .... 12(9)	Reid, A .... 6(1)
Edgar, S .... 29(7)	Martin, A .... 4(5)	Reid, N .... 1(2)
Elder, G .... 12(2)	Martin, P 28	Rossiter, B .... 26(1)

Tyrrell, P .... 15(4)   Whelan, J 8

League Goals (41): Edgar 7, Carmichael 6, Finlayson K 6, Martin P 6, Brown 3, Graham 2, Caven 1, Elder 1, Ferry 1, Whelan 1, Little 1, McGill 1, McGuffie 1, Orr 1, Parks 1, Opponents 2.
League Cup Goals (1): Graham 1. **Scottish Cup Goals (6):** Edgar 2, Brown 1, Finlayson K 1, Graham 1, Parks 1.

ROSS COUNTY

Ground: Victoria Park Stadium, Dingwall. **Capacity:** 5,320.
Telephone: 01349 860860. **Colours:** Navy blue and white. **Nickname:** County.

Adams, D 4	Herd, W .... 5(2)	McKee, C .... –(1)
Campbell, C .... 1(7)	Higgins, G .... 1(2)	Meldrum, C 2
Den Bieman, I 2	Hunter, M .... 3(3)	Munro, G 1
Escalon, F .... 17(1)	Kinnaird, P 10	Ross, D .... 19(9)
Ewing, G .... 1(2)	Mackay, D .... 16(4)	Stewart, G 1
Ferguson, S 26	Mackay, S .... –(2)	Tarrant, N .... 27(6)
Ferries, K .... 15(7)	MacLeod, B .... 1(2)	Taylor, A .... 24(8)
Furphy, W .... 6(4)	Matheson, D 7	Tully, C 8
Gilbert, K 25	Maxwell, J 36	Walker, J 31
Golabek, S .... 18(5)	McBain, R 33	Williamson, R .... 1(2)
Haro, M 26	McGlashan, J .... 16(1)	Wood, G .... 12(15)
Hart, R 1		

League Goals (87): Ferguson 17, Tarrant 17, Wood 12, Ross 7, McGlashan 6, McBain 5, Ferries 4, Taylor 4, Adams 3, Maxwell 3, Golabek 2, Escalon 1, Haro 1, Kinnaird 1, Opponents 4.
League Cup Goals (8): Adams 5, Tarrant 2, Ross 1. **Scottish Cup Goals (6):** Tarrant 5, McBain 1.

STENHOUSEMUIR

Ground: Ochilview Park, Stenhousemuir. **Capacity:** 2,354.
Telephone: 01324 562992. **Colours:** Maroon and white. **Nickname:** Warriors.

Armstrong, G 35	Gibson, J .... 17(5)	Lansdowne, A .... 10(7)
Banks, A .... 20(7)	Graham, T .... 22(2)	Lawrence, A 33
Baptie, C .... 25(2)	Hall, M .... 15(3)	McKinnon, C .... 6(1)
Brown, S .... –(1)	Hamilton, L 34	Middlemist, R .... –(1)
Budinauckas, K 2	Hamilton, R .... 34(1)	Miller, K 11
Christie, M 3	Huggon, R .... –(2)	Sprott, A .... 17(13)
Craig, A 32	Hunter, P .... –(2)	Watters, W .... 18(11)
Davidson, G .... 23(1)	Hutchison, G 2	Wood, D .... 5(3)
Fisher, J 29	Kane, K .... 3(3)	

League Goals (62): Hamilton R 11, Watters 9, Lawrence 8, Miller 8, Craig 7, Graham 4, Gibson 3, Sprott 3, Armstrong 2, McKinnon 2, Banks 1, Baptie 1, Christie 1, Huggon 1, Wood 1.
League Cup Goals (1): Watters 1. **Scottish Cup Goals (6):** Craig 2, Miller 2, Hall 1, Watters 1.

F.A. CARLING PREMIERSHIP

CLUB DETAILS AND PLAYING STAFFS 1999-2000

(as notified at time of going to press)

ARSENAL

Ground: Arsenal Stadium, Highbury, London, N5 1BU.
Telephone: 0171 704 4000 **Clubcall:** 0891 413 3366.
Club Nickname: The Gunners.
First-choice colours: Red shirts; white shorts; white and red stockings.
Record transfer fee: £7,500,000 to Internazionale for Dennis Bergkamp, June 1995.
Record fee received: £5,000,000 from West Ham Utd. for John Hartson, February 1997.
Record attendance: At Highbury: 73,295 v Sunderland March 1935. At Wembley: 73,295 v Lens (Champions League) November 1998.
Capacity for 1999-2000: 38,500.
Average home League attendance 1998-99: 38,023.
Sponsors: Sega.
League Championship: winners 1930-31, 1932-33, 1933-34, 1934-35, 1937-38, 1947-48, 1952-53, 1970-71, 1988-89, 1990-91, 1997-98.
F.A. Cup: winners 1930, 1936, 1950, 1971, 1979, 1993, 1998.
League Cup: winners 1987, 1993.
European Competitions: winners Fairs Cup: 1969-70, Cup Winners Cup: 1993-94.
Finishing positions in Premiership: 1992-93 10th, 1993-94 4th, 1994-95 12th, 1995-96 5th, 1996-97 3rd, 1997-98 1st, 1998-99 2nd.
Biggest win: 12-0 v Loughborough Town, Div. 2, 12.3.1900.
Biggest defeat: 0-8 v Loughborough Town, Div. 2, 12.12.1896.
Highest League scorer in a season: Ted Drake, 42, 1934-35.
Most League goals in aggregate: Cliff Bastin, 150, 1930-47.
Most capped player: Kenny Sansom (England) 77.
Longest unbeaten League sequence: 26 matches (April 1990).
Longest sequence without a League win: 23 (September 1912).
History: Founded as Dial Square in 1886 by workers at the Royal Arsenal, turned professional 1891 and played on Plumstead Common as Royal Arsenal and Woolwich Arsenal before moving to Highbury in 1913 to avoid competition with Charlton Athletic. Nott'm. Forest supplied the new Dial Square club with a set of red shirts and a ball. Legendary manager **Herbert Chapman** persuaded London Electric Railway officials to put Arsenal on London's tube map by changing the name from Gillespie Road in November, 1932. The team celebrated with a 7-1 win over Wolves the same day.

HIGHBURY PLAYING STAFF

Name	Height ft. in.	Previous Club	Birthplace	Birthdate
Goalkeepers				
Lukic, John	6. 4	Leeds Utd.	Chesterfield	11.12.60
Manninger, Alex	6. 2	Casino Graz, Aus.	Salzburg, Aus.	4.06.77
Seaman, David	6. 4	Q.P.R.	Rotherham	19.09.63
Taylor, Stuart	–	–	Romford	28.11.80
Defenders				
Adams, Tony	6. 3	–	Romford	10.10.66
Cole, Ashley	–	–	Stepney	20.12.80
Dixon, Lee	5. 8	Stoke City	Manchester	17.03.64
Grimandi, Gilles	5. 9	AS Monaco, Fra.	Gap, Fra.	11.11.70

Keown, Martin	6. 1	Everton	Oxford	24.07.66
Luzhny, Oleg	6. 0	Dynamo Kiev	Ukraine	5.08.68
Silvinho	–	Corinthians	Brazil	
Upson, Matthew	6. 0	Luton Town	Hartismere	18.04.79
Winterburn, Nigel	5. 8	Wimbledon	Nuneaton	11.12.63
Midfield				
Boa-Morte, Luis	5.10	Sporting Lisbon	Lisbon, Por.	4.08.77
Hughes, Stephen	6. 0	–	Wokingham	18.09.76
Lincoln, Greg	–	–	Cheshunt	23.03.80
Ljungberg, Fredrick	5.10	Halmstads, Swe.	Sweden	16.04.77
Malz, Stefan	6. 0	1860 Munich, Ger.	Ludwigshafen, Ger.	15.06.72
Mendez-Rodrigues, Alberto	5.11	Feucht, Ger.	Nuremberg, Ger.	24.10.74
Parlour, Ray	5.10	–	Romford	7.03.73
Petit, Emmanuel	6. 0	AS Monaco, Fra.	Dieppe, Fra.	22.09.70
Overmars, Marc	5. 8	Ajax, Hol.	Emst, Hol.	29.03.73
Vernazza, Paolo	–	–	Islington	1.11.79
Vieira, Patrick	6. 3	AC Milan	Dakas, Sen.	23.06.76
Forward				
Anelka, Nicolas	6. 1	Paris St Germain	Versailles, Fra.	14.03.79
Bergkamp, Dennis	6. 0	Inter Milan	Amsterdam, Hol.	10.05.69
Kanu, Nwankwo	6. 3	Inter Milan	Owerri, Nig.	1.08.76
Riza, Omer	–	–	Edmonton	8.11.79
Wreh, Christopher	5. 9	AS Monaco, Fra.	Monrovia, Lib.	14.05.75

ASTON VILLA

Ground: Villa Park, Trinity Road, Birmingham City, B6 6HE.
Telephone: 0121 327 2299 **Clubcall:** 0891 121148.
Club Nickname: Villans.
First-choice colours: Claret and blue shirts; white shorts; claret and blue stockings.
Record transfer fee: £7,000,000 to Liverpool for Stan Collymore, May 1997.
Record fee received: £5,500,000 for David Platt from Bari, July 1991.
Record attendance: 76,588 v Derby Co. (F.A. Cup 6) 2 March 1946.
Capacity for 1999-2000: 39,217.
Average home League attendance 1998-99: 36,936.
Sponsors: Reebok.
League Championship: winners 1893-94, 1895-96, 1896-97, 1898-99, 1899-1900, 1909-10, 1980-81.
F.A. Cup: winners 1887, 1895, 1897, 1905, 1913, 1920, 1957.
League Cup: winners 1961, 1975, 1977, 1994, 1996.
European Competitions: Winners European Cup 1981-82, European Super Cup 1982-83.
Finishing positions in Premiership: 1992-93 2nd, 1993-94 10th, 1994-95 18th, 1995-96 4th, 1996-97 5th, 1997-98 7th, 1998-99 6th.
Biggest win: 12-2 v Accrington, Div. 1, 12.3.1892, 11-1 v Charlton Athletic, Div. 2, 24.11.1959, 10-0 v Sheffield Wed., Div. 1, 5.10.1912 and v Burnley, Div. 1, 29.8.1925.
Biggest defeat: 0-7 in five League matches from Blackburn Rov., Div. 1, 19.10.1889 to Manchester Utd., Div. 1, 24.10.1964.
Highest League scorer in a season: 'Pongo' Waring, 49, 1930-31.
Most League goals in aggregate: Harry Hampton, 215, 1904-1915.
Most capped player: Paul McGrath (Ireland) 51.
Longest unbeaten League sequence: 15 matches (January 1897, December 1909 and March 1949).
Longest sequence without a League win: 12 matches (November 1973 and December 1986).

History: Cricket-playing members of Villa Cross Wesleyan Chapel, Aston, Birmingham, decided to form their own football club during the winter of 1873-74 because there were few local clubs to join. In their first game against Aston Brook St. Mary's Rugby team, they played one half rugby and the other half soccer. Villa Park, the club's home since 1897, was a 1966 world cup venue and is regularly used for F.A. Cup semi-finals. England have also staged internationals there on six occasions.

VILLA PARK PLAYING STAFF

Name	Height ft. in.	Previous Club	Birthplace	Birthdate
Goalkeepers				
Enckelman, Peter	–	–	Finland	–
Ghent, Matthew	6. 3	–	Burton on Trent	5.10.80
James, David	6. 5	Liverpool	Welwyn	1.08.70
Oakes, Michael	6. 2	–	Northwich	30.10.73
Rachel, Adam	5.11	–	Birmingham	10.12.76
Defenders				
Barry, Gareth	5.11	–	Hastings	23.02.81
Calderwood, Colin	6. 0	Tottenham	Stranraer	20.01.65
Delaney, Mark	5.11	Cardiff City	Haverfordwest	13.05.76
Ehiogu, Ugo	6. 2	W.B.A.	London	3.11.72
Hazell, Reuben	5.11	–	Birmingham	24.04.79
Hughes, David	6. 4	–	Wrexham	1.02.78
Jaszczun, Tommy	5.10	–	Kettering	16.09.77
Ridley, Martin	–	–	–	–
Scimeca, Riccardo	6. 1	–	Leamington Spa	13.06.75
Southgate, Gareth	6. 0	Crystal Palace	Watford	3.09.70
Wright, Alan	5. 4	Blackburn Rov.	Ashton-under-Lyme	28.09.71
Midfield				
Curtolo, David	5. 9	Vasteras	Stockholm, Swe.	30.09.80
Draper, Mark	5.10	Leicester City	Long Eaton	11.11.70
Ferraresi, Fabio	5. 9	Cesena, Ita.	Fano, Ita.	24.05.79
Grayson, Simon	5.11	Leicester City	Ripon	16.12.69
Joachim, Julian	5. 6	Leicester City	Boston	20.09.74
Lescott, Aaron	5. 8	–	Birmingham	2.12.78
Melaugh, Gavin	5. 7	–	Derry	9.07.81
Samuel, Jay Lloyd	–	–	–	24.05.79
Standing, Michael	5.10	–	Shoreham	20.03.81
Stone, Steve	5. 8	–	Gateshead	20.08.71
Taylor, Ian	6. 1	Sheffield Wed.	Birmingham	4.06.68
Thompson, Alan	6. 0	Bolton Wand.	Newcastle	22.12.73
Watson, Steve	6. 0	Newcastle Utd.	North Shields	1.04.74
Forwards				
Blackwood, Michael	5.10	–	Birmingham	30.09.79
Byfield, Darren	5.11	–	Birmingham	22.09.76
Collymore, Stan	6. 2	Liverpool	Stone	22.01.71
Dublin, Dion	6. 1	Coventry City	Leicester	22.04.69
Hendrie, Lee	5.10	–	Birmingham	18.05.77
Merson, Paul	6. 0	Middlesbrough	Harlesden	20.03.68
Middleton, Darren	6. 0	–	Lichfield	28.12.78
Tarrant, Neil	6. 0	Ross County	Darlington	24.06.79
Vassell, Darius	5. 7	–	Birmingham	30.06.80
Walker, Richard	6. 0	–	Birmingham	8.11.77

BRADFORD CITY

Ground: The Pulse Stadium, Valley Parade, West Yorkshire, BD8 7DY.
Telephone: 01254 698888 **Clubcall:** 0891 121179.

Club Nickname: Bantams.
First-choice colours: Claret and amber shirts; amber shorts; claret stockings.
Record transfer fee: £1,400,000 to Leeds Utd. for David Wetherall, July 1999.
Record fee received: £2,000,000 from Newcastle Utd. for Des Hamilton, March 1997.
Record attendance: 39,146 v Burnley (F.A. Cup 4) March 1911.
Capacity for 1999-2000: 18,018.
Average home League attendance 1998-99: 14,265.
Sponsors: JCT 600.
League Championship: (best) 5th 1910-11.
F.A. Cup: winners 1911.
League Cup: (best) 5th round 1965, 1989.
Biggest win: 11-1 v Rotherham Utd., Div. 3N, 25.8.1928.
Biggest defeat: 0-8 v Manchester City, Div. 2, 7.5.1927.
Highest League scorer in a season: David Layne, 34, 1961-62.
Most League goals in aggregate: Bobby Campbell, 121, 1981-84, 1984-86.
Most capped player: Harry Hampton (Northern Ireland) 9.
Longest unbeaten League sequence: 21 matches (January 1969).
Longest sequence without a League win: 16 matches (August 1948).
History: Financial difficulties in 1903 persuaded members of Manningham RFC, a local rugby side, to found a football club and they re-named themselves Bradford City. The Football League quickly accepted Bradford City's application for membership of the Second Division, hoping that the new club would spread football into Yorkshire's rugby heartland. Bradford City is one of only two clubs to enter the Football League without playing a senior fixture – Chelsea is the other. Striker **Albert Whitehurst** scored seven goals in an 8–0 win over Tranmere Rov. in March, 1929 (Div. 3N) and his club record of 24 League goals lasted 30 years until beaten by John McCole's 28 in the 1958–59 season.

VALLEY PARADE PLAYING STAFF

Name	Height ft. in.	Previous Club	Birthplace	Birthdate
Goalkeepers				
Clarke, Matt	6. 4	Sheffield Wed.	Sheffield	3.11.73
Prudhoe, Mark	6. 0	Stoke City	Washington, USA	8.11.63
Walsh, Gary	6. 3	Middlesbrough	Wigan Athletic	21.03.68
Defenders				
Bower, Mark	5.10	–	Bradford	23.01.80
Dreyer, John	6. 1	Stoke City	Alnwick	11.06.63
Halle, Gunnar	5.11	Leeds Utd.	Oslo, Nor.	11.08.65
Jacobs, Wayne	5. 8	Rotherham Utd.	Sheffield	3.02.69
Moore, Darren	6. 2	Doncaster Rov.	Birmingham	22.04.74
Myers, Andy	5. 9	Chelsea	Hounslow	3.11.73
O'Brien, Andy	5.10	–	Harrogate	29.06.79
Todd, Lee	5. 7	Southampton	Hartlepool	7.03.72
Westwood, Ashley	6. 0	Crewe Alexandra	Bridgnorth	31.08.76
Wetherall, David	6. 4	Leeds Utd.	Sheffield	14.03.71
Wright, Stephen	5.10	Glasgow Rangers	Belshill	27.08.71
Midfielders				
Beagrie, Peter	5. 9	Manchester City	Middlesbrough	28.11.65
Lawrence, Jamie	5.10	Leicester City	Balham	8.03.70
McCall, Stuart	5. 6	Glasgow Rangers	Leeds	10.06.64
Patterson, Andrew		–	Kirkcaldy	26.11.80
Sharpe, Lee	6. 0	Leeds Utd.	Halesowen	27.05.71
Whalley, Gareth	5.10	Crewe Alexandra	Manchester	19.12.73
Forwards				
Blake, Robbie	5. 9	Darlington	Middlesbrough	4.03.76
Grant, Gareth		–	Leeds	6.09.80
Mills, Lee	6. 1	Port Vale	Mexborough	10.07.70

Rankin, Isiah	5.10	Arsenal	London	22.05.78
Watson, Gordon	5.10	Southampton	Sidcup	20.03.71
Windass, Dean	5.10	Oxford Utd.	Hull	1.04.69

CHELSEA

Ground: Stamford Bridge Stadium, London SW6 1HS.
Telephone: 0171 385 5545 **Clubcall:** 0891 121159.
Club Nickname: The Blues.
First-choice colours: Blue shirts; blue shorts; white stockings.
Record transfer fee: £10,000,000 to Blackburn Rov. for Chris Sutton, July 1999.
Record fee received: £2,200,000 from Tottenham for Gordon Durie, July 1991.
Record attendance: 82,905 v Arsenal, 12 October 1935.
Capacity for 1999-2000: 34,845.
Average home League attendance 1998-99: 34,751.
Sponsors: Autoglass.
League Championship: winners 1954-55.
F.A. Cup: winners 1970, 1997.
League Cup: winners 1965, 1998.
European Competitions: winners Cup Winners' Cup 1997-98.
Finishing positions in Premiership: 1992-93 11th, 1993-94 14th, 1994-95 11th,
   1995-96 11th, 1996-97 6th, 1997-98 4th, 1998-99 3rd.
Biggest win: 7-0 in four League matches from Lincoln City, Div. 2, 29.10.1910 to
   Walsall, Div. 2, 4.2.1989. Also 9-2 v Glossop N.E. Div. 2, 1.9.1906.
Biggest defeat: 1-8 v Wolves, Div. 1, 26.9.1923. Also 0-7 v Leeds Utd., Div. 1,
   7.10.1967 and v Nott'm For. Div. 1, 20.4.1991.
Highest League scorer in a season: Jimmy Greaves, 41, 1960-61.
Most League goals in aggregate: Bobby Tambling, 164, 1958-70.
Most capped player: Ray Wilkins (England) 24.
Longest unbeaten League sequence: 27 matches (October 1988).
Longest sequence without a League win: 21 matches (November 1987).
History: Chelsea FC was formed in 1905 and gained swift admission to the Football
   League second division after being rejected by the Southern League. The Chelsea
   story could have been over before it began if Fulham had taken up the Stamford
   Bridge landowner's offer to rent them the ground. The ground, now being updated
   and redeveloped, staged England internationals in 1913, 1929 and 1932.

STAMFORD BRIDGE PLAYING STAFF

Name	Height ft. in.	Previous Club	Birthplace	Birthdate
Goalkeepers				
De Goey, Ed	6. 6	Feyenoord, Hol.	Gouda, Hol.	20.12.66
Hitchcock, Kevin	6. 1	Mansfield Town	Custom House	5.10.62
Defenders				
Babayaro, Celestine	6. 0	Anderlecht, Bel.	Kadun, Nig.	29.08.78
Clement, Neil	5.10	–	Reading	3.10.78
Desailly, Marcel	6. 1	AC Milan	Accra, Gha.	17.09.68
Duberry, Michael	6. 2	–	Enfield	14.10.75
Ferrer, Albert	5. 7	Barcelona	Barcelona, Spa.	6.06.70
Hogh, Jes	–	Fenerbahce	Denmark	
Hughes, Paul	5.11	–	London	19.04.76
Lambourde, Bernard	5.10	Bordeaux	Pointe-a-Pitre, Fra.	11.05.71
Lebouef, Frank	6. 1	Strasbourg, Fra.	Paris, Fra.	22.01.68
Le Saux, Graeme	5.10	Blackburn Rov.	Jersey	17.10.68
Melchiot, Mario	–	Ajax, Hol.	Amsterdam, Hol.	4.11.76

Midfield

Dalla Bona, Samuele	–	Atalanta, Ita.	Italy	6.02.81
Deschamps, Didier	5. 9	Juventus	Bayonne, Fra.	15.10.68
Di Matteo, Roberto	5.10	Lazio	Berne, Swi.	29.05.70
Goldbaek, Bjarne	–	Copenhagen, Den.	Nykoebing, Den.	6.10.68
Harley, Jon	5. 8	–	London	26.09.79
Morris, Jody	5. 4	–	London	22.12.78
Newton, Eddie	5.11	–	Hammersmith	13.12.71
Petrescu, Dan	5. 9	Sheffield Wed.	Bucharest, Rom.	22.12.67
Poyet, Gustavo	6. 0	Real Zaragoza, Spa.	Monteviedo, Uru.	15.11.67
Wise, Dennis	5. 6	Wimbledon	Kensington	16.12.66

Forwards

Casiraghi, Pierluigi	5.10	Lazio	Monza, Ita.	4.03.69
Crittenden, Nick	5. 7	–	Ascot	11.11.78
Flo, Tore Andre	6. 3	Brann Bergen, Nor.	Norway	15.06.73
Forssell, Mikael	–	HJK Helsinki, Fin.	Steinfurt, Ger.	15.03.81
Hampshire, Steve	5.10	–	Edinburgh	17.10.79
Nicholls, Mark	5. 9	–	Hillingdon	3.05.77
Sheerin, Joe	–	–	Hammersmith	8.11.77
Sutton, Chris	6. 3	Blackburn Rov.	Nottingham	10.03.73
Zola, Gianfranco	5. 6	Parma, Ita.	Sardinia, Ita.	7.07.66

COVENTRY CITY

Ground: Highfield Road Stadium, King Richard Street, Coventry CV2 4FW.
Telephone: 01203 234000 **Clubcall:** 0891 121166.
Club Nickname: Sky Blues.
First-choice colours: Sky blue shirts, sky blue shorts; sky blue stockings.
Record transfer fee: £3,500,000 to Grasshoppers for Viorel Moldovan, December 1997.
Record fee received: £5,750,000 from Aston Villa for Dion Dublin, November 1998.
Record attendance: 51,455 v Wolves, 29.4.1967.
Capacity for 1999-2000: 23,627.
Average home League attendance 1998-99: 20,778.
Sponsors: Subaru.
League Championship: (best) 6th 1969-70.
F.A. Cup: winners 1987.
League Cup: (best) semi-finals 1981, 1990.
European Competitions: (best) UEFA Cup 2nd round 1970-71.
Finishing positions in Premiership: 1992-93 15th, 1993-94 11th, 1994-95 16th, 1995-96 16th, 1996-97 17th, 1997-98 11th, 1998-99 15th.
Biggest win: 9-0 v Bristol City, Div. 3 (S), 28.4.1934.
Biggest defeat: 2-10 v Norwich City, Div. 3 (S), 15.3.1930.
Highest League scorer in a season: Clarrie Bourton, 49 1931-32.
Most League goals in aggregate: Clarrie Bourton, 171, 1931-37.
Most capped player: Dave Clements (N.Ireland) and Ronnie Rees (Wales) 21 each.
Longest unbeaten League sequence: 25 matches (November 1966).
Longest sequence without a League win: 19 matches (August 1919).
History: Workers at the city's Singer cycle factory formed a club called Singers F.C. in 1883. Their success in the Birmingham Junior Cup in 1891 led to their admission to the Birmingham and District League three years later. They became Coventry City in 1898, moved to Highfield Road a year later and joined the Southern League in 1908. Highfield Road became England's first all-seater ground in 1977 but terraces were soon reintroduced at the request of supporters. Coventry City are among the top flight's longest serving continuous members, having gained promotion to the old first division in 1967. Defender **George Curtis** made a record 538 appearances between 1955 and 1970 as the club rose from division four to division one in eight years (1959-1967). **Alf Wood** turned out for the club against Plymouth Argyle in an F.A.

Cup second round tie in December 1958 aged 44 years 207 days. In August 1982, **Perry Suckling** faced Southampton in a division one match aged 16 years 321 days.

HIGHFIELD ROAD PLAYING STAFF

Name	Height ft. in.	Previous Club	Birthplace	Birthdate
Goalkeepers				
Hedman, Magnus	6. 3	IFK Stockholm, Swe	Stockholm, Swe	19.03.73
Hyldgaard, Morten	6. 1	Ikast	Denmark	27.04.76
Kirkland, Christopher	6. 3	–	Leicester	2.05.81
Ogrizovic, Steve	6. 3	Shrewsbury Town	Mansfield	12.09.57
Defenders				
Breen, Gary	6. 1	Birmingham City	London	12.12.73
Brightwell, Ian	5.10	Manchester City	Lutterworth	9.04.68
Burrows, David	5.10	Everton	Dudley	25.10.68
Burrows, Mark	6. 3	–	Kettering	14.08.80
Daish, Liam	6. 2	Birmingham City	Portsmouth	23.09.68
Edworthy, Marc	5. 8	Crystal Palace	Barnstaple	24.12.72
Hall, Marcus	6. 1	–	Coventry	24.03.76
Konjic, Mohammed	6. 1	Monaco, Fra.	Bosnia	14.05.70
Shaw, Richard	5. 9	Crystal Palace	Brentford	11.09.68
Williams, Paul	6. 0	Derby Co.	Burton-on-Trent	26.03.71
Midfield				
Barnett, Christopher	5.11	–	Derby	20.12.78
Boateng, George	5. 9	Feyenoord, Hol.	Nkawkan, Gha.	5.09.75
Boland, Willie	5. 9	–	Ennis, Ire.	6.08.75
Devaney, Martin	5.10	–	Cheltenham	1.06.80
Eustace, John	5.11	–	Solihull	3.11.79
Froggatt, Steve	5.10	Wolves	Lincoln	9.03.73
McAllister, Gary	6. 1	Leeds Utd.	Motherwell	25.12.64
Quinn, Barry	6. 0	–	Dublin	9.05.79
Shilton, Sam	5.11	–	Nottingham	21.07.78
Soltvedt, Trond Egil	6. 1	Rosenborg, Nor.	Voss, Nor.	15.02.67
Strachan, Gavin	5.10	–	Aberdeen	23.12.78
Telfer, Paul	5. 9	Luton Town	Edinburgh	21.10.71
Forwards				
Aloisi, John	6. 0	Portsmouth	Australia	5.02.76
Hall, Paul	5. 9	Portsmouth	Manchester	3.07.72
Huckerby, Darren	5.11	Newcastle Utd.	Nottingham	23.04.76
Whelan, Noel	6. 2	Leeds Utd.	Leeds	30.12.74

DERBY COUNTY

Ground: Pride Park Stadium, Derby Co. DE24 8XL.
Telephone: 01332 667503 **Clubcall:** 0891 121187.
Club Nickname: The Rams.
First-choice colours: White shirts; black shorts; white stockings.
Record transfer fee: £3,000,000 to Crewe Alexandra for Seth Johnson, May 1999.
Record fee received: £5,300,000 from Blackburn Rov. for Christian Dailly, August 1998.
Record attendance: At Pride Park: 32,913 v Liverpool, Premier League 1999. At Baseball Ground: 41,826 v Tottenham, Division 1, 1969.
Capacity for 1999-2000: 33,000.
Average home League attendance 1998-99: 29,194.
Sponsors: EDS.
League Championship: winners 1971-72, 1974-75.

F.A. Cup: winners 1946.
League Cup: semi-finals 1968.
European Competitions: European Cup, semi-finals 1972-73.
Finishing positions in Premiership: 1996/97 12th, 1997/98 9th, 1998/99 8th.
Biggest win: 9-0 v Wolves, Div. 1, 10.1.1891, v Sheffield Wed., Div. 1, 21.1.1899. Also 12-0 v Finn Harps, UEFA Cup 1st Rd 1st Leg, 15.9.76.
Biggest defeat: 0-8 v Blackburn Rov. Div. 1, 3.1.1891 and v Sunderland Div. 1, 1.9.1894. Also 2-11 v Everton, FA Cup 1st Rd 1889-90.
Highest League scorer in a season: Jack Bowers, 37, 1930-31 and Ray Straw, 37, 1956-57.
Most League goals in aggregate: Steve Bloomer, 292, 1892-1906 and 1910-14.
Most capped player: Peter Shilton (England) 34.
Longest unbeaten League sequence: 22 matches (March 1969).
Longest sequence without a League win: 20 matches (December 1990).
History: Founded in 1884 by members of the Derbyshire County Cricket Club following a boom in football in the area. The Cricket Club believed that the foundation of Derby Co. FC would swell finances for the cricket season. **Steve Bloomer** netted six times in the 9-0 win over Sheffield Wed. in 1899. After 102 years Derby left the Baseball Ground for the newly-constructed Pride Park.

PRIDE PARK PLAYING STAFF

Name	Height ft. in.	Previous Club	Birthplace	Birthdate
Goalkeepers				
Hoult, Russell	6. 4	Leicester City	Ashby	22.11.72
Knight, Richard	6. 1	Burton Albion	Burton-on-Trent	3.08.79
Oakes, Andy	6. 1	Hull City	Northwich	11.01.77
Poom, Mart	6. 5	Portsmouth	Tallinn, Est.	3.02.72
Defenders				
Boertien, Paul	5.10	Carlisle Utd.	Carlisle	21.01.79
Borbokis, Vassilis	5.11	Sheffield Utd.	Serres, Gre.	10.02.69
Carbonari, Horacio	6. 3	Rosario Central, Arg.	Argentina	2.05.73
Delap, Rory	6. 0	Carlisle Utd.	Birmingham	6.07.76
Dorigo, Tony	5. 9	Torino, Ita.	Melbourne, Aus.	31.12.65
Jackson, Richard	5. 9	Scarborough	Whitby	18.04.80
Johnson, Seth	5.10	Crewe Alexandra	Birmingham	12.03.79
Prior, Spencer	6. 1	Leicester City	London	24.04.71
Schnoor, Stefan	6. 1	Hamburg, Ger.	Germany	24.04.71
Stimac, Igor	6. 2	Hadjuk Split, Cro.	Vejle, Cro.	6.09.67
Midfield				
Bridge-Wilkinson, Marc	5. 6	Carlisle Utd.	Coventry	16.03.79
Bohinen, Lars	6. 1	Blackburn Rov.	Vadso, Nor.	8.09.69
Eranio, Stefano	5.10	AC Milan, Ita.	Genoa, Ita.	29.12.68
Murray, Adam	5. 9	–	Birmingham	30.09.81
Powell, Darryl	6. 0	Portsmouth	Lambeth	15.11.71
Forwards				
Baiano, Francesco	5. 6	Fiorentina, Ita.	Napoli, Ita.	24.02.68
Beck, Mikkel	6. 1	Middlesbrough	Aarhus, Den.	4.05.73
Burton, Deon	5. 9	Portsmouth	Reading	25.10.76
Christie, Malcolm	5.10	Middlesbroughugh	Nuneaton	11.04.79
Harper, Kevin	5. 7	Hibernian	Oldham	15.01.76
Robinson, Marvin	5.11	–	Crewe	11.04.80
Sturridge, Dean	5. 8	–	Birmingham	27.07.73
Wanchope, Paulo	6. 4	Herediano, Cos.	Costa Rica	31.07.76

EVERTON

Ground: Goodison Park, Liverpool L4 4EL.
Telephone: 0151 330 2200 **Clubcall:** 0891 121199.
Club Nickname: Toffees.
First-choice colours: Blue shirts; white shorts; blue stockings.
Record transfer fee: £5,750,000 to Middlesbrough for Nick Barmby.
Record fee received: £8,000,000 from Fiorentina for Andrei Kanchelskis.
Record attendance: 78,299 v Liverpool, Div. 1, September 1948.
Capacity for 1999-2000: 40,200.
Average home League attendance 1998-99: 36,202.
Sponsors: One2One.
League Championship: winners 1890-91, 1914-15, 1927-28, 1931-31, 1938-39, 1962-63, 1969-70, 1984-85, 1986-87.
F.A. Cup: winners 1906, 1933, 1966, 1984, 1995.
League Cup: runners up 1977, 1984.
European Competitions: winners Cup-Winners' Cup 1984-85.
Finishing positions in Premiership: 1992-93 13th, 1993-94 17th, 1994-95 15th 1995-96 6th 1996-97 15th 1997-98 17th 1998-99 14th.
Biggest win: 9-1 v Manchester City, Div. 1, 3.9.1906, v Plymouth Argyle, Div. 2, 27.12.1930. Also 11-2 v Derby Co., F.A. Cup 1st rd, 18.1.1890.
Biggest defeat: 4-10 v Tottenham, Div. 1, 11.10.1958.
Highest League scorer in a season: Ralph 'Dixie' Dean, 60, 1927-28.
Most League goals in aggregate: Ralph 'Dixie' Dean, 349, 1925-37.
Most capped player: Neville Southall (Wales) 92.
Longest unbeaten League sequence: 20 matches (April 1978).
Longest sequence without a League win: 14 matches (March 1937).
History: Everton began life in 1878 as St Domingo's. They were founder members of the Football League and the former church side won their first championship three years after joining. In 1892 they left their Anfield ground after a row with the landlord and moved across Stanley Park to Goodison. This ground has staged a dozen England internationals and was also a 'home' base for Ireland when they played Wales in 1973. It was the scene of England's first home defeat by overseas opponents when Ireland won 2-0 in 1950. The stadium was a 1966 world cup venue. In 1985 Everton came agonisingly close to completing a treble; winning the League then the European Cup Winners Cup before losing to Manchester Utd. in extra-time in the FA Cup final.

GOODISON PARK PLAYING STAFF

Name	Height ft. in.	Previous Club	Birthplace	Birthdate
Goalkeepers				
Gerrard, Paul	6. 2	Oldham Athletic	Heywood	22.01.73
Myhre, Thomas	6. 4	Viking Stavanger, Nor.	Sarpsborg, Nor.	16.10.73
Simonsen, Steve	6. 3	Tranmere Rov.	South Shields	3.04.79
Defenders				
Ball, Michael	5.10	–	Liverpool	2.11.79
Bilic, Slaven	6. 3	West Ham Utd.	Croatia	11.09.68
Cleland, Alex	5.10	Glasgow Rangers	Glasgow	10.12.70
Dunne, Richard	6. 2	–	Dublin	21.09.79
Farley, Adam	6. 2	–	Liverpool	12.01.80
Gough, Richard	6. 0	San Jose Clash, USA	Stockholm, Swe.	5.04.62
O'Kane, John	5.10	Manchester Utd.	Nottingham	15.11.74
Phelan, Terry	5. 6	Chelsea	Manchester	16.03.67
Short, Craig	6. 2	Derby Co.	Bridlington	25.06.68
Regan, Carl	6. 0	–	Liverpool	14.01.80
Unsworth, David	6. 1	Aston Villa	Chorley	16.10.73
Ward, Mitch	5. 8	Sheffield Utd.	Sheffield	

Watson, Dave	6. 1	Norwich City	Liverpool	20.11.61
Weir, David	6. 3	Heart of Midlothian	Falkirk	10.05.70
Midfield				
Barmby, Nick	5. 8	Middlesbrough	Hull	11.02.74
Collins, John	5. 8	Monaco, Fra.	Galashiels	31.01.68
Degn, Peter	5.11	Aarhus, Den.	Denmark	6.04.77
Farrelly, Gareth	6. 0	Aston Villa	Dublin	28.08.75
Gemmill, Scot	5. 9	Nott'm. Forest	Paisley	2.01.71
Grant, Tony	5.10	–	Liverpool	14.11.74
Hutchison, Don	6. 1	Sheffield Utd.	Gateshead	9.05.71
McKay, Matt	6. 0	Chester City	Warrington	21.01.81
Milligan, Jamie	5. 7	–	Blackpool	3.01.80
Oster, John	5. 9	Grimsby Town	Boston	8.12.78
Parkinson, Joe	6. 0	Bournemouth	Eccles	11.06.71
Williamson, Danny	6. 1	West Ham Utd.	West Ham	5.12.73
Forwards				
Branch, Michael	5.11	–	Liverpool	18.11.78
Cadamateri, Danny	5. 9	–	Bradford	21.10.79
Jeffers, Francis	5.10	–	Liverpool	25.01.81
Jevons, Phil	5.11	–	Liverpool	1.08.79

LEEDS UNITED

Ground: Elland Road, Leeds LS11 OES.
Telephone: 0113 2266000 **Clubcall:** 0891 121180.
Club Nickname: Whites.
First-choice colours: White shirts; white shorts; white stockings.
Record transfer fee: £4,500,000 to Manchester Utd. for Lee Sharpe, August 1996.
Record fee received: £3,500,000 from Everton for Gary Speed, June 1995.
Record attendance: 57,892 v Sunderland, 15 March 1967.
Capacity for 1999-2000: 40,000.
Average home League attendance 1998-99: 35,845.
Sponsors: Packard Bell.
League Championship: winners 1968-69, 1973-74, 1991-92.
F.A. Cup: winners 1972.
League Cup: winners 1968.
European Competitions: winners Fairs Cup 1967-68, 1970-71. runners-up European Cup 1974-75, Cup winners cup 1972-73.
Finishing positions in Premiership: 1992-93 17th, 1993-94 5th, 1994-95 5th, 1995-96 13th, 1996-97 11th, 1997-98 5th, 1998-99 4th.
Biggest win: 8-0 v Leicester City, Div. 1, 7.4.1934.
Biggest defeat: 1-8 v Stoke City, Div. 1, 27.8.1934.
Highest League scorer in a season: John Charles, 42 1953-54.
Most League goals in aggregate: Peter Lorimer, 168, 1965-79 and 1983-86.
Most capped player: Billy Bremner (Scotland) 54.
Longest unbeaten League sequence: 34 matches (October 1968).
Longest sequence without a League win: 17 matches (February 1947).
History: When the Leeds City club was wound up by the F.A. in 1919 following allegations of illegal payments to players, solicitor Alf Masser called a meeting at which Leeds Utd. was formed. They participated in the Midland League. Merger talks were held with financially stretched Huddersfield Town but they broke down. Leeds Utd. developed from a mediocre second division side into a major European force during the reign of **Don Revie** (1961-1974). Revie even changed the official colours from yellow and blue to all white to resemble Real Madrid. He also introduced player numbers on stocking tops and made Elland Road one of the most feared grounds in the country for opponents. Revie captured a host of trophies but also suffered notable setbacks like an F.A. Cup upset at Colchester Utd. and an even greater upset in the

1973 F.A. Cup Final against second division Sunderland. One of Revie's favourites was Scotland winger **Peter Lorimer** who set records as both the youngest and oldest player to appear for the club. He made his debut aged 15 years 289 days against Southampton 29.9.1962 and also appeared against Barnsley on 27.10.1985 aged 38 years 317 days.

ELLAND ROAD PLAYING STAFF

Name	Height ft. in.	Previous Club	Birthplace	Birthdate
Goalkeepers				
Martyn, Nigel	6. 2	Crystal Palace	St. Austell	11.08.66
Robinson, Paul	6. 4	–	Beverley	15.10.79
Defenders				
Evans, Gareth	6. 0	–	Leeds Utd.	15.02.81
Evans, Kevin	6. 2	–	Carmarthen	16.12.80
Granville, Danny	6. 1	Chelsea	London	19.01.75
Harte, Ian	6. 0	–	Drogheda, Ire.	31.08.77
Hiden, Martin	6. 1	Rapid Vienna, Aus	Stainz, Aus.	11.03.73
Jackson, Mark	6. 0	–	Barnsley	30.09.77
Kelly, Gary	5. 8	Home Farm	Drogheda, Ire.	09.07.74
Lanns, Jason	5. 8	Birmingham City	Birmingham	2.11.81
Loughran, Anthony	6. 0	–	Liverpool	11.11.81
Lynch, Damian	5.10	–	Dublin	31.07.79
Martin, Alan	5.11	–	Dublin	21.11.81
Maybury, Alan	5. 9	–	Dublin	8.08.78
McChrystal, Brian	6. 4	–	Dundalk	20.01.81
Mills, Danny	5.11	Charlton Athletic	Norwich	18.05.77
Molenaar, Robert	6. 2	Volendam, Hol.	Zaamdam, Hol.	27.02.69
Radebe, Lucas	6. 1	Kaizer Chiefs, S.A.	Johannesburg, S.A.	12.04.69
Robertson, David	5.11	Glasgow Rangers	Aberdeen	17.10.68
Shepherd, Paul	5.11	–	Leeds	17.11.77
Woodgate, Jonathan	6. 2	–	Middlesbrough	22.01.80
Midfield				
Bakke, Eirik	6. 4	Sogndal, Nor.	Sogndal, Nor.	13.09.77
Batty, David	5. 8	Newcastle Utd.	Leeds	2.12.68
Bowyer, Lee	5. 9	Charlton Athletic	London	3.01.77
Cawley, Alan	6. 2	–	Sligo	3.01.82
Dixon, Kevin	5. 9	Chelsea	Easington	27.06.80
Haaland, Alf-Inge	6. 1	Nott'm. Forest	Stavanger, Nor.	23.11.72
Hopkin, David	6. 1	Crystal Palace	Greenock	21.08.70
Jones, Matthew	5.11	–	Llanelli	1.09.80
Knarvik, Tommy	5. 8	Skjerjard, Nor.	Bergen, Nor.	1.11.79
Lagan, Brian	5. 5	–	County Derry	3.10.80
McPhail, Stephen	5.11	–	London	9.12.79
O'Brien, Carl	5. 9	–	Dublin	6.11.81
Ribeiro, Bruno	5. 8	Vitoria de Setubal, Por.	Setubal, Por.	22.10.75
Watson, Simon	5. 9	–	Strabane	22.09.80
Forwards				
Boyle, Wesley	5.11	–	Portadown	30.03.79
Crawford, Dale	5. 9	Middlesbrough	Sunderland	14.09.81
Feeney, Warren	5.10	–	Belfast	17.01.81
Hackworth, Anthony	6. 2	–	Durham	19.05.80
Hasselbaink, Jimmy Floyd	6. 0	Boavista, Por.	Surinam	27.03.72
Kennedy, Alan	5. 8	–	Dublin	17.10.81
Kewell, Harry	6. 0	New South Wales Soccer Academy	Sydney, Aus.	22.09.78
Lennon, Anthony	5. 9	Manchester Utd.	Leeds	16.05.82

The Red Devils.
ours: Red shirts, white shorts, black stockings.
fee: £12,600,000 to Aston Villa for Dwight Yorke, August 1998.
ived: £7,000,000 from Internazionale for Paul Ince, June 1995.
nce: Club: 70,504 v Aston Villa, 27 December 1920, F.A. Cup
76,962, Wolves v Grimsby Town, 25 March, 1939. Note: 83,260 saw
td. v Arsenal, Div. 1, 17 January 1948 at Maine Road. Old Trafford was
through bomb damage.
9-2000: 56,024.
eague attendance 1998-99: 55,188.
.
onship: winners 1907-08, 1910-11, 1951-52, 1955-56, 1956-7,
66-67, 1992-93, 1993-94, 1995-96, 1996-97, 1998-99.
s 1909, 1948, 1963, 1977, 1983, 1985, 1990, 1994, 1996, 1999.
nners 1992.
etitions: winners European Cup 1967-68, 1998-99, Cup Winners'
uropean Super Cup 1991.
ns in Premiership: 1992-93 1st, 1993-94 1st, 1994-95 2nd, 1995-96
7 1st, 1997-98 2nd,1998-99 1st.
hile Newton Heath) 10-1 v Wolves, Div.1, 15.10.1892, (as Manchester
pswich Town, FAPL, 4.3.1995. Europe: 10-0 v Anderlecht, European
ound, 26.9.1956.
0-7 v Wolves Div 2, 26.12.1931, v Aston Villa, Div. 1, 27.11.1930 and
Rov. Div. 1, 10.4.1926.
scorer in a season: Dennis Viollet, 32, 1959-60.
als in aggregate: Bobby Charlton, 199, 1956-73.
ayer: Bobby Charlton (England) 106.
n League sequence: 26 matches (February 1956).
ce without a League win: 16 matches (November 1928 and April 1930).
in 1902 following the bankruptcy of their predecessors Newton Heath.
n date is usually given as 1878 when carriage and waggon workers at the
nd Yorkshire Railway Company formed Newton Heath L and YR Cricket
Club. Newton Heath were admitted to the Second Division in 1892
r Manchester City victory in 1886. Matt Busby, a former Manchester City
erminded the rise of the club to a world power during a 14-year spell as
wned by European Cup triumph over Benfica at Wembley in 1968. Alex
ulated this feat when Utd. beat Bayern Munich in Barcelona in May
completing a domestic League and F.A. Cup double. Both men were
n February 6, 1958, seven Utd. players perished when their aircraft
m a European Cup tie with Red Star Belgrade crashed on take-off at
rt after a refuelling stop. England's Duncan Edwards died later in hospital
eceived the last rites but later recovered from serious injuries.

RD PLAYING STAFF

Height ft. in.	Previous Club	Birthplace	Birthdate
6. 3	York City	York	6.07.76
6. 2	–	Sheffield	1.11.76
6. 3	Vitesse Arnhem, Hol.	Oldenzaal, Hol.	24.03.63
6. 1	Aston Villa	Sydney, Aus.	13.01.72
6. 0	Blackburn Rov.	Eidsvell, Nor.	1.09.69
6. 1	–	Manchester	13.10.79
5. 8	–	Ashton-under-Lyne	3.07.77
5.10	–	Nuneaton	3.09.78
5. 9	–	Bolton	3.10.81

Name	Height ft. in.	Previous Club	Birthplace	Birthdate
Lilley, Derek	5.11	Greenock Morton	Paisley	9.02.74
Matthews, Lee	6. 2	–	Middlesbrough	6.01.79
Porter, Graeme	5. 6	–	Liverpool	24.11.81
Singh, Harpal	5. 7	–	Bradford	15.09.81
Wijnhard, Clyde	6. 0	Willem II, Hol.	Surinam	9.11.73
Wright, Anthony	5. 6	–	Leeds	21.10.78

LEICESTER CITY

Ground: City Stadium, Filbert Street, Leicester City LE2 7FL.
Telephone: 0116 291 5000 Clubcall: 0891 121185.
Club Nickname: Foxes.
First-choice colours: Blue shirts; white shorts; blue stockings.
Record transfer fee: £2,000,000 to Chelsea for Frank Sinclair, August 1998, and to Bolton Wand. for Arnar Gunnlaugsson, February 1999.
Record fee received: £3,250,000 from Aston Villa for Mark Draper, July 1995.
Record attendance: 47,298 v Tottenham (F.A. Cup 5) February 1928.
Capacity for 1999-2000: 21,500.
Average home League attendance 1998-99: 20,468.
Sponsors: Walkers.
League Championship: (best) 2nd 1928-29.
F.A. Cup: (best) runners up 1949, 1961, 1963, 1969.
League Cup: winners 1964, 1997.
European Competitions: (best) Cup winners cup, second round, 1961-62.
Finishing positions in Premiership: 1994-95 21st, 1996-97 9th, 1997-98 10th, 1998-99 10th.
Biggest win: 10-0 v Portsmouth, Div. 1, 20.10.1928.
Biggest defeat: 0-12 v Nott'm. Forest, Div. 1, 21.4.1909.
Highest League scorer in a season: Arthur Rowley, 44, 1956-57.
Most League goals in aggregate: Arthur Chandler, 259, 1923-35.
Most capped player: John O'Neill(Northern Ireland) 39.
Longest unbeaten League sequence: 19 matches (February 1971).
Longest sequence without a League win: 18 matches (April 1975).
History: A whip round to buy a ball for ninepence (less than 4p) among old boys of Wyggeston School sparked the club's birth in 1884. Membership was also fixed at ninepence. At that historic meeting in a garden shed they formed Leicester Fosse FC, a bold move in an area dominated by rugby union. Four years later they signed their first professional player, Harry Webb from Stafford Rangers, for 2s 6d (12p) per week plus travelling expenses. The name change to Leicester City occurred in 1919. The club produced two of England's longest serving post-war goalkeepers. Gordon Banks was a 1966 world cup winner and won 73 caps. He was succeeded at Filbert Street by Peter Shilton who played in a record 125 England internationals.

FILBERT STREET PLAYING STAFF

Name	Height ft. in.	Previous Club	Birthplace	Birthdate
Goalkeepers				
Andrews, Ian	6. 2	Bournemouth	Nottingham	1.12.64
Arphexad, Pegguy	6. 2	Racing Club, Lens, Fra.	Guadeloupe	28.05.73
Hodges, John	6. 1	–	Leicester	22.01.80
Keller, Kasey	6. 2	Millwall	Washington, USA	29.11.69
Defenders				
Branston, Guy	6. 1	–	Leicester	6.01.79
Elliott, Matt	6. 3	Oxford Utd.	Roehampton	1.11.68
Goodwin, Tommy	6. 1	–	Leicester	8.11.79
Impey, Andy	5. 8	West Ham Utd.	Hammersmith	13.09.71

Name	ft. in.		Birthplace	Date
Kaamark, Pontus	6. 1	IFK Gothenburg, Swe.	Vasteras, Swe.	5.04.69
Sinclair, Frank	5. 9	Chelsea	Lambeth	3.12.71
Taggart, Gerry	6. 1	Bolton Wand.	Belfast	18.10.70
Walsh, Steve	6. 3	Wigan Athletic	Fulwood	3.11.64
Midfield				
Campbell, Stuart	5.10	–	Corby	9.12.77
Guppy, Steve	5.11	Port Vale	Winchester	29.03.69
Izzet, Mustafa	5.10	Chelsea	Hackney	31.10.74
Lennon, Neil	5. 9	Crewe Alexandra	Belfast	25.06.71
McCann, Tim	5. 8	–	Belfast	22.03.80
Mitchell, Ross	5.11	–	Halifax	24.08.78
Oakes, Stefan	5.11	–	Leicester	6.09.79
Parker, Garry	6. 0	Aston Villa	Oxford	7.03.65
Savage, Robbie	5.11	Crewe Alexandra	Wrexham	18.10.74
Taylor, Scott	5. 9	Reading	Portsmouth	23.11.70
Ullathorne, Robert	5. 8	Osasuna, Spa.	Wakefield	11.10.71
Wilson, Stuart	5. 8	–	Leicester	16.09.77
Zagorakis, Theo	5. 9	PAOK Salonika, Gre.	Kavala, Gre.	27.10.71
Forwards				
Cottee, Tony	5. 8	Selangor, Mal.	West Ham	11.07.65
Dudfield, Lawrence	6. 0	Kettering Town	London	7.05.80
Fenton, Graham	5.11	Blackburn Rov.	Wallsend	22.05.74
Gunnlaugsson, Arnar	5.11	Bolton Wand.	Akranes, Ice.	6.03.73
Heskey, Emile	6. 2	–	Leicester	11.01.78
Marshall, Ian	6. 2	Ipswich Town	Liverpool	20.03.66
Neil, Gary	6. 0	–	Glasgow	16.08.78

LIVERPOOL

Ground: Anfield Road, Liverpool L4 0TH.
Telephone: 0151 263 2361 **Clubcall:** 0891 121184.
Club Nickname: Reds or Pool.
First-choice colours: Red shirts; red shorts; red stockings.
Record transfer fee: £8,500,000 to Nott'm. Forest for Stan Collymore, June 1995.
Record fee received: £7,000,000 from Aston Villa for Stan Collymore, May 1997.
Record attendance: 61,905 v Wolves, 2 February 1952.
Capacity for 1999-2000: 45,362.
Average home League attendance 1998-99: 43,321.
Sponsors: Carlsberg.
League Championship: winners 1900-01, 1905-06, 1921-22, 1922-23, 1946-47, 1963-64, 1965-66, 1972-73, 1975-76, 1976-77, 1978-79, 1979-80, 1981-82, 1982-83, 1983-84, 1985-86, 1987-88, 1989-90.
F.A. Cup: winners 1965, 1974, 1986, 1989, 1992.
League Cup: winners 1981, 1982, 1983, 1984, 1995.
European Competitions: winners European Cup 1976-77, 1977-78, 1980-81, 1983-84 UEFA Cup 1972-73, 1975-76 European Super Cup 1977.
Finishing positions in Premiership: 1992-93 6th, 1993-94 8th, 1994-95 4th, 1995-96 3rd, 1996-97 4th, 1997-98 3rd, 1998-99 7th.
Biggest win: 10-1 v Rotherham Utd., Div. 2, 18.2.1896. Europe: 11-0 v Stromsgodset, CWC, 17.9.1974.
Biggest defeat: 1-9 v Birmingham City, Div. 2, 11.12.1954.
Highest League scorer in a season: Roger Hunt, 41, 1961-62.
Most League goals in aggregate: Roger Hunt, 245, 1959-69.
Longest unbeaten League sequence: 31 matches (May 1987).
Longest sequence without a League win: 14 (December 1953).
History: A dispute with Everton and their landlord in 1892 led to the formation of the club. Everton left Anfield for Goodison Park leaving landlord John Houlding to form

Liverpool Association FC in 1892. Scot **B**
emergence from second division mediocrity
1960's. During his 15 years at the helm Liver
and carried off the UEFA Cup twice. Success
his nine years in charge, winning two Europe
Liverpool have won a record 18 League Ch
victories in European competitions.

ANFIELD PLAYING STAFF

Name	ft. in.	Previous Club
Goalkeepers		
Friedel, Brad	6. 3	Columbus Crew,
Nielsen, Jorgen	6. 0	Hvidovre, Den.
Westerveld, Sander	6. 2	Vitesse Arnhem,
Defenders		
Babb, Phil	6. 0	Coventry City
Bjornebye, Stig Inge	5.10	Rosenborg, Nor.
Heggem, Vegard	5.11	Rosenborg, Nor.
Henchoz, Stephane	6. 1	Blackburn Rov.
Hyypia, Sammy	6. 4	Willem II, Hol.
Jones, Eifion	6. 3	–
Kippe, Frode	6. 4	Lillestrom, Nor.
Kvarme, Bjorn	5.11	Rosenborg, Nor.
Matteo, Dominic	6. 1	–
Traore, Djimi	6. 3	Laval, Fra.
Song, Rigobert	6. 0	Salernitana, Ita.
Staunton, Steve	6. 1	Aston Villa
Wright, Stephen	6. 0	–
Midfielders		
Berger, Patrik	6. 1	Borussia Dortmund
Carragher, Jamie	6. 1	–
Ferri, Jean-Michel	6. 0	Istanbulspor, Tur.
Gerrard, Steven	6. 1	–
Ince, Paul	5.10	Inter Milan, Ita.
Leonhardsen, Oyvind	5.10	Wimbledon
Maxwell, Layton	5. 8	–
Murphy, Danny	5. 9	Crewe Alexandra
Partridge, Richie	5. 8	–
Redknapp, Jamie	6. 0	Bournemouth
Smicer, Vladimir	–	Lens
Thompson, David	5. 7	–
Forwards		
Camara, Titi	6. 0	Marseille, Fra.
Dundee, Sean	6. 1	Karlsruhe, Ger.
Fowler, Robbie	5.11	–
Gudnason, Haukar	5.11	Keflavik, Ice.
Meijer, Erik	6. 3	Bayer Leverkusen
Newby, John	6. 0	–
Owen, Michael	5. 8	–
Riedle, Karlheinz	5.11	Borussia Dortmu Ger.

MANCHESTER

Ground: Old Trafford Stadium, Sir Matt Busby Wa
Telephone: 0161 872 1661 **Clubcall:** 0891 121

Club Nickname
First-choice c
Record transfe
Record fee re
Record attend
(semi-final)
Manchester
out of actio
Capacity for 1
Average home
Sponsors: Sha
League Cham
1964-65,
F.A. Cup: winn
League Cup: w
European Com
1990-91,
Finishing posi
1st, 1996-
Biggest win: 5
Utd.) 9-0 v
Cup prelim
Biggest defeat
v Blackburn
Highest Leagu
Most League g
Most capped p
Longest unbea
Longest seque
History: Form
The format
Lancashire
and Footba
following th
player, mas
manager c
Ferguson in
1999 after
knighted.
returning f
Munich Air
and Busby

OLD TRAFF

Name
Goalkeepers
Culkin, Nick
Gibson, Paul
Van der Gouw
Raimond
Bosnich, Ma
Defenders
Berg, Hennin
Brown, Wesle
Clegg, Micha
Curtis, John
Strange, Gare

Higginbotham, Danny	6. 1	–	Manchester	29.12.78
Irwin, Dennis	6. 2	Oldham Athletic	Cork	31.10.65
Johnsen, Ronny	6. 3	Besiktas, Tur.	Sandefjord, Nor.	10.06.69
May, David	6. 0	Blackburn Rov.	Oldham	24.06.70
Neville, Gary	5.11	–	Bury	18.02.75
Neville, Phil	5.11	–	Bury	21.01.77
O'Shea, John	6. 3	Waterford Bohemians	Waterford	30.04.81
Ryan, Michael	5.11	–	Stockport Co.	3.10.79
Stam, Japp	6. 3	PSV Eindhoven, Hol.	Kampen, Hol.	17.07.72
Teather, Paul	6. 0	–	Rotherham	28.12.77
Wallwork, Ronnie	5.10	–	Manchester	10.09.77
Midfield				
Beckham, David	6. 0	–	Leytonstone	2.05.75
Butt, Nicky	5.10	–	Manchester	21.01.75
Cosgrove, Stephen	5. 9	–	Glasgow	29.12.80
Keane, Roy	5.11	Nott'm. Forest	Cork	10.01.71
Evans, Wayne	5. 9	–	Carmarthen	23.10.80
Ford, Ryan	5. 9	–	Worksop	3.09.78
Jordic, Bojand	–	Bromma-Pojakama	Sweden	–
Scholes, Paul	5. 7	–	Salford	16.11.74
Stewart, Michael	5.11	–	Edinburgh	26.02.81
Thorrington, John	5. 7	US College Soccer	Johannesburg, S.A.	17.10.79
Twiss, Michael	5.11	–	Salford	26.12.77
Wellens, Richard	5. 9	–	Manchester	26.03.80
Wilson, Mark	6. 0	–	Scunthorpe	9.02.79
Forwards				
Cole, Andy	5.10	Newcastle Utd.	Nottingham	15.10.71
Cruyff, Jordi	6. 1	Barcelona, Spa.	Amsterdam, Hol.	9.02.74
Blomqvist, Jesper	5. 9	Parma, Ita.	Umeaa, Swe.	5.02.74
Fitzpatrick, Ian	5. 9	–	Manchester	22.09.80
Giggs, Ryan	5.11	–	Cardiff	29.11.73
Greening, Jonathan	6. 0	York City	Scarborough	2.01.79
Healey, David	5. 8	–	Downpatrick	5.08.79
Nevland, Erik	5.10	Viking Stavanger, Nor.	Stavanger, Nor.	10.11.77
Notman, Alex	5. 7	–	Edinburgh	10.12.79
Sheringham, Teddy	6. 0	Tottenham	Highams Park	2.04.66
Solskjaer, Ole Gunnar	5.10	Molde, Nor.	Kristiansund, Nor.	26.02.73
Webber, Danny	5. 9	–	Manchester	28.12.81
Wheatcroft, Paul	5. 8	–	Manchester	22.11.80
Wood, Jamie	5.10	–	Salford	21.09.78
Yorke, Dwight	5.10	Aston Villa	Canaan, Tob.	3.11.71

MIDDLESBROUGH

Ground: Cellnet Riverside Stadium, Middlesbrough, Cleveland TS3 6RS.
Telephone: 01642 877700 **Clubcall:** 0891 42400.
Club Nickname: Boro.
First-choice colours: Red shirts; white shorts; red stockings.
Record transfer fee: £7,000,000 to Juventus for Fabrizio Ravanelli.
Record fee received: £12,000,000 from Atletico Madrid for Juninho, July 1997.
Record attendance: At Riverside Stadium: 34,687 v Tottenham (Premier League) February 1999. At Ayresome Park: 53,596 v Newcastle Utd. (Div.1) December 1949.
Capacity for 1999-2000: 35,000.
Average home League attendance 1998-99: 34,389.
Sponsors: Cellnet.
League Championship: 3rd 1913-14.
F.A. Cup: runners up 1997.

League Cup: runners up 1997, 1998.
Finishing positions in Premiership: 1992-93 21th 1995-96 12th, 1996-97 19th 1998-99 9th.
Biggest win: 9-0 v Brighton & H.A., Div 2, 23.8.1958.
Biggest defeat: 0-9 v Blackburn Rov., Div 2, 6.11.1954.
Highest League scorer in a season: George Camsell, 59, 1926-27.
Most League goals in aggregate: George Camsell, 326, 1925-39.
Longest unbeaten League sequence: 24 matches (September 1973).
Longest sequence without a League win: 19 matches (October 1981).
Most capped player: Wilf Mannion (England) 26.
History: Middlesbrough FC was formed by members of the Middlesbrough Cricket Club at a meeting in the Albert Park Hotel in 1875. The belief that the club was founded at a tripe supper at the Corporation Hotel has proved to be little more than a good story. The Club played at Ayresome Park for 92 years from 1903 when they left the Linthorpe Road Ground to 1995 when they moved to the state of the art Riverside Stadium. During the 1966 World Cup, Ayresome Park's reputation was such that it was selected as a host venue. Middlesbrough made their first ever appearance at Wembley in 1997 when they lost to Leicester City in the League Cup Final. Having broken their duck they returned in that year's F.A. Cup final and the following season's League Cup Final. On both occasions however they lost to Chelsea. In 1997-88 Middlesbrough broke two post-war records. They fielded 36 players and 20 of them scored during the course of the season.

RIVERSIDE PLAYING STAFF

Name	Height ft. in.	Previous Club	Birthplace	Birthdate
Goalkeepers				
Beresford, Marlon	6. 1	Burnley	Lincoln	2.06.69
Jones, Bradley	6. 3	–	Australia	19.03.82
Roberts, Ben	6. 2	–	Bishop Auckland	22.06.75
Schwarzer, Mark	6. 5	Bradford City	Sydney, Aus.	6.10.72
Defenders				
Baker, Steve	6. 0	–	Pontefract	8.09.78
Cooper, Colin	5.11	Nott'm. Forest	Sedgefield	28.02.67
Festa, Gianluca	5.11	Inter Milan, Ita.	Cagliari, Ita.	15.03.69
Fleming, Curtis	5.10	St. Patrick's Athletic	Manchester	8.10.68
Gavin, Jason	6. 0	–	Dublin	14.03.80
Gordon, Dean	6. 0	Crystal Palace	Thornton Heath	10.02.73
Hanson, Christian	6. 1	–	Middlesbrough	3.08.81
Harrison, Craig	6. 0	–	Gateshead	10.11.77
Kinder, Vladimir	5. 9	Slovan Bratislava, Cze.	Bratislava, Cze.	9.03.69
Pallister, Gary	6. 5	Manchester Utd.	Ramsgate	30.06.65
Stockdale, Robbie	6. 0	–	Redcar	30.11.79
Vickers, Steve	6. 2	Tranmere Rov.	Bishop Auckland	13.10.67
Midfield				
Cummins, Michael	6. 0	–	Dublin	1.06.78
Gascoigne, Paul	5.10	Glasgow Rangers	Gateshead	27.05.67
Kell, Richard	6. 1	–	Bishop Auckland	15.09.79
Maddison, Neil	5.10	Scunthorpe Utd.	Darlington	2.10.69
Moore, Alan	5.10	Rivermount	Dublin	25.11.74
Mustoe, Robbie	6. 0	Oxford Utd.	Oxford	28.08.68
O'Loughlin, John	5. 8	Bruncrana Hearts	Letterkenny	31.01.79
Ormerod, Anthony	5.11	–	Middlesbrough	31.03.79
Prunty, Sean	5. 9	Belvedere	Dublin	10.07.80
Stamp, Phil	5.11	–	Middlesbrough	12.12.75
Summerbell, Mark	5.11	–	Durham	30.10.76
Townsend, Andy	6. 0	Aston Villa	Maidstone	27.07.63
Walklate, Steve	5.11	–	Durham	27.09.79

Forwards

Name	Height ft. in.	Previous Club	Birthplace	Birthdate
Armstrong, Alun	6. 0	Stockport Co.	Gateshead	22.02.75
Campbell, Andy	6. 0	–	Middlesbrough	18.04.79
Canavan, Michael	6. 1	–	South Shields	17.09.80
Deane, Brian	6. 3	Benfica, Por.	Leeds	7.02.68
Jones, Thomas	5.10	–	Middlesbrough	26.03.80
O'Neill, Keith	6. 1	Norwich City	Dublin	16.02.79
Ricard, Hamilton	6. 1	Deportivo Cali, Por.	Choco, Col.	12.01.74

NEWCASTLE UNITED

Ground: St James' Park, Newcastle-upon-Tyne, NE1 4ST.
Telephone: 0191 201 8400 **Clubcall:** 0891 121190.
Club Nickname: Magpies.
First-choice colours: Black and white shirts; black shorts; black stockings.
Record transfer fee: £15,000,000 to Blackburn Rov. for Alan Shearer, July 1996.
Record fee received: £6,250,000 from Manchester Utd. for Andy Cole, January 1995.
Record attendance: 68,386 v Chelsea (Div. 1) September 1930.
Capacity for 1999-2000: 36,610.
Average home League attendance 1998-99: 36,665.
Sponsors: Newcastle Breweries.
League Championship: winners 1904-05, 1906-07, 1908-09, 1926-27.
F.A. Cup: winners 1910, 1924, 1932, 1951, 1952, 1955.
League Cup: runners up 1976.
European Competitions: winners Fairs Cup 1968-69, Anglo-Italian Cup 1972-73.
Finishing positions in Premiership: 1993-94 3rd 1994-95 6th 1995-96 2nd 1996-97 2nd 1997-98 13th 1998-99 13th.
Biggest win: 13-0 v Newport County, Div. 2, 5.10.1946.
Biggest defeat: 0-9 v Burton Wanderers, Div. 2, 15.4.1895.
Highest League scorer in a season: Hughie Gallacher, 36, 1926-27.
Most League goals in aggregate: Jackie Milburn, 177, 1946-57.
Most capped player: Alf McMichael (Northern Ireland) 40.
Longest unbeaten League sequence: 14 matches (April 1950).
Longest sequence without a League win: 21 matches (January 1978).
History: The Magpies origins can be traced to Stanley, a club formed in 1881. In October 1882 Stanley changed their name to Newcastle East End to avoid confusion with two other local clubs, Stanley Nops and Stanley Albion. And in 1892, members of the recently defunct Newcastle West End, invited the Magpies to play at St James' Park. They accepted the offer and after a meeting at Bath Lane Hall changed their name to Newcastle Utd. **Len Shackleton** scored six times as Newcastle Utd. beat Newport 13-0 in a second division match in 1946. Receipts totalled £83,000 when Newcastle Utd. faced Liverpool in a testimonial match for **Kevin Keegan** in May 1984. Newcastle Utd. established a formidable reputation as F.A. Cup experts during the early 1950's when they won the trophy three times in five years.

ST JAMES' PARK PLAYING STAFF

Name	Height ft. in.	Previous Club	Birthplace	Birthdate
Goalkeepers				
Given, Shay	6. 2	Blackburn Rov.	Lifford, Ire.	20.04.76
Harper, Steve	6. 2	Seaham Redstar	Easington	3.02.70
Perez, Lionel	6. 0	Sunderland	Bagnol Ceze, Fra.	24.04.67
Defenders				
Barton, Warren	5.11	Wimbledon	Stoke Newington	19.03.69
Beharall, David	6. 0	–	Newcastle	8.03.79
Domi, Didier	5. 8	Paris St Germain, Fra.	Sarcelles, Fra.	2.05.78

Howey, Steve	6. 1	–	Sunderland	26.10.71
Charvet, Laurent	5.11	Cannes, Fra.	Beziers, Fra.	8.05.73
Hughes, Aaron	6. 0	–	Magherafelt	8.11.79
Griffin, Andy	5. 8	Stoke City	Wigan	17.03.79
Goma, Alain	6. 0	Paris St Germain, Fra.	Sault, Fra.	5.12.72
Marcelino, Elena	6. 2	Real Mallorca, Spa.	Santander, Spa.	26.09.73
Pistone, Alessandro	5.11	Inter Milan, Ita.	Milan, Ita.	27.07.75
Serrant, Carl	5.11	Oldham Athletic	Bradford	12.09.75
Midfield				
Brady, Gary	5.10	Tottenham	Glasgow	7.09.76
Glass, Stephen	5. 9	Aberdeen	Dundee	23.05.76
Hamilton, Des	5.11	Bradford City	Bradford	15.08.76
Hamann, Dieter	6. 2	Bayern Munich, Ger.	Munich, Ger.	27.08.73
Lee, Robert	5.11	Charlton Athletic	West Ham	1.02.66
Maric, Silvio	5.10	Croatia Zagreb. Cro.	Zagreb, Cro.	20.03.75
McClen, Jamie	5. 8	–	Newcastle	13.03.79
Solano, Nolberto	5. 9	Boca Juniors, Arg.	Lima, Per.	12.12.74
Speed, Gary	5. 9	Everton	Mancot	8.09.69
Forwards				
Andersson, Andreas	5. 8	AC Milan, Ita.	Osterhoninage, Swe.	10.04.74
Ferguson, Duncan	6. 3	Everton	Stirling	27.12.71
Ketsbaia, Temuri	5. 8	AEK Athens, Gre.	Gale, Geo.	18.03.68
Shearer, Alan	6. 0	Blackburn Rov.	Newcastle	13.08.70

SHEFFIELD WEDNESDAY

Ground: Hillsborough, Sheffield S6 1SW.
Telephone: 0114 2212121 **Clubcall:** 0891 121186.
Club Nickname: The Owls.
First-choice colours: Blue and white striped shirts, black shorts, black stockings.
Record transfer fee: £4,700,000 to Celtic for Paulo Di Canio, August 1997.
Record fee received: £2,650,00 from Blackburn Rov. for Paul Warhurst, September 1993.
Record attendance: 72,841 v Manchester City, 17 February 1934.
Capacity for 1999-2000: 39,859.
Average home League attendance 1998-99: 26,745.
Sponsors: Sanderson.
League Championship: winners 1902-03, 1903-04, 1928-29, 1929-30.
F.A. Cup: winners 1896, 1907, 1935. **Biggest win:** 12-0 v Halliwell, R1, 17.1.1891.
League Cup: winners 1991.
European Competitions: (best) UEFA Cup qf 1963-64.
Finishing positions in Premiership: 1992-93 14th, 1993-94 7th, 1994-95 13th, 1995-96 15th, 1996-97 7th, 1997-98 16th, 1998-99 12th.
Biggest win: 9-1 v Birmingham City, Div. 1, 13.12.1930 and 8-0 v Sunderland, Div. 1, 26.12.1911.
Biggest defeat: 0-10 v Aston Villa, Div. 1, 5.10.1912.
Highest League scorer in a season: Derek Dooley, 46, 1951-52.
Most League goals in aggregate: Andy Wilson, 199, 1900-20.
Most capped player: Nigel Worthington (Northern Ireland) 50.
Longest unbeaten League sequence: 19 matches (December 1960).
Longest sequence without a League win: 20 matches (October 1954).
History: Founded in 1867 by members of Sheffield Wed. Cricket Club. The footballers occasionally used Sheffield Utd.'s Bramall Lane ground before settling at Owlerton (later Hillsborough) in 1899. It has staged two England internationals, was a 1966 world cup venue and is regularly selected for F.A. Cup semi-finals. In 1989, 96 Liverpool fans died as a result of overcrowding at the Leppings Lane end during an abandoned semi-final with Nott'm. Forest. Everton's visit to the ground in April 1902

attracted a record low crowd of only 2,500. Wednesday scored seven first half goals during their 8-0 win over Sunderland on Boxing Day 1911 but **Doug Hunt** holds the individual club record for goalscoring in a single match with six against Norwich City in division two, 19.11.1938.

HILLSBOROUGH PLAYING STAFF

Name	Height ft. in.	Previous Club	Birthplace	Birthdate
Goalkeepers				
Jones, Stuart	–	Weston-super-Mare	Bristol	24.10.77
Pressman, Kevin	6. 1	–	Fareham	6.11.97
Srnicek, Pavel	6. 2	Banik Ostrava, Cze	Ostrava, Cze	10.03.68
Defenders				
Barrett, Earl	5.10	Everton	Rochdale	28.04.67
Billington, David	5. 7	Peterborough Utd.	Oxford	15.10.80
Hinchcliffe, Andy	5. 1	Everton	Manchester	5.02.69
Newsome, Jon	6. 2	Norwich City	Sheffield	6.09.70
Nolan, Ian	6. 0	Tranmere Rov.	Liverpool	9.07.70
Stefanovic, Dejan	6. 2	RS Belgrade, Yug	Nis, Yug	28.10.74
Thome, Emerson	6. 1	Benfica, Por	Porto Alegra, Bra	30.03.72
Walker, Des	5.11	Sampdoria, Ita	Hackney	26.11.65
Midfield				
Agogo, Manuel	5. 9	–	Accra, Ghana	1.08.79
Alexandersson, Niclas	6. 2	IFK Gothenburg, Swe	Halmstad, Swe	29.12.71
Atherton, Peter	5.11	Coventry City	Wigan	6.04.70
Carbone, Benito	5. 6	Inter Milan, Ita	Begnara, Ita	14.08.71
Haslam, Steven	–	–	Sheffield	6.09.79
Jonk, Wim	6. 1	PSV Eindhoven, Hol	Netherlands	12.10.66
Rudi, Petter	6. 1	Molde, Nor	Kristiansund, Nor	17.09.73
Scott, Phillip	5. 9	St Johnstone	Perth	14.11.74
Sonner, Danny	5.11	Ipswich Town	Wigan	9.01.72
Forwards				
Booth, Andy	6. 1	Huddersfield Town	Huddersfield	17.03.73
Briscoe, Lee	5.11	–	Pontefract	30.09.75
Cresswell, Richard	6. 0	York City	Bridlington	20.09.77
Humphreys, Richie	5.10	–	Sheffield	30.11.77
McKeever, Mark	5.10	Peterborough Utd.	Derry	16.11.78
Morrison, Owen	–	–	–	–
Oakes, Scott	5.11	Luton Town	Leicester	5.08.72
Quinn, Alan	5. 9	Cherry Orchard	Dublin	13.06.79
Sanetti, Francesco	6. 1	Genoa, Ita	Rome, Ita	11.01.79
Whittingham, Guy	5.10	Aston Villa	Evesham	10.11.64

SOUTHAMPTON

Ground: The Dell, Milton Road, Southampton, Hampshire SO15 2XH.
Telephone: 01703 220505 **Clubcall:** 0891 121178.
Club Nickname: Saints.
First-choice colours: Red and white striped shirts; black shorts; red and white stockings.
Record transfer fee: £2,000,000 to Sheffield Wed. for David Hirst, October 1997.
Record fee received: £7,500,000 from Blackburn Rov. for Kevin Davies, June 1998.
Record attendance: 31,044 v Manchester Utd. (Div. 1) October 1969.
Capacity for 1999-2000: 15,250.
Average home League attendance 1998-99: 15,139.
Sponsors: Friends Provident.
League Championship: 2nd 1983-84.

FA Cup: winners 1976.

League Cup: runners-up 1979.

European Competitions: (best) Fairs Cup round 3, 1969-70, Cup Winners' Cup round 3(QF), 1976-77.

Finishing positions in Premiership: 1992-93 18th 1993-94 18th 1994-95 10th 1995-96 17th 1996-97 16th 1997-98 12th 1998-99 17th.

Biggest win: 8-0 v Northampton Town, Div. 3S, 24.12.1921.

Biggest defeat: 0-8 v Tottenham, Div. 2, 28.3.1936 and v Everton Div. 1, 20.11.1971.

Highest League scorer in a season: Derek Reeves, 39, 1959-60.

Most League goals in aggregate: Mike Channon, 185, 1966-77, 1979-82.

Most capped player: Peter Shilton (England) 49.

Longest unbeaten League sequence: 19 matches (September 1921).

Longest sequence without a League win: 20 matches (August 1969).

History: Formed as Southampton St Mary by a group of church goers with a curate as their first president, the club reached the FA Cup finals of 1900 and 1902 as a Southern League side. After playing on the Antelope and County cricket grounds, Southampton settled into the Dell in 1898. They joined the new Third Division in 1920 and won promotion within two years. Southampton's greatest day came at Wembley in 1976. They were then a second division side but a **Bobby Stokes** goal upset mighty Manchester Utd. and allowed them to carry off the FA Cup for the first time. Winger **Terry Paine**, who won 19 England caps, made a total of 809 appearances (713 League) for the club in an 18-year career between 1956 and 1974. Only 1,875 spectators turned up to watch Southampton play Port Vale in Division 2 on 30 March 1936.

THE DELL PLAYING STAFF

Name	Height ft. in.	Previous Club	Birthplace	Birthdate
Goalkeepers				
Bevan, Scott	6. 7	–	Southampton	16.09.79
Jones, Paul	6. 3	Stockport Co.	Stockport	18.04.67
Moss, Neil	6. 3	Bournemouth	New Milton	10.05.75
Stensgaard, Michael	6. 2	Copenhagen	Denmark	–
Defenders				
Colleter, Patrick	5. 8	Marseille	France	6.11.65
Collins, Chris	6. 1	–	Chatham	26.09.79
Dodd, Jason	5.10	–	Bath	2.11.70
Dryden, Richard	6. 1	Bristol City	Stroud	14.06.69
Hiley, Scott	5. 9	Manchester City	Plymouth	27.09.68
Jenkins, Steve	6. 3	–	Bristol	2.01.80
Lundekvam, Claus	6. 4	Brann Bergen	Brann, Nor.	22.03.73
Marshall, Scott	6. 1	Arsenal	Edinburgh	1.05.73
Monk, Gary	6. 1	Torquay Utd.	Bedford	6.03.79
Monkou, Ken	6. 3	Chelsea	Surinam	29.11.64
Warner, Phil	5.10	–	Southampton	2.02.79
Midfield				
Benali, Francis	5. 9	–	Southampton	30.12.68
Beresford, John	5. 8	Newcastle Utd.	Sheffield	4.09.66
Gibbens, Kevin	5.11	–	Southampton	4.11.79
Howells, David	6. 0	Tottenham	Guildford	15.12.67
Hughes, David	5.11	–	St. Albans	30.12.72
Kachloul, Hassan	6. 1	Metz, Fra.	Agadir, Alg.	19.02.73
Marsden, Chris	6. 0	Birmingham City	Sheffield	3.01.69
Oakley, Matthew	5.11	–	Peterborough	17.08.77
Sims, Adam	5.10	–	Bristol	–
Forwards				
Beattie, James	6. 1	Blackburn Rov.	Lancaster	27.02.78
Bradley, Shayne	6. 0	–	Gloucester	8.12.79

Bridge, Wayne	5.11	–	Southampton	5.08.80
Hirst, David	5.11	Sheffield Wed.	Barnsley	7.12.67
Hughes, Mark	5.10	Chelsea	Wrexham	1.11.63
Le Tissier, Matthew	6. 1	–	Guernsey	14.10.68
Ostenstad, Egil	5.11	Viking Stavanger, Nor.	Haugesund, Nor.	2.01.72
Pahars, Marian	5. 9	Skonto Riga, Lat	Riga, Latvia	–
Paul, Mark	5. 7	–	Peterborough	–
Ripley, Stuart	6. 0	Blackburn Rov.	Middlesbrough	20.11.67
Rodrigues, Dani	5.10	Farense, Por.	Portugal	–
Williams, Andrew	5.10	–	Bristol	8.10.77

SUNDERLAND

Ground: Stadium of Light, Sunderland, Tyne and Wear SR5 1BT.
Telephone: 0191 5515000. **Clubcall:** 01716 136000.
Club Nickname: None.
First-choice colours: Red and white shirts; black shorts, black stockings.
Record transfer fee: £2,500,000 to Newcastle Utd. for Lee Clark, June 1997.
Record fee received: £3,000,000 from Fulham for Lee Clark, July 1999.
Sponsors: Reg Vardy.
Average home League attendance 1998-99: 38,745.
Capacity for 1999-2000: 42,000.
Record attendance: (Roker Park) 75,118 v Derby Co. (F.A. Cup 6) 8 March 1933.
(Stadium of Light) 41,634 v Birmingham City (Div. 1) 9 May 1999.
League Championship: winners 1891-92, 1892-93, 1894-95, 1901-02, 1912-13, 1935-36.
F.A. Cup: winners 1937, 1973.
League Cup: runners up 1985.
European Competitions: Cup Winners' Cup R2, 1973-74.
Finishing positions in Premiership: 1996-97 18th.
Biggest win: 9-1 v Newcastle Utd. Div. 1, 5.12.1908. **F.A. Cup:** 11-1 v Fairfield, round one, 2.2.1895.
Biggest defeat: 0-8 v Sheffield Wed., Div. 1, 26.12.1911, v West Ham Utd., Div. 1, 19.10.1968, v Watford, Div. 1, 25.9.1982.
Highest League scorer in a season: Dave Halliday, 43, 1928-29.
Most League goals in aggregate: Charlie Buchan, 209, 1911-25.
Most capped player: Charlie Hurley (Republic of Ireland) 38.
Longest unbeaten League sequence: 19 matches (May 1998).
Longest sequence without a League win: 14 matches (April 1985).
History: Scottish schoolmaster James Allan formed The Sunderland and District Teachers' Association FC in 1879 for members of the teaching profession. Financial difficulties forced the club to allow others from outside the profession to join, and in October 1880 the club was re-named Sunderland AFC. Sunderland used five different grounds in their early years before settling at Roker Park 1898. It was their home until 1997 when they left for the Stadium of Light. The club sprang one of the greatest F.A. Cup Final upsets of all time when, as a second Division club, they defeated a formidable Leeds Utd. side in the 1973 showpiece when managed by Bob Stokoe. **Kevin Phillips**, who completed a run of scoring in seven successive matches in January 1998, broke Brian Clough's post-war scoring record with 35 in all competitions during the 1997-98 season.

STADIUM OF LIGHT PLAYING STAFF

Name	Height ft. in.	Previous Club	Birthplace	Birthdate
Goalkeepers				
Marriott, Andy	6. 0	Wrexham	Sutton-in-Ashfield	11.10.70

Sorensen, Thomas	6. 4	Odense BK, Den.	Odense, Den.	
Weaver, Luke	6. 2	Leyton Orient	Woolwich	26.06.79
Defenders				
Bould, Steve	6. 4	Arsenal	Stoke on Trent	16.11.62
Butler, Paul	6. 2	Bury	Manchester	2.11.72
Craddock, Jody	6. 0	Cambridge Utd.	Redditch	25.07.75
Dickman, Elliot	5.10	–	Hexham	11.10.78
Gray, Michael	5. 7	–	Sunderland	3.08.74
Harrison, Gerry	5.10	Burnley	Lambeth	15.04.72
Holloway, Darren	6. 0	–	Bishop Auckland	3.10.77
Makin, Chris	5.11	Oldham Athletic	Manchester	8.05.73
Scott, Martin	5.10	Bristol City	Sheffield	7.01.68
Williams, Darren	5.10	York City	Middlesbrough	28.04.77
Midfielders				
Aiston, Sam	6. 0	Newcastle Utd.	Newcastle	21.11.76
Ball, Kevin	5. 9	Portsmouth	Hastings	12.11.64
Butler, Thomas	6. 0	–	Dublin	2.04.81
Fredgaard, Carsten	6. 0	Lyngby, Den.		
Johnston, Allan	5.11	Rennes, Fra.	Glasgow	14.12.73
McCann, Gavin	5.11	Everton	Blackpool	10.01.78
Rae, Alex	5. 9	Millwall	Glasgow	30.09.69
Summerbee, Nicky	5.11	Manchester City	Altrincham	26.08.71
Thirlwell, Paul	5.11	–	Newcastle	13.02.79
Wainwright, Neil	6. 0	Wrexham	Warrington	4.11.77
Forwards				
Beavers, Paul	6. 3	–	Hastings	2.10.78
Bridges, Michael	6. 1	–	North Shields	5.08.78
Dichio, Danny	6. 3	Sampdoria	Hammersmith	19.10.74
Phillips, Kevin	5. 7	Watford	Hitchin	25.07.73
Quinn, Niall	6. 4	Manchester City	Dublin	6.10.66

TOTTENHAM HOTSPUR

Ground: 748 High Road, Tottenham, London N17 OAP.
Telephone: 0181 3655010 **Clubcall:** 0891 335555.
Club Nickname: Spurs.
First-choice colours: White shirts, navy blue shorts, white stockings.
Record transfer fee: £6,000,000 to Newcastle Utd. for Les Ferdinand, July 1997.
Record fee received: £5,500,000 from Lazio for Paul Gascoigne, May 1992.
Record attendance: 75,038 v Sunderland (F.A. Cup 6) 5 March 1938.
Capacity for 1999-2000: 36,214.
Average home League attendance 1998-99: 34,153.
Sponsors: Holsten.
League Championship: winners 1950-51, 1960-61.
F.A. Cup: winners 1901, 1921, 1961, 1962, 1967, 1981, 1982, 1991.
League Cup: winners 1971, 1973.
European Competitions: winners Cup Winners' Cup 1962-63, UEFA Cup 1971-72, 1983-84.
Finishing positions in Premiership: 1992-93 8th, 1993-94 15th, 1994-95 7th, 1995-96 8th, 1996-97 10th, 1997-98 14th, 1998-99 11th.
Biggest win: 9-0 v Bristol Rov., Div.2, 22.10.1977, F.A. Cup 13-2 v Crewe Alexandra, round four replay, 3.2.1960, Europe 9-0 v Keflavik, UEFA Cup, round one, 28.9.1971.
Biggest defeat: 0-7 v Liverpool, Div.1, 2.9.1979.
Highest League scorer in a season: Jimmy Greaves, 37, 1962-63.
Most League goals in aggregate: Jimmy Greaves, 220, 1961-70.
Most capped player: Pat Jennings (Northern Ireland) 74.

Longest unbeaten League sequence: 22 matches (August 1949).
Longest sequence without a League win: 16 matches (December 1934).
History: Formed from a cricket club in 1882, many of the founding members of the Hotspur Football Club were old boys of St.John's Presbyterian School and Tottenham Grammar School. The club's original home ground was Tottenham marshes but after three years they moved to Northumberland Park and arrived at White Hart Lane four years later. The ground staged three England internationals in the 1930's and another in 1949. They won the F.A. Cup as a non-League club in 1901 but the 1961 League Championship and F.A. Cup double under **Bill Nicholson** was their finest achievement. Three European trophies followed. Despite their relegation to Division two for the 1977-78 season Tottenham quickly recovered their status as one of the biggest clubs in the land. Four players have scored five goals in a single Tottenham League match: Viv Woodward, Ted Harper, Alf Stokes and Bobby Smith. **Steve Perryman** made 864 appearances in various competitions for the club between 1969 and 1986.

WHITE HART LANE PLAYING STAFF

Name	Height ft. in.	Previous Club	Birthplace	Birthdate
Goalkeepers				
Baardsen, Espen	6. 5	San Francisco All Blacks, USA	San Rafael, USA	7.12.77
Segers, Hans	5.11	Wolves	Eindhoven, Hol.	30.10.61
Walker, Ian	6. 1	–	Watford	31.10.71
Defenders				
Campbell, Sol	6. 1	–	Newham	18.09.74
Carr, Stephen	5. 8	–	Dublin	29.08.76
Edinburgh, Justin	5.10	Southend Utd.	Basildon	18.12.69
King, Ledley	6. 1	–	London	12.10.80
Perry, Chris	5. 8	Wimbledon	Carshalton	26.04.73
Scales, John	6. 0	Liverpool	Harrogate	4.07.66
Taricco, Mauricio	5. 8	Ipswich Town	Buenos Aires, Arg.	10.03.73
Thelwell, Alton	5.11	–	London	5.09.80
Tramezzani, Paolo	6. 0	Piacenza, Ita.	Reggio-Emilia, Ita.	30.07.70
Vega, Ramon	6. 3	Cagliari, Ita.	Zurich, Swi.	14.06.71
Young, Luke	5.11	–	Harlow	19.07.79
Midfield				
Anderton, Darren	6. 1	Portsmouth	Southampton	3.03.72
Clemence, Stephen	5.11	–	Liverpool	31.03.78
Fox, Ruel	5. 6	Newcastle Utd.	Ipswich Town	14.01.68
Freund, Steffen	5. 9	Borussia Dortmund, Ger.	Brandenburg, Ger.	19.01.70
Ginola, David	6. 0	Newcastle Utd.	Gassin, Fra.	25.01.67
Korsten, Willem	5.11	Vitesse Arnhem, Hol.	–	
Nielsen, Allan	5. 8	Brondby, Den.	Esbjerg, Denmark	13.03.71
Saib, Moussa	5. 8	Valencia, Spa.	Theniet-el-Had, Alg.	5.03.69
Sherwood, Tim	6. 1	Blackburn Rov.	St. Albans	2.02.69
Forwards				
Allen, Rory	5.11	–	Beckenham	17.10.77
Armstrong, Chris	6. 0	Crystal Palace	Newcastle	19.06.71
Dominguez, Jose	5. 3	Sporting Lisbon, Por.	Lisbon, Por.	16.02.74
Ferdinand, Les	5.11	Newcastle Utd.	Ladbroke Grove	18.12.66
Iversen, Steffen	5.10	Rosenborg, Nor.	Oslo, Nor.	10.11.76
McVeigh, Paul	5. 6	–	Belfast	6.12.77

WATFORD

Ground: Vicarage Road Stadium, Vicarage Road, Watford, Herts WD1 8ER.
Telephone: 01923 496000 **Clubcall:** 0891 104104.

Club Nickname: Hornets.
First-choice colours: Yellow shirts; red shorts, red stockings.
Record transfer fee: £550,000 to AC Milan for Luther Blissett.
Record fee received: £2,300,000 from Chelsea for Paul Furlong.
Record attendance: 34,099 v Manchester Utd. (F.A. Cup 4) February 1969.
Capacity for 1999-2000: 22,763.
Average home League attendance 1998-99: 11,822.
Sponsors: Phones 4U.
League Championship: (best) 2nd 1982-83.
F.A. Cup: (best) runners-up 1984.
League Cup: (best) semi-final 1979.
European Competitions: (best) UEFA Cup, round three, 1983-84.
Biggest win: 8-0 v Sunderland, Div. 1, 25.9.1982. F.A. Cup 10-1 v Lowestoft Town, first
   round, 27.11.1926.
Biggest defeat: 1-8 v Crystal Palace, Div 4, 23.9.1959, v Aberdare, Div 3S, 2.1.1926
   and 0-7 v Port Vale, Div 3S, 15.9.1947. F.A. Cup 0-10 v Wolves round one,
   13.12.1912.
Highest League scorer in a season: Cliff Holton, 42, 1959-60.
Most League goals in aggregate: Luther Blissett, 148, 1976-83, 1984-88, 1991-92.
Most capped player: John Barnes (England) and Kenny Jackett (Wales) both 31.
Longest unbeaten League sequence: 22 matches (October 1996).
Longest sequence without a League win: 19 matches (November 1971).
History: Originally formed as Watford Rov. in 1881, the club was re-named Watford in
   1898 after merging with local rivals Watford St Mary's. The Hornets became founder
   members of the Third Division when they joined the Football League in 1920. And
   they remained there until joining the newly created Fourth Division 38 years later.
   Enjoyed their best days under **Graham Taylor** who piloted the club's dramatic rise from
   division four to runners-up in the first division in six years. Singer-chairman Elton
   John wept tears of disappointment in the Wembley VIP box after Watford's 1984 F.A.
   Cup Final defeat by Everton. When Taylor left for Aston Villa in 1987, the club lost
   stability under four managers in four years. **Duncan Welbourne** made 457 appearances
   in all comptitions between 1963 and 1974. He missed only two League games in
   four seasons. **Joe Calvert** played for Watford aged 41 years and 25 days.

VICARAGE ROAD PLAYING STAFF

Name	Height ft. in.	Previous Club	Birthplace	Birthdate
Goalkeepers				
Chamberlain, Alec	6. 2	Sunderland	March	20.06.64
Day, Chris	6. 4	Crystal Palace	Walthamstow	28.07.75
Defenders				
Gibbs, Nigel	5. 7	–	St. Albans	20.11.65
Iroha, Ben	5. 8	Elche, Nig.	Calabar, Nig.	29.11.69
Langston, Matthew	6. 2	–	Brighton	2.04.81
Lyttle, Des	5. 8	Nott'm Forest	Wolverhampton	26.09.71
Millen, Keith	6. 2	Brentford	Croydon	26.09.66
Page, Robert	6. 0	–	Llwynipia	9.09.74
Palmer, Steve	6. 1	Ipswich Town	Brighton	31.03.68
Panayi, James	5.11	–	Hammersmith	24.01.80
Perpetuini, David	5. 9	–	Hitchin	26.09.79
Pluck, Colin	6. 0	–	London	6.09.78
Robinson, Paul	5. 9	–	Watford	14.12.78
Ward, Darren	6. 3	–	Harrow	13.09.78
Williams, Mark	6. 0	Chesterfield	Cheshire	28.09.70
Yates, Dean	6. 2	Derby Co.	Leicester	26.10.67
Midfield				
Bakalli, Adrian	5.10	RW Molenbeek, Bel.	Belgium	–
Bonnot, Alex	5. 8	SC Angers, Fra.	Poissy, Fra.	31.07.73

Easton, Clint	5.11	–	Barking	1.11.77
Gudmundsson, Johann	6. 0	Keflavik, Ice.	Rekjavik, Ice.	5.12.77
Hazan, Alon	6. 1	Ironi Ashdod, Isr.	Ashdod, Isr.	14.09.67
Hyde, Micah	5.10	Cambridge Utd.	Newham	10.11.74
Johnson, Lee	5. 7	–	Newmarket	7.06.81
Johnson, Richard	5.10	Newcastle Utd., Aus.	Kurri Kurri, Aus	27.04.74
Kennedy, Peter	5.10	Notts Co.	Lisburn	10.09.73
Forwards				
Brooker, Stephen	5.10	–	Newport Pagnell	21.05.81
Mooney, Tommy	5.11	Southend Utd.	Middlesbrough	11.08.71
Ngonge, Michel	6. 0	Samsunspor, Tur.	Huy, Zai.	10.01.67
Noel-Williams, Gifton	6. 1	–	London	21.01.80
Smart, Allan	6. 2	Carlisle Utd.	Perth	8.07.74
Smith, Tommy	5. 9	–	Hemel Hempstead	22.05.80
Wright, Nick	5.10	Carlisle Utd.	Derby	15.10.75

WEST HAM UNITED

Ground: Boleyn Ground, Green Street, Upton Park, London E13 9AZ.
Telephone: 0181 548 2748 **Clubcall:** 0891 121165.
Club Nickname: Hammers.
First-choice colours: Claret and sky blue shirts; white shorts; claret stockings.
Record transfer fee: £4,200,000 to Lens for Marc Viven Foe, January 1999.
Record fee received: £7,000,000 from Wimbledon for John Hartson, January 1999.
Record attendance: 43,322 v Tottenham, Div. 1, October 1970.
Capacity for 1999-2000: 26,014.
Average home League attendance 1998-99: 25,683.
Sponsors: Dr Martens.
League Championship: (best) 3rd 1985-86.
F.A. Cup: winners 1964, 1975, 1980.
League Cup: runners up 1966, 1981.
European Competitions: winners Cup Winners' Cup 1964-65.
Finishing positions in Premiership: 1993-94 13th 1994-95 14th 1995-96 10th 1996-97 14th 1997-98 8th 1998-99 5th.
Biggest win: 8-0 v Rotherham Utd., Div 2, 8.3.1958 and v Sunderland, Div 1, 19.10.1968. League Cup 10-0 v Bury, round 2, 25.10.1984.
Biggest defeat: 0-7 v Sheff. Wed., Div 1, 28.11.1959, v Everton, Div 1, 22.10.1927 and v Barnsley, Div 2, 1.9.1919.
Highest League scorer in a season: Vic Watson, 42, 1929-30.
Most League goals in aggregate: Vic Watson, 298, 1920-35.
Most capped player: Bobby Moore (England) 108.
Longest unbeaten League sequence: 27 matches (December 1980).
Longest sequence without a League win: 17 matches (January 1976).
History: Started as Thames Ironworks founded by shipbuilding yard employees based at Chatham, Kent, in 1895. The club failed for lack of funds and was wound up in June 1900 but relaunched a month later as West Ham Utd. They made their Football League debut in 1919. Featured in the first Wembley F.A. Cup final staged at Wembley in 1923 – but were beaten by Bolton Wand. after spectators were cleared from the pitch by a policeman on a white horse. West Ham Utd. provided the backbone of England's 1966 world cup winning team with **Bobby Moore**, **Martin Peters** and **Geoff Hurst** all appearing in the 4-2 victory over West Germany. Hurst, who started the competition as a reserve, remains the only man ever to score a hat-trick in the world cup final. West Ham Utd. have had only eight managers in their entire League history. **Ron Greenwood**, who later managed England, was the most successful winning the F.A. Cup twice and the European Cup Winners' Cup. **Geoff Hurst** and **Vic Watson** each scored six goals in a single first division match for the club. Hurst's came against Sunderland in 1968 and Watson's against Leeds Utd. in 1929.

UPTON PARK PLAYING STAFF

Name	Height ft. in.	Previous Club	Birthplace	Birthdate
Goalkeepers				
Bywater, Stephen	6. 5	Rochdale	Manchester	7.06.81
Forrest, Craig	6. 4	Chelsea	Vancouver	20.09.67
Hislop, Shaka	6. 4	Newcastle Utd.	Hackney	22.02.69
Sealey, Les	6. 1	Leyton Orient	Bethnal Green	29.11.57
Defenders				
Coyne, Chris	6. 0	Perth	Brisbane, Aus.	20.12.78
Ferdinand, Rio	6. 2	–	Peckham	8.11.78
Iriekpen, Ezomo	6. 0	–	London	14.05.82
Margas, Javier	6. 1	Universidad, Chi.	Chile	10.05.69
Minto, Scott	5.10	Benfica, Por.	Cheshire	6.08.71
Pearce, Ian	6. 3	Blackburn Rov.	Bury St. Edmunds	7.05.74
Potts, Steve	5. 7	–	Hartford, USA	7.05.67
Ruddock, Neil	6. 2	Liverpool	Wandsworth	9.05.68
Vivien-Foe, Marc	6. 2	Lens, Fra,	Cameroon	1.05.75
Midfield				
Cole, Joe	5. 8	–	London	8.11.81
Keller, Marc	5. 8	Karlsruhe, Ger.	Colmar, Fra.	14.01.68
Lampard, Frank	6. 0	–	Romford	20.06.78
Lomas, Steve	6. 0	Manchester City	Hanover, Germany	14.03.72
Moncur, John	5. 7	Swindon Town	Mile End	22.09.66
Forwards				
Abou, Samassi	6. 1	Cannes, Fra.	Gagnoa, Iv. Co.	4.05.73
Alexander, Gary	6. 0	–	London	15.08.79
Bullard, Jimmy	5.10	Gravesend	Newham	23.10.78
Di Canio, Paolo	5. 9	Sheffield Wed.	Rome	9.07.68
Holligan, Gavin	6. 0	Kingstonian	Lambeth	13.06.80
Kitson, Paul	5.11	Newcastle Utd.	Murton	9.01.71
Lazaridis Stan	5. 9	West Adelaide, Aus.	Perth, Aus.	16.08.72
Omoyinmi, Emmanuel	5. 7	–	Nigeria	28.12.77
Sinclair, Trevor	5.10	Q.P.R.	Dulwich	2.03.73
Wright, Ian	5.10	Arsenal	Woolwich	3.11.63

WIMBLEDON

Ground: Selhurst Park, Norwood, London SE25 6PY.
Telephone: 0181 771 2233 **Clubcall:** 0891 121175.
Club Nickname: The Dons, The Crazy Gang.
First-choice colours: Navy blue shirts; navy blue shorts; navy blue stockings.
Record transfer fee: £7,000,000 to West Ham Utd. for John Hartson.
Record fee received: £4,000,000 from Newcastle Utd. for Warren Barton, June 1995.
Record attendance: 30,115 v Manchester Utd., May 1993.
Capacity for 1999-2000: 26,309.
Average home League attendance 1998-99: 18,235.
Sponsors: Elonex.
League Championship: (best) 1993-94 6th.
F.A. Cup: winners 1988.
League Cup: (best) semi-finals 1996-97, 1998-99.
Finishing positions in Premiership: 1992-93 12th, 1993-94 6th, 1994-95 9th, 1995-96 14th, 1996-97 8th, 1997-98 15th, 1998-99 16th.
Biggest win: 6-0 v Newport County, Div 3, 3.9.1983.
Biggest defeat: 1-6 v Carlisle Utd., Div 2, 23.3.1985. League Cup 0-8 v Everton, round 2, 29.8.1978.

Highest League scorer in a season: Alan Cork, 29, 1982-83.
Most League goals in aggregate: Alan Cork, 145, 1977-92.
Most capped player: Kenny Cunningham (Republic of Ireland) 23.
Longest unbeaten League sequence: 22 matches (January 1983).
Longest sequence without a League win: 14 matches (February 1980 and September 1995).
History: Wimbledon FC was founded in 1889 as Wimbledon Old Centrals by old boys from Central School. The club played in the Clapham League before moving to the Southern Suburban League in 1902. Gained election to the Football League in 1977 and were a top flight side by 1986, completing a 10-year dash from the Southern League. Provided probably the greatest post-war F.A. Cup final upset when they overcame strong favourites Liverpool with a **Lawrie Sanchez** goal at Wembley in 1988 to complete an unusual 'double'. They had won the F.A. Amateur Cup in 1963 when **Eddie Reynolds** scored all their goals with headers in a 4-2 victory over Sutton Utd. Wimbledon left their outdated Plough Lane home in 1991 to groundshare with Crystal Palace at Selhurst Park.

SELHURST PARK PLAYING STAFF

Name	Height ft. in.	Previous Club	Birthplace	Birthdate
Goalkeepers				
Davis, Kelvin	6. 1	Luton Town	Bedford	29.09.76
Heald, Paul	6. 2	Leyton Orient	Rotherham	20.09.68
Sullivan, Neil	6. 0	Sutton Utd.	Sutton	24.02.70
Defenders				
Blackwell, Dean	6. 1	–	Camden	5.12.69
Cunningham, Kenny	5.11	Millwall	Dublin	28.06.71
Hawkins, Peter	6. 0	–	Maidstone	18.09.78
Hodges, Danny	6. 0	–	Greenwich	14.09.76
Jupp, Duncan	6. 0	Fulham	Guildford	25.01.75
Kimble, Alan	5.10	Cambridge Utd.	Poole	6.08.66
McAllister, Brian	5.11	–	Glasgow	30.11.70
Pedersen, Tore	6. 1	Eintract Frankfurt	Fredrikstad, Nor.	20.09.69
Thatcher, Ben	5.11	Millwall	Swindon	30.11.75
Willmott, Chris	6. 2	Luton Town	Bedford	30.09.77
Midfield				
Ainsworth, Gareth	5.10	Port Vale	Blackburn	10.05.73
Ardley, Neil	5. 8	–	Epsom	1.09.72
Castledine, Stewart	6. 1	–	Wandsworth	22.01.73
Earle, Robbie	5. 9	Port Vale	Newcastle-u-Lyme	27.01.65
Francis, Damien	6. 0	–	Wandsworth	27.02.79
Hughes, Ceri	5.10	Luton Town	Pontypridd	26.01.71
Hughes, Michael	5. 6	West Ham Utd.	Belfast	2.08.71
Roberts, Andy	5.10	Crystal Palace	Dartford	20.03.74
Forwards				
Agyemang, Patrick	6. 1	–	Walthamstow	29.09.80
Cort, Carl	6. 4	–	London	1.11.77
Ekoku, Efan	6. 2	Norwich City	Manchester	8.06.67
Euell, Jason	5.11	–	London	6.02.77
Goodman, Jon	5.11	Millwall	Walthamstow	2.06.71
Hartson, John	6. 1	West Ham Utd.	Swansea	5.04.75
Leaburn, Carl	6. 3	Charlton Athletic	Lewisham	30.03.69

NATIONWIDE LEAGUE PLAYING STAFF
1999-2000

DIVISION ONE

BARNSLEY

Name	Height ft. in.	Previous Club	Birthplace	Birthdate
Goalkeepers				
Bullock, Anthony	6. 1	Leek	Warrington	18.02.72
Watson, David	5.11	–	Barnsley	10.11.73
Defenders				
Appleby, Matthew	5.10	Darlington	Middlesbrough	16.04.72
Barnard, Darren	5.10	Bristol City	Rintein, Ger.	30.11.71
Bassinder, Gavin	6. 0	–	Mexborough	24.09.79
Eaden, Nicholas	5.10	–	Sheffield	12.12.72
Jones, Scott	5.10	–	Sheffield	1.05.75
Krizan, Ales	5. 8	Branik Maribor, Slo.	Maribor, Slo.	25.07.71
Markstedt, Peter	5.11	Vasteras SK, Swe.	Vasteras, Swe.	11.01.72
Morgan, Chris	5.10	–	Barnsley	9.11.77
Moses, Adrian	6. 1	–	Doncaster	4.05.75
Midfielders				
Bullock, Martin	5. 4	Eastwood Town	Derby	5.03.75
Dudgeon, James	6. 2	–	Newcastle	19.03.81
Fumaca	6. 0	Colchester Utd.	Belem Parz, Bra.	15.07.76
Gregory, Andrew	5. 8	–	Barnsley	8.10.76
Marcelle, Clint	5. 4	Felgueiras, Por.	Port of Spain, Tri.	9.11.68
McClare, Sean	5. 9	–	Rotherham	12.01.78
Richardson, Kevin	5. 7	Southampton	Newcastle	4.12.62
Smith, Andrew	5. 7	–	Blackpool	31.01.80
Thomas, Geoff	6. 1	Nott'm Forest	Manchester	5.08.64
Tinkler, Eric	6. 2	Cagliari, Ita.	Roodepoort, S.A.	30.07.70
Van Der Laan, Robin	5.11	Derby Co.	Schiedam, Hol.	5.09.68
Forwards				
Bagshaw, Paul	5. 7	–	Sheffield	29.05.79
Dyer, Bruce	6. 0	Crystal Palace	Ilford	13.04.75
Hignett, Craig	5. 9	Aberdeen	Whiston	12.01.70
Hristov, Gjorgi	6. 0	Partizan Belgrade, Yug.	Bitola, Yug.	30.01.76
Parkin, Johnathan	6. 4	–	Barnsley	30.12.81
Rose, Karl	5. 8	–	Barnsley	12.10.78
Sheron, Mike	5. 9	Q.P.R.	Liverpool	11.01.72
Turner, Mike	6. 2	Bilston Town	Stoke on Trent	2.04.76

BIRMINGHAM CITY

Name	Height ft. in.	Previous Club	Birthplace	Birthdate
Goalkeepers				
Bennett, Ian	6. 0	Peterborough Utd.	Worksop	10.10.71
Poole, Kevin	5.10	Leicester City	Bromsgrove	21.07.63
Defenders				
Ablett, Gary	6. 2	Everton	Liverpool	19.11.65
Bass, Jonathan	6. 0	–	Weston-Super-Mare	1.01.76
Charlton, Simon	5. 8	Southampton	Huddersfield	25.10.71
Dyson, James	6. 2	–	Wordsley	20.04.79
Gill, Jeremy	5.11	Yeovil Town	Clevedon	8.09.70

Name	Height ft. in.	Previous Club	Birthplace	Birthdate
Grainger, Martin	5.10	Brentford	Enfield	23.08.72
Holdsworth, David	6. 1	Sheffield Utd.	Walthamstow	8.11.68
Johnson, Michael	5.11	Notts Co.	Nottingham	4.07.73
Marsh, Simon	5.11	Oxford Utd.	Ealing	29.01.77
Purse, Darren	6. 2	Oxford Utd.	Stepney	14.02.77
Rea, Simon	6. 1	–	Coventry	20.09.76
Rowett, Gary	6. 0	Derby Co.	Bromsgrove	6.03.74
Wassall, Darren	6. 0	Derby Co.	Birmingham	27.06.68
Midfielders				
Holland, Chris	5. 9	Newcastle Utd.	Whalley	11.09.75
Hughes, Bryan	5. 9	Wrexham	Liverpool	19.06.76
Hyde, Graham	5. 7	Sheffield Wed.	Doncaster	10.11.70
McCarthy, Jon	5. 9	Port Vale	Middlesbrough	18.08.70
O'Connor, Martin	5. 8	Peterborough Utd.	Walsall	10.12.67
Robinson, Steve	5. 9	–	Nottingham	17.10.75
Forwards				
Adebola, Dele	6. 3	Crewe Alexandra	Lagos, Nig.	23.06.75
Forinton, Howard	5.11	Yeovil Town	Boston	18.09.75
Furlong, Paul	6. 0	Chelsea	London	27.01.65
Johnson, Andrew	6. 0	–	Bedford	10.02.81
Ndlovu, Peter	5. 8	Coventry City	Buluwayo, Zim.	25.02.73

BLACKBURN ROVERS

Name	Height ft. in.	Previous Club	Birthplace	Birthdate
Goalkeepers				
Fettis, Alan	6. 2	Nott'm Forest	Belfast	1.02.71
Filan, John	5.11	Coventry City	Sydney, Aus.	8.02.70
Flowers, Tim	6. 3	Southampton	Kenilworth	3.02.67
Williams, Anthony	6. 1	–	Ogwr	20.09.77
Defenders				
Broomes, Marlon	6. 1	–	Meriden	28.11.77
Croft, Gary	5. 8	Grimsby Town	Stafford	17.02.74
Dailly, Christian	6. 0	Derby Co.	Dundee	23.10.73
Davidson, Callum	5.10	St. Johnstone	Stirling	26.06.76
Kenna, Jeff	5.11	Southampton	Dublin	27.08.70
Peacock, Darren	6. 1	Newcastle Utd.	Bristol	3.02.68
Taylor, Martin	6. 4	–	Ashington	9.11.79
Midfielders				
Carsley, Lee	5. 9	Derby Co.	Birmingham	28.02.74
Corbett, Jimmy	5.10	Gillingham	Hackney	6.07.80
Dunn, David	5.10	–	Blackburn	27.12.79
Flitcroft, Garry	6. 0	Manchester City	Bolton	6.11.72
Gill, Wayne	5.10	–	Chorley	28.11.75
Gillespie, Keith	5.10	Newcastle Utd.	Larne	18.02.75
Johnson, Damien	5.10	–	Lisburn	18.11.78
McAteer, Jason	5.11	Liverpool	Birkenhead	18.06.71
McKinlay, Billy	5. 8	Dundee Utd.	Glasgow	22.04.69
McNamee, David	5.11	St. Mirren	Glasgow	10.10.80
O'Brien, Burton	5.11	St. Mirren	South Africa	10.06.81
Forwards				
Blake, Nathan	6. 0	Bolton Wand.	Bolton	27.01.72
Davies, Kevin	6. 0	Southampton	Sheffield	26.03.77
Duff, Damien	5. 8	–	Ballyboden	2.03.79
Gallacher, Kevin	5. 8	Coventry City	Clydebank	23.11.66
Jansen, Matt	5.11	Crystal Palace	Carlisle	20.10.77
Thomas, James	6. 0	–	Swansea	16.01.79

| Ward, Ashley | 6.1 | Barnsley | Manchester | 24.11.70 |
| Wilcox, Jason | 6.0 | – | Bolton | 15.07.71 |

BOLTON WANDERERS

Name	Height ft. in.	Previous Club	Birthplace	Birthdate
Goalkeepers				
Banks, Steve	5.11	Blackpool	Hillingdon	9.02.72
Branagan, Keith	6. 0	Millwall	Fulham	10.07.66
Jaaskelainen, Jussie	6. 4	–	Vaasa, Fin.	17.04.75
Defenders				
Aljofree, Hansey	6. 0	–	Manchester	11.07.78
Bergsson, Gudni	6. 1	Tottenham	Iceland	21.07.65
Cox, Neil	6. 0	Middlesbrough	Scunthorpe	8.10.71
Elliott, Robbie	5.10	Newcastle Utd.	Newcastle	25.12.73
Fish, Mark	6. 4	Lazio, Ita.	Cape Town, SA.	14.03.74
Phillips, Jimmy	6. 0	Middlesbrough	Bolton	8.02.66
Spooner, Nicky	5.10	–	Manchester	5.06.71
Todd, Andy	5.10	Middlesbrough	Derby	21.09.74
Warhurst, Paul	6. 0	Crystal Palace	Stockport	26.09.69
Whitlow, Mike	6. 0	Leicester City	Northwich	13.01.68
Midfielders				
Doherty, Martin	6. 1	–	Urmston	17.10.78
Frandsen, Per	6. 1	Copenhagen, Den.	Copenhagen, Den.	6.02.70
Gardner, Ricardo	5. 9	Harbour View, Jam.	St Andrews, Jam.	25.09.78
Jensen, Claus	5.11	Lyngby, Den.	Nykobing, Den.	
Johansen, Michael	5. 6	Copenhagen, Den.	Glostrup, Den.	22.07.72
Morrison, Peter	5.11	–	Manchester	29.06.80
Staton, Luke	5. 0	Blackburn Rov.	Doncaster	10.03.79
Forwards				
Corrigan, Noel	5.10	–	Belfast	29.12.79
Dawson, Chris	5.10	–	Coventry	22.08.79
Gudjohnson, Eidur	6. 0	PSV Eindhoven, Hol.	Rekjavic, Ice.	15.09.78
Hansen, Bo	6. 1	Brondby, Den.	Denmark	16.06.72
Holdsworth, Dean	5.11	Wimbledon	Walthamstow	8.11.68
Potter, Lee	5.11	–	Salford	3.09.78
Taylor, Bob	5.10	W.B.A.	Horden	3.02.67
Xiourouppa, Costas	5.11	–	Dudley	11.09.79

CHARLTON ATHLETIC

Name	Height ft. in.	Previous Club	Birthplace	Birthdate
Goalkeepers				
Ilic, Sasa	6. 4	St. Leonards Stamcroft	Melbourne, Aus.	18.07.72
Kiely, Dean	6. 0	Bury	Salford	10.10.70
Royce, Simon	6. 2	Southend Utd.	Forest Gate	9.09.71
Salmon, Michael	6. 2	Wrexham	Leyland	14.06.64
Turner, John	6. 1	–	Pontypool	9.09.80
Defenders				
Allman, Anthony	5. 9	–	Sidcup	14.12.80
Barness, Anthony	5.11	Chelsea	London	25.03.73
Brown, Steve	6. 1	–	Brighton	13.05.72
Fortune, Jon	6. 2	–	Islington	23.08.80
Konchesky, Paul	5.10	–	Barking	15.05.81
Poole, Gary	6. 0	Birmingham City	Stratford	11.09.67
Powell, Chris	5.10	Derby Co.	Lambeth	8.09.69
Rufus, Richard	6. 1	–	Lewisham	12.01.75
Tiler, Carl	6. 2	Everton	Sheffield	11.08.70

402

Youds, Eddie	6. 1	Bradford City	Liverpool	3.05.70
Midfielders				
Holmes, Matthew	5. 7	Blackburn Rov.	Luton	1.08.69
Izzet, Kemal	5. 8	–	Whitechapel	29.09.80
Jones, Keith	5.11	Southend Utd.	Dulwich	17.03.70
Kinsella, Mark	5. 9	Colchester Utd.	Dublin	12.08.72
Newton, Shaun	5. 8	–	Camberwell	20.08.75
Parker, Scott	5. 9	–	Lambeth	13.10.80
Redfearn, Neil	5. 8	Barnsley	Dewsbury	20.06.65
Robinson, John	5.10	Brighton & H.A.	Bulawayo, Zim.	29.08.71
Stuart, Graham	5. 8	Sheffield Utd.	Tooting	24.10.70
Forwards				
Hales, Leigh	5.10	–	Gillingham	1.05.81
Hunt, Andy	6. 0	Thurrock	West Bromwich	9.06.70
James, Kevin	5. 9	–	Southwark	3.01.80
Jones, Steve	5.11	West Ham Utd.	Cambridge	17.03.70
Lisbie, Kevin	5. 9	–	Hackney	17.10.78
MacDonald, Charlie	5. 9	–	Southwark	13.02.81
McCammon, Mark	6. 2	Cambridge City	Barnet	7.08.78
Mendonca, Clive	5.10	Grimsby Town	Islington	9.09.68
Pringle, Martin	6. 2	Benfica, Por.	Gothenburg, Swe.	18.11.70

CREWE ALEXANDRA

Name	Height ft. in.	Previous Club	Birthplace	Birthdate
Goalkeepers				
Kearton, Jason	6. 1	Everton	Ipswich, Aus.	9.07.69
Defenders				
Bignot, Marcus	5. 9	Kidderminster Har.	Birmingham	28.08.74
Foran, Mark	6. 3	Peterborough Utd.	Aldershot	30.10.73
Foster, Steve	5.11	–	Warrington	10.09.80
Lightfoot, Chris	6. 1	Wigan Athletic	Penketh	1.04.70
Macauley, Steve	6. 1	Fleetwood	Lytham	4.03.69
Smith, Shaun	5.10	Emley	Leeds	9.04.71
Walton, Dave	6. 2	Shrewsbury Town	Bellingham	10.04.73
Wright, David	5.11	–	Warrington	1.05.80
Midfielders				
Charnock, Phil	5.10	Liverpool	Southport	14.02.75
Lunt, Kenny	5.10	–	Runcorn	20.11.79
Unsworth, Lee	5.11	Ashton Utd.	Eccles	25.02.73
Wright, Jermaine	5.10	Wolves	Greenwich	21.10.75
Forwards				
Collins, James	5. 8	–	Liverpool	28.05.78
Jack, Rodney	5. 7	Torquay Utd.	Kingston, Jam.	28.09.72
Little, Colin	5.10	Hyde Utd.	Wythenshawe	4.11.72
Rivers, Mark	6. 0	–	Crewe	26.11.75
Smith, Peter	5.10	–	Rhuddlan	15.09.78
Street, Kevin	5.10	–	Crewe	25.11.77

CRYSTAL PALACE

Name	Height ft. in.	Previous Club	Birthplace	Birthdate
Goalkeepers				
Digby, Fraser	6. 1	Swindon Town	Sheffield	23.04.67
Gregg, Matt	5.11	Torquay Utd.	Cheltenham	30.11.78
Miller, Kevin	6. 1	Watford	Falmouth	15.03.69
Ormshaw, Gareth	6. 0	Ramblers, S.A.	Durban, S.A.	8.07.79

Defenders

Name	Height ft. in.	Previous Club	Birthplace	Birthdate
Austin, Dean	5.11	Tottenham	Hemel Hempstead	26.04.70
Harris, Richard	5.11	–	Croydon	23.10.80
Hibburt, Jamie	5. 9	–	Spelthorne	13.10.79
Jihai, Sun	5. 6	Dalian Wanda, Chi.	Dalian, Chi.	30.09.77
Linighan, Andy	6. 4	Arsenal	Hartlepool	18.06.62
Mullins, Hayden	5.11	–	Reading	27.03.79
Smith, Jamie	5. 8	Wolves	Birmingham	17.09.74
Tuttle, David	6. 2	Sheffield Utd.	Reading	6.02.72
Woozley, David	6. 0	–	Berkshire	6.12.79
Zhiyi, Fan	5.11	Shanghai Shenhua, Chi.	Shanghai, Chi.	22.01.70

Midfielders

Name	Height ft. in.	Previous Club	Birthplace	Birthdate
Carlisle, Wayne	5. 7	–	Lisburn	9.09.79
Evans, Stephen	6. 0	–	Caerphilly	25.09.80
Foster, Craig	5.11	Portsmouth	Melbourne, Aus.	15.04.69
Frampton, Andrew	5.11	–	Wimbledon	3.09.79
Fullarton, Jamie	5.11	–	Belshilll	20.07.74
Graham, Gareth	5. 7	–	Belfast	6.12.78
Rodger, Simon	5. 9	–	Shoreham	3.10.71

Forwards

Name	Height ft. in.	Previous Club	Birthplace	Birthdate
Bradbury, Lee	6. 0	Manchester City	Isle of Wight	3.07.75
Harries, Paul	6. 1	Portsmouth	Sydney, Aus.	20.10.77
Martin, Andrew	6. 0	–	Cardiff	28.02.80
McKenzie, Leon	5.10	–	Croydon	17.05.78
Morrison, Clinton	5.10	–	Tooting	14.05.79
Rizzo, Nicky	5. 4	Liverpool	Sydney, Aus.	9.06.79
Svensson, Mathias	6. 0	FC Tirol, Austria	Boras, Swe.	24.09.74

FULHAM

Name	Height ft. in.	Previous Club	Birthplace	Birthdate
Goalkeepers				
Arendse, Andre	6. 4	Cape Town Tottenham, S.A.	Cape Town, S.A.	27.06.67
Hahnemann, Marcus	–	Colorado Rapids	–	–
Taylor, Maik	6. 3	Southampton	Hildeshein, Ger.	4.09.71
Defenders				
Brevett, Rufus	5. 8	Q.P.R.	Derby Co.	24.09.69
Coleman, Chris	6. 2	Blackburn Rov.	Swansea	10.06.70
McAnespie, Steve	5. 9	Bolton Wand.	Kilmarnock	1.02.72
McGuckin, Ian	6. 2	Hartlepool Utd.	Middlesbrough	24.04.73
Melville, Andy	6. 1	Sunderland	Swansea	29.11.68
Morgan, Simon	5.10	Leicester City	Birmingham	5.09.66
Neilson, Alan	5.11	Southampton	Wegburg, Ger.	26.09.72
Palmer, Ryan	6. 1	–	Dulwich	02.02.80
Symons, Christopher	6. 1	Manchester City	Basingstoke	8.03.71
Uhlenbeek, Gus	5.10	Ipswich Town	Paramaribo, Sur.	20.08.70
Midfielders				
Clark, Lee	5. 8	Sunderland	Wallsend	27.10.72
Collins, Wayne	6. 0	Sheffield Wed.	Manchester	4.03.69
Davis, Sean	5.11	–	Clapham	20.09.79
Hayward, Steve	5.11	Carlisle Utd.	Walsall	8.09.71
Selley, Ian	5. 9	Arsenal	Chertsey	14.06.74
Smith, Neil	5. 8	Gillingham	Lambeth	30.09.71
Trollope, Paul	6. 0	Derby Co.	Swindon	3.06.72
Forwards				
Betsy, Kevin	6. 1	Woking	Seychelles	20.03.78
Brooker, Paul	5. 8	–	Hammersmith	25.11.76

Cornwall, Luke	5.11	–	Lambeth	23.07.80
Finnan, Steve	5. 9	Notts Co.	Chelmsford	20.04.76
Hayles, Barry	5. 9	Bristol Rov.	London	17.04.72
Horsfield, Geoff	6. 0	Halifax Town	Barnsley	1.11.73
Peschisolido, Paul	5. 7	W.B.A.	Scarborough, Can.	25.05.71
Salako, John	5. 9	Bolton Wand.	Nigeria	11.02.69

GRIMSBY TOWN

Name	Height ft. in.	Previous Club	Birthplace	Birthdate
Goalkeepers				
Croudson, Stephen	6. 0	–	Grimsby	24.11.80
Love, Andrew	6. 1	–	Grimsby	28.03.79
Defenders				
Bloomer, Matthew	6. 1	–	Grimsby	3.11.78
Butterfield, Daniel	5. 9	–	Boston	21.11.79
Chapman, Ben	5. 7	–	Scunthorpe	2.03.79
Gallimore, Tony	5.10	Carlisle Utd.	Crewe Alexandra	21.02.72
Handyside, Peter	6. 1	–	Dumfries	31.07.74
Lever, Mark	6. 3	–	Beverley	29.03.70
McDermott, John	5. 7	–	Middlesbrough	3.02.69
Smith, Richard	6. 0	Leicester City	Lutterworth	3.10.70
Midfielders				
Black, Kingsley	5. 8	Nott'm Forest	Luton	22.06.68
Buckley, Adam	5. 9	–	Nottingham	2.08.79
Burnett, Wayne	6. 0	Huddersfield Town	Lambeth	4.09.71
Coldicott, Stacy	5.11	W.B.A.	Redditch	29.04.74
Donovan, Kevin	5. 7	W.B.A.	Halifax	17.12.71
Groves, Paul	5.11	W.B.A.	Derby	28.02.66
Smith, David	5. 8	W.B.A.	Stonehouse	29.03.68
Forwards				
Ashcroft, Lee	5.10	Preston N.E.	Preston	7.09.72
Clare, Daryl	5. 9	–	Jersey	1.08.78
Lester, Jack	5. 9	–	Sheffield	8.10.75
Livingstone, Steve	6. 1	Chelsea	Middlesbrough	8.09.69

HUDDERSFIELD TOWN

Name	Height ft. in.	Previous Club	Birthplace	Birthdate
Goalkeepers				
Cuss, Paul	6. 1	–	Hanover, Ger.	17.04.79
Vaesen, Nico	6. 3	Brugge, Bel.	Belgium	28.09.69
Defenders				
Armstrong, Craig	5.11	Nott'm Forest	South Shields	23.05.75
Crossley, Ryan	6. 0	–	Halifax	23.07.80
Dyson, Jon	6. 1	–	Mirfield	18.12.71
Edmondson, Darren	6. 0	Carlisle Utd.	Coniston	4.11.71
Gray, Kevin	6. 0	Mansfield Town	Sheffield	7.01.72
Jenkins, Steve	5.11	Swansea City	Merthyr	16.07.72
Lucketti, Chris	6. 0	Bury	Littleborough	28.09.71
Scott, Paul	6. 0	–	Wakefield	5.11.79
Vincent, Jamie	5.11	Bournemouth	Wimbledon	1.01.79
Midfielders				
Baldry, Simon	5.11	–	Huddersfield	12.02.76
Beech, Chris	5.10	Hartlepool Utd.	Blackpool	16.09.74
Beresford, David	5. 8	Oldham Athletic	Middleton	11.11.76
Dalton, Paul	5.11	Plymouth Argyle	Middlesbrough	25.04.67
Donis, Georgio	6. 2	AEK Athens, Gre.	Greece	29.10.69

Edwards, Rob	5. 9	Crewe Alexandra	Manchester	23.02.70
Heary, Thomas	5.10	Sheriff, Ire.	Dublin	14.02.79
Horne, Barry	5.10	Birmingham City	St Asaph	18.05.62
Irons, Kenny	5.10	Tranmere Rov.	Liverpool	4.11.80
Johnson, Grant	5.10	Dundee Utd.	Dundee	24.03.72
Richardson, Lee	5.11	Oldham Athletic	Halifax	12.03.69
Sellars, Scott	5. 8	Bolton Wand.	Leeds	27.11.65
Thornley, Ben	5. 7	Manchester Utd.	Bury	21.04.75

Forwards
Allison, Wayne	6. 1	Swindon Town	Huddersfield	16.10.68
Facey, Delroy	6. 0	–	Huddersfield	22.04.80
Schofield, Danny	6. 0	Brodsworth	Doncaster	10.04.80
Stewart, Marcus	5.10	Bristol Rov.	Bristol	7.11.72

IPSWICH TOWN

Name	Height ft. in.	Previous Club	Birthplace	Birthdate
Goalkeepers				
Wright, Richard	6. 2	–	Ipswich	5.11.77
Defenders				
Bramble, Titus	6. 1	–	Ipswich	31.07.81
Brown, Wayne	6. 0	–	Barking	20.08.77
Kennedy, John	5. 8	–	Cambridge	19.08.78
Mowbray, Tony	6. 1	Celtic	Saltburn	22.11.63
Thetis, Jean-Manuel	6. 3	Sevilla, Spa.	Gold Coast	5.11.71
Venus, Mark	6. 1	Wolves	Hartlepool	6.04.67
Wilnis, Fabian	5.10	De Graafschap, Hol.	Surinam	23.08.70
Midfielders				
Clapham, Jamie	5. 9	Tottenham	Lincoln	7.12.75
Dyer, Kieron	5. 7	–	Ipswich	29.12.78
Holland, Matt	5. 9	Bournemouth	Bury	11.04.74
Holster, Marco	5. 7	Heracles, Hol.	Weesp, Hol.	4.01.71
Keeble, Chris	5.10	–	Colchester	17.09.78
Logan, Stewart	5.10	–	Bury St Edmunds	11.04.83
Magilton, Jim	6. 0	Sheffield Wed.	Belfast	6.05.69
Niven, Stuart	5.11	–	Glasgow	24.12.78
Petta, Bobby	5. 7	Feyenoord, Hol.	Rotterdam, Hol.	6.08.74
Stockwell, Micky	5. 9	–	Chelmsford	14.02.65
Tanner, Adam	6. 0	–	Maldon	25.10.73
Forwards				
Friars, Sean	5. 8	Arsenal	Derry	15.05.79
Johnson, David	5. 6	Bury	Kingston, Jam.	15.08.76
Midgley, Neil	5.11	–	Cambridge	21.10.78
Naylor, Richard	6. 1	–	Leeds	28.02.77
Scowcroft, Jamie	6. 1	–	Bury St Edmunds	15.11.75

MANCHESTER CITY

Name	Height ft. in.	Previous Club	Birthplace	Birthdate
Goalkeepers				
Hodgson, Stephen	5.11	–	Macclesfield	23.12.81
Weaver, Nick	6. 3	Mansfield Town	Sheffield	2.03.79
Wright, Tommy	5.11	Nott'm Forest	Belfast	29.08.63
Defenders				
Crooks, Lee	6. 1	–	Wakefield	14.01.78
Duff, Greg	5.11	–	Manchester	16.10.80
Edghill, Richard	5. 9	–	Oldham	23.09.74
Fenton, Nick	6. 1	–	Preston	23.11.79

Holmes, Shaun	5. 9	–	Londonderry	27.12.80
Jobson, Richard	6. 2	Leeds Utd.	Holderness	9.05.63
Morrison, Andy	5.11	Huddersfield Town	Inverness	30.07.70
Shelia, Murtaz	6. 0	Alania Vladikavkaz, Rus.	Georgia	7.09.68
Tiatto, Danny	5. 8	Baden, Ger.	Melbourne, Aus.	22.05.73
Tskhadadze, Kakhaber	6. 1	Frankfurt, Ger.	Rustavi	7.09.68
Vaughan, Tony	6. 1	Ipswich Town	Manchester	11.10.75
Wiekens, Gerard	6. 0	Veendam, Hol.	Tolhuiswyk, Hol.	25.02.73
Midfielders				
Bishop, Ian	5.10	West Ham Utd.	Liverpool	29.05.65
Brown, Michael	5. 9	–	Hartlepool	25.01.77
Dunfield, Terry	5. 7	–	Canada	20.02.82
Horlock, Kevin	6. 0	Swindon Town	Erith	1.11.72
Kennedy, Mark	5.11	Wimbledon	Dublin	15.05.76
Laycock, David	5.10	–	Hull	1.10.80
Mason, Gary	5. 8	–	Edinburgh	15.10.79
Pollock, Jamie	6. 0	Bolton Wand.	Stockton-on-Tees	16.02.74
Reilly, Alan	5.11	–	Dublin	22.08.80
Whitley, Jeff	5. 9	–	Zambia	28.01.79
Whitley, Jim	5. 9	–	Zambia	14.04.75
Forwards				
Allsopp, Danny	6. 0	Port Melbourne, Aus.	Melbourne, Aus.	10.08.78
Bailey, Alan	5.11	–	Macclesfield	1.11.78
Cooke, Terry	5. 8	Manchester Utd.	Birmingham	5.08.76
Dickov, Paul	5. 5	Arsenal	Glasgow	1.11.72
Garfield, Darren	5. 9	–	Tameside	27.01.81
Goater, Shaun	6. 0	Bristol City	Bermuda	25.02.70
Greenacre, Chris	5.11	–	Halifax	23.12.77
Killen, Chris	5.11	Miramar Rangers, N.Z.	New Zealand	8.10.81
Kneen, Jason	5.10	–	Stockport Co.	20.10.80
Mike, Leon	6. 0	–	Manchester	4.09.81
Russell, Craig	5.10	Sunderland	Jarrow	4.02.74
Taylor, Gareth	6. 1	Sheffield Utd.	Weston-Super-Mare	25.02.73
Wright-Phillips, Shaun	5. 6	–	London	25.10.81

NORWICH CITY

Name	Height ft. in.	Previous Club	Birthplace	Birthdate
Goalkeepers				
Green, Robert	6. 2	–	Chertsey	18.01.80
Marshall, Andy	6. 2	–	Bury	14.04.75
Defenders				
Fleming, Craig	6. 0	Oldham Athletic	Calder	6.10.71
Fuglestad, Erik	5.11	Viking Stavanger, Nor.	Randaberg, Nor.	13.08.74
Jackson, Matt	6. 1	Everton	Leeds	19.10.71
Joynson, Matthew	5. 9	–	Liverpool	21.03.81
Kenton, Darren	5.10	–	Wandsworth	13.09.78
Mackay, Malcolm	6. 2	Celtic	Glasgow	19.02.72
Scott, Kevin	6. 3	Tottenham	Easington	17.12.66
Sutch, Daryl	6. 0	–	Lowestoft	11.09.71
Wilson, Che	5.10	–	Ely	17.01.79
Midfielders				
Anselin, Cedric	5. 8	Bordeaux, Fra.	Lens, Fra.	24.07.77
Carey, Shaun	5. 9	–	Rushden	13.05.76
Fitzsimon, Ross	5.10	Tottenham	Edgware	26.09.80
Grant, Peter	5. 9	Celtic	Glasgow	30.08.65
Marshall, Lee	6. 1	Enfield	Islington	21.01.79
Milligan, Mike	5. 8	Oldham Athletic	Manchester	20.02.67

Mulryne, Philip	5.10	Manchester Utd.	Belfast	1.01.78
Russell, Darel	5.11	–	Mile End	22.10.80
Way, Darren	5. 7	–	Plymouth	21.11.79
Forwards				
Bellamy, Craig	5. 8	–	Cardiff	13.07.79
Coote, Adrian	6. 2	–	Great Yarmouth	30.09.78
Dalglish, Paul	5.10	Newcastle Utd.	Glasgow	18.02.77
Eadie, Darren	5. 8	–	Chippenham	10.06.75
Forbes, Adrian	5. 8	–	Greenford	23.01.79
Llewellyn, Chris	5.11	–	Swansea	28.08.79
Parker, Kevin	5.10	–	Plymouth	10.09.79
Roberts, Iwan	6. 3	Wolves	Bangor	26.06.68

NOTTINGHAM FOREST

Name	Height ft. in.	Previous Club	Birthplace	Birthdate
Goalkeepers				
Beasant, Dave	6. 4	Southampton	Willesden	20.03.59
Crossley, Mark	6. 0	–	Barnsley	16.06.69
Defenders				
Bonalair, Thierry	5. 9	Neuchatel Xamax, Swi.	Paris, Fra.	14.06.66
Chettle, Steve	6. 1	–	Nottingham	27.09.68
Doig, Chris	6. 2	–	Dumfries	13.02.81
Edwards, Christian	6. 2	Swansea City	Caerphilly	23.11.75
Hjelde, Jon-Olav	6. 2	Rosenborg, Nor.	Levanger, Nor.	30.07.72
Mattsson, Jesper	6. 0	Halmstads, Swe.	Sweden	18.04.68
Rogers, Alan	5.10	Tranmere Rov.	Liverpool	3.01.77
Midfielders				
Allou, Bernard	5. 8	Grampus Eight, Jap.	Ivory Coast	19.06.75
Bart-Williams, Chris	5.10	Sheffield Wed.	Sierra Leone	16.06.74
Burns, John	5. 8	Belvedere	Dublin	4.12.77
Gray, Andy	6. 1	–	Harrogate	15.11.77
Johnson, Andy	6. 0	Norwich City	Bristol	2.05.74
Melton, Stephen	5.11	–	Lincoln	3.10.78
Merino, Carlos	5. 8	–	Urdaneta, Spa.	15.03.80
Palmer, Carlton	6. 2	Southampton	Oldbury	5.12.65
Quashie, Nigel	6. 0	Q.P.R.	Nunhead	20.07.78
Woan, Ian	5.10	Runcorn	Wirral	14.12.67
Forwards				
Guinan, Steve	6. 1	–	Birmingham	24.12.75
Freedman, Dougie	5. 9	Wolves	Glasgow	21.01.74
Harewood, Marlon	6. 1	–	Hampstead	25.08.79
Shipperley, Neil	6. 1	Crystal Palace	Chatham	30.10.74

PORTSMOUTH

Name	Height ft. in.	Previous Club	Birthplace	Birthdate
Goalkeepers				
Flahavan, Aaron	6. 1	–	Southampton	15.12.75
Knight, Alan	6. 0	–	Balham	03.06.61
Petterson, Andy	6. 1	Charlton Athletic	Fremantle Aust.	29.09.69
Tardiff, Christopher	6. 0	–	Guernsey	19.09.79
Defenders				
Awford, Andy	5. 9	–	Worcester	14.07.72
Crowe, Jason	5. 7	Arsenal	Sidcup	30.09.78
Cundy, Jason	6. 0	Ipswich Town	Wimbledon	12.11.69
Fenton, Anthony	5.10	Manchester City	Preston	23.11.79
Perrett, Russell	6. 3	Lymington	Barton-on-Sea	18.06.73

Waterman, David	5.10	–	Guernsey	16.05.77
Whitbread, Adrian	6. 2	West Ham Utd.	Epping	22.10.71
Midfielders				
Durnin, John	5.10	Oxford Utd.	Bootle	18.08.65
Igoe, Sammy	5. 6	–	Spelthorne	30.09.75
McLoughlin, Alan	5. 8	Swindon Town	Manchester	20.04.67
Miglioranzi, Stefani	6. 0	St. John's College Soccer, USA	Pacos de Caldaf, Bra.	20.09.77
Peron, Jeff	6. 2	Walsall	Barton-on-Sea	18.06.73
Phillips, Martin	5.11	Manchester City	Exeter	13.03.76
Robinson, Matt	5.11	Southampton	Exeter	23.12.74
Simpson, Fitzroy	5. 8	Bristol City	Bradford-on-Avon	26.02.70
Thogerson, Thomas	6. 1	Brondby, Den.	Copenhagen, Den.	2.04.68
Vlachos, Mihalis	5.10	AEK Athens, Gre.	Athens, Gre.	20.09.67
Forwards				
Claridge, Steve	5.11	Wolves	Portsmouth	10.04.66
Nightingale, Luke	5.10	–	Portsmouth	22.12.80

PORT VALE

Name	Height ft. in.	Previous Club	Birthplace	Birthdate
Goalkeepers				
Musselwhite, Paul	6. 2	Scunthorpe Utd.	Portsmouth	22.12.68
Pilkington, Kevin	6. 1	Manchester Utd.	Hitchin	8.03.74
Defenders				
Barnett, Dave	6. 1	Dunfermline Athletic	London	16.04.67
Burns, Liam	6. 1	–	Belfast	30.10.78
Butler, Tony	6. 2	Blackpool	Stockport	28.09.72
Carragher, Matt	5.10	Wigan Athletic	Liverpool	14.01.76
Gardner, Anthony	6. 5	–	Tittenson	18.08.81
Snijders, Mark	6. 1	AZ 67 Alkmaar, Hol.	Alkmaar, Hol.	12.03.72
Walsh, Michael	6. 0	Scunthorpe Utd.	Rotheram	5.08.77
Midfielders				
Bogie, Ian	5. 9	Leyton Orient	Newcastle	6.12.67
Brammer, David	5. 9	Wrexham	Bromborough	28.02.75
Brisco, Neil	6. 0	Manchester City	Wigan	26.01.78
Corden, Wayne	5.10	–	London	6.07.80
Eyre, Richard	5.11	–	Hull	9.10.74
Minton, Jeff	5. 6	Brighton & H.A.	Hackney	28.12.73
O'Callaghan, George	6. 1	–	Cork, Ire.	5.09.79
Talbot, Stuart	6. 0	–	Birmingham	14.06.63
Widdrington, Tommy	5. 8	Grimsby Town	Newcastle	1.10.71
Forwards				
Bent, Marcus	6. 3	Crystal Palace	Hammersmith	19.05.78
Foyle, Martin	5.11	Oxford Utd.	Salisbury	2.05.78
Griffiths, Carl	5.10	Leyton Orient	Oswestry	15.07.71
Naylor, Tony	5. 7	Crewe Alexandra	Manchester	29.03.67
Rougier, Tony	6. 0	Hibernian	Tinidad and Tobago	17.07.71

QUEENS PARK RANGERS

Name	Height ft. in.	Previous Club	Birthplace	Birthdate
Goalkeepers				
Harper, Lee	6. 1	Arsenal	London	30.10.71
Hurst, Richard	6. 0	–	Hammersmith	23.12.76
Miklosko, Ludek	6. 5	West Ham Utd.	Protesov, Cze.	9.12.61
Defenders				
Baraclough, Ian	6. 1	Notts Co.	Leicester	4.12.70

Breacker, Tim	5.11	West Ham Utd.	Bicester	2.07.65
Darlington, Jermaine	5. 6	Aylesbury Utd.	Clapton	11.04.74
Heinola, Antti	6. 0	Heracles, Fin.	Helsinki, Fin.	20.02.73
Maddix, Danny	5.10	Tottenham	Ashford	11.10.67
Morrow, Steve	5.11	Arsenal	Belfast	2.07.70
Ord, Richard	6. 2	Sunderland	Easington	3.03.70
Perry, Mark	5.10	–	London	19.10.78
Plummer, Chris	6. 0	–	Isleworth	12.10.76
Ready, Karl	6. 0	–	Neath	14.08.72
Rose, Matthew	5.11	Arsenal	Dartford	24.09.75
Rowland, Keith	5.10	West Ham Utd.	Portadown	1.09.71
Yates, Steve	5.11	Bristol Rov.	Bristol	29.01.70
Midfielders				
Bruce, Paul	5. 1	–	London	18.02.78
Graham, Mark	5. 1	–	Newry	24.10.74
Graham, Richard	5. 3	–	Newry	5.08.79
Jeanne, Leon	5. 6	–	Cardiff	17.11.80
Kulcsar, George	6. 0	Bradford City	Budapest, Hun.	12.08.67
Langley, Richard	5.10	–	London	27.12.79
Mahoney-Johnson, Michael	5.10	–	Paddington	6.11.76
Murray, Paul	5. 8	Carlisle Utd.	Carlisle	31.08.76
Peacock, Gavin	5. 8	Chelsea	Eltham	18.11.67
Scully, Tony	5. 7	Manchester City	Dublin	12.06.76
Forwards				
Dowie, Ian	6. 1	West Ham Utd.	Hatfield	9.01.65
Gallen, Kevin	5.11	–	Hammersmith	21.09.75
Kiwomya, Chris	5.10	Arsenal	Huddersfield	2.12.69
Lusardi, Mario	5. 9	–	Islington	27.09.79
Purser, Wayne	5. 9	–	Basildon	13.04.80
Slade, Steve	5.11	Tottenham	Romford	6.10.75
Weare, Ross	5.10	East Ham Utd.	Perivale	19.03.77

SHEFFIELD UNITED

Name	Height ft. in.	Previous Club	Birthplace	Birthdate
Goalkeepers				
Kelly, Alan	6. 3	Preston N.E.	Preston	11.08.68
Tracey, Simon	6. 0	Wimbledon	Woolwich	9.12.67
Walker, Leigh	5.10	–	Sheffield	27.02.81
Defenders				
Dellas, Traianos	6. 4	Thesalonikas, Gre.	Salonika, Gre.	31.01.76
Doane, Ben	5.10	–	Sheffield	22.12.79
Jacobsen, Anders	6. 3	IK Start, Nor.	Oslo, Nor.	18.04.68
Kozluk, Rob	5. 8	Derby Co.	Sutton-in-Ashfield	5.08.77
Marker, Nicky	6. 0	Blackburn Rov.	Exeter	3.05.65
O'Connor, Jon	6. 0	Everton	Darlington	29.10.76
Sandford, Lee	6. 0	Stoke City	Basingstoke	22.04.68
Camm, Mark	5. 8	–	Mansfield	1.10.81
McAughtrie, Craig	6. 2	–	Burton-on-Trent	3.03.81
Midfielders				
Cullen, Jon	6. 0	Hartlepool Utd.	Durham	10.01.73
Davies, Kevin	6. 0	–	Sheffield	15.11.78
Derry, Shaun	5.10	Notts Co.	Nottingham	6.12.77
Ford, Bobby	5. 8	Oxford Utd.	Bristol	22.9.74
Hamilton, Ian	5.10	W.B.A.	Stevenage	14.12.67
Hunt, Jonathan	5.10	Derby Co.	London	2.11.71
Quinn, Wayne	5.10	–	Truro	19.11.76

Name	ft. in.		Previous Club	Birthplace	Birthdate
Whitehouse, Dane	5.10	–		Sheffield	14.10.70
Woodhouse, Curtis	5. 8	–		Driffield	17.04.80
Burley, Adam	5.10	–		Sheffield	27.11.80
Forwards					
Devlin, Paul	5. 8	Birmingham City		Birmingham	14.04.72
Katchouro, Petr	6. 0	Dinamo Minsk, Bel.		Minsk, Bel.	2.08.72
Marcelo	6. 0	Alaves, Por.		Niteroi, Bra.	11.10.69
Morris, Lee	5.10	–		Driffield	30.04.80
Burke, Paul	5.10	–		Doncaster	17.07.81

STOCKPORT COUNTY

Name	Height ft. in.	Previous Club	Birthplace	Birthdate
Goalkeepers				
Gray, Ian	6. 2	Rochdale	Manchester	25.02.75
Nash, Carlo	6. 5	Crystal Palace	Bolton	13.09.73
Defenders				
Connelly, Sean	5.10	–	Sheffield	26.06.70
Dinning, Tony	6. 0	Newcastle Utd.	Wallsend	12.04.75
Flynn, Mike	6. 0	Preston N.E.	Oldham	23.05.69
Gannon, James	6. 2	Sheffield Utd.	Southwark	7.09.68
Johnson, Ben	6. 1	–	–	–
McIntosh, Martin	6. 3	Hamilton	East Kilbride	19.03.71
Nicholson, Shane	5.10	Chesterfield	Newark	3.06.70
Woodthorpe, Colin	6. 0	Aberdeen	Ellesmere Port	31.01.69
Midfielders				
Bennett, Tom	5.11	Wolves	Falkirk	12.12.69
Byrne, Chris	5. 9	Sunderland	Manchester	9.02.75
Cook, Paul	5.11	Tranmere Rov.	Liverpool	22.06.67
Mannion, Sean	5. 8	–	Dublin	3.03.80
Smith, David	5.10	Oxford Utd.	Liverpool	26.12.70
Forwards				
Angell, Brett	6. 2	Sunderland	Marlborough	20.08.68
Cooper, Kevin	5. 8	Derby Co.	Derby	8.02.75
Ellis, Tony	5.11	Bury	Salford	20.10.64
Matthews, Rob	6. 0	Bury	Slough	14.10.70
Moore, Ian	5.11	Nott'm Forest	Birkenhead	26.08.76
Wilbraham, Aaron	6. 3	–	Knutsford	21.10.79

SWINDON TOWN

Name	Height ft. in.	Previous Club	Birthplace	Birthdate
Goalkeepers				
Flanagan, Alan	5.11	–	Drogheda, Ire.	9.10.80
Glass, Jimmy	6. 1	Bournemouth	Epsom	1.08.73
Mildenhall, Stephen	6. 5	–	Swindon	13.05.78
Talia, Francesco	6. 1	Blackburn Rov.	Melbourne, Aus.	20.07.72
Defenders				
Campagna, Sam	6. 1	–	Worcester	19.11.80
Colbertson, Ricky	6. 0	–	Ballymena	10.08.80
Davies, Gareth	6. 1	Reading	Hereford	11.12.73
Davis, Sol	5. 8	–	Cheltenham	4.09.79
Hall, Gareth	5. 8	Sunderland	Croydon	20.03.69
Reeves, Alan	6. 0	Wimbledon	Birkenhead	19.11.67
Robinson, Mark	5. 9	Newcastle Utd.	Rochdale	21.11.68
Taylor, Craig	6. 1	Dorchester Town	Plymouth	24.01.74
Williams, James	5. 9	–	Liverpool	15.07.80
Willis, Adam	5.11	Coventry City	Nuneaton	21.09.76

Midfielders

Name	ft. in.	Previous Club	Birthplace	Birthdate
Collins, Lee	5. 7	Albion Rov.	Bellshill	3.02.74
Cuervo, Philippe	5.11	St Etienne, Fra.	Calais, Fra.	13.08.69
Gooden, Ty	5. 8	Wycombe Wand.	Canvey Island	23.10.72
Howe, Bobby	5. 7	Nott'm Forest	Newcastle	6.11.73
Hulbert, Robin	5. 9	–	Plymouth	14.03.80
Leitch, Scott	5. 9	Hearts	Motherwell	6.10.69
McAreavey, Paul	5.10	–	Belfast	3.12.80
McHugh, Frazer	5.11	–	Nottingham	24.07.81
Mills, Jamie	5.10	–	Swindon	31.03.81
Walters, Mark	5. 1	Southampton	Birmingham	2.06.64

Forwards

Name	ft. in.	Previous Club	Birthplace	Birthdate
Burke, Nicky	5. 9	–	Watford	3.01.81
Cowe, Steve	5. 7	Aston Villa	Gloucester	29.09.74
Grazioli, Giuliano	5.11	Peterborough Utd.	London	23.03.75
Griffin, Charlie	5.10	Chippenham	Bath	25.06.79
Hay, Chris	5.11	Celtic	Glasgow	28.08.74
Ndah, George	6. 1	Crystal Palace	Dulwich	23.12.74
Onuora, Iffy	6. 1	Gillingham	Glasgow	28.07.67

TRANMERE ROVERS

Name	Height ft. in.	Previous Club	Birthplace	Birthdate
Goalkeepers				
Achterberg, John	6. 1	PSV Eindhoven, Hol.	Utrecht, Hol.	8.07.71
Murphy, Joe	6. 1	–	Dublin	21.08.81
Defenders				
Allen, Graham	6. 0	Everton	Bolton	8.04.77
Challinor, Dave	6. 1	Bromborough Pool	Chester	2.10.75
Frail, Stephen	5.11	Hearts	Glasgow	10.08.69
Hill, Clinton	6. 0	–	Liverpool	19.10.78
Hinds, Richard	6. 2	–	Sheffield	22.08.80
Joy, Ian	5.10	–	San Diego, USA	14.07.81
McGreal, John	6. 1	–	Liverpool	2.06.72
Morgan, Alan	5. 9	–	Aberystwyth	2.11.73
Santos, George	6. 3	Toulon, Fra.	Marseille, Fra.	15.08.70
Sharps, Ian	6. 3	–	Warrington	23.10.80
Thompson, Andy	5. 5	Wolves	Cannock	9.01.67
Midfielders				
Black, Michael	5. 8	Arsenal	Chigwell	6.10.76
Gibson, Neil	5.11	–	St. Asaph	10.10.79
Koumas, Jason	5.10	–	Wrexham	25.09.79
Mahon, Alan	5. 9	–	Dublin	4.04.78
Rogers, Peter	5.10	–	Dublin	5.12.80
Forwards				
Jones, Gary	6. 3	–	Chester	10.05.75
Jones, Lee	5. 8	Liverpool	Wrexham	29.05.73
Kelly, David	5.11	Sunderland	Birmingham	25.11.65
Parkinson, Andy	5. 8	Liverpool	Liverpool	27.05.79
Taylor, Perry	5.11	–	Birkenhead	29.01.81
Taylor, Scott	5.10	Bolton Wand.	Chertsey	5.05.76
Williams, Ryan	5. 4	Mansfield Town	Chesterfield	31.08.78

WALSALL

Name	Height ft. in.	Previous Club	Birthplace	Birthdate
Goalkeepers				
Emberson, Carl	6. 1	Colchester Utd.	Epsom	13.07.73

Walker, James	5.11	Notts Co.	Nottingham	9.07.73

Defenders

Gadsby, Matthew	6. 0	–	Sutton Coldfield	6.09.79
Green, Richard	6. 1	Gillingham	Wolves	22.11.67
Marsh, Chris	6. 0	–	Dudley	14.01.70
Roper, Ian	6. 4	–	Nuneaton	20.06.77
Viveash, Adrian	6. 1	Barnsley	Swindon	30.09.69
Wrack, Darren	5. 9	Shrewsbury Town	Cleethorpes	5.05.76

Midfielders

Brissett, Jason	5.11	Bournemouth	Redbridge	7.09.74
Daley, Tony	5. 8	Watford	Birmingham	18.10.67
Evans, Wayne	5.10	Welshpool	Abermule	25.08.71
Keister, John	5. 7	Tigres	Manchester	11.11.70
Larusson, Bjarni	5.11	Hibernian	Reykjavik	11.03.76
Thomas, Wayne	5.11	–	Walsall	28.08.78

Forwards

Eyjolfsson, Siggy	6. 1	I.A Akranes,Ice.	Iceland	1.12.73
Mavrak, Darko	5.10	Fazenburg	–	19.01.69
Platt, Clive	6. 4	–	Wolves	27.10.77
Rammell, Andy	6. 2	Southend Utd.	Nuneaton	10.02.67
Ricketts, Michael	6. 2	–	Birmingham	4.12.78
Watson, Andy	5. 9	Blackpool	Leeds	1.04.67

WEST BROMWICH ALBION

Name	Height ft. in.	Previous Club	Birthplace	Birthdate

Goalkeepers

Adamson, Chris	5.11	–	Ashington	4.11.78
Miller, Alan	6. 3	Middlesbrough	Epping	29.03.70
Whitehead, Phil	6. 2	Oxford Utd.	Halifax	17.12.69

Defenders

Burgess, Daryl	5.11	–	Birmingham	24.01.68
Carbon, Matthew	6. 2	Derby Co.	Nottingham	8.06.75
Gabbidon, Daniel	5.10	–	Cwmbran	8.08.79
Holmes, Paul	5.10	Everton	Stocksbridge	18.02.68
Mardon, Paul	6. 0	Birmingham City	Bristol	14.09.69
McDermott, Andy	5. 9	Q.P.R.	Sydney, Aus.	24.03.77
Murphy, Shaun	6. 1	Notts Co.	Sydney, Aus.	5.11.70
Potter, Graham	6. 1	Southampton	Solihull	20.05.75
Raven, Paul	6. 1	Doncaster Rov.	Salisbury	28.07.70
Van Blerk, Jason	6. 1	Manchester City	Sydney, Aus.	16.03.68

Midfielders

Flynn, Sean	5. 8	Derby Co.	Birmingham	13.03.68
Kilbane, Kevin	6. 0	Preston N.E.	Preston	1.02.77
Maresca, Enzo	5.11	Cagliari, Ita.	Salerno	10.02.80
Quinn, James	6. 1	Blackpool	Coventry	15.12.74
Sneekes, Richard	5.11	Bolton Wand.	Amsterdam, Hol.	30.10.68

Forwards

De Freitas, Fabian	6. 1	Osasuna, Spa.	Paramaribo, Hol.	28.07.72
Evans, Mike	6. 0	Southampton	Plymouth	1.01.73
Hughes, Lee	5.10	Kidderminster Har.	Birmingham	22.05.76
Oliver, Adam	5. 9	–	West Bromwich	25.10.80
Quailey, Brian	6. 1	Nuneaton Borough	Leicester	21.08.78
Richards, Justin	5.10	–	West Bromwich	16.10.80

WOLVERHAMPTON WANDERERS

Name	Height ft. in.	Previous Club	Birthplace	Birthdate
Goalkeepers				
Stowell, Mike	6. 2	Everton	Portsmouth	19.04.65
Defenders				
Bazeley, Darren	5. 8	Watford	Northampton	5.10.72
Curle, Keith	6. 0	Manchester City	Bristol	14.11.63
Green, Ryan	5. 8	–	Cardiff	20.10.80
Muscat, Kevin	5.11	Crystal Palace	Crawley	7.08.73
Naylor, Lee	5. 8	–	Bloxwich	19.03.80
Sedgley, Steve	6. 1	Ipswich Town	Enfield	26.05.68
Williams, Adrian	6. 2	Reading	Reading	11.08.66
Midfielders				
Corica, Steve	5. 8	Leicester City	Cairns, Aus.	24.03.73
Emblen, Neil	6. 1	Millwall	Bromley	19.06.71
Ferguson, Darren	5.10	Manchester Utd.	Glasgow	9.02.72
Niestroj, Robert	5.10	Fortuna Dusseldorf, Ger.	Oppein, Ger.	2.12.74
Osborn, Simon	5.10	Q.P.R.	New Addington	19.01.71
Robinson, Carl	5.10	–	Llandrindod	13.10.76
Sinton, Andy	5. 8	Tottenham	Newcastle	19.03.66
Forwards				
Bull, Steve	5.11	W.B.A.	Tipton	28.03.65
Flo, Havard	6. 2	Werder Bremen, Ger.	Volda, Nor.	4.04.70
Jones, Mark	5.10	–	Walsall	7.09.79
Keane, Robbie	5. 9	–	Dublin	8.07.80

DIVISION TWO

BLACKPOOL

Name	Height ft. in.	Previous Club	Birthplace	Birthdate
Goalkeepers				
Barnes, Philip	6. 1	Rotherham Utd.	Rotherham	2.03.79
Caig, Tony	6. 1	Carlisle Utd.	Whitehaven	11.04.74
Defenders				
Bardsley David	5.10	Q.P.R.	Manchester	11.09.64
Beesley, Paul	6. 1	Port Vale	Liverpool	21.07.65
Bryan, Marvin	6. 0	Q.P.R.	Paddington	2.08.75
Carlisle, Clarke	6. 1	–	Preston	14.10.79
Hills, John	5. 8	Everton	Blackpool	21.04.78
Hughes, Ian	5.10	Bury	Bangor	2.08.74
Robinson, Phil	5. 9	–	Manchester	28.09.80
Shuttleworth, Barry	5. 8	Rotherham Utd.	Accrington	9.07.77
Thompson, Phil	5.11	–	Blackpool	1.04.81
Midfielders				
Bushell, Steve	5. 9	York City	Manchester	28.12.72
Clarkson, Phil	5.10	Scunthorpe Utd.	Garstang	13.11.68
Couzens, Andy	5.10	Carlisle Utd.	Shipley	4.06.75
Forsyth, Richard	5.11	Stoke City	Dudley	3.10.70
Garvey, Steve	5. 9	Crewe Alexandra	Stalybridge	22.11.73
Forwards				
Aldridge, Martin	5.11	Oxford Utd.	Northampton	4.12.74
Bent, Junior	5. 5	Bristol City	Huddersfield	1.02.70
Conroy, Michael	6. 0	Fulham	Glasgow	31.12.65
Nowland, Adam	5.11	–	Preston	6.07.81
Ormerod, Brett	5.11	Accrington Stanley	Blackburn	18.10.76

AFC BOURNEMOUTH

Name	Height ft. in.	Previous Club	Birthplace	Birthdate
Goalkeepers				
Colgan, Nick	6. 1	Chelsea	Drogheda	19.09.73
Ovendale, Mark	6. 2	Barry Town	Leicester	22.11.73
Stewart, Gareth	6. 0	Blackburn Rov.	Preston	2.02.80
Defenders				
Broadhurst, Karl	6. 0	–	Halling Island	26.04.80
Cox, Ian	6. 0	Crystal Palace	Croydon	25.03.71
Day, Jamie	5. 7	Arsenal	Bexley	13.09.79
Howe, Eddie	5.11	–	Bournemouth	29.11.77
Young, Neil	5. 8	Tottenham	Harlow	31.08.73
Midfielders				
Bailey, John	5. 8	Enfield	London	6.05.69
Beardsmore, Russell	5. 6	Manchester Utd.	Wigan	28.09.68
Dean, Michael	5.10	–	Bournemouth	9.03.78
Fletcher, Carl	5.10	–	Surrey Heath	7.04.80
Huck, William	–	Arsenal	–	–
Hughes, Richard	5. 9	Arsenal	Glasgow	25.06.79
O'Neil, Jon	5.10	Celtic	Glasgow	3.01.74
Rawlinson, Mark	5.10	Manchester Utd.	Bolton	9.06.75
Robinson, Steve	5. 9	Tottenham	Mile End	15.11.77
Tindall, Jason	5. 8	Leyton Orient	Lisburn	10.12.74
Forwards				
Fletcher, Steven	6. 2	Hartlepool Utd.	Hartlepool	26.06.72
Hayter, James	5. 9	–	Newport	9.04.79
Stein, Mark	5. 6	Chelsea	Cape Town, S.A.	28.01.66
Warren, Chris	5.10	Fulham	Bournemouth	10.10.74

BRENTFORD

Name	Height ft. in.	Previous Club	Birthplace	Birthdate
Goalkeepers				
Pearcey, Jason	6. 1	Grimsby Town	Leamington Spa	23.07.71
Woodman, Andy	6. 3	Northampton Town	Camberwell	11.08.71
Defenders				
Anderson, Ijah	5. 8	Southend Utd.	Hackney	30.12.75
Boxall, Danny	5. 8	Crystal Palace	Croydon	24.08.77
Cullip, Danny	6. 1	Fulham	Bracknell	17.09.76
Hreidarsson, Hermann	6. 1	Crystal Palace	Iceland	11.07.74
Jenkins, Stephen	6. 1	Southampton	Bristol	2.01.80
Powell, Darren	6. 2	Hampton	Hammersmith	10.03.76
Quinn, Robert	5.11	Crystal Palace	Sidcup	8.11.76
Theobald, David	6. 2	Ipswich Town	Cambridge	15.12.78
Midfielders				
Clark, Dean	5.10	–	Hillingdon	31.03.80
Evans, Paul	5. 7	Shrewsbury Town	Oswestry	1.09.74
Folan, Tony	6. 0	Crystal Palace	Lewisham	18.09.78
Mahon, Gavin	6. 0	Hereford Utd.	Birmingham	2.01.77
Rowlands, Martin	5. 8	Farnborough Town	London	8.02.79
Forwards				
Bryan, Derek	5.10	Hampton	London	11.11.74
Owusu, Lloyd	6. 0	Slough Town	Slough	12.12.76
Scott, Andy	6. 1	Sheffield Utd.	Epsom	2.08.72
Partridge, Scott	5. 9	Torquay Utd.	Leicester	13.10.74

BRISTOL CITY

Name	Height ft. in.	Previous Club	Birthplace	Birthdate
Goalkeepers				
Andersen, Bo	6. 0	Lyngby	Slagelse, Den.	26.03.76
Naylor, Stuart	6. 4	W.B.A.	Leeds	6.12.62
Phillips, Steve	6. 1	Paulton Rov.	Bath	6.05.78
Defenders				
Bell, Mickey	5. 8	Wycombe Wand.	Newcastle	15.11.71
Brennan, Jim	5. 9	Sora Lazio	Toronto, Can.	8.05.77
Edwards, Rob	6. 0	Carlisle Utd.	Kendal	1.07.73
Hill, Matthew	5. 7	–	Bristol	26.03.81
Jordan, Andrew	5.11	–	Manchester	14.12.73
Langan, Kevin	5.11	–	Jersey	7.04.78
Locke, Adam	5.11	Colchester Utd.	Croydon	20.08.70
Sebok, Vilmos	6. 3	Ujpest Dozsa	Budapest	13.06.73
Shail, Mark	6. 1	Yeovil Town	Sandvikhen, Swe.	15.10.66
Taylor, Shaun	6. 1	Swindon Town	Plymouth	26.02.63
Midfielders				
Carey, Louis	5.10	–	Bristol	22.01.77
Doherty, Tommy	5. 8	–	Bristol	17.03.79
Hewlett, Matthew	6. 2	–	Bristol	25.02.76
Hutchings, Carl	6. 0	Brentford	London	24.09.74
Murray, Scott	5.10	Aston Villa	Aberdeen	26.05.74
Tistimetanu, Ivan	5.10	FC Zimbru	Moldova	27.04.74
Tinnion, Brian	5.11	Bradford City	Stanley	23.02.68
Forwards				
Akinbiyi, Ade	6. 1	Gillingham	Hackney	10.10.74
Andersen, Soren	5.11	Aalborg	Aarhaus, Den.	31.01.70
Brown, Aaron	5.10	–	Bristol	14.03.80
Goodridge, Greg	5. 6	Q.P.R.	Barbados	10.07.71
Munhasser, Jehad	5.10	Arsenal	Libya	26.07.78
Thorpe, Tony	5. 9	Fulham	Leicester	10.04.74
Torpey, Steve	6. 3	Swansea City	Islington	8.12.70
Wright, Ben	5.11	Kettering Town	Northampton	3.11.77

BRISTOL ROVERS

Name	Height ft. in.	Previous Club	Birthplace	Birthdate
Goalkeepers				
Johnston, Ray	6. 1	–	Bristol	5.05.81
Jones, Lee	6. 3	Swansea City	Pontypridd	9.08.70
Kuipers, Michel	6. 2	–	Amsterdam	26.06.74
Defenders				
Andreasson, Marcus	6. 4	Osters I.F., Swe.	Liberia	13.07.78
Challis, Trevor	5. 8	Q.P.R.	Paddington	23.10.75
Foster, Stephen	6. 1	Woking	Mansfield	3.12.74
Leoni, Stephane	5. 9	Metz, Fra.	Metz, Fra.	1.09.76
Pethick, Robbie	5.10	Portsmouth	Tavistock	8.09.70
Pritchard, David	5. 7	Telford Utd.	Wolves	27.05.72
Smith, Mark	6. 0	–	Bristol	13.09.79
Thomson, Andrew	6. 3	Portsmouth	Swindon	28.03.74
Tillson, Andrew	6. 2	Q.P.R.	Huntingdon	30.06.66
Trought, Michael	6. 2	–	Bristol	19.10.80
White, Thomas	5.11	–	Bristol	26.01.76
Midfielders				
Hillier, David	5.10	Portsmouth	Blackheath	19.12.69
Holloway, Ian	5. 7	Q.P.R.	Bristol	12.03.63

Mauge, Ronnie	5.10	Plymouth Argyle	Islington	10.03.69
Meaker, Michael	5. 8	Reading	Greenford	18.08.71
Shore, Jamie	5. 9	Norwich City	Bristol	1.09.77
Trees, Robert	5.10	Witton Albion	Manchester	18.12.77
Zabek, Lee	6. 0	–	Bristol	13.10.78
Forwards				
Bennett, Frankie	5. 7	Southampton	Birmingham	13.01.69
Cureton, Jamie	5. 7	Norwich City	Bristol	28.08.75
Ellington, Nathan	5.10	Walton & Hersham	Bradford	2.07.81
Penrice, Gary	5. 8	Watford	Bristol	23.03.64
Roberts, Jason	6. 1	Wolves	Park Royal	25.01.78
Zamora, Robert	6. 1	–	London	16.01.81

BURNLEY

Name	Height ft. in.	Previous Club	Birthplace	Birthdate
Goalkeepers				
Crichton, Paul	6. 1	W.B.A.	Pontefract	3.10.68
Mawson, Craig	6. 0	–	Keighley	16.05.79
Defenders				
Armstrong, Gordon	6. 0	Bury	Newcastle	15.07.67
Brass, Christopher	5. 9	–	Easington	24.07.75
Davis, Steve	6. 2	Luton Town	Hexham	30.10.68
Devenney, Michael	5. 8	–	Bolton	8.02.80
Heywood, Matthew	6. 3	–	Chatham	26.08.79
Jepson, Ronnie	6. 0	Oldham Athletic	Stoke City	12.05.63
Mellon, Michael	5. 9	Tranmere Rov.	Paisley	18.03.72
Scott, Christopher	5.11	–	Burnley	12.02.80
Vindheim, Rune	5.11	Bergen, Nor.	Hoyancuer, Nor.	18.05.72
Williamson, John	6. 2	–	Derby	3.03.81
Midfielders				
Johnrose, Lenny	5.10	Bury	Preston	29.11.69
Little, Glen	6. 3	Glentoran	Wimbledon	15.10.75
Maylett, Bradley	5. 8	–	Manchester	24.12.80
Robertson, Mark	5. 9	Marconi, Aus.	Sydney, Aus.	6.04.77
Smith, Ian	6. 1	–	Leeds	22.07.76
Weller, Paul	5. 8	–	Brighton	6.03.75
Forwards				
Branch, Graham	6. 3	Stockport Co.	Liverpool	12.02.72
Cooke, Andrew	5.11	Newtown	Stoke	20.01.74
Lee, Alan	6. 2	Aston Villa	Galway	21.08.78
Payton, Andy	5. 9	Huddersfield Town	Burnley	23.10.67
Swan, Peter	6. 2	Bury	Leeds	28.09.66

BURY

Name	Height ft. in.	Previous Club	Birthplace	Birthdate
Goalkeepers				
Blackwell, Kevin	5.11	Plymouth Argyle	Luton	21.12.58
Kenny, Patrick	6. 0	Bradford Park Ave.	Halifax	17.05.78
Defenders				
Barrick, Dean	5. 8	Preston N.E.	Hemsworth	30.09.68
Billy, Chris	6. 0	Notts Co.	Huddersfield	2.01.73
Debenham, Robert	5. 8	Doncaster Rov.	Doncaster	28.11.79
Redmond, Steve	6. 0	Oldham Athletic	Liverpool	2.11.67
Souter, Ryan	5.10	Bedford	Weston Super-Mare	5.02.78
Swailes, Chris	6. 3	Ipswich Town	Gateshead	19.20.70
Wilcox, Robert	5. 9	–	Bury	7.11.79

417

Williams, Paul	5. 7	Gillingham	Leicester	11.09.69
Woodward, Andy	5.10	Crewe Alexandra	Stockport	23.09.73
Midfielders				
Borg, John	5. 7	Doncaster Rov.	Salford	22.02.80
Bullock, Darren	5. 8	Swindon Town	Worcester	12.02.69
Donnelly, Mark	6. 0	Doncaster Rov.	Leeds	22.12.79
Forrest, Martyn	5.10	–	Bury	2.01.79
Preece, Andy	6. 1	Blackpool	Evesham	27.03.67
Reed, John	5.10	Blackpool	Rotherham	27.08.72
Forwards				
Barnes, Paul	5.10	Huddersfield Town	Leicester	16.11.67
D'Jaffo, Laurent	6. 0	Ayr Utd.	Bazas, France	5.11.70
James, Lutel	5.11	–	Bury	2.06.72
Jemson, Nigel	5.11	Oxford Utd.	Preston	10.08.69
Littlejohn, Adrian	5. 9	Oldham Athletic	Wolves	26.09.70

CAMBRIDGE UNITED

Name	Height ft. in.	Previous Club	Birthplace	Birthdate
Goalkeepers				
Marshall, Shaun	6. 1	–	Fakenham	3.10.78
Van Heusden, Arjan	6. 0	Port Vale	Alphen, Hol.	11.12.72
Defenders				
Ashbee, Ian	6. 1	Derby Co.	Birmingham	6.09.76
Chenery, Ben	6. 0	Luton Town	Ipswich	28.01.77
Duncan, Andrew	6. 0	Manchester Utd.	Hexham	20.10.77
Eustace, Scott	6. 0	Mansfield Town	Leicester	13.06.75
Joseph, Marc	6. 0	–	Leicester	10.11.76
McAvoy, Lawrence	5. 8	–	Lambeth	7.09.79
McNeil, Martin	6. 1	–	Rutherglenn, Sco.	28.09.80
Wilde, Adam	5.10	–	Southampton	22.05.79
Midfielders				
Armstrong, Dean	5. 8	–	Chiswick	7.09.79
Ingham, Andrew	5. 7	–	Leeds	21.08.81
Mustoe, Neil	5. 8	Wigan Athletic	Gloucester	5.11.76
Preece, David	5. 6	Derby Co.	Bridgnorth	28.05.63
Russell, Alex	5. 8	Rochdale	Crosby	17.03.73
Wanless, Paul	6. 0	Lincoln City	Banbury	14.12.73
Forwards				
Benjamin, Trevor	6. 2	–	Kettering	8.02.79
Butler, Martin	5.11	Walsall	Wordsley	15.09.74
Cockrill, Darren	6. 1	–	Great Yarmouth	28.02.80
Kyd, Michael	5. 8	–	Hackney	21.05.77
Taylor, John	6. 3	Luton Town	Norwich	24.10.64
Youngs, Tom	5. 8	–	Bury St Edmunds	31.08.79

CARDIFF CITY

Name	Height ft. in.	Previous Club	Birthplace	Birthdate
Goalkeeper				
Hallworth, Jon	6. 1	Oldham Athletic	Stockport	26.10.65
Defenders				
Eckhardt, Jeff	6. 0	Stockport Co.	Sheffield	7.10.65
Jarman, Lee	6. 3	–	Cardiff	16.12.77
Legg, Andy	5. 8	Peterborough Utd.	Neath	28.07.66
Phillips, Lee	6. 1	–	Abermule	18.03.79
Midfielders				
Boland, Willie	5. 9	Coventry City	Ennis	6.08.75

Bonner, Mark	5. 9	Blackpool	Ormskirk	7.06.74
Bowen, Jason	5. 6	Reading	Merthyr Tydfil	24.08.72
Brazier, Matthew	5. 8	Fulham	Whipps Cross	2.07.76
Cadette, Nathan	5. 6	–	Cardiff	6.01.80
Carpenter, Richard	5.10	Fulham	Sheerness	30.09.72
Fowler, Jason	6. 1	Bristol City	Bristol	20.08.74
Middleton, Craig	5. 9	Cambridge Utd.	Nuneaton	10.09.70
Ramasut, Tom	5. 9	Bristol Rov.	Cardiff	30.08.77
Young, Scott	6. 1	–	Pontypridd	14.01.76
Forwards				
Earnshaw, Robert	5. 7	–	Zambia	6.04.81
Nugent, Kevin	6. 1	Bristol City	Edmonton	10.04.69
Roberts, Chris	5.11	–	Cardiff	22.10.79
Thomas, David	5.10	Watford	Caerphilly	26.09.75

CHESTERFIELD

Name	Height ft. in.	Previous Club	Birthplace	Birthdate
Goalkeepers				
Leaning, Andrew	6. 2	Lincoln City	York	18.05.63
Mercer, Billy	6. 1	Sheffield Utd.	Liverpool	22.05.69
Defenders				
Blatherwick, Steven	6. 1	Burnley	Nottingham	20.09.73
Breckin, Ian	5.11	Rotherham Utd.	Rotherham	24.02.75
Simpkins, Michael	6. 0	Sheffield Wed.	Sheffield	28.11.78
Midfielders				
Beaumont, Chris	5.11	Stockport Co.	Sheffield	5.12.65
Carss, Anthony	5.10	Cardiff City	Alnwick	31.03.76
Curtis, Tom	5. 8	Derby Co.	Exeter	1.03.73
Ebdon, Marcus	5.10	Peterborough Utd.	Pontypool	17.10.70
Hewitt, Jamie	5.10	–	Chesterfield	17.05.68
Holland, Paul	5.11	Sheffield Utd.	Lincoln	8.07.73
Pearce, Greg	5. 9	–	Bolton	26.05.80
Willis, Roger	6. 0	Peterborough Utd.	Islington	17.06.67
Forwards				
Howard, Jonathan	5.11	Rotherham Utd.	Sheffield	7.10.71
Lee, Jason	6. 3	Watford	Forest Gate	9.05.71
Reeves, David	6. 0	Preston N.E.	Birkenhead	19.11.67
Wilkinson, Steven	5.11	Preston N.E.	Lincoln	1.09.68

COLCHESTER UNITED

Name	Height ft. in.	Previous Club	Birthplace	Birthdate
Goalkeepers				
–	–	–	–	–
Defenders				
Burton, Sagi	6. 3	Crystal Palace	Birmingham	25.11.77
Greene, David	6. 3	Luton Town	Luton	26.10.73
Farley, Craig	6. 1	Watford	–	17.03.81
Keith, Joe	6. 1	West Ham Utd.	–	1.10.78
Richard, Fabrice	6. 1	Martigues, Fra.	France	16.08.73
Skelton, Aaron	6. 0	Luton Town	Welwyn Garden	22.11.74
Wiles, Ian	6. 0	–	Epping	28.04.80
Wilkins, Richard	6. 0	Hereford	Streatham	25.05.65
Midfielders				
Aspinall, Warren	5. 9	Brentford	Wigan	13.09.67
Dozzell, Jason	6. 2	Northampton Town	Ipswich	9.12.67
Forbes, Steve	6. 2	Millwall	Stoke Newington	24.12.75

Gregory, David	5.10	Peterborough Utd.	Polestead	23.01.70
Launders, Brian	5.10	Derby Co.	Dublin	8.01.76
Pinault, Thomas	5.11	Cannes	France	4.12.81
Webster, Adrian	5.10	Charlton Athletic	–	11.10.80
Williams, Geraint	5. 8	Ipswich Town	Cwmparc	5.01.62

Forwards

Duguid, Karl	5.11	–	Letchworth	21.03.78
Germain, Steve	5.10	Cannes	–	22.06.81
Gregory, Neil	6. 0	Ipswich Town	Zambia	7.10.72
Moralee, Jamie	5.11	Brighton & H.A.	Wandsworth	2.12.71
Sale, Mark	6. 5	Mansfield Town	Burton-on-Trent	27.02.72
Lua Lua, Tresor	5. 7	–	Zaire	28.12.80

GILLINGHAM

Name	Height ft. in.	Previous Club	Birthplace	Birthdate
Goalkeepers				
Bartram, Vince	6. 2	Arsenal	Birmingham	7.08.68
Stannard, Jim	6. 2	Fulham	London	16.10.62
Defenders				
Ashby, Barry	6. 1	Brentford	London	2.11.70
Butters, Guy	6. 2	Portsmouth	Hillingdon	30.10.69
Bryant, Matt	6. 0	Bristol City	Bristol	21.09.70
Carr, Darren	6. 2	Chesterfield	Bristol	4.09.68
Edge, Roland	5.10	–	Gillingham	25.11.78
Masters, Neil	6. 0	Wolves	Lisburn	25.05.72
Patterson, Mark	5. 9	Plymouth Argyle	Leeds	13.07.68
Pennock, Adrian	6. 0	Borenmouth	Ipswich	27.03.71
Statham, Brian	5. 8	Brentford	Zimbabwe	21.05.69
Midfielders				
Browning, Marcus	6. 0	Huddersfield Town	Bristol	22.04.71
Galloway, Mick	5.10	Notts Co.	Nottingham	13.10.74
Hessenthaler, Andy	5. 7	Watford	Gravesend	17.06.65
Nosworthy, Nayron	5.10	–	Brixton	11.10.80
Saunders, Mark	5.10	Plymouth Argyle	Reading	23.07.71
Smith, Paul	5.10	Brentford	East Ham	18.09.71
Southall, Nicky	5. 9	Grimsby Town	Middlesbrough	28.01.72
Forwards				
Asaba, Carl	6. 1	Reading	London	28.01.73
Hodge, John	5. 7	Walsall	Ormskirk	1.04.69
Pinnock, James	5. 8	–	Dartford	1.08.78
Taylor, Robert	6. 1	Brentford	Norwich	30.04.71

LUTON TOWN

Name	Height ft. in.	Previous Club	Birthplace	Birthdate
Goalkeepers				
Ward, Scott	6. 2	–	Brent	5.10.81
Tate, Daniel	5.11	–	Bedford	12.11.80
Defenders				
Ayres, James	6. 3	–	Luton	18.09.80
Boyce, Emmerson	5.11	–	Aylesbury	24.09.79
Doherty, Gary	6. 2	–	Donegal	31.01.80
Fraser, Suart	5. 9	–	Edinburgh	9.01.80
James, Julian	5.10	–	Tring	22.03.70
Johnson, Marvin	6. 1	–	Wembley	29.10.68
McGowan, Gavin	5.10	Arsenal	Blackheath	16.01.76

Taylor, Matthew	5.11	–	Oxford	27.11.81
Thomas, Mitchell	6. 2	West Ham Utd.	Luton	2.10.64
White, Alan	6. 2	Middlesbrough	Darlington	22.03.76

Midfielders

Jerry, Moses	5. 9	–	Kampala, Uganda	22.02.81
McIndoe, Michael	5. 9	–	Edinburgh	2.12.79
McKinnon, Ray	5.10	Dundee Utd.	Dundee	5.08.70
McLaren, Paul	6. 1	–	High Wycombe	17.11.76
Scarlett, Andre	5. 4	–	Brent	11.01.80
Spring, Matthew	5.11	–	Harlow	17.11.79
Zahana-Oni, Landry	5.10	Bromley	Ivory Coast	8.08.76

Forwards

Douglas, Stuart	5. 8	–	London	9.04.78
Fotiadis, Andrew	5.11	–	Hitchin	6.09.77
George, Liam	5. 9	–	Luton	2.02.79
Gray, Phil	5. 9	Fortuna Sittard	Belfast	2.10.68
Kandol, Tresor	6. 2	–	Banga, Zaire	30.08.81

MILLWALL

Name	Height ft. in.	Previous Club	Birthplace	Birthdate
Goalkeepers				
Smith, Phil	5.10	–	Harrow	14.12.79
Spink, Nigel	6. 2	W.B.A.	Chelmsford	8.08.58
Defenders				
Cook, Andy	5. 9	Portsmouth	Romsey	10.08.69
Cort, Leon	6. 2	Dulwich Hamlet	London	11.09.79
Dolan, Joe	6. 2	–	Harrow	27.05.80
Dyche, Sean	6. 0	Bristol City	Kettering	28.06.71
Fitzgerald, Scott	6. 0	Wimbledon	London	13.08.69
Hicks, Mark	5. 8	–	Ireland	24.07.81
Law, Brian	6. 2	Wolves	Merthyr Tydfil	1.01.70
McLeary, Alan	5.11	Bristol City	Lambeth	6.10.64
Nethercott, Stuart	6. 0	Tottenham	Chadwell Heath	21.03.73
Ryan, Robbie	5.10	Huddersfield Town	Dublin	6.05.77
Stuart, Jamie	5.10	Charlton Athletic	Southwark	15.10.76
Midfielders				
Bircham, Marc	5.10	–	Brent	11.05.78
Bowry, Bobby	5. 8	Crystal Palace	Croydon	19.05.71
Cahill, Tim	5.10	–	Sydney, Aus.	6.12.79
Carter, Jimmy	5.10	Portsmouth	Hammersmith	9.11.65
Gilkes, Michael	5. 8	Wolves	Hackney	20.07.65
Ifill, Paul	5.11	–	Brighton	20.10.79
Newman, Ricky	5.10	Crystal Palace	Guildford	5.09.70
Neill, Lucas	6. 1	–	Sydney, Aus.	9.03.78
Odunsi, Leke	5. 8	–	London	
Reid, Steven	5.11	–	Kingston	10.03.81
Forwards				
Grant, Kim	5.10	Luton Town	Ghana	25.07.72
Harris, Neil	5.11	Cambridge City	Orsett	12.07.77
Hockton, Danny	6. 0	–	Barking	7.02.79
Moody, Paul	6. 3	Fulham	Portsmouth	13.06.67
Sadlier, Richard	6. 2	–	Dublin	14.01.79
Shaw, Paul	5.11	Arsenal	Burnham	4.09.73

NOTTS COUNTY

Name	Height ft. in.	Previous Club	Birthplace	Birthdate
Goalkeepers				
Gibson, Paul	6. 2	Manchester Utd.	Sheffield	1.11.76
Ward, Darren	5.11	Mansfield Town	Worksop	11.05.74
Defenders				
Dyer, Alex	5.11	Huddersfield Town	Forest Gate	14.11.65
Liburd, Richard	5.10	Carlisle Utd.	Nottingham	26.09.73
Pearce, Dennis	5. 9	Wolves	Wolves	10.09.74
Redmile, Matthew	6. 3	–	Nottingham	12.11.76
Warren, Mark	5. 9	Leyton Orient	Clapton	12.11.74
Midfielders				
Bolland, Paul	5.10	Bradford City	Bradford	23.12.79
Hughes, Andy	5.11	Oldham Athletic	Stockport	2.01.78
Marshall, Ben	6. 0	–	Sutton	5.09.79
Murray, Shaun	5. 7	Bradford City	Newcastle	7.02.70
Owers, Gary	5.10	Bristol City	Newcastle	3.10.68
Richardson, Ian	5.10	Birmingham City	Bolton	22.10.70
Robson, Mark	5. 7	Charlton Athletic	Newham	22.05.69
Tierney, Fran	5.10	Crewe Alexandra	Liverpool	10.09.75
Forwards				
Beadle, Peter	6. 0	Port Vale	Lambeth	13.05.72
Darby, Duane	5.11	Hull City	Birmingham	17.10.73
Farrell, Sean	6. 0	Peterborough Utd.	Watford	28.02.69
Rapley, Kevin	5. 9	Brentford	Reading	21.09.77
Stallard, Mark	6. 0	Wycombe Wand.	Derby	24.10.74

OLDHAM ATHLETIC

Name	Height ft. in.	Previous Club	Birthplace	Birthdate
Goalkeepers				
Cherry, Steve	6. 1	Mansfield Town	Nottingham	5.08.60
Kelly, Gary	5.11	Bury	Preston	3.08.66
Miskelly, David	6. 0	–	Ards	3.09.79
Defenders				
Garnett, Shaun	6. 2	Swansea City	Wallasey	22.11.69
Graham, Richard	6. 2	–	Dewsbury	28.11.74
Holt, Andy	6. 1	–	Stockport	21.04.78
Innes, Mark	5.10	–	Bellshill	27.09.78
McNiven, Scott	5.10	–	Leeds	27.05.79
Salt, Philip	5.11	–	Huddersfield	2.03.70
Midfielders				
Duxbury, Lee	5. 8	Bradford City	Keighley	7.10.69
Hotte, Mark	5.11	–	Bradford	27.09.78
Reid, Paul	5. 9	Huddersfield Town	Oldbury	19.01.68
Rickers, Paul	5.10	–	Leeds	9.05.75
Swan, Iain	6. 3	–	Glasgow	16.10.79
Forwards				
Allott, Mark	5.11	–	Manchester	2.10.77
Clitheroe, Lee	5.10	–	Chorley	18.11.78
Dudley, Craig	5.10	Notts Co.	Newark	12.09.79
McNiven, David	5.10	–	Leeds	27.05.78
Tipton, Matthew	5.10	–	Bangor	29.06.80

OXFORD UNITED

Name	Height ft. in.	Previous Club	Birthplace	Birthdate
Goalkeepers				
Lundin, Paul	6. 4	Osters IF, Swe.	Stockholm, Swe.	7.03.72
Defenders				
Davis, Steve	6. 0	Barnsley	Birmingham	26.07.65
Gilchrist, Phil	5.11	Hartlepool Utd.	Stockton	25.08.73
Robinson, Les	5. 8	Doncaster Rov.	Shirebrook	1.03.67
Whelan, Phil	6. 4	Middlesbrough	Stockport	7.03.72
Midfielders				
Fear, Peter	5.10	Wimbledon	Sutton	10.09.73
Lewis, Mickey	5. 8	Derby Co.	Birmingham	15.02.65
Murphy, Matt	5.10	Corby Town	Northampton	20.08.71
Powell, Paul	5. 9	–	Wallingford	30.06.78
Tait, Paul	6. 1	Northampton Town	Sutton Coldfield	31.07.71
Watson, Mark	5.10	Walsall	Vancouver, Can.	8.09.70
Forwards				
Anthrobus, Steve	6. 0	Crewe Alexandra	Lewisham	10.11.68
Banger, Nicky	5. 9	Oldham Athletic	Southampton	25.02.71
Beauchamp, Joey	5.10	Swindon Town	Oxford	13.03.71
Cook, Jamie	5.10	–	Oxford	2.08.79
Folland, Robert	6. 0	–	Swansea	16.09.74
Francis, Kevin	6. 7	Birmingham City	Birmingham	6.12.67
Thomson, Andy	5.10	Southend Utd.	Motherwell	1.04.71
Weatherstone, Simon	5. 9	–	Reading	5.09.79

PRESTON NORTH END

Name	Height ft. in.	Previous Club	Birthplace	Birthdate
Goalkeepers				
Lucas, David	6. 0	–	Chapletown	23.11.77
Moilanen, Tuevo	6. 1	Jaro, Fin.	Oulu, Fin.	12.12.73
Defenders				
Alexander, Graham	5.10	Luton Town	Coventry	10.10.71
Eaton, Adam	5. 9	Everton	Wigan	2.05.80
Jackson, Michael	5.11	Bury	Chester	4.12.73
Kidd, Ryan	5.11	Port Vale	Radcliffe	6.10.71
Ludden, Dominic	5. 8	Watford	Basildon	30.02.74
Morgan, Paul	5.11	–	Belfast	23.10.78
Murdock, Colin	6. 1	Manchester Utd.	Ballymena	2.07.75
Parkinson, Gary	5.10	Burnley	Thornaby	10.01.68
Midfielders				
Appleton, Michael	5. 9	Manchester Utd.	Salford	4.12.75
Gregan, Sean	6. 0	Darlington	Guiseborough	29.03.74
King, Stuart	5. 9	–	Londonderry	20.03.81
McKenna, Paul	5. 7	–	Chorley	23.10.78
Rankine, Mark	5. 7	Wolves	Doncaster	30.09.69
Forwards				
Basham, Steve	5. 9	Southampton	Southampton	2.12.77
Cartwright, Lee	5. 8	–	Rossendale	19.09.72
Eyres, David	5.10	Burnley	Liverpool	26.02.64
Harris, Jason	6. 0	Leyton Orient	London	24.11.76
Macken, Jonathan	5. 9	Manchester Utd.	Manchester	7.09.77
Nogan, Kurt	5.10	Burnley	Cardiff	9.09.70
Wright, Mark	5.10	–	Chorley	4.09.81

READING

Name	Height ft. in.	Previous Club	Birthplace	Birthdate
Goalkeepers				
Hammond, Nicky	6. 0	Plymouth Argyle	Hornchurch	7.09.67
Howie, Scott	6. 3	Motherwell	Motherwell	4.01.72
Mautone, Steve	6. 2	West Ham Utd.	Australia	10.08.70
Van der Kwaak, Peter	6. 4	FC Dordrecht, Hol.	Haarlem, Holl.	12.10.68
Defenders				
Barras, Tony	6. 4	York City	Stockton	29.03.71
Bernal, Andy	5.10	Sydney Olympic	Canberra	16.07.66
Casper, Chris	6. 0	Manchester Utd.	Burnley	28.04.75
Gray, Stuart	5.11	Celtic	Harrogate	18.12.73
Gurney, Andy	5.11	Torquay Utd.	Bristol	25.01.74
Hunter, Barry	6. 3	Wrexham	Coleraine	18.11.68
Kromheer, Elroy	6. 4	FC Volendam, Hol.	Amsterdam	15.01.70
Polston, John	6. 0	Norwich City	Walthamstow	10.06.68
Primus, Linvoy	6. 0	Barnet	Forest Gate	14.09.73
Midfielders				
Brebner, Grant	5.10	Manchester Utd.	Edinburgh	6.12.77
Caskey, Darren	5. 8	Tottenham	Basildon	21.08.74
Crawford, Jimmy	5.11	Newcastle Utd.	Chicago	1.05.74
Evers, Sean	5. 9	Luton Town	Hitchin	10.10.77
Glasgow, Byron	5. 5	–	London	18.02.79
Hodges, Lee	5.10	Barnet	Epping	4.09.73
McLaren, Andy	5.10	Dundee Utd.	Glasgow	5.06.73
Murty, Graeme	5.10	York City	Saltburn	13.11.74
Parkinson, Phil	6. 0	Bury	Chorley	1.12.67
Forwards				
Brayson, Paul	5. 5	Newcastle Utd.	Newcastle	16.09.77
Forster, Nicky	5. 9	Birmingham City	Caterham	8.09.73
McIntyre, Jim	5.11	Kilmarnock	Alexandria	24.05.72
Sarr, Mass	5.10	Hadjuk Split	Liberia	6.02.73
Scott, Keith	6. 3	Wycombe Wand.	Westminster	9.06.67
Williams, Martin	5. 9	Luton Town	Luton	12.07.73

SCUNTHORPE UNITED

Name	Height ft. in.	Previous Club	Birthplace	Birthdate
Goalkeepers				
Clarke, Tim	6. 3	York City	Stourbridge	19.09.68
Evans, Thomas	6. 0	Crystal Palace	Doncaster	31.12.76
Defenders				
Fickling, Ashley	5.10	Grimsby Town	Sheffield	15.11.72
Graves, Wayne	5. 8	–	Scunthorpe	18.09.80
Hope, Chris	6. 1	Nott'm Forest	Sheffield	14.11.72
Housham, Steven	5.10	–	Gainsborough	24.02.76
Laws, Brian	5. 9	Darlington	Wallsend	14.10.61
Logan, Richard	6. 1	Plymouth Argyle	Barnsley	24.05.69
McAuley, Sean	6. 0	Hartlepool Utd.	Sheffield	23.06.72
Stanton, Nathan	5. 9	–	Nottingham	6.05.81
Wilcox, Russ	6. 0	Preston N.E.	Hemsworth	25.03.64
Midfielders				
Calvo-Garcia, Alex	5.11	Eibar	Ordizia, Spa.	1.01.72
Dawson, Andrew	5. 9	Nott'm Forest	Northallerton	20.10.78
Harsley, Paul	5. 8	Grimsby Town	Scunthorpe	29.05.78
Marshall, Lee	5. 9	Eastwood Town	Nottingham	1.08.75
Walker, Justin	5.10	Nott'm Forest	Nottingham	6.09.75

Forwards

Name	Height ft. in.	Previous Club	Birthplace	Birthdate
Bull, Gary	5.10	York City	West Bromwich	12.06.66
Gayle, John	6. 2	Northampton Town	Bromsgrove	30.07.64
Sheldon, Gareth	5.11	–	Barnsley	8.05.80
Stamp, Darryn	6. 3	Hessle	Beverley	21.09.78

STOKE CITY

Name	Height ft. in.	Previous Club	Birthplace	Birthdate
Goalkeepers				
Fraser, Stuart	6. 0	–	Cheltenham	1.08.78
Muggleton, Carl	6. 2	Leicester City	Leicester	13.09.68
Ward, Gavin	6. 3	Bolton Wand.	Sutton Coldfield	30.06.70
Defenders				
Collins, Lee	6. 1	Aston Villa	Birmingham	10.09.77
Clarke, Clive	5.11	–	Dublin	14.01.80
Kavanagh, Jason	5. 9	Wycombe Wand.	Birmingham	23.11.71
Mohan, Nicky	6. 1	Wycombe Wand.	Middlesbrough	6.10.70
Petty, Ben	6. 0	Aston Villa	Solihull	22.03.77
Short, Chris	5.10	Sheffield Utd.	Munster,Ger.	9.05.70
Sigurdsson, Larus	6. 0	Thor SC,Ice.	Akureyri,Ice	4.06.73
Small, Bryan	5. 9	Bolton Wand.	Birmingham	15.11.71
Wooliscroft, Ashley	5.10	–	Stoke	28.12.79
Midfielders				
Cartwright, Jamie	5. 6	–	Lichfield	11.10.79
Godbold, Jamie	5. 4	–	Great Yarmouth	10.01.80
Heath, Robert	5. 8	–	Stoke	31.08.78
Kavanagh, Graham	5.10	Middlesbrough	Dublin	3.12.73
Mackenzie, Neil	6. 2	–	Birmingham	15.04.76
O'Connor, James	5. 7	–	Dublin	1.09.79
Robinson, Phil	5.10	Notts. Co	Stafford	6.01.67
Forwards				
Connor, Paul	6. 1	Middlesbrough	Bishop Auckland	12.01.79
Crowe, Dean	5. 5	–	Stockport	6.06.79
Lightbourne, Kyle	6. 2	Walsall	Bermuda	29.09.68
Oldfield, David	6. 0	Luton Town	Perth, Aus.	30.05.68
Taaffe, Stephen	5. 5	–	Stoke	10.09.79
Thorne, Peter	6. 0	Swindon Town	Manchester	21.06.73

WIGAN ATHLETIC

Name	Height ft. in.	Previous Club	Birthplace	Birthdate
Goalkeepers				
Carroll, Roy	6. 2	Hull City	Enniskillen	30.09.77
Nixon, Eric	6. 4	Stockport Co.	Manchester	4.10.62
Defenders				
Balmer, Stuart	6. 0	Charlton Athletic	Falkirk	20.09.69
Bradshaw, Carl	5.10	Norwich City	Sheffield	2.10.68
Fitzhenry, Neil	6. 0	–	Billinge	24.09.78
Green, Scott	5.10	Bolton Wand.	Walsall	15.01.70
Griffiths, Gareth	6. 4	Port Vale	Winsford	10.04.70
McGibbon, Pat	6. 2	Manchester Utd.	Lurgan	6.09.73
Sharp, Kevin	5. 9	Leeds Utd.	Canada	19.09.74
Midfielders				
Kilford, Ian	5.10	Nott'm Forest	Bristol	6.10.73
Martinez, Roberto	5.11	CF Balaguer, Spa.	Balaguer, Spa.	13.07.73
McLaughlin, Brian	5. 4	Dundee Utd.	Bellshill	14.05.74
Nicholls, Kevin	6. 0	Charlton Athletic	Newham	2.01.79

O'Neill, Michael	5.11	Coventry City	Portadown	5.07.69
Porter, Andy	5. 9	Port Vale	Holmes Chapel	17.09.68
Forwards				
Barlow, Stuart	5.10	Oldham Athletic	Liverpool	16.07.68
Haworth, Simon	6. 1	Coventry City	Cardiff	30.03.77
Jones, Graeme	6. 0	Doncaster Rov.	Gateshead	13.03.70
Lee, David	5. 7	Bolton Wand.	Whitefield	5.11.67
Liddell, Andy	5. 6	Barnsley	Leeds	28.06.73

WREXHAM

Name	Height ft. in.	Previous Club	Birthplace	Birthdate
Goalkeepers				
Cartwright, Mark	6. 1	Stockport Co.	Chester	13.01.73
Dearden, Kevin	5.11	Huddersfield Town	Luton	8.03.70
Rogers, Christian	6. 0	–	Chester	7.10.80
Walsh, Dave	6. 1	–	Wrexham	29.04.79
Defenders				
Brace, Deryn	5. 9	Norwich City	Haverfordwest	15.03.75
Carey, Brian	6. 2	Leicester City	Cork	31.05.68
Hardy, Phil	5. 8	–	Chester	9.04.73
Humes, Tony	5.11	Ipswich Town	Blyth	19.03.66
McGregor, Mark	5.10	–	Chester	30.04.78
Ridler, David	6. 0	–	Liverpool	12.03.76
Ryan, Michael	5.11	Manchester Utd.	Stockport	3.10.79
Midfielders				
Barrett, Paul	5. 9	Newcastle Utd.	Newcastle	13.04.78
Chalk, Martin	5. 6	Stockport Co.	Louth	30.08.69
Gibson, Robin	5. 8	–	Crewe	15.11.79
Owen, Gareth	5. 8	–	Chester	21.10.71
Roberts, Steven	6. 0	–	Wrexham	24.02.80
Thomas, Steve	5.10	–	Hartlepool	23.06.79
Williams, Daniel	6. 1	Liverpool	Wrexham	12.07.79
Forwards				
Connolly, Karl	5. 9	–	Prescot	9.02.70
Edwards, Jake	6. 0	–	Manchester	11.05.76
Lowe, David	5.10	Wigan Athletic	Liverpool	30.08.65
Morrell, Andy	5.11	Newcastle Bluestar	Doncaster	28.09.74
Roberts, Paul	5.11	–	Bangor	29.07.77
Roberts, Neil	5.10	–	Wrexham	7.04.78
Russell, Kevin	5. 8	Notts Co.	Portsmouth	6.12.66
Spink, Dean	5.11	Shrewsbury Town	Birmingham	22.01.67

WYCOMBE WANDERERS

Name	Height ft. in.	Previous Club	Birthplace	Birthdate
Goalkeepers				
Osborn, Mark	6. 0	–	Bletchley	19.06.81
Taylor, Martin	6. 0	Derby Co.	Tamworth	9.12.66
Westhead, Mark	6. 3	Kidderminster	Blackpool	19.07.75
Defenders				
Bates, Jamie	6. 1	Brentford	Croydon	24.02.68
Beeton, Alan	5.11	–	Watford	4.10.78
Cousins, Jason	5.11	Brentford	Hayes	14.10.70
Lawrence, Matthew	6. 1	Fulham	Northampton	19.06.74
Lee, Martin	5. 7	–	Guildford	10.08.80
Leach, Martin	5.11	–	Hemel Hempstead	30.01.81
McCarthy Paul	6. 0	Brighton & H.A.	Cork	4.08.71

Rogers, Mark	5.11	Vancouver	Beulph, Can.	3.11.78
Vinnicombe, Chris	5. 9	Burnley	Exeter City	20.10.70
Midfielders				
Brown, Steve	6. 1	Northampton Town	Northampton	6.07.66
Carroll, Dave	6. 0	Ruslip Manor	Paisley	20.09.66
Holsgrove, Lee	6. 2	Millwall	Wendover	13.12.79
Ryan, Keith	6. 0	Berkhamsted	Northampton	25.06.70
Simpson, Michael	5. 9	Notts. Co.	Nottingham	28.02.74
Wraight, Gary	5. 6	–	Epping	5.03.79
Forwards				
Baird, Andrew	6. 1	–	East Kilbride	18.01.79
Bulman, Danny	5. 9	Ashford	Ashford	24.01.79
Devine, Sean	6. 0	Barnet	Lewisham	6.09.72
Emblen, Paul	5.11	Charlton Athletic	Bromley	3.04.76
Harkin, Maurice	5.10	–	Derry	16.08.79
McSporran, Jermaine	5.10	Oxford City	Abingdon	1.01.77
Senda, Danny	5.11	Southampton	Harrow	17.04.81
Thompson, Richard	5. 8	Crawley Town	Lambeth	2.05.74

DIVISION THREE

BARNET

Name	Height ft. in.	Previous Club	Birthplace	Birthdate
Goalkeepers				
Harrison, Lee	6. 2	Fulham	Billericay	12.09.71
Defenders				
Arber, Mark	6. 1	Tottenham	South Africa	9.10.77
Basham, Mike	6. 2	Peterborough Utd.	Barking	27.09.73
Chapman, Danny	5.11	–	London	16.08.77
Goodhind, Warren	5.11	–	Johannesburg, S.A.	16.08.77
Hackett, Warren	6. 0	Mansfield Town	Plaistow	16.12.71
Heald, Greg	6. 1	Peterborough Utd.	Enfield	26.09.71
Sawyers, Robert	5.10	Wolves	Dudley	20.11.78
Stockley, Sam	5. 8	Southampton	Tiverton	5.09.77
Midfielders				
Brown, Danny	5.10	Leyton Orient	London	12.09.80
Currie, Darren	5. 9	Plymouth Argyle	Hampstead	29.11.74
Doolan, John	6. 1	Mansfield Town	Liverpool	7.05.74
Gledhill, Lee	5. 9	–	Woolwich	7.11.80
Searle, Steve	5.10	Sittingbourne	Lambeth	7.03.77
Toms, Fraser	5.11	Charlton Athletic	Ealing	13.09.79
Wilson, Paul	5. 9	Barking	Forest Gate	26.09.64
Forwards				
Barnes, Steve	5. 4	Birmingham City	Harrow	5.01.76
Charley, Ken	6. 1	Stockport Co.	Stepney	28.11.64
King, Marlon	6. 0	–	London	26.04.80
McGleish, Scott	5. 9	Leyton Orient	Barnet	10.02.74
Strevens, Ben	5.10	Wingate and Finchley	Hendon	24.05.86

BRIGHTON AND HOVE ALBION

Name	Height ft. in.	Previous Club	Birthplace	Birthdate
Goalkeepers				
Ormerod, Mark	6. 0	–	Bournemouth	5.02.76
Parkin, Brian	6. 1	Notts. Co.	Birkenhead	12.10.65
Walton, Mark	6. 4	Fulham	Merthyr Tydfil	1.06.69

Defenders

Name	Height ft. in.	Previous Club	Birthplace	Birthdate
Andrews, Ben	6.10	–	Burton-on-Trent	18.11.80
Arnott, Andy	6. 1	Fulham	Chatham	18.10.73
Culverhouse, Ian	5.10	Swindon Town	Bishop's Stortford	22.09.64
Hobson, Gary	6. 1	Hull City	Hull	12.11.72
Johnson, Ross	6. 0	–	Brighton	2.01.76
McPherson, Keith	5.11	Reading	Greenwich	11.09.63
Watson, Paul	5. 8	Brentford	Hastings	4.01.75

Midfielders

Name	Height ft. in.	Previous Club	Birthplace	Birthdate
Armstrong, Paul	5.10	–	Dublin	5.10.78
Bissett, Nicky	6. 2	Fulham	Fulham	5.04.68
Campbell, Jamie	6. 1	Cambridge Utd.	Birmingham	21.10.72
Hinshelwood, Danny	5. 9	Portsmouth	Bromley	4.12.75
Mayo, Kerry	5.10		Pearcehaven	21.09.77
Oatway, Charlie	5. 8	Brentford	Hammersmith	28.11.73

Forwards

Name	Height ft. in.	Previous Club	Birthplace	Birthdate
Davies, Lawrence	6. 1	Bradford City	Abergavenny	3.09.77
Freeman, Darren	5.11	Brentford	Brighton	22.08.73
Hart, Gary	5. 9	Stanstead	Harrow	21.09.76
Thomas, Rod	5. 7	Chester City	Brent	10.10.70
Westcott, John	5. 6	–	Eastbourne	31.05.79

CARLISLE UNITED

Name	Height ft. in.	Previous Club	Birthplace	Birthdate
Goalkeepers				
Keen, Peter	6. 1	Newcastle Utd.	Middlesbrough	16.11.76
Defenders				
Barr, Billy	5.11	Crewe Alexandra	Halifax	21.01.69
Bowman, Rob	6. 1	Rotherham Utd.	Durham	21.11.75
Brightwell, David	6. 2	Northampton Town	Lotterworth	7.01.71
Clark, Peter	6. 1	Arsenal	Romford	16.12.79
Pitts, Matthew	6. 1	Sunderland	Middlesbrough	25.12.79
Reid, Paul	6. 2	–	Carlisle	18.02.82
Whitehead, Stuart	6. 0	Bolton Wand.	Bromsgrove	17.07.76
Midfielders				
Anthony, Graham	5. 7	Plymouth Argyle	South Shields	9.08.75
Hopper, Tony	5.11	–	Carlisle	31.05.76
Prokas, Richard	5. 9	–	Penrith	22.01.76
Searle, Damon	5.10	Stockport Co.	Cardiff	26.10.71
Skelton, Gavin	5. 7	–	Penrith	27.03.81
Thorpe, Jeff	5.11	–	Cockermouth	17.11.72
Thurstan, Mark	6. 2	–	Carlisle	10.02.80
Forwards				
Dobie, Scott	6. 2	–	Workington	10.10.78
Douglas, Andrew	5. 9	–	Penrith	27.05.80
Tracey, Richard	5.11	Rotherham Utd.	Muirfield	9.07.79

CHELTENHAM TOWN

Name	Height ft. in.	Previous Club	Birthplace	Birthdate
Goalkeepers				
Book, Steve	6. 2	Forest Green	Bournemouth	7.07.69
Higgs, Shane	6. 0	Worcester City		
Defenders				
Banks, Chris	6. 2	Bath City	Stone	22.11.65
Brough, John	6. 0	Hereford Utd.	Ilkeston	8.01.73
Duff, Michael	5.11	–	Belfast	11.01.78

Freeman, Mark	5.10	Gloucester City	Walsall	27.01.70
Victory, Jamie	5. 8	Bournemouth	London	14.11.75
Walker, Richard	5.11	Hereford Utd.	Derby	9.11.71
Midfielders				
Bloomer, Bob	6. 0	Bristol Rov.	Sheffield	21.06.66
Howells, Lee	5. 8	Brisbane Utd.	Brisbane, Aus.	
Jackson, Michael	5.10	–	Cheltenham	26.06.80
Milton, Russell	5.11	Dover Athletic	Folkestone	12.01.69
Yates, Mark	6. 0	Kidderminster	Birmingham	24.01.70
Forwards				
Bailey, Dennis	5.10	Farnborough	Lambeth	13.11.65
Grayson, Neil	6. 0	Hereford Utd.	York	1.11.64
Hopkins, Gareth	5.10	–	Cheltenham	14.06.80
Watkins, Dale	5. 9	Gloucester City	Peterborough	4.11.71

CHESTER CITY

Name	Height ft. in.	Previous Club	Birthplace	Birthdate
Goalkeepers				
Brown, Wayne	6. 0	Bristol City	Southampton	14.01.77
Cutler, Neil	6. 1	Crewe Alexandra	Birmingham	3.09.76
Defenders				
Crosby, Andy	6. 2	Darlington	Rotheram	3.03.73
Davidson, Ross	5. 9	Sheffield Utd.	Chertsey	13.11.73
Woods, Mattie	6. 0	Everton	Gosport	9.09.76
Midfielders				
Clench, Philip	6. 0	–	Chester	23.03.79
Cross, Jon	5.10	Wrexham	Wallasey	2.03.75
Fisher, Neil	5.10	Bolton Wand.	St Helens	7.11.70
Flitcroft, David	5.10	Preston N.E.	Bolton	14.01.74
Priest, Chris	5. 8	Everton	Leigh	18.10.73
Reid, Shaun	5. 8	Bury	Huyton	13.10.65
Richardson, Nick	6. 0	Bury	Halifax	11.04.67
Shelton, Andy	6. 0	–	Sutton Coldfield	19.06.80
Shelton, Gary	5. 7	Bristol City	Nottingham	21.03.58
Forwards				
Bennett, Gary	5.10	Wigan Athletic	Sheffield	20.09.63
Jones, Jon	5. 9	–	Wrexham	27.10.78
Murphy, John	6. 3	–	Whiston	18.10.76
Wright, Darren	5. 8	–	Warrington	7.09.79

DARLINGTON

Name	Height ft. in.	Previous Club	Birthplace	Birthdate
Goalkeepers				
Preece, David	6. 2	Sunderland	Sunderland	28.08.76
Samways, Mark	6. 2	York City	Doncaster	11.11.68
Defenders				
Bennett, Gary	6. 0	Scarborough	Manchester	4.12.61
Hope, Richard	6. 2	Blackburn Rov.	Stockton	22.06.78
Liddle, Craig	5.11	Middlesbrough	Chester-le-Street	21.10.71
Stephenson, Ashley	6. 2	Waterford	South Africa	6.07.74
Naylor, Glenn	5.11	York City	York	11.08.72
Tutill, Steve	6. 1	York City	York	1.10.69
Midfielders				
Atkinson, Brian	5. 9	Sunderland	Darlington	19.01.71
Brumwell, Phillip	5. 7	Sunderland	Darlington	8.08.75
Campbell, Paul	6. 1	–	Middlesbrough	29.01.80

Gaughan, Steve	5.11	Chesterfield	Doncaster	14.04.70
Gray, Martin	5. 9	Oxford Utd.	Stockton	17.08.71
Reed, Adam	6. 0	Blackburn Rov.	Bishop's Auckland	18.02.75

Fowards

Carruthers, Martin	5.11	Peterborough Utd.	Nottingham	7.08.72
Dorner, Mario	5.10	Motherwell	Austria	21.03.70
Gabbiadini, Marco	5.10	Stoke City	Nottingham	20.01.68
Himsworth, Gary	5. 7	York City	Pickering	19.12.69
Hunt, David	5.10	–	Durham	5.03.80
Roberts, Darren	5.10	Chesterfield	Birmingham	12.10.69

EXETER CITY

Name	Height ft. in.	Previous Club	Birthplace	Birthdate
Goalkeepers				
Fox, Peter	5.11	Stoke City	Scunthorpe	5.07.57
Potter, Danny	6. 0	Colchester Utd.	Ipswich Town	18.03.79
Defenders				
Blake, Noel	6. 2	Dundee	Kingston, Jam.	12.01.62
Curran, Chris	5.11	Plymouth Argyle	Birmingham	17.09.71
Gale, Shaun	6. 1	Barnet	Reading	8.10.69
Gittens, Jon	6. 0	Torquay Utd.	Birmingham	22.01.64
Power, Graeme	5.10	Bristol Rov.	Pinner	7.03.77
Richardson, Jon	6. 0	–	Nottingham	29.08.75
Midfielders				
Breslan, Geoff	5. 7	–	Torquay	4.06.80
Buckle, Paul	5.10	Colchester Utd.	Hatfield	16.12.70
Holloway, Christopher	5.10	–	Swansea	5.02.80
Rees, Jason	5. 6	Cambridge Utd.	Aberdare	22.12.69
Smith, Peter	5.11	–	Liverpool	31.10.80
Forwards				
Flack, Steve	6. 2	Cardiff City	Cambridge	29.05.71
McConnell, Barry	5.10	–	Exeter	1.01.77
Rowbotham, Darren	5.11	Shrewsbury Town	Cardiff	22.10.66
Speakman, Robert	5. 9	–	Swansea	5.12.80
Waugh, Warren	6. 1	–	London	9.10.80
Wilkinson, John	5.10	–	Exeter	24.08.79

HALIFAX TOWN

Name	Height ft. in.	Previous Club	Birthplace	Birthdate
Goalkeepers				
Parks, Tony	5.11	Scarborough	London	28.01.63
Defenders				
Bradshaw, Mark	5.10	Macclesfield Town	Ashton-under-Lyme	7.09.69
Jules, Mark	5. 7	Chesterfield	Bradford	5.09.71
Lucas, Richard	5.10	Hartlepool Utd.	Chapeltown	22.09.70
Murphy, Jamie	6. 0	Cambridge Utd.	Manchester	25.02.73
Overson, Vince	6. 2	Burnley	Kettering	15.05.62
Sertori, Mark	6. 1	Scunthorpe Utd.	Manchester	1.09.78
Stansfield, James	6. 2	Huddersfield Town	Dewsbury	18.09.78
Stoneman, Paul	6. 0	Blackpool	Whitley Bay	26.02.73
Wills, Dave	5. 6	Manchester City	Manchester	9.05.71
Midfielders				
Paterson, Jamie	5. 4	Scunthorpe Utd.	Dumfries	26.04.73
Butler, Peter	5. 9	W.B.A.	Halifax	27.08.66
Hulme, Kevin	5.10	Macclesfield Town	Farnworth	7.12.67
Murphy, Stephen	5.11	Huddersfield Town	Dublin	5.04.78

	Height ft. in.	Previous Club	Birthplace	Birthdate
n, Steve	5.11	Lincoln City	Southend	6.12.73
on, Richard	6. 3	Stockport Co.	Worthing	22.03.70

NSFIELD TOWN

	Height ft. in.	Previous Club	Birthplace	Birthdate
eepers				
ng, Ian	6. 3	Bradford City	Sheffield	27.07.65
ders				
yce, Ian	6. 3	Welling	Bolton	9.06.75
, Daniel	6. 0	–	–	–
l, Robert	5.10	–		
s, Stuart	6. 2	Hereford Utd.	Derby	4.06.80
ns, Lee	5. 6	Tranmere Rov.	Wolves	8.05.66
			Birmingham	3.02.73
ders				
Darrell	5. 9	–	Mansfield	16.12.77
ony	5. 9	Barrow	Grimsby	14.05.59
vid	5.11	Manchester City	Dumfries	6.09.74
Jason	5.10	–	Peterborough	5.08.79
Michael	5. 8		Mansfield	24.11.78
ary	5.11	Kilmarnock	Drogheda	5.09.73
Tony	6. 0	Preston N.E.	Ashington	29.10.70
Lee	6. 0	Carlisle Utd.	Paisley	9.10.76
nathan	5.10	–	–	

MPTON TOWN

	Height ft. in.	Previous Club	Birthplace	Birthdate
h	6. 1	Bristol City	Bolton	3.10.68
n	5,10	Stoke City	Solihull	4.12.70
y	6. 1	W.B.A.	Coventry	5.02.69
	5. 9	Birmingham City	Birmingham	8.10.68
	6. 0	Notts Co.	Ilford	5.12.71
	6. 3	Burnley	Sunderland	1.04.69
d	6. 2	Darlington	Stockton	22.06.78
y	6. 0	–	Birmingham	14.11.68
	5. 9	Norwich City	Salisbury	17.02.76
	5. 8	Notts Co.	Derby	17.12.76
an	5.10	W.B.A.	Saltburn	29.10.73
	5.11	Burnley	Islington	23.09.70
	5.10	Doncaster Rov.	Wrexham	14.03.72
can	6. 1	Millwall	Dublin	30.07.73
	6. 1	Southampton	Frimley	7.09.77
	5.10	Plymouth Argyle	Canada	25.12.71
	6. 3	Hartlepool Utd.	Durham	10.05.76
	6. 2	Doncaster Rov.	Aylesbury	8.10.76
	6. 1	Millwall	Louth	30.10.64
	5. 8	Walsall	Banbury	18.04.61
	5. 7	Wycombe Wand.	North Walsham	24.01.69
	5. 9	–	Bangor	5.10.80

	Height ft. in.	Previous Club	Birthplace	Birthdate
Newton, Chris	6. 0	–	Leeds	5.11.79
Richards, Ian	5. 9	Blackburn Rov.	Barnsley	5.10.79
Forwards				
Jackson, Justin	5.10	Notts Co.	Nottingham	10.12.74
Power, Lee	5. 8	Hibernian	Wallingford	30.06.72
Tate, Chris	6. 0	Scarborough	York	27.12.77
Clarke, Matthew	6. 3	Wolves	Leeds	18.12.80

HARTLEPOOL UNITED

Name	Height ft. in.	Previous Club	Birthplace	Birthdate
Goalkeepers				
Dibble, Andy	6. 3	Altrincham	Cwmbran	8.05.65
Downey, Gareth	6. 1	–	Sunderland	8.02.81
Hollund, Martin	6. 0	–	Stord, Norway	11.08.74
Defenders				
Barron, Michael	5.11	–	Lumley	22.12.74
Downey, Glen	6. 1	–	Newcastle	20.09.78
Ingram, Denny	5.11	–	Sunderland	27.06.76
Knowles, Darren	5. 6	–	Sheffield	8.10.70
Lake, Craig	5.11	–	Stockton	10.02.80
Lee, Graeme	6. 2	–	Middlesbrough	31.05.78
Miller, Tommy	6. 1	–	Easington	8.01.79
Robinson, Mark	5. 9	–	Guisborough	24.07.81
Strodder, Gary	6. 2	Notts Co.	Mirfield	1.04.65
Westwood, Chris	5.11	Wolves	Dudley	13.02.77
Midfielders				
Briggs, John	5.11	–	Stockton	9.11.79
Clark, Ian	5.10	–	Stockton	23.10.74
Cooper, Paul	5. 9	–	Easington	8.10.80
Di Lella, Gus	5. 9	–	Buenos Aires, Arg.	6.10.73
Evans, Nicky	5. 8	–	Carmarthen	12.05.80
Forster, Richard	5.11	–	Easington	16.8.81
Hughes, Danny	5.10	Wolves	Bangor	13.02.80
Smith, Jeff	5.10	–	Middlesbrough	28.06.80
Forwards				
Dunwell, Michael	5.11	–	Stockton	6.01.80
Freestone, Chris	5.10	Northampton Town	Nottingham	4.09.71
Hay, Andy	5.11	–	North Shields	20.10.80
Henderson, Kevin	5.11	Burnley	Ashington	8.06.74
Jones, Gary	6. 1	Notts Co.	Huddersfield	6.04.69
Midgley, Craig	5. 7	–	Bradford	24.05.76
Stephenson, Paul	5.10	–	Wallsend	2.01.68

HULL CITY

Name	Height ft. in.	Previous Club	Birthplace	Birthdate
Goalkeepers				
Baker, Matthew	6. 0	–	Claro	18.12.79
Wilson, Stephen	5.10	–	Hull	24.04.74
Defenders				
Dewhurst, Robert	6. 3	Blackburn Rov.	Keighley	10.09.71
Edwards, Michael	6. 0	–	Hull	25.04.80
Greaves, Mark	6. 1	Brigg Town	Hull	22.01.75
Morley, Ben	5. 9	–	Hull	22.12.80
Perry, Jason	5.11	Lincoln City	Caerphilly	22.04.70
Swales, Stephen	5. 9	Reading	Scarborough	26.12.73
Whitney, Jonathan	5.10	Lincoln City	Nantwich	23.12.70

Name	Height ft. in.	Previous Club	Birthplace	Birthdate
Whittle, Justin	6. 1	Stoke City	Derby	18.03.71
Whitworth, Neil	6. 0	Kilmarnock	Wigan	12.04.72
Midfielders				
Bolder, Adam	5. 9	–	Hull City	25.10.80
Brabin, Gary	5.11	Blackpool	Liverpool	9.12.70
D'Auria, David	5. 8	Scunthorpe Utd.	Swansea	26.03.70
French, Jonathan	5.10	Bristol Rov.	Bristol	25.09.76
Hawes, Steven	5. 8	Sheffield Utd.	High Wycombe	17.07.78
Joyce, Warren	5. 9	Burnley	Oldham	20.01.65
Mann, Neil	5.10	Grantham Town	Nottingham	19.11.72
McGinty, Brian	6. 1	Rangers	East Kilbride	10.12.76
Williams, Gareth	6. 0	Scarborough	Isle of Wight	12.03.67
Forwards				
Alcide, Colin	6. 2	Lincoln City	Huddersfield	14.04.72
Blythe, Michael	6. 1	–	Hull	21.09.80
Brown, David	5.10	Manchester Utd.	Bolton	2.10.78
Ellington, Lee	5.10	–	Bradford	8.07.80
Eyre, John	6. 0	Scunthorpe Utd.	Hull	9.10.74
Tucker, Dexter	6. 1	–	Pontefract	22.09.79
Wilson, Paul	5.10	–	Hull	24.04.74

LEYTON ORIENT

Name	Height ft. in.	Previous Club	Birthplace	Birthdate
Goalkeepers				
Andrews, Barry	6. 1	Q.P.R.	Dublin	30.08.80
Bayes, Ashley	6. 1	Exeter City	Lincoln	19.04.72
Barrett, Scott	6. 0	Cambridge Utd.	Ilkeston	2.04.63
Defenders				
Harris, Andy	5.10	Southend Utd.	South Africa	26.02.77
Hicks, Stuart	6. 1	Scarborough	Peterborough	30.05.67
Joseph, Matthew	5. 8	Cambridge Utd.	Bethnal Green	30.09.72
Joseph, Roger	5.11	W.B.A.	Paddington	24.12.65
Lockwood, Matthew	5. 9	Bristol Rov.	Southend	17.10.76
Smith, Dean	6. 1	Hereford Utd.	West Bromwich	19.03.71
Midfielders				
Ampadu, Kwame	5.10	Swansea City	Bradford	20.12.70
Beall, Matthew	5. 7	Cambridge Utd.	Enfield	4.12.77
Canham, Scott	5. 9	Brentford	Newham	5.11.74
Ling, Martin	5. 8	Swindon Town	West Ham	15.07.66
Low, Josh	6. 1	Bristol Rov.	Bristol	15.02.76
Martin, John	5. 6	–	Bethnal Green	15.07.81
Morrison, David	5.11	Peterborough Utd.	Waltham Forest	30.11.74
Shorey, Nicky	5. 8	–	Romford	19.02.81
Walschaerts, Wim	5.10	Tielen	Antwerp	5.11.72
Forwards				
Baker, Joe	5. 8	Charlton Athletic	London	19.04.77
Christie, Iyseden	5.10	Mansfield Town	Coventry	14.11.76
Curran, Danny	5. 8	–	Basildon	13.06.81
Inglethorpe, Alex	5.11	Watford	Epsom	14.10.71
Richards, Tony	5.11	Cambridge Utd.	Newham	17.09.73
Simba, Amara	6. 0	Leon, Mex.	Senegal	23.12.61
Watts, Steve	6. 0	Fisher Athletic	Peckham	11.07.76

LINCOLN CITY

Name	Height ft. in.	Previous Club	Birthplace
Goalkeepers			
Richardson, Barry	6. 1	Preston N.E.	Newcastle
Vaughan, John	5.11	Preston N.E.	Isleworth
Defenders			
Austin, Kevin	6. 1	Leyton Orient	Hackney
Barnett, Jason	5. 9	Wolves	Shrewsbury
Bimson, Stuart	5.11	Bury	Liverpool
Brown, Grant	6. 0	Leicester City	Sunderland
Holmes, Steven	6. 2	Preston N.E.	Middlesbroug
Wilkins, Ian	5.11		Lincoln
Midfielders			
Finnigan, John	5. 8	Nott'm Forest	Wakefield
Fleming, Terry	5. 8	Preston N.E.	Birmingham
Gain, Peter	5. 9	Tottenham	London
Miller, Paul	6. 0	Bristol Rov.	Bisley
Peacock, Richard	6. 1	Hull City	Sheffield
Phillips, David	5.10	Huddersfield Town	RAF Wegl
Philpott, Lee	5.11	Blackpool	Barnet
Smith, Paul	5.11	Nott'm Forest	Hastings
Stones, Craig	5.10		Scunth
Forwards			
Battersby, Tony	6. 0	Bury	Doncas
Gordon, Gavin	6. 2	Hull City	Manch
Stant, Phil	5.11	Bury	Bolton
Thorpe, Lee	6. 0	Blackpool	Wolve

MACCLESFIELD TOWN

Name	Height ft. in.	Previous Club	Bir
Goalkeepers			
Clyde, Glyn	6. 2	Barnsley	D
Price, Ryan	6. 4	Birmingham City	C
Defenders			
Da Costa, Nelson	5.10	Stockport Co.	
Hitchen, Steve	5. 8	Blackburn Rovers	
Ingram, Rae	5.11	Manchester City	
Payne, Steve	5.11		
Rioch, Greg	5.11	Hull City	
Sodje, Efetobore	6. 1	Stevenage Borough	
Tinson, Darren	5.10		
Ware, Paul	5. 9	Hednesford	
Midfielders			
Brown, Greg	5.10	Chester City	
Collins, Simon	5.11	Plymouth Argyle	
Davies, Simon	6. 0	Luton Town	
Durkan, Kieron	5.10	Stockport Co.	
Sedgemore, Ben	5.10	Mansfield Town	
Whittaker, Stuart	5. 7	Bolton Wand.	
Wood, Steve	5. 8	–	
Forwards			
Askey, John	6. 0		
Bailey, Alan	5. 9	Manchester Ci	
Barclay, Dominic	5.10	Bristol City	
Barker, Richie	6. 0	Brighton & H	

Brow...
Land...

MA...

Name		Previous Club
Goal...		Bowli
Defen...		
Allard		Bacon
Hasse		
Watkis		
Willian		
Midfiel...		
Clarke,		
Ford, T		
Kerr, D		
Seolan		
Sission		
Tallon,		
Forwards		
Lormer,		
Peacock,		
Milner, J		

NORTHA...

Name		Previous Club	Bir
Goalkeepers			
Welch, Keit			
Defenders			
Clarkson, Ia			
Dobson, Ia			
Frain, John			
Hendon, Ian			
Howey, Lee			
Hope, Richar			
Hughes, Garr			
Midfielders			
Gibb Alistair			
Hunt, James			
Hunter, Roy			
Matthew Dam			
Parrish, Jason			
Savage, Dave			
Spedding, Dur			
Forwards			
Corazzin, Carlo			
Howard, Steve			
Lee, Chris			
Wilkinson, Paul			
Wilson, Kevin			
McGavin, Steve			
Morrow, Andy			

PETERBOROUGH UNITED

Name	Height ft. in.	Previous Club	Birthplace	Birthdate
Goalkeepers				
Connor, Daniel	6. 2	–	Dublin	31.01.81
Griemink, Bart	6. 3	Birmingham City	Holland	29.03.72
Tyler, Mark	5.11	–	Norwich	2.04.77
Defenders				
Campbell, James	6. 2	–	Kent	16.11.79
Chapple, Phil	6. 2	Charlton Athletic	Norwich	26.11.79
Drury, Adam	5.10	–	Cambridge	29.08.78
Edwards, Andy	6. 2	Birmingham City	Epping	17.09.71
Haley, Grant	5. 8	–	Bristol	20.09.79
Hooper, Dean	5.10	Kingstonian	Harefield	13.04.71
Jelleyman, Gareth	5.10	–	Hollywell	14.11.80
Kenna, Warren	6. 1	–	Southampton	18.05.80
Lyttle, Gerrard	5. 7	Celtic	Glasgow	6.02.78
Wicks, Matthew	6. 2	Crewe Alexandra	Reading	8.09.78
Midfielders				
Castle, Steve	5.10	Birmingham City	Ilford	17.05.66
Danielsson, Helgi	5.11	Fylkir, Ice.	Reykjavik, Ice.	13.07.81
Davies, Simon	5.10	–	Haverford West	23.10.79
French, Daniel	5.11	–	Peterborough	25.11.79
Gill, Matthew	6. 0	–	Cambridge	8.11.80
Hanlon, Ritchie	5.10	Rushden & D.	Kenton	26.05.78
Inman, Niall	5. 9	–	Wakefield	6.02.78
Koogi, Anders	5.10	–	Roskilde, Den.	8.09.79
Scott, Richard	5. 9	Shrewsbury Town	Dudley	29.09.74
Shields, Tony	5. 7	–	Londonderry	4.06.80
Forwards				
Broughton, Drewe	6. 3	Brentford	Hitchin	25.10.78
Clarke, Andy	5.10	Wimbledon	Islington	22.02.67
Cleaver, Chris	5.11	–	Hitchin	24.03.79
Etherington, Matthew	6. 0	–	Truro	14.08.81
Farrell, David	5. 9	Wycombe Wand.	Birmingham	11.11.71
Green, Francis	5.11	Ilkeston Town	Derby Co.	23.04.80
Hann, Matthew	5. 9	–	Saffron Walden	6.09.80
Martin, Jae	5.11	Lincoln City	London	5.02.76

PLYMOUTH ARGYLE

Name	Height ft. in.	Previous Club	Birthplace	Birthdate
Goalkeepers				
Dungey, James	5. 8	–	Plymouth	7.02.78
Sheffield, John	5.11	Peterborough Utd.	Bedworth	1.02.69
Defenders				
Adams, Steve	6. 0	–	Plymouth	25.09.80
Ashton, Jon	6. 0	–	Plymouth	4.08.79
Beswetherick, Jon	5.11	–	Liverpool	15.01.78
Gibbs, Paul	5.10	Torquay Utd.	Gorleston	26.10.72
Heathcote, Mick	6. 2	Cambridge Utd.	Durham	10.09.65
Rowbotham, Jason	5. 9	Wycombe Wand.	Cardiff	3.01.69
Midfielders				
Barlow, Martin	5. 7	–	Barnstaple	25.06.71
Hargreaves, Chris	5.11	Hereford	Cleethorpes	12.05.72
McCall, Steve	5.11	Torquay Utd.	Carlisle	15.10.60
McGovern, Brendan	5.10	–	Camborne	9.02.80
Wills, Kevin	5. 8	–	Paignton	15.10.80

Wotton, Paul	5.11	–	Plymouth	17.08.77
Forwards				
Belgrave, Barrington	5. 8	Norwich City	Bedford	16.09.80
Ford, Liam	5. 7	–	Bradford	8.09.79
Marshall, Dwight	5. 7	Luton Town	Jamaica	3.10.65
McCarthy, Sean	6. 1	Oldham Athletic	Bridgend	12.09.67
McGregor, Paul	5.10	Nott'm Forest	Liverpool	17.12.74
Morrison-Hill, Jamie	5. 8	–	Plymouth	8.06.81
Phillips, Lee	5.10	–	Penzance	16.09.80
Stonebridge, Ian	6. 0	Tottenham	Lewisham	30.08.81

ROCHDALE

Name	Height ft. in.	Previous Club	Birthplace	Birthdate
Goalkeepers				
Edwards, Neil	5. 8	Stockport Co.	Aberdare	5.12.70
Key, Lance	6. 3	Blackburn Rov.	Kettering	13.05.68
Priestley, Phil	–	–	–	–
Defenders				
Barlow, David	5. 8	Blackpool	Oldham	24.11.65
Bayliss, Dave	5.11	–	Liverpool	8.06.76
Hill, Keith	6. 1	Plymouth Argyle	Bolton	17.05.69
Johnson, Alan	6. 0	Hong Kong	Wigan	19.02.71
Monington, Mark	6. 1	Rotherham Utd.	Mansfield	21.10.70
Stokes, Dean	5. 8	Port Vale	Birmingham	23.05.70
Midfielders				
Carden, Paul	5. 9	Blackpool	Liverpool	29.03.79
Farrell, Andy	5.11	Wigan Athletic	Colchester	7.10.65
Jones, Gary	5.11	Swansea City	Birkenhead	3.06.77
Peake, Jason	5.11	Bury	Leicester	29.09.71
Stoker, Gareth	5. 9	Cardiff City	Bishop Auckland	22.02.73
Forwards				
Holt, Michael	5.10	Preston N.E.	Burnley	28.07.77
Lancashire, Graham	5. 9	Wigan Athletic	Blackpool	19.10.72
Morris, Andy	6. 4	Chesterfield	Sheffield	17.11.67
Painter, Robbie	5.10	Darlington	Wigan	26.01.71

ROTHERHAM

Name	Height ft. in.	Previous Club	Birthplace	Birthdate
Goalkeepers				
Pollitt, Mike	6. 4	Sunderland	Bolton	29.02.72
Pettinger, Paul	6. 0	Leeds Utd.	Sheffield	1.10.75
Defenders				
Artell, David	6. 1	–	Rotherham	
Beech, Chris	5.10	Cardiff City	Congleton	5.11.75
Dillon, Paul	5. 9	–	Limerick	22.10.78
Hurst, Paul	5. 4	–	Sheffield	25.09.74
Roden, Craig	6. 1	–	Rotherham	4.11.80
Varty, Will	6. 0	Carlisle Utd.	Workington	1.10.76
Warner, Vance	6. 0	Nott'm Forest	Leeds	3.09.74
Williams, Mark	6. 0	Rochdale	Liverpool	10.11.78
Wilsterman, Brian	6. 1	Oxford Utd.	Surinam	19.11.66
Midfielders				
Berry, Trevor	5. 6	Aston Villa	Halsmere	1.08.74
Garner, Darren	5. 9	Dorchester	Plymouth	10.12.71
Hudson, Danny	5. 9	–	Mexborough	25.06.79
Ingledow, Jamie	5. 7	–	Barnsley	23.08.80

Name	Height ft. in.	Previous Club	Birthplace	Birthdate
Turner, Andy	5.11	Crystal Palace	London	23.03.75
Forwards				
Fortune-West, Leo	6. 4	Brentford	Stratford	9.04.71
Glover, Lee	5.11	Nott'm Forest	Kettering	24.04.70
Martindale, Gary	6. 1	Notts Co.	Liverpool	24.06.71
Monkhouse, Andy	6. 0	–	Leeds	23.10.80
Scott, Robert	6. 1	Fulham	Epsom	15.08.73
Sedgwick, Chris	5.11	–	Sheffield	28.04.80
Warne, Paul	5. 8	Wigan Athletic	Norwich	8.05.73
White, Jason	6. 1	Northampton Town	Birmingham	19.10.71

SHREWSBURY TOWN

Name	Height ft. in.	Previous Club	Birthplace	Birthdate
Goalkeepers				
Cooksey, Scott	6. 3	Hednesford Town	Birmingham	24.06.72
Edwards, Paul	6. 0	Crewe Alexandra	Liverpool	22.02.65
Thompson, Glyn	6. 3	–	Shrewsbury	24.02.81
Defenders				
Drysdale, Leon	5. 9	–	Walsall	3.02.81
Hanmer, Gareth	5. 6	W.B.A.	Shrewsbury	12.10.73
Herbert, Craig	5.10	W.B.A.	Coventry	9.11.75
Seabury, Kevin	5.10	–	Shrewsbury	24.11.73
Tretton, Andrew	6. 0	Derby Co.	Derby	9.10.76
Whelan, Spencer	6. 2	Chester City	Liverpool	17.09.71
Wilding, Peter	6. 1	Telford Utd.	Shrewsbury	28.11.68
Midfielders				
Berkley, Austin	5. 9	Swindon Town	Gravesend	28.01.73
Craven, Dean	5. 6	W.B.A.	Shrewsbury	17.02.79
Jobling, Kevin	5. 8	Grimsby Town	Sunderland	1.01.68
Preece, Roger	5. 8	Telford Utd.	Much Wenlock	9.06.68
Forwards				
Brown, Michael	5. 9	Preston N.E.	Birmingham	8.02.68
Jagielka, Steve	5. 8	Stoke City	Manchester	10.03.78
Jones, Matthew	6. 0	–	Shrewsbury	11.10.80
Kerrigan, Steve	6. 1	Ayr Utd.	Bailleston	9.10.72
Steele, Lee	5. 8	Northwich Victoria	Liverpool	2.12.73

SOUTHEND UNITED

Name	Height ft. in.	Previous Club	Birthplace	Birthdate
Goalkeepers				
Capelton, Melvin	6. 0	Leyton Orient	Hackney	24.10.73
Margetson, Martyn	6. 0	Manchester City	West Neath	8.09.71
Spitle, Stephen	6. 3	–	Walsall	9.04.81
Defenders				
Beard, Mark	5.10	Sheffield Utd.	Roehampton	8.10.74
Booty, Martyn	5. 8	Reading	Kirby Muxloe	30.05.71
Coleman, Simon	6. 0	Bolton Wand.	Mansfield	13.06.68
Cross, Gary	–			10.07.80
Jones, Nathan	5. 7	Numencia,Spa	Cardiff	28.05.73
Livett, Simon	5.10	Cambridge Utd.	Newham	8.01.69
Morley, David	–	Manchester City	St. Helens	25.09.77
Newman, Rob	6. 2	Norwich City	Bradford-on-Avon	13.12.63
Perkins, Chris	5.11	–	London	1.03.80
Roget, Leo	6. 1	–	Ilford	1.08.77
Midfielders				
Byrne, Paul	5.11	Celtic	Dublin	30.06.72

Clarke, Adrian	5. 9	Arsenal	Cambridge	28.09.74
Gridelet, Phil	5.11	Barnsley	Edgeware	30.04.67
Hails, Julian	5.10	Fulham	Fulham	20.11.67
Houghton, Scott	5. 5	Peterborough Utd.	Htichin	22.10.71
Maher, Kevin	5.11	Tottenham	Ilford	17.10.76
Nielsen, John	5. 9	Ikast	Denmark	7.04.72
Forwards				
Burns, Alex	5. 8	SC Heracles, Hol.	Bellshill, Scot.	4.08.73
Campbell, Neil	5.10	York City	Middlesbrough	26.01.77
Conlon, Barry	6. 3	Manchester City	Dublin	1.10.78
Connelly, Gordon	6. 0	York City	Glasgow	1.11.76
Fitzpatrick, Trevor	6. 1	–	Surrey	19.02.80
Patterson, Mark	5. 8	Sheffield Utd.	Darwen	24.05.65
Roach, Neville	5.10	Reading	Reading	29.09.78
Tolson, Neil	6. 3	York City	Wordley	25.10.73
Whyte, David	5. 8	Bristol Rov.	Greenwich	20.04.71

SWANSEA CITY

Name	Height ft. in.	Previous Club	Birthplace	Birthdate
Goalkeepers				
Freestone, Roger	6. 3	Chelsea	Newport	19.08.68
Jones, Jason	6. 2	Liverpool	Wrexham	10.05.79
Defenders				
Bound, Matthew	6. 2	Stockport Co.	Melksham	6.11.72
Clode, Mark	5.10	Plymouth Argyle	Plymouth	24.02.73
Howard, Mike	5. 9	Tranmere Rov.	Birkenhead	2.12.78
Jones, Steve	5.11	Cheltenham Town	Bristol	25.12.70
O'Leary, Kristian	5.11	–	Neath	30.08.77
Smith, Jason	6. 3	Tiverton Town	Birmingham	6.09.74
Walker, Keith	6. 0	St Mirren	Edinburgh	17.04.66
Midfielders				
Appleby, Richie	5. 8	Ipswich Town	Middlesbrough	18.09.75
Coates, Jon	5. 8	–	Swansea	27.06.75
Cusack, Nick	6. 0	Fulham	Rotherham	24.12.65
Jenkins, Lee	5. 9	–	Pontypool	28.06.79
Lacey, Damien	5. 9	–	Bridgend	3.08.77
Price, Jason	6. 2	Aberaman, Wal.	Pontypridd	12.04.77
Roberts, Stuart	5. 6	–	Llanelli	22.07.80
Thomas, Martin	5. 8	Fulham	Lymington	12.09.73
Forwards				
Alsop, Julian	6. 4	Bristol Rov.	Nuneaton	28.05.73
Bird, Tony	5.10	Barry Town	Cardiff	1.09.74
Casey, Ryan	6. 1	–	Coventry	3.01.79
Newhouse, Aidan	6. 2	Fulham	Wallasey	23.05.72
Watkin, Steve	5.10	Wrexham	Wrexham	16.06.71

TORQUAY UNITED

Name	Height ft. in.	Previous Club	Birthplace	Birthdate
Goalkeepers				
Southall, Neville	6. 1	Stoke City	Llandudno	16.09.58
Defenders				
Aggrey, Jimmy	6. 5	Fulham	London	26.10.78
Gomm, Richard	5. 7	–	Torbay	24.05.79
Herrera, Robbie	5. 7	Fulham	Torquay	12.06.70
Russell, Lee	5.11	Portsmouth	Southampton	3.09.69
Thomas, Wayne	5.11	–	Gloucester	17.05.79

Name	Height ft. in.	Previous Club	Birthplace	Birthdate
Tully, Steve	5. 7	–	Torbay	10.02.80
Watson, Alex	6. 1	Gillingham	Liverpool	5.04.68
Midfielders				
Clayton, Gary	5.10	Plymouth Argyle	Sheffield	2.02.63
Hadley, Shaun	5. 7	–	Birmingham	6.02.80
Hapgood, Leon	5. 6	–	Torquay	8.02.80
Leadbitter, Chris	5. 9	Plymouth Argyle	Middlesbrough	17.10.67
McGorry, Brian	5.10	Hereford Utd.	Liverpool	16.04.70
Forwards				
Bedeau, Tony	5.10	–	Hammersmith	24.03.79
Donaldson, O'Neill	6. 1	Stoke City	Birmingham	24.11.69
Hill, Kevin	5. 8	–	Exeter	6.03.76
McFarlane, Andy	6. 3	Scunthorpe Utd.	Wolves	30.11.66
Platts, Mark	5. 8	Sheffield Wed.	Sheffield	23.05.79
Williams, Eifion	6. 0	Barry Town		

YORK CITY

Name	Height ft. in.	Previous Club	Birthplace	Birthdate
Goalkeepers				
Mimms, Bobby	6. 2	Rotherham Utd.	York	12.10.63
Defenders				
Bullock, Lee	6. 0	–	Stockton	22.05.81
Dawson, Andrew	6. 1	–	York	8.12.79
Fairclough, Chris	5.11	Notts Co.	Nottingham	12.04.64
Fox, Christian	5. 9	–	Auchenbrae	11.04.81
Hall, Wayne	5. 9	–	Rotherham	25.10.68
Hocking, Matt	5.11	Hull City	Boston	30.01.78
Jones, Barry	6. 0	Wrexham	Prescot	20.06.70
McMillan, Andy	5.10	–	South Africa	22.06.68
Reed, Martin	6. 1	–	Scarborough	10.01.78
Rennison, Graham	6. 0	–	Northallerton	2.10.78
Thompson, Neil	5.11	Barnsley	Beverley	2.10.63
Midfielders				
Agnew, Steve	5. 9	Sunderland	Shipley	9.11.65
Garratt, Martin	5.10	–	York City	22.02.80
Jordan, Scott	5. 9	–	Newcastle	19.07.75
Pouton, Alan	6. 0	Newcastle Utd.	Newcastle	1.02.77
Skinner, Craig	5. 8	Wrexham	Bury	21.10.70
Tinkler, Mark	5.11	Leeds Utd.	Bishop Auckland	24.10.74
Walters, Steve	5. 8	–	York	6.12.80
Forwards				
Rowe, Rodney	5. 8	Huddersfield Town	Plymouth	30.07.75
Dibie, Michael	5.10	–	Nigeria	20.03.81
Turley, James	5. 8	–	Manchester	24.06.81
Williams, Marc	5. 8	Halifax Town	Bangor	8.02.73

SCOTTISH LEAGUE
SQUADS 1999-2000

PREMIER LEAGUE

ABERDEEN: Russell Anderson, Paul Bernard, Baldur Bett, Calum Bett, Martin Buchan, Christopher Clark, Andrew Dow, Russell Duncan, Ryan Esson, Richard Gillies, Iain Good, James Hamilton, Michael Hart, John Inglis, Eoin Jess, Ilian Kiriakov, Malcolm Kpedekpo, James Leighton, Darren MacKie, Steven Marwick, Andreas Mayer, James McAllister, Stuart McCaffrey, Philip McGuire, Kevin Milne, Michael Newell, Colin Pepper, Mark Perry, David Rowson, Kevin Rutkiewicz, Gary Smith, Fergus Tiernan, Tzanko Tzvetanov, Derek Whyte, Robert Winters, Dennis Wyness, Darren Young, Derek Young. **Manager:** Ebbe Skovdahl.

CELTIC: Enrico Annoni, Reginald Blinker, Thomas Boyd, Harald Brattbakk, Mark Burchill, Craig Burley, Mark Casey, Marc Cocozza, John Convery, Barry Corr, Marco Cortani, Stephen Crainey, Barry Elliot, Allan Fraser, James Gallagher, James Goodwin, Jonathan Gould, Colin Healy, Thomas Johnson, Liam Keogh, James Kerr, Paul Lambert, Henrik Larsson, Stephane Mahe, Shaun Maloney, Kevin McBride, Ryan McCann, Brian McColligan, Jon McGovern, Thomas McKinlay, Stephen McManus, Jackie McNamara, Liam Miller, Stephen Miller, Johan Mjallby, Lubomir Moravcik, Tadg Moriarty, Allan Morrison, Bryan Prunty, Marc Rieper, Vidar Riseth, Alessandro Sanna, James Smith, Alan Stubbs, Vincent Sullivan, Mark Viduka, Morten Wieghorst. **Manager:** John Barnes.

DUNDEE: Dariusz Adamczuk, Iain Anderson, Edward Annand, Graham Bayne, Gavin Beith, Steven Boyack, Paul Clark, Thomas Coyne, Robert Douglas, James Earlie, John Elliott, William Falconer, Barry Forbes, Eric Garcin, Keith Gibson, Finn Gilfillan, James Grady, Brian Irvine, Jonathan Kelly, James Langfield, Lee Maddison, Lee Mair, Shaun McSkimming, Mark Melling, William Miller, Steven Milne, Richard Montgomery, Michael O'Neill, Stephane Pounewatchy, Gavin Rae, Robert Raeside, David Riley, Hugh Robertson, Lee Sharp, Mark Slater, Barry Smith, Derek Soutar, Jonathan Thompson, Graeme Thomson, Steven Tweed, Lee Wilkie, Michael Yates. **Manager:** Jocky Scott.

DUNDEE UNITED: Julian Alsford, James Bruce, Alan Combe, Marc Cooper, Lee Curran, Gareth Dailly, Hugh Davidson, Jason De Vos, Sieb Dijkstra, William Dodds, Stuart Duff, John Duffy, Craig Easton, Jose Espinoza, Steven Fallon, Joaquim Miguel Ferraz, Paul Gallacher, Christopher Gentile, David Hannah, Paul Jarvie, Iain Jenkins, Sigurdur Jonsson, Maurice Malpas, Goran Marklund, Alexander Mathie, Stephen McConalogue, David McCracken, Scott McCulloch, Stephen McCulloch, Jamie McCunnie, Kevin McDonald, Jonathan McKeith, Ryan McMullan, Mark McNally, Gary Middleton, Joseph Miller, Tonny Mols, Mariano Montefiori, Michael Neil, David Partridge, Bernard Pascual, James Paterson, Darren Patterson, Erik Pedersen, Colin Reilly, Magnus Skoldmark, James Smith, Steven Thompson, David Winters, David Worrell. **Manager:** Paul Sturrock.

HEART OF MIDLOTHIAN: Stephane Adam, Colin Cameron, Bobby Clyde, Ryan Davidson, Craig Findlay, Thomas Flogel, Stephen Fulton, Darren Goldie, Alisdair Graham, Markus Holemar, Derek Holmes, Robert Horn, Darren Jackson, Kevin James, Leigh Jenkinson, Paul Kaczan, Andrew Kirk, Gary Locke, Lee Makel, Alan McIlroy, Roderick McKenzie, Robert McKinnon, Gary McSwegan, Kenneth Milne, Grant Murray, Gary Naysmith, Craig Neeson, Robbie Neilson, Steven O'Donnell, Kris O'Neil, Juanjo Perez, Steven Pressley, Jose Quitongo, Paul Ritchie, Gilles Rousset, Stefano Salvatori, Christian Schandl, Scott Severin, Stephen Simmons, Barry Smith, Grant Smith, Scott Strang. **Manager:** James Jefferies.

HIBERNIAN: Scott Bannerman, Richard Barr, Lloyd Beaton, Emilio Bottiglieri, Kris Brown, John Campbell, Derek Collins, Scott Cormack, Stephen Crawford, Allan Dempsie, Mark Dempsie, Shaun Dennis, Jamie Ewart, Craig Gibson, Olafur Gottskalksson, Paul Hartley, Paul Hilland, Paul Holsgrove, Russel Huggon, John Hughes,

Martin Hughes, Ross Jeffrey, Russell Latapy, Barry Lavety, Paul Lindsay, Stuart Lovell, Paul Lovering, Alexandre Marinkov, Patrick McGinlay, Thomas McManus, Kenneth Miller, Colin Morton, Garry O'Connor, Liam O'Sullivan, Mika-Matti Paatelainen, John Paterson, Thomas Phillips, Alan Reid, Michael Renwick, Derek Riordan, Franck Sauzee, Justin Skinner, Thomas Smith. **Manager:** Alex McLeish.

KILMARNOCK: David Bagan, Martin Baker, Christopher Boyle, Alexander Burke, Peter Canero, Stuart Davidson, Paul Di Giacomo, Ian Durrant, James Fowler, Garry Hay, John Henry, Gary Holt, Christopher Innes, Dylan Kerr, James Lauchlan, Rodney Lennox, James Lundie, Angus MacPherson, Alan Mahood, Gordon Marshall, Alistair McCoist, Gary McCutcheon, Gary McDonald, Kevin McGowne, Kevin McNeill, Colin Meldrum, Alistair Mitchell, Ross Moffat, Martin O'Neill, Mark Reilly, Mark Roberts, Graeme Smith, Jerome Vareille, David Williams, Paul Wright. **Manager:** Bobby Williamson.

MOTHERWELL: Derek Adams, Gerard Brannan, Stephen Craigan, William Davies, Greig Denham, Michel Doesburg, David Doherty, Patrick Fitzpatrick, Donald Goodman, Andrew Goram, Stephen Halliday, Mikko Kaven, Holm Kraska, Keith Lasley, Rob Matthaei, Edward May, Brian McClair, Lee McCulloch, Jamie McGowan, Stephen McMillan, Jan Michels, Patrick Nevin, Steven Nicholas, Kai Nyyssonen, Douglas Ramsay, Ian Ross, Eliphas Shivute, John Spencer, Shaun Teale, Tony Thomas, Derek Townsley, Kevin Twaddle, Simo Valakari, Stephen Woods. **Manager:** Billy Davies.

RANGERS: Jorg Albertz, Gabriel Amato, Lorenzo Amoruso, Joachim Bjorklund, Mark Brown, Stephen Carson, Iain Chalmers, Lionel Charbonnier, Ross Currie, Gary Dewar, Gordon Durie, Lee Feeney, Barry Ferguson, Ian Ferguson, Darren Fitzgerald, James Gibson, William Gibson, Edward Hendry, Jonatan Johansson, Andrei Kanchelskis, Stuart Kelly, Stefan Klos, Peter MacDonald, Robert Malcolm, Steven McAdam, Stuart McCall, Neil McCann, Allan McGregor, Paul McHale, Derek McInnes, Paul McKnight, Steven McLean, Charles Miller, Craig Moore, Marco Negri, Barry Nicholson, Antti Niemi, Arthur Numan, Sergio Porrini, Daniel Prodan, Claudio Reyna, Maurice Ross, Sebastian Rozental, Stale Stensaas, Michael Stone, Giovanni van Bronckhorst, Peter van Vossen, Antony Vidmar, Rodney Wallace, Kirk Willoughby, Scott Wilson, David Young. **Manager:** Dick Advocaat.

ST. JOHNSTONE: Gary Bauld, Gary Bollan, Patrick Connolly, Christopher Conway, Brendan Crozier, Kevin Cuthbert, Nick Dasovic, Darren Dods, Allan Ferguson, Ross Forsyth, Martyn Fotheringham, Andrew Goldie, Roderick Grant, Daniel Griffin, Kieran Guy, Paul Kane, Darren Kearney, Alexander Keddie, Alan Kernaghan, Martin Lauchlan, Aaron Lofting, Nathan Lowndes, Alan Main, Stuart Malcolm, Steven McAllister, Kieran McAnespie, John McBride, Stuart McCluskey, Marc McCulloch, Michael McDowall, Gerard McMahon, John McQuillan, George O'Boyle, Keith O'Halloran, John O'Neil, Keigan Parker, Allan Preston, Stephen Robertson, David Scott, Miguel Simao, Daryn Smith, Stephen Stewart, Barry Thompson, James Weir, Andrew Whiteford. **Manager:** Sandy Clark.

FIRST DIVISION

AIRDRIEONIANS: James Dick, Stewart Easton, Gareth Evans, David Farrell, Gerard Farrell, Edward Forrest, Stuart Ingram, Paul Jack, Forbes Johnston, Henry McCann, John McClelland, Brian McCloy, Stephen McCormick, David McGuire, Stephen McKeown, Allan Moore, Alexander Neil, James Sandison, Alexander Stewart, William Struthers, Stuart Taylor, Scott Thomson. **Manager:** Gary MacKay.

AYR UNITED: Gareth Armstrong, Alexander Bone, Gary Bowman, John Bradford, Gordon Burns, Mark Campbell, David Castilla, David Clapperton, Stephen Cooper, David Craig, Mark Crilly, John Davies, Cornelius Duffy, Mark Duthie, Colin Frye, Keith Hogg, Glynn Hurst, Russell Kelly, Andrew Lyons, Craig Nelson, John Kenneth Nolan, Barry Prenderville, Michael Reynolds, John Robertson, David Rogers, Neil Scally, Gary Teale, John Traynor, Andrew Walker, Steven Welsh, Marvyn Wilson. **Manager:** Gordon Dalziel.

CLYDEBANK: Andrew Brown, Stephen Docherty, Robert Gardner, Graeme Love, Ian McCall, Daniel McKelvie, James McKinstrey, Joseph McLaughlin, Derek McWilliams, Scott Murdoch, Colin Scott, Fraser Wishart. **Manager:** Ian McColl.

DUNFERMLINE ATHLETIC: David Barnett, Philip Bermingham, Thomas Bone, Steven Boyle, Lee Butler, Owen Coyle, Jason Dair, James Dolan, Craig Faulconbridge, Hamish French, David Graham, David Hay, Richard Huxford, Craig Ireland, David Linighan, Craig Martin, Christopher McGroarty, Marc Millar, Colin Nish, Stewart Petrie, Brian Reid, Greg Shields, Andrew Smith, James Squires, Christopher Templeman, Scott Thomson, Andrew Tod, Ian Westwater. **Manager:** Dick Campbell.

FALKIRK: Kevin Christie, Martyn Corrigan, Scott Crabbe, Ivo Den Bieman, Alan Gray, David Hagen, Darren Hill, Myles Hogarth, Gareth Hutchison, Allan Jones, Marino Keith, Mark Kerr, Andrew Lawrie, Kevin McAllister, Colin McDonald, Scott McKenzie, Scott McLean, James McQuilken, Garry McStay, Ian Morris, David Moss, David Nicholls, Gerard O'Hara, Charles Pearson, Steven Rennie, Grant Richardson, Andrew Seaton, David Sinclair, Paul Tweedie, Richard Waddell. **Manager:** Alex Totten.

GREENOCK MORTON: Stephen Aitken, Derek Anderson, John Anderson, Owen Archdeacon, Andrew Carlin, Henry Curran, Paul Fenwick, Ian Ferguson, Warren Hawke, Brian Kerr, Ross Matheson, Alastair Maxwell, Craig McPherson, Andrew Millen, David Murie, Bryan Slavin, Kevin Thomas, Garry Tweedie, Stephen Whalen, Keith Wright. **Manager:** William Stark.

INVERNESS CALEDONIAN THISTLE: Andrew Allan, James Calder, Paul Cherry, Charles Christie, David Craig, Gary Farquhar, Leslie Fridge, Martin Glancy, Stuart Golabek, Richard Hastings, David Hind, Scott Kellacher, Iain MacArthur, Robert Mann, Mark McCulloch, Scott McLean, Grant Munro, Michael Newlands, Barry Robson, Duncan Shearer, Paul Sheerin, Iain Stewart, Michael Teasdale, Ross Tokely, Barry Wilson. **Manager:** Steven W Paterson.

LIVINGSTON: Neil Alexander, Colin Allison, Darren Baillie, John Bennett, David Bingham, Sean Clark, Graham Coughlan, Thomas Courts, Paul Deas, Craig Feroz, Derek Fleming, Patrick Kelly, Charles King, Ian Little, Christopher Love, Ian McCaldon, Mark McCormick, David McEwan, Allan McManus, Brian McPhee, John Millar, John Robertson, James Sherry, Sean Sweeney, Gregg Watson. **Manager:** Ray Stewart.

RAITH ROVERS: Paul Agnew, Marvin Andrews, Kenneth Black, Paul Browne, Alexander Burns, Andrew Clark, Craig Coyle, Steven Craig, Craig Dargo, Laurence Ellis, George Fotheringham, Kevin Fotheringham, Kevin Gaughan, Paul Hampshire, David Kirkwood, Roderick Maughan, Greig McCulloch, Craig McEwan, David McInally, James McKenzie, Kevin McLeish, Christopher Mill, Stuart Morrison, Kevin Nicol, George Penman, Paul Shields, Craig Smart, Jay Stein, Allan Stewart, Paul Tosh, Steven Tosh, Guido Van De Kamp, Ross Venables, Colin Waldie, Kevin Webster. **Manager:** John McVeigh.

ST. MIRREN: Ryan Witkowski, Davide Xausa, Sergei Baltacha, Thomas Brown, Colin Drew, Stephen Gallacher, Kieran Gallagher, Christopher Kerr, Steven McGarry, Barry McLaughlin, Ronald McQuilter, Norman McWhirter, Junior Mendes, Hugh Murray, Iain Nicolson, Ryan Robinson, Ludovic Roy, Paul Rudden, Derek Scrimgour, Thomas Turner, Scott Walker, Mark Yardley. **Manager:** Tom Hendrie.

SECOND DIVISION

ALLOA ATHLETIC: Gilbert Allan, David Beaton, Stewart Bovill, Mark Cairns, Martin Cameron, Derek Clark, Mark Cowan, Mark Donaghy, William Irvine, Paul McAneny, Gregor McKechnie, David Menelaws, Mark Nelson, Raymond Sharp, Craig Valentine, Mark Wilson. **Manager:** Terry Christie.

ARBROATH David Arbuckle, Thomas Bryce, David Butler, Craig Cooper, Jonathan Crawford, Christopher Devine, Barry Donachie, Steven Florence, John Gallagher, Craig Hinchcliffe, Kenneth Jones, John McAulay, Colin McGlashan, Mark McWalter, James Mercer, Brian Mitchell, Scott Peters, Walter Scott, Barry Sellars, Darren Spink, James Thomson, Neil Thomson, Kevin Tindal, Colin Wares, Craig Wight. **Manager:** David Baikie.

CLYDE: John Barrett, Brian Carrigan, Steven Convery, Craig Cranmer, Terence Farrell, Allan Grant, Paul Hay, Patrick Keogh, Andrew McClay, Richard McCusker, Ian McDonald, Graham McGhee, Mark McGraw, Gordon McIntyre, Martin McLauchlan, Jamie Mitchell, Darren Murray, John Ross, Bryan Smith, John Spittal, Thomas Woods, David Wylie. **Manager:** Allan Maitland.

HAMILTON ACADEMICAL: Martin Bonnar, Gary Clark, Edward Cunnington, William Davidson, Paul Gaughan, Darren Henderson, Nicholas Henderson, Christopher Hillcoat, Ryan Kelly, Gary Lynn, Ian MacFarlane, Ross MacLaren, Michael Martin, Ian McAulay, Steven McCormick, David McFarlane, Colin Miller, Michael Moore, Dean Muir, Graham Potter, Christopher Reid, Steven Renicks, Allan Russell, Steven Thomson, Gary Wales. **Manager:** Colin Miller.

PARTICK THISTLE: Alan Archibald, Kenneth Arthur, Steven Bonar, Kenneth Brannigan, Thomas Callaghan, Stephen Dallas, Gavin Duncan, Robert Dunn, Andrew Frame, William Howie, Thomas McAllister, Kevin McCann, Edward McGuinness, Desmond McKeown, Scott Miller, Andrew Morgan, Richard Newall, Eric Paton. **Manager:** John Lambie.

QUEEN OF THE SOUTH: Charles Adams, Andrew Aitken, Lee Bailey, Denis Boyle, Bryan Caldwell, Marc Cleeland, Kenneth Eadie, Steven Leslie, David Lilley, Stephen Mallan, David Mathieson, John McCaig, Russel McGuffie, Adam Moffat, Thomas Muirhead, John Rowe, Christopher Strain, Mark Weir. **Manager:** George Rowe.

ROSS COUNTY: Connor Campbell, Neale Cooper, Franck Escalon, Garry Ewing, Steven Ferguson, Kenneth Gilbert, David MacKay, Steven MacKay, Brian MacLeod, Ian Maxwell, Roy McBain, John McGlashan, Graham Munro, David Ross, Craig Tully, Joseph Walker, Garry Wood. **Manager:** Neale Cooper.

STENHOUSEMUIR: Graeme Armstrong, Alan Banks, Scott Brown, Ross Carlow, Albert Craig, Stewart Croly, Aaron Cummings, Graeme Davidson, James Fisher, John Gibson, Thomas Graham, Michael Hall, Lindsay Hamilton, Ross Hamilton, Paul Kerr, Alan Lawrence, David Lorimer, Colin McKinnon, Paul Miller, Richard Perriss, Grant Stronach, William Watters, David Wood. **Manager:** Graeme Armstrong.

STIRLING ALBION: Alan Aitken, David Bell, Patrick Clark, Graeme Donald, Garry Gow, Alastair Graham, Brian Martin, Kevin McCallion, David McCallum, Mark McGeown, Paul Mortimer, Gareth Munro, Andrew Paterson, John Philliben, Scott Sinclair, William Stuart, Craig Taggart, Christopher Wood. **Manager:** John Philliben.

STRANRAER: Steven Abbott, Robert Bell, Thomas Black, Alan Blaikie, Gordon Bruce, Derek Cahoon, Duncan George, Ian Harty, Allan Jenkins, Douglas Johnstone, Keith Knox, Grant McMartin, Allan Mitchell, Paul Ronald, James Smith, Paul Walker, Paul Watson, Fraser Wright, Gordon Young, Jason Young. **Manager:** Billy McLaren.

THIRD DIVISION

ALBION ROVERS: Douglas Bruce, James Coulter, Ian Diack, Euan Donaldson, Graham Duncan, Robert Greenock, James Hamilton, Martin Harty, Martin Lannigan, Scott McArthur, Kevin McBride, Neil McGowan, John McIntyre, Mark McLean, James McLees, Ryan McMillan, Stephen McMullen, John McStay, Martin Melvin, Alexander Nesovic, John Ramage, Robert Reid, Gary Scanlan, Martin Shaw, Christopher Silvestro, Jordan Smith, Gary Sturrock, David Sutherland. **Manager:** Mark Shanks.

BERWICK RANGERS: John Baigrie, Kenneth Buglass, Michael Burgess, Colin Campbell, John Clark, Paul Forrester, Graeme Fraser, Lloyd Haddow, Murray Hunter, Kevin Kane, Moray Leask, Kevin Magee, David McCole, Joseph McLeod, Grant McNicoll, Gavin Murray, Martin Neil, Alan Neill, Gary O'Connor, Brian Quinn, Kenneth Rafferty, Iain Ramage, David Reilly, Innes Ritchie, Gregory Shaw, Craig Sinclair, Darren Smith, Paul Smith, David Watt. **Manager:** Paul Smith.

BRECHIN CITY: Kevin Bain, Roddy Black, Paul Boylan, Robert Brown, Garry Buick, James Butter, Henry Cairney, Stephen Campbell, Graeme Christie, Douglas Coulston, Marcus Dailly, Marco De-Barros, John Dickson, Stuart Garden, Andrew Hutcheon, Steven Kerrigan, Kevin Laing, Iain MacLeod, James McKellar, Paul Riley, Greig Smith, Stuart Sorbie, Karl Williamson. **Manager:** John Young.

COWDENBEATH: Peter Bannatyne, Neil Berry, Darren Blair, Mark Bradley, Graeme Brown, John Burns, Grant Carnie, Robert Clark, Lee Cuthbert, Ryan Dinse, Andrew Donlevy, Graeme Findlay, Ross Godfrey, Callum Graham, Stuart Grieve, Alistair Hamilton, Stephen Hutchison, Kevin Hutt, Derek Johnston, Ross Johnston, Shaun King, Christopher Kirkcaldy, Alan Letham, Keith McCulloch, Murray McDowell, Craig McMillan, Adam Melvin, Paul Millar, Wesley Mitchell, Darren Murray, Roy Ness, David

Paver, Michael Perry, Malcolm Robertson, Peter Smith, Scott Snedden, William Stewart, Richard Thomson, Murray Urquhart, Martin Ward, David White, Craig Winter, Craig Young. **Manager:** Craig Levein.

DUMBARTON: Alan Barnes, Derek Barnes, Craig Brittain, Daniel Brooks, Alan Brown, Jamie Bruce, Richard Chang, Robert Cudahy, Christopher Dalrymple, Peter Dennison, Michael Dickie, Mark Docherty, Paul Finnigan, Patrick Flannery, Alexander Grace, Stephen Jack, Andrew Kilpatrick, Thomas King, David Lindsay, Sean Marner, Ross McCuaig, Scott McHarg, David Meechan, Kenneth Meechan, Martin Melvin, William Melvin, Keith Millar, Ritchie Paterson, John Rennie, Joseph Robertson, Christopher Smith, Hugh Ward, Barry Wilkinson. **Manager:** James Brown.

EAST FIFE: John Cusick, Ryan Dignan, Richard Gibb, Kieran Grattan, Thomas Harrison, David Hay, Ben Honeyman, Stephen Kirk, Raymond Logan, Stuart MacKay, John Martin, William McCulloch, Scott McIntosh, Grant McPherson, Barrie Moffat, Ryan Mooney, Kenneth Munro, Steven Ramsay, Graham Robertson, Andrew Stewart, Gavin Tinley. **Manager:** Steve Kirk.

EAST STIRLINGSHIRE: Khalid Abdulrahman, Anthony Barr, Colin Bowsher, Murray Brown, Martin Hardie, David Hendry, Gary Higgins, Stewart Jaffa, Steven Laidlaw, Gary MacMillan, Gordon McDougall, William McNeill, David Muirhead, Paul Patterson, Neil Ramage, Brian Ross, Gordon Russell, Jamie Shirra, Andrew Storrar, Barry Stuart. **Manager:** Hugh McCann.

FORFAR ATHLETIC: John Allison, Ralph Brand, Andrew Cargill, Paul Catto, Sean Christie, Douglas Craig, Graeme Ferguson, Stuart Glennie, Andrew Harrow, George Johnston, Scott Lammie, Bradley Lowe, Graeme McCheyne, Paul McIllravey, Barry McLean, Craig Milne, Jonathan Mitchell, James Moffat, James Nairn, Alan Rattray, Craig Russell, Sean Taylor. **Manager:** Ian PcPhee.

MONTROSE: Benjamin Andrew, Christopher Collie, Mark Craib, Michael Craig, Craig Farnan, Graeme Ferris, Frazer Fitzpatrick, Craig Mailer, Keith McHattie, Ross McWilliam, Graham Meldrum, Mark Murray, Kristopher Niddrie, Jerry O'Driscoll, Gary Paterson, Martin Shand, Craig Stevenson, Scott Taylor, Stefan Winiarski. **Manager:** Kevin Drinkell.

QUEEN'S PARK: James Brown, Derek Carmichael, Ross Caven, Denis Connaghan, Barry Cook, Scott Edgar, Graeme Elder, Paul Ferguson, Daniel Ferry, Mark Gallagher, Joseph Geoghegan, David Graham, Alexander Martin, Paul Martin, Barry McColl, Martin McFadyen, David McGhee, Kevin McGoldrick, Ryan McGuffie, Brian O'Donnell, Stewart Orr, Alan Paterson, Alan Reid, Nicholas Reid, Barry Rossiter, Allan Smith, Mark Travers, Paul Tyrrell, Jonathan Whelan. **Manager:** John McCormack.

QUOTE – UNQUOTE

'Despite all the snidey things that have been said about me I'd hate to think I have contributed wittingly, or unwittingly, to damaging our game' – **Graham Kelly** on quitting as FA Chief Executive in the so-called 'cash-for-votes' scandal.

'I've been in the game 30 years and I'd like to stay in it. I've had messages of support but no offers yet. Some people feel they have to ring me, others want to ring me. You know the difference' – **Graham Kelly** on the reaction to his resignation from the FA.

'We have to get rid of any sleaze associated with us through our World Cup bid and trips abroad' – FA acting chairman **Geoff Thompson**.

'There will be nothing unethical happening while I'm in charge' – FA acting chairman **Geoff Thompson**.

'Stressed out? Try telling that to a 29-year-old at somewhere like Rochdale with three months left on his contract, a wife, three kids and a mortgage. What would someone in that predicament think of it all?' – Aston Villa manager **John Gregory** on learning his star striker Stan Collymore was suffering from stress.

LEAGUE FIXTURES 1999-2000

Saturday, 7 August
F.A. Carling Premiership
Arsenal v Leicester City
Chelsea v Sunderland
Coventry City v Southampton
Leeds Utd. v Derby Co.
Middlesbrough v Bradford City
Newcastle Utd. v Aston Villa
Sheffield Wed. v Liverpool
Watford v Wimbledon
West Ham Utd. v Tottenham

Nationwide League Division One
Birmingham City v Fulham
Blackburn Rov. v Port Vale
Charlton Athletic v Barnsley
Crystal Palace v Crewe Alexandra
Grimsby Town v Stockport Co.
Ipswich Town v Nott'm. Forest
Portsmouth v Sheffield Utd.
Q.P.R. v Huddersfield Town
Tranmere Rov. v Bolton Wand.
Walsall v Swindon Town
W.B.A. v Norwich City

Nationwide League Division Two
Bournemouth v Cambridge Utd.
Blackpool v Wrexham
Bristol Rov. v Brentford
Bury v Gillingham
Cardiff City v Millwall
Chesterfield v Colchester Utd.
Notts Co. v Luton Town
Oldham Athletic v Preston N.E.
Reading v Bristol City
Stoke City v Oxford Utd.
Wigan Athletic v Scunthorpe Utd.
Wycombe Wand. v Burnley

Nationwide League Division Three
Brighton & H.A. v Mansfield Town
Carlisle Utd. v Leyton Orient
Cheltenham v Rochdale
Chester City v Barnet
Exeter City v Hull City
Halifax Town v Darlington
Lincoln City v Rotherham Utd.
Macclesfield Town v Northampton Town
Peterborough Utd. v Hartlepool Utd.
Shrewsbury Town v Torquay Utd.
Southend Utd. v Plymouth Argyle
York City v Swansea City

Sunday, 8 August
F.A. Carling Premiership
Everton v Manchester Utd.

Nationwide League Division One
Manchester City v Wolves

Monday, 9 August
F.A. Carling Premiership
Tottenham v Newcastle Utd.

Tuesday, 10 August
F.A. Carling Premiership
Sunderland v Watford
Wimbledon v Middlesbrough
Derby Co. v Arsenal

Wednesday, 11 August
F.A. Carling Premiership
Aston Villa v Everton
Leicester City v Coventry City
Liverpool v West Ham Utd.
Manchester Utd. v Sheffield Wed.
Southampton v Leeds Utd.

Friday, 13 August
Nationwide League Division One
Huddersfield Town v Blackburn Rov.

Saturday, 14 August
F.A. Carling Premiership
Bradford City v Sheffield Wed.
Derby Co. v Middlesbrough
Leicester City v Chelsea
Liverpool v Watford
Manchester Utd. v Leeds Utd.
Sunderland v Arsenal
Tottenham v Everton
Wimbledon v Coventry City

Nationwide League Division One
Barnsley v Crystal Palace
Bolton Wand. v Q.P.R.
Crewe Alexandra v Charlton Athletic
Fulham v Manchester City
Norwich City v Birmingham City
Nott'm. Forest v Grimsby Town
Port Vale v W.B.A.
Sheffield Utd. v Walsall
Stockport Co. v Tranmere Rov.
Wolves v Portsmouth

Nationwide League Division Two
Brentford v Oldham Athletic
Bristol City v Bournemouth

Burnley v Chesterfield
Cambridge Utd. v Reading
Colchester Utd. v Notts Co.
Gillingham v Bristol Rov.
Luton Town v Blackpool
Millwall v Wigan Athletic
Oxford Utd. v Cardiff City
Preston N.E. v Stoke City
Scunthorpe Utd. v Wycombe Wand.
Wrexham v Bury

Nationwide League Division Three
Barnet v Exeter City
Darlington v Macclesfield Town
Hartlepool Utd. v Halifax Town
Hull City v Lincoln City
Leyton Orient v Brighton & H.A.
Mansfield Town v Cheltenham
Northampton Town v Peterborough Utd.
Plymouth Argyle v Shrewsbury Town
Rochdale v Southend Utd.
Rotherham Utd. v Chester City
Swansea City v Carlisle Utd.
Torquay Utd. v York City

Sunday, 15 August
F.A. Carling Premiership
Southampton v Newcastle Utd.

Nationwide League Division One
Swindon Town v Ipswich Town

Monday, 16 August
F.A. Carling Premiership
Aston Villa v West Ham Utd.

Friday, 20 August
Nationwide League Division One
W.B.A. v Nott'm. Forest

Saturday, 21 August
F.A. Carling Premiership
Chelsea v Aston Villa
Coventry City v Derby Co.
Everton v Southampton
Leeds Utd. v Sunderland
Middlesbrough v Liverpool
Newcastle Utd. v Wimbledon
Sheffield Wed. v Tottenham
Watford v Bradford City
West Ham Utd. v Leicester City

Nationwide League Division One
Birmingham City v Port Vale
Blackburn Rov. v Barnsley
Charlton Athletic v Norwich City
Crystal Palace v Swindon Town
Grimsby Town v Fulham
Ipswich Town v Bolton Wand.
Manchester City v Sheffield Utd.
Portsmouth v Stockport Co.

Q.P.R. v Wolves
Tranmere Rov. v Huddersfield Town
Walsall v Crewe Alexandra

Nationwide League Division Two
Bournemouth v Colchester Utd.
Blackpool v Gillingham
Bristol Rov. v Oxford Utd.
Bury v Brentford
Cardiff City v Wrexham
Chesterfield v Cambridge Utd.
Notts Co. v Scunthorpe Utd.
Oldham Athletic v Burnley
Reading v Luton Town
Wigan Athletic v Bristol City
Wycombe Wand. v Preston N.E.

Nationwide League Division Three
Brighton & H.A. v Torquay Utd.
Carlisle Utd. v Hartlepool Utd.
Cheltenham v Hull City
Chester City v Northampton Town
Exeter City v Rotherham Utd.
Halifax Town v Plymouth Argyle
Lincoln City v Barnet
Macclesfield Town v Swansea City
Peterborough Utd. v Leyton Orient
Shrewsbury Town v Darlington
Southend Utd. v Mansfield Town
York City v Rochdale

Sunday, 22 August
F.A. Carling Premiership
Arsenal v Manchester Utd.

Nationwide League Division Two
Stoke City v Millwall

Monday, 23 August
F.A. Carling Premiership
Leeds Utd. v Liverpool

Tuesday, 24 August
F.A. Carling Premiership
Middlesbrough v Leicester City
Watford v Aston Villa

Wednesday, 25 August
F.A. Carling Premiership
Coventry City v Manchester Utd.
Everton v Wimbledon
Newcastle Utd. v Sunderland
Sheffield Wed. v Derby Co.
West Ham Utd. v Southampton
Arsenal v Bradford City

Friday, 27 August
Nationwide League Division One
Stockport Co. v Birmingham City

Saturday, 28 August
F.A. Carling Premiership
Aston Villa v Middlesbrough
Bradford City v West Ham Utd.
Derby Co. v Everton
Liverpool v Arsenal
Southampton v Sheffield Wed.
Tottenham v Leeds Utd.
Wimbledon v Chelsea

Nationwide League Division One
Barnsley v Portsmouth
Bolton Wand. v Manchester City
Crewe Alexandra v Grimsby Town
Fulham v Charlton Athletic
Huddersfield Town v Crystal Palace
Norwich City v Blackburn Rov.
Nott'm. Forest v Q.P.R.
Port Vale v Tranmere Rov.
Sheffield Utd. v Ipswich Town
Swindon Town v W.B.A.
Wolves v Walsall

Nationwide League Division Two
Brentford v Blackpool
Bristol City v Bury
Burnley v Stoke City
Cambridge Utd. v Notts Co.
Colchester Utd. v Reading
Gillingham v Wycombe Wand.
Luton Town v Cardiff City
Millwall v Chesterfield
Oxford Utd. v Oldham Athletic
Preston N.E. v Wigan Athletic
Scunthorpe Utd. v Bournemouth
Wrexham v Bristol Rov.

Nationwide League Division Three
Barnet v York City
Darlington v Brighton & H.A.
Hartlepool Utd. v Cheltenham
Hull City v Macclesfield Town
Leyton Orient v Halifax Town
Mansfield Town v Carlisle Utd.
Northampton Town v Lincoln City
Plymouth Argyle v Peterborough Utd.
Rochdale v Exeter City
Rotherham Utd. v Shrewsbury Town
Swansea City v Southend Utd.
Torquay Utd. v Chester City

Sunday, 29 August
F.A. Carling Premiership
Sunderland v Coventry City

Monday, 30 August
F.A. Carling Premiership
Leicester City v Watford
Manchester Utd. v Newcastle Utd.

Nationwide League Division One
Birmingham City v Crewe Alexandra
Blackburn Rov. v Bolton Wand.
Charlton Athletic v Stockport Co.
Crystal Palace v Wolves
Grimsby Town v Swindon Town
Ipswich Town v Barnsley
Manchester City v Nott'm. Forest
Portsmouth v Huddersfield Town
Q.P.R. v Port Vale
Tranmere Rov. v Sheffield Utd.
Walsall v Norwich City
W.B.A. v Fulham

Nationwide League Division Two
Bournemouth v Luton Town
Blackpool v Oxford Utd.
Bristol Rov. v Burnley
Bury v Colchester Utd.
Cardiff City v Scunthorpe Utd.
Chesterfield v Bristol City
Notts Co. v Brentford
Oldham Athletic v Millwall
Reading v Preston N.E.
Stoke City v Gillingham
Wigan Athletic v Cambridge Utd.
Wycombe Wand. v Wrexham

Nationwide League Division Three
Brighton & H.A. v Hull City
Carlisle Utd. v Plymouth Argyle
Cheltenham v Barnet
Chester City v Rochdale
Exeter City v Mansfield Town
Halifax Town v Torquay Utd.
Lincoln City v Swansea City
Macclesfield Town v Rotherham Utd.
Peterborough Utd. v Darlington
Shrewsbury Town v Hartlepool Utd.
Southend Utd. v Leyton Orient
York City v Northampton Town

Friday, 3 September
Nationwide League Division One
Port Vale v Grimsby Town

Saturday, 4 September
Nationwide League Division One
Barnsley v Tranmere Rov.
Crewe Alexandra v W.B.A.
Fulham v Portsmouth
Huddersfield Town v Ipswich Town
Norwich City v Manchester City
Nott'm. Forest v Walsall
Sheffield Utd. v Crystal Palace
Stockport Co. v Q.P.R.
Swindon Town v Blackburn Rov.
Wolves v Charlton Athletic

Nationwide League Division Two
Brentford v Cardiff City
Bristol City v Blackpool
Burnley v Bournemouth
Cambridge Utd. v Stoke City
Colchester Utd. v Wigan Athletic
Gillingham v Oldham Athletic
Luton Town v Bury
Millwall v Reading
Oxford Utd. v Wycombe Wand.
Preston N.E. v Chesterfield
Scunthorpe Utd. v Bristol Rov.
Wrexham v Notts Co.

Nationwide League Division Three
Barnet v Macclesfield Town
Darlington v Exeter City
Hartlepool Utd. v Southend Utd.
Hull City v Chester City
Leyton Orient v Shrewsbury Town
Mansfield Town v Peterborough Utd.
Northampton Town v Carlisle Utd.
Plymouth Argyle v Brighton & H.A.
Rochdale v Halifax Town
Rotherham Utd. v York City
Swansea City v Cheltenham
Torquay Utd. v Lincoln City

Sunday, 5 September
Nationwide League Division One
Bolton Wand. v Birmingham City

Friday, 10 September
Nationwide League Division One
Barnsley v Stockport Co.

Saturday, 11 September
F.A. Carling Premiership
Arsenal v Aston Villa
Chelsea v Newcastle Utd.
Coventry City v Leeds Utd.
Liverpool v Manchester Utd.
Middlesbrough v Southampton
Sheffield Wed. v Everton
Sunderland v Leicester City
West Ham Utd. v Watford
Wimbledon v Derby Co.

Nationwide League Division One
Birmingham City v W.B.A.
Blackburn Rov. v Tranmere Rov.
Charlton Athletic v Bolton Wand.
Grimsby Town v Walsall
Manchester City v Crystal Palace
Norwich City v Crewe Alexandra
Port Vale v Fulham
Portsmouth v Ipswich Town
Q.P.R. v Sheffield Utd.
Swindon Town v Nott'm. Forest
Wolves v Huddersfield Town

Nationwide League Division Two
Bournemouth v Reading
Bristol City v Millwall
Cambridge Utd. v Brentford
Chesterfield v Stoke City
Colchester Utd. v Scunthorpe Utd.
Luton Town v Wrexham
Notts Co. v Blackpool
Oldham Athletic v Bury
Oxford Utd. v Gillingham
Preston N.E. v Burnley
Wigan Athletic v Bristol Rov.
Wycombe Wand. v Cardiff City

Nationwide League Division Three
Carlisle Utd. v Lincoln City
Chester City v Exeter City
Halifax Town v Brighton & H.A.
Macclesfield Town v Southend Utd.
Mansfield Town v Leyton Orient
Northampton Town v Hartlepool Utd.
Plymouth Argyle v Rotherham Utd.
Rochdale v Darlington
Swansea City v Barnet
Torquay Utd. v Hull City
York City v Peterborough Utd.

Sunday, 12 September
F.A. Carling Premiership
Bradford City v Tottenham

Nationwide League Division Three
Cheltenham v Shrewsbury Town

Saturday, 18 September
F.A. Carling Premiership
Aston Villa v Bradford City
Derby Co. v Sunderland
Everton v West Ham Utd.
Leicester City v Liverpool
Manchester Utd. v Wimbledon
Southampton v Arsenal
Watford v Chelsea

Nationwide League Division One
Bolton Wand. v Barnsley
Crewe Alexandra v Swindon Town
Crystal Palace v Grimsby Town
Fulham v Q.P.R.
Huddersfield Town v Norwich City
Ipswich Town v Birmingham City
Sheffield Utd. v Charlton Athletic
Stockport Co. v Port Vale
Tranmere Rov. v Portsmouth
Walsall v Manchester City
W.B.A. v Blackburn Rov.

Nationwide League Division Two
Blackpool v Bournemouth
Brentford v Luton Town
Bristol Rov. v Oldham Athletic

Burnley v Colchester Utd.
Bury v Wycombe Wand.
Cardiff City v Notts Co.
Gillingham v Preston N.E.
Millwall v Cambridge Utd.
Reading v Chesterfield
Scunthorpe Utd. v Bristol City
Stoke City v Wigan Athletic
Wrexham v Oxford Utd.

Nationwide League Division Three
Barnet v Northampton Town
Brighton & H.A. v Chester City
Darlington v Mansfield Town
Exeter City v York City
Hartlepool Utd. v Plymouth Argyle
Hull City v Swansea City
Leyton Orient v Torquay Utd.
Lincoln City v Macclesfield Town
Peterborough Utd. v Cheltenham
Rotherham Utd. v Rochdale
Shrewsbury Town v Carlisle Utd.
Southend Utd. v Halifax Town

Sunday, 19 September
F.A. Carling Premiership
Leeds Utd. v Middlesbrough
Newcastle Utd. v Sheffield Wed.
Tottenham v Coventry City

Nationwide League Division One
Nott'm. Forest v Wolves

Saturday, 25 September
F.A. Carling Premiership
Arsenal v Watford
Coventry City v West Ham Utd.
Derby Co. v Bradford City
Leeds Utd. v Newcastle Utd.
Leicester City v Aston Villa
Manchester Utd. v Southampton
Middlesbrough v Chelsea
Sunderland v Sheffield Wed.

Nationwide League Division One
Barnsley v Huddersfield Town
Birmingham City v Q.P.R.
Blackburn Rov. v Walsall
Bolton Wand. v Nott'm. Forest
Fulham v Crewe Alexandra
Port Vale v Swindon Town
Portsmouth v Grimsby Town
Sheffield Utd. v Wolves
Stockport Co. v Norwich City
Tranmere Rov. v Charlton Athletic
W.B.A. v Crystal Palace

Nationwide League Division Two
Bournemouth v Bury
Blackpool v Wycombe Wand.

Brentford v Preston N.E.
Bristol City v Burnley
Cambridge Utd. v Gillingham
Cardiff City v Wigan Athletic
Luton Town v Oxford Utd.
Millwall v Colchester Utd.
Notts Co. v Bristol Rov.
Reading v Oldham Athletic
Scunthorpe Utd. v Chesterfield
Wrexham v Stoke City

Nationwide League Division Three
Brighton & H.A. v Cheltenham
Chester City v Lincoln City
Darlington v Plymouth Argyle
Exeter City v Macclesfield Town
Halifax Town v Carlisle Utd.
Hull City v York City
Leyton Orient v Hartlepool Utd.
Mansfield Town v Shrewsbury Town
Rochdale v Swansea City
Rotherham Utd. v Northampton Town
Southend Utd. v Peterborough Utd.
Torquay Utd. v Barnet

Sunday, 26 September
F.A. Carling Premiership
Wimbledon v Tottenham

Nationwide League Division One
Ipswich Town v Manchester City

Monday, 27 September
F.A. Carling Premiership
Liverpool v Everton

Friday, 1 October
Nationwide League Division One
Nott'm. Forest v Barnsley

Saturday, 2 October
F.A. Carling Premiership
Aston Villa v Liverpool
Bradford City v Sunderland
Everton v Coventry City
Sheffield Wed. v Wimbledon
West Ham Utd. v Arsenal

Nationwide League Division One
Charlton Athletic v Birmingham City
Crystal Palace v Portsmouth
Grimsby Town v Ipswich Town
Huddersfield Town v Sheffield Utd.
Manchester City v Port Vale
Norwich City v Fulham
Q.P.R. v Blackburn Rov.
Swindon Town v Bolton Wand.
Walsall v Stockport Co.
Wolves v W.B.A.

Nationwide League Division Two
Bristol Rov. v Blackpool
Burnley v Brentford
Bury v Cardiff City
Chesterfield v Bournemouth
Colchester Utd. v Wrexham
Gillingham v Millwall
Oldham Athletic v Notts Co.
Oxford Utd. v Bristol City
Preston N.E. v Cambridge Utd.
Stoke City v Scunthorpe Utd.
Wigan Athletic v Luton Town
Wycombe Wand. v Reading

Nationwide League Division Three
Barnet v Hull City
Carlisle Utd. v Southend Utd.
Cheltenham v Rotherham Utd.
Hartlepool Utd. v Darlington
Lincoln City v Exeter City
Macclesfield Town v Torquay Utd.
Northampton Town v Rochdale
Peterborough Utd. v Brighton & H.A.
Plymouth Argyle v Leyton Orient
Shrewsbury Town v Halifax Town
Swansea City v Mansfield Town
York City v Chester City

Sunday, 3 October
F.A. Carling Premiership
Chelsea v Manchester Utd.
Newcastle Utd. v Middlesbrough
Tottenham v Leicester City
Watford v Leeds Utd.

Nationwide League Division One
Crewe Alexandra v Tranmere Rov.

Monday, 4 October
F.A. Carling Premiership
Southampton v Derby Co.

Friday, 8 October
Nationwide League Division One
Walsall v Birmingham City

Saturday, 9 October
Nationwide League Division One
Charlton Athletic v Blackburn Rov.
Crewe Alexandra v Sheffield Utd.
Crystal Palace v Ipswich Town
Grimsby Town v W.B.A.
Huddersfield Town v Port Vale
Manchester City v Portsmouth
Norwich City v Barnsley
Nott'm. Forest v Fulham
Q.P.R. v Tranmere Rov.
Swindon Town v Stockport Co.
Wolves v Bolton Wand.

Nationwide League Division Two
Bristol Rov. v Cardiff City
Bury v Notts Co.
Chesterfield v Blackpool
Colchester Utd. v Brentford
Gillingham v Wrexham
Oldham Athletic v Luton Town
Oxford Utd. v Millwall
Preston N.E. v Bristol City
Stoke City v Reading
Wigan Athletic v Bournemouth
Wycombe Wand. v Cambridge Utd.

Nationwide League Division Three
Barnet v Rochdale
Carlisle Utd. v Brighton & H.A.
Cheltenham v Southend Utd.
Hartlepool Utd. v Hull City
Lincoln City v Darlington
Macclesfield Town v Halifax Town
Northampton Town v Torquay Utd.
Peterborough Utd. v Chester City
Plymouth Argyle v Mansfield Town
Shrewsbury Town v Exeter City
Swansea City v Rotherham Utd.
York City v Leyton Orient

Sunday, 10 October
Nationwide League Division Two
Burnley v Scunthorpe Utd.

Saturday, 16 October
F.A. Carling Premiership
Arsenal v Everton
Coventry City v Newcastle Utd.
Derby Co. v Tottenham
Leeds Utd. v Sheffield Wed.
Leicester City v Southampton
Liverpool v Chelsea
Manchester Utd. v Watford
Wimbledon v Bradford City

Nationwide League Division One
Barnsley v Wolves
Birmingham City v Crystal Palace
Blackburn Rov. v Grimsby Town
Bolton Wand. v Huddersfield Town
Fulham v Swindon Town
Ipswich Town v Q.P.R.
Port Vale v Norwich City
Portsmouth v Charlton Athletic
Sheffield Utd. v Nott'm. Forest
Stockport Co. v Crewe Alexandra
Tranmere Rov. v Manchester City
W.B.A. v Walsall

Nationwide League Division Two
Bournemouth v Stoke City
Blackpool v Bury
Brentford v Oxford Utd.
Cambridge Utd. v Colchester Utd.

Cardiff City v Oldham Athletic
Luton Town v Gillingham
Millwall v Burnley
Notts Co. v Wycombe Wand.
Reading v Wigan Athletic
Scunthorpe Utd. v Preston N.E.
Wrexham v Chesterfield

Nationwide League Division Three
Brighton & H.A. v York City
Chester City v Macclesfield Town
Darlington v Cheltenham
Exeter City v Carlisle Utd.
Halifax Town v Peterborough Utd.
Hull City v Northampton Town
Leyton Orient v Lincoln City
Mansfield Town v Hartlepool Utd.
Rochdale v Plymouth Argyle
Rotherham Utd. v Barnet
Southend Utd. v Shrewsbury Town
Torquay Utd. v Swansea City

Sunday, 17 October
F.A. Carling Premiership
Middlesbrough v West Ham Utd.

Nationwide League Division Two
Bristol City v Bristol Rov.

Monday, 18 October
F.A. Carling Premiership
Sunderland v Aston Villa

Tuesday, 19 October
Nationwide League Division One
Barnsley v Swindon Town
Birmingham City v Manchester City
Bolton Wand. v Crewe Alexandra
Fulham v Wolves
Ipswich Town v Charlton Athletic
Port Vale v Nott'm. Forest
Portsmouth v Walsall
Sheffield Utd. v Norwich City
Stockport Co. v Huddersfield Town
Tranmere Rov. v Grimsby Town
W.B.A. v Q.P.R.

Nationwide League Division Two
Bournemouth v Bristol Rov.
Blackpool v Oldham Athletic
Brentford v Gillingham
Bristol City v Colchester Utd.
Cambridge Utd. v Burnley
Cardiff City v Stoke City
Luton Town v Wycombe Wand.
Millwall v Preston N.E.
Notts Co. v Chesterfield
Scunthorpe Utd. v Oxford Utd.
Wrexham v Wigan Athletic

Nationwide League Division Three
Brighton & H.A. v Shrewsbury Town
Chester City v Cheltenham
Darlington v Carlisle Utd.
Exeter City v Swansea City
Halifax Town v York City
Hull City v Plymouth Argyle
Leyton Orient v Barnet
Mansfield Town v Northampton Town
Rochdale v Macclesfield Town
Rotherham Utd. v Hartlepool Utd.
Southend Utd. v Lincoln City
Torquay Utd. v Peterborough Utd.

Wednesday, 20 October
Nationwide League Division One
Blackburn Rov. v Crystal Palace

Nationwide League Division Two
Reading v Bury

Saturday, 23 October
F.A. Carling Premiership
Aston Villa v Wimbledon
Bradford City v Leicester City
Chelsea v Arsenal
Everton v Leeds Utd.
Sheffield Wed. v Coventry City
Southampton v Liverpool
Tottenham v Manchester Utd.
West Ham Utd. v Sunderland

Nationwide League Division One
Charlton Athletic v W.B.A.
Crewe Alexandra v Barnsley
Crystal Palace v Tranmere Rov.
Grimsby Town v Birmingham City
Huddersfield Town v Fulham
Manchester City v Blackburn Rov.
Nott'm. Forest v Stockport Co.
Q.P.R. v Portsmouth
Swindon Town v Sheffield Utd.
Walsall v Ipswich Town
Wolves v Port Vale

Nationwide League Division Two
Bristol Rov. v Notts Co.
Burnley v Bristol City
Bury v Bournemouth
Chesterfield v Scunthorpe Utd.
Colchester Utd. v Millwall
Gillingham v Cambridge Utd.
Oldham Athletic v Reading
Oxford Utd. v Luton Town
Preston N.E. v Brentford
Stoke City v Wrexham
Wigan Athletic v Cardiff City
Wycombe Wand. v Blackpool

Nationwide League Division Three
Barnet v Torquay Utd.
Carlisle Utd. v Halifax Town
Cheltenham v Brighton & H.A.
Hartlepool Utd. v Leyton Orient
Lincoln City v Chester City
Macclesfield Town v Exeter City
Northampton Town v Rotherham Utd.
Peterborough Utd. v Southend Utd.
Plymouth Argyle v Darlington
Shrewsbury Town v Mansfield Town
Swansea City v Rochdale
York City v Hull City

Sunday, 24 October
F.A. Carling Premiership
Watford v Middlesbrough

Nationwide League Division One
Norwich City v Bolton Wand.

Monday, 25 October
F.A. Carling Premiership
Newcastle Utd. v Derby Co.

Tuesday, 26 October
Nationwide League Division One
Charlton Athletic v Tranmere Rov.
Crewe Alexandra v Fulham
Crystal Palace v W.B.A.
Grimsby Town v Portsmouth
Huddersfield Town v Barnsley
Manchester City v Ipswich Town
Norwich City v Stockport Co.
Swindon Town v Port Vale
Walsall v Blackburn Rov.
Wolves v Sheffield Utd.

Wednesday, 27 October
Nationwide League Division One
Nott'm. Forest v Bolton Wand.
Q.P.R. v Birmingham City

Saturday, 30 October
F.A. Carling Premiership
Arsenal v Newcastle Utd.
Derby Co. v Chelsea
Leeds Utd. v West Ham Utd.
Leicester City v Sheffield Wed.
Manchester Utd. v Aston Villa
Middlesbrough v Everton
Sunderland v Tottenham
Wimbledon v Southampton

Nationwide League Division One
Barnsley v Nott'm. Forest
Birmingham City v Charlton Athletic
Blackburn Rov. v Q.P.R.
Bolton Wand. v Swindon Town
Fulham v Norwich City
Ipswich Town v Grimsby Town

Port Vale v Manchester City
Portsmouth v Crystal Palace
Sheffield Utd. v Huddersfield Town
Stockport Co. v Walsall
Tranmere Rov. v Crewe Alexandra
W.B.A. v Wolves

Sunday, 31 October
F.A. Carling Premiership
Coventry City v Watford

Monday, 1 November
F.A. Carling Premiership
Liverpool v Bradford City

Tuesday, 2 November
Nationwide League Division Two
Brentford v Reading
Bristol Rov. v Bury
Burnley v Wrexham
Cambridge Utd. v Scunthorpe Utd.
Cardiff City v Blackpool
Gillingham v Bristol City
Millwall v Luton Town
Oldham Athletic v Wycombe Wand.
Oxford Utd. v Colchester Utd.
Preston N.E. v Bournemouth
Wigan Athletic v Chesterfield

Nationwide League Division Three
Carlisle Utd. v York City
Darlington v Leyton Orient
Halifax Town v Cheltenham
Hartlepool Utd. v Barnet
Lincoln City v Peterborough Utd.
Macclesfield Town v Mansfield Town
Northampton Town v Swansea City
Plymouth Argyle v Exeter City
Rochdale v Hull City
Rotherham Utd. v Torquay Utd.
Shrewsbury Town v Chester City
Southend Utd. v Brighton & H.A.

Wednesday, 3 November
Nationwide League Division Two
Stoke City v Notts Co.

Friday, 5 November
Nationwide League Division One
Port Vale v Crewe Alexandra

Saturday, 6 November
F.A. Carling Premiership
Aston Villa v Southampton
Bradford City v Coventry City
Chelsea v West Ham Utd.
Liverpool v Derby Co.
Manchester Utd. v Leicester City
Middlesbrough v Sunderland
Sheffield Wed. v Watford
Tottenham v Arsenal

Nationwide League Division One
Barnsley v Sheffield Utd.
Blackburn Rov. v Ipswich Town
Bolton Wand. v Crystal Palace
Charlton Athletic v Walsall
Huddersfield Town v Swindon Town
Norwich City v Nott'm. Forest
Portsmouth v Birmingham City
Q.P.R. v Manchester City
Stockport Co. v Fulham
Tranmere Rov. v W.B.A.
Wolves v Grimsby Town

Nationwide League Division Two
Bournemouth v Cardiff City
Blackpool v Wigan Athletic
Bristol City v Cambridge Utd.
Bury v Stoke City
Chesterfield v Oldham Athletic
Colchester Utd. v Preston N.E.
Luton Town v Burnley
Notts Co. v Gillingham
Scunthorpe Utd. v Millwall
Wrexham v Brentford
Wycombe Wand. v Bristol Rov.

Nationwide League Division Three
Barnet v Darlington
Brighton & H.A. v Hartlepool Utd.
Cheltenham v Carlisle Utd.
Chester City v Plymouth Argyle
Exeter City v Southend Utd.
Hull City v Rotherham Utd.
Leyton Orient v Northampton Town
Mansfield Town v Lincoln City
Peterborough Utd. v Shrewsbury Town
Swansea City v Halifax Town
Torquay Utd. v Rochdale
York City v Macclesfield Town

Sunday, 7 November
F.A. Carling Premiership
Wimbledon v Leeds Utd.

Nationwide League Division Two
Reading v Oxford Utd.

Monday, 8 November
F.A. Carling Premiership
Newcastle Utd. v Everton

Friday, 12 November
Nationwide League Division Two
Gillingham v Bournemouth

Saturday, 13 November
Nationwide League Division One
Birmingham City v Blackburn Rov.
Crewe Alexandra v Wolves
Crystal Palace v Q.P.R.
Fulham v Barnsley

Grimsby Town v Charlton Athletic
Ipswich Town v Tranmere Rov.
Manchester City v Stockport Co.
Sheffield Utd. v Bolton Wand.
Swindon Town v Norwich City
Walsall v Port Vale
W.B.A. v Portsmouth

Nationwide League Division Two
Brentford v Scunthorpe Utd.
Bristol Rov. v Reading
Burnley v Blackpool
Cambridge Utd. v Luton Town
Cardiff City v Chesterfield
Millwall v Wrexham
Oldham Athletic v Colchester Utd.
Oxford Utd. v Bury
Preston N.E. v Notts Co.
Stoke City v Bristol City
Wigan Athletic v Wycombe Wand.

Nationwide League Division Three
Carlisle Utd. v Peterborough Utd.
Darlington v Torquay Utd.
Halifax Town v Exeter City
Hartlepool Utd. v Chester City
Lincoln City v York City
Macclesfield Town v Brighton & H.A.
Northampton Town v Cheltenham
Plymouth Argyle v Barnet
Rochdale v Mansfield Town
Rotherham Utd. v Leyton Orient
Shrewsbury Town v Swansea City
Southend Utd. v Hull City

Sunday, 14 November
Nationwide League Division One
Nott'm. Forest v Huddersfield Town

Saturday, 20 November
F.A. Carling Premiership
Arsenal v Middlesbrough
Derby Co. v Manchester Utd.
Everton v Chelsea
Leeds Utd. v Bradford City
Leicester City v Wimbledon
Southampton v Tottenham
Sunderland v Liverpool
Watford v Newcastle Utd.

Nationwide League Division One
Barnsley v Birmingham City
Blackburn Rov. v Fulham
Bolton Wand. v Grimsby Town
Charlton Athletic v Manchester City
Huddersfield Town v W.B.A.
Norwich City v Ipswich Town
Port Vale v Crystal Palace
Portsmouth v Crewe Alexandra
Q.P.R. v Walsall
Stockport Co. v Sheffield Utd.

Tranmere Rov. v Nott'm. Forest
Wolves v Swindon Town

Sunday, 21 November
F.A. Carling Premiership
West Ham Utd. v Sheffield Wed.

Monday, 22 November
F.A. Carling Premiership
Coventry City v Aston Villa

Tuesday, 23 November
Nationwide League Division One
Crewe Alexandra v Blackburn Rov.
Crystal Palace v Norwich City
Fulham v Bolton Wand.
Grimsby Town v Q.P.R.
Ipswich Town v Wolves
Manchester City v Barnsley
Sheffield Utd. v Port Vale
Swindon Town v Charlton Athletic
Walsall v Huddersfield Town
W.B.A. v Stockport Co.

Nationwide League Division Two
Bournemouth v Brentford
Blackpool v Millwall
Bristol City v Oldham Athletic
Bury v Wigan Athletic
Chesterfield v Bristol Rov.
Colchester Utd. v Cardiff City
Luton Town v Preston N.E.
Notts Co. v Oxford Utd.
Scunthorpe Utd. v Gillingham
Wrexham v Cambridge Utd.
Wycombe Wand. v Stoke City

Nationwide League Division Three
Barnet v Carlisle Utd.
Brighton & H.A. v Lincoln City
Cheltenham v Plymouth Argyle
Chester City v Southend Utd.
Exeter City v Northampton Town
Hull City v Halifax Town
Leyton Orient v Rochdale
Mansfield Town v Rotherham Utd.
Peterborough Utd. v Macclesfield Town
Swansea City v Darlington
Torquay Utd. v Hartlepool Utd.
York City v Shrewsbury Town

Wednesday, 24 November
Nationwide League Division One
Birmingham City v Tranmere Rov.
Nott'm. Forest v Portsmouth

Nationwide League Division Two
Reading v Burnley

Friday, 26 November
Nationwide League Division One
Walsall v Fulham

Saturday, 27 November
F.A. Carling Premiership
Arsenal v Derby Co.
Coventry City v Leicester City
Everton v Aston Villa
Leeds Utd. v Southampton
Middlesbrough v Wimbledon
Newcastle Utd. v Tottenham
Sheffield Wed. v Manchester Utd.
Watford v Sunderland
West Ham Utd. v Liverpool

Nationwide League Division One
Birmingham City v Swindon Town
Blackburn Rov. v Stockport Co.
Charlton Athletic v Port Vale
Crystal Palace v Nott'm. Forest
Ipswich Town v Crewe Alexandra
Manchester City v Huddersfield Town
Portsmouth v Bolton Wand.
Q.P.R. v Barnsley
Tranmere Rov. v Wolves
W.B.A. v Sheffield Utd.

Nationwide League Division Two
Bournemouth v Millwall
Blackpool v Cambridge Utd.
Bristol Rov. v Luton Town
Bury v Preston N.E.
Cardiff City v Gillingham
Chesterfield v Oxford Utd.
Notts Co. v Bristol City
Oldham Athletic v Wrexham
Reading v Scunthorpe Utd.
Stoke City v Colchester Utd.
Wigan Athletic v Burnley
Wycombe Wand. v Brentford

Nationwide League Division Three
Brighton & H.A. v Northampton Town
Carlisle Utd. v Rotherham Utd.
Cheltenham v Leyton Orient
Chester City v Swansea City
Exeter City v Torquay Utd.
Halifax Town v Mansfield Town
Lincoln City v Rochdale
Macclesfield Town v Hartlepool Utd.
Peterborough Utd. v Barnet
Shrewsbury Town v Hull City
Southend Utd. v Darlington
York City v Plymouth Argyle

Sunday, 28 November
F.A. Carling Premiership
Chelsea v Bradford City

Nationwide League Division One
Grimsby Town v Norwich City

Friday, 3 December
Nationwide League Division One
Wolves v Manchester City

Saturday, 4 December
F.A. Carling Premiership
Aston Villa v Newcastle Utd.
Bradford City v Middlesbrough
Derby Co. v Leeds Utd.
Leicester City v Arsenal
Manchester Utd. v Everton
Southampton v Coventry City
Sunderland v Chelsea
Wimbledon v Watford

Nationwide League Division One
Barnsley v Charlton Athletic
Bolton Wand. v Tranmere Rov.
Crewe Alexandra v Crystal Palace
Fulham v Birmingham City
Huddersfield Town v Q.P.R.
Norwich City v W.B.A.
Port Vale v Blackburn Rov.
Sheffield Utd. v Portsmouth
Stockport Co. v Grimsby Town
Swindon Town v Walsall

Nationwide League Division Two
Brentford v Bristol Rov.
Bristol City v Reading
Burnley v Wycombe Wand.
Cambridge Utd. v Bournemouth
Colchester Utd. v Chesterfield
Gillingham v Bury
Luton Town v Notts Co.
Millwall v Cardiff City
Oxford Utd. v Stoke City
Preston N.E. v Oldham Athletic
Scunthorpe Utd. v Wigan Athletic
Wrexham v Blackpool

Nationwide League Division Three
Barnet v Chester City
Darlington v Halifax Town
Hartlepool Utd. v Peterborough Utd.
Hull City v Exeter City
Leyton Orient v Carlisle Utd.
Mansfield Town v Brighton & H.A.
Northampton Town v Macclesfield Town
Plymouth Argyle v Southend Utd.
Rochdale v Cheltenham
Rotherham Utd. v Lincoln City
Swansea City v York City
Torquay Utd. v Shrewsbury Town

Sunday, 5 December
F.A. Carling Premiership
Liverpool v Sheffield Wed.

Nationwide League Division One
Nott'm. Forest v Ipswich Town

Monday, 6 December
F.A. Carling Premiership
Tottenham v West Ham Utd.

Saturday, 11 December
Nationwide League Division Two
Blackpool v Reading
Brentford v Chesterfield
Bristol Rov. v Colchester Utd.
Bury v Cambridge Utd.
Cardiff City v Bristol City
Gillingham v Burnley
Luton Town v Stoke City
Notts Co. v Bournemouth
Oldham Athletic v Wigan Athletic
Oxford Utd. v Preston N.E.
Wrexham v Scunthorpe Utd.
Wycombe Wand. v Millwall

Nationwide League Division Three
Brighton & H.A. v Rochdale
Carlisle Utd. v Torquay Utd.
Cheltenham v Macclesfield Town
Darlington v Chester City
Halifax Town v Rotherham Utd.
Hartlepool Utd. v Swansea City
Leyton Orient v Exeter City
Mansfield Town v York City
Peterborough Utd. v Hull City
Plymouth Argyle v Lincoln City
Shrewsbury Town v Northampton Town
Southend Utd. v Barnet

Friday, 17 December
Nationwide League Division One
Wolves v Birmingham City

Saturday, 18 December
F.A. Carling Premiership
Arsenal v Wimbledon
Aston Villa v Sheffield Wed.
Bradford City v Newcastle Utd.
Leicester City v Derby Co.
Liverpool v Coventry City
Middlesbrough v Tottenham
Sunderland v Southampton
Watford v Everton
West Ham Utd. v Manchester Utd.

Nationwide League Division One
Barnsley v Walsall
Bolton Wand. v Stockport Co.
Crystal Palace v Fulham
Huddersfield Town v Grimsby Town
Ipswich Town v W.B.A.
Manchester City v Swindon Town
Nott'm. Forest v Crewe Alexandra
Portsmouth v Port Vale
Q.P.R. v Charlton Athletic
Tranmere Rov. v Norwich City

Nationwide League Division Two
Bournemouth v Oxford Utd.
Bristol City v Wycombe Wand.
Burnley v Cardiff City
Cambridge Utd. v Oldham Athletic
Chesterfield v Gillingham
Colchester Utd. v Luton Town
Millwall v Notts Co.
Preston N.E. v Blackpool
Reading v Wrexham
Scunthorpe Utd. v Bury
Stoke City v Bristol Rov.
Wigan Athletic v Brentford

Nationwide League Division Three
Barnet v Mansfield Town
Chester City v Halifax Town
Exeter City v Hartlepool Utd.
Hull City v Carlisle Utd.
Lincoln City v Shrewsbury Town
Macclesfield Town v Leyton Orient
Northampton Town v Plymouth Argyle
Rochdale v Peterborough Utd.
Rotherham Utd. v Darlington
Swansea City v Brighton & H.A.
Torquay Utd. v Cheltenham
York City v Southend Utd.

Sunday, 19 December
F.A. Carling Premiership
Chelsea v Leeds Utd.

Nationwide League Division One
Sheffield Utd. v Blackburn Rov.

Sunday, 26 December
F.A. Carling Premiership
Coventry City v Arsenal
Derby Co. v Aston Villa
Everton v Sunderland
Leeds Utd. v Leicester City
Manchester Utd. v Bradford City
Newcastle Utd. v Liverpool
Sheffield Wed. v Middlesbrough
Southampton v Chelsea
Tottenham v Watford
Wimbledon v West Ham Utd.

Nationwide League Division One
Birmingham City v Sheffield Utd.
Blackburn Rov. v Nott'm. Forest
Charlton Athletic v Crystal Palace
Crewe Alexandra v Huddersfield Town
Fulham v Ipswich Town
Grimsby Town v Barnsley
Norwich City v Q.P.R.
Port Vale v Bolton Wand.
Stockport Co. v Wolves
Swindon Town v Portsmouth
Walsall v Tranmere Rov.
W.B.A. v Manchester City

Nationwide League Division Two
Blackpool v Stoke City
Brentford v Bristol City
Bristol Rov. v Millwall
Bury v Burnley
Cardiff City v Reading
Gillingham v Colchester Utd.
Luton Town v Chesterfield
Notts Co. v Wigan Athletic
Oldham Athletic v Scunthorpe Utd.
Oxford Utd. v Cambridge Utd.
Wrexham v Preston N.E.
Wycombe Wand. v Bournemouth

Nationwide League Division Three
Brighton & H.A. v Barnet
Carlisle Utd. v Rochdale
Cheltenham v Exeter City
Darlington v Hull City
Halifax Town v Lincoln City
Hartlepool Utd. v York City
Leyton Orient v Swansea City
Mansfield Town v Chester City
Peterborough Utd. v Rotherham Utd.
Plymouth Argyle v Torquay Utd.
Shrewsbury Town v Macclesfield Town
Southend Utd. v Northampton Town

Tuesday, 28 December
F.A. Carling Premiership
Arsenal v Leeds Utd.
Bradford City v Everton
Leicester City v Newcastle Utd.
Liverpool v Wimbledon
Sunderland v Manchester Utd.
Watford v Southampton
West Ham Utd. v Derby Co.

Nationwide League Division One
Barnsley v Port Vale
Bolton Wand. v W.B.A.
Crystal Palace v Walsall
Huddersfield Town v Charlton Athletic
Ipswich Town v Stockport Co.
Manchester City v Grimsby Town
Nott'm. Forest v Birmingham City
Portsmouth v Blackburn Rov.
Q.P.R. v Crewe Alexandra
Sheffield Utd. v Fulham
Tranmere Rov. v Swindon Town
Wolves v Norwich City

Nationwide League Division Two
Bournemouth v Wrexham
Bristol City v Luton Town
Burnley v Oxford Utd.
Cambridge Utd. v Cardiff City
Chesterfield v Bury
Colchester Utd. v Wycombe Wand.
Millwall v Brentford

Preston N.E. v Bristol Rov.
Reading v Notts Co.
Scunthorpe Utd. v Blackpool
Stoke City v Oldham Athletic
Wigan Athletic v Gillingham

Nationwide League Division Three
Barnet v Halifax Town
Chester City v Leyton Orient
Exeter City v Peterborough Utd.
Hull City v Mansfield Town
Lincoln City v Hartlepool Utd.
Macclesfield Town v Carlisle Utd.
Northampton Town v Darlington
Rochdale v Shrewsbury Town
Rotherham Utd. v Brighton & H.A.
Swansea City v Plymouth Argyle
Torquay Utd. v Southend Utd.
York City v Cheltenham

Wednesday, 29 December
F.A. Carling Premiership
Chelsea v Sheffield Wed.
Aston Villa v Tottenham
Middlesbrough v Coventry City

Monday, 3 January, 2000
F.A. Carling Premiership
Coventry City v Chelsea
Derby Co. v Watford
Everton v Leicester City
Leeds Utd. v Aston Villa
Manchester Utd. v Middlesbrough
Newcastle Utd. v West Ham Utd.
Sheffield Wed. v Arsenal
Southampton v Bradford City
Tottenham v Liverpool
Wimbledon v Sunderland

Nationwide League Division One
Birmingham City v Huddersfield Town
Blackburn Rov. v Wolves
Charlton Athletic v Nott'm. Forest
Crewe Alexandra v Manchester City
Fulham v Tranmere Rov.
Grimsby Town v Sheffield Utd.
Norwich City v Portsmouth
Port Vale v Ipswich Town
Stockport Co. v Crystal Palace
Swindon Town v Q.P.R.
Walsall v Bolton Wand.
W.B.A. v Barnsley

Nationwide League Division Two
Blackpool v Colchester Utd.
Brentford v Stoke City
Bristol Rov. v Cambridge Utd.
Bury v Millwall
Cardiff City v Preston N.E.
Gillingham v Reading
Luton Town v Scunthorpe Utd.

Notts Co. v Burnley
Oldham Athletic v Bournemouth
Oxford Utd. v Wigan Athletic
Wrexham v Bristol City
Wycombe Wand. v Chesterfield

Nationwide League Division Three
Brighton & H.A. v Exeter City
Carlisle Utd. v Chester City
Cheltenham v Lincoln City
Darlington v York City
Halifax Town v Northampton Town
Hartlepool Utd. v Rochdale
Leyton Orient v Hull City
Mansfield Town v Torquay Utd.
Peterborough Utd. v Swansea City
Plymouth Argyle v Macclesfield Town
Shrewsbury Town v Barnet
Southend Utd. v Rotherham Utd.

Saturday, 8 January
F.A. Carling Premiership
Bradford City v Chelsea

Nationwide League Division Two
Bournemouth v Notts Co.
Bristol City v Cardiff City
Burnley v Gillingham
Cambridge Utd. v Bury
Chesterfield v Brentford
Colchester Utd. v Bristol Rov.
Millwall v Wycombe Wand.
Preston N.E. v Oxford Utd.
Reading v Blackpool
Scunthorpe Utd. v Wrexham
Stoke City v Luton Town
Wigan Athletic v Oldham Athletic

Nationwide League Division Three
Barnet v Southend Utd.
Chester City v Darlington
Exeter City v Leyton Orient
Hull City v Peterborough Utd.
Lincoln City v Plymouth Argyle
Macclesfield Town v Cheltenham
Northampton Town v Shrewsbury Town
Rochdale v Brighton & H.A.
Rotherham Utd. v Halifax Town
Swansea City v Hartlepool Utd.
Torquay Utd. v Carlisle Utd.
York City v Mansfield Town

Wednesday, 12 January
F.A. Carling Premiership
Chelsea v Tottenham

Saturday, 15 January
F.A. Carling Premiership
Arsenal v Sunderland
Chelsea v Leicester City
Coventry City v Wimbledon

Everton v Tottenham
Leeds Utd. v Manchester Utd.
Middlesbrough v Derby Co.
Newcastle Utd. v Southampton
Sheffield Wed. v Bradford City
Watford v Liverpool
West Ham Utd. v Aston Villa

Nationwide League Division One
Birmingham City v Norwich City
Blackburn Rov. v Huddersfield Town
Charlton Athletic v Crewe Alexandra
Crystal Palace v Barnsley
Grimsby Town v Nott'm. Forest
Ipswich Town v Swindon Town
Manchester City v Fulham
Portsmouth v Wolves
Q.P.R. v Bolton Wand.
Tranmere Rov. v Stockport Co.
Walsall v Sheffield Utd.
W.B.A. v Port Vale

Nationwide League Division Two
Bournemouth v Bristol City
Blackpool v Luton Town
Bristol Rov. v Gillingham
Bury v Wrexham
Cardiff City v Oxford Utd.
Chesterfield v Burnley
Notts Co. v Colchester Utd.
Oldham Athletic v Brentford
Reading v Cambridge Utd.
Stoke City v Preston N.E.
Wigan Athletic v Millwall
Wycombe Wand. v Scunthorpe Utd.

Nationwide League Division Three
Brighton & H.A. v Leyton Orient
Carlisle Utd. v Swansea City
Cheltenham v Mansfield Town
Chester City v Rotherham Utd.
Exeter City v Barnet
Halifax Town v Hartlepool Utd.
Lincoln City v Hull City
Macclesfield Town v Darlington
Peterborough Utd. v Northampton Town
Shrewsbury Town v Plymouth Argyle
Southend Utd. v Rochdale
York City v Torquay Utd.

Saturday, 22 January
F.A. Carling Premiership
Aston Villa v Chelsea
Bradford City v Watford
Derby Co. v Coventry City
Leicester City v West Ham Utd.
Liverpool v Middlesbrough
Manchester Utd. v Arsenal
Southampton v Everton
Sunderland v Leeds Utd.

Tottenham v Sheffield Wed.
Wimbledon v Newcastle Utd.

Nationwide League Division One
Barnsley v Blackburn Rov.
Bolton Wand. v Ipswich Town
Crewe Alexandra v Walsall
Fulham v Grimsby Town
Huddersfield Town v Tranmere Rov.
Norwich City v Charlton Athletic
Nott'm. Forest v W.B.A.
Port Vale v Birmingham City
Sheffield Utd. v Manchester City
Stockport Co. v Portsmouth
Swindon Town v Crystal Palace
Wolves v Q.P.R.

Nationwide League Division Two
Brentford v Bury
Bristol City v Wigan Athletic
Burnley v Oldham Athletic
Cambridge Utd. v Chesterfield
Colchester Utd. v Bournemouth
Gillingham v Blackpool
Luton Town v Reading
Millwall v Stoke City
Oxford Utd. v Bristol Rov.
Preston N.E. v Wycombe Wand.
Scunthorpe Utd. v Notts Co.
Wrexham v Cardiff City

Nationwide League Division Three
Barnet v Lincoln City
Darlington v Shrewsbury Town
Hartlepool Utd. v Carlisle Utd.
Hull City v Cheltenham
Leyton Orient v Peterborough Utd.
Mansfield Town v Southend Utd.
Northampton Town v Chester City
Plymouth Argyle v Halifax Town
Rochdale v York City
Rotherham Utd. v Exeter City
Swansea City v Macclesfield Town
Torquay Utd. v Brighton & H.A.

Saturday, 29 January
Nationwide League Division One
Birmingham City v Stockport Co.
Blackburn Rov. v Norwich City
Charlton Athletic v Fulham
Crystal Palace v Huddersfield Town
Grimsby Town v Crewe Alexandra
Ipswich Town v Sheffield Utd.
Manchester City v Bolton Wand.
Portsmouth v Barnsley
Q.P.R. v Nott'm. Forest
Tranmere Rov. v Port Vale
Walsall v Wolves
W.B.A. v Swindon Town

Nationwide League Division Two
Bournemouth v Scunthorpe Utd.
Blackpool v Brentford
Bristol Rov. v Wrexham
Bury v Bristol City
Cardiff City v Luton Town
Chesterfield v Millwall
Notts Co. v Cambridge Utd.
Oldham Athletic v Oxford Utd.
Reading v Colchester Utd.
Stoke City v Burnley
Wigan Athletic v Preston N.E.
Wycombe Wand. v Gillingham

Nationwide League Division Three
Brighton & H.A. v Darlington
Carlisle Utd. v Mansfield Town
Cheltenham v Hartlepool Utd.
Chester City v Torquay Utd.
Exeter City v Rochdale
Halifax Town v Leyton Orient
Lincoln City v Northampton Town
Macclesfield Town v Hull City
Peterborough Utd. v Plymouth Argyle
Shrewsbury Town v Rotherham Utd.
Southend Utd. v Swansea City
York City v Barnet

Saturday, 5 February
F.A. Carling Premiership
Aston Villa v Watford
Bradford City v Arsenal
Derby Co. v Sheffield Wed.
Leicester City v Middlesbrough
Liverpool v Leeds Utd.
Manchester Utd. v Coventry City
Southampton v West Ham Utd.
Sunderland v Newcastle Utd.
Tottenham v Chelsea
Wimbledon v Everton

Nationwide League Division One
Barnsley v Ipswich Town
Bolton Wand. v Blackburn Rov.
Crewe Alexandra v Birmingham City
Fulham v W.B.A.
Huddersfield Town v Portsmouth
Norwich City v Walsall
Nott'm. Forest v Manchester City
Port Vale v Q.P.R.
Sheffield Utd. v Tranmere Rov.
Stockport Co. v Charlton Athletic
Swindon Town v Grimsby Town
Wolves v Crystal Palace

Nationwide League Division Two
Brentford v Notts Co.
Bristol City v Chesterfield
Burnley v Bristol Rov.
Cambridge Utd. v Wigan Athletic

Colchester Utd. v Bury
Gillingham v Stoke City
Luton Town v Bournemouth
Millwall v Oldham Athletic
Oxford Utd. v Blackpool
Preston N.E. v Reading
Scunthorpe Utd. v Cardiff City
Wrexham v Wycombe Wand.

Nationwide League Division Three
Barnet v Cheltenham
Darlington v Peterborough Utd.
Hartlepool Utd. v Shrewsbury Town
Hull City v Brighton & H.A.
Leyton Orient v Southend Utd.
Mansfield Town v Exeter City
Northampton Town v York City
Plymouth Argyle v Carlisle Utd.
Rochdale v Chester City
Rotherham Utd. v Macclesfield Town
Swansea City v Lincoln City
Torquay Utd. v Halifax Town

Saturday, 12 February
F.A. Carling Premiership
Arsenal v Liverpool
Chelsea v Wimbledon
Coventry City v Sunderland
Everton v Derby Co.
Leeds Utd. v Tottenham
Middlesbrough v Aston Villa
Newcastle Utd. v Manchester Utd.
Sheffield Wed. v Southampton
Watford v Leicester City
West Ham Utd. v Bradford City

Nationwide League Division One
Birmingham City v Bolton Wand.
Blackburn Rov. v Swindon Town
Charlton Athletic v Wolves
Crystal Palace v Sheffield Utd.
Grimsby Town v Port Vale
Ipswich Town v Huddersfield Town
Manchester City v Norwich City
Portsmouth v Fulham
Q.P.R. v Stockport Co.
Tranmere Rov. v Barnsley
Walsall v Nott'm. Forest
W.B.A. v Crewe Alexandra

Nationwide League Division Two
Bournemouth v Burnley
Blackpool v Bristol City
Bristol Rov. v Scunthorpe Utd.
Bury v Luton Town
Cardiff City v Brentford
Chesterfield v Preston N.E.
Notts Co. v Wrexham
Oldham Athletic v Gillingham
Reading v Millwall

Stoke City v Cambridge Utd.
Wigan Athletic v Colchester Utd.
Wycombe Wand. v Oxford Utd.

Nationwide League Division Three
Brighton & H.A. v Plymouth Argyle
Carlisle Utd. v Northampton Town
Cheltenham v Swansea City
Chester City v Hull City
Exeter City v Darlington
Halifax Town v Rochdale
Lincoln City v Torquay Utd.
Macclesfield Town v Barnet
Peterborough Utd. v Mansfield Town
Shrewsbury Town v Leyton Orient
Southend Utd. v Hartlepool Utd.
York City v Rotherham Utd.

Saturday, 19 February
Nationwide League Division One
Barnsley v Q.P.R.
Bolton Wand. v Portsmouth
Crewe Alexandra v Ipswich Town
Fulham v Walsall
Huddersfield Town v Manchester City
Norwich City v Grimsby Town
Nott'm. Forest v Crystal Palace
Port Vale v Charlton Athletic
Sheffield Utd. v W.B.A.
Stockport Co. v Blackburn Rov.
Swindon Town v Birmingham City
Wolves v Tranmere Rov.

Nationwide League Division Two
Brentford v Wycombe Wand.
Bristol City v Notts Co.
Burnley v Wigan Athletic
Cambridge Utd. v Blackpool
Colchester Utd. v Stoke City
Gillingham v Cardiff City
Luton Town v Bristol Rov.
Millwall v Bournemouth
Oxford Utd. v Chesterfield
Preston N.E. v Bury
Scunthorpe Utd. v Reading
Wrexham v Oldham Athletic

Nationwide League Division Three
Barnet v Peterborough Utd.
Darlington v Southend Utd.
Hartlepool Utd. v Macclesfield Town
Hull City v Shrewsbury Town
Leyton Orient v Cheltenham
Mansfield Town v Halifax Town
Northampton Town v Brighton & H.A.
Plymouth Argyle v York City
Rochdale v Lincoln City
Rotherham Utd. v Carlisle Utd.
Swansea City v Chester City
Torquay Utd. v Exeter City

Saturday, 26 February
F.A. Carling Premiership
Arsenal v Southampton
Bradford City v Aston Villa
Chelsea v Watford
Coventry City v Tottenham
Liverpool v Leicester City
Middlesbrough v Leeds Utd.
Sheffield Wed. v Newcastle Utd.
Sunderland v Derby Co.
West Ham Utd. v Everton
Wimbledon v Manchester Utd.

Nationwide League Division One
Barnsley v Bolton Wand.
Birmingham City v Ipswich Town
Blackburn Rov. v W.B.A.
Charlton Athletic v Sheffield Utd.
Grimsby Town v Crystal Palace
Manchester City v Walsall
Norwich City v Huddersfield Town
Port Vale v Stockport Co.
Portsmouth v Tranmere Rov.
Q.P.R. v Fulham
Swindon Town v Crewe Alexandra
Wolves v Nott'm. Forest

Nationwide League Division Two
Bournemouth v Blackpool
Bristol City v Scunthorpe Utd.
Cambridge Utd. v Millwall
Chesterfield v Reading
Colchester Utd. v Burnley
Luton Town v Brentford
Notts Co. v Cardiff City
Oldham Athletic v Bristol Rov.
Oxford Utd. v Wrexham
Preston N.E. v Gillingham
Wigan Athletic v Stoke City
Wycombe Wand. v Bury

Nationwide League Division Three
Carlisle Utd. v Shrewsbury Town
Cheltenham v Peterborough Utd.
Chester City v Brighton & H.A.
Halifax Town v Southend Utd.
Macclesfield Town v Lincoln City
Mansfield Town v Darlington
Northampton Town v Barnet
Plymouth Argyle v Hartlepool Utd.
Rochdale v Rotherham Utd.
Swansea City v Hull City
Torquay Utd. v Leyton Orient
York City v Exeter City

Saturday, 4 March
F.A. Carling Premiership
Aston Villa v Arsenal
Derby Co. v Wimbledon
Everton v Sheffield Wed.

Leeds Utd. v Coventry City
Leicester City v Sunderland
Manchester Utd. v Liverpool
Newcastle Utd. v Chelsea
Southampton v Middlesbrough
Tottenham v Bradford City
Watford v West Ham Utd.

Nationwide League Division One
Bolton Wand. v Charlton Athletic
Crewe Alexandra v Norwich City
Crystal Palace v Manchester City
Fulham v Port Vale
Huddersfield Town v Wolves
Ipswich Town v Portsmouth
Nott'm. Forest v Swindon Town
Sheffield Utd. v Q.P.R.
Stockport Co. v Barnsley
Tranmere Rov. v Blackburn Rov.
Walsall v Grimsby Town
W.B.A. v Birmingham City

Nationwide League Division Two
Blackpool v Notts Co.
Brentford v Cambridge Utd.
Bristol Rov. v Wigan Athletic
Burnley v Preston N.E.
Bury v Oldham Athletic
Cardiff City v Wycombe Wand.
Gillingham v Oxford Utd.
Millwall v Bristol City
Reading v Bournemouth
Scunthorpe Utd. v Colchester Utd.
Stoke City v Chesterfield
Wrexham v Luton Town

Nationwide League Division Three
Barnet v Swansea City
Brighton & H.A. v Halifax Town
Darlington v Rochdale
Exeter City v Chester City
Hartlepool Utd. v Northampton Town
Hull City v Torquay Utd.
Leyton Orient v Mansfield Town
Lincoln City v Carlisle Utd.
Peterborough Utd. v York City
Rotherham Utd. v Plymouth Argyle
Shrewsbury Town v Cheltenham
Southend Utd. v Macclesfield Town

Tuesday, 7 March
Nationwide League Division One
Crewe Alexandra v Port Vale
Crystal Palace v Bolton Wand.
Fulham v Stockport Co.
Grimsby Town v Wolves
Ipswich Town v Blackburn Rov.
Manchester City v Q.P.R.
Sheffield Utd. v Barnsley
Swindon Town v Huddersfield Town

Walsall v Charlton Athletic
W.B.A. v Tranmere Rov.

Nationwide League Division Two
Brentford v Wrexham
Bristol Rov. v Wycombe Wand.
Burnley v Luton Town
Cambridge Utd. v Bristol City
Cardiff City v Bournemouth
Gillingham v Notts Co.
Millwall v Scunthorpe Utd.
Oldham Athletic v Chesterfield
Oxford Utd. v Reading
Preston N.E. v Colchester Utd.
Wigan Athletic v Blackpool

Nationwide League Division Three
Carlisle Utd. v Cheltenham
Darlington v Barnet
Halifax Town v Swansea City
Hartlepool Utd. v Brighton & H.A.
Lincoln City v Mansfield Town
Macclesfield Town v York City
Northampton Town v Leyton Orient
Plymouth Argyle v Chester City
Rochdale v Torquay Utd.
Rotherham Utd. v Hull City
Shrewsbury Town v Peterborough Utd.
Southend Utd. v Exeter City

Wednesday, 8 March
Nationwide League Division One
Birmingham City v Portsmouth
Nott'm. Forest v Norwich City

Nationwide League Division Two
Stoke City v Bury

Saturday, 11 March
F.A. Carling Premiership
Aston Villa v Coventry City
Bradford City v Leeds Utd.
Chelsea v Everton
Liverpool v Sunderland
Manchester Utd. v Derby Co.
Middlesbrough v Arsenal
Newcastle Utd. v Watford
Sheffield Wed. v West Ham Utd.
Tottenham v Southampton
Wimbledon v Leicester City

Nationwide League Division One
Barnsley v Manchester City
Blackburn Rov. v Crewe Alexandra
Bolton Wand. v Fulham
Charlton Athletic v Swindon Town
Huddersfield Town v Walsall
Norwich City v Crystal Palace
Port Vale v Sheffield Utd.
Portsmouth v Nott'm. Forest
Q.P.R. v Grimsby Town

Stockport Co. v W.B.A.
Tranmere Rov. v Birmingham City
Wolves v Ipswich Town

Nationwide League Division Two
Bournemouth v Preston N.E.
Blackpool v Cardiff City
Bristol City v Gillingham
Bury v Bristol Rov.
Chesterfield v Wigan Athletic
Colchester Utd. v Oxford Utd.
Luton Town v Millwall
Notts Co. v Stoke City
Reading v Brentford
Scunthorpe Utd. v Cambridge Utd.
Wrexham v Burnley
Wycombe Wand. v Oldham Athletic

Nationwide League Division Three
Barnet v Hartlepool Utd.
Brighton & H.A. v Southend Utd.
Cheltenham v Halifax Town
Chester City v Shrewsbury Town
Exeter City v Plymouth Argyle
Hull City v Rochdale
Leyton Orient v Darlington
Mansfield Town v Macclesfield Town
Peterborough Utd. v Lincoln City
Swansea City v Northampton Town
Torquay Utd. v Rotherham Utd.
York City v Carlisle Utd.

Saturday, 18 March
F.A. Carling Premiership
Arsenal v Tottenham
Coventry City v Bradford City
Derby Co. v Liverpool
Everton v Newcastle Utd.
Leeds Utd. v Wimbledon
Leicester City v Manchester Utd.
Southampton v Aston Villa
Sunderland v Middlesbrough
Watford v Sheffield Wed.
West Ham Utd. v Chelsea

Nationwide League Division One
Birmingham City v Barnsley
Crewe Alexandra v Portsmouth
Crystal Palace v Port Vale
Fulham v Blackburn Rov.
Grimsby Town v Bolton Wand.
Ipswich Town v Norwich City
Manchester City v Charlton Athletic
Nott'm. Forest v Tranmere Rov.
Sheffield Utd. v Stockport Co.
Swindon Town v Wolves
Walsall v Q.P.R.
W.B.A. v Huddersfield Town

Nationwide League Division Two
Brentford v Bournemouth
Bristol Rov. v Chesterfield
Burnley v Reading
Cambridge Utd. v Wrexham
Cardiff City v Colchester Utd.
Gillingham v Scunthorpe Utd.
Millwall v Blackpool
Oldham Athletic v Bristol City
Oxford Utd. v Notts Co.
Preston N.E. v Luton Town
Stoke City v Wycombe Wand.
Wigan Athletic v Bury

Nationwide League Division Three
Carlisle Utd. v Barnet
Darlington v Swansea City
Halifax Town v Hull City
Hartlepool Utd. v Torquay Utd.
Lincoln City v Brighton & H.A.
Macclesfield Town v Peterborough Utd.
Northampton Town v Exeter City
Plymouth Argyle v Cheltenham
Rochdale v Leyton Orient
Rotherham Utd. v Mansfield Town
Shrewsbury Town v York City
Southend Utd. v Chester City

Tuesday, 21 March
Nationwide League Division One
Barnsley v Fulham
Bolton Wand. v Sheffield Utd.
Charlton Athletic v Grimsby Town
Huddersfield Town v Nott'm. Forest
Norwich City v Swindon Town
Port Vale v Walsall
Portsmouth v W.B.A.
Stockport Co. v Manchester City
Tranmere Rov. v Ipswich Town
Wolves v Crewe Alexandra

Nationwide League Division Two
Bournemouth v Gillingham
Blackpool v Burnley
Bristol City v Stoke City
Bury v Oxford Utd.
Chesterfield v Cardiff City
Colchester Utd. v Oldham Athletic
Luton Town v Cambridge Utd.
Notts Co. v Preston N.E.
Scunthorpe Utd. v Brentford
Wrexham v Millwall
Wycombe Wand. v Wigan Athletic

Nationwide League Division Three
Barnet v Plymouth Argyle
Brighton & H.A. v Macclesfield Town
Cheltenham v Northampton Town
Chester City v Hartlepool Utd.
Exeter City v Halifax Town

Hull City v Southend Utd.
Leyton Orient v Rotherham Utd.
Mansfield Town v Rochdale
Peterborough Utd. v Carlisle Utd.
Swansea City v Shrewsbury Town
Torquay Utd. v Darlington
York City v Lincoln City

Wednesday, 22 March
Nationwide League Division One
Blackburn Rov. v Birmingham City
Q.P.R. v Crystal Palace

Nationwide League Division Two
Reading v Bristol Rov.

Saturday, 25 March
F.A. Carling Premiership
Arsenal v Coventry City
Aston Villa v Derby Co.
Bradford City v Manchester Utd.
Chelsea v Southampton
Leicester City v Leeds Utd.
Liverpool v Newcastle Utd.
Middlesbrough v Sheffield Wed.
Sunderland v Everton
Watford v Tottenham
West Ham Utd. v Wimbledon

Nationwide League Division One
Barnsley v Grimsby Town
Bolton Wand. v Port Vale
Crystal Palace v Charlton Athletic
Huddersfield Town v Crewe Alexandra
Ipswich Town v Fulham
Manchester City v W.B.A.
Nott'm. Forest v Blackburn Rov.
Portsmouth v Swindon Town
Q.P.R. v Norwich City
Sheffield Utd. v Birmingham City
Tranmere Rov. v Walsall
Wolves v Stockport Co.

Nationwide League Division Two
Bournemouth v Wycombe Wand.
Bristol City v Brentford
Burnley v Bury
Cambridge Utd. v Oxford Utd.
Chesterfield v Luton Town
Colchester Utd. v Gillingham
Millwall v Bristol Rov.
Preston N.E. v Wrexham
Reading v Cardiff City
Scunthorpe Utd. v Oldham Athletic
Stoke City v Blackpool
Wigan Athletic v Notts Co.

Nationwide League Division Three
Barnet v Brighton & H.A.
Chester City v Mansfield Town
Exeter City v Cheltenham

Hull City v Darlington
Lincoln City v Halifax Town
Macclesfield Town v Shrewsbury Town
Northampton Town v Southend Utd.
Rochdale v Carlisle Utd.
Rotherham Utd. v Peterborough Utd.
Swansea City v Leyton Orient
Torquay Utd. v Plymouth Argyle
York City v Hartlepool Utd.

Saturday, 1 April
F.A. Carling Premiership
Coventry City v Liverpool
Derby Co. v Leicester City
Everton v Watford
Leeds Utd. v Chelsea
Manchester Utd. v West Ham Utd.
Newcastle Utd. v Bradford City
Sheffield Wed. v Aston Villa
Southampton v Sunderland
Tottenham v Middlesbrough
Wimbledon v Arsenal

Nationwide League Division One
Birmingham City v Wolves
Blackburn Rov. v Sheffield Utd.
Charlton Athletic v Q.P.R.
Crewe Alexandra v Nott'm. Forest
Fulham v Crystal Palace
Grimsby Town v Huddersfield Town
Norwich City v Tranmere Rov.
Port Vale v Portsmouth
Stockport Co. v Bolton Wand.
Swindon Town v Manchester City
Walsall v Barnsley
W.B.A. v Ipswich Town

Nationwide League Division Two
Blackpool v Preston N.E.
Brentford v Wigan Athletic
Bristol Rov. v Stoke City
Bury v Scunthorpe Utd.
Cardiff City v Burnley
Gillingham v Chesterfield
Luton Town v Colchester Utd.
Notts Co. v Millwall
Oldham Athletic v Cambridge Utd.
Oxford Utd. v Bournemouth
Wrexham v Reading
Wycombe Wand. v Bristol City

Nationwide League Division Three
Brighton & H.A. v Swansea City
Carlisle Utd. v Hull City
Cheltenham v Torquay Utd.
Darlington v Rotherham Utd.
Halifax Town v Chester City
Hartlepool Utd. v Exeter City
Leyton Orient v Macclesfield Town
Mansfield Town v Barnet

Peterborough Utd. v Rochdale
Plymouth Argyle v Northampton Town
Shrewsbury Town v Lincoln City
Southend Utd. v York City

Saturday, 8 April
F.A. Carling Premiership
Arsenal v Sheffield Wed.
Aston Villa v Leeds Utd.
Bradford City v Southampton
Chelsea v Coventry City
Leicester City v Everton
Middlesbrough v Manchester Utd.
Sunderland v Wimbledon
Watford v Derby Co.
West Ham Utd. v Newcastle Utd.

Nationwide League Division One
Barnsley v W.B.A.
Bolton Wand. v Walsall
Crystal Palace v Stockport Co.
Huddersfield Town v Birmingham City
Ipswich Town v Port Vale
Manchester City v Crewe Alexandra
Nott'm. Forest v Charlton Athletic
Portsmouth v Norwich City
Q.P.R. v Swindon Town
Sheffield Utd. v Grimsby Town
Tranmere Rov. v Fulham
Wolves v Blackburn Rov.

Nationwide League Division Two
Bournemouth v Oldham Athletic
Bristol City v Wrexham
Burnley v Notts Co.
Cambridge Utd. v Bristol Rov.
Chesterfield v Wycombe Wand.
Colchester Utd. v Blackpool
Millwall v Bury
Preston N.E. v Cardiff City
Reading v Gillingham
Scunthorpe Utd. v Luton Town
Stoke City v Brentford
Wigan Athletic v Oxford Utd.

Nationwide League Division Three
Barnet v Shrewsbury Town
Chester City v Carlisle Utd.
Exeter City v Brighton & H.A.
Hull City v Leyton Orient
Lincoln City v Cheltenham
Macclesfield Town v Plymouth Argyle
Northampton Town v Halifax Town
Rochdale v Hartlepool Utd.
Rotherham Utd. v Southend Utd.
Swansea City v Peterborough Utd.
Torquay Utd. v Mansfield Town
York City v Darlington

Sunday, 9 April
F.A. Carling Premiership
Liverpool v Tottenham

Saturday, 15 April
F.A. Carling Premiership
Coventry City v Middlesbrough
Derby Co. v West Ham Utd.
Everton v Bradford City
Leeds Utd. v Arsenal
Manchester Utd. v Sunderland
Newcastle Utd. v Leicester City
Sheffield Wed. v Chelsea
Southampton v Watford
Tottenham v Aston Villa
Wimbledon v Liverpool

Nationwide League Division One
Birmingham City v Nott'm. Forest
Blackburn Rov. v Portsmouth
Charlton Athletic v Huddersfield Town
Crewe Alexandra v Q.P.R.
Fulham v Sheffield Utd.
Grimsby Town v Manchester City
Norwich City v Wolves
Port Vale v Barnsley
Stockport Co. v Ipswich Town
Swindon Town v Tranmere Rov.
Walsall v Crystal Palace
W.B.A. v Bolton Wand.

Nationwide League Division Two
Blackpool v Scunthorpe Utd.
Brentford v Millwall
Bristol Rov. v Preston N.E.
Bury v Chesterfield
Cardiff City v Cambridge Utd.
Gillingham v Wigan Athletic
Luton Town v Bristol City
Notts Co. v Reading
Oldham Athletic v Stoke City
Oxford Utd. v Burnley
Wrexham v Bournemouth
Wycombe Wand. v Colchester Utd.

Nationwide League Division Three
Brighton & H.A. v Rotherham Utd.
Carlisle Utd. v Macclesfield Town
Cheltenham v York City
Darlington v Northampton Town
Halifax Town v Barnet
Hartlepool Utd. v Lincoln City
Leyton Orient v Chester City
Mansfield Town v Hull City
Peterborough Utd. v Exeter City
Plymouth Argyle v Swansea City
Shrewsbury Town v Rochdale
Southend Utd. v Torquay Utd.

Saturday, 22 April
F.A. Carling Premiership
Aston Villa v Leicester City
Bradford City v Derby Co.
Chelsea v Middlesbrough
Everton v Liverpool
Newcastle Utd. v Leeds Utd.
Sheffield Wed. v Sunderland
Southampton v Manchester Utd.
Tottenham v Wimbledon
Watford v Arsenal
West Ham Utd. v Coventry City

Nationwide League Division One
Charlton Athletic v Portsmouth
Crewe Alexandra v Stockport Co.
Crystal Palace v Birmingham City
Grimsby Town v Blackburn Rov.
Huddersfield Town v Bolton Wand.
Manchester City v Tranmere Rov.
Norwich City v Port Vale
Nott'm. Forest v Sheffield Utd.
Q.P.R. v Ipswich Town
Swindon Town v Fulham
Walsall v W.B.A.
Wolves v Barnsley

Nationwide League Division Two
Bristol Rov. v Bristol City
Burnley v Millwall
Bury v Blackpool
Chesterfield v Wrexham
Colchester Utd. v Cambridge Utd.
Gillingham v Luton Town
Oldham Athletic v Cardiff City
Oxford Utd. v Brentford
Preston N.E. v Scunthorpe Utd.
Stoke City v Bournemouth
Wigan Athletic v Reading
Wycombe Wand. v Notts Co.

Nationwide League Division Three
Barnet v Rotherham Utd.
Carlisle Utd. v Exeter City
Cheltenham v Darlington
Hartlepool Utd. v Mansfield Town
Lincoln City v Leyton Orient
Macclesfield Town v Chester City
Northampton Town v Hull City
Peterborough Utd. v Halifax Town
Plymouth Argyle v Rochdale
Shrewsbury Town v Southend Utd.
Swansea City v Torquay Utd.
York City v Brighton & H.A.

Monday, 24 April
F.A. Carling Premiership
Coventry City v Everton
Derby Co. v Southampton
Liverpool v Aston Villa

Manchester Utd. v Chelsea
Middlesbrough v Newcastle Utd.
Sunderland v Bradford City
Wimbledon v Sheffield Wed.

Nationwide League Division One
Barnsley v Norwich City
Birmingham City v Walsall
Blackburn Rov. v Charlton Athletic
Bolton Wand. v Wolves
Fulham v Nott'm. Forest
Ipswich Town v Crystal Palace
Port Vale v Huddersfield Town
Portsmouth v Manchester City
Sheffield Utd. v Crewe Alexandra
Stockport Co. v Swindon Town
Tranmere Rov. v Q.P.R.
W.B.A. v Grimsby Town

Nationwide League Division Two
Bournemouth v Chesterfield
Blackpool v Bristol Rov.
Brentford v Burnley
Bristol City v Oxford Utd.
Cambridge Utd. v Preston N.E.
Cardiff City v Bury
Luton Town v Wigan Athletic
Millwall v Gillingham
Notts Co. v Oldham Athletic
Reading v Wycombe Wand.
Scunthorpe Utd. v Stoke City
Wrexham v Colchester Utd.

Nationwide League Division Three
Brighton & H.A. v Peterborough Utd.
Chester City v York City
Darlington v Hartlepool Utd.
Exeter City v Lincoln City
Halifax Town v Shrewsbury Town
Hull City v Barnet
Leyton Orient v Plymouth Argyle
Mansfield Town v Swansea City
Rochdale v Northampton Town
Rotherham Utd. v Cheltenham
Southend Utd. v Carlisle Utd.
Torquay Utd. v Macclesfield Town

Tuesday, 25 April
F.A. Carling Premiership
Arsenal v West Ham Utd.
Leeds Utd. v Watford
Leicester City v Tottenham

Saturday, 29 April
F.A. Carling Premiership
Aston Villa v Sunderland
Bradford City v Wimbledon
Chelsea v Liverpool
Everton v Arsenal
Newcastle Utd. v Coventry City
Sheffield Wed. v Leeds Utd.

Southampton v Leicester City
Tottenham v Derby Co.
Watford v Manchester Utd.
West Ham Utd. v Middlesbrough

Nationwide League Division One
Charlton Athletic v Ipswich Town
Crewe Alexandra v Bolton Wand.
Crystal Palace v Blackburn Rov.
Grimsby Town v Tranmere Rov.
Huddersfield Town v Stockport Co.
Manchester City v Birmingham City
Norwich City v Sheffield Utd.
Nott'm. Forest v Port Vale
Q.P.R. v W.B.A.
Swindon Town v Barnsley
Walsall v Portsmouth
Wolves v Fulham

Nationwide League Division Two
Bristol Rov. v Bournemouth
Burnley v Cambridge Utd.
Bury v Reading
Chesterfield v Notts Co.
Colchester Utd. v Bristol City
Gillingham v Brentford
Oldham Athletic v Blackpool
Oxford Utd. v Scunthorpe Utd.
Preston N.E. v Millwall
Stoke City v Cardiff City
Wigan Athletic v Wrexham
Wycombe Wand. v Luton Town

Nationwide League Division Three
Barnet v Leyton Orient
Carlisle Utd. v Darlington
Cheltenham v Chester City
Hartlepool Utd. v Rotherham Utd.
Lincoln City v Southend Utd.
Macclesfield Town v Rochdale
Northampton Town v Mansfield Town
Peterborough Utd. v Torquay Utd.
Plymouth Argyle v Hull City
Shrewsbury Town v Brighton & H.A.
Swansea City v Exeter City
York City v Halifax Town

Saturday, 6 May
F.A. Carling Premiership
Arsenal v Chelsea
Coventry City v Sheffield Wed.
Derby Co. v Newcastle Utd.
Leeds Utd. v Everton
Leicester City v Bradford City
Liverpool v Southampton
Manchester Utd. v Tottenham
Middlesbrough v Watford
Sunderland v West Ham Utd.

Wimbledon v Aston Villa

Nationwide League Division Two
Bournemouth v Wigan Athletic
Blackpool v Chesterfield
Brentford v Colchester Utd.
Bristol City v Preston N.E.
Cambridge Utd. v Wycombe Wand.
Cardiff City v Bristol Rov.
Luton Town v Oldham Athletic
Millwall v Oxford Utd.
Notts Co. v Bury
Reading v Stoke City
Scunthorpe Utd. v Burnley
Wrexham v Gillingham

Nationwide League Division Three
Brighton & H.A. v Carlisle Utd.
Chester City v Peterborough Utd.
Darlington v Lincoln City
Exeter City v Shrewsbury Town
Halifax Town v Macclesfield Town
Hull City v Hartlepool Utd.
Leyton Orient v York City
Mansfield Town v Plymouth Argyle
Rochdale v Barnet
Rotherham Utd. v Swansea City
Southend Utd. v Cheltenham
Torquay Utd. v Northampton Town

Sunday, 7 May
Nationwide League Division One
Barnsley v Crewe Alexandra
Birmingham City v Grimsby Town
Blackburn Rov. v Manchester City
Bolton Wand. v Norwich City
Fulham v Huddersfield Town
Ipswich Town v Walsall
Port Vale v Wolves
Portsmouth v Q.P.R.
Sheffield Utd. v Swindon Town
Stockport Co. v Nott'm. Forest
Tranmere Rov. v Crystal Palace
W.B.A. v Charlton Athletic

Sunday, 14 May
F.A. Carling Premiership
Aston Villa v Manchester Utd.
Bradford City v Liverpool
Chelsea v Derby Co.
Everton v Middlesbrough
Newcastle Utd. v Arsenal
Sheffield Wed. v Leicester City
Southampton v Wimbledon
Tottenham v Sunderland
Watford v Coventry City
West Ham Utd. v Leeds Utd.

SCOTTISH LEAGUE FIXTURES 1999-2000

(Copyright © The Scottish Football League 1999)

Saturday, 31 July
Premier League
Aberdeen v Celtic
Dundee Utd. v Dundee
Hibernian v Motherwell
Rangers v Kilmarnock
St. Johnstone v Heart of Midlothian

Saturday, 7 August
Premier League
Celtic v St. Johnstone
Dundee v Hibernian
Heart of Midlothian v Rangers
Kilmarnock v Aberdeen
Motherwell v Dundee Utd.

First Division
Clydebank v Airdrieonians
Dunfermline Ath. v Inverness Cal. Th.
Falkirk v Morton
Livingston v Raith Rov.
St. Mirren v Ayr Utd.

Second Division
Clyde v Alloa Athletic
Partick Thistle v Stenhousemuir
Queen of the South v Arbroath
Ross County v Hamilton Acad.
Stirling Albion v Stranraer

Third Division
Albion Rov. v Dumbarton
East Fife v Berwick Rangers
Forfar Athletic v Brechin City
Montrose v Cowdenbeath
Queen's Park v East Stirlingshire

Saturday, 14 August
Premier League
Aberdeen v Dundee
Dundee Utd. v Celtic
Hibernian v Heart of Midlothian
Rangers v Motherwell
St. Johnstone v Kilmarnock

First Division
Airdrieonians v Dunfermline Athletic
Ayr Utd. v Livingston
Inverness Cal. Th. v Falkirk
Morton v Clydebank
Raith Rov. v St. Mirren

Second Division
Alloa Athletic v Partick Thistle
Arbroath v Clyde
Hamilton Acad. v Queen of the South

Stenhousemuir v Stirling Albion
Stranraer v Ross County

Third Division
Berwick Rangers v Albion Rov.
Brechin City v Queen's Park
Cowdenbeath v Forfar Athletic
Dumbarton v Montrose
East Stirlingshire v East Fife

Saturday, 21 August
Premier League
Dundee v Celtic
Heart of Midlothian v Aberdeen
Kilmarnock v Motherwell
Rangers v Dundee Utd.
St. Johnstone v Hibernian

First Division
Clydebank v Raith Rov.
Dunfermline Athletic v Morton
Falkirk v Ayr Utd.
Livingston v Airdrieonians
St. Mirren v Inverness Cal. Th.

Second Division
Clyde v Stranraer
Partick Thistle v Arbroath
Queen of the South v Alloa Athletic
Ross County v Stenhousemuir
Stirling Albion v Hamilton Acad.

Third Division
Albion Rov. v Brechin City
East Fife v Dumbarton
Forfar Athletic v East Stirlingshire
Montrose v Berwick Rangers
Queen's Park v Cowdenbeath

Saturday, 28 August
Premier League
Aberdeen v St. Johnstone
Celtic v Heart of Midlothian
Dundee Utd. v Kilmarnock
Hibernian v Rangers
Motherwell v Dundee

First Division
Airdrieonians v Raith Rov.
Ayr Utd. v Inverness Cal. Th.
Clydebank v St. Mirren
Dunfermline Athletic v Falkirk
Morton v Livingston

467

Second Division
Alloa Athletic v Hamilton Acad.
Clyde v Stirling Albion
Partick Thistle v Queen of the South
Ross County v Arbroath
Stenhousemuir v Stranraer

Third Division
Berwick Rangers v Queen's Park
Brechin City v Dumbarton
East Fife v Montrose
East Stirlingshire v Cowdenbeath
Forfar Athletic v Albion Rov.

Saturday, 4 September
First Division
Falkirk v Clydebank
Inverness Cal. Th. v Morton
Livingston v Dunfermline Athletic
Raith Rov. v Ayr Utd.
St. Mirren v Airdrieonians

Second Division
Arbroath v Alloa Athletic
Queen of the South v Clyde
Stirling Albion v Ross County
Stranraer v Partick Thistle

Third Division
Albion Rov. v East Fife
Cowdenbeath v Brechin City
Dumbarton v Berwick Rangers
Montrose v East Stirlingshire
Queen's Park v Forfar Athletic

Sunday, 5 September
Second Division
Hamilton Acad. v Stenhousemuir

Saturday, 11 September
Premier League
Dundee Utd. v Hibernian
Heart of Midlothian v Dundee
Kilmarnock v Celtic
Rangers v Aberdeen
St. Johnstone v Motherwell

First Division
Ayr Utd. v Airdrieonians
Dunfermline Athletic v St. Mirren
Falkirk v Livingston
Inverness Cal. Th. v Clydebank
Morton v Raith Rov.

Second Division
Alloa Athletic v Ross County
Arbroath v Stirling Albion
Clyde v Partick Thistle
Hamilton Acad. v Stranraer
Queen of the South v Stenhousemuir

Third Division
Albion Rov. v Montrose
Berwick Rangers v Cowdenbeath
Brechin City v East Stirlingshire
Dumbarton v Queen's Park
East Fife v Forfar Athletic

Saturday, 18 September
Premier League
Aberdeen v Dundee Utd.
Celtic v Rangers
Dundee v St. Johnstone
Hibernian v Kilmarnock
Motherwell v Heart of Midlothian

First Division
Airdrieonians v Falkirk
Clydebank v Ayr Utd.
Livingston v Inverness Cal. Th.
Raith Rov. v Dunfermline Athletic
St. Mirren v Morton

Second Division
Partick Thistle v Hamilton Acad.
Ross County v Clyde
Stenhousemuir v Arbroath
Stirling Albion v Alloa Athletic
Stranraer v Queen of the South

Third Division
Cowdenbeath v East Fife
East Stirlingshire v Dumbarton
Forfar Athletic v Berwick Rangers
Montrose v Brechin City
Queen's Park v Albion Rov.

Saturday, 25 September
Premier League
Dundee Utd. v Heart of Midlothian
Hibernian v Celtic
Kilmarnock v Dundee
Motherwell v Aberdeen
Rangers v St. Johnstone

First Division
Dunfermline Athletic v Ayr Utd.
Falkirk v St. Mirren
Inverness Cal. Th. v Raith Rov.
Livingston v Clydebank
Morton v Airdrieonians

Second Division
Alloa Athletic v Stenhousemuir
Arbroath v Stranraer
Clyde v Hamilton Acad.
Partick Thistle v Ross County
Queen of the South v Stirling Albion

Third Division
Albion Rov. v East Stirlingshire
Berwick Rangers v Brechin City
Dumbarton v Cowdenbeath

468

East Fife v Queen's Park
Montrose v Forfar Athletic

Montrose v Dumbarton
Queen's Park v Brechin City

Saturday, 2 October
Premier League
Aberdeen v Hibernian
Celtic v Motherwell
Dundee v Rangers
Heart of Midlothian v Kilmarnock
St. Johnstone v Dundee Utd.

First Division
Airdrieonians v Inverness Cal. Th.
Ayr Utd. v Morton
Clydebank v Dunfermline Athletic
Raith Rov. v Falkirk
St. Mirren v Livingston

Second Division
Hamilton Acad. v Arbroath
Ross County v Queen of the South
Stenhousemuir v Clyde
Stirling Albion v Partick Thistle
Stranraer v Alloa Athletic

Third Division
Brechin City v East Fife
Cowdenbeath v Albion Rov.
East Stirlingshire v Berwick Rangers
Forfar Athletic v Dumbarton
Queen's Park v Montrose

Saturday, 9 October
Second Division
Hamilton Acad. v Ross County

Saturday, 16 October
Premier League
Celtic v Aberdeen
Dundee v Dundee Utd.
Heart of Midlothian v St. Johnstone
Kilmarnock v Rangers
Motherwell v Hibernian

First Division
Clydebank v Morton
Dunfermline Athletic v Airdrieonians
Falkirk v Inverness Cal. Th.
Livingston v Ayr Utd.
St. Mirren v Raith Rov.

Second Division
Clyde v Arbroath
Partick Thistle v Alloa Athletic
Queen of the South v Hamilton Acad.
Ross County v Stranraer
Stirling Albion v Stenhousemuir

Third Division
Albion Rov. v Berwick Rangers
East Fife v East Stirlingshire
Forfar Athletic v Cowdenbeath

Saturday, 23 October
Premier League
Aberdeen v Kilmarnock
Dundee Utd. v Motherwell
Hibernian v Dundee
Rangers v Heart of Midlothian
St. Johnstone v Celtic

First Division
Airdrieonians v Clydebank
Ayr Utd. v St. Mirren
Inverness Cal. Th. v Dunfermline Ath.
Morton v Falkirk
Raith Rov. v Livingston

Second Division
Alloa Athletic v Clyde
Arbroath v Queen of the South
Stenhousemuir v Partick Thistle
Stranraer v Stirling Albion

Third Division
Berwick Rangers v East Fife
Brechin City v Forfar Athletic
Cowdenbeath v Montrose
Dumbarton v Albion Rov.
East Stirlingshire v Queen's Park

Saturday, 30 October
Premier League
Aberdeen v Rangers
Celtic v Kilmarnock
Dundee v Heart of Midlothian
Hibernian v Dundee Utd.
Motherwell v St. Johnstone

First Division
Airdrieonians v Ayr Utd.
Clydebank v Inverness Cal. Th.
Livingston v Falkirk
Raith Rov. v Morton
St. Mirren v Dunfermline Athletic

Second Division
Partick Thistle v Clyde
Ross County v Alloa Athletic
Stenhousemuir v Queen of the South
Stirling Albion v Arbroath
Stranraer v Hamilton Acad.

Third Division
Cowdenbeath v Berwick Rangers
East Stirlingshire v Brechin City
Forfar Athletic v East Fife
Montrose v Albion Rov.
Queen's Park v Dumbarton

Saturday, 6 November
Premier League
Dundee Utd. v Aberdeen
Heart of Midlothian v Motherwell
Kilmarnock v Hibernian
Rangers v Celtic
St. Johnstone v Dundee

First Division
Ayr Utd. v Clydebank
Dunfermline Athletic v Raith Rov.
Falkirk v Airdrieonians
Inverness Cal. Th. v Livingston
Morton v St. Mirren

Second Division
Alloa Athletic v Stirling Albion
Arbroath v Stenhousemuir
Clyde v Ross County
Hamilton Acad. v Partick Thistle
Queen of the South v Stranraer

Third Division
Albion Rov. v Queen's Park
Berwick Rangers v Forfar Athletic
Brechin City v Montrose
Dumbarton v East Stirlingshire
East Fife v Cowdenbeath

Saturday, 13 November
Premier League
Aberdeen v Heart of Midlothian
Celtic v Dundee
Dundee Utd. v Rangers
Hibernian v St. Johnstone
Motherwell v Kilmarnock

First Division
Airdrieonians v St. Mirren
Ayr Utd. v Raith Rov.
Clydebank v Falkirk
Dunfermline Athletic v Livingston
Morton v Inverness Cal. Th.

Second Division
Alloa Athletic v Arbroath
Clyde v Queen of the South
Partick Thistle v Stranraer
Ross County v Stirling Albion
Stenhousemuir v Hamilton Acad.

Third Division
Berwick Rangers v Dumbarton
Brechin City v Cowdenbeath
East Fife v Albion Rov.
East Stirlingshire v Montrose
Forfar Athletic v Queen's Park

Saturday, 20 November
Premier League
Dundee v Motherwell
Heart of Midlothian v Celtic

Kilmarnock v Dundee Utd.
Rangers v Hibernian
St. Johnstone v Aberdeen

First Division
Falkirk v Dunfermline Athletic
Inverness Cal. Th. v Ayr Utd.
Livingston v Morton
Raith Rov. v Airdrieonians
St. Mirren v Clydebank

Second Division
Arbroath v Ross County
Hamilton Acad. v Alloa Athletic
Queen of the South v Partick Thistle
Stirling Albion v Clyde
Stranraer v Stenhousemuir

Third Division
Albion Rov. v Forfar Athletic
Cowdenbeath v East Stirlingshire
Dumbarton v Brechin City
Montrose v East Fife
Queen's Park v Berwick Rangers

Saturday, 27 November
Premier League
Dundee Utd. v St. Johnstone
Hibernian v Aberdeen
Kilmarnock v Heart of Midlothian
Motherwell v Celtic
Rangers v Dundee

First Division
Dunfermline Athletic v Clydebank
Falkirk v Raith Rov.
Inverness Cal. Th. v Airdrieonians
Livingston v St. Mirren
Morton v Ayr Utd.

Second Division
Alloa Athletic v Stranraer
Arbroath v Hamilton Acad.
Clyde v Stenhousemuir
Partick Thistle v Stirling Albion
Queen of the South v Ross County

Third Division
Albion Rov. v Cowdenbeath
Berwick Rangers v East Stirlingshire
Dumbarton v Forfar Athletic
East Fife v Brechin City
Montrose v Queen's Park

Saturday, 4 December
Premier League
Aberdeen v Motherwell
Celtic v Hibernian
Dundee v Kilmarnock
Heart of Midlothian v Dundee Utd.
St. Johnstone v Rangers

First Division
Airdrieonians v Morton
Ayr Utd. v Dunfermline Athletic
Clydebank v Livingston
Raith Rov. v Inverness Cal. Th.
St. Mirren v Falkirk

Second Division
Hamilton Acad. v Clyde
Ross County v Partick Thistle
Stenhousemuir v Alloa Athletic
Stirling Albion v Queen of the South
Stranraer v Arbroath

Third Division
Brechin City v Berwick Rangers
Cowdenbeath v Dumbarton
East Stirlingshire v Albion Rov.
Forfar Athletic v Montrose
Queen's Park v East Fife

Saturday, 11 December
Premier League
Aberdeen v Celtic
Dundee Utd. v Dundee
Hibernian v Motherwell
Rangers v Kilmarnock
St. Johnstone v Heart of Midlothian

First Division
Airdrieonians v Livingston
Ayr Utd. v Falkirk
Inverness Cal. Th. v St. Mirren
Morton v Dunfermline Athletic
Raith Rov. v Clydebank

Saturday, 18 December
Premier League
Celtic v Dundee Utd.
Dundee v Aberdeen
Heart of Midlothian v Hibernian
Kilmarnock v St. Johnstone
Motherwell v Rangers

First Division
Clydebank v Airdrieonians
Dunfermline Ath. v Inverness Cal. Th.
Falkirk v Morton
Livingston v Raith Rov.
St. Mirren v Ayr Utd.

Second Division
Clyde v Alloa Athletic
Partick Thistle v Stenhousemuir
Queen of the South v Arbroath
Ross County v Hamilton Acad.
Stirling Albion v Stranraer

Third Division
Albion Rov. v Dumbarton
East Fife v Berwick Rangers
Forfar Athletic v Brechin City

Montrose v Cowdenbeath
Queen's Park v East Stirlingshire

Monday, 27 December
Premier League
Aberdeen v Dundee Utd.
Celtic v Rangers
Dundee v St. Johnstone
Hibernian v Kilmarnock
Motherwell v Heart of Midlothian

First Division
Ayr Utd. v Airdrieonians
Dunfermline Athletic v St. Mirren
Falkirk v Livingston
Inverness Cal. Th. v Clydebank
Morton v Raith Rov.

Second Division
Alloa Athletic v Queen of the South
Arbroath v Partick Thistle
Hamilton Acad. v Stirling Albion
Stenhousemuir v Ross County
Stranraer v Clyde

Third Division
Berwick Rangers v Montrose
Brechin City v Albion Rov.
Cowdenbeath v Queen's Park
Dumbarton v East Fife
East Stirlingshire v Forfar Athletic

Monday, 3 January 2000
First Division
Airdrieonians v Falkirk
Clydebank v Ayr Utd.
Livingston v Inverness Cal. Th.
Raith Rov. v Dunfermline Athletic
St. Mirren v Morton

Second Division
Partick Thistle v Hamilton Acad.
Ross County v Clyde
Stenhousemuir v Arbroath
Stirling Albion v Alloa Athletic
Stranraer v Queen of the South

Third Division
Cowdenbeath v East Fife
East Stirlingshire v Dumbarton
Forfar Athletic v Berwick Rangers
Montrose v Brechin City
Queen's Park v Albion Rov.

Saturday, 8 January
First Division
Falkirk v Clydebank
Inverness Cal. Th. v Morton
Livingston v Dunfermline Athletic
Raith Rov. v Ayr Utd.
St. Mirren v Airdrieonians

Saturday, 15 January
First Division
Airdrieonians v Raith Rov.
Ayr Utd. v Inverness Cal. Th.
Clydebank v St. Mirren
Dunfermline Athletic v Falkirk
Morton v Livingston

Second Division
Alloa Athletic v Ross County
Arbroath v Stirling Albion
Clyde v Partick Thistle
Hamilton Acad. v Stranraer
Queen of the South v Stenhousemuir

Third Division
Albion Rov. v Montrose
Berwick Rangers v Cowdenbeath
Brechin City v East Stirlingshire
Dumbarton v Queen's Park
East Fife v Forfar Athletic

Saturday, 22 January
Premier League
Dundee Utd. v Hibernian
Heart of Midlothian v Dundee
Kilmarnock v Celtic
Rangers v Aberdeen
St. Johnstone v Motherwell

First Division
Dunfermline Athletic v Ayr Utd.
Falkirk v St. Mirren
Inverness Cal. Th. v Raith Rov.
Livingston v Clydebank
Morton v Airdrieonians

Second Division
Alloa Athletic v Stenhousemuir
Arbroath v Stranraer
Clyde v Hamilton Acad.
Partick Thistle v Ross County
Queen of the South v Stirling Albion

Third Division
Albion Rov. v East Stirlingshire
Berwick Rangers v Brechin City
Dumbarton v Cowdenbeath
East Fife v Queen's Park
Montrose v Forfar Athletic

Saturday, 5 February
Premier League
Aberdeen v St. Johnstone
Celtic v Heart of Midlothian
Dundee Utd. v Kilmarnock
Hibernian v Rangers
Motherwell v Dundee

First Division
Airdrieonians v Inverness Cal. Th.
Ayr Utd. v Morton

Clydebank v Dunfermline Athletic
Raith Rov. v Falkirk
St. Mirren v Livingston

Second Division
Hamilton Acad. v Arbroath
Ross County v Queen of the South
Stenhousemuir v Clyde
Stirling Albion v Partick Thistle
Stranraer v Alloa Athletic

Third Division
Brechin City v East Fife
Cowdenbeath v Albion Rov.
East Stirlingshire v Berwick Rangers
Forfar Athletic v Dumbarton
Queen's Park v Montrose

Saturday, 12 February
Premier League
Dundee v Celtic
Heart of Midlothian v Aberdeen
Kilmarnock v Motherwell
Rangers v Dundee Utd.
St. Johnstone v Hibernian

First Division
Clydebank v Raith Rov.
Dunfermline Athletic v Morton
Falkirk v Ayr Utd.
Livingston v Airdrieonians
St. Mirren v Inverness Cal. Th.

Second Division
Alloa Athletic v Hamilton Acad.
Clyde v Stirling Albion
Partick Thistle v Queen of the South
Ross County v Arbroath
Stenhousemuir v Stranraer

Third Division
Berwick Rangers v Queen's Park
Brechin City v Dumbarton
East Fife v Montrose
East Stirlingshire v Cowdenbeath
Forfar Athletic v Albion Rov.

Saturday, 19 February
Second Division
Arbroath v Alloa Athletic
Hamilton Acad. v Stenhousemuir
Queen of the South v Clyde
Stirling Albion v Ross County
Stranraer v Partick Thistle

Third Division
Albion Rov. v East Fife
Cowdenbeath v Brechin City
Dumbarton v Berwick Rangers
Montrose v East Stirlingshire
Queen's Park v Forfar Athletic

Saturday, 26 February
Premier League
Aberdeen v Hibernian
Celtic v Motherwell
Dundee v Rangers
Heart of Midlothian v Kilmarnock
St. Johnstone v Dundee Utd.

First Division
Airdrieonians v Dunfermline Athletic
Ayr Utd. v Livingston
Inverness Cal. Th. v Falkirk
Morton v Clydebank
Raith Rov. v St. Mirren

Second Division
Alloa Athletic v Partick Thistle
Arbroath v Clyde
Hamilton Acad. v Queen of the South
Stenhousemuir v Stirling Albion
Stranraer v Ross County

Third Division
Berwick Rangers v Albion Rov.
Brechin City v Queen's Park
Cowdenbeath v Forfar Athletic
Dumbarton v Montrose
East Stirlingshire v East Fife

Saturday, 4 March
Premier League
Dundee Utd. v Heart of Midlothian
Hibernian v Celtic
Kilmarnock v Dundee
Motherwell v Aberdeen
Rangers v St. Johnstone

First Division
Airdrieonians v Ayr Utd.
Clydebank v Inverness Cal. Th.
Livingston v Falkirk
Raith Rov. v Morton
St. Mirren v Dunfermline Athletic

Second Division
Clyde v Stranraer
Partick Thistle v Arbroath
Queen of the South v Alloa Athletic
Ross County v Stenhousemuir
Stirling Albion v Hamilton Acad.

Third Division
Albion Rov. v Brechin City
East Fife v Dumbarton
Forfar Athletic v East Stirlingshire
Montrose v Berwick Rangers
Queen's Park v Cowdenbeath

Saturday, 11 March
Premier League
Celtic v St. Johnstone
Dundee v Hibernian

Heart of Midlothian v Rangers
Kilmarnock v Aberdeen
Motherwell v Dundee Utd.

Second Division
Partick Thistle v Clyde
Ross County v Alloa Athletic
Stenhousemuir v Queen of the South
Stirling Albion v Arbroath
Stranraer v Hamilton Acad.

Third Division
Cowdenbeath v Berwick Rangers
East Stirlingshire v Brechin City
Forfar Athletic v East Fife
Montrose v Albion Rov.
Queen's Park v Dumbarton

Saturday, 18 March
Premier League
Aberdeen v Dundee
Dundee Utd. v Celtic
Hibernian v Heart of Midlothian
Rangers v Motherwell
St. Johnstone v Kilmarnock

First Division
Ayr Utd. v Clydebank
Dunfermline Athletic v Raith Rov.
Falkirk v Airdrieonians
Inverness Cal. Th. v Livingston
Morton v St. Mirren

Second Division
Alloa Athletic v Stirling Albion
Arbroath v Stenhousemuir
Clyde v Ross County
Hamilton Acad. v Partick Thistle
Queen of the South v Stranraer

Third Division
Albion Rov. v Queen's Park
Berwick Rangers v Forfar Athletic
Brechin City v Montrose
Dumbarton v East Stirlingshire
East Fife v Cowdenbeath

Saturday, 25 March
Premier League
Dundee Utd. v Aberdeen
Heart of Midlothian v Motherwell
Kilmarnock v Hibernian
Rangers v Celtic
St. Johnstone v Dundee

First Division
Falkirk v Dunfermline Athletic
Inverness Cal. Th. v Ayr Utd.
Livingston v Morton
Raith Rov. v Airdrieonians
St. Mirren v Clydebank

Second Division
Arbroath v Ross County
Hamilton Acad. v Alloa Athletic
Queen of the South v Partick Thistle
Stirling Albion v Clyde
Stranraer v Stenhousemuir

Third Division
Albion Rov. v Forfar Athletic
Cowdenbeath v East Stirlingshire
Dumbarton v Brechin City
Montrose v East Fife
Queen's Park v Berwick Rangers

Saturday, 1 April
Premier League
Aberdeen v Rangers
Celtic v Kilmarnock
Dundee v Heart of Midlothian
Hibernian v Dundee Utd.
Motherwell v St. Johnstone

First Division
Airdrieonians v St. Mirren
Ayr Utd. v Raith Rov.
Clydebank v Falkirk
Dunfermline Athletic v Livingston
Morton v Inverness Cal. Th.

Second Division
Alloa Athletic v Arbroath
Clyde v Queen of the South
Partick Thistle v Stranraer
Ross County v Stirling Albion
Stenhousemuir v Hamilton Acad.

Third Division
Berwick Rangers v Dumbarton
Brechin City v Cowdenbeath
East Fife v Albion Rov.
East Stirlingshire v Montrose
Forfar Athletic v Queen's Park

Saturday, 8 April
Premier League
Dundee v Motherwell
Heart of Midlothian v Celtic
Kilmarnock v Dundee Utd.
Rangers v Hibernian
St. Johnstone v Aberdeen

First Division
Airdrieonians v Morton
Ayr Utd. v Dunfermline Athletic
Clydebank v Livingston
Raith Rov. v Inverness Cal. Th.
St. Mirren v Falkirk

Second Division
Hamilton Acad. v Clyde
Ross County v Partick Thistle
Stenhousemuir v Alloa Athletic

Stirling Albion v Queen of the South
Stranraer v Arbroath

Third Division
Brechin City v Berwick Rangers
Cowdenbeath v Dumbarton
East Stirlingshire v Albion Rov.
Forfar Athletic v Montrose
Queen's Park v East Fife

Saturday, 15 April
Premier League
Aberdeen v Heart of Midlothian
Celtic v Dundee
Dundee Utd. v Rangers
Hibernian v St. Johnstone
Motherwell v Kilmarnock

First Division
Dunfermline Athletic v Clydebank
Falkirk v Raith Rov.
Inverness Cal. Th. v Airdrieonians
Livingston v St. Mirren
Morton v Ayr Utd.

Second Division
Alloa Athletic v Stranraer
Arbroath v Hamilton Acad.
Clyde v Stenhousemuir
Partick Thistle v Stirling Albion
Queen of the South v Ross County

Third Division
Albion Rov. v Cowdenbeath
Berwick Rangers v East Stirlingshire
Dumbarton v Forfar Athletic
East Fife v Brechin City
Montrose v Queen's Park

Saturday, 22 April
Premier League
Aberdeen v Motherwell
Celtic v Hibernian
Dundee v Kilmarnock
Heart of Midlothian v Dundee Utd.
St. Johnstone v Rangers

First Division
Airdrieonians v Clydebank
Ayr Utd. v St. Mirren
Inverness Cal. Th. v Dunfermline Ath.
Morton v Falkirk
Raith Rov. v Livingston

Second Division
Alloa Athletic v Clyde
Arbroath v Queen of the South
Hamilton Acad. v Ross County
Stenhousemuir v Partick Thistle
Stranraer v Stirling Albion

Third Division
Berwick Rangers v East Fife
Brechin City v Forfar Athletic
Cowdenbeath v Montrose
Dumbarton v Albion Rov.
East Stirlingshire v Queen's Park

Saturday, 29 April
Premier League
Dundee Utd. v St. Johnstone
Hibernian v Aberdeen
Kilmarnock v Heart of Midlothian
Motherwell v Celtic
Rangers v Dundee

First Division
Clydebank v Morton
Dunfermline Athletic v Airdrieonians
Falkirk v Inverness Cal. Th.
Livingston v Ayr Utd.
St. Mirren v Raith Rov.

Second Division
Clyde v Arbroath
Partick Thistle v Alloa Athletic
Queen of the South v Hamilton Acad.
Ross County v Stranraer
Stirling Albion v Stenhousemuir

Third Division
Albion Rov. v Berwick Rangers
East Fife v East Stirlingshire
Forfar Athletic v Cowdenbeath
Montrose v Dumbarton
Queen's Park v Brechin City

Saturday, 6 May
Premier League
Celtic v Aberdeen
Dundee v Dundee Utd.

Heart of Midlothian v St. Johnstone
Kilmarnock v Rangers
Motherwell v Hibernian

First Division
Airdrieonians v Livingston
Ayr Utd. v Falkirk
Inverness Cal. Th. v St. Mirren
Morton v Dunfermline Athletic
Raith Rov. v Clydebank

Second Division
Alloa Athletic v Queen of the South
Arbroath v Partick Thistle
Hamilton Acad. v Stirling Albion
Stenhousemuir v Ross County
Stranraer v Clyde

Third Division
Berwick Rangers v Montrose
Brechin City v Albion Rov.
Cowdenbeath v Queen's Park
Dumbarton v East Fife
East Stirlingshire v Forfar Athletic

Saturday, 13 May
Premier League
Aberdeen v Kilmarnock
Dundee Utd. v Motherwell
Hibernian v Dundee
Rangers v Heart of Midlothian
St. Johnstone v Celtic

Saturday, 20 May
Premier League
Celtic v Dundee Utd.
Dundee v Aberdeen
Heart of Midlothian v Hibernian
Kilmarnock v St. Johnstone
Motherwell v Rangers

NATIONWIDE CONFERENCE
FIXTURES 1999-2000

These fixtures are the copyright of the Nationwide Conference and are reproduced with their permission.

Saturday, August 14
Altrincham v Stevenage Borough
Doncaster Rov. v Forest Green Rov.
Kettering Town v Northwich Victoria
Kidderminster Harr. v Dover Athletic
Morecambe v Rushden & D.
Nuneaton Borough v Hayes
Scarborough v Yeovil Town
Southport v Woking
Sutton Utd. v Hereford Utd.
Telford Utd. v Kingstonian
Welling Utd. v Hednesford Town

Monday, August 16
Stevenage Borough v Doncaster Rov.

Tuesday, August 17
Altrincham v Hednesford Town
Hayes v Welling Utd.
Hereford Utd. v Nuneaton Borough
Northwich Victoria v Morecambe
Rushden & D. v Telford Utd.
Southport v Scarborough
Woking v Kettering Town
Yeovil Town v Kidderminster Harr.

Wednesday, August 18
Forest Green Rov. v Sutton Utd.
Kingstonian v Dover Athletic

Saturday, August 21
Dover Athletic v Nuneaton Borough
Forest Green Rov. v Scarborough
Hayes v Morecambe
Hednesford Town v Sutton Utd.
Hereford Utd. v Kettering Town
Kingstonian v Southport
Northwich Victoria v Welling Utd.
Rushden & D. v Kidderminster Harr.
Stevenage Borough v Telford Utd.
Woking v Doncaster Rov.
Yeovil Town v Altrincham

Tuesday, August 24
Doncaster Rov. v Southport
Dover Athletic v Hayes
Kettering Town v Kingstonian
Morecambe v Hereford Utd.
Nuneaton Borough v Yeovil Town
Scarborough v Hednesford Town
Sutton Utd. v Stevenage Borough
Telford Utd. v Forest Green Rov.

Welling Utd. v Woking

Saturday, August 28
Doncaster Rov. v Hayes
Hednesford Town v Morecambe
Kidderminster Harr. v Woking
Kingstonian v Altrincham
Nuneaton Borough v Northwich Victoria
Scarborough v Stevenage Borough
Southport v Forest Green Rov.
Sutton Utd. v Rushden & D.
Telford Utd. v Dover Athletic
Welling Utd. v Hereford Utd.
Yeovil Town v Kettering Town

Monday, August 30
Altrincham v Southport
Dover Athletic v Sutton Utd.
Forest Green Rov. v Kidderminster Harr.
Hayes v Kingstonian
Hednesford Town v Nuneaton Borough
Hereford Utd. v Telford Utd.
Morecambe v Scarborough
Northwich Victoria v Doncaster Rov.
Rushden & D. v Welling Utd.
Stevenage Borough v Kettering Town
Woking v Yeovil Town

Saturday, September 4
Altrincham v Dover Athletic
Forest Green Rov. v Nuneaton Borough
Hayes v Southport
Hereford Utd. v Doncaster Rov.
Kettering Town v Sutton Utd.
Morecambe v Telford Utd.
Northwich Victoria v Rushden & D.
Scarborough v Kingstonian
Stevenage Borough v Kidderminster Harr.
Welling Utd. v Yeovil Town
Woking v Hednesford Town

Monday, September 6
Hednesford Town v Kettering Town

Tuesday, September 7
Doncaster Rov. v Altrincham
Rushden & D. v Hayes
Yeovil Town v Hereford Utd.

Saturday, September 11
Dover Athletic v Doncaster Rov.
Hednesford Town v Stevenage Borough

Kettering Town v Forest Green Rov.
Kidderminster Harr. v Scarborough
Kingstonian v Northwich Victoria
Nuneaton Borough v Welling Utd.
Rushden & D. v Woking
Southport v Hereford Utd.
Sutton Utd. v Altrincham
Telford Utd. v Hayes
Yeovil Town v Morecambe

Monday, September 13
Kidderminster Harr. v Nuneaton Borough

Tuesday, September 14
Doncaster Rov. v Hednesford Town
Hayes v Yeovil Town
Hereford Utd. v Forest Green Rov.
Kettering Town v Rushden & D.
Northwich Victoria v Scarborough

Saturday, September 18
Altrincham v Woking
Doncaster Rov. v Kettering Town
Forest Green Rov. v Kingstonian
Hednesford Town v Hayes
Hereford Utd. v Stevenage Borough
Morecambe v Kidderminster Harr.
Northwich Victoria v Dover Athletic
Rushden & D. v Southport
Scarborough v Nuneaton Borough
Welling Utd. v Telford Utd.
Yeovil Town v Sutton Utd.

Tuesday, September 21
Sutton Utd. v Welling Utd.

Wednesday, September 22
Kingstonian v Yeovil Town

Saturday, September 25
Dover Athletic v Hereford Utd.
Hednesford Town v Rushden & D.
Kettering Town v Morecambe
Kidderminster Harr. v Doncaster Rov.
Nuneaton Borough v Altrincham
Scarborough v Hayes
Southport v Sutton Utd.
Stevenage Borough v Kingstonian
Telford Utd. v Yeovil Town
Welling Utd. v Forest Green Rov.
Woking v Northwich Victoria

Tuesday, September 28
Welling Utd. v Kingstonian

Wednesday, September 29
Forest Green Rov. v Northwich Victoria

Saturday, October 2
Altrincham v Rushden & D.
Doncaster Rov. v Welling Utd.
Forest Green Rov. v Stevenage Borough

Hayes v Kidderminster Harr.
Hereford Utd. v Scarborough
Kingstonian v Kettering Town
Morecambe v Woking
Northwich Victoria v Hednesford Town
Nuneaton Borough v Southport
Sutton Utd. v Telford Utd.
Yeovil Town v Dover Athletic

Saturday, October 9
Doncaster Rov. v Nuneaton Borough
Dover Athletic v Scarborough
Hednesford Town v Forest Green Rov.
Kettering Town v Hayes
Kidderminster Harr. v Yeovil Town
Rushden & D. v Kingstonian
Southport v Welling Utd.
Stevenage Borough v. Morecambe
Sutton Utd. v Northwich Victoria
Telford Utd. v Altrincham
Woking v Hereford Utd.

Saturday, October 23
Dover Athletic v Hednesford Town
Hereford Utd. v Hayes
Kidderminster Harr. v Kettering Town
Morecambe v Kingstonian
Northwich Victoria v Stevenage Borough
Nuneaton Borough v Sutton Utd.
Scarborough v Rushden & D.
Telford Utd. v Doncaster Rov.
Welling Utd. v Altrincham
Woking v Forest Green Rov.
Yeovil Town v Southport

Monday, November 1
Hednesford Town v Kidderminster Harr.

Tuesday, November 2
Kettering Town v Welling Utd.
Nuneaton Borough v Rushden & D.
Sutton Utd. v Kingstonian

Saturday, November 6
Altrincham v Hereford Utd.
Forest Green Rov. v Morecambe
Hayes v Northwich Victoria
Hednesford Town v Yeovil Town
Kingstonian v Welling Utd.
Rushden & D. v Dover Athletic
Southport v Kettering Town
Stevenage Borough v Scarborough
Sutton Utd. v Doncaster Rov.
Telford Utd. v Kidderminster Harr.
Woking v Nuneaton Borough

Saturday, November 13
Doncaster Rov. v Woking
Dover Athletic v Forest Green Rov.
Hayes v Stevenage Borough
Hereford Utd. v Northwich Victoria

Kettering Town v Altrincham
Kidderminster Harr. v Southport
Morecambe v Hednesford Town
Nuneaton Borough v Kingstonian
Scarborough v Telford Utd.
Welling Utd. v Sutton Utd.
Yeovil Town v Rushden & D.

Saturday, November 20
Altrincham v Morecambe
Forest Green Rov. v Hayes
Kingstonian v Doncaster Rov.
Northwich Victoria v Kidderminster Harr.
Nuneaton Borough v Telford Utd.
Rushden & D. v Hednesford Town
Scarborough v Kettering Town
Southport v Dover Athletic
Stevenage Borough v Hereford Utd.
Sutton Utd. v Yeovil Town
Woking v Welling Utd.

Tuesday, November 30
Altrincham v Nuneaton Borough

Saturday, December 4
Doncaster Rov. v Stevenage Borough
Dover Athletic v Altrincham
Hayes v Rushden & D.
Hednesford Town v Woking
Hereford Utd. v Southport
Kettering Town v Telford Utd.
Kidderminster Harr. v Kingstonian
Morecambe v Sutton Utd.
Nuneaton Borough v Forest Green Rov.
Welling Utd. v Scarborough
Yeovil Town v Northwich Victoria

Saturday, December 11
Altrincham v Hayes
Forest Green Rov. v Hednesford Town
Kingstonian v Hereford Utd.
Northwich Victoria v Nuneaton Borough
Rushden & D. v Yeovil Town
Scarborough v Kidderminster Harr.
Southport v Doncaster Rov.
Stevenage Borough v Dover Athletic
Sutton Utd. v Kettering Town
Telford Utd. v Welling Utd.
Woking v Morecambe

Saturday, December 18
Altrincham v Forest Green Rov.
Kettering Town v Dover Athletic
Kidderminster Harr. v Morecambe
Kingstonian v Hednesford Town
Scarborough v Hereford Utd.
Southport v Northwich Victoria
Stevenage Borough v Woking
Sutton Utd. v Nuneaton Borough
Telford Utd. v Rushden & D.

Welling Utd. v Doncaster Rov.
Yeovil Town v Hayes

Monday, December 27
Doncaster Rov. v Scarborough
Dover Athletic v Welling Utd.
Forest Green Rov. v Yeovil Town
Hayes v Sutton Utd.
Hednesford Town v Telford Utd.
Hereford Utd. v Kidderminster Harr.
Morecambe v Southport
Northwich Victoria v Altrincham
Nuneaton Borough v Kettering Town
Rushden & D. v Stevenage Borough
Woking v Kingstonian

Monday, January 3, 2000
Altrincham v Northwich Victoria
Kettering Town v Nuneaton Borough
Kidderminster Harr. v Hereford Utd.
Kingstonian v Woking
Scarborough v Doncaster Rov.
Southport v Morecambe
Stevenage Borough v Rushden & D.
Sutton Utd. v Hayes
Telford Utd. v Hednesford Town
Welling Utd. v Dover Athletic
Yeovil Town v Forest Green Rov.

Saturday, January 8
Doncaster Rov. v Sutton Utd.
Dover Athletic v Yeovil Town
Forest Green Rov. v Altrincham
Hayes v Kettering Town
Hednesford Town v Scarborough
Hereford Utd. v Rushden & D.
Kingstonian v Telford Utd.
Morecambe v Stevenage Borough
Nuneaton Borough v Kidderminster Harr.
Welling Utd. v Northwich Victoria
Woking v Southport

Saturday, January 15
Altrincham v Scarborough
Dover Athletic v Kettering Town
Kidderminster Harr. v Welling Utd.
Kingstonian v Nuneaton Borough
Northwich Victoria v Hereford Utd.
Rushden & D. v Morecambe
Stevenage Borough v Forest Green Rov.
Sutton Utd. v Hednesford Town
Telford Utd. v Southport
Woking v Hayes
Yeovil Town v Doncaster Rov.

Tuesday, January 18
Telford Utd. v Morecambe

Saturday, January 22
Doncaster Rov. v Kingstonian
Forest Green Rov. v Rushden & D.